Gender in

Cross-Cultural

Perspective

FOURTH EDITION

Gender in Cross-Cultural Perspective

Edited by

Caroline B. Brettell

and

Carolyn F. Sargent

Southern Methodist University

PEARSON

Prentice Hall

Upper Saddle River, New Jersey 07458

Library of Congress Cataloging-in-Publication Data

Gender in cross-cultural perspective / edited by Caroline B. Brettell and
Carolyn F. Sargent.
   —4th ed. p. cm.
  ISBN 0-13-184971-9
  1. Sex role—Cross-cultural studies. I. Brettell, Caroline. II. Sargent,
  Carolyn Fishel, 1947–

GN479.65.G4634 2005
305.3—dc22

2004006679

Publisher: Nancy Roberts
Editorial Liaison: Sharon Chambliss
Production Liaison: Marianne Peters-Riordan
Director of Marketing: Beth Gillette Mejia
Marketing Assistant: Adam Laitman
Manufacturing Buyer: Mary Ann Gloriande
Cover Art Director: Jayne Conte
Cover Design: Suzanne Behnke
Cover Illustration/Photo: Fresh Paint Studios/Stock Illustration Source
Composition/Full-Service Project Management: Pine Tree Composition
Printer/Binder: Phoenix Book Tech

Credits and acknowledgments borrowed from other sources and reproduced, with permission,
in this textbook appear on appropriate page within text.

Pearson Education LTD., London
Pearson Education Singapore, Pte. Ltd
Pearson Education, Canada, Ltd
Pearson Education–Japan
Pearson Education Australia PTY, Limited

Pearson Education North Asia Ltd
Pearson Educación de Mexico, S.A. de C.V.
Pearson Education Malaysia, Pte. Ltd
Pearson Education, Upper Saddle River, New Jersey

10 9 8 7 6 5 4 3 2 1
ISBN 0-13-184971-9

For Richard Brettell and David Freidel, men who have given new meaning to the gendered division of labor, with gratitude for the intellectual and emotional support that they have provided for many years.

Contents

Preface

The initial idea for this reader came from the experience of teaching undergraduate courses in gender and anthropology. In reviewing the textbooks available for an introductory course, we came to the conclusion that there was a need for a readable text that built on the classic contributions of the 1970s while incorporating the more recent and diverse literature on gender roles and ideology around the world. Although a number of sophisticated theoretical works devoted to this subject existed, we felt there was a dearth of classroom material available in one volume and appropriate for less advanced students, whether undergraduates or beginning graduate students.

We have had five goals in mind as we selected materials for the fourth edition. First, as in previous editions, we want to introduce students to the most significant topics in the field of the anthropology of gender. These include the study of men and women in prehistory; the relationship between biology and culture; the cultural construction of masculinity, femininity, sexuality, personhood, and the body; variations in the sexual division of labor and economic organization; women's involvement in ritual and religion; and the impact on gender issues of various forces of change such as colonialism, the rise of the state, the global economy, and migration.

Second, we think it is important to maintain the broad cross-cultural coverage evident in earlier editions. This breadth encourages comparative analysis of the themes under discussion and allows us to address issues of gender in industrial society as well as in developing societies.

Third, we have expanded our efforts to complement research on women's lives with articles that deal with masculinity and male gender roles. Feminist theory is increasingly being applied to the study of men and we have tried to represent some of this research in our volume.

Fourth, we have always been committed to combining theoretically and ethnographically based articles in each section of the book. We hope that we have compiled a volume that can stand alone or, if the instructor so desires, can be complemented by the use of full ethnographies.

Fifth, in every edition we have included introductions to each section that review as clearly as possible some of the significant issues debated in particular subject areas in the anthropology of gender. These introductions, updated for the current edition, are intended to orient students to the articles in the section and to provide a context in which readers can more fully understand each article. Each introduction concludes with a list of references that can be used by teachers and students to examine further the questions raised in that section.

We do not expect all instructors to assign the sections in the order that they appear in the text although for this edition we have rearranged the sections slightly. The order makes sense to us, but our ultimate goal is to provide for maximum flexibility in teaching. Indeed, there are articles in some sections that can be related to articles in other sections. We also have no intention of imposing a particular theoretical perspective, although our own predilections may be apparent to some readers. We include readings that reflect a variety of theoretical orientations to enable instructors to emphasize their own approach to the subject.

The text concludes with a list of recommended films organized by sections of this book. We have reviewed many of these films, and we hope that all of them will successfully complement the readings in the text.

ACKNOWLEDGMENTS

Many people have contributed substantially to the preparation and development of this book. For the first edition, Andrew Webb provided invaluable clerical and organizational assistance. The undergraduate students in Professor Sargent's course "Gender and Sex Roles: A Global Perspective" have consistently offered valuable criticisms of selected articles. Their opinions continue to influence us enormously in the final selection process. John Phinney acted as an invaluable library of knowledge for obscure references; Sue Linder-Linsley offered indispensable computer advice and tirelessly scanned in text to save us time in the preparation of the second edition; and Sue Racine and Scott Langley contributed clerical assistance. Tim Benner and Louann Miller worked conscientiously to help us complete the third edition. For this edition we have had the assistance of Melissa Nibungco. We are also grateful to Southern Methodist University for various forms of support over the years.

We want to thank the reviewers of the original manuscript and the professors around the world who have used previous editions and offered valuable suggestions for improvements to the fourth edition. We are also grateful to our project assistant John Shannon who answered numerous queries during the spring and summer of 2004. Finally, we wish to acknowledge Nancy Roberts and Sharon Chambliss of Prentice-Hall for their confidence in our judgment and their constant support of this project. We have a wonderful partnership!

Caroline B. Brettell
Carolyn F. Sargent

About the Authors

Caroline Brettell received her BA degree from Yale University and her MA and Ph.D. degrees from Brown University. She joined the faculty of the Department of Anthropology at Southern Methodist University in 1988, and in 2003 was named Dedman Family Distinguished Professor. From 1989-1994 she served as Director of Women's Studies and from 1994-2004 she served as Chair of the Department of Anthropology. She is the author of *Men Who Migrate, Women Who Wait: Population and History in a Portuguese Parish* (1986), *We Have Already Cried Many Tears: The Stories of Three Portuguese Migrant Women* (1982, 1995), *Writing Against the Wind: A Mother's Life History* (1999) and *Anthropology and Migration: Essays on Transnationalism, Ethnicity and Identity* (2003); co-author with Richard Brettell of *Painters and Peasants in the 19th Century* (1983); editor of *When The Read What We Write: The Politics of Ethnography* (1993); co-editor of *International Migration: The Female Experience* (1986), *Gender in Cross-Cultural Perspective* (Prentice-Hall 1993, 1997, 2001, 2005), *Gender and Health: An International Perspective* (1996), and *Migration Theory: Talking Across Disciplines* (2000). She is also the author of numerous book chapters and articles. She currently is Principal Investigator on a project funded through the Cultural Anthropology Program of the National Science Foundation titled "Immigrants, Rights and Incorporation in a Suburban Metropolis." Professor Brettell has served as a member of NIH Study Section-SNEM 3, and several selection panels for the Social Science Research Council and the NEH. She has served as President of the Society for the Anthropology of Europe and of the Social Science History Association.

Carolyn Sargent received her Bachelors degree from Michigan State University, her MA degree from the University of Manchester, and her Ph.D. from Michigan State University. She joined the faculty of the Department of Anthropology at Southern Methodist University in 1979. She has been serving as Director of Women's Studies since 1994. She is currently a research fellow at the University of Paris V. Sargent is the author of *The Cultural Context of Therapeutic Choice: Obstetrical Decisions Among the Bariba of Benin* (1982), and *Maternity, Medicine and Power: Reproductive Decisions in Urban Benin* (1989); and coeditor of *Medical Anthropology: A Handbook of Theory and Method, Gender in Cross-Cultural Perspective* (Prentice-Hall 1993, 1997, 2001, 2005), *Gender and Health: An International Perspective* (1996); *Childbirth and Authoritative Knowledge* (1997), and *Small Wars: The Cultural Politics of Childhood.* In addition to several book chapters, she has also authored numerous articles, many of them published in *Medical Anthropological Quarterly* and *Social Science and Medicine.* She is the recipient of many research grants and fellowships and is currently Principal Investigator of a project funded through the Cultural Anthropology Program of the National Science Foundation titled "Reproduction and Representations of Family among Malian Migrants in Paris." She is currently serving on a Senior Advisory Panel of the National Science Foundation and on the Executive Board for the Society for Medical Anthropology. In Dallas she serves as a Community Representative for both Parkland and Baylor Hospitals.

Gender in Cross-Cultural Perspective

I

Biology, Gender, and Human Evolution

What is the role of biology in human behavior? To what extent are differences between men and women explained by biology, by culture, or by an interaction between the two? Is there a biological basis for the sexual division of labor? These questions are hotly debated in the United States as we struggle with such issues as why men dominate the fields of math and science, whether women are equipped for war and combat, and the implications for child development of female participation in the labor force. When issues of gender are considered in a cross-cultural context, we explore whether women are universally subordinated to men and to what extent biological differences explain the allocation of roles and responsibilities between men and women.

The relative importance of biology, or nature, versus culture, or nurture, is an enduring dilemma. This issue was addressed by anthropologist Margaret Mead early in the twentieth century. Using data drawn from her fieldwork in Samoa and New Guinea, Mead (1928, 1935) set out to establish the significance of culture or environment in molding gender differences. She wanted to offer an alternative to the powerful intellectual principles of biological determinism and eugenics (biological engineering) that dominated academic circles in the 1920s. She also hoped to demonstrate to North American women that a range of possibilities was open to them and that the social roles of housework and childrearing were not their inevitable lot. In her view, anatomy was not destiny.

Mead's work was challenged in the 1980s by Derek Freeman (1983). Freeman accused Mead of cultural determinism (that is, giving priority to culture over biology) and opened a lively debate within academic and nonacademic circles (Holmes 1987; Leacock 1993; Orans 1996; Rensberger 1983; Scheper-Hughes 1987; Schneider 1983). For some, Freeman's book was taken (erroneously) as new support for the sociobiological approach to an understanding of human behavior, an approach formulated by Edward Wilson (1975) that contends that there is a genetic basis for all social behavior.

Although few people deny the anatomical and hormonal differences between men and women, they disagree about the importance of these differences for gender roles and personality attributes. A significant body of research, much of it conducted by psychologists, suggests that male and female infants cannot be significantly distinguished by their degree of dependence on parents, their visual and verbal abilities, or their aggression as measured by activity level (Bleier 1984; Fausto-Sterling 1985;

Renzetti and Curran 1989). These characteristics tend to emerge later in the development process, indicating the importance of environment.

One controversy centers on how the brain is organized and to what extent brain lateralization is related to sex differences. One position holds that women are left-brain dominant, giving them superior verbal skills, while men are right-brain dominant, giving them superior visual-spatial skills. While research on variations in the structure and development of male and female brains continues, there are those who contend that to date "there is little evidence indicating that the sexual differentiation of the brain, if it occurs in humans, consequently predisposes males and females to behave in gender-specific ways" (Renzetti and Curran 1989: 33; see also Fausto-Sterling 1985: 44–53).

Within anthropology the role of biology in explaining differences between men and women, including social behaviors such as the division of labor and the tendency for women to be subordinated to men, has been explored within an evolutionary framework. Evolutionary theories fall roughly into four categories: male strength hypotheses, male aggression hypotheses, male bonding hypotheses, and women's childbearing hypotheses. Male strength hypotheses argue that men are physically stronger than women and this gives them superiority. They are larger, and they have stronger muscles and less fat, a pelvis better adapted for sprinting, larger hearts and lungs, and so forth. These physical differences between the males and females of a species are referred to as sexual dimorphism.

Several anthropologists have studied nonhuman primates in order to explore the evolutionary origins of sexual dimorphism (differences in morphology, such as weight and body dimensions) and, by analogy, sexual asymmetry, the sexual division of labor, and the emergence of the nuclear family (Fedigan 1992; Zihlman 1993). This research is part of a large body of literature that uses animals as models for understanding human behavior. One of the earliest statements was Leibowitz's (1975) discussion of the evolution of sex differences. Leibowitz challenged the tendency to link sexual dimorphism to particular sex role patterns by demonstrating enormous variations among different species of primates. Rather than explaining greater male size and strength solely as an adaptation to the roles of protection and provisioning associated with hunting, Leibowitz urged consideration of the reproductive advantage to women of the cessation of growth soon after sexual maturity is reached. In the process, she asked us to reconsider what we mean by strength. She also cautioned that our stereotypes of human male attributes have been drawn from one of the most sexually dimorphic species of nonhuman primates, the plains baboon. As Sperling observed, "This use of the baboon troop as model for ancestral human populations was very influential in forming both sexist and anthropomorphic views of monkeys in popular culture" (1991: 210). Sperling, Fedigan (1986), and Leibowitz have all emphasized the inappropriateness of the "baboonization" of early human life, given the distant relationship between humans and baboons. If we are going to draw comparisons with nonhuman primates, it would be preferable to draw analogies with the great apes, particularly the chimpanzees.

In this book, biologist Marlene Zuk takes up the question of animal models in gender studies, exploring the biological roots of sex differences. She argues forcefully that we should not succumb to stereotypes that would make us pawns of our evolutionary heritage. She cites current research that supports the idea of female preference for particular types of males as a major force in evolution. But she also stresses that there is a great deal of diversity and variation in sexual selection in the animal world and that this variation should offer lessons for how we understand the biological basis of sex differences and mating practices in humans. Even the non-human primate world is characterized by this variation.

A second line of argument attempts to explain male dominance with reference to the biological basis of aggression. Many studies of aggression contend that men are more aggressive than women (Wilson 1975; see Fedigan 1992:71ff for a critique of this position), and often link this difference to levels of male hormones (testosterone). According to Fausto-Sterling (1985: 126), "Many societies, including our own, have tested this belief by castrating men who have a history of violent or anti-social behavior." Scientific research has demonstrated that there is no connection between castration and aggression.

It has also been argued that male aggressive tendencies are an adaptation to the male role in defense (Martin and Voorhies 1975) among both human and nonhuman primates. The problem with any line of argument that links male dominance or male social roles to male aggression is that it ignores the wide variation in behaviors and personalities not only between the sexes, but also within them (Renzetti and Curran 1989: 38). This is certainly true of non-human primates. Smuts (1986), for example, argues that both males and females in various species are capable of opportunistic alliances and defense of victims, depending on the circumstances.

Cross-cultural ethnographic data indicate that human societies also differ in culturally appropriate levels of aggression expressed by men and women (Burbank 1994; Counts, Brown, and Campbell 1992). Richard Lee's (1979) study of conflict and violence among the !Kung San, a relatively egalitarian and peace-loving people, addresses the issue of aggression among men and women. He lends support to the argument that both men and women are aggressive in different ways. !Kung women engage in verbal abuse, but homicides are disproportionately committed by men. Lee compares trends in !Kung violence to those in several other societies. Although his statistics are from the 1950s and 1960s, more recent research indicates that the patterns remain similar. Statistics on criminal activity in the United States indicates that while violent offenses committed by women increased between the mid-1970s and the mid-1980s, they were still predominantly committed by men (Morris 1987: 35). Between 1986 and 1991, the proportion of violent offenses among female prison inmates declined from 40.7 percent to 32.2 percent. Corresponding figures for males were from 55.2 percent and 47.4 percent (U.S. Department of Justice 1991). In 1991, 24 percent of male prison inmates and 20 percent of female prison inmates in England and Wales were incarcerated for "violence against a person" (Lynch et al. 1994). In 2000 in the United States 83 percent of convicted criminals were male and 17 percent were female. In the United Kingdom the comparable figures were 82 percent and 18 percent. While there has been a convergence in recent years between men and women in theft offenses there is little convergence for violent offenses (Austin 1993). A comparison between the !Kung and modern industrial societies suggests that the reasons for gender differences in aggressive behavior are complex. In addition to biological factors, access to weapons, culturally approved expressions of hostility, and the role of the state in the evolution of social control should also be considered.

Among the !Kung the victims of violent crimes tend to be other men, a finding that supports Maccoby and Jacklin's (1974) observation that primate males in general demonstrate more aggression against one another than against females. Dominance of men over women through aggression is thereby brought into question, as is the concept of aggression itself. As Fedigan (1992: 89) suggests, aggression "is such a heterogeneous category of behaviors and interactions that 'amount of aggression' is not a very useful concept." Fausto-Sterling (1985: 129) concurs and points to the fact that no studies on hormone levels and aggression use female subjects or compare men and women. She raises fundamental questions regarding the causal relationship between testosterone levels and aggression.

A third body of evolutionary theory attempts to explain male domination in terms of their supposedly greater ability to form social bonds among themselves (Tiger 1969). This ability is presumed to be genetically programmed and associated with the evolutionary adaptation to hunting. Women, conversely, are thought to lack the genetic code for bonding and are therefore unsuited to the kinds of cooperative and political endeavors that give men power and prestige.

Ehrenberg (in this book) explores this bonding issue in its relation to the development of the sexual division of labor among early humans. She suggests that women were often the social center of groups. They fostered sociability and sharing. Ehrenberg also addresses a much wider debate about the relative contributions of men and women to human evolution. She provides an alternative to what has been labeled the "coattails theory" of biological evolution—"Traits are selected for in males and women evolve by clinging to the men's coattails" (Fedigan 1986: 29). The male bias reflected in this approach has been equally evident in analyses of cultural development, especially in the emphasis on hunting, a male activity, as the distinctive human activity (Lee and DeVore 1968). In her reevaluation of a discussion that essentially omitted half of humanity from the story of evolution, Ehrenberg suggests that hunting probably evolved from the physical, technological, and social innovations associated with gathering (a female activity).

In this book, Lucinda Peach explores how the ideas about male strength, male bonding, and male aggression have shaped the debate in the United States about women in the military. Women are barred from almost all assignments involving the operation of offensive, line-of-sight weapons as well as from all positions involving ground fighting. She suggests that such exclusions are based on assumptions and stereotypes about female "nature" rather than on verifiable gender differences that clearly demonstrate women's inability to perform competently specific combat duties. Warfare is a masculine arena; women need to be protected; women lack the necessary physical strength to perform adequately; the presence of women in combat units would undermine unit cohesion by disrupting male bonding— these are some of the arguments that are put forward to justify the banishment of women from specific military activities. One result, by extension, is that women are denied certain opportunities for promotion that are predicated on active combat service.

A fourth body of theory linking biology to gender difference and gender hierarchy explains the absence of women from cooperative and political activity in the non-domestic sphere (hence their subordination) in terms of their reproductive roles. A corollary of this argument is the idea that women possess a maternal instinct. The fact that women bear children and lactate has been the basis of assertions that women innately experience an attachment to their children that forms the foundation of effective mothering, while men lack a similar capacity to nurture (Peterson 1983; Rossi 1977, 1978). This attachment may be the result of such factors as hormone levels (O'Kelly 1980: 30) or of the experiences of pregnancy, labor, and nursing (Whitbeck 1983: 186). In contrast, Collier and Rosaldo (1981: 315) argue that "there are no facts about human sexual biology that, in and of themselves, have immediate social meanings or institutional consequences. Mothering is a social relation, much like fathering, judging, or ruling, whose meaning and organization must be understood with reference to a particular configuration of relationships within a complex social whole."

The article by Scheper-Hughes (in this book) illustrates this assertion. She examines the inevitability of maternal-infant attachment among mothers in the shantytowns of northeast Brazil. In an environment of poverty, chronic hunger, and economic exploitation, Scheper-Hughes finds that mothers adopt a strategy of delayed attachment and neglect of weaker children thought unlikely to survive. Such attitudes of resignation and fatalism toward the death of children are documented in historical studies of other cultures as well; for example, Ransel's account of child abandonment in Russia relates the passive attitude toward childhood death to child death rates in the 50 percent range (1988: 273; see also Boswell 1988). Parental attitudes are reflected in an entire category of lullabies with the motif of wishing death on babies; women sang these lullabies to infants who were sickly, weak, or crippled (Ransel 1988: 273). Thus, mother love seems less a "natural and universal maternal script" than a luxury reserved for the strongest and healthiest children. In the context of frequent infant death, maternal attachment means grief, and mother love emerges as culturally and socially constructed, rather than as an innate emotion.

Hewlett (in this book) offers a somewhat different perspective on the question of maternal instinct by exploring the role of fatherhood among the Aka pygmies, a group of foragers who live in the tropical forest regions of central Africa. Aka fathers spend a significant portion of their day caring for and nurturing their children. A good father, among the Aka, is a man who stays near his children, shows them affection, and assists the mother with her work. Indeed Aka male–female relations are very egalitarian. Women and men each contribute significantly to subsistence; while Aka men hold all the named positions of status, women challenge men's authority regularly and play a decisive role in all kinds of decision making; physical violence is infrequent, and violence against women is rare (Hewlett 1991). Hewlett suggests that strong father–infant attachment among the Aka can be explained by a range of ecological, social, ideological, and demographic factors. The implications of the Aka example, especially for alternate parenting models in the United States, are clear. As Hewlett argues, "The Aka demonstrate that there are cultural systems where men can be active, intimate and nurturing caregivers" (Hewlett 1991: 171).

Research on nonhuman primates has shown that role variability and plasticity are deeply rooted in the evolutionary history of primates. Cross-cultural data suggest a similar plasticity among humans. The evidence from this section should support the argument that biology merely sets the parameters for a broad range of human behaviors. Thus, biological differences between men and women have no uniform and universal implication for social roles and relations. As Rosaldo and Lamphere (1974: 4) contend, biology, for humans, takes on meaning as it is interpreted in human culture and society.

REFERENCES

Austin, Roy L. 1993. "Recent Trends in Official Male and Female Crime Rates: The Convergence Controversy," *Journal of Criminal Justice* 21: 447–466.

Bleier, Ruth. 1984. *Science and Gender: A Critique of Biology and Its Theories on Women.* New York: Pergamon Press.

Boswell, John. 1988. *The Kindness of Strangers: The Abandonment of Children in Western Europe from Late Antiquity to the Renaissance.* New York: Pantheon Books.

Burbank, Victoria Katherine. 1994. *Fighting Women. Anger and Aggression in Aboriginal Australia.* Berkeley: University of California Press.

Collier, Jane E., and Michelle Z. Rosaldo. 1981. "The Politics of Gender in Simple Societies," In Sherry S. Ortner and Harriet Whitehead (eds.). *Sexual Meanings,* pp. 275–330. Cambridge: Cambridge University Press.

Counts, D, J. Brown, and J. Campbell (eds.). 1992. *Sanctions and Sanctuary: Cultural Perspectives on the Beating of Wives.* Boulder: Westview Press.

Fausto-Sterling, A. 1985. *Myths of Gender.* New York: Basic Books.

Fedigan, Linda Marie. 1986. "The Changing Role of Women in Models of Human Evolution," *Annual Review of Anthropology* 15:25–66.

———. 1992. *Primate Paradigms: Sex Roles and Social Bonds.* Chicago: University of Chicago Press.

Freeman, Derek. 1983. *Margaret Mead and Samoa: The Making and Unmaking of an Anthropological Myth.* Cambridge: Harvard University Press.

Hewlett, Barry S. 1991. *Intimate Fathers: The Nature and Context of Aka Pygmy Paternal Infant Care.* Ann Arbor: University of Michigan Press.

Holmes, Lowell D. 1987. *Quest for the Real Samoa: The Mead/Freeman Controversy and Beyond.* South Hadley, MA: Bergin Garvey

Leacock, Eleanor. 1993. "Women in Samoan History: A Further Critique of Derek Freeman," In Barbara Diane Miller (ed.). *Sex and Gender Hierarchies,* pp. 351–365. Cambridge: Cambridge University Press.

Lee, Richard. 1979. *The !Kung San: Men, Women, and Work in a Foraging Society.* Cambridge: Cambridge University Press.

Lee, Richard S., and Irven DeVore (eds.). 1968. *Man the Hunter.* New York: Aldine.

Leibowitz, Lila. 1975. "Perspectives on the Evolution of Sex Differences," In Rayna Rapp (ed.). *Toward an Anthropology of Women,* pp. 20–35. New York: Monthly Review.

Lynch, James P., Steven K. Smith, Helen A. Graziadei, and Tanutda Pittayathikhun. 1994. "Profiles of Inmates in the United States and in England and Wales," U.S. Department of Justice, Office of Justice Programs, Bureau of Justice Statistics, NFJ-145863.

Maccoby, E.E., and C.N. Jacklin. 1974. *The Psychology of Sex Differences.* Stanford: Stanford University Press.

Martin, M. Kay, and Barbara Voorhies. 1975. *Female of the Species.* New York: Columbia University Press.

Mead, Margaret. 1928. *Coming of Age in Samoa.* New York: Dell.

———. 1935. *Sex and Temperament in Three Primitive Societies.* New York: Dell.

Morris, Allison. 1987. *Women, Crime and Criminal Justice.* Oxford: Basil Blackwell.

O'Kelly, Charlotte. 1980. *Women and Men in Society.* New York: D. Van Nostrand Co.

Orans, Martin. 1996. *Not Even Wrong: Margaret Mead, Derek Freeman and the Samoans.* New York: Chandler and Sharp.

Peterson, Susan Rae. 1983. "Against 'Parenting'," In Joyce Trebilcot (ed.). *Mothering: Essays in Feminist Theory,* pp. 41–62. Totowa, NJ: Rowman and Allanheld.

Ransel, David L. 1988. *Mothers of Misery: Child Abandonment in Russia.* Princeton: Princeton University Press.

Rensberger, Boyce. 1983. "Margaret Mead: The Nature-Nurture Debate: From Samoa to Sociobiology," *Science* 83: 28–46.

Renzetti, Clair M., and Daniel J. Curran. 1989. *Women, Men and Society: The Sociology of Gender.* Needham Heights, Mass: Allyn and Bacon.

Rosaldo, Michelle Z., and Louise Lamphere (eds.). 1974. *Woman, Culture, and Society.* Stanford: Stanford University Press.

Rossi, Alice. 1977. "A Biosocial Perspective on Parenting." *Daedalus* 106: 1–31.

———. 1978. "The Biosocial Side of Parenthood." *Human Nature* 1: 72–79.

Scheper-Hughes, Nancy. 1987. "The Margaret Mead Controversy: Culture, Biology and Anthropological Inquiry," In Herbert Applebaum (ed.). *Perspectives in Cultural Anthropology,* pp. 443–454. Albany: State University of New York Press.

Schneider, David. 1983. "The Coming of a Sage to Samoa," *Natural History* 92(6): 4–10.

Smuts, Barbara. 1986. "Gender, Aggression, and Influence," In Barbara Smuts, Dorothy L. Cheney, Robert Seyfarth, Richard Wrangham and Thomas Struhsaler (eds.). *Primate Societies*, pp. 400–412. Chicago: University of Chicago Press.

Sperling, Susan. 1991. "Baboons with Briefcases vs. Langurs in Lipstick. Feminism and Functionalism in Primate Studies," In Micaela di Leonardo (ed.). *Gender at the Crossroads of Knowledge: Feminist Anthropology in the Postmodern Era*, pp. 204–234. Berkeley: University of California Press.

Tiger, Lionel. 1969. *Men in Groups.* New York: Random House.

Trebilcot, Joyce (ed.). 1983. *Mothering: Essays in Feminist Theory.* Totowa, NJ: Rowman and Allanheld.

U.S. Department of Justice. 1991. *Women in Prison,* Bureau of Justice Statistics, Special Report. Washington D.C.: U.S. Department of Justice.

Whitbeck, Caroline. 1983. "The Maternal Instinct," In Joyce Trebilcot (ed.). *Mothering: Essays in Feminist Theory,* pp. 185–192. Totowa, NJ: Rowman and Allenheld.

Wilson, Edward O. 1975. *Sociobiology: The New Synthesis.* Cambridge: Harvard University Press.

Zihlman, Adrienne L. 1993. "Sex Differences and Gender Hierarchies among Primates: An Evolutionary Perspective," In Barbara Diane Miller (ed.). *Sex and Gender Hierarchies,* pp. 32–56. Cambridge: Cambridge University Press.

Animal Models and Gender

Marlene Zuk

The notion that biology, particularly evolutionary biology, can explain much about gender differences in humans raises hackles in many people. The fear is that science will be used to justify sexism, so that men are "naturally" dominant and women submissive, men natural philanderers and women naturally inclined to stop them from straying. These stereotypes are often said to arise from the animal kingdom, apparently leaving us with no other choices than to accept our evolutionary heritage and resign ourselves to a life of oppression, or reject the idea that biology has any relevance to explaining gender in modern day humans.

In this chapter I hope to counter this impression, both by explaining how biologists view the evolution of sex differences in animals and by showing how understanding the connection between our sexual behavior and that of other species can be liberating rather than restrictive. It is possible to use evolution to inform us about gender without either succumbing to the old stereotypes or substituting new ones; a caricature of a nature-girl is just as damaging as one that stays barefoot and pregnant. Much of the material here is discussed in more detail in Zuk (2002). Numerous other authors have attempted to link feminism and evolutionary biology, and provide feminist critiques of biology from a scientific perspective, perhaps most notably Patricia Gowaty (1997, 2003), but also including Hrdy (1986, 1997, 1999), Keller (1985), Fausto-Sterling (1987, 2003), Liesen (1995), and many others. Here I focus on studies from animals, rather than examining the field of biology as a whole, and examine the use of animal models in studies of gender.

SEXUAL SELECTION

Sex differences in animals are of much interest to biologists, and the body of theory commonly accepted as the explanation of how these differences evolve is called sexual selection. Like its relative natural selection, sexual selection relies on individual differences in the likelihood of leaving genes in succeeding generation, but unlike natural selection, the differential reproduction due to sexual selection occurs because of an individual's ability to acquire the best and/or most mates, not because of survival ability. Thus a bird with a long ungainly tail that attracts more females than his shorter-tailed counterparts is at a sexual selection advantage, even if he has a harder time flying and cannot escape predators as easily.

Also like natural selection, the theory of sexual selection has its origin in the work of Charles Darwin. When Darwin began to develop his ideas about the origin of species, he attempted to explain the evolution of traits that differ between the sexes, but are not necessary for the physical act of reproduction, such as the mane on male lions or the antlers of male deer. Darwin devoted an entire book, *The Descent of Man and Selection in Relation to Sex*, published in 1871, to explaining such traits, which he called secondary sexual characters, and noted that in many cases they simply could not seem to have arisen through natural selection because they are often costly to produce and make their bearers more conspicuous to predators.

Darwin suggested that secondary sexual characters could evolve in one of two ways. First, they could be useful to one sex, usually males, in fighting for access to members of the other sex. Hence, the antlers and horns on male ungulates, such as bighorn sheep, or on the aptly named male rhinoceros beetles. These are weapons, and they are advantageous because better fighters are presumed to get more mates and have more offspring. The second way was more problematic. Darwin noted that females often pay attention to traits like long tails and elaborate plumage during courtship, and he concluded that the traits evolved because the females preferred them. Peahens find peacocks with long tails attractive, just like we do. The sexual selection process, then, consisted of two components: male–male competition, which results in weapons, and female choice, which results in ornaments.

While competition among males for the rights to mate with a female seemed reasonable enough to Darwin's Victorian contemporaries, virtually none of them could swallow the idea that females—of any species, but especially the so-called dumb animals—could possibly do anything so complex as discriminating between males with slightly different plumage colors. Alfred Russell Wallace, who also independently arrived at some of the same conclusions about evolution and natural selection that Darwin did, was particularly vehement in his objections (Wallace 1889). He, and many others, simply found it absurd that females could make the sort of complex decision required by Darwin's theory; it would require the female to possess an aesthetic sense like that of humans, an idea they were unwilling to accept. According to the thinking of his time, even among humans only those of the upper social classes could appreciate aesthetic things like art and music, so it seemed ridiculous to imagine that animals could do something many humans—particularly non Englishmen—could not.

Largely because of this opposition to the idea of female choice, sexual selection as a theory lay dormant for several decades. This time lag meant that while sexual selection and natural selection were introduced at about the same time, sexual selection has not received the same continuous scrutiny by scientists. In some ways, therefore, the study of sex differences is a younger science than the study of species origin and diversity. It was not until the late 1960s that interest in the evolution of sex differences was revived, and the most important contribution to the new theory was a 1972 paper by Robert Trivers, who argued that selection acts differently on males and females because of how they allocate resources into succeeding generations. Females are limited by the number of offspring they can successfully produce and rear. Because they are the sex that supplies the nutrient-rich egg, and often the sex that cares for the young, they have an upper limit set at a relatively low number. They leave the most genes in the next generation by having the highest quality young they can. Which male they mate with could be very important, because a mistake in the form of poor genes or no help with the young could mean that they have lost their whole breeding effort for an entire year.

Males, on the other hand, can leave the most genes in the next generation by fertilizing as many females as possible. Because each mating requires relatively little investment from him, a male who mates with many females sires many more young than a male mating with only one female. Hence, males are expected to compete among themselves for access to females, and females are expected to be choosy, and to mate with the best possible male they can. In addition, females were often referred to as "coy," with the implication that the impetus for sex came largely from males, who fought among themselves to get to the females and allow the choices to occur.

This, of course, is the same division of sexual selection that Darwin originally proposed, and Trivers had given it a new rationale. What he did, too, was bring female choice back to the forefront of sexual selection, and suggest a more modern underlying advantage to it. Furthermore, ideas about the evolution of behavior had advanced enough that scientists no longer worried about an "aesthetic sense" in animals; it didn't matter how females recognized particular males, just that if they did, and it was beneficial, the genes associated with the trait females were attracted to would become more common in the population than the genes of less-preferred traits. Evolutionary biologists, therefore, could ignore questions about motivation and get to the more testable issue of how discrimination among males might result in the evolution of ornamental traits that did not function either in day-to-day life or in male combat.

Current work on female behavior in many species of animals has confirmed Trivers'— and Darwin's—basic idea about female preference for particular types of males being a major force in evolution (Andersson 1994). Again and again, females have been shown to be able to distinguish small differences among available mates, and to prefer to mate with those individuals bearing the most

exaggerated characters. In some cases those males are also more healthy and vigorous, so that ornaments appear to indicate not just attractiveness but the ability to survive.

One of the most well-known examples can be found in peacocks, often used as the symbol of sexual selection with their huge elaborate tails. English gentry have kept peacocks (more correctly, peafowl, as the term peacock strictly speaking refers only to the male) for many years, and British biologist Marion Petrie studied the behavior of flocks that were allowed to range freely in a park in England (Petrie 1994, Petrie and Halliday 1994). She discovered that females did indeed prefer males with greater numbers of eyespots on their tail feathers, and that this preference could be manipulated by cutting the eyespots off of some males' tails and gluing them onto others; females lost interest in the dubbed peacocks, and became attracted to the augmented ones. Even more interesting, she allowed females to mate with males that had variable numbers of eyespots, and then reared all of the offspring in communal incubators to control for differences in maternal care. The chicks fathered by the more ornamented males weighed more than the other chicks, an attribute usually connected with better survival in birds. Indeed, when the individually marked chicks were then released into the park and recaptured the following year, the ones with the more attractive fathers also were more likely to evade predators and survive in the seminatural conditions.

The notion that females are "coy" has not survived so well, as it has been amply demonstrated that females frequently seek out matings with multiple males, and that they often take an active part in many kinds of sexual interactions (Andersson 1994; Jennions and Petrie 2000, 1997; Gowaty and Buschhaus 1998). The reasons behind such behaviors are the subject of intensive study by biologists, and ideas are changing all the time. Nevertheless, the concept of sexual selection, and the core ideas of reproductive competition and mate choice, appears to explain a great deal about animal sexual differences.

The Philandering Male, the Coy Female, and Other Myths

What about humans? Does this mean that males are designed by evolution to be indiscriminate in seeking sex, and females are forever conscribed by the need to raise children alone? The answer is an emphatic no, and to understand why it is important to understand how animal models are used in biology.

First of all, even among animals a great deal of variation exists in the manifestation of the basic principles of sexual selection. For example, male elephant seals come ashore at isolated beaches along the Pacific coast during late summer. The males can weigh up to three tons, more than twice the size of females, and spend several weeks fighting among themselves for dominance. Females arrive after the males, and after they come ashore the dominant males attempt to sequester groups of females and keep them from rival males; the females themselves, although they do exert some degree of choice, are constrained in their movements by the males (Le Boeuf and Reiter 1988, Galimberti et al. 2002). The male competition aspect of sexual selection appears to prevail in this species.

In contrast, female bowerbirds have virtually total control over mating. This group of several species of birds is found in Australia and New Guinea. The males construct elaborate structures out of twigs, grass and other objects, and then decorate them with ornaments that can include plastic items as well as fruit, flowers, bones, and shells (Borgia 1995, Uy et al. 2001, Madden 2003). Each species has a characteristic bower type. After the bowers are made, males wait for females to visit; the bowers are generally rather widely separated, so males cannot hear or see each other when they are tending their bowers. A female generally visits the bowers of several males before choosing one of them. When a female arrives, the male courts her with elaborate vocal and visual displays, but he cannot prevent a female from leaving to sample additional males, something the females commonly do. Eventually a female selects a male, mates with him, and leaves to lay her eggs and rear her chicks alone. The bower is not a nest, and males take no part in rearing offspring. Female choice, rather than male competition, is paramount among bowerbirds.

These two systems illustrate completely different "solutions" to the same problem of reproduction faced by all species. Other examples, including substantial male contributions to offspring, extreme female aggression and competition, and sexual behavior outside the fertile period, could also be cited. Among bonobos, small relatives of chimpanzees, sexual activity occurs between virtually all members of a social group, including members of the same sex. This point is an important one: although male competition and female choice are the basic elements of sexual selection, even among animals tremendous diversity exists in how they are implemented. Those unfamiliar with the behavior of animals in the wild often do not realize that animal family life, or lack of it, is not a simplified version of human existence, even human existence in an imaginary early hunter–gatherer society. It is simply incorrect to suggest that finding a link between our gender-related behavior and that of other animals would inevitably mean a link to a male-dominated social system. A single animal model for the origin of sex roles does not exist, even if we were to accept that finding such a model would make it impossible to act outside of it.

Note that this diversity also precludes claiming that women are naturally caring, verbal, peace loving, or sexually adventurous. Substituting one stereotype, of a strong Amazon, for the more traditional one of a coy stay at home mom uninterested in sex, does not solve the problem. We may like the previously unappreciated female bonobo, with her overt sexuality, more than another animal model, but it is important to remember that the animals are model systems for understanding a range of behaviors, and not role models.

How, then, can we learn from animals about gender and sex roles? Below I detail two examples of topics that are often discussed in the context of animal behavior, maternal instinct and mate fidelity. I hope to show that we can learn from biology without either succumbing to old stereotypes or substituting new ones for them.

MATERNAL INSTINCT
AND MOTHER LOVE

One of the cornerstones of popular belief in a biological basis for gender-based behavior is that females instinctively care for their young. If maternal care-giving behavior is natural, then presumably all women want to do it, know how to do it without learning how, and feel deprived if they do not. A modern version of the maternal instinct is the mother–infant bond, this mysterious connection that supposedly naturally occurs between a woman and her child soon after birth.

How fixed is this bond, and how ingrained in a female's psyche is the ability—and even the desire—to care for her young? It would seem reasonable to assume that animals should show a behavior that women are supposed to have inherited, and it is therefore instructive to look at research from the 1950s and 1960s using rhesus macaques, the monkeys used in numerous medical and behavioral studies; the "Rh" in Rh-positive or Rh-negative blood types comes from the name of this species. Two psychologists named Harry and Margaret Harlow were interested in understanding the effects of social deprivation on humans, the kind of deprivation that arises through abuse, neglect, and warfare. The Harlows wanted to know how these problems arose and thus perhaps gain insight into correcting them. They could not, of course, perform controlled experiments on human children, and so they used an animal model and manipulated the early rearing environment of groups of macaques so that deprived youngsters could be compared to more normally raised controls. The Harlows' research is expertly analyzed by Deborah Blum (2002), who also raises some of the interesting ethical issues that arise from the treatment of the monkeys.

The infant macaques were taken from their mothers at birth, and raised under one of several different sets of conditions. For example, some were allowed access to a monkey-sized, wire-covered model that had a bottle attached to it approximately where the nipple of a mother monkey might be. The bottle was filled with milk and the cages cleaned at appropriate intervals by human caretakers who had no contact with the monkeys. Other baby macaques had the wire-covered model with the food, and in addition were given another model covered with terrycloth. In some instances, the monkeys saw or contacted other equally deprived infants during their development, while in others they were kept in isolation. As the monkeys grew up, they were used in a variety of tests to examine their social behavior and eventually their ability to mate and have offspring of their own.

To the surprise of few, the socially deprived monkeys did not exhibit normal behavior. They were more fearful when new stimuli were introduced to their cages, they did not interact with other juvenile monkeys the way that babies raised with their mothers did, and they showed numerous other signs of psychological abnormality. Interestingly, however, the babies given the cloth-covered model "mother" were better adjusted than those given only the wire model, and when a novel and potentially frightening object was introduced into the cage, they ran not to the source of food but to the source of what the Harlows called "contact comfort." In other words, clinging to a soft object is more soothing than returning to the place where essential nourishment is found.

The Harlows went on from these studies to discuss a number of fascinating theories about the need for this contact comfort and its potential value in helping children with minimal resources develop more normally. Their ideas have been thoroughly dissected—and in some cases debunked—by developmental psychologists. For my purposes here, however, a more relevant finding was the discovery that females raised with the models had difficulties in mating with male monkeys once they reached sexual maturity. They simply did not know how to have sex— they didn't know the postures, the signals, the responses. Even more significant, if they were artificially inseminated and became pregnant, they were incapable of caring for the resulting young, and their infants had to be removed from their mothers lest they be seriously injured. The mothers did get better with experience, so that subsequent young fared better, but the early babies were as foreign as extra-terrestrials to their mothers.

These results seem to flatly contradict the notion of a simple maternal instinct. Even mother monkeys, animals very similar to ourselves, do not automatically feel bonded to their infants, much less know how to take care of them. The mystical mother–child relationship is shattered when the mother is raised without others of her kind. This situation is clearly unusual, of course. The monkeys are not usually raised by wire models, and under natural circumstances they can relate to their offspring perfectly well. This, however, is precisely my point: even a behavior supposedly as sacrosanct at the love a mother will have for her child depends on the environment. And therefore it is also clear that the evidence does not support assuming a particular behavior in humans is "natural," even one as supposedly biological as mothering.

The consequences of acknowledging this fact are many. If one is freed from the idea of the maternal instinct, one is also freed from equating being female to being a mother, as if no other role was possible or important. Examining female behavior, in humans or animals, is therefore enriched by abandoning the stereotype. Females can exhibit all kinds of behavior, and females, human or not, are not only defined by their relationship to their offspring. One can also start dissecting maternal behavior itself, asking questions about what kind and how much of an investment would benefit mothers under different circumstances. The "maternal-infant bond" becomes a malleable behavior rather than a fixed biological entity.

The idea of variable mothering leads to some interesting and sometimes startling predictions. For example, the eminent anthropologist Sarah Blaffer Hrdy has found that infanticide can be adaptive for monkeys and other mammals that exhibit it (Hausfater and Hrdy 1984). While I hasten to point out that this hardly justifies the behavior in humans, it does suggest that an analysis that does not focus exclusively on the stereotypical nurturing mother can be enlightening.

ADULTERY AND PHILANDERING MALES

Infidelity, again whether in humans or animals, is a topic of great interest to those wanting to understand whether animals show us our own biologically based behaviors. The classic stereotype of male nature is of the man seeking multiple sexual partners while the woman is content to remain with a single partner for her entire life. Infidelity has also recently become a subject of interest to scientists, because the advent of genetic testing has allowed us to sample the DNA from a set of chicks in a nest and compare it to the DNA of the male and female associated with the young. As it turns out, so-called extra-pair paternity is quite common among birds; estimates of the proportion of offspring sired by males other than the one attending a female and her nest range from 0 in snow geese to a whopping 90% in a species of fairy wren, brilliantly colored tiny birds from Australia (Griffith et al. 2002, Griffith and Montgomerie 2003). Although frequently only one male and one female are seen associating, including feeding and protecting the young, it has become apparent that additional males fathered offspring in the nest. In mammals that have multiple young in a litter, the young may also have more than one father, though mammals are less likely to appear to be monogamous in the first place.

This discovery was quite a shock to scientists, because outwardly it had appeared that most birds were monogamous. If this was not the case, many questions arose. What are the advantages to females of having multiple fathers for her brood? Do males attempt to deter females from such multiple mating, since it is costly to them to help rear offspring not their own? Why, given the apparent disparity of investment of males and females in offspring, should females pursue quantity rather than quality of mates? Questions like these are currently the subject of ongoing research in a variety of species.

The occurrence of extra-pair mating is also rather surprising to non-scientists, perhaps because the birds unwittingly had served as something of a role model for human marriage. It is tempting to conclude that if warblers, robins, and other models of monogamy are doing it, we should admit that extra-pair copulation, or adultery—or whatever term you prefer—is natural, expected, and maybe we should stop making such a fuss about it and resign ourselves to our evolutionary heritage.

But the problem is that the birds are not "cheating," they are just doing what they do, and they did not invent the rules about the pair bond between a male and female, we did. It isn't cheating if there are no rules to break. Some animals are monogamous, some are not, and one mating system is no more "natural," or "biological," than the other. Certainly multiple mating appears to be favored in many species, more species than had previously been believed, but that does not argue for the death of fidelity. Instead, it suggests a reexamination of sexual selection theory, something that is already occurring among scientists. This brings up an important point about the use of animal models for human behavior. Animals are useful for showing us what kinds of solutions exist to the common biological problems involved in survival and reproduction. How does the environment influence the costs and benefits of multiple mating? This is an interesting and relevant question—whether human males are biologically destined to cheat on their wives is not. As with maternal behavior, in mating systems multiple solutions are virtually always the norm, and there is no single natural male or female role.

What about the primates, our closest relatives? Here too, the sex role stereotypes are

crumbling. Male dominance was viewed as the major force in primate societies when most monkeys and apes were studied in the middle of the twentieth century (Strum and Fedigan 2000), with females viewed as relatively uninterested in sex outside the time when they were most likely to become pregnant. However, probably not coincidentally with the growing numbers of women entering primatology, as more species were studied more intensively, it soon became clear that male-female relationships were more complex and furthermore that females often sought out sex (sometimes with both males and females) outside the period of maximum fertility (Smuts 1999, Strum and Fedigan 2000). In olive baboons, some males and females became what primatologist Barbara Smuts called "friends," with bonds of association that went beyond the brief act of sex itself (Smuts 1999). This complexity argues against the caricature of sex-crazed males and demure females that people sometimes thinks constitutes our heritage from other animals.

Studying a diversity of human cultures is also of interest once we recognize this multiplicity of solutions in other animals. What patterns of courtship and marriage seem to be universal, and what patterns depend on environmental attributes such as food availability and distribution?

Model Systems and Role Models

It is also important to remember not to substitute one stereotype for another; it would be just as fallacious to conclude that all women are sexual adventuresses as to adhere to the old model of the frigid female. Deciding that biology is relevant to understanding gender does not mean that we imitate the species we prefer; model systems like the fruit flies used in genetics are useful tools for generalizing because we understand a great deal about them, but, as I mentioned earlier, they should not be confused with role models. Animals tell us that females can be assertive, but perhaps more important they tell us that females are variable. Furthermore, like many other biologists, I urge caution in interpreting nature.

The naturalistic fallacy holds that what is natural is good, but what is natural can't be inherently "good" any more than it can be inherently amusing, inherently painful, or more likely to keep your hair shiny. Finding out that some animals eat their young says no more about the ethics of infanticide than finding out that some animals are yellow says about fashion trends.

As a scientist studying animals, not humans, I am also concerned about how our verdict of cheating affects our views of the animals themselves. Some of the early papers on extra-pair paternity in birds are interestingly divided in whom is portrayed as the active party in the behavior. Initially, there seemed to be two approaches, neither one particularly favorable to females. Either the males were roaming around taking advantage of hapless females waiting innocently in their own territories for the breadwinner males to come home with the worms, or else females were brazen hussies, seducing blameless males who otherwise would not have strayed from the path of moral righteousness into turpitude. One scientist refers rather peevishly to "female promiscuity" in blackbirds. Several papers, including one published in the prestigious journal *Nature*, call young birds fathered by males not paired with the mother as "illegitimate," as if their parents had tiny avian marriage licenses and chirped their vows (Gyllensten et al. 1990, Hassequist et al. 1995, Bjornstad and Lifjeld 1997). Scientists, of course, are subject to social influences just like other people, but we should try not to allow our prejudices to influence our interpretation of what we see the animals doing. A paper on Tasmanian native hens, birds with a rather complex set of relationships between the sexes, discussed what appears to be polyandry, multiple males associated with a single female (Maynard Smith and Ridpath 1972). The paper refers to this behavior as "wife-sharing," but I have never seen multiple females associated with a male, its mirror image, and a common mating pattern, called "husband-sharing." Making the males the active parties (they "share" the female, as if she were a six-pack of beer) may reduce the likelihood of noticing what the females do, of seeing things from their point of view. Similarly, if we only see female baboons as mothers, we are less likely to notice that in fact their relationships, not those of males, determine troop structure and movement (Smuts 1999).

CONCLUSIONS

It is no surprise that many people get twitchy when they hear about any so-called "biological" explanations of behavior in humans. They are also nervous when scientists study behaviors in animals that seem to occur in humans, for the reasons I described above. Here I have tried to ameliorate this fear, though at least in part it should be replaced with caution and awareness. Biology has great potential for harming women, but it is through our misbehavior, not the science itself. Biology can extend the boundaries of our thinking about gender as it can for so many other ideas. Contrary to popular belief, biology does not set limits, it demolishes them.

It is also important to remember that discoveries of mate fidelity, male tenderness or female sexual violence do not argue for a human nature that includes or excludes them. Evolution is an important explanation for the origin and diversity of life on earth, including human life. It helps us understand how organisms are related to each other, how the species that occur on a coral reef got there, whether a reed warbler female is likely to have any surviving young in a given year, how the members of chimpanzee groups sometimes benefit by being kind to one another, and why diet may help determine the probability of getting heart disease. Suggesting that evolutionary biology is irrelevant to human lives is as foolish as suggesting that it is irrelevant to the lives of fruit flies. Men and women are not the same, both from the standpoint of physiology and evolution. Neither are male and female goldfish, or fruit flies, or weasels. But this does not mean that men and women inherit templates of irreversible behavior.

REFERENCES

Andersson, M. 1994. Sexual selection. Princeton University Press, Princeton.

Bjornstad, G. and Lifjeld, J.T. 1997. High frequency of extra-pair paternity in a dense and synchronous population of Willow Warblers *Phylloscopus trochilus*. J. Avian Biol. 28 (4): 319–324.

Blum, D. 2002. Love at Goon Park. Perseus Publishing, New York.

Borgia, G. 1995. Why do bowerbirds build bowers? Amer. Sci. 83: 542–547.

Darwin, C. 1871. The Descent of Man and Selection in Relation to Sex. Modern Library reissue, New York.

Fausto-Sterling, A. 1987. Myths of gender: Biological Theories about Women and Men. Basic Books, New York.

Fausto-Sterling, A. 2003. Science matters, culture matters. Perspec. Biol. Med. 46:109–124.

Galimberti, F., Fabiani, A. and Sanvito, S. 2002. Measures of breeding inequality: a case study in southern elephant seals. Can. J. Zool. 80: 1240–1249.

Gowaty, P.A. and Buschhaus, N. 1998. Ultimate causation of aggressive and forced copulation in birds: Female resistance, the CODE hypothesis, and social monogamy. Amer. Zool. 38: 207–225.

Gowaty, P.A. (ed.) 1997. Feminism and evolutionary biology: boundaries, intersections, and frontiers. Chapman and Hall, New York.

Gowaty, P.A. 2003. Sexual natures: How feminism changed evolutionary. Signs 28: 901–921.

Griffith, S.C., Owens I.P.F., and Thuman K.A. 2002. Extra pair paternity in birds: a review of interspecific variation and adaptive function. Molec. Ecol. 11: 2195–2212.

Griffith S.C. and Montgomerie, R. 2003. Why do birds engage in extra-pair copulation? Nature 422: 833–833.

Gyllensten, U.B., Jakobsson, S., and Temrin, H. 1990. No evidence for illegitimate young in monogamous and polygynous warblers. Nature 343: 168–170.

Hasselquist, D., Bensch, S. and von Schantz, T. 1995. Low frequency of extrapair paternity in the polygynous great reed warbler *Acrocephalus arundinaceus*. Behav. Ecol. 6: 27–38.

Hausfater, G. and Hrdy, S.B. (eds.) 1984. Infanticide: Comparative and Evolutionary Perspectives. Aldine de Gruyter, New York.

Hrdy, S.B. 1986. Empathy, polyandry, and the myth of the coy female. In: Feminist approaches to science, R. Bleier, ed. Pergamon Press, NY.

Hrdy, S.B. 1997. Raising Darwin's consciousness— Female sexuality and the prehominid origins of patriarchy. Human Nature 8:1–49.

Hrdy, S.B. 1999. Mother nature. Pantheon, New York.

Jennions, M.D. and Petrie, M. 2000. Why do females mate multiply? A review of the genetic benefits. Biol. Rev. Cam. Phil. Soc. 75: 21–64.

Jennions, M.D. and Petrie, M. 1997. Variation in mate choice and mating preferences: A review of causes and consequences. Biol. Rev. Cam. Phil. Soc. 72: 283–327

Keller, E.F. 1985. Reflections on gender and science. Yale University Press, New Haven.

Le Boeuf, B.J. and Reiter, J. 1988. Lifetime reproductive success in northern elephant seals. pp 344–362 in Reproductive Success: studies of individual variation in contrasting breeding systems, T.H. Clutton-Brock, ed. University of Chicago Press, Chicago.

Liesen, L.T. 1995. Feminism and the politics of reproductive strategies. Politics Life Sci. 14:145–162.

Madden, J.R. 2003. Male spotted bowerbirds preferentially choose, arrange and proffer objects that are good predictors of mating success. Behav. Ecol. Sociobiol. 53 (5): 263–268.

Maynard Smith, J. and Ridpath, M.G. 1972. Wife sharing in the Tasmanian native hen, *Tribonyx mortierii*: a case of kin selection? Amer. Nat. 106:447–452.

Petrie, M. 1994. Improved growth and survival of offspring of peacocks with more elaborate trains. Nature 371: 598–599.

Petrie, M. and Halliday, T. 1994. Experimental and natural changes in the peacock's (*Pave cristatus*) train can affect mating success. Behav. Ecol. Sociobiol. 35: 213–217.

Smuts, B.B. 1999. Sex and friendship in baboons. 2nd ed. Harvard University Press, Cambridge, MA.

Strum, S.C. and Fedigan, L.M. (eds.) 2000. Primate encounters: Models of science, gender, and society. University of Chicago Press, Chicago.

Trivers, R.L. 1972. Parental investment and sexual selection. Pp 136–179 In B. Campbell, ed., Sexual selection and the descent of man, 1871–1971. Heinemann, London.

Uy, J.A.C., Patricelli, G.L. and Borgia, G. 2001. Complex mate searching in the satin bowerbird *Ptilonorhynchus violaceus*. Amer. Nat. 158: 530–542.

Wallace, A.R. 1889. Darwinism: an exposition of the theory of natural selection with some of its applications. MacMillan Press, London.

Zuk, M. 2002. Sexual selections: what we can and can't learn about sex from animals. University of California Press, Berkeley.

The Role of Women in Human Evolution

Margaret Ehrenberg

Human evolution has traditionally been discussed in terms of the role which "Man the Hunter" played in devising weapons and tools for catching and slaughtering animals for food, how he needed to walk upright on two feet to see his prey above the tall savanna grass, and how he was more successful than other species in his hunting exploits because he teamed up with other men and learnt the value of co-operation. And what of "woman", meanwhile? Was she sitting at home, twiddling her thumbs, waiting for "man" to feed her and increase his brain capacity and abilities until he became "*Homo sapiens sapiens*?" The argument went that as human evolution progressed, more and more time was needed to look after infants, so females no longer had time to hunt, and male co-operative hunting became essential in order that the men could bring enough food home to feed the family. As a result, male-female bonding in monogamous unions was an essential and a very early development. While most accounts of human evolution have assumed that all the advances in human physical and cultural development were led by men, a number of recent studies suggest alternative possibilities and have pointed out the vital role which must have been played by women.

Research into the earliest stages of human evolution is based on three strands of evidence. Physical anthropologists study the remains of early human skeletons, to assess the way in which they developed. For example, it is possible to tell from the structure of the legs and back whether an individual would have walked upright on two legs, or used the forearms for balance. Changes in the size of the skull through time give an indication of brain capacity. Secondly, the study of the behavior of other animals, and especially primates, particularly those species closest to humans such as apes and chimpanzees, reveals some patterns that may have been shared by the earliest humans before cultural norms began to play an overriding part. For example, chimpanzees may be studied to see if males and females eat or collect different foods, or to find out whether they share any of the differences in child-care practices seen in human women and men. Thirdly, archaeological evidence for tools, settlements, environment and diet sheds light on the social and cultural development of the earliest humans.

Some scholars within all these three areas have turned away from the traditional male-dominated view of evolution and have begun to formulate an alternative model, allowing that female primates and hominids have played an important part, if not the key role, in the development of human behavior. Different authors have stressed different factors in this development. Adrienne Zihlman[1] argues that changes in the environment were crucial in necessitating social and economic changes in human populations in order to exploit this environment efficiently. Sally Slocum[2] points out that the only division of labor by sex amongst other primates is that females take primary care of their young, while males tend to dominate in protecting the group. She argues that a division of labor in food collecting is therefore unlikely to have been a key feature of early human behavior. Other feminist writers[3] suggest that the female's choice of a co-operative and gentle mate was a critical factor in human evolution, as the chances of survival were improved by caring more closely for near relatives; in all mammals, and especially in primates, this is much more a female task or trait.

Among the physical changes which took place in the early stages of human evolution were increases in the size of the brain and the teeth; a decrease in sexual dimorphism (difference in size between males and females); increased hairlessness over the body; and bipedalism, or walking on two feet, rather than using the forelimbs for support, as chimpanzees and apes do. While an infant chimpanzee can cling to its mother's cover of body hair, leaving her hands free for walking or carrying food, a young human or early hairless hominid would need to be carried by the mother: this seems a much more likely stimulus both to bipedalism and to the invention of tools for carrying the infant as well as food than is the need to see prey animals over tall savanna grass and to throw simple weapons at them, which has been the traditional explanation for these changes.

A key aspect of the debate about the evolution of sex-role behavior centers on food collection, and the way in which females and males may have foraged for different foods. Many discussions, including those written by some feminist anthropologists, assume that from a very early stage in evolution females primarily gathered plant foods, while males mainly hunted animals, the pattern usual in modern hunter-gatherer societies. Many recent arguments about other aspects of the role played by females in human social and technological evolution depend on this belief, even though it is rarely argued out fully. At one end of the scale other primates show little evidence for differences in food collecting behavior between females and males, while at the other all modern foragers apparently divide subsistence tasks on the basis of sex. The question, therefore, is when and why this difference came about, and whether looking after young offspring would have a limiting effect on hunting by females. One view[4] suggests that

although males unburdened by young might have caught meat more often than females, a regular division of labor would probably have come quite late in human evolution, as the physical differences between females and males are insufficient to make one sex or the other more suitable for either task. Recent work has also questioned whether meat actually filled a significant part of the early human diet, suggesting that this would have been far more like that of other primates, based almost entirely on a wide range of plant foods. What meat was eaten in the earliest phases of the Paleolithic was probably scavenged, rather than hunted. Both these factors are problematic for the traditional view, as they suggest that hunting was neither an important factor in physical evolution, nor in the social and economic balance between female and male activities. Both sexes would have obtained vegetable foods and occasional meat, and brought some of their day's collection back to the homebase for sharing.

If there was little division of labor in the earliest phase of human development, when and why did it become usual? Two chronological points may have provided possible contexts. Initially, hominids would have been content to catch small game or to scavenge meat caught by other animals, or to collect those that had died naturally, but perhaps around 100,000 years ago they developed suitable tools and techniques for hunting large animals. While hunting small game would not have been hazardous, big-game hunting might often have resulted in death or injury to the hunter rather than the hunted. In small societies, such as these early human groups and present-day forager societies, every unexpected death is a serious blow to the viability of the community, particularly the death of women of child-bearing age. Mobility would also have been more important in hunting large game; the hunter would have to move rapidly and quietly, with hands free to throw a spear or shoot an arrow. It would not be possible to do this while carrying a bag or basket of gathered food, nor a young child, who might cause an additional hazard by making a noise at a crucial moment. Thus gathering and hunting become incompatible as simultaneous occupations; pregnant women and those carrying very small infants would have found hunting difficult, though gathering is quite easily combined with looking after young children. It is therefore possible that at this stage women began to hunt less, until a regular pattern of dividing subsistence tasks was established.[5]

Another possible context for the origin of the division of labor[6] is the change in environment which hominids found when they first entered Europe. It is argued that this spread could not have occurred until the perceptual problems of coping with a new environment had been resolved, by splitting food foraging into separate tasks. During the Lower Paleolithic in East Africa, plants and animals would have been abundant, so vegetable foods and small game would have provided plenty of easily obtainable food with only the occasional large game caught to supplement the diet. As the hominid population increased and went in search of new territory, some hominids moved north into Europe. There they encountered colder conditions in which plant foods were harder to come by, so meat would have formed a more significant part of their diet. If this problem was not serious enough to necessitate a solution when hominids first moved into Europe, it would have become so with the onset of the last glaciation when conditions became very much colder and vegetation more sparse (this period equates archaeologically with the Upper Paleolithic). The time and danger involved in hunting large animals became more worthwhile, but would not have provided a regular, guaranteed source of food, and would have been more dangerous. A solution might have been for only part of the community to concentrate on hunting, while the rest continued gathering plants and small animals. It is likely that this division would usually have been on a female-male basis for the reasons already suggested.

On the other hand, more detailed studies of chimpanzee behavior suggest that there may be slight differences in the food collecting behavior of females and males of non-human primates, which could argue for an early gathering/hunting division.[7] Although chimpanzees eat very little animal flesh, males make nearly all the kills and eat more of the meat; however, termite fishing, involving the use of sticks as fishing rods to poke into the termite mounds, a skilled task requiring patience and simple tool use, is far more commonly carried out by females. Whether the "changing environment" theory or the latter argument is preferred, both hypotheses suggest that a division of labor on the basis of sex would have been an early development in human history.

Tool-using was once thought to be a distinctly human attribute, but in simple form it is now known to be shared with several of the higher primates, and even other animals and birds. Most early theories suggested that tool-using by humans was intimately linked with hunting, which in turn was assumed to be a male task, and that the earliest tools would have been spears for hunting animals and stone knives or choppers for butchery. This idea was partly encouraged by the archaeological evidence of the early stone tools, most of which are thought to have had such functions. However, this is partly a circular argument, as on the one hand the function of these tools is far from certain, and many would have been just as useful for cracking nuts or digging roots, and on the other, the very earliest tools would almost certainly have been made of wood, skins or other perishable material. Artifacts such as digging sticks, skin bags, nets, clubs and spears can be made entirely of organic materials, and would not have survived, so the extant stone tools are probably quite late in the sequence of hominid tool use. The evidence of tool use by other primates and by modern foragers, combined with a more balanced theoretical view, suggests that other factors and possibilities need to be considered.

One of the most significant human tools must be the container. Whether it be a skin bag, a basket, a wooden bowl or pottery jar, it allows us to carry items around or store them safely in one place. The container may have been one of the earliest tools to be invented, though unfortunately there is little archaeological evidence to demonstrate this. Chimpanzees can carry things in the skinfold in their groin, but when hominids became bipedal this skin was stretched and the fold was lost. The use of a large leaf or an animal skin, carried over one arm or the developing shoulder, or tied to the waist, might have replicated this lost natural carrier.[8] One of the most important things that a female hominid would need to carry would be her young offspring. The complex interaction of bipedalism, food gathering, the loss of hair for the infant to cling to, and changes in the structure of the toes which made them useless for clinging to its mother would have made it necessary for the mother to carry the child. The development of a sling for supporting the infant, found in almost all modern societies, including foraging groups, is likely to have been among the earliest applications of the container.

The first tools to aid in foraging and preparing foodstuffs are perhaps more likely to have been used in connection with plant foods and small animals than in the hunting of large mammals. The tools and actions required for termite fishing, for example, are not unlike those required for digging up roots more easily. Modern foraging groups often choose a particularly suitable stone to use as an anvil for cracking nuts, which they leave under a particular tree and then return to it on subsequent occasions. Higher primates also use stones for cracking nuts, so it is very likely that early hominids would have done this even before tools were used for hunting. The role of women as tool inventors, perhaps contributing many of the major categories of tools that are most essential even today, cannot be dismissed.

The introduction of food gathering, as opposed to each individual eating what food was available where it was found, was another significant advance which would both have necessitated and been made possible by the invention of the container. More food might be gathered than was needed immediately by one individual, either for giving to someone else or for later consumption. With the exception of parents feeding very young offspring,

this behavior is unusual among other animals and presumably would not have been common amongst the very earliest hominids, but gradually developed to become a hallmark of human behavior. Another change would have involved carrying this food to a base, which would imply both conceptual and physical changes, made possible by the use of containers, and may also have made it necessary to walk on two legs, leaving the hands free to carry the food, either directly or in containers. The development of consistent sharing, not only with offspring but also with others in the group, and exchanging food brought from different environments of savanna and forest would have been a stage towards living in regular social groups.

Environmental changes would also have led to social changes within early hominid groups. In savanna grassland, as opposed to forest, it would have been more difficult to find safe places to sleep overnight, and water would have been harder to obtain. Once a suitable location was discovered, there would have been a greater tendency to remain there as long as possible rather than sleeping in a different place each night, thus introducing the idea of a homebase.

Women also played a key role in social development. A major difference between human development and that of other animals is the greater length of time during which infants need to be cared for and fed: this has probably contributed to a number of human characteristics, including food sharing and long-term male–female bonding. The sharing of food between mother and offspring would necessarily have continued for longer in early hominids than in other primates, and it is argued that when a mammal too large to be consumed by the hunters alone was killed, the males would have shared it with those who had shared with them in their youth, that is their mothers and sisters, rather than with their sexual partners. This argument is supported by a primate study[9] that shows that banana sharing almost always takes place within matrifocal groups rather than between sexual partners. This has important implications for the primacy or otherwise of monogamy and marriage. Several scholars have also pointed out that in this situation the female would choose to mate with a male who was particularly sociable and willing to share food with his partner while she was looking after a very young infant. As well as preferring those most willing to share, females would choose those males who appeared to be most friendly. Not surprisingly, female chimpanzees will not mate with males who are aggressive towards them. The more friendly-looking males would probably have been smaller, or nearer in size to the female, and would have had less pronounced teeth, and therefore have been less aggressive-looking. Over thousands of years this female sexual preference would have led to gradual evolutionary changes in favor of smaller, less aggressive, males.

The stronger tie between mother and offspring caused by the longer period of time during which human infants need to be cared for would have resulted in closer social bonds than are found in other species. The primary bond between mother and offspring would be supplemented by sibling ties between sisters and brothers growing up together. Older offspring would be encouraged or socialized to contribute towards the care of younger siblings, including grooming, sharing food, playing and helping to protect them. The natural focus of such a group would clearly be the mother rather than, as is so often supposed, any male figure. Moreover, this group behavior would lead to increased sociability in the male as well as in the species in general. The role of the female, both in fostering this increased sociability in the species and as the primary teacher of technological innovations during this long period of caring, must be recognized.

An increase in human sociability, and particularly female sociability, would have had a number of other positive side-effects. As a result of a mutual willingness to share food and food resources, each individual would have had more access to overlapping gathering areas when a particular resource was abundant. This in turn might greatly increase the chances of the offspring being well fed and therefore surviving, and thus of the survival of the species in general. As the ability to communicate precisely increased with the development of language, it would have become possible for humans to have ordered social relationships with more individuals and other groups. This would have evolved into a pattern very similar to that found in modern foraging groups, many of which include distant relations who regularly meet up with other groups in the course of their annual movements. Males who had moved out of the matrifocal group in order to mate would have learnt a pattern of friendly contact with their ancestral females when they met them in the course of their foraging.

It can therefore be argued that the crucial steps in human development were predominantly inspired by females. These include economic and technological innovations, and the role of females as the social center of groups. This contrasts sharply with the traditional picture of the male as protector and hunter, bringing food back to a pair-bonded female. That model treats masculine aggression as normal, assumes that long-term, one-to-one, male–female bonding was a primary development, with the male as the major food provider, and that male dominance was inherently linked to hunting skills. None of these patterns, however, accords with the behavior of any but the traditional Western male. Other male primates do not follow this pattern, nor do non-Western human groups, in particular those foraging societies whose lifestyle in many ways accords most closely with putative early human and Paleolithic cultural patterns.

NOTES

1. Zihlman, 1981.
2. Slocum, 1975.
3. For example, Tanner, 1981; Martin and Voorhies, 1975.
4. Zihlman, 1981; Isaac and Crader, 1981.
5. Zihlman, 1978; the same arguments are used by Friedl, 1975 and 1978, who explains in more detail than here why present-day foragers divide food collecting tasks along gender lines.
6. Dennell, 1983, 55.

7. McGrew, 1981; Goodall, 1986.
8. Tanner and Zihlman, 1976.
9. McGrew, 1981, 47.

REFERENCES

Dennell, R. 1983. *European Economic Prehistory.* London: Academic Press.

Friedl, E. 1975. *Women and Men: An Anthropologist's View.* New York: Holt, Rinehart and Winston.

———. 1978. "Society and sex roles." *Human Nature* 1: 68–75.

Goodall, J. 1986. *The Chimpanzees of Gombe: Patterns of Behavior.* Cambridge, MA: Harvard University Press.

Isaac, G. and Crader, D. 1981. "To what extent were early hominids carnivorous?" In Teleki, G. (ed.). *Omnivorous Primates: Gathering and Hunting in Human Evolution.* New York: Columbia University Press.

Martin, M.K. and Voorhies, B. 1975. *Female of the Species.* New York: Columbia University Press.

McGrew, W. 1981. "The female chimpanzee as a human evolutionary prototype." In Dahlberg, Frances (ed.). *Woman The Gatherer.* New Haven: Yale University Press.

Slocum, S. 1975. "Woman the gatherer: male bias in anthropology." In Reiter, Rayna R. (ed.). *Toward an Anthropology of Women.* New York: Monthly Review Press.

Tanner, N. 1981. *On Becoming Human.* Cambridge: Cambridge University Press.

Tanner, N. and Zihlman, A. 1976. "Woman in evolution. Part 1: Innovation and selection in human origins." *Signs* 1(3): 585–608.

Zihlman, A. 1978. "Women in evolution. Part 2: Subsistence and social organization among early hominids." *Signs* 4: 4–20.

———. 1981. "Woman as shapers of human adaption." In Dahlberg, Frances (ed.). *Woman the Gatherer.* New Haven: Yale University Press.

Gender and War: Are Women Tough Enough for Military Combat?

Lucinda J. Peach

INTRODUCTION

Women's participation in the U.S. military was spotlighted during the Persian Gulf War. Since that time, military personnel, government officials, public policy makers, and members of the public have given increased scrutiny to the issue of whether women should participate in military combat.

A number of arguments have been made over the years to justify the exclusion of women from military combat. Although certain positions in the military designated as "combat" have been opened up to women in recent years, especially on combat aircraft and naval vessels (except for submarines), the

vast majority of combat positions remain closed to them.

The definition of "direct ground combat" that was adopted in 1993 bars women from units that engage the enemy with weapons on the ground while exposed to hostile fire and which involve substantial probability of direct physical contact with hostile forces (see Schmitt 1994a; Schmitt 1994b: A18; Lancaster 1994: A1; Pine 1994: A5). Under the new policy, exposure to risk, alone, is an insufficient ground for excluding women from a particular assignment. Nevertheless, women are barred from almost all assignments that involve operating offensive, line-of-sight weapons, and from all positions involving ground fighting. This includes armor, infantry, and field artillery, the three specialties that are considered the core of

Original material prepared for this text.

combat (see Schmitt 1994b; Schmitt 1994: A7). In consequence, women have been excluded from certain benefits and opportunities for promotion and advancement within (and outside) the military that are available only to those with combat experience. The exclusion also functions to limit the numbers of women who can participate in military service (because of the relatively small percentage of positions that are available to them). In addition, the exclusion of women from combat contributes to other forms of discrimination against women, both within and outside of the military.

In this essay, I will argue that all of these arguments have been based more on "gender ideology"—that is, on assumptions, prejudices, stereotypes and myths about male and female "natures" and "natural" or "proper" sex roles and behaviors (see Code 1991: 196)—than on empirically verifiable gender differences that demonstrate women's inability to competently perform combat roles in the U.S. military.

Two ideological myths about gender in particular underlie many of the arguments against according combat positions to women. First, identification of the military as masculine makes males the standard by which females are assessed. The male standard operates, sometimes explicitly, but more often implicitly, to perpetuate the stereotype that women are out of place in the military, particularly in combat. Throughout history, war has been a theater in which men could prove their masculinity, and in which masculinity has been deemed a necessary prerequisite to success. During his 1992 presidential election campaign, for example, Bill Clinton's lack of military experience received a lot of attention, some of it based on the view that Clinton's lack of exposure to war made him unfit for presidential leadership. The perception that the virtues of "manliness" are necessary for effective combat soldiering, and that women are incapable or ill-suited to the development of these virtues, has contributed to the maintenance of women's exclusion from most combat assignments.

The second myth used as a rationale to exclude women from combat duty suggests that the purpose for which men fight is to pro-

tect women (see Stiehm 1989: 6–7; Kornblum 1984). Women, according to the myth, are the weaker sex and need to be protected by strong men; they are victims dependent upon men rather than autonomous agents who are competent to defend themselves. Members of the military have expressed "a special regard for women who must be protected as the symbolic vessel of femininity and motherhood" (Karst 1991: 536).

These myths are supported by the argument that integrating women into combat would be deleterious to combat effectiveness and the military's ability to mobilize in time of war (Hooker 1989: 36; Kelly 1984: 103; Mitchell 1989: 159; Marlowe 1983: 194; Rogan 1981: 21). Women's supposed physical, physiological, and psychological characteristics are offered as the basis for this argument. Although none of these rationales, alone or combined, provides an adequate ethical basis for maintaining the combat restrictions for women, their popularity and prominence makes it important to note how each of them is based on ideological notions of gender that frequently are inconsistent with the realities of gender difference.

The most common arguments in support of the view that the inclusion of women would diminish combat readiness and effectiveness are that: (1) women lack the necessary physical strength to perform adequately; (2) their capacity for pregnancy and childbearing makes them inappropriate combatants; and (3) women's participation in combat units would reduce unit cohesion by disrupting male bonding and promoting sexual fraternization. Let us examine each of these arguments in greater detail.

PHYSICAL STRENGTH

Military effectiveness is often said to be compromised by women's lack of physical strength and stamina relative to men (Mitchell 1989: 156–62; Kantrowitz 1991; Gordon and Ludvigson 1991: 20–22, D'Amico 1990: 6). Military personnel have testified before Congress that few women would meet the physical standards for combat duty (Hackworth 1991: 25; Appropriations Hearings 1991; Cramsie 1983: 562). Women's purported inferior physical capability is voiced especially loudly by enlisted men, who deny that women have the strength necessary for fighting on the front lines (see Kantrowitz 1991: 23). For example, one of the reasons integrated basic training was ended in the Army in 1982 was because of enlisted men's complaints that women were holding them back (see Coyle, 1989; Stiehm 1985b: 209; Rogan 1981: 27). A study of enlisted service personnel's attitudes toward women in the Army in 1975 indicated that only about 50 percent of men interviewed thought women had the physical strength for combat (see Mitchell 1989: 157–58; Stiehm 1989: 102).

There is no question that, in general, most men are physically stronger than most women. Military studies document that men have some advantages in upper body and leg strength, cardiovascular capacity, and lean muscle, which make men "more fitted for physically intense combat" (see Mitchell 1989: 157; Kelly 1984: 100–101; Marlowe 1983: 190; Hooker 1989: 44). However, these tests generally do not also indicate the fact that some women are capable of meeting the standards established for men. Nor do they typically take into consideration the disparities in prior physical training and physical conditioning that men and women have undergone. Army reports reveal that some women do have the requisite upper body strength to qualify for combat. In addition, some women are stronger than some men. Women have performed well in the limited number of combat-type situations in which they have been tested. However, because the combat exclusion has precluded the possibility of obtaining data about women's physical performance under actual combat conditions, gender-based assumptions and prejudices have dominated policy discussions.

The assumption that women lack the physical strength necessary for combat is ideological because it often persists in the face of direct evidence to the contrary. The nature of modern combat, with its emphasis on high-technology equipment, makes the issue of physical strength far less important than it was in an era when war involved primarily hand-to-hand combat. Physical size and strength are of minimal, if any, consideration, when weapons are being fired at the touch of a button from a location far removed from the combat theatre. As Judith Stiehm argues, the question should not be "how strong women are, but how strong they need to be" (1989: 219). The positive experiences with using women in traditionally all-male fields, such as police and fire fighting forces, which require similar skills to combat, support the conclusion that women are capable of performing satisfactorily in physical defense of self and others in situations involving the use of lethal force (see McDowell 1992; Segal 1982: 286; Karst 1991: 539; Kornblum 1984: 392–93).

Nonetheless, skeptics point out that "there is no real evidence that technology has in fact reduced the need for physical strength among military men and women. What evidence there is shows that many military jobs still require more physical strength than most women possess" (Mitchell 1989: 157). To the contrary, although there are some combat positions that most women are unable to perform satisfactorily because of inadequate physical strength, there is a considerable range of combat positions that many, if not most, women are qualified to perform. Although sheer physical strength may occasionally be an issue when technology fails to function properly, more often than not, the physical strength issue is no longer a legitimate reason for excluding women from combat duty. In addition, physical strength is only one of many factors that needs to be assessed in determining the capability of persons for military combat.

Several proposals have been forwarded, by military personnel and others, to assign combat positions on the basis of the physical strength required to perform them, as at least one of several relevant criterion, rather than exclusively on the basis of gender (Appropriations Hearings 1991: 865;

Roush 1990: 11–12; Coyle 1989: 31; Proxmire 1986: 110; Segal 1983: 110; Segal 1982: 270–71; Nabors 1982: 51; Rogan 1981: 306).[1] Such proposals would result in a fairer and more accurate measure of "fit" between persons and assignments than the current reliance on gender difference. The main rationale used by military officers for their failure to implement such a gender-neutral scheme is that it may not be "cost-effective" (see Association 1991: 54; Rogan 1981: 20). However, the military's failure to demonstrate how gender-neutral standards for assignments would be financially infeasible suggests that the maintenance of the combat exclusion is based more on the continuing force of gender ideology than on financial expense or damage to military effectiveness.

Sometimes the protection myth serves to reinforce the physical strength argument by portraying women as "the weaker sex" who need to be protected from the risks of being raped and physically violated in war. It is sometimes argued that the presence of women in combat would cause male soldiers to respond by becoming more concerned about protecting them than fighting the enemy, thus compromising combat effectiveness (see Barkalow 1990: 260 (quoting Colonel Houston's comment that men's emotional commitment to recapture POW women would be so intense and extreme as to cause fighting to escalate); Beecraft 1989: 43; Van Creveld 1993). Here, the protection rationale is dominant.

During the Gulf War, the press raised the argument that women soldiers would be psychologically unable to handle being taken as prisoners of war, especially because of the greater possibility that they would be raped and otherwise sexually abused (see Nabors 1982: 59; Rogan 1981: 26). Here, the assumption is that women are less stable than men emotionally, and are thus less well equipped to handle the extreme psychological stresses of combat (Mitchell 1989: 7, 182–92; Marlowe 1983: 195).

There is no factual basis for the conclusion that female combatants would be any weaker or more vulnerable than men under such circumstances. To the contrary, the experience of military women such as Air Force Major Rhonda Cornum, a flight surgeon whose aircraft was shot down during the Gulf War, reveals a very matter-of-fact attitude about survival in the face of physical injury and sexual abuse at the hands of her captors. Cornum's response stands as a testament to the ability of military women to cope as POWs (see Cornum 1992).

The notion that women in the military are in need of protection is based on stereotypes of male machismo and female weakness and vulnerability. Further, the assumption that males are able to protect military women is itself a myth, since women are too integrated throughout the armed forces to be protected by their exclusion from combat. (Providing women soldiers with arms and training in self-defense would provide a measure of protection against sexual violence that they would not otherwise have.) The rationale that women need to be protected from becoming POWs because of the risk that their torture would include sexual abuse ignores the reality that men as well as women are raped in war, and that women are already subject to such sexual violence at home or by their fellow soldiers on or near the field of combat. In addition, military women are susceptible to being captured and raped during war, regardless of whether they are themselves engaged in combat.

Also related to the physical strength argument is the assumption that men are naturally more aggressive than women, and that the "natural aggressiveness" of males would be "softened" by women's participation in battle (Mitchell 1989: 7; Marlowe 1983: 191; Tuten 1982: 255). More recently, some scholars have challenged the argument that women are innately less aggressive than men (see Rosoff 1991; Sunday 1991; Marquit 1991), while others observe the lack of evidence regarding women's psychological weakness (see Gordon and Ludvigson 1991; Dillingham 1990: 227–28; Kornblum 1984: 398–99).

Many of those who conclude that men are "naturally" more aggressive than women rely on incomplete studies of primates, not humans, conducted by anthropologist Lionel

Tiger. Tiger observed that male primates in the wild spend much of their time in groups organized to fight with outsiders, whereas female primates were engaged in grooming activities in pairs. Tiger's research has since been largely discredited by further research. Subsequent studies have revealed that females also engaged in collective aggressive action to protect their young, and that both males and females spend much of their time grooming (see Appropriations Hearings 1991: 981; Holm 1982: 95).

The evidence to support the claim of women's lesser aggression is very tenuous, especially after women soldiers demonstrated their competence in performing the psychologically demanding tasks required in combat duty during the Gulf War. But even assuming that women are less aggressive than men, there is still no evidence that it stems from biological causes rather than culture and socialization, which are malleable. The military has not offered empirical evidence to demonstrate that women cannot be trained to exhibit the same degree of aggressiveness that men exhibit. Nonetheless, the assumption that women are less aggressive continues to strengthen the myth of combat as a masculine institution of which only men are capable.

PREGNANCY AND MOTHERHOOD

One specific aspect of women's physiology that some have argued disrupts unit cohesion and consequently hampers combat effectiveness is pregnancy (Nabors 1982: 56–58; see Barkalow 1990: 238–41; Shields 1988: 108; Stiehm 1985b: 226; Rogan 1981: 256). The Army has expressed concern with the effects of pregnancy on "readiness," "mission accomplishment," and "deployability" (Mitchell 1989: 6, 166–71; see Tuten 1982: 251; Rogan 1981: 26; Stiehm 1985a). Until 1975, women were automatically discharged from the military as soon as their pregnancy was discovered. This contributed to high attrition rates for women in the armed services. In 1975, the Department of Defense (DOD) made such

discharge for pregnancy voluntary (see Segal 1983: 207; Treadwell 1954: 200).

Pregnancy also arguably interferes with the ability of the armed forces to rapidly mobilize troops for combat, since it cannot be predicted in advance which women will be pregnant, and thus unavailable for deployment. Pregnancy continues to be an issue of concern, both in the military and among the public. A Newsweek poll conducted in 1991 revealed that 76 percent of the public is concerned about military women becoming pregnant and putting the fetus at risk (Hackworth 1991: 27). Pregnancy does account for a significant percentage of women's lost time, although military women lose less service time overall than do men for illness, drug and alcohol abuse, and disability (see D'Amico 1990: 8; Coyle 1989: 39; Shields 1988: 109; Kornblum 1984: 417–18).

Because of the way military units are currently structured, pregnancy does present a genuine difficulty in the full integration of all women into combat forces. Since military policy, at least in the Army, does not provide temporary replacements for pregnant personnel, the presence of pregnant women in a unit increases everyone else's work load, and consequently brings with it the risk of breeding resentment among coworkers. In addition, although there is no certainty that women desiring to get pregnant will be successful, some opponents of women combatants contend that enlisted women will use pregnancy as a means of avoiding combat duty.

Therefore, pregnancy may be a legitimate reason to exclude women from actually engaging in some forms of combat. However, excluding all women from all positions designated as combat is far too extreme a response. Most women are not pregnant most of the time. Only about ten percent of servicewomen are pregnant at any given time (see Gordon and Ludvigson 1991: 22–23; Hackworth 1991: 27). Further, the experience of pregnancy varies widely in affecting a woman's job performance. Some women are able to carry on their normal activities into the latter stages of pregnancy. Most logistical problems relating to pregnancy, such as deployment plans, etc., can be satisfactorily surmounted by careful planning.

The protection myth also operates here to call into question the propriety of risking the safety of the nation's child bearers by exposing them to the risks of combat. As with the lack of data on gender-integrated units, there have been no studies of the actual impact of pregnancy on military effectiveness because the combat exclusion has precluded the possibility of gathering data. Pregnancy is one consideration that needs to be factored into the analysis of how and whether to integrate women into certain combat roles. But it does not justify the stringency of the current restrictions.

Related to the pregnancy issue is the symbolic, if not actual, role of women as mothers. Motherhood and women's responsibilities to their families are viewed as antithetical to effective combat soldiering. The assumption underlying this view is that women's proper role is to be the center of family life. According to this perspective, women not only bear the children, but are also primarily responsible for their care and nurture (see Mitchell 1989: 6, 171–76; Rogan 1981: 26; Segal 1982: 274–75, 281–82; Costin 1983: 305). The media's promulgation of images of women soldiers kissing their infants goodbye before going off to the Gulf War, and its stories about fathers left at home to care for children emphasized the unnaturalness of female soldiers going off to combat (see Enloe 1993: 201–27).

The influence of gender ideology on this issue is evident in the view of Alexander Webster, a chaplain for the Army National Guard, who speculates about the "identity confusion that must confront any would-be woman warrior who pauses for a moment to consider her potential for motherhood." Webster also surmises that the paradigm of the citizen soldier may have been destroyed by the "social disruption and havoc among families wreaked by the mobilization and deployment of mothers of young children to the theater of operations in the Persian Gulf" (1991: 29). Webster continues: "Disturbing images on television and in the print media of mothers wrenched from their offspring may be the most enduring from the Persian Gulf War" (24–25). According to these ideological notions of gender, women need special protection because they are responsible, in turn, for protecting their children. Notably missing from this assessment is consideration of the consequences of *fathers* being "wrenched from their offspring," thus perpetuating the identification of women as the primary parent. Such testimony assumes that mothers are more responsible for family life than are fathers, so that it is women's military involvement that is questionable, not men's, whenever families are concerned.

Such ideological assumptions about the gender of parenthood are widespread. Surveys reveal that the public continues to be more willing to send young fathers into combat than young mothers. Even supporters of combat roles for women have assumed that mothers would be more reluctant to risk their lives in combat than would men (see Campbell 1992: 18; Lieberman 1990: 219). Attrition and reenlistment data for women indicate that motherhood is a primary reason why women leave the military. And surveys indicate that the large majority of service women do want to have children (see Shields 1988: 109). Former Secretary of Defense Richard Cheney argued that exempting all single parents and dual service-career couples from deployment would weaken military capability (see Campbell 1992: 18, 20). This problem impacts more heavily on women, who comprise the larger percentage of single parents in the military. Women's family obligations may thus present a practical problem for women's ability to carry out combat assignments, particularly for single mothers.

Several other factors need to be considered, however. Many military women are not mothers, and have no plans to become mothers. Most women entering the military are not (yet) mothers. The belief that women are essentially mothers is an outdated ideological assumption. It leads to the irrational result that men who are fathers can be required to participate in combat whereas women who are not mothers cannot (see Association 1991: 25; Segal 1982: 283).

Such beliefs underlie the former Army prohibition on the enlistment of women who had children in certain age groups (see Treadwell 1954: 496).[2]

Further, although most women traditionally *have* taken primary responsibility for protecting and providing for their children, not all mothers are primary caretakers. Many families include alternative arrangements for childcare that do not make the mother primarily responsible. Finally, tradition should not determine who *should* be responsible for national defense in time of war. Fathers have equal responsibility for protecting and providing for their children. Yet, since the Korean War, they have not been exempted from combat duty. In addition, the legislation mandating women's exclusion from combat does not exempt them from military service in time of war. Children of military parents are just as much in need of care and protection during wartime, regardless of whether their mothers are assigned to combat duty or some other position. In the absence of evidence indicating that combat jobs are more incompatible with being a wife and mother than a husband and father, families should be entitled to make their own decisions about child care in the event that the mother is called to serve in combat duty. Current military policy provides that if both parents are in the services, one can claim an exemption in the event that troops are deployed. There is no rational basis for the government to preempt the parents' right to choose based on a set of assumptions about motherhood.

UNIT COHESION AND MALE BONDING

Unit or troop "cohesion" is a function of interpersonal relationships between military leaders and their troops, and the leader's ability to create and sustain "those interpersonal skills that allow him to build strong ties with his men" (Gabriel 1982: 172–73). The argument that male soldiers will lose the camaraderie and team spirit necessary for unit cohesion if they are required to share their duties with women has been advanced as a reason to exclude women from military combat. For example, former Marine Corps Commandant Robert Barrows defends the notion of male bonding as a "real . . . cohesiveness," a "mutual respect and admiration," and a "team work" that would be destroyed by the inclusion of women. "If you want to make a combat unit ineffective," he said, "assign some women to it" (Appropriations Hearings 1991: 985–96).

Although the argument about the indispensability of cohesion to effectiveness is persuasive, the view that the presence of women will damage the "male bonding" linked to that cohesion is exaggerated by the influence of gender ideology. This "influence" is often supported by outdated and anecdotal evidence, such as Tiger's largely discredited research (Mitchell 1989; Golightly 1987; Rogan 1981: 25; Hooker 1989: 45). In addition, the military has not studied the impact that integration of the forces has had on "male bonding" in actual combat for the past several years, nor has it made efforts to instill male–female or female–female bonding in its soldiers (see Stiehm 1989: 236; Stiehm 1985a: 172).

The experience with female soldiers in the Persian Gulf War, as well as the limited studies that have been done in simulated combat and field conditions, indicate that the presence of women in combat units does not adversely affect combat effectiveness. The Army Research Institute conducted two of these studies, labeled "REFWAC" and "MAXWAC" (Johnson 1978; United States Army Research Institute 1977). MAXWAC results showed that female ratios varying from 0 to 35 percent had no significant effect on unit performance. REFWAC results similarly showed that the presence of 10 percent female soldiers on a REFORGER ("Return of Forces to Germany") ten-day field exercise made no difference in the performance of combat support and combat service support units.

In addition, Navy Commander Barry Boyle, participating in Navy squadron preparations, Charles Moskos, observing an

Army exercise in Honduras, and Constance Devilbliss, participating in rigorous Army exercises, reached similar conclusions that integrated units performed as effectively, if not more so, than all-male units (see Coyle 1989; Moskos 1985; Devilbliss 1985). Experience with women in combat in other nations, as well as the successful integration of women into police and other traditionally male-only professions, also provide useful analogies indicating that the participation of American military women in combat would not hamper unit or troop cohesion (Association 1991; Appropriations 1991; Goldman 1982a, b).

FRATERNIZATION

Women in uniform represent an anomaly to traditional social ordering based on traditional sex-gender distinctions, and thus to traditional sexual morality. Thus, in addition to their supposedly detrimental effect on male bonding, including women in combat roles is sometimes alleged to diminish troop effectiveness because of the inevitable sexual attraction and behavior that would follow from having mixed-gender units. Some express a fear that men will be preoccupied with winning the sexual favors of women rather than concentrating on their mission (Mitchell 1989: 176–78; Golightly 1987: 46; Rogan 1981: 27).

The fraternization argument ignores the capability of the sexes to interact with one another in nonsexual ways, particularly under the exigent circumstances of combat. The limited studies that have been conducted under simulated combat conditions indicate that fraternization does not hamper combat readiness or troop effectiveness. Studies show that gender-integrated combat units are as effective as all-male units, and that members of gender-integrated units develop brother-sister bonds rather than sexual ones.

Fraternization is most likely to be a problem where there is ineffective leadership. It is likely that unit bonding depends more on shared experiences, including sharing of risks and hardships, than on gender distinctions (see Karst 1991: 537, 543; Devilbliss 1985: 519; Opinion 1988: 138). Experience has shown that actual integration diminishes prejudice and fosters group cohesiveness more effectively than any other factor. It is thus likely that women's integration into combat forces would parallel that of black men into previously all-white forces during the 1950s and 1960s (see Moskos 1990: 74; Kornblum 1984: 412, 422; Segal 1983: 203–04, 206; Holm 1982: 257).

As the preceding discussion reveals, none of the primary rationales that have been forwarded to exclude women from combat roles provides a legitimate basis for maintaining the current restrictions on women's participation in combat. The analysis of these rationales suggests that the resistance of Congress, the courts, the military, and the public to removing the combat restrictions results more from gender ideology than from demonstrated evidence of women's inability to perform combat roles effectively.

Once outdated stereotypes and myths about women's capabilities and deficiencies are eliminated from consideration of the ethics of women in military combat, the current restrictions on combat roles for women are revealed to lack persuasive foundations. Only when the military begins assigning women to positions on the basis of gender-neutral standards for evaluating the degree of physical strength, psychological fortitude, bonding and troop cohesiveness necessary to perform combat roles can the issue of women in combat be addressed without the undue influence of ideological notions of gender.

NOTES

1. A standard based on physical strength rather than gender could be waived in emergency situations where rapid mobilization is necessary and individual testing would be inefficient (see Segal 1982: 270–71).

2. This policy was reversed in Crawford v. Cushman, 531 F.2d 1114 (2d Cir. 1976).

REFERENCES

Association of the Bar of the City of New York, "The Combat Exclusion Laws: An Idea Whose Time Has Gone," *Minerva,* Vol. 9, No. 4 (Winter, 1991), pp. 1–55 (Association).

Barkalow, Carol, *In the Men's House* (New York: Poseidon Press, 1990).

———. "Women Have What It Takes," *Newsweek* (August 5, 1991), p. 30.

Beecraft, Carolyn, "Personnel Puzzle," *Proceedings* (*of the U.S. Naval Institute*), Vol. 115, No. 4 (April, 1989), pp. 41–44.

Campbell, D'Ann, "Combatting the Gender Gulf," Temple Political and Civil Rights Law Review, Vol. 1, No. 2 (Fall, 1992), reprinted in *Minerva,* Vol. X, Nos. 3–4 (Fall/Winter 1992), pp. 13–41.

Code, Lorraine, *What Can She Know? Feminist Theory and the Construction of Knowledge* (Ithaca, NY: Cornell University Press, 1991).

Cornum, Rhonda, *She Went to War: The Rhonda Cornum Story* (Novato, CA: Presidio Press, 1992).

Costin, Lela, "Feminism, Pacifism, Nationalism, and the United Nations Decade for Women," in Judith Stiehm (ed.), *Women and Men's Wars* (Oxford: Pergamon Press, 1983), pp. 301–16.

Coyle, Commander Barry, U.S. Navy, "Women on the Front Lines," *Proceedings* (*of the U.S. Military Institute*), Vol. 115, No. 4 (April, 1989), pp. 37–40.

Cramsie, Jodie, "Gender Discrimination in the Military: The Unconstitutional Exclusion of Women From Combat," *Valparaiso Law Review,* Vol. 17 (1983), pp. 547–88.

D'Amico, "Women at Arms: The Combat Controversy," *Minerva,* Vol. 8, No. 2 (1990), pp. 1–19.

Devilbliss, M. C., "Gender Integration and Unit Deployment: A Study of G.I. Jo," *Armed Forces and Society,* Vol. 11, No. 3 (1985), pp. 523–52.

Dillingham, Wayne, "The Possibility of American Military Women Becoming Prisoners of War: Justification for Combat Exclusion Rules?" *Federal Bar News and Journal,* Vol. 37, No. 4 (1990), pp. 223–30.

Enloe, Cynthia, *The Morning After: Sexual Politics at the End of the Cold War* (Berkeley, CA: University of California Press, 1993).

Gabriel, Richard, *To Serve With Honor: A Treatise on Military Ethics and the Way of the Soldier* (Westport, CT: Greenwood Press, 1982).

Goldman, Nancy Loring (ed.), *Female Soldiers— Combatants or Noncombatants? Historical and Contemporary Perspectives* (Westport, CT: Greenwood Press, 1982a).

———. *The Utilization of Women in Combat: An Historical and Social Analysis of Twentieth-Century Wartime and Peacetime Experience* (Alexandria, VA: U.S.A.R.I., 1982b).

Golightly, Lieutenant Neil L., U.S. Navy, "No Right to Fight," *Proceedings* (*of the U.S. Naval Institute*), Vol. 113, No. 12 (1987), pp. 46–49.

Gooch, Master Chief Sonar Technician Robert H., U.S. Navy, "The Coast Guard Example," *Proceedings* (*of the U.S. Naval Institute*), Vol. 114, No. 5 (May, 1988), pp. 124–33.

Gordon, Marilyn and Mary Jo Ludvigson, "A Constitutional Analysis of the Combat Exclusion for Air Force Women," *Minerva: Quarterly Report on Women and the Military,* Vol. 9, No. 2 (1991), pp. 1–34.

Hackworth, Colonel David, "War and the Second Sex," *Newsweek* (August 5, 1991), pp. 24–28.

Holm, Maj. Gen. Jeanne, U.S.A.F. (Ret.), Women in the Military (Novato, CA: Presidio Press, 1982).

Hooker, Richard, "Affirmative Action and Combat Exclusion: Gender Roles in the U.S. Army," *Parameters: U.S. War College Quarterly,* Vol. 19, No. 4 (1989), pp. 36–50.

Hunter, Anne E. (ed.), *Genes and Gender VI: On Peace, War, and Gender: A Challenge to Genetic Explanations* (New York: Feminist Press, 1991).

Johnson, Cecil, et al., *Women Content in the Army:* REFORGER (REFWAC 77) (Alexandria, VA: U.S.A.R.I., 1978).

Kantrowitz, Barbara, "The Right to Fight," *Newsweek* (August 5, 1991), pp. 22–23.

Karst, Kenneth, "The Pursuit of Manhood and the Desegregation of the Armed Forces," *U.C.L.A. Law Review,* Vol. 38, No. 3 (1991), pp. 499–581.

Kelly, Karla, "The Exclusion of Women From Combat: Withstanding the Challenge," *Judge Advocate General Journal,* Vol. 33, No. 1 (1984), pp. 77–108.

Kornblum, Lori, "Women Warriors in a Men's World: The Combat Exclusion," *Law and Inequality,* Vol. 2 (1984), pp. 351–445.

Lancaster, John, *Washington Post* (January 13, 1994), pp. A1, A7.

Lieberman, Jeanne, "Women in Combat," *Federal Bar News and Journal,* Vol. 37, No. 4 (1990), pp. 215–22.

Marlowe, David, "The Manning of the Force and the Structure of Battle: Part 2—Men and Women," in Robert Fullinwider (ed.), *Conscripts and Volunteers: Military Requirements, Social Justice, and the All-Volunteer Force* (Totowa, NJ: Rowman & Allanheld, 1983), pp. 189–99.

Marquit, Doris and Erwin Marquit, "Gender Differentiation, Genetic Determinism, and the Struggle for Peace," in Anne E. Hunter (ed.), *Genes and Gender VI: On Peace, War, and Gender: A Challenge to Genetic Explanations* (New York: Feminist Press, 1991), pp. 151–62.

McDowell, Jeanne, "Are Women Better Cops?" *Time* (February 17, 1992), pp. 70–72.

Mitchell, Brian, *The Weak Link: The Feminization of the American Military* (Washington, DC: Regnery Gateway, 1989).

Moskos, Charles, "Female GI's in the Field," *Society*, Vol. 22, No. 6 (1985), pp. 28–33.

———. "Army Women," *Atlantic Monthly*, Vol. 266, No. 2 (August, 1990), pp. 70–78.

———. "How Do They Do It? *The New Republic* (August 5, 1991), pp. 16–20.

Nabors, Major Robert, "Women in the Army: Do They Measure Up?" *Military Review* (October, 1982), pp. 50–61.

Newsweek Staff, "Women in the Armed Forces," *Newsweek*, Vol. 95 (February 18, 1980), pp. 34–42.

"No Right to Fight?" *Proceedings (of the U.S. Naval Institute)*, Vol. 114, No. 5 (May, 1988), pp. 134–39.

Pine, Art, "Women Will Get Limited Combat Roles," *Los Angeles Times* (January 14, 1994), p. A5.

Proxmire, Senator William, "Three Myths About Women and Combat," *Minerva*, Vol. 4, No. 4 (Winter, 1986), pp. 105–19.

Rogan, Helen, *Mixed Company: Women in the Modern Army* (New York: G.P. Putnam's Sons, 1981).

Rosoff, Betty, "Genes, Hormones, and War," in Hunter (ed.), *Genes and Gender VI: On Peace, War, and Gender: A Challenge to Genetic Explanations* (New York: Feminist Press, 1991), pp. 39–49.

Roush, Paul, "Combat Exclusion: Military Necessity or Another Name For Bigotry?" *Minerva*, Vol. 13, No. 3 (Fall, 1990), pp. 1–15.

Schmitt, Eric, "Generals Oppose Combat by Women" *Newsweek* (June 17, 1994a) pp. A1, A18.

Schmitt, Eric, "Army Will Allow Women in 32,000 Combat Posts" *New York Times* (July 28, 1994b), p. A5.

Segal, Mady Wechsler, "The Argument for Female Combatants," in Goldman (ed.), *Female Soldiers—Combatants or Noncombatants? Historical and Contemporary Perspectives* (Westport, CT: Greenwood Press, 1982), pp. 267–90.

———. "Women's Roles in the U.S. Armed Forces: An Evaluation of Evidence and Arguments for Policy Decisions," in Robert Fullinwider (ed.), *Conscripts and Volunteers: Military Requirements, Social Justice, and the All-Volunteer Force* (Totowa, NJ: Rowman & Allanheld, 1983), pp. 200–13 .

Shields, Patricia, "Sex Roles in the Military," in Charles Moskos and Frank Wood (eds.), *The Military—More Than Just a Job?* (Washington, DC: Pergamon Basseys, 1988), pp. 99–111.

Stiehm, Judith Hicks, "Women's Biology and the U.S. Military," in Virginia Sapiro (ed.), *Women, Biology, and Public Policy* (Beverly Hills: SAGE Publications, 1985a), pp. 205–32.

———. "Generations of U.S. Enlisted Women," *Signs: Journal of Women in Culture and Society*, Vol. 11, No. 1 (1985b), pp. 155–75.

———. *Arms and the Enlisted Woman* (Philadelphia: Temple University Press, 1989).

Sunday, Suzanne R., "Biological Theories of Animal Aggression," in Hunter (ed.), *Genes and Gender VI: On Peace, War, and Gender: A Challenge to Genetic Explanations* (New York: Feminist Press, 1991), pp. 50–63.

Treadwell, Mattie, *The Women's Army Corps, in World War II Special Studies,* Vol. 8 (Washington, DC: Office of the Chief of Military History of the Army, 1954).

Tuten, Jeff, "The Argument Against Female Combatants," in Goldman (ed.), *Female Soldiers—Combatants or Noncombatants? Historical and Contemporary Perspectives* (Westport, CT: Greenwood Press, 1982), pp. 237–66.

United States Army Research Institute, *Women Content in Units Force Deployment Test* (MAXWAC) (Alexandria, VA: U.S.A.R.I., 1977).

United States Senate, Hearings before the Committee on Appropriations, DOD Appropriations, 102d Cong., 1st Sess., H.R. 2521, Pts. 4 & 6, *Utilization of Women in the Military Services* (Washington, DC: Government Printing Office, 1991) (Appropriations Hearings).

Van Creveld, Martin, "Why Israel Doesn't Send Women into Combat," *Parameters,* Vol. 23, No. 1 (Spring, 1993), pp. 5–9.

Webster, Alexander, "Paradigms of the Contemporary American Soldier and Women in the Military," *Strategic Review* (Summer 1991), pp. 22–30.

Lifeboat Ethics: Mother Love and Child Death in Northeast Brazil

Nancy Scheper-Hughes

I have seen death without weeping.
The destiny of the Northeast is death.
  Cattle they kill.
To the people they do something worse.

Anonymous Brazilian singer (1965)

"Why do the church bells ring so often?" I asked Nailza de Arruda soon after I moved into a corner of her tiny mud-walled hut near the top of the shantytown called the Alto do Cruzeiro (Crucifix Hill). I was then a Peace Corps volunteer and a community development/health worker. It was the dry and blazing hot summer of 1965, the months following the military coup in Brazil, and save for the rusty, clanging bells, of N. S. das Dores Church, an eerie quiet had settled over the market town that I call Bom Jesus da Mata. Beneath the quiet, however, there was chaos and panic. "It's nothing," replied Nailza, "just another little angel gone to heaven."

Nailza had sent more than her share of little angels to heaven, and sometimes at night I could hear her engaged in a muffled but passionate discourse with one of them, two-year-old Joana. Joana's photograph, taken as she lay propped up in her tiny cardboard coffin, her eyes open, hung on a wall next to one of Nailza and Zé Antonio taken on the day they eloped.

Nailza could barely remember the other infants and babies who came and went in close succession. Most had died unnamed and were hastily baptized in their coffins. Few lived more than a month or two. Only Joana, properly baptized in church at the close of her first year and placed under the protection of a powerful saint, Joan of Arc, had been

Reprinted with permission from *Natural History* 98(10): 8-16, 1989. Copyright Nancy Scheper–Hughes.

expected to live. And Nailza had dangerously allowed herself to love the little girl.

In addressing the dead child, Nailza's voice would range from tearful imploring to angry recrimination: "Why did you leave me? Was your patron saint so greedy that she could not allow me one child on this earth?" Zé Antonio advised me to ignore Nailza's odd behavior, which he understood as a kind of madness that, like the birth and death of children, came and went. Indeed, the premature birth of a stillborn son some months later "cured" Nailza of her "inappropriate" grief, and the day came when she removed Joana's photo and carefully packed it away.

More than fifteen years elapsed before I returned to the Alto do Cruzeiro, and it was anthropology that provided the vehicle of my return. Since 1982 I have returned several times in order to pursue a problem that first attracted my attention in the 1960s. My involvement with the people of the Alto do Cruzeiro now spans a quarter of a century and three generations of parenting in a community where mothers and daughters are often simultaneously pregnant.

The Alto do Cruzeiro is one of three shantytowns surrounding the large market town of Bom Jesus in the sugar plantation zone of Pernambuco in Northeast Brazil, one of the many zones of neglect that have emerged in the shadow of the now tarnished economic miracle of Brazil. For the women and children of the Alto do Cruzeiro the only miracle is that some of them have managed to stay alive at all.

The Northeast is a region of vast proportions (approximately twice the size of Texas) and of equally vast social and developmental problems. The nine states that make up the region are the poorest in the country and are representative of the Third World within a dynamic and rapidly industrializing nation.

Despite waves of migrations from the interior to the teeming shantytowns of coastal cities, the majority still live in rural areas on farms and ranches, sugar plantations and mills.

Life expectancy in the Northeast is only forty years, largely because of the appallingly high rate of infant and child mortality. Approximately one million children in Brazil under the age of five die each year. The children of the Northeast, especially those born in shantytowns on the periphery of urban life, are at a very high risk of death. In these areas, children are born without the traditional protection of breast-feeding, subsistence gardens, stable marriages, and multiple adult caretakers that exists in the interior. In the hillside shantytowns that spring up around cities or, in this case, interior market towns, marriages are brittle, single parenting is the norm, and women are frequently forced into the shadow economy of domestic work in the homes of the rich or into unprotected and oftentimes "scab" wage labor on the surrounding sugar plantations, where they clear land for planting and weed for a pittance, sometimes less than a dollar a day. The women of the Alto may not bring their babies with them into the homes of the wealthy, where the often-sick infants are considered sources of contamination, and they cannot carry the little ones to the riverbanks where they wash clothes because the river is heavily infested with schistosomes and other deadly parasites. Nor can they carry their young children to the plantations, which are often several miles away. At wages of a dollar a day, the women of the Alto cannot hire baby sitters. Older children who are not in school will sometimes serve as somewhat indifferent caretakers. But any child not in school is also expected to find wage work. In most cases, babies are simply left at home alone, the door securely fastened. And so many also die alone and unattended.

Bom Jesus da Mata, centrally located in the plantation zone of Pernambuco, is within commuting distance of several sugar plantations and mills. Consequently, Bom Jesus has been a magnet for rural workers forced off their small subsistence plots by large landowners wanting to use every available piece of land for sugar cultivation. Initially, the rural migrants to Bom Jesus were squatters who were given tacit approval by the mayor to put up temporary straw huts on each of the three hills overlooking the town. The Alto do Cruzeiro is the oldest, the largest, and the poorest of the shantytowns. Over the past three decades many of the original migrants have become permanent residents, and the primitive and temporary straw huts have been replaced by small homes (usually of two rooms) made of wattle and daub, sometimes covered with plaster. The more affluent residents use bricks and tiles. In most Alto homes, dangerous kerosene lamps have been replaced by light bulbs. The once tattered rural garb, often fashioned from used sugar sacking, has likewise been replaced by store-bought clothes, often castoffs from a wealthy *patrão* (boss). The trappings are modern, but the hunger, sickness, and death that they conceal are traditional, deeply rooted in a history of feudalism, exploitation, and institutionalized dependency.

My research agenda never wavered. The questions I addressed first crystallized during a veritable "die-off" of Alto babies during a severe drought in 1965. The food and water shortages and the political and economic chaos occasioned by the military coup were reflected in the handwritten entries of births and deaths in the dusty, yellowed pages of the ledger books kept at the public registry office in Bom Jesus. More than 350 babies died in the Alto during 1965 alone—this from a shantytown population of little more than 5,000. But that wasn't what surprised me. There were reasons enough for the deaths in the miserable conditions of shantytown life. What puzzled me was the seeming indifference of Alto women to the death of their infants, and their willingness to attribute to their own tiny offspring an aversion to life that made their death seem wholly natural, indeed all but anticipated.

Although I found that it was possible, and hardly difficult, to rescue infants and toddlers from death by diarrhea and dehydration with a simple sugar, salt, and water solution (even bottled Coca-Cola worked fine), it was more difficult to enlist a mother herself in the rescue of a child she perceived as ill-fated for life or better off dead, or to convince her to take back into her threatened and besieged home a baby she had already come to think of as an angel rather than as a son or daughter.

I learned that the high expectancy of death, and the ability to face child death with stoicism and equanimity, produced patterns of nurturing that differentiated between those infants thought of as thrivers and survivors and those thought of as born already "wanting to die." The survivors were nurtured, while stigmatized, doomed infants were left to die, as mothers say, a mingua, "of neglect." Mothers stepped back and allowed nature to take its course. This pattern, which I call mortal selective neglect, is called passive infanticide by anthropologist Marvin Harris. The Alto situation, although culturally specific in the form that it takes, is not unique to Third World shantytown communities and may have its correlates in our own impoverished urban communities in some cases of "failure to thrive" infants.

I use as an example the story of Zezinho, the thirteen-month-old toddler of one of my neighbors, Lourdes. I became involved with Zezinho when I was called in to help Lourdes in the delivery of another child, this one a fair and robust little tyke with a lusty cry. I noted that while Lourdes showed great interest in the newborn, she totally ignored Zezinho who, wasted and severely malnourished, was curled up in a fetal position on a piece of urine- and feces-soaked cardboard placed under his mother's hammock. Eyes open and vacant, mouth slack, the little boy seemed doomed.

When I carried Zezinho up to the community day-care center at the top of the hill, the Alto women who took turns caring for one another's children (in order to free themselves for part-time work in the cane fields or washing clothes) laughed at my efforts to save Zé, agreeing with Lourdes that here was a baby without a ghost of a chance. Leave him alone, they cautioned. It makes no sense to fight with death. But I did do battle with Zé, and after several weeks of force-feeding (malnourished babies lose their interest in food), Zé began to succumb to my ministrations. He acquired some flesh across his taut chest bones, learned to sit up, and even tried to smile. When he seemed well enough, I returned him to Lourdes in her miserable scrap-material lean-to, but not without guilt about what I had done. I wondered whether returning Zé was at all fair to Lourdes and to his little brother. But I was busy and washed my hands of the matter. And Lourdes did seem more interested in Zé now that he was looking more human.

When I returned in 1982, there was Lourdes among the women who formed my sample of Alto mothers—still struggling to put together some semblance of life for a now grown Zé and her five other surviving children. Much was made of my reunion with Zé in 1982, and everyone enjoyed retelling the story of Zé's rescue and of how his mother had given him up for dead. Zé would laugh the loudest when told how I had had to force-feed him like a fiesta turkey. There was no hint of guilt on the part of Lourdes and no resentment on the part of Zé. In fact, when questioned in private as to who was the best friend he ever had in life, Zé took a long drag on his cigarette and answered without a trace of irony, "Why my mother, of course!" "But of course," I replied.

Part of learning how to mother in the Alto do Cruzeiro is learning when to let go of a child who shows that it "wants" to die or that it has no "knack" or no "taste" for life. Another part is learning when it is safe to let oneself love a child. Frequent child death remains a powerful shaper of maternal thinking and practice. In the absence of firm expectation that a child will survive, mother love as we conceptualize it (whether in popular terms or in the psychobiological notion of maternal bonding) is attenuated and delayed with consequences for infant survival. In an environment already precarious to young life, the emotional detachment of mothers toward some of their babies contributes even further to the spiral of high mortality—high fertility in a kind of macabre lock-step dance to death.

The average woman of the Alto experiences 9.5 pregnancies, 3.5 child deaths, and 1.5 stillbirths. Seventy percent of all child deaths in the Alto occur in the first six months of life, and 82 percent by the end of the first year. Of all deaths in the community each year, about 45 percent are of children under the age of five.

Women of the Alto distinguish between child deaths understood as natural (caused by diarrhea and communicable diseases) and those resulting from sorcery, the evil eye, or other magical or supernatural afflictions. They also recognize a large category of infant deaths seen as fated and inevitable. These hopeless cases are classified by mothers under the folk terminology "child sickness" or "child attack." Women say that there are at least fourteen different types of hopeless child sickness, but most can be subsumed under two categories—chronic and acute. The chronic cases refer to infants who are born small and wasted. They are deathly pale, mothers say, as well as weak and passive. They demonstrate no vital force, no liveliness. They do not suck vigorously; they hardly cry. Such babies can be this way at birth or they can be born sound but soon show no resistance, no "fight" against the common crises of infancy: diarrhea, respiratory infections, tropical fevers.

The acute cases are those doomed infants who die suddenly and violently. They are taken by stealth overnight, often following convulsions that bring on head banging, shaking, grimacing, and shrieking. Women say it is horrible to look at such a baby. If the infant begins to foam at the mouth or gnash its teeth or go rigid with its eyes turned back inside its head, there is absolutely no hope. The infant is "put aside"—left alone—often on the floor in a back room, and allowed to die. These symptoms (which accompany high fevers, dehydration, third-stage malnutrition, and encephalitis) are equated by Alto women with madness, epilepsy, and worst of all, rabies, which is greatly feared and highly stigmatized.

Most of the infants presented to me as suffering from chronic child sickness were tiny, wasted famine victims, while those labeled as victims of acute child attack seemed to be infants suffering from the deliriums of high fever or the convulsions that can accompany electrolyte imbalance in dehydrated babies.

Local midwives and traditional healers, praying women, as they are called, advise Alto women on when to allow a baby to die. One midwife explained: "If I can see that a baby was born unfortuitously, I tell the mother that she need not wash the infant or give it a cleansing tea. I tell her just to dust the infant with baby powder and wait for it to die." Allowing nature to take its course is not seen as sinful by these often very devout Catholic women. Rather, it is understood as cooperating with God's plan.

Often I have been asked how consciously women of the Alto behave in this regard. I would have to say that consciousness is always shifting between allowed and disallowed levels of awareness. For example, I was awakened early one morning in 1987 by two neighborhood children who had been sent to fetch me to a hastily organized wake for a two-month-old infant whose mother I had unsuccessfully urged to breast-feed. The infant was being sustained on sugar water, which the mother referred to as soro (serum), using a medical term for the infant's starvation regime in light of his chronic diarrhea. I had cautioned the mother that an infant could not live on soro forever.

The two girls urged me to console the young mother by telling her that it was "too bad" that her infant was so weak that Jesus had to take him. They were coaching me in proper Alto etiquette. I agreed, of course, but asked, "And what do you think?" Xoxa, the eleven-year-old, looked down at her dusty flip-flops and blurted out, "Oh, Dona Nanci, that baby never got enough to eat, but you must never say that!" And so the death of hungry babies remains one of the best-kept secrets of life in Bom Jesus da Mata.

Most victims are waked quickly and with a minimum of ceremony. No tears are shed, and the neighborhood children form a tiny procession, carrying the baby to the town graveyard where it will join a multitude of others. Although a few fresh flowers may be scattered over the tiny grave, no stone or wooden cross will mark the place, and the same spot will be reused within a few months' time. The mother will never visit the grave, which soon becomes an anonymous one.

What, then, can be said of these women? What emotions, what sentiments motivate them? How are they able to do what, in fact, must be done? What does mother love mean in this inhospitable context? Are grief, mourning, and melancholia present, although deeply repressed? If so, where shall we look for them? And if not, how are we to understand the moral visions and moral sensibilities that guide their actions?

I have been criticized more than once for presenting an unflattering portrait of poor Brazilian women, women who are, after all, themselves the victims of severe social and institutional neglect. I have described these women as allowing some of their children to die, as if this were an unnatural and inhuman act rather than, as I would assert, the way any one of us might act, reasonably and rationally, under similarly desperate conditions. Perhaps I have not emphasized enough the real pathogens in this environment of high risk: poverty, deprivation, sexism, chronic hunger, and economic exploitation. If mother love is, as many psychologists and some feminists believe, a seemingly natural and universal maternal script, what does it mean to women for whom scarcity, loss, sickness, and deprivation have made that love frantic and robbed them of their grief, seeming to turn their hearts to stone?

Throughout much of human history—as in a great deal of the impoverished Third World today—women have had to give birth and to nurture children under ecological conditions and social arrangements hostile to child survival, as well as to their own well-being. Under circumstances of high childhood mortality, patterns of selective neglect and passive infanticide may be seen as active survival strategies.

They also seem to be fairly common practices historically and across cultures. In societies characterized by high childhood mortality and by a correspondingly high (replacement) fertility, cultural practices of infant and childcare tend to be organized primarily around survival goals. But what this means is a pragmatic recognition that not all of one's children can be expected to live. The nervousness about child survival in areas of northeast Brazil, northern India, or Bangladesh, where a 30 percent or 40 percent mortality rate in the first years of life is common, can lead to forms of delayed attachment and a casual or benign neglect that serves to weed out the worst bets so as to enhance the life chances of healthier siblings, including those yet to be born. Practices similar to those that I am describing have been recorded for parts of Africa, India, and Central America.

Life in the Alto do Cruzeiro resembles nothing so much as a battlefield or an emergency room in an overcrowded inner city public hospital. Consequently, morality is guided by a kind of "lifeboat ethics," the morality of triage. The seemingly studied indifference toward the suffering of some of their infants, conveyed in such sayings as "little critters have no feelings," is understandable in light of these women's obligation to carry on with their reproductive and nurturing lives.

In their slowness to anthropomorphize and personalize their infants, everything is mobilized so as to prevent maternal overattachment and, therefore, grief at death. The bereaved mother is told not to cry, that her tears will dampen the wings of her little angel so that she cannot fly up to her heavenly home. Grief at the death of an angel is not only inappropriate, it is a symptom of madness and of a profound lack of faith.

Infant death becomes routine in an environment in which death is anticipated and bets are hedged. While the routinization of death in the context of shantytown life is not hard to understand, and quite possible to empathize with, its routinization in the formal institutions of public life in Bom Jesus is not as easy to accept uncritically. Here the social production of indifference takes on a different, even a malevolent cast.

In a society where triplicates of every form are required for the most banal events (registering a car, for example), the registration of infant and child death is informal, incomplete, and rapid. It requires no documentation, takes less than five minutes, and demands no witnesses other than office clerks. No questions are asked concerning the circumstances of the death, and the cause of death is left blank, unquestioned and unexamined. A neighbor, grandmother, older sibling, or common-law husband may register the death. Since most infants die at home, there is no question of a medical record.

From the registry office, the parent proceeds to the town hall, where the mayor will give him or her a voucher for a free baby coffin. The full-time municipal coffinmaker cannot tell you exactly how many baby coffins are dispatched each week. It varies, he says, with the seasons. There are more needed during the drought months and during the big festivals of Carnaval and Christmas and São Joao's Day because people are too busy, he supposes, to take their babies to the clinic. Record keeping is sloppy.

Similarly, there is a failure on the part of city-employed doctors working at two free clinics to recognize the malnutrition of babies who are weighed, measured, and immunized without comment and as if they were not, in fact, anemic, stunted, fussy, and irritated starvation babies. At best the mothers are told to pick up free vitamins or a health "tonic" at the municipal chambers. At worst, clinic personnel will give tranquilizers and sleeping pills to quiet the hungry cries of "sick-to-death" Alto babies.

The church, too, contributes to the routinization of, and indifference toward, child death. Traditionally, the local Catholic church taught patience and resignation to domestic tragedies that were said to reveal the imponderable workings of God's will. If an infant died suddenly, it was because a particular saint had claimed the child. The infant would be an angel in the service of his or her heavenly patron. It would be wrong, a sign of a lack of faith, to weep for a child with such good fortune. The infant funeral was, in the past, an event celebrated with joy. Today, however, under the new regime of "liberation theology," the bells of N. S. das Dores parish church no longer peal for the death of Alto babies, and no priest accompanies the procession of angels to the cemetery where their bodies are disposed of casually and without ceremony. Children bury children in Bom Jesus da Mata. In this most Catholic of communities, the coffin is handed to the disabled and irritable municipal gravedigger, who often chides the children for one reason or another. It may be that the coffin is larger than expected and the gravedigger can find no appropriate space. The children do not wait for the gravedigger to complete his task. No prayers are recited and no sign of the cross made as the tiny coffin goes into its shallow grave.

When I asked the local priest, Padre Marcos, about the lack of church ceremony surrounding infant and childhood death today in Bom Jesus, he replied: "In the old days, child death was richly celebrated. But those were the baroque customs of a conservative church that wallowed in death and misery. The new church is a church of hope and joy. We no longer celebrate the death of child angels. We try to tell mothers that Jesus doesn't want all the dead babies they send him." Similarly, the new church has changed its baptismal customs, now often refusing to baptize dying babies brought to the back door of a church or rectory. The mothers are scolded by the church attendants and told to go home and take care of their sick babies. Baptism, they are told, is for the living; it is not to be confused with the sacrament of extreme unction, which is the anointing of the dying. And so it appears to the women of the Alto that even the church has turned away from them, denying the traditional comfort of folk Catholicism.

The contemporary Catholic Church is caught in the clutches of a double bind. The new theology of liberation imagines a kingdom of God on earth based on justice and equality, a world without hunger, sickness, or childhood mortality. At the same time, the church has not changed its official position on sexuality and reproduction, including its sanctions against birth control, abortion, and sterilization. The padre of Bom Jesus da Mata recognizes this contradiction intuitively, although he shies away from discussions on the topic, saying that he prefers to leave questions of family planning to the discretion and the "good consciences" of his impoverished parishioners. But this, of course, sidesteps the extent to which those good consciences have been shaped by traditional church teachings in Bom Jesus, especially by his recent predecessors. Hence, we can begin to see that the seeming indifference of Alto mothers toward the death of some of their infants is but a pale reflection of the official indifference of church and state to the plight of poor women and children.

Nonetheless, the women of Bom Jesus are survivors. One woman, Biu, told me her life history, returning again and again to the themes of child death, her first husband's suicide, abandonment by her father and later by her second husband, and all the other losses and disappointments she had suffered in her long forty-five years. She concluded with great force, reflecting on the days of Carnaval '88 that were fast approaching:

No, Dona Nanci, I won't cry, and I won't waste my life thinking about it from morning to night. . . . Can I argue with God for the state that I'm in?

No! And so I'll dance and I'll jump and I'll play Carnaval! And yes, I'll laugh and people will wonder at a pobre like me who can have such a good time.

And no one did blame Biu for dancing in the streets during the four days of Carnaval—not even on Ash Wednesday, the day following Carnaval '88 when we all assembled hurriedly to assist in the burial of Mercea, Biu's beloved *casula*, her last-born daughter who had died at home of pneumonia during the festivities. The rest of the family barely had time to change out of their costumes. Severino, the child's uncle and godfather, sprinkled holy water over the little angel while he prayed: "Mercea, I don't know whether you were called, taken, or thrown out of this world. But look down at us from your heavenly home with tenderness, with pity, and with mercy." So be it.

The Cultural Nexus of Aka Father–Infant Bonding

Barry S. Hewlett

Despite a steady increase in the quantity and quality of studies of infants, young children and motherhood in various parts of the world (e.g., LeVine et al. 1994), we know relatively little about the nature of father–child relations outside of the U.S. and Western Europe (see Hewlett 1992 for some exceptions). In general, mother-oriented theories of infant and child development have guided cross-cultural research. The majority of these theories view the mother-infant relationship as the prototype for subsequent attachments and relationships (Ainsworth 1967, Bowlby 1969, Freud 1938, and Harlow 1961). According to Freud and Bowlby, for instance, one had to have a trust-

Adapted for this text from Barry S. Hewlett, *Intimate Fathers: The Nature and Context of Aka Pygmy Paternal-Infant Care* (Ann Arbor: University of Michigan Press, 1991). Copyright © 1991 by the University of Michigan Press.

ing, unconditional relationship with his or her mother in order to become a socially and emotionally adjusted adult. These influential theorists generally believed that the father's role was not a factor in the child's development until the Oedipal stage (3–5 years old). The field methods to study infancy reflected this theoretical emphasis on mother. Observations were either infant or mother-focused and conducted only during daylight hours; father-focused and evening observations were not considered. Also, standardized questionnaires and psychological tests were generally administered only to the mother. One consistent result from the cross-cultural studies was that fathers provided substantially less direct care to infants than mothers. In fact, all cross-cultural studies to date indicate that a number of other female caretakers (older female siblings, aunts, grandmothers) provide more direct care to infants than do fathers. Since fathers are not as conspicuous as mothers and other females during daylight hours researchers tend to emphasize a "deficit" model of fathers (Cole and Bruner 1974); that is, fathers are not around much and therefore do not contribute much to the child's development.

Given the paucity of systematic research outside of the U.S. on father's interactions with children, it is ironic that this variable (i.e., the degree of father vs. mother involvement with children) should be so consistently invoked as an explanatory factor in the literature. It is hypothesized to be related, for example, to gender inequality (Chodorow 1974), universal sexual asymmetry (Rosaldo and Lamphere 1974), and the origin of the human family (Lancaster 1987).

FATHER–INFANT BONDING

Bowlby's (1969) theory, mentioned above, suggested that an early secure attachment (or "bonding") between infant and caregiver (usually mother) was crucial for normal development. Lack of bonding between mother and infant led to the infant's protest, despair, detachment, and eventual difficulty in emotional and social development. Most studies of attachment have focused on mother–infant bonding, but an increasing number of studies in the U.S. and Europe have tried to understand if and when infants become attached to fathers. Numerous psychological studies now indicate that infants are attached to their fathers and that the infants become attached to fathers at about the same age as they do to mothers (8–10 months of age) (Lamb 1981). But how does this bonding take place if infant bonding to mother is known to develop through regular, sensitive, and responsive care? American fathers are seldom around to provide this type of care. The critical factor that has emerged in over 50 studies of primarily middle-class American fathers is vigorous play. The physical style of American fathers is distinct from that of American mothers, is evident three days after birth, and continues

throughout infancy. The American data have been so consistent that some researchers have indicated a biological basis (Clarke-Stewart 1980). The idea is that mother–infant bonding develops as a consequence of the frequency and intensity of the relationship, while father–infant bonding takes place because of this highly stimulating interaction. British, German, and Israeli studies generally support this hypothesis. This chapter examines the process of father–infant bonding among the Aka, a hunter–gatherer group living in the tropical forest of central Africa.

THE AKA

There are about 30,000 Aka hunter–gatherers in the tropical rain forests of southern Central African Republic and northern Congo-Brazzaville. They live in camps of 25–35 people and move camp every two weeks to two months. Each nuclear family has a hut, and each camp generally has 5–8 huts arranged in a circle. The circle of huts is about 12 meters in diameter and each hut is about 1.5 meters in diameter. Each hut has one bed of leaves or logs on which everyone in the family sleeps. The Aka have patriclans and many members of a camp belong to the same patriclan (generally a camp consists of brothers, their wives and children, and unrelated men who are doing bride service for the sisters of the men in camp). The Aka have high fertility and mortality rates: A woman generally has five to six children during her lifetime, and one-fifth of the infants die before reaching 12 months and 43 percent of children die before reaching 15 years.

Life in the camp is rather intimate. While the overall population density is quite low (less than one person per square kilometer), living space is quite dense. Three or four people sleep together on the same 4-feet-long by 2-feet-wide bed, and neighbors are just a few feet away. The 25–35 camp members live in an area about the size of a large American living room. The Aka home represents the "public" part of life, while time outside of camp tends to be relatively "private." This is the reverse of the American pattern (i.e., home is usually considered private). The camp is relatively young as half of the members of the camp are under 15 and most women have a nursing child throughout their childbearing years.

The Aka use a variety of hunting techniques, but net hunting, which involves men, women, and children, is the most important and regular hunting technique. Women generally have the role of tackling the game in the net and killing the animal. Game captured is eventually shared with everyone in camp. Some parts of the game animal are smoked and eventually traded to Bantu and Sudanic farmers for manioc or other domesticated foods. The Aka have strong economic and religious ties to the tropical forest. The forest is perceived as provider and called friend, lover, mother, or father.

Sharing and cooperation are pervasive and general tenets of Aka camp life. Food items, infant care, ideas for song and dance, and material items such as pots and pans are just some of the items that are shared daily in the camp. An Ngandu farmer describes Aka sharing:

> Pygmies [the Ngandu use the derogatory term Babinga to refer to the Aka] are people who stick together. Twenty of them are able to share one single cigarette. When a pygmy comes back with only five roots she shares them all. It is the same with forest nuts; they will give them out to everybody even if there are none left for them. They are very generous.

The Aka are also fiercely egalitarian. They have a number of mechanisms to maintain individual, intergenerational, and gender equality. The Ngandu villager mentioned above describes his concerns about Aka intergenerational egalitarianism:

> Young pygmies have no respect for their parents; they regard their fathers as their friends. . . . There is no way to tell whether they are talking to their parents because they always use their first names. Once I was in a pygmy camp and several people were sitting around and a son said to his father "Etobe your balls are hanging out of your loincloth" and everyone started laughing. No

respect, none, none, none. . . . It's real chaos because there is no respect between father and son, mother and son or daughter. That's why pygmies have such a bad reputation, a reputation of being backward.

Three mechanisms that promote sharing and egalitarianism are prestige avoidance, rough joking and demand sharing. The Aka try to avoid drawing attention to themselves, even if they have killed an elephant or cured someone's life-threatening illness. Individuals who boast about their abilities are likely to share less or request more from others in the belief that they are better than others. If individuals start to draw attention to themselves, others in the camp will use rough and crude jokes, often about the boastful person's genitals, in order to get the individuals to be more modest about their abilities. Demand sharing also helps to maintain egalitarianism: if individuals like or want something (cigarettes, necklace, shirt) they simply ask for it, and the person generally gives it to them. Demand sharing promotes the circulation of scarce material goods (e.g., shoes, shirt, necklaces, spear points) in the camp.

Gender egalitarianism is also important. For instance, there are male and female roles on the net hunt, but role reversals take place daily and individuals are not stigmatized for taking the roles of the opposite sex. If one does the task poorly, regardless of whether it is a masculine or feminine task, then one is open to joking and teasing by others (e.g., when the anthropologist chases the game in the wrong direction).

The rough joking mentioned above is also linked to another feature of Aka culture—playfulness. There is no clear separation between "work" and "play" time. Dances, singing, net hunting, male circumcision, sorcery accusations all include humorous mimicking, practical jokes, and exaggerated storytelling. Aka life is informal because of egalitarianism and the playful activity that occurs throughout the day by both adults and children. Play is an integral part of both adult and child life and contributes to enhanced parent–child and adult–child communication. Parents and adults have an extensive repertoire of play, and can and do communicate cultural knowledge to children through their playful repertoire.

Greater ethnographic detail on the Aka can be found in Hewlett (1991) or Bahuchet (1985).

AKA INFANCY

The infant lives with a relatively small group of individuals related through his or her father (unless the infant is the first born in which case the family is likely to be in the camp of the wife for the purposes of bride service) and sleeps in the same bed as mother, father, and other brothers and sisters.

Cultural practices during infancy are quite distinct from those found in European and American cultures. Aka parents are indulgent as infants are held almost constantly, nursed on demand (breast-fed several times per hour), attended to immediately if they fuss, and are seldom, if ever, told "no! no!" if they misbehave (e.g., get into food pots, hit others, or take things from other children). An Aka father describes Aka parenting and contrasts it with parenting among his Ngandu farming neighbors:

> We, Aka look after our children with love, from the minute they are born to when they are much older. The villagers love their children only when they are babies. When they become children they get beaten up badly. With us, even if the child is older, if he is unhappy, I'll look after him, I will cuddle him.

Older infants are allowed to use and play with knives, machetes, and other "adult" items. They are allowed to crawl into a parent's lap while the parent is engaged in economic (e.g., butchering animal, repairing net) or leisure (e.g., playing a harp or drum) activity. While older infants are given considerable freedom to explore the house and camp, parents do watch infants to make sure they do not crawl into the fire.

Extensive multiple caregiving of 1 to 4-month-old infants (Hewlett 1989) exists, especially while the Aka are in the camp. Individuals other than mother (infant's father, brothers, sisters, aunts, uncles, grand-mothers) hold the infant the majority of the time (60 percent) in this context, and the infant is moved to different people about seven times per hour. Mothers' holding increases to 85 percent and the transfer rate drops to two transfers per hour outside of the camp (i.e., on net hunt or in fields).

Infancy is very active and stimulating. Infants are taken on the hunt and are seldom laid down. They are held on the side of the caregiver rather than on the caregiver's back as in many farming communities so there are opportunities for caregiver–infant face-to-face interaction and communication. The infant can also breast feed by simply reaching for the mother's breast and can nurse while mother walks. While out on the net hunt the infant sleeps in the sling as the caregiver walks, runs, or sits.

THE STUDY

I started working with the Aka in 1973 so by the time I started the father–infant study in 1984 I was familiar with specific Aka families and Aka culture in general. Since I wanted to test some of the psychological hypotheses regarding father–infant relations, I incor-porated psychological methods into my research. The quantitative psychological methods consisted of systematically observing 15 Aka families with infants from 6 A.M. to 9 P.M. (the observations focused either on the father or the infant). This enabled me to say precisely how much time Aka versus American fathers held or were near their infants and precisely describe how American versus Aka styles of interaction were similar or different. Informal discussions while on the net hunt and in camp were also utilized to develop structured interviews. Men and women, young and old, were asked about their feelings regarding relations with their mothers, fathers, and other caregivers.

The study focused on two domains important for trying to understand father–infant bonding: the degree of father involvement and mother's versus father's parenting style. For degree of father involvement I wanted to know: How often do fathers actually interact with their infants, how often are fathers available to their infants, if fathers are not involved with infants what other activities are they involved in, how do children characterize the nature of their involvement with their father? Questions regarding paternal versus maternal parenting style included: Are there distinctions between the mother's and the father's play behavior with their infants, do mothers and fathers hold their infants for different purposes, what do mothers and fathers do while they hold the infant, do infants show different types of attachment behavior to mothers and fathers, how do children view their mother's and father's parenting styles?

WHY ARE AKA FATHERS SO INVOLVED WITH THEIR INFANTS? THE CULTURAL NEXUS OF FATHER–INFANT BONDING

Although few cross-cultural studies of father-child relations have been conducted, Aka father involvement in infancy is exceptional, if not unique. Aka fathers are within an arm's reach (i.e., holding or within one meter) of their infant more than 50 percent of 24-hour periods. Table 1.1 demonstrates that Aka fathers hold their very young infants during the day at least five times more than fathers in other cultures, while Table 1.2 indicates Aka fathers are available to their infants at least three times more frequently than fathers in other cultures. American and European fathers hold their infants, on average, between 10 and 20 minutes per day (Lamb et al. 1987) while Aka fathers, on average, hold their infants about one hour during daylight hours and about 25 percent of the time after the sun goes down. At night fathers sleep with mother and infant, whereas American fathers seldom sleep with their infants. While Aka father care is extensive, it is also highly context dependent—fathers provide at least four times as much care while they are in the camp setting than they do while out of camp (e.g., out on the net hunt or in the villagers' fields). What factors influence this high level of paternal emotional and physical involvement among the Aka?

Aka father–infant bonding is embedded within a cultural nexus—it influences and is influenced by a complex cultural system. This brief overview describes some of the cultural facets linked to Aka father–infant bonding.

Like many other foragers, the Aka have few accumulable resources that are essential for survival. "Kinship resources," the number of brothers and sisters in particular, are probably the most essential "resource" for survival, but are generally established at an early age. Food resources are not stored or accumulated, and Aka males and females contribute similar percentages of calories to the diet. Cross-cultural studies have demonstrated that in societies where resources essential to survival can be accumulated or where males are the primary

TABLE 1.1 Comparison of Father Holding in Selected Foraging Populations

POPULATION	AGE OF INFANTS (MOS.)	FATHER HOLDING (PERCENT OF TIME)	SOURCE
Gidgingali	0–6	3.4	Hamilton (1981)
	6–18	3.1	
!Kung	0–6	1.9	West and Konner (1976)
	6–24	4.0	
Efe Pygmies	1–4	2.6	Winn et al. (1990)
Aka Pygmies	1–4	22.0	Hewlett (1991)
	8–18	14.0	

NOTE: All observations were made in a camp setting (Table from Hewlett 1991).

TABLE 1.2   Comparison of Father Presence with Infants or Children Among Selected Foraging and Farming Populations

POPULATION	LOCATION	SUBSISTENCE	PERCENT TIME FATHER PRESENT/IN VIEW	PRIMARY SETTING OF OBSERVATIONS	SOURCE
Gusii	Kenya	farming	10	house/yard & garden	1
Mixteca	Mexico	farming	9	house/yard	1
Ilocano	Philippines	farming	14	house/yard	1
Okinawan	Japan	farming	3	public places & house/yard	1
Rajput	India	farming	3	house/yard	1
!Kung	Botswana	foraging	30	camp	2
Aka Pygmies	Central African Republic	foraging	88	forest camp	3
Logoli	Kenya	farming	5	house/yard	4
Newars	Nepal	farming	7	house/yard	4
Samoans	Samoa	farming	8	house/yard	4
Carib	Belize	farming	3	house/yard	4
Ifaluk	Micronesia	farm-fish	13	house/yard	5

Sources (Table from Hewlett 1991):
1. Whiting and Whiting 1975
2. West and Konner 1976
3. Hewlett 1991
4. Munroe and Munroe 1992
5. Betzig, Harrigan, and Turke 1990

contributors to subsistence, fathers invest more time competing for these resources and, consequently, spend less time with their children. In contrast, where resources are not accumulable or men are not the primary contributors to subsistence, men generally spend more time in the direct care of their children. Katz and Konner (1981: 174) found that father–infant proximity (degree of emotional warmth and physical proximity) is closest in gathering-hunting populations (gathered foods by females are principal resources, meat is secondary) and most distant in cultures where herding or advanced agriculture is practiced. In the latter cultures, cattle, camels, and land are considered the essential accumulable resources necessary for survival. These findings are consistent with Whiting and Whiting's (1975) cross-cultural study of husband–wife intimacy. They found husband–wife intimacy to be greatest in cultures without accumulated resources or capital investments. While there are other factors to consider (the protection of resources and the polygyny rate), there is a strong tendency for

fathers/husbands to devote more time to their children/wives if there are no accumulable resources.

Three additional factors seem to be especially influential in understanding the extraordinarily high level of Aka paternal care. First, the nature of Aka subsistence activity is rather unique cross-culturally. Usually mens' and womens' subsistence activities take place at very different locations. The net hunt and other subsistence activities, such as caterpillar collecting, involve men, women, and children. If men are going to help with infant care on a regular basis they have to be near the infant a good part of the day. The net hunt makes this possible. The net hunt also requires that men and women walk equal distances during the day. In most foraging societies, females do not travel as far from camp as males. Older siblings are not useful for helping their mothers because of the extensive labor involved in walking long distances with an infant. If a mother is to receive help on the net hunt, it needs to come from an adult. Most of the other adult females carry baskets full of food and have their own infants or young children to carry since fertility is high. Fathers are among the few alternative caregivers regularly available on the net hunt to help mothers. While fathers do carry infants on the net hunt, especially on the return from the hunt when the mothers' baskets are full of meat, collected nuts, and fruit, father–infant caregiving is much more likely to occur in the camp.

Another influential factor is the nature of husband–wife relations. The net hunt contributes substantially to the time husband and wife spend together and patterns the nature of that time spent together. Observations in the forest and village indicate husbands and wives are within sight of each other 46.5 percent of daylight hours. This is more time together than in any other known society, and it is primarily a result of the net hunt. This percentage of course increases in the evening hours. But, husbands and wives are not only together most of the day, they are actively cooperating on the net hunt. They have to know each other well to communicate and cooperate throughout the day. They work together to set up the family net, chase game into the net, butcher and divide the game and take care of the children. Husbands and wives help each other out in a number of domains, in part because they spend so much time together. Husband–wife relations are many-stranded; that is, social, economic, ritual, parenting, and leisure activities are shared and experienced in close proximity. When they return to camp the mother has a number of tasks—she collects firewood and water, and prepares the biggest meal of the day. The father has relatively few tasks to do after returning from the hunt. He may make string or repair the net, but he is available to help with infant care. He is willing to do infant care, in part, because of the many-stranded reciprocity between husband and wife. In many societies men have fewer tasks to do at the end of the day, while women have domestic tasks and prepare a meal. Men are available to help out with childcare, but seldom provide much assistance, in part, due to the more distant husband–wife relationship.

The third important factor in understanding Aka fathers' involvement with infants is father-infant bonding. Father and infant are clearly attached to each other. Fathers seek out their infants and infants seek out their fathers. Fathers end up holding their infants frequently because the infants crawl to, reach for, or fuss for their fathers. Fathers pick up their infants because they intrinsically enjoy being close to their infants. They enjoy being with them and carry them in several different contexts (e.g., out in the fields drinking palm wine with other men).

While the factors described above are especially influential, other cultural factors also play a part. Gender egalitarianism pervades cultural beliefs and practices: Men do not have physical or institutional control over women, violence against women is rare or nonexistent, both women and men are valued for their different but complementary roles, there is flexibility in these gender roles, and holding infants is not perceived as being feminine or "women's work." Sharing, helping out, and generosity are central concepts in Aka life; this applies to subsistence and parenting spheres. Aka ideology of good and bad fathers reiterates the importance of father's proximity—a good father shows love for his children, stays near them, and assists mother with caregiving when her workload is heavy. A bad father abandons his children and does not share food with them. There is no organized warfare and male feuding is infrequent, so men are around camp and help with subsistence rather than being away at battle. Fertility is high, so most adult women have nursing infants and there are few other adult women around to help out. Finally, the Aka move their camps several times a year and consequently do not accumulate material goods that need to be defended.

The point here is that Aka father-infant relations have to be viewed in a complex cultural nexus. Some cultural factors are somewhat more influential than others—net hunting, husband–wife relations, for instance—but even these cultural features take place in a web of other cultural beliefs and practices that contribute to the intimate nature of Aka father–infant relations.

FATHER–INFANT BONDING IN THE AKA AND UNITED STATES

Over 50 studies of European and American fathers indicate that father's interactions with infants and young children are clearly distinguished from mother's interactions in that fathers are the vigorous rough and tumble playmates of infants and young children, while mothers are sensitive caregivers. The American literature suggests that this rough and tumble play is how infants become attached to fathers ("bond") and develop social competence (Lamb et al. 1987). The Aka father–infant study is not consistent with the American studies that emphasize the importance of father's vigorous play. Aka fathers rarely, if ever, engage in vigorous play with their infants; only one episode of vigorous play by a father was recorded during all 264 hours of systematic observation. Informal observations during more than 10 field visits over the last 20 years are also consistent with this finding. The quantitative data indicate that by comparison to mothers, Aka fathers are significantly more likely to hug, kiss, or soothe a fussy baby while they are holding the infant.

While Aka fathers do not engage in vigorous play with their infants, they are slightly more playful than mothers; fathers are somewhat more likely to engage in minor physical play (e.g., tickling) with their one- to four-month-old infants than are mothers. But characterizing the Aka father as the infant's playmate would be misleading. Other caretakers, brothers and sisters in particular, engage in play with the infant while holding much more frequently than fathers or mothers. Mothers have more episodes of play over the course of a day than fathers or other caretakers because they hold the infant most of the time. The Aka father–infant relationship might be better characterized by its intimate and affective nature. Aka fathers hold their infants more than fathers in any other human society known to anthropologists, and Aka fathers also show affection more frequently while holding than do Aka mothers.

So how can vigorous play be a significant feature in American studies of father–infant bonding, but not among the Aka? Four factors appear to be important for understanding the process of Aka father–infant bonding: familiarity with the infant; knowledge of caregiving practices (how to hold an infant, how to soothe an infant); the degree of relatedness to the infant; and cultural values and parental goals.

First, due to frequent father-holding and availability, Aka fathers know how to communicate with their infants. Fathers know the early signs of infant hunger, fatigue, and illness as well as the limits in their ability to soothe the infant. They also know how to stimulate responses from the infant without being vigorous. Unlike American fathers, Aka wait for infants to initiate interaction. Aka caregivers other than mothers and fathers are less familiar with the infants and the most physical in their play, suggesting a relationship between intimate knowledge of the infant's cues and the frequency of vigorous play while holding. Consistent with this is the finding that working mothers in the U.S. are more likely to engage in vigorous play than are stay-at-home mothers.

Second, knowledge of infant caregiving practices seems to play a role in determining how much play is exhibited in caretaker–infant interactions. Child caretakers were the most physical and the loudest (singing) in their handling of infants. Children were not restricted from holding infants, but they were closely watched by parents. While "other" caretakers were more playful than mothers or fathers, younger fathers and "other" caretakers were more physical than older ones, probably because they did not know how to handle and care for infants as well as adult caretakers.

A third factor to consider is the degree of relatedness of the caretaker to the infant. If vigorous play can assist in developing attachment, more closely related individuals may have a greater vested interest in establishing this bond than distantly related individuals. Attachment not only enhances the survival of the infant, but it can potentially increase the related caretaker's survival and fitness. Aka mothers and fathers establish attachment by their frequent caregiving; vigorous play is not necessary to establish affective saliency. Brothers and sisters, on the other hand, might establish this bond through physical play. Aka brothers and sisters, in fact, provided essentially all of the physical play the focal infants received; cousins and unrelated children were more likely to engage in face-to-face play with the infant instead of physical play.

Finally, cultural values and parental goals of infant development should be considered. American culture encourages individualistic aggressive competition; Aka culture values cooperation, nonaggression, and prestige avoidance (one does not draw attention to oneself even, for instance, if one kills an elephant). Apparently, Americans tolerate—if not actually encourage—aggressive rough-and-tumble types of play with infants. Also, due to the high infant mortality rate, the primary parental goal for Aka is the survival of their infants. The constant holding and immediate attention to fussing reflect this goal. In the United States, infant mortality rates are markedly lower and, as a result, parental concern for survival may not be as great. The Aka infant is taken away from a caretaker who plays roughly with the infant, in part because it could be seen as aggressive behavior, but also because the pervasive aim of infant care practices is survival of the infant, and rough-and-tumble play could risk the infant's safety.

These factors tentatively clarify why Aka fathers do not engage in vigorous play like American fathers, but do participate in slightly more physical play than Aka mothers (but not more than other caretakers). American fathers infrequently participate directly in infant care and consequently are not as familiar with infant cues. To stimulate interaction and (possibly) bonding, they engage in physical play. Aka brothers and sisters are also much less physical in their play with infants than American fathers (Aka never tossed infants in the air or swung them by their arms), again suggesting that Aka children know their infant brother or sister and the necessary infant caregiving skills better than American fathers. These observations are obviously speculative and need further empirical study.

Sociologists LaRossa and LaRossa (1981) also describe stylistic differences between American mothers' and fathers' interactions with their infants. They list a number of male–female role dichotomies that reflect different parenting styles. One distinction they make is role distance versus role embracement. Fathers are more likely to distance themselves from the parenting role while mothers are more likely to embrace the parenting role. American women generally want to remain in primary control of the children, and while fathers may show interest in caregiving, they are more likely to distance themselves from caregiving while embracing their roles as the breadwinners. LaRossa and LaRossa also suggest that fathers generally have low intrinsic value and relatively high extrinsic value, while mothers have the reverse.

> The intrinsic value of something or someone is the amount of sheer pleasure or enjoyment that one gets from experiencing an object or person. The extrinsic value of something or someone is the amount of social rewards (e.g., money, power, prestige) associated with having or being with the object or person. (64)

They use this dichotomy to explain why fathers are more likely to carry or hold an infant in public than in private. Fathers receive extrinsic rewards from those in public settings, while this does not happen in the home. According to LaRossa and LaRossa,

> Fathers will roughhouse with their toddlers on the living-room floor, and will blush when hugged or kissed by the one-year-olds, but when you really get down to it, they just do not have that much fun when they are with their children. If they had their druthers, they would be working at the office or drinking at the local pub. (65)

These role dichotomies may be useful for understanding American mother–father parenting styles, but they have limited value in characterizing Aka mother–father distinctions. Aka mothers and fathers embrace the parenting role. Generally, mothers and fathers want to hold their infants, and certainly they derive pleasure from infant interactions. As indicated earlier, fathers were in fact more likely to show affection while holding than mothers. Fathers also offered their nipples to infants who wanted to nurse, cleaned mucus from their infants' noses, picked lice from their infants' hair, and cleaned their infants after they urinated or defecated (often on the father). Fathers' caregiving did not appear any more or less perfunctory than mothers'. Aka fathers are not burdened with infant care; if a father does not want to hold or care for the infant he gives the infant to another person. Overall, Aka fathers embrace their parenting role as much as they embrace their hunting role.

The intrinsic–extrinsic role dichotomy does not fit well with Aka mother–father parenting styles either. Again, both Aka mothers and fathers place great intrinsic value and little extrinsic value on parenting. The fathers' intrinsic value is demonstrated above, but the lack of extrinsic value among the Aka can best be seen by comparing Aka and Ngandu fathers (the Ngandu are the horticulturalist trading partners of the Aka). When a Ngandu father holds his infant in public he is "on stage." He goes out of his way to show his infant to those who pass by, and frequently tries to stimulate the infant while holding it. He is much more vigorous in his interactions with the infant than are Aka men. The following experience exemplifies Ngandu fathers' extrinsic value towards their infants. An Ngandu friend showed me a 25-pound fish he had just caught, and I asked to take a photograph of him with his fish. He said fine, promptly picked up his nearby infant, and proudly displayed his fish and infant for the photograph. His wife was also nearby but was not invited into the photograph. Aka fathers, on the other hand, are matter-of-fact about their holding or transporting of infants in public places. They do not draw attention to their infants. Aka fathers also hold their infants in all kinds of social and economic contexts.

CONCLUSION

This paper has examined the cultural nexus of Aka father–infant bonding and has made some comparisons to middle-class American father–infant relations. American fathers are characterized by their vigorous play with infants, while Aka fathers are characterized by their affectionate and intimate relations with their infants. Aka infants bond with their fathers because they provide sensitive and regular care, whereas American infants bond to their fathers, in part, due to their vigorous play. The purpose of this paper is not to criticize American fathers for their style of interaction with their infants; physical play is important in middle-class American context because it is a means for fathers who are seldom around their infants to demonstrate their love and interest in the infant. Vigorous play may also be important to American mothers who work outside the home; studies indicate they are also more likely than stay-at-home mothers to engage in vigorous play with their infants. The Aka study does imply that father–infant bonding does not always take place through physical play, and it is necessary to explore a complex cultural nexus in order to understand the nature of father-infant relations.

Aka fathers are very close and affectionate with their infants, and their attachment processes, as defined in Western bonding theory, appear to be similar to that of mothers. While Aka mother– and father–infant relations are similar they are not the same. Fathers do spend substantially less time with infants than do mothers, and the nature of their interactions is different. Aka and American fathers bring something qualitatively different to their children; father's caregiving pattern is not simply a variation of mother's pattern. More research is needed on the unique features of father involvement so we can move away from a "deficit" model of fathering.

Finally, this paper identifies cultural factors that influence father–infant bonding; biological forces are not considered. This is unusual in that mother–infant bonding generally mentions or discusses the biological basis of mother's attachment to the infant. The release of prolactin and oxytocin with birth and lactation is said to increase affectionate feelings and actions toward the infant. These same hormones exist in men but endocrinologists generally believe they have no function in men. Is there a biology of fatherhood, or is motherhood more biological and fatherhood more cultural? This is a complex question as both men and women probably have evolved ("biological") psychological mechanisms that influence their parenting, but if one just focuses on endocrinology, few data exist on the endocrinology of fatherhood. For instance, Gubernick et al. (unpublished paper) found that men's testosterone levels decreased significantly two weeks after the birth of their children; the decrease was not linked to decline in sexual behavior, increased stress, or sleep deprivation. Another small study of American fathers indicated significant increases in plasma prolactin levels after fathers held their 3-month-old infants on their chest for 15 minutes (Hewlett and Alster, unpublished data). The few biological studies that do exist suggest that biology can and does influence fatherhood. More studies of the biocultural nexus of fatherhood are needed.

While biology probably influences both mothers' and fathers' parenting to some degree, this chapter has demonstrated that the cultural nexus is a powerful force that profoundly shapes the nature and context of father–infant bonding. Aka father–infant bonding takes place through regular and intimate (i.e., hugging, kissing, soothing) care while American father–infant bonding takes place through vigorous play. American fathers often do not know their infants very well and try to demonstrate their love and concern through vigorous play. American mothers that work outside the home also tend to be more vigorous with their infants. American fathers are not necessarily "bad" fathers because they do not do as much direct caregiving as the Aka fathers. Fathers around the world "provide" and enrich the lives of their children in diverse ways (e.g., physical and emotional security, economic well-being). The Aka data do suggest that there are alternative processes by which father–infant bonding can and does

take place and that Americans and others might learn from this comparative approach as policy decisions about parental leave and other topics are considered.

REFERENCES

Ainsworth, M.D.S. 1967. *Infancy in Uganda: Infant Care and the Growth of Love.* Baltimore: Johns Hopkins Press.

Bahuchet, S. 1985. *Les Pygmées Aka et la Fôret Centrafricaine.* Paris: Selaf.

Betzig, L., A. Harrigan, and P. Turke. 1990. "Childcare on Ifaluk." *Zeitscrift fur Ethnologie* 114.

Bowlby, J. 1969. *Attachment and Loss Vol. 1: Attachment.* New York: Basic Books.

Chodorow, N. 1974. "Family Structure and Feminine Personality." In *Woman, Culture, and Society,* ed. Michelle Zimbalist Rosaldo and Louise Lamphere. Stanford, CA: Stanford University Press.

Clarke-Stewart, K.A. 1980. "The Father's Contribution to Children's Cognitive and Social Development in Early Childhood." In *The Father–Infant Relationship,* ed. S.A. Pedersen. New York: Praeger.

Cole, M., and J.S. Bruner. 1974. "Cultural Differences and Inferences about Psychological Processes." In *Culture and Cognition,* ed. J.W. Berry and P.R. Dasen. London: Methuen.

Freud, S. 1938. *An Outline of Psychoanalysis.* London: Hogarth.

Gubernick, D.J., C.M. Worthman, and J.F. Stallings. "Hormonal Correlates of Fatherhood in Men." Unpublished paper.

Hamilton, A. 1981. *Nature and Nurture: Aboriginal Child-Rearing in North-Central Arnhem Land.* Canberra: Australian Institute of Aboriginal Studies.

Harlow, H.F. 1961. "The Development of Affectional Patterns in Infant Monkeys." In *Determinants of Infant Behavior,* Vol. 1, ed. B.M. Foss. London: Methuen.

Hewlett, B.S. 1989. "Multiple Caretaking Among African Pygmies. *American Anthropologist* 91:186–191.

———. 1991. *Intimate Fathers: The Nature and Context of Aka Pygmy Paternal-Infant Care.* Ann Arbor, MI: University of Michigan Press.

———. 1992 (ed.). *Father-Child Relations: Cultural and Biosocial Perspectives.* NY: Aldine de Gruyter.

Hewlett, B.S. and D. Alster. "Prolactin and Infant Holding among American Fathers." Unpublished manuscript.

Katz, M.M., and Melvin J. Konner. 1981. "The Role of Father: An Anthropological Perspective." In *The Role of Father in Child Development*, ed. Michael E. Lamb. New York: John Wiley and Sons.

Lamb, M.E., ed. 1981. *The Role of the Father in Child Development*, 2nd ed. New York: John Wiley & Sons.

Lamb, M.E., J.H. Pleck, E.L. Charnov, and J.A. LeVine. 1987. "A Biosocial Perspective on Paternal Behavior and Involvement." In *Parenting Across the Lifespan*, ed. J.B. Lancaster, J. Altmann, A. Rossi, L.R. Sherrod. Hawthorne, NY: Aldine.

Lancaster, J.B., and C.S. Lancaster. 1987. "The Watershed: Change in Parental-Investment and Family Formation Strategies in the Course of Human Evolution." In *Parenting Across the Life Span*, ed. J.B. Lancaster, J. Altmann, A.S. Rossi, and L.R. Sherrod. Hawthorne, NY: Aldine.

LaRossa, R., and M.M. LaRossa. 1981. *Transition to Parenthood: How Infants Change Families*. Beverly Hills: Sage Publications.

LeVine, R.A., S. Dixon, S. LeVine, A. Richman, P.H. Leiderman, C.H. Keefer, and T.B. Brazelton. 1994. *Child Care and Culture: Lessons from Africa*. New York: Cambridge University Press.

Munroe, R.H., and R.L. Munroe. 1992. "Fathers in Children's Environments: A Four Culture Study." In *Father-Child Relations: Cultural and Biosocial Contexts*, Barry S. Hewlett, ed. New York: Aldine de Gruyter.

Rosaldo, M.Z., and L. Lamphere, eds. 1974. *Woman, Culture and Society*. Stanford, CA: Stanford University Press.

West, M.M., and M.J. Konner. 1976. "The Role of Father in Anthropological Perspective." In *The Role of the Father in Child Development*. 2nd ed., M.E. Lamb, ed. New York: John Wiley and Sons.

Whiting, B.B., and J.W.M. Whiting. 1975. *Children of Six Cultures*. Cambridge, MA: Harvard University Press.

Winn, S., G.A. Morelli, and E.Z. Tronick. 1990. "The Infant in the Group: A Look at Efe Caretaking Practices." In *The Cultural Context of Infancy*, J.K. Nugent, B.M. Lester, and T.B. Brazelton, eds. Norwood, NJ: Ablex.

II

Gender and Prehistory

A popular introductory archaeology text began its career thirty years ago with the title *Men of the Earth* (Fagan 1974). For the last ten editions (Fagan 1977–2004) it has been called *People of the Earth*. This change is deliberate and illustrates a growing sensitivity on the part of some archaeologists to the importance of considering the contribution of women, as well as men, to the history of our species (Claassen and Joyce 1997; Wright 1996; Wylie 1991, 1992; Gero and Conkey 1991; Seifert 1991). An archaeological focus on gender provides a lens for reassessing modern myths about the past that single out men as the agents of cultural change. As some archaeologists seek to reinstate women as agents and as subjects, widely held assumptions about "mankind" and "man's past" are challenged by a focus on women's involvement in production, politics, and the generation of symbol systems in past societies. In contrast to earlier archaeological orientations (see Gero and Conkey 1991 for a review of archaeological approaches) an "engendered" archaeology proposes that the process of adaptation throughout human history has of necessity involved a collaborative effort between men and women. Those who advocate a feminist-informed archaeology have explored such issues as women's participation in the creation of wealth (for example, women's production of textiles or ceramics and power relations among craft producers), women's' roles in the dynamics of state formation, representations of powerful women in prehistoric art in relation to gender inequality and identity, and women's roles in the development of agriculture (see Wright 1996 for a collection of articles representing a range of methodologies and theoretical orientations applied to the "archaeologies of gender"; also Spielmann 1995; Simon and Ravesloot 1995).

Questions of fundamental importance regarding the sexual division of labor in past societies can only be resolved from an archaeological perspective that includes explicit methods of identifying the material traces of women's political interests. Rather than assuming that it is simply a natural given that the "earliest human groups were conscious of and elaborated sex differences into differentially valued, gender-exclusive task groups," Spector and Whelan (1989: 73) suggest that an archaeology of gender needs to begin by raising questions about the origins of a sexual division of labor and by determining what gender differentiation might have accomplished among early human populations (Spector and Whelan 1989: 72–73; see also Ehrenberg 1989).

As Conkey (this book) suggests, in the study of gender in archaeology, we are reminded of the importance of confronting presuppositions and values that guide our work, however "scientific" we presume our methodologies to be. Conkey outlines a number of challenges for future archaeological research. First, archaeologists must recognize and eliminate biased reconstructions of past gender roles that derive from our own cultural assumptions. Second, they must pay more attention to theories about gender in analyzing their data. Third, archaeologists need to use their data to make explicit inferences about men and women in prehistory. Finally, Conkey points out biases not only in analysis but also in the very practice of archaeology. Eliminating gender bias from archaeology, as Conkey suggests, will require a major commitment to the same critical reflection that has characterized other branches of anthropology. As Nelson and Kehoe (1990: 4) observe, "disentangling our culture-bound assumptions from the actual archaeological record will be a long and wrenching procedure."

Nelson's discussion of Upper Paleolithic "Venus" figurines in archaeology textbooks (1990) illustrates the potential for distortion in the archaeological record when cultural values affect archaeological analysis. She demonstrates that most textbooks convey the same ideological message in their treatment of Venus figurines—that adult male humans are fascinated by women's bodies and view them as signs of fertility. The widely held assumption that Upper Paleolithic figurines possibly depicting human females are fertility fetishes is, according to Nelson, poorly founded. Feminist analysis of the figurines suggests alternative explanations regarding their production, functions, and symbolism, and serves as a warning that "reinforcing present cultural stereotypes by projecting them into the past allows whole generations of students to believe that our present gender constructs are eternal and unchanging" (Nelson 1990: 19; see also Rice 1991; Wright 1996:9).

Similarly, Galloway (in this book) argues that ethnocentric bias has shaped archaeological interpretations of menstrual seclusion structures in late prehistoric Southeastern Indian societies. She suggests that the search for evidence of menstrual practices is a direct route to finding women in the archaeological record. Menstrual seclusion may be an important correlate of social organization, indicating the probability of matrilineal kinship. Accordingly, investigation of menstrual structures may provide a means of testing for matriliny archaeologically. In spite of the likelihood that there are thousands of menstrual structures in the Southeast, so far none has been reliably reported from an archaeological context. Galloway argues that discomfort with the topic has produced its erasure from scientific discourse, and urges archaeologists both to reinterpret existing data and search for new evidence on these "women's houses," and the artifactual evidence of ritual elements and requirements of daily life associated with them.

In an effort to better explain contemporary gender relations, archaeological evidence has offered a means of understanding the present by reconstructing our evolutionary past. Scholarly and public imaginations have been drawn to the possibility that archaeological data might document the existence of a matriarchal society in which women occupied a privileged position as rulers. If powerful women could be found in history or prehistory, this would serve as evidence that male dominance is not inevitable.

Myths of past matriarchy exist in both western and nonwestern societies. Nineteenth-century evolutionists such as J.J. Bachofen (1967) described a history of humankind that passed from a state of primitive communal marriages, through mother right, or a rule of women, to patriarchy. Similar myths of matriarchy have been recorded in several South American societies (Bamberger 1974: 266). According to Bamberger these myths share a common theme, that of women's loss of power through moral failure. The myths describe a past society in which women held power; however, through their incompetence, the rule of women was eventually replaced by patriarchal leadership.)

Rather than representing historical events, the myths of matriarchy serve as a tool to keep "woman" bound to her place. They reinforce current social relations by justifying male dominance (Bamberger 1974: 280). There is no historical or archaeological evidence of matriarchal societies in which women systematically and exclusively dominated men. In spite of the absence of such evidence the idea remains popular, precisely because it conveys the possibility of a future society characterized by female dominance that is reminiscent of the matriarchal past.

We can avoid projecting our common assumptions and wishful fantasies about gender roles in the past by paying more careful attention to a range of sources at our disposal in the archaeological record. The reconstruction of gender roles and relations in ancient societies may be facilitated by representations of women and men in burials, images, and written texts. The oldest writing tradition in the world is found in the cities of the Sumerian civilization in southern Iraq. Four thousand year old literary texts pertaining to early Sumer portray women in supportive, nurturing roles, acting to further the interests of male political rulers or heroes (Pollock 1991). In some texts, women are also described as political officeholders, or queens. Pollock concludes that some women seem to have had significant political and economic power, although few of them were written about compared to the number of men in such positions whose lives were more fully recorded. Sumerian women also held offices in the temple hierarchy as priestesses; it is possible that these were the primary positions of power available to women. An informative example is that of the priestess Enheduanna, installed at Ur by her father King Sargon. Literary texts suggest that she acted to further her father's political ambitions as well as her own authority (Pollock 1991). These texts, as well as burials and images, suggest that Sumerian women were not pawns to be manipulated by men, but were able to attain positions of high status and power.

Similarly, recent access to Maya history by decipherment of glyphic texts on public monuments has shown that some royal women played politically central roles in their kingdoms. Hypogamy, or the marriage of higher-status women to lower-status men, insured the alliance of these lower-status men to higher-status men of their wives' families. Hypergamy, or the marriage of lower-status women to higher-status men, also occurred. More importantly, the women involved in marriage alliance and royal politics were anything but passive pawns in the games of men. Guenter and Freidel (in this book) look at the lives and exploits of powerful Maya women, demonstrating that Maya royal women were important political players. The translation of glyphic texts has also shown that royal women can emerge as extraordinarily heroic figures and great politicians when their stories are known. Guenter and Freidel review the exploits of several Classic period royal women who had central roles in the unfolding history of their civilization. They focus on the saga of one of these women, a queen at Yaxchilan, who rose to full partnership with her king in matters of war and statecraft and saw to it that her son succeeded to the throne despite the rivalry to a younger queen's child. Lady K'ab'al Xook's success resulted not only from a forceful personality, but from religious and political currents in Maya culture that were thrusting women into the forefront of regional struggles for imperial power. The various forms of power exercised by these women suggest that although there were no matriarchies in the past, women could control important resources and influence the course of public events. Little is known about the lives of commoner women, whose exploits are less visible in texts and other representations. The limited information available on commoner Maya women highlights the need for innovative conceptual and methodological approaches to the archaeological record that will help reconstruct gender roles in past societies.

Conkey and Spector discuss the general problem of the prehistoric "archaeo-logical invisibility" of women (1984: 5), which, they contend, is more the result of a false notion of objectivity and of the gender paradigms archaeologists use than of an inherent invisibility of such data (Conkey and Spector 1984:6). Questions that would elicit information about prehistoric gender behavior or organization are too infrequently asked, while researchers "bring to their work preconceived notions about what each sex ought to do, and these notions serve to structure the way artifacts are interpreted"—for example, the presumption of linkages between projectile points with men and pots with women (Conkey and Spector 1984: 10). In contrast, goals for feminist archaeologies would include gender-inclusive reconstructions of past human behavior, the development of a specific paradigm for the study of gender, and an explicit effort to eliminate androcentrism in the content and mode of presentation of archaeological research (Conkey and Spec-tor 1984: 15). As Brian Fagan has observed, "an engendered archaeology ventures into new territory, using innovative approaches to present the multiple voices of the past . . . " (2004:23).

REFERENCES

Bachofen, Johann. 1967. *Myth, Religion and Mother Right* [Die Mutterrecht 1861 orig.]. London: Routledge and Kegan Paul.

Bamberger, Joan. 1974. "The Myth of Matriarchy: Why Men Rule in Primitive Society." In Michelle Z. Rosaldo and Louise Lamphere (eds.). *Woman, Culture, and Society*, pp. 263–281. Stanford: Stanford University Press.

Claassen, Cheryl and Rosemary A. Joyce (eds.) 1997. *Women in Prehistory*. Philadelphia: University of Pennsylvania Press.

Conkey, Margaret W. and Janet Spector. 1984. "Archaeology and the Study of Gender." In Michael B. Schiffer (ed.). *Advances in Archaeological Method and Theory*, Vol. 7, pp. 1–29. New York: Academic Press.

Ehrenberg, Margaret. 1989. *Women in Prehistory*. Norman, Oklahoma: University of Oklahoma Press.

Fagan, Brian. 1974. *Men of the Earth*. Boston: Little, Brown and Co.

———. 2004. *People of the Earth*. Upper Saddle River, N.J.: Prentice Hall.

Gero, J.M. and Margaret W. Conkey (eds.). 1991. *Engendering Archaeology: Women in Prehistory*. Oxford: Basil Blackwell.

Nelson, Sarah M. 1990. "Diversity of the Upper Paleolithic Venus Figurines and Archeologi-cal Mythology." In Sarah M. Nelson and Alice B. Kehoe (eds.). *Powers of Observation: Alter-native Views in Archeology*, pp. 11–23. *Archeological Papers of the American Anthropological Association*, Number 2.

Nelson, Sarah M. and Alice B. Kehoe. 1990. "Introduction." In Sarah M. Nelson and Alice B. Kehoe (eds.). *Powers of Observation: Alternative Views in Archeology*, pp. 1–10. *Archeological Papers of the American Anthropological Association*, Number 2.

Pollock, Susan. 1991. "Women in a Men's World: Images of Sumerian Women." In Joan Gero and Margaret Conkey (eds.). *Engendering Archaeology: Women and Prehistory*. Oxford: Basil Blackwell.

Rice, Patricia. 1991. "Prehistoric Venuses: Symbols of Motherhood or Womanhood?" *Journal of Anthropological Research* 37(4): 402–414.

Seifert, Donna J. (ed.). 1991. "Gender in Historical Archaeology." *Historical Archeology* (spe-cial issue) 25(4): 1–132.

Simon, Arleyn W. and John C. Ravesloot. 1995. "Salado Ceramic Burial Offerings: A Consid-eration of Gender and Social Organization." *Journal of Anthropological Research* 51(2): 103–124.

Spector, Janet D. and Mary K. Whelan. 1989. "Incorporating Gender into Archaeology Courses." In Sandra Morgen (ed.). *Gender and Anthropology: Critical Reviews for Research and Teaching*, pp. 65–95. Washington, DC: American Anthropological Association.

Spielmann, Katherine A. 1995. "Glimpses of Gender in the Prehistoric Southwest." *Journal of Anthropological Research* 51(2): 91–102.

Wright, Rita P. (ed.) 1996. *Gender and Archaeology*. Philadelphia: University of Pennsylvania Press.

Wylie, Alison, 1991. "Feminist Critiques and Archaeological Challenges." In D. Walde and N. Willows (eds.). *The Archaeology of Gender*, pp. 17–23. Calgary: The Archaeological Association of Calgary.

———. 1992. "The Interplay of Evidential Constraints and Political Interests: Recent Archaeological Research on Gender." *American Antiquity* 57(1): 15–35.

The Archaeology of Gender Today: New Vistas, New Challenges

Margaret W. Conkey

The *entire village* left the next day in about 30 canoes, leaving us alone with the *women and children* in the abandoned houses.

> Levi-Strauss 1936, *as cited by Michard-Marshale and Ribery 1982, in Eichler and Lapointe 1985: 11.*

When we close our eyes and think about the human societies and individuals who lived thousands of years ago, what kinds of people do we "see"? What are they doing? What kinds of roles and relationships do we imagine? Is everyone clearly identifiable as either a man or a woman, or are there other social persons, as well? If one really thinks about this, it should be apparent that there must have been many different roles and relationships, ones that even shifted during the course of any one person's lifetime, or with varied circumstances. There must have been men and women of power, men with children, women as decision-makers, men making pots, women making stone tools, men and women working together in the fields or elsewhere, men in trance, and women as

healers. And in many societies it was likely that there were other social persons; perhaps ritual undertakers who were neither "just" men or women, but those who served to mediate between the living and the dead (Hollimon 1997), or perhaps pre-adolescent young people who did not yet bear the social signifiers of any one more particularly gendered person (Joyce 2000a). Yes, we must recognize that a " two genders" system is not likely to have been everywhere and throughout time.

Yet all too often archaeological accounts, and especially the popular reconstructions of past societies that appear in magazines or coffee table books, suggest a much simpler picture: only men hunt while women gather plants or hover in the background; the men are making the tools, and, if women are depicted at all, they are almost always the ones with children, carrying out a limited range of activities: bringing firewood or scraping hides (Gifford-Gonzalez 1993). Why do we have such simple and yet rather familiar kinds of reconstructions? Certainly part of the explanation is that, until relatively recently, archaeologists had not done much that explicitly asked about gender, yet we had developed models or reconstructions that implicate or involve gender. These reconstructions derive from a variety of problematic sources: from ethnographic accounts that are gender-biased (such as the opening quote from Levi-Strauss) or from the beliefs that twentieth century (mostly western, white, male) archaeologists hold about gender, about men and women, about sexuality and about the division of labor, and about how prehistoric societies "worked" and changed.

We are all, of course, understandably susceptible to our own cultural ideals, ideas, and ideologies, although its not very anthropological to just dismiss certain general activities from being plausible—such as women performing as ritual artists in a past society—based on our presuppositions and cultural biases and beliefs. Most North American archaeologists have taken somewhat longer to be as reflexive and self-critical about this than some of their anthropological colleagues.

Thus, to think about the people of prehistoric societies and to think about their gender roles, gender ideologies, engendering practices, and gender relations raises several archaeological challenges. First, there is the challenge of recognizing and stripping away as much as possible the biased or implied gender reconstructions. It has been said about the study of gender in archaeology that it is not so much a matter of adding gender but of re-gendering the narratives or re-thinking gender. Second, there is the matter of understanding more explicitly what gender is about so we can develop theories of gender—or, as some would argue, theories about identity and difference—that are useful in archaeological research. Third, there is the challenge of making explicit inferences about gender, and about men and women, using archaeological data to help answer questions concerning what might have happened in prehistory and in the historical past. For some, this is a methodological challenge: after all, how can we infer gender and social relations if we cannot "see" the people in action, or talk to them about what their lives are like, what their rituals and symbols might mean, or

how they conceptualize what might be "gender" and other aspects of personal identity and social practice?

While archaeologists clearly came late to the field of gender studies and to using insights from feminist theory, the past fifteen years have been explosive in the amount and diversity of studies and literature that explicitly take up aspects of gender in the human past. The first major paper that reviewed archaeology and the study of gender (Conkey and Spector 1984) came more than ten years after the first major books in sociocultural anthropology, but even then it was clear that archaeological accounts were already "saturated" with gender, albeit accounts that were androcentric (male-centered). Furthermore, these were accounts with a delimited notion of "gender," one that considered gender to be simply another variable or an attribute that could be straightforwardly lined up with being male or being female, rather than the current views that approach gender as a much more fluid, complex, even performative process that is entangled with other aspects of social personhood. Ten years ago, one might have said that at least half of the task of thinking about men and women in prehistory was to question the gendered accounts that pervaded our reconstructions of past societies. And while today we must still be very attentive to the ways in which androcentric (male-centered) and gynecentric (female-centered) accounts are perpetuated, there are, nonetheless, many explicit archaeologies of gender and abundant archaeological studies that have taken on critical and insightful analyses of all sorts of social practices and processes—from craft-specializations, to rock art, to trading systems, to mortuary practices, to queenships, among others—with an explicit concern for their gendered natures and gendered effects.

Twenty years ago, it would have been a challenge to "find" many women in our accounts of the prehistoric past, or, if there, they were usually depicted in a passive way: they were rarely the ones who had made or used the "fancy" ritual objects, even if the objects had been found in a female's grave (Winters 1968). Indeed, the first impulse of a gender-aware archaeology was to "find" the women of the past who had been missing, to make women visible. Today, there are dozens of studies about women and prehistory, women in prehistory, women and production in prehistory. But there are also studies that have pushed archaeological scholarship in other directions as well: archaeologies of sexuality, of mothering, of childhood, of gender transformations, and of the inter-sectionalities of gender with other dimensions of identity, such as race, class, and ethnicity. Many of these studies have taken up topics that were unimagined by the scholars who first proposed a more gender sensitive, critical and feminist-informed archaeology, but this is a good indicator of a healthy and robust field of inquiry.

In the following brief essay, I will try to give something of a historical account of how, despite the many challenges, the archaeological study of gender has come to be so robust and so prevalent in contemporary archaeology. As one author has noted, in referring to the 1991 collection of papers on engendering archaeology (Gero and Conkey 1991), this was "possibly the most influential book published on archaeological theory in the last decade" (Johnson 1999). That the archaeological study of gender could "come from behind" with such success is a testimony to the ways in which dozens of scholars have succeeded in not just providing compelling critiques of previous archaeological work but primarily by engaging in theoretically-informed and empirically-substantiated ways with archaeological materials that can allow valid and insightful inferences about many dimensions of "gender" in the human past.

In writing a short essay like this more than ten years ago (Conkey 1992), the main headings for the essay were: "Challenging Gender Bias" and "Making Gender Explicit in Archaeological Research." Here the two headings will be: "Why an Archaeology of Gender has Emerged" and "Why Gender Matters." In both sections, the challenges

that have been faced and that archaeologists continue to grapple with will be highlighted. But one thing is for sure, not only has the concern for gender in archaeological studies opened all sorts of perspectives on the human past, but also, it has promoted (if not initiated) a genuine concern with the everyday lives, the on-the-ground *people* of the past instead of the more abstract concerns with prehistoric "cultural systems" "groups" or "societies."

WHY AN ARCHAEOLOGY OF GENDER HAS EMERGED

Although it was not immediately apparent to most archaeologists of the 1970s, just a little bit of critical work made it painfully obvious that our archaeological accounts were androcentric, highlighting topics of research that were gendered male in contemporary societies, such as technological innovations and achievements, politics and rulers, warfare and conquest. Hunting (by males) was said to have "caused" the evolutionary success of humans as a species, and the "male-provisioning" of stay-at-home females with children was pushed back to our earliest hominid ancestors (Lovejoy 1981), millions of years ago. At a more subtle level, the ways in which archaeologists represented the males and females of the past was readily shown to be androcentric as well. Men were described with more detail and in more active terms, using active verbs, while women, if portrayed or mentioned, were presented as passive, and by the use of more passive language.

As the substantive critiques of archaeological accounts accumulated, and as studies of language, of the illustrations used to show the people of the past, and of the preferred research topics pointed out all sorts of biases and omissions, over and over again, no one could deny that we had been producing differential representations of men and women in the human past. Our accounts were very archaeo-*logical* because they "made sense" and were logical, given, of course, a certain specific western male-centered point-of view. Further-more, by ascribing considerable antiquity to such things as a sex-based division of labor—with active risk-taking adventurous males, and passive, "home-making," maternally-restricted females—these social relations and arrange-ments were legitimated and naturalized. Even though it was admitted that women might have had, for example, more to do, as a group, with plants (as in "woman the gatherer"), when it came to explaining the "origins of agricul-ture"—considered to be one of the most signif-icant transformations in human history—some scholars went to great lengths to disassociate women from the acts and processes of plant domestication (Watson and Kennedy 1991), suggesting, for example, that (male) shamans cultivated the gourds they needed for their rat-tles, or that the plant seeds that accumulated in refuse heaps around living sites basically domesticated themselves.

It became clear that bias can creep into archaeological (and other) accounts when the analysts do not consciously reflect upon their assumptions nor explicitly use some the-oretical models about gender and social iden-tity. Archaeology, like all other research, is influenced by and embedded in the social and political worlds within which it is prac-ticed. There is now a very well established body of literature that shows how the values, cultural assumptions, and social contexts of the researchers can and do strongly affect the kind of science that is practiced; the produc-tion of knowledge is always situated (Haraway 1988). All sciences are social; every fact has a factor, a maker, who is a person of a certain identity, a certain nationality, race, class, gen-der, ethnicity, status, experience and pers-pective within their profession or field of research. In addition to the substantive cri-tiques of the archaeological accounts as pri-marily androcentric—and androcentric in many different dimensions—early studies in the practice of archaeology that looked at *who* it is that produces archaeological accounts showed the gender differentials and inequities that had favored males.

It is not just Indiana Jones who is the archaeologist-hero; children's drawings of who an archaeologist is confirm the deep-seated assumptions that men are archaeolo-gists (and scientists). One archaeologist once said there were two types of archaeologists: the "hairy chested" or the "hairy chinned" (Ascher 1960). The statistics about who actually is an archaeologist would show that until well into the 1980's archaeology in North America was a predominantly white male enterprise. Although there has been a notable increase in women archaeologists (Zeder 1997), the ethnic diversification of the disci-pline is slower to take place. Throughout the past two decades of explosive work on gender in archaeology, concerns with equity issues have been side-by-side with the archaeological research. Of course, it was not merely the case that there were many more male archaeolo-gists, but it was shown that they received many more of the major research grants to carry out the highly-valued fieldwork and excavation projects, while women archaeologists, as Gero (1994) has shown, had been more relegated to the "housework" of archaeology, such as in the lab, or carrying out the specialist studies rather than directing the "big dig." In other research, Gero has shown (1993) how the studies of American Paleoindian cultures have been dominated by male archaeologists and how the primary picture of Paleoindian life-ways is one that focuses almost exclusively on activities presumed to be male, especially the hunting of big game, with all the associated tools and strategies.

The point of studies like Gero's is not merely to "expose" and critique androcentric thinking and practice. It is, of course, a seri-ous charge to note that the nature of archae-ological (or any other) knowledge is directly created by the topics that are given research priority and that these can be influenced by the gender, race, class, ethnicity and national-ity of the practitioners (and of those who fund archaeology). Rather, the point of such studies is to understand how such factors work, how they do or might bias our archaeo-logical understandings, and to ask critical questions, such as " where *do* archaeologists get assumptions about gender and social life that underlie their interpretations?"

While these studies exposed bias and enhanced a critical reflection about archaeological research and the structure of the discipline, these alone were not enough to bring a genuine concern for gender into archaeology. In addition, of course, we needed to show that we could make inferences about gender, about men and women, and even about other gender systems and roles, that were based on archaeological evidence, or "evidential constraints" (Wylie 1992). This continues to be a genuine challenge. On the one hand, we could not just replace a male-centered view with a female-centered one, even though some of these have been crucial in revealing the biases of the androcentric accounts (e.g., Slocum 1975). On the other hand, this could not be accomplished by merely "adding women" to the story somehow, or by finding some methodological breakthrough that would enable us to "see" gender in the human past. Many researchers have made important and productive contributions by pursuing how we might attribute gender to certain artifacts or burials or living spaces (such as identifying men's houses, or women's work spaces, or women's artifacts), but others have argued that while this was an important step in the re-gendering of archaeology, there were many additional studies and perspectives to take.

For example, while using ethnohistoric information that associated Aztec women with cooking and weaving, Brumfiel (1991) not only made these women more "visible" in the archaeology by drawing on relevant texts and not on our modern assumptions about women's work, but she also considered the ways in which women's labor was being used and deployed in the service of the functioning of the Aztec state. The required cloth tribute, it appears, was provided either directly by women weavers or indirectly by those women who purchased cloth using the funds they raised by selling large amounts of food at the markets, as inferred by the large size of the cooking vessels in archaeological contexts. For Brumfiel, the question at hand is not so much that of doing a remedial archaeology that makes "women visible" but how do systems of social inequality work and how do they draw upon and structure the daily and gendered practices of local people?

Within twenty years or less, the literature that has critiqued gender biases, made women visible, and inquired into the gendered nature of past human cultural lives and processes is rich and diverse: studies have looked at rock art sites as likely female initiation sites, or as bearing heretofore undiscussed images that relate to women's mythologies and social statuses (Hays-Gilpin 2003); all sorts of aspects of gendered power relations have been identified and discussed in a wide variety of past societies (e.g., in Sweely 1999); human skeletal remains have been used to make valid inferences about gendered work practices (e.g., Peterson 2002), and, for example, about violence and skeletal trauma among women, men and "other genders" in the archaeological record of the northern Plains (USA) (Hollimon 2001). The ambiguity of gender in many prehistoric settings (e.g., Klein 2001; Crass 2001; Schmidt 2000) or at certain points in human lifecycles (Joyce 1996, 2001) has shown how we can not really look only for "men" or "women"; rather that gender is more of a process (always being performed, always in the process of becoming) or a relation (one "becomes" gendered in the context of relationships to others or to certain cultural events and practices) than a stable, unchanging given "fact" of life. But this is to jump ahead a bit to talk about why gender matters in our archaeological accounts.

The overall trajectory of gender research in archaeology, then, over the past few decades has been first, to critique our biased accounts and the disciplinary practices of archaeology that might have promoted or at least tolerated such biases. This work must still go on, but we have been building on this necessary foundation. The next major spurt of research was to indeed "make women visible," given that the single most apparent gender bias was against the active presence of women in the human past. Many studies for many parts of the world are still concerned with "finding" women and demonstrating not only their presence but their active contributions to the archaeological record—their tools, spaces, accomplishments—and thus, to the human societies of the past. But in addition, what this quest has brought forth has been a spate of all sorts of new questions, new perspectives, and perhaps even some new archaeologies, both in terms of what questions we ask, what accounts we can give of the human past and various events, and how we therefore "do" archaeology.

As one archaeologist once noted, when he had the "ah ha" experience of realizing that gender was a crucial aspect of human life that, as an explicit and theoretically informed concept, had been quite missing from archaeology, much—he actually said "most"—of the archaeological record must have been in all or in large part the work of women, especially when one is working with the remains of residences, work patios, ceramics, and such. While we no longer can assume that "the domestic" exists as a separate space (as had been the case among Victorian societies and later anthropologists, see Lamphere, this volume, and Rosaldo 1980)), there is no doubt that the hearths, the residential refuse, and many of the day-to-day activities of human societies that were carried out in the sites that are most often more visible to and more substantial in contents for archaeologists most likely contain evidence of gendered work and gendered life, often gendered predominantly female. When we have very complete archaeological records due to exceptional preservation (e.g., Hamlin 2001), we can get a much more nuanced understanding of the various activities and tasks carried out at sites of everyday life, including the recognition of not just "men" and "women" but also sub-adults, children, and even infants. In fact, if there is one major contribution of a gender-sensitive archaeology, it has been to augment and expand our understandings of everyday life, and the micro-scale level of archaeology. When added to the often prevalent interests in macro-scale archaeology that seeks to understand large scale cultural processes, such as population expansions, state-formation, or the origins of certain technologies (metals, agriculture), this refined micro-scale archaeology and archaeology of the everyday makes for a more complete archaeology, a veritable multi-scalar archaeology.

WHY GENDER MATTERS

Just as we note that social and political concerns can affect our science and our anthropology, couldn't it be said that this robust interest in gender and in reclaiming women as active agents in the making of culture and culture history is primarily a political and social act, set in the wake of the second and third wave feminist movements of western society? Is this archaeology of gender of such interest because gender issues are (or at least ought to be, given persistent inequities) among some of more important and widespread interests of our times, in our societies? Perhaps this is partly true, and, to the extent that our research has almost always been influenced by what our interests are and what resonates with our concerns and social needs are, then the engagement with, and even the passion for an engendered archaeology can be accounted for in terms of our present-day interests. Is it no surprise that, for the most part, the scholars who have really focused on gender in archaeology have been women? Does this, however, tend to make this subfield something of a marginalized "ghetto" of scholars or at least more liable to be marginalized? These are long-standing concerns, and have led some archaeologists of gender (e.g., Stig-Sorenson 2000) to distance themselves, and the field of gender archaeology, from any politics at all. We could go much further in discussing this topic, and it is one well worth discussing, but in the short space that remains, I would like to emphasize instead what an engendered archaeology has led to, and what, no matter what the inspiration for the research, a concern with gender can do and has done for our archaeology and for our understandings of the human past.

First, as noted above, the "gender focus" has led not only to even more emphasis on the micro-scale and the archaeology of everyday life, it has also allowed for/encouraged a link with other theoretical interests that have been re-shaping archaeological inquiry. In particular, a concern with gender has fit well with and enhanced the adoption of some aspects of what is called "practice theory" by archaeologists, in which, simplistically put, the concern is for understanding the everyday, often unacknowledged social practices that not only constituted the social formations and "cultures" of the past, but that also constituted the identities and social personae of the people of the past. How our practices inform our identities and notions of self and how these might have worked in the past are fascinating, somewhat new questions. They are fundamental questions if we want to understand even the large-scale events or processes that shaped past societies. Some of the most exciting and provocative of studies in an engendered archaeology have drawn explicitly from practice and performance theories (e.g., Joyce 1998, 2000b).

Second, we can perhaps better understand "gender" as a phenomenon in the contemporary world not by assuming it has always been there or always been more-or-less the same, but by explicitly questioning the concept, and by accepting that perhaps—as archaeologists are beginning to show—"our" understandings of gender and our ways of using gender ideologies to structure social relations are not the only possibilities. As Henrietta Moore once said (1995: 53), "it is the archaeologists [rather than the post modernists] to whom we look to sustain our awareness of the plurality of social times." That is, archaeological inquiry into "gender"—if it existed, how it was practiced, what it might have signified, how it was defined and performed, what varieties of gender might have been "at work" in past societies—has shown some of the ways in which a single notion of gender—usually that there are 2 biological sexes who perform associated gender roles (those of men and those of women)—cannot be sustained for all human societies. For those who do have political concerns about inequality in the present, this is important evidential information that can be helpful in challenging some of the "givens" of present day society. If there is one "fact" about gender that archaeologists have shown, it is

that gender is mutable, and, as a distinct social concept, may not have existed in the same terms as today, if it even existed at all.

Furthermore, what a concern with gender also facilitated was an increasing archaeological interest in and engagement with broader social processes that archaeologists had heretofore often considered in simplistic terms. For example, some feminist archaeologists (e.g., Meskell 2001, 2003) would suggest that archaeological concerns are thus with "identity" and difference, how this was constructed in the past, and how gender, as third wave feminists demonstrated (e.g., Moraga and Anzaldua 1981), cannot be understood as distinct from other dimensions of identity and social position and practice. For many contemporary researchers, their concerns have been with the intersections among gender, race, class, ethnicity (e.g., Collins 1999). These may not always be the relevant "categories" for societies in the past, but it is increasingly clear that aspects of one's identity, such as age, social positions (but not necessarily socioeconomic class, as in capitalist societies), kinship, wealth, sexual orientations, experience, as well as something we might broadly consider to be "genders," were integral to how one's social status was determined and how societies "worked." Many of these processes, how they worked, changed, and shaped societies are crucial even to understanding large scale sociopolitical processes and cultural change, long the favorite topics of archaeologists.

If one really wants to better understand how human systems—social, political, economic, etc—work and changed, the workings of such phenomena as "gender, class and faction" (Brumfiel 1992), and their intersections, are of enormous relevance: that it was the work of women making *chicha* (corn-based beer) that "fed" the politics of the Inka state (Hastorf 1991); that it was the net-making knowledge and practices, most likely by women, that allow us to infer their role in making the famous Ice Age female figurines (Soffer, et al. 2000); that certain stone tool making practices were crucial to the redefinition of Aboriginal masculinities and the maintenance of a viable identity in the face of colonial impacts (Harrison 2002); that there were many possible ways in which women gained legitimate as well as covert political powers (Marcus 2001). These are all examples of how archaeological work has not only made women visible, but added to the more nuanced understandings of how gender and social relations are at work in social stability and transformation. These archaeologies add to the evidence that has toppled the once-prevalent notion that we could talk about "the" cross-cultural status of women, which is now shown to be so variable in its forms, processes, and practices.

Gender, or something akin to what we mean by gender, almost has to be in existence in some forms or another in many human societies since the appearance of symbol-using, socially-bound modern humans. If archaeology does not consider how gender, age and other factors have been instrumental in the formation and definition of such fundamental human social practices as the division of labor and the construction of iden-tity-consciousness by individuals and social groups, we will surely miss a lot about how human societies worked, "got on" and changed, changing others on the way.

Looking at gender has also prompted more engaged attention to other dimensions of human life that have rarely been in the archaeological focus, such as sexuality, chil-dren, and mothering. After all, all of these were surely part of prehistoric life and soci-eties; without them, there would be no us, no descendants! Yet, some may ask, how can we ever "see" sexuality, or "find" the activities of children? These have become some of the new archaeological challenges, now that much archaeology has turned its attention to the people of the past, as much as to the cul-tural processes. Of course, these are not likely to be aspects of life that we can make infer-ences about in every situation, with every archaeological record, for every site or "cul-ture." But we now know more about such things as the African-American midwife and mothering practices in the late 19th century southern United States (Wilkie 2003), or

about the strategies of women and their female partners in forging identities in a colo-nial women's prison in Tasmania (Casella 2000), or about how the imposition of new architectures and uses of space on native Californians by colonizing Spaniards must have re-structured their intimate interper-sonal lives (Voss 2000).

Even if one makes the move, then, from what might have started out as a somewhat straightforward inquiry into the archaeology of (just two?) genders, especially by "adding women," into some of the multiple related domains of social life—sexual orientation and identity; the construction of difference of all sorts and in varying contexts; the prac-tices of mothering; the place, roles and practices of children; a more intense look at the everyday lives; the micro-scale; the household lives and labors of everyone—archaeology has gained in our understand-ings of not just past social life, social formations, social transformations and change. We also gain a more expanded understanding of what these social proc-esses, categories and practices are about in contemporary life and in human soci-eties more broadly. Archaeologists have expanded their theoretical resources beyond a good grasp on how humans and their environments inter-relate to how social life is enacted and could be defined and how humans not only develop a sense of dif-ference, but institutionalize and challenge such differences, at many scales of their lives. This then is an archaeology that con-tinues to have challenges; after all, it is not easy to make valid inferences about issues that we have difficulty with even when we can participate in a living society or inter-view selected informants. And it is not easy to change the persistence of biases, the dis-ciplinary structures that prefer and reward certain kinds of research over others, and that are part of wider institutional and social settings that are still marked by inequities and differential access to resources and social value.

What we have seen is that once made aware of just some of the more blatant androcentric archaeologies, in content and in practice, many archaeologists not only re-assessed their own work and interpretations, but took up the challenges of "finding women," then questioning the concepts of "gender," trying to infer aspects of sexuality, mothering, and other gendered practices, and using gender as a stepping stone in concept and method to broaden our archaeological horizons, contribute to defining what we now see to be richly varied tableau of human social arrangements and cultural ways of being in the world.

REFERENCES

Ascher, Robert. 1960. Archaeology and the public image. *American Antiquity* 25(3): 402–403.

Brumfiel, Elizabeth. 1991. Weaving and cooking: Women's production in Aztec Mexico. In Joan Gero and Margaret Conkey (eds). *Engendering Archaeology: Women and Prehistory*, pp. 224–254. Oxford: Basil Blackwell.

———. 1992. Breaking and entering the ecosystem: Gender, class and faction steal the show. *American Anthropologist* 94(3): 551–567.

Casella, Eleanor. 2000. Bulldaggers and gentle ladies: Archaeological approaches to female homosexuality in convict-era Australia. In Robert Schmidt and Barbara Voss (eds). *Archaeologies of Sexuality*, pp. 143–159, London and New York: Routledge.

Collins, Patricia Hill. 1999. Moving beyond gender. Intersectionality and scientific knowledge. In M.M. Ferree, Judith Lorber, and B.B. Hess (eds). *Revisioning Gender*, pp. 261–284. Thousand Oaks, CA: Sage.

Conkey, Margaret. 1992. Men and women in prehistory: An archaeological challenge. In Caroline Brettell and Carolyn Sargent (eds). *Gender in Cross-Cultural Perspective* pp. 41–50, New York: Prentice-Hall.

Conkey, Margaret and Janet Spector. 1984. Archaeology and the study of gender. In Michael B. Schiffer (ed.) *Advances in Archaeological Method and Theory*, Vol. 7, pp. 1–38, New York: Academic Press.

Crass, Barbara A. 2001. Gender and mortuary analysis: What can grave goods really tell us? In Bettina Arnold and Nancy L. Wicker (eds). *Gender and the Archaeology of Death*, pp. 105–118, Walnut Creek, CA: Alta Mira Press.

Eichler, Margrit and Jeanne Lapointe. 1985. *On the Treatment of the Sexes in Research*. Ottawa: Social Sciences and Humanities Research Council of Canada.

Gero, Joan. 1993. The social world of prehistoric facts: gender and power in Paleoindian research. In Hilary du Cros and Laurajane Smith (eds.). *Women in Archaeology, A Feminist Critique, Occasional Papers in Prehistory*, No. 23, pp. 31–40, Canberra: Australian National University, Department of Prehistory.

———. 1994. Excavation bias and the woman-at-home ideology. In Margaret Nelson, Sarah M. Nelson, and Alison Wylie (eds.). *Equity Issues for Women in Archaeology, Archaeology Papers of the American Anthropological Association, Number 5*, pp. 37–42, Washington, DC: American Anthropological Association.

Gero, Joan and Margaret Conkey (eds.). 1991. *Engendering Archaeology: Women and Prehistory*. Oxford: Basil Blackwell.

Gifford-Gonzalez, Diane. 1993. You can hide, but you can't run. Representations of women's work in illustrations of Paleolithic life. *Visual Anthropology Review* 9(1): 3–21.

Hamlin, Christine. 2001. Sharing the Load: Gender and Task Division at the Windover Site. In Bettina Arnold and Nancy L. Wicker (eds.). *Gender and the Archaeology of Death*, pp. 119–136, Walnut Creek, CA: Alta Mira Press.

Haraway, Donna. 1988. Situated knowledges: The science question in feminism and the privilege of partial perspective. *Feminist Studies* 14(3): 575–599.

Harrison, Rodney. 2002. Archaeology and the colonial encounter: Kimberly spearpoints, cultural identity and masculinity in the north of Australia," *Journal of Social Archaeology*, 2(3): 352–377.

Hastorf, Christine. 1991. Gender, space and food in prehistory. In Joan Gero and Margaret Conkey (eds.). *Engendering Archaeology: Women and Prehistory*, pp. 132–162, Oxford: Basil Blackwell.

Hays-Gilpin, Kelly. 2003. *Ambiguous Images: Gender and Rock Art*. Walnut Creek, CA: Alta Mira Press.

Hollimon, Sandra. 1997. The third gender in California: Two-spirit undertakers among the Chumash and their neighbors. In Cheryl Claassen and Rosemary Joyce (eds.). *Women in Prehistory. North America and Mesoamerica*, pp. 173–188, Philadelphia: University of Pennsylvania Press.

———. 2001. Warfare and gender in the northern Plains: Osteological evidence of trauma reconsidered. In Bettina Arnold and Nancy

L. Wicker (eds.). *Gender and the Archaeology of Death*, pp. 179–194, Walnut Creek, CA: Alta Mira Press.

Johnson, Matthew. 1999. *Archaeological Theory*. Oxford: Basil Blackwell.

Joyce, Rosemary. 1996. The construction of gender in classic Maya monuments. In Rita B. Wright (ed.). *Gender and Archaeology*, pp. 167–198, Philadelphia: University of Pennsylvania Press.

———. 1998. Performing the body in prehispanic Central America. *Res: Anthropology and Aesthetics* Vol. 33 (spring): 147–165.

———. 2000a. Girling the girl and boying the boy: The production of adulthood in ancient Mesoamerica. *World Archaeology* 31(3): 473–483.

———. 2000b. *Gender and Power in Prehispanic Mesoamerica*. Austin, TX: University of Texas Press.

———. 2001. Negotiating sex and gender in Mesoamerican society. In Cecelia Klein (ed.). *Gender in Pre-hispanic America*, pp. 109–142, Washington, DC: Dumbarton Oaks Research Library and Collection.

Klein, Cecelia. 2001. None of the above: Gender ambiguity in Nahua ideology. In Cecelia Klein (ed.). *Gender in Pre-hispanic America*, pp. 109–142, Washington, DC: Dumbarton Oaks Research Library and Collection.

Levi-Strauss, Claude. 1936. Contributions á l' étude de l'organization sociale des Indiens Bororo. *Journal de la Société des Americanistes de Paris* 28: 269–304.

Lovejoy, Owen. 1981. The origin of man. *Science* 211: 341–350.

Marcus, Joyce. 2001. Breaking the glass ceiling: The strategies of royal women in ancient states. In Cecelia Klein (ed.). *Gender in Pre-hispanic America*, pp. 305–340, Washington, DC: Dumbarton Oaks Research Library and Collection.

Meskell, Lynn. 2001. Archaeologies of identity. In Ian Hodder (ed.). *Archaeological Theory Today*, pp. 187–211, Cambridge: Polity Press.

———. 2003. Feminist archaeologies of identity and difference. In special feature: Revisiting Feminism and Anthropology Across the Four Fields. *VOICES: A Publication of the Association for Feminist Anthropology*, volume 6(1): 5, 13, 14.

Michard-Marshale, Claire and Claudine Ribery. 1982. *Sexisme et Science Humaine*. Lille: Presses Universitaires de France.

Moore, Henrietta. 1995. The problems of origins: Poststructuralism and beyond. In Ian Hodder, Michael Shanks, Alexandra Alexandri, Victor Buchli, John Carman, Jonathan Last, and Gavin Lucas (eds.), *Interpreting Archaeology:*

Finding Meaning in the Past. pp. 51–53, London and New York: Routledge.

Moraga, Cherrie and Gloria Anzaldua eds. 1981. *This Bridge Called My Back. Writings by Radical Women of Color*. Watertown, MA: Persephone.

Peterson, Jane. 2002. *Sexual Revolutions: Gender and Labor at the Dawn of Agriculture*. Walnut Creek, CA: Alta Mira Press.

Rosaldo, Michelle. 1980. The use and abuse of anthropology. Reflections on feminism and cross-cultural understanding, *SIGNS: Journal of Women in Culture and Society*, 5(3):389–417.

Schmidt, Robert. 2000. Shamans and northern cosmology: The direct historical approach to Mesolithic sexuality. In Robert Schmidt and Barbara Voss (eds.), *Archaeologies of Sexuality*, pp. 220–235. London and New York: Routledge.

Slocum, Sally. 1975. Woman the gatherer: Male bias in anthropology. In Rayna Rapp Reiter (ed.). *Toward an Anthropology of Women*, pp. 36–50, New York and London: Monthly Review Press.

Soffer, Olga, James Adovasio and D. C. Hyland. 2000. The "Venus" figurines: Textiles, basketry, gender and status in the Upper Paleolithic. *Current Anthropology* 41(4): 511–537.

Stig-Sorenson, Marie-Louise. 2000. *Gender Archaeology*. Cambridge: Polity Press.

Sweely, Tracy L. (ed.). 1999. *Manifesting Power. Gender and the Interpretation of Power In Prehistory*. London and New York: Routledge.

Voss, Barbara. 2000. Colonial sex: Archaeology, structured space, and sexuality in Alta California's Spanish-colonial missions. In Robert Schmidt and Barbara Voss (eds.), *Archaeologies of Sexuality*, pp. 35–61. London and New York: Routledge.

Watson, Patty Jo and Mary C. Kennedy. 1991. The development of horticulture in the eastern woodlands of North America: Women's role. In Joan Gero and Margaret Conkey (eds.). *Engendering Archaeology: Women and Prehistory*, pp. 255–275, Oxford: Basil Blackwell.

Wilkie, Laurie. 2003. *The Archaeology of Mothering. An African-American Midwife's Tale*. London and New York: Routledge.

Winters, Howard. 1968. Value-systems and trade cycles of the late archaic in the Midwest. In S. R. Binford and L. R. Binford (eds.). *New Perspectives in Archaeology*, pp. 175–222. Chicago: Aldine.

Wylie, Alison. 1992. The interplay of evidential constraints and political interests: Recent archaeological research on gender. *American Antiquity* 57(1): 15–35.

Zeder, Melinda. 1997. *The American Archaeologist: A Profile*. Walnut Creek, CA: Alta Mira Press.

Where Have All the Menstrual Huts Gone? The Invisibility of Menstrual Seclusion in the Late Prehistoric Southeast

Patricia Galloway

OVERTURE

> . . . she invariably had three things with her on the ledge of her ground-floor box: her opera-glass, a bag of sweets, and a bouquet of camellias. For twenty-five days of the month the camellias were white, and for five they were red; no one ever knew the reason for this change of colour, which I mention though I can not explain it.
>
> *Alexandre Dumas fils*

"She," of course, was Alexandre Dumas fils's Camille, the Lady of the Camellias, a very expensive Parisian courtesan who renounced everything for love. Today the best-selling line of French "sanitary napkins" is brandnamed "Camellia," but then that is the kind of mildly smutty public discourse that straitlaced Americans would expect from the French. And it is a far cry, indeed, from a high-flown literary allusion to the grubby term "menstrual hut"—or is it? Both terms were coined by Western cultures, and both share the tendency to hide female practices accommodating the "wound that does not heal." As archaeologists we are deluding ourselves if we think our own professional practice is unaffected by that same tendency. If the most basic move toward engendering archaeology is finding women in the archaeological record, the search for evidence of menstrual practices is about as direct a way to do it as there could be. Yet it is a search that pretty clearly has not been made. This is unfortunate, since anthropological studies suggest

From C. Claussen and R. Joyce, eds. *Women in Prehistory: North America and Mesoamerica*, pp. 47–62. 1997, University of Pennsylvania Press.

that menstrual seclusion may be an important correlate of social organization, and social organization is just what researchers concerned with the late prehistoric Southeast have all been claiming to be interested in.

LITERATURE REVIEW

The term "menstrual hut" is already very evocative; why not "house" or simply "structure"? We know in a general way that in historic period Southeastern nonstate societies women subject to rules of ritual seclusion during menses withdrew to specific structures for the duration of their period of "pollution." But Southeastern archaeologists do not find menstrual huts routinely, even when investigating settlements; they have apparently assumed that the structures reserved for that purpose were too squalid and temporary to leave evidence worth looking for, and the term "hut" is an index of that assumption. But why have such assumptions been made? Is this really the reliable import of the ethnographic literature?

In the first place, "the ethnographic literature" for the early historic period in the Southeast is almost exclusively limited to the work of John R. Swanton. We should remember in dealing with the information he provides that this is the same John Swanton who presented the explicit sexual material in *Myths and Tales of the Southeastern Indians* (1929) in Latin, and his reticence in dealing with reproductive matters with most of his contemporary informants is reflected in the fact that his sources on the topic of menstruation are mostly limited to the fortuitous testimonies of eighteenth-century male European missionaries and colonists and (for the Creeks) other ethnologists of his own time. Neither Swanton nor his colleagues obtained information about menstrual huts from female informants, so all that we have regarding this matter, even now, amounts to external observation at best. A sample of Swanton's evidence for menstrual practices and taboos follows:

1. *Timucua:* fish and venison food restrictions, prohibition of fire kindling; similar food restrictions after childbirth (Swanton 1946:713). Note that Swanton's source for making of "a separate fire" by women during menses is its listing as a superstitious sin in the 1613 *Confessionario of Francisco Pareja* (Milanich et al. 1972:25).

2. *Creek:* menstrual seclusion in house "by herself" for four days (as at childbirth); utensils for food preparation and consumption reserved for use during menses; prohibition on consumption of meat from large animals and on presence in garden; bathing required downstream from men, prohibition on presence upwind of men; required bath and change of clothes for purification at the end of menses. Early-twentieth-century informants and ethnologists referred to "a house," a "seclusion lodge," "a separate tent or house," and "a small house near some spring or stream" (Swanton 1928:358–360, 1947:714).

3. *Chickasaw:* menstrual huts, built far from dwellings but near enough to the village to be safe from enemies, used monthly and at childbirth; required bath and change of clothing afterward; food restrictions during pregnancy, also couvade practices (abstention from work, avoidance by other men) by the husband after birth. Adair refers to the relevant structures as "small huts" (Swanton 1928:358–359, 1946:715–716).

4. *Choctaw:* small cabin "apart" monthly and for childbirth; food restrictions at childbirth; covade practices (food restrictions) (Swanton 1946:716). Note that this comes from only one source, the ca. 1730s French "Anonymous Relation."

5. *Natchez:* A brief remark taken from the descriptions of marriage by the missionary Father Le Petit notes that during menstruation there was a prohibition on marital intercourse; Swanton notes nothing further for the Natchez on this subject (1911:97).

Thus where information is available for Southeastern Indian groups, it all definitely points to ritual seclusion during menses carried out publicly, generally in a structure specifically reserved for the purpose, with accompanying taboos. It is relevant that where such ritual seclusion took place for menstruation, it was also required along with many of the same taboos for childbirth, often apparently in the same structure. Unfortunately the evidence is rather vague on the details of such structures, suggesting that many of those who reported them may not have seen one. The overwhelming evidence for such structures makes it all the more curious that none has been found by archaeologists.

THE ANTHROPOLOGY OF MENSTRUATION

The topic of menstrual practices has served along with female puberty initiations and childbirth practices as a hobbyhorse for nearly every strain of anthropological thought (see Buckley and Gottlieb 1988b). Lately, as a result of attention from feminists, menstrual practices have come in for a good deal of popularizing "anthropological" and "psychological" treatment, being linked with the old notion of primal matriarchies and the New Age "goddess" movement in several popular books (cf. Delaney et al. 1976; Shuttle and Redgrove 1978; even Weideger 1976 overgeneralizes from very poor anthropological evidence). However praiseworthy a clear-eyed look at menstruation as experienced by modern women is, these books have not clarified matters by viewing menstrual seclusion as "universal" and a "cruelty" imposed by patriarchal authority jealous of "women's mysteries," and in any case they all virtually ignore prehistoric cultures.

Several relatively recent serious anthropological studies are, I think, much more helpful in thinking about prehistory because they grapple with the problem of how menstrual seclusion works within cultures and its possible correlation with social organization. Paige and Paige (1981) have treated the topic as part of an analysis of the sociopolitical functioning of "fraternal interest groups" under a version of exchange theory; Douglas (1966) and Schlegal (1972) have analyzed menstrual seclusion as part of cross-cultural studies of pollution and male domination, respectively; several of the essays edited by Buckley and Gottlieb (1988a) focus on the experience of the practice itself and on its advantages to women; while Martin's (1992) work on Western female embodiment stresses the usefulness of menstrual taboos to modern women. These rather heterogeneous studies appear to agree that menstrual seclusion and its accompanying practices are advantageous to women and are characteristic of societies where husbands and males in general are not particularly dominant, especially matrilineal societies where residence rules are generally matrilocal. Paige and Paige (1981) go on to generalize that such societies—societies with "weak fraternal internal groups"—are characterized by a subsistence base that is not valuable enough to require defense, such as shifting agriculture with hunting and gathering. This is not inappropriate as a description of the historic tribes of the Southeast, but it is more problematic as a characterization of the rather aggressive chiefdom model now accepted for the late prehistoric societies that preceded them.

Kinship and residence in Mississippian societies have been more assumed about than understood. Knight (1990) has recently discussed the relation of kinship to sociopolitical structure in some detail, foregrounding the problematic nature of ethnohistorically attested kinship forms in the early colonial Southeast, but concludes that archaeological correlates "are yet to be worked out." And although Paige and Paige (1981:121) argue generally that matrilineal, matrilocal societies do not have an abundant and rich resource base, they have discussed one example of an advanced agricultural society, the Nayar of India (which is matrilineal and matrilocal), that practices menstrual seclusion and is even characterized by non-resident husbands.

Clearly much more work remains to be done in understanding whether menstrual seclusion does actually correlate reliably with matrilineality/matrilocality, since the cross-cultural sample used by Paige and Paige (1981) was based on largely androcentrically biased ethnographies and coding practices (cf: Buckley 1988: 192–193). It is, for example, quite possible that matrilineality/matrilocality in the Southeast was an artifact of the protohistoric disease holocaust period: Harris (1988:34–37) suggests that warfare or other disruption is a strong pressure for matrilocality, and it stands to reason that since matrilineages would select for female children to expand the lineage and attract bridewealth, they would also favor population increase and prove an ideal vehicle for post-catastrophe population recovery.

Still, it is not beyond the bounds of possibility that the known population expansion of the Mississippian period might also be explained in this manner; that the Natchez model, at least for matrilines, is correct for the Mississippian period; and that Mississippian societies might thus be characterized by the same practices—which should be marked materially by the presence of "menstrual huts." If, on the other hand, Mississippian societies did not practice menstrual seclusion, it is quite possible that their kinship organization was not matrilineal, and their residence practice not matrilocal. If that possibility is admitted, then a thorough reexamination of our dependence on post-contact ethnographies is in order. The point is that the correlation between menstrual seclusion and matrilineal kinship seems to be good enough that it should be possible to test for matrilineal kinship archaeologically if we can just figure out what a "menstrual hut" ought to look like in the ground.

MENSTRUAL TABOOS AND MODERN ARCHAEOLOGY

If the ethnographic evidence and the matrilineal model are correct, there must have been thousands of menstrual huts constructed in the Southeast, just from the colonial period from which they are certainly attested. Yet so far no menstrual hut has been reliably reported from a Southeastern archaeological context. The few identifications from elsewhere are unfortunately problematic. J. Heilman's identification of a "women's house" (House II/77) at the Fort Ancient Sunwatch site is the right period, but it remains unpublished and details are lacking (J. Heilman, personal communication, 1992); furthermore, the structure in question is located within the village, which would contradict the need for spatial separation. Robson Bonnichsen (1973:281) suggested a "menstrual retreat" as one possible explanation for apparently female-occupied tent remains at a contemporary multiple-structure Cree camp, but this and the other two candidate explanations proved false when the camp owner was interviewed. Finally, Lewis Binford's half-hearted identification of a possible menstrual hut in the Hatchery West report (1970:40–41), was based solely on the fact that it was a small and anomalous structure. Why "anomalous"? Perhaps simply because menstruation is marked as "polluting" and "dangerous" in our own society's dominant male discourse, and that prejudice is transferred to other societies, including prehistoric ones, without much reflection. I am suggesting, in short, that the influence of modern taboos on ethnocentric archaeologists, whether male or female, should not be ignored; just as women rarely menstruate in Western literature, so menstruation is generally ignored in considering women's lives archaeologically, as though women in all times and places similarly hid the condition of menstruation—indeed hid it so effectively that it became invisible in the archaeological record.

The symptoms of this ethnocentricity are not far to seek. Charles Hudson, in his influential normative summary of Southeastern menstrual seclusion practices in 1976, matter-of-factly drew on uniformitarian generalization when he offered the following assertion, now discounted by cross-cultural studies (Hudson's reference in this passage is to Paige's 1973 popular article, which was actually about how Western women are socialized to suffer during menstruation):

> The Southeastern Indians may have recognized at least implicitly some sound social and psychological principles. Psychologists have amply verified what folk knowledge tells us about menstruation, namely that women become depressed, hostile, anxious, and even socially disruptive just before and during menstruation. (Hudson 1976:320)

There is very good reason for anthropologists and archaeologists enculturated in Western societies to believe assertions like Hudson's and to experience "negative affect" associated with the very topic of menstruation, despite mounting evidence for the social origin of most of the negative behavioral correlates observed in Western societies (Martin 1992:92–138). Because Western societies practice the hiding of menstruation (as do many "primitive" societies like the Manus of New Guinea [Mead 1939:157–158]), the topic itself is treated with reticence by females, discomfited derision by males, and with pollution anxieties, in many instances, by both. Being seen in public to bleed from the vagina is still one of the most profound humiliations a Western female can experience, despite the fact that at least a majority of American women value their menstrual periods as a sign of their identity as women and of their continuing fertility (Martin 1992).

Beginning with the commodification of disposable "sanitary" supplies in 1921, advertisements for them have stressed invisibility, security of protection from staining, and suppression of menstrual odor, without once using the word "menstruation." These advertisements have frequently featured women wearing white or light-colored clothing (though white clothing is the very last thing a menstruating Western woman would choose to wear or especially the expensive formal clothing worn on highly public and therefore dangerously exposed) occasions. Even in the 1990s, very little has changed in terms of the language used (menstruation and blood are almost never mentioned explicitly), although much more frankness in the portrayal of the product (particularly comparative photographs of sanitary napkins, for example) is evident. The fact remains that despite all the pop-psychology discussion of premenstrual syndrome, or PMS, menstruating Western women are still not supposed to betray the fact in public and may still be subject to specific restrictions in private on grounds of religious or other belief (Martin 1992:97–98). And although most Western males do not go so far as John Milton, whose wife had to sleep on the floor while menstruating rather than pollute the marriage bed, many are reluctant to have sexual intercourse with menstruating women.

This is not a trivial issue. The whole topic of menstruation in modern Western cultures is still so avoided by women through shame, or trivialized by men through PMS jokes (even scientific ones), that our discomfort with it may blind us even to paying attention to its significance in other cultures or in subcultures within our own. Modern Miccosuki women use paper plates and plastic utensils in the tribal cafeteria during their periods, while men and nonmenstruating women use china and stainless steel (Pat Kwachka, personal communication, 1992), and the same practice is followed in conservative Creek households (Bell 1990:334). Orthodox Jewish women around the world are forbidden to prepare food while menstruating and are required to take a ritual bath at the termination of the menstrual cycle. I suggest, therefore, that discomfort with the topic and its resulting erasure from scientific discourse are the simple reasons that no one has proposed a model for the archaeological correlates of menstrual seclusion practices.

Cultural practices that deal with areas of life that the dominant culture does not mark as shameful (and that are the domain of men and, therefore, "unmarked") can be looked at in public, and this is nowhere more graphically obvious than in the treatment of blood: we have become accustomed to gallons of blood and gore from wounds inflicted by (generally male) violence, whether on the evening news or in our entertainment, and even we as archaeologists have exhibited endless fascination with evidence for wounds on skeletal remains. Yet advertisements depicting the absorptive capabilities of "sanitary" supplies prudishly use a thin *blue* liquid for demonstration. Examples of treatment of blood from the female genital area in current entertainment media include horror films (both *Carrie* and *The Exorcist* treat the alleged enormously magnified telekinetic powers of young girls at menarche) and decidedly unusual European films (in both Ingmar Bergman's *Cries and Whispers* and the soft-porn French film *Going Places*, women mutilate their vaginas, in the first case possibly to simulate menstruation and avoid intercourse, and in the second to recover menstrual function lost during a prison sentence). In none of these films is menstruation treated as something that happens ordinarily to every woman, and in the very few television shows that have treated it so (*All in the Family, Cosby Show, I'll Fly Away*), the theme is taken up only once or twice, and blood has been notable for its invisibility.

CONSIDERATIONS FOR AN ARCHAEOLOGICAL MODEL

The same kind of gender discrimination, I suggest, carries over into the treatment of archaeological features. Features created by male-dominated or gender-neutral activities, even if they were designed for purification from ritual pollution, do not suffer from invisibility. Indeed several instances of putative sweat lodges are reported in the Southeastern literature (for example, the Fredericks site sweat lodge reported in Ward and Davis 1988). Yet for at least half of the population, the so-called menstrual huts were equally important for ritual purification, both monthly and after childbirth. This helps make an argument for their being more than flimsy "huts."

To suggest something of the possible existential force of the taboos connected with the menstrual-seclusion practice in the prehistoric Southeast, let me offer a specific example from the early eighteenth century, in which a male adult Creek was observed to vomit the sagamité he had eaten before learning that it had been prepared by a menstruating woman; he then claimed to see red specks in the remaining food in the pot (Swanton 1931). His European guest thought he was overreacting, but the nineteenth- and twentieth-century Creek materials that Swanton presented and that Bell has confirmed by recent fieldwork—which indicate persistent beliefs that menstruating women should not touch men or gardens and that it was dangerous for men to smell menstruating women, to bathe downstream of them, or to walk where they had walked—indicate that this was likely normal behavior, however androcentrically interpreted. If people in Southeastern societies indeed believed that menstruating women were capable of introducing disruption and disaster at frequent and regular intervals, it was cost-effective for the societies to be serious about their precautions and to provide substantial structures for containing the danger, as other societies have done.

Because of this fear of pollution, the location where menstruating women should be secluded, according to all the testimony offered, had to be at a distance from where men carried on their ordinary activities, and ought to have been downstream from the primary village or hamlet water source (Swanton 1928). Restrictions on contact with males and with agricultural fields dictated that historic period menstrual huts were placed on the outskirts of the villages, at what might be seen as the village/fields boundary, and the taboo was observed no matter what. In the 1750s, Chickasaw women who so isolated themselves in the face of attacks by pro-French enemies were recognized as valorous, because their action helped to preserve their husbands' virility (Bossu 1962:171). This locational practice can be compared with an example from the South Seas, the Ulithi, who placed the communal menstrual structure parallel to the shore (Paige and Paige 1981:213), thus also at the village/subsistence-source boundary.

Another issue that needs to be addressed when considering how many menstrual huts there were, and how substantial they were, is the average frequency of menstruation for late prehistoric Southeastern women. There is still great difficulty in addressing the issue of birth regulation archaeologically, but modern studies of women without access to medicalized birth control measures show that women can and do regulate birth frequency by means of extended lactation after a birth and complex socially institutionalized practices of abstention from intercourse. Although it is finally being recognized that the Western frequency of regular menstrual periods is unusual and perhaps unprecedented, it is not true that fertile non-Western women were always pregnant. Thus it is possible that if menstrual seclusion was practiced in the late prehistoric Southeast, at any given time as many as one-eighth to one-tenth of the fertile adult female population might have been so secluded. What the women did during their ritual seclusion from village life should be of interest, both because it would suggest what kind of structure was involved and because it would account for a significant expenditure of time. Pollution restrictions would have meant that there were many things menstruating women could not do (evidence for which would therefore not be found): produce household necessities like pottery or cloth, work at cultivation, perhaps take care of children, or cook for the household. With a wide range of activities barred, most of them the very activities that constituted the enormous visible economic contribution of women to Southeastern societies, what was left?

Although, most frequently, "menstrual huts" were also used for all the other activities related to female biological reproduction—including puberty rituals, childbirth, and the purification rituals following it—details of what went on inside them are noticeably missing for the colonial period Southeast as elsewhere (cf. Buckley and Gottlieb 1988b:12–13). Yet it is unlikely that fertile women spent one-fourth to one-fifth of their time while not pregnant or lactating sleeping or looking at the wall. Part of that notion may arise from the general assumption that women were alone in their huts.

There is another possibility worth considering, which is that more than one woman from the same household might be spending the same time in ritual seclusion. The tendency of women who live together or work together in close proximity to synchronize menses is now widely attested medically as well as anecdotally (see McClintock 1971 for the *locus classicus;* Knight 1988:233 lists references from recent medical literature; Knight 1991 builds an entire theory of the origins of culture on the phenomenon). Menstrual synchrony would surely have been experienced by the menstruating women, all of them related, in the extended matrilineage households postulated as the dominant residential mode in the late prehistoric Southeast. The ethnographic evidence from historic Southeastern tribes is not at all clear on how many of these huts there were at any given time, but the possibility of menstrual synchrony suggests that perhaps each lineage had its own women's house, a structure as substantial as any other.

Much has been made of the hard and unremitting work of women in the aboriginal agricultural Southeast, as opposed, to the episodic hunting and defense activities of men. Although that picture is surely skewed, no one who works hard is going to mind getting up to a week off once a month, as Hudson has suggested (1976:320; cf. Martin 1992:98). But it is likely that such time would be spent doing something. Even if societies themselves articulate the male-segregated activities as "sacred" and the female-segregated activities as "polluting" (though this is usually attributable to a Western reading of the evidence), that does not mean that there are no activities at all. Instead, it would seem reasonable to suggest that a similar range of activities might take place in the structures dedicated to both and that archaeological correlates might be suggested for them. Buckley's (1988) work on Yurok menstrual practices suggests that they could be seen as directly parallel to the male purification activities aimed at the accumulation of spiritual power, and that the structures used for menstrual seclusion could be as important as men's houses.

Since male ethnographers have been invited to partake of the activities in "men's houses," we do know something of what

goes on in them. Men carry out ritual activities or preparation for ritual activities, tell stories about hunting and women, sleep, and make ceremonial items, weapons or boats, or items of personal adornment. Although not restricted to the interior of the men's house by pollution restrictions, the ceremonial items are frequently restricted to use within the men's house because of secrecy requirements. And because male ethnographers are telling the tale, the talking that goes on is usually dignified as instructive for younger men or as reinforcing societal conventions (or, in case the stories go beyond societal conventions, as encouraging innovation). It is rarely trivialized as gossip.

If activities in the women's house paralleled such men's house activities, certainly women must have spent time resting as men did; certainly they also spent time talking and telling stories that could be similarly dignified as instruments of societal regulation. Other social activities, such as gambling, are documented ethnographically (Underhill 1936). We know they ate, because there is evidence that they had to use special vessels that could not be used elsewhere; indeed the Beng women of the Ivory Coast prepare a particularly prized and delectable dish only when menstruating (Gottlieb 1988:71–72). Because they did bleed, they may have had bloodstained breechcloths or other absorbent materials to dispose of by burning or burial. Is there any reason why it would have been unlikely that they participated in ritual activities? Certainly the sun worship that dominated Southeastern ritual practice is connected with fertility, and women in their period of ritual seclusion would at a minimum be concerned with the continuing fertility that their very seclusion proclaimed.

At this point I take a side trip into Southeastern myth to emphasize the connections between women, blood, and fertility by retelling the common story from the region of the origin of corn, with its overtones of the dominance of hunting-gathering by agriculture. In this tale there is a family consisting of a father, Hunter; a mother, Corn; and two boys, one a son of Hunter and Corn and one an adopted son who had been made from discarded deer's blood. After the boys had in mischief released game animals from the secret place where their father kept them, thereby making them scarce and hard to find, they became interested in how it was that their mother was able to provide corn and beans for them to eat instead. One day they spied on her activities within the storehouse and discovered that the corn and beans came from her body. Thinking her a witch, they decided to kill her. Seeing them refuse the food she offered, which they now considered polluted, she guessed their plan and instructed them on how they should do it: clear a large piece of ground and drag her dead body over it seven times. The boys killed her after having cleared only small patches of ground and then dragged her body over it only twice. As a result, corn sprang up only where her blood touched the cultivated earth, and it would make only two crops per year ever after (paraphrased from the Cherokee version as presented in Lankford 1987:148–151; cf. Bell 1990:335 for the relevance of this myth to Creek social reproduction).

This is as clear a connection as could be desired between female fertility, of which blood is the sign, and agricultural fertility, of which female blood is the cause. I would suggest that it may even include a mythical explanation of the origin of menstrual seclusion in the Southeast. I take the liberty of imagining that this connection would have been celebrated and ritualized somehow and, further, that it must have been part of at least some rites connected with the "women's house." It seems to me that the widespread attestation of the existence of "women's languages" in the Southeast (cf. Bell 1990:341 n. 1), correlated as it is with the practice of menstrual seclusion from the community, may also argue for the existence of a "women's house" institution with ritual characteristics that has simply been missed in the ethnohistorical literature for the reasons suggested above.

What might this possibility of ritual activity mean for archaeological correlates? We have had a hard time trying to decide how to identify other structures connected with Southeastern ritual; temple structures are known not only by their division into multiple rooms and the presence of a hearth, but almost indispensably by location on a mound. Clearly a "women's house" would be distinguished by the locational considerations I have discussed, and structurally it would require a hearth, because women would be staying there for several days, but little else of a structural nature can be suggested.

The story would, however, be different with reference to artifacts. If ritual artifacts such as statuettes or pipes or everyday items like pottery vessels, which might have been specially decorated to ensure their recognition and avoidance by others, were used inside the women's house, pollution restrictions would keep them there, where they would likely be found.

ARCHAEOLOGICAL IMPLICATIONS

What we have to look for, therefore, would be much like any other Mississippian house of wattle and daub or thatch. It would be spatially distinguished because it would be at whatever distance from living areas and field or forest that ritual purity demanded. The pattern of its location might select for nearness to running water because of its requirement for ritual cleansing. It would be downstream from the village or hamlet. If the disposal of soiled garments or pads had to be provided for by burning or burial—as we know was the case with the placenta—evidence of such disposal would be found within the house or nearby. Furthermore, if we reconceive the "menstrual hut" as a "women's house," then the complex of artifactual evidence would be much expanded to include ritual elements—structures, artifacts—and more of the long-term requirements of daily life. The presence of artifacts symbolically associated with females, fertility, and agriculture would fit this scenario, as would a distinctive ceramic assemblage with limited distribution. Both sorts of evidence are habitually assigned to (male) ritual contexts, as at the BBB Motor site (Emerson 1989; Pauketat and Emerson 1991) and the Sponemann site (Jackson et al. 1992) in the America Bottom, but in light of this discussion it might be worth reevaluating the evidence to see if another explanation might deal equally parsimoniously with the evidence.

I am suggesting, of course, that the red bauxite Birger and Keller figurines at the BBB Motor site, portraying kneeling women occupied in agricultural pursuits, and the similar Sponemann, Willoughby, and West figurines from Sponemann may be a clue that there is another possible interpretation not only for the "temple" complexes on both sites but for Ramey ceramics as well. Emerson's (1989:65) interpretation of Ramey motifs as "involving fertility and life forces" could hardly be more apposite to such an interpretation. Pauketat and Emerson interpret the symbolism of the Ramey jar, seen from above, as the cosmos (the decorative field) surrounding an orifice symbolizing the Underworld, such that the contents of the jar were seen as "associated with feminine life forces—earth, fertility, Under World—or female activities (e.g., agriculture, food preparation)" (Pauketat and Emerson 1991:933) But why not then see the orifice as the vaginal opening, and the contents of the pots (perhaps that dangerous red-flecked sagamité?) as coming from the body of the Corn Mother? Certainly pottery with "broad, simple designs. . . highly visible at a distance" (Pauketat and Emerson 1991:922) would be easily avoidable; designs "meant for a special purpose rather than simply being decorations for the elite" (Emerson 1989:63) could be meant to warn of pollution. The care taken in the execution of Ramey pottery, which Emerson (1989:66–67) argues was by "potters who were associated with each specific lineage/community ritual group," would be appropriate to a ware made by women not burdened by daily tasks (note that there is

enough variation in Ramey ceramics that highly restricted specialist production is not suggested), and its relative scarcity fits well with a ware used for periodic seclusion. Such a "'utilitarian' ritual ware" (Emerson 1989:65) might well be included in mortuary offerings (especially for childbirth deaths), would appear in midden and garbage deposits, and would be distributed through all levels of the social hierarchy (since all women menstruate and most give birth).

It is worth noting that the BBB Motor site also exhibited other finds that could be reinterpreted in the direction of women's house practices: systematically reexcavated pit features; red ocher pigment and a large quartz crystal with a dramatic red impurity (which Emerson compares to a Cherokee story of a man who regularly fed such a crystal with blood!); and Datura stramonium, which could have been used for abortion or difficult childbirths. Finally, the site was separated from the surrounding land by water and marshes during the period of its use. None of this evidence is conclusive, but I suggest that it is worth a thorough reevaluation, especially the sexing of the burials.

The occurrence of figurines similar to those at BBB Motor made a "ceremonial" interpretation inevitable for the Sponemann "Ceremonial Complex" of architectural and pit remains, which includes a "temple" and an adjoining structure interpreted as the temple-keeper's lodging. Because the figurines were evidently intentionally "killed" by being broken into fragments, and because the spread of those fragments coincides closely with the burned "temple," Fortier argues that the figurines had been broken outside the structure and most of the fragments placed within it before its intentional destruction by fire. This destruction supposedly marked a final "purification" step in an episode of "busk" ceremonialism focused on this "household temple" structure, which Fortier identifies by analogy with temples described by Du Pratz for the Natchez (Jackson et al. 1992:52–70).

Again, however, it would seem that an alternative interpretation connected with women's house ceremonialism and especially purification practices might be appropriate, at least for the "Ceremonial Complex" portion of the site. Fortier suggests that the destruction of the figurines and the "temple" building was part of a ritual act terminating a "year-end busk celebration" and representing "a symbolic act of regeneration and perhaps purification of the sacred busk complex." Further, he suggests that the "sanctity of this act and the busk ground itself" is signified by the fact that the site was not reoccupied after the destruction episode (Jackson et al. 1992:303). Yet if the "temple" and adjoining "lodging" were interpreted as a women's house complex accommodating menstrual-seclusion facilities and fertility ceremonialism, it would seem that abandonment might be as much the product of notions of pollution as of sacredness, and the apparently inauspicious location of the site in a low clayey swale (Jackson et al. 1992:49) would then suggest that it was chosen because of its proximity to water needed for purification.

In both the "ceremonial" and "residential" precincts of the Sponemann site small quantities of Ramey ceramics were found, although the concentration of small sherds in pits, especially in the "ceremonial" precinct, gave Fortier grounds for the suggestion that they were part of assemblages that represented the sweeping out of structures as another part of a "purification" practice. Certainly this kind of distribution for Ramey ceramics—whether associated with menstrual practices or not—helpfully raises the question of whether a possible distinctive "menstrual ware" might not also appear in an ordinary domestic setting, where vessels might be stored or used to obtain cooked foods destined for women in menstrual seclusion. This last surmise shows that finding evidence of distinctive women's houses will not be uncomplicated, but it will not be done at all unless we ask the questions.

There is no way we are going to understand late prehistoric Southeastern cultures until we come to grips with the basic issues of kinship organization and the role of women. Nor can we completely ignore a substantial portion of Southeastern women's lives, particularly one so strikingly connected with the central arcana of Mississippian ceremonialism. Ethnohistorical evidence can only take us so far back; after that, archaeology must serve as time machine. Here, however, ethnographic analogy gives us an actual structure to look for, and it is time we stopped being too ethnocentric to do so.

ACKNOWLEDGMENTS

I am indebted to Cheryl Claassen for inviting me to reprise and polish this essay, which was first presented in a less developed form at the 1990 Southeastern Archaeological Conference meeting in Jackson, Mississippi. Since that presentation, I have received many helpful suggestions from colleagues and friends, including Amy Bushnell, Penelope Drooker, James Heilman, Bonnie McEwan, Charles McNutt, LeAnne Howe, Pat Kwachka, Mary Powell, John Scarry, and Bruce Smith. It is interesting to note that whereas female colleagues took this essay seriously from the outset, some male colleagues initially behaved as though they considered it a joke. I am happy to say that they no longer seem to do so.

REFERENCES

Bell, Amelia Rector. 1990. "Separate People: Speaking of Creek Men and Women." *American Anthropologist* 92:332–345.

Binford, Lewis R. 1970. "Archaeology at Hatchery West." *Memoirs of the Society for American Archaeology* 24.

Bonnichsen, Robson. 1973. "Millie's Camp: An Experiment in Archaeology." *World Archaeology* 4:227–291.

Bossu, Jean-Bernard. 1962. *Travels in the Interior of North America*, 1751–1762. Translated and edited by Seymour Feiler. Norman: University of Oklahoma Press.

Buckley, Thomas. 1988. "Menstruation and the Power of Yurok Women." In *Blood Magic: The Anthropology of Menstruation*, edited by Thomas Buckley and Alma Gottlieb, 188–209. Berkeley: University of California Press.

Buckley, Thomas, and Alma Gottlieb (editors). 1988a. *Blood Magic: The Anthropology of Menstruation*. Berkeley: University of California Press.

———. 1988b. "A Critical Appraisal of Theories of Menstrual Symbolism." In *Blood Magic: The Anthropology of Menstruation*, edited by Thomas Buckley and Alma Gottlieb, 3–50. Berkeley: University of California Press.

Delaney, Janice, Mary Jane Lupton, and Emily Toth. 1976. *The Curse: A Cultural History of Menstruation*. New York: E. P. Dutton.

Douglas, Mary. 1966. *Purity and Danger*. London: Pelican.

Emerson, Thomas E. 1989. "Water, Serpents, and The Underworld: An Exploration into Cahokian Symbolism." In *The Southeastern Ceremonial Complex: Artifacts and Analysis*, edited by Patricia Galloway, 45–92. Lincoln: University of Nebraska Press.

Gottlieb, Alma. 1988. "Menstrual Cosmology among the Beng of Ivory Coast." In *Blood Magic: The Anthropology of Menstruation*, edited by Thomas Buckley and Alma Gottlieb, 55–74. Berkeley: University of California Press.

Harris, Marvin. 1988. *Culture, People, Nature: An Introduction to General Anthropology*. 5th ed. New York: Harper and Row.

Hudson, Charles. 1976. *The Southeastern Indians*. Knoxville: University of Tennessee Press.

Jackson, Douglas K., Andrew C. Fortier, and Joyce A. Williams. 1992. *The Sponemann Site 2: The Mississippian Oneota Occupations (II-Ms–517)*. American Bottom Archaeology, FAI–270 Site Reports, No. 24. Urbana: University of Illinois Press.

Knight, Chris. 1988. "Menstrual Synchrony and the Australian Rainbow Snake" In *Blood Magic: The Anthropology of Menstruation*, edited by Thomas Buckley and Alma Gottlieb, 232–255. Berkeley: University of California Press

———. 1991. *Blood Relations: Menstruation and the Origins of Culture*. New Haven: Yale University Press.

Knight, Vernon James. 1990. "Social Organization and the Evolution of Hierarchy in Southeastern Chiefdoms." *Journal of Anthropological Research* 46:1–23.

Lankford, George. 1987. *Native American Legends*. Little Rock: August House.

Martin, Emily. 1992. *The Woman in the Body: A Cultural Analysis of Reproduction*. 2nd ed. Boston: Beacon Press.

McClintock, Martha K. 1971. "Menstrual Syndrome and Suppression." *Nature* 229(5282): 244–245.

Mead, Margaret. 1939. *From the South Seas: Studies of Adolescence and Sex in Primitive Societies*. New York: William Morrow and Company.

Milanich, Jerald, William C. Sturtevant, and Emilio Moran (editors and translators). 1972. *Francisco Pareja's 1613 Confessionario: A Documentary Source for Timucuan Ethnography*. Tallahassee: Florida Division Archives, History, and Records Management.

Paige, Karen Ericksen, and Jeffrey M. Paige. 1981. *The Politics of Reproductive Ritual*, Berkeley: University of California Press.

Pauketat, Timothy R., and Thomas E. Emerson. 1991. "The Ideology of Authority and the Power of the Pot." *American Anthropologist* 93:919–941.

Schlegal, Alice. 1972. *Male Dominance and Female Autonomy*. New Haven: HRAF Press.

Shuttle, Penelope, and Peter Redgrove. 1978. *The Wise Wound: Eve's Curse and Everywoman*. New York: Richard Marek.

Swanton, John R. 1911. *Indians of the Lower Mississippi Valley and Adjacent Coast of the Gulf of Mexico*. Bureau of American Ethnology Bulletin 43. Washington, D.C.

———. 1928. *"Social Organization and Social Usages of the Indian of the Creek Confederacy."* Bureau of American Ethnology 42nd Annual Report (1925), 43–472. Washington, D.C.

———. 1929. *Myths and Tales of the Southeastern Indians*. Bureau of American Ethnology Bulletin 88. Washington, D.C.

———. 1931. *Source Material for the Social Ceremonial Life of the Choctaw Indians*. Bureau of American Ethnology Bulletin 103. Washington, D.C.

———. 1946. *Indians of the Southeastern United States*. Bureau of American Ethnology Bulletin 137. Washington, D.C.

Underhill, Ruth. 1936. *The Autobiography of a Papago Woman*. Memoir 46, American Anthropological Association.

Ward, Trawick, and Steve Davis. 1988. "Archaeology of the Historic Occaneechi Indians." *Southern Indian Studies* 36–37.

Weideger, Paula. 1976. *Menstruation and Menopause: The Physiology and Psychology, The Myth and Reality*. New York: Knopf.

Warriors and Rulers: Royal Women of the Classic Maya

Stanley P. Guenter and David A. Freidel

INTRODUCTION

The Classic Maya civilization of southern Mexico and northern Central America, encompassed some 80,000 sq km of tropical lowland country at its height in 750 AD. With only stone tool technology and no beasts of burden, Maya men and women created dozens of cities with towering pyramids and sprawling palaces. They turned forested swamps and rolling hills into flourishing agricultural fields capable of feeding millions and also producing vast quantities of cotton and cacao for export trade. Most importantly, the Maya recorded their religion, histories, and advanced astronomical knowledge in their unique hieroglyphic writing system. Although all but a handful of Maya paper books perished centuries before modern scholars could read them, texts sculptured on stone monuments, painted on walls and pottery vases, and incised on bone, shell, and jade, have survived to reveal the outlines of the Pre-Columbian world's only literate society. While most archaeologists have to construct models of past gender relations without the aid of writing, the Classic Maya elite themselves now provide insight into how they conceived of women's roles at the pinnacles of power.[1] However, there is a price to be paid for the unique window on the past that textual information can afford. In order to discuss these historical figures, their names, titles and achievements, we cannot avoid using the actual Mayan words. Where we can, we use glosses in English for the titles, and sometimes the decipherment of the texts has not progressed sufficiently to yield actual names and experts are still using "nicknames" for some people. But just as historians

"Warriors and Rulers: Royal Women of the Classic Maya," by Stanley P. Guenter and David A. Freidel. Used with permission.

use the actual names of people in ancient Egypt, Greece, Rome, Mesopotamia, and China, so we must use the actual names of Maya women, their husbands, and children. To do otherwise is not only poor scholarship, but also a disservice to these people, who played important roles in shaping the history and destiny of their world. So we encourage readers not to get hung up on the pronunciation of the names or their exotic character and concentrate on the exploits of their owners. Someday, just as people accept Cleopatra VI and her consort Julius Caesar as named historical figures, perhaps they will accept the names of the great women of Maya civilization as part of common knowledge among educated Americans.

The Roles of Women

There are many millions of people today in Mexico and Central America who speak a Maya language and are culturally related to the ancient Maya who lived in this country. The great majority of these people reckon kinship through the male line and men generally dominate public affairs. Women, however, can have important roles in the preparation of religious festivals and in the performance of ritual activities in homes. Moreover, there are numerous women curers, midwives, and diviners, specialists with access to supernatural powers that make them deeply respected and influential in their communities.[2] While the Maya world was, and remains, quite patriarchal and most Pre-Columbian Classic royal women merit mention in glyphic texts only as mothers of kings, it is clear that noble women were barred from few, if any, principal courtly roles. For example, a text painted upon a fine ceramic vessel informs us that the mother of a sixth century king of the great lowland capital of Tikal was a "scribe,"[3] indicating that at least some women were literate in the hieroglyphic writing system. Recent analyses of Marc Zender and Alfonso Lacadena suggest that some Maya women were priests in the ecclesiastical hierarchy.[4] This suggests that Maya noble women carried out rituals to honor and care for the gods on behalf of their subjects, as did their male counterparts.

Most royal titles actually had female variants. Thus we read of "Lady First-of-the-Earth," "Lady Ruler" and "Lady Supreme Warlord."[5] Most experts gloss this last title as "emperor" because it is clearly superior to that of king. It clearly had military connotations and one variant of the glyph portrays the storm god wielding an axe. So a fair gloss of this title is thus "supreme warlord" and a number of important queens took this title. Lady K'ab'il, a seventh century princess of Calakmul, was one of these, and as Supreme Warlord she actually held a higher status than her husband, the king of El Peru-Waka'.

Lady Warlords: A Case Study from Yaxchilan

Classic Maya history is dominated by the political and military competition between Supreme Warlord level lords. On the other hand, the site of Yaxchilan, situated above the Usumacinta River in the western Maya lowlands, provides one of the most intriguing stories of the competition between aspiring Supreme Warlords both male and female, *within* the same kingdom. Yaxchilan had languished underneath the domination of its northern neighbor, Piedras Negras, throughout the late sixth and entire seventh centuries. In 713, however, in the 32nd year of his long reign, king Itzamnaaj B'ahlam III reasserted Yaxchilan's independence in battle, and was thus in later years referred to as the kingdom's "first supreme warlord."[6]

Structure 23, the first great construction of Itzamnaaj B'ahlam III's reign was built ten years later yet extolled not his own great feats, but those of his principal wife, Lady K'ab'al Xook. Like her husband, she took the title "western supreme warlord,'" a reference to Yaxchilan's intention to rule the western Maya lowlands. Structure 23 contained three beautifully carved

lintels featuring the queen performing in a related series of rituals, apparently associated with her role as a Lady supreme warlord. The lintels are large stone slabs that held up the heavy masonry over the doorways. The carved surfaces could only be viewed by the gods and the privileged few nobility who paused and looked up as they passed through the doors. Carved lintels were a typical way that the Maya elite used to dedicate buildings. The first, Lintel 24, shows the queen on the day of her husband's coronation, performing self-sacrifice by pulling a thorn-studded rope through her tongue. Her husband, the new king, is shown as an attendant, raising a flaming torch above her to illuminate the gruesome scene.

The second, central doorway, lintel (Lintel 25) portrays Lady K'ab'al Xook experiencing a vision of a serpent, out of whose open mouth emerges a warrior. Until recently, everyone thought that the warrior was a male, an ancestor of the king. However, a closer reading of the accompanying text shows that this is actually the queen herself[7] emerging as a goddess named "Lady Heart of the *Wite' Naah*."[8] *Wite' Naah* is an enigmatic place associated with royal dynasties and the city of Teotihuacán in Mexico. It appears to refer to a sacred fire temple deeply infused with political and religious symbolism of Teotihuacan.[9]

It is important to note here that the warrior figure emerging armed with battle shield and spear, the elementary symbols of Maya warfare, is said in the inscription to be the queen herself and not her husband. We may never know if royal women actually went to battle, but Lady K'ab'al Xook is certainly given credit in this temple for the religious and political legitimacy of war prosecuted by her husband. The final lintel in this series, Lintel 26, highlights the queen's role as source of military power, as a Lady supreme warlord, by depicting Lady K'ab'al Xook handing her husband his war gear, including shield, spear and jaguar-headed, feather-crested battle helmet.

Lady K'ab'al Xook's position as the Lady western supreme warlord of her kingdom secured her power as leading lady and primary queen, positions she held throughout the reign of her husband. She may well have given birth to his heir, king Yopaat B'ahlam II. This king remains a shadowy figure as he in turn was succeeded by another son of Itzamnaaj B'ahlam III, a famous king name Yaxuun B'ahlam IV. Yaxuun B'ahlam IV was born in the 28th year of his father's reign and when his mother, a princess of Calakmul named Lady Eveningstar, was at least 38 years old. Certainly a very junior member of the royal family, Yaxuun B'ahlam was a great warrior and struggled long and hard, likely against Yopaat B'ahlam II, to finally secure the throne ten years after his father died.

By this time his mother and, more importantly, her co-wife Lady K'ab'al Xook, had also passed away. In his retrospective history, Yaxuun B'ahlam portrayed his mother as a primary queen during the reign of Itzamnaaj B'ahlam III. Lady Eveningstar, who is said to have been a high priestess,[10] is also accorded the title of eastern supreme warlord, in reference to her coming from Calakmul, northeast of Yaxchilan. While we have no contemporary records of Lady Eveningstar, a junior wife of Itzamnaaj B'ahlam, she left a lasting impression with her son who went to great pains once he had finally secured the kingship for himself to credit his mother as not only a great queen but also a Lady supreme warlord on par with Lady K'ab'al Xook.

Foreign Princesses: Lady Six Sky at Naranjo and Lady Batz' Ek' at Caracol

It can thus been seen that certain remarkable and forceful women appeared as the ultimate wielders of power within their kingdoms. Lady Six Sky of Dos Pilas, a small but highly strategic and famous royal capital in southern Peten, Guatemala, is another of these. She was the daughter of a great Dos Pilas warrior-king and she established herself at the city of Naranjo to the northeast where she appears on monuments with all the prerogatives of sole ruler in the early eighth century AD. Her son, born five years after her arrival at Naranjo, became the next king of this city. While Lady Six Sky herself never claimed the title of ruler of that city (she was always referred to as a princess of Dos Pilas), she was certainly the *de facto* ruler until her son was old

enough to take command of the armies himself. The father of her son was apparently never mentioned in the site's history but her son did regularly pair his own monuments with ones dedicated to his mother.

The tropical environment and the vagaries of history have destroyed or damaged most of the historical records that the Classic Maya left to posterity and our current understanding of their past still remains, and always shall remain, fragmentary. What information that has survived the passage of centuries, the heat and humidity, and looters, both ancient and modern, provides but random facts and insights into Classic Maya individual lives. Thus, while we know a lot about Lady Six Sky's actions at Naranjo as dowager queen, we cannot even state how old she was when she arrived at her new home, nor how long she lived and ruled there as neither her tomb nor a mention of her death having yet been found.[11]

In order to arrive at a fuller view of the lives of Classic Maya royal women we must compare the snippets of biographical information for various queens and princesses to come up with cultural norms. Lady Batz' Ek', who married into the royal family of Caracol, a huge city in the Maya mountains of Belize and Naranjo's arch-rival for dominance of the eastern Peten, provides a close parallel to the life of Lady Six Sky. Lady Batz' Ek' was born in 566 AD as a princess of a little known dynasty related to that of Calakmul, a city in southern Campeche, Mexico, and the most powerful Maya kingdom of the Classic Maya civilization. At the age of 18 she journeyed to Caracol to marry its king. He was a relatively old man and he had already been on the throne for 31 years, during which time he had switched his allegiance from the powerful city of Tikal in Peten, Guatemala, to its arch-rival, Calakmul in Mexico. His new princess bride, Lady Batz' Ek' was proof of his newfound allegiance in flesh and blood. Marriage alliances of this sort were common throughout the Classic period and undoubtedly in both the periods preceding and following this, periods for which we do not have written records.

Lady Batz' Ek' was not her husband's first wife. As we saw in the case at Yaxchilan, the polygamous marriages of Maya kings often lead to competition between their wives for the position of primary queen and the ability to place one of their children on the throne. Providing the king with children, especially sons, was one of the keys to success for his wives. Lady Batz' Ek' gave birth to a son, Sak Witzil B'aah ("White Mountain Gopher"), four years after her arrival. In 599 the king died and was succeeded by his elder son, Knot Ajaw. Prince Sak Witzil B'aah was only eleven years old at the time and while Lady Batz' Ek' bided her time, she groomed her son for the throne. This must have taken considerable skill and intelligence, as Sak Witzil B'aah was a threat and rival to his half-brother, the new king. We will never know the full story of this tense situation but after a reign of 18 years, Knot Ajaw disappears from the historical record and Sak Witzil B'aah finally gained the throne as king K'an II, arguably the greatest king of Caracol.

Our vision of Lady Batz' Ek' guiding her son to the throne and being his major backer is not merely modern speculation. It is the portrait that K'an II wished painted of the foundation of his rule. One of the major monuments of his reign is largely devoted to recording her personal history and mentions the crucial information that she was a 'witness' to his accession, a position usually associated with political authority and agency. The devotion of K'an II to his mother extended even in death. Her probable tomb, bearing a painted date of 634, was located deep inside Temple B–19, the central pyramid atop the largest building at Caracol and the tallest ancient structure in all of Belize. That this foreign princess should be accorded such incredible honor in her adopted home bespeaks the success of her life, the love of her son and subjects, and provides an excellent example of just how lofty the achievements of Classic Maya royal women could be.

An Assertive Queen: Lady Winikhaab' Ajaw at Piedras Negras

On the other side of the Maya world, at Piedras Negras on the Usumacinta River, we read of the story of Lady Winikhaab' Ajaw,[12] a princess from the small, neighboring kingdom of Maan. Texts on monumental carved stone stelae tell us that at the age of twelve she was married to the Piedras Negras heir who shortly thereafter succeeded his father as king. This king had a long reign but appears to have been a weak ruler. While he raised many monuments at his home city, texts from foreign centers document the failures in warfare that Piedras Negras suffered during his reign. Within twenty years, this king's realm consisted of little more than the immediate vicinity of his capital. Gradually in the course of his reign, his wife took an increasingly prominent role. Finally, the text on the rear of Stela 3 records that on the occasion of the king's 25th anniversary of accession his wife "took (possession of) the throne." Just what this seizure of power entailed is hard to discern from archaeology, but the recording of it in public history is quite remarkable.

Lady Winikhaab' Ajaw's source of power is unknown but the birth of her daughter, Lady Huntahn Ahk is given special prominence on the same monument recording her seizure of power and the events may be linked. The king does not appear to have had a son, and Lady Huntahn Ahk may have been his first (and possibly only) child and, hence, heir. The future husband of this princess stood to gain a kingdom and by overseeing the marriage of her daughter, Lady Winikhaab' Ajaw became very influential and the source of considerable power over the future of Piedras Negras. Although living in a patriarchal society, Classic Maya women could adroitly use the system to achieve success and positions of power.

The Ruling Queens of Palenque

When situations arose in which no clear male heir was available to assume the throne it was possible, at least in certain kingdoms, for royal women to assume the status and position of actual ruler. At Palenque in the far west of the lowlands, we have chronicles that record the accession of a Lady Yohl Ik'nal in 584. She went on to reign for two decades and was considered so important by her illustrious descendant, K'inich Janaab' Pakal I (the Great), that she was given two portraits on the latter's famous sculptured sarcophagus, an honor otherwise reserved only for the king's parents. Unfortunately, no contemporary evidence of her reign has survived to the present and we are left with only Pakal's retrospective accounts as a document to this woman.

The reason for the lack of any records from the reign of Lady Yohl Ik'nal, or from any reign prior to that of Pakal the Great, is that for a decade (and perhaps even longer) following this great woman's reign, the site of Palenque was subject to a series of devastating attacks by its neighbors and foreign enemies. The worst of these took place in 611 when the king of Calakmul marched his army hundreds of kilometers to the west to sack Palenque. The Temple of the Inscriptions at Palenque records the results of these military disasters in poetic form: "lost is the queen, lost is the king,"[13] an apparent reference to the capture or even (sacrificial?) deaths of the royal family.

In the aftermath of this dynastic catastrophe a new lineage came to the throne of Palenque. Curiously, the first new ruler who acceded in 612 AD took the same name as that of the local variant of the Maize (Corn) God, Muwaan Mat. Mythological texts from Palenque record that Muwaan Mat was born in 3121 BC and gave birth to the site's triad of patron deities before acceding in 2325 BC. This primordial accession is recorded as Muwaan Mat's "first," the implication being that the Muwaan Mat who acceded in 612 AD was a reincarnation of the deity.

There has been considerable controversy among epigraphers as to who the human behind the divine façade of Muwaan Mat really was. As the Maize God is normally portrayed in Classic Maya art as a male, some scholars have sought a male to fill this role. However, maize is traditionally conceived of by modern Maya as female and one portrait of the Maize Deity in the Dresden Codex, identified by this god's distinctive name glyph, is clearly a woman complete with an exposed breast. In fact, the Maize "God" now appears to best be described as a hermaphroditic Maize Deity.[14]

If one accepts that as Maize Deity Muwaan Mat was both male and female, there can no longer be any objection to seeing a woman behind this ruler. In fact, the most common costume for Maya royal women was as the Maize Deity, a costume also worn by men (a fact which has led to considerable confusion in the study of Classic Maya concepts of gender). The most likely candidate for Muwaan Mat is the mother of Pakal I, Lady Sak K'uk' ("White Quetzal"). She is the one shown on the Oval Palace Tablet (set behind the royal throne) passing the royal crown to her son at his accession, which took place only three years after the accession to the throne of the reincarnated Muwaan Mat. Pakal's Sarcophagus Lid, which provides an account of the deaths of all of this king's predecessors, includes that of his mother in the royal position expected for the ruler/deity Muwaan Mat.

It can thus be seen that Lady Sak K'uk', likely a princess from the earlier dynastic line whose primary members had been "lost" in the wars of the early seventh century, came to the throne under the guise of Muwaan Mat, to "divinely" restart the dynasty. After three years as sole ruler she elevated her 12-year old son, Pakal I, as king and co-ruler. Lady Sak K'uk' was undoubtedly the driving force in this royal duo throughout the early years of his reign and it is not until after her death that we really see Pakal emerging as a ruler in his own right.

Queens as Viceroys

While at least one Maya queen seems to have seized control of her adopted home city, and others assumed the throne peacefully in the absence of male heirs, still others appear to have been sent by imperial kings to vassal cities to rule in the name of their royal families. The Dallas Panel, from the ancient vassal city of *Sak Nikte'* in northwestern Guatemala records the "arrivals" (the establishment in authority) of three royal women of the Snake Kingdom over a period of two centuries beginning in 520 AD. The Snake Kingdom, Kan, one of the mightiest of the ancient Maya polities, had successive capitals at the sites Dzibanche in southeastern Quintana Roo, and then Calakmul in southern Campeche, during the course of the Classic period. The mightiest Snake King of the Classic period, celebrated his 20-year anniversary in power at Sak Nikte' and he may have used it as a southern base-of-operations in his long and ultimately successful war of imperial expansion against his arch-enemy, the kingdom of Tikal. His daughter was one of the royal Snake women mentioned on the Dallas Panel (she married the local lord, a vassal of her father's).

The rituals that she and the other royal women from Kan are said to have carried out at Sak Nikte' include those usually reserved for the ruler himself. Indeed evidence suggests that the Dallas Panel was originally placed in a wall of a throne room where the queens ruled. The images on the panel show women standing in front of their thrones framed by gods and war beasts. It may well be that these women actually ruled in place of their husbands and it is interesting that during their time, there is little evidence for the actions of any local rulers, who were likely preempted by these foreign queens.

A similar practice may be in evidence at Calakmul's great enemy, the kingdom of Tikal. Altar 5 of that city portrays two lords dressed in deathly costumes and kneeling to either side of a stack of bones and a skull. The text on this monument has long puzzled scholars, but clearly revolves around a woman, Lady Tuunte' Kaywak. She is said to have accompanied Tikal's king to the small island site of Topoxte, southeast of Tikal. This island was in the jurisdiction of Yaxha's capital city on the other side of the same lake. The kingdom of Yaxha was allied with Tikal and Lady Tuunte' Kaywak may have been a wife of the Tikal king sent by her husband to govern a vassal royal court. We have reason to suspect that the skull and bones prominently displayed on this altar are hers, retrieved from the kingdom of Yaxha because they were threatened with desecration by the king of Narjano, son of Lady Six Sky. Archaeologists discovered a skull and long bones underneath the stela portraying the Tikal king next to the altar. These may well be the re-interred bones of the queen whose burial dedicated and sanctified these monuments.

CONCLUDING THOUGHTS

The study of Maya texts and their correlation with archaeology is just beginning to yield information relevant to gender studies in this civilization. It is already clear to us, however, that Maya royal women were major players on their historical stage. As role models for other elite women of their world, powerful royal women may well have encouraged a certain gender parity among the nobility that does not yet seem evident to us among the commoner classes. However, 50 years ago, no Maya archaeologists believed that royal women wielded such power. Future breakthroughs in research may show that ordinary Maya women enjoyed modest versions of the religious and political roles of noble women, analogous to the women shamans, healers, and midwives of the modern Maya peoples.

NOTES

1. There are many recent publications on gender roles in ancient Maya civilization. Rosemary Joyces's *Gender and Power in Prehispanic Mesoamerica* (2000) is a clearly written introduction to the general theme with special chapters on the Maya. *Ancient Maya Women* (2002) is an edited book with more technical and advanced discussions covering important aspects of the topic.
2. See Barbara Tedlock's *Time and the Highland Maya* 1982, chapter 3, for a good review of Maya men and women specialists in the supernatural.
3. The term scribe is *aj tz'ihb'* in ancient Mayan.
4. The *ajk'uhuun* title, carried by a few Maya royal women, was a priestly title according to Alfonso Lacadena (personal communication, 2002) and Marc Zender, 2003, *A Study of Classic Maya Priesthood,* unpublished Ph. D. dissertation, University of Calgary.
5. Maya scribes formed female titles by simply prefixing the female agentive *ix* to the title itself. Thus we read of *ix b'akab'* ("Lady First-of-the-Earth", *ix ajaw* ("Lady Ruler") and *ix kaloomte'* Supreme Warlord.
6. The phrase is *natal kaloomte* in ancient Mayan.
7. Personal communication from Marc Zender, 2001.
8. *Ix Yohl Wite' Naah* in ancient Mayan.

9. Karl Taube (1999) makes the argument that the *Wite' Naah* is a fire temple. See also the article by David Stuart (1999)

10. *ix ajk'uhuun* in ancient Mayan.

11. An hieroglyphic bench from Lady Six Sky's hometown of Dos Pilas has long been thought to mention her death in 741. However, a closer analysis by Stanley Guenter and Federico Fahsen has noted that the eroded name of a Dos Pilas princess on this monument only resembles in part that of Lady Six Sky and is almost certainly another woman, perhaps a sister of Lady Six Sky and probably the wife of Dos Pilas Ruler 3.

12. Traditionally known as Lady Katun Ahau.

13. *satay k'uhul ixik satay ajaw,* in ancient Mayan.

14. See Mathew Looper "Women Men (and Men-Women): Classic Maya Rulers and the Third Gender" in Ancient Maya Women, T. Adren editor 2002 for a related argument on the Maize god and the Moon goddess.

III

Domestic Worlds and Public Worlds

In 1974, in an attempt to document a universal subordination of women, Michelle Rosaldo (1974: 18) proposed a paradigm relating "recurrent aspects of psychology and cultural and social organization to an opposition between the 'domestic' orientation of women and the extradomestic or 'public' ties, that, in most societies, are primarily available to men." The domestic-public model led Rosaldo to suggest that women's status is highest in societies in which the public and domestic spheres are only weakly differentiated, as among the Mbuti pygmies. In contrast "women's status will be lowest in those societies where there is a firm differentiation between domestic and public spheres of activity and where women are isolated from one another and placed under a single man's authority, in the home. Their position is raised when they can challenge those claims to authority . . . " (Rosaldo 1974: 36). According to this argument, women may enhance their status by creating a public world of their own or by entering the men's world. In addition, the most egalitarian societies will be those in which men participate in the domestic domain.

Correspondingly, writing in the same volume (Rosaldo and Lamphere 1974), Sanday (1974) suggested that women's involvement in domains of activity such as subsistence or defense may be curtailed because of their time and energy commitment to reproduction and mothering. Men, on the other hand, are free to form broader associations in the political, economic, and military spheres that transcend the mother-child unit. While the linkage of women with the domestic and men with the public domains may imply a biological determinism based on women's reproductive roles, Rosaldo (1974: 24) argued that the opposition between domestic and public orientations is an intelligible but not a necessary arrangement.

One aspect of women's domestic responsibilities is that it is women who primarily raise children. Nancy Chodorow (1974) developed a theory linking adult sex role behavior to the fact that children's early involvement is with their female parent. Chodorow contended that girls are integrated through ties with female kin into the world of domestic work. Age, rather than achievement, may define their status, while boys must "learn" to be men. Unlike girls, boys have few responsibilities in childhood and are free to establish peer groups that create "public" ties. To become an adult male a boy is often obliged to dissociate himself from the home and from female kin. According to Rosaldo (1974: 26), "the fact that children virtually everywhere grow up with their mothers may well account for characteristic differences in male and female psychologies" as well as set the stage for adult organization of activities.

As scholarship devoted to an understanding of gender issues has evolved, the influential domestic-public model has been the focus of considerable controversy, revolving around three related issues: whether male domination is universal, whether male domination is explained by the domestic-public dichotomy, and whether—and under what conditions—the concept of domestic-public has relevance.

Lamphere (in this book) reviews the formulation of the domestic-public model, and discusses the subsequent critiques of its validity and applicability. Rosaldo herself, rethinking her original position, said that although male dominance appears widespread, it does not "in actual behavioral terms assume a universal content or a universal shape. On the contrary, women typically have power and influence in political and economic life, display autonomy from men in their pursuits, and rarely find themselves confronted or constrained by what might seem the brute fact of male strength" (1980: 394). Although the domestic-public opposition has been compelling, Rosaldo suggested that the model assumes too much rather than helping to illuminate and explain.

As Lamphere observes, it has become increasingly clear that the domestic-public opposition is the heir to nineteenth-century social theory rooted in a dichotomy contrasting home and woman, with a public world of men, and reflecting an understanding of political rights based on sex. The domestic/public dichotomy emerged from the industrial revolution and the separation of home and workplace. Conceptualizing social life as dichotomized into domestic and public domains does not make sense in societies in which management of production occurs within the household and in which household production itself involves the management of the "public" economy (Leacock 1978: 253).

In contrast, in an industrial society, where home and workplace are clearly demarcated, the domestic-public opposition may have explanatory value. For example, Murcott (in this book) analyzes one domestic task, cooking, as part of an exploration of economic relations in the family and of the division of labor between spouses. Interviews with Welsh housewives indicate that ideas about home cooking reflect understandings of the relationship between domestic and paid labor. An analysis of the production of meals illuminates the allocation of responsibility for different domestic tasks, the gendered control of decision making and the distribution of power and authority in marriage. The informants shared the view that proper eating must occur at home and that a cooked dinner is necessary to family health and well-being. Murcott suggests that the emphasis on having a proper dinner waiting for the husband when he comes in from work underscores the symbolic importance of the return home: "the cooked dinner marks the threshold between the public domains of school or work and the private sphere behind the closed front door" (Murcott, this volume).

In his analysis of fatherhood in the United States, Townsend (in this book) contends that in the United States, an industrialized society, it is often assumed that parenting represents a simple division of labor in which men are engaged in the public sphere of paid labor and politics, while women are involved in the domestic sphere of childcare and reproduction. His research demonstrates, however, that the domestic and public spheres interpenetrate and that arrangements made in one sphere influence behavior in another. Parenting, he argues, is deeply gendered. This means not only that fathers and mothers "do" different things, but that fatherhood has different meanings for men and women. Men interviewed in his research claimed to want greater involvement as fathers than their own fathers had experienced. They saw "marriage and children" as a package deal; for these men, a relationship with a woman was necessary for a man to see himself as a father.

Correspondingly, Townsend shows that women are often influential in men's decisions about when to have children. Women are the "default parent" while men are in a more "optional" position with their role as disciplinarian or "fun dad" shaped by the interests of their children's mother. Thus women, as wives and mothers, mediate and facilitate fatherhood. Moreover, the structural division of labor placing men in the labor force and women at home has been maintained by strong cultural themes that continue to emphasize women's involvement in their children's lives, even with women's increasing labor force participation.

Townsend shows that in the United States, an ideological association of men with the public and women with the domestic does not accurately represent the interpenetration of these spheres. Similarly, in Andalusia, in southern Spain, women are ideologically associated with the home, and men with public places, yet the reality is more complex (Driessen 1983). According to widely held ideals, the woman should be virtuous, docile, and devoted to husband and children; the ideal man is the head of the household, tough, but seldom at home. However, in actuality, the involvement of men in the private sphere and women in the public sphere varies according to social class. Among agricultural laborers, women's labor is critical to the household economy. It is common for women to be employed, while their men are unemployed. This contradiction produces tensions that are reflected in men's sociability patterns. The bar offers men the opportunity to display their masculinity by heavy drinking and sexual banter. Men's sociability is best understood as a response to the vulnerability of unemployed men to women who contribute substantially to the family income through wage labor. This results in blurred idealized distinctions between male and female identities and responsibilities.

Research on the public/private distinction has implications for the interplay among gender, status, and power. Whereas traditional conceptions of power emphasized formal political behavior and authority associated with a status conferring the "right" to impose sanctions (Lamphere 1974: 99), informal power strategies such as manipulation and maneuvering are also important aspects of political activity. Cynthia Nelson (1974) examined the concept of power, focusing on images of women and power in the domestic and public domains in the societies of the Middle East. Ethnographies of this region have commonly differentiated two social worlds, a woman's private world and a man's public world. Women's concerns are domestic, men's political. Nelson argues that the assignment of private and public reflects the imposition of western cultural categories on the Middle East; the meaning of power is influenced by these categorizations, as well as by the limitations of data obtained by male ethnographers from male informants.

This is a point made forcefully by Annette Weiner (1976) in her reanalysis of Trobriand exchange. She argues that "we unquestioningly accept male statements about women as factual evidence for the way a society is structured. . . . Any study that does not include the role of women—as seen by women—as part of the way the society is structured remains only a partial study of that society. Whether women are publicly valued or privately secluded, whether they control politics, a range of economic commodities, or merely magic spells, they function within that society, not as objects, but as individuals with some measure of control" (228).

Similarly, Nelson argues that by asking such questions as "How do women influence men?" "Who controls whom about what?" "How is control exercised?" it becomes apparent that women exercise a greater degree of power in social life than is often appreciated. In addition, she challenges the idea that the social worlds of men and women are reducible to private and public domains, with power limited to the public arena. Nelson's review of ethnographies addressing the role and position of women in Middle Eastern society indicates that women play a crucial role as structural links between kinship groups in societies in which family and kinship are fundamental institutions. Women are in a position to influence men through ritual means, to channel information to male kin, and to influence decision making about alliances; consequently, women do participate in "public" activities, and women's exclusive solidarity groups exercise considerable social control and political influence. The conceptions of power as defined by the western observer are particularly challenged by literature on women written by women who offer multiple perspectives on the experiences of Middle Eastern women, derived from the actors themselves.

In the course of her critique of the application of the domestic-public opposition to social organization in the Middle East, Nelson challenges longstanding assumptions regarding women's subordination and male dominance and calls into question the association between political power and a public domain that excludes women. Similarly, in studies of peasant societies Rogers (1975) and others (Friedl 1967; Riegelhaupt 1967) contend that the sector of life over which peasant women have control—the household—is in fact the key sphere of activity, socially, politically, and economically. Men occupy public and prestigious positions of authority within the village sphere, but these activities do not have the impact on daily life that household activities have. In light of these analyses demonstrating women's power and influence, we are reminded that the universality of male dominance appears untenable.

Similarly, Brenner (1995) questions the value of totalizing models of gender-based power and prestige in her study of gender ideologies in Java. Her analysis critiques the stereotyped, male-centered visions of male power pervasive in Javanese cultural representations and in ethnographic accounts. The ethnographic record has emphasized male-focused gender ideologies while neglecting alternative conceptions of gender voiced by women. She shows that the home and market, both associated with women in Javanese thought, are not only sites of economic production, but also sites where conflicting understandings of male and female nature are symbolically negotiated. According to the gendered division of domestic power, the wife should defer to her husband as head of the household but in reality, women's power may far outweigh that of their husbands. Moreover, the dominance of women in the household is often linked to economic power within and outside the home. Yet in spite of their economic power, central ideologies devalue women precisely because of their commercial pursuits, which are held to detract from prestige. to master their passions. This analysis suggests that although women are identified with the domestic, their activities are central to the production of the family's status in the broader society.

In her chapter "Cities of Women," Weismantel also explores the interpenetration of domestic and public spheres, using the case of Andean women's domination of the produce market. Weismantel challenges the universality of an opposition between a feminine private domain and a masculine outside world, although some scholars have asserted that this dichotomy characterizes Latin America. Rather, she contends that the market exists as a highly gendered institution, a public space that is dramatically feminine, in spite of the idealized boundary between domestic and commercial work. Men find women's domination of this public space unnerving, in contrast to the generalized masculinization of public life in Andean communities. This study also demonstrates that market women are not merely "women serving men," but are social actors engaged in pursuing their own needs and goals, as well as those of other women. For these women, home and domesticity do not necessarily represent a private female domain but rather, a patriarchal territory. Market work is both domestic and commercial, generating income for the vendors while producing food for housewives, thus shaping the workload for women in the home. Weismantel's analysis of Andean market women illustrates how the line between work and family, the public and domestic, is erased in conjunction with the domesticity of the market and the commodification of private life.

In reflecting on feminist research in anthropology, Rosaldo critiques the very tendency to look for universal truths and origins. Rather, anthropologists need to develop theoretical perspectives that analyze the relationships of men and women in a broader social context (Rosaldo 1980: 414), involving inequality and hierarchy. As Henrietta Moore emphasizes, although women in many societies share some experiences and problems, women have had very different encounters with racism, colonialism, the penetration of capitalism, and international development. We need to move from assumptions of the shared experience of "women" to a critical analysis of the differences among them (1988: 9). Assuming the universality of dichotomous domestic and public spheres constrains our exploration of gendered social space and the interconnections between home and workplace.

REFERENCES

Brenner, Suzanna A. 1995. "Why Women Rule the Roost: Rethinking Javanese Ideologies of Gender and Self-Control." In Aihwa Ong and Michael Peletz (eds.) *Bewitching Women, Pious Men: Gender and Body Politics in Southeast Asia.* Berkeley: University of California Press.

Chodorow, Nancy. 1974. "Family Structure and Feminine Personality." In Michelle Z. Rosaldo and Louise Lamphere (eds.). *Woman, Culture, and Society,* pp. 43–67. Stanford: Stanford University Press.

Driessen, Henk. 1983. "Male Sociability and Rituals of Masculinity in Rural Andalusia." *Anthropological Quarterly* 56(3): 125–133.

Friedl, Ernestine. 1967. "The Position of Women: Appearance and Reality." *Anthropological Quarterly* 40: 97–108.

Lamphere, Louise. 1974. "Strategies, Cooperation, and Conflict Among Women in Domestic Groups." In Michelle Z. Rosaldo and Louise Lamphere, (eds.). *Woman, Culture, and Society,* pp. 97–113. Stanford: Stanford University Press.

Leacock, Eleanor. 1978. "Women's Status in Egalitarian Society. Implications for Social Evolution." *Current Anthropology* 19(2): 247–275.

Moore, Henrietta L. 1988. *Feminism and Anthropology.* Minneapolis: University of Minnesota Press.

Nelson, Cynthia. 1974. "Public and Private Politics: Women in the Middle Eastern World." *American Ethnologist* 1(3):551–563.

Riegelhaupt, Joyce. 1967. "Saloio Women: An Analysis of Informal and Formal Political and Economic Roles of Portuguese Peasant Women." *Anthropological Quarterly* 40: 109–126.

Rogers, Susan Carol. 1975. "Female Forms of Power and the Myth of Male Dominance: A Model of Female/Male Interaction in Peasant Society." *American Ethnologist* 2: 727–756.

Rosaldo, Michelle Z. 1974. "Theoretical Overview." In Michelle Z. Rosaldo and Louise Lamphere (eds.). *Woman, Culture, and Society,* pp. 17–43. Stanford: Stanford University Press.

———. 1980. "The Use and Abuse of Anthropology: Reflections on Feminism and Cross-Cultural Understanding." *Signs* 5(3): 389–418.

Sanday, Peggy R. 1974. "Female Status in the Public Domain." In Michelle Z. Rosaldo and
    Louise Lamphere (eds.). *Woman, Culture, and Society,* pp. 189–207. Stanford: Stanford
    University Press.
Weiner, Annette B. 1976. *Women of Value, Men of Renown: New Perspectives in Trobriand
    Exchange.* Austin: University of Texas Press.

The Domestic Sphere of Women and the Public World of Men: The Strengths and Limitations of an Anthropological Dichotomy

Louise Lamphere

Since 1974 there has been a burgeoning interest within anthropology in the study of women, sex roles, and gender. Anthropology has long been a discipline that contained important women (Elsie Clews Parsons, Ruth Benedict, and Margaret Mead among the most famous) and a field in which women have been studied as well (e.g., Kaberry 1939, 1952; Landes 1938, 1947; Leith-Ross 1939; Underhill 1936; and Paulme 1963). However, with the publication of *Woman, Culture, and Society* (Rosaldo and Lamphere 1974) and *Toward an Anthropology of Women* (Reiter 1975a) women scholars, many of whom were identified as feminists, began to critique the androcentric bias in anthropology, to explore women's status in a wide variety of societies, and to provide explanatory models to understand women's position cross-culturally.

One of the most powerful and influential models was proposed by Michelle Rosaldo in her introductory essay to *Woman, Culture, and Society* (1974). Her argument began by asserting that although there is a great deal of cross-cultural variability in men's and women's roles, there is a pervasive, universal asymmetry between the sexes. "But what is perhaps most striking and surprising," Rosaldo writes, "is the fact that male, as opposed to

female, activities are always recognized as predominantly important, and cultural systems give authority and value to the roles and activities of men" (Rosaldo 1974:19).

One of the quotes we chose to appear at the beginning of the book, a passage from Margaret Mead's *Male and Female,* sums up what we saw in 1974 in all the ethnographies and studies we examined. "In every known society, the male's need for achievement can be recognized. Men may cook, or weave, or dress dolls or hunt hummingbirds, but if such activities are appropriate occupations of men, then the whole society, men and women alike, votes them as important. When the same occupations are performed by women, they are regarded as less important" (Mead 1949:125). Not only were there differential evaluations of women's activities, but, Rosaldo argues, "everywhere men have some authority over women, that [is] they have culturally legitimated right to her subordination and compliance" (1974:21).

Having argued for a pervasive sexual asymmetry across cultures, not just in terms of cultural values, but also in terms of power and authority, Rosaldo accounted for this difference between men and women in terms of a dichotomy.[1] She argued that women are associated with a "domestic orientation," while men are primarily associated with extradomestic, political, and

Original material prepared for this text.

military spheres of activity. By "domestic" Rosaldo meant "those minimal institutions and modes of activity that are organized immediately around one or more mothers and their children." In contrast, the "public" referred to "activities, institutions, and forms of association that link, rank, organize, or subsume particular mother-child groups. Put quite simply, men have no single commitment as enduring, time-consuming, and emotionally compelling—as close to seeming necessary and natural—as the relation of a woman to her infant child; and so men are free to form those broader associations that we call 'society,' universalistic systems of order, meaning, and commitment that link particular mother-child groups."

Rosaldo, along with Sherry Ortner and Nancy Chodorow who also wrote essays in *Woman, Culture, and Society,* insisted that the connection between women's role in reproduction (the fact that women everywhere lactate and give birth to children) and their domestic orientation is not a necessary one. In other words biology is not destiny. Women's domestic orientation was structurally and culturally constructed and "insofar as woman is universally defined in terms of a largely maternal and domestic role, we can account for her universal subordination" (Rosaldo 1974:7).

"Although" Rosaldo writes, "I would be the last to call this a necessary arrangement or to deny that it is far too simple as an account of any particular empirical case, I suggest that the opposition between domestic and public orientations (an opposition that must, in part, derive from the nurturant capacities of women) provides the necessary framework for an examination of male and female roles in any society" (Rosaldo 1974:24).

For Rosaldo, then, women were involved in the "messiness" of daily life; they were always available for interruption by children. Men could be more distanced and may actually have separate quarters (such as men's houses) away from women's activities. Men could thus "achieve" authority and create rank, hierarchy, and a political world away from women. The confinement of women to the domestic sphere and men's ability to create and dominate the political sphere thus accounted for men's ability to hold the greater share of power and authority in all known cultures and societies.

At the time Rosaldo wrote her overview and in the introduction we both wrote, we were faced with building a framework where none existed. Despite the number of monographs on women, Margaret Mead's work and that of Simone de Beauvoir (1953) were the most provocative, and perhaps the only, theoretical works we knew.[2] The argument for universal sexual asymmetry followed in a long tradition in anthropology where scholars have sought to look for what is broadly "human" in all cultures. In addition to language, anthropologists have discussed the universality of the incest taboo, marriage, and the family. The notion that women might be universally subordinate to men thus made sense as a first attempt at theory building in this newly revived "subfield" within anthropology.

Although Rosaldo argued for universal subordination, she was careful to make clear that women are not powerless. They exercise informal influence and power, often mitigating male authority or even rendering it trivial (Rosaldo 1974:21). In addition, there are important variations in women's roles in different cultures, and variation was discussed in most of the rest of the articles in the collection. For example, Sanday and Sacks compared women's status in a number of different societies, while Leis examined the structural reasons why women's associations are strong in one Ijaw village in Nigeria, yet absent in another. Finally, in my own article I examined the differences in women's strategies within domestic groups in a number of societies, which related to the relative integration or separation of domestic and political spheres.

Since 1974 the hypothesis of universal subordination of women and the dichotomous relationship between women in the domestic sphere and men in the public sphere have been challenged and critiqued by a number of feminist anthropologists. As appealing as this dichotomy seemed in the abstract, it turned out to be difficult to apply when actually looking at examples of women's activities in different cultures. For example, in an important article written about the same time as Rosaldo's introduction, Rayna Reiter (now Rayna Rapp) described women's and men's distinct lives in a small French village in the south of France. "They inhabited different domains, one public, one private. While men fraternized with whomever they found to talk to in public places, women were much more enmeshed in their families and their kinship networks" (Reiter 1975b:253). However, two categories of public space fell into women's domain: the church and three shops, including the local bakery. Men tended to avoid women's places, entering the bakery, for example, only when several men were together and joking, "Let's attack now" (Reiter 1975b:257).

Reiter argues that men and women use public space in different ways and at different times. "The men go early to the fields, and congregate on the square or in the cafes for a social hour after work. Sometimes they also fraternize in the evenings. These are the times when women are home cooking and invisible to public view. But when the men have abandoned the village for the fields, the women come out to do their marketing in a leisurely fashion. The village is then in female hands. In the afternoon, when the men return to work, the women form gossip groups on stoops and benches or inside houses depending on the weather" (Reiter 1975b:258). Despite the powerful imagery—women associated with the private or domestic domain and men with public space—the description also shows that the dichotomy is not neat. After all women are in public a great deal; they have taken over, in some sense, the Church and the shops and even the public square in the middle of the day.

In Margery Wolf's description of women in a Taiwanese village based on data she collected in the late 1950s, she emphasizes that because researchers have focused on the dominance of patrilineal descent in the family, they have failed to see women's presence. "We have missed not only some of the system's subtleties but also its near-fatal weaknesses" (Wolf 1972:37). Women have different interests than men and build uterine families—strong ties to their daughters, but primarily to their sons who give their mothers loyalty and a place in the patrilineal extended family. Outside the

family in the community women formed neighborhood groups—around a store, at a platform where women washed their clothes in the canal, or under a huge old tree. In a village strung out between a river and a canal, there was no central plaza dominated by men as in the South of France.

In Peihotien Wolf did not describe a cultural geography where women were in a private sphere and men in the public one; rather there was more of a functional separation—men and women had different activities and interests. They were often located in the same places but had a different relationship to the patrilineal extended family and the male-dominated community. Women's lack of power led them to different strategies, different tactics that often undermined male control of the household and even the community. As Sylvia Yanagisako (1987:111) has pointed out the notion of domestic-public entails both a spatial metaphor (of geographically separated or even nested spaces) and a functional metaphor (of functionally different activities or social roles) in the same conceptual dichotomy. Analysts often "mix" these different metaphors in any particular analysis—sometimes using domestic-public spatially and at other times functionally.

Even in the Middle East, the association of women with a private domain (and a lack of power) and men with a public domain (and the center of politics) was too simple, as Cynthia Nelson pointed out in her article, "Public and Private Politics: Women in the Middle Eastern World" (1974). Because they are born into one patrilineal group and marry into another, women are important structural links between social groups and often act as mediators. Because there are segregated social worlds, all-female institutions are important for enforcing social norms: Women fill powerful ritual roles as sorceresses, healers, and mediums; women are important sources of information for their male kin; and women act as "information brokers," mediating social relations within both the family and the larger society.

From Rosaldo's point of view, these aspects of women's power are primarily "informal" and very different from the public, legitimate roles of men. Nevertheless, even though Nelson affirms the separation of male and female worlds (both spatially and functionally), what is "domestic" has public ramifications (the arrangement of a marriage, the transmission of highly charged political information) and the shadow of the family and kin group (the "domestic") is present in even the most "public" of situations. What at first seemed like a simple straightforward dichotomy, in light of actual case material seems very "slippery" and complex.

Furthermore, in many cultures, particularly those with an indigenous band or tribal structure, a separation of "domestic" and "public" spheres makes no sense because household production was simultaneously public, economic, and political. Leacock pointed out the following after reviewing the literature on the Iroquois during the seventeenth and eighteenth century:

> Iroquois matrons preserved, stored, and dispensed the corn, meat, fish, berries, squashes, and fats that were buried in special pits or kept in the long house. Brown (1970:162) notes that women's control over the dispensation of the foods they produced, and meat as well, gave them de facto power to veto declarations of war and to intervene to bring about peace. . . . Women also guarded the "tribal public treasure" kept in the long house, the wampum quill and feather work, and furs. . . . The point to be stressed is that this was "household management" of an altogether different order from management of the nuclear or extended family in patriarchal societies. In the latter, women may cajole, manipulate, or browbeat men, but always behind the public facade; in the former case, "household management" was itself the management of the "public economy." (Leacock 1978:253)

Sudarkasa has made much the same point about women in West African societies such as the Yoruba. She argues that many of the political and economic activities anthropologists discuss as public are actually embedded in households (Sudarkasa 1976, as quoted in Rapp 1979:509). Furthermore, "in West Africa, the 'public domain' was not conceptualized as 'the world of men.' Rather, the public domain was one in which both sexes were

recognized as having important roles to play" (Sudarkasa 1986:99).

A more appropriate conception would be to recognize two domains, "one occupied by men and another by women, both of which were internally ordered in a hierarchical fashion and both of which provided 'personnel' for domestic and extradomestic (or public) activities" (Sudarkasa 1986:94).

Furthermore, a careful examination of "domestic domain" indicates that the categories of "woman" and "mother" overlap in Western society, but the meaning of motherhood may be vastly different in another society. Women may not be exclusively defined as mothers and childrearers in terms of their status and cultural value (see Moore 1988:20–29 for a discussion of this point).

In addition to the issue of whether the domestic-public dichotomy can provide an adequate *description* of men's and women's spatial and functional relationships in our own and other societies, the model has problems as an *explanation* of women's status. One of these problems is the inherent circularity of the model. A central point is to account for the nature of these domains, yet they are already assumed to exist widely and are treated as categories in terms of which women's activities (such as food preparing, cooking, childcare, washing) can be classified (as opposed to male hunting, warfare, political councils). Comaroff says that the model "can only affirm what has already been assumed—that is, that the distinction between the domestic and politico-jural is an intrinsic, if variable, fact of social existence" (Comaroff 1987:59). When the model is used to explain women's positions in different societies in relation to these two orientations, the reasoning is equally circular. To put it in the words of Yanagisako and Collier, "The claim that women become absorbed in domestic activities because of their role as mothers is tautological given the definition of 'domestic' as 'those minimal institutions and modes of activity that are organized immediately around one or more mothers and their children'" (Yanagisako and Collier 1987:19).

Finally, we have come to realize that the concepts of domestic and public were bound up in our own history and our own categories grounded particularly in a Victorian heritage. Rosaldo, in a thoughtful reevaluation of her model, came to argue this position herself.

> The turn-of-the-century social theorists whose writings are the basis of most modern social thinking tended without exception to assume that women's place was in the home. In fact, the Victorian doctrine of separate male and female spheres was, I would suggest, quite central to their sociology. Some of these thinkers recognized that modern women suffered from their association with domestic life, but none questioned the pervasiveness (or necessity) of a split between the family and society. (Rosaldo 1980:401–402)

Rosaldo traced the historical roots of domestic-public from the nineteenth century evolutionists through twentieth-century structural functionalists to her own work. Instead of two opposed spheres (different and apart), Rosaldo suggested an analysis of gender relationships, an examination of inequality and hierarchy as they are created particularly through marriage (Rosaldo 1980:412–413).

The dichotomy has been usefully employed in several ways since 1974. First, several authors have shown us how it works in Western societies (e.g., France and the United States, where it arose historically and still has an important ideological function) (Reiter 1975b; Collier, Rosaldo, and Yanagisako 1982). In a related way, analysts have explored the meanings surrounding domestic activities of women, putting together a much more complex picture of women's relation to men in this sphere (Chai 1987; and Murcott 1983, reprinted in this book). Second, anthropological analysis has helped us to understand the historical development of domestic-public spheres in societies under colonialism. John Comaroff's analysis of the Tshidi chiefdom in South Africa during the early twentieth century is an excellent example of this approach (1987:53–85). Finally, some analysts have used the cultural concepts of other societies to critique our own model of domestic-public orientations. Sylvia Yanagisako's essay on the clear separation of "inside-outside" domains (a spatial metaphor) and "work-family" activities (a functional dichot-

omy) in Japanese American culture demonstrates how the anthropological model of domestic-public mixes these metaphors, which has made analysis confusing and difficult (Yanagisako 1987).

Despite these useful attempts at examining women's lives through the lens of a domestic-public opposition, many of us would agree with Rayna Rapp's 1979 summary of the problems with this dichotomy.

> We cannot write an accurate history of the West in relation to the Rest until we stop assuming that our experiences subsume everyone else's. Our public/private conflicts are not necessarily the same as those of other times and places. The specific oppression of women cannot be documented if our categories are so broad as to decontextualize what "womanness" means as we struggle to change that definition. A Tanzanian female farmer, a Mapuche woman leader, and an American working-class housewife do not live in the same domestic domain, nor will the social upheavals necessary to give them power over their lives be the same. We must simultaneously understand the differences and the similarities, but not by reducing them to one simple pattern. (Rapp 1979:511)

Thus, many of us have tired of the domestic-public dichotomy. We feel it is constraining, a "trap," while new approaches try to get away from dichotomous thinking. These approaches do one of several things. Often they take history seriously, examining women's situation as it has evolved, often in a colonial context. Furthermore, they treat women as active agents and following Collier (1974), as people who have interests, often divergent from men, and who act on them. Third, they often focus on gender relationships, rather than only on women. Finally, they do not treat all women as part of a single universal category of "woman." Rather women are usually analyzed in terms of their social location. Age, class, race, ethnicity, and kinship are all likely to divide women, so newer analyses examine women's strategies and identities as they are differently shaped. Several examples will illustrate some of the different approaches taken in recent years.

Collier's examination of Comanche, Cheyenne, and Kiowa gender relationships (1988) illustrates the recent focus on gender and on the multiple positions that men and women hold in societies in which the domestic-public dichotomy seems inappropriate. This is because these "spheres" are integrated, and there is no firm line between domestic and public space (see Lamphere 1974 and Leacock 1978).

The Comanche are an example of a bride service society in which, like many hunter-gatherer societies, men and women were relatively autonomous, the concept of femininity was not elaborated, and the greatest status differences were between unmarried and married men. Marriage established men as having something to achieve (e.g., a wife), leaving women without such a cultural goal. Young men, through providing meat for their in-laws (bride service), become equal adults, and older men, through egalitarian relations and generosity, become the repositories of wisdom and knowledge. Politics focused on the issue of sexuality and on male–male relationships, which often erupted in conflict and violence. Women celebrated their health and sexuality, and hence the roles of "woman the gatherer" or even "woman the mother" did not emerge as cultural themes.

Among the Cheyenne, an equal bridewealth society, and among the Kiowa, an unequal bridewealth society, marriage relationships were structured in a much different way in the nineteenth century, so gender relationships had a much different content, politics were more hierarchical, and ideology played a different role. Collier's interest is not in the subordination of women in these three societies, because in all three there are several kinds of inequality: between men and women, between older women and girls, between unmarried men and married men, and between kin and affines. An interest in "spheres" and "domains" has been replaced by an emphasis on relationships and an analysis that focuses on the ways in which inequality gets reproduced through marriage transactions, claims on the labor of others, and giving and receiving of gifts. Dominance and subordination become a much more layered,

contextualized phenomenon—more interesting than the simple assertion that women are universally subordinated. The processes through which women's inequality (and that of young men) is constructed are laid bare, rather than flatly asserted.

Mary Moran's study of civilized women (1990) explores the historical beginnings and present-day construction of the category "civilized," which does confine educated women among the Glebo of southeastern Liberia to a "domestic sphere." The dichotomy between "civilized" and "native" (or even tribal or country) is a result of missionization and has created a status hierarchy differentially applied to men and to women. Men, once educated and with a history of paid wage work, never lose their status as "civilized," while women, even though married to a "civilized man," may lose their status if they do not dress correctly, keep house in specific ways, and refrain from farming and marketing. Native women, who market or have farms, are more economically independent but occupy positions of lower prestige. Here we see not only the importance of historical data in examining how cultural categories evolve, but also the ways in which both civilized and native women actively manage their status positions. Civilized women, through the practice of fosterage, recruit younger women to their households to carry out the more elaborate household routines in which they must engage and to train these fostered daughters to become civilized themselves.

The civilized-native dichotomy represents the juxtaposition of two systems. One is a parallel-sex system in which native men and women are represented by their own leaders in two linked but relatively autonomous prestige hierarchies (as suggested by Sudarkasa 1986). The other is a single-sex system (based on a Western model) in which men in political positions represent both sexes, and women have little access to prestige except through their husbands. Thus, this is a much more complex system than one based on a domestic-public dichotomy. There are dichotomous categories—civilized-native, male-female—but they do not fit neatly together. Moran speaks of categories as "gender sensitive" and suggests that "The Glebo have inserted gender into the civilized/native dichotomy to the point that women's status is not only more tenuous and vulnerable than men's but also very difficult to maintain without male support." In some respects civilized women trade off dependency for prestige, but Moran provides a sympathetic picture of how both civilized and native women manage their lives.

Lila Abu-Lughod's study (1986) of Bedouin women's ritual poetry gives us further insights into the complexity of women who in 1974 we would have simply thought of as "confined to a domestic sphere." Among the Bedouin, women's marriages are arranged; wives wear black veils and red belts (symbolizing their fertility); and women must behave within a code of behavior that emphasizes family honor and female modesty and shame. When confronted with loss, poor treatment, or neglect, the public discourse is one of hostility, bitterness, and anger. In the case of lost love the discourse is of militant indifference and denial of concern. In contrast, Bedouin poetry, a highly prized and formally structured art, expresses sentiments of devastating sadness, self-pity, attachment, and deep feeling (Abu-Lughod 1986:187). Although both men and women recite poetry for women, it may express conflicting feelings concerning an arranged marriage, a sense of loss over a divorce, or sentiments of betrayal when a husband marries a new wife. The poems are used to elicit sympathy and get help, but they also constitute a dissident and subversive discourse. Abu-Lughod sees ritual poetry as a corrective to "an obsession with morality and an overzealous adherence to the ideology of honor. . . . Poetry reminds people of another way of being and encourages, as it reflects, another side of experience. . . . And maybe the vision [offered through poetry] is cherished because people see that the costs of this system, in the limits it places on human experiences, are just too high" (Abu-Lughod 1986:259). Bedouin women in this portrait are not simply victims of patriarchy confined to a domestic sphere; they are active individuals who use a highly valued cultural form to express their deepest sentiments, acknowledge an alternative set of values, and leave open the possibility of subverting the system in which they are embedded.

A large number of studies have been conducted in the United States that loosely focus on what used to be termed the domestic sphere and the public world of work. As in the Native American, African, and Middle Eastern cases cited previously, when one begins to examine a topic in detail, global notions like domestic-public seem too simple to deal with the complexities of women's lives. Clearly work and home are distinctly separated spheres in the United States. Women who have been employed in the paid labor force have experienced the disjunction of spending eight or more hours of the day in a place of employment where they are "female workers" and the rest of their time in the home where they are daughters, wives, and/or mothers. With this comes responsibilities for cooking, cleaning, and providing nurturance, care, and intimacy for other family members. Several recent studies have examined the contradictions women face when combining work and family, the impact of paid employment on family roles, and vice versa. I will refer to only three examples of this growing literature.

Patricia Zavella's research on Chicana cannery workers examines women's networks that link the workplace and the family (Zavella 1987). Calling these "work-related networks," Zavella describes groups of friends who saw each other outside work and who were members of a kin network employed in the same cannery. Women used work-related networks as sources of exchange for information, baby sitters, and emotional support. Networks operated in more political ways as workers organized a women's caucus and filed a complaint with the Fair Employment Practices Commission. Women's cannery work was seasonal and had relatively little impact on power relations in the family or the household division of labor. On the other hand work-related networks of friends or kin were an important "bridging mechanism" helping women to deal with the contradictions and demands that came from two different spheres.

Karen Sacks' study of hospital workers at the Duke Medical center examines the ways in which black and white women brought family notions of work, adulthood, and responsibility to work with them and used these values to organize a walk out and subsequent union drive (1988). Sacks focuses on the activities of "center women"—leaders in the union drive. Unlike the men who were often the public speakers at rallies and events, the center women organized support on an interpersonal, one-to-one basis. Rather than emphasizing the bridging aspect of women's networks, Sacks shows how the family is "brought to work" or in the old terminology how the "domestic" influences the "public."

In my own research I have traced the changes in the relationship between women, work, and family historically through the study of immigrant women in a small industrial community, Central Falls, Rhode Island (Lamphere 1987). Using the twin notions of productive and reproductive labor, I examined the rise of the textile industry in Rhode Island and the recruitment of working daughters and later of working mothers to the textile industry and to the other light industries that have replaced it since World War II. Rather than seeing production and reproduction as a rigid dichotomy (like public and domestic), I have used these categories to study relationships and to examine the kinds of strategies that immigrant women and their families forged in confronting an industrial system where wage work was a necessity and where working-class families had no control over the means of production. Such an approach revealed a great deal of variability both between and within ethnic groups—the Irish, English, French-Canadian, and Polish families who came to Central Falls between 1915 and 1984 and the more recent Colombian and Portuguese immigrants. Examination of strikes and walkouts in the 1920s and 1930s and my own experience as a sewer in an apparel plant in 1977 led me to emphasize the strategies of resistance the women workers used on the job, as well as the impact of women's paid labor on the family itself. When daughters were recruited as workers in textile mills, the internal division of labor within the household did not materially change because wives and mothers continued to do much of the reproductive labor necessary to maintain the household. Fathers, teenage sons, and daughters worked for wages. In the current period, in contrast, as more wives have become full-time workers, immigrant men have begun to do some reproductive labor, particularly child care. Immigrant couples often work different shifts and prefer to care for children themselves rather than trust baby sitters from their own ethnic group. In my study I argue that "the productive system as constituted in the workplaces has shaped the family more than issues of reproduction have shaped the workplace" (Lamphere 1987:43).

More recently Patricia Zavella, Felipe Gonzalez, and I have found that young working mothers in sunbelt industries have moved much further than Cannery women or New England industrial immigrant women in changing the nature of the household division of labor (Lamphere, Zavella, Gonzalez, and Evans 1993). These new committed female workers have been employed since high school and do not drop out of the labor force for long periods of time to have children. Thus, they and their husbands construct a family life around a two-job household. Although some couples have a "traditional" division of housework (women do the cooking and the majority of the cleaning and husbands take out the garbage, do minor repairs, and fix the car), many husbands participate in "female chores" and do substantial amounts of childcare (often caring for children while the wife is at work). Here we see the impact of what we used to call the "public sphere" on the domestic one, but in our analysis we have focused more on the varied ways that Anglos and Hispanics (including single mothers) have negotiated household and childcare arrangements, viewing husbands and wives as mediating contradictions. Subtle similarities and differences among and between working class Anglo and Hispanic women have emerged from this analysis, making it clear that the impact of work in the public world is not a monolithic but a variegated process.

In summary the dichotomy between the public world of men and domestic world of women was, in 1974, an important and useful starting point for thinking about women's roles in a cross-cultural perspective. As anthropologists have written more detailed and fine-grained studies of women's lives in a wide variety of other cultures and in our own society, we have gone beyond the use of dichotomies to produce analyses of the complex and layered structure of women's lives. We now treat women more historically, viewing them as social actors and examining the variability among women's situations within one culture and in their relationship to men.

NOTES

1. Rosaldo says that "the opposition does not *determine* cultural stereotypes or asymmetries in the evaluations of the sexism, but rather underlies them, to support a very general . . . identification of women with domestic life and of men with public life" (Rosaldo 1974:21–22). Thus, I would argue, Rosaldo did not attempt to *explain* women's subordination through the dichotomy, but saw it as an underlying structural framework in any society that supported subordination and that would have to be reorganized to change women's position.

2. It is interesting that we did not know of Elsie Clews Parsons' extensive feminist writing during 1910 to 1916, much of which is reminiscent of the kind of position we took in *Woman, Culture, and Society*. In another article I have noted the similarities between Shelly's prose and that of Parsons (see Lamphere 1989 and Parsons 1913, 1914, 1915).

REFERENCES

Abu-Lughod, Lila. 1986. *Veiled Sentiments: Honor and Poetry in a Bedouin Society*. Berkeley and Los Angeles: University of California Press.

Brown, Judith. 1970. Economic organization and the position of women among the Iroquois. *Ethnohistory* 17(3/4):131–167.

Chai, Alice Yun. 1987. Freed from the elders but locked into labor: Korean immigrant women in Hawaii. *Women's Studies* 13:223–234.

Collier, Jane. 1974. Women in politics. In Michelle Z. Rosaldo and Louise Lamphere (eds.). *Woman, Culture, and Society*. Stanford: Stanford University Press.

———. 1988. *Marriage and Inequality in Classless Societies*. Stanford: Stanford University Press.

Collier, Jane, Michelle Rosaldo, and Sylvia Yanagisako. 1982. Is there a family? New anthropological views. In Barrie Thorne and Marilyn Yalom (eds.). *Rethinking the Family: Some Feminist Questions*. New York and London: Longman.

Comaroff, John L. 1987. Sui genderis: Feminism, kinship theory, and structural "domains." In Jane Fishburne Collier and Sylvia Junko Yanagisako (eds.). *Gender and Kinship: Essays Toward a Unified Analysis*. Stanford: Stanford University Press.

de Beauvoir, Simone. 1953. *The Second Sex*. New York: Alfred A. Knopf. Originally published in French in 1949.

Kaberry, Phyllis M. 1939. *Aboriginal Women, Sacred and Profane*. London: G. Routledge.

———. 1952. *Women of the Grassfields*. London: H. M. Stationery Office.

Lamphere, Louise. 1974. Strategies, cooperation, and conflict among women in domestic groups. In Michelle Z. Rosaldo and Louise Lamphere (eds.). *Woman, Culture, and Society*. Stanford: Stanford University Press.

———. 1987. *From Working Daughters to Working Mothers: Immigrant Women in a New England Industrial Community*. Ithaca, NY: Cornell University Press.

———. 1989. Feminist anthropology: The legacy of Elsie Clews Parsons. *American Ethnologist* 16(3):518–533.

Lamphere, Louise, Patricia Zavella, Felipe Gonzales and Peter Evans 1993. *Sunbelt Working Mothers: Reconciling Family and Factory*. Ithaca, NY: Cornell University Press.

Landes, Ruth. 1938. *The Ojibwa Woman, Part 1: Youth*. New York: Columbia University. Contributions to Anthropology, Vol. 31.

———. 1947. *The City of Women: Negro Women Cult Leaders of Bahia*, Brazil. New York: Macmillan.

Leacock, Eleanor. 1978. Women's status in egalitarian society: Implications for social evolution. *Current Anthropology* 19(2):247–275.

Leith-Ross, Sylvia. 1939. *African Women: Study of the Ibo of Nigeria*. London: Faber and Faber.

Mead, Margaret. 1949. *Male and Female*. New York: William Morrow and Co.

Moran, Mary H. 1990. *Civilized Women: Gender and Prestige in Southeastern Liberia*. Ithaca, NY: Cornell University Press.

Moore, Henrietta L. 1988. *Feminism and Anthropology*. Minneapolis: University of Minnesota Press.

Murcott, Anne. 1983. "It's a pleasure to cook for him": Food, mealtimes and gender in some South Wales households. In Eva Gamarnikow, D.H.J. Morgan, June Purvis, and Daphne Taylorson (eds.). *The Public and the Private*. London: Heinemann Educational Books.

Nelson, Cynthia. 1974. Public and private politics: Women in the Middle East. *American Ethnologist* 1:551–563.

Ong, Aihwa. 1987. *Spirits of Resistance and Capitalist Discipline.* Albany, NY: State University of New York Press.

Parsons, Elsie Clews. 1913. *The Old Fashioned Woman.* New York: G. P. Putnam's Sons.

———. 1914. *Fear and Conventionality.* New York: G. P. Putnam's Sons.

———. 1915. *Social Freedom: A Study of the Conflicts Between Social Classifications and Personality.* New York: G. P. Putnam's Sons.

Paulme, Denise (ed.). 1963. *Women of Tropical Africa.* Berkeley: University of California Press.

Rapp, Rayna. 1979. Anthropology. *Signs* 4(3): 497–513.

Reiter, Rayna (ed.). 1975a. *Toward an Anthropology of Women.* New York: Monthly Review Press.

———. 1975b. Men and women in the South of France: Public and private domains. In Rayna Reiter (ed.). *Toward an Anthropology of Women.* New York: Monthly Review Press.

Rosaldo, Michelle. 1974. Woman, culture and society: A theoretical overview. In Michelle Z. Rosaldo and Louise Lamphere (eds.). *Woman, Culture, and Society.* Stanford: Stanford University Press.

———. 1980. The uses and abuses of anthropology. *Signs* 5(3): 389–417.

Rosaldo, Michelle Z. and Louise Lamphere (eds.). 1974. *Woman, Culture, and Society.* Stanford: Stanford University Press.

Sacks, Karen. 1988. *Caring by the Hour: Women, Work, and Organizing at the Duke Medical Center.* Urbana and Chicago: University of Illinois Press.

Sudarkasa, Niara. 1976. Female employment and family organization in West Africa. In Dorothy McGuigan (ed.). *New Research on Women and Sex Roles.* Ann Arbor: Center for Continuing Education of Women.

———. 1986. The status of women in indigenous African Societies. *Feminist Studies* 12: 91–104.

Underhill, Ruth. 1936. *Autobiography of a Papago Woman. Supplement to American Anthropologist* 38(3), Part II. Millwood, NY: American Anthropological Association.

Wolf, Margery. 1972. *Women and the Family in Rural Taiwan.* Stanford: Stanford University Press.

Yanagisako, Sylvia Junko. 1987. Mixed metaphors: Native and anthropological models of gender and kinship domains. In Jane Fishburne Collier and Sylvia Junko Yanagisako (eds.). *Gender and Kinship: Essays Toward a Unified Analysis.* Stanford: Stanford University Press.

Yanagisako, Sylvia Junko and Jane Fishburne Collier. 1987. Toward a unified analysis of gender and kinship. In Jane Fishburne Collier and Sylvia Junko Yanagisako (eds.). *Gender and Kinship: Essays Toward a Unified Analysis.* Stanford: Stanford University Press.

Zavella, Patricia. 1987. *Women's Work and Chicano Families: Cannery Workers of the Santa Clara Valley.* Ithaca, NY: Cornell University Press.

"It's a Pleasure to Cook for Him": Food, Mealtimes, and Gender in Some South Wales Households

Anne Murcott

INTRODUCTION

I think it lets him know that I am thinking about him—as if he knows that I am expecting him. But it's not as if "oh I haven't got anything ready.". . . Fair play, he's out all day . . . he doesn't ask for that much . . . you know it's not as if he's been very demanding or—he doesn't come home and say "oh, we've got chops again," it's really a pleasure to cook for

Reprinted with permission from Eva Gamarnikow, David H. J. Morgan, June Purvis, and Daphne Taylorson (eds.), The Public and the Private (London: Heinemann Educational Books, Ltd., 1983), pp. 78–90. Copyright ©1983 British Sociological Association.

him, because whatever you. . . oh I'll give him something and I think well, he'll like this, he'll like that. And he'll always take his plate out. . . and he'll wash the dishes without me even asking, if I'm busy with the children. Mind, perhaps his method is not mine.

Every now and then an informant puts precisely into words the results of the researcher's analytic efforts—providing in the process a quotation suitable for the title! The extract reproduced above, explaining the importance of having the meal ready when her husband arrives home, comes from one of a series of interviews on which this paper is based.[1] The discussion starts by remembering that "everyone knows" that women do the cooking: all the women interviewed—and the few husbands/boyfriends or mothers who came in and out—took it for granted that cooking was women's work. Informants may not enjoy cooking, or claim not to be good at it; they may not like the arrangement that it is women's work, or hanker after modifying it. But all recognize that this is conventional, some volunteer a measure of approval, most appeared automatically to accept it, a few resigned themselves and got on with it.

Studies of the organization of domestic labor and marital role relationships confirm that cooking continues to be a task done more by women than men; this is also the case cross-culturally (Stephens, 1963; Murdock and Provost, 1973). Emphasis in the literature has shifted from Young and Willmott's (1975) symmetrical view of sharing and marital democracy. Now rather more thoroughgoing empirical study suggests their assessment is little more than unwarranted optimism (Oakley, 1974a and b; Edgell, 1980; Leonard, 1980; Tolson, 1977). This work improves on earlier studies of the domestic division of labor by going beyond behaviorist enquiry about "who does which tasks" to consider the meanings attached to them by marital partners. The distribution of work turns out not to correlate neatly with assessments of importance or allocation of responsibility. (Oakley, 1974b; Edgell, 1980).

Part of this effort (in particular, Oakley, 1974a and b) has in addition attempted to analyze domestic work as a "job like any other," considering housewives' work satisfaction, routines, supervision and so on. While this line of enquiry has undoubtedly made visible much of women's lives conventionally rendered invisible, it has perhaps not gone far enough. The study of housework as an occupation needs to attend in addition to features such as quality control, timekeeping, client as well as worker satisfaction, and perhaps further consideration of who, if anyone, is a housewife's boss. As will be seen, each of these is implicated in the discussion that follows.

These occupational aspects of housework provide, moreover, additional means of examining the relationship of the domestic division of labor to the economic structure as a whole. Recent commentary has also proposed that the view of the family as stripped of all but the residual economic function of consumption is ill-conceived and over-simplified. Domestic laborers refresh and sustain the existing labor force and play a key part in reproducing that of the future—as well as providing a reserve of labor themselves. The precise manner in which the political economy is to be accounted continues to be debated (West, 1980; Fox, 1980; Wajcman, 1981). For the moment, however, the general drift of that discussion can be borne in mind by recalling the everyday terminology of eating; food is consumed, meals have to be produced. The language favored in cookbooks echoes that of industry and the factory (Murcott, 1983a). Homecooking may nicely embody the terms in which the family and household's place in the division of labor has to be seen. It may also provide a convenient arena for the further exploration of the economic and labor relations in the family and the relation of the marital partners to the means of production of domestic labor (Middleton, 1974).

Examination of the household provision of meals in these terms is, however, some way in the future. This paper does no more than offer some empirical foundation on which such study might build. It brings together informants' ideas about the importance of cooking, their notions of propriety of household eating, and indicates their relation to gender. It starts with views of the significance of good cooking for home life, and goes on to deal with the place of cooking in the domestic division of labor. The familiar presumption that women are the cooks is extended to show that their responsibility in this sphere is tempered with reference to their husband's, not their own, choice. The paper concludes with brief comment on possible ways these data may illuminate some of the questions already raised.

HOME COOKING

> Aside from love, good food is the cornerstone of a happy household . . . (Opening lines of a 1957 cookbook called *The Well Fed Bridegroom*).

Right through the series of interviews three topics kept cropping up; the idea of a proper meal, reference to what informants call a "cooked dinner" and the notion that somehow home is where proper eating is ensured. Moreover, mention of one like as not involved mention of another, sometimes all three. The composite picture that emerges from the whole series suggests that these are not merely related to one another in some way, but virtually equated.

It first needs to be said that informants seemed quite comfortable with a conception of a proper meal—indeed the very phrase was used spontaneously—and were able to talk about what it meant to them. Effectively a proper meal is a cooked dinner. This is one which women feel is necessary to their family's health, welfare and, indeed, happiness. It is a meal to come home to, a meal which should figure two, three, or four times in the week, and especially on Sundays. A cooked dinner is easily identified—meat, potatoes, vegetables and gravy. It turns out that informants displayed considerable unanimity as to what defines such a dinner, contrasting it to, say, a "snack" or "fried." In so doing they made apparent remarkably clear rules not only for its composition but also its preparation and taking. I have dealt with their detail and discussed their implications in full elsewhere (Murcott, 1982). But in essence these rules can be understood as forming part of the equation between proper eating and home cooking. And, as will be noted

in the next section, they also provide for the symbolic expression of the relationship between husband and wife and for each partner's obligation to their home.

The meal for a return home is, in any case, given particular emphasis—a matter which cropped up in various contexts during the interviews. Thus, for some the very importance of cooking itself is to be expressed in terms of homecoming. Or it can provide the rationale for turning to and making a meal, one to be well cooked and substantial—not just "beans on toast . . . thrown in front of you."

The actual expression "home cooking"—as distinct from "cooking for homecoming"—received less insistent reference. Informants were straightforward, regarding it as self-evident that people preferred the food that they had at home, liked what they were used to and enjoyed what they were brought up on. Perhaps untypically nostalgic, one sums up the point:

> When my husband comes home . . . there's nothing more he likes I think than coming in the door and smelling a nice meal cooking. I think it's awful when someone doesn't make the effort. . . . I think well if I was a man I'd think I'd get really fed up if my wife never bothered. . . .

What was prepared at home could be trusted—one or two regarded the hygiene of restaurant kitchens with suspicion, most simply knew their chips were better than those from the local Chinese take-away or chippy. Convenience foods had their place, but were firmly outlawed when it came to a cooked dinner. In the ideal, commercially prepared items were ranged alongside snacks, and light, quick meals: lunches and suppers in contrast to proper dinners. Informants talked about home cooking, but used this or some such phrase infrequently; the following is an exception:

> I'd like to be able to make home-made soups and things, it's just finding the time and getting organized, but at the moment I'm just not organized. . . . I think it would probably be more good for us than buying. . . . I suppose it's only—I'd like to be—the image of the ideal housewife is somebody who cooks her own food and keeps the household clean and tidy.

The sentiments surrounding her valuation of home-made food are not, however, an exception. Time and again informants linked not only a view of a proper meal for home-coming, but a view of the proper parts husband and wife are to play on this occasion. So cooking is important when you are married.

> you must think of your husband . . . it's a long day for him at work, usually, . . . even if they have got a canteen at work, their cooking is not the same as coming home to your wife's cooking. . . . I think every working man should have a cooked meal when he comes in from work. . . .

Cooking is important—though not perhaps for everybody "like men who don't cook"—for women whose "place [it is] to see the family are well fed."

In this section, I have indicated that informants virtually treat notions of proper meals, home-based eating, and a cooked dinner, as equivalents. The stress laid on the homecoming not only underlines the symbolic significance attached to both the meal and the return home. It simultaneously serves as a reminder of the world beyond the home being left behind for that day. Put another way, the cooked dinner marks the threshold between the public domains of school or work and the private sphere behind the closed front door. In the process of describing these notions of the importance of cooking in the home, it becomes apparent that the familiar division of labor is assumed.

COOKING IN THE DOMESTIC DIVISION OF LABOR

As noted in an earlier section, all those interviewed took it for granted that it is the women who cook. What they had to say refers both to conventions in general, and themselves and their circumstances in particular.[2] There are two important features of their general presumption that women are the cooks; one indicates the terms in which it is modifiable, the other locates it firmly as a matter of marital justice and obligation. The upshot of each of these is to underline the manner in which the domestic preparation of meals is securely anchored to complementary concepts of conduct proper to wife and husband.

To say that women cook is not to say that it is only women who ever do so. It is, however, to say that it is always women who daily, routinely, and as a matter of course are to do the cooking. Men neither in the conventional stereotype nor in informants' experience ever cook on a regular basis in the way women do.[3] Husband/boyfriends/fathers are "very good really"; they help informants/their mothers with carrying the heavy shopping, preparing the vegetables, switching the oven on when told, doing the dishes afterwards (cf. Leonard, 1980). Such help may be offered on a regular enough basis, notably it is available when the women are pregnant, dealing with a very young infant, unwell or unusually tired. But none of this is regarded as men doing the cooking.

More significantly, it is not the case that men do not cook—in the strict sense of taking charge of the transformation of foodstuffs to some version of a meal. They may make breakfast on a Sunday, cook only "bacon-y" things, can do chips or "his" curries: all examples, incidentally, of foods that do not figure in the proper cooked dinner (Murcott, 1983c).

For some, however, competence in the kitchen (and at the shops) is suspect: he'll "turn the potatoes on at such and such a time. . . but leave him he's hopeless" and another just "bungs everything in." For others, it is men who make better domestic cooks than women, are more methodical, less moody. Another couple jokingly disagree: she "not taken in" by Robert Carrier on TV, he claiming that "the best chefs are men." The point is that either way, of course, informants do regard gender as relevant to the question of who is to cook.

It is not even the case that all men cannot cook the proper, homecoming meal. One or two, when out of work for a while, but his wife still earning (this only applied to those having a first baby) might start the meal or even have it ready for her return. But once he is employed again he does not continue to take this degree of responsibility, reverting either to "helping" or waiting for her to do it. Now and again, wives have learned to cook not at school or from their mothers, but from their husbands. But it was still assumed that it was for the woman to learn. This was even so in one instance where the informant made a "confession . . . my husband does the cooking." But now that she was pregnant and had quit paid work she would take over; "it would be a bit lazy not to." Like others for whom the cooking may have been shared while both were employed, cooking once again became the home-based wife's task (cf. Bott, 1957, p. 225; Oakley, 1980, p. 132).

The issue is, however, more subtle than an account of who does what, or who takes over doing what. Men and women's place involve mutual obligation. "I think a woman from the time she can remember is brought up to cook. . . Whereas most men are brought up to be the breadwinner." The question of who does the cooking is explicitly a matter of justice and marital responsibility. A woman talks of the guilt she feels if she does not, despite the greater tiredness of late pregnancy, get up to make her husband's breakfast and something for lunch—"he's working all day." Another insists that her husband come shopping with her so he knows the price of things—he's "hopeless" on his own—but she has a clear idea of the limits of each person's responsibility: each should cook only if the wife *has* to earn rather than chooses to do so.

Here, then, I have sought to show that informants subscribed in one way or another to the convention that it is women who cook. In the process it transpired that it is certain sorts of cooking, i.e., routine, homecoming cooking, which are perennially women's work. The meal that typically represents "proper" cooking is, of course, the cooked dinner. Its composition and prescribed cooking techniques involve prolonged work and attention; its timing, for homecoming, prescribes when that work shall be done. To do so demands the cook be working at it, doing wifely work, in time that corresponds to time spent by her husband earning for the family (Murcott, 1982). This is mirrored in Eric Batstone's (1983) account of the way a car worker's lunch box prepared by his wife the

evening before is symbolic of the domestic relationship which constitutes the rationale for his presence in the workplace; he endures the tedium of the line in order to provide for his wife and family. It transpired also that men do cook in certain circumstances, but such modification seems to reveal more clearly the basis for accounting cooking as part of a wife's responsibility (to the family) at home corresponding to the husband's obligation (to the family) at work, i.e., their mutual responsibilities to each other as marriage partners.

WHO COOKS FOR WHOM?

At this point I introduce additional data which bear on cooking's relation to the question of marital responsibility. Repeatedly informants indicated that people do not cook for themselves; evidently it is not worth the time and effort.[4] But the data suggest implications beyond such matters of economy. Two interrelated features are involved: one is the distinction already alluded to in the previous section, between cooking in the strict sense of the word and cooking as preparation of a particular sort of meal. The other enlarges on the following nicety. To observe that people do not cook for themselves can mean two things. First it can imply that a solitary person does not prepare something for themselves to eat while on their own. But it can also imply that someone does not do the cooking on their own behalf, but in the service of some other(s). Examination of the transcripts to date suggests that not only could informants mean either or both of these, but also that each becomes elided in a way that underlines the nuances and connotations of the term cooking.

The question of a lone person not cooking themselves a meal unsurprisingly cropped up most frequently with reference to women themselves, but men, or the elderly, were also thought not to bother.

Informants are clear, however, that not cooking when alone does not necessarily mean going without. Women "pick" at something that happens to be in the house, have a bar of chocolate or packet of crisps later in the evening or a "snack." Men will fry something, an egg or make chips. No one said that a man would go without altogether (though they may not know), whereas for themselves—and women and girls in general—skipping a meal was thought common enough. Men—and occasionally women—on their own also go back to their mother's or over to their sister's for a meal. One informant was (the day of my interview with her) due to go to her mother's for the evening meal, but fearful of being alone in the house at night, she was also due to stay there for the next few days while her husband was away on business.

The suggestion is, then, that if a person is by themselves, but is to have a proper meal, as distinct from "fried" or a "snack" then they join a (close) relation's household. The point that it is women who cook such meals receives further emphasis. Indeed, when women cook this particular meal, it is expressly for others. In addition to the temporary lone adults just noted who return to mothers or sisters, women in turn may cook for the older generation, as well as routinely cooking for children or for men home at "unusual" times if unemployed or temporarily or a different shift.

This conventional requirement that women cook for others is not always straightforward in practice. At certain stages in an infant's life the logistics of producing meals for husband and child(ren) there as well meant the woman felt difficulties in adequately meeting the obligations involved. And not all informants enjoyed cooking; most just accepted that it needed doing, though there were also those who took positive, creative pleasure in it (cf. Oakley, 1974b). Part of this is expressed in the very satisfaction of providing for others something they should be getting, and in turn will enjoy.

More generally cooking can become tiresome simply because it has to be done day-in, day-out. The pleasure in having a meal prepared for you becomes all the more pointed if routinely you are cooking for others.[5] In the absence of any data for men, it can only be a guess that going out for a meal is thus specially enjoyable for women. But for those who on occasion did eat out this clearly figures in their pleasure. Even if it rarely happened, just the idea of having it put in front of you meant a treat: "it's nice being spoiled."

The question "who cooks for whom?" can now begin to be answered. Apparently it is women who cook for others—effectively, husbands and children. If husbands and children are absent, women alone will not "cook," indeed many may not even eat. It is the others' presence that provides the rationale for women's turning to and making a proper meal—that is what the family should have and to provide it is her obligation. Men—and children—have meals made for them as a matter of routine: but for women it is a treat. That solitary men do not "cook" for themselves either, and may go to a relative's for meals (cf. Rosser and Harris, 1965; Barker, 1972), or that a woman on her own may also do so does not detract from the main proposal that it is women who cook for others. For it is not only that informants or their husbands will go temporarily back to their mother's, not their father's, home-cooking. It is also that both men and women revert to the status of a child for whom a woman, a mother, cooks. The mother may actually be the adult's parent, but they—and I with them—may stretch the point and see that she may be mother to the adult's nieces or nephews or indeed, as in the case of cooking for the elderly, she may be mother to the adult's grandchildren.

The appreciation that it is women who cook for others elaborates the more familiar convention, discussed above, that in the domestic division of labor cooking is women's work. First of all it indicates that this work is service work. Cooking looks increasingly like a task quite particularly done for others. Second, when cooking for others women are performing a service to those who are specifically related (sic) rather than for a more generalized clientele known only by virtue of their becoming customers. The marital—and parental—relationship defines who is server, who served.

That said, there remains the question of deciding what the server shall serve. As already discussed in an earlier section, the conventional expectation shared, it seems, by both woman and man, is that meals shall be of a certain sort—a cooked dinner for a certain occasion, most commonly the return home from work, or the celebration of Sunday, a work-free day. The "rules" involved are not entirely hard and fast, or precisely detailed. Cooked dinners are neither daily nor invariable affairs (Murcott, 1982). And the cooked dinner itself can properly comprise a number of alternative meats (and cuts) and range of different vegetables. What then, determines the choice of meat and vegetables served on any particular day? Some of the factors involved, as will be seen in the next section, once again echo ideas of responsibility and mutual obligation.

DECIDING WHAT TO HAVE

A number of factors feature in deciding what to have for a particular day's meal.[6] First, a question of cost was taken for granted. This does not necessarily mean keeping expenditure to a minimum—eating in the customary manner despite hard times was highly and expressly valued by some. Second, the conventional provision of proper dinners itself contributed to the determination of choice. These two factors present themselves as marking the limits within which the finer decisions about what the precise components of the day's dinner are to be. Here reference to their husband's—and, to a lesser extent, children's—preferences was prominent in informants' discussion of such detailed choices.

It was indicated earlier that in an important sense women's cooking is service work. This sort of work has two notable and interrelated aspects affecting decisions and choice: is it the server or served who decides what the recipient is to want? Exploring the mandate for professionals' work, Everett Hughes (1971, p. 424) highlights a key question: "professionals do not merely serve: they define the very wants they serve." Servants, and service workers such as waitresses (Whyte, 1948; Spradley and Mann, 1975) compliantly provide for the wants identified by the served. On the face of it, then, the professional has

total and the waitress nil autonomy. Examples reflecting this sort of range occurred among informants, varying from one woman apparently always deciding, through to another always making what he wants for tea. But in the same way that the maximum autonomy of the professional is continually, to a certain degree, a matter of negotiation and renegotiation with clients, and that, similarly, the apparent absence of autonomy is modified by a variety of more or less effective devices waitresses use to exert some control over customers, so a simple report of how meal decisions are reached can, I propose, either conceal negotiations already complete, or reveal their workings.

Thus informants interested in trying new recipes still ended up sticking to what they usually made because their husbands were not keen. Others reported that "he's very good" or "never complains" while some always asked what he wanted. A non-committal reply however did not necessarily settle the matter, for some discovered that being presented with a meal she had then decided on could provoke adverse and discouraging remarks. But it was clear that even those who claimed not to give their husbands a choice were still concerned to ensure that he agreed to her suggestion. It is almost as if they already knew what he would like, needed to check out a specific possibility every now and then but otherwise continued to prepare meals within known limits. Deciding what to have already implicitly took account of his preferences so that the day-to-day decision seemed to be hers.

The material presented in this section provides only a glimpse of this area of domestic decision-making. Other aspects need consideration in future work. For instance, what degree of importance do people attach to the matter (cf. Edgell, 1980, pp. 58–9)? Attention also needs to be paid to wider views of the legitimacy of choice in what one eats. In what sense do restaurant customers choose and mentally subnormal patients not? Does a child that spits out what it is fed succeed in claiming a choice or not? And in apparently acquiescing to their husband's choice, are wives circumscribing their own? But it looks as if deciding what to have is of a piece with a shared view of marital responsibility whereby he works and so deserves, somehow, the right to choose what she is to cook for him.

GENDER AND THE PRODUCTION OF MEALS

I know a cousin of mine eats nothing but chips, in fact his mother-in-law had to cook him chips for his Christmas dinner and she went berserk . . .

This "atrocity story" recapitulates various elements of the preceding discussion. Such unreasonableness is, no doubt, unusual but its artless reporting emphasizes a number of points already made. Not only do chips break the rules of what should properly figure in a Christmas meal, superior even to the Sunday variant of a cooked dinner, but it remains, however irksome, up to the woman to prepare what a man wants. The burden of this paper, then, may be summarized as revealing allegiance to the propriety of occasion such that a certain sort of meal is to mark home (male) leisure versus (male) work-time, and that such meals are cooked by women for others, notably husbands, in deference, not to the woman's own, but to men's taste.

This examination of cooking, mealtimes and gender within the household has implications for the continuing analysis of domestic work as work. While it does not shed light on why such work is women's, only reasserting that conventionally this is so, it clearly casts the work of meal provision as service work.

The everyday way of describing dishing up a meal as serving food is embedded in a set of practices that prescribe the associated social relationships as of server and served. As already observed this involves two interrelated matters: control over the work, and decisions as to what are the "wants" the worker shall serve, what the work shall be. Each is considered in turn.

Oakley (1974a and b) reports that one of the features of housewifery that women value is the feeling of autonomy. Care is needed, though, not to treat such attitudes as tantamount to their analysis. Just because housewives express their experiences in terms of enjoying being their own boss does not mean that their conditions of work can be analyzed in terms of a high degree of autonomy. The material presented in this paper suggests that doing the cooking is not directed by the woman herself, but is subject to various sorts of control.

First of these is the prescription for certain kinds of food for certain occasions. The idea of the cooked dinner for a homecoming is just such an example of cultural propriety. Related to this is a second control, namely that the food is to be ready for a specific time. Mealtimes construed in this way may exert just the same sort of pressure on the cook as any other production deadline in industry. Third, control is also exerted via the shared understanding that it is the preferences of the consumer which are to dictate the exact variant of the dinner to be served. What he fancies for tea constrains the cook to provide it. These kinds of control in the domestic provision of meals find their counterpart in the industrial concerns of quality control, timekeeping and market satisfaction. A woman cooking at home may not have a chargehand "breathing down her neck" which is understandably a source of relief to her. But this does not mean to say that she enjoys autonomy—simply perhaps that other controls make this sort of oversight redundant. Evidence either way is extremely sparse, but Ellis (1983) suggests that failing to cook according to her husband's wishes can contribute to a wife's battering.

Linked to the issue of control of domestic cooking is the question of decision-making. Edgell (1980) has drawn attention to the degree of importance couples attach to different aspects of family living about which decisions have to be made. He distinguishes assessments of importance from, first, whether the decision is mainly the wife's or husband's responsibility and second, from the frequency with which the decision has to be made. So, for instance, moving is the husband's decision, perceived to be very important and infrequent, a contrast to the matter of spending on food. What Edgell does not make clear, however, is quite what either his informants or he mean by "importance." As an analytic device, the idea does not distinguish between family matters which partners may identify as both important and somehow major or permanent such as moving, and those identified as mundane, or fleeting but important nonetheless, such as daily eating. Like refuse collection or sewage work which is regarded as vital but low-status, the importance attached to meals may not be remarked in the general run of things, though noticed particularly if absent. But that does not necessarily mean that both husband and wife regard it as unimportant. And, harking back to the question of autonomy in decision-making, reports such as Edgell's that food spending, cooking or whatever is regarded as the wife's responsibility, cannot, of itself, be seen as evidence of her power and freedom from control in those areas. For as Jan Pahl (1982, p. 24) has so cogently observed, "being able to offload certain decisions and certain money-handling chores on to the other spouse can itself be a sign of power." The delegate may be responsible for execution of tasks, but they are answerable to the person in whom the power to delegate is originally vested.

The preliminary analysis offered in this paper has theoretical and political implications concerning power and authority in marriage and the relation between domestic and paid work. The exploration of ideas about cooking and mealtimes starts to provide additional approach to detailing the means of domestic production. And the sort of work women are to do to ensure the homecoming meal provides a critical instance of the juncture between the control of a worker and the (his) control of his wife. The meal provides one illustration not only of a point where the public world of employment and the private world of the home meet one another; it also shows how features of the public take precedence within the private. For the stress informants lay on this mealtime offers an interesting way of understanding how the industrial rhythms which circumscribe workers are linked to the rhythms which limit women's domestic work (cf. Rotenberg, 1981).

And women's continual accommodation to men's taste can also be seen as a literal expression of wives' deference to husbands' authority (Bell and Newby, 1976; Edgell, 1980, p. 70). This acquiescence to his choice provides the cultural gloss to the underlying economic relationship whereby industry produces amongst other things both the wage, and the raw materials it buys, for the domestic to produce what is needed to keep the industrial worker going. Part of the conjugal contract that each in their own way provide for the other, it does indeed become "a pleasure to cook for him."

ACKNOWLEDGMENTS

I am very grateful to all those necessarily anonymous people who made the research possible and who generously gave their time to answer my questions. I should like to record my appreciation of conversations with Tony Coxon, Sara Delamont, Robert Dingwall, Rhian Ellis, Bill Hudson and Phil Strong at various stages during the preparation of this paper and of the computing help and advice Martin Read provided. Only I and not they are to blame for its deficiencies. And I must thank Lindsey Nicholas, Joan Ryan, Sheila Pickard, Myrtle Robins and Margaret Simpson very much, despite flu all round, and an unusually scrawly manuscript, for their help in typing both drafts.

NOTES

1. In order to begin remedying sociology's neglect (Murcott, 1983b) of food beliefs and of the social organization of eating, I conducted a single-handed exploratory study (supported by a grant from the SSRC) holding unstructured tape-recorded interviews with a group of 37 expectant mothers attending a health center in a South Wales valley for antenatal care (22 pregnant for the first time), 20 of whom were interviewed again after the baby's birth. No claim is made for their representativeness in any hard and fast sense, though they represent a cross-section of socio-economic groups. For present

purposes the data are treated as providing a composite picture. The prime concern here is to indicate the range and variety of evidence gathered. An instance that occurs once only thus becomes as interesting as one occurring 30 times. This is reflected in the discussion by the deliberate use of phrases such as "some informants" rather than "6 out of 37." In any case reference to numbers of instances is no more exact, and risks implying a spurious representativeness.

These qualifications are most important. But for the sake of a tolerably readable account I do not hedge every other sentence with reminder of these limitations. Yet they do actively have to be taken as read.

2. Informants referred not only to themselves but also to mothers, sisters, sisters-in-law and women friends doing cooking.

3. No informant who had children old enough to cook currently shared the household with them.

4. Market researchers know how to trade on such reports. During the period of interviewing a TV commercial was running which sought to persuade busy housewives not to neglect themselves but have a frozen ready-cooked meal at lunchtime.

5. Interestingly, no one talked of hospital meals put in front of them as a treat. (None had a home delivery.) Rather it was the quality of the food provided which informants concentrated on. Institution cooking could not be home cooking.

6. It might have been expected that nutritional criteria would figure in these decisions. Analysis so far suggests that cultural prescriptions for proper eating at home override what is known about healthy eating. (Murcott, 1983d).

REFERENCES

Barker, D.L. 1972. "Keeping close and spoiling," *Sociological Review*, 20(4), 569–590.

Batstone, E. 1983. "The hierarchy of maintenance and the maintenance of hierarchy: Notes on food and industry," in A. Murcott (ed.), *The Sociology of Food and Eating*, Gower.

Bell, C. and Newby, H. 1976. "Husbands and wives: The dynamics of deferential dialectic," in D.L. Barker and S. Allen (eds.), *Dependence and Exploration in Work and Marriage*, Longmans.

Bott, E. 1957. *Family and Social Network*, Tavistock.

Edgell, S. 1980. *Middle Class Couples: A Study of Segregation, Domination and Inequality in Marriage*, Allen and Unwin.

Ellis, R. 1983. "The way to a man's heart . . . ," in A. Murcott (ed.), *The Sociology of Food and Eating*, Gower.

Fox, B. (ed.). 1980. *Hidden in the Household*, Toronto: Women's Press.

Hughes, E.C. 1971. "The humble and the proud," in *The Sociological Eye: Selected Papers*, Aldine-Atherton.

Leonard, D. 1980. *Sex and Generation*, Tavistock.

Middleton, C. 1974. "Sexual inequality and stratification theory," in E. Parkin (ed.), *The Social Analysis of Class Structure*, Tavistock.

Murcott, A. 1982. "On the social significance of the 'cooked dinner' in South Wales," *Social Science Information*, 21(4/5), 677–695.

———. 1983a. "Women's place: Cookbook's image of technique and technology in the British Kitchen," *Women's Studies International Forum*, 6(1): 33–40.

———. (ed.) 1983b. *The Sociology of Food and Eating*, Gower.

———. 1983c. "Cooking and the cooked," in A. Murcott (ed.), *The Sociology of Food and Eating*, Gower.

———. 1983d. "Menus, meals and platefuls," *International Journal of Sociology and Social Policy* (forthcoming).

Murdock, G.P. and Provost, C. 1973. "Factors in the division of labour by sex: A cross-cultural analysis," *Ethnology*, XII(2), 203–225.

Oakley, A. 1974a. *Housewife*, Penguin.

———. 1974b. *The Sociology of Housework*, Martin Robertson.

———. 1980. *Women Confined: Towards a "Sociology of Childbirth,"* Martin Robertson.

Pahl, J. 1982. "The allocation of money and the structuring of inequality within marriage," *Board of Studies in Social Policy and Administration*, University of Kent, mimeo.

Rosser, C. and Harris, C. 1965. *The Family and Social Change*, Routledge and Kegan Paul.

Rotenberg, R. 1981. "The impact of industrialisation on meal patterns in Vienna, Austria," *Ecology of Food and Nutrition*, 11(1), 25–35.

Spradley, J.O. and Mann, B.J. 1975. *The Cocktail Waitress: Women's Work in a Man's World*, John Wiley.

Stephens, W.N. 1963. *The Family in Cross-Cultural Perspective*, Holt, Rinehart and Winston.

Tolson, A. 1977. *The Limits of Masculinity*, Tavistock.

Wajcman, J. 1981. "Work and the family: Who gets "the best of both worlds?"" in Cambridge Women's Studies Group, *Women in Society*, Virago.

West, J. 1980. "A political economy of the family in capitalism: Women, reproduction and wage labour," in T. Nichols (ed.), *Capital and Labour: A Marxist Primer,* Fontana.

Whyte, W.F. 1948. *Human Relations in the Restaurant Industry,* McGraw-Hill.

Young, M. and Willmott, P. 1975. *The Symmetrical Family,* Penguin.

Fatherhood and the Mediating Role of Women

Nicholas W. Townsend

In this chapter I confront an apparent paradox in men's accounts of fatherhood. Men say they want to be involved fathers but they do not seem to be acting that way.

Nearly all the men I talked to in my research said they wanted to be more involved as fathers than their own fathers had been, and this stated desire is very common for men in the United States. But men in the United States do not put much time into domestic work or child care (Coltrane, 1996), and after divorce many men in the United States pay very little or nothing in child support and frequently maintain no contact with their children (Furstenberg and Cherlin, 1991; Arendell, 1995). I argue that we can understand some of this paradox if we consider what men do as fathers as well as what they do not do, and if we listen to what they have to say about being fathers.

Parenting is deeply gendered. And by this I do not mean only that fathers and mothers do different things, though that is clearly the case, but also that being a parent means different things to mothers and fathers, and that being a father means different things to men and women. Parenting is also gendered in other ways, such as men's stated preference for sons and the ways they treat daughters and sons differently. I have discussed these aspects of fatherhood elsewhere (Townsend, n.d.). In this chapter, I am focusing on the gendered relationship between fathers and mothers. Seeing men and their accounts as gendered

Original material prepared for this text

in this way helps us to understand how men think about being fathers and about relationships in general.

In the first section below I describe how men see "marriage and children" as elements of a "package deal" which cannot be easily separated. Conceptually, a relationship with a woman is necessary for a man to see himself as a father or "family man." In the subsequent sections, I show how women are often the "driving force" behind men's decisions about when to have children; that a structural division of labor that places men in the labor force and women at home is maintained and supported by cultural work in the face of women's increasing labor force participation; and that parenting itself is gendered, with women being the "default parents" who maintain schedules and routines, while men are in a more "optional" position, with their participation as "fun dads" or "enforcers" mediated by their children's mothers.

It has been easy to see the gendered division of labor in parenting as a simple division in which men are engaged in the public sphere of paid work and politics and women are involved in the domestic sphere of child care and reproduction.[1] What my description shows, however, is that these two spheres interpenetrate, and that arrangements made in one sphere influence behavior in another. For instance, we shall see that cultural ideas about the division of paid labor and about who should provide for families have an impact on ideas about who should do what for children.

My discussion in this chapter is based on talking to men who graduated from the same high school in 1972 and were in their late thirties when I interviewed them.[2] Because they all graduated from the same high school, I was able to learn a lot about the community in California in which they grew up, the events of their youth, and the opportunities they faced as adults. I can speak with confidence about the attitudes these men shared, and about the differences between them, and I would argue that these men are in many ways typical of men in the United States, but these men's experiences and meanings cannot be used to support universal or essential ideas about "male" experience or fathering as a universal pattern of behavior.[3]

What emerged from my conversations is that, for the men I talked to, the father–child relationship could not be described or thought about independent of the relationship between husband and wife. When I ask men about their parents, they talk mostly about their fathers, but when I ask them about becoming fathers they talk about their wives. Some of the paradoxes of men's relations to their children may be resolved by understanding the relative positions of men, women, and children, and specifically the crucial linking or mediating role of women.

Appreciating the linking role of women is not the same as saying that men do not care about children, or that they think that children are entirely women's business. Certainly becoming a parent is more separated from biological reproduction for men than for women. One can scarcely imagine a woman saying, as one of my male informants did: "Actually I have had a child before, although through very strange circumstances I didn't know I had a child before he was a year old and someone sent me a Christmas card saying: 'This is your baby.'" Equally certainly, men consider childbearing and child rearing to be predominantly women's responsibility. This is not to say that men are indifferent to having children. They have strong feelings about the number, timing, and kind of children they want, but at crucial points in their lives they find that their paternity depends on the cooperation of women. The men are not passively dependent on women's motivations—they actively select and try to persuade, pressure, and coerce women, but the mediating link provided by women remains crucial.

It is not just that men need, and realize that they need, a woman's physical cooperation in order to become fathers. There is also an asymmetry in the ways that men and women think about becoming parents. For instance, many women are prepared to think about single parenthood as a possible, though usually less desirable, route to motherhood; the men I talked to, on the other hand, do not even register it as a possibility. Many single, childless women are able to think and talk directly about whether they want to have children. In doing so, and in reading the advice and examples they are offered in books and magazines, it is clear that they see having a child on one's own as an option. It is an option with definite emotional, social, and financial drawbacks as well as opportunities, and it is an option that they may well reject, but it remains a possibility. That having a child on her own is a possibility to be considered means that women are able to weigh and articulate their specific desire for children outside the matrix of family and relationship with a man. The relationship between mother and child, the activity of mothering, and the transformation of self into a mother, are things women can think about directly and in isolation. The men I talked to could not talk about having children without talking about "having a family" or "being a family man." For these men, "having children" is part of "being married and having a family." They can only conceptualize the relationship between father and children within the matrix of family relationships.

Of course, the relationships between men and their wives are very important in their own right, but my interest here is in the way that marital relationships are structurally important for men's relationships with their children. Women, as wives and mothers, mediate and facilitate fatherhood. The word "mediate" describes women's role in the relationship between men and children because it captures, in its various meanings, some of the complexity of that role. Women are in the middle of this relationship, they frequently do mediate in the most literal sense of operating as go-betweens or negotiators between their husbands and their children, and their presence and activity makes possible the reproduction, both biological and social, that is at the heart of fatherhood.

For men, having children is a reproduction of fatherhood—a patrilineal process of the movement of males through the statuses of son, father, and grandfather and of child, adult, and old man (Townsend, 1998). There are five moments, phases, or aspects of reproduction at which women's mediating role is most apparent: at marriage, when decisions are made about the timing and number of children, in the structural division of labor after children are born, in gendered parenting, and after divorce.

MARRIAGE AND CHILDREN: WIFE AND MOTHER

"We always knew we wanted to get married and have a family" was a frequent comment of men who married women they had known in high school. For my informants, marriage is almost always considered to be a relationship that will involve having children. In most first marriages, husbands say they either "knew" or "assumed" that their wives would want children. For the men, marriage meant getting a "wife and family" as a sort of package deal.

As is often the case, it is when obstacles to meeting a norm arise that its existence is made most clear. Several men told me that they did not marry women with whom they had "good relationships" because those women did not want or could not have children. Conversely, men who had actually wanted to have children told me that they had ended relationships with women they did not want to marry by telling them that they did not want to have children. That this was an excuse is made clear by the rapidity with which they subsequently met, married, and had children with other women. Regardless of whether the particular men or women in any relationship or marriage really wanted children or not, the point is that the cultural idea that marriage and children go together was so clear to all that it could be used as a reason to end a relationship without rejecting the other person by saying: "I don't want to marry you." Men are making a simultaneous decision about "a wife and a mother to my children."

Greg, an earnest man with two children who worked as a programmer in a software company, had married at age twenty-nine, a fact that was very significant to him and to which he returned repeatedly. To him, twenty-nine was old to be getting married, and he did not want to be too old to be a vigorous father to his children. He felt, however, that waiting until he was twenty-nine had not been a bad thing:

> I kind of got everything out of my system before I got married. And then, when I did get married I wanted it to be forever, as they say, and I was ready to have kids. When I got married I was ready to have kids. I probably had it planned in my mind. "We'll get married and we'll have children."

Although Greg linked marriage with having children, he said that he and his wife had not talked explicitly before their marriage about having children, but that it was "Just something you kind of know."

> I had seen a lot of women over a period of years. You see all kinds of women out there. I mean, there are some smart ones, but most of them are—they don't know if they're coming or going, you know. Maggie's very intelligent, which I like, very kind, and very funny. That's very important to me, a sense of humor. It is kind of hard to explain exactly why you know that that's the person, but she had all the factors that I was looking for. I remember telling myself: "I can live with this girl for the rest of my life. I mean I can actually do it through the day to day." I just had the inner feeling that I could be comfortable with her for basically the rest of my life.

Greg's choice of a wife was, however, not based simply on personal compatibility: "If

I knew that she did not want to have children," he added, "I would not have married her."

Gordon, an engineer with three sons, had married his wife two years after they met, and two years later, while he was still in college, his first son was born. Gordon told me early on that: "before we got married we had a goal of three and when we finally got three, I just said: 'I don't have enough for any more.'" Later, when I asked him if he had always wanted children, he replied, after a pause: "I never felt that I would not have children. But, you know, up until I found the person I wanted to marry and live with, I never thought 'I really want kids.' I don't think I consciously said that." And when I asked him if children are needed to complete a family he immediately responded: "That's not the reason we had children, but I believe that's a true statement. Not to say that a couple is incomplete, but I think you're *more married* if you have children." His predisposition to have children, and his liking for children (he taught Sunday School before he was married) had not gelled into a firm plan to have children of his own until he met the person he wanted to marry. Marriage and children were inextricably linked in his thinking, as they were in another man's comment that "Getting married and not having kids at all, seems kind of incomplete. I can see you being a single person and not having kids. I can understand that more now. If you're married it would be odd not having children."

A deliberately childless marriage is definitely a thing to be negotiated beforehand. At least normatively, inability to bear children is not grounds for divorce, but one partner's unwillingness to have them might cause the other partner to hesitate or to refuse to enter into marriage in the first place. Several men said that in order to marry a woman who did not want children "you would have to love her a lot." There is an implication here that a marriage without children requires a stronger love than a marriage with children. But I think it is closer to these men's meanings that children provide structure and cohesion to a marriage, and that romantic love alone, without the cement of shared parenting and the

economic partnership of working to support home and family, is a slender thread on which to hang a lifetime together.

During the 1970s and early 1980s, when the men I interviewed were aged between eighteen and thirty, the divorce rate for childless couples was higher than for couples who had children (Wienberg, 1988). Divorces of childless couples also proceeded more rapidly than the divorces of couples with children (White, et al., 1986). Conversely, the birth of a first child within marriage drastically reduced the divorce rate for the next year (Waite, et al., 1985). Although subsequent births did not have this effect, the presence of children in a marriage did appear to slow the process of divorce (White, et al., 1986).[4] Of the men I talked to, those who had been through divorces in which children had been involved reported more protracted divorces, with separations and reconciliations, whereas the divorces that did not involve children were more rapid and clear-cut. The direction of causation in these relationships between fertility and divorce is not always clear. It may be that having children makes a marriage less likely to end in divorce, but it may also be that couples who think their marriage is in trouble are less likely to embark on childbearing.

The men I talked to recognized that having a child may both strengthen and undermine the relationship between husband and wife. On the one hand, they appreciated the problems of fatigue, busy schedules, and restrictions on shared leisure that children create for marriages. On the other hand, they stressed the responsibility they felt toward maintaining an intact family and also mentioned the new connections with their wives that came from enjoying their children and from sharing activities with them. Having children certainly made divorce harder to think about. They would, they said, stay married through hard times and routine times.

The comments I heard are consistent with the statistical picture that fertility within marriage reduces the incidence and slows the process of divorce. They also indicate that childlessness within marriage is not a common goal, and would demand of a marriage something qualitatively different than is expected in a reproductive union. Several men described a couple they knew who were married soon after high school graduation but deliberately had no children. After their divorce, both partners remarried and had children. The interpretation put on this by their friends is that the marriage without children could not sustain itself, but that subsequent marriages to people with whom they were ready to have children were likely to be satisfying and successful. Childlessness, in this account, is presented as both a consequence of doubts about the marriage and a cause of its failure.

The men I spoke to depend on a marital relationship with a woman for a paternal relationship with children. In the contemporary United States, the availability of effective contraception and a relaxation of the standard of sexual chastity for brides means that a man's girlfriend, his premarital sexual partner, the woman he lives with, and his wife may all be the same person, but are not necessarily so—the roles and the individuals filling them are uncoupled. A wife, however, is unique in the formalization of her social position and in the way that she links a man to other social persons by virtue of that social position and not merely by virtue of her personal qualities and associations.

Barry, balding and hospitable, lived in a new house in a new subdivision. As we sat on his deck, watching his young children from his second marriage play in the wading pool, he told me a story that encapsulated the connection between marriage and children:

> It's funny, I knew this one girl that I worked with. She was living with her boyfriend. She never took any birth control. For probably years, she never did. Never got pregnant. But they finally got married, and like their wedding night, she got pregnant. It was kind of a psychological thing, you know? Like: "Geez, I can't get pregnant, I'm not married. Well, now I'm married, it's OK."

In both his own marriages, Barry had drawn the same distinction between living together (and therefore not having children) and being married (and having or planning children).

> The first time, you just get married because it was the thing to do, so to speak. The second time you're a little bit wiser and more cautious. The first time I was twenty-one and my wife had just turned nineteen. We were married for a couple of years. And what's interesting is that she was raised in a very strict Catholic background so living together was kind of taboo. So we never lived together. We basically got married and we found out that what she wanted and what I wanted were really different. We talked about children. Nothing real serious, but like: "Down the road here, we should have children." So it's a good thing that we didn't. We were using birth control. It wasn't to the point where we decided "Let's try" and we weren't successful. We weren't ready at that time.

The second time he got married, Barry proceeded very differently. Even his sentence structure and word choice when telling me about it expressed his greater deliberation:

> We both had our own separate homes and lifestyles when we first met and we spent a lot of time together. We decided we had a pretty lasting relationship going and that we should live together and consolidate. That way we could really tell, by living together, whether or not we could live together forever. Because you just don't know people until you actually live with them. So we lived together for a while. And then we decided to get married and have children. In fact, that was kind of interesting. My wife—one of her comments that kind of surprised me was: "Geez, we don't need to get married to have children." And that really kind of took me by surprise because I've kind of had different morals than that. If you're going to have children, at least plan children, then you need to be married. Obviously there are times when things are not planned and you're not married. But the way I believe, if you're going to plan to have children, you should be married. She was very insistent that that didn't need to be the case. . . . She likes children, and I like children, so it was kind of a—We discussed it and decided "Let's get married and we'll have children" instead of just having children and not getting married.

Barry attributed his surprise at his wife's suggestion that they did not need to get married to have children to "different morals," but when his comments are taken as a whole, we can see that his association of children and marriage is not so much moral as conceptual. His picture of family life, his conceptual framework for social relationships, was one that included the possibility of living together and that separated sexual relations from procreation, but equated having children with being married. In this, and in the difference between him and his wife, Barry was typical. In order to be a father, he had to be married. His fatherhood, therefore, conceptually depends on his having a marital relationship with a woman. Once married, the timing of his children's births would depend on his wife's willingness and initiative.

"THE DRIVING FORCE": WOMEN, TIMING, AND BIRTH CONTROL

In general, the men I talked to assumed that, in their own lives, conception and birth were events that could be controlled. They assumed that sexual intercourse without pregnancy was a reasonable expectation, so that premarital sex, a space of time between marriage and their first birth, a controlled space between their children's births, and a cessation of childbearing were all things to be reasonably expected and planned for. Their confidence in their ability to plan was, to a certain extent, justified by the technological innovations of the birth control pill, the IUD, and safe and easy techniques for male and female sterilization.

Previous fertility declines and control, at the level of populations and of couples, have depended on a mix of methods, including heavy reliance on abstinence and withdrawal (Schneider and Schneider, 1996). These are methods that involve at least the participation, if not the active initiation, of men. The Pill and the IUD, by contrast, are methods that are used by women and that do not require contraceptive action by men or women at the time of intercourse. They are, particularly for men, much less psychically costly than withdrawal or abstinence. For men in the United States, these methods

have had the double effect of enabling a conceptual and physical separation between sexual activity and reproduction and of moving control over reproduction to women. Control over reproduction was seen as not only technically, but also morally, women's responsibility.

Barry, for example, does not say the decision about when to have children was his wife's alone, but he does put the primary responsibility on her.

> She was probably the driving force. Again, I wanted children too. So it wasn't like: "OK, I'll just give in. If you want children, we'll have children." But she was probably more the driver of that issue than myself. I could have been content to wait a couple years. But again, we both wanted children. It wasn't just because she wanted children. If she would have been very insistent against it, it would have been something we probably would have had to talk about. It's really hard to say, but I think I wanted to have children also, but not to the same degree as she did. It would have been nice to have them, but if I didn't, I could have lived without them. It wouldn't have been a decision I may have regretted.

Notice that while she is the "driving force" behind the timing, he also makes it clear that he too wanted children. But he then questions his own desire when he says "I think I wanted to have children" and "I could have lived without them." In the face of this uncertainty, he placed the initiative with his wife.

The norm expressed by all the men I talked to is that there should be a period at the beginning of married life when the couple have "time for themselves as a couple." This norm may be violated by early conception, or by a period of living together followed by marriage and rapid subsequent conception.

Marvin, a large, easygoing man, who worked in purchasing, told me that he and his wife had children sooner than he would have liked. His plan had been to graduate from college and buy a house before having children. His wife had taken the initiative and had persuaded him that they should have children while he was still in college.

> I wasn't all that hot about the idea. I was not sure I could handle all the responsibilities. I probably thought, in fact I did think, about how they develop and how you grow along with them. It's "Oh gosh, what am I gonna do when they're teenagers?" that sort of thing. So I wasn't all that hot about having kids. My wife convinced me that yeah, it's probably not all that tough. I should say now I know how tough it is. It's very hard. It's a never-ending challenge. But we finally agreed that we'd go ahead and have kids. And so we did. I wanted to make sure I had a house, which we didn't at the time. And go ahead and have college for me, which I didn't. So that was a kind of unsettling thing, to go from following this nice neat path to success. And here's the time to have kids. Here's the time to do this, to do that. I couldn't do that. So that kind of bothered me.

In the event, Marvin had not finished college, but he told me that had not been a real obstacle in his career, and he and his wife had bought a house with help from his wife's parents.

Men discuss their decisions about timing in terms of their "readiness" to become fathers.[5] Readiness is presented as a psychological state that does not necessarily coincide with the birth of the first child. Men may realize that they are "ready" when their first child is born, but they may also feel "not ready," causing personal anxiety and strain on their marriage. Several men told me that they only became ready to be fathers some time after the birth of their first child, usually at a point when they felt they could relate to their children.[6] On the other hand, other men have reported "being ready" before their wives were, and then embarking on campaigns to persuade them to become pregnant. For these men, it was not women's enthusiasm that drove the decision, but their reluctance or hesitation that put women in a position to control the realization of men's plans for fatherhood.

The men I talked to discussed the timing of births as if they were under perfect control, and difficulties getting pregnant, as well as unplanned pregnancies, were seen as surprising. From my perspective as an observer who knows something about the variability of human biology, this sense of being in perfect control was itself surprising. But being in control is a central organizing element of my informants' stories in all areas. Being out of control is an explanation for the bad things that happen, and a good deal of rhetorical effort is expended to create a life story characterized by control and the realization of intentions.[7] Men are actively involved in decisions about timing, but contraception during the childbearing years is overwhelmingly by female methods and men are dependent on the cooperation of their wives. But their dependence is not inevitable or driven simply by the use of female contraceptive methods. These men are actually *relinquishing* control and presenting the situation as if their wives were the only ones responsible.

Alfred, for instance, had wanted only one child, but he delayed his vasectomy after the birth of his first child. He reported that his wife then "surprised" him with a set of twins, but he delayed his vasectomy again. He only got around to sterilization after she "surprised" him with a second set. He is an exceptional example only because of the extreme personal and demographic consequences of his dependence on imperfect methods and his reluctance to assume responsibility for birth control. Alfred's position, however, underlines the centrality of effective birth control for the realization of these men's fertility plans and life plans in general. With five children under the age of six, he found himself living in too small a house, with bills higher than he had expected, and with no financial leeway. He worked as a skilled technician, but his skills were being made obsolete by technological change, and he was not in a position to make the expenditure, or take the cut in pay, necessary to acquire new skills or to move into a job with prospects of promotion. His high fertility, in fact, had effects on his work, his place of residence, and the division of labor in his marriage, and will continue to have effects in the future.

MEN AT WORK, WOMEN AT HOME: THE STRUCTURAL DIVISION OF LABOR

The archetypical picture of family life in the United States has been of a nuclear household, composed of a married heterosexual couple and their children, in which the man is the breadwinner and the woman is the homemaker. This has not, of course, been an accurate picture of the family lives of many people, but it has been a cultural archetype, or hegemonic image, that shapes people's perceptions even when it does not represent their reality.[8] Even when they become very common, however, behaviors that do not conform to hegemonic cultural norms continue to be perceived as "exceptions." When people's lives diverge from cultural norms they have to do cultural work to deny, explain, or reinterpret, this divergence. Some husbands of employed women who wanted to emphasize that they were the primary providers for their families explained that their wives' incomes were used for "extras" or "luxuries." Others described their wives' work as something they did mainly for variety, social contacts, or to "get away from the kids." But in either case they were doing cultural work to interpret their arrangements as conforming to a hegemonic picture of the structural division of labor in marriage. In support of this division of labor, the men I talked to made three interlocking arguments: that they liked or chose the arrangement, that it was best for the children, and that it was natural.

Gordon, the engineer with three sons who felt "more married" once he had children, expressed very clearly the structural division of labor between parents: one parent should stay home to raise the children, and it should be the mother.

> I think it's wrong to have kids and then lock them in daycare centers while you're working. That's why I'm really grateful that my wife can stay home. And although at times we were real tight for money, and I told her she might have to start looking for a job if we were going to make ends

meet, I was grateful when things worked out and she didn't have to. Because this is really the place the kids need a full-time mother, to watch them.

This arrangement works, Gordon says, because "She's not the working type." This gendered division of labor between husband and wife is a reproduction of his parents' pattern. His father had been a skilled machinist, his mother, with a college degree, had stayed home and not worked outside the home until her children were in high school. Gordon explains the arrangement he has with his wife as the result of their "choice" and in accord with his wife's personality. Although Gordon described both the division of labor and the fact that he followed his father into working on machines as "natural," this couple is an instance of a social fact: in the overwhelming number of cases where one of a couple works full time, it is the husband.

Like Gordon, Marvin attributes the division of labor in his marriage to his wife's preference. She has worked off and on, he says, selling products from the home and working as a teacher's aide for the local school district, which "gives her a lot of flexibility." When I asked him if she had ever wanted to work full-time, he said:

> She seems to have wanted more to be a good mother. And she was the type of person that when we got married, she had this view of herself as not "Super Mom," but "Nice Mom" that does the things that Moms do and takes the kids and gets involved in things. And that was a really big thing to her.

Marvin is articulating what Garey (1999) points to as a dominant cultural image of mothers as oriented either to work or to family. Garey argues that many employed mothers downplay their aspirations to "career" or to being "Super Mom" and practice "maternal visibility" by making a point of being seen as doing "the things that Moms do."

Paul went a step beyond Gordon and Marvin in his defense of a structural gendered division of labor, turning it into a timeless and natural pattern. Paul is a serious, almost intense man who talks quietly but displays a fierce protectiveness of his family. He works a night shift with lots of overtime and shift differential pay. He and his wife, who was employed full time, lived with their two sons, ages six and eight, in a townhouse near his work. The children were cared for by his wife's mother during the day, but she was about to move away and Paul's plan was for his wife to reduce her hours of employment and work part time.

> I was thinking about trying to buy a [single family] house over here, but if it's going to cause me to be away from the family, or cause [my wife] to have to work all the time, I think we're gonna back out. If I can't afford a house on my pay alone, and make it, if we can't do it on my paycheck alone, we're not gonna do it. Because that's just basic. It's just the way it's been since time began. Women stay home. I'm not trying to be chauvinist by any—but if you're gonna have a family, that's the way it works best.

The gendered division of labor, then, puts women in the home as the mothers of men's children, and this division of labor is reinforced by cultural work that emphasizes men's responsibility as providers and women's involvement in their children's lives. Such a division of labor is presented as natural and equal, but it is a product of a particular economic structure and social organization of work, and it works to the advantage of men in giving them more control over their leisure time (though less over the large amount of their lives they spend at work). The gendered division of labor at the structural level also has profound implications for the daily activity of parenting.

DISCIPLINE, CARING, AND PROVIDING: GENDERED PARENTING

In parenting and child rearing men once again place women between themselves and their children. Their interactions with their children are controlled, arranged, or supervised by their wives. Women have most of the responsibility for arranging and enforcing children's activities, with men exerting their influence through their wives. Some men do put a lot of energy into their children's activities, especially into their athletic activities, and even more express the desire to do so, especially to do more with their children than their fathers did with them. But studies of time use continue to find differences between working husbands and wives in the total number of hours worked when paid labor, childcare, and housework are combined.[9]

Not only is there a difference in the number of hours men and women spend in child rearing, but fathers and mothers approach parenting very differently. The men I talked to express the belief that mothers are the "default parent." They act on this belief and by their actions make it true. Being the default parent means being on terms of greater intimacy, being the one to whom a child turns first, and being the one with the responsibility for knowing what the child's needs and schedules are. The default parent, ultimately, is the one who has to be there, to whom parenting is in no sense optional (Walzer, 1998). For example, fathers may go to meetings at their children's schools or take their children to sports practice, but it is usually mothers who keep track of when the meetings and practices are, and who are, therefore, the default parents. Lareau (2000a, 2000b) reports that fathers are very vague and general in their accounts of their children's daily routine, in contrast to the detailed and specific responses of mothers. In general, my informants indicated that it was their wives who kept the mental and physical calendar, and I would simply add that the person who keeps track of scheduling has a good deal of control over what is scheduled.

Even in the area of discipline and punishment, where it would seem that the father's position as ultimate authority was secure, mothers are the gatekeepers or mediators. Consider the proverbial threat of mothers to their children: "Just you wait until your father gets home!" This expression was used as an example by a number of men to express that they were deeply involved in their children's lives. It was meant to indicate that they were the source of discipline even if they were not in a position of direct supervision most of the time. On closer examination, however, the expression indicates a very different relationship, for it is the mother who decides when and what the father is told, and thus when he can act. Rather than being in an immediate disciplinary relationship with his children, he is a resource to be mobilized by his wife in her dealings with the children, and thus in a relationship mediated by his wife.

The disciplinary dynamic in families can take several forms, but two are common. While they may seem very different, in both of them the wife and mother is ultimately responsible for discipline. In the first, the husband is an authority figure and disciplinarian who sees himself as supporting or backing up his wife. In the second, the husband is allowed to be fun because his wife is the disciplinarian.

Both Ralph and Terry used the word "enforcer" to describe their role in their children's discipline. Neither of them liked this, though both accepted it as their responsibility to support their wives. Ralph had two children and was one of the most impressive men I met doing this research. He had had a troubled adolescence, but since then he had worked his way to a highly responsible job in public service and was universally admired by his former classmates. Ralph told me that there had been one disciplinarian in his family when he was growing up, and that it was the same in his marriage:

> One parent seems like the disciplinarian and the other one is not. And in my family I am. And my wife doesn't understand: "Why won't the children listen to me?" Because it's always: "I'm gonna tell your father." She had to call me here [at work]. I've had to talk to them on the phone. And they straighten right up.

Ralph felt that his wife should be more consistent in her discipline so that the children would not ignore her threats and make her lose her temper. She, on the other hand, sometimes felt overwhelmed and told him

that if she were to hit the children instead of threatening: "I'd beat them to death. I'd be constantly hitting them."

Terry, the father of two boys, is also critical of his wife's treatment of the children, but he too accepts his role as enforcer.

> The thing is, you've gotta be the enforcer. The man has to be the enforcer and that's the only thing that sometimes irritates me. I come home from working a hard day and my wife right off "Terry, he's done this, he's done that." And I get mad and I go in there and yell at him. That's where a lot of times I would like to say "You're the mother. Handle it. If you want to restrict him, restrict him. If you want him to be whupped, do it." She's home every day. She knows exactly what's going on. I think she ought to handle it more herself.

For both Ralph and Terry, the structural division of labor, their position at work, and their wives' presence at home, means that their wives are the ones who determine what is expected of their children and who know what they are doing. The women then decide what to tell their husbands and so determine the kinds of interactions fathers and children will have. Terry yells at his children and Ralph spanks his, but their wives, as the default parents, mediate the flow of information and expectation between fathers and children. Women's mediation should not, however, be seen as deliberately manipulative. The gendered division of discipline is not an individual choice or decision, but part of a whole gendered system of division of labor.

Gordon's situation is a rather different manifestation of the same gendered system. In Gordon's family, he is the one who can relax and have fun with his sons because his wife is protective and strict. When it comes to parenting, he says:

> My wife does a better job. Although she is very protective of the kids. Like my eleven-year-old, she won't drop off at baseball practice. She'll stay and wait until it's over. And even though sitting in a car, she's always there. She won't leave the kids anywhere alone. . . . I think she's just worried about something happening to them.

Not having an accident, like falling off of something, but with all the crazies out there, she's just worried about losing one of them. Which is—I mean, it's a real-life concern. I can't blame her for that, but it gets a little excessive sometimes. And she does discipline them better, they mind her better, she's more sensitive to their feeling and that kind of thing. It's the insensitive dad, sometimes. . . . I don't treat my kids the way [my father] treated us. He was a very heavy disciplinarian and we were afraid of him when we grew up. I don't want my kids to be afraid of me.

Partly because he does not want his children to fear him as he feared his father, and partly because his wife is watching over them, protecting them, and disciplining them, he feels he can let them run a little wild: "When they're just goofing off and it's Friday night, I'm not going to crack the whip and put them to bed." He laughs, "It wouldn't work anyway."

Edward's position as a "fun dad" to his three children is also mediated by his wife, who ran a child care business in her home when the youngest was a toddler and now teaches at the private school the children attend. She is very involved in the lives of children in general and her own children in particular, and part of her involvement is in scheduling her husband's time with his children. Edward says that: "When there are three there, it's tough. They're all vying for your attention." So his wife intervened and he now says to his children: "'Your Mom says it's your turn.' So each time I do something I take a different child with me. And it works out two ways. It's a lot cheaper for one. And also I get that one-on-one with my kids." Many of the things he does with his children are recreational activities that he enjoys, such as baseball and basketball games. While his wife is orchestrating this activity, Edward gets to be the fun father, spending quality time with his children doing something they can enjoy together. Edward also gets to be spontaneous with the whole family. Several times he told me that he would, "on the spur of the moment," sweep the family up and drive to the beach:

Like I get them going at seven in the morning up to Santa Cruz and I'll bring my camping stuff and we'll cook breakfast and we'll just have breakfast and when other people are coming, we're leaving and coming back home. We do stuff off the wall like that. Spur-of-the-moment type things. On Friday afternoon I'll tell everyone to pack their suitcase and we'll go to Monterey for a night and things like that. I think that's pretty neat.

Overall, Edward emphasized the fun and spontaneity of his relations with his children: "Age wise, I'm probably considered an adult, but you talk to my kids and I'm probably the biggest kid around. I'm not kidding. I'm a big kid at heart. I love sports. I love my kids." It is important to notice that Edward's ability to be spontaneous and to have fun with his children, just like his one-on-one time with his children, is dependent on the routine, day-by-day, planned, and conscientious work of his wife.

The gendered division of labor in parenting not only distributes work and fun differentially between fathers and mothers, it also distributes who gets taken for granted, and who gets the credit for what they do. Hochschild shows how couples negotiate not only a material division of labor, but also an economy of gratitude (1989): people do not just want to be appreciated, they want to be appreciated for the contributions they think are important. Psychologists Carolyn and Philip Cowan (1999) observed that, for men, paid employment "counts" as childcare—when men work they are seen as doing something for their children. In addition, wives see their husbands' attention to their children as contributions to the marriage relationship. Women's employment, on the other hand, is seen as detracting from their mothering, and their husbands do not see the care mothers give their children as couple time or as building the marriage. For the men I talked to, their fathers' employment was remembered and appreciated, while their mothers' employment was minimized or forgotten. In addition, their mothers' parenting was taken for granted, while their fathers' more occasional attention was treasured.

Even though he said his father did not spend much time with him—"Dad was working. I remember when my father worked three jobs"—Edward appreciated the hard work his father had done to build a financially stable foundation for his family: "My Dad's helped me out financially, he's helped every single one of his kids out. Financially and every other way." Edward also remembered "the few vacations we had" with his father. His fond memories of those rare occasions was one motivation for his own spontaneous family trips. But his memories of his mother are less precise and more matter-of-fact. I asked him if his mother had worked:

> I know she worked off and on because she worked at [an electronics company] for the longest time. Yeah, she did work. I'm just trying to remember. There was a time when I know she didn't because I know when I was in elementary school I remember coming home at lunchtime and she would have lunch for me. So maybe when the kids were smaller she didn't work. And then she started working. I remember her working at [the electronics company] a long time. Then went to [a computer manufacturer] and retired from there.

In fact, his mother had also worked full-time before the family moved to Orchardtown when Edward was six, but the point to notice is not so much whether she worked or not as that her son did not see her work as part of her identity, and certainly not as part of her parenting, which was represented by that daily routine of having lunch ready. On the other hand, for her husband work was central to his being a father. The financial help Edward received from his parents (both of whom were working full time when he was a young man) is reported as coming from his father, and the family activities he points to are a handful of family vacations with his father.

Mothers who are supervising and caring for their children may well know more about those children, about their hopes and insecurities, than fathers who are there to have occasional fun. They are then in a position to relay or to hold back knowledge about their children, and mothers are the ones who both fathers and children talk to about the other. Edward told me a typical story of an incident

between him and his daughter about which both of them had, independently, talked to his wife. Their communication about the event, and its resolution in Edward's mind, was very directly mediated by the mother.

> I just talked to my wife the other night. My oldest daughter, somehow I felt like she wasn't communicating with me lately, the last couple weeks. I was asking my wife if there was anything wrong. What particular things had happened at school. I went to pick up my son and she was gonna go somewhere else and I saw her and I know she saw me, but she didn't acknowledge me being there. So I was kind of hurt because usually they'll come up "Hi Dad!" And my wife goes "It had nothing to do with her not wanting—" What it was, I guess, her friends were wearing makeup and she knows I'm against girls at this age wearing makeup and I guess that was why she didn't come and talk to me. So that's fine. I can see why she didn't want to talk to me.

These examples illustrate that the structural division of labor, in which men are seen as providers and women as homemakers, is connected to a gendered division of parenting. Mothers not only do more child care and domestic work, they also know more about what their children are doing and feeling, they talk to them more, and they control the flow of information between fathers and children. They also schedule their children's lives and the interactions they have with their fathers. As part of this gendered system, the relationship that mothers have with their children even influences the quality of the interactions men have with their children. Mothers may invoke their husbands as disciplinarians and enforcers, so that the fathers are stricter or sterner than they might otherwise be. Or mothers may maintain the structure of family life, giving men the space to be spontaneous and fun.

Within this gendered system of parenting, men and women act out and reinforce gender stereotypes. Men are expected to play more actively with children than women do, and as a general rule they do so. Mothers, so I was told, control male exuberance, calming people down and discouraging dangerous or over-exuberant play. It is mothers, I am told, who set limits on the activity of men and children. By doing so, they constrain themselves or, rather, are constrained by an entire system of expectations from being "fun" in quite the same way that men are. Men's playfulness and men's anger, their distance and their sense of inadequacy, are reproduced in the daily interactions of family life. A crucial element of these interactions is the mediating position of women, as wives and mothers.

CONCLUSION

The question arises of whether women jealously guard their control over the family or whether men relegate women to the less prestigious area of domestic work and childcare. At the level of family life and the lives of individual men and women, clearly both are going on (Coltrane, 1989; Cowan and Cowan, 1999; Hertz, 1986: 64–65; Walzer, 1998: 45 ff). The gendered division of labor in parenting is part of an "arrangement between the sexes" (Goffman, 1977)—a constructed and continually reinforced division of being between men and women. Men certainly develop a learned or deliberate incompetence in certain areas. It is a joke among both men and women that after a man has once done the laundry with mixed whites and coloreds and turned everything pink, or fixed a meal and turned the kitchen into a disaster area, or looked after the children for a weekend during which they ate nothing but pizza and never bathed, it is easier for women to do these things themselves. But men also develop different ways of doing things—playing more aggressively, teasing, and challenging children to take risks or break out of routines. Both men and women live out and perform stereotypes, frequently performing them while acknowledging that, in some sense at least, they should not do so. So a woman who says: "I know I should learn how to check the oil in the car, but I let my husband do it," or a man who, like me, sheepishly excuses himself from making social arrangements because "My

wife keeps track of the calendar," is perpetuating a particular gendered division of labor at the same time that his words are explicitly criticizing it.

This process of negotiating gender, which is often referred to as "doing gender" (West and Zimmerman, 1987) to describe gender as an activity rather than an intrinsic quality that people have, is complex and often internally contradictory. In this chapter I have shown how the cultural norm of men's public labor force participation and their role in the domestic sphere as family providers is maintained by cultural work done by men (and women) to emphasize the importance of fathers' earnings although mothers are also playing vital roles in the work force and public sphere. I have also shown that, within the domestic area, there is a gendered division of parenting, and of the meaning of being a parent, that continues to be very important even when both parents are involved in the day-to-day activities of their children. Fathering, like all human activity, is both a pattern of behavior and a set of meanings. Behavior and meaning sometimes reinforce each other, sometimes contradict each other, and sometimes work together to cover over contradictions or to make sense of changing circumstances.

In family life in the United States, as men, women, and children move back and forth between the public areas of employment and school and the domestic areas of home life and care giving, cultural ideas of what is gender-appropriate function to make sense of change and to provide meaningful continuity and coherence.

NOTES

1. A large amount of human activity is carried on in an area that is neither strictly domestic nor public. Areas of life such as friendship, visiting, kinship, and socializing cut across the public/domestic divide. In a study of community in nineteenth-century New England, Hansen (1994) proposes the term "social" for this third sphere of action.

2. The interviews involved an interaction between my personal situation, the perceptions of the men I talked to, and my conclusions (Townsend, 1999). I refer to all the men by pseudonyms. The quotations are taken from the transcripts of tape-recorded interviews. I have not changed or added to what men said, but because I do not want to distract attention from the content of what they told me, I have not presented all the "ers," "ums," and "you knows" with which real speech is studded. In the quotations, a dash (–) indicates an incomplete sentence or change of topic, ellipsis (. . .) indicates that I have omitted words or sentences from a quotation.

3. I do not mean to imply that all men, or all women, think and feel alike. Certainly, fatherhood means something different to men in the contemporary United States than it does to men in India, in the Congo basin, or in New Guinea. Fatherhood also has different meanings to men in the United States now than it did to men in the nineteenth century or in the colonial period. Fatherhood also means different things to different groups of men in the contemporary United States. Fathers in the upper classes, for instance, have concerns about inheritance and family status that are very different from those of fathers in the middle class who are worried about their children's college education and the dangers of downward mobility, or from working class fathers whose positions in families are being transformed by declining real wages and an increasing family dependence on two incomes.

4. The birth of children before marriage is associated with a marital disruption rate 57 to 80 percent higher than for couples without premarital births for cohorts of white women married between 1970 and 1985 (Martin and Bumpass, 1989: 42). This association may be because of greater strains on the early marriage, because couples who have a child before marriage have less normative commitment to marriage, or because some of the births were the biological children of men other than the husband and so do not have an "own children" effect on his behavior. My assertion of the connectedness of marriage and children, however, by the lack of association between premarital conception and marital disruption (Billy, et al., 1986).

5. Leone's (1986) discussion of the key values invoked by middle class white women in the United States to describe and explain their childbearing decisions reveals the importance of "readiness" for women as well as for men.

6. Ehrensaft (1990: 119–122) interviewed couples who had decided to share the work of parenting their children. She describes the men's reactions of "falling in love with" their children. For women, "the gap between the anticipation and the reality [of children] was smaller" and the major surprise was the absorbing day-to-day reality of parenthood. For men, the anticipation was more anxious and the realization of parenthood marked a greater break. In the terms of my discussion, the paternal relationship, the paternal sentiment, and the sense of being a father is something that is brought about, that happens, and that is not taken for granted or inevitably linked to the biological events of conception or birth. (In an absolute sense, the same is true of women. "Maternal bonding" is a cultural event also, but it is an unquestioned event of our culture in a way that "paternal bonding" is not.)

7. Langer (1983) has analyzed the psychology of "perceived control" and its importance for both a sense of well-being and the actual outcome of events.

8. The "father breadwinner, mother homemaker" family has been both historically recent and short-lived as a dominant pattern. From 1850 until the Second World War, the decline of farm families was matched by an increase in the percentage of children in "father breadwinner, mother homemaker, nonfarm families" which reached almost 60 percent by 1930 and then fluctuated around that level until 1960, when it began a rapid drop to 27 percent by 1989. From 1950 onward, the declines in farm and father breadwinner families has been matched by a rise in the percentage of children in dual-earner and one-parent families, which was approaching 70 percent by 1990. Since 1970, less than half of the children in the United States have been in families of the father breadwinner, mother homemaker type (Hernandez, 1993: 103).

9. Hochschild (1989: 3–4 and 271–273) summarized studies that concluded that there was a difference of ten to twenty hours of total work between working husbands and wives. Other studies have found that men and women spend approximately equal amounts of time on the combination of housework and paid work (Ferree, 1991; Pleck, 1985; Schor, 1991), but certain domestic tasks continue to be overwhelmingly women's work (Coltrane, 1996; Shelton, 1992), and men's contribution to housework still tends to be thought of, by both

husbands and wives, as helping (Coltrane, 1989; Walzer, 1998). When married couples have children, the division of domestic labor tends to become more traditionally gendered (Cowan and Cowan, 1999) and women spend less time in the paid labor force while men spend more (Shelton, 1992).

REFERENCES

Arendell, Terry. 1995. *Men and Divorce*. Thousand Oaks, CA: Sage.

Billy, John H.G., Nancy S. Landale, and Steven D. McLaughlin. 1986. "The Effect of Marital Status at First Birth on Marital Dissolution Among Adolescent Mothers." *Demography* 23:329–49.

Coltrane, Scott. 1989. "Household Labor and the Routine Production of Gender." *Social Problems* 36:473–90.

———. 1996. *Family Man: Fatherhood, Housework, and Gender Equity*. New York: Oxford University Press.

Cowan, Carolyn Pape and Philip A. Cowan. 1999. *When Partners Become Parents: The Big Life Change for Couples*. Mahwah, NJ: Lawrence Erlbaum.

Ehrensaft, Diane. 1990. *Parenting Together: Men and Women Sharing the Care of Their Children*. Urbana: University of Illinois Press.

Ferree, Myra Marx. 1991. "The Gender Division of Labor in Two-Earner Marriages: Dimensions of Variability and Change." *Journal of Family Issues* 12:158–80.

Furstenberg, Frank F. and Andrew Cherlin. 1991. *Divided Families: What Happens to Children When Parents Part*. Cambridge: Harvard University Press.

Garey, Anita Ilta. 1999. *Weaving Work and Motherhood*. Philadelphia: Temple University Press.

Goffman, Erving. 1977. "The Arrangement Between the Sexes." *Theory and Society* 4:301–36.

Hansen, Karen V. 1994. *A Very Social Time: Crafting Community in Antebellum New England*. Berkeley: University of California Press.

Hernandez, Donald J. 1993. *America's Children: Resources from Family, Government, and the Economy*. New York: Russell Sage Foundation.

Hertz, Rosanna. 1986. *More Equal Than Others: Women and Men in Dual-Career Marriages*. Berkeley: University of California Press.

Hochschild, Arlie. 1989. *The Second Shift: Working Parents and the Revolution at Home*. New York: Viking.

Langer, Ellen J. 1983. *The Psychology of Control*. Beverly Hills: Sage.

Lareau, Annette. 2000a. "Vague Answers: Reflections on Studying Fathers' Contributions to Children's Care." Paper presented at "Work and Family, Expanding the Horizons," University of California, Berkeley.

———. 2000b. "Social Class and the Daily Lives of Children: A Study from the United States," *Childhood* 7 (2): 155–171.

Leone, Catherine L. 1986. "Fairness, Freedom, and Responsibility: The Dilemma of Fertility Choice in America," Unpublished Ph.D. dissertation in Anthropology, Washington State University.

Martin, Teresa Castro and Larry L. Bumpass. 1989. "Recent Trends in Marital Disruption." *Demography* 26:37–51.

Pleck, Joseph. 1985. *Working Wives/Working Husbands*. Beverly Hills, CA: Sage.

Schneider, Jane C. and Peter Schneider. 1996. *Festival of the Poor: Fertility Decline and the Ideology of Class in Sicily, 1860–1980*. Tucson: University of Arizona Press.

Schor, Juliet B. 1991. *The Overworked American: The Unexpected Decline of Leisure*. New York: Basic Books.

Shelton, B.A. 1992. *Women, Men, Time*. New York: Greenwood.

Townsend, Nicholas W. 1998. "Fathers and Sons: Men's Experience and the Reproduction of Fatherhood," pp. 363–76 in *Families in the U.S.: Kinship and Domestic Politics*, edited by Karen V. Hansen and Anita Ilta Garey. Philadelphia: Temple University Press.

———. 1999. "Fatherhoods and Fieldwork: Intersections Between Personal and Theoretical Positions." *Men and Masculinities* 2(1):89–99.

———. n.d. *The Package Deal: Marriage, Work, and Fatherhood in Men's Lives*.

Waite, Linda, Gus Haggstrom, and David Kanouse. 1985. "The Consequences of Parenthood for the Marital Stability of Young Adults." *American Sociological Review* 50:850–57.

Walzer, Susan. 1998. *Thinking About the Baby: Gender and Transitions Into Parenthood*. Philadelphia: Temple University Press.

West, Candace and Don H. Zimmerman. 1987. "Doing Gender." *Gender & Society* 1(2):125–51.

White, Lynn, Alan Booth, and John Edwards. 1986. "Children and Marital Happiness: Why the Negative Relationship?" *Journal of Family Issues* 7:131–48.

Wienberg, Howard. 1988. "Duration Between Marriage and First Birth and Marital Stability." *Social Biology* 35:91–102.

Cities of Women

Mary Weismantel

INTRODUCTION: SEXING THE MARKET

In her influential essay "Democracy for a Small Two-Gender Planet", Mexican anthropologist Lourdes Arizpe surveys a wide range of politically active women, including "Bolivian peasant[s] . . . Chilean trade unionists, mothers . . . in Argentina . . . and the women leaders of the poor neighborhoods and shanty towns in São Paolo, Lima, and other Latin American cities" (1990:xvi), and finds one underlying commonality. All of these women struggled to gain access to the public life of their societies. Regardless of class, race, or nationality, she asserts, the opposition between a feminine private domain and the masculine outside world is fundamental to the social geography of the continent. Arizpe goes on to provide an illuminating analysis of political activism at the end of the century; but the gendered geography from which she begins is not as universal as she claims. Throughout the Andean nations of Ecuador, Peru and Bolivia, (and elsewhere in Latin America as well, including some regions of Arizpe's own Mexico), every small town and big city is home to one kind of public space dominated by women—the produce market.

The Andean marketplace is unmistakably female. Men drive the trucks, buses and taxis that move sellers and products in and out of the market, and they control the wholesale end of the business, where most of the money is made. But by far the largest numbers of people who work in the market are vendors, and almost all of these are women. In my own research on markets in the Ecuadorian city of Cuenca, at least ninety percent of the vendors

in the two central markets were women. Ownership of the prized interior stalls was almost 100% female. Similar patterns obtain throughout the highlands. Bromley found that eighty-five to ninety-five percent of the retailers of fresh fruits, vegetables, meat and fish in the highland Ecuadorian markets in the early 1970s were women (1981). Blumberg and Colyer, too, estimated that eighty-five percent of the vendors in the Saquisilí main market in the late 1980s were women (1990:255), results that I confirmed throughout the 1980s and 1990s for all of the major markets of Cotopaxi Province. In Peru, women comprised seventy percent of all vendors in metropolitan Lima in 1976 (Bunster and Chaney 1985) and eighty percent of all sellers in the Huaraz market in the 1980s (Babb 1989). In Bolivia, this occupation has been "almost exclusively" female throughout the latter half of the century (Buechler and Buechler 1996:223).

That such a large, old and well-established institution could remain invisible to analysts like Arizpe, allowing her to speak unconditionally of Latin America as a society without public spheres for women, illustrates just how anomalous the market is within dominant sexual geographies. The markets are flamboyantly female and unabashedly public, yet they exist within a larger world in which the public sphere is masculine, while feminine realms are enclosed and hidden away from the intrusive eyes of strangers. The existence of this highly gendered institution highlights the masculinity of other public spaces, even as, for market women themselves, it reverses the gendering of both public and private space. And for every household that consumes its products, the market, and the variety of cooked and uncooked foods it provides, troubles the boundary between domestic and commercial work—between a labor of love and working for money.

Adapted from *Cholas and Pistacos: Stories of Race and Sex in the Andes* and reprinted with permission from Mary Weismantel. *Cholas and Pistacos: Stories of Race and Sex in the Andes* (Chicago: University of Chicago Press, 2001, pp. 45–80. Copyright 2001. The University of Chicago Press.

THE TWO PLAZAS

The incompatibility between femininity and public space is, of course, inflected by race and class. For the most part, working-class women have not been afforded the protection—or suffered the imprisonment—of seclusion within the private domain to the same extent as elite and middle-class women. Ethnicity, too, changes how South Americans think about women's mobility. In the rural Quichua-speaking community of Zumbagua, in Cotopaxi province, Ecuador, where I have done fieldwork for ten years now, the sunburnt farmwomen of the parish spend most of their waking hours outdoors, among the sheep and the barleyfields. Their physical presence within the parish—the way in which they move, work, and talk in public—is strikingly masculine by comparison with other Latin American social contexts.

The cities are different. Gender is deeply inscribed in the plan of the Latin city, which exalts the difference between public and private. Traditional homes are often walled, turned inwards to protect family life within a generous but totally enclosed space. Public life occurs within a city plan dominated by a central square, typically bearing a name like "Plaza de Armas," "Plaza de la República," or "Plaza de la Independencia." As a physical representation of victories by and for European men, the Plaza de Armas defines itself against those it excludes: Indian leaders dethroned and banished to the peripheries of empire, Africans deracinated and forced into slavery, and women of all races disenfranchised and contained within houses and convents.

The central plaza is designed to present a visually overwhelming image of the power of the state, the glory of the wealthy, and the honor of men. It is clean and barren and masculine, an open space surrounded by the closed and forbidding architecture of state power. But the Plaza de Armas is not the only plaza to be found in Andean cities. Each of them also boasts another plaza: the messy and feminine space where the produce markets are held. In rural towns, these two different plazas occupy the same space: once a week the market takes over the civic plaza, temporarily re-defining its purpose. In larger cities, civil authorities try to keep the two spaces separate, designating specific squares, streets, and buildings around the periphery of the city as officially sanctioned markets, and sending the police to cleanse the main plaza of vendors and *ambulantes*. The public authorities in Andean cities and towns are perpetually at work to contain the constant, organic growth of this feminine, vernacular space within spatial and temporal limits, and so to protect the dignity of the city's public persona.

The masculinity of the public sphere, we are told, is everywhere under attack. In the global society occupied by the professional classes, it has become a commonplace to speak of women's success in entering the worlds of business and politics. But the inclusion of women as full-fledged members of such communities remains tentative and incomplete, giving rise to a popular discourse about glass ceilings and a legal wrangle over hostile environments. These architectural metaphors are apt: the buildings erected by governments, banks and corporations, like the central plazas around which these buildings are arrayed, are white male spaces, within which femininity continues to be a stigma that marks the interloper. Inside the markets, it is elite men who are made to feel peripheral, like women and the poor in the "other" public spaces. They enter with hesitation and leave quickly, afraid that people are laughing at them behind their backs. The market is made up of individual stalls, row upon row piled with fresh food. Whether the display of food is simple or elaborate, at its center sits the marketwoman herself, a rounded vertical form rising from flat rectangles piled with goods. Repeated again and again across the open expanse of the plaza, or under the enormous metal roofs of the municipal market building, the female bodies of the vendors take on an almost architectonic function. Stationary in the midst of the tumult, these are the pivotal figures who give the market its shape and purpose. This public visibility of the female form, on display not for male delectation but for other purposes entirely, presents a symbolic inversion of the dominant sexual order that some men find profoundly unsettling.

When travel writer Henry Shukman entered the municipal market building of a small town on the altiplano, he was stung by the silent stares of the sellers. They appeared indifferent to him; even their clothing— "absurd, wide, ballerina-like skirts and derby hats"— expressed an apparent unconcern with attracting masculine desire that he found frankly terrifying. Nonplussed, he translated what he saw there into a total reversal of the patriarchal order. These women "hold a frightening dominion over the men" of the town, he asserts hyperbolically. Upset by their unreadable expressions, appalled by the absence of other men, he hastened to leave. "[T]hey didn't want me here," he writes, apparently astonished at the notion (1989:53).

Constrained by the bold gaze of a myriad of women, men in the markets temporarily lose what they have previously taken for granted: the freedom to move about in public with relative unself-consciousness. The sight of so many women so completely at ease in a public sphere of their own making, creates a corresponding unease in men momentarily bereft of a hitherto unquestioned privilege.

This unease has its origins not merely in the fact that this space is dominated by women, but in its dedication to "women's work"—activities normally hidden from view. The visual impression created by the market mimics the intimate spaces and informal organization of domestic life; rather than the empty formality of the masculine plaza, here impromptu constructions criss-crossed with ephemeral passageways fill every available space. This is a haphazardly vernacular architecture, with hand-made, open-walled structures that invite the passerby to look, touch, and taste. The atmosphere is redolent with the smells of food and cooking, as well as of garbage and ordure.

Public life derives its masculine air of dignified display, from its contrast with the secluded existence of its necessary complement: the private world of the family. In erasing this opposition, the placeras' daily activities undermine the plaza's self-importance, making low comedy of high drama. The sight of bloody carcasses and dirty potatoes, the sound of voices calling out "Escobas!Escobas!", "Chochoooos! Chochoooos!", the loudspeakers extolling Jesus or toilet paper, the bustle of women cooking dinner, washing dishes, emptying the slop bucket—all of these bring the mundane and even the unmentionable into open view.

Nor can the activities here be subsumed under the category of women serving men, for the women at work here are very publicly engaged in serving their own needs and one another's needs as well—including the bodily needs that are strictly excluded from other public spaces. In Cuenca, I saw market women urinating in a public park, using their full skirts to hide their genitals, but completely unabashed about the nature of the act itself. In this, they resemble country women; in Zumbagua, too, women squat down unashamedly to urinate beside a road or a path, just as men turn their backs to do the same. (It is a surprisingly modest act for individuals of either sex wearing traditional clothing: women's full skirts cover them from exposure just as men's long ponchos do.) This matter-of-factness about a physical need that bourgeois women never acknowledge in public, may enable us to see that their attitude towards another bodily function, eating, is also rather extraordinary.

Market women eat in public with gusto. Older women, especially, display a self-congratulatory indulgence in the physical pleasures of eating that is more reminiscent of eighteenth century English novels like Tom Jones, than of prevalent attitudes towards public consumption today. In contrast to the manners thought appropriate to fine dining— not to mention the epidemic of disorders that make it impossible for many American women to eat in public at all—public eating in the markets is a proud display of financial success and physical well-being. In a public display of power, important women eat with relish, licking their fingers, sucking on ripe mangoes or greasy chicken bones—even, in one memorable scene in a Quito market last year, eating the brains out of a goat's head with a spoon.

The unequal relationships between older and younger, richer and poorer women take on physical form in the plates of food that move between stalls. Established vendors— big women with rolls of flesh—sit behind their piles of merchandise and watch while younger, thinner women who approach them timidly with plates of food. "Por si acaso . . ." the young women offer timidly, "If perhaps this might please you a little . . . ." Grudgingly, the older woman accepts, and sit back eating slowly and with relish while her younger associates wait on customers. Occasionally the she stops her meal to make change for her helpers, pulling out an enormous roll of bills of different denominations.

The overall impression is not one of comic vulgarity, however: the women who gossip, eat, and take naps in public, shell beans and make soup, clean fish and fry pork, do so with a dignified self-confidence that makes it difficult to take them lightly. When travel writer Eric Lawlor was brought to the La Paz markets by a Bolivian women friend, he had a series of alarming encounters with the women working there, which culminated when he accidentally knocked over a pail of *refresco* belonging to a vendor who specialized in these flavored beverages. "The woman glared with such ferocity that, before I quite knew what I was doing, I had pressed all my money into her hand and fled," he recalled. "To be frank, marketwomen unnerved me" (1989:32).

This surface appearance of the market as an independent city of women can mislead. Relationships with men and with masculine institutions set invisible boundaries everywhere. Socially, women live within neighborhoods and extended families dominated by men; in their businesses, marketwomen depend upon the male wholesalers, truckers and drivers who bring them their merchandise; politically, the relentless intervention of the state wears a masculine face and uniform—that of the policeman. The many faceted and heavy-handed effort by all the Andean states to control the markets, which includes draconian measures to limit their growth economically and spatially, as well as abusive police tactics against individual vendors, is itself an indication that, however limited the freedoms it offers to women, the market nevertheless offers a pro-

found threat to the social order. The market provides the women who work there not only with a job, but with a vantage point from which to critique, to reject—and even to transform— the domestic unit that is the building block of civil society.

REJECTIONS

Travelers' impressions of the Andean marketplace as a profoundly female, even an antimasculine zone, are supported by a recent life history, *In The World of Sofia Velasquez: The autobiography of a Bolivian market vendor* (1996), published by anthropologists Hans and Judith-Maria Buechler. Unlike the alienating sea of identical female faces described by male writers, the market in Sofia's book is a richly heterogeneous territory. She speaks with affection, antagonism, familiarity and irritation of many different kinds of women: her fellow vendors, with whom she must negotiate for room to sell; the female restaurant owners who buy her pork, eggs and cheeses; the women who loan her money and those who are indebted to her. While men—especially her brother Pedro—are never entirely absent from the story of her life, they are far overshadowed by the dozens if not hundreds of female partners, competitors, customers, relatives, neighbors, friends and enemies who populate Sofia's busy world.

The working lives of professional women in offices are still largely defined by their relationships with men, whether as subordinates or colleagues. But Sofia, asked about what it means to be a woman, emphasizes the opportunities for homosociality that the produce market provides:

> I see friendships between women sitting next to one another. They become friends or comadres. I frequently see them talk to one another or go and drink together. They lend one another money and they are concerned about what is happening in each other's lives.

For women who work in such intimacy with other women, the home has a different meaning than it does for women who work in male-dominated contexts—or who do not work outside the home at all. For market vendors, domesticity does not appear as the one definitively and unambiguously female domain, where women can feel at home and in control; far from it. In a radical inversion of this gender paradigm, domestic life with husbands, fathers and brothers appears in market women's testimonies as an ominously patriarchal territory controlled and dominated—often violently—by men.

In Sofia Velasquez's account, domesticity and the market are twin magnetic poles pulling women in opposite directions, towards men and away from them. Throughout her story, two family members stand for these opposite worlds. Her mother represents a happily feminine life of buying and selling, while her brother Pedro emerges as a repressive figure, forever attempting to shape her behavior to conform to masculine ideals which Sofia does not attempt to refute, but which she nevertheless refuses to live by. When she first became an ambulante, conflict with Pedro erupted almost immediately.

> [O]ne afternoon, my brother Pedro saw me selling on the street. . . . [and] said, 'I will tell my sister that she is no longer my sister. It is shameful for her to be selling on the street.'. . . He said that it was unseemly for me to sit in the street and that his friends would criticize him. . . . But . . . I liked to sell. Selling was pleasant. I could go and sell whenever I wanted and I was earning money. (20–21)

At this young age, Sofia's turn to marketing involved staking out her gender loyalties, rejecting male authority and looking to other women for support. "I won't stop, Mother," I told her. 'Let him go ahead and say that I am not his sister. It's fine with me. They (the other vendors) will help me.' And so I continued to sell . . . (21)"

To Pedro, as to other working-class men of La Paz, it is especially inappropriate for married women to sell. Sofia repeatedly tells of women leaving the market at the behest of husbands, especially newlyweds (often to

reappear when family finances dictate). One of her most richly enjoyed victories over Pedro's meddling, occurs when his own finances take a downturn and his wife joins Sofia selling on the street.

If family life sometimes pulls women from the marketplace, it has just as often pushed them into it. This feminine workplace not only provides women with an income when male wages are insufficient; it also acts as a refuge when a home falls apart, or becomes too dangerous. Sociologists Bunster and Chaney, in their 1985 study of working-class women in Lima, heard many tales of domestic tragedy when they interviewed recent immigrants from the highlands. Some women had been abandoned, like Alicia, who said, "I had separated from my husband because he ran off with another woman. That was the reason I came to Lima. In the sierra I couldn't support myself . . . I came alone. . . ." Or Edelmira, who explained that "I didn't have anything, my husband went off with another woman. I came here when I was two months pregnant." Another woman fled "the sexual advances of her stepfather after her mother's death" (19xx:40–41). Anthropologist Leslie Gill, who wrote an engaging study of domestic workers in La Paz, also met many young immigrants escaping family violence: "Six-year-old Zenobia Flores fled to La Paz with her mother in 1972 to escape the drunken rages of her father, who regularly beat up his wife and children" (1994: 65).

The opposition between the market and the home in these accounts is strikingly gendered; while some women described fleeing an abusive stepmother, most were escaping fathers and husbands. Inasmuch as it provides them with a source of income, the market clearly gives women some independence. Perhaps as importantly, it places them within a collectivity of other women, one that, in the central markets, is highly organized. This position enables them to pass collective judgment about what goes on within the domestic sphere, and even to intervene. When married women work in the market, their co-workers claim the right to protest marital abuse, speaking on behalf of marketwomen in general.

Sofia Velasquez recalled: "My secretary of organization, Rosa Espinosa, was beaten by her husband. One day, I called her husband and told him that I didn't like the fact that he was beating his wife". But Sofia admits that the vendor's ability to protect one another is limited. The story of one woman, Ventura, ends tragically: "We [the market women's union] dealt with the matter, but the man killed her anyway, by beating her."

In the Mercado 10 de Agosto, a municipal market in the center of Cuenca, most of the socias [members] had inherited their professions, and sometimes even their stalls, from mothers, aunts or grandmothers. Rosa Loja, for example, who sells peppers, has been a market vendor for forty-four years. Her mother was a *frutera,* a seller of fruit, in the now-defunct Mercado San Francisco. Women who do not inherit this job have little chance of joining an association like the 10 de Agosto's, but they still come to the markets by the thousands trying to develop a successful career as a vendor. Economic, political and military upheavals have driven record numbers of rural peasants to the cities in recent decades, but this migration takes gender-specific forms. Women make their way to the markets along well-established routes, one of the most common of which is an initial flight from one's own rural family, followed by a second escape from the oppressive life of a domestic. "The sexual harassment and abuse of household workers is one of the enduring features of female domestic service in La Paz" (Gill 74). Speaking to Bunster and Chaney in Peru, and to Gill in Bolivia, market women explained their choice of occupation by describing themselves as psychologically unable to bear the repressive and abusive situations they had encountered previously as domestics. In another life history from the Andes, Gregorio Condori Mamami's wife Asunta, a vendor of cooked food in the Cuzco market in the 1970s, recalled her earlier employment as a domestic with distaste. The husband of the woman who employed her, she said, was "un diablo" who tried to rape her whenever he found her alone in the house (1977).

The market can offer temporary respite from the violent excesses of male violence, or a permanent escape from patriarchal domination. While some vendors suffer execrable relationships with men, others terminate relationships that are abusive, seek transitory rather than permanent alliances, or insist upon more egalitarian relationships with husbands and lovers. Some women reject heterosexual partnerships with men completely.

My interest in the domestic arrangements of women who work in the markets was first aroused by two women who had succeeded in opening establishments not in the market square itself, but in small buildings on its periphery. Heloisa Huanotuñu was the owner of a tiny but much-frequented tavern on the edge of the square where the Zumbagua weekly market is held; her friend Elena had turned her kitchen into a lunch room popular with the white school teachers, doctors, and nurses who worked in the parish school and clinic. The two were inseparable, Heloisa's tall black-clad figure a counterpoise to stout little Elena, who always wore one of the frilly shawls that the Irish nuns had taught local women to crochet. Heloisa and Elena were well-respected businesswomen by the standards of the town, and both were popular there; their establishments were central clearing houses for news, as well as crucibles where public opinion was forged—Heloisa's a gathering place for indigenous farmers, as Elena's was for the town's tiny white bourgeoisie.

The two were interesting personalities in their own right, but I was especially fascinated because they did not conform to the image of rural Andean women promulgated in social-science textbooks, in which heterosexual marriage is described as mandatory (see for example Bolton and Mayer 1977). Neither had ever been married. Although they maintained separate (but adjacent) households, it was Elena who provided Heloisa with companionship, in the early morning, at meals, in the slow hours of the afternoon, and at night in bed. (In the cold mountain towns of the Andes, sleeping together in the same bed is a common practice and does not necessarily imply sexual intimacy. It is extremely unusual for either children or adults to sleep alone, and the need for a sleeping companion for warmth and to prevent loneliness is universally acknowledged. Nevertheless, people in town speculated that the two were indeed lovers.)

I never heard either woman express the slightest desire for adult male companionship beyond that of their brothers—indeed, quite the reverse. They spoke of the married women they knew in voices that mixed sympathy, pity, and a slight but unmistakable contempt.

Far to the south in Bolivia, living in a bustling capital city rather than in a remote rural periphery, Sofia Velasquez grew up knowing women like Heloisa and Elena. As a child, Sofia was resentful of her older brothers' control over her, and quick to note that some of her friends lived in all-women households. As though to foreshadow the adult relationships between women that would be so important to her later on, the first page of Sofia's life story introduces a childhood friend, Yola, who lived in an exclusively female household:

> She doesn't have a father. [Her mother] lived with a friend called Agustina Quiñones. They came from Peru together. . . . To this day, neither one of them is married and they are still living together. They are inseparable friends. (1996:1)

Later in the text, she describes them as Yola's "two mothers."

Explaining her decision to work in the market, Sofia begins by stating that she had never had any desire to marry, or to live with men. In drawing the connection between working in the market and escaping domestic life with men so explicitly, she inadvertently makes her brother's relentless opposition to her marketing more understandable. Like Sofia, Pedro sees the market as the antithesis of patriarchal domesticity—and thus as a direct threat to his own attempts to control the women in his life, both sisters and wives.

There appears to be a popular recognition that the markets make these alternative domesticities possible. Consider the words of Bolivian working-class men in the early 1990s, who repeatedly described market women to anthropologist Robert Albro as "varonil", manlike, or the traditional belief, widespread in parts of Bolivia as well as in southern Ecuador, that market women lived in "matriarchal" households. Or the exchanges between Cuzco market vendors and other working-class women recorded by Linda Seligman a decade earlier. In one argument, a market woman snapped at a customer, "Watch out or I'll slap you one." The other woman replied, "And you? Who are you to have to slap me? Don't I already have a husband who slaps me? Perhaps you [formal] don't have one who would slap you" (Seligman 1993:196).

Despite the provisional freedoms it permits from male domination, hierarchies of other kinds permeate the markets; relationships between market vendors and their employees can be as exploitative and abusive as the domestic situations that initially brought young women to the market looking for work. Zenobia Flores, for example, who ran away from employment as a child maid, told Leslie Gill that she was

> taken home by a chola woman, who saw her crying and walking aimlessly down a street, and for a year Zenobia worked for this woman, grinding chilies into powder and selling in a small dry-goods store. She was never paid and frequently went hungry, and the woman eventually abandoned her on a street corner. (Gill 63)

But without patriarchal or legal pressures binding the parties together, poor women are more easily able to leave oppressive situations if better opportunities arise; indeed, other women often urge them to do so.

> Julia Yapita came to La Paz with her female cousins when she was twelve years old. For over a year, she lived with an older sister, who resided in one of the sprawling immigrant neighborhoods in the Alto. The sister sold food on the street and knit sweaters for tourists. Julia assisted her in these tasks but resented always being ordered about. "My sister bossed me around a lot", Julia explained, "and my aunts, who lived next door, told me to find a job,

because my sister was never going to buy me clothes. They knew of a chola . . . who wanted a maid and took me to meet her. She wore a pollera . . . and sold salteñas. I started working for her that day." (Gill 68–9)

Without men to define the limits of female behavior, Julia is free to become like the older, more independent women she sees around her—and to successfully resist their attempts to control her.

This independence explains why Pedro considered his sister's work to be indecent, calling it "shameful" and "disgraceful". The source of this immorality lies in an apparent rejection of domesticity, an act which, Arizpe tells us, would place them outside of the norm for Latin American women of all classes and races. However, this marginality does not render their understanding of the home as a patriarchal space, irrelevant. Don Kulick observes that such marginality can allow members of a subculture to "distill and clarify" aspects of sexuality and gender of profound and pervasive importance in Latin America (1997:582). Like the prostitutes with whom Kulick worked, market women are not alone in their perceptions, but their perspective gives them a greater clarity of vision.

In recent Peruvian fiction by two very different male authors, Mario Vargas Llosa and Jaime Bayly, childhood memories of well-to-do homes are characterized by an all-pervasive and terrifyingly violent paternal order (Ellis 1998). Nor do working-class homes appear to be domains controlled by women: the title of Wendy Weiss's doctoral dissertation sums up working-class Quiteños domesticity with the phrase, "Es El Que Manda". But while women of wealth and poor women alike resent the autocratic behavior of husbands and fathers, they imagine themselves to be without alternatives. Male authors, too, write of vaguely imagined temporary refuges, such as an escape into nature or a few hours in a whorehouse. In contrast, the markets are full of women who slammed the door on oppressive domestic lives, in active pursuit of viable permanent alternatives. When wealthy Bolivian girls, sent away to college in the United States or Europe, began coming home in the 1970s filled with new feminist ideas about living outside of marriage, they found that such a move had meanings within the Andes that it did not have elsewhere. To reject sexist domestic arrangements would not be seen as a radical innovation, but as a scandalous abandonment of one's class and race position: an educated woman choosing to live like a market vendor (Gill 1994:87).

AT HOME IN THE MARKET

Market vendors, then, are public scandals: women without men, working the streets. Many of the women who work in the market are in fact married, or live in consensual unions with men; most of them are mothers; and all of them, except the truly destitute, have homes. But market women, even when earning money to support their husbands, fathers, and sons, evoke images of wicked women rather than of the good wife. The negativity that attaches to the woman of the plaza, is a measure of the positive valuation given to the woman at home.

The only problem with this picture, is that the street market is less an antithesis to the domestic kitchen, than its raucous twin. The public market exists in close economic symbiosis with the unseen interiors of the private homes that surround it, and which it daily provisions. The home and the home-maker are the market to which produce vendors sell their goods: The world of the plaza exists to provide services for the domestic sphere. 'Casera', 'casera', shout the marketwomen to potential customers: 'homemaker', 'homemaker'.

Visitors from other countries are often charmed and surprised by the incongruous domesticity of scenes in the market: a man sits at his sewing machine, ready to patch your trousers or catch up a fallen hem; a woman spreads a wooden table with a bright-colored plastic tablecloth, and offers to sell you anything from a Coca-cola to a four-course *almuerzo*, complete with dessert. Nor is this commercial domesticity a mirage: workmen and students cultivate special relations with particular market women, eating at their stalls day after day, taking comfort in the familiarity of the woman's voice, her steady supply of gossip, and her knowledge of their particular tastes and appetites. Real and fictitious family relationships abound. Some customers are distant relatives—perhaps the son of a country cousin, sent to the city to attend high school with a strict enjoinder to eat all his meals "*donde su tía*" [where your aunt is]. No one who eats at a particular stall for any length of time remains a stranger; regular customers are inexorably drawn into the domestic dramas between the women who work there, and are ruthlessly—albeit sympathetically—interrogated about their own lives and kin.

Cooking is not the only housewifely work that market women do. Like women who shop for their families, they bring the products of male producers and wholesalers into a feminine realm where these can be transformed into meals for individual families. Babb observes that market women's labor is wrongly characterized as strictly distributive in nature. In fact, many kinds of food processing take place in the market that would readily be interpreted as productive if done in a factory. Vendors break down bulk quantities into smaller portions; shell beans and peas; peel fruit and vegetables; chop herbs and grate onions. They even make small ready-to-cook soup packages, filled with combinations of raw legumes, herbs and vegetables in exact proportions. Many stalls feature a single product offered in every stage of preparation, from unpeeled and dirty, to washed and sliced, to cooked and ready to eat.

Heloisa's trago shop is a case in point. She buys contraband cane alcohol in large quantities from the men who bring it up from the western jungle by mule and llama train. The little caravans arrive at her home in the early hours of the morning, and she and the men pour the alcohol from saddlebags into big plastic containers that once held kerosene. Customers occasionally buy entire barrels of the stuff for weddings or funerals, or to bootleg over the mountains for resale in the white towns to the east. Most people bring smaller containers—gallon jars, empty liquor bottles—that are filled by a hose and closed with a fragment from a plastic bag. As the morning wears on, other customers appear looking for a shot to be consumed on the spot. Heloisa or another family member is ready to oblige, siphoning the liquor directly from a fifty-gallon drum into a tiny glass.

Sometimes a group of people makes an impromptu celebration there; in that case, Heloisa can provide soft drinks for the children, and stale bread for everyone. She does not cook for her customers, but can always use her extensive social network to rustle up snacks or cooked food, as well as a variety of other services: a child to run an errand or deliver a message, a decoy to keep enemies away—and, not least in importance, her own physically and psychologically imposing presence to prevent the arguments that develop among drunks, from getting out of hand.

If work done in the market strikes economists as somehow too informal, too feminine, too unimportant to be recognized as productive, it is at the same time too commercial in nature to be properly domestic. The same activities, done inside the home, do not count as labor at all; in economic terms, they become invisible. But for housewives, the existence of inexpensive market labor radically re-shapes the work load within the home. Women come to buy big quantities of corn already cooked into *mote* for a family dinner, or a little bag of it with hot sauce on top for immediate snacking. They may purchase a whole cooked pig or a single slice of roast pork. Some vendors sell enormous wheels of *panela* [turbinado sugar] dark and strong-smelling, wrapped in banana leaves; but they will also cut you off a little chunk to eat like candy.

Histories of the American consumer describe the advent of ready-to-eat foods as a recent innovation made possible by enormous technological advances. The willingness of working women and their families to eat prepackaged food, or to dine in restaurants, is described as a fundamental change in twentieth century social life. Arizpe describes this as a pernicious penetration of the capitalist market into women's traditional sphere of authority, one that has usurped their most valuable "function" and left them "empty handed" (xv). These visions of history are too narrow in both class and geographical perspectives. In Latin America, the presence of the markets, with their abundance of precooked foods, is old rather than new. Some industrial technologies have filtered into the plaza: many factory-made foods are sold there; beverage stall counters are lined with electric blenders; the small stores that ring the market occasionally invest in a refrigerator for milk and cheese. But for the most part, this enormous system of provisioning works through the simplest of technologies: knives to slice and peel, ropes to carry bundles, cooking pots and wooden spoons to boil and stir. The fact that it is human labor, not capital investment or technological innovation, that adds value to the products there, is transparently obvious. The fact that this labor is predominantly feminine, has limited the ability of scholars and policy-makers to understand, or even perceive it.

Working-class women depend upon the ready availability of meals and ingredients from the markets; in small cities and towns this attitude extends to professional women as well. Travelling the back roads of Cotopaxi Province with a car full of Ecuadorian anthropologists, I was surprised when one passenger insisted that we drop in for lunch on an old school friend he had not seen in some time. Her feelings would be hurt, he insisted, when she found out he had been in the town and had not let her give his friends a midday meal. How, I wondered, could this unknown woman cope with a half dozen unexpected lunch guests? The market provided the answer: our hostess disappeared within minutes of our arrival, then returned to usher us in with fanfare to a dining room laden with local specialties: potato pancakes, roast pork, tomato salad, fresh corn. Beaming, she boasted of knowing all the best market stalls in town: without her, she insisted, we would never have been able to eat well in a strange place.

The willingness of market women to perform any sort of food preparation, and the eagerness of housewives and domestic servants to avail themselves of these services, mediates the boundary between the loving work of caring for a family, and the paid labor of strangers. Men and children eating a meal within the house, consume the work not only of their own wife and mother, but of other women as well. In order to be the ideal housewife who knows how to provision her family, women must create and keep good relations with the women of the market and of the small shops that surround it. Thus even for women who do not work there, the markets demand a degree of female homosociality which customers find alternately maddening and rewarding. Market women foster affective relations with their customers, capturing their loyalty, blurring the line between business and friendship. An expatriate American scholar who lives in Cuenca spoke to me fondly about "her egg ladies", whose stall was a regular stop on her Saturday morning excursions around town. But personal relationships are always risky. When Sofia Velasquez, an "egg lady" herself, got on the wrong side of one of a restaurant owner who bought large quantities of eggs from her on a weekly basis, she found herself scrambling for new customers—and missing the tasty sandwiches the woman's husband used to sell her, as well.

The relationship between a market woman and her customers has its own arcana. Many a gringa who has lived in the Andes for an extended period of time, recalls with pride her first 'yapa'—the first time that, as a repeat customer, she earned a little 'extra' scoop of flour or beans, poured into her bag after it has been weighed and the price figured. Marketwomen who sell to Indians often keep a bag of cheap, brightly colored candies with which they 'yapa' their customers, preferring to offer these treats rather than any of the more expensive dry goods or produce they sell. The result is a subtle insult, masked as a kindness: are these candies for the purchaser's children, or is the Indian woman herself being treated as a child? Why is it that the seller, pretending friendship, nevertheless insists that Indians—unlike their white customers—pay full price for every ounce of merchandise?

I vividly remember archaeologist Clark Erickson and his wife Kay Chandler's return to the United States, after spending almost three years in a small, isolated community on the Peruvian Altiplano near Lake Titicaca. They ruefully recalled to me their first attempts at creating good relations with local shopkeepers. Anxious not to offend, the couple had tried to alternate making purchases between each of the two small stores that sold dry goods—the only source of food on the days in between the weekly market. The women who owned the shops, miffed that Kay had not cultivated a special friendship with one or the other of them in accordance with local mores, responded by refusing to sell them anything at all—and temporarily succeeded in turning the market women against them as well. Within a few months, however, Kay had learned to behave appropriately enough to create a completely different relationship with 'her' chosen shop owner: by the end of their stay, the woman carefully tucked away specially chosen eggs and cheeses for 'her' special gringa to buy.

From the market woman's perspective, maintaining the proper degrees of intimacy with customers is among the most complicated and delicate of tasks—and the one that separates an inept from a successful entrepreneur. My landlady in Zumbagua, Rosa Quispe, operated a cooked-food stall in the Saturday market there for a while, but gave it up in disgust. "It costs me more than I earn," she explained to me. "The entire family comes to the market and expects me to feed them for free, but I have to buy all my ingredients in Latacunga the day before, and there I pay cash."

Successful market women, too, find the boundary between market and domestic relations impossible to maintain. What distinguishes professional women like the stall-owners in the Cuenca municipal markets from amateurs like Rosa is their ability to make profit out of their personal relationships, while using their commercial ties to benefit themselves and those they care about. For the true professional, the line between public and private, commercial and familial

disappear almost completely. The Buechlers comment about Sofia Velasquez, that she and her co-workers, unlike the Bolivian middle class, eat out all the time. The domestic expertise upon which mothers and wives pride themselves, is among market women translated into knowledge of especially tasty or reasonably-priced meals cooked by others. They collect coveted relationships with restaurant owners who give free meals, wholesalers who add on a generous yapa "just for the family", and growers who reserve choice produce for friends and intimates.

Sofia Velaquez, for example, reminisces about sharing meals with her daughter, but not because she had stayed home and cooked for her. Rather, returning home after a long overnight journey to make purchases at a rural fair, she recalls that "We would always arrive hungry and would go to eat salchipapas together" at a favorite stall that stayed open late into the night (204).

CONCLUSIONS: COOKING FOR LOVE AND MONEY

In the late afternoons, when the market is quiet, the market in Cuenca is a drowsy place. There are almost no customers. The big metal doors of the market are pulled down part-way, making the interior dim and cool. Young assistants and relatives have been sent home; only the older women, owners of the stalls, lounge in them half-asleep, reading newspapers or taking naps as though in their own living rooms. They take out their reading glasses, their crocheting, and their slippers, wrap themselves in their shawls and prop their feet up on a sack of potatoes or noodles.

If the market is literally a domestic space for these women, whose work brings them there seven days a week from the middle of the night till mid-afternoon, their homes, in turn, become staging sites for commercial and productive operations. Sra. Loja, the rocoto seller, didn't mind that her daughters had not followed exactly in the footsteps of their mother and grandmother. They sell clothing rather than food, and recently began to manufacture some items at home. "They have turned the house into a factory", she remarked with satisfaction.

In La Paz, Pedro complains that Sofia uses the family home, inherited from their mother, as a source of income. He doesn't mind that she has filled the bedrooms with boarders, as her mother had done before her. What upsets him is that Sofia rents out the courtyard to her fellow vendors as storage space. It is stacked with folding tables, portable stoves, piles of raw produce, and even—much to Pedro's disgust, and eliciting complaints from the long-suffering tenants—loads of freshly slaughtered meat.

Heloisa Huanotuñu lives in her trago shop. The counter and shelves, table and chairs serve both as her kitchen and the bar's furniture. Her bed, partly curtained with a sheet of plastic, and the small storage areas above and below it, are the only semi-private spaces within the one-room building. Much of her emotional life is centered elsewhere, in the family farmstead up above town, where her brothers and sisters and nieces and nephews live. She spends many hours there, cooking and eating, listening to complaints and giving advice, loaning money and demanding help. But she does not sleep there. She, too, then, has arranged working, sleeping, eating, and loving in ways that cannot readily be reduced to a single dichotomy of public and private.

Henry Shukman and Pedro Velasquez are separated by race, class, and nationality, but united in their embrace of the idea that family life, the home and domesticity should be a single unit, defined by its contrast to the public spheres of work, business and politics. In rejecting this pattern, market women do not challenge universal or essential sexual patterns, or even Hispanic or Mediterranean cultural patterns. Rather, they are rejecting a pattern specific to modern capitalism, which fetishizes the home as the realm of affective relations (Moore 1988:23). Market women, although they live completely within the commercial and urban spheres of capitalism, are as resistant to this, its central tenet, as are the Indian peasants who live on its fringes. Women vendors do not merely leave the realm of the domestic in order to enter commercial life;

they drag domesticity into public in order to make money, and embrace a commodification of private life that is more unnerving still to a bourgeois sensibility.

The domesticity of the market stall and the industrialization of the home erase the line between work and family. If some market vendors have unconventional domestic partnerships, all of them create intergenerational relationships that violate bourgeois notions about love. It is in their relations with children—the individuals with whom vendors typically form their most enduring and intimate relationships—that market women violate the norms of bourgeois capitalism most egregiously.

Their intergenerational relationships are manifestly as commercial and industrial as they are emotional and social. In Cuenca, young women helped older ones in relationships that were either actually or fictively the kinship relations of mother and daughter, or aunt and niece—but were also those of employer and employee, banker and debtor, investor and fledgling entrepreneur. Sofia Velasquez provides a detailed, decades-long account of how such relationships develop. She began life as her mother's dependent, but quickly became her employee, then her partner. In her eyes, there is no contradiction between financial and emotional investment—and no shame in the expectation of both immediate and long-term return. Remembering the loans her mother made to get her started as in her own independent business, and the careful accounting of interest payments each night, she says fondly and with pride, "She made a really good profit from me in those years."

Today, she explains her love for her own daughter—and her daughter's love for her—by detailing the girl's labors as her employee.

Rocio is helping me at home for two years now. . . . She gets up at 4:30, dresses warmly and goes out to light the kerosene stoves and prepares the food . . . . I get up at 5:00 just to see what she has done. At 6:30 she packs up the food and has it transported with the stevedore to my sales site on the street . . . at 7:30 she leaves for school. (210–11).

Here, the bourgeois convention of cooking as an expression of female affection for loved ones, is translated into a commercial proposition. In Sofia's experience, mothers and daughters cook for one another, not in intimate, lovingly-produced meals removed from the uncaring relations of the commercial world, but in bulk, as cheaply and efficiently as possible, because they are business partners hoping to turn a profit.

The market, then, challenges the sexual geography of the Americas on several fronts at once. It brings women and women's work into the public sphere; and it allows some women to reject the patriarchal domination exerted over the private sphere as well. The most profound challenge it offers, however, is to the very separation of private and public spaces, and of commercial and familial relations. It threatens to create a domesticity without walls, drawing household members outside into the plaza for the satisfaction of their social, emotional and bodily needs, while invading the domestic kitchen with commoditized relationships between the marketwomen who work for money, and the housewives who buy their labor when they might have done the work themselves.

As Sofia Velasquez' brother Pedro seems all too aware, the market undermines the foundations of Andean patriarchy, including the authority and privilege extended to men within the home—an authority backed up, when necessary, with violence. More unsettling still is the erosion of a distinction between highly valued male wage labor, and the unpaid domestic labor performed by women. And worst of all is the market woman's insistence on defining her emotional work in raising children, as well as her remunerative work in the commercial sphere, not as selfless giving for the good of her family, but as activities from which she herself enjoys multiple returns—in love and friendship, money and security, and in the immediate physical pleasures of eating and drinking, talking and laughing in the company of other women.

Today, large American-style supermarket chains are beginning to undermine the importance of the open-air produce market in the Andes, a process that will no doubt accelerate in years to come. Many of the daughters of Cuenca's market women are abandoning not only the plazas where their mothers sell, but the city, the nation, and the region as a whole, emigrating to the United States in droves. These girls grew up in households in which the lines between profit and pleasure, domesticity and public life, friendship and commerce were configured in defiance of the dominant sexual geographies of the Americas; what they will do with this intimate and embodied knowledge as they move into spheres far removed from the produce markets of the Andes, we can only wait to discover.

REFERENCES

Arizpe, Lourdes
1990   Democracy for a small two-gender planet. Forward *to Women and Social Change in Latin America*. Pps. xiv-xix. London: Zed Books.

Babb, Florence
1989   *Between Field and Cooking Pot: The political economy of marketwomen in Peru*. Austin: University of Texas Press

Bolton, Ralph and Enrique Mayer, eds.
1977   Andean Kinship and Marriage. Washington, D.C.: American Anthropological Association. Special Publication Number 7.

Blumberg, Rae Lesser and Dale Colyer
1990   Social Institutions, Gender and Rural Living Conditions. Pps. 247–266 in *Agriculture and Economic Survival: The Role of Agriculture in Ecuador's Development*. Morris D. Whitaker and Dale Colyer, eds. Boulder: Westview Press.

Bromley, Ray
1981   Market Center and Market Place in Highland Ecuador: A Study of Organization, Regulation, and Ethnic Discrimination. Pp. 233–259 in *Cultural Transformations and Ethnicity in Modern Ecuador*. Norman E. Whitten, Jr., editor. Urbana: University of Illinois Press.

Buechler, Hans and Judith-Maria Buechler
1996   *The World of Sofía Velasquez: The Autobiography of a Bolivian Market Vendor*. New York: Columbia University Press.

Bunster, Ximena and Elsa M. Chaney
1985   Sellers and Servants: Working Women in Lima, Peru. New York: Praeger.

Ellis, Robert
1998   The Inscription of Masculinity and Whiteness in the Autobiography of Mario Vargas Llosa. *Bulletin of Latin American Research* 17(2).

Gill, Leslie
1994   *Precarious Dependencies: Gender, Class and Domestic Service in Bolivia.* New York: Columbia University Press.

Kulick, Don
1997   The Gender of Brazilian Transgendered Prostitutes. *American Anthropologist* 99(3): 574–585.

Lawlor, Eric
1989   *In Bolivia: An adventurous odyssey through the Americas' least-known nation.* New York: Vintage Press.

Moore, Henrietta L.
1988   *Feminism and Anthropology.* Minneapolis: University of Minnesota Press.

Seligman, Linda J.
1989   To Be In Between: The Cholas as Market-women. *Comparative Studies in Society and History* 31(4):694–721

1993   Between Worlds of Exchange: Ethnicity among Peruvian Market Women. *Cultural Anthropology* 8(2):187–213.

Shukman, Henry
1989   *Sons of the Moon: A Journey in the Andes.* New York: Charles Scribner's Sons.

Valderrama Fernandez, Ricardo and Carmen Escalante Gutierrez
1977   Gregorio Condori Mamani: Autobiografía. Cuzco: Centro de estudios rurales andinos bartolomé de las casas".

IV

Equality and Inequality: The Sexual Division of Labor and Gender Stratification

In most societies certain tasks are predominantly assigned to men while others are assigned to women. In European and American cultures it used to be considered "natural" for men to be the family breadwinners; women were expected to take care of the home and raise the children. An underlying assumption of this division of labor was that men were dominant because their contribution to the material well-being of the family was more significant than that of women. Women were dependent on men and therefore automatically subordinate to them.

The "naturalness" of this division of labor has been called into question as women increasingly enter the labor force. However, has this significantly altered the status of women within their families and in the wider society? Or has it simply meant that women are now working a double day, performing domestic tasks that are negatively valued and not considered work once they get home from their "real" day's work? If employment enhances the social position of women, why is it that women still earn less than men earn for the same work? Why is there still a high degree of occupational segregation by gender? What precisely is the relationship between the economic roles of women and gender stratification? Cross-cultural research on the sexual division of labor attempts not only to describe the range of women's productive activities in societies with different modes of subsistence, but also to assess the implications of these activities for the status of women.

In many parts of the world women contribute significantly, if not predominantly, to subsistence. This is perhaps most apparent among hunting and gathering or foraging populations, and for this reason such groups have been labeled the most egalitarian of human societies. Hunters and gatherers used to form the bulk of the human population, but today only a small number remain. They are found in relatively isolated regions; they possess simple technology and therefore make little effort to alter the environment in which they live. They tend to be characterized by a division of labor whereby men hunt and women gather. Friedl (1975: 18) outlines four reasons for this division: the variability in the supply of game, the different skills required for hunting and gathering, the incompatibility between carrying burdens and hunting, and the small size of semi-nomadic foraging populations. Friedl (1975) further argues that in foraging societies in which gathering contributes more to the daily diet than hunting, women and men share equal status (see also Lee 1979; Martin and Voorhies 1975). Conversely, in societies in which hunting and fishing predominate (such as among the Inuit), the status of women is lower. It seems that female productive activities enhance the social position of women in society, but Sanday (1974) cautions that participation in production is a necessary but not sufficient precondition. Control over the fruits of their labor and a positive valuation of this labor are other factors to consider, as is the extent to which women are involved in at least some political activities. In addition, the absence of a sharp differentiation between public and private domains (Draper 1975) and the fact that there is no economic class structure and no well-defined male-held political offices (Leacock 1975) have been cited as explanations for the relative egalitarianism in foraging societies compared to more complex societies.

Despite the common assumption that men hunt and women gather, in some foraging societies the division of labor is not sharply defined. This often provides the basis for the highest degree of egalitarianism. Among the Tiwi, Australian aborigines who live on Melville Island off the coast of northern Australia, both men and women hunt and gather. Goodale (1971) demonstrates that resources and technology, rather than activities, are divided into male domains and female domains. Although the big game that Tiwi men hunt provides most of the meat to the group and therefore gives them a dominant position in the society, Tiwi women, who hunt and gather, provide more than half of the food consumed; they share in both the comradery and the spoils of their endeavors. As major provisioners, women are economic assets and a source of wealth and prestige for men in this polygynous society. Despite the fact that their opportunities for self-expression may be more limited than those of men, with age women acquire social status and can be politically influential. In general Goodale suggests that Tiwi culture emphasizes the equality of men and women in society.

Among the Agta Negritos of northeastern Luzon, the Philippines, women enjoy even greater social equality with their men than among the Tiwi. This is a society in which the division of labor and the battle of the sexes appear to be virtually absent. Agta women hunt game animals and fish just as men do. Not only do they make significant contributions to the daily food supply, but they also control the distribution of the foods they acquire, sharing them with their families and trading them in the broader community. The Griffins (in this book) argue that these roles are clearly the basis for female authority in decision-making within families and residential groups.

The Agta case challenges the widely held notion that in foraging societies pregnancy and child care are incompatible with hunting (Friedl 1978: 72). Agta women have developed methods of contraception and abortion to aid them in spacing their children. After becoming pregnant, they continue hunting until late in the pregnancy and resume hunting for several months after the birth of the child. There are always some women available to hunt, during which time children may be cared for by older siblings, grandparents, or other relatives. Reproduction is clearly not a constraint on women's economic roles in this society.

In horticultural societies, in which cultivation is carried out with simple hand-tool technology and slash-and-burn methods of farming, women also play important roles in production (Boserup 1970; Bossen 1989). One theory argues that the economic importance of female production in horticultural societies emerged from women's gathering activities in foraging groups. Horticultural societies vary in the degree to which men participate in crop cultivation as well as whether this cultivation is supplemented by hunting, fishing, and raising livestock. In addition, many horticultural societies are matrilineal (reckoning descent through the female line), and in these societies women tend to have higher status than in patrilineal societies. Lepowsky (in this book) points to gender egalitarianism among the horticultural and matrilineal people of the Pacific island of Vanatinai. In this society, men are not dominant over women either in practice or ideologically. Like men, women on this island can gain both prestige and power through engaging in exchange activities and the sponsorship of feasts where valuable goods are distributed. As a result of these activities, they can become "big women" as men can become "big men." Thus, Lepowsky argues that "the prominent positions of women in Vanatinai exchange and other activities outside of household and subsistence indicate as well as reinforce generally egalitarian relations between women and men. Vanatinai women have access to power both through their control of the economic capital of land and the subsistence and surplus production of yams and through their accumulation of symbolic capital in exchange and mortuary ritual" (1993:38).

Despite descent systems and economic roles that enhance the status and power of women among horticulturalists such as the people of Vanatinai, Friedl (1975) cautions that women's status is not universally high in such societies. Male control of valued property and male involvement in warfare (an endemic feature in many of these societies) can be mitigating factors that provide the basis for male dominance over women. For example, among horticulturalists in highland New Guinea, women raise staple crops but men raise prestige crops that are the focus of social exchange. This cultural valuation is the foundation for gender stratification that is then reinforced by gender ideologies of male superiority and a high degree of sexual antagonism between men and women (Brown and Buchbinder 1976; Herdt and Poole 1982; Strathern 1988). Among the Hua, for example, Meigs (1990) describes a "chauvinistic" ideology that is rooted in men's roles as warriors.

Among the Mundurucú, an Amazonian horticultural society who were also once involved in fierce warfare (Murphy and Murphy 1985), the division is such that men hunt, fish, and fell the forest area for gardens while women plant, harvest, and process manioc. In their daily tasks women form cooperative work groups, have authority, and are the equals of men. To the extent that their work "draws women together and isolates them from the immediate supervision and control of the men, it is also a badge of their independence" (Murphy and Murphy 1985: 237). However, according to a male-dominated ideology, women are subservient to men. Despite the contributions that Mundurucú women make to subsistence, what men do is assigned more value. As Murphy and Murphy state, "Male ascendancy does not wholly derive from masculine activities but is to a considerable degree prior to them" (234). Male domination among the traditional Mundurucú is symbolic. As the Mundurucú become increasingly drawn into a commercial economy based on the rubber trade, men, with their rights to rubber trees and to trading, may gain a more complete upper hand. "The women may well discover that they have traded the symbolic domination of the men, as a group, over the women, as a group, for the very real domination of husbands over wives" (238).

Although women's labor is clearly important in horticultural societies, it has been argued that it becomes increasingly insignificant relative to that of men with the development of intensive agriculture. Intensive agriculture is based on the use of the plow, draft animals, fertilizers, and irrigation systems. In a survey of 93 agricultural societies, Martin and Voorhies (1975: 283) demonstrate that 81 percent delegate farming to men who then achieve primacy in productive activities. One explanation for the decline in female participation in agriculture is that the female domestic workload tends to increase when root crops are replaced by cereal crops and when animal labor replaces manual labor (Martin and Voorhies 1975). Cereal crops require more extensive processing, and field animals must be cared for. Both these activities fall to women. In addition, the kin-based units of production and consumption become smaller, and this too adds to the burden on individual women.

Concomitant with the presumably declining importance of women in agricultural activities is a supposed decline in social status (Boserup 1970). Women's value is defined by their reproductive abilities rather than by their productive activities. It has been suggested that the lesser status of women in some agricultural societies, particularly those of Eurasia, compared to some horticultural societies, as in sub-Saharan Africa, is reflected in the contrast between systems of bridewealth and systems of dowry (Goody 1976). Bridewealth is a compensation to the bride's parents or her kin for the productive and reproductive rights of the bride; dowry, as a form of inheritance, provides a bride with land and other wealth and helps her to attract a husband (see Stone and James in this book).

Despite arguments describing a decline in women's status and their relegation to the domestic sphere in association with the emergence of intensive agriculture, cross-cultural data indicate that women in agricultural societies lead much more diverse and complex lives than some theories suggest (Bossen 1989). In northwestern Portugal women do most of the agricultural activity, inherit property equally, and are often the recipients of a major inheritance that generally includes the parental household (Brettell 1986). This division of labor has emerged because men have been assigned the role of emigrants. Another exception is rural Taiwan, where, despite the patriarchal and patrilineal character of Chinese society, women construct a familial network that gives them a good deal of power and influence in later life (Wolf 1972). Finally, in rural Ireland today, women have become active partners in the farm business (O'Hara 1998).

Another economic adaptation is that of pastoralism or herding. Some pastoralists are fully nomadic, moving their entire communities in accordance with the demands of the herd. Others are involved in cultivation and are therefore transhumant. They engage in seasonal migration. Among pastoralists the ownership, care, and management of herds are generally in the hands of men. Though there are exceptions, male domination of herding tends to be reflected in other aspects of social organization—the near universality of patrilineal descent and widespread patrilocal residence. Pastoral societies are also generally characterized by patriarchy and a dichotomization of the sexes, both symbolically and socially. Segregation of the sexes and gender stratification, in other words, are fundamental attributes of many pastoral societies.

The symbolic opposition between men and women is apparent among the Sarakatsani, a group of transhumant shepherds who live in the mountainous regions of the province of Epirus in Greece. According to Campbell (1964) the life of pastoral Sarakatsani revolves around three things: sheep, children (particularly sons), and honor. "The sheep support the life and prestige of the family, the sons serve the flocks and protect the honour of their parents and sisters, and the notion of honour presupposes physical and moral capacities that fit the shepherds for the hard and sometimes dangerous work of following and protecting their animals" (18). Gender ideology is embedded in these three valued items, especially in the parallel oppositions between sheep and goats on the one hand and men and women on the other. The practical division of labor parallels this symbolic opposition. Women give assistance in the care of animals and make major contributions to their families. The economic roles of husband and wife are complementary. Nevertheless, Sarakatsani husbands have ultimate authority over their wives; obedience to a husband is a moral imperative for a wife. As among the Mundurucú, ideology assigns women to a lesser status, in spite of their economic complementarity.

Rasmussen (in this book) reviews many of these aspects of men's and women's roles among pastoralists, but her essay focuses most closely on the Tuareg, a seminomadic, Islamic, socially stratified people who live in Niger, Mali, Burkina Faso, and Algeria. The Tuareg, in her view, offer variations to standard interpretations of gender in pastoral nomadic societies. For example, the frequent absence of Tuareg men from home (in raiding activities in the past and in separatist warfare against the central state governments of Mali and Niger more recently), as well as men's peaceful trading activities, have necessitated women's independence in work and the education of children. Tuareg women are not sequestered, they do not veil their faces (although Tuareg men do), and they do not engage in gestures of subservience to their husbands such as kneeling or bowing their heads. Men and women regularly meet and socialize in public and women regularly entertain male visitors (although not necessarily lovers) when their husbands are absent. Although Tuareg women are generally consulted by men about matters that affect the life of the camp or village, there are contexts in which women defer to men—before Islamic scholars, important chiefs, and elders on the patrilineal side. Much of the status of Tuareg women is sustained by their rights of ownership in livestock.

Rasmussen concludes with a discussion of the impact of increasing sedentarization on the roles of Tuareg men and women. Sedentarization has increased women's workloads and altered their bases of property. A shift to virilocal patterns of residence (living with the husband and his kin) has increasingly isolated women from the support of their own kin networks. And, for all Tuareg, sedentarization has reduced autonomy as it has opened new opportunities for work in cooperative agencies.

In more recent years anthropologists have begun to exam the roles of poor urban men and women in a variety of developing countries (Nelson 1979; Smith 1989). Bossen (1989:348) points out that most of this research shows "that men have a distinct advantage in obtaining a variety of formal, higher paying jobs, while women are concentrated in the less profitable informal service sectors, where the competition is intense". Often these women are involved in small-scale trading and marketing activities (Babb 1985, Weismantel this volume). Babb's chapter in this volume takes up the subject of women's roles in the urban economy, examining their participation in several urban cooperatives as well as in home production and petty sales in the barrios of Managua. She describes the challenges that women have faced in keeping cooperative enterprises going, as well as the competing demands on their time that result from their income-producing and domestic responsibilities. She observes that while poor urban Nicaraguan women contribute virtually all their income to collective household needs, men do not and that it is women who help to absorb the shocks to household finances generated by economic and political instability. Indeed Babb demonstrates how men and women in Nicaragua have been differentially impacted by the international economy, by internal conflicts such as the Contra War of the 1980s, and by post War structural adjustments that have eroded many of the gains of the Sandinista period.

Generalizations are often made about the status of women according to different modes of adaptation. However, the readings in this section demonstrate that there is a great deal of diversity within each subsistence strategy. For example, in foraging societies women may hunt as well as gather; in intensive agricultural and pastoral societies not all women are powerless, dependent, and relegated to the domestic sphere. Although women's contributions to subsistence are important to gender stratification, a number of other factors need to be considered. These include leadership roles in family and kinship units and in the wider community; inheritance of property; control of the distribution and exchange of valued goods; authority in child-rearing; and participation in ritual activities. In addition, the ideological definitions of women's roles and valuations of their economic activities are often powerful determinants of status.

To fully understand gender stratification, both ideology and participation in production must be taken into account. As Atkinson (1982: 248) states, "It is too facile to deny the significance of sexual stereotypes or to presume that women's influence in one context cancels out their degradation in another. Just as we know that women's status is not a unitary phenomenon across cultures, we need to be reminded that the intracultural picture is equally complex."

REFERENCES

Arensberg, Conrad M., and Solon T. Kimball. 1940. *Family and Community in Ireland.* Cambridge, Mass.: Harvard University Press.

Atkinson, Jane. 1982. "Review: Anthropology." *Signs* 8: 236–258.

Babb, Florence. 1985. "Middlemen and 'Marginal' Women: Marketers and Dependency in Peru's Informal Sector." In Stuart Plattner (ed.). *Markets and Marketing.* Lanham, Md: University Press of America.

Babb, Florence, 1986. "Producers and Reproducers: Andean Marketwomen in the Economy." In June Nash and Helen Safa (eds.). *Women and Change in Latin America.* South Hadley, Mass: Bergin and Garvey.

Boserup, Esther. 1970. *Women's Role in Economic Development.* London: G. Allen and Unwin.

Bossen, Laurel. 1989. "Women and Economic Institutions." In Stuart Plattner (ed.). *Economic Anthropology*, pp. 318–350. Stanford: Stanford University Press.

Brettell, Caroline B. 1986. *Men Who Migrate, Women Who Wait: Population and History in a Portuguese Parish.* Princeton: Princeton University Press.

———. 1995. *We Have Already Cried Many Tears: The Stories of Three Portuguese Migrant Women.* Prospect Heights, IL: Waveland Press.

Brown, Paula, and Georgeda Buchbinder (eds.). 1976. *Man and Woman in the New Guinea Highlands.* Washington, D.C. : American Anthropological Association.

Campbell, John K. 1964. *Honour, Family and Patronage.* Oxford: Oxford University Press.

Draper, Patricia. 1975. "!Kung Women: Contrasts in Sexual Egalitarianism in Foraging and Sedentary Contexts." In Rayna Reiter (ed.). *Toward an Anthropology of Women*, pp. 77–109. New York: Monthly Review Press.

Friedl, Ernestine. 1975. *Women and Men: An Anthropologist's View.* New York: Holt, Rinehart and Winston.

———. 1978. "Society and Sex Roles." *Human Nature* April: 68–75.

Goodale, Jane C. 1971. Tiwi *Wives: A Study of the Women of Melville Island, North Australia.* Seattle: University of Washington Press.

Goody, Jack. 1976. *Production and Reproduction*. Cambridge: Cambridge University Press.

Herdt, Gilbert, and Fitz Poole (eds.). 1982. "Sexual Antagonism, Gender, and Social Change in Papua New Guinea." *Social Analysis* (special issue), Volume 12.

Leacock, Eleanor. 1975. "Class, Commodity, and the Status of Women." In Ruby Rohrlich-Leavitt (ed.). *Women Cross-Culturally: Change and Challenge*, pp. 601–616. The Hague: Mouton.

———. 1978. "Women's Status in Egalitarian Society: Implications for Social Evolution." *Current Anthropology* 19(2): 247–275.

Lee, Richard. 1979. *The !Kung San*. Cambridge: Cambridge University Press.

Lepowsky, Maria. 1993. *Fruit of the Motherland: Gender in an Egalitarian Society*. New York: Columbia University Press.

Martin, M. Kay, and Barbara Voorhies. 1975. *Female of the Species*. New York: Columbia University Press.

Meigs, Anna. 1990. Multiple Gender Ideologies and Statuses. In Peggy Sanday and Ruth Goodenough (eds.). *Beyond the Second Sex: New Directions in the Anthropology of Gender*, pp. 99–112. Philadelphia: University of Pennsylvania Press.

Murphy, Yolanda, and Robert F. Murphy. 1985. *Women of the Forest*. New York: Columbia University Press.

Nelson, Nici. 1979. "How Women and Men Get By: The Sexual Division of Labour in the Informal Sector of a Nairobi Squatter Settlement." In Ray Bromley and Chris Gerry (eds.). *Casual Work and Poverty in Third World Cities*. New York: John Wiley & Sons.

O'Hara, Patricia. 1998. *Partners in Production? Women, Farm and Family in Ireland*. New York: Berghahn Books.

Sanday, Peggy Reeves. 1974. "Female Status in the Public Domain." In Michelle Z. Rosaldo and Louise Lamphere (eds.). *Woman, Culture, and Society*, pp. 189–206. Stanford: Stanford University Press.

Smith, M. Estellie. 1989. "The Informal Economy." In Stuart Plattner (ed.). *Economic Anthropology*, pp. 292–317. Stanford: Stanford University Press.

Strathern, Marilyn. 1988. *The Gender of the Gift: Problems with Women and Problems with Society in Melanesia*. Berkeley: University of California Press.

Wolf, Margery. 1972. *Women and the Family in Rural Taiwan*. Stanford: Stanford University Press.

Woman the Hunter: The Agta

Agnes Estioko-Griffin and P. Bion Griffin

Among Agta Negritos of northeastern Luzon, the Philippines, women are of special interest to anthropology because of their position in the organization of subsistence. They are substantial contributors to the daily subsistence of their families and have considerable authority in decision making in the family and in residential groups. In addition, and in contradiction to one of the sacred canons of anthropology, women in one area frequently hunt game animals. They also fish in the rivers with men and barter with lowland Filipinos for goods and services.[1]

In this chapter, we describe women's roles in Agta subsistence economy and discuss the relationship of subsistence activities, authority allocation, and egalitarianism. With this may come an indication of the importance of the Agta research to the anthropology of women and of hunter-gatherers in general. . . .

Women, especially women in hunting-gathering societies, have been a neglected domain of anthropological research. The recent volume edited by Richard Lee and Irven DeVore (1976) and the *!Kung of Nyae Nyae* (Marshall 1976) begin to remedy the lack but focus solely on the !Kung San of southern Africa. Other works are either general or synthetic (Friedl 1975; Martin and Voorhies 1975), or report narrowly bounded topics (Rosaldo and Lamphere 1974). Sally Slocum, writing in *Toward an Anthropology of Women* (Reiter 1975), has provided impetus for the Agta study. Slocum points out a male bias in studying hunter-gatherers, showing how approaching subsistence from a female view gives a new picture. From the insights of Slocum we have sought to focus on Agta women, to compare the several dialect groups, and to begin investigating the nature and implications of women as not "merely" gatherers but also hunters.

THE AGTA

The Agta are Negrito peoples found throughout eastern Luzon, generally along the Pacific coast and up rivers into the Sierra Madre interior. . . . Although perhaps fewer in numbers, they are also located on the western side of the mountains, especially on the tributary rivers feeding the Cagayan. In general terms, the Agta of Isabela and Cagayan provinces are not dissimilar to other present and past Philippine Negritos. (See Vanoverbergh 1925, 1929–30, 1937–38; Fox 1952; Garvan 1964; and Maceda 1964 for information on Negritos outside the present study area.) In the more remote locales, hunting forest game, especially wild pig, deer, and monkey, is still important. Everywhere, collection of forest plant foods has been eclipsed by exchange of meat for corn, rice, and cultivated root crops. Fishing is usually important throughout the dry season, while collection of the starch of the caryota palm (*Caryota cumingii*) is common in the rainy season. An earlier paper (Estioko and Griffin 1975) gives some detail concerning the less settled Agta; both Bennagen (1976) and Peterson (1974, 1978*a*, *b*, n.d.)

closely examine aspects of subsistence among Agta in the municipality of Palanan.

A brief review of Agta economic organization will be sufficient for later discussion of women's activities. Centuries ago all Agta may have been strictly hunter-gatherers. Since at least A.D. 1900 the groups near the towns of Casiguran (Headland and Headland 1974) and Palanan have been sporadic, part-time horticulturalists, supplementing wild plant foods with sweet potatoes, corn, cassava, and rice. The more remote, interior Agta, sometimes referred to as *ebuked* (Estioko and Griffin 1975), plant small plots of roots, a few square meters of corn, and a banana stalk or two. They usually plant only in the wet season, harvesting an almost immature crop when staples are difficult to obtain by trade. *Ebuked* neglect crop production, preferring to trade meat for grains and roots.

Lee and DeVore (1968:7) argue that women produce much of the typical hunter-gatherers' diet and that in the tropics vegetable foods far outweigh meat in reliability and frequency of consumption. The Dipagsanghang and Dianggu-Malibu Agta strikingly contradict this idea. They are superb hunters, eat animal protein almost daily, and, as noted above, may have both men and women hunting. (The Tasaday, to the south in Mindanao, may represent an extreme nonhunting adaptation, one in which plant food collection is very dominant [Yen 1976].) Hunting varies seasonally and by techniques used among various groups, but is basically a bow and arrow technology for killing wild pig and deer, the only large game in the Luzon dipterocarp forests. Monkey, although not large, is a reliable rainy season prey. Among Agta close to Palanan and Casiguran, hunting is a male domain. Many hunters pride themselves on skill with bow and arrow; less able hunters may use traps. Dogs to drive game are very desirable in the dry season when the forest is too noisy for daylight stalking of animals.

The collecting of wild plant food is not a daily task. Most Agta prefer to eat corn, cassava, and sweet potatoes, and neglect the several varieties of roots, palm hearts, and greens procurable in the forest. . . . Forest foods are difficult to collect, necessitate residence moves over long distances, and do not taste as good as cultivated foods. Emphasis of trade networks with lowland farmers favors deemphasis of forest exploitation of plants. Only in the rainy season do Agta actively process a traditional resource, the sago-like caryota palm. Fruits are often picked on the spur of the moment; seldom do parties leave camp solely for their collection.

Trade with farmers is practiced by all Agta known to us. Rumors of Agta "farther into the mountains" who never trade (or cultivate) seem to be without substance. In the report of the Philippine Commission (1908:334), evidence of lowland-Agta trade around 1900 indicates the *ibay* trade partner relationship to have some antiquity. As the lowlander population has increased since World War II, trade has also increased. Agta are more and more dependent on goods and foodstuffs gained from farmers; adjustments of Agta economic behavior continue to be made, with labor on farms being one aspect of change. Agta formerly simply traded meat for carbohydrates. Around Palanan they may now work for cash or kind when residing close to farmers' settlements. Hunting decreases as the demands of cultivation are met. A cycle is created, and further withdrawal from forest subsistence occurs. Farmers live in areas once solely owned by Agta. Debts to farmers increase with economic dependence; freedom of mobility and choice of activity decrease; and Agta in farming areas become landless laborers.

At the same time, Agta seek to get out of the cycle by emulating the farmers. Many Agta within ten kilometers of Palanan Centro are attempting to become farmers themselves. While the success rate is slow, the attempt is real. Again, when questioned by an early American anthropologist, Agta close to Palanan Centro claimed to be planting small rainy season plots with corn, roots, and upland rice (Worcester 1912:841). Living informants confirm the long practice of cultivation, but suggest a recent expansion of Agta fields and commitment to abandoning

forest nomadism (especially over the last fifteen years). Around the areas of Disuked-Dilaknadinum and Kahanayan-Diabut in Palanan, Agta are well known for their interest in swidden cultivation. Even the most unsettled Agta farther upriver claim small fields and sporadically plant along the rivers well upstream of lowland farmsteads.

The horticultural efforts of the Agta appear less than is the case, since the social organization and settlement patterns are very different from those of the farmers. Agta throughout Isabela and Cagayan are loosely organized into extended family residential groups. A group, called a *pisan*, is seldom less than two nuclear families and very rarely more than five (in the dry season—perhaps slightly higher average during the wet season). The nuclear family is the basic unit of Agta society, being potentially self-sufficient under usual circumstances. The residential group is organized as a cluster of nuclear families united either through a common parent or by sibling ties. Non-kin friends may be visitors for several weeks, and any nuclear family is able to leave and join another group of relatives at will.

As is typical of hunting-gathering societies, no formal, institutionalized authority base exists. The nuclear family is the decision maker concerning residence, work, and relations with other people. Older, respected individuals, often parents and grandparents of group members, may be consulted, but their opinions are not binding. Often group consensus is desired; people who disagree are free to grumble or to leave.

The settlement pattern is determined, in part, by the seasonal cycle of rains and sunny weather, and by these influences on the flora and fauna exploited for food. Rainy season flooding restricts forest travel, brings hardships in exchange, but is compensated by good condition of the game animals. The dry season permits travel over greater distances and into the remote mountains. Predictable fish resources enhance the advantages of human dispersal; only the need to carry trade meats to farmers inhibits distant residence placement.

WOMEN'S ACTIVITIES

Women participate in all the subsistence activities that men do. Women trade with farmers, fish in the rivers, collect forest plant foods, and may even hunt game animals. Tasks are not identical, however; a modest sexual division of labor does exist. Furthermore, considerable variation is found among the groups of Agta of Isabella and Cagayan provinces. These differences may possibly be ascribed to the degree of adjustment of Agta to lowland Filipino culture. Some differences may be due to unique culture histories and to little contact.

Although in Isabela most Agta women do not hunt with bow and arrows, with machetes, or by use of traps, most are willing to assist men in the hunt. Not uncommonly, women help carry game out of the forest. Since mature pig and deer are heavy and the terrain is difficult, this is no small accomplishment. Even in areas around Palanan and Casiguran, women are known to accompany men and dogs into the forest and to guide the dogs in the game drive. Some women are famous for their abilities to handle dogs; one informant, a girl about fifteen years of age, was especially skilled. In Palanan and Casiguran, women and men laugh at the idea of women hunting. Such a practice would be a custom of wild, uncivilized Agta (*ebuked*) far in the mountains, they say. Many of the attributes of ebuked seem to be old-fashioned customs still practiced by interior groups.

Two groups studied as part of the present research do have women who hunt. Among the Dipagsanghang Agta, several mature women claim to have hunting skills; they learned these in their unmarried teen years. They only hunt under extreme circumstances, such as low food supplies or great distances from farmers and a supply of corn. All these Agta are found in southern Isabela between Dipagsanghang and Dinapiqui.

In the northernmost section of Isabela and well into Cagayan province, women are active and proficient hunters. While we have termed the Agta here as the Dianggu-Malibu group, we are actually referring to speakers of the southeast Cagayan dialect who live on the river drainage areas of the Dianggu and Malibu rivers.[2] Both the dialect and women who hunt are found over a considerably greater territory, according to informants, reaching north to Baggao, Cagayan, and at least to the Taboan River.

Among the Dianggu-Malibu women some variation, perhaps localized, perhaps personal, is found. On the Dianggu, some of the women questioned, and observed hunting, carried machetes and were accompanied by dogs. They claim to prefer the machete to the bow and arrow, allowing dogs to corner and hold pigs for sticking with the knife. Our sample of actual observations is too small to argue that only immature pigs are killed, but we do know that in the dry season adult male pigs are dangerous in the extreme. Dogs may be killed during hunts. Since Agta dogs are seldom strong animals, we wonder if mature pigs are acquired only occasionally. On the other hand, so many dogs are owned by these Agta that sheer numbers may favor large kills. We have observed two Agta women with as many as fifteen dogs. Other Dianggu women prefer the bow.

On the Malibu River, Agta women are expert bow and arrow hunters. On both of our brief visits to this group, women were observed hunting. They claim to use bows always, and they seek the full range of prey animals. Wild pig is most desired, while deer are often killed. Future work must quantify the hunting details, but women seem to vary slightly from men in their hunting strategies. Informants say they hunt only with dogs. On closer questioning they admit to knowing techniques that do not involve dogs—for example, they may climb trees and lie in wait for an animal to approach to feed on fallen fruit. Among all Agta, hunting practices vary considerably between the rainy and dry seasons. Our fieldwork in Malibu has been confined to the dry season, when dogs are important. In the rainy season solitary stalking is practiced. Field observations should eventually provide quantitative data on women hunting in this season; we must stress that our data are primarily from interview and brief observation. We have not resided among Cagayan Agta long enough to advance quantitatively based generalizations.

Women not only hunt but appear to hunt frequently. Like men, some enjoy hunting more than others. The more remotely located Agta seem most to favor hunting. Even among Agta certain males and females are considered lacking in initiative, a fault that may not be confined to hunting.

Informant data indicate that while women may make their own arrows, the actual blacksmithing of the metal projectile points is a male activity. More field research is necessary to confirm the universality of this detail. Other items of interest pertain to the composition of hunting parties. Most people in any one residence group are consanguineally or affinely related. We have observed several combinations of hunting parties. Men and women hunt together or among themselves. Often sisters, or mother and daughter, or aunt and niece hunt together. At Malibu, two sisters, co-wives of one male, hunt together, and either or both sisters join the husband to hunt. When young children exist, one of the two wives may stay at the residence while the husband and the other wife hunt and fish. Also, sisters and brothers cooperate on the hunt. A woman would not hunt with, for example, a cousin's husband unless the cousin were along.

The only real argument, in our opinion, that has been advanced to support the contention that women must gather and men hunt relates to childbearing and nurture. Among the Agta, during late pregnancy and for the first few months of nursing, a woman will not hunt. In spite of the small size of each residential group, however, some females seem always to be around to hunt, although one or more may be temporarily withdrawn from the activity. Women with young children hunt less than teenagers and older women. On the occasion of brief hunts—part of one day—children are cared for by older siblings, by grandparents, and by other relatives. Occasionally a father will tend a child. Only infants are closely tied to mothers.

Girls start hunting shortly after puberty. Before then they are gaining forest knowledge but are not strong. Boys are no different. We have no menopause data, but at least one woman known to us as a hunter must have passed childbearing age. She is considered an older woman, but since she is strong, she hunts. The pattern is typical of men also. As long as strength to travel and to carry game is retained, people hunt. Our best informant, a young grandmother, hunts several times a week.

Both Agta men and women fish. In fact, from early childhood until the infirmity of old age all Agta fish. If most adults are gone on a hunting trip for several days, the remaining adults and children must obtain animal protein by themselves. Only women in late pregnancy, with young infants, or into old age, withdraw from fishing, which makes considerable demands of endurance as well as skill. Some men excel at working in rough, deep, and cold waters. The everyday techniques for fishing are limited to underwater spear fishing. Glass-lensed wooden goggles, a heavy wire spear or rod varying according to size of fish sought, and an inner-tube rubber band complete the equipment. To fish, people simply swim underwater, seeking fish in the various aquatic environments known for each species. Girls in their teens are very capable at fishing. When fishing individually, women may be major contributors to the daily catch.

When group fishing is undertaken, a drive is conducted. In this operation, a long vine is prepared by attaching stones and banners of wild banana stalks. Two people drag the vine, one on each end and on opposite sides of the river, while the people in the water spear fish startled by the stones and stalks. Women join men in the drives, with older men and women dragging the vine while all able-bodied youths and adults work in the water.

Difficulty of fishing may be characterized as a gradient upon which men and women become less and less able as age and debilities increase. The elderly, when mobile, may still be productive, but instead of true fishing, their activities may be termed collecting. Both the coastal reef areas and freshwater rivers and streams have abundant shellfish, shrimp, and amphibians that may be caught by hand. Elderly women and grandchildren are especially eager to harvest these resources. Older men are not ashamed to follow suit, although the enthusiasm of others for the task seldom gives old men incentive. Men are much less eager to give up riverine fishing after middle age than are women. Clearly some emphasis on males securing protein is found among Agta. Women, however, seem to have traditionally been active in fishing. Interestingly, as a few Agta adopt lowland fishing technology, especially nets, women seldom participate. Like their female counterparts in lowland society, women are deemed not appropriate in net fishing.

One might expect that, on the basis of worldwide comparison, tropic hunters would really be gatherers, and that women would be the steady and substantial providers. Agta do not fit the generalizations now accepted. Few Agta women regularly dig roots, gather palm hearts, seek fruit, or pick greens. Most Agta daily consume domesticated staples grown by the farmers. Women are, however, very knowledgeable concerning flora and its use, and among the less settled Agta, young girls are still taught all traditional forest lore. Brides-to-be among these Agta are partially evaluated on the basis of their knowledge, skill, and endurance in collecting jungle plant foods.

Roots are collected by women whenever more desirable food is unobtainable, when several wild pigs have been killed and the men want to eat "forest food" with pig fat, or when a visit to relatives or friends calls for a special treat. The interior groups may actually combine meat and wild roots for weeks when camped so far from farmers that exchange for corn is impossible. Downriver Agta consider such a practice a real hardship, not to be willingly endured. Men are known to dig roots, even though they say it is women's work. On long-distance hunts men do not as a rule carry food, and they may occasionally dig roots to alleviate the all meat-fish diet.

As hunting is thought of as a "sort of" male activity among many Agta (in Isabela),

processing the starch of the caryota palm is a female activity. Women cruise the forest searching for trees containing masses of the starch; they also chop down the trees, split the trunks, adze out the pith, and extract the flour. Often parties of women and girls work together, speeding up the laborious task. On occasion, men will assist. Extracting the flour starch is moderately heavy work, and tiring. Husbands may help when wives have a pressing need to complete a task quickly. Since much of the final product is given in gift form, the need for haste occurs frequently. Perhaps most important to note is the male participation. Sexual division of labor is tenuously bounded among all Agta. Emphases may exist, but a man can even build a house (i.e., tie the fronds to the frame—a female task).

As noted at the beginning, trade, exchange, and horticulture are not new to Agta. Informants, early photographs, and writings indicate that all but the most remote Agta were not "pure" hunter-gatherers after about A.D. 1900. Since the mountains have been a final retreat—from the earliest Spanish attempts to conquer the Cagayan Valley until the present—Agta must have been in contact with former farmers/revolutionaries in hiding. Keesing (1962), summarizing the peoples of northern Luzon, documents several societies of pagan swiddeners adjacent to or in Negrito territory. The Palanan River drainage area was inhabited by farmers before Spanish contact in the sixteenth century. Doubtless, Agta have participated in economic exchange and social intercourse for centuries. Agta now have institutionalized trade partnerships, at least in Palanan and Casiguran municipalities. Trade partners are called ibay (Peterson [1978a, b] discussed the *ibay* relationship in detail), and partnerships may last between two families over two or more generations. *Ibay* exchange meat for grains and roots, or meat for cloth, metal, tobacco, beads, and other goods. Services may be exchanged, especially in downriver areas. Fields may be worked by Agta, who then borrow a carabao, receive corn or rice, and satisfy any of a number of needs. What is important in relation to this chapter is that

Agta women may engage in *ibay* partnerships. Among the lowland farmers almost all *ibay* are males. An Agta woman may be an *ibay* with a lowland man. According to our data, an Agta husband often is not also *ibay* with his wife's *ibay*, but he must treat the farmer as he would his own *ibay*. Of course Agta men and women trade with any farmer they choose, but such exchange is without the consideration given to an *ibay*. (Considerations include credit, acts of friendship, and first choice/best deal on goods.) Not only do women have *ibay*, but they very frequently are the most active agents of exchange. In areas where the trade rests mostly on meat and where men do most of the hunting, women are likely to carry out the dried meat and bring back the staple. They therefore gain experience in dealing with the farmers. We should note that many farmers attempt to cheat the Agta by shortchanging them on counts or weights, but they do so on the basis of gullibility or naiveté of the Agta, not on the basis of sex. Agta women are actually more aggressive traders than are men, who do not like confrontation.

Among the Dipagsanghang Agta, women seldom hunt today, and infrequently dig roots. They do carry out meat to trade. They seem to have an easier life, with emphasis on corn, rice, and roots instead of gathering wild foods. However, downriver, close to farmers, Agta women have reversed this trend, and are working harder and longer hours.[3] Intensification of the ibay relationship and need to own and cultivate land has forced women to become horticulturalists and wage laborers for farmers. On their own family plots (family-owned, not male- or female-owned) they, together with adult males and youths, clear land, break soil, plant, weed, and harvest. When clearing virgin forest of large trees, women do not participate. They do clear secondary growth in fallowed fields.

In the families that reside close to Palanan . . . men and women work almost daily in the fields of farmers. Women go to the forest to collect the lighter raw materials for house construction, mats, betel chews, medicines, and so on. Men follow a similar pattern, giving up hunting for field labor and a corn and sweet potato diet supplemented by small fish. Again we see a remarkable parallel in the activities of males and females.

Looking more closely at specialized women's activities, one may suggest increasing importance in downriver areas. Women have several domains that they use to gain cash or kind income. As just stated, income from labor in fields adds to the economic power of women. A small-scale traditional pursuit, shared by men and women, is the gathering of copal, a tree resin common to trees (*Agathis philippinensis*) found scattered in the Sierra Madre. Women often collect and carry the resin out to lowland "middlemen," who sell it to the depot in town. While corn and cash may be sought in exchange, cloth is desired in order to make skirts. Medicine and medical treatments for ailing children may be paid for by copal collection. Another example of entrepreneurship by females is a small-scale mobile variety store effort. After working in fields for cash and building a surplus, families may cross the Sierra Madre to the towns of San Mariano, Cauayan, and Ilagan. There Agta, often women, purchase in markets and stores goods for use and resale in Palanan. Palanan Centro itself has no real market, only several small general stores selling goods at highly marked up prices. Since no road reaches Palanan, all manufactured supplies must enter town by airplane from Cauayan or boat from Baler. Freight costs are high. Some Agta women are very eager to hike outside to get tobacco, which always commands a high price and a ready market.

DISCUSSION

The role of women in Agta economic activities has been reviewed. Assessment of an hypothesized egalitarian position of women may be more difficult, and rests on assertions and interpretations drawn from the economic roles. First, drawing in part from Friedl (1975), an argument can be made that women in Agta society have equality with men because they have similar authority in decision making. The authority could be based on the equal contribution to the subsistence resources. Working back, we see that among many Agta, women do contribute heavily to the daily food supply, do perform maintenance tasks with men, and may initiate food acquisition efforts through their own skills. They do control the distribution of their acquired food, sharing first with their own nuclear family and extended family, then trading as they see fit. They may procure nonfood goods as they desire. Men may do the same; generally spouses discuss what work to do, what needs should be satisfied, and who will do what. Whole residential groups frequently together decide courses of action. Women are as vocal and as critical in reaching decisions as are men. Further examples could strongly validate the hypothesis that women do supply a substantial portion of foods, and the assertion that women have authority in major decision making. Two questions arise. May we accept a causal relationship between percentage of food production and equality? Certainly there are cases to the contrary. According to Richard A. Gould (personal communication), Australian Aboriginal women in various areas collected the bulk of the food, yet remained less than equal (as we will define equality). Second, we may ask if Agta males and females are actually "equal."

Two avenues may suffice in answering this question. First, one might explore a definition of equality, surely a culturally loaded concept. Since Agta women have authority or control of the economic gain of their own labor, they may be equal in this critical domain. Equality must surely be equated with decision-making power and control of one's own production. The second avenue of equality validation by the scientist may be to examine the female's control over herself in noneconomic matters. These could include selection of marriage partner, lack of premarital sexual intercourse proscription, spacing of children, ease of divorce, and polygyny rules.

In marriage, two forms are typical of Agta. One, the less common, is elopement by young lovers. While such marriages admittedly are fragile, elopement is not uncommon. In this case both partners must be willing. Rape and abduction are rare. Rape by Agta men is not known to the authors. Abduction must involve a slightly willing female, and is not done by young people. A mature man might abduct a married woman, crossing the mountains to a safe locale. To abduct a young girl would be difficult. Parents of eloping couples may be enraged, but usually reconcile themselves to the marriage. If the newlyweds stay together, no more is made of it.

The proper form of marriage is one arranged by customary meetings and discussions, as well as exchange of goods between two families. Often neither the bride nor the groom has had much say in the matter, although serious dislike by either would probably kill the negotiations before the marriage. Mothers are the most important in choosing who will marry whom. Even when their children are young, they are looking about for good partners. Word filters around when a young girl is marriageable, and efforts are made to get the appropriate young man and his family into negotiations before an undesirable family appears. Once any family with a prospective groom formally asks, a rejection is given only for strong and good reasons, since the denied family loses considerable face and may be angry enough to seek revenge.[4]

Criteria for choice of a marriage partner are varied. Often a young man in his early twenties marries a girl about fifteen. Girls entering marriage before puberty are not uncommon. In such cases the husband may help raise the girl until the time the marriage is consummated and full wifehood is recognized. Other combinations are seen. One much discussed case was the marriage of a woman in her forties to a man in his mid-twenties. The couple seemed very happy, with the wife paying rather special attention to her husband. The man's mother, a friend of the wife's, decided that the marriage was peculiar but acceptable.

Premarital female chastity is not an idea of much currency. Agta close to farmers will pay lip service to the idea, but should a girl become pregnant she will take a husband. There are no illegitimate Agta children, although an occasional rape of an Agta by a lowland male may produce a child. Since by the time a girl is fertile she likely will be married, illegitimacy is not the issue. Although some data are difficult to collect concerning sex, almost certainly girls are able to engage in sexual activity with relative ease; promiscuity is not favored in any circumstance. Males may have as little or great difficulty in engaging in sex as females. The Agta are widely dispersed in extended family groups; hence appropriate sexual partners are seldom seen. No homosexuality is known to exist.

Agta gossip suggests that many Agta, male and female, married and unmarried, constantly carry on extramarital sexual relations. This may be a function of gossip and a gross exaggeration. Whatever reality, neither males nor females seem to be especially singled out for criticism.

Women say they space their children. The practice certainly varies hugely from person to person, as does fecundity and luck in keeping children alive. The Agta use various herbal concoctions that supposedly prevent conception, cause abortions shortly after conception, and have several functions related to menstruation. These medicines are known to all Agta and are frequently used. Our census data indicate that some women seem to be successful in spacing births. Other cases note high infant mortality yet no infanticide, female or male. All Agta abhor the idea.

Divorce is infrequent among Agta, with elopement being more prone to failure than are arranged marriages. Divorce does happen often enough, however, for us to look at the causes and relate them to an inquiry into female equality. First, either sex may divorce the other with equal ease. Agta have no possessions. Some gift giving between the two families establishes the marriage, but most of the gifts are food. Cloth, kettles, and minor items make up the rest. Return of marriage gifts is unlikely. Spouses simply take their personal possessions and return to the residential group of close relatives.

Causes for divorce are mainly laziness or improvidence, excessive adultery, or personality clashes and incompatibility, usually caused by a combination of the first two conditions. Skill and success in subsistence activities is of primary importance to marriage. While some Agta are less industrious and less skilled than others, all Agta expect a mate to work hard at all appropriate tasks. Should a male fail, divorce is likely. Occasionally, very young couples experience extra difficulties. These may be accentuated by displeased parents of either party.

Polygamy is not found in most of Isabela. Census data collected to date reveal only monogamy or serial monogamy. That is, spouses may be divorced or widow(er)ed several times in a lifetime. In Cagayan the data are incomplete but startling. Probably some of the strongest support for the equality of women hypothesis, when added to the facts of women as hunters, comes from a study of Agta polygamy. We noted earlier that two co-wives, sisters, hunted together in Malibu. South of Malibu at Blos, another husband and two sisters/co-wives arrangement was found. In the same residential unit we recorded a woman residing with her two co-husbands. They were not brothers; one was older than the wife, one younger. The other women considered this arrangement as humorous, but acceptable. An insight into the male sexual jealousy found in many societies worldwide is the comment of a Palanan Agta man. This old man, when told of the polyandrous marriage to the north, thought for a moment and commented, "Well, perhaps one man with two wives is OK, but a woman with two husbands? I find that totally bad." The women laughed at him.

NOTES

1. Although the authors have worked among the Agta about fourteen months, visits to the northerly group in the Dianggu-Malibu area have been brief. The practice of women hunting was first observed during a survey trip in 1972. We again visited the Dianggu group in 1975.

In August 1978 we returned for one week to Dianggu and Malibu, where we verified in greater detail the subsistence activities of women. Data were collected using the Palanan Agta dialect and Ilokano.

2. Dianggu and Malibu are river names used by Agta and nearby Malay Filipinos. On the Board of Technical Surveys and Maps (Lobod Point, Philippines), the Dianggu is named the Lobod and the Malibu is named the Ilang.

3. Peterson (n.d.) argues that "downriver" Agta women are highly variable in their devotion to labor, older women being hardworking and young mothers not at all industrious.

4. Thomas Headland tells us that rejection of a prospective spouse may be a less serious matter among Casiguran Agta than among those we know.

REFERENCES

Bennagen, Ponciano. 1976. Kultura at Kapaligiran: Pangkulturang Pagbabago at Kapanatagan ng mga Agta sa Palanan, Isabela. M.A. thesis, Department of Anthropology, University of the Philippines, Diliman, Quezon City.

Briggs, Jean L. 1974. Eskimo women: makers of men. In *Many sisters: women in cross-cultural perspective,* ed. Carolyn J. Matthiasson, pp. 261–304. New York: Free Press.

Estioko, Agnes A., and P. Bion Griffin. 1975. The Ebuked Agta of northeastern Luzon. *Philippines Quarterly of Culture and Society* 3(4):237–44.

Flannery, Regina. 1932. The position of women among the Mescalero-Apache. *Primitive Man* 10:26–32.

———. 1935. The position of women among the eastern Cree. *Primitive Man* 12:81–86.

Fox, Robert B. 1952. The Pinatubo Negritos, their useful plants and material culture. *Philippine Journal of Science* 81:113–414.

Friedl, Ernestine. 1975. *Women and men: an anthropologist's view.* New York: Holt, Rinehart and Winston.

Garvan, John M. 1964. *The Negritos of the Philippines,* ed. Hermann Hochegger, Weiner beitrage zur kulturgeschichte und linguistik, vol. 14. Horn: F. Berger.

Goodale, Jane C. 1971. *Tiwi wives: a study of the women of Melville Island, north Australia.* Seattle, Wash.: University of Washington Press.

Gough, Kathleen. 1975. The origin of the family. In *Toward an anthropology of women,* ed. Rayna

R. Reiter, pp. 51–76. New York: Monthly Review Press.

Hammond, Dorothy, and Alta Jablow. 1976. *Women in cultures of the world.* Menlo Park, Calif.: Benjamin/Cummings.

Harako, Reizo. 1976. The Mbuti as hunters—a study of ecological anthropology of the Mbuti pygmies. *Kyoto University African Studies* 10:37–99.

Headland, Thomas, and Janet D. Headland. 1974. *A Dumagat (Casiguran)–English dictionary.* Pacific Linguistics Series C. No. 28. Australian National University, Canberra: Linguistics Circle of Canberra.

Howell, F. Clark. 1973. *Early man,* rev. ed. New York: Time-Life Books.

Isaac, Glynn L. 1969. Studies of early culture in East Africa. *World Archaeology* 1:1–27.

———. 1971. The diet of early man: aspects of archaeological evidence from lower and middle Pleistocene sites in Africa. *World Archaeology* 2: 278–98.

———. 1978. The food-sharing behavior of protohuman hominids. *Scientific American* 238(4): 90–109.

Jenness, Diamond. 1922. *The life of the Copper Eskimos. Report of the Canadian Arctic Expedition* 1913–1918, vol. XII, pt. 9. Ottawa: Acland.

Keesing, Felix. 1962. *The ethnohistory of northern Luzon.* Stanford, Calif.: Stanford University Press.

Lancaster, Jane B. 1978. Carrying and sharing in human evolution. *Human Nature* 1(2):82–89.

Landes, Ruth. 1938. *The Ojibwa Woman.* New York: Columbia University Press.

Lee, Richard B., and Irven DeVore. 1968. Problems in the study of hunters and gatherers. In *Man the Hunter,* ed. Lee and DeVore. Chicago: Aldine.

———. 1976. *Kalahari hunter-gatherers: studies of the !Kung San and their neighbors.* Cambridge, Mass.: Harvard University Press.

Maceda, Marcelino M. 1964. *The culture of the mamanuas (northeast Mindanao) as compared with that of the other Negritos of Southeast Asia.* Manila: Catholic Trade School.

Marshall, Lorna. 1976. *The !Kung of Nyae Nyae.* Cambridge, Mass.: Harvard University Press.

Martin, M. Kay, and Barbara Voorhies. 1975. *Female of the species.* New York: Columbia University Press.

Peterson, Jean Treloggen. 1974. An ecological perspective on the economic and social behavior of Agta hunter-gatherers, northeastern Luzon, Philippines. Ph.D. dissertation, University of Hawaii at Manoa.

————. 1978*a*. Hunter-gatherer farmer exchange. *American Anthropologist* 80:335–51.

————. 1978*b*. The ecology of social boundaries: Agta foragers of the Philippines. *Illinois Studies in Anthropology No. 11.* University of Illinois, Urbana-Champaign, Ill.

————. n.d. Hunter mobility, family organization and change. In *Circulation in the Third World*, ed. Murray Chapman and Ralph Mansell Prothero. London: Routledge & Kegan Paul.

Philippine Commission. 1908. *8th Annual Report of the Philippine Commission: 1907.* Bureau of Insular Affairs, War Department. Washington, D.C.: Government Printing Office.

Quinn, Naomi. 1977. Anthropological studies on women's status. In *Annual review of anthropology*, ed. Bernard J. Siegel, pp. 181–225. Palo Alto, Calif.: Annual Reviews.

Reiter, Rayna R., ed. 1975. *Toward an anthropology of women.* New York: Monthly Review Press.

Rosaldo, Michelle Zimbalist, and Louise Lamphere, eds. 1974. *Woman, culture, and society.* Stanford, Calif.: Stanford University Press.

Slocum, Sally. 1975. Woman the gatherer: male bias in anthropology. In *Toward an anthropology of women*, ed. Rayna R. Reiter, pp. 36–50. New York: Monthly Review Press.

Tanner, Nancy, and Adrienne Zihlman. 1976. Women in evolution. Part I: Innovations and selection in human origins. *Signs: Journal of Women in Culture and Society* 1:585–608.

Tanno, Tadashi. 1976. The Mbuti net-hunters in the Ituri Forest, Eastern Zaire—their hunting activities and band composition. *Kyoto University African Studies* 10:101–35.

Turnbull, Colin M. 1965. *Wayward servants: the two worlds of the African pygmies.* Garden City, NY: Natural History Press.

Vanoverberg, Maurice. 1925. Negritos of northern Luzon. *Anthropos* 20:148–99.

————. 1929–30. Negritos of northern Luzon again. *Anthropos* 24:1–75, 897–911; 25:25–71, 527–656.

————. 1937–38. Negritos of eastern Luzon. *Anthropos* 32:905–28; 33:119–64.

Washburn, Sherwood L., and C. S. Lancaster. 1968. The evolution of hunting. In *Man the hunter,* ed. Richard B. Lee and Irven DeVore, pp. 293–303. Chicago: Aldine.

Worcester, Dean C. 1912. Head-hunters of northern Luzon. *National Geographic* 23(9):833–930.

Yen, D. E. 1976. The ethnobotany of the Tasaday: III. Note on the subsistence system. In *Further studies on the Tasaday,* ed. D. E. Yen and John Nance. Makati, Rizal: PANAMIN Foundation Research Series No. 2.

The Sexual Division of Labor on Vanatinai

Maria Lepowsky

THE SEXUAL DIVISION OF LABOR

The sexual division of labor for Vanatinai adults, young people, and children features a marked overlap between the tasks considered appropriate for men and for women, as predicted for egalitarian societies.[1] Both Vanatinai women and men tend and harvest yams, the most highly valued cultigen, sweet potato, taro, manioc, banana, and other garden crops, and individuals of both sexes know various forms of garden magic, includ-

From Maria Lepowsky, *Fruit of the Motherland: Gender in an Egalitarian Society,* Columbia University Press, 1993.

ing the magic used in the annual yam planting ritual.

A woman is referred to by both sexes as "the owner of the garden," or *ghuma tanuwagai.* Women and men together agree on where and when to clear land for a new yam garden and on how big it needs to be for subsistence and exchange purposes. Men cut tall forest trees to clear land for new gardens, but the work party is comprised of men and women, and the women cut the smaller trees and shrubs and supervise the burning of the forest cover. Men normally loosen the soil to form mounds for planting yams using eight-foot digging sticks, but I have observed women performing this task. Women generally do the actual preparation and planting of seed yams, and they take the major responsibility for maintaining the gardens.

Both sexes plan the nature and extent of the coming year's gardens and plant them, but women do most of the daily garden maintenance, although certain men too are renowned for their industry in gardening. Food is harvested, usually by individual women, when it is ready. Yams are the only annual crop, and the only root crop which it is possible to store for many months. They are harvested by both women and men along with the appropriate magic and may be stored in small yam houses constructed either in the garden or near the hamlet.

Men weed and harvest gardens according to individual temperament and household needs. Men have primary responsibility for working sago. They do most of the pounding of the sago pith to extract the starch, a major dietary staple, but again the work party is usually mixed, and women supervise the drying of cakes of sago starch over a low fire.

Both women and men forage for a wide variety of wild nuts, legumes, tubers, fruits, and leaves in the rain forest, although women generally spend more time foraging than most men. Foraging, and being in the forest, is considered more enjoyable than weeding gardens in the hot sun.

Both women and men collect shellfish, fish in the lagoon with monofilament line from shore or from a canoe, use derris root to stun and collect fish trapped in shallow pools in the coral, and fish in the inland streams for freshwater fish, prawns, and eel. Men fish with spears in the lagoon at low tide during the day and using torches of dead coconut leaf at night. More rarely, men hunt crocodiles at night with torches and spears, or spear dugong in the lagoon shallows. The amount of time a person spends fishing and collecting shellfish varies tremendously according to whether the individual likes to fish and not according to sex.

Both men and women care for domestic pigs. If a woman owns and raises a pig, it is she who decides whether or not to contribute for a memorial feast or other occasion to satisfy her personal exchange obligations.

Killing human beings with spears or greenstone axes was a former monopoly of men. Hunting with spears, for wild pig, dugong, and crocodile, is also an exclusively male activity. But Vanatinai women hunt as well, without using spears. They hunt opossum, flying foxes, and fruit bats by climbing forest trees or tall coconuts to sneak up on the slow-moving nocturnal marsupials. Women also hunt monitor lizards, which grow to four feet in length, by climbing tall mangrove trees or by setting traps for them.[2]

In many parts of the Pacific, women are not supposed to climb trees, but on Vanatinai women climb not only to hunt but to obtain coconuts or betel nuts. Women fish using a fishing line or derris root, a fish poison. Formerly both sexes fished using nets woven by men of the fibrous aerial root of the wild pandanus palm. Both women and men gather shellfish in streams and along the fringing reef. Both dive in the lagoon for giant Tridacna clams. More rarely women dive for the blacklip or goldlip pearlshell, which may be sold to traders, or for the red-rimmed oyster-like shells made by both men and women into the shell-disc necklaces that circulate throughout the Louisiade Archipelago and the kula ring as far as the Trobriand Islands.

Men do most of the work of building houses. Women participate by collecting sago leaves for roofing and by weaving sago leaves for one type of wall. They must also provide the builders with cooked food. A few men also make outrigger paddling canoes and, more rarely, sailing canoes, but both men and women paddle and sail them. Although men and male youths more frequently make up the crews of sailing canoes, some women are expert sailors and make trips on their own or with other women to gardens and water sources. Both sexes frequently paddle and pole canoes. In the East Calvados Islands, with their strong maritime orientation, women spend most of their time in garden work while men sail to trade, fish, and make sago on nearby islands.

Men carve ceremonial axe handles and lime spatulas of wood and delicate tortoise-shell lime spatulas. Both men and women manufacture shell-disc necklaces. Women weave pandanus sleeping mats, fine coconut-leaf betel nut baskets, and coconut-leaf skirts. All these items circulate in interisland exchange and during mortuary feasts.

Daily cooking, washing, fetching water and firewood, and sweeping are primarily female tasks, but men occasionally perform each of them. Men and women both fetch water and firewood and cook during feasts and other communal occasions such as roofing or yam planting. Men butcher and boil pork, scrape coconut meat, and prepare the boiled sago and green coconut pudding. Women prepare the stone oven for roasting vegetable food.

It is always the woman's job to clean up pig droppings around the hamlet every morning, using a piece of sago bark and a coconut-rib broom. In many cases they are the owners of the pigs. An angry meeting of village men took place to complain when a teacher in the primary school at Griffin Point, who came from another part of Papua New Guinea, assigned both boys and girls to clean up pig droppings from the school grounds, and the job was afterward given only to the girls.

Women are responsible for sweeping the hamlet ground, or bakubaku, every morning, for cooking, for fetching water, fetching salt-water (for salting food), gathering firewood, washing dishes and clothes, and caring for children, a responsibility that is often delegated to older siblings or grandparents. Older brothers, fathers, mother's brothers, grandfathers, and other male relatives often play with children and carry them around, but they do this only when they feel like it.

Both men and women are tender and indulgent parents, but the care of young children is primarily the responsibility of women. Because a father and child belong to different lineages, his nurturing is perceived as a gift rather than an obligation of kinship. Men are frequently seen carrying around their offspring or maternal nieces or nephews, and they often take older boys and girls with them to the garden for the day or on gathering expeditions. People explain that the reason why a father's matrilineal kin must be compensated with valuables when someone dies is that the deceased excreted upon the father as an infant and the father cleaned it up uncomplainingly.

EXCHANGE AND THE LIFE CYCLE

Every individual from young adulthood to old age has obligations to contribute labor, food, pigs, or ceremonial valuables upon certain occasions, particularly to aid kin and affines who may be hosting or attending a mortuary feast. Death comes early to many people on Vanatinai, from infant and child mortality due to malaria, from childbirth, and from infectious diseases such as pneumonia and tuberculosis (Lepowsky 1990). Genealogies often show that half the offspring of one couple died in infancy or childhood, and young adults and middle-aged people occasionally die suddenly and mysteriously. It is likely therefore that by the time an individual reaches adulthood he or she will have lost several close kin or affines and participated in the year-long series of mourning restrictions and feasts.

Young people begin their exchange careers by producing foodstuffs and household goods for use at feasts, for less spectacular exchange purposes dictated by kin responsibilities, and for home consumption: yams and garden produce, sago, pigs, skirts, mats, and baskets. All of these objects may be generated by the labor of an industrious young man or woman, who by doing so gains a reputation as a hard worker and therefore as a desirable marriage partner.

The unmarried young in their teens and early twenties are also expected to work hard at the many tasks of the zagaya itself. Sometimes their kin or the host of a feast will reward their effort with a valuable such as a greenstone axe blade. Every worker is fed well and given uncooked food to take home afterward. Young adults may request ceremonial valuables from their matrilineal kin, father's kin, or parents' closest exchange partners to contribute to a ritual obligation such as a feast or bridewealth. They will be expected to repay the debt with an equivalent valuable at a later time when asked. Another way in which a young person of either sex enters the ceremonial system is by raising a pig to maturity and contributing it to a feast or in exchange for valuables such as greenstone axe blades.

There is no difference in the obligations of men and women to provide food or valuables upon ceremonial occasions. When an exchange obligation arises, women as well as men may set off in quest of ceremonial valuables, leaving children, husbands, gardens, and household responsibilities behind.

A few adults refuse to participate at all in exchange. Some people of both sexes choose to contribute only the minimum expected by custom. Others strive to give more yams, more bundles of sago, more pigs, and more valuables and to host and organize more feasts for dead kin or affines, earning the title *gia*. The amount of energy that men and women expend in exchange-activities is largely a function of individual personality. But the offspring of big men and big women—people with successful exchange careers and generally people with rights to large tracts of good garden land—have an advantage. They will inherit the land, ceremonial valuables, and exchange partners of their parents and matrilineal kin.

They will also closely observe successful exchange activities and their nuances from an early age. The ten-year-old daughter of one big man had already circumnavigated Vanatinai on her father's sailing canoe three times, accompanying him on exchange expeditions and attending feasts. She had also visited several of the East Calvados Islands. By contrast, some middle-aged people from the Jelewaga area had never visited the eastern settlements of the island or any neighboring islands.

A reputation as a big man or big woman is not gained by any one act of generosity in exchange or even by hosting one memorial feast or *zagaya*. A cycle of personal exchange activities develops as an individual matures and takes on new social responsibilities. By their twenties many young people, married and unmarried, contribute ceremonial valuables as well as foodstuffs to feasts as individuals and develop their personal networks of exchange partners. But people in their thirties to early sixties tend to be most widely known for their wealth, skill, and knowledge about exchange.

Not only the mothers but the fathers of young children are inhibited by the fear that envious sorcerers or witches may take revenge by injuring or killing their children. Parents of young children also refrain from extensive exchange activities because of their extra subsistence and childcare obligations.

Women on Vanatinai have the opportunity, if they wish, to build their personal reputations as *giagia* through exchange activities. If they do not choose to exert the effort, they, like Vanatinai men who do not choose to build their reputations through the exchange of valuables, may gain the respect of their peers by taking good care of their families, growing good gardens, or helping their neighbors through their skill in healing.

Mortuary and other exchanges on Vanatinai are a primary means of gaining prestige and symbolic capital available to both men and women, but it is up to the individual to decide whether regionwide renown and influence is worth the trouble. Experts in exchange, healing, or gardening must be "strong," whether they are male or female: willing to take risks and engage in persistent hard work beyond the demands of substinence. They must seek out and learn the magic or ritual knowledge without which they will not succeed, exposing not only themselves but their families to the risk of illness or death through the sorcery or witchcraft of envious competitors.

Vanatinai adults of both sexes show a wide range of personality differences, and they occupy their days with a variety of activities, accommodating the demands of subsistence, sharing with others, and maintaining their reputations as strong and reliable kinspeople and neighbors according to their personal desires and preferences. The degree of personal autonomy and privileges of women and men are largely symmetrical in freedom of movement, choosing marriage partners or divorcing them, launching careers as prominent exchangers of valuables, and acquiring supernatural knowledge and power. Their society values autonomy and tolerates idiosyncrasy and variation among women and men. It also values the same qualities of strength, wisdom, and generosity in both sexes.

NOTES

1. Sanday (1974, 1981) hypothesizes that where men and women contribute equally to subsistence, women's status will be higher and suggest that the mingling of the sexes in the tasks of daily life works against the rise of male dominance. Similarly Bacdayan (1977) sees "task interchangeability" between the sexes as an important correlation of high status of women in a particular society.
2. Female hunting is relatively rare worldwide, but it has been reported among foragers and horticulturists in various parts of the world, such as Australian aborigines of the Kimberleys and Melville Island (Kaberry 1939, Goodale 1971), the Agta of the Philippines (Estioko-Griffin and Griffin 1981, 1985) and the Ojibwa, Montagnais-Naskapi, and Rock Cree of Canada (Landes 1938, Leacock 1978, Brightman 1993).

REFERENCES

Bacdayan, Albert. 1977. "Mechanistic Cooperation and Sexual Equality Among the Western Bontoc." In Alice Schlegel, ed., *Sexual Stratification: A Cross-Cultural View.* New York: Columbia University Press.

Brightman, Robert. 1993. "Biology, Taboo, and Gender Politics in the Sexual Division of Foraging Labor." Department of Anthropology, Reed College, Manuscript.

Estioko-Griffin, Agnes, and P. Bion Griffin. 1981. "Woman the Hunter." In Frances Dahlberg, ed., *Woman the Gatherer.* New Haven, CT: Yale University Press.

Estioko-Griffin, Agnes, and P. Bion Griffin. 1985. "Woman Hunters: The Implications for Pleistocene Prehistory and Contemporary Ethnography." In Madeleine Goodman, ed., *Women in Asia and the Pacifica: Towards an East-West Dialogue.* Honolulu: Women's Studies Program, University of Hawaii.

Goodale, Jane. 1971. *Tiwi Wives.* Seattle: University of Washington Press.

Kaberry, Phyllis. 1939. *Aboriginal Woman: Sacred and Profane.* London: Routledge

Landes, Ruth. 1938. *The Ojibwa Woman.* New York: Columbia University Press.

Leacock, Eleanor. 1978. "Women's Status in Egalitarian Society: Implications for Social Evolution." *Current Anthropology* 19: 247–276.

Lepowsky, Maria. 1990. "Sorcery and Penicillin: Treating Illness on Papua New Guinea Island." *Social Science and Medicine* 30 (10): 1049–1063.

Sanday, Peggy. 1974. "Female Status in the Public Domain." In Michelle Rosaldo and Louise Lamphere, eds., *Woman, Culture and Society.* Stanford, Calif.: Stanford University Press.

Sanday, Peggy. 1981. *Female Power and Male Dominance: On the Origins of Sexual Inequality.* Cambridge: Cambridge University Press.

Pastoral Nomadism and Gender: Status and Prestige, Economic Contribution, and Division of Labor Among the Tuareg of Niger

Susan Rasmussen

INTRODUCTION: GENDER IN ANTHROPOLOGY

This is a discussion of women's perceived economic contributions in relation to status,

Original material prepared for this text.

prestige, and division of labor in a traditionally pastoral nomadic, stockbreeding society, the Tuareg of the African Sahara and Sahel. I also offer a critique of some interpretations of gender and pastoralism in predominantly seminomadic communities moving toward sedentarization and migrant labor. First, I situate my own analysis in current approaches to gender in anthropology, and present an overview of studies of women's and men's roles in pastoral society. Following this section, I focus upon the Tuareg, a seminomadic, Islamic, socially stratified people who live in Niger, Mali, Burkina Faso, and Algeria, with an emphasis on data from my research among the Air Tuareg of northern Niger Republic.[1] I conclude with a brief discussion of socioeconomic and political transformations that impinge upon Tuareg gender, relations between the sexes, and issues raised for the future.

Gender is socially and culturally constructed, and can usefully be understood as a comparative, relational concept (Di Leonardo 1990; Butler 1990:6; Davison 1997). Critical to gender structuring are intertwined modalities: social variables such as ethnicity, class, religion, and age, among many (Ortner and Whitehead 1981; Di Leonardo 1990). Regional variations may also impinge on inter- and intragender identities and relationships (Meena 1992; Gaidzanwa 1985; Mannathoko 1992; Davison 1997). Each of these modalities, singly or in combination, interacts dialectically with gender in a given society at a specific point in time, altering the way women and men are perceived and how they perceive themselves and each other. Constructions of gender therefore depend heavily upon positionality.[2]

In recent years, a number of scholars have called for studies that treat gender dynamically, as occurring in processes generated by discrete locales and through particular histories; they assert that gender is not fixed either across time or in location (di Lauretis 1984; Scott 1988,1992; Kondo 1990; Probyn 1990; Butler 1992; Flax 1993; Barlow 1996). Thus although I use the term "women," I also try to make clear that the Tuareg women about whom I write do not constitute an undifferentiated category of "essentialized woman." They interact with men, and are defined by their age, social origins, occupations, kinship roles, and other locations

in Tuareg society. I insist that specifics of time and place are critical; I aim to tease out the relationship of historical and social contexts to certain configurations of gender.[3] My point is not to argue for some timeless, quintessentially Tuareg sense of woman, but to show how gender and knowledge are constructed in a particular place and time, namely, of seminomadism: in a pastoralist nomadic community undergoing transitions whose directions are difficult to predict over the long term, but who now include some sedentary oasis gardening and migrant labor, within a larger, multiethnic nation-state experiencing ecological disaster, economic crisis, and political tensions.

WOMEN AND MEN IN PASTORAL NOMADISM

Some researchers (Barth 1961; Martin and Voorhies 1975:332–366) view pastoralism as one extreme on a continuum of dependence upon herd animals and cultivation for subsistence, in which segments of sedentary tilling communities may, during periods of scarce resources (i.e., droughts, overpopulation) come to depend increasingly on the products of their herd animals for subsistence. Much Tuareg data, however, contradicts this: in the difficulties of drought, many Tuareg have been pressured to become more sedentary, and to depend increasingly on products of their oasis gardens rather than herd animals for subsistence. Despite this, however, a pastoralist ideology persists. Many Tuareg yearn to return to pastoral nomadism but realize the necessity today for mixing subsistence modes of herding, oasis gardening, caravan and other itinerant trading, and migrant labor, and among the more specialized artisan social strata, arts/crafts production (Rasmussen 1992, 1994, 1996). Martin and Voorhies also observe that during periods of plenty, when the size of herds becomes cumbersome or provides the wherewithal for purchase of arable land, pastoral segments may be repatriated to villages. But among the Tuareg, exactly the opposite occurs: during periods of stress and deprivation when herds become greatly diminished or even depleted, population segments tend to be repatriated to villages.

Tuareg patterns therefore suggest the need to modify or refine some prevalent representations of the cyclical pattern of pastoralism (Martin and Voorhies 1975:334). They offer contradictions, or at least variations, of some previous interpretations of gender in pastoral nomadic societies, and show the need to deconstruct concepts in both pastoralist and gender studies. In a classic study, Martin and Voorhies (1975:351) acknowledge that it is difficult to point to any single pattern of economic adaptation or social juxtaposition of the sexes among pastoralists as a whole, and correlations cannot always be converted to causal connections. Based upon their ethnological, cross-cultural and historical secondary data, these authors make several tentative generalizations. They note that the sexual division of labor seems related to the degree and nature of mobility required for the successful execution of subsistence activities (Martin and Voorhies 1975:352). They argue that gender variations among pastoralists are influenced by at least three factors: (1) their specific adaptation to a given environment (settlement pattern, interaction of herding and cultivation); (2) cultural history of society (common culture areas such as sedentary community origins in Africa south of the Sahara correlate with economic independence, the hoe, polygyny, and sexual freedom; those in the Middle East and of agricultural origins display the opposite pattern); and (3) recent diffusion of ideas rather than cultural origins (Islam, for example—although the Tuareg are an exception to other Muslim pastoralists, in demonstrating less emphasis on the patriarchal family and on gender inequalities) (Martin and Voorhies 1975:365–366).

From their study of forty-four pastoral societies, Martin and Voorhies conclude that the female contribution to the diet of herders is small. Men do almost all herding and women dairy in only about one-third of societies. Men also do most of the cultivation

in half of their sample, however, where cultivation is based on horticultural techniques, women are either the exclusive cultivators, or men and women share equally in cultivation (Martin and Voorhies 1975:339–343; O'Kelly and Carney 1986:66). Martin and Voorhies and O'Kelly and Carney suggest that among herders with a high dependence on crops, variations found in the gender division of labor may be a result of the influence of the parent cultural community out of which pastoral society developed. Hence it is instructive to acknowledge the cultures of neighbors. However, the reverse also holds true. Cultural flows are multidirectional, and Tuareg influences are also present in their neighboring sedentary farming cultures. Thus it is difficult to determine the direction of cultural and social influences, and it is not easy to generalize that all nomadic cultures with a horticultural background are more likely to share tasks, or that all those with an agricultural background are more likely to assign primary productive tasks to men.

O'Kelly and Carney (1986:66) argue that gender division of labor within many pastoral societies is "tipped toward male dominance" of economically productive tasks. These authors explain this in terms of the strength required to handle large animals. Males tend to be exclusive herders of large animals. Females may, however, herd smaller animals and serve as dairy maids for large and small species. Women and children contribute by gathering food, carrying water, and processing byproducts such as milk, wool, hides, and dung. But the lack of firm differentiation between domestic and public spheres encourages gender egalitarianism. Where women have some economic control, women's status may be raised. Boulding (1976:288–299) argues that women participate more fully in the total life of these societies than they do in settled agricultural communities. But Martin and Voorhies (1975) argue that male dominance of economic production gives rise to male dominance in the wider culture and social structure of pastoral societies. Lois Beck, on the other hand, found a flexible division of labor, economic interdependence between genders, and a low degree of gender segregation among the Qashqai of Iran (Beck in Beck and Keddie 1978:365–367). Furthermore, because of the small size of independent households of these pastoralists, males and females were partners in economically independent units, and neither males nor females formed strong separate solidarity groups.

Many authors agree that, however diverse the forms it takes, the division of labor among herders does not create a sharp dichotomy between domestic and public spheres. Women's tasks are more likely to take place in camp than men's tasks, but they do not isolate women in the household. Much women's work is done in cooperation with other women. Both men and women participate in collective work patterns with other members of the same gender. Camps are typically divided into women's spaces and men's spaces, but almost all activities are carried out in the open, avoiding development of private domestic spheres for women versus public spheres for men (O'Kelly and Carney 1986:67). Women's work may be household work, but it is public household work; public/domestic domains thus emerge as overly rigid and bound to western cultures.[4]

In many pastoral nomadic societies, ownership and control over the disposition of livestock appear to be predominantly in male hands. However, females are sometimes at least nominal owners of some livestock through inheritance, dowries, or purchase (O'Kelly and Carney 1986:68). But even owners of livestock cannot usually dispose freely of their animals: they are bound by an intricate web of kinship-based exchanges, which requires giving periodically large numbers of animals to close kin, as bridewealth to the bride's family, dowries to the groom, and as compensation for violation of certain rules, for example, homicide (Evans-Pritchard 1956; Hutchinson 1996) and adultery (Rasmussen 1998a). Furthermore, certain animals in a herd may be held

jointly with others or in their interest, and are subject to many limitations on use and disposal. Males who control large herds thus do not necessarily derive significant economic power from these herds; rather, use rights are important considerations. But large herds bring prestige and influence to owners.

Other factors influencing gender are the defense needs and warfare practices of herders and patricentric kinship systems. In terms of Peggy Sanday's (1981:181) typology, many pastoralists appear to fall under the rubric of "real male dominance," because in most cases the environment is sufficiently dangerous for the society to depend on the strength and aggressiveness of their men for survival. Sanday argues that under such conditions of stress, for the sake of social and cultural survival, women "accept real male dominance." Once again, the Tuareg data suggest modifications of this hypothesis. Tuareg men's frequent absence from home in past raiding and more recent separatist warfare against the central state governments of Mali and Niger, and also men's peaceful trading, have encouraged, indeed necessitated women's independence in some domains of activity (education of children and work). However, some high-status men remain at home and control official political decisions. Thus a warrior aristocracy does not produce gender inequality in all respects; rather, there is a mixed bag here. In fact, some authors report legends of "warrior queens" in Tuareg and other pastoralist nomadic cultures (Boulding 1976:303–312; Rodd 1926:170).[5] While difficult to verify, they suggest that women's elevated position in the class structure may modify their gender roles; thus class cross-cuts gender (Ortner and Whitehead 1981; Di Leonardo 1990).

The pastoral-nomadic/gender relationship is therefore complex, and defies facile generalizations or typologies. There are numerous cross-cultural contradictions and forces that tend toward both gender egalitarianism and male dominance. These suggest the importance of examining local cultures and histories.

THE TUAREG CASE

Tuareg Gender Roles and Relations Between the Sexes: Women's Status and Prestige

Tuareg pastoral nomads today are predominantly seminomadic and practice, to varying degrees, mixed subsistence patterns. Most Tuareg live in the central Sahara and along its borders, in the Sahel. More nomadic Tuareg herd camels, sheep, goats, cattle, and donkeys. They are Muslims of Berber origin. Most Tuareg of the Air Mountain region in Niger originated in the Fezzan and other areas of Libya. Eight politically distinct descent groups (drum groups) all speak mutually intelligible dialects of a Berber-derived language, Tamajaq, and are designated by geographic region. Two of these, Kel Ajjer and Kel Ahaggar, are the northern Tuareg in Algeria. The other six—Kel Adar, Kel Air, and Kel Geres, Iwllemmeden Kel Dennek, and Iwllemmeden Kel Ataram, and Kel Tademaket—live on the southern fringes of desert in Mali, Niger, and Burkina Faso, and are the southern Tuareg. Within the Kel Air are the political confederations of Kel Ewey, Kel Ferwan, and Kel Fadey, those groups emphasized in the present essay. Precolonial social organization was divided into free nobles, religious scholars, tributaries, smiths/artisans, and servile peoples. In most regions, slavery was abolished by the mid-twentieth century.

In general, many Tuareg women enjoy considerable rights and privileges. They are not sequestered, do not veil their faces (although Tuareg men do), and have much social and economic independence and freedom of movement. Separation of the sexes is relatively minimal. Men and women regularly meet and socialize in public. Women are singers and musicians, and organizers of many social events, such as drum playing and dance gatherings, which feature much flirting and courtship. Throughout their lives, many Tuareg women enjoy freedom of choice in sexual involvement and actively pursue romantic preferences (King 1903:280; Rodd 1926:174–175). They may regularly have male visitors, though not always lovers, when their husbands are absent (Rodd 1926:174–175); Nicolas 1946:225; Lhote 1955:335; Murphy 1964; Claudot-Hawad 1993).

Although many of these gender roles and relationships apply to most Tuareg, there is the need to refine and specify, rather than generalize, interpretation of some aspects of Tuareg women's status. Many Tuareg groups display variation in gender arrangements according to relative degrees of nomadism and sedentarization, devotion to official Islam, and regional and confederational differences, as well as age, kinship roles, and social stratum origins. The Kel Ewey *ineslemen* clans of maraboutique Islamic scholars, for example, attempt to control their women slightly more by placing greater emphasis upon virginity and application of Koranic inheritance laws. Even among these clans, however, women own property, are not secluded, and go about unveiled and relatively freely visit and receive male visitors, and although extramarital affairs are less tolerated, men, not women, are fined or punished in reprisals (Rasmussen 1994, 1998a, 1998b).

There are gender transformations over the life course: for example, age and marital status make a difference in women's status, prestige, and property ownership, as well as work and economic independence. Older women enjoy security as mothers-in-law and grandmothers. They specialize in herbal medicine, divination, and bone-setting healing specialties. Urbanization and nation-state policies also influence Tuareg women's status, roles, prestige, and economic bases of power. For example, much property in the Saharan town of Agadez is not independently owned by the married woman, but merged together with that of her husband in civic records.

There are, moreover, seasonal variations in residential spatial arrangements that symbolically convey gender-related socioeconomic processes. In seminomadic carvanning Air villages, the basic residential unit, *eghiwan,* is highly flexible, undergoing fission and fusion according to season and subsistence strategy. Men are often gone from five to seven months a year on caravan trade and migrant labor. Young, unmarried girls and older post-childbearing-age women often go out and establish temporary camps with their herds, intermittently for four months during the dry season; elderly women in the rainy season leave for several weeks to gather leaves and roots and grasses for sauces, and herbal healers are often absent on trips to collect medicines from trees on Mount Bagzan.

During the cold, dry caravanning season, women construct their tent doors to face outward, toward the compounds of their female relatives, the more matrifocal or matricentric space reflecting these women's greater cooperation and sharing at this time. In contrast, in the hot and rainy seasons while many men are at home, the women close these doors and construct doors opening onto the interior courtyard of the nuclear-household compound; the emphasis here is more patrifocal, and patricentric, reflecting greater focus within the nuclear household. Ties with maternal female kin become less emphasized during this time (women visit each other less, and do more housework such as cooking within their own kitchen while husbands are at home).

Most women prefer monogamous unions, and polygyny is a rare occurrence, except among some prominent chiefs, Islamic scholars, and prosperous, more sedentarized gardeners and merchants. I frequently heard women in monogamous marriages tease those who were co-wives about polygyny, and many women initiate divorce upon husbands' attempts to contract polygynous marriages. Polygynous men try to avoid co-wives' jealousy by installing wives in separate compounds and even distant villages. Co-wives never share cooking facilities or sleep in the same compound. A widow or divorcee may become a household head in advanced age; if younger, she usually returns to her parental household.

There is a tendency toward late marriages and preference for political marriages within the descent group or *tawsit* and chiefly among families in many noble groups. The idea in Tuareg marriage is an enduring relationship based upon romantic love. Tuareg often say they prefer to marry cross-cousins because the joking relationship that ordinarily obtains between them is conducive to a strong marital bond (Bernus 1981:149). On the other hand, some such marriages do not last because some Tuareg say close cousins continue to "feel like brother and sister" (Nicolaisen 1963; Murphy 1964). As the marriage stabilizes, the joking relationship is supposed to become a more serious relationship of mutual respect, with some aspects of a respect/reserve relationship in public between the spouses. Name avoidance does not entail wife-to-husband deference among the Tuareg as Schlegel (1975:167–168) inferred from the data available on Tuareg through the HRAF (Human Relations Area Files). The use of teknonymy and sobriquets is symmetric, applying to both sexes. The term for a new spouse is "friend," and later on, "wife" and "husband." Wife-to-husband deference is not a feature of Tuareg society, as it is among the Hausa, for example, where a wife ritually kneels when serving her husband. Tuareg women do not ritually kneel, bow their heads, or engage in any other extreme gestures of subservience to their husbands. Husbands, at least ideally, should regularly "defer" to their wives' wishes about as much as wives to husbands, in a mutual-respect relationship. One man, for example, commented that he had been considering polygyny, but had decided to refrain from taking a co-wife in deference to his wife's wishes, because he "respected" her. A woman may show her contempt for her husband's behavior by returning to her mother's camp, removing the tent and its contents, and leaving the man without a shelter. Direct expression of anger on the part of a man toward his wife is considered shameful.

The creation of a home and its furnishing in nomadic societies is usually part of the dowry institution: this occurs in the context of marriage. Tuareg women receive their nuptial tent as part of their dowry. It is constructed communally on the evening of the wedding by elderly female relatives of the bride, and torn down and reconstructed to be larger on each successive evening of the seven-day wedding ritual (Ramussen 1997). A tent thus comes into being with the wedding ritual, and is a metaphor for the institution of the family. Because descent is bilateral and the tent is matrilineally defined and transmitted, the tent also becomes a metaphor for matriliny and an allegory for maternity (Prussin 1995:92). A woman has the same status in her own tent as she has in her mother's; she is at home in both. Conversely, a man is a guest in his wife's tent.

The wedding tent, which after the marriage will be the tent of the newly married couple's residence, is erected near the camp of the bride's family. For seven days, this tent remains empty during the day, occupied by the couple only at night. The two spouses subsequently may choose to move with their tent to the husband's family camp. Since the tent is inherited matrilineally, it moves from one camp to another, as when the bride's relatives bring her tent to her husband's camp or village. An unmarried man usually lives in a straw and mat conical building called *tettrem*, or in more sedentarized communities, in an adobe mud house. These single men's buildings are located either within or just adjacent to their parents' compound. Traditionally, the only men who owned their own tent were noble drum-group chiefs. So Tuareg men and women do not inhabit tents in the same way. In general, only a married woman can have a tent. Thus the number of tents in a camp or village generally indicates the number of married women.

In Tuareg culture, the nuptial tent is therefore women's property, brought to the marriage as dowry, a central symbol in the wedding, and used as the married couple's sleeping room, but also much more: it symbolizes the traditional ideal of monogamy. Recently, however, many men have been constructing adobe mud houses that the married man owns. These houses now often stand next to the tent owned by a married woman within the married couple's household compound (Rasmussen 1994, 1996, 1997). The more nomadic Tuareg groups still count women as

owners of compounds, as well as tents, in identifying the household compounds. But the semisedentarized Kel Ewey have begun to identify compounds by the names of husbands, as belonging to men, as they do the men's adobe mud houses in many of these compounds, standing next to the women's tents. These processes indicate some important changes in gender roles, status, and power upon sedentarization, which disrupts the property balance between the sexes. To what extent, then, does the tent confer women's control? The key issue, as Moore (1988:52–53) points out, is the relationship between women's productive and reproductive roles, in the descent and inheritance system.

LEGAL/JURAL RIGHTS, PROPERTY, DESCENT, AND INHERITANCE

The Tuareg official political structure is male-dominated. Among the more nomadic groups, the camping group (*eghiwan*) is an extended family headed by a male elder (*amghar*). In more sedentarized, seminomadic groups this term *eghiwan* refers to the village or hamlet, which may include a number of families, many of whom are related, and today often also includes households whose members vary in occupation and degree of nomadism, sometimes combining or alternating between several different subsistence forms (for example, a man of diverse social stratum origins might practice caravan trade, herding, oasis gardening, and migrant labor within a single lifetime, in different seasons). Allied descent groups comprise a drum group or confederation under the power of a drum chief called *ettebel*, a legitimate male successor from the dominant noble group within it. The confederation is socially stratified into noble and vassal named groups.

Most Tuareg descent groups are bilateral, combining patrilineal influences from Islam with local matrilineal institutions. Many descent groups trace their origins matrilineally to female ancestresses or culture heroines, although some more devoutly Muslim groups and men in general tend to downplay these ancestresses and emphasize patrilineal descent and male ancestors or culture heroes. For example, many Kel Ewey Tuareg men and marabouts in rural Aïr communities where I conducted research mentioned Boulkhou, a patrilineal ancestor of the current *ettebel*, as their important founder. He had sunk the first well, built a mosque, and resisted enemies in battles in that region. By contrast, many women tended to emphasize Tagurmat, the female ancestor of the Kel Igurmaden descent group within the Kel Ewey confederation, who in a myth gave birth to twin daughters who founded the professions of herbalism and Islamic/Koranic healing. The Kel Fadey say their people descend from two sisters who came from the east, bringing with them livestock, herds, and a large wooden drum (the drum, kept by the chief's wife, is used to call the tribal sections together for political or military action) (Worley 1992:56). The Kel Fadey reckon their most important kinship connections through women (matrilineally), so a child's closest relationships are usually with his or her mother's people, especially the mother's brother. In the past, both property inheritance and succession to the chieftainship followed maternal lines, from a man to his sister's sons and daughters.

A recurring question in Tuareg ethnography has been the extent to which Tuareg practice matrilineal inheritance and descent and succession. In matriliny, theoretically, mothers and sisters of heirs enjoy status. A problem here is the use of the term to mean certain institutions, or "society" and "culture" in general (Oxby 1977). Also often ignored are variations among the different Tuareg groups and according to social context. Thus the issue becomes, which kin links are most important and what factors other than kinship are important in determining relationships between the generations and the sexes? Descent group (*tawsit*) allegiance is, in practice, through the mother. Ideally, however, political office passes from father to son in all groups but the Kel Geres, where it goes from maternal uncle to sister's son. Hence both matrilateral and patrilateral kin ties are important. There are also important criteria apart from kinship in

political leadership: for example, wealth and personal qualities of leadership.

Women's property is passed down mainly from mother to daughter; men's, from father to son. Objects acquired by women before marriage include jewelry, blankets, a bed, other household items, and sometimes cloth and sandals. In the past, noble women brought a slave to their married household; today, rural noble women still inherit an attached smith/artisan client family. Inheritance of livestock is predominantly Koranic: daughters receive one-third to one-half of sons' shares. Children are considered, among most Aïr Tuareg, more important heirs than spouses and siblings. If there are only daughters, a brother receives the son's share. The mother's brother is a less significant figure in some groups than in others, but everywhere the mother's brother/sister's son tie features, at minimum, affection, and frequent gifts, and security in assistance. The sibling tie in fact sometimes competes with the husband-wife tie. Each spouse, regardless of postmarital residence, if possible spends much time during the day (for example, eating meals) at the residence of his/her own kin. Individuals often try to return to maternal kin in latter years of life. Women often refuse to follow husbands to remote places, for example, to start new gardens, and divorce often ensues (although this may be changing recently). Men are present with their sisters during the funeral sacrifice of meat in the event of their sisters' children's death. An older sister is described as "like a mother" to her younger brother; older brothers are supposed to take care of younger sisters, accompanying them on travel and assisting them in legal cases. Brothers and sisters are supposed to be allies, and brothers ideally should look out for sisters' legal and other interests. Often, brothers do support sisters upon the divorce, and also contribute to the support of widowed sisters' children. The father's sibling group is equated with the father, as a source of authority and possible conflict; the mother's sibling group, by contrast, is a source of love and aid, generosity, and support. A man has the right to take domestic animals from his true and classificatory mother's brothers. He must inform them of this act through a third party.

Some Tuareg say, "It is the stomach that colors the child." Another source of shared maternal identity is breast milk: those who are nursed by the same woman cannot marry. Possession by spirits not curable by Koranic verses is believed to be inherited matrilineally from mother to daughter in breast milk. Formerly, matrilineal clans were associated with specific totems. Sultan Goma allotted land to noble women in these clans in order to prevent it from passing out of the clan's ownership (Nicolaisen 1963; Norris 1972,1975). Many Tuareg believe that the maternal nephew inherits intelligence from his maternal uncle. But Kel Ewey do not use separate kinship terms for a maternal versus paternal nephew; they refer to both as *tegazay*.

Nowadays, however, the concept of maternal kinship identity tends to be submerged in most legal practice. Koranic and patrilineal influence extend to naming, ideas about children's affiliation and identity, and marriage. Men refer to the offspring of a polygynous man and one of his co-wives as the "children of men." They tend to disparage an older form of naming a girl "daughter of" (*oult*) as "only done with an illegitimate child." Rural women are now called Madame plus the name of husband's father as surname, in postal addresses, clinic rosters, and school registration. Illegitimacy is considered shameful, antisocial, and greatly stigmatizing to the mother. A child belongs to the descent group or clan of his or her father. Men insist that the secret, Tamajaq name which older female relatives bestow on the child in the unofficial naming ritual the evening before the official Islamic naming by the father and marabout at the mosque, is "not important, it means nothing," but women dispute this, saying the latter name is as important to the child's identity as the Arabic, Koranic name. Women's property is sometimes subject to dispute and challenge in Koranic-based rulings by marabouts. For example, although a woman has the right to eject her husband from her tent, a woman's bridewealth is only reimbursed to the person

the marabout rules is not at fault in divorce; many marabouts rule the woman at fault if she requests divorce to protest polygyny.

Nonetheless women's opinions are highly valued, and they are normally consulted by men on decisions that affect the life of the camp or village (Bernus 1981:146–147). Yet there are some contexts in which women defer to some men: namely, before Islamic scholars and important chiefs, and toward elders in general, particularly those on the patrilineal side. Female herbal medicine women, for example, referred patients to marabouts for diagnosis of illness, more often than vice versa. But women participate in public discussions over matters of concern to the group, represent themselves in legal cases, and exert great influence in the public sphere. For example, a smith/artisan woman in Agadez held a position as head of a smith/artisan women's cooperative, and also gave radio addresses on women's health issues.

Tuareg women generally enjoy a high degree of economic independence, since they own significant property in livestock. Under optimum conditions, therefore, livestock does constitute great security for women. But this can fluctuate according to climate and nation-state conditions. During droughts and armed conflicts, many herds were diminished, lost, or dispersed. Elderly women often survive off herds of donkeys, which are easy to care for (only requiring salt licks and free roaming for water) and which they sell off gradually at markets. A number of authors (Bernus 1981; Casajus 1987; Claudot-Hawad 1993; Keenan 1977; Lhote 1955; Murphy 1964), correctly I believe, have noted the importance of a custom among the Tuareg that allows women to acquire more property in livestock, and sometimes date palms, than they would normally have right to under Koranic law. This practice, known as *akh hudderan*, allows an individual to make a pre-inheritance gift of livestock to female relatives, usually daughters, sisters, and nieces, which they then own and control corporately. This property cannot be sold or otherwise disposed of.

Additionally, Tuareg women accumulate livestock through important gifts (*alkhalal*) from both parents and other relatives after birth, which form the basis of their own herds. Women may receive outright gifts of livestock from consanguine kin throughout their lives, and in all marriages after the first, it is usually the wife herself who accepts the bridewealth (*taggalt*). As a result of these gifts and pre-inheritance practices, therefore, some women under optimum conditions (of plentiful pasture, regular rainfall, cooperative male kin and spouses, and peace) may indeed become quite wealthy in livestock. Even in the recent droughts and warfare, some women manage to support themselves. In more prosperous and peaceful eras, it was not uncommon for a woman to be wealthier than her husband. But it is difficult to assess the extent to which women still enjoy these ideal property arrangements, in the light of recent upheavals. More nomadic nobles, in particular, have lost much property over the past twenty years. But these losses affect both sexes, not solely women. There are strong pressures to settle down and practice oasis gardening more extensively, and there is evidence that women's bases of property are increasingly altered by all these processes. In semisedentarized communities, for example, men's houses complicate property disputes on divorce. For example, after the divorce of Aghaly and Mariama (pseudonyms), Aghaly retained his mud house and Mariama her tent in the same compound on the same land. At first, the ex-husband did not want to leave his house. The couple took their case to the secular courts in Agadez, which ruled a compromise: each party changed the door on his or her respective structure, so that the buildings faced the exterior, rather than the interior courtyard. Aghaly ate his meals at his mother's home. This solution divided the property and also saved the divorced couple from daily interaction. Aghaly eventually moved back into his old house adjacent to his parents' compound in a neighboring village (Rasmussen 1996:18).

Some married women residing virilocally (with the husband's family) have very different spatial and social arrangements in their new home, which affect work and authority patterns. In initial postmarital uxorilocality (residence with the wife's family), most visiting and sharing of resources and work occurs between maternally related women (mothers and sisters and daughters); whereas in virilocal residence, the wife is more isolated from her own kin, and more dependent upon her husband and his family. She is also subject to a strict reserve relationship with her parents-in-law. She also obtains a bit less assistance with household tasks from her sisters-in-law than she would from her own sisters.

SEXUAL DIVISION OF LABOR

Domestic work in more nomadic groups takes a minimum of women's time. Mothers can support pregnancy and breastfeed children while performing the physically demanding work of pastoralism, milking the livestock, and packing and moving the tents they own. One noble woman in a seminomadic village, the daughter of a local chief, has managed her own small store since 1997. Another woman has a small restaurant on a road from Agadez into the rural area. Older children usually watch small children and toddlers. Infants may be carried on the mother's back while she is working. There is little house cleaning to contend with. The tent needs to have the wall mats adjusted several times a day as the direction of the wind changes (Worley 1988:278), and it is swept out occasionally. Fresh clean sand is gathered at intervals for the tent floor. Grinding and sifting and crushing millet and other cereals is arduous work that all women, nowadays, do (in the past, slaves did this labor). In nomadic Kel Fadey camps, Worley reported that this task takes approximately two hours a day (Worley 1988: 278); in the seminomadic villages of the Kel Ewey Tuareg, I noticed, pounding millet took up far more of women's time, up to approximately 90 percent of their day's work. In more sedentarized communities, therefore, women's time is taken up more extensively with food-processing work within the compound than is more nomadic women's time; these latter, by contrast, often circulate more widely away from the compound herding their own livestock at outlying pastures. Other cereal grains were traditionally crushed on a flat stone. Recently, several mills have been built in this area and women no longer crush corn and wheat on flat stone as I had observed them do earlier in my research (in the 1970s and 1980s). In all Tuareg rural communities, women's communal work parties do mat and tent construction and repair, together in reciprocal gatherings called gaya (derived from Hausa).

Subsistence work regularly takes many women outside the village or camp for the collection of firewood, gathering of wild grains, berries, and other plants, and the daily drawing of water at a well, which may be several miles from the camp. Women view these tasks differently, however: some welcome tasks such as herding and gathering for the freedom they confer; others, however, view going to the well and herding as hot, arduous tasks. In semisedentarized communities around Mount Bagzan, some women are described as "housewives" (called by the French term *menageres*). These women have given up herding (though not always herd ownership), and have relegated this task to kinspersons. A few gardeners' wives have even given up their tents. Reasons given for this included scarcity of materials, and also no further need for a tent, in the presence of a husband's house. But most women still own and use tents, even alongside men's houses, and still own herds. Some women married to gardeners are giving up herding and (if smiths) leatherwork, as well. Very few women individually own gardens, which are traditionally inherited and owned mostly by men (though a few women have date-palms through matrilineal *akh huderan* inheritance). Upon herds' depletion in drought, theft, or war, women are at a disadvantage because livestock herds are more difficult to reconstitute than oasis gardens. Traditionally, planting was done by men and harvesting done only by elderly women; recently, however, over the summer of 1998 I noticed some hints of change in

these patterns. A development agency had established a women's garden cooperative, and some women had begun enclosing and gardening in this designated space, known as the "women's garden (enclosure)" (*afarag n tchidoden*). In order to prevent erosion, a fence was being constructed: each woman is paid an amount to participate in the work party, provide wood, and construct the fence. A female "president" supervises this project, in which the women take up a collection (250 CFA or approximately 50 cents each) from each household to build a well (cost: 25,000 CFA, approximately $50). When the well is completed, the project organization will give the group an animal. Women have also recently been involved in projects selling millet on the market in Agadez. It remains to be seen how extensively Tuareg women will pursue gardening tasks on these semisedentarized oases. This may constitute a significant departure from women's traditional work patterns, and become a new property base and source of economic power.

Many women who own animals, however, continue to herd small livestock—goats, sheep, and donkeys, and on occasion, camels when men are absent. Women milk the small livestock and process the milk into cheese and butter, consuming them within the household and also selling some of the surplus to travelers and other local residents. Women's subsistence work is considered critical in Tuareg pastoral production, and they must be capable of taking over some of the men's work on occasion when men are absent. In the 1960s, 1970s, and 1980s, for example, many young men left in exile from the droughts of 1973 and 1984, in search of jobs. In 1990, the Tuareg rebellion broke out. Therefore many young marriageable men became marginalized economically and politically, resisted some elders' efforts to arrange matches, or found it difficult to raise bridewealth to marry at all. A few men are beginning to sell Tuareg silver and leatherwork items abroad in international art fairs. Other men work on farms in Italy and Libya. Male migrant workers are forbidden by Libya to send or bring money home to

Niger, however. So they must hide it, and/or wives must support their families on their own at home. Many women, not solely smith/artisans, do this by making basketry and embroidery for sale in craft shops in Niger and France, though very few Tuareg women travel to France.

Smith/artisan men and women derive much income from arts and crafts. Metal and woodworking are smith men's work; most leatherworking is smith women's work. Women of diverse social origins tan hides, but mostly smith/artisan women cut and embroider them. Smith/artisan women in rural areas obtain cash and food gifts through leatherworking and rites-of-passage services for nobles. In Saharan towns, women smiths continue to do leatherwork, but with fewer raw materials, which cost more in the sedentarized setting, and also fewer customers, for demand there is lower than in rural communities where herders and gardeners need hide containers and implements, and tourists and functionaries buy more metal jewelry than leatherwork. Recently, some religious and human rights and aid organizations in France purchased millet while it was at a low price and gave it to Air Tuareg groups to store during the period of higher millet prices. These organizations also bring art objects made in workshops (by both men and women specialists) to sell in France at fairs. They sponsor women's basketry and weaving workshops, where artists modify traditional designs for sale in France.

CONCLUSIONS

Socioeconomic and Political Changes; Implications; Issues and Questions Raised for Future Trends

One of the key changes affecting the organization of nomadic pastoralism is the nomads' loss of autonomy after incorporation into sedentary nation-states, in the wake of the military advantage of sedentary states and revolutions in transportation technology during the past century (Barfield 1993:207).

Upon sedentarization, there is disruption of traditional ties and undermining of important sources of defense and security. As men are increasingly obliged to travel as migrant laborers and children are sent to school, the workload of women extends from their traditional routines to a heavier involvement in supplementary tasks. In Niger, colonial and postcolonial eras saw pastoralist border zones farmed, depleting the soil and disrupting ecological and socioeconomic balance and relations between groups and lands. Mobility has been curtailed, censuses, schools and taxes imposed by colonial governments, and by postcolonial central state governments. Sometimes these have imposed a patrilineal bias. Tuareg are unique among pastoralists in the enduring significance their matrilineal institutions have for gender roles and relations between the sexes. Although these remain significant in the bilateral system, there is evidence that matriliny is under duress. This is shown by the transformations in property balance described in this article and elsewhere (Rasmussen 1994,1996,1997,1998). It is also shown in Gast's (1992: 151–172) description of Tuareg cultural encounters with more powerful neighbors: nation-state policies toward Tuareg nomads brought many workers, functionaries, soldiers, and tourists into rural Tuareg communities. Often, they were ignorant of and disrespectful toward traditional beliefs and practices; for example, they misunderstood evening festival and courtship customs as opportunities to seduce women, whereas traditionally, Tuareg cultural values emphasize music, poetry, flirting, visits, and conversation without necessarily including sexual intercourse. Some camps along routes became labeled by outsiders as places of license and prostitution (Gast 1996:169). In some respects, then, Tuareg women appear to have become the wards of men in encounters with outside males, and in national systems of registration/naming, food relief and medical distribution programs, taxation and census counts. However, as shown, there are also new opportunities—in new cooperative agencies and projects offering some benefits for women, as well as men.

The question raised is how nomadic pastoral Tuareg women actively respond to forces of sedentization, urbanization, and nationalism. Do they gain or lose? How? For example, women can use the urban setting to escape from an extended household ruled over by a mother-in-law. It is therefore hazardous to generalize too sweepingly about pastoralism, women, and gender, or to base observations solely upon structural as opposed to situational meanings and practices. Pastoral nomadic societies display a wide range of variation in economics, culture, and gender relations, and divergent transformations. Rather than building models and typologies, anthropologists need to deconstruct and refine pastoral and gender-related categories and processes.

NOTES

1. In these projects—on spirit possession, aging and the life course, herbal healers, and rural and urban smith/artisans, I gratefully acknowledge assistance from Fulbright Hays (1983,1998); Wenner Gren Foundation for Anthropological Research (1991,1995,1998); Social Science Research Council (1995); National Geographic Society for Research and Exploration (1995, 1998); Indiana University (1983), and University of Houston (1991).

2. For example, Mohanty (1992) criticizes western feminists for essentializing women's experience regardless of race, class, or nationality. Mohanty faults western feminists for universalizing women's oppression, as well. She argues that western feminists psychologize complex and often contradictory historical and cultural realities that mark differences among women. Differences among women need to be engaged rather than transcended. She also warns against globalizing women as victims; there is the need to acknowledge women's active agency. Yet feminists in these areas are diverse; they come from various schools of thought depending on their national and cultural orientations.

3. Despite very valuable work on women and gender in the Muslim world, there have been some tendencies to deploy "Islam" and "Muslim" as a gloss for very diverse cultural interpretations of official religion, their sharing of common themes notwithstanding. Mernissi's (1987)

famous analysis of gender relations in Moroccan society is complemented and enriched by perspectives from scholars on other Muslim societies in Africa, for example Afonja (1986).

4. Pastoralist societies therefore break down the assumed dichotomy of private/public or domestic/public domains, a tenacious concept in some early feminist anthropology (Rosaldo and Lamphere 1974) later critiqued in more recent anthropology of gender studies (Ong 1987).

5. These observations raise interesting issues. For example, traditionally, men's honor depended upon women's praise music upon their victorious return from battles; thus women control men's reputations. Women's praise songs of men often welcomed them after successful raids or migrant labor or caravan trade, but women could also mock and scorn men who returned less victorious or without money. Women still hold power over men's reputations, but many men have not returned victorious or wealthy in recent years. Some men have attempted to find social recognition through participation in the 1990–95 nationalist/separatist military conflict. Much new music of the Tuareg rebellion composed by both sexes, as well as women's traditional songs, perhaps is responding to these new predicaments and in effect, conveys men's and women's efforts to reconstruct social prestige and independent socioeconomic status in Tuareg gender-role relationships.

REFERENCES CITED

Afonja, S. 1986. Changing Modes of Production and the Sexual Division of Labor among the Yoruba. In *Women's Work*, E. Leacock and H. Safa, eds. South Hadley, MA: Bergin and Garvey.

Barfield, Thomas J. 1993. *The Nomadic Alternative.* Upper Saddle River, NJ: Prentice Hall.

Barlow, Tani. 1996. Theorizing Women: Funu, Guojia, Jiating. (Chinese Women, Chinese State, Chinese Family). In *Feminism and History*, Joan W. Scott, ed. Oxford: Oxford University Press.

Barth, Fredrik. 1961. *Nomads of South Persia: The Basseri Tribe of the Khamseh Confederacy.* Oslo: Oslo University Press.

Beck, Lois. 1978. Women among Qashqai Nomadic Pastoralist in Iran. In *Women in the Muslim World*, Lois Beck and Nikki Keddie, eds. Cambridge, MA.: Harvard University Press.

Bernus, Edmond. 1981. *Touaregs Nigeriens: Unité Culturelle et Diversité Regionale d'un Peuple Pasteur*. Paris: Office de la Recherche Scientifique et Technique Outre-Mer.

Boulding, Elise. 1976. *The Underside of History*. Boulder, CO: Westview Press.

Butler, Judith. 1990. *Gender Trouble*. New York: Routledge Press.

Casajus, Dominique. 1987. *La Tente dans l'Essuf*. London and Paris: Cambridge.

Claudot-Hawad, Hélène 1993. *Les Touaregs: Portrait en Fragments*. Aix-en-Provence: Edisud.

Davison, Jean. 1997. *Gender, Lineage, and Ethnicity in Southern Africa*. Boulder, CO: Westview Press.

di Lauretis, Teresa. 1984. *Alice Doesn't: Feminism, Semiotics, Cinema*. Bloomington: Indiana University Press.

Di Leonardo, Michaela. 1990. *Gender at the Crossroads of Knowledge*. Berkeley: University of California Press.

Evans-Pritchard, E.E. 1956 *Nuer Religion*, Oxford: Oxford University Press.

Flax, Jane. 1993. *Disputed Subjects: Essays on Psychoanalysis, Politics, and Philosophy*. New York: Routledge.

Gaidzanwa, R. B. 1985. *Images of Women in Zimbabwean Literature*. Harere: College Press.

Gast, Marcel. 1992. Relations Amoureuses chez les Kel Ahaggar. In *Amour, Phantasmes, et Sociétés en Afrique du Nord et au Sahara*, Tassadit Yacine, ed. Paris: L'Harmattan-Awal.

Hutchinson, Sharon. 1996. *Nuer Dilemmas*. Berkeley: University of California Press.

Keenan, Jeremy. 1977. *Tuareg: People of Ahaggar*. New York: St. Martins Press.

King, William J. Harding. 1903. *A Search for the Masked Tawaraks*. London: Smith, Elder and Co.

Kondo, Dorinne. 1990. *Crafting Selves*. Chicago: University of Chicago Press.

Lhote, Henri. 1955. *Les Touaregs du Hoggar*. Paris: Payot.

Mannathoko, C. 1992. Feminist Theories and the Study of Gender in Southern Africa. In *Gender in Southern Africa*, R. Meena, ed. Harare: SAPES Books.

Martin, M. Kay, and Barbara Voorhies 1975. *Female of the Species*. New York: Columbia University Press.

Meena, R. 1992. Gender Research/Studies in Southern Africa: An Overview. In *Gender in Southern Africa: Conceptual and Theoretical Issues*, R. Meena, ed. Harare: SAPES Books.

Mernissi, Fatima. 1987. *Beyond the Veil: Male-Female Dynamics in Modern Muslim Society*. Bloomington: Indiana University Press.

Mohanty, C.T. 1992. Feminist Encounter: Locating the Politics of Experience. In *Destabilizing Theory: Contemporary Feminist Debates*, M. Barrett and A. Phillips, eds. Palo Alto: Stanford University Press.

Moore, Henrietta. 1988. *Feminism and Anthropology*. Minneapolis: University of Minnesota Press.

Murphy, Robert. 1964. Social Distance and the Veil. *American Anthropologist* 66:1257–1274.

Nicolaisen, Johannes. 1963. *Ecology and Culture of the Pastoral Tuareg*. Copenhagen: Royal National Museum.

Nicolas, Francis. 1946. *Tamesna: Les Ioullemmeden de l'Est, ou Tuareg Kel Dinnik, Cercle de T'awa—Colonie du Niger*. Paris: Imprimerie Nationale.

Norris, H.T. 1972. *Saharan Myth and Saga*. Oxford: Clarendon Press.

———. 1975. *The Tuaregs: Their Islamic Legacy and its Diffusion in the Sahel*. Warminster, England: Aris and Phillips.

O'Kelly, Charlotte G. and Larry S. Carney 1986. *Women and Men in Society: Cross-Cultural Perspectives on Gender Stratification*. Belmont, CA: Wadsworth Publishing Company.

Ong, Aihwa. 1987. *Spirits of Resistance and Capitalist Discipline: Factory Women in Malaysia*. Albany: State University of New York Press.

Ortner, Sherry. and Harriet Whitehead, eds. 1981. *Sexual Meanings*. Cambridge: Cambridge University Press.

Oxby, Clare. 1978. *Sexual Division and Slavery in a Tuareg Community*. Ph.D. dissertation, London School of Economics.

Probyn, Elspeth. 1990. Travels in the Postmodern: Making Sense of the Local. In *Feminism/Postmodernism*, Linda J. Nicholson, ed. New York: Routledge.

Prussin, LaBelle. 1995. *African Nomadic Architecture: Space, Place, and Gender*. Washington, DC: Smithsonian Institution Press.

Rasmussen, Susan. 1992. Disputed Boundaries: Tuareg Discourse on Class and Ethnicity. *Ethnology* 31: 351–366.

———. 1994. Female Sexuality, Social Reproduction, and Medical Intervention: Kel Ewey Tuareg Perspectives. *Culture, Medicine, and Psychiatry* 18:433–462.

———. 1995. *Spirit Possession and Personhood among the Kel Ewey Tuareg*. Cambridge: Cambridge University Press.

———. 1996. Tuareg Tent as Field Space and Cultural Symbol. *Anthropological Quarterly*, 69:14–27.

———. 1997. *The Poetics and Politics of Tuareg Aging: Life Course and Personal Destiny in Niger*. DeKalb, IL: Northern Illinois University Press.

————. 1998a. Within the Tent and at the Crossroads: Travel and Gender Identity among the Tuareg of Niger. *Ethos* 26:153–182.

————. 1998b. Only Women Know Trees: Medicine Women and the Role of Herbal Healing in Tuareg Culture. *Journal of Anthropological Research* 54:147–171.

Rodd, Francis, Lord of Rennell. 1926. *People of the Veil.* London: MacMillan and Co.

Rosaldo, Michele, and Louise Lamphere, eds. 1974. *Women, Culture, and Society.* Stanford: Stanford University Press.

Sanday, Peggy. 1981. *Female Power and Male Dominance: On the Origins of Sexual Inequality.* Cambridge: Cambridge University Press.

Schlegel, Alice. 1975. *Three Styles of Domestic Authority: A Cross-Cultural Study. In Being Female: Reproduction, Power, and Change,* Dana Raphael, ed. The Hague, Paris: Mouton Publishers.

Scott, Joan W. 1988. *Gender and the Politics of History.* New York: Columbia University Press.

Scott, Joan W. 1992. Experience. In *Feminists Theorize the Political,* Judith Butler and Joan W. Scott, eds. New York: Routledge.

Worley, Barbara. 1988. Bed Posts and Broad Swords: Tuareg Women's Work Parties and the Dialectics of Sexual Conflict. In *Dialectics and Gender: Anthropological Approaches,* Richard R. Randolph, David M. Schneider, and May N. Diaz, eds. Boulder: Westview Press.

————. 1992. Where All the Women Are Strong. *Natural History* 101 (11):54–64.

Women and Work in a Postrevolutionary Society: Urban Cooperatives and the Informal Economy in Nicaragua

Florence E. Babb

Throughout Latin America, governments introduced economic stabilization and structural adjustment programs during the 1980s in an effort to bring rampant inflation under control. In Nicaragua, the Sandinista revolutionary government implemented adjustment programs late in the decade, but harsher measures mandated by the International Monetary Fund and the World Bank came more recently, after the 1990 elections ushered in the government of Violeta Chamorro de Barrios. A debate emerged in the country over the consequences of these measures for the most vulnerable social groups. In Nicaragua as elsewhere, the poor, women, and children were hit hardest by these policies. Yet in Nicaragua the recent history of

social mobilization prepared these sectors in distinct ways to confront the harsh effects of these economic programs, setting the country apart from others in Latin America. Low-income urban women have been among those affected most by the political change of the past fifteen years, and they have responded by actively confronting difficult conditions both at work and at home.

In this essay, I first consider some of the general consequences of structural adjustment policies for Third World women and men and then turn to examine the effects these policies have had in Nicaragua, particularly for women in formal and informal work in small industries and commerce in the capital city of Managua. I concentrate on the situation of women in several urban cooperatives I followed over the years of my

Used with permission.

research, and then discuss the growing number of women conducting informal activities, often out of the front rooms of their homes in the city's working-class and poor barrios.

Several authors have led the way toward a critical and gendered perspective on the recent effects of development policies that rely on stabilization and adjustment measures (e.g., Elson 1991; Benería and Feldman 1992; Afshar and Dennis 1992). They have called for attention to the household, where women are functioning as shock absorbers for these measures, and they have argued that adjustment plans extend women's unpaid work in the home in ways that must be assessed. I suggest that while turning to the household and women's unpaid work—the emphasis of most feminist research in this area—has brought about a needed transformation in our thinking about economic development, it is equally important at this point to assess the gender-specific ways that women are experiencing adjustment and absorbing the shock through their paid work in and outside the home. Indeed, women's unpaid and paid work are highly interconnected, and just as women's expanding work in the household may constrain their participation in the labor force, their increasingly difficulties in earning a livelihood make the new demands at home that much harder to meet. In taking this position, I hope to complement other feminist analyses of economic policy based on structural adjustment, demonstrating through the Nicaraguan case the need for greater attention to forms of women's economic and political participation that extend beyond the home.

WOMEN AND THE INTERNATIONAL ECONOMY

In her examination of male bias in the development process, Diane Elson (1991: 164) writes that "macro-economic problems, such as large balance of payments deficits, high inflation rates and very low growth rates, have devastated many countries in Asia, Africa,

Latin America and the Caribbean." She notes that these problems stem from both internal and external problems and that many countries have no choice but to look to the International Monetary Fund (IMF) and the World Bank for financial assistance. Elson was among the first to challenge the supposedly gender-neutral programs of economic stabilization and structural adjustment that are introduced as conditions of international assistance. These include plans to reduce inflation, privatize industry, increase export production, decontrol prices, and cut public expenditures.

As Elson and others (Benería and Feldman 1992; Afshar and Dennis 1992) have noted, adjustment programs that are designed to streamline economies and enhance competitiveness are based on macroeconomic concepts that apply to economies overall rather than to particular enterprises or households. Therefore, they rarely examine the disproportionate number of women who are located in the small industries and informal businesses that are apt to suffer most from the new policies. Nor are they likely to notice that when unemployment rises, food costs go up, and health care and education become less widely available, it is women who must adjust to meet pressing family needs. Because the work of stretching household budgets, caring for the ill, and in general managing to get along under conditions of economic and psychological stress are unpaid services that do not apparently affect the market, they are overlooked by development planners. Yet there is increasing evidence that women's ability to cushion the blow of economic adjustment is not without limits, and many households are suffering serious consequences from the crises produced by recent policies.

Research has shown that where men are present as contributors to households in Third World countries, they typically offer a smaller portion of what they earn to meet family expenses and keep more for personal spending than women, even though their incomes are generally higher; in contrast, whether or not women are the sole providers in their families, they tend to turn almost all their income to collective needs (Blumberg 1991). Gender inequality in unpaid service to families is even more apparent, with women performing far more of the work of family maintenance. Unequal economic power is frequently accompanied by domestic conflict and violence against women, a serious social problem that is now coming to public attention largely because of women's activism. Thus, if we are interested not only in aggregate measures of economic development but also in social justice, we need to disaggregate the household to discover patterns of resource allocation, the gender division of labor, and gender relations in the home (Tinker 1990).

In an analysis that considers the microdynamics of class and gender as households respond to structural adjustment at the macroeconomic level, Benería (in Benería and Feldman 1992: viii) describes the deepening inequalities that are emerging. While she notes the significant absence of proposed alternatives to structural adjustment, she judges that, given women's key roles in the household and beyond, they will be instrumental in efforts to resolve current problems. In fact, she and others (e.g., Elson 1992; Pérez-Alemán et al. 1992) point to evidence of women's organizing in grassroots social movements in ways that may ultimately transform societies. In the Nicaraguan case, women contributed significantly in the period of social revolution and they have demonstrated a determination to play a similar role even under drastically changed circumstances since 1990.[1]

THE NICARAGUAN ECONOMY IN THE SANDINISTA PERIOD

When the Sandinistas came to power in 1979 following their long struggle against the Somoza dictatorship, they faced almost insurmountable problems of underdevelopment, among them an impoverished population, poorly managed resources, and inadequate health care and education. In their first few years in government they carried out a broad program of agrarian reform, created a mixed economy and improved working conditions, made medical care and education widely avail-

able, and addressed issues of gender inequality as perpetuated through the media, the law, and other social institutions. Through the Nicaraguan Women's Association (AMNLAE), they worked with women in both the rural and the urban sectors to promote social participation in support of the revolution.

Within a few years, however, the conflict known as the Contra War required the development of a wartime economy that left little in the budget to sustain the development that was under way. Analysts have described the Sandinista period as a decade of both enormous hope and deep disappointment as the country struggled to bring about structural change while defending itself against internal and external aggression.[2] Until 1983, the economy experienced growth and social services expanded, but the strain produced by the war and by a U.S. economic embargo became great enough that by 1985 an economic adjustment was imposed to try to stabilize the economy. As the formal economy crumbled, the informal sector of unregulated small enterprises expanded, serving as a safety valve for rising unemployment.

The high cost of defending the country and continuing to subsidize social services such as health care and education had contributed to spiraling inflation and a large deficit. Attempting to reverse the trend, the government implemented the 1988 Stabilization and Adjustment Program—shifting from domestic production and consumption to export-oriented production, devaluing the currency, laying off thousands of workers in the public sector (a measure known as *compactación*), and drastically cutting social services. The government continued to provide food packages of sugar, beans, and rice to state employees, as well as subsidies for basic needs such as transportation, electricity, and water. Even so, the social cost of the adjustment was high and women were affected most adversely by the measures both as workers in less secure jobs and as family members responsible for child care and household maintenance (Brenes et al. 1991).

During this period of economic crisis, when households needed income earners, more women sought to enter the labor market. As the formal sector shrank, many urban women sought employment in the informal sector, where they found increased competition. As early as 1985, 60 percent of employed women were in the informal sector, compared with 49 percent of employed men (Pérez-Alemán et al. 1992: 245). Women continued to experience higher levels of unemployment and lower wages and other earnings than men, an especially critical disparity given the large proportion of female-headed households (conservatively estimated at about 45 percent in Managua). Women were also hit harder as artisans and as workers in small industries, since most available inputs were directed to large private and state industries, and credit was tightened.

Thus, when the Sandinista government brought about a devaluation of the national currency and massive cuts in the public sector, the results were severe for the majority of the population and especially for low-income women. This accounts in significant part for the Sandinistas' electoral loss two years later and for the gender gap in the vote, with more women than men supporting the opposition. Nevertheless, the adjustment programs adopted by the postrevolutionary governments since 1990 have had even more severe consequences. Privatization, cuts in social spending, and a reduction of the state sector are familiar by now as key elements in the structural adjustment program, but in Nicaragua, the rate at which these measures have been implemented has been crushing—particularly for a country that had grown accustomed to the state providing a safety net for those most vulnerable in the society.

THE POST-SANDINISTA PERIOD

Soon after taking power, the Chamorro government embraced the structural adjustment model in an effort to stabilize the economy. Key components of the program have included reducing government spending (cutting back state sector employment and eliminating government subsidies of food, public utilities, and transportation), increasing the sales tax (affecting the poor most, since they spend a greater proportion of their income on goods that are taxed), devaluing the currency, increasing interest rates and reducing access to credit, privatizing state enterprises, promoting assembly plants in the free trade zone (largely textiles), and eliminating import tariffs (allowing cheaper imported goods to undercut national production). As a result of these harsh measures, 700,000 Nicaraguans left the country to seek work elsewhere, whenever possible sending home remissions to allow their families to escape the worst economic hardship.[3]

A new monetary plan in 1991 included a major currency devaluation that caused sharp socioeconomic dislocations as real wages fell and prices of many basic goods rose out of reach for the majority. That year, the Occupational Conversion Plan, funded by the Agency for International Development (AID), offered up to US$2,000 in severance pay to state-sector workers who would give up their jobs "voluntarily." Some 30,000 left by 1993 (25 percent of the total, and disproportionately women) and many more did so in the next couple of years. Some paid off debts and many more began selling food and other household items informally from their homes—having the intended effect of shifting workers from the public to the private sector.[4] By 1992, the "Year of Reactivation," privatization of industries and export-oriented production were proceeding apace. Inflation was brought under control, yet all indicators showed that Nicaragua had never had a worse depression, with levels of unemployment and poverty unprecedented in the country's history. Formal-sector employment dropped 18 percent in two years, with many workers leaving jobs in health, education, and other public services. Unemployment rose to 19 percent and underemployment to 45 percent (Envío, 1992a: 18–20). The figures reached 20 percent and 54 percent respectively by 1995, making the unemployment rate twice that of 1990 and ten times that of 1984 (Arana 1997:84).

An agreement known as the ESAF (Enhanced Structural Adjustment Facility) was signed in 1994 with the International Monetary Fund (IMF). In return for balance of payment stability, broad and stringent conditions had to be met. At the macroeconomic level there were signs of growth and recovery, but new problems emerged a year later when the country could not meet the requirements set by the IMF. The foreign debt reached over $11 billion, the highest per capita debt in the world. Furthermore, the wide gap between rich and poor remained, with poverty conditions unabated, and the high social cost of the plan came to be viewed as a key political issue.

With the rapid entry of competing foreign industries and products, cuts in credit available to national industry, and the removal of subsidies and some price controls, small producers and sellers faced a shortage of the primary materials needed in their work and a declining demand for the items they offer for sale. The strategy of establishing free-trade zones and favoring large industries that are more competitive in the world market, as well as sharply reducing protective tariffs on imported goods, has driven out many small industries and threatens to weaken many more in Nicaragua. As a result, the informal sector has expanded to absorb displaced workers from industries and from the shrinking, "more efficient" state sector.

Viewed by Western development analysts, the Nicaraguan government, and even some critics as inevitable, structural adjustment has curbed inflation while contributing to high levels of unemployment, declining real wages, and a sharply falling standard of living. Access to basic health care and education, available to all during the Sandinista period, became a privilege for the middle class. Although many new products, including luxury items, have entered the market, few people have the resources to buy them.

Once widely considered gender-neutral, structural adjustment has had particularly harsh consequences for women—something that has received attention in Nicaragua (Fundación Internacional para el Desafío Económico Global—FIDEG, 1991a). Researchers have noted that the redistributive impact has been largely at the expense of women (Stahler-Sholk 1997; Metoyer 1997). Often, when men made up the majority of the newly unemployed, women were more numerous among the underemployed (Renzi and Agurto 1993). Since women made up the majority of state workers, they were disproportionately affected by cuts in the public sector, which sent many of them into the informal sector (Evans 1995). At work and in the family, women have often provided the cushion needed when resources are in short supply. Women seek new sources of income, stretch household budgets, and take up the slack by offering services that are no longer provided by the government. Thus, any success that structural adjustment may have in contributing to "productivity" and "efficiency" depends on a longer working day for women, who carry the major responsibility for maintaining their families. And this, of course, leaves in place the underlying structural basis of economic crises and gender inequality.

WOMEN AND URBAN COOPERATIVES

Changes in economic policy in Nicaragua have had particularly adverse consequences for low-income women. Throughout the country, women have worked harder to earn a livelihood and support their families, and in the capital city of Managua many have turned to small industries and commerce, organized formally or informally and based outside or within their homes. The government offered little assistance to small and medium-size enterprises or the informal sector, where the majority of Nicaraguans find employment, and instead relied on market forces which favored larger industries. When assistance was offered to small enterprises, the impact was limited.

During the Sandinista period, many small-scale producers were organized into cooperatives in the urban sector, just as in the rural, agricultural sector. The cooperatives were part of the state project to formalize and collectivize small industries to increase production and build class unity among workers. These co-ops benefited from the distribution of low-cost materials and from the state's assistance in marketing their products. Women were drawn into the newly formed cooperatives for the same reasons men were, but also as part of the deliberate effort to include women in the revolutionary process.[5] Unfortunately, while women were drawn into cooperatives as well as mass organizations, traditional gender relations persisted at home, making it difficult for women to carry out many new responsibilities and avoid men's criticism that they were not fulfilling their family "duty." Many men, even those who in principle supported women's right and responsibility to engage in the wider economy, feared that their wives were beyond their control as they gained access to space in the public sphere. Implicit or explicit was the traditional invocation of women's proper place in the home (*en la casa*) and not in the "street" (*en la calle*). Some women bowed to the challenge to their propriety as wives and mothers and left work in cooperatives, but many others actively engaged in economic and political work that took them outside the household. Unfortunately, economic policy in the postrevolutionary period generally has not favored small industry, instead encouraging foreign investment and larger industries that can better compete in the global market. As a result, many small industries (estimated at over half nationwide) failed in the early 1990s, and those that remained have struggled in the new political economic context (*Barricada Internacional*, 1993).

My ethnographic research in Managua sought to provide in-depth local-level studies of working women as a window through which to view the effects of the dramatically shifting policy and the responses of women to these changes. Although women working in small industries and commerce form the majority of employed urban women in the country, they have rarely been the focus of research. The four urban cooperatives I discuss here formed after the Sandinista victory, one as late as 1991. Two of the co-ops were made up exclusively of women, while women

figured prominently in the other two. Two involved women in traditional gender roles, in the preparation of clothing and food, and the others in nontraditional ones, in welding and artisanry. All felt the impact of the changing economic policies, and the women interviewed noted the adjustments that they themselves were making at work and at home in order to get by. These are frequently viewed as coping or survival strategies, but they should also be understood as women's response to economic policies that are transferring work from the public to the private sector. In their workplaces and in the household, women absorb the shock of the economic crisis, and in so doing they underwrite the very policies that adversely affect them.

WOMEN'S UNITED TEXTILE COOPERATIVE

The Women's United Textile Cooperative formed in 1982 as a service co-op, made up of women sewing clothing at home who came on a rotating basis to sell their clothes from a small store in Managua's Mercado Oriental (Eastern Market) district. Like other service co-ops formed under the Sandinista government, they benefited from the availability of lower-priced materials, in their case fabric and thread. They enjoyed the friendships they made with other women workers, and along with many other cooperatives they joined the National Chamber of Medium- and Small-Scale Industry (CONAPI), which allocated supplies and offered other support.

The co-op began with 68 members, but by 1991 its membership had declined to 29. Many of the remaining women were among the founders, now middle-aged or older women, who regarded the co-op as a sort of family to which they owed their loyalty. Like others in small industries, they identified the problems they were experiencing as stemming from postrevolutionary government support of large industries and elimination of assistance to small industries in the name of the "free market." The garment producers were particularly hard hit, however, as imported new and used clothing from the United States and elsewhere began flooding the market and underselling them. For those who retained active membership in the co-op, the altered conditions and slower sales stalled their production, and many sought other sources of income. Some began selling soft drinks or other items from their homes, and some, ironically, entered in the business of selling used clothing. As one woman put it, "The *compañeras* understand that I do it out of necessity."

The first half of 1992 saw an even more serious downturn for this cooperative. Its store, which had displayed racks of clothing made at home by members, stood nearly bare, and almost no customers came to make purchases. The women continued taking turns coming to the store but mainly to safeguard their property and to share a midday meal that they prepared together; everyone ate, regardless of ability to pay, and they had each other's company at a time when the mood was grim. Some expressed resentment that CONAPI had used them as a "battle horse" for the organization, praising the women's relatively long history and commitment, but saying nothing when times were hard. They were particularly bitter because the new president of CONAPI had been in the garment industry himself but changed to another business in time to avoid the problems they were facing. They felt that he had had a responsibility to advise them but instead had only looked out for his own interests.

The cooperative dealt in isolation with the difficult question of whether to sell its store and dissolve the co-op or to hang on a while longer. On my last visit to the store that year, I found the women in low spirits, feeling defeated, with a single rack of clothing for sale. Sadly, the items were imported second-hand clothing from the United States. One woman summed up the situation by saying, "The truth is, our chances of surviving here are slim." Indeed, when I returned to Nicaragua early in 1993 I was surprised to find that the store had simply vanished. Upon questioning, I learned that the co-op members had sold the store to a neighboring clothing retailer, who had absorbed the space to enlarge his own establishment. It took me several weeks to locate members who still identified actively with the cooperative and worked on some basis from their homes or in the streets. These women spoke of trying to find a new space in which to work together again, but in the meantime they were changing leadership and preparing to carry out business from the new coordinator's home.

Although the co-op's clothing production has dropped off sharply since that time, some members have put more time into attracting sales by selling to clients from their homes and from market stalls in the streets. Some have added shoes or other merchandise to their offerings. Still others concentrate on working to meet the seasonal demand for new school uniforms or Easter dresses. Those who continue to sew find that locating acceptable-quality fabric and thread at reasonable prices is more difficult, and therefore more time is put into searching for supplies. Several women travel regularly to other Central American countries to purchase sewing supplies or ready-made apparel at lower prices.

If economic policies that favor large garment factories and imported clothing have not yet put the women of this cooperative out of business, they are nonetheless struggling harder to retain sales. They extend their hours of work, diversify their production and their market, and travel greater distances to purchase materials and to make sales. In all these ways, they not only support themselves and their families but also underwrite the process of structural adjustment through their resolve to work harder and withstand its force. In spite of all their efforts, the women who continue to identity as members of the cooperative are still threatened with the prospect of failure.

INDUSTRIAL BAKERS OF MANAGUA

The largest service cooperative of bakeries, Industrial Bakers of Managua, was established in 1979. More men than women became members, but many had wives who worked closely with them, and a number of women owners of bakeries were represented as well. As members of the trade union organization CONAPI, they benefited from the co-op's provision of basic materials such as flour at lower cost. The co-op owned ample office space in a working-class neighborhood, where meetings were held regularly by the leadership.

Bread producers would seem to have the advantage of engaging in a business that would have a constant demand. Yet, as more bakeries open there is more competition, with larger enterprises having more chance of success. Some bakers reported changing with the times to offer popular items like pizza or sweet pastries. In one bakery where I conducted interviews, the family is proud of its college-educated daughter, who handles the bookkeeping and manages the enterprise, no doubt contributing to its success. Another family in the bakery business has cornered the market in one city neighborhood, with the mother doing business near a major traffic circle and her daughter managing her own bakery just a block away. The daughter has space for a half-dozen tables where customers can sit down to enjoy pastry and something to drink, thus drawing more people to the bakery. But even in these more fortunate enterprises production was declining sharply and the loss of income was threatening families' economic survival.

In early 1992, the cooperative ceased to function, having been driven out of operation when suppliers of flour began selling directly to the bakeries at favorable prices. Unable to compete, the co-op put its offices up for sale, and the bakeries I visited began viewing their enterprises as independent. They saw little advantage in affiliating with a trade-union organization that was itself struggling for survival. A year later the co-op's property remained unsold, and the formerly active secretary came periodically to sell a small quantity of bread there, half hoping that the co-op could be revived—a prospect that looked less and less likely. Bakery owners in general were divided between those who adopted the

government attitude regarding the desirability of open competition and others who looked back nostalgically on the more protective policies of the Sandinista goverment. All appeared critical of CONAPI, noting its lack of support for the co-ops, whether or not they favored the continuation of the bakery cooperative. And all were demoralized by the economic situation that further reduced bread consumption as many families bought tortillas and even bananas as cheaper substitutes.

This cooperative's experience suggests that while some individuals place responsibility for their present difficulties on CONAPI or on the bakers' co-op itself, their problems stem from increasing competition and lack of government support in the market-driven economy. Like the garment producers, the bakers are highly resourceful, yet both are reporting that production is being cut dramatically, often by 50 percent, as sales dwindle.

FRANCISCO ESTRADA COOPERATIVE

Five jewelry makers and five bark-work artisans came together in 1987, working out of the home of one woman, a German who had come to Nicaragua in solidarity with the revolution during its early years. They founded the Francisco Estrada cooperative, named for an artisan and national hero, and became active within CONAPI. The men and women who made up their workshop included experienced jewelers who worked with silver, malachite, and black coral, resources found in the country, as well as a woman who specialized in making ornamental wall hangings and other items from the bark of trees found on the Atlantic coast. The latter trained several other women who became part of the co-op, though she herself left to work independently. Despite the high quality of their work, sales have remained low, limited to foreigners in Nicaragua seeking unusual artisans' crafts and the small number of Nicaraguans who can afford ornamental items. Two men, jewelry makers, left the co-op in 1992, and the other members explained their departure by saying that the men could not accept the crisis conditions that they were collectively facing. In response to these conditions, members began slowing down production and seeking new markets to increase sales.

As in the sewing cooperative described above, members of this co-op substituted time spent in marketing their products for production time. Often, several members would take an afternoon off to visit hotels or shops that might sell their jewelry or bark items. They also explored possibilities of exporting their work to European markets, however these efforts did not result in many opportunities to expand their sales. Another strategy has been to try new techniques and designs to capture the interest of the buying public. This has sometimes backfired, however, as when two of the women invested many hours and costly materials to create several folding room screens with detailed bark work—and then the client, who had commissioned the work with a down payment, failed to come up with the remaining money owed. The co-op considered whether the bark workers should be apprenticed as jewelers (one already had been), since jewelry sales were somewhat better.

By 1993, however, the two remaining bark workers had left the co-op to return to their homes. Both said that the needs of their husbands and children demanded more of their time. Certainly another factor in the women's decisions was the very low level of their sales. They had virtually been subsidized by the jewelry makers for some time and may have considered themselves a liability to the co-op. In better times they might not have faced this difficult decision. More recently, the cooperative sought and received financial support to build a separate workshop and expand its productive capacity. Following months of effort requiring many visits to various offices, CONAPI and a Norwegian nongovernmental organization (NGO) gave the co-op the loan they needed for the construction. The artisans hope that as their visibility and their productive capacity grow, so will their sales. They have apprenticed several new women in jewelry making

and have stepped up efforts to find markets outside Nicaragua. They acknowledge that they are taking a risk in incurring debts as they expand production, but morale has improved as they enjoy their spacious new workshop and the new equipment they have acquired.

As in the first two cooperatives described, this one has had some internal problems, but in general members have worked hard to build a successful working environment and viable business. The artisans in the Francisco Estrada co-op are recognized for the high quality and design of their products, but sales are down at a time when international travel to Nicaragua is low, few Nicaraguans purchase ornamental items, and those who do find better buys in imported jewelry and other artisanry from neighboring countries. While some government officials claim that so many small industries are failing because of the poor quality of their products and poor managerial skills, the examples offered here suggest ways in which new policies favoring larger industries and imported goods undermine the best efforts of many small producers.

WELDERS' COOPERATIVE

Finally, a fourth cooperative is one of welders that formed in 1991 after a group of ten formerly unemployed women completed a trade-school course. The women's preparation included not only ten months of technical training in welding but also consciousness-raising workshops organized by the vocational program INATEC (National Technical Institute) to ready them as women for nontraditional work. A sample of their work was displayed at an International Women's Day festival and soon afterward they inaugurated their workshop with a gala opening in one of Managua's women's centers, sponsored by AMNLAE. In high spirits, the women began their work with support from local organizations, making wrought-iron chairs and tables, plant stands, and security bars for windows and doors.

Jobs kept them busy in the early months, but then work tapered off and interpersonal problems developed over how work was shared. Some felt that the co-coordinators were lacking in necessary leadership skills. Other differences emerged when CONAPI sought their participation and the director of the AMNLAE center where they worked resisted this decision on feminist grounds, saying that the women would lose their autonomy under the male-dominated leadership. By mid1992 only two welders from the original group remained active in the co-op. One of the co-coordinators, judged by others to be too much of an individualist for the cooperative, left to work in partnership with a male welder. Lack of work and heavy family responsibilities kept some women away, including a few who hoped to resume their work later. Eight new women began a training course, but within a few months only three remained. The continuing coordinator of the co-op surmised that the cost of transportation to the training center was prohibitive when the women lacked paid employment.

Despite these setbacks, the remaining welders devised several strategies for the survival of their co-op. Besides training new women, they consulted with several individuals regarding the promotion of their work. One woman, the designated advertising manager, polled the others concerning ways of becoming better-known around the city. The women continued to receive a few jobs by word of mouth and through INATEC. Given the competitive nature of work in welding and the discrimination against women in the field, the future looked uncertain. Those remaining in the co-op depended, for the most part, on other sources of family support to get through that difficult period. The women talked about refashioning the co-op as a microenterprise—a legal entity of up to five workers promoted by the government—to increase their likelihood of receiving a loan. During this time, two Peace Corps volunteers became involved with the welders, offering them workshops designed for women in small businesses and encouraging them to apply for development grants. To take this suggestion,

however, they would have needed to invest more unpaid time before seeing a return, something they could ill afford.

By 1993 the welders' co-op had disbanded. Citing the family obligations of the other women, the former coordinator (the only single woman among them) expressed disappointment at their failure to continue working together. The lack of work and an unresolved disagreement over the use of space in the women's center surely entered into the decision of the women to return home, though the coordinator emphasized the "jealousy of husbands." Her own passionate commitment to welding led her to join briefly with several male welders, but the relationship was a tenuous one. Her outlook during our last meeting was grim.

In this cooperative, the only one of the four discussed here that had ceased to function by 1993, family needs and expectations were often cited as drawing women back home and away from their paid work. This was also the case for the two women doing bark work in the last co-op mentioned. While this might be interpreted as the result of individual circumstances rather than changing economic and political conditions, I would maintain that the two are intertwined. As I have noted, structural adjustment has often resulted in heavier responsibilities for women at home when social services are cut, health care and education costs rise, and household incomes drop. The competing demands on women's time and energy, often divided between the family and the workplace, become especially acute when conditions of austerity and adjustment combine with a conservative social ideology. At a certain point the day can be stretched no farther and women must negotiate "personal" solutions to their collective problems.

WOMEN IN THE URBAN INFORMAL SECTOR

As women in cooperatives and other formal-sector employment are losing ground in Managua, many are turning to a precarious livelihood in the urban informal sector. There, small-scale production and commerce, often based in the home, do not benefit from protective legislation or the representation of a trade-union organization. While earnings are typically quite low, there is great diversity within the informal sector in terms of economic activities and the individuals who perform them (Chamorro, Chávez, and Membreño, 1991).

The urban informal sector has for some time included over half of Managua's economically active population, but there has been significant growth in recent years. Under the Sandinista government, some informal workers were "formalized" as they joined cooperatives and state enterprises. Now that these are being reduced in the interest of streamlining the economy, people are falling back on independent and informal activities. Recent policy has had the effect of transferring even more workers from the public to the private sector. The Plan for Occupational Reconversion, mentioned before, was introduced to encourage public-sector employees to leave their jobs and set up small businesses. Many who left public-sector jobs were Sandinistas, considered undesirable by the new government, or women, viewed as appropriately turning their attention back home. Home is no refuge, however, when women must work double time to take care of families and earn incomes by undertaking a host of small-scale informal activities in manufacturing and commerce. Far from supporting sustainable enterprises, one result of the plan was an abundance of freezer purchases allowing people to sell drinks or ice out of their homes.

The Managua barrio where I stay is known for its high concentration of artisans and sellers and a smaller number of professionals. I have found city blocks in which a majority of households are also small commercial establishments, operating both informally and formally. Small restaurants, barbershops, and carpenters', tailors', and mechanics' workshops are among the most visible. Less obvious from the street are the many households engaged in selling small quantities of fruit,

vegetables, soft drinks, or other goods out of their homes' front rooms. In the poorest families, children add to the family income by selling in the streets or by asking for tips for guarding parked cars.

Interviews with people in this barrio often led from conversations about declining business and deteriorating standards of living to discussions of how women are attempting to survive crisis conditions. The stories told in people's homes were often poignant. A young woman I spoke with one morning as her two children sat nearby was employed as a teacher but seeking other sources of income to support her family. Her husband's business had failed four years before, around the time her second child was born. Under the Sandinistas they had received the package of support for state workers that included rice, beans, and sugar. Now they received no such benefits. Her husband had been deeply affected by his unemployment, consulting a psychologist and later converting to an evangelical faith that had finally brought him some peace of mind.

Another young woman I visited lived with her three children, selling ice cream, soap, and chlorine from her home to support them. Her brother, who had once lived with them, had taken his life two months earlier out of despair over the economic situation they faced. The woman talked on for a time, distraught and clearly needing to unburden herself. She blamed privatization and other changes in the country for her brother's suicide, adding that women were the most affected, especially because many did not have the support of men at home.

A visit with another woman in the barrio led to a conversation with a number of family members. In all, 30 people were living in the four rooms of her home. Besides her husband and five children, her mother and several sisters and their husbands shared the household, as did their many children. This woman had been an active Sandinista and her husband had been part of the revolutionary insurrection. Their hardship by the early 1990s was clearly demonstrated by their surroundings and their dress. When I visited, they had no water or electricity, since they could not pay the bills. Their lack of a functioning refrigerator affected not only their eating habits but also their ability to sell food or drink items from their home. Their close quarters were unbearably hot, with no fan to relieve them, and they had to carry water in pails from a park a few blocks away. As they took me through their very crowded house, they indicated the number of people who slept in each of the beds and joked self-consciously about the sorry state of their inexpensive shoes.

The sources of family income in this household included the husband's low salary as a police officer, a son-in-law's employment as a typographer, another son-in-law's earnings as a market porter, and a daughter-in-law's sales of cooked ears of corn, candy, and gum in the street in front of their home. A teen-aged daughter who worked part-time helping in meal preparation and cleaning in the home of a neighbor may have been the top income-earner in the family, making just over $100 a month; she lost the job soon after my visit, however, when she was caught stealing from her employer. While three of the older children in the family attended college, most of the children had dropped out of school because of new fees and the rising cost of uniforms and shoes.

With little money even for food, the family sometimes had nothing to eat. They tried to feed the youngest ones first, when possible. In the morning, they generally had coffee; when there was no milk, the children drank sugared water. Other foods they bought included rice, eggs, cheese, and tortillas, but rarely beans since the price had risen so high. In the past they had shopped in a supermarket to save money, but by this point they were purchasing just a little at a time at a corner market to save on transportation costs and because they had little cash on hand at any given time. With medical costs rising, they made few trips to see doctors, and their general level of health appeared rather poor.

Like many in the barrio, members of this family expressed the view that things were far better before the Sandinistas lost the elections in 1990. They mentioned the distribution of basic foods, the better employment situation, and the active part they had played in neighborhood politics. "Now there is nothing," they said. When I asked if men and women were affected differently, they first said no, but then the senior woman added that women suffered more because they cared for the children and had to see that low incomes stretched to meet family needs.

Another woman who had lived in the barrio for many years was in somewhat better circumstances. Several adults, including her grown children, contributed income to her household. She herself managed a front-room store, selling items that she advertised with a number of makeshift signs displayed outside her door along with Sandinista campaign posters left over from the 1990 elections. The signs suggested the range of goods that she had sold at one time or another: cheese, cream, beans, bread, and snacks, ice and ice cream, soft drinks, *chicha*, black dye, used clothes. She smiled when I asked if she sold all of these items, saying that she was currently selling just a few things, including bread, cheese, cream, eggs, soft drinks, and beer.

Beginning in 1960, she and her husband sold materials for shoemaking, but the business was declining by the late 1970s. With the "Triumph" in 1979, they started the store she has today and during the next decade they expanded to sell basic grains. Yet by 1988–1989, this business was also suffering, and by 1993 they were even worse off. She attributed the economic problems of the Sandinista government to the war and the blockade and said that at least people had had something to eat, since the government had provided basic foods at lower prices. Before, there were loans for small businesses, but now those who could get them had to pay high interest rates for short-term loans. With no money circulating and high unemployment caused by the poor leadership of the new government, she told me, the situation was critical.

This woman described for me how she and her family got along during a recent "difficult time" when her sales were low. Although she is skilled as a seamstress and still has a sewing machine in her front room where she used to sew for clients, she now sews mainly for family. Her husband's small retirement income helped, as did the food and other needed supplies brought by friends from time to time. Much of the personal support that she counted on, however, came from her long-time political commitment to a group of women whose relatives had been killed or disappeared during the revolutionary insurrection. As a community leader she had a wide network of friends and acquaintances who met often, and she told me that this helped relieve some of the psychological pressure that is prevalent in the country as a consequence of the economic crisis. Her story suggests the importance of women's organizing to confront current political and economic conditions and to maintain a safety net of social support.

STRUCTURAL ADJUSTMENT OR STRUCTURAL CHANGE?

Women in Managua's barrios did not all share the same political views, but many of them sounded critical of the postrevolutionary government as they commented on the ways in which they were coping at home and at work with low earnings, rising prices, and inadequate services. Many noted that their families' eating habits had changed; instead of waking up to large meals of rice, beans, eggs, and cheese, they just had a bit of *gallopinto* (mixed rice and beans) and coffee. Instead of having three abundant meals, including meat, each day, they included meat in their diet only about once a week. They looked longer and harder for less expensive foods. Other women cut back on transportation costs, opting to walk to places where they had formerly taken buses. Some who had had the resources in the past to hire other women to wash and iron their clothes were doing this work themselves. Those who had always done this work themselves were restricting it to once or twice a week to save on soap and electricity. In addition, with an apparent

deterioration of physical and mental health in the country, women were taking on the care of family members in ill health. These household responses to the crisis conditions brought on by adjustment policies in Nicaragua have parallels in a number of other Third World countries.

What is distinct about Nicaragua is the way in which the fast pace and devastating effects of these policies have eroded the gains brought about with the Sandinista revolution. Yet, also distinct is the readiness of the population to mobilize in opposition to these policies. The decade of broad participation left a legacy of expectations that has been challenged but not eliminated since 1990. The persistent determination of Nicaraguans to take part in the political process and to retain their hard-won rights is expressed in everyday strategies of resistance to the economic crisis, as well as through organized social protests.

I suggested at the beginning of this essay that we need to reexamine women's strategies for confronting crisis conditions in their paid work as well as at home. By offering examples of women working in urban cooperatives and in the urban informal sector, I have shown that even in instances where production and sales have slowed down, working women often step up their efforts to get by. They often work longer hours to find affordable materials, to acquire the skills they need, and to gain access to markets for their products. The strain of surviving under conditions that are driving many small industries and commercial enterprises out of business surely affects their ability to carry out family responsibilities, too. Therefore, we need to examine the interconnectedness of women's unpaid and paid work as both are extended in response to current economic policies.

Almost half of the households in Nicaragua's cities are headed by women, and women make up at least 44 percent of the economically active population. Policies that do not take gender into account stand to have serious effects on the health and well-being of these women and their children. My work and that of others (Afshar and Dennis, 1992; Benería and Feldman, 1992; Elson, 1991) presents evidence that structural adjustment is cushioned by women whose discretionary time and energy are already extremely limited. The human cost of recent policies will be seen in the long term if the consequences of these policies are not considered now.

Structural adjustment, by introducing new competition and reducing national demand, has led to the decline of many urban cooperatives and small industries established under the Sandinistas in Nicaragua. A report by CONAPI (*Barricada Internacional,* 1993) indicated that some 7,000 small and medium-sized industries and services closed in 1992 alone, leaving just 3,000 shops registered with the Ministry of Economy. Since women have been disproportionately represented in the co-ops and industries, the decline has hit them particularly hard.

Some writers have argued that more enlightened approaches to structural adjustment would lower the high cost exacted among the most vulnerable sectors in Third World countries (Cornia, Jolly, and Stewart, 1987; UNICEF, 1989). However, they overlook the adverse effects of adjustment programs on both men and women in broad sectors of the population and the ways in which structural inequalities of gender, class, and race serve to underwrite economic "stabilization." We have seen that women, in particular, subsidize the cost of national development through their extended workdays. Other analysts more in line with the view presented here have been more critical of structural adjustment and have called for discussion of more far-reaching structural transformation (Gladwin, 1991). Such discussion should be informed by the experiences of countries such as Nicaragua that have broken away—for a time—from the dominant economic development models.

In Nicaragua, a nation that has seen the structural transformation of the 1980s rolled back to a significant degree since the 1990 election, discussion of alternatives to the current economic model has begun (*Envío,*1992b). During a brief period, the country went through two major transitions, from a market economy dominated by the Somoza family dictatorship to a state-regulated economy under the Sandinistas and back to a market-driven program under postrevolutionary governments. These were not simple shifts between capitalist and socialist models, however, but rather negotiated processes that often allowed for unexpected economic juxtapositions. While state intervention in the market characterized the Sandinista period, the current period is also marked by a significant degree of market regulation by the government (Spoor, 1994). The political lines from the 1980s to the present have been no less complicated. Just as some Sandinistas became critical of the party and adopted a supportive stance in relation to government policy, some business elites supported the Sandinistas in the past and currently oppose undercutting national production through structural adjustment. While it was widely expected that the gains of the revolution would be dismantled in the post-Sandinista period, the transition has been considerably more complex (Spalding, 1994: 157).

Not surprisingly, women are among the most vocal in questioning the current economic model and pressing for substantive change. As active participants in the Nicaraguan revolution, they claimed a space in which to assert their rights to full citizenship. In the late 1980s these women found new ways to organize and confront difficult conditions as the demands on their time increased both in the labor force and at home. Although women's participation in political organizations declined in the 1990s, their engagement in the labor movement grew stronger (Pérez-Alemán et al., 1992: 250). In the postrevolutionary period, there have been new openings for women's activism despite the deepening problems the country is facing. While AMNLAE no longer plays a strong leadership role, emergent feminist and women's organizations are growing along with NGOs and social movements. Thus, while women in Managua's urban cooperatives and informal economy are experiencing tough economic conditions in their workplaces and their homes, through their struggle for better lives and livelihoods these women are also challenging Nicaraguans to seek alternative national policies that will benefit all of society.

NOTES

1. For further discussion of the impact of structural adjustment on women in Nicaragua since 1990, see Babb 1996, 2001, Metoyer 2000, and Fernández Poncela 1996.
2. A number of writers have offered extensive analyses of this decade of revolutionary government in Nicaragua (e.g., Booth 1985; Spalding 1987; Walker 1986, 1991; Martínez Cuenca 1992). A few have considered the situation of women in the revolutionary process (Randall 1981; Molyneux 1986; Padilla, Murguialday, and Criquillon 1987; Collinson 1990; Kampwirth 2002). See Babb 1996 and Criquillon 1995 for discussion of emergent feminism in Nicaragua in the postrevolutionary period.
3. A summary of the effects of neoliberalism and structural adjustment is offered by Nicholson in the newsletter *Nicaraguan Developments* 7(1):4–5 (1999).
4. In his discussion of structural adjustment programs under the Sandinista and post-Sandinista governments, Stahler-Sholk (1997) indicates that while Violeta Chamorro de Barrios's government made some attempt to soften the blow of adjustment by offering limited support for employment, this barely offset the growing rate of unemployment.
5. See Montoya 1996 for a useful discussion of women's involvement in two rural cooperatives organized during the Sandinista period and the mixed success they had due to difficulties faced by many cooperatives as well as persistent male bias against women's participation in the economy and society beyond the household. Her work examines the general problems women faced as they made claims to public space usually controlled by men. See also Pérez Alemán 1990 for discussion of women's participation in rural cooperatives in the Sandinista period and the

This essay is adapted from chapter five of my book, *After Revolution: Mapping Gender and Cultural Politics in Neoliberal Nicaragua* (University of Texas Press 2001). I am most grateful for the cooperation of many Nicaraguans who made this work possible.

difficulty of carrying the burden of housework and childcare as women performed more agricultural work.

REFERENCES

Afshar, Haleh and Carolyne Dennis (eds.). 1992. *Women and Adjustment Policies in the Third World.* New York: St. Martin's Press.

Arana, Mario. 1997. "General Economic Policy." In *Nicaragua without Illusions: Regime Transition and Structural Adjustment in the 1990s.* Thomas Walker, ed. Pp. 82–96. Wilmington, DE: SR Books.

Babb, Florence E. 1996. "Women's Movements and Feminism." In *Cross-Cultural Research for Social Science.* Carol R. Ember and Melvin Ember, eds. Pp. 23–40. Englewood Cliffs, NJ: Prentice Hall.

———. 2001. *After Revolution: Mapping Gender and Cultural Politics in Neoliberal Nicaragua.* Austin, TX: University of Texas Press.

Barricada Internacional. 1993. "Recession decimates small businesses." 13 (January): 7.

Benería, Lourdes and Shelley Feldman, eds. 1992. *Unequal Burden: Economic Crises, Persistent Poverty, and Women's Work.* Boulder, CO: Westview Press.

Blumberg, Rae Lesser. 1991. "Income under female versus male control: hypotheses from a theory of gender stratification and data from the Third World." In *Gender, Family, and Economy: The Triple Overlap.* Rae Lesser Blumberg, ed.. Pp. 97–127. Newbury Park, CA: Sage.

Booth, John A. 1985. *The End and the Beginning: The Nicaraguan Revolution.* Boulder, CO: Westview Press.

Brenes, Aria Julia, Ivania Lovo, Olga Luz Restrepo, Sylvia Saakes, and Flor de Maria Zuniga. 1991. *La Mujer Nicaragüense en los Años 80.* Managua, Nicaragua: Nicarao.

Chamorro, Amalia, Mario Chávez, and Marcos Membreño. 1991. "El Sector Informal en Nicaragua." In *Informalidad Urbana en Centroamérica: Entre la Acumulación y la Subsistencia.* J.P. Pérez Sáinz and R. Menjívar Larín, eds. Pp. 217–257.

Collinson, Helen, ed. 1990. *Women and Revolution in Nicaragua.* London: Zed Books.

Cornia, Giovanni Andrea, Richard Jolly, and Frances Stewart (eds.). 1987. *Adjustment with a Human Face.* New York: Oxford University Press.

Criquillon, Ana. 1995. "The Nicaraguan Women's Movement: Feminist Reflections From Within." *The New Politics of Survival: Grassroots Movements in Central America.* Minor Sinclair, ed. Pp. 209–237. New York: Monthly Review Press.

Elson, Diane. 1992. "From Survival Strategies to Transformation Strategies: Women's Needs and Structural Adjustment." In *Unequal Burden: Economic Crises Persistent Poverty and Women's Work.* Lourdes Benería and Shelley Feldman, eds. pp. 26–48. Boulder, CO: Westview Press.

Elson, Diane, ed. 1991. *Male Bias in the Development Process.* Manchester, England: Manchester University Press.

Envío. 1992a. "Economic takeoff: the little train that couldn't." 11 (October): 18–20.

———. 1992b. "A national project." 11 (December): 31–40.

Evans, Trevor. 1995. *La transformación neoliberal del sector público.* Managua, Nicaragua: CRIES (Coordinadora Regional de Investigaciones Económicas y Sociales).

Fernández Poncela, Anna M. 1996. The Disruptions of Adjustment: Women in Nicaragua. *Latin American Perspectives* 23(1):49–66.

Gladwin, Christina (ed.). 1991. *Structural Adjustment and African Women Farmers.* Gainesville, FL: University of Florida Press.

Kampwirth, Karen. 2002. *Women and Guerrilla Movements: Nicaragua, El Salvador, Chiapas, Cuba.* University Park, PA: The Pennsylvania State University Press.

Metoyer, Cynthia Chávez. 1997. "Nicaragua's Transition of State Power: Through Feminist Lenses." In *The Undermining of the Sandinista Revolution* Gary Prevost and Harry Vanden, eds., pp. 114–140. New York: St. Martine Press.

———. 2000. *Women and the State in Post-Sandinista Nicaragua.* Boulder, CO: Lynne Rienner.

Molyneux, Maxine. 1986. "Mobilization without emancipation? Women's interests, state, and revolution," pp. 280–302 in Richard R. Fagen, Carmen Diana Deere, and José-Luis Coraggio (eds.), *Transition and Development: Problems of Third World Socialism.* New York: Monthly Review Press.

Montoya, Rosario. 1996. *Fractured Solidarities: Utopian Projects and Local Hegemonies among a Sandinista Peasantry, Nicaragua, 1979–1995.* Ph.D. dissertation, University of Michigan.

Padilla, Martha Luz, Clara Murguialday, and Ana Criquillon. 1987. "Impact of the Sandinista Agrarian Reform on Rural Women's Subordination." In *Rural Women and State Policy: Feminist Perspectives on Latin American Agricultural Development.* Carmen Diana Deere and Magdalena León, eds. Pp. 124–141. Boulder, CO: Westview Press.

Pérez-Alemán, Paola. 1990. *Organización, identidad y cambio.* Managua, Nicaragua: Editorial Vanguardia.

Pérez-Alemán, Paola. 1992. Economic Crisis and Women in Nicaragua. In *Unequal Burden: Economic Crises, Persistent Poverty, and Women's Work.* Lourdes Beneria and Shelley Feldman, eds. pp. 239–258. Boulder, CO: Westview Press.

Randall, Margaret. 1981. *Sandino's Daughters: Testimonies of Nicaraguan Women in Struggle.* Vancouver, BC: New Star Books.

Renzi, María Rosa, and Sonia Agurto. 1993. *Que hace la mujer nicaragüense ante la crisis económica?* Managua, Nicaragua: FIDEG (Fundación Internacional para el Desafio Económico Global).

Spalding Rose J. 1987. *The Political Economy of Revolutionary Nicaragua.* Boulder, CO: Westview Press.

———. 1994. *Capitalists and Revolution in Nicaragua: Opposition and Accommodation, 1979–1993.* Chapel Hill: University of North Carolina Press.

Spoor, Max. 1994. "Issues of state and market: from interventionism to deregulation of food markets in Nicaragua." *World Development* 22 (4): 567–578.

Stahler-Sholk, Richard. 1997. "Structural Adjustment and Resistance: The Political Economy of Nicaragua under Chamorro." In *The Undermining of the Sandinista Revolution.* Gary Prevost and Harry Vanden, eds. Pp. 74–113. New York: St. Martin's Press.

Tinker, Irene (ed.). 1990. *Persistent Inequalities: Women and World Development.* New York: Oxford University *Press.*

UNICEF. 1989. *The Invisible Adjustment: Poor Women and the Economic Crisis.* Santiago, Chile: UNICEF.

Walker, Thomas W. 1986. *Nicaragua: The Land of Sandino.* Boulder, CO: Westview Press.

Walker, Thomas W. (ed.). 1991. *Revolution and Counterrevolution in Nicaragua.* Boulder: Westview Press

———. 1997. Nicaragua Without Illusions: Regime Transition and Structural Adjustment in the 1990s. Wilmington, DE: SR Books.

V

The Cultural Construction of Gender and Personhood

We all live in a world of symbols that assign meaning and value to the categories of male and female. Despite several decades of consciousness raising in the United States, advertising on television and in the print media perpetuates sexual stereotypes. Although "house beautiful" ads are less prominent as women are increasingly shown in workplace contexts, "body beautiful" messages continue to be transmitted. In children's cartoons, women are still the helpless victims that the fearless male hero must rescue. Toys are targeted either for little boys or little girls and are packaged appropriately in colors and materials culturally defined as either masculine or feminine (see Swedlund and Urla in the next section of this book).

To what extent are these stereotypes of men and women and the symbols with which they are associated universal? If they are universal, to what extent are they rooted in observed differences in the biological nature of men and women that are made culturally significant? These questions have interested scholars as they have attempted to account for both similarity and difference among the people of the world. Making the assumption that the subordination of women exists in all societies—a "true universal"—Ortner (1974: 67) sought to explain the pervasiveness of this idea not in the assignation of women to a domestic sphere of activity, but in the symbolic constructions by which women's roles are evaluated. Ortner argues that women, because of their reproductive roles, are universally viewed as being closer to nature while men are linked with culture. She defines culture as "the notion of human consciousness, or . . . the products of human consciousness (i.e., systems of thought and technology), by means of which humanity attempts to assert control over nature" (72). That which is cultural and subject to human manipulation is assigned more worth than that which is natural; hence, women and women's roles are denigrated or devalued, whether explicitly or implicitly.

The nature–culture dichotomy is a useful explanatory model in the United States where, according to Martin (1987: 17), "Women are intrinsically closely involved with the family where so many 'natural,' 'bodily' (and therefore lower) functions occur, whereas men are intrinsically closely involved with the world of work where (at least for some) 'cultural,' 'mental,' and therefore higher functions occur. It is no accident that 'natural' facts about women, in the form of claims about biology, are often used to justify social stratification based on gender."

Although this model may be applicable in some cultures, its universality has been challenged not only by those who point out that nature–culture is a dichotomy of western thought in particular (Bloch and Bloch 1980; Jordanova 1980; Moore 1988), but also by those who provide ethnographic data to indicate its lack of salience in other cultures around the world (Strathern 1980). Similarly, the assumption that women are universally subordinated while men are dominant (Ortner 1974: 70) appears questionable when viewed through the lens of recent ethnographic analysis. The critique of the concepts of universal subordination and of the nature–culture dichotomy has stimulated significant research on how gender identity and gender roles are constructed in particular cultural contexts (Errington and Gewertz 1987; Ortner and Whitehead 1981; Weiner 1976). Whether and under what conditions social asymmetry between men and women emerges in the process of this construction is open to empirical investigation.

The cultural construction of gender in a particular society involves definitions of what it means to be masculine or feminine, and these definitions vary cross-culturally. Gilmore (in this book) takes up this topic by examining cross-cultural variations in what it means to be a man. He finds a recurring notion that "real manhood is different from simple anatomical maleness, that it is not a natural condition that comes about spontaneously through biological maturation but rather is a precarious or artificial state that boys must win against powerful odds" (1990: 11). To Gilmore the answer to the manhood puzzle lies in culture. He examines a post-Freudian understanding of masculinity as a category of self-identity, showing how boys face special problems in separating from their mother. A boy's separation and individuation is more perilous and difficult than a girl's, whose femininity is reinforced by the original unity with her mother. Thus, to become separate the boy must pass a test, breaking the chain to his mother. Ultimately, Gilmore concludes that manhood ideologies force men to shape up "on penalty of being robbed of their identity." Men are not innately different from women, but they need motivation to be assertive.

Herdt (in this book) also focuses on the manhood, examining how it is constructed in the context of ritual among the Sambia of New Guinea. The Sambia, like many other societies in New Guinea (Biersack 2001; Brown and Buchbinder 1976; Herdt 1982; Meigs 1984; Roscoe 2001), are characterized by a high degree of segregation and sexual antagonism between men and women, both of which are reinforced by powerful taboos. These taboos, and other facets of Sambian male identity including that of the warrior, are inculcated during a series of initiation rituals whereby boys are "grown" into men. As Herdt observes, the Sambia "perceive no imminent, naturally driven fit between one's birthright sex and one's gender identity or role" (1982: 54). Indeed, Sambian boys and men engage in what some societies would label homosexual activity, yet they do it to create masculinity. It is precisely for this reason that an analytical distinction is often made between "sex" as a biological classification and "gender" as a set of learned social roles.

Through the rituals of manhood Sambian boys are progressively detached from the world of women, a world they occupied for the first six or seven years of their lives and which they must now learn to both fear and devalue. This process of detachment has been identified by Chodorow (1974) as a major phase of human male development. If it is unmarked and therefore ambiguous in most western cultures, it is marked in many nonwestern cultures and often associated with male circumcision. Among the Mende of Sierra Leone (Little 1951), for example, boy initiates are seized from their homes by the force of spirits—men wearing masks and long raffia skirts. In this act they are dramatically and suddenly separated from their childhood, and carried into the bush where they will spend several weeks in seclusion and transition before they reemerge as men.

Initiation rituals that prepare girls for their roles as women and instruct them in what it means to be a woman in a particular cultural context can also be found in various societies around the world (Brown 1963; Richards 1956). However, the transition to womanhood is often part of a more subtle and continuous process of enculturation and socialization. In a description of Hausa socialization Callaway (1987) demonstrates how girls in this society learn how to behave in culturally appropriate ways. The Hausa are an Islamic people who live in northern Nigeria. Historically, ruling-class Hausa women had significant authority and social standing, but with the expansion of Islam this position was eroded and a sexually segregated society characterized by female subordination emerged. Hausa girls marry young, generally upon reaching puberty. At that time they enter kulle, or seclusion. In seclusion, the social roles of women are specifically defined and their sexual activities are limited. Though a Hausa woman becomes part of her husband's family, her place is secured only by bearing sons, and all her children belong to her husband. Hausa women are taught the expected life course from early childhood. In Hausa society, Callaway (1987: 22) claims, "the reproduction of 'masculine' and 'feminine' personalities generation after generation has produced psychological and value commitments to sex differences that are tenaciously maintained and so deeply ingrained as to become central to a consistent sense of self." This self is defined by reproductive roles and by deference to men; thus a good daughter-in-law gives her first-born child to her husband's mother, an act that strengthens family ties.

Conceptions of the self or personhood are, as Henrietta Moore (1988: 39) has observed, "cross-culturally as variable as the concepts of 'woman' and 'man.'" Personhood is constituted by a variety of attributes. In addition to gender, it may comprise age, status in the family and in the community, and physical appearance or impairment. In many cultures naming is also an important mechanism for constructing personhood. In the United States, for instance, the use of Ms. to replace Mrs. and Miss is an acceptable option. It is increasingly common for married women to retain the name that they were born with rather than replace it with one that only gives them an identity in relation to someone else—their husband.

Among the Chambri of New Guinea, initial identity or personhood is gained through a totemic name given by a child's patrilineal and matrilateral relatives. According to Errington and Gewertz (1987: 32, 47), "these names both reflect and affect the transactions which constitute a person's fundamental social relationships and identity. . . . Totemic names allow both men and women to pursue respectively their culturally defined preoccupations of political competition and the bearing of children. The totemic names available to men, however, convey different sorts of power and resources than do those available to women. . . . Men seek to augment their own power through gaining control of the names of others. . . . The power conveyed by [women's] names cannot shape social relationships as does the power of names men hold, but, instead, ensures reproduction."

Women's names among the Chambri work in different ways from those of men, but they nonetheless enable women to claim personhood in Chambri society. The married Chinese women described by Watson (in this book) have an entirely different experience. They are denied individuating names, and through this denial their personhood is in question. They remain, says Watson, "suspended between the anonymous world of anybodies and the more sharply defined world of some-bodies." In contrast with the namelessness of Chinese women, men in Chinese culture acquire numerous names as they pass through the life cycle. Nowhere is the difference more apparent than at marriage—a time when a man acquires a name that symbolizes his new status and public roles and a woman loses her girlhood name and becomes the "inner person." Like the Hausa women who assume an identity with respect to their husbands, Chinese women begin newly married life by learning the names and kinship terms for all their husbands' ancestors and relatives. Namelessness follows them to the grave—anybodies in life, they become nobodies at death.

Personhood is also encoded in the language that men and women use. Indeed anthropologists and others have focused on the relationship between language and gender, building on the pioneering work of Lakoff (1975) and, more recently, Deborah Tannen (1990). In many cultures around the world, speech styles differ between men and women while in others there are no distinctions (Keenan 1974; Sherzer 1987). Sometimes these differences are associated with the relative equality/inequality between the sexes, and hence with power. As Susan Gal (1990:177) has written, "some linguistic strategies and genres are more highly valued and carry more authority than others". McElhinney (this book) takes up the topic of gendered language and its relation to authority and personhood in her research on the Pittsburgh police department. She links gender to race and class, offering a complex analysis of how police officers talk about the use of physical force and how this has affected the integration of women into the police profession, a traditionally male occupation. Equally at issue is the extent to which women police officers use "tough talk" and whether this usage results in them being described as more masculine or less feminine, as well as more or less competent as police officers.

In many societies personhood for women is also associated with conceptions of the body (Conklin 2001; Diemberger 1993). Lamb (in this book) addresses the gendered nature of the body and how it makes and unmakes the social ties of Bengali Indian women over the life course. Purity among Bengalis is associated with touching and the controlled exchange of bodily fluids. Women are considered more impure than men and hence must bathe more often and must observe cultural practices that discipline their bodies—spatial seclusion, cloth covering, etc. Their bodies are more open and hence more vulnerable; menstruation marks the beginning of openness—a sign of readiness for marriage and reproduction. At her wedding, a time when her personal identity is changing, a Bengali woman must absorb substances originating from her husband's body and household. This also represents a severing of ties with her natal family and a forging of ties with her husband's family. Similarly later in life, and as a widow, women begin to unmake ties. When a woman loses her husband she becomes half a person and if young, Lamb tells us, "not merely a sexual hazard, but also a repulsive anomaly." In old age, when they are past reproduction their bodies close and cool and they regain purity. Postmenopausal women become "like men" and enjoy many of the freedoms that men enjoy.

The readings in this section of the book all emphasize that the biological categories of male and female are foundations upon which culturally-defined and culturally-appropriate gender roles and gender identities are constructed by both men and women in any society. What it means to be masculine or feminine varies across cultures, across social locations defined by such factors as class, ethnicity, or employment sector, and over the life course.

REFERENCES

Biersack, Aletta. 2001. "Reproducing Inequality; The Gender Politics of Male Cults in the Papua New Guinea Highlands and Amazonia." In Thomas A. Gregor and Donald Tuzin (eds.), *Gender in Amazonia and Melanesia,* pp. 69–90. Berkeley: University of California Press.

Bloch, Maurice and Jean Bloch. 1980. "Women and the Dialectics of Nature in Eighteenth-Century French Thought." In Carol MacCormack and Marilyn Strathern (eds.). *Nature, Culture and Gender,* pp. 25–41. Cambridge: Cambridge University Press.

Brown, Judith K. 1963. "A Cross-Cultural Study of Female Initiation Rites Among Pre-Literate Peoples." *American Anthropologist* 65(4): 837–853.

Brown, Paula and Georgeda Buchbinder. 1976. *Man and Woman in the New Guinea Highlands.* Washington, DC: American Anthropological Association, Special Publication, number 8.

Buckley, Thomas. 1982. "Menstruation and the Power of Yurok Women: Methods in Cultural Reconstruction." *American Ethnologist* 9: 47–60.

Buckley, Thomas and Alma Gottlieb (eds.). 1988. Blood Magic: *The Anthropology of Menstruation.* Berkeley: University of California Press.

Callaway, Barbara J. 1987. *Muslim Hausa Women in Nigeria: Tradition and Change.* Syracuse: Syracuse University Press.

Chodorow, Nancy. 1974. "Family Structure and Feminine Personality." In Michele Z. Rosaldo and Louise Lamphere (eds.). *Woman, Culture, and Society,* pp. 43–67. Stanford: Stanford University Press.

Conklin, Beth. 2001. "Women's Blood, Warriors' Blood, and the Conquest of Vitality in Amazonia." In Thomas A. Gregor and Donald Tuzin (eds.), *Gender in Amazonia and Melanesia,* pp. 141–174. Berkeley: University of California Press.

Diemberger, Hildegard. 1993. "Blood, Sperm, Soul and the Mountain. Gender Relations, Kinship and Cosmovision among the Khumbo (NE Nepal). In Teresa del Valle (ed.), *Gendered Anthropology,* pp. 88–127. London and New York: Routledge.

Douglas, Mary. 1966. *Purity and Danger: An Analysis of Concepts of Pollution and Taboo.* London: Routledge and Kegan Paul.

Errington, Frederick and Deborah Gewertz. 1987. *Cultural Alternatives and a Feminist Anthropology: An Analysis of Culturally Constructed Gender Interests in Papua New Guinea.* Cambridge: Cambridge University Press.

Gal, Susan. 1991. "Between Speech and Silence: The Problematics of Research on Language and Gender." In Micaela di Leonardo (ed.), *Gender at the Crossroads of Knowledge:Feminist Anthropology in the Modern Era,* pp. 175–203. Berkeley: University of California Press.

Gottlieb, Alma. 1982. "Sex, Fertility and Menstruation Among the Beng of the Ivory Coast: A Symbolic Analysis." *Africa* 52(4): 34–47.

Herdt, Gilbert. 1982. *Rituals of Manhood: Male Initiation in Papua New Guinea.* Berkeley and Los Angeles: University of California Press.

Keenan, Elinor Ochs. 1974. "Norm-makers and Norm-breakers: Uses of Speech by Men and Women in a Malagasy Community." In Richard Bauman and Joel Sherzer (eds.), *Explorations in the Ethnography of Speaking,* pp. 125–143. New York: Cambridge University Press.

Jordanova, L. J. 1980. "Natural Facts: A Historical Perspective on Science and Sexuality." In Carol MacCormack and Marilyn Strathern (eds.). *Nature, Culture and Gender,* pp. 42–69. Cambridge: Cambridge University Press.

Keesing, Roger. 1985. "Kwaio Women Speak: The Micropolitics of Autobiography in a Solomon Island Society." *American Anthropologist* 87: 27–39.

Lakoff, Robin. 1975. *Language and Women's Place.* New York: Harper and Row.

Lawrence, Denise. 1988. "Menstrual Politics: Women and Pigs in Rural Portugal." In Thomas Buckley and Alma Gottlieb (eds.). *The Anthropology of Menstruation,* pp. 117–136. Berkeley: University of California Press.

Little, Kenneth L. 1951. *The Mende of Sierra Leone: A West African People in Transition.* London: Routledge and Kegan Paul.

Martin, Emily. 1987. *The Woman in the Body: A Cultural Analysis of Reproduction*. Boston: Beacon Press.

Meggitt, M. J. 1964. "Male-Female Relationships in the Highlands of Australian New Guinea." *American Anthropologist* 66(4, part 2): 204–224.

Meigs, Anna S. 1984. *Food, Sex, and Pollution: A New Guinea Religion*. New Brunswick, NJ: Rutgers University Press.

Moore, Henrietta. 1988. *Feminism and Anthropology*. Minneapolis: University of Minnesota Press.

Ortner, Sherry. 1974. "Is Female to Male as Nature to Culture?" In Michelle Z. Rosaldo and Louise Lamphere (eds.). *Woman, Culture, and Society*, pp. 66–87. Stanford: Stanford University Press.

Ortner, Sherry and Harriet Whitehead. 1981. *Sexual Meanings: The Cultural Construction of Gender and Sexuality*. Cambridge: Cambridge University Press.

Powers, Marla. 1986. *Oglala Women*. Chicago: University of Chicago Press.

Richards, Audrey I. 1956. *Chisungu: A Girls' Initiation Ceremony among the Bemba of Northern Rhodesia*. London: Faber and Faber.

Rosaldo, Michelle. 1974. "Woman, Culture, and Society: A Theoretical Overview." In Michelle Z. Rosaldo and Louise Lamphere (eds.). *Woman, Culture, and Society*, pp. 17–42. Stanford: Stanford University Press.

Roscoe, Paul. 2001. "Strength and Sexuality: Sexual Avoidance and Masculinity in New Guinea and Amazonia." In Thomas A. Gregor and Donald Tuzin (eds.), *Gender in Amazonia and Melanesia*, pp. 279–308. Berkeley: University of California Press.

Shahshahani, Soheila. 1986. "Women Whisper, Men Kill: A Case Study of the Mamasani Pastoral Nomads of Iran." In Leela Dube, Eleanor Leacock, and Shirley Ardener (eds.). *Visibility and Power: Essays on Women in Society and Development*, pp. 85–97. Delhi: Oxford University Press.

Sherzer, Joel. 1987. "A Diversity of Voices: Men's and Women's Speech in Ethnographic Perspective," In S. Philips, S Steel, and C. Tanz (eds.), *Language, Gender and Sex in Comparative Perspective*, pp. 95–120. New York: Cambridge University Press.

Strathern, Marilyn. 1980. "No Nature, No Culture: The Hagen Case." In Carol MacCormack and Marilyn Strathern (eds.). *Nature, Culture and Gender*, pp. 174–222. Cambridge: Cambridge University Press.

Tannen, Deborah. 1990. *You Just don't Understand. Women and Men in Conversation*. New York: William Morrow.

Weiner, Annette. 1976. *Women of Value, Men of Renown*. Austin: University of Texas Press.

The Manhood Puzzle

David D. Gilmore

> There are continuities of masculinity that transcend cultural differences.
>
> —*Thomas Gregor, Anxious Pleasures*

Are there continuities of masculinity across cultural boundaries, as the anthropologist

Reprinted with permission from David D. Gilmore, *Manhood in the Making* (New Haven: Yale University Press, 1990), pp. 9–29. Copyright ©1990 Yale University Press.

Thomas Gregor says (1985:209)? Are men everywhere alike in their concern for being "manly?" If so, why? Why is the demand made upon males to "be a man" or "act like a man" voiced in so many places? And why are boys and youths so often tested or indoctrinated before being awarded their manhood? These are questions not often asked in the growing literature on sex and gender roles. Yet given the recent interest in sexual stereotyping, they are ones that need to be considered if we are to understand both sexes and their relations.

Regardless of other normative distinctions made, all societies distinguish between male and female; all societies also provide institutionalized sex-appropriate roles for adult men and women. A very few societies recognize a third, sexually intermediary category, such as the Cheyenne *berdache*, the Omani *xanith*, and the Tahitian *mahu* . . . but even in these rare cases of androgynous genders, the individual must make a life choice of identity and abide by prescribed rules of sexual comportment. In addition, most societies hold consensual ideas—guiding or admonitory images—for conventional masculinity and femininity by which individuals are judged worthy members of one or the other sex and are evaluated more generally as moral actors. Such ideal statuses and their attendant images, or models, often become psychic anchors, or psychological identities, for most individuals, serving as a basis for self-perception and self-esteem (D'Andrade 1974:36).

These gender ideals, or guiding images, differ from culture to culture. But, as Gregor and others (e.g., Brandes 1980; Lonner 1980; Raphael 1988) have argued, underlying the surface differences are some intriguing similarities among cultures that otherwise display little in common. Impressed by the statistical frequency of such regularities in sexual patterning, a number of observers have recently argued that cultures are more alike than different in this regard. For example, Gregor (1985:200) studied a primitive Amazonian tribe and compared its sex ideals to those of contemporary America. Finding many subsurface similarities in the qualities expected of men and women, he concludes that our different cultures represent only a symbolic veneer masking a bedrock of sexual thinking. In another study, the psychologist Lonner (1980:147) echoes this conclusion. He argues that culture is "only a thin veneer covering an essential universality" of gender dimorphism. In their comprehensive survey of sex images in thirty different cultures, Williams and Best (1982:30) conclude that there is "substantial similarity" to be found "panculturally in the traits ascribed to men and women."

Whether or not culture is only a thin veneer over a deep structure is a complicated question: as the rare third sexes show, we must not see in every culture "a Westerner struggling to get out" (Munroe and Munroe 1980:25). But most social scientists would agree that there do exist striking regularities in standard male and female roles across cultural boundaries regardless of other social arrangements (Archer and Lloyd 1985:283–84). The one regularity that concerns me here is the often dramatic ways in which cultures construct an appropriate manhood—the presentation or "imaging" of the male role. In particular, there is a constantly recurring notion that real manhood is different from simple anatomical maleness, that it is not a natural condition that comes about spontaneously through biological maturation but rather is a precarious or artificial state that boys must win against powerful odds. This recurrent notion that manhood is problematic, a critical threshold that boys must pass through testing, is found at all levels of sociocultural development regardless of what other alternative roles are recognized. It is found among the simplest hunters and fishermen, among peasants and sophisticated urbanized peoples; it is found in all continents and environments. It is found among both warrior peoples and those who have never killed in anger.

Moreover, this recurrent belief represents a primary and recurrent difference from parallel notions of femaleness. Although women, too, in any society are judged by sometimes stringent sexual standards, it is rare that their very status as woman forms part of the evaluation. Women who are found deficient or deviant according to these standards may be criticized as immoral, or they may be called unladylike or its equivalent and subjected to appropriate sanctions, but rarely is their right to a gender identity questioned in the same public, dramatic way that it is for men. The very paucity of linguistic labels for females echoing the epithets "effete," "unmanly," "effeminate," "emasculated," and so on, attest to this archetypical difference between sex judgments worldwide. And it is far more assaultive (and frequent) for men to be challenged in this way than for women.

Perhaps the difference between male and female should not be overstated, for "femininity" is also something achieved by women who seek social approval. But as a social icon, femininity seems to be judged differently. It usually involves questions of body ornament or sexual allure, or other essentially cosmetic behaviors that enhance, rather than create, an inherent quality of character. An authentic femininity rarely involves tests or proofs of action, or confrontations with dangerous foes: win-or-lose contests dramatically played out on the public stage. Rather than a critical threshold passed by traumatic testing, an either/or condition, femininity is more often construed as a biological given that is culturally refined or augmented.

TESTS OF MANHOOD: A SURVEY

Before going any further, let us look at a few examples of this problematic manhood. Our first stop is Truk Island, a little atoll in the South Pacific. Avid fishermen, the people of Truk have lived for ages from the sea, casting and diving in deep waters. According to the anthropologists who have lived among them, the Trukese men are obsessed with their masculinity, which they regard as chancy. To maintain a manly image, the men are encouraged to take risks with life and limb and to think "strong" or "manly" thoughts, as the natives put it (Marshall 1979). Accordingly, they challenge fate by going on deep-sea fishing expeditions in tiny dugouts and spearfishing with foolhardy abandon in shark-infested waters. If any men shrink from such challenges, their fellows, male and female, laugh at them, calling them effeminate and childlike. When on land, Trukese youths fight in weekend brawls, drink to excess, and seek sexual conquests to attain a manly image. Should a man fail in any of these efforts, another will taunt him: "Are you a man? Come, I will take your life now" (Marshall 1979:92).

Far away on the Greek Aegean island of Kalymnos, the people are also stalwart seafarers, living by commercial sponge fishing (Bernard 1967). The men of Kalymnos dive into deep water without the aid of diving equipment, which they scorn. Diving is therefore a gamble because many men are stricken and crippled by the bends for life. But no matter: they have proven their precious manhood by showing their contempt for death (119). Young divers who take precautions are effeminate, scorned and ridiculed by their fellows.

These are two seafaring peoples. Let us move elsewhere, to inland Africa, for example, where fishing is replaced by pastoral pursuits. In East Africa, young boys from a host of cattle-herding tribes, including the Masai, Rendille, Jie, and Samburu, are taken away from their mothers and subjected at the outset of adolescence to bloody circumcision rites by which they become true men. They must submit without so much as flinching under the agony of the knife. If a boy cries out while his flesh is being cut, if he so much as blinks an eye or turns his head, he is shamed for life as unworthy of manhood, and his entire lineage is shamed as a nursery of weaklings. After this very public ordeal, the young initiates are isolated in special dormitories in the wilderness. There, thrust on their own devices, they learn the tasks of a responsible manhood: cattle rustling, raiding, killing, survival in the bush. If their long apprenticeship is successful, they return to society as men and are only then permitted to take a wife.

Another dramatic African case comes from nearby Ethiopia: the Amhara, a Semitic-speaking tribe of rural cultivators. They have a passionate belief in masculinity called wand-nat. This idea involves aggressiveness, stamina, and bold "courageous action" in the face of danger; it means never backing down when threatened (Levine 1966:18). To show their wand-nat, the Amhara youths are forced to engage in whipping contests called buhe (Reminick 1982:32). During the whipping ceremonies, in which all able-bodied male adolescents must participate for their reputations' sake, the air is filled with the cracking of whips. Faces are lacerated, ears torn open, and red and bleeding welts appear (33). Any sign of weakness is greeted with taunts and mockery. As if this were not enough, adolescent Amhara boys are wont to prove their virility by scarring their arms with red-hot embers (Levine 1966:19). In these rough ways the boys actualize the exacting Amhara "ideals of masculinity" (Reminick 1976:760).

Significantly, this violent testing is not enough for these virile Ethiopians. Aside from showing physical hardihood and courage in the buhe matches, a young man must demonstrate his potency on his wedding night by waving a bloody sheet of marital consummation before the assembled kinsmen (Reminick 1996: 760–61). As well as demonstrating the bride's virginity, this ceremonial defloration is a talisman of masculinity for the Amhara groom. The Amhara's proof of manhood, like that of the Trukese, is both sexual and violent, and his performances both on the battlefield and in the marriage bed must be visibly displayed, recorded, and confirmed by the group; otherwise he is no man.

Halfway around the world, in the high mountains of Melanesia, young boys undergo similar trials before being admitted into the select club of manhood. In the New Guinea Highlands, boys are torn from their mothers and forced to undergo a series of brutal masculinizing rituals (Herdt 1982). These include whipping, flailing, beating, and other forms of terrorization by older men, which the boys must endure stoically and silently. As in Ethiopia, the flesh is scored and blood flows freely. These Highlanders believe that without such hazing, boys will never mature into men but will remain weak and childlike. Real men are made, they insist, not born.

PARALLELS

To be sure, there are some contextual similarities in these last few examples. The Amhara, Masai, and New Guinea Highlanders share one feature in common beyond the stress on manhood: they are fierce warrior peoples, or were in the recent past. One may argue that their bloody rites prepare young boys for the idealized life of the warrior that awaits them. So much is perhaps obvious: some Western civilizations also subject soft youths to rough hazing and initiations in order to toughen them up for a career of soldiering, as in the U.S. Marines (Raphael 1988). But these trials are by

no means confined to militaristic cultures or castes. Let us take another African example.

Among the relatively peaceful !Kung Bushmen of southwest Africa (Thomas 1959; Lee 1979), manhood is also a prize to be grasped through a test. Accurately calling themselves "The Harmless People" (Thomas 1959), these nonviolent Bushmen have never fought a war in their lives. They have no military weapons, and they frown upon physical violence (which, however, sometimes does occur). Yet even here, in a culture that treasures gentleness and cooperation above all things, the boys must earn the right to be called men by a test of skill and endurance. They must single-handedly track and kill a sizable adult antelope, an act that requires courage and hardiness. Only after their first kill of such a buck are they considered fully men and permitted to marry.

Other examples of stressed manhood among gentle people can be found in the New World, in aboriginal North America. Among the nonviolent Fox tribe of Iowa, for example, "being a man" does not come easily (Gearing 1970:51). Based on stringent standards of accomplishment in tribal affairs and economic pursuits, real manhood is said to be "the Big Impossible," an exclusive status that only the nimble few can achieve (51–52). Another American Indian example is the Tewa people of New Mexico, also known as the Pueblo Indians. These placid farmers, who are known today for their serene culture, gave up all warfare in the last century. Yet they subject their boys to a severe hazing before they can be accounted men. Between the ages of twelve and fifteen, the Tewa boys are taken away from their homes, purified by ritual means, and then whipped mercilessly by the Kachina spirits (their fathers in disguise). Each boy is stripped naked and lashed on the back four times with a crude yucca whip that draws blood and leaves permanent scars. The adolescents are expected to bear up impassively under the beating to show their fortitude. The Tewa say that this rite makes their boys into men, that otherwise manhood is doubtful. After the boys' ordeal, the Kachina spirits tell them, "You are now a man. . . . You are made a man" (Hill 1982:220). Although Tewa girls have their own (nonviolent) initiations, there is no parallel belief that girls have to be *made* women, no "big impossible" for them; for the Tewa and the Fox, as for the other people above, womanhood develops naturally, needing no cultural intervention, its predestined arrival at menarche commemorated rather than forced by ritual (Hill 1982:209–10).

Nor are such demanding efforts at proving oneself a man confined to primitive peoples or those on the margins of civilization. In urban Latin America, for example, as described by Oscar Lewis (1961:38), a man must prove his manhood every day by standing up to challenges and insults, even though he goes to his death "smiling." As well as being tough and brave, ready to defend his family's honor at the drop of a hat, the urban Mexican, like the Amhara man, must also perform adequately in sex and father many children. Such macho exploits are also common among many of the peasant and pastoral peoples who reside in the cradle of the ancient Mediterranean civilizations. In the Balkans, for instance, the category of "real men" is clearly defined. A real man is one who drinks heavily, spends money freely, fights bravely, and raises a large family (Simic 1969). In this way he shows an "indomitable virility" that distinguishes him from effeminate counterfeits (Denich 1974:250). In eastern Morocco, true men are distinguished from effete men on the basis of physical prowess and heroic acts of both feuding and sexual potency; their manly deeds are memorialized in verses sung before admiring crowds at festivals, making manhood a kind of communal celebration (Marcus 1987:50). Likewise, for the Bedouin of Egypt's Western Desert, "real men" are contrasted with despicable weaklings who are "no men." Real Bedouin men are bold and courageous, afraid of nothing. Such men assert their will at any cost and stand up to any challenge; their main attributes are "assertiveness and the quality of potency" (Abu-Lughod 1986:88–89). Across the sea, in Christian Crete, men in village coffee shops proudly sing paeans to their own virility, their self-promotion having been characterized as the "poetics of manhood" by Michael Herzfeld (1985:15). These Cretans must demonstrate their "manly selfhood" by stealing sheep, procreating large families, and besting other men in games of chance and skill.

Examples of this pressured manhood with its almost talismanic qualities could be given almost indefinitely and in all kinds of contexts. Among most of the peoples that anthropologists are familiar with, true manhood is a precious and elusive status beyond mere maleness, a hortatory image that men and boys aspire to and that their culture demands of them as a measure of belonging. Although this stressed or embattled quality varies in intensity, becoming highly marked in southern Spain, Morocco, Egypt, and some other Mediterranean-area traditions, true manhood in other cultures frequently shows an inner insecurity that needs dramatic proof. Its vindication is doubtful, resting on rigid codes of decisive action in many spheres of life: as husband, father, lover, provider, warrior. Because it is a restricted status, there are always men who fail the test. These are the negative examples, the effete men, the men-who-are-no-men, held up scornfully to inspire conformity to the glorious ideal.

Perhaps these stagy routes to manhood seem bizarre to us at first glance. But none of them should surprise most Anglophone readers, for we too have our manly traditions, both in our popular culture and in literary genres. Although we may choose less flamboyant modes of expression than the Amhara or Trukese, we too have regarded manhood as an artificial state, a challenge to be overcome, a prize to be won by fierce struggle: if not "the big impossible," then certainly doubtful.

For example, let us take a people and a social stratum far removed from those above: the gentry of modern England. There, young boys were traditionally subjected to similar trials on the road to their majority. They were torn at a tender age from mother and home, as in East Africa or in New Guinea, and sent away in age sets to distant testing grounds that sorely took their measure. These were the public boarding schools, where a cruel "trial by ordeal," including physical violence and terrorization by elder males, provided a passage to a "social state of manhood" that their parents thought could be achieved in no other way (Chandos 1984:172). Supposedly, this harsh training prepared young Oxbridge aristocrats for the self-reliance and fortitude needed to run the British Empire and thereby manufactured "a serviceable elite as stylized as Samurai" (346). Even here, in Victorian England, a culture not given over to showy excess, manhood was an artificial product coaxed by austere training and testing.

Similar ideas motivated educators on both sides of the Atlantic, for example, the founders of the Boy Scouts. Their chartered purpose, as they put it in their pamphlets and manuals, was to "make big men of little boys" by fostering "an independent manhood," as though this were not to be expected from nature alone (cited by Hantover 1978:189). This obsessive moral masculinization in the English-speaking countries went beyond mere mortals of the day to Christ himself, who was portrayed in turn-of-the-century tracts as "the supremely manly man," athletic and aggressive when necessary, no "Prince of Peace-at-any-price" (Conant 1915:117). The English publicist Thomas Hughes dilated rhapsodically about the manliness of Christ (1879), while his colleagues strove to depict Christianity as the "muscular" or "manly" faith. Pious and articulate English Protestants loudly proclaimed their muscular religion as an antidote to what Charles Kingsley derided as the "fastidious maundering, die-away effeminacy" of the High Anglican Church (cited in Gay 1982:532). Boys, faiths, and gods had to be made masculine; otherwise there was doubt. The same theme runs through much British literature of the time, most notably in Kipling, as for example in the following lines from the poem "If":

If you can fill the unforgiving minute
With sixty seconds worth of distance run,
Yours is the Earth, and everything that's in it,
And—which is more—you'll be a Man, my son!

Consequent only to great deeds, being a Kiplingesque man is more than owning the Earth, a truly imperial masculinity consonant with empire building. The same theme of "iffy" heroism runs through many aspects of popular middle-class American culture today. Take, for example, the consistent strain in U.S. literature of masculine *Bildungsroman*— the ascension to the exalted status of manhood under the tutelage of knowledgeable elders, with the fear of failure always lurking menacingly in the background. This theme is most strongly exemplified by Ernest Hemingway, of course, notably in the Nick Adams stories, but it is also found in the work of such contemporaries as William Faulkner and John Dos Passos, and in such Hemingway epigones as Studs Terkel, Norman Mailer, James Dickey, Frederick Exley, and—the new generation—Robert Stone, Jim Harrison, and Tom McGuane. This "virility school" in American letters (Schwenger 1984:13), was sired by Papa Hemingway (if one discounts Jack London) and nurtured thereafter by his acolytes, but it is now in its third or fourth generation and going strong (for a feminist view see Fetterly 1978).

In contemporary literary America, too, manhood is often a mythic confabulation, a Holy Grail, to be seized by long and arduous testing. Take, for example, this paradigmatic statement by Norman Mailer (1968:25): "Nobody was born a man; you earned manhood provided you were good enough, bold enough." As well as echoing his spiritual forebears, both British and American, Mailer articulates here the unwritten sentiments of the Trukese, the Amhara, the Bushmen, and countless other peoples who have little else in common except this same obsessive "quest for male validation" (Raphael 1988:67). Although some of us may smile at Mailer for being so histrionic and sophomoric about it, he nevertheless touches a raw nerve that pulsates through many cultures as well as our own. Nor is Mailer's challenge representative of only a certain age or stratum of American society. As the poet Leonard Kriegel (1979:14) says in his reflective book about American manhood, "In every age, not just our own, manhood was something that had to be won."

Looking back, for instance, one is reminded of the cultural values of the antebellum American South. Southerners, whatever their class, placed great stress on a volatile manly honor as a defining feature of the southern character, a fighting principle. Indeed, Bertram Wyatt-Brown, in his book *Southern Honor* (1982), has argued convincingly that this touchy notion was a major element behind southern secessionism and thus an important and underrated political factor in U.S. history. A defense of southern "manliness" was in fact offered by Confederate writers of the time, including the South Carolina firebrand Charles C. Jones, as one justification for regional defiance, political separation, and, finally, war (cited in McPherson 1988:41). And of course similar ideals are enshrined in the frontier folklore of the American West, past and present, as exemplified in endless cowboy epics.

This heroic image of an achieved manhood is being questioned in America by feminists and by so-called liberated men themselves (Pleck 1981; Brod 1987). But for decades, it has been widely legitimized in U.S. cultural settings ranging from Italian-American gangster culture to Hollywood Westerns, private-eye tales, the current Rambo imagoes, and children's He-Man dolls and games; it is therefore deeply ingrained in the American male psyche. As the anthropologist Robert LeVine (1979:312) says, it is an organization of cultural principles that function together as a "guiding myth within the confines of our culture." But given the similarities between contemporary American notions of manliness and those of the many cultures discussed above, can we drop LeVine's qualifying phrase about "the confines of our culture"? Can we speak instead of an archetype or "deep structure" of masculinity, as Andrew Tolson (1977:56) puts it? And if so, what explains all these similarities? Why the trials and the testing and the seemingly gratuitous agonies of man-playing? Why is so much indoctrination and motivation needed in all these cultures to make real men? What is there about "official" manliness that requires such effort, such challenge, and such investment? And why should manhood be so desirable a state and at the same time be conferred so grudgingly in so many societies? These are

some of the questions I want to consider here. Only a broadly comparative approach can begin to answer them.

MANHOOD AND GENDER ROLE

Let us pause at this point to take stock. What do we know so far about the origins of such gender imagery? Until very recently, studies of male and female were wedded to a persistent paradigm derived from mechanistic nineteenth-century antecedents. Most pervasive was the idea of generic types, a Universal Man counterpoised to a Universal Woman—a sexual symmetry supposedly derived from self-evident dualisms in biology and psychology (Katchadourian 1979:20). Freud, for example, held that anatomy was destiny, and Jung (1926) went so far as to develop universal principles of masculinity and femininity which he conveyed as "animus" and "anima," irreducible cores of sexual identity. Western literature and philosophy are full of such fundamental and supposedly immutable dualisms (Bakan 1966); they are also found in some Asian cosmologies, for example, the Chinese Yin and Yang, and in countless sets of binary oppositions both philosophical and scientific (e.g., Ortner 1974). What could be a neater polarity than sex? Our view of manhood in the past was often a simple reflection of these polar views of male and female "natures" or "principles." This view had some scientific support among biologists and psychologists, many of whom held that the aggressiveness of masculinity, including the testing and proving, was merely a consequence of male anatomy and hormones: men seek challenges because they are naturally aggressive. That is simply the way they are; women are the opposite. Period.

The way we look at sex roles, however, has changed drastically in the past two decades. Although appealing to many, sex dualisms and oppositions are definitely out of fashion, and so are sexual universals and biological determinisms. Part of the reason, aside from the recent movement away from static structural dualisms in the social sciences generally, lies in the feminist revolution of the past twenty years. Starting in the 1960s, the feminist attack on the bipolar mode of sexual thinking has shaken this dualistic edifice to its roots; but to be fair, it was never very sturdy to begin with. For example, both Freud and Jung accepted an inherent mixture of masculinity and femininity within each human psyche. Although he distinguished male and female principles, Jung to his credit admitted the existence of animus and anima to degrees in all people; bisexuality was in fact one of the bedrocks of Freud's psychological reasoning. In every human being, Freud (1905:220) remarks, "pure masculinity or femininity is not to be found either in a psychological or a biological sense. Every individual on the contrary displays a mixture."

Moreover, feminists of various backgrounds and persuasions (see, for example, Baker 1980; Sanday 1981; Otten 1985) have convincingly demonstrated that the conventional bipolar model based on biology is invalid and that sex (biological inheritance) and gender (cultural norms) are distinct categories that may have a relationship but not an isomorphic identity. Most observers would agree that hormones and anatomy do have an effect on our behavior. The biological anthropologist Melvin Konner has convincingly shown this in his book, *The Tangled Wing* (1982). Assessing the latest scientific and clinical literature in this highly acclaimed survey, Konner concludes that testosterone (the main male sex hormone) predisposes males to a slightly higher level of aggressivity than females (see also Archer and Lloyd 1985; 138–39). But, as Konner freely admits, biology does not determine all of our behavior, or even very much of it, and cultures do indeed vary to some degree in assigning sex roles, measured in jobs and tasks. Discrete concepts of masculinity and femininity, based on secondary sex characteristics, exist in virtually all societies, but they are not always constructed and interfaced in the same way. Gender is a symbolic category. As such, it has strong moral overtones, and therefore is ascriptive and culturally relative—potentially changeful. On the other hand, sex is rooted in anatomy and is

therefore fairly constant (Stoller 1968). It is now generally accepted, even among the most traditional male researchers, that masculine and feminine principles are not inherent polarities but an "overlapping continuum" (Biller and Borstelmann 1967: 255), or, as Spence and Helmreich put it (1979:4), "orthogonal dimensions."

Still, as we have seen from the previous examples, there exists a recurrent cultural tendency to distinguish and to polarize gender roles. Instead of allowing free play in sex roles and gender ideals, most societies tend to exaggerate biological potentials by clearly differentiating sex roles and by defining the proper behavior of men and women as opposite or complementary. Even where so-called "third sexes" exist, as for example the Plains Indian *berdache* and the Omani *xanith,* conventional male and female types are still strongly differentiated. So the question of continuities in gender imaging must go beyond genetic endowment to encompass cultural norms and moral scripts. If there are archetypes in the male image (as there are in femininity), they must be largely culturally constructed as symbolic systems, not simply as products of anatomy, because anatomy determines very little in those contexts where the moral imagination comes into play. The answer to the manhood puzzle must lie in culture; we must try to understand why culture uses or exaggerates biological potentials in specific ways.

PREVIOUS INTERPRETATIONS

Some feminists and other relativists have perceived the apparent contradiction between the theoretical arbitrariness of gender concepts and the empirical convergence of sex roles. Explanations have therefore been offered to account for it. The existing explanations are interesting and useful, and I do not argue against them on the grounds of logical consistency. Rather, I think that the wrong questions have been asked in this inquiry. Most explanations have been phrased in one of two ways, both ideologically satisfying depending upon one's point of view, but neither getting us very far analytically.

First, the question has been phrased by the more doctrinaire Marxists and some radical feminists in an idiom of pure conflict theory. They see gender ideology as having a purely exploitative function. Thus they ask, inevitably, cui bono? Since many male ideologies include an element of gender oppressiveness, or at least hierarchy (in the view of liberated Western intellectuals), some of these radicals regard masculine ideologies as masks or justifications for the oppression of women. They see male ideologies as mystifications of power relationships, as examples of false consciousness (see, for example, Ortner 1981; Godelier 1986). This explanation is probably true for some cases, at least as a partial explanation, especially in some extreme patriarchies where male dominance is very pronounced. But it cannot be true as a universal explanation, because it cannot account for instances in which males are tested for manhood but where there is relative sexual equality. We have seen one example of this in the African Bushmen (Thomas 1959; Lee 1979; Shostak 1981). Although these nonsexist foragers are often held up by feminists as a model of sexual egalitarianism (Shostak 1981), Bushmen boys must prove their manhood by hunting prowess. They must also undergo tests of hardiness and skill from which girls are excluded. . . . Their manhood is subject to proof and, conceptually, to diminishment or loss. The same is true of the Fox and the Tewa of North America. So if a conception of manhood has no oppressive function in these societies, what is it doing there? It seems that the conflict theorists are missing something.

The second idiom of explanation is equally reductionistic. Here, biological or psychological processes are given analytical priority. There are two forms of biopsychological reductionist argument. The first is biological/evolutionary à la Lionel Tiger in *Men in Groups* (1971). Tiger holds that men worry about manhood because evolutionary pressures have predisposed them to do so.

Once we were all hunters, and our success and therefore the survival and expansion of the group depended upon our developing genetically determined "masculine tendencies," aggression and male bonding being principal among them. This sociobiological argument is useful in certain cases, again, most notably in the violent patriarchies. But it is demonstrably false as a universal explanation because there are many societies where "aggressive" hunting never played an important role, where men do not bond for economic purposes, where violence and war are devalued or unknown, and yet where men are today concerned about demonstrating manhood. Further, this argument commits the historical fallacy of proposing a historical explanation for a cultural trait that persists under changed circumstances.

The second genetic reductionism is the standard psychoanalytic one about male psychic development. It is based squarely on an orthodox reading of Freud's Oedipus complex and its derivative, castration anxiety. This orthodoxy has been challenged recently with a neo-Freudian viewpoint stressing other aspects of male development, which I find much more powerful. . . . The standard psychoanalytic view holds that men everywhere are defending against castration fears as a result of identical oedipal traumas in psychosexual development. Masculinity cults and ideals are compensations erected universally against such fears (Stephens 1967; Kline 1972).

In this view, the norms of masculinity are projected outward from the individual psyche onto the screen of culture; public culture is individual fantasy life writ large. I think this explanation is useful in some cases but supererogatory. More damaging, it fails to give proper weight to social constraints that enforce male conformity to manhood ideals; as we shall see, boys have to be encouraged—sometimes actually forced—by social sanctions to undertake efforts toward a culturally defined manhood, which by themselves they might not do. So the explanation cannot be one based solely on psychic projections. Moreover, the orthodox psychoanalytic view can also be demonstrated to be false at a universal level, for there are empirical exceptions to the culture of manhood. There are a few societies that do not place the usual stress on achieving a masculine image; in these exceptional "neuter" societies, males are freed from the need to prove themselves and are allowed a basically androgynous script, which, significantly, they find congenial. As these exceptions do exist, . . . the answer to the masculinity puzzle must have a social side to it, because formal variation cannot be explained on the basis of a psychological constant such as castration anxiety.

SOME HELP FROM
THE POST-FREUDIANS

At this point we have to call upon some alternative models of male psychosexual development that accommodate social and relational factors. A psychological theory of masculinity that I find useful derives in part from recent work by the post-Freudian ego psychologists. The list of relevant theorists and their works is long but may be reduced here to Erik Erikson, Ralph Greenson, Edith Jacobson, Margaret Mahler, Gregory Rochlin, Robert Stoller, and D. W. Winnicott.

The basic idea here concerns the special problems attached to the origin of masculinity as a category of self-identity distinct from femininity. The theory begins with the assumption that all infants, male and female, establish a primary identity, as well as a social bond, with the nurturing parent, the mother. This theory already departs from the classic Freudian assumption that the boy child has from the first a male identity and a natural heterosexual relationship with his mother that culminates in the oedipal conflict, that the boy's identity as male is axiomatic and unconflicted. This new theory goes on to posit an early and prolonged unity or psychic merging with the mother that Freud (1914) discussed under "primary narcissism," a period when the infant fails to distinguish between self and mother. The argument is that the physical separation of child and mother at birth does not bring with it a psychological separation of equivalent severity or finality.

As the child grows, it reaches the critical threshold that Mahler (1975) has called separation-individuation. At this juncture its growing awareness of psychic separateness from the mother combines with increased physical mobility and a motoric exercise of independent action, for example, walking, speaking, manipulating toys. These independent actions are rewarded socially both by parents and by other members of the group who want to see the child grow up (Erikson 1950). Boys and girls alike go through these same trial stages of separation, self-motivation, encouragement and reward, and proto-personhood; and both become receptive to social demands for gender-appropriate behavior. However, according to this theory, the boy child encounters special problems in the crucible of the separation-individuation stage that impede further progression toward independent selfhood.

The special liability for boys is the different fate of the primal psychic unity with the mother. The self-awareness of being a separate individual carries with it a parallel sense of a gender identity—being either a man or a woman, boy or girl. In most societies, each individual must choose one or the other unequivocally in order, also, to be a separate and autonomous person recognizable as such by peers and thus to earn acceptance. The special problem the boy faces at this point is in overcoming the previous sense of unity with the mother in order to achieve an independent identity defined by his culture as masculine—an effort functionally equivalent not only to psychic separation but also to creating an autonomous public persona. The girl does not experience this problem as acutely, according to this theory, because her femininity is reinforced by her original symbiotic unity with her mother, by the identification with her that precedes self-identity and that culminates with her own motherhood (Chodorow 1978). In most societies, the little boy's sense of self as independent must include a sense of the self as different from his mother, as separate from her both in ego-identity and in social role. Thus for the boy the task of separation and individuation carries an added burden and peril. Robert Stoller (1974:358) has stated this problem succinctly:

> While it is true the boy's first love object is heterosexual [the mother], he must perform a great deed to make this so: he must first separate his identity from hers. Thus the whole process of becoming masculine is at risk in the little boy from the day of birth on; his still-to-be-created masculinity is endangered by the primary, profound, primeval oneness with mother, a blissful experience that serves, buried but active in the core of one's identity, as a focus which, throughout life, can attract one to regress back to that primitive oneness. That is the threat latent in masculinity.

To become a separate person the boy must perform a great deed. He must pass a test; he must break the chain to his mother. He must renounce his bond to her and seek his own way in the world. His masculinity thus represents his separation from his mother and his entry into a new and independent social status recognized as distinct and opposite from hers. In this view the main threat to the boy's growth is not only, or even primarily, castration anxiety. The principal danger to the boy is not a unidimensional fear of the punishing father but a more ambivalent fantasy-fear about the mother. The ineradicable fantasy is to return to the primal maternal symbiosis. The inseparable fear is that restoring the oneness with the mother will overwhelm one's independent selfhood.

Recently, armed with these new ideas, some neo-Freudians have begun to focus more specifically on the puzzle of masculine role modeling cults. They have been less concerned with the questions of gender identity and castration anxiety than with the related questions of regression and its relation to social role. In a recent symposium on the subject, the psychoanalyst Gerald Fogel (1986:10) argues that the boy's dilemma

goes "beyond castration anxiety" to a conflicted effort to give up the anaclitic unity with the mother, which robs him of his independence. In the same symposium, another psychoanalyst (Cooper 1986:128) refers to the comforting sense of omnipotence that this symbiotic unity with the mother affords. This sense of omnipotence, of narcissistic completeness, sensed and retained in fantasy as a blissful experience of oneness with the mother, he argues, is what draws the boy back so powerfully toward childhood and away from the challenge of an autonomous manhood. In this view, the struggle for masculinity is a battle against these regressive wishes and fantasies, a hard-fought renunciation of the longings for the prelapsarian idyll of childhood.

From this perspective, then, the manhood equation is a "revolt against boyishness" (Schafer 1986:100). The struggle is specifically "against regression" (100). This revisionist theory provides us with a psychological key to the puzzle of manhood norms and ideals. Obviously, castration fear is also important from an individual point of view. But manhood ideologies are not only intrapsychic; they are also collective representations that are institutionalized as guiding images in most societies. To understand the meaning of manhood from a sociological point of view, to appreciate its social rather than individual functions and causes, regression is the more important variable to consider. The reason for this is that, in aggregate, regression poses a more serious threat to society as a whole. As we shall see, regression is unacceptable not only to the individual but also to his society as a functioning mechanism, because most societies demand renunciation of escapist wishes in favor of a participating, contributing adulthood. Castration anxiety, though something that all men may also need to resolve, poses no such aggregate threat to social continuity. In sum, manhood imagery can be interpreted from this post-Freudian perspective as a defense against the eternal child within, against puerility, against what is sometimes called the Peter Pan complex (Hallman 1969).

REFERENCES

Abu-Lughod, Lila. 1986. *Veiled Sentiments: Honor and Poetry in a Bedouin Society.* Berkeley: University of California Press.

Archer, John, and Barbara Lloyd. 1985. *Sex and Gender.* Cambridge: Cambridge University Press.

Bakan, David. 1966. *The Duality of Human Existence.* Chicago: University of Chicago Press.

Baker, Susan W. 1980. Biological influences on human sex and gender. *Signs* 6:80–96.

Bernard, H. Russell. 1967. Kalymnian sponge diving. *Human Biology* 39:103–30.

Biller, Henry B., and Lloyd Borstelmann. 1967. Masculine development: An integrative view. *Merrill-Palmer Quarterly* 13:253–94.

Brandes, Stanley H. 1980. *Metaphors of Masculinity: Sex and Status in Andalusian Folklore.* Philadelphia: University of Pennsylvania Press.

Brod, Harry (ed.). 1987. *The Making of Masculinities: The New Men's Studies.* Boston: Allen and Unwin.

Chandos, John. 1984. *Boys Together: English Public Schools, 1800–1864.* New Haven: Yale University Press.

Chodorow, Nancy. 1978. *The Reproduction of Mothering.* Berkeley: University of California Press.

Conant, Robert W. 1915. *The Virility of Christ.* Chicago: no publisher.

Cooper, Arnold M. 1986. What men fear: The facade of castration anxiety. In *The Psychology of Men: New Psychoanalytic Perspective,* ed. Gerald Fogel, F. M. Lane, and R. S. Liebert, pp. 113–30. New York: Basic Books.

D'Andrade, Roy G. 1974. Sex differences and cultural institutions. In *Culture and Personality: Contemporary Readings,* ed. Robert A. LeVine, pp. 16–39. Chicago: Aldine.

Denich, Bette. 1974. Sex and power in the Balkans. In *Women, Culture, and Society,* ed. Michelle Rosaldo and Louise Lamphere, pp. 243–62. Stanford: Stanford University Press.

Erikson, Erik. 1950. *Childhood and Society.* New York: Norton.

Fetterly, Judith. 1978. *The Resisting Reader: A Feminist Approach to American Fiction.* Bloomington, Ind.: Indiana University Press.

Fogel, Gerald I. 1986. Introduction: Being a man. In *The Psychology of Men: New Psychoanalytic Perspectives,* ed. Gerald Fogel, F. M. Lane, and R. S. Liebert, pp. 3–22. New York: Basic Books.

Freud, Sigmund. 1905. *Three Essays on the Theory of Sexuality, III: The Transformations of Puberty.* Standard Edition, ed. James Strachey 7:207–30. London: Hogarth Press (1975).

———. 1914. *On narcissism.* Standard Edition, ed. James Strachey, 14:67–102. London: Hogarth Press (1975).

Gay, Peter, 1982. Liberalism and regression. *Psychoanalytic Study of the Child* 37:523–45. New Haven: Yale University Press.

Gearing, Frederick O. 1970. *The Face of the Fox.* Chicago: Aldine.

Godelier, Maurice. 1986. *The Making of Great Men.* Cambridge: Cambridge University Press.

Gregor, Thomas. 1985. *Anxious Pleasures: The Sexual Life of an Amazonian People.* Chicago: University of Chicago Press.

Hallman, Ralph, 1969. The archetypes in Peter Pan. *Journal of Analytic Psychology* 14:65–73.

Hantover, Jeffrey P. 1978. The Boy Scouts and the validation of masculinity. *Journal of Social Issues* 34:184–95.

Herdt, Gilbert H. 1982. Fetish and fantasy in Sambia initiation. In *Rituals of Manhood,* ed. Gilbert H. Herdt, pp. 44–98. Berkeley: University of California Press.

Hertzfeld, Michael. 1985. Gender pragmatics: agency, speech and bride-theft in a Cretan mountain village. *Anthropology* 9:25–44.

Hill, W. W. 1982. *An Ethnography of Santa Clara Pueblo, New Mexico,* ed. and annotated by Charles H. Lange, Albuquerque, N. Mex.: University of New Mexico Press.

Hughes, Thomas. 1879. *The Manliness of Christ.* London: Macmillan.

Jung, Carl. 1926. *Psychological Types.* New York: Harcourt, Brace and Co.

Katchadourian, Herant A. 1979. The terminology of sex and gender. In *Human Sexuality: Comparative and Developmental Perspectives,* ed. Herant A. Katchadourian, pp. 8–34. Berkeley: University of California Press.

Kline, Paul. 1972. Fact and Fantasy in *Freudian Theory.* London: Methuen.

Konner, Melvin. 1982. *The Tangled Wing: Biological Constraints on the Human Spirit.* New York: Harper Colophon Books.

Kriegel, Leonard, 1979. *On Men and Manhood.* New York: Hawthorn Books.

Lee, Richard B. 1979. *The !Kung San: Men, Women, and Work in a Foraging Society.* Cambridge: Cambridge University Press.

Levine, Donald N. 1966. The concept of masculinity in Ethiopian culture. *International Journal of Social Psychiatry* 12:17–23.

LeVine, Robert A. 1979. Anthropology and sex: Developmental aspects. In *Human Sexuality:*

Comparative and Developmental Perspectives, ed. Herant A. Katchadourian, pp. 309–31. Berkeley: University of California Press.

Lewis, Oscar. 1961. *The Children of Sanchez.* New York: Random House.

Lonner, Walter J. 1980. The search for psychological universals. In *Handbook of Cross-Cultural Psychology,* ed. Harry C. Triandis and William W. Lambert, 1:143–204. Boston: Allyn & Bacon.

McPherson, James M. 1988. *Battle Cry of Freedom: The Civil War Era.* New York: Oxford University Press.

Mahler, Margaret, et al. 1975. *The Psychological Birth of the Human Infant.* New York: Basic Books.

Mailer, Norman. 1968. *Armies of the Night.* New York: New American Library.

Marcus, Michael. 1987. "Horsemen are the fence of the land": Honor and history among the Ghiyata of eastern Morocco. In *Honor and Shame and the Unity of the Mediterranean,* ed. David D. Gilmore, pp. 49–60. Washington, D.C.: American Anthropological Association, Special Pub. no. 22.

Marshall, Mac. 1979. *Weekend Warriors.* Palo Alto, CA: Mayfield.

Munroe, Robert L. and Ruth H. Munroe. 1980. Perspectives suggested by anthropological data. In *Handbook of Cross-Cultural Psychology,* ed. Harry C. Triandis and William W. Lambert 1:253–317. Boston: Allyn and Bacon.

Ortner, Sherry B. 1974. Is female to male as nature is to culture? In *Woman, Culture, and Society,* ed. Michelle Z. Rosaldo and Louise Lamphere, pp. 67–88. Stanford: Stanford University Press.

———. 1981. Gender and sexuality in hierarchical societies: The case of Polynesia and some comparative implications. In *Sexual Meanings,* ed. Sherry B. Ortner and Harriet Whitehead, pp. 359–409. Cambridge: Cambridge University Press.

Otten, Charlotte M. 1985. Genetic effects on male and female development and on the sex ratio. In *Male-Female Differences: A Bio-Cultural Perspective,* ed. Roberta L. Hall, pp. 155–217. New York: Praeger.

Pleck, Joseph. 1981. *The Myth of Masculinity.* Cambridge, Mass.: MIT Press.

Raphael, Ray. 1988. *The Men from the Boys: Rites of Passage in Male America.* Lincoln, Nebr.: University of Nebraska Press.

Reminick, Ronald A. 1976. The symbolic significance of ceremonial defloration among the Amhara of Ethiopia. *American Ethnologist* 3:751–63.

———. 1982. The sport of warriors on the wane: a case of cultural endurance in the face of social change. In *Sport and the Humanities,* ed. William H. Morgan, pp. 31–36. Knoxville, Tenn.: Bureau of Educational Research and Service, University of Tennessee Press.

Sanday, Peggy R. 1981. *Female Power and Male Dominance: On the Origins of Sexual Inequality.* Cambridge: Cambridge University Press.

Schafer, Roy. 1986. Men who struggle against sentimentality. In *The Psychology of Men: New Psychoanalytic Perspectives,* ed. Gerald I. Fogel, L. M. Lane, and R. S. Liebert, pp. 95–110. New York: Basic Books.

Schwenger, Peter. 1984. *Phallic Critiques: Masculinity and Twentieth-Century Literature.* London: Routledge and Kegan Paul.

Shostak, Marjorie. 1981. *Nisa: The Life and Words of a !Kung Woman.* Cambridge, Mass.: Harvard University Press.

Simic, Andrei. 1969. Management of the male image in Yugoslavia. *Anthropological Quarterly* 42: 89–101.

Spence, Janet, and Robert L. Helmreich. 1979. *Masculinity and Femininity: Their Psychological Dimensions, Correlates and Antecedents.* Austin, Tex.: University of Texas Press.

Stephens, William N. 1967. A cross-cultural study of menstrual taboos. In *Cross-Cultural Approaches,* ed. Clellan S. Ford, pp. 67–94. New Haven: HRAF Press.

Stoller, Robert. 1968. *Sex and Gender.* New York: Science House.

———. 1974. Facts and fancies: An examination of Freud's concept of bisexuality. In *Women and Analysis,* ed. Jean Strouse, pp. 343–64. New York: Dell.

Thomas, Elizabeth Marshall. 1959. *The Harmless People.* New York: Vintage Books.

Tiger, Lionel. 1971. *Men in Groups.* New York; Random House.

Tolson, Andrew. 1977. *The Limits of Masculinity: Male Identity and the Liberated Woman.* New York: Harper and Row.

Williams, John E., and Deborah L. Best. 1982. *Measuring Sex Stereotypes: A Thirty-Nation Study.* Beverly Hills: Sage Publications.

Wyatt-Brown, Bertram. 1982. *Southern Honor: Ethics and Behavior in the Old South.* New York: Oxford University Press.

Rituals of Manhood: Male Initiation in Papua New Guinea

Gilbert H. Herdt

Sambia are a mountain-dwelling hunting and horticultural people who number some 2,000 persons and inhabit one of New Guinea's most rugged terrains. The population is dispersed through narrow river valleys over a widespread, thinly populated rain forest; rainfall is heavy; and even today the surrounding mountain ranges keep the area isolated. Sambia live on the fringes of the Highlands, but they trace their origins to the Papua hinterlands; their culture and economy thus reflect a mixture of influences from both of those areas. Hunting still predominates as a masculine activity through which most meat protein is acquired. As in the Highlands, though, sweet potatoes and taro are the staple crops, and their cultivation is for the most part women's work. Pigs are few, and they have no ceremonial or exchange significance; indigenous marsupials, such as possum and tree kangaroo, provide necessary meat prestations for all initiations and ceremonial feasts (cf. Meigs 1976).

Sambia settlements are small, well-defended, mountain clan hamlets. These communities comprise locally based descent groups organized through a strong agnatic idiom. Residence is patrivirilocal, and most men actually reside in their father's hamlets. Clans are exogamous, and one or more of them together constitute a hamlet's landowning corporate agnatic body. These men also form a localized warriorhood that is sometimes allied with other hamlets in matters of fighting, marriage, and ritual. Each hamlet contains one or two men's clubhouses, in addition to women's houses, and the men's ritual life centers on their clubhouse. Marriage is usually by sister exchange or infant betrothal,

although the latter form of prearranged marriage is culturally preferred. Intrahamlet marriage is occasionally more frequent (up to 50 percent of all marriages in my own hamlet field site) than one would expect in such small segmentary groupings, an involutional pattern weakened since pacification.

Sambia male and female residential patterns differ somewhat from those of other Highlands peoples. The nuclear family is an important subunit of the hamlet-based extended family of interrelated clans. A man, his wife, and their children usually cohabit within a single, small, round hut. Children are thus reared together by their parents during the early years of life, so the nuclear family is a residential unit, an institution virtually unknown to the Highlands (Meggitt 1964; Read 1954). Sometimes this unit is expanded through polygyny, in which case a man, his cowives, and their children may occupy the single dwelling. Girls continue to reside with their parents until marriage (usually near the menarche, around fifteen to seventeen years of age). Boys, however, are removed to the men's clubhouse at seven to ten years of age, following their first-stage initiation. There they reside exclusively until marriage and cohabitation years later. Despite familial cohabitation in early childhood, strict taboos based on beliefs about menstrual pollution still separate men and women in their sleeping and eating arrangements.

Warfare used to be constant and nagging among Sambia, and it conditioned the values and masculine stereotypes surrounding the male initiatory cult. Ritualized bow fights occurred among neighboring hamlets, whose members still intermarried and usually initiated their sons together. At the same time, though, hamlets also united against enemy tribes and in staging war parties against them. Hence, warfare, marriage, and initiation were interlocking institutions; the effect of this political instability was to reinforce tough, strident masculine performance in most arenas of social life. "Strength" (*jerundu*) was—and is—a pivotal idea in this male ethos. Indeed, strength, which has both ethnobiological and behavioral aspects, could be aptly translated as "maleness" and "manliness." Strength has come to be virtually synonymous with idealized conformity to male ritual routine. Before conquest and pacification by the Australians, though, strength had its chief performative significance in one's conduct on the battlefield. Even today bitter reminders of war linger on among the Sambia; and we should not forget that it is against the harsh background of the warrior's existence that Sambia initiate their boys, whose only perceived protection against the inconstant world is their own unbending masculinity.

Initiation rests solely in the hands of the men's secret society. It is this organization that brings the collective initiatory cycle into being as jointly performed by neighboring hamlets (and as constrained by their own chronic bow fighting). The necessary feast-crop gardens, ritual leadership, and knowledge dictate that a handful of elders, war leaders, and ritual experts be in full command of the actual staging of the event. Everyone and all else are secondary.

There are six intermittent initiations from the ages of seven to ten and onward. They are, however, constituted and conceptualized as two distinct cultural systems within the male life cycle. First-stage (*moku,* at seven to ten years of age), second-stage (*imbutu,* at ten to thirteen years), and third-stage (*ipmangwi,* at thirteen to sixteen years) initiations—bachelorhood rites—are collectively performed for regional groups of boys as age-mates. The initiations are held in sequence, as age-graded advancements; the entire sequel takes months to perform. The focus of all these initiations is the construction and habitation of a great cult house (*moo-angu*) on a traditional dance ground; its ceremonialized building inaugurates the whole cycle. Fourth-stage (*nuposha:* sixteen years and onward), fifth-stage (*taiketnyi*), and sixth-stage (*moondangu*) initiations are,

conversely, individually centered events not associated with the confederacy of interrelated hamlets, cult house, or dance ground. Each of these initiations, like the preceding ones, does have its own ritual status, social role, and title, as noted. The triggering event for the latter three initiations, unlike that for the bachelorhood rites, is not the building of a cult house or a political agreement of hamlets to act collectively but is rather the maturing femininity and life-crisis events of the women assigned in marriage to youths (who become the initiated novices). Therefore, fourth-stage initiation is only a semipublic activity organized by the youths' clansmen (and some male affines). Its secret purificatory and other rites are followed by the formal marriage ceremony in the hamlet. Fifth-stage initiation comes at a woman's menarche, when her husband is secretly introduced to additional purification and sexual techniques. Sixth-stage initiation issues from the birth of a man's wife's first child. This event is, de jure, the attainment of manhood. (The first birth is elaborately ritualized and celebrated; the next three births are also celebrated, but in more truncated fashion.) Two children bring full adulthood (*aatmwunu*) for husband and wife alike. Birth ceremonies are suspended after the fourth birth, since there is no reason to belabor what is by now obvious: a man has proved himself competent in reproduction. This sequence of male initiations forms the basis for male development, and it underlies the antagonistic tenor of relationships between the sexes.

It needs stating only once that men's secular rhetoric and ritual practices depict women as dangerous and polluting inferiors whom men are to distrust throughout their lives. In this regard, Sambia values and relationships pit men against women even more markedly, I think, than occurs in other Highlands communities (cf. Brown and Buchbinder 1976; Meggitt 1964; Read 1954). Men hold themselves as the superiors of women in physique, personality, and social position. And this dogma of male supremacy permeates all social relationships and institutions, likewise coloring domestic behavior among the sexes (cf. Tuzin 1980 for an important contrast). Men fear not only pollution from contact with women's vaginal fluids and menstrual blood but also the depletion of their semen, the vital spark of maleness, which women (and boys, too) inevitably extract, sapping a man's substance. These are among the main themes of male belief underlying initiation.

The ritualized simulation of maleness is the result of initiation, and men believe the process to be vital for the nature and nurture of manly growth and well-being. First-stage initiation begins the process in small boys. Over the ensuing ten to fifteen years, until marriage, cumulative initiations and residence in the men's house are said to promote biological changes that firmly cement the growth from childhood to manhood. Nature provides male genitals, it is true; but nature alone does not bestow the vital spark biologically necessary for stimulating masculine growth or demonstrating cold-blooded self-preservation.

New Guinea specialists will recognize in the Sambia belief system a theme that links it to the comparative ethnography of male initiation and masculine development: the use of ritual procedures for sparking, fostering, and maintaining manliness in males (see Berndt 1962; Meigs 1976; Newman 1964, 1965; Poole 1981; Read 1965; Salisbury 1965; Strathern 1969, 1970). Sambia themselves refer to the results of first-stage collective initiation—our main interest—as a means of "growing a boy"; and this trend of ritual belief is particularly emphatic.

Unlike ourselves, Sambia perceive no imminent, naturally driven fit between one's birthright sex and one's gender identity or role.[1] Indeed, the problem (and it is approached as a situation wanting a solution) is implicitly and explicitly understood in quite different terms. The solution is also different for the two sexes: men believe that a girl is born with all of the vital organs and fluids necessary for her to attain reproductive competence through "natural" maturation. This conviction is embodied in cultural perceptions of the girl's development beginning with the sex assignment at birth. What distinguishes a girl (*tai*) from a boy (*kwulai'u*) is

obvious: "A boy has a penis, and a girl does not," men say. Underlying men's communications is a conviction that maleness, unlike femaleness, is not a biological given. It must be artificially induced through secret ritual; and that is a personal achievement.

The visible manifestations of girls' fast-growing reproductive competence, noticed first in early motor coordination and speech and then later in the rapid attainment of height and secondary sex traits (e.g., breast development), are attributed to inner biological properties. Girls possess a menstrual-blood organ, or *tingu*, said to precipitate all those events and the menarche. Boys, on the other hand, are thought to possess an inactive *tingu*. They do possess, however, another organ—the *kere-ku-kereku*, or semen organ—that is thought to be the repository of semen, the very essence of maleness and masculinity; but this organ is not functional at birth, since it contains no semen naturally and can only store, never produce, any. Only oral insemination, men believe, can activate the boy's semen organ, thereby precipitating his push into adult reproductive competence. In short, femininity unfolds naturally, whereas masculinity must be achieved; and here is where the male ritual cult steps in.

Men also perceive the early socialization risks of boys and girls in quite different terms. All infants are closely bonded to their mothers. Out of a woman's contaminating, life-giving womb pours the baby, who thereafter remains tied to the woman's body, breast milk, and many ministrations. This latter contact only reinforces the femininity and female contamination in which birth involves the infant. Then, too, the father, both because of postpartum taboos and by personal choice, tends to avoid being present at the breast-feedings. Mother thus becomes the unalterable primary influence; father is a weak second. Sambia say this does not place girls at a "risk"—they simply succumb to the drives of their "natural" biology. This maternal attachment and paternal distance clearly jeopardize the boys' growth, however, since nothing innate within male maturation seems to resist the inhibiting effects of mothers' femininity. Hence boys must be traumatically separated—wiped clean of their female contaminants—so that their masculinity may develop.

Homosexual fellatio inseminations can follow this separation but cannot precede it, for otherwise they would go for naught. The accumulating semen, injected time and again for years, is believed crucial for the formation of biological maleness and masculine comportment. This native perspective is sufficiently novel to justify our using a special concept for aiding description and analysis of the data: masculinization (Herdt 1981:205 ff). Hence I shall refer to the overall process that involves separating a boy from his mother, initiating him, ritually treating his body, administering homosexual inseminations, his biological attainment of puberty, and his eventual reproductive competence, as *masculinization*. (Precisely what role personal and cultural fantasy plays in the negotiation of this ritual process I have considered elsewhere: see Herdt 1981: chaps. 6, 7, and 8.)

A boy has female contaminants inside of him which not only retard physical development but, if not removed, debilitate him and eventually bring death. His body is male: his tingu contains no blood and will not activate. The achievement of puberty for boys requires semen. Breast milk "nurtures the boy," and sweet potatoes or other "female" foods provide "stomach nourishment," but these substances become only feces, not semen. Women's own bodies internally produce the menarche, the hallmark of reproductive maturity. There is no comparable mechanism active in a boy, nothing that can stimulate his secondary sex traits. Only semen can do that; only men have semen; boys have none. What is left to do, then, except initiate and masculinize boys into adulthood?

NOTE

1. I follow Stoller (1968) in adhering to the following distinctions: the term *sex traits* refers to purely biological phenomena (anatomy, hormones, genetic structure, etc.), whereas *gender* refers to those psychological and cultural attributes that compel a person (consciously or unconsciously) to sense him- or herself, and other persons, as belonging to either the male or female sex. It follows that the term gender role (Sears 1965), rather than the imprecise term sex role, refers to the normative set of expectations associated with masculine and feminine social positions.

REFERENCES

Berndt, R. M. 1962. *Excess and Restraint: Social Control among a New Guinea Mountain People.* Chicago: University of Chicago Press.

Brown, P., and G. Buchbinder (eds.). 1976. *Man and Woman in the New Guinea Highlands.* Washington, D.C.: American Anthropological Association.

Herdt, G. H. 1981. *Guardians of the Flutes: Idioms of Masculinity.* New York: McGraw-Hill.

Meggitt, M. J. 1964. Male-female relationships in the Highlands of Australian New Guinea. In New Guinea: The Central Highlands, ed. J. B. Watson, *American Anthropologist,* 66, pt. 2 (4):204–224.

Meigs, A. S. 1976. Male pregnancy and the reduction of sexual opposition in a New Guinea Highlands society. *Ethnology* 15 (4):393–407.

Newman, P. L. 1964. Religious belief and ritual in a New Guinea society. In New Guinea: The Central Highlands, ed. J. B. Watson, *American Anthropologist* 66, pt. 2 (4):257–272.

———. 1965. *Knowing the Gururumba.* New York: Holt, Rinehart and Winston.

Poole, F. J. P. 1981. Transforming "natural" woman: female ritual leaders and gender ideology among Bimin-Kuskumin. *In Sexual Meanings,* ed. S. B. Ortner and H. Whitehead. New York: Cambridge University Press.

Read, K. E. 1954. Cultures of the Central Highlands, New Guinea. *Southwestern Journal of Anthropology* 10 (1):1–43.

———. 1965. *The High Valley.* London: George Allen and Unwin.

Salisbury, R. F. 1965. The Siane of the Eastern Highlands. In *Gods, Ghosts, and Men in Melanesia,* P. Lawrence and M. J. Meggitt, pp. 50–77. Melbourne: Melbourne University Press.

Sears, R. R. 1965. *Development of gender role. In Sex and Behavior,* ed. F. A. Beach, pp. 133–163. New York: John Wiley and Sons.

Stoller, R. J. 1968. *Sex and Gender*. New York: Science House.

Strathern, A. J. 1969. Descent and alliance in the New Guinea Highlands: some problems of comparison. Royal Anthropological Institute, *Proceedings*, pp. 37–52.

———. 1970. Male initiation in the New Guinea Highlands societies. *Ethnology* 9(4):373–379.

Tuzin, D. F. 1980. *The Voice of the Tambaran: Truth and Illusion in Ilahita Arapesh Religion*. Berkeley, Los Angeles, and London: University of California Press.

The Named and the Nameless: Gender and Person in Chinese Society

Rubie S. Watson

In Chinese society names classify and individuate, they have transformative powers, and they are an important form of self-expression. Some names are private, some are chosen for their public effect. Many people have a confusing array of names while others are nameless. The theory and practice of personal naming in Chinese society is extremely complex and unfortunately little studied.

For the male villagers of rural Hong Kong, naming marks important social transitions: the more names a man has the more "socialized" and also, in a sense, the more "individuated" he becomes. To attain social adulthood a man must have at least two names, but most have more. By the time a male reaches middle age, he may be known by four or five names. Village women, by contrast, are essentially nameless. Like boys, infant girls are named when they are one month old, but unlike boys they lose this name when they marry. Adult women are known (in reference and address) by kinship terms, teknonyms, or category terms such as "old woman."

In Chinese society personal names constitute an integral part of the language of joking, of boasting, and of exhibiting one's education and erudition. The Chinese themselves are fascinated by personal names: village men enjoy recounting stories about humorous or

clumsy names, educated men appreciate the elegance of an auspicious name, and all males worry about the quality of their own names and those of their sons. To a large extent women are excluded from this discourse. They cannot participate because in adulthood they are not named, nor do they name others. Until very recently the majority of village women were illiterate and so could not engage in the intellectual games that men play with written names. Women were not even the subjects of these conversations.

The namelessness of adult women and their inability to participate in the naming of others highlights in a dramatic way the vast gender distinctions that characterize traditional Chinese culture. The study of names gives us considerable insight into the ways in which gender and person are constructed in Chinese society. Judged against the standard of men, the evidence presented here suggests that village women do not, indeed cannot, attain full personhood. The lives of men are punctuated by the acquisition of new names, new roles, new responsibilities and new privileges; women's lives, in comparison, remain indistinct and indeterminate.

In his essay "Person, Time, and Conduct in Bali," Clifford Geertz argues that our social world "is populated not by anybodies . . . but by somebodies, concrete classes of determinate persons positively characterized and appropriately labeled" (1973:363). It is this process by which anybodies are converted into somebodies that concerns me here. Do men and women become "somebodies" in the same way? Are they made equally determinate, positively characterized and labeled?

Although this discussion is based primarily on field research carried out in the Hong Kong New Territories, examples of naming practices have been drawn from other areas of Chinese culture as well. It is difficult to determine the extent to which the patterns described in this paper are indicative of rural China in general.[1] Available evidence suggests that there is considerable overlap between Hong Kong patterns of male naming and those of preliberation Chinese society and present-day rural Taiwan (see for example Eberhard 1970; Kehl 1971; Sung 1981; Wu 1927). Unfortunately, there have been no studies that specifically examine the differences between men's and women's naming, although brief references in Martin Yang's study of a Shantung village (1945:124) and in Judith Stacey's account of women in the People's Republic (1983:43, 131) suggest that the gender differences discussed here are not unique to Hong Kong. In making these statements I do not wish to suggest that there are no substantial differences in personal naming between rural Hong Kong and other parts of China. A general survey of personal naming in China, especially one that takes the postrevolution era into account, has yet to be done.

This paper draws heavily on ethnographic evidence gathered in the village of Ha Tsuen, a single-lineage village located in the northwest corner of the New Territories. All males in Ha Tsuen share the surname Teng and trace descent to a common ancestor who settled in this region during the 12th century (see R. Watson 1985). For most villagers postmarital residence is virilocal/patrilocal. The Ha Tsuen Teng practice surname exogamy, which in the case of a single-lineage village means that all wives come from outside the community. These women arrive in Ha Tsuen as strangers and their early years of marriage are spent accommodating to a new family and new community. The Teng find this completely natural; "daughters," they say, "are born looking out; they belong to others."

Patrilineal values dominate social life in Ha Tsuen. Women are suspect because they are outsiders. As Margery Wolf points out, Chinese women are both marginal and essential to the families into which they marry (1972:35). They are necessary because they produce the next generation, yet as outsiders their integration is never complete. Women are economically dependent on the family estate, but they do not have shareholding rights in that estate. Half the village land in Ha Tsuen is owned by the lineage (see R. Watson 1985:61–72), and the other half is owned by private (male) landlords. Women have no share in this land; they do not own immovable property nor do they have rights to inherit it. Few married women are employed in wage labor, and since the villagers gave up serious agriculture in the 1960s, most women are dependent on their husbands' paychecks for family income. At the time I conducted my research (1977–78) Ha Tsuen had a population of approximately 2500—all of whom are Cantonese speakers.

NAMING AN INFANT

Among the Cantonese a child's soul is not thought to be firmly attached until at least 30 days after its birth. During the first month of life the child and mother are secluded from all but the immediate family. After a month has passed, the child is considered less susceptible to soul loss and is introduced into village life. The infant is given a name by his or her father or grandfather at a ceremony called "full month" (*man yueh*). If the child is a son, the "full month" festivities will be as elaborate as the family can afford; if, on the other hand, a girl is born, there may be little or no celebration (except, perhaps, a special meal for family members). The naming ceremony for a boy normally involves a banquet for neighbors and village elders, along with the distribution of red eggs to members of the community. The first name a child is given is referred to as his or her *ming*.[2]

This name (*ming*) may be based on literary or classical allusions. It may express a wish for the child's or family's future, or it may enshrine some simple event that took place at or near the time of the child's birth. Examples of this kind of naming are found not only in Ha Tsuen but in other areas of China as well. Arlington, in an early paper on Chinese naming, describes how the name "sleeve" was given to a girl of his acquaintance who at the time of her birth had been wrapped in a sleeve (1923:319). In the People's Republic of China, people born during the Korean War might be called "Resist the United States" (Fan-mei) or "Aid Korea" (Pang-ch'ao). Alternatively, children may be given the name of their birthplace, for example, "Born in Anhwei" (Hui-sheng) or "Thinking of Yunnan" (Hsiang-yun). In the past girl babies might be named Nai ("To Endure"). This name was given to infant girls who survived an attempted infanticide. One way of killing an infant was to expose it to the elements. If a girl survived this ordeal, she might be allowed to live. In these cases the name Nai commemorated the child's feat of survival.[3]

A child's name may express the parents' desire for no more children. For instance, in Taiwan a fifth or sixth child may be named Beui, a Hokkien term meaning "Last Child." Alternatively, a father may try to ensure that his next child will be a son by naming a newborn daughter "Joined to Brother" (Lien-ti). There are several girls with this name in Ha Tsuen. A father or grandfather might express his disappointment or disgust by naming a second or third daughter "Too Many" (A-to)[4] or "Little Mistake" (Hsiao-t'so) or "Reluctant to Feed" (Wang-shih). A sickly child might be given the name of a healthy child. My informants told me that a long-awaited son may be given a girl's name to trick the wandering ghosts into thinking the child had no value and therefore could be ignored (see also Sung 1981:81–82). For example, a Ha Tsuen villager, who was the only son of a wealthy family (born to his father's third concubine), was known by everyone as "Little Slave Girl" (in Cantonese, Mui-jai).

In most cases the infant receives a ming during the full month ceremony but this name is little used. For the first year or two most children are called by a family nickname ("milk name" or *nai ming*). Babies are sometimes given milk names like "Precious" (A-pao), or A-buh (mimicking the sounds infants make) or "Eldest Luck," or "Second Luck," indicating sibling order.

Some care and consideration is given to a child's *ming*, especially if it is a boy. By referring to the Confucian classics or by alluding to a famous poem, the name may express the learning and sophistication of the infant's father or grandfather. The name, as we will see, may also save the child from an inauspicious fate. Commonly girls' names (*ming*) are less distinctive and less considered than are boys' names. And, as we have seen, girls' names may also be less flattering: "Too Many" or "Little Mistake." Often a general, classificatory name is given to an infant girl; Martin Yang reports from rural Shantung that Hsiao-mei ("Little Maiden") was a "generic" girls' name in his village (1945:124).

Most Chinese personal names are composed of two characters, which follow the one character surname (for example, Mao Tse-tung or Teng Hsiao-ping). One of the characters of the *ming* may be repeated for all the children of the same sex in the family or perhaps all sons born into the lineage during one generation (for example, a generation or sibling set might have personal names like Hung-hui, Hung-chi, Hung-sheng, and so on). Birth order may also be indicated in the child's name. In these cases part of the name indicates group affiliation and sibling order. However, one of the characters is unique to the individual and so the child is distinguished from his siblings. A variation on this theme occurs when a parent or grandparent selects a name for all sons or grandsons from a group of characters that share a single element (known as the radical—a structured component found in every Chinese character). For example, Margaret Sung (1981:80) in her survey of Chinese naming practices on Taiwan notes that in some families all son's names may be selected from characters that contain the "man" radical (for example, names like "Kind" [Jen], "Handsome" [Chun], or "Protect" [Pao]).

Individuation of the name, Sung points out, is very strong in Chinese society (1981:88). There is no category of words reserved specifically for personal names and care is taken to make names (particularly boys' names) distinct. The Chinese find the idea of sharing one's given name with millions of other people extraordinary.[5] In Taiwan, Sung notes that individuation of one's name is so important that the government has established a set of rules for name changes (1981:88). According to these regulations a name can be changed when two people with exactly the same name live in the same city or county or have the same place of work. "Inelegant" names or names shared with wanted criminals can also be changed.

In Ha Tsuen a boy might be named, in Cantonese, Teng Tim-sing, which translates Teng "To Increase Victories"; another person could be called Teng Hou-sing, "Reliably Accomplish" (Teng being the shared surname). Parents, neighbors, and older siblings will address the child or young unmarried adult (male or female) by his or her *ming* or by a nickname. Younger siblings are expected to use kin terms in addressing older siblings. It should be noted that, in contrast to personal names, Chinese surnames do not convey individual meaning. When used in a sentence or poem, the character *mao* (the same character used in Mao Tse-tung) means hair, fur, feathers, but when it is used as a surname it does not carry any of these connotations.

THE POWER OF NAMES: NAMES THAT CHANGE ONE'S LUCK

Names classify people into families, generational sets, and kin groups. Ideally, Chinese personal names also have a unique quality. Personal names carry meanings; they express wishes (for more sons or no more daughters), mark past events ("Sleeve" or "Endure"), and convey a family's learning and status. Beyond this rather restricted sense there is, however, another level of meaning. According to Chinese folk concepts each person has a unique constitution—a different balance of the five elements (fire, water, metal, earth, and wood). When the child is about one month old a family will usually have a diviner cast the child's horoscope. The horoscope consists of eight characters (*pa tzu*)—two each for the hour, day, month, and year of birth. The combination of these characters determines in part what kind of person one is (what kind of characteristics one has) and what will happen in future years. However, the *pa tzu* do not represent destiny; one is not bound to act out this fate.

By means of esoteric knowledge a person's fate can be changed. Perhaps the most common method of accomplishing such a change is through naming. For example, if one of the five elements is missing from a person's constitution or is not properly balanced with other elements, the name (*ming*) may then include a character with the radical for that element. In the event of illness the diviner may suggest that the patient suffers from an imbalance of wood and that the radical for this element be added to the child's name. In such a case the character *mei* (plum), for example, may replace one of the original characters of the ming and thus save the child from a bad fate, illness, or perhaps death. *Mei* achieves this astounding feat not because there is anything intrinsically wood-like about *mei* but because the written character *mei* has two major components: *mu*, the radical for wood and another symbol that is largely phonetic. It is the written form of the character that is important here; in spoken Chinese there is nothing that suggests that *mei* has within it the element wood. I will return to this point later.

Significantly, it is not only one's own horoscope that matters; one must also be in balance with the horoscopes of parents, spouses, and offspring. It is particularly important that the five elements of mother and child be properly matched to ensure mutual health.[6] If conditions of conflict arise and nothing is done to resolve this conflict, the child may become ill and even die. A name change, however, can rectify the situation. It is obvious that Chinese personal names *do* things: they not only classify and distinguish but also have an efficacy in their own right.

GENDER DIFFERENCES AND THE WRITTEN NAME

As noted above, even in childhood there are important gender distinctions in naming. Girls nearly always have less elaborate full month rituals than their brothers, and less care is taken in choosing girls' names. The greatest difference between the sexes, however, pertains not to the aesthetics of naming but to the written form of the name.

Until the 1960s in Ha Tsuen and in rural Hong Kong generally births were seldom registered with government agencies. Except in cases of a bad fate, there was no compelling reason for girls' names ever to appear in written form. There was rarely any need to attach their names to legal documents. Girls did not inherit land, they had no rights in property, and their given names were not entered in genealogies (on this point see also Hazelton 1986) or on ancestral tablets (see below). Until the 1960s girls rarely attended primary schools. Consequently, nearly all village women born prior to 1945 cannot write or recognize their own names.

Commenting on the role of nicknames, Wolfram Eberhard makes the point that in spoken Chinese with its many homonyms, a two-word combination may fail to express clearly what the speaker wants to convey. The intended meaning of a name (that is, the two-character *ming*) is only apparent when it is written. Nicknames, Eberhard notes, are not normally meant to be written and, hence, are usually longer (often three or four characters) than a person's *ming* (1970:219). Given the ambiguities, a great deal of play is possible with the spoken form of names. For example, Hsin-mei can mean "New Plum" or "Faithful Beauty" depending on the tones that one uses in pronouncing the characters. In the written form the meaning of this name is perfectly clear, but in the spoken form it can be misunderstood or misconstrued, sometimes with disastrous consequences. The Manchu (Ch'ing) authorities played the naming game when they changed the written form of one of Sun Yat-sen's many names. During Sun's long political career, he used a variety of names and aliases (see Sharman 1934), one being Sun Wen (*wen* translates as "elegant," "civil," "culture"). In Manchu attacks on Sun the character *wen* pronounced with a rising tone (elegant, culture) was replaced by another character *wen* pronounced

with a falling tone (which translates as "defile"). The change was effected simply by adding the water radical to the term for elegant. *Wen* (defile), it should be noted, was also the name of a famous criminal in southern China during the last years of Manchu rule.

Upon seeing a person's written name, the beholder may comment on the beauty, the refinement, the auspicious connotations of the characters. As long as it is simply spoken, however, it is in a sense "just a name." Although women have names, these do not convey as much information as do men's names, for the obvious reason that the former were rarely written. Until recently New Territories women were not given names with a view to their written effect. The written form of "Too Many" may be offensive or unpleasant in a way that the spoken form is not.

Given that it is the written form of names that has force, that informs, that can be used to change a bad fate, there is justification for thinking that those whose names are rarely or never written are at some disadvantage. Girls, it would appear, did not have names in the same way that boys did.[7] It is also clear that girls' names are less expressive, less individuating than their brothers' names are. Fathers strove to make son's names distinctive, unique—whereas girls' names tended to classify (for example, Endure, Little Maiden) or to be used as a vehicle for changing circumstances external to the girl herself (for example, Joined to Brother). Many girls of course had names like Splendid Orchid, Morning Flower, Resembling Jade, but in general they were more likely than were their brothers to be given negative names, stereotypic names, or goal-oriented names. These gender distinctions are significant, but the contrast between men and women becomes even more dramatic when we consider adult naming practices.

MEN'S NAMING

When a Ha Tsuen man marries, he is given or takes (often he chooses the name himself) a marriage name, or *tzu*. Considering the importance of the written name it is significant that *tzu* is the same character that is commonly used for "word" or "ideograph." The marriage name is given in a ceremony called *sung tzu,* which literally means "to deliver written characters." This ceremony is an integral part of the marriage rites and is held after the main banquet on the first day of wedding festivities.

In Ha Tsuen, the marriage name (always two characters) is written on a small rectangular piece of red paper and is displayed in the main reception hall of the groom's house (alternatively, it may be hung in the groom's branch ancestral hall). This name is chosen with regard to its effect in the written form. Great care is taken in choosing the characters; they often have origins in the Confucian classics. In Ha Tsuen one of the two characters of this marriage name is usually shared by a lineage generational set. In some kin groups a respected scholar may be asked to choose a poem or aphorism to be used in generational naming. Each generation will then take in turn one character of the poem as part of their (*tzu*) name. Of course, this makes the selection of an auspicious, learned name more difficult and also more intellectually challenging. Naming at this level can become a highly complicated game.

In choosing a marriage name (*tzu*) the groom demonstrates his sophistication, learning, and goals. Among the people I studied, the possession of a marriage name is essential for the attainment of male adulthood, which gives a man the right to participate in important lineage and community rituals. In Ha Tsuen the correct way to ask whether a man has full ritual rights in the lineage is to inquire, "Does X have a *tzu*?" not "Is X married?" Marriage names are not used as terms of address; they may, however, appear in lineage genealogies and in formal documents.

By the time a man is married he will have acquired a public nickname (*wai hao,* literally an "outside name"). This is usually different from the family nickname he had in infancy or the "school name" given to him by a teacher.[8] Nicknames are widely used as terms of address and reference for males in the village; in fact, a man's birth and marriage names may be largely unknown.

In a discussion of naming among the Ilongot, Renato Rosaldo emphasizes the process by which names come into being (1984:13). Rosaldo argues that names are negotiated, and that naming, like other aspects of Ilongot social life, is a matter of give and take, challenge and response (1984:22). Rosaldo's approach is particularly useful for understanding Chinese nicknaming. *Ming* (birth names) are formally bestowed by one's seniors, one chooses the *tzu* (marriage name) and, as we will see, the *hao* (courtesy name) oneself. Nicknames (*wai hao*), however, are negotiated; both the namer and the named play the game. By setting up this dichotomy between nicknames and other given names, I do not mean to suggest that these two categories have no common features or that *ming,* marriage names, and courtesy names are simply the consequence of a set of rigidly applied rules and structures. It is clear, however, that nicknames fit into the transactional world of local politics, friendship, and informal groups more comfortably than do formal names.

In Chinese society, one can gain a reputation for cleverness by giving nicknames that are particularly apt or make witty literary allusions. Chinese nicknames are highly personalized and often refer to idiosyncratic characteristics. They may also be derogatory or critical, whereas one's formal names would never be intentionally unflattering (especially for a man). Nicknames may refer to a physical quality (for example, "Fatty") or a personal quality ("Stares at the Sky" for someone who is a snob). Nicknames may also protect ("Little Slave Girl") or they may equalize, at least temporarily, unequal relationships. The richest and most powerful man in one New Territories village was nicknamed "Little Dog." In one respect this was a useful nickname for an extremely wealthy man whose political career depended on being accepted by everyone in the community. Rather than rejecting his derogatory nickname he embraced it.

In Ha Tsuen when a man reaches middle age or when he starts a business career, he usually takes a *hao*—"style" or "courtesy" name. A man chooses this name himself. Sung notes that such names are "usually disyllabic or polysyllabic, and [are] selected by oneself bas[ed] upon whatever one would like to be" (1981:86). Some people have more than one courtesy name. The *hao* is a public name par excellence. Such names, Eberhard points out, are often used on occasions when a man wants "to make his personal identity clear without revealing his personal name (*ming*)" (1970:219). In the past, and to some extent today,[9] the *ming* was considered to be too intimate, too personal to be used outside a circle of close friends and kin (Eberhard 1970:218). "The Chinese I know hide their names," writes Maxine Hong Kingston in *Woman Warrior;* "sojourners take new names when their lives change and guard their real names with silence" (1977:6).

Sung notes that *hao* names are no longer popular in present-day Taiwan except among high government officials (1981:86). However, in Hong Kong *hao* are still widely used; they are commonly found, for example, on business cards, and of course many painters or writers sign their work with a *hao*.

In one sense courtesy names are different from birth and marriage names. One achieves a courtesy name. They are a mark of social and economic status, and a poor man who gives himself such a name may be accused of putting on airs. Any man may take a *hao* but if he is not a "man of substance," the *hao* is likely to remain unknown and unused. With poor men or politically insignificant men these names, if they have them at all, may appear only in genealogies or on tombstones.

Some Ha Tsuen men have posthumous names (*shih-hao*) that they take themselves or have conferred upon them by others. Among the imperial elite posthumous names or titles were given to honor special deeds. In the village, however, taking or giving a *shih-hao* is left to individual taste. The practice has declined in recent years.

The preceding discussion suggests that names mark stages in a man's social life. The possession of a birth name, school name, nickname, marriage name, courtesy name, and posthumous name attest to the fact that a man has passed through the major stages of social adulthood. By the time a man reaches

middle age he has considerable control over his names and naming. He names others (his children or grandchildren, for example) and he chooses his own marriage, courtesy, and posthumous names. He also has some control over the use of these names. This is especially true of a successful businessman or politician whose business associates may only know his courtesy name, his drinking friends one of his nicknames, his lineage-mates his birth name, and so on. The use of names is situational and involves some calculation both on the part of the named and those with whom he interacts.

Beidelman, in an article on naming among the Kaguru of Tanzania, emphasizes the point that the choice of name reflects the relation between the speaker and the person to whom he speaks (1974:282; see also Willis 1982). The choice of one name or another, or the use of a kin term rather than a personal name, is a tactical decision. In Ha Tsuen the use of nicknames, pet names, birth names, courtesy names is, like the use of kin terms, highly contextual. Intimates may address each other by a nickname when they are among friends but not when strangers are present; family nicknames may be used in the household but not outside of it; birth names and surnames with titles may be used in formal introductions but not in other settings. A man might be addressed by a kin term or a nickname depending on the speaker's goals. One can give respect by using a courtesy name or claim intimacy by using a nickname. In a single lineage village like Ha Tsuen, where all males are agnatic kinsmen, the strategic use of kin terms and personal names provides a fascinating glimpse into social relationships.

Surprisingly, however, this flexibility does not continue into old age. When a man reaches elderhood at age 61, his ability to control his names diminishes just as his control over his family and corporate resources weakens. In Ha Tsuen and in China generally men often hand over headship of the family when they become elders. The village code of respect requires that male elders be addressed by a kin term (for example, in Cantonese *ah baak,* FeB, or a combination of the given name and kin term, for example, *ah Tso baak*). Only an exceptional man, a scholar or wealthy businessman, will continue to be called by one of his personal names after his 60th birthday. For example, no villager would dare refer to or address the 93-year-old patriarch of the wealthiest family in Ha Tsuen as *ah baak*. In general, however, with advancing age the playful aspects of names and naming are taken away as is a man's power to transact his name. In old age a man has little control over what he is called, and in this respect his situation is similar to that of a married woman. As with wives, old men have left (or are leaving) the world of public and financial affairs to become immersed in the world of family and kinship where they are defined not by a set of distinctive names but by their relationship to others.

"NO NAME" WOMEN

At one month a Ha Tsuen girl is given a name (*ming*); when she marries this name ceases to be used. Marriage is a critical rite of passage for both men and women, but the effect of this rite on the two sexes is very different. Just as a man's distinctiveness and public role are enhanced by his marriage and his acquisition of a marriage name, the marriage rites relegate the woman to the inner world of household, neighborhood, and family. On the one hand, the marriage rites seek to enhance the young bride's fertility, but on the other hand, and in a more negative vein, they also dramatize the bride's separation from her previous life and emphasize the prohibitions and restrictions that now confine her. When the young bride crosses her husband's threshold, what distinctiveness she had as a girl is thrust aside. It is at this point that she loses her name and becomes the "inner person" (nei jen), a term Chinese husbands use to refer to their wives.

While the groom is receiving his marriage name on the first day of marriage rites, his bride is being given an intensive course in kinship terminology by the elderly women of Ha Tsuen. Marriage ritual provides a number of occasions for the formal, ritualized exchange of kin terms (for a description of marriage rites in Ha Tsuen see R. Watson 1981). These exchanges, which always feature the bride, instruct the new wife and daughter-in-law in the vast array of kin terms she must use for her husband's relatives. The prevalence of virilocal/patrilocal residence means that the groom remains among the kin with whom he has always lived. It is the bride who must grasp a whole new set of kin terms and learn to attach these terms to what must seem a bewildering array of people. Two women residents in the groom's village (called in Cantonese *choi gaa*, "bride callers") act as the bride's guides and supporters during the three days of marriage rites, and it is their responsibility to instruct the bride in the kin terminology she will need in order to survive in her new environment.

These ritualized exchanges of kin terms do more, however, than serve as a pedagogic exercise; they also locate and anchor the bride in a new relational system. As the groom acquires his new marriage name—a name, it should be noted, that denotes both group or category membership *and* individual distinctiveness—the bride enters a world in which she exists only in relation to others. She is no longer "grounded" by her own special name (*ming*), however prosaic that name might have been; after marriage she exists only as someone's eBW or yBW or as Sing's mother, and so on. Eventually even these terms will be used with decreasing frequency; as she approaches old age, she will be addressed simply as "old woman" (*ah po*) by all but her close kin.

When I first moved into Ha Tsuen, I quickly learned the names of the male residents (mostly nicknames). But for the women I, like other villagers, relied on kin terms or category terms. Significantly, the rules that govern the use of these terms are not dependent on the age of the women themselves, but rather are a function of the lineage generation of their husbands. Women married to men of an ascending generation to the speaker (or the speaker's husband) may be addressed as *ah suk po* (a local expression meaning FyBW) or by the more formal *ah sam* (also meaning FyBW). For women married to men of one's own generation (male ego) the terms *ah sou* (eBW) or, if one wanted to give added respect, *ah sam* (FyBW) may be used.

A woman may also be referred to by the nickname of her husband plus "leung" (for example, ah Keung leung), or by a teknonym. For their part married women ordinarily use kin terms for their husbands' agnates and for other women in the village. I was told that a woman must use kin terms for men older in age or generation than her husband. Between husband and wife teknonyms are often used so that the father of Tim-sing might address his wife as *ah Sing nai* (ah is a prefix denoting familiarity, *Sing* is part of the son's *ming,* nai is "mother" or, literally, "milk"). In addressing their husbands, women might use nicknames; my neighbor always called her husband "Little Servant."[10]

Although there is some flexibility in deciding what to call a woman, the reference and address terms used for women in Ha Tsuen are very rigid compared to those employed for men. Furthermore, among women there is no possibility of self-naming. Men name themselves, women are named by others. Similarly, Ha Tsuen women are more restricted than their husbands in the tactical use they can make of names and kin terms. Whereas a man may refer to or address his neighbor by his nickname ("Fatty"), his *ming* (*ah Tim*), or by a kin term, decorum dictates that his wife use either a kin term appropriate to her husband's generation or one appropriate to her children. In Cantonese society, and presumably in China generally, adults often address and refer to each other by a version of the kin term their children would use for that person. I suspect, but at this point cannot document, that women are far more likely to do this than are men.

While it is true that a man has little choice in the reference or address terms he uses for women, he does have considerable freedom in distinguishing among his male acquaintances, friends, and kin. Women, as outlined previously, have a restricted repertoire for both sexes. In this sense adult women may be said to carry a particularly heavy burden for guarding the kinship and sexual order. No adult woman is free to act alone or to be treated as if she were independent. The terms by which she is addressed and the terms she uses to address others serve as constant reminders of the hierarchical relations of gender, age, and generation.

As men grow older, as they become students, marry, start careers, take jobs, and eventually prepare for ancestorhood, their new names anchor them to new roles and privileges. These names are not, however, only role markers or classifiers. Ideally, they assign people to categories and at the same time declare their uniqueness. The pattern of naming in Chinese society presents an ever changing image of men. Viewed from this perspective Chinese males are always growing, becoming, accumulating new responsibilities and new rights.

Peasant women, on the other hand, experience few publicly validated life changes, and those that they do undergo link them ever more securely to stereotyped roles. Women's naming leaves little room for individuation or self-expression. Unlike males, whose changes are marked by both ascribed (for example, elderhood) *and* achieved criteria (such as student, scholar, businessman, writer, politician), a woman's changes (from unmarried virgin to married woman, from nonmother to mother, from reproducer to nonreproducer) are not related to achievement outside the home. Instead of acquiring a new name at marriage or the birth of a first child, women's changes are marked by kin terminology or category shifts. At marriage the bride loses her *ming* and becomes known by a series of kin terms. At the birth of a child she may add a teknonym ("Sing's mother"), and as she approaches and enters old age more and more people will address her simply as "old woman" (*ah po*).

The most dramatic changes that women make are the shift from named to unnamed at marriage and the gradual shift from kin term to category term as their children mature and marry.[11] It would appear that as a woman's reproductive capacity declines, she becomes less grounded in the relational system. She becomes, quite simply, an "old woman" much like any other old woman. Of course, family members continue to use kin terms for these elderly women, especially in reference and address, but gradually their anonymity increases. Unlike men, women do not become elders. There is no ceremony marking their entry into respected old age. They move from reproductively active mother to sexually inactive grandmother with no fanfare and with little public recognition of their changed status.

Even in death a woman has no personal name. On the red flag that leads the spirit of the deceased from the village to the grave is written the woman's father's surname (for example, *Lin shih,* translated "Family of Lin"); no personal name is added. For men, the deceased's surname plus his courtesy and/or posthumous name is written on the soul flag. Neither do women's personal names appear on the tombstone where, here again, only the surname of the woman's father is given ("Family of Lin"). In Ha Tsuen women do not have separate ancestral tablets; if they are commemorated at all, they appear as minor appendages on their husbands' tablets. And, once more, they are listed only under the surnames of their fathers. In subsequent generations whatever individuating characteristics a woman might have had are lost—not even a name survives as testimony of her existence as a person.

CONCLUSIONS

If one were to categorize Ha Tsuen villagers on a social continuum according to the number and quality of their names, married peasant women would stand at the extreme negative pole.[12] To my knowledge they share this dubious distinction with no other group. In the past even male slaves (*hsi min*) and household servants had nicknames (see J. Watson 1976:365). They may not have had *ming* or surnames as such but they did possess names that distinguished them from others. It is important to note that it is not only the possession of multiple names that matters but also the fact that, at one end of the continuum, people have no control over their own names while, at the other end, they name themselves and others.

At marriage women find themselves enmeshed in the world of family and kinship. It is a world, as noted in the introduction, that they belong to but do not control. In Ha Tsuen brides arrive as outsiders but quickly, one might even say brutally, they become firmly entrenched in their new environment. Village women can only be identified within the constellation of male names or within the limits of kinship terminology. Unlike their husbands and brothers, women—having no public identity outside the relational system—are defined by and through others.

In Ha Tsuen women are excluded from participation in most of the formal aspects of lineage or community life and they are not involved in decision making outside the home. Ha Tsuen women do not inherit productive resources; they are also restricted in the uses to which they can put their dowries (R. Watson 1984). Furthermore, women in Ha Tsuen cannot become household heads and, even today, they do not vote in local elections. They do not worship in ancestral halls nor do they join the cult of lineage ancestors after death. Although individual peasant women may attain considerable power within their households, they are said to have gained this power by manipulation and stealth. Women by definition cannot hold positions of authority.

In a discussion of male and female naming among the Omaha Sioux, Robert Barnes writes: "The names of Omaha males provide men with distinctive individuality, while also linking each unmistakably to a recognized collectivity. The possibility of acquiring multiple names in adulthood enhances individual prominence for men" (1982:220). Barnes goes on to say that women's names "barely rescue them from a general anonymity, neither conferring uniqueness nor indicating group membership" (1982:22). As among the Sioux, personal naming among Chinese men is a sign of both individual distinctiveness and group membership, while naming practices among village women simply confirm their marginality.

In Ha Tsuen the practice of personal naming reflects and facilitates the passage from one social level to another. Names establish people in social groups and give them certain rights within those groups. With each additional name, a man acquires new attributes. Maybury-Lewis has argued that among many Central Brazilian societies names give humans their "social persona and link [them] to other people" (1984:5; see also Bamberger 1974). Names, Maybury-Lewis writes, "transform individuals into persons" (1984:7). Naming may not be as central to Chinese social organization and ideology as it is among the societies of Central Brazil, yet there is no doubt that, for Chinese men, names have a transformative power that binds them as individuals to society.

In Ha Tsuen the ultimate goal of all males is to produce an heir, to have a grandson at one's funeral, to leave property that guarantees the performance of one's ancestral rites. The possession of many names testifies to the fact that a man has completed the cycle of life. Full personhood is not acquired at birth, at marriage, or even at the death of one's father. It is a process that continues throughout life and is punctuated by the taking and bestowing of names. One might argue that it is a process that extends even beyond death as the named ancestor interacts with the living. If, as Grace Harris suggests, personhood involves a process of social growth "in the course of which changes [are] wrought by ceremony and ritual" (1978:49), then Chinese women never approximate the full cycle of development that their menfolk experience.[13] In stark contrast to men, women become less distinct as they age. The changes they undergo remain largely unrecognized and unnoticed.

In Chinese society, as in other societies, there is a tension between the notion of the unique individual (the individual as value) and the notion of the person tied to society.[14] In some sense the great philosophical systems of Taoism and Confucianism represent these

two poles. Among men, naming involves a dual process through which they achieve personhood by being bound to society, while at the same time they acquire an enhanced sense of individuality and distinctiveness. The peasant women described in this paper seem to have been largely excluded from the individuating, individualizing world of personal naming. The situation with regard to personhood is, however, another matter. It would be wrong to say that peasant wives are nonpersons; rather, they are not persons in the same sense or to the same degree as are husbands and sons. Viewed from the perspective of names, peasant women are neither fully individuated nor "personed." In life as in death they remain suspended between the anonymous world of anybodies and the more sharply defined world of somebodies.

ACKNOWLEDGMENTS

The research for this study was conducted in 1977–78 and was made possible by a grant from the Social Science Research Council (Great Britain) and by the University of London Central Research Fund. An earlier version of this paper was presented at the 1984 American Anthropological Association Annual Meetings. Versions of this paper were also presented at the University of London Intercollegiate Anthropology Seminar and at the University of Rochester's Anthropology Colloquium. I thank the members of those seminars for their suggestions and criticisms. I owe a special debt to Jack Dull, Hsu Cho-yun, Sun Man-li, Roderick MacFarquhar, and James Watson, all of whom have helped in this project. Deborah Kwolek, Judy Tredway, and Martha Terry of the Asian Studies Program at the University of Pittsburgh helped in the preparation of the manuscript and I thank them for their assistance.

Cantonese terms are in Yale romanization and Mandarin terms follow the Wade-Giles system.

This paper is dedicated to the memory of my friend and fellow anthropologist Judith Strauch (1942–85).

NOTES

1. There are bound to be regional, temporal, urban-rural, and class differences in Chinese naming practices. A general discussion of Chinese naming awaits further research.
2. In Taiwan the *ming* is the legal name (it appears in the official household register) and is sometimes called the *cheng ming* (correct name) (Sung 1981:70). In Hong Kong this name may or may not be the name used on legal documents.
3. I am grateful to Professor Jack Dull for pointing out to me the significance and frequency of the personal name Nai among Chinese women.
4. In a similar vein a fifth or sixth child might be named "To End" or "To Finish." One can find such names in the Hong Kong and Taipei telephone directories (see also Sung 1981:81).
5. In China there are no given names like John that are shared by millions of people; on this point see Sung 1981:85.
6. In a discussion of the cosmic relationship between mother and child Marjorie Topley writes of her Cantonese informants:

    The constitutional imbalance of a child with a queer fate may also involve other parties. First, the child may be polarized in the same direction as someone with whom it has a continuous relationship. Then both parties may suffer from continual illness. This may be corrected by adding an element to the child's name so it is compatible with that of the other party [1974:240].

7. This is changing now that girls go to school and their births are registered.
8. In the past when village boys started school at age five or six (girls did not attend school until the 1960s), the schoolmaster gave each student a school or "study name" (*hsueh-ming*). School names are no longer very important in the New Territories.
9. In the past officials' *ming* could not be used except by intimates (see Eberhard 1970 and Sung 1981).
10. After I gained some insight into the micropolitics of my neighbor's household, the name seemed well chosen.
11. Once a son marries reproduction becomes a matter for the younger generation, and in Ha Tsuen it was considered shameful for the mother of a married son to become pregnant.
12. It should be noted here that men do not constitute a uniform category in this regard. Highly literate men make up one extreme but many poorly educated or uneducated men fall somewhere between the two extremes. Like the names of their sisters, their names may be inelegant and rarely seen in written form, but unlike adult women, they do retain their names after marriage.
13. On this point see also LaFontaine 1985:131.
14. For discussions of the concept of the individual as value and the self in Chinese society see for example de Bary 1970; Shiga 1978:122; and more recently Elvin 1985; Munro 1985 (especially essays by Hansen, Yu, Munro, and de Bary).

REFERENCES

Arlington, L. C. 1923. The Chinese Female Names. *China Journal of Science and Arts* 1(4):316–325.

Bamberger, Joan. 1974. Naming and the Transmission of Status in a Central Brazilian Society. *Ethnology* 13:363–378.

Barnes, Robert B. 1982. Personal Names and Social Classification. In *Semantic Anthropology*. David Parkin, ed., pp. 211–226. London: Academic Press.

Beidelman, T. O. 1974. Kaguru Names and Naming. *Journal of Anthropological Research* 30:281–293.

de Bary, William Theodore. 1970. Individualism and Humanitarianism in Late Ming Thought. In *Self and Society in Ming Thought*. Wm. Theodore de Bary, ed., pp. 145–247. New York: Columbia University Press.

Eberhard, Wolfram. 1970. A Note on Modern Chinese Nicknames. In *Studies in Chinese Folklore and Related Essays*. Wolfram Eberhard, ed., pp. 217–222. Indiana University Folklore Institute Monograph Series, Vol. 23. The Hague: Mouton.

Elvin, Mark. 1985. Between the Earth and Heaven: Conceptions of the Self in China. In *The Category of the Person*. Michael Carrithers, Steven Collins, Steven Lukes, eds., pp. 156–189. Cambridge: Cambridge University Press.

Geertz, Clifford. 1973. Person, Time, and Conduct in Bali. In *The Interpretation of Cultures*. pp. 360–411. New York: Basic Books.

Harris, Grace. 1978. *Casting Out Anger: Religion among the Taita of Kenya*. Cambridge: Cambridge University Press.

Hazelton, Keith. 1986. Patrilines and the Development of Localized Lineages: The Wu of Hsiu-ming City, Hui-chou, to 1528. In *Kinship Organization in Late Imperial China*. Patricia B. Ebrey and James L. Watson, eds., pp. 137–169. Berkeley: University of California Press.

Kehl, Frank. 1971. Chinese Nicknaming Behavior: A Sociolinguistic Pilot Study. *Journal of Oriental Studies* 9:149–172.

Kingston, Maxine Hong. 1977. *The Woman Warrior: Memories of a Girlhood among Ghosts*. New York: Vintage Books. (Originally published in hardcover by Alfred Knopf, 1976.)

La Fontaine, Jean. 1985. Person and Individual: Some Anthropological Reflections. In *The Category of the Person*. Michael Carrithers, Steven Collins, and Steven Lukes, eds., pp. 123–140. Cambridge: Cambridge University Press.

Maybury-Lewis, David. 1984. Name, Person, and Ideology in Central Brazil. In *Naming Systems*. Elisabeth Tooker, ed., pp. 1–10. 1980 Proceedings of the American Ethnological Society. Washington, DC: American Ethnological Society.

Munro, Donald (ed.). 1985. *Individualism and Holism: Studies in Confucian and Taoist Values*. Ann Arbor: University of Michigan Press.

Rosaldo, Renato. 1984. Ilongot Naming: The Play of Associations. *In Naming Systems*. Elisabeth Tooker, ed., pp. 11–24. 1980 Proceedings of the American Ethnological Society. Washington, DC: American Ethnological Society.

Sharman, Lyon. 1934. *Sun Yat-sen: His Life and Its Meaning*. Stanford, CA: Stanford University Press.

Shiga, Shuzo. 1978. Family Property and the Law of Inheritance in Traditional China. In *Chinese Family Law and Social Change*. David Buxbaum, ed., pp. 109–150. Seattle: University of Washington Press.

Stacey, Judith. 1983. *Patriarchy and Socialist Revolution in China*. Berkeley: University of California Press.

Sung, Margaret M. Y. 1981. Chinese Personal Naming. *Journal of the Chinese Language Teachers Association* 16(2):67–90.

Topley, Marjorie. 1974. Cosmic Antagonisms: A Mother-Child Syndrome. In *Religion and Ritual in Chinese Society*. Arthur Wolf, ed., pp. 233–249. Stanford, CA: Stanford University Press.

Watson, James L. 1976. Chattel Slavery in Chinese Peasant Society: A Comparative Analysis. *Ethnology* 15:361–375.

Watson, Rubie S. 1981. Class Differences and Affinal Relations in South China. *Man* 16:593–615.

———. 1984. Women's Property in Republican China: Rights and Practice. *Republican China* 10(12):1–12.

———. 1985. *Inequality Among Brothers: Class and Kinship in South China*. Cambridge: Cambridge University Press.

Willis, Roy. 1982. On a Mental Sausage Machine and other Nominal Problems. In *Semantic Anthropology*. David Parkin, ed., pp. 227–240. London: Academic Press.

Wolf, Margery. 1972. *Women and the Family in Rural Taiwan*. Stanford, CA: Stanford University Press.

Wu, Ching-chao. 1927. The Chinese Family: Organization, Names, and Kinship Terms. *American Anthropologist* 29:316–325.

Yang, Martin C. 1945. *A Chinese Village: Taitou, Shantung Province*. New York: Columbia University Press.

Gender and the Stories Pittsburgh Police Officers Tell About Using Physical Force

Bonnie McElhinny

When most people think of work on language and gender, they probably think of works like linguist Deborah Tannen's *You Just Don't Understand* or perhaps even psychologist John Gray's

Adapted from Bonnie McElhinny, "Fearful, Forceful Agents of the Law: Ideologies about Language and Gender in Police Officers' Narratives about the Use of Physical Force," *Pragmatics* 13 (2003): 253–284. Reprinted with permission of publisher.

Men are From Mars, Women are from Venus, studies of "miscommunications" between women and men in heterosexual couples. Despite an increasing number of different approaches, in studies of language and gender in North America the focus on cross-sex miscommunication remains influential and, at its best, insightful.[1] There are, however, a number of increasingly controversial theoretical assumptions about gender often implicitly embedded in this approach, including the notions that the study of gender is closely wedded to the study of heterosexual relations, that gender is an attribute rather than a practice, and that the study of gender is the study of individuals (McElhinny 2003). Studying gender in heterosexual dyads can suggest that "gendered talk is mainly a personal characteristic or limited to the institution of the family" (Gal 1991:185). It also draws attention away from the importance of studying the ways that gender is a structural principle organizing social institutions such as workplaces, schools, courts, and the state and the patterns they display in the recruitment, treatment, and mobility of different men and women (Gal 1991). Gender, like class and racialized ethnicity, nationality, age and sexuality, is an axis for the organization of inequality, a principle for allocating access to resources, though the way each of these axes work may have their own distinctive features (Scott 1986:1054). In this chapter, I talk about how gender structures policing, a type of work that has been traditionally reserved in the United States for men, especially working- class White men. In 1991–1992 I spent twelve months patrolling with the Pittsburgh police department, and recorded 182 hours of police officer interaction. This department was, at the time of my resarch, one of the most racially and sexually diverse big-city police departments in the United States, with 25% female officers and 25% Black officers. This was largely due to a court-enforced affirmative action program in place from 1975–1991 which mandated the hiring of gender and ethnic quotas: each time the department hired a class of recruits, the class was 25% Black women, 25% White women, 25% Black men and 25% White men. The Pittsburgh police force, like many other public sector jobs, was also shaped by a veterans' hiring preference program. Each veteran who took the civil service exam for policing had ten percent added to the score achieved. This practice tended to benefit men, perhaps especially White men (see McElhinny 2000). Even though this workplace was increasingly diverse, it was still perceived as "men's work." The gender of a workplace is determined not only by the presence, or even predominance, of women or men in it but also by cultural norms and interpretations of gender that dictate who is best suited for different sorts of employment. Female police officers routinely found themselves addressed as "sir." My research investigates what the dominant kind of masculinity was in this workplace, and the ways that different officers adopted, adapted or rejected this way of defining policing.

In this chapter, I examine narratives told by male and female, Black and White police officers in Pittsburgh about moments when they found it necessary to use physical force. Policing is a job predominantly staffed by men, and the dominant style of policing is understood as masculine. Nonetheless, in this study I do not assume that men and women are different. Rather, I ask what advantages and disadvantages accrue to men and women embracing different interactional strategies at different moments, when these are associated with gender, and the ways they are associated with dominant institutional norms and practices. I believe that, "interpretations of maleness, manhood, or masculinity are not neutral, but rather all such attributions have political entailments. In any given situation, they may align men against women, some men against other men, some women against other women, or some men and some women against others. In short, the processes of gendering produce difference and inequality" (Cornwall and Lindisfarne 1994:10).

---

[1] It is perhaps significant that Deborah Tannen's later work, focusing on men and women at work, did not receive the same public attention as her work on men and women in couples. This suggests that work which matches certain prevailing assumptions about how gender works is amplified and widely circulated, while other kinds of research are not.

"ACTING CRAZY" AS A THEORY OF AGENCY AND MODEL OF PERSONHOOD

Many male and some female police officers in Pittsburgh understand themselves as fighting a "war" on crime. These police officers believe that the only way to earn respect from citizens is by "acting crazy", a phrase they use to describe their efforts to instill fear in others so that they will not try to push them around. Acting crazy is also a useful strategy for gaining control over an interactional situation since it entails a refusal to negotiate. The construction of authority by using displays of anger raises certain dilemmas that "acting crazy", as a theory of agency and model of personhood, is meant to solve. First, police officers find it important to distinguish between acting crazy and being crazy.

> **You're not really a hard person, but you have to act that way**, because they'll brick you. [PO 30A, Black male, 30, 2 years on the job]

(For details on the transcription conventions used for these recordings, please see Appendix A.) Certain officers, often portrayed as male and older, are seen as "going off", or "blowing their tops" that is, breaking out into unexpected rages that they are not in control of. Though the suddenness of their anger is similar to "acting crazy", other officers distinguish their actions by suggesting that some of these older male officers ARE crazy, rather than ACTING crazy. The difference, then, is that police officers portray other officers as out of control even when they are in control, while understanding themselves as in control even when out of control. Second, in order to justify fear-inspiring actions which they fully realize are controversial, police officers describe the wild, dirty, terrifying world of "the streets" which they must react to. Some officers themselves come to seem inordinately fearful as they tell these stories. As a result, at the very moments when police officers exercise the most force they portray themselves as most helpless: "What else could I do?" "Acting crazy" is thus a way of simultaneously claiming and denying responsibility for action.

Although the necessity for "acting crazy" is not extensively challenged by police officers in Pittsburgh, not all police officers support or value this style of interaction. Some officers perceive themselves more like bureaucrats or social workers than street fighters, and these beliefs lead to different models of agency and personhood (McElhinny 1995). Nonetheless a focus on fighting crime, often called the *crime control* model of policing (Walker 1977) predominates. The *crime-control* model, also known as the crime fighter or militarized model, "characterizes the typical police officer as a crime fighter extraordinaire, a seasoned, well-armed, professional soldier in an unending and savage war on crime" (Appier 1998:160). Between World War II and the early 1970s, women were not seen as appropriate for policing jobs because they were thought incapable of being combat soldiers. The ideal police officer was aggressive and tough, authoritative and male. However, with the advent of affirmative action hiring programs in police departments in the early 1970s (McElhinny n.d.), the gendered ideal shifted a bit. For this reason, not all proponents of a crime-fighting ideology are men: we will look at the narratives of several women below too. A far greater percentage of men, however, embraced such a model, for a variety of complex historical and institutional reasons. At the end of this chapter, I consider what the implications of how police officers talk about the use of physical force are. I am particularly interested in understanding whether and how the integration of women into a traditionally masculine occupation like policing leads to the reinscription or transformation of certain ideologies about how interaction should proceed.

USING NARRATIVES TO STUDY GENDER AND IDEOLOGY

Analyzing narratives is particularly helpful for elucidating how police officers' make sense of their experiences in particular. First, narratives are *event-centered*, that is, they focus on human action and interaction. Second, narratives are *experience-centered*, and thus allow us to infer something about what it feels like to be in the story world. Third, narratives are *performative, seductive and evocative*. That is, narratives do not merely refer to past experience but create experiences for their audience, and they try to persuade listeners by seducing them into the world portrayed. Narratives make an argument about what happened as part of describing what happened (Mattingly 1998:31). Analyses of narratives helps us to understand how stories are given shape by their tellers but also how stories shape the way tellers see and experience themselves, how people become the stories they tell about their lives. Police officers who embrace a crime control model frequently rehearse how they will behave in certain situations if confronted with a recalcitrant husband, or drunken prisoner, or fleeing burglar. They also frequently review the moments in which they have found themselves embroiled in such situations. Narratives allow officers to simultaneously present their own views on past conflicts, shape the on-going interaction (here, with an anthropologist), and rehearse how they would, ideally, talk in the future. The very reiteration of these stories serves to keep alive for these officers the need to be prepared, always, to use force. Stories thus can provide crucial insights into how ideologies around certain styles of policing are forged or reinforced on the ground by police officers.

ALL OF A SUDDEN: RAPID ACTION, REASONABLENESS, AND ROBOCOP.

Rapid, perhaps unpredictable, behavior is a central feature of most police officers' stories about the use of force. In the following narrative, a White female officer is describing the actions of a towering young Black officer ("David") who has come to be called "Robocop" by some of the people in the neighborhood, in part because of his weight-lifter's physique, in part because he's six foot three inches tall, and in part because of his policing style.[2]

> I was working behind a desk last um, last SPRING. . . . David's brought these two people in, a guy and a girl and the guy he had handcuffed to a chair and the girl he had handcuffed to the other chair and the guy's . . . was talking and ta::lking and talking and talking and David's like "SHUT UP." He told him like twenty times and Zellini's sitting behind me . . . singing these little songs like <<in song-song voice>> "You better shut u:::p, David's gonna get ma:::d." (LAUGHS) and like right when he says that **all of a sudden** David PICKED this guy up, chair and all and just like **slammed** him down to the ground. He's like "I told you to SHUT THE FUCK UP. NOW SHUT UP." (LAUGHS) and then he comes over to me afterwards he goes <<she mimics him mumbling under his breath>>, "I'm sorry. I lost my temper." He goes "I can't- I can't stand when I do that you know." (LAUGHS) I'm like, "That's cool David y::- you don't have to apologize." He's like "I didn't mean to swear that much in front of you." He's like real polite and stuff too you know but- They call him Robocop. [PO 25A, White female, 28, 3 years on the job]

Although the narrator concludes by suggesting that David's size and strength alone are enough to intimidate the public, the story suggests otherwise. He (even he) needs to construct a police persona. This female officer portrays him as being unpredictable, crazy, wild. "All of a sudden" is an adverbial phrase which marks Robocop's transition from one condition to another, and which describes him as being out of control. "Slammed", with its connotations of violence, noise and unexpectedness, is used to similar effect, as are the profanity and shouting in David's reported speech. Although David's

---

[2] I have chosen to use the terms *Black* and *White* throughout this paper because they are the terms which police officers usually use. Female officers tend to use *policeman* or *police officer* to describe their own role; male officers tend to use *policeman*. I have opted to use *police officer* as the default term throughout, adding a description of gender where it seems relevant.

action is portrayed as perhaps being sudden from the handcuffed man's point of view, it is also portrayed as intelligible and even predictable from a police officer's point of view. The narrator manages this by portraying the actions of the handcuffed man as unreasonable (*"he was talking and ta::lking and talking and talking*).

What, however, is the point of this story? Skillful narratives often include an evaluation that indicates why a story was told and what the narrator was getting at. Evaluations may be external (in which the point is made explicitly) or internal (in which the narrative dramatizes this information). Here the narrator's laughter throughout the story draws our attention to the hilarious juxtaposition of the fearsome giant with the pussycat who then apologizes to the young female officer. The juxtaposition itself implicitly suggests that David's actions are not an intrinsic part of his character, but part of a display. Indeed the narrator, here relying on the U.S. folk ideology which associates people's real selves with those they display to family and friends, may even be suggesting that the real man is the "real polite" man and not the real angry man. Such a story thus minimizes the actions that "Robocop" takes while acting out his violent role.

ARMED ROBBERS AND AGENCY

If this story begins to illustrate the theory of personhood associated with acting crazy, the stories of Jay, a White officer in his mid-20s from a policing family (his Dad and his wife are also officers) elucidate the interactional and professional dilemmas for which "acting crazy" is a solution. One of Jay's principal fears—and it was a fear he articulated repeatedly even in the few days I rode with him—was that his firearm would be wrestled from him in a fight, or that the firearm of another officer would be taken and used against him. Even if most policing doesn't require guns or physical force, Jay repeatedly pointed out that it only takes one incident to get him killed. Jay justifies police force by describing it

entirely in terms of self-defense, as a reaction to other actions. Portraying the use of force as self-defense contributes to a siege mentality. Any struggle between a police officer and another person is seen merely as a fight between individuals rather than one between an individual and an institution. Jay offers one example of series of events which were, he says, distorted by the "liberal media".

> I caught an armed robber on Polka Street. Guy runs out. "Hey some black guy-" had a big knife, runs at the car. I say, "Hey, what the fuck are you doing?" Andy sees <the robber> hiding between these homes, crouched down. I hear Andy yell. Guy was supposed to be armed so Andy had his gun on him. Guy could have gone straight up on this porch. Andy couldn't see his hands—he said, "Show me your hands, real slow, or you're gonna get whacked." **Now we're in a fist fight, he got his ass beat,** <community members> saw this brutal act, by a police man, was a bunch of shit. This brutal police man. Man falsely accused. He was the guy that robbed the place. He wouldn't show Andy his hands. Community leaders saw it, and they said it's wrong. "You police man are wrong." [PO 114B, White male, 26, 5 years on the job]

In the part of the narrative where Jay is catching the robber, he regularly uses historic present tense ("*I say*", "*Andy sees*", "*I hear*") and leaves "guy" unmodified by a definite or indefinite article. This iconically captures and conjures up the breathless rapidity with which events happen and with which officers must make decisions about appropriate actions. The suddenness of the movement from threat to force ("*Now we're in a fist fight*") emphasizes the danger of police work, and justifies the rapidity with which he too must make a transition from one emotional state to another. Most surprising here is the vagueness at a crucial moment: Who exactly initiated the fist fight? Although police officers have a kind of discretionary power over others' freedom that would justify a portrayal of themselves as super agents, they often downplay their own agency. "Now we're in a fist fight" and "He got his ass beat" leave unmarked the agent or agents of the acts. Jay consistently blames the other person for escalating interactions from a polite to an impolite one, from a verbal interaction to one which is physically threatening, from an interaction in which a physical threat is implicit to one in which it is explicit.

If Jay accounts for his actions in terms of the activities he must respond to, Frank, a burly man who looks like Hollywood's stereotype of an Irish policeman, justifies his actions in terms of the character of the people he must deal with. He half-jokes, "Anymore when someone asks me what I do for a living, I say garbageman" [9A]. He uses other metaphors for criminals ("vermin" and "maggots") which serve to downplay the agency and humanity of those he interacts with. He portrays his actions as inevitable, as entirely determined by the situation rather than his own agency.

> I don't usually confess up to too many things, but the one time I did beat a man I didn't really have to, whereas we get a call for child molestation. We could look in the window we could see this little girl about four years old bleeding from the vagina-area. This maggot's in the corner, crying. I hit him. More than once. **What am I supposed to do**. [PO 9B, White male, 39/40, 13 years on the job]

Frank offers no apologies for actions that he sees as natural, in the circumstances. Like Jay, he sees his role as reaction, not action.

Even in seemingly frank descriptions of the emotional distress the job causes him, Frank uses agency-masking grammatical devices. After he described this child abuse call, I ask if it was difficult not to take the job home.

> Not to sound like a wimp, but more than once I've gone home and cried. I don't see myself as a wimp but . . . **it catches up to you**. One time I had to take little girls, I didn't actually take them, I helped carry them out of the fire, they'd died. That bothered me. Thinking of those girls—nobody gets a break on a fire hydrant. [PO 9B, White male, 39/40, 13 years on the job]

Though he does say "I've cried", "it catches up to you" doesn't even give him the relative passive role of experiencer (compare "I felt").

Frank also moves quickly away from a discussion of how the job affects him to describing the sort of tough professional action he takes as a result (writing tickets for people illegally parked near fire hydrants).

"Between a Rock and a Hard Place": The Dilemmas of Being a Black Police Officer

So far the stories considered here have been stories told by White officers, but a crime fighter ideology is not limited to these officers. Doug, a young African-American officer, came on the job with a college degree but no street experience. He notes that when he first became a police officer, he tried to be polite and nice (a strategy he calls being "Officer Friendly"), but these strategies did not work. He says that police officers cannot simply let others tell them what to do. Instead, he says, police officers need to take control of situations:

> **If you more or less yell at them**, tell them "Get the hell outta here, we're not gonna have this", they'll get real quiet, they'll get real soft, and everything else [PO 30A, Black male, 30, 2 years on the job]

"If you more or less yell at them" uses a hedge to downplay the police officer's action. The use of impersonal "you" ("*If you more or less yell. . . .*") rather than "I" has a similar effect.

Doug uses many military metaphors to describe his work. He describes the drug trade in Pittsburgh as a "drug war", and says that the job of policing sometimes becomes so overwhelming that police men become "just like Vietnam vets—they need to get away." He describes his own style of policing as aggressive. In the accounts of officers like Doug, there often seems to be a surprisingly thin edge between displays of anger and aggression and accounts of fear. Doug himself is most aware of this when discussing other officers. As part of his training period, he worked with a White officer who was tense every time he found himself around a group of Blacks. Though Doug is critical of such White officers' actions, he also excuses them to some extent by suggesting that they're not "mean," just "scared." He reserves his harshest critique for the supervisors who deploy their officers without sensitivity to what they can and cannot do.

Like Jay, Doug argues that people's critiques of cops arise because they do not fully understand what it is like "out here", not because people might have different moral or legal views about force. Doug's comments arose when we were talking about his reaction to the beating of African-American motorist Rodney King by white police officers in Los Angeles. He quickly noted that he believed the L.A. police officers were wrong, but followed that with comments on the ways that people tend to misinterpret police actions. His comments condense a number of the strategies discussed thus far in this paper.

> Say for instance you would like be in a window and you would see me run up on some kids you seen right across the street. And you- they don't look like they're doing anything to you. But I go up and choke one of them, just running out of my car and and I go up and choke one of them. It seems like for no reason at all. It would be hard for me to explain that I told them to get off the street, I knew they were dealing drugs, I wouldn't have it, I told them if I came back, you know. Now if they would have pulled him out of the car and somebody would have shot that saying that "Oh they just beat him." Now how do they know he didn't have a gun or whatever? Now like I said, that <<the beating of Rodney King>> was excessive force, and that was ridiculous, to beat a guy like that. But I mean if they would have beat him a couple times or whatever and that was filmed, it would look kinda one-sided. See as a police officer, you have enough problems worrying about yourself (pause) being ali- getting, you know, being shot, being- existing out on the street. But to worry about if you're gonna get sued, if your family's gonna, you know if you're gonna lose your house and all that stuff. Every time you question something, or move you make, it could cost you your life. If you're afraid that someone is watching you, you're afraid you don't want to hit this guy or snatch him up, and then he turns around and stabs you, and kills you. You're between a rock and a hard place. [PO 30A, Black male, 30, 2 years on the job]

Doug is torn. He wants to critique what happened in L.A., but reserve the right to use force for himself. He wants to critique outsiders' views of policing at the same time that he is an outsider to what happened in L.A. In this brief passage a cluster of grammatical features mark anxious preoccupation and serve to heighten the officer's message about his double bind, how immobilized he feels by needing to balance a need for self-defense with a concern for citizens' rights. There is a cluster of verbs and adjectives that describes worry and fear, though note that here again the officer does not construct himself as the agent or actor or even the experiencer ("*to worry about if you're gonna get sued, if you're afraid*"). The author also piles up the potential consequences of any act, with a series of "if" clauses that together imagine the worse that could happen: *if you're gonna get sued, if your family's gonna, if you're afraid*. Finally, impersonal "you" serves to distance these concerns from him in the second half of his account: "*if you're afraid*", "*you're between a rock and a hard place*". If Jay largely emphasizes the physical dangers of policing, Doug adds to these concerns a preoccupation with the moral and legal hazards of the job. This spiral of panic may reflect the particular dilemmas that being Black and being a police officer pose.

Girls Who Freak: Turning Rapport Talk on Its Head

After having repeatedly heard how masculine Cissy was, I was eager to meet her. I was startled to find she was a short, plump White woman with long, curly black hair. Though following department regulations would have meant pulling her hair up into a bun, she wore it loose down on her shoulders. It was the week before Halloween and she was wearing a pumpkin tie pin. Though regulation socks are dark blue, her socks had pumpkins on them. She looked like a PTA mother. My surprise at the fact that she was perceived as masculine reflects some dominant gender ideologies that link femininity and masculinity to appearance. For police officers, however, it is interaction which is a more salient characteristic, in part because interactions are so carefully scrutinized by the public and by supervisors, but also because interactions shape the work environment for other officers. Cissy's enthusiasm for "acting crazy" led to her being perceived as masculine, and is evidence that the crime control ideology is gendered as masculine, regardless of who embraces it. There was, however, a stronger negative connotation in labelling her as masculine than in labelling male officers as such. Other officers saw Cissy as an impatient, impetuous officer who did not treat people right. More than any of the other officers I rode with, Cissy's image of the kind of police officer she was differed from my observations and from the perceptions of other officers. Cissy repeatedly painted herself as an active officer who was interested in helping people, and who had a knack for establishing rapport with the public. She describes the way people in a racially-mixed, lower-to-middle income neighborhood reacted to her and her female partner.

[I]t was funny cause they would see two females come down in the car and it was like, "We're not afraid of you" so you kinda had to get real hard-nosed with them at first, but it was funny cause after you like really got out of the car and you show them this is the way it's gonna be, they kinda like you. **You got a rapport going** with them, where when they would see your car, they would just leave. We have worked out **such a good rapport** with those people down there. I've NE:VER had no problems. Those other officers they go down there and they give them a real hard time. . . . I had one problem and after that. "I'm not moving, you're not nothing." I'm like, "Oh yeah. We're something. Let's go." And we were out of the car. And it was like, "**Those girls are CRA:zy.** They'll actually make you move." [PO 11A, White female, mid-30s, 2 years on the job]

In the literature on language and gender, seeking rapport has been largely associated with women's talk. Tannen (1990:77) defines rapport-talk as a way of establishing connections and negotiating relations in which emphasis is placed on displaying similarities and matching experiences. She contrasts this with report-talk, in which she maintains many men display knowledge or skills as a way to preserve independence and status in a hierarchical social order. Cissy's definition of rapport is much more like Tannen's definition of report-talk. For her, rapport seems to be understood as everyone recognizing her right and ability to use verbal and physical force, and fearing that possibility.

The extent to which women officers are licensed to use physical force and tough talk is at least partly linked to the class and ethnic persona they present, and to stereotypes about White and Black femininity in the U.S. Though Cissy was seen in a negative light, as "too masculine", Ayanna, a young Black woman who was seen as ready, willing, and able to use force, did not receive similar sanctions. Ayanna was one of the few young female police officers who received the accolade of "knows her way around out there" from older White male officers. She was in her mid-20s and had been on the force for 2 years. She was a slight African-American woman (weighing about 100 pounds, she confessed, and trying to gain more), with tightly cropped hair. Though many smaller women were ignored or babied by male officers, Ayanna was, at the time I rode with her, being actively recruited by the City's Drug Task Force, which at the time of my fieldwork had no female officers. She tells stories about fights with relish.

We had to chase this guy . . . when I first came on. We had to chase him cause they were going on a drug bust . . . and they wanted him and Jimmy Baker. . . . We got a tip right, we had to chase these boys, they were supposed to be armed. . . . We really didn't know if they were armed or not. Police officers been chasing them for months and they been lying to them, blowing them off. Me and my partner caught these guys. . . . When I finally caught them I had these fake nails on. I used to go and get my nails done every week. Broke my nail. Fifty dollars. When I seen he broke my nail, I **freaked.** I said, "You broke my nail!" I **pounded** him in his head, **acting like I was crazy.** "I can't believe you broke my nail!" I'm **tripping** over my nail right. I'm still huffing and puffing from the run. Was fun. We had a great time that day. [PO 58A, Black female, early 20s, 2 years on the job]

In a curious reversal of feminine stereotypes, here a broken fingernail does not reduce a woman to ineffectiveness, but rather leads to the use of physical force. Though a fake fingernail is a symbol of femininity, perhaps especially a symbol of a certain kind of Black femininity, her physical reaction is precisely that of other officers whose authority is questioned in any way. Again verbs mark a sudden change of state ("*was tripping*", "*freaked*", "*pounded*"). Like the male officers above, she describes her actions as a masquerade ("*acting like I was crazy*"). Ayanna also invoked the necessity for "acting crazy" in other, rather different circumstances. She was on her way to a call that had been described by the dispatcher as "complainant says her boyfriend's on the way over to her house and she expects trouble." As Ayanna drove to the largely White working-class area she said that this was an area where people were known for fighting police officers, and for their dislike of Black officers. She described the strategy she would try to adopt to handle the call ("*First I'll try to start off nice*"), but points out that sometimes "you gotta act crazy" to be recognized as an authority in such a neighborhood.

It is clear from these descriptions that women, too, can embrace a crime control ideology, and that younger women in particular are likely to do so. They are not trying to establish a distinctively feminine or womanly style of policing as a way of creating space for themselves in this predominantly masculine workplace, as women did at the turn of the century when they saw policing as an extension of social work (Appier 1998). Instead, these younger women choose to assimilate to, and reinscribe the power of, the dominant ideology of how to act, and interact, as a police officer, in ways that end up allying them with certain male officers, and against older female officers who often adopt a more critical stance towards the crime control model. Indeed, younger women argue that

older women may have been qualified for the job, but they took it for the wrong reasons: "they only do it for the money." Many of the older women did enter policing at times of financial hardship (e.g. a divorce, a husband's loss of a job in a steel mill), and they do not describe policing as a job they had always dreamed of doing. Because they "only took the job for the money" they are not seen as professional. Younger women distance themselves from the problems faced by the first female officers, many of whom are still on the job, understanding them as difficulties faced by particular individuals rather than challenges linked to breaking down the barriers to women working on this job. They tend to see measures such as affirmative action as unnecessary. Young women therefore tend to overestimate the extent to which simply being a "good" police officer allows them to succeed on the job, and to under-estimate the ways that their presence on the job was and is supported by certain institutional measures (like affirmative action). Their views do not allow them to see the ways that gender remains linked to the definition of what being a good police officer is, albeit in a less marked way that when women were seen as incapable of becoming police officers.

CONCLUSIONS

The wide distribution of the ideology of police officer as crime fighter among Pittsburgh police officers is partial evidence for its dominant status among Pittsburgh police officers. Police officers who espouse it may be White or Black, men or women. Some have college educations and others have high school educations, some are veterans and some are not, some are rookies and some have been on the force for close to fifteen years. Among those who espouse the ideology there is, perhaps, an unusually high cluster of people who come from policing families. And yet the crime fighter ideology remains associated with a certain kind of masculinity, irrespective of the people who hold it. This makes it difficult for women, and men who have not traditionally been police officers, to be perceived as competent, and thus gives them a tenuous foothold within the job. In addition, those who challenge the dominant ideology may not be judged as policing effectively. Rather than "acting crazy" some officers focus on constructing another persona, that of the rational, calm, cool bureaucrat. Officers who orient towards this way of thinking about policing tend to be women (especially older women), or Black men, or White men with college educations. These officers may be portrayed by others as unwilling or unable to do "real" police work. Still, those who fall in with dominant norms may not be seen as effective police officers either. As affirmative action hiring plans have been rolled back in police departments in recent years, hirings of women and (to a lesser extent) minority men have immediately dropped because they still are not seen by administrators as fully capable of doing the job. Recent redefinitions of policing as community policing, or as "social work in combat boots" do offer a significant challenge to the crime-fighter ideology, and may create more permanent niches for women and minority men in policing. In Pittsburgh, however, community policing has not been embraced by either administrators or police officers.

When the police officers tell stories, to themselves or to the public or to me, about moments when the use of force was necessary, they are not merely describing those experiences, but recreating them, seducing themselves and others into believing that the sequence of events that they describe was not only justified, but inevitable. Given the emotional power of these stories, simply instructing officers to behave in other ways, where their actions are perceived as inappropriate, seems unlikely to be a productive strategy for changing the way they approach these scenarios. Activists have repeatedly found that in numerous settings presenting research which suggests to people that their beliefs are "false" is not sufficient for engendering support for change, or even agreement that the activists are right. One needs, instead, to find a way of restructuring these ways of feeling.

The discursive strategies which accompany these officers' descriptions of and justifications

for their use of force focus on the ways they elicit respect and fear by acting crazy, and by acting in abrupt and unpredictable ways. These narrators also (with attentiveness to public perceptions of the use of force) often de-emphasize their own role as agents of the law. This denial of agency may be one of the defining features of legal and medical institutional talk in many settings, and one of the key ways that authority and power not only justified but disguised (see also Briggs 1997). Many of these officers' stories about the use of force are accompanied by sheer fear about the potential crumbling of their police power. By emphasizing the danger they face "out here", they justify the use of force in self-defense. Other working class jobs—mining, construction, agriculture—are, in fact, more dangerous than police work but police officers' constant sense of fear distinguishes them from these workers (Reuss-Ianni 1983:19–20). The discourse on fear here shares with studies of colonial violence, where talk about fear of the dominated was used to justify suppression, as well as a way of bargaining with other elites for resources and support needed to face down the purported threat (see Abu-Lughod and Lutz 1990:14). It does not seem inconsequential for understanding the particular stances towards violence expressed here that veterans of the U.S. military receive preference in hiring as police officers (McElhinny 2000), or that my fieldwork was conducted during a period when the U.S. government saw itself as waging a "war on drugs" both in the U.S. and in Latin and South America. Perhaps what is most striking about the worldview of police officers is precisely the ways in which they assume that social interactions are built around conflict and mayhem. They repeatedly insist that the world is violent and that no one is trustworthy. Though some may lament the loss of innocence and trust that comes with repeatedly dealing with violence, most police officers were convinced that the Hobbesian view of human nature which this led them to have was much more accurate than the blinkered and rosier view of others. The stories they tell about instances in which they use physical force, and the justifications which they offer for it, are built around this linguistic and social ideology. For them, instances of lying, conflict and violence are not extraordinary, but ordinary, everyday occurrences. Indeed, for many police officers, violence and deception define humanity.

ACKNOWLEDGMENTS

Research and writing were supported by the National Science Foundation (NSF Graduate Fellowship and NSF Dissertation Improvement Grant), the Mellon Foundation, the Wenner Gren Foundation for Anthropological Research (Pre-Doctoral Grant, and Richard Carley Hunt Post-doctoral Grant), the Stanford Humanities Center, the University of Pittsburgh Women's Studies Program, the Stanford Center for the Study of Conflict and Negotiation, and the Department of Anthropology at the University of Toronto.

APPENDIX A. TRANSCRIPTION CONVENTIONS

Each transcribed example is followed by information about the tape that the example can be found on, as well as the police officer's sex (male or female), ethnicity (Black, White, Mixed ethnicity) and years of work on the Pittsburgh police force (where available). For example, [PO 11A, White female, mid-30s, 2 years on the job] indicates that the transcribed example is on side A of PO 11. The officer is White, female, and in her mid-30s. She has worked as a police officer for two years. This paper also draws on the following transcription conventions:

(pause)	**All pauses are marked between parentheses.**
We were walk-	A dash marks a word or phrase broken off before it is finished.
LOUD	Capital letters indicate increased volume.
eve::ry	Semi-colon marks lengthened sound.
(laughs)	Laughter is marked between single parentheses.
" quote "	Indicates quoted speech.
<text>	Parentheses surround barely audible speech for which the transcription is uncertain
. . . .	Three or four dots indicate that some material from the original transcript has been omitted.
<<comment>>	Double brackets enclose transcriber comments.
bold	Part of transcript highlighted for analyst's purposes

REFERENCES

Abu-Lughod, Lila and Catherine Lutz. 1990. Introduction: Emotion, discourse and the politics of everyday life. In Catherine Lutz and Lila Abu-Lughod (eds.), *Language and the politics of emotion*. Cambridge: Cambridge University Press, 1–23.

Appier, Janis. 1998. *Policing women: The sexual politics of law enforcement and the LAPD*. Philadelphia: Temple University Press.

Briggs, Charles (1997) Introduction: From the ideal, the ordinary, and the orderly to conflict and violence in pragmatic research. Special issue of *Pragmatics* on "Conflict and violence in pragmatic research." Volume 7(4): 451–459.

Capps, Lisa and Elinor Ochs. 1995. *Constructing panic: The discourse of agoraphobia*. Cambridge: Harvard University Press.

Cornwall, Andrea and Nancy Lindisfarne. 1994. Dislocating masculinity: Gender, power, and anthropology. In Andrea Cornwall and Nancy Lindisfarne (eds.), Dislocating Masculinities: Comparative Ethnographies. NY: Routledge 11–47.

Gal, Susan. 1991. Between speech and silence: The problematics of research on language and gender. In Micaela di Leonardo (ed.), *Gender at the crossroads of knowledge*. Berkeley: University of California Press, 175–203.

Mattingly, Cheryl. 1998. *Healing dramas and clinical plots: The narrative structure of experience*. Cambridge: Cambridge University Press.

McElhinny, Bonnie. 1995. Challenging hegemonic masculinities: Female and male police officers handling domestic violence. In Kira Hall and Mary Bucholtz (eds.), *Gender articulated: Language and the socially constructed self*. New York: Routledge, 217–243.

McElhinny, Bonnie. 2000. Affirmative action and veterans' hiring preferences: Two quota systems. *Voices: Newsletter of the association for feminist anthropology.* July, 4(1): 1–6.

McElhinny, Bonnie. 2003. Theorizing gender in sociolinguistics and linguistic anthropology. In Janet Holmes and Miriam Meyerhof (eds.), *Handbook of language and gender.* Oxford: Basil Blackwell. pp. 21–42.

McElhinny, Bonnie. n.d. *Policing language and gender.* Book ms.

Reuss-Ianni, E. 1983. *The two cultures of policing: Street cops and management cops.* New Brunswick NJ: Transaction Books.

Scott, Joan. 1986. Gender: A useful category of historical analysis. *American Historical Review.* 91(5): 1053–75.

Tannen, Deborah. 1990. *You just don't understand: Women and men in conversation.* New York: William Morrow.

Walker, Samuel. 1977. *A critical history of police reform: The emergence of professionalism.* Lexington, MA: Lexington Books.

Woolard, Kathryn. 1998. Introduction: Language ideology as a field of inquiry. In Bambi Schieffelin, Kathryn Woolard and Paul Kroskrity (eds.), *Language ideologies: Practice and theory.* Oxford: Oxford University Press, 3–50.

The Making and Unmaking of Persons: Gender and Body in Northeast India

Sarah Lamb

A principal theme in sociocultural studies of South Asia[1] over the past several decades has been the investigation of South Asian notions of what a "person" or "self" is.[2] One of the most interesting insights of much of this research has been the suggestion that Indians view persons as relatively fluid and open in nature. Research produced by McKim Marriott, Ronald Inden and E. Valentine Daniel, for instance, has suggested that Indian persons are not thought to be bound and self-contained individuals, but rather connected *substantially* with the other people, places, and things of their lived-in worlds. By means of transactions with other persons, such as through sex, childbirth, living together, feeding, touching, and exchanging words, people are thought to absorb and give out parts of themselves. Thus it is possible—indeed, inevitable—for persons to establish substantial relations with other people (such as sexual partners, household and community members) and with the places (land, village,

houses) in which they live. It may then make sense to describe Indian or South Asian persons as composite and hence "dividual" or divisible in nature, Marriott and later other scholars suggested; by contrast, Europeans and Americans view persons as relatively closed, contained and solid "*in*dividuals."[3]

One deficiency in early studies of personhood in South Asia, however, was the relatively scant attention paid to gender. This was true not only of the work on the person in South Asia, but also of the wider anthropological literature on personhood. What is striking is that although anthropological interest in personhood developed contemporaneously with the anthropology of gender (from about the 1970s on), there has been little attempt to bring these two fields of inquiry together. As Henrietta Moore observes: "Indigenous concepts of the person and self are presented, most often, as gender neutral, but on closer examination it is clear that the implicit model for the person in much ethnographic writing is, in fact, an adult male" (1994:28). This gives the misleading impression that person and self are ontologically prior to and separate from gender identity.

"The Making and Unmaking of Persons: Notes on Aging and Gender in North India." *Ethos* 25(3): 279–302. Used with permission.

This chapter explores gendered aspects of personhood[4] for Bengali Indians, focusing on the gendered nature of the body and its implications for the making and unmaking of women's ties over the life course. Although Bengalis regard both men and women as relatively fluid and open in nature, they view women as being significantly more so, especially during their postpubertal and premenopausal years. This has important implications both for the ways women manage their daily interactions, and for the ways women's ties are made, unmade and remade over the course of their lives.

The chapter draws primarily on fieldwork done in the village of Mangaldihi in the northeast Indian state of West Bengal, where I lived for a year and a half in 1989–90 and for a brief revisit in 2003. Mangaldihi is a large, predominantly Hindu village of about 1,700, in the gently undulating terrain of the Birbhum District, about 150 kilometers northwest of Kolkata.

OPEN PERSONS AND SUBSTANTIAL EXCHANGES

The people I know in Mangaldihi (consistent in many ways with previous models of South Asian personhood) do feel themselves to be inherently relational, each person functioning as a nexus within a "net" (*jal*) of ties shared with people (especially kin), places, and things. By sharing and exchanging bodily and other substances through acts such as sex, touching, living together, sharing food, owning things, and eating the fruits of village soil, people see themselves as forming substantial-emotional bonds with their kin, homes, possessions, and land— all of which together make up a "person" (or *lok*).[5] Bengalis commonly refer to these kinds of relations as *maya,* a polyvalent term often translated by scholars as "illusion," but locally more often equated with affects like attachment, affection, compassion, and love.[6] The concept of maya entails integrally both material and what we might call emotional or sentimental dimensions. Maya is often imaged as a "net" (*jal, mayajal*), the strands of which are constituted both of shared bodily substance, as

well as of emotional attachments such as affection, love, and compassion.

Such an understanding of persons as relatively open and unbound was at first especially apparent to me in practices surrounding "mutual touching" (*choyachuyi*) and the management of "impurity" (*asuddhata*) in daily life. People in Mangaldihi are concerned about whom and what they touch because touching involves a mutual transfer of substantial qualities from one person or thing to the next. High-caste Hindus avoid touching low-caste Hindus; Hindus avoid touching Muslims; and people of all castes frequently avoid touching those who are in states of "impurity" because of recent activities (e.g., defecating, visiting a hospital, or riding on a crowded bus of mixed castes and unknown substances). To be sure, people often touch one another in the course of their daily affairs. But when they do, each considers that substantial properties from the other have permeated his or her own body, and the person who is in the "higher" or more "pure" position will often feel it necessary to change clothes and bathe to rid him or herself from the effects of the contact. Further, some forms of contact—such as regularly sharing food or living together—are regarded as being so intimate and extensive that they cannot be erased simply by bathing: a person's substance and nature will have changed. (This is, in fact, how some relations of kinship are formed.)

As I happened to reside in a neighborhood of Brahmans—the highest Hindu caste and those tending to be most concerned about matters of purity—I was taught early on as part of my bodily training as an anthropologist to carefully manage my own touching, or bodily influxes and outflows. I was pressed to be careful about whom and what I interacted with, and to bathe and change my clothes after coming into contact with "impure" (*asuddha*) persons and things. On some days it seemed I had to bathe almost continuously—after I defecated (which unfortunately could happen more than once, especially when suffering from mild dysentery), or visited a lower-caste neighborhood, or came into contact accidentally with some dog-doo, or returned from a bus trip, or accidentally touched the outside panel of a truck carrying a dead person to the cremation ground, and on and on—so that I felt I could get almost nothing else done.

I am chagrined to confess, however, that for my first several months in the village, I did not notice that women were much more vulnerable than men to such daily impurities, and thus more frequently subjected to bathing rituals. Then one day quite by chance as I was having a casual conversation with an older Brahman man, he told me that, in fact, men (Brahman or otherwise) do not have to bathe after coming into cursory contact with impure things. They can if they *wish* to, that is if they desire to be particularly "pure" for the purposes of entering a temple or some such; but they do not *have* to—no harm (*dos*) will occur if they do not. It is only *women* who must so often bathe. I was astounded, not only because I realized that a male anthropologist in Mangaldihi would not have had to spend so many seemingly futile hours bathing, but also because I had been so oblivious to this crucial difference in men's and women's daily practices. I spent the next several weeks asking everyone, men and women, why it is that women are more vulnerable to impurity than men, and their answers led me to some crucial differences in the ways people conceive of men's and women's bodies and personhoods.

GENDERED BODIES AND EVERYDAY PRACTICES

Key here are differences perceived in the biologies of the two sexes. In the predominant patrilineal discourses of Mangaldihi, women's bodies are taken to be naturally more "open" (*khola*) than men's—especially because of their involvement in the processes of menstruation, marriage, sexuality, and childbirth—all processes that entail, for women, substances going into and out of the body. This means that women can be viewed as more dangerously vulnerable to impurity, sexual violations, and receipts from the outside than are men, and also as more exudative.

For instance, a woman is especially open, and also impure (*asuddha*), during her menstrual period. A girl's first menstruation marks the beginnings of a state of openness, and thus her readiness for marriage, sexual relations, and pregnancy. Many women practice closing and containing techniques during their periods, such as refraining from touching household deities and food intended for superiors, and binding their hair tightly in a braid or bun. Sexual intercourse also involves opening a woman, and virgins are sometimes described as *bandha*, or closed. Intercourse, say Bengalis, takes place within the woman and outside the man. Sexual fluids leave the man at the moment of ejaculation to enter and permeate the woman: once she has slept with a man, a woman contains some of his substance within her permanently, although a man can sleep with a woman with no real lasting effect. A woman's sexual "heat" also makes her open (to sexuality, fertility, and other mixings); and many across India say that women have even more sexual heat and desire than men (unlike popular American conceptions).[7] Childbirth as well makes women impure and leaves them dangerously open for a period of one month after they give birth or experience a late miscarriage or abortion. To remedy this condition—to close and "dry out" (*sukote*) her body and womb—a woman has to undergo a drying, self-containing, and separative period of birth impurity (*asauc*), similar to that occurring after a death in the family.[8]

Village women themselves express clear ideas about the relative openness and impurity of women's bodies. A married Brahman woman, Subradi, told me: "Women are always impure (*apabitra*), because everything happens to them—menstruation, childbirth. These don't happen to men. For this reason if men touch a Muslim[9] or defecate, no harm (*dos*) happens to them, and they don't have to wash their clothes or bathe. But harm happens to a woman." My closest companion Hena (then soon to be married, in her early twenties) offered similar comments: "Men are always pure. They don't menstruate or give birth. Women menstruate, give birth—all that happens to them. Men only defecate, and nothing else." As Subradi and Hena both put it, things "happen" to women—menstruation, childbirth, defecation, and so on. As passive receivers of action, women have a greater vulnerability to outside agents. One common north Indian saying illustrates this notion of the openness or permeability of women particularly vividly: Women are like unglazed earthen water jugs, which are permeable and become easily contaminated to such depth that they cannot be purified. Men are like impermeable brass jugs, which are difficult to contaminate and easy to purify (cf. Dube 1975:163, 1988:16; Jacobson 1978:98).

A final point made to me about women's relative openness emphasized not their receptivity but their diffusion. It is women, people told me, who nurse children, cook, fetch water, feed and care for household gods, and handle on a daily basis all sorts of household things. That is why women, rather than men, must take the most care in regulating their mixings with others, lest they exude impurity or unwanted substances onto the household things and members they feed and care for.

Because of the perceived potential dangers of their openness, women and girls in the Mangaldihi region are taught by their senior kin to discipline their bodies—to attempt selectively (in certain contexts, especially in public and around men) to close themselves. They rely not only on bathing, but also on spatial seclusion, cloth coverings, binding the hair, and the like. These disciplining techniques seem to aim primarily at controlling and channeling a woman's powers toward desired ends within a patrilineage. Dominant discourses indicate that a woman's body is in most need of control or containment between the onset of puberty and marriage, as well as during the early years of marriage, because a woman is most vulnerable to violations—sexual and otherwise—of her body and household during these times. So women, when possible, confine their movements to the home, sending men or young children to the store for needed goods instead of going themselves, refraining from attending the entertaining plays and videos that periodically come through the village, and traveling only when accompanied by close male kin to

visit natal homes or married daughters. They also cover their bodies carefully with saris, modestly pull a sari end over their heads when around senior and unknown men, and keep their hair bound (for "open" hair signifies looseness, in morality and body).

Not all women accept such expectations fully or without critique. For instance, I have known village women to venture out with friends to see a play or take a trip to town, or embark on a pilgrimage while (impurely) menstruating, or engage in an extra-marital romances (see Lamb 2000:194–197). Others speak of women's impurity and openness with an air of critical sarcasm, indicating a sense of the system's injustice. For instance, Mona exclaimed sarcastically, when I asked about women's need to bathe, "A Brahman man can even drink alcohol and sleep with a Leather-working woman [the lowest Hindu caste in Mangaldihi], and no harm happens. A woman never could! This is just the human [or male] system (*manuser bidhan*)."[10] Nonetheless, dominant understandings across genders and castes in Mangaldihi are that women are more "open" than men and need thus to practice some containment.

Such notions about the relative openness of women's bodies are not uncommon cross-culturally. Thus Carol Delaney (1991:38) finds that in Turkish society the male body is viewed as self-contained whereas the female body is relatively unbounded. Renee Hirschon (1978:76–80) writes about the ambiguous nature of female "openness" in Greek society, while Jean Comaroff (1985:81) notes the relative lack of closure of female bodies among the Tswana of South Africa. But we must remember that in this community of northeast India, even the male body is not usually considered to be wholly bound; it is only *relatively* bound compared to the greater openness of the female body.

GENDERED LIFE COURSES

The same traits of openness and permeability that mean that women are dangerously open to impurities also impact the ways women's bodily-emotional ties—of kinship, love, attachment, or maya—are made and unmade over the life course. The main argument I wish to make here is that women's personhood is unique, in that their ties are disjoined and then remade, while men's ties are extended and enduring. Feminist theorists such as Nancy Chodorow (1978) and Carol Gilligan (1982) have challenged the adequacy of models of the autonomous individual to explain women's experiences (in the United States, at least), arguing that American women's self-conceptions tend to focus more on connectedness to others than men's do. Such a contrast, however, does not really hold for Bengalis. *Both* men and women in Mangaldihi define themselves strongly in terms of their relations with others. But there are significant differences in the way women and men find themselves to be constituted via relational ties over their lives.

These contrasts can be said to begin with the differences perceived in the biologies of the two sexes, differences magnified by practices in upbringing and marriage. The contrasts can also be said to derive from patrilineality and virilocal postmarital residence, which favor the continuity of men and the transformation of incoming women. These perceptions and practices continually lead to contrary treatments of the genders: the most important connections of males are made but once and intended to endure throughout and beyond their lifetimes, while those of females are repeatedly altered—first made, then unmade and remade, then often again unmade. Women are said to be capable of such changes because of the natural "openness" of their bodies. One piece of proverbial wisdom states that a woman will fare best if she is malleable like clay, to be cast into a shape of his choice by the potter (her husband), discarding earlier loyalties, attributes, and ties to become absorbed into her husband's family.

Infants of both sexes are marked and initially connected with their kin and the village by a first feeding of rice ceremony (*annaprasana*). Males are differentiated, however, by the greater scale and elaboration of that ceremony, and among Brahmans by

several other subsequent ceremonies of "marking" or "refining" (*samskara*). Among Brahmans, marriage thus might be the eighth connection-making ceremony for a boy, but only the second for a girl. In many castes, the male child is identified as a growing node of his enduring patrilineage (*bamsa,* literally a "bamboo"), while a girl might be spoken of as a mere temporary sojourner awaiting her departure in marriage. A phrase I would often hear was, "A daughter is nothing at all. You just raise them for a few days, and then to others you give them away." People speak of daughters as "belonging not to us but to others" (cf. Dube 1988; Jeffery and Jeffery 1996; Narayan 1986:69–70).

Among the many urban Bengali families who have settled in Kolkata apartments upon fleeing East Pakistan (now Bangladesh) at the time of partition between India and Pakistan, or moved abroad to the United States for work, *men* also speak of having been forced painfully to cut apart the ties of their maya prematurely—like a woman does in marriage—viewing the "modern" era following partition and globalization as a very "separate," "independent" and "maya-reducing" time (c.f. Lamb 2002). However, men in Mangaldihi and other nearby villages still usually reside—save perhaps for brief periods of urban work—within the same community and on the same soil where they were born. That is why, some men say, it is so difficult for them to loosen their ties of maya at the end of a lifetime when facing death; for they have become so deeply embedded within a family, community, home, soil.

For girls in Mangaldihi, it is through marriage that they receive their most markings and that the ties of their personhood are substantially unmade and remade. Throughout the three-day wedding, the bride is made to absorb substances originating from her husband's body and household. She rubs her body with turmeric paste with which he has first been anointed, she eats leftover food from his plate, she absorbs his sexual fluids (which are described as permeating her body), she moves to his place of residence, and there mingles with his kin and mixes with the substances of his soil. The bride's surname and patrilineal membership (*bamsa*) are also formally changed to those of her husband. In this way, her marriage is generally interpreted as obscuring and greatly reducing, although not obliterating, the connections she once enjoyed with her natal home. She will no longer refer to persons of her natal family as her "own people" (*nijer lok*), but rather as her husband does—as her "relatives by marriage" (*kutumbs*), for she is said to have become by marriage the "half body" (*ardhangini*) of her husband.

For a girl, then, preparing to marry is like a first confrontation with mortality. Anticipating the pain of cutting so many ties with their natal families, homes, and friends, young brides spoke to me with dread, not comprehending how they would ever survive such an ordeal. These conversations struck me as resembling the ways I heard older people speak of impending separations at death. During the months before her wedding, my companion Hena would say to me through tears, "Your father gives you away. He makes you other. He wipes out the relation." She would also purposefully pick quarrels with me and other friends and kin in Mangaldihi in order, she said, "to cut the maya" of bodily-emotional ties before her actual departure.

Mothers at least as much as fathers in Mangaldihi stress the transience of a daughter's connections with her natal place. Most mothers have known such separations from personal experience, and at each visit after marriage—their own or others'—they might relive their earlier feelings. Many tell of feeling always the pain of having the ties of their girlhood and family downgraded or ignored in their husbands' homes. Yet all agree that however disused, violated, or abused their earlier ties might be after marriage, a connection does remain forever between mother and child. Most said they continue to "feel a pull (*tan*) of maya," "of blood," or "of the womb."

A WIDOW'S BONDS

High-caste families' responses to the deaths of husbands often do even more than marriages to unmake women, and do so again

mainly through stopping their interpersonal connections. Having lost many earlier relationships in marriage, most women rightly dread widowhood as another, similar phase of disconnection that will occur in their later lives. They expect such a phase since girls are married at younger ages, generally outlive their husbands, and usually do not remarry.

The legal option of remarriage for widows in West Bengal was sanctioned by British legislation in 1856 and has been exercised by widows in cities, but never by a high-caste widow in Mangaldihi. On the other hand, a man who loses his wife is usually encouraged to remarry, unless already senior with grown children. Thus in Mangaldihi's 335 households in 1990 there were only 13 unremarried widowers, but 69 unremarried widowed women. Childless young widows of Mangaldihi's lower castes are generally remated swiftly by a simpler ritual called "joining" (*sanga kara*), which does not require or attempt their removing the marks and ties of their first husbands; for even among these groups, a woman can ordinarily go through a true marriage ceremony (*biye*) but once.

Women of the higher castes who are widowed in Mangaldihi are pressed by their husbands' kin to minimize their transactions. While varying in strictness from group to group, this set of restrictive practices includes wearing white clothing, avoiding "hot" foods (such as fish, onions, garlic), limiting rice intake to only once a day (an amount considered almost equivalent to fasting), living in celibacy, avoiding participation in any auspicious ceremony, and often (because of their other dietary restrictions) cooking their food separately. Until recently, most families also required their widows to keep the head shaved (a practice some of the most senior Mangaldihi widows still observe) and to sleep on the ground.

One hears these practices recommended because they will reduce the widow's sexual desires and thus also reduce the husband's family's vulnerability to the slander and sexual marking that would occur were the widow to engage in liaisons with others. It is also striking that these are the very same practices that persons suffering death impurity (*asauc*) observe when a family member dies. Death impurity, however, lasts for just a limited period, whereas the widow's condition persists forever.

I first began to compare the condition of widows with that of others suffering death impurity because of their many similarities. Like a widow, persons suffering death impurity are expected to remain celibate; avoid "hot," non-vegetarian food; limit intake of boiled rice; restrict sharing of food with others; and avoid participating in auspicious rituals. Males suffering from death impurity, like older, more traditional widows, also have their heads shaved. These are all practices that reduce the likelihood that personal properties will be transferred among people.[11] During the transitional phase of death impurity, the survivors limit their interactions, both in order to separate themselves from the deceased person and to avoid infecting others in the community with their condition. The aim is to cut the lingering bodily emotional connections between the survivors and the deceased, so that both the departed spirit and the survivors can move on to form new relationships. For other survivors, the practices of impurity end with the final funeral rites after 10 to 30 days (cf. D. Mines 1990).

But the incapacity and inauspicious (*asubha*) condition of the widow is permanent due, it appears, to her having become, through her putatively indissoluble merger with him in marriage, the "half body" (*ardhangini*) and lifelong soul mate of her husband. When he is dead, her living bodily presence makes her, if young, not merely a sexual hazard, but also a repulsive anomaly. Until her own death, she can be seen as either the remnant, leftover half-body of a corpse, or as a faithless companion who has abandoned her husband by remaining on earth. She is also sometimes spoken of as a deficient wife whose lapses must have hastened her husband's death. Feared then for her defects as a devouring witch by some (as in Bandyopadhyay 1990), or as a vulture, she is often peripheralized within the family, if not expelled.

The asymmetry generally thus assumed in the high-caste marital relation is extreme, for the husband is not considered to be the wife's half-body, and unlike her, is not said to be diminished by (or responsible for) his partner's death. If she dies first, his person remains whole and free to remarry, his temporary incapacity of death impurity lasting no more than that of other close survivors. On the other hand, people tell me that even if the woman dies first, then although her surviving husband may be free, *her* spirit still remains bound to him and wanders around near him until the time of his funeral, when her soul will be merged under his name into the line of his male ancestors.

If people in Mangaldihi view persons, then, to be constituted of networks of relations, then women are in a peculiar position because their connections are made, remade, and unmade at several critical junctures over their lives: in girlhood, marriage, widowhood, and death. A daughter has to attenuate painfully ties with her natal family and place, so that she can move on to form new ties within her husband's home. A woman's ties to others as an ancestor are also uncertain, as she is ritually merged indistinguishably with her husband after death. The only tie for a high-caste woman that seems to be unambiguously unseverable, within the dominant patrilineal discourse of Mangaldihi, is the one she shares with her husband. This bond, which defines a woman's very bodily substance and identity, is one that a married woman cannot cut, even if her husband dies. This underlies why the majority of women in Mangaldihi endure such singular existences as widows as the last phase of their lives.

THE CHANGES OF AGE

Old age, however, brings important changes to the bodies and social identities of both widows and married women. Anthropological studies of women, in South Asia and elsewhere, have tended to focus on women in their married, domestic and reproductive years, with very little attention paid to how women's bodies may be perceived to change in old age. Although I have described female bodies as relatively open—making possible the somatic-social conditions that women must contend with, such as impurity and the capacity to mix profoundly with a husband—women's bodies are believed to become much cooler, dryer and more contained as they grow old.

According to villagers, it is as women enter into post reproductive phases of life that they experience a relative closing and cooling of the body. Women say that after menopause, their bodies become cool and dry and they no longer feel the heat of sexual desire. The cessation of childbearing entails an important bodily closing as well; and it is expected that women, like men, will become celibate as they age and their children marry, a further closing. An older widowed Brahman woman, Mejo Ma, described: "When you get old, everything becomes closed or stopped (*bandha*). That which happens between husband and wife stops. Menstruation stops. And then when your husband dies, eating all hot food stops as well. This is so that the body will dry out and not be hot." Bhogi Bagdi, an elderly lower caste widow, spoke as well of the cooling and drying of her body. She enjoyed sitting in the narrow, dusty lane in front of her house talking about sex, using vulgar language, and teasing the young people who visited her about their sexual practices. So I asked her one day if *she* still had sexual desire. She answered quickly, "No, of course not! After the blood stopped, my body dried out. Even if I wanted to [have sex], I wouldn't be able to. I had four kids, then my blood dried up, and then my body dried up. Now I have desire only for food."

Such somatic transitions bring women to a state of increased purity and boundedness, making them similar in some respects, people say explicitly, to men. The perception that postmenopausal women are in significant ways "like men" can also be found elsewhere in India (e.g., Flint 1975) and in other societies, such as the Kel Ewey Tuareg of northeastern Niger (Rasmussen 1987) and the Bedouins of Egypt (Abu-Lughod 1986:131, 133). When I would ask *why,* village women would explain that old women no longer menstruate, no longer give birth, no longer have sex, and (especially if they are upper-caste widows) no longer eat hot, non-vegetarian foods. This makes them relatively closed and "pure" (*suddha*) like men ordinarily are. Upper caste *widowed* women are further at times described as so "pure" (*suddha*) that they are "like gods" (*thakurer moto*), presumably because they are categorically free from the hot and female activities of sexuality and wifehood, and observing for life a radically cooling, separative, and minimally transacting code for conduct. It might warrant explaining here that daily impurities due to mixing and openness (*asuddhata*) are *not* the same as the death impurity that kin experience following a death (*asauc*), although the two terms are both traditionally glossed by Indologists as "impurity." In fact, by observing the set of minimally transacting practices prescribed for death-impure persons and widows, a person can become highly "pure" (*suddha*) in the everyday sense, because he or she will be made quite separate from others.

Young and older women alike in Mangaldihi speak of the processes of aging, stopping menstruation and becoming more like a man as a positive one. These somatic transitions mean that older women can take on some of the freedoms and privileges that men enjoy throughout their lives, such as exposing their calves and even chests on hot days, their saris simply wrapped around the waist in the style of a man, and wandering freely beyond the home—to visit friends or daughters, play cards on open temple platforms, watch village plays, dance care freely with young men at festivals, and sit on front stoops gossiping and watching the passers-by. Because their bodies have become naturally cool and dry, older widows are not even compelled to follow the strict widow's code for conduct, some say; because these restrictions are meant especially to curb the heat, sexual desire and openness of a *young* widow's body. The older widows I know nonetheless observe such restrictions—out of habit, fear of slander, and/or a desire to respect "tradition" or their husbands—but many do enjoy the other "male-like" freedoms of old age. Thus, suspended amid the countervailing currents of restraint and freedom, inauspiciousness and auspiciousness, the greater portion of Mangaldihi women live the last phases of their lives.

CONCLUSION

We have seen, then, that for those in Mangaldihi, understandings of personhood are profoundly gendered and intricately tied to the body. This ethnographic material challenges the tendency—which has been widespread in anthropological literature on personhood—to examine person and self as ontologically prior to or separate from gender identity. Conceptions of personhood, I would argue, cannot be understood in isolation from conceptions about gendered selves.

We also see how a focus on age and the life course can illuminate our understandings of gendered personhood. For Bengalis, contrary to assumptions found in much existing literature, gender is not a constant determined by dichotomous and fixed physical differences between men and women. Instead, the qualities of openness and permeability that all bodies and persons possess to relative degrees fluctuate significantly over the life course. This means that what it is to be a woman—the nature of a woman's body, personhood, and ties with others—is profoundly different at different life phases. By paying attention to age, we can train our gaze on this kind of flux in the ways the body is used to create gendered identities, and thereby gain a much more nuanced and complex understanding of the plural and evolving nature of gender and personhood conceptions.

NOTES

1. The subcontinent of South Asia includes the contemporary nations of India, Nepal, Pakistan, Bangladesh, Sri Lanka, Assam, and Bhutan. Sometimes Afghanistan—also part of British "India"—is included as South Asia, as well. Work on India has often dominated South Asian studies, and some scholars use "India" and "South Asia" somewhat interchangeably.

2. Studies of person or self in South Asia include Daniel 1984; Dissanayake 1996; Dumont 1980; Ewing 1990, 1991; Lamb 1997, 2000; Marriott 1976, 1990; Marriott and Inden 1974, 1977; McHugh 1989; M. Mines 1988, 1994; Nabakov 2000; Ortner 1995; Ostor et al. 1982; Parish 1994; Parry 1989; Shweder and Bourne 1984.

3. Marriott (1976) was the first to posit more or less "open" persons whose capacities for exchanging properties make them composite and "*dividual*" (rather than individual)—a suggestion that has spread in Melanesian as well as in South Asian studies (see also Marriott 1990; Strathern 1988:13, 15, 348–349n). Clifford Geertz suggests that the Western notion of the bounded and autonomous "individual" is, in fact, "a rather peculiar idea within the context of the world cultures" (1983:59).

4. "Personhood" refers to beliefs and practices surrounding what it is to be a person, or human being. Conceptions about personhood vary profoundly cross-culturally, and are constituted via a variety of elements. These elements might include some or all of the following: a subjective sense of self; the nature of the body, mind, emotions, and/or spirit; forms of power and status; age and the shape of the life course; relationships with others; karma or fate (perhaps ingrained in or written on the body or soul in some way); and significantly in most, if not all, contexts—sex and gender. For those living in the northeastern Indian state of West Bengal, gender is a very salient dimension of personhood.

5. The Bengali (and Sanskrit) term *lok* can also mean "world." These overlapping meanings of "world" and "person" connote the openness and nonindividuality of persons, as well as the common notion of the person as a microcosm of the world.

6. Among the Newars of Nepal, maya similarly refers to "love" or the "web of relatedness" (Bennett 1983:39; Parish 1994:156 ff). Gold (1991, 1992, 1999) also compellingly explores the complex, intertwining meanings of maya as "illusion" and as love for women, creative divine grace, delusive magicians' skills, and binding attachments to the relationships of this world.

7. For perspectives on the comparative sexual heat and capacities of women and men in various parts of India, see Daniel 1984: 171–72, Lamb 2000:187–92, Marglin 1985:60, Vatuk and Vatuk 1979:215.

8. For more on menstrual, birth and death impurities (which are distinct), see Lamb 2000:183–87, 164–69, 229–31; Marglin 1996; and D. Mines 1990.

9. Hindus in Mangaldihi commonly use the example of "touching a Muslim" to describe how people become impure (*asuddha*). Although Mangaldihi is a predominantly Hindu village, it is surrounded by smaller Muslim villages, and the Hindus there are especially concerned with preserving their own separateness.

10. As in English, the Bengali term for "man" (*manus*) can refer either to males in particular or to humankind in general.

11. Together these practices constitute what McKim Marriott (1976) would call a "minimal transactional strategy."

REFERENCES

Abu-Lughod, Lila. 1986. *Veiled Sentiments: Honor and Poetry in a Bedouin Society*. Berkeley: University of California Press.

Bandyopadhyay, Tarashankar. 1990. "The Witch." In Kalpana Bardhan (trans. and ed.). *Of Women, Outcastes, Peasants and Rebels: A Selection of Bengali Short Stories*, pp. 110–123. Berkeley: University of California Press.

Bennett, Lynn. 1983. *Dangerous Wives and Sacred Sisters: Social and Symbolic Roles of High-Caste Women in Nepal*. New York: Columbia University Press.

Chodorow, Nancy. 1978. *The Reproduction of Mothering: Psychoanalysis and the Sociology of Gender*. Berkeley: University of California Press.

Comaroff, Jean. 1985. *Body of Power, Spirit of Resistance: The Culture and History of South African People*. Chicago: University of Chicago Press.

Daniel, E. Valentine. 1984. *Fluid Signs: Being a Person the Tamil Way*. Berkeley: University of California Press.

Delaney, Carol. 1991. *The Seed and the Soil: Gender and Cosmology in Turkish Village Society*. Berkeley: University of California Press.

Dissanayake, Wimal, ed. 1996. *Narratives of Agency: Self-Making in China, India, and Japan*. Minneapolis: University of Minnesota Press.

Dube, Leela. 1975. "Woman's Worlds—Three Encounters." In A. Beteille and T.N. Madan (eds.). *Encounter and Experience: Personal Accounts of Fieldwork*, pp. 157–177. Delhi: Vikas.

———. 1988. "On the Construction of Gender: Hindu Girls in Patrilineal India." *Economic and Political Weekly* 23(18): 11–19.

Dumont, Louis. 1980. *Homo Hierarchicus*. Chicago: University of Chicago Press.

Ewing, Katherine P. 1990. "The Illusion of Wholeness: Culture, Self, and the Experience of Inconsistency." *Ethos* 18: 251–278.

———. 1991. "Can Psychoanalytic Theories Explain the Pakistani Woman? Intrapsychic Autonomy and Interpersonal Engagement in the Extended Family." *Ethos* 19: 131–160.

Flint, Marcha. 1975. "The Menopause: Reward or Punishment?" *Psychosomatics* 16: 161–163.

Geertz, Clifford. 1983. "'From the Native's Point of View': On the Nature of Anthropological Understanding." In *Local Knowledge: Further Essays in Interpretive Anthropology*, pp. 55–70. New York: Basic Books.

Gilligan, Carol. 1982. *In a Different Voice: Psychological Theory and Women's Development*. Cambridge, MA: Harvard University Press.

Gold, Ann Grodzins. 1991. "Gender and Illusion in a Rajasthani Yogic Tradition." In Arjun Appadurai, Frank Korom, and Margaret Mills (eds.). *Gender, Genre, and Power in South Asian Expressive Traditions*, pp. 102–135. Philadelphia: University of Pennsylvania Press.

———. 1992. *A Carnival of Parting: The Tales of King Bharthari and King Gopi Chand as Sung and Told by Madhu Natisar Nath of Ghatiyali, Rajasthan*. Berkeley: University of California Press.

———. 1999. "Maya." In Serinity Young (ed.). *Encyclopedia of Women and World Religion* 2: 635–636. New York: Macmillan.

Hirschon, Renee. 1978. "Open Body/Closed Space: The Transformation of Female Sexuality." In Shirley Ardener (ed.). *Defining Females: The Nature of Women in Society*, pp. 66–88. London: St. Martin's Press.

Jacobson, Doranne. 1978. "The Chaste Wife: Cultural Norm and Individual Experience." In Sylvia Vatuk (ed.). *American Studies in the Anthropology of India*, pp. 95–138. New Delhi: Manohar.

Jeffery, Patricia and Roger Jeffery. 1996. *Don't Marry Me to a Plowman! Women's Everyday Lives in Rural North India*. Boulder, Colo.: Westview Press.

Lamb, Sarah. 1997. "The Making and Unmaking of Persons: Notes on Aging and Gender in North India." *Ethos* 25(3): 279–302.

———. 2000. *White Saris and Sweet Mangoes: Aging, Gender, and Body in North India*. Berkeley: University of California Press.

———. 2002. "Intimacy in a Transnational Era: The Remaking of Aging among Indian Americans." *Diaspora* 11(3). In press.

Marglin, Frederique Apffel. 1985. "Female Sexuality in the Hindu World." In Clarissa W. Atkinson, C.H. Buchanan, and M.R. Miles (eds.). *Immaculate and Powerful: The Female in Sacred Image and Social Reality,* pp. 39–60. Boston: Beacon Press.

———. 1996. "Rationality, the Body, and the World: From Production to Regeneration." In Frederique Apffel Marglin and Stephen A. Marglin (eds.). *Decolonizing Knowledge: From Development to Dialogue,* pp. 142–181. Oxford: Clarendon Press.

Marriott, McKim. 1976. "Hindu Transactions: Diversity without Dualism." In Bruce Kapferer (ed.). *Transaction and Meaning: Directions in the Anthropology of Exchange and Symbolic Behavior,* pp. 109–142. Philadelphia: Institute for the Study of Human Issues.

———. 1990. "Constructing an Indian Ethnosociology." In McKim Marriott (ed.). *India through Hindu Categories,* pp. 1–39. Delhi: Sage Publications.

Marriott, McKim and Ronald Inden. 1974. "Caste Systems." *Encyclopedia Britannica, Macropaedia* 3: 982–991. Chicago: H. Benton.

———. 1977. "Toward an Ethnosociology of South Asian Caste Systems." In Kenneth David (ed.). *The New Wind: Changing Identities in South Asia,* pp. 227–238. The Hague: Mouton Publishers.

McHugh, Ernestine. 1989. "Concepts of the Person among the Gurungs of Nepal." *American Ethnologist* 16: 75–86.

Mines, Diane Paull. 1990. "Hindu Periods of Death 'Impurity.'" In McKim Marriott (ed.). *India through Hindu Categories,* pp. 103–130. New Delhi: Sage Publications.

Mines, Mattison. 1988. "Conceptualizing the Person: Hierarchical Society and Individual Autonomy in India." *American Anthropologist* 90: 568–579.

———. 1994. *Public Faces, Private Voices: Community and Individuality in South India.* Berkeley: University of California Press.

Moore, Henrietta. 1994. *A Passion for Difference: Essays in Anthropology and Gender.* Bloomington: Indiana University Press.

Nabokov, Isabelle. 2000. *Religion against the Self: An Ethnography of Tamil Rituals.* New York: Oxford University Press.

Narayan, Kirin. 1986. "Birds on a Branch: Girlfriends and Wedding Songs in Kangra." *Ethos* 14: 47–75.

Ortner, Sherry B. 1995. "The Case of the Disappearing Shamans, or No Individualism, No Relationism." *Ethos* 23: 355–390.

Ostor, Akos, Lina Fruzzetti, and Steve Barnett, eds. 1982. *Concepts of Person: Kinship, Caste, and Marriage in India.* Cambridge, MA: Harvard University Press.

Parish, Steven M. 1994. *Moral Knowing in a Hindu Sacred City: An Exploration in Mind, Emotion, and Self.* New York: Columbia University Press.

Parry, Jonathan P. 1989. "The End of the Body." In Michel Feher, with Ramona Naddaff and Nadia Tazi (eds.). *Fragments for a History of the Human Body, Part Two,* pp. 490–517. New York: Zone.

Rasmussen, Susan. 1987. "Interpreting Androgynous Woman: Female Aging and Personhood among the Key Ewey Tuareg." *Ethnology* 26: 17–30.

Shweder, Richard A., and Edmund J. Bourne. 1984. "Does the Concept of the Person Vary Cross-Culturally?" In Richard A. Shweder and Robert A. LeVine (eds.). *Culture Theory: Essays on Mind, Self, and Emotion,* pp. 158–199. Cambridge: Cambridge University Press.

Strathern, Marilyn. 1988. *The Gender of the Gift: Problems with Women and Problems with Society in Melanesia.* Berkeley: University of California Press.

Vatuk, Ved Prakash, and Sylvia Jane Vatuk. 1979. "The Lustful Stepmother in the Folklore of North-Western India." In Ved Prakash Vatuk (ed.). *Studies in Indian Folk Traditions,* pp. 190–221. New Delhi: Manohar.

VI

Culture, Sexuality, and the Body

The study of sexuality in anthropology is a relatively recent research emphasis. Classic anthropological monographs have reported exotic sexual practices in the course of ethnographic description. For example, we learn in Malinowski's *The Sexual Life of Savages* (1929) that the Trobriand islanders may bite each others' eyelashes in the heat of passion, but other than occasional esoterica, the naturalistic, biological bias has dominated the study of sexuality. However, as Vance observes (1984: 8), "although sexuality, like all human cultural activity, is grounded in the body, the body's structure, physiology, and functioning do not directly or simply determine the configuration or meaning of sexuality." Rather, sexuality is in large part culturally constructed. Moreover, the body itself has been the focus of feminist analysis. Feminist theorists have argued that historical, social, and political influences "produce" the body; the lived experience of the body is gendered and culturally diverse. Just as we may inquire into the culturally variable meanings of masculinity and femininity, we may examine the ways in which sexuality and the body are invested with meaning in particular societies (Ortner and Whitehead 1981: 2).

Sexuality, as a topic of analysis, links the personal and the social, the individual and society. To Americans sex may imply the body, medical facts, Freud, and erotic techniques, but all of these aspects of sexuality are socially shaped and sexual activity is inevitably curbed. Within every culture there are measures for the management of sexuality and gender expression (Ortner and Whitehead 1981: 24–25) and sanctions for those who break the rules.

These sanctions may be imposed at the level of the family, the lineage, the community, or the state. Indeed, Foucault (1981) has suggested that a feature of the recent past is the increasing intervention of the state in the domain of sexuality. In this regard Ross and Rapp (1981: 71) conclude that it is not accidental that contemporary western culture conceptualizes sex as a thing in itself, isolated from social, political, and economic context: "The separation with industrial capitalism of family life from work, of consumption from production, of leisure from labour, of personal life from political life, has completely reorganized the context in which we experience sexuality. . . . Modern consciousness permits, as earlier systems of thought did not, the positing of 'sex' for perhaps the first time as having an 'independent' existence." However, Caplan (1987: 24) warns that while western culture may have a concept of sexuality divorced from reproduction, marriage, or other social domains, it is not possible to analyze sexuality without reference to the economic, political, and cultural matrix in which it is embedded.

A comparative perspective informs us that the attributes of the body seen as sexual and erotic vary cross-culturally. For example, scarification, the corseted waist, bound feet, and the subincised penis are admired and provocative in particular cultures. Such attributes as these are not only physical symbols of sexuality, but indicators of status. Similarly, Sudanese women practice infibulation, a form of female genital cutting, causing serious pain and health risks to young women, for the honor of the family and as a sign of virtue. In the name of power, young men applied as recruits to the palace eunuch staff in Imperial China carrying their genitals in jars (Ortner and Whitehead 1981: 24). These examples are reminders of the impact of social concerns and cultural meanings in the domain of sexuality.

Abu-Lughod (in this book) explores the cultural construction of sexuality and local meanings of Islam through an analysis of wedding rituals in a Bedouin community in Egypt's Western Desert. Weddings produce and transform people's experiences of sexuality and gender relations, and serve as a marker of cultural identity. Whereas sexuality in North America is considered something essentially private, separate from society and social power, to these Bedouin the wedding involves sexuality that has a public and participatory element. The defloration of the bride is a ritualized encounter between the bride and groom and including the women and men who congregate around them. Central to the ritual is the bride's virginity, which represents her family's honor; her body and the emphasis on opening the bride's vagina thus become a matter of public interest. Connections to kin and control of the kinship group are symbolized in these wedding rites. The sexual politics of gender relations were formerly portrayed in women's wedding songs and dances that represented the encounter between male and female as a contest of wills. Changing power relations have led to a de-emphasis of this mechanism for challenging male power. As Bedouins are drawn into the wider Egyptian state and economy, weddings increasingly are seen as entertainment and spectacle, rather than as the ritual reproduction of the social and political dynamics of the community, symbolized in the sexual contest surrounding the bride's virginity.

Research in hunting and gathering societies also shows that sexual intercourse, while personal, can be a political act. In such societies, claims to women are central to men's efforts to achieve equal status with others (Collier and Rosaldo 1981: 291). Through sexual relations with women, men forge relationships with one another and symbolically express claims to particular women. Shostak (1981) presents the perspective of a !Kung woman, Nisa, on sex, marriage, and fertility in the broader context of a hunting and gathering society in which women have high status.

The !Kung believe that without sex, people can die, just as without food, one would starve. Shostak observes that "talk about sex seems to be of almost equal importance [to eating]. When women are in the village or out gathering, or when men and women are together, they spend hours recounting details of sexual exploits. Joking about all aspects of sexual experience is commonplace" (1981: 265). According to Nisa, "If a woman doesn't have sex . . . her thoughts get ruined and she is always angry" (Shostak 1981: 31). Nisa's characterization of sexuality among the !Kung suggests that for both men and women, engaging in sex is necessary to maintaining good health and is an important aspect of being human.

In contrast, for the past 150 years Anglo-American culture has defined women as less sexual than men. This represents a major shift from the widespread view prior to the seventeenth century that women were especially sexual creatures. By the end of the nineteenth century the increasingly authoritative voice of male medical specialists argued that women's bodies were characterized by sexual anesthesia

(Caplan 1987: 3). Victorian ideas about male sexuality emphasized the highly sexed and baser nature of men. In contrast, Muslim concepts of female sexuality (Mernissi 1987: 33) cast the woman as aggressor and the man as victim. Imam Ghazali, writing in the eleventh century, describes an active female sexuality in which the sexual demands of women appear overwhelming and the need for men to satisfy them is a social duty (Mernissi 1987: 39). Women symbolize disorder and are representative of the dangers of sexuality and its disruptive potential.

The example of the Kaulong of New Guinea further illustrates the extent to which understandings of male and female bodies and sexual desires are cultural products (Goodale 1980). Both sexes aspire to immortality through the reproduction of identity achieved through parenting. Sexual intercourse, which is considered animal-like, is sanctioned for married people. Animals are part of the forest and nature, so the gardens of married couples are in the forest. The only sanctioned purpose of sex and marriage is reproduction; sex without childbearing is viewed as shameful. Suicide was formerly considered an acceptable recourse for a childless couple. Sexual activity is thought to be dangerous to men and women in different ways: polluting for men and leading to dangers of birth for women. Goodale notes that girls are encouraged to behave aggressively toward men, to initiate sex, and to choose a husband. In contrast, men are reluctant to engage in sex, are literally "scared to death of marriage," and rarely take the dominant role in courtship (1980: 135). Thus, the Kaulong view seems to reverse the western idea of the passive woman and the active man (Moore 1988: 17).

For the Kaulong, as among numerous groups in New Guinea, men's anxiety about contact with the body of a woman is heightened by the understanding that menstrual blood is dangerously polluting. A man who had sexual contact with a menstruating woman would risk serious physical and mental harm. Men engage in a range of symbolic behaviors—for example, tongue scraping and smokehouse purification—to cleanse themselves of what they believe are the harmful effects of contact with women's bodies. The Mae Enga, for instance, believe that "contact with [menstrual blood] or a menstruating woman will, in the absence of appropriate countermagic, sicken a man and cause persistent vomiting, turn his blood black, corrupt his vital juices so that his skin darkens and wrinkles as his flesh wastes, permanently dull his wits, and eventually lead to a slow decline and death" (Meggitt 1964: 207).

Concern about the symbolic dangers of women's bodies is not limited to New Guinea, but rather, has been documented in diverse cultures (Buckley and Gottlieb 1988). Research on such symbolic dangers and the body as ritually polluting has often focused on menstruation. Buckley (1982) has addressed male bias and the female perspective on menstruation in his discussion of menstrual beliefs and practices among the Yurok Indians of North America. In his reanalysis of Yurok data Buckley found that while pre-contact Yurok men considered women, through their menstrual blood, to be dangerous, Yurok women viewed menstruation as a positive source of power. Rather than looking on the forced monthly seclusion as isolating and oppressive, women viewed it as a source of strength and sanctuary.

In her chapter in this book, Gottlieb notes that most early anthropological writings on menstruation were overly simplistic in assuming that menstrual blood was necessarily a source of mystical contamination. Works such as Buckley's study of Yurok menstruation and also Buckley and Gottlieb's 1988 classic collection on menstrual practices cross-culturally were groundbreaking in furthering our understanding of the diversity of women's bodily experiences and how body practices are shaped by culture and history. Gottlieb describes the growing feminist literature that focuses on menstruation and on the body in general. Recent scholarship includes accounts by anthropologists who gained first-hand knowledge of women's menstrual houses by means of participant observation. In addition, scholars have emphasized the agency of menstruating women—for example, their use of menstrual blood to engage in magical procedures to deceive their husbands or to attract sexual advances, the use of herbal and other methods to regulate menstruation, or the use of diverse techniques to induce abortions. Gottlieb's analysis reminds us that women shape their own menstrual experiences and are not bound to a solely biological or cultural script.

Such biological or cultural scripts are equally influential in defining two, and only two gender identities, the masculine and the feminine, leaving little room for culturally defined variance. This is true in popular thought in the United States but other cultures provide for alternative gender constructs as well as acknowledgement of physical variation. Some research suggests at least three phenotypic sexes in human cultures: female, male, and androgynous or hermaphroditic individuals. This classification refers to characteristics observable to the naked eye rather than to medical classifications of sex types based on chromosomal evidence (Jacobs and Roberts 1989: 440). Linguistic markers for gender reveal culturally specific epistemological categories (Jacobs and Roberts 1989: 439). Accordingly, in English one may distinguish woman, lesbian, man, or gay male. The Chuckchee counted seven genders—three female and four male—while the Mohave reportedly recognize four genders—a woman, a woman who assumes the roles of men, a man, or a male who assumes the roles of women (Jacobs and Roberts 1989: 439–440). Thus, cross-cultural research suggests that we need to use categories of sex and gender that reflect the evidence of diversity rather than rigid classification systems.

In any culture gender, sex, and body are recognized, named, and given meaning in accordance with the culture's rules or customs (Jacobs and Roberts 1989: 446). When a baby is born people generally rely on the appearance of the infant's external genitalia to determine whether that child will be treated as female or male. As a child grows, more criteria come into play, such as the phenotypic expression of sex—facial hair, voice, and breast development. In some societies, social and sexual identities may be created by means of modifying the physical body. One such example is the *hijras* of Indian society. The *hijra* role attracts people who in the West might be called eunuchs, homosexuals, transsexuals, transvestites, or hermaphrodites. *Hijras* are primarily phenotypic men who have chosen to sacrifice their genitalia in return for the power to bless or curse others with fertility or infertility.

The *hijra* role is deeply rooted in Indian culture, and it accommodates a variety of sexual needs, gender behaviors and identities, and personalities. Reddy and Nanda (in this book) show that Hinduism encompasses ambiguities and contradictions in gender categories without trying to resolve them. *Hijras,* have been identified as a "third sex" or "intersexed" identity—in Nanda's terms, "neither men nor women" (1990), situated within a larger continuum of sexual and gender configurations. In Hindu myths, rituals, and art, the theme of the powerful man-woman is significant; mythical figures who are androgynous figure in popular Indian culture. Islam also reinforces the construct of alternative genders by means of the historical role of the eunuch in the Muslim court culture of India. Although the popular understanding of *hijras* is as an alternative sex and gender, their identities are also constructed through spirituality, religious affiliation, and political action. As political candidates, some *hijras* have used their sexual and physical ambiguities as a symbolic asset in their campaign platforms.

Additional examples of cultures that tolerate gender ambiguity are found in Native American societies, in which a male who felt an affinity for female occupation, dress, and attributes could choose to become classified as a two-spirit, sometimes known as a berdache. Williams (1986) discusses alternative gender identities for Native American women whom he calls amazons. According to Williams' use of the term, an amazon is a woman who has manifested an unfeminine character from infancy, has shown no interest in heterosexual relations, and might have expressed a wish to become a man. Such women were known for their bravery and skill as warriors. For example, Kaska Indians would select a daughter to be a son if they had none; after a transformation ritual the daughter would dress like a man and be trained for male tasks. Ingalik Indians also recognize such a status; in this society the amazons even participated in male-only sweat baths. The woman was accepted as a man on the basis of her gender behavior (Williams 1986).

The assignment of this changed gender "operates independently of a person's morphological sex and can determine both gender status and erotic behavior" (Williams 1986: 235). In some societies a woman could choose to be a man, as among the Kutenai Indians. The "manlike woman" was greatly respected, although the Kutenai did not recognize a similar status for men. A tribe with an alternative gender role for one sex did not necessarily have one for the other, and the roles were not seen as equivalent. The Mohave also recognized this alternative, subjecting these women to a ritual that authorized them to assume the clothing, sexual activity, and occupation of the opposite, self-chosen sex. It is sometimes believed that such women do not menstruate because menstruation is a crucial part of the definition of a woman. However, the category of amazon is distinct from that of men or women. It is another gender status. Thus, some Native American cultures have a flexible recognition of gender variance, and they incorporate fluidity in their world view.

In western culture today sexuality is thought to comprise an important part of one's identity, the core of self (Caplan 1987: 2). In her discussion of women's intimate friendships, Blackwood (this book) notes that although from a Western viewpoint, sexuality and sexual identity are held to comprise stable, coherent categories, comparative evidence from other cultures challenges this assumption. Based on case studies of women's same sex relations in southern Africa, aboriginal Australia, China, New Guinea, Surinam and Sumatra, she argues that human sexuality takes its form through social processes such as religion, ethnicity, class, family, and reproduction, as well as the material conditions of everyday life. The ethnographic data suggest that sexuality is neither a static state nor a fixed identity. In Lesotho, for example, intimate schoolgirl friendships called "mummy-baby" relationships draw on a tradition of girls' initiations, strong social networks for women, and cultural notions of women's agency in their own sexuality. Close bonds between young women are constructed as an aspect of maturing, and are believed to shape girls' sexuality as they enter into heterosexual relations. Blackwood contends that cultural systems of gender construct different sexual beliefs and practices for men and women, and frame sexual desire within cultural systems of meaning.

As Blackwood points out, in American society sexuality is an integral part of identity on a personal and a social level. Sexuality not only classifies one as male or female, but is an aspect of adult identity. In the United States, where heterosexual relations are the norm, the dominant ideology suggests that heterosexuality is innate and natural. Correspondingly, lesbianism may be threatening to male dominance, while male homosexuality threatens male solidarity and the sense of masculine identity. The linkage of sexual identity and gender leads to an identification of gay men and lesbians in terms of their homosexuality, although they do not necessarily change their gender. In the U.S., a lack of fit between sexual anatomy, gender, and sexuality may cause suspicion. In other cultures, however, gender and sexuality are conceptually separate. For example, Shepherd (1987) shows that for Swahili Muslims of Mombasa, Kenya, being in a homosexual relationship does not change one's gender, which is essentially assigned by biological sex.

If some scholars, through their cross-cultural research, are attempting to show us significant variation in gender identities as well as attitudes toward sexuality and the body, others have focused on the heightened standardizing and regulation of the "ideal" woman's body in industrialized societies. This is precisely the question that Urla and Swedlund (in this book) address in their exploration of how images of the ideal body in 21st century North America are represented and shaped by the popular and controversial cultural icon, the Barbie doll. Barbie symbolizes the appropriately gendered female body, and conveys the significance of appearance for success in the "rituals of heterosexual teenage life." As the first teen fashion doll, Barbie personifies the sexy girl but at the same time the clean-cut teen who does not actually have sex. Barbie, her wardrobe and other accessories exemplify the commodification of the body and of gender itself. To achieve the feminine ideal that Barbie represents requires constant vigilance, and endless financial investments, physical adornments and interventions. The glamorous doll serves as a reminder that women—and even young girls—often experience their bodies as defective and embark on lifelong quests in pursuit of an inaccessible ideal. Urla and Swedlund describe attempts to scientifi-cally define an "average" U.S. female body in the late 19th and early 20th centuries in relation to an implicit male prototype. Conforming to gendered norms of fitness and weight are now identified with social and moral worth. The disciplined body, beautiful, sexually appealing, and embedded in consumerism, exists in the fantasy world of Barbie.

The articles in this section reveal that there are multiple culturally acceptable gendered and sexual identities (Caplan 1987: 22) as well as diverse constructs of the ideal gendered body. Although western categorizations impose a particular rigidity on concepts of gender, sexuality and the body, cross-cultural data demonstrate that these identities are not fixed and unchangeable. This realization necessitates a critique of these western classifications and provokes a number of stimulating ques-tions: Are heterosexuality and homosexuality equally socially constructed? Is there cross-cultural variation in the extent to which sexuality represents a core feature of human identity? Is there a timeless, universal, normative body?

REFERENCES

Buckley, Thomas. 1982. "Menstrution and the power of Yurok Women: Methods in Cultural Reconstruction." *American Ethnologist* 9:47–60.

Buckley, Thomas and Alma Gottlieb (eds.). 1988. Blood Magic: *The Anthropology of Menstrua-tion.* Berkeley: University of California Press.

Caplan, Pat. 1987. "Introduction." In Pat Caplan (ed.). *The Cultural Construction of Sexuality,* pp. 1–31. London: Tavistock.

Collier, Jane E. and Michelle Z. Rosaldo. 1981. "Politics and Gender in Simple Societies." In Sherry Ortner and Harriet Whitehead (eds.). *Sexual Meanings: The Cultural Construction of Gender and Sexuality,* pp. 275–330. Cambridge: Cambridge University Press.

Foucault, Michel, 1981. *The History of Sexuality.* Harmondsworth: Penguin.

Goodale, Jane C. 1980. "Gender, Sexuality and Marriage: A Kaulong Model of Nature and Culture." In Carol P. MacCormack (ed.). *Nature, Culture and Gender,* pp. 119–143. Cambridge: Cambridge University Press.

Jacobs, Sue-Ellen and Christine Roberts. 1989. "Sex, Sexuality, Gender, and Gender Variance." In Sandra Morgen (ed.). *Gender and Anthropology: Critical Reviews for Research and Teaching*, pp. 438–462. Washington, DC: American Anthropological Association.

Malinowski, Bronislaw. 1929. *The Sexual Life of Savages in Northwestern Melanesia*. New York: Harvest Books.

Meggitt, M. J. 1964. "Male–Female Relationships in the Highlands of Australian New Guinea," *American Anthropologist* 66(4, Part 2): 204–227.

Mernissi, Fatima. 1987. *Beyond the Veil: Male–Female Dynamics in Modern Muslim Society*. Bloomington and Indianapolis: Indiana University Press.

Moore, Henrietta L. 1988. *Feminism and Anthropology*. Minneapolis: University of Minnesota Press.

Nanda, Serena. 1990. *Neither Man Nor Woman: The Hijras of India*. Belmont, California; Wadsworth, Inc.

Nelson, Nici. 1987. "'Selling her Kiosk': Kikuyu Notions of Sexuality and Sex for Sale in Mathare Valley, Kenya." In Pat Caplan (ed.). *The Cultural Construction of Sexuality*, pp. 217–240. London: Tavistock.

Ortner, Sherry B. and Harriet Whitehead. 1981. "Introduction: Accounting for Sexual Meanings." In Sherry Ortner and Harriet Whitehead (eds.). *Sexual Meanings: The Cultural Construction of Gender and Sexuality*, pp. 1–29. Cambridge: Cambridge University Press.

Ross, E. and R. Rapp. 1981. "Sex and Society: A Research Note from Social History and Anthropology." *Comparative Studies in Society and History* 20: 51–72.

Shepherd, Gill. 1987. "Rank, Gender, and Homosexuality: Mombasa as a Key to Understanding Sexual Options." In Pat Caplan (ed.). *The Cultural Construction of Sexuality*, pp. 240–271. London: Tavistock.

Shostak, Marjorie. 1983. Nisa: *The Life and Words of a !Kung Woman*. Cambridge, MA: Harvard University Press.

Vance, Carole S. 1984. "Pleasure and Danger: Toward a Politics of Sexuality." In Carole S. Vance (ed.). *Pleasure and Danger: Exploring Female Sexuality*, pp.1–29. Boston: Routledge and Kegan Paul.

Williams, Walter L. 1986. *The Spirit and The Flesh*. Boston: Beacon Press.

Is There a Muslim Sexuality? Changing Constructions of Sexuality in Egyptian Bedouin Weddings

Lila Abu-Lughod

The project of defining the nature of Muslim Arab sexuality—what it is or what it should be—has engaged many people with different stakes and interests. Western discourses have tended to contrast the negative sexuality of "the East" with the positive sexuality of the West. French colonial settlers in Algeria depicted Algerian women in pornographic postcards that suggested a fantastic Oriental world of

Original material prepared for this text.

perverse and excessive sexuality (Alloula 1986). Western feminists concerned with global issues dwell on veiling and other practices like clitoridectomy found in the Muslim Arab world as signs of the repressive control over or exploitation of women's sexuality (e.g., Daly 1978).

From the Muslim world itself come other discourses on Arab Muslim sexuality. These include religious and legal texts and pronouncements, but also, more recently, some critical studies by intellectuals and scholars.

How different the understandings can be is clear from two important books. One, by a Tunisian scholar with a background in psychoanalytic thought, argues that the misogynist practices of sexuality in the Muslim world are corruptions of the ideals of the Quran and other religious texts (Bouhdiba 1985). The second, by a Moroccan sociologist, argues from a feminist perspective that the legal and sacred texts themselves, like the erotic texts that flourished in the medieval period, carry negative messages about and perpetuate certain consistent attitudes toward the bodies and behavior of Muslim women (Sabbah 1984).

What these various discourses on Arab Muslim sexuality, by outsiders and insiders, defenders and critics, share is the presumption that there is such a thing as a "Muslim sexuality." An anthropologist like myself, familiar with the tremendous variety of communities to be found in the regions composing the Muslim Arab world, would have to question this presumption. Neither Islam nor sexuality should be essentialized—taken as things with intrinsic and transhistorical meanings. Rather, both the meaning of Islam and the constructions of sexuality must be understood in their specific historical and local contexts.[1]

To show why I argue this, I will analyze wedding rituals in a community of Awlad 'Ali Bedouin in Egypt's Western Desert—a community I worked in over a period of twelve years. Weddings are the highlight of social life, awaited with anticipation and participated in with enthusiasm. Each wedding is different. And each wedding is a personal affair of great moment for the bride and groom, even if only one dramatic event in what will be their marriage, lasting for years. Yet public rituals in face-to-face societies are also arenas where people play out their social and political relations. There are other discourses and practices related to sexuality in this Bedouin community but none so powerfully seek to produce, and are now transforming, people's experiences of sexuality and gender relations as weddings do. Without pretending that a symbolic analysis exhausts the meaning of weddings for the individuals involved, I would still insist that such an analysis of Awlad 'Ali weddings is useful: It reveals both how sexuality is constructed by the symbols and practices of members of particular communities and how these symbols and practices themselves are open to change and political contestation. Islam, it will be seen, figures not so much as a blueprint for sexuality as a weapon in changing relations of power.

SEXUALITY AND CULTURAL IDENTITY

In the twelve years between 1978 and 1990 that I had been regularly returning to this community of Arab Muslim sedentarized herders in Egypt, the same questions had been asked of me, sometimes even by the same people, as were asked in the first month of my stay. Usually in the context of a gathering of older women, one old woman would lean toward me and ask if I were married. After a short discussion of the fact that I was not, she or another older woman would ask me the next intense question: "Where you come from, does the bridegroom do it with the finger or with 'it'?" The first time they asked me this, I did not know what they meant by "it" and they had a good laugh. The question that followed inevitably in such conversations was, "And do they do it during the daytime or at night?" They were asking about weddings and particularly about the defloration of the virgin bride, which is for them the central moment of a wedding.[2]

In the obsessive concern with whether they do it with the finger or "it," at night or during the daytime, is a clue to one of the things the discourse on this aspect of sexuality has become as the Awlad 'Ali Bedouins have greater contact and interaction with outsiders, primarily their Egyptian peasant and urban neighbors. Whatever its former or current meaning within the community, meanings I will analyze in the following section, the central rite of weddings has now also become a marker of cultural identity—essential to the Awlad Ali's self-defining discourse on what makes them distinctive.

Individuals vary in how they evaluate their differences from their compatriots. When I met the Bedouin representative to the Egyptian Parliament, a sophisticated man in sunglasses whose long contact with other Egyptians showed in his dialect, he assured me that there were a few Bedouin practices that were wrong: One was that they used the finger in the daytime. But he defended the practice by saying that it reminded girls to be careful. Another respected man of the community explained to me that "entering" with the finger was wrong. "We're the only ones who do it this way," he noted. Then he added, "Nothing in our religion says you should." By way of excuse, though, he said, "But the faster the groom does it, the better—the more admired he is because it means he wasn't timid or cowardly." Even women occasionally complained that it was stupid how the female wedding guests waited and waited, just to see that drop of blood. But they too defended the ceremony, saying that the defloration had to take place in the afternoon so that everyone could see and there would be no doubts about the reputation of the girl. Their horror at the idea that the groom would use "it" came from their fear that it would be more painful for the bride.

Besides asking whether they do it with the finger or "it," day or night, the women I knew often asked whether, where I came from, there was anyone with the bride to hold her down. They were surprised to hear that she needed no one and marveled that she wasn't afraid to be alone with the man. Among themselves, they almost always had a few older women, usually aunts or close neighbors of the groom and bride, in the room with the bride when the groom came to her. There in theory to hold the bride, these women also end up giving advice to the groom and making sure that he knew what to do so that everything—the display of the blood on the cloth—would turn out right.

For their part, somewhat like most Europeans and Americans, non-Bedouin Egyptians and assimilated Awlad 'Ali from the agricultural areas find Bedouin weddings scandalous and distasteful. Bedouin women are not unaware of these views and the men discussed

previously were probably reacting defensively to them. These outsiders may laugh at some customs but they are embarrassed by others. After one wedding in the community in which I was living, the bride's aunt, who had spent most of her life in a non-Bedouin provincial town, talked about the wedding and some of the customs she had witnessed that made her laugh "until her stomach hurt." She obviously considered her new in-laws backward.[3]

What seemed to disturb her most was the public nature of what she felt should be private. She thought it humiliating, for example, that at night, the young men from the community (peers of the bridegroom) hung around the room, listening, shining a flashlight under the door and through the window, and generally being disruptive. More horrible to her was the public display of the blood-stained cloth. "It was incredible," she exclaimed. "After the defloration didn't you hear my son saying to his aunt when she went to hang the cloth on the tent ropes, 'It's shameful, my aunt, it's shameful to put the cloth out for people to see.'" Like other urban and rural Egyptians, she thought that the bride and groom should be brought together at night and left alone.

Although other Egyptians and Americans might feel that such privacy is more civilized, the Awlad 'Ali women I knew did not see it that way. Bedouin women were scandalized by the secrecy of night deflorations, the immediate and explicit link such weddings make between marriage and sexual intercourse, and what they view as either the total vulnerability of the poor bride forced to be alone with a man or, even worse, the bride's immodest desire for a man. They knew that instead of struggling, the Egyptian bride has her photo taken with her husband-to-be, she sits with him at weddings where the sexes mix, and she dresses in make-up and fancy clothes for all to see. Because poorer Bedouin men sometimes marry young women from peasant areas, whether they are of Egyptian stock or long-sedentarized Bedouin involved in agriculture, the Bedouin women also knew that unmarried sisters accompanied the bride. They interpreted this practice as a shameful attempt to display and "sell" marriageable daughters. They also knew that such brides sometimes arrived bringing a cooked duck or goose to feed a new husband; they took this as a sign of the bride's unseemly eagerness to please the groom.

Egyptian weddings, much like American ones, construct the couple as a separate unit, distinct from families or ties to members of the same gender group. At their center is a sexual joining that is private and intimate. For the Awlad 'Ali, this is a strange thing. The secrecy of private sex, in the dark, behind closed doors, and preferably in the foreign or anonymous setting (for the honeymoon) produces sexuality as something personal, intensely individual, apparently separate from society and social power. It produces sexuality as something belonging in an inviolable private sphere—the bedroom—a sphere in which others cannot interfere with whatever pleasure or violence and coercion accompanies it. One of the consequences of this construction of sexuality is that we, and perhaps Egyptians, come to think there is a part of oneself that is not social or affected by the prevailing power relations in society.[4]

The three crucial elements in the Bedouin discourse on differences between their weddings and those of other groups are (1) whether the defloration is public and participatory, (2) whether it involves sexual intercourse, and (3) whether it is seen as a contest, especially between bride and groom. These elements also had meaning within the local context. In Bedouin weddings the ways in which sexuality is related to power relations and the social order were clear. Marriages have been the occasion for people to collectively enact and reproduce this social order and the individual's place in it. And the individual's place was, until recently, very much a part of the group—whether the kin group or the group defined by gender.

WEDDINGS AS PUBLIC RITES: THE POWER OF KINSHIP AND GENDER

The participants in Awlad 'Ali Bedouin weddings instantiate, by means of a bride and groom, the relations between families or kin groups on the one hand, and the relations between men and women on the other. A symbolic analysis of the central rite, the defloration, enacted in a homologous fashion on the bodies of the bride and groom and on the collective bodies of the gathered kin and friends, reveals that it produces an understanding of sexuality as something public and focused on crossing thresholds, opening passages, and moving in and out. There are no strong messages of mingling or joining or even interchange in a private sexual act. The emphasis is on opening the bride's vagina by breaking the hymen and bringing out or making visible what was in there. And although people say that deflorations should be done during the daytime so everyone can see the cloth, the fact that in the rhythm of daily life morning and daytime generally are times of opening and going out from home or camp, while evening is a time of returning inward, cannot but reinforce the auspiciousness of this time for opening and taking outward.[5]

That this opening is a prelude to the insemination which should eventuate in childbirth is suggested by some practices associated with the blood-stained virginity cloth. It is taken out of the room by the groom and thrown to the women gathered just outside. It is said that if the cloth is then brought back into the room without the bride having exited first—if, as they say, the cloth enters upon her—it will block her from conceiving.[6] Young women are told to save their virginity cloths; if they have trouble conceiving, they must bathe in water in which they have soaked the cloth.

Everything in the rites and the songs that accompany them suggests that the individuals engaged in this opening and being opened, taking out and showing, and having something taken out and shown, embody both their kin groups and their gender groups. The connection to kin, and control by the kin group, is clear in the key role they have in arranging and negotiating marriages and is reflected in the songs the groom's female relatives sing as they go to fetch the bride from her father's household. It is also reinforced in the songs the bride's female kin sing to greet these people. Most of the songs compliment the social standing of the families of the bride and groom.

Even the practices and movements of the wedding itself perpetuate the identifications with kin groups. Most brides, even today, are brought from their fathers' households completely covered by a white woolen woven cloak (*jard*) that is the essential item of men's dress. The cloak must belong to the girl's father or some other male kinsman. So, protected and hidden by her father's cloak, she is brought out of her father's protected domain and carried to her husband's kin group's domain. There she is rushed, still hidden, into the room (or in the past, the tent) which she will share with her husband. Although nowadays the woven cloak is usually removed once she enters the room, in the past the bride remained under her father's cloak and was not revealed even to the women gathered around her until after the defloration.

The virginity of the bride is also constructed as something inseparable from her family's honor. Although one unmarried girl explained the importance of the blood-stained cloth in terms of her own reputation, she stressed the effect it would have on others.

> For us Bedouins, this is the most important moment in a girl's life. No matter what anyone says afterward, no one will pay attention as long as there was blood on the cloth. They are suspicious of her before. People talk. "She went here, she went there." "She looked at So-and-so." "She said hello to So-and-so." "She went to the orchard." But when they see this blood the talk is cut off. . . . When they see the cloth, she can come and go as she pleases. They love her and everything is fine.

The best way to get a sense of who has a stake in the girl's virginity and why is to listen to the conventional songs sung wildly outside the door of the bride's room as the defloration is underway. Unmarried girls and some young married women clap and sing rhyming songs that refer to the effect of the proof of the bride's virginity on various members of her family and community.

> Make her dear Mom happy, Lord
> Hanging up her cloth on the tent ropes
> O Saint 'Awwaam on high
> Don't let anyone among us be shamed

Older women sing more serious songs that take up similar themes:

> When the people have gathered
> O Generous One favor us with a happy ending . . .
> Behind us are important men
> who ask about what we are doing . . .

Relatives of the bride show their support and faith in the bride in songs like this:

> I'm confident in the loved one
> you'll find it there intact . . .

Even the groom's behavior during the defloration reflects on his relatives. One song a relative of his might sing as he arrives or is inside with the bride is the following:

> Son, be like your menfolk
> strong willed and unafraid . . .

After the virginity cloth is brought out by the groom and thrown to the women, a different set of songs is sung. These praise the cloth and the honor of the girl who had remained a virgin. The songs reflect on who is affected by her purity and who is proud. At one wedding a female relative of the bride sang to a nephew nearby:

> Go tell your father, Said
> the banner of her honor is flying high . . .

About the bride a woman might sing:

> Bravo! She was excellent
> she who didn't force down her father's eyelashes . . .

Given this group investment in the bride's virginity, the central rite of the wedding becomes a drama of suspense and relief that must powerfully shape people's experiences of sexuality as something that belongs to the many, and especially to one's family. The wedding is also, importantly, an occasion when families find themselves in some rivalry, the honor of each at stake. This was more apparent in the past when the young men celebrated all night on the eve of the wedding and expressed the rivalry through singing contests that sometimes broke out into actual fights between lineages.

Kinship is not the only power-laden aspect of social life that finds itself reflected and reinforced in the wedding. The second set of power relations weddings play with are those of gender. The bride and groom in the wedding rite enact the charged relations between men and women as distinct genders in a kind of battle of the sexes. Although most activities in the community are informally segregated by gender, at weddings—in part because there are non-family members present—the sexual segregation is more obvious and fixed, women and men forming highly separate collectivities for nearly all events.

Given this separation of the sexes, the defloration, taking place in the middle of the day when all are gathered in their distinct places, becomes a ritualized and extreme form of encounter between both the bride and groom and the women and men who surround each of them. The movements of the groom and his age-mates as they penetrate the crowd of women surrounding the bride mirror the groom's penetration of his bride, who forms a unit with the women in the room with her. The young men stand just outside the door, sometimes dancing and singing, ready to fire off guns in celebration when the groom emerges. They rush him back away from the women. This mirroring is expressed in the ambiguity of the term used for both moments of this event: the entrance (*khashsha*) refers both to the entry with the finger and the whole defloration process when the groom enters the bride's room, which can be thought of as his kin group's womb.

The encounter between male and female takes the form of a contest. The groom is encouraged to be fearless. He is expected to finish the deed in as short a time as possible. The bride is expected to try valiantly to fight him off. Taking the virginity she has been so careful to guard and thus opening the way for his progeny is the groom's victory; the bride doesn't give it up without a struggle. Calling this, as the literature often does, a virginity test is a misnomer in that it misses this combative dimension of the ritualized act. The way people describe what happens even on the wedding night suggests again that the groom and bride are involved in a contest. The rowdy young men who listen outside the marital chamber want to know "who won." They know this, some adolescent girls informed me, not just by whether the groom succeeds in having intercourse with his bride (a rare event), but by whether the groom succeeds in making his bride talk to him and answer his questions. This is, perhaps, another kind of opening up.

There is other evidence that weddings provoke a heightened attention to issues of gender and sexual mixing. One of the most revealing and intriguing is the spontaneous cross-dressing that sometimes happens at weddings. At several weddings I attended one woman in our community actually put on men's clothes, a fake mustache and beard, and covered her head in a man's headcloth. Amidst much hilarity she came out to dance in front of the bride. Others expressed some disapproval and called this woman a bit mad. But they laughed riotously anyway. One woman who thought it excessive described someone else who she thought was quite funny: All she did was dance in front of the bride with a shawl bunched up in front like male genitalia. Sometimes it was reported that the unmarried men and young boys had celebrated the night before the wedding by dressing up a boy with women's bracelets and a veil and dancing in front of him as if he were a bride.

SEXUAL TRANSFORMATIONS

Many Awlad 'Ali claim that their rituals are changing. In this final section, I want to explore how in these changed wedding practices we can begin to track changes in the nature of power and social relations. This is further support for my initial argument that constructions of sexuality cannot be understood apart from understandings of particular forms of social power. Most people talked about changes in weddings over the last twenty years or so in terms of what had been lost. Many said weddings were not fun any more. As far as I could determine, the main element that seems to have been lost is the celebration the night before the wedding (*saamir*). Not only do the young men no longer sing back and forth, but no longer is it even thinkable that a young woman from the community would come out to dance in front of them. This is what used to happen and the change is crucial for Bedouin gender relations.

What happened in the past was that an unmarried sister or cousin of the groom would be brought out from among the women by a young boy. She would dance amidst a semi-circle of young men. Her face veiled and her waist girded with a man's white woven cloak, like the one the bride would come covered in the following day, she danced with a stick or baton in her hands. According to one man who described this to me, the young men tried to "beg" the stick from her, sometimes using subterfuges like pretending to be ill; she would often bestow the stick, he said, on someone she fancied. But according to the women I spoke with, the young men would sometimes try to grab the stick from her and she would, if they were too aggressive, get angry with them and leave. The young men took turns singing songs that welcomed the dancer and then described her every feature in flattering terms. The standard parts praised in such songs were her braids, her eyes, her eyebrows, her cheeks, her lips, her tattoos, her neck, her breasts, her arms, her hands, and her waist—most of which, it should be remembered, because of the way she was dressed were not actually visible. Thus in a sense the dancer was, through men's songs, made into the ideal woman, attractive object of men's desires.

The dancer must be seen as the bride's double or stand-in, an interpretation supported by the other occasion on which a young woman danced in front of men. In the days before cars, brides were carried from their fathers' households to their husbands' on camel-back, completely cloaked and sitting hidden inside a wooden litter (*karmuud*) covered in red woven blankets. Another woman always preceded her on foot, dancing as young men sang to her and shot off guns near her.

In both cases, the dancer as bride and as ideal womanhood went out before men who complimented and sought her. What is crucial to notice is how the women described the dancer. They attributed to her a special bravery and described her actions as a challenge to the young men. One wedding in which a young woman was accidentally wounded by a poorly aimed gun was legendary. The wedding went on, the story went, as a second dancer who had been near her merely wiped the blood from her forehead and continued to dance. More telling is the ritualized struggle over the stick, which one anthropologist who worked with a group in Libya has argued is associated with virginity (Mason 1975). A woman explained to me, "If the dancer is sharp they can't take the stick from her. They'll be coming at her from all sides but she keeps it."

But perhaps some of the short songs traditionally exchanged between the women (gathered in a tent some distance away from the young men standing in a line near the dancer) and the young men, make clearest the ways in which a challenge between the sexes was central to weddings. One especially memorable competitive exchange was the following. As her sister danced a woman sang of her:

> A bird in the hot winds glides
> and no rifle scope can capture it . . .

A man responded with the song:

> The heart would be no hunter
> if it didn't play in their feathers . . .

In the loss and delegitimation of this whole section of the wedding ritual, an important piece of the construction of Bedouin sexual relations has disappeared. Today, all that is left in a ritual that was a highly charged and evenly matched challenge between the sexes is the enactment of the men's hunt. The groom is the hunter, the bride his prey. Decked out in her make-up and white satin dress, she is brought from her father's house and her "virginity" taken by her groom in a bloody display.

Wedding songs, only sung by women now, reinforce this construction of the bride as vulnerable prey. They liken the bride to a gazelle. This is a compliment to her beauty but also suggests her innocence and defenselessness. Other songs liken the groom to a falcon or hunter. This is no longer balanced by women's former powers to create desire but elude capture.

The disappearance of the female dancer can thus be seen to have shifted the balance such that women's capacities to successfully challenge men have been de-emphasized. Although the sexes are still pitted against each other, the contest is no longer represented as even.

There is a second important point to be made about the dancer that relates to some transformations in constructions of power and sexuality. For it is not completely true that women no longer dance in front of men at Awlad 'Ali weddings. It has become unacceptable for respectable young kinswomen to dance, but there are now some professional dancers. They accompany musical troupes hired to entertain at weddings of the Bedouin nouveau riche. These women may or may not be prostitutes but they are certainly not considered respectable.[7] In that sense, and in the fact that ordinary women go nowhere near the areas where these musicians and dancers perform, one cannot any longer claim that the dancer represents Woman or enacts women's challenge of men. The opposite may be true. This new kind of wedding may be introducing a new view of women, one quite familiar to us in the United States but quite strange to the Awlad 'Ali: women as sexual commodities stripped of their embeddedness in their kin groups or the homosocial world of women.

The professionalization of weddings as entertainment and spectacle (if spectacles that retain vestiges of the participatory in that young men seize the microphone to sing songs) may also be signaling a fundamental shift in the relationship of the construction of sexuality and the construction of the social order. What seems to be disappearing is the participation of the whole community in the responsibility of ritually reproducing the fundamental social and political dynamics of the community. Does this indicate the emergence of a new kind of power? One that works differently? One whose nexus is perhaps the individual rather than the kin group or gender group? This new form of wedding is not being adopted universally in the Bedouin region since the poor cannot afford it and the respectable condemn it as undignified and inappropriate for pious Muslims. Nevertheless, as a public discourse it must enter and shape the field of sexuality for all.

The third and final historical shift I will discuss comes out in the comments women made about what had happened to weddings. One old woman reminisced about weddings of the past. She shook her head and laughed, "No, the things they did before you can't do anymore. Nowadays weddings are small, like a shrunken old man. People used to really celebrate, staying up all night, for days! But they have become like the Muslim Brothers now." The younger woman she was talking to had explained for me. "They say it is wrong. Now everything is forbidden. People before didn't know. They were ignorant." She used a term with connotations of the pre-Islamic era.

These women's invocations of Islam and the proper behavior of the pious in the contexts of weddings mark some significant changes in power relations. It has always been important to the Awlad 'Ali that they are Muslims and that they are good Muslims. And these two women themselves were devout. They prayed regularly and the old one had been on the pilgrimage to Mecca. Yet when they and other women brought up the religious wrongness of their traditional wedding practices, it was with some ambivalence since they were also nostalgic for the richer days of the past. After one wedding there was a hint of disapproval in women's gossip about one aunt in the community. Someone with a good voice who usually sang at weddings, she had just returned from the pilgrimage to Mecca and had refused this time. "It is wrong," she told them. They thought she was being self-righteous—and selfish.

What is really at stake comes out clearly from women's discussions of a happy wedding that had taken place in my absence. I was told that, as usual, for days before the wedding the women and girls had been celebrating by themselves every evening, drumming and singing. The older men of the community wanted them to stop and instructed them that at least once the guests (non-relatives) had begun to arrive, they would have to stop. It was shameful to sing in front of people, the men insisted. On the eve of the wedding as the women and girls gathered and began to sing and dance in celebration, the groom's father came in to greet his visiting female relatives. He also wanted to try to silence the group of women. When he entered the tent, he saw his own older sister, a dignified woman in her sixties, dancing. "Hey, what's this?" he said. "Rottenest of days, even you, Hajja?" He called her by the respectful title reserved for those who have performed the pilgrimage to Mecca. "That's right," she answered definitely, "even me!" Everyone laughed then and each time they retold the story.

Women still refuse to be stopped from celebrating weddings. But the older men, armed with religious righteousness, are clearly trying to assert authority over them in domains that were previously inviolable. Weddings, like the discontinued sheep-shearing festivities to which they are often likened, were always before classified as occasions where young men and young women could express desires. Elder men were not to interfere. At sheep-shearing festivities young men used to sing with impunity oblique sexual songs to flirt with the women present. The songs often insulted the patriarch whose herds the young men were shearing. Similarly, at weddings young men sang to women, not just the dancer. Even more important, women sang back—songs of love and desire. Older men made sure they were not in the vicinity.[8]

Now, not only have the exchanges between young men and women stopped but older men seem to be trying to assert control over the separate women's festivities. Their motives for this intervention are irrelevant. They may genuinely believe they are encouraging their families to live up to an interpretation of Islam that denounces such frivolity as impious. The effect, however, on women and young men, is

that by means of this discourse of Islamic propriety wielded by older men, they are being displaced as the prime actors in the rites that produced and reproduced Bedouin constructions of sexuality and desire.

If, as I have tried to show, in a small Bedouin community in Egypt, sexuality can come to be a crucial marker of cultural identity, and if the construction of sexuality is so closely tied to the organization of kinship and gender and changes as the community is transformed by such broad processes as its incorporation into the wider Egyptian nation and economy, then it seems impossible to assert the existence of a Muslim sexuality that can be read off texts or shared across communities with very different histories and ways of life. Instead, we need to think about specific constructions of sexuality and, in the case of the Muslim Arab world, about the variable role discourses on religion can play in those constructions.

AUTHOR'S NOTE

Most of the research in Egypt on which this article is based was supported by an NEH Fellowship for College Teachers and a Fulbright Award under the Islamic Civilization Program. I am grateful to Samia Mehrez for inviting me to present an early version at Cornell University. I am more grateful to the women and men in the Awlad 'Ali community who shared their lives, including their weddings, with me.

NOTES

1. The literature, especially the feminist literature, on sexuality has become vast in the last decade or two. A helpful early text is Vance (1984). Anthropologists have recently begun to pay more attention to constructions of sexuality and their cross-cultural perspective should contribute to our understanding of the way that sexuality is constructed. For a good introduction to some of that work, see Caplan (1987).
2. For this reason the weddings of divorcees or widows are not celebrated with as much enthusiasm and are considered somewhat ordinary affairs.

3. For example, she described what is known as the *dayra* (the circling). On the evening of the wedding day, they had seated the bride and groom on a pillow, back to back. A neighbor carrying a lamb on his back, holding one foreleg in each of his hands, had walked around and around them—seven times. She mimicked the audience counting: "Hey, did you count that one? One, two, three, four." "Thank God," she said at one point, "there were no outsiders (non-relatives) from back home with us. How embarrassing it would have been."

4. The theorist who has most developed this notion of the effects on subjectivity and sense of individuality of the Western discourses on sexuality is Michel Foucault (1978, 1985).

5. For an analysis of similar kinds of symbolic constructions of gender and sexuality, see Bourdieu's (1977) work on Algerian Kabyles. My analysis of the meaning of this rite differs significantly from that of Combs-Schilling (1989), who worked in Morocco.

6. For more on rituals related to fertility and infertility, see my *Writing Women's Worlds* (1993). Boddy (1989) has analyzed for Muslim Sudanese villagers the extraordinary symbolic stress on women's fertility over their sexuality.

7. As Van Nieuwkerk (1995) has documented, this is generally true about professional dancers in Egypt.

8. Peters (1990) describes a similar avoidance by elders of wedding celebrations among the Bedouin of Cyrenaica in the 1950s.

REFERENCES

Abu-Lughod, Lila. 1993. *Writing Women's Worlds: Bedouin Stories*. Berkeley and Los Angeles: University of California Press.

Alloula, Malek. 1986. *The Colonial Harem*. Myran and Wlad Godzich, trans. Minneapolis: University of Minnesota Press.

Boddy, Janice. 1989. *Wombs and Alien Spirits: Women, Men, and the Zar Cult in Northern Sudan*. Madison, WI: University of Wisconsin Press.

Bouhdiba, Abdelwahab. 1985. *Sexuality in Islam*. London and Boston: Routledge & Kegan Paul.

Bourdieu, Pierre. 1977. *Outline of a Theory of Practice*. Cambridge: Cambridge University Press.

Caplan, Patricia, ed. 1987. *The Cultural Construction of Sexuality*. London and New York: Tavistock Publications.

Combs-Schilling, M.E. 1989. *Sacred Performances: Islam, Sexuality and Sacrifice*. New York: Columbia University Press.

Daly, Mary. 1978. *Gyn/ecology, the Metaethics of Radical Feminism*. Boston: Beacon Press.

Foucault, Michel. 1978. *The History of Sexuality: Volume 1: An Introduction*. New York: Random House.

———. 1985. *The Use of Pleasure*. Vol. 2 of *The History of Sexuality*. New York: Pantheon.

Mason, John. 1975. "Sex and Symbol in the Treatment of Women: The Wedding Rite in a Libyan Oasis Community." *American Ethnologist* 2: 649–61.

Peters, Emrys. 1990. *The Bedouin of Cyrenaica*. Edited by Jack Goody and Emanuel Marx. Cambridge: Cambridge Univeristy Press.

Sabbah, Fatna A. 1984. *Woman in the Muslim Unconscious*. New York and Oxford: Pergamon Press.

Vance, Carole. 1984. *Pleasure and Danger: Exploring Female Sexuality*. Boston and London: Routledge & Kegan Paul.

Van Nieuwkerk, Karin. 1995. *"A Trade Like Any Other": Female Singers and Dancers in Egypt*. Austin, TX: University of Texas Press.

From Pollution to Love Magic: The New Anthropology of Menstruation

Alma Gottlieb

Consider this story: A college student—we'll call him Eddie—is having difficulty in his love life. Girls are so keyed into feminism these days, Eddie's concluded, that they rarely

---

"Bloody Mess, Blood Magic, or Just Plain Blood? Anthropological Perspectives on the Menstrual Experience"

(adaptation/elaboration of "Afterword", Ethnology 41 (4): 381–390

consider boys worthy of their affection. How to seduce a girl of this feminist generation? One day, our frustrated student is inspired: Even the staunchest feminist might be excited at the thought of a prospective boyfriend who himself professes an interest in feminist theory, he ventures. Eddie decides to make use of campus resources and scours the bookstores for the most unabashedly, even outrageously feminist book he can find. He chooses a scholarly tome called *Blood Magic: The Anthropology of Menstruation*, a collection of essays about the ways that women around the world experience their periods (Buckley and Gottlieb 1988a). Eddie buys the volume, brings it home, and places the unread prop strategically on his coffee table before inviting his next date to his apartment, then hopes for the book to have its anticipated effect.[1]

In planning his strategy, the model Eddie used was an old one, although he was undoubtedly unaware of its pedigree: he was relying on menstrual blood—or its textual representation—as a seduction technique, a form of "love magic." This use of menstrual blood to secure sexual favors (or fidelity) is well documented in other cultural contexts (Hoskins 2002); in fact, a (semi-fictionalized) folk example from southen Illinois is even mentioned in the introduction to the very book Eddie was displaying on his coffee table.

However, most previously documented forms of menstrual-blood-as-love-magic involve women manipulating the substance either to seduce men, or to bind straying husbands or lovers to them; Eddie had reversed the more usual gender pattern. Using cunning and deceit, he had acted as the initiator of the sexual relationship. In his plan, he upheld the usual patriarchal structure of Western gender relations of men taking advantage of women by exercising differential access to power of one sort or another. Thus if Eddie's unexpected use

of a feminist book about menstrual experiences spoke to a documented ethnographic practice, it also represented a violation of the feminist intention of the analytic project of understanding those practices. Eddie's story signals how far scholars still have to go in furthering the widespread understanding of feminism and how it can lead us to understand women's lives and bodily-based experiences.

When the book Eddie was using as a quasi-fetish in his flirtation repertoire was first published (Buckley and Gottlieb 1988b), anthropological works about menstruation were few and far between. Moreover, most early anthropological writings on menstruation tended to confirm a simplistic agenda suggesting that menstrual blood is generally taken as a source of what anthropologists call symbolic pollution (Douglas 1966). In other words, menstrual blood was assumed to be seen as mystically contaminating, hence something to be avoided at all costs by anyone who is not menstruating—and especially by men.[2] Feminism had not yet made serious inroads into the comparative, cultural study of women's bodies in general. And systematic cross-cultural fieldwork with consultants concerning the topic of menstruation, let alone with menstruating women themselves about their own perspectives on their somatic lives, was still a rarity. In assembling our collection of anthropological essays about menstrual practices cross-culturally, Buckley and I hoped to be followed by a new generation of writings that would both add new data to our existing knowledge of women's experiences of their bodies, and that would pose a range of new models inspired in one way or another by feminist theory. These future works would, we thought, investigate how women's experiences of the menstrual cycle—as with other body practices—are profoundly shaped by culture and history. For this to occur, we

---

[1] The story was shared with me by my husband, writer Philip Graham, who heard it from a writing student of his who was "Eddie's" roommate. The writing student was visiting our home for a class party and, after noticing a copy of *Blood Magic* on my bookshelf, relayed the above narrative to his amused professor.

[2] For a critical review of earlier works informed by this and other problematic perspectives, see Buckley and Gottlieb (1988a).

needed to be followed by a new generation of ethnographers committed to conducting fieldwork-based studies on somatic processes such as menstruation that seemed to belong exclusively to the domain of biology but that were nevertheless deeply defined by systems of cultural values and historical factors alike.

During the fifteen years that have elapsed since *Blood Magic* appeared, feminism has indeed made exciting inroads into the comparative, cultural study of women's bodies in general. Accordingly, systematic cross-cultural fieldwork with consultants concerning the topic of menstruation in particular, and with menstruating women themselves about their own perspectives on their somatic lives, is no longer such a rarity. Indeed, in the past decade-and-a-half, there has been a groundswell of published work, both within and outside anthropology, that focuses on menstruation as well as other aspects of reproduction in particular and the body in general. Originally, these writings emphasized *women's* bodily experiences. In many ways launched by Emily Martin's award-winning work, *The Woman in the Body* (1987), a host of books and articles have brilliantly explored the culturally and historically produced nature of a wide gamut of reproduction experiences previously assumed to be regulated by biology alone.[3] Increasingly, scholars have begun to explore cultural and historical constructions of *men's* bodily experiences as well (e.g. Gardiner 2002, Gutmann 1996, Kimmel 1987, Lugo and Maurer 2000). Contemporary authors now writing about the menstrual experience cross-culturally are thus in conversation with a larger cohort of colleagues bringing fresh perspectives to the dynamic interface between body, person, gender identity, and society.

[3] For an excellent review of earlier work, see Ginsburg and Rapp (1991). More recent works include: Bledsoe and Banja (2002), Davis-Floyd (1992), Davis-Floyd and Sargent (1997), Davis-Floyd, Cosminsky and Pigg (2002), Davis-Floyd and Dumit (1997), Feldman-Savelsberg (1999), Franklin and Ragoné (1998), Ginsburg and Rapp (1995), Handwerker (1990), Héritier (1994, 1996), Inhorn (1994, 1995), Jordan (1993), Morgan (1999), Nourse (1999), Owen (1993), Ragoné (1994), Rapp (1999), Roth (2002), Sargent (1989), and M. Strathern (1992).

In this chapter, I will especially focus on one recent collection of essays that offers an especially rich selection of practices, beliefs and values concerning menstrual cycle cross-culturally (Hoskins 2002a). Some important themes run through the essays in that collection. For example, the in/famous *menstrual hut* is drastically revisioned in this new writing. Long conceived as an architectural instantiation of female oppression, the "menstrual hut" in much classic anthropological literature was usually described as a lonely and flimsy structure in which women were consigned to spend their menstruating days alone—bored, self-loathing (allowed only to scratch an itch on their contaminated bodies using the infamous "scratching sticks" to avoid auto-pollution), and in virtual (if temporary) exile. This anthropologically vaunted, somewhat mystical space was surrounded by decades of disciplinary speculation that was, however, rarely based on relevant fieldwork. The menstrual buildings described in current anthropological writings inhabit an entirely different universe.

Janet Hoskins (2002b) occupies an especially privileged position from which to understand the experiences of women while inside a menstrual residence. While living among the Huaulu people in eastern Indonesia, Hoskins herself was expected to spend time in the menstrual hut every month while she had her period. Her account runs parallel to that of another ethnographer, Wynne Maggi, who has recently conducted participant observation research in menstrual houses every month over the course of fieldwork with the (largely non-Muslim) Kalasha community in Pakistan and has written a first-person account of her experiences (Maggi 2001: 125–133). Having conducted fieldwork in societies with active menstrual shelters and a number of explicit menstrual expectations, both Hoskins and Maggi were afforded rare opportunities to gain firsthand knowledge of the occupants' activities and the general atmosphere inside the houses, and thus to demystify women's actual experiences.

Perhaps the greatest challenge posed by both the Huaulu and the Kalasha to the infamous image of the menstrual-hut-as-prison concerns the personnel. Due to the now fairly well documented but still-little-understood phenomenon of menstrual synchrony—the likelihood of co-resident women starting their periods on the same day each month (often at the new moon or full moon)[4]—there is usually a lively gathering of several simultaneously menstruating women inside both Huaulu and Kalasha menstrual huts, rather than the stereotyped single, lonely woman. Moreover, among the Huaulu, beyond the menstruating women themselves, one is also likely to find some of their young children—both boys and girls—and on occasion some visiting women friends as well. Hoskins intrigues us with her account of all manner of pleasurable female activity occurring inside the collectivity temporarily inhabiting the hut. Singing and playing instruments, telling stories, doing craftwork, relaxing, breastfeeding, caring for young children—all these occur each month inside the menstrual residence. Indeed, the sociable nature of the chamber lends itself to charismatic personalities: one Huaulu woman even turned the hut into a performance space in which she recounted lively stories, building up political reputations village-wide from her narrative skills.

Elsewhere, women do not maintain a complete monopoly over the menstrual residence. Among the Pangia of the New Guinea highlands, such buildings may also legitimately shelter *men* (Stewart and Strathern 2002). This occurs on the rare occasion that a man is said by members of the local community to be pregnant because he inadvertently ingested menstrual blood. In such a disastrous situation, the unfortunate man is said to be cured by a ritual that he undergoes inside the menstrual hut shelter—now empty of women. Writing of less legitimate cases elsewhere in New Guinea, Stewart and Strathern (ibid.) also mention in passing the possibility of *menstrual adultery* occurring in the private space of the menstrual hut. This is an under-discussed but surely fruitful topic for comparative inquiry, especially where menstrual seclusion is practiced. Both these Melanesian

cases serve as a powerful reminder to the outsider that, as anthropology so often teaches us about nearly every other aspect of social life, nothing may be assumed: in this case, in any given menstrual residence, even the gender of the occupants may be variable.

In Indonesia, Hoskins (2002b) further notes that the Huaulu menstrual building shelters women not only when they are menstruating but also while they are in labor. Such dual-use structures—for both menstruation and childbirth—are reported elsewhere as well (e.g., Maggi 2001). In such cases where the menstrual shelter also serves as the birth clinic, perhaps even the term "menstrual hut" (or "house") is misleading and ought to be replaced by a more culturally inclusive term—"women's reproduction house" or even just "women's house," echoing the "men's houses" that are documented among many groups in Melanesia, Africa and South America. Such a semantic shift would be in keeping with the fact that menstruation may not always be singled out for special treatment in complete contrast to all other bodily fluids and processes.

The emphasis on *agency* in contemporary works about menstruation extends beyond the menstrual shelter to the experience of menstruating women, whether or not they inhabit a special building reserved for the occasion. Thus, the agency of the individual woman-as-menstruator is stressed in several recent essays. From Hoskins (2002b), for example, we learn of Kodi women on Sumba in eastern Indonesia who deploy menstrual blood to deceive their husbands in a variety of disempowering ways, effectively manipulating the secret powers of menstrual blood at the expense of their men. The flip side to such actions is exercised by Huaulu women, who manage the more public powers of menstruation for the *protection* of their men.

Elsewhere in Indonesia, Balinese women may make use of menstrual blood in manufacturing more friendly forms of "love magic". At the same time, in a provocative narrative, Pedersen (2002) illustrates how the individual menstruator's own perceptions of her state can complicate seemingly simple ideologies of menstruation-as-pollution when she cites a Balinese consultant who claims that

---

[4]For ethnographic and historic examples of menstrual synchrony, see Buckley (1988) Knight (1988, 1991); and Lamp (1988).

sitting on a garbage heap while menstruating makes her feel royal. Other Balinese women knowingly violate menstrual taboos by illicitly entering a temple while menstruating but apparently feel no remorse or guilt. As analyzed by Pedersen, such women employ psychological techniques to counterbalance the spiritual pollution they should in theory cause by their violation. Here we see how ideologies of pollution, where they exist, should be the beginning—not the end—of ethnographic analysis. Women's own views of a patriarchal ideology can strikingly offer an alternative reading of that ideology, sometimes affording women a form of personal resistance to a degrading cultural script, or allowing them to reinterpret it entirely.

The agency of the individual is explicitly stressed by Phyllis Morrow writing about the native American Yupik of central Alaska. Morrow (2002) explores how the Yupik generally emphasize individual responsibility in maintaining cultural expectations. Thus the Yupik allow latitude for individuals to find their own comfort level in adhering to rules, or "teachings" (as Morrow sometimes translates the Yupik word), for personal behavior—including those that pertain to menstruation. This is an apt case of an indigenous or "folk" model of social life pointing productively to an appropriate analytic model. The conjunction between indigenous and analytic models serves as a humble reminder that local systems of knowledge exist on the same level as do "scientific" ones, and each can speak productively to the other (cf. Rosaldo 1989).

Another means to deploy agency in the menstrual experience involves the use of *emenagogues:* herbal and other practical methods that women throughout the world and throughout history have devised to regulate the timing of their periods. Sometimes these techniques have been used to promote fertility, at other times, they have been used (usually furtively) to induce abortions. In either case, using such techniques may constitute a more secular effort by women to regulate their menstrual flow, thereby allowing them to exercise general control over their bodies.

Writing of Bali, for example, Pedersen (2002) mentions that women may prepare a dish with uncooked pig's blood to hasten the onset of their menstrual periods. This observation echoes abundant information contained in a new collection of essays (Renne and van der Walle 2001) reporting an impressive variety of emenagogues cross-culturally and historically. Once again, we encounter the theme of agency, as women deliberately shape their own menstrual experience rather than seeing themselves as scripted actors reading from either a biologically *or* culturally mandated text.

All these cases demonstrate how close attention to individual perspectives deconstructs the classic, monolithic view of menstrual taboos and cultural expectations as preprogrammed models from which actual subjects may never diverge. Such testimonies are theoretically critical insofar as they challenge the image that anthropologists have long held of menstrual culture—perhaps as an extension of a more general model inherited from such early scholars as Lucien Lévy-Bruhl (1985) and others, that cultural traditions in general exert a certain deadening, conservative force. This is a perspective that is very much challenged in the recent work on menstruation.

The individual manipulation of menstrual taboos and expectations speaks at another level to intracultural variation via subgroups with structurally divergent agendas or even ambiguity or ambivalence among members of a given society regarding women's menstrual activities. When Buckley (1988) first suggested that among the native North American Yurok of California, men and women, as well as aristocrats and commoners, may perceive menstruation differently from one another, it was a somewhat novel proposal. Several recent essays provide extended studies of situations that are likewise complex in their own ways. Menstruation emerges from these societies as a process that is perceived differentially according to multiple subject positions.

Writing of Bali, for example, Pedersen charts how the deeply structured system of rank adapted from the Hindu caste system has a significant impact on how girls and women experience their periods. Whereas high-ranking Balinese women may find menstrual taboos to be empowering, low-ranking girls and women may experience menstrual taboos as simply one more painful sign of their inferior status. Social change adds further layers to the entanglements of rank. Pederson notes that "'modern' working women are more prone than any to 'take advantage' of the leverage provided by the exempting options." If such options are more available to higher-ranked women than to lower-ranked ones, this would perpetuate, and perhaps even magnify, the divide between women at different ends of the system of social hierarchy. Here we see the complexity of class and gender as they work against each other. Ironically, women's bodies—which might (seemingly) serve as a foundation for female solidarity—can be culturally manipulated in such a way as to divide rather than unite women of diverse class and prestige backgrounds. The menstrual experience speaks here to broader feminist concerns: sadly, the empowerment of some women often comes at the expense of the oppression of others.

Ironically, the opposite effects of the relationship between class and menstrual symbolism are found in Bengal. In this region of Hindu India, as analyzed by Hanssen (2002), the Brahmanic view is that menstrual blood is polluting. However, when men and women of the low-ranked leatherworker caste become "renouncers" through a particular religious sect—the Vaishnava Baul group—they embrace a major precept of the sect: that menstrual blood contains a life force or "seed" within it—as with other bodily fluids in the Baul scheme of life, but even more so. Taking into account such symbolic potency, some of the "renouncers" with whom Hanssen conducted research may on occasion ingest menstrual blood so as to regain spiritual strength. Here we see the symbolic potency to menstrual fluid being harnessed not for nefarious goals, as is reported in much of the classic literature, but for regenerative purposes. Again, the menstrual pollution model is effectively challenged.

Another subgroup meriting particular attention is that of *unmarried girls*. The menstrual blood of this group—defined variously as virgins and/or unmarried—is held up for special ritual treatment in several societies that are the focus of the articles I have been discussing. For example, Stewart and Strathern (2002) report that the Duna people of Melanesia addressed societal disruptions that were said to be caused by a mischievous spirit by offering the spirit the menstrual blood of a virginal girl. The consequences to the girl chosen to supply this critical ritual ingredient were drastic: as an adult, she was not allowed ever to bear children. In exploring the individual nuances of such cases here and elsewhere, there may be a subject ripe for new, comparative analysis.

Indeed, the experiences of girls undergoing menarche in general are still under-reported by anthropologists. Scholars in history, cultural studies, nursing, journalism, and other disciplines are embarrassingly ahead of anthropologists here, inasmuch as the menarcheal histories of girls in the U.S. are now well documented by scholars in adjacent fields (e.g., Golub 1992, Houppert 1999, Lee and Coen 1996). A few current works by anthropologists do address the issue, however. Thus Pedersen (2002) recounts intriguing menarcheal histories of Balinese women that are at great variance from those reported for contemporary North American girls. Whereas in the U.S., many women and girls still feel great shame concerning their first periods (and regarding menstruation in general), and they attest to the continuing existence of a virtual taboo against discussion of the subject in most contexts, this is not the case in Bali. Intriguingly, Pederson reports that Balinese of all ages and both genders feel comfortable in discussing menstruation quite casually, and all females with whom Pederson conversed about the subject recalled that they enjoyed their first periods, even when they were surprised by or afraid of their first flow. Such discussions of the menarcheal experiences of non-Western girls reminds us that the more negative experiences of contemporary North American and other Western girls, while now well reported, cannot be taken as universal.

Surely it is time for more anthropologists to conduct systematic fieldwork with menstruating—as well as pre-menarcheal—girls to hear their own perspectives on this crucial life passage. At a more structural level, such discussions may enable us to think about *deconstructing* the category of "menstrual blood" itself. Are we talking about a unified semantic field when we analyze the blood flow of young girls and that of married women in the same way, if a given society singles out the menstrual blood of unmarried/virginal girls as harboring special capacities that the menstrual blood of adult women does not bear?

In short, from recent work it is clearer than ever that we can no longer talk of "the" (single or hegemonic) view or model of menstruation in a particular society. Rather, it is now clear that before assuming generality, we must interrogate the *range* of views and experiences that menstruation may produce across the social divides that structure women's lives.

Related to the previous points, one notices in the essays I have been discussing an insistence that the meanings of menstrual blood and menstruating women are decidedly *plural* in a given locale depending on the particular context. The classic menstrual-blood-as-pollution model that permeated so much early writing by anthropologists is definitively discarded here in favor of much more situationally nuanced understandings. In particular, the symbolically constituted relation of menstrual blood to both *fertility and infertility*, as well as to other cultural matrices, emerges as an especially critical theme in these papers (for an earlier example, see Gottlieb 1988).

Thus Stewart and Strathern (2002) propose a dramatic re-visioning of the hegemonic, disciplinary model of menstruation-as-pollution as it was foundationally conceptualized. Taking us to the heartland of classical anthropological thinking about menstruation— the highlands of Papua New Guinea—they draw on A. Strathern's recent, stimulating book, *Body Thoughts* (1996) to ground their

discussion of menstruation in broader issues relating the body and society. Their description (from Sainsbury) of the menarcheal Siane girl who is celebrated and courted for her induction into life as a menstruator is at striking odds with the classic pollution model that permeated much early anthropological writing about gender relations in New Guinea. Stewart and Strathern then produce in effect a counterfactual model, imagining what regional ethnography might have been like over the past three decades had Sainsbury's ethnography—rather than that of other Melanesianists such as Mervyn Meggitt— prevailed as the orienting study.[5]

But Stewart and Strathern's *What if. . . ?* line of thinking is not purely conjectural: they argue that the Siane would indeed serve as a more appropriate model for the New Guinea highlands. Drawing on additional Melanesian ethnography, Stewart and Strathern (2002) propose that a complementary rather than antagonistic model of gender relations is more relevant to much of Melanesia than previous ethnography suggested. Stewart and Strathern's disarmingly reorienting survey should serve to reinscribe the anthropological imagining of that cultural region with new models steeped in subtlety well beyond the classic statements. Moreover, their proposed model of complementary gender relations resonates with contemporary discussions of complementary and egalitarian models of gender being developed for a variety of independent, non-Western groups elsewhere before state conquest (e.g. Du 2002). Here we see how menstruation theory can speak to, and even inform, gender theory more broadly. This is the case insofar as menstruation is deeply implicated in a wide array of social matrices, from religion (most obviously) to such disparate spheres as architecture, political economy and beyond.

---

[5] Their fantasy reminds one of Mary Douglas' long-ago published wondering what Africanist ethnography would look like had the British scholar, Sir E. Evans-Pritchard, studied the Dogon of francophone West Africa and the French scholar, Marcel Griaule, studied the Nuer of anglophone northeast Africa (Douglas 1975).

Indeed, the necessity for a contextual approach highlighting what anthropologist Victor Turner might have called *positionality*—an approach that would produce a wide-ranging analysis of how menstrual practices relate to other ritual and social forces at play in a given society—becomes quite pressing from all the work I have been discussing. Most of the societies that are the subject of the articles I have discussed—the Yupik of Alaska, several Melanesian groups, the eastern Indonesian Huaulu, and the Balinese—expect women to adhere carefully to culturally delimited menstrual restrictions; at the same time, the members of these societies orient these practices around conceptual models that are far from a simple pollution framework. Thus all the authors of the works I have discussed remind us that menstrual restrictions are best seen as one of many types of ritual and/or somatic restrictions in the lives of all who practice them. Depending on the society, the proper context for understanding menstrual restrictions may necessitate understanding comparable restrictions in the lives of both males and females, old and young, laypersons and ritual specialists alike. The language of pollution misleads here, these authors all observe; as Morrow (2002) points out, Mary Douglas' early hypothesis that menstrual pollution indexes underlying sociological ambiguity concerning women does not necessarily apply.

At the same time, writing of the Kodi, Hoskins (2002b) points out that the *absence* of menstrual taboos belies a deep-seated conviction that menstrual blood is exceedingly *potent*. Her insight signals that a lack of explicitly religious *taboos* concerning menstrual practice does not necessarily signal a lack of culturally shaped thinking about menstruation. The current outpouring of ethnographies of modern urban life speaks powerfully to this point: secular culture is still culture, these ethnographies remind us—even science is grounded in a set of cultural assumptions

that appeal to deeply held but unverifiable beliefs about the nature of reality.[6] As Clifford Geertz cautioned some time ago (1983), what passes for "common sense" is not necessarily common, as peoples everywhere forge their own distinctive notion of common sense as the basis for reality. A contextual approach to social life borrowed from Turner, highlighting positionality, offers a fruitful method for teasing out local nuances that seeming similarities across cultures might otherwise conceal.

As with other taboos, the longstanding anthropological and popular images alike of menstrual taboos is that they have somehow existed since time immemorial and that their origins are untraceable. In the recent writings I have been discussing, we learn otherwise. In taking into account the press of *history and social change*, it becomes clear that menstrual practices engage with a variety of modernities. Earlier studies tended to treat the body either as an artifact of biology—i.e., more or less immutable, hence anthropologically boring—or, more recently, as cultural constructions that were nevertheless conceived as static. More recent discussions have taken up the insistence—persuasively argued by the French scholar, Michel Foucault, and others—that bodily regimes are as much subject to historical shifts as are political regimes. In keeping with this productive direction for scholarly research, in the essays I have been considering, the authors offer discussions of how menstrual practices have—or in some surprising instances have not—transformed within the recent past. Indeed, in some places, rather than insistent continuity, radical changes in menstrual practices have been documented.

Not only may their histories be knowable, but menstrual practices have weakened in some places whereas—in contrast to what modernization theory would have predicted—they have intensified in other regions. Among the Pangia in Melanesia, for example, Stewart and Strathern (2002) inform us that menstrual huts, far from having existed since some primeval *ur*-time, were first introduced to the group along with

---

[6] For some examples of ethnographic accounts of contemporary scientific culture, see Gusterson (1996), Haraway (1990), Martin (1994), and Toumey (1996).

performances dedicated to a regional female spirit cult. This spirit is widely respected as promoting fertility; Stewart and Strathern treat it as an index of a more general model of gender complementarity. The traceable co-introduction of female spirit cult performances and the practice of menstrual seclusion raises fascinating questions about changing gender roles during an earlier era of Pangia history. The case suggests that we might question the seemingly unchanging history of other menstrual practices elsewhere. Assuming that contemporary menstrual practices are a permanent feature of a given social landscape makes no more sense than assuming that any other aspect of a society—say, its political structure, or its economic base—has existed unchanged for millennia.

Moreover, in those cases where cultural continuity *is* demonstrable, its meanings are not necessarily transparent. On Bali, Pedersen (2002) tells us, menstrual taboos continue in strong force even in the face of available new menstrual technologies (industrially produced sanitary pads and tampons). However, the continuity of menstrual restrictions does not imply a thoroughgoing neglect of, or resistance to, modernity; the practices of menstrual culture can also acknowledge and even adapt to changing medical science. Thus nowadays, some Balinese women take birth control pills in order to delay the onset of their periods; precisely timing the menstrual cycle in this way can allow women to participate in traditional temple rituals from which menstruating women are still actively banned. In this menstrual culture that persists in the face of active engagement with the Western world, even tourists are subject to regulations . . . as the English-language signs at Balinese temples forbidding entrance by menstruating women remind foreign visitors. The Balinese case teaches us that apparent cultural conservatism may be maintained self-consciously for reasons engaging with modernity. Contemporary factors such as ethnic pride and nationalism in the face of international pressure to Westernize may become as relevant as

insistent maintenance of tradition might have been in a previous era.

In short, tracing menstrual histories can serve to remind us that, as with other current social practices, what we observe at any given moment in the field *may* represent continuity—but it may also be an aberration, a variation, or a rejection of what has occurred in the recent or distant past. In the colonized world in particular, the ravages brought by the triple invasion of soldiers, traders and missionaries likely produced upheavals in the way that the body is culturally read and produced. *Precolonial* somatic regimes will of course be much more of a challenge to reconstruct, but oral histories, and in some cases colonial records, should help us to understand pivotal moments in history when the gendered body may have been re-thought and re-experienced. Through such records, can we begin to account for *why* menstrual taboos have relaxed in some areas whereas they have rigidified in others under varying colonial and post-colonial regimes, as indigenous populations endeavor to forge their own futures in the face of an increasingly engulfing modernity? This question contains a promising set of issues for researchers to continue to pursue.

THE FUTURE OF MENSTRUAL STUDIES

For over fifteen years, a pedagogical engagement with menstruation has allowed me to construct a classroom-based ethnographic portrait that affords some insight into contemporary U.S. college students' perceptions and experiences of the menstrual cycle. At my home university, I have regularly taught an undergraduate course on "Cultural Images of Women" which always includes a section on menstrual practices in cross-cultural perspective. Learning of the obfuscatory terms by which American female students (who are largely but not exclusively female) still refer to their periods ("the curse," "Aunt Flo," "on the rag," and so on)—which are typically identical to terms that have been documented for the U.S. for much of the twentieth century—is a depressing exercise. For the striking continuity in such terms speaks to the continuing existence of strong menstrual taboos and a polluting image of menstruation at the heart of the supposedly rationalized and secular (and, dare one hope, decreasingly patriarchal) mainstream North American society.

However, another student exercise in this course often reveals a different, and more hopeful, portrait of the current generation of American students' attitudes towards toward menstruation. In choosing among several options for final exam essays, the most popular choice is often the essay question that invites students to design a new menstrual ritual for an imagined future daughter or niece, based on what students know from the menstrual experiences of their friends, relatives, and themselves, as well as what they have learned about women's menstrual experiences elsewhere from class readings. In writing their final essays, students year after year have proposed empowering rituals that harness the menstrual cycle to inspire menarcheal girls to feel pride rather than shame at their new somatically acquired status. One student, for example, envisioned a long ritual process of educating her not-yet-conceived daughter into the wonders of the menstrual cycle. During one portion of the imagined ritual, the author and her future husband would, she planned, "throw confetti into the air in celebration" (Schroeder 2001:2). This and other festive acts would serve to teach their future daughter to feel comfortable with her menstrual identity: "She would never once feel she had to hide the box of tampons in her bathroom or avoid the clerk's gaze while purchasing pads at the local grocery store" (ibid.:6–7).

Year after year, imagined rituals such as these have testified to a hunger by my students to revision menstruation in general,

and menarche in particular, from a stigmatized to a celebrated event in contemporary North America. If my students' responses are typical, menstrual experiences offer a rich site from which to understand the embodied subject as a place in which gender, power and representation intersect in personally forceful ways. In particular, my students' writings suggest that at least some of the contemporary generation of young women is motivated to rethink their own menstrual histories and enjoys imagining menstrual futures offering ritualized revelry rather than secrecy and shame.

Meanwhile, current anthropological writings offer a range of models of menstrual practices that some of the world's women have forged. Together, these work constitute an exceedingly provocative set of writings that point to the exciting state that characterizes current comparative research into menstruation and that signal the fresh, *multiple* intellectual roads down which the anthropology of menstruation—as an exemplar of the embodied subject—is now traveling.

ACKNOWLEDGMENTS

A short version of this chapter was first presented at the 99th Annual Meeting of the American Anthropological Association (San Francisco, 2000), and a somewhat different version was published in *Ethnology* 41(4) (2002) (special issue: "Blood Mysteries: Beyond Menstruation as Pollution," ed. Janet Hoskins). Many thanks to Janet Hoskins for comments on the earlier version.

REFERENCES

Bledsoe, Caroline with Fatoumatta Banja
2002   *The Contingent Life Course: Reproduction, Time and Aging in West Africa.* Chicago: University of Chicago Press.
Buckley, Thomas
1988   Menstruation and the Power of Yurok Women. In *Blood Magic: The Anthropology of Menstruation*, ed. Thomas Buckley and

Alma Gottlieb. Berkeley: University of California Press, pp. 187–209.

—— and Alma Gottlieb

1988a A Critical Appraisal of Theories of Menstrual Symbolism. In *Blood Magic: The Anthropology of Menstruation*, ed. Thomas Buckley and Alma Gottlieb. Berkeley: University of California Press, pp. 1–53.

—— and ——, eds.

1988b *Blood Magic: The Anthropology of Menstruation*. Berkeley: University of California Press.

Davis-Floyd, Robbie E.

1992 *Birth as an American Rite of Passage*. Berkeley: University of California Press.

——, Sheila Cosminsky and Stacy Leigh Pigg, eds.

2002 Daughters of Time: The Shifting Identities of Contemporary Midwives. Special issue of *Medical Anthropology* 20 (3).

—— and Joe Dumit, eds.

1997 *Cyborg Babies: From Techno Tots to Techno Toys*. New York: Routledge.

Davis-Floyd, Robbie E. and Carolyn F. Sargent, eds.

1997 *Childbirth and Authoritative Knowledge: Cross-Cultural Perspectives*. Berkeley: University of California Press.

Douglas, Mary

1975 [1967] If the Dogon. . . ? In *Mary Douglas, Self-Evidence: Essays in Anthropology*. London: Routledge & Kegan Paul, pp. 124–141.

Du, Shanshan

2002 *"Chopsticks Always Work in Pairs": Gender Unity and Gender Equality among the Lahu of Southwest China*. New York: Columbia University Press.

Feldman-Savelsberg, Pamela

1999 *Plundered Kitchens, Empty Wombs: Threatened Reproduction and Identity in the Cameroon*. Ann Arbor: University of Michigan Press.

Franklin, Sarah and Helena Ragoné, eds.

1998 *Reproducing Reproduction: Kinship, Power, and Technological Innovation*. Philadelphia: University of Pennsylvania Press.

Gardiner, Judith Kegan, ed.

2002 *Masculinity Studies and Feminist Theory: New Directions*. New York: Columbia University Press.

Geertz, Clifford

1983 [1975] Common Sense as a Cultural System. In Clifford Geertz, *Local Knowledge: Further Essays in Interpretive Anthropology*. New York: Basic Books, pp. 73–93.

Ginsburg, Faye and Rayna Rapp

1991 The Politics of Reproduction. *Annual Review of Anthropology* 20: 311–343.

Ginsburg, Faye and Rayna Rapp, eds.

1995 *Conceiving the New World Order: The Global Politics of Reproduction*. Berkeley: University of California Press.

Golub, Sharon

1992 *Periods: From Menarche to Menopause*. London: Sage.

Gottlieb, Alma

1988 Menstrual Cosmology among the Beng of Ivory Coast. In *Blood Magic: The Anthropology of Menstruation*, ed. Thomas Buckley and Alma Gottlieb. Berkeley: University of California Press, pp. 55–74.

Gusterson, Hugh

1996 *Nuclear Rites: A Weapons Laboratory at the End of the Cold War*. Berkeley: University of California Press.

Gutmann, Matthew C.

1996 *The Meanings of Macho: Being a Man in Mexico City*. Berkeley: University of California Press.

Handwerker, W. P., ed.

1990 *Births and Power: Social Change and the Politics of Reproduction*. Boulder: Westview Press.

Hanssen, Kristen.

2002 "Ingesting Menstrual Blood: Notions of Health and Bodily Fluids in Bengal," *Ethnology* 41(4): 365–380.

Haraway, Donna

1990 *Primate Visions: Gender, Race and Nature in the World of Modern Science*. New York: Routledge.

Héritier, Françoise

1994 *Les deux soeurs et leur mère*. Paris: Editions Odile Jacob.

1996 *Masculin/féminin: La pensée de la différence*. Paris: Editions Odile Jacob.

Hoskins, Janet

2002a "Blood Mysteries: Beyond Menstruation as Pollution." *Ethnology*, special issue, Volume 41, No 4.

Hoskins, Janet

2002b "The Menstrual Hut and the Witch's Lair in Two Indonesian Societies" *Ethnology* 41(4), 317–334.

Houppert, Karen

1999 *The Curse—Confronting the Last Unmentionable Taboo: Menstruation*. New York: Farrar, Straus, Giroux.

Inhorn, Marcia

1994 *Quest for Conception: Gender, Infertility, and Egyptian Medical Traditions*. Philadelphia: University of Pennsylvania Press.

1995   *Missing Motherhood: Infertility, Patri-archy and the Politics of Gender in Egypt.* Philadelphia: University of Pennsylvania Press.

Jordan, Brigitte
1993 [1978]   *Birth in Four Cultures: A Cross-Cultural Investigation of Childbirth in Yucatan, Holland, Sweden and the United States.* Robbie Davis-Floyd, ed. 4th ed. Prospect Heights, IL: Waveland Press.

Kimmel, Michael S., ed.
1987   *Changing Men: New Directions in Research on Men and Masculinity.* Beverly Hills, CA: Sage.

Knight, Chris
1988   Menstrual Synchrony and the Australian Rainbow Snake. In *Blood Magic: The Anthropology of Menstruation*, ed. Thomas Buckley and Alma Gottlieb. Berkeley: University of California Press, pp. 232–255.
1991   *Blood Relations: Menstruation and the Origins of Culture.* New Haven: Yale University Press.

Lamp, Frederick
1988   Heavenly Bodies: Menses, Moon, and Rituals of License among the Temne of Sierra Leone. In *Blood Magic: The Anthropology of Menstruation*, ed. Thomas Buckley and Alma Gottlieb. Berkeley: University of California Press, pp. 210–231.

Lee, Janet and Jennifer Sasser-Coen
1996   *Blood Stories: Menarche and the Politics of the Female Body in Contemporary U.S. Society.* New York: Routledge.

Lévy-Bruhl, Lucien
1985 [1922]   *How Natives Think.* Lilian A. Clare, transl. Princeton: Princeton University Press.

Lugo, Alejandro and Bill Maurer, eds.
2000   *Gender Matters: Rereading Michelle Z. Rosal-do.* Ann Arbor: University of Michigan Press.

Maggi, Wynne
2001   *Our Women Are Free: Gender and Ethnicity in the Hindukush.* Ann Arbor: University of Michigan Press.

Martin, Emily
1987   *The Woman in the Body: A Cultural Analysis of Reproduction.* Boston: Beacon Press.
1994   *Flexible Bodies: Tracking Immunity in Ameri-can Culture—From the Days of Polio to the Age of AIDS.* Boston: Beacon Press.

Morgan, Lynne, ed.
1999   *Fetal Subjects, Feminist Positions.* Philadel-phia: University of Pennsylvania Press.

Morrow Phyllis
2002   "The Woman's Vapor: Yupik Bodily Powers in Southwest Alaska," *Ethnology* 41(4): 335–348.

Nourse, Jennifer W.
1999   *Conceiving Spirits: Birth Rituals and Contested Identities Among Laujé of Indonesia.* Washing-ton, D.C.: Smithsonian Institution Press.

Owen, Lara
1993   *Her Blood Is Gold: Celebrating the Power of Menstruation.* San Francisco: Harper San Francisco.

Pedersen, Lene
2002   "Ambiguous Bleeding: Purily and Sacri-fice in Bali," *Ethonology* 41(4): 303–316.

Ragoné, Helena
1994   *Surrogate Motherhood: Conception in the Heart.* Boulder: Westview Press.

Rapp, Rayna
1999   *Testing Women, Testing the Fetus: The Social Impact of Amniocentesis in America.* New York: Routledge.

Renne, Elisha and Etienne van der Walle, eds.
2001   *Regulating Menstruation: Beliefs, Practice, Interpretations.* Chicago: University of Chicago Press.

Rosaldo, Renato
1989   *Culture and Truth: The Remaking of Social Analysis.* Boston: Beacon Press.

Roth, Denise.
2002   *Managing Motherhood, Managing Risk: Fertility and Danger in West Central Tanzania.* Ann Arbor: University of Michigan Press. In press.

Sargent, Garolyn
1989   *Maternity, Medicine, and Power: Reproductive Decisions in Urban Benin.* Berkeley: Univer-sity of California Press.

Schroeder, Annica
2001   A "Rite"ful Passage into Womanhood for Little Gabriella. Paper for ANTH 262, University of Illinois at Urbana-Champaign, December 6, 2001. Unpublished manuscript.

Stewart, Pamela J. and Andrew Strathern
2002   "Power and Placement in Blood Prac-tices," *Ethnology* 41(4): 349–367.

Strathern, Andrew
1996   *Body Thoughts.* Ann Arbor: University of Michigan Press.

Strathern, Marilyn
1992   *Reproducing the Future: Anthropology, Kin-ship, and the New Reproductive Technologies.* New York: Routledge.

Toumey, Christopher P.
1996   *Conjuring Science: Scientific Symbols and Cul-tural Meanings in American Life.* New Brunswick, NJ: Rutgers University Press.

Women's Intimate Friendships and Other Affairs: An Ethnographic Overview

Evelyn Blackwood

Anthropological evidence constitutes an important source for theorizing about women's sexualities. It allows us to go beyond European and American cultures and sexual categories to view sexuality from different perspectives. From a Western viewpoint sexuality appears to be an essential or core attribute of identity; Europeans and Americans tend to think that individuals have fixed sexual identities or orientations. The sexual practices and identities of the United States and Europe, however, often bear little resemblance to sexual relationships and practices in other cultures. The cultural evidence shows the richness and diversity of women's sexualities, and the importance of sociocultural factors in the construction of sexuality.

Social construction theory asserts that sexual acts only have meaning within the context of particular cultures and their beliefs about the self and the world. Human sexual potential takes its form through a number of social processes, including ideologies of religion or ritual, ethnicity, class, gender, family, and reproduction, as well as the material and social conditions of everyday life. These processes provide the interpretive context for sexual feelings, desires and longings. In this article I first take a number of case studies of women's same-sex relations in non-Western societies to illustrate the way particular sociocultural processes frame sexual desire within cultural schemas of meaning. Then I explore how cultural systems of gender construct different sexual beliefs and practices for men and women. In the third section I use two detailed examples of female sexualities, one from Suriname and one from West Sumatra, to argue that sexuality is neither a static category nor a fixed identity. I conclude the essay

From Journal of Social Issues. Reprinted by permission of Blackwell Publishers.

by exploring some broad patterns at work in framing women's sexualities across cultures.

CULTURAL CONTEXTS OF SEXUALITY

Female same-sex sexuality has been noted in a number of indigenous groups since the beginning of European imperialism (Blackwood 1986b; Blackwood and Wieringa 1999a).[1] The kinds of relationships that appear in the anthropological record include affective or intimate friendships between adult heterosexually married women, adolescent sex play, ritual same-sex practices, and erotic relations between a woman and a transgender female (a female-bodied man) (see Blackwood 1999).[2] In this section I discuss several case studies of women's same-sex relations to illuminate the sociocultural processes that construct particular sexualities. I take three different types of relationships—intimate friendship, erotic ritual practice, and adolescent sex play—to represent both the variety of sexualities as well as the complexities of the social processes involved.

INTIMATE FRIENDSHIPS

In Lesotho, a small country surrounded by the nation of South Africa, school girls have intimate friendships that they call mummy-baby relationships (Gay 1986). The "mummy-baby" relation is an institutionalized friendship between younger and older girls and women; it became popular throughout much of black southern African starting in the 1950s (Blacking 1978). Prior to this time, young women in rural communities were educated for adult life in initiation schools run by women. The neighboring Venda people organized an initiation school for a group of girls when they reached puberty. Each initiate was appointed a "mother," an older girl who helped her "child" through initiation. This practice established strong ties between the two age sets of young women, ties that were maintained through visits and exchanges of gifts for many years after (Blacking 1978). As a result of missionary efforts to stop this form of education, the schools are now virtually abandoned. The majority of young women attend public or boarding schools in neighboring towns or urban areas. Yet the bond between initiates serves as a cultural model for the mummy-baby relations of contemporary school girls.

In the contemporary mummy-baby relationship, two young women start a relationship by arranging private encounters and exchanging love letters and gifts. The older one, who becomes the mummy, might already have a boyfriend, or other babies, while the younger one, the baby, can only have one mummy. The mummies, being older, usually arrange when to get together and are the ones to give gifts to their babies. They are also a source of "advice on sex and protection from aggressively courting young men" (Gay 1986, 104). The couple treat the friendship like an affair, or romance; hugging, kissing and sexual relations are part of it (Gay 1986).[3] Many of the girls in these relationships are in their teens and only separated in age by a couple of years, but some young women who work or attend schools in distant towns establish relationships with older married women in those towns. For the girls who became mummies and babies to each other, their relationship is part of the romantic drama of growing up and learning the pleasures and responsibilities of relationships. As they become older, they may become mummies to their own babies, and they may begin to have boyfriends as well. Usually the intensity of mummy-baby relations ends with marriage, when a woman's attention is turned toward domestic responsibilities, but many women maintain the bonds of friendship with other women after marriage (Gay 1986). These adult friendships provide important emotional and economic ties for women within rural communities.

Mummy-baby relationships are constructed from a number of cultural sources. The similarities between mummy-baby relationships and those established in initiation schools mentioned earlier are quite strong. Older girls or women are relied on (and constructed) as an important source of friendship and social connection into adulthood. In a culture where it is taboo for a mother to talk about sexuality with a daughter, older girls in initiation schools and now "mummies" at school are the culturally sanctioned source for this information.

Cultural ideologies of sexuality constitute another element in the construction of mummy-baby relationships. Although in Lesotho men's sexuality is represented as being dominant and assertive, certain cultural practices define women as having agency in their own sexuality. In the past both married women and men had sexual partners other than their spouses (Nthunya 1997); their sexuality was not considered the sole property of their partner. Young girls were trained for adult sexual relations in initiation schools, and on their own practiced lengthening the labia, which women believe makes them "hotter." Although sexual ideology makes virginity important for Lesotho girls brought up under the influence of the Roman Catholic church, Gay argues that "female sensuality is both encouraged and restrained, but it is never denied" (Gay 1986, 101).

The mummy-baby relationship also draws on a tradition of rural women's special affective and gift exchange partnerships.[4] Women of an earlier generation in rural Lesotho established intimate friendships with other women called *motsoalle* (special friend) (Kendall 1999). These special friendships were long-term, loving, and erotic relationships that coexisted with heterosexual marriage. In this patrilineal country, in which family inheritance and property move from father to sons and women are legal minors, a woman at marriage moves to her husband's house and village. One woman, Nthunya, who had a *motsoalle,* was a poor, rural farmer most of her life (Nthunya 1997). When she married her husband, she moved to where her husband's family lived. She worked on their farm, raising sheep and growing maize. Her husband worked with her when he was home but was often away on road construction or other wage labor jobs. Together they had six children. During her marriage, she established a *motsoalle* relationship with another married woman, which she describes as follows:

> It's like when a man chooses you for a wife, except when a man chooses, it's because he wants to share the blankets with you. The woman chooses you the same way, but she doesn't want to share the blankets. She wants love only. When a woman loves another woman, you see, she can love her with a whole heart. (Nthunya 1997, 69)

Their relationships was celebrated by gift-giving and feasting that involved the whole community. For the feast, a sheep was slaughtered, gifts were exchanged, and neighbors and kin from throughout the village came to eat, drink, and dance. This ritual feast publicly validated the commitment of the two women to each other. A relationship with a *motsoalle* was neither an alternative nor a threat to marriage. According to Nthunya, her husband and her *motsoalle's* husband were both supportive of their relationship. Such friendships had many benefits. Nthunya said, "In the old days friendship was very beautiful—men friends and women friends. Friendship was as important as marriage. Now this custom is gone; everything is changing" (Nthunya 1997, 72).

The poverty of Lesotho and the migration of husbands have often been used as explanations for women's intimate friendships in southern Africa. Such explanations assume that women are loving each other because they are deprived of heterosexual outlets. This deprivation thesis assumes that an underlying sexual urge must be satisfied even when husbands are absent. But the cultural context of Lesotho makes better sense of women's intimate friendships. As the preceding case suggests, sexuality for women of Lesotho is constructed through a number of sociocultural processes. These include the institution of women's friendships, which develop and maintain strong social networks for women, and the cultural tradition of age mates, in which groups of slightly older and more experienced girls provide advice, support, and protection for younger girls. Older girls are seen as appropriate sources of advice and guidance about heterosexual relations and also as appropriate partners in one's first romantic and sexual encounters. A cultural ideology of sexuality positions women as sexual actors and not the property of their spouses. These processes shape sexual intimacies with other girls as a way to develop and manage their own sexual feelings. Consequently, close emotional and intimate bonds between young women are constructed as part of growing up and an important source of social ties in adulthood.

EROTIC RITUAL PRACTICES

The homoerotic ritual practices of aboriginal Australian women constitute another case that does not fall easily within a Western framework of sexual identities. Prior to interference from white Australians, aborigines were seminomadic, egalitarian foragers who lived in small camps. Their complex kinship system defined who was a potential marriage partner and who was not. Extramarital heterosexual relations as well as same-sex relations were the norm for both women and men (Roheim 1933).

Young girls were initiated into their adult roles at first menstruation through a process of training and ritual. Initiation ceremonies conveyed a number of messages about the configuration of tribal land, kinship categories, and proper social action. Included in these ceremonies were homoerotic dances between the women and the initiates. Earlier anthropologists, who were reluctant to discuss this aspect of initiation performances, described the movements of the women dancers as sexually suggestive, culminating in what was called "simulated intercourse" (Kaberry 1939). The intent of this performance was said to ensure heterosexual success (getting or keeping a husband or male lover). Since the 1950s such ceremonies are rarely performed in north Australia, but, according to Povinelli (1992), they continue to unnerve Anglo audiences and confuse young aboriginal women, who are now familiar with the Anglo gay identity. Older Belyuen women, however, are not troubled by the homoerotic "digging" (*yedabetj*) of the ritual performances. For them it is erotic play that initiates young women into the complex social and kin categories that circumscribe their lives as married adults (Povinelli 1992).[5]

For Australian aboriginal groups the social processes that produce erotic ritual play include a cultural ideology of women's sexuality in which women have agency, and beliefs in the power of ritual to influence and control human action. Adult women teach adolescent girls about proper kin relations and appropriate sexual partners through ritual practices between women; they also learn how to work magic for sexual success.

ADOLESCENT SEX PLAY

Adolescent heterosexual play is well documented for many cultures. Its practice is closely tied to ideas about childhood, sexuality, and virginity. For girls it is more typical (or visible) in societies where virginity is not given heavy weight, such as the !Kung San of the Kalahari Desert of southern Africa. Few !Kung now live their nomadic foraging lifestyle, having been forced to settle in one place by colonial authorities and the postcolonial state, but one !Kung woman, Nisa, has recounted a life history that sheds light on adolescent sexual practices (Shostak 1983).

The egalitarian !Kung lived in small communities of kin that moved with the rains and availability of food. Each family had few possessions. The adult couple shared a small grass dwelling with their children, and in such close quarters waited until their children fell asleep to engage in sex. Adults insisted that they disapproved of childhood sex play (to disapproving missionaries, perhaps), but when children played in their mock villages

or in the bush, they played at the things their parents did, including keeping house and experimenting sexually. !Kung children and adolescents engaged in both heterosexual and homosexual play. Nisa recounted how she watched older girls play sexually with each other and then did the same with her girlfriends as she approached adolescence. The girls would use saliva to enhance the glide of genitals over genitals. As the girls got older, they were expected to play sexually with the boys, although Nisa describes herself as initially reluctant to do so. All the young girls Nisa knew later married men. For these !Kung women, however, marriage did not become the only locus of sexuality, since, according to Nisa, both men and women have sexual relations with partners other than their spouses. In adulthood the bonds of adolescence remain strong, providing women with loyal friends throughout their lifetimes.

The !Kung have constructed an adolescent phase of sexual experimentation that includes both same-sex and other-sex partners. This construction of sexuality is framed through several sociocultural processes, including ideologies of gender, family, and childhood. !Kung gender ideology is egalitarian, which means that in terms of families, neither marriage partner has exclusive sexual rights over the other. The learning period of childhood extends to developing adolescents, who are expected to engage in sexual play as a way to learn their sexual feelings and desires. Each of these factors combine to produce an adolescent sexuality in which experiences with both boys and girls are possible. Adolescence is constituted as a sexual "learning" period that precedes heterosexual marriage. In this period sexuality between young women is understood as part of their sexual exploration.

CONSTRUCTING MEN'S AND WOMEN'S SEXUALITIES

In this section I explore how gender ideologies construct men's and women's sexualities. By gender ideologies, I mean the set of ideas about men and women, their appropriate behaviors and attributes, and their relations to each other. These ideas in some cases structure very different sexualities for women and men. In the following examples from Papua New Guinea and patriarchal China, the sexual ideologies for men are quite distinct from those for women.

Among the Sambia of Papua New Guinea, for example, young boys are inseminated through oral sex with adult men during the initiation rituals of adolescence (Herdt 1981). This practice is understood as a means to ensure the proper development of masculine traits. According to Western definitions, such a practice would be considered "homosexual." In this Papua New Guinea culture, however, it is explicitly linked to notions of the efficacy of fluids for human development and the necessity of ritual insemination for the development of masculinity (Elliston 1995). Sambian boys are not said to go through a phase of homosexual behavior but rather to undergo ritual measures through sexual means to ensure masculinity and reproductive competence. Once properly inseminated to achieve their full masculinity, these young men are then ready for heterosexual marriage. In contrast, Sambian girls are thought to possess inherent femininity and reproductive competence, and hence, have no need to be given their femininity ritually. From all accounts, young girls do not engage in ritual "homosexual" practices. But although girls' sexual development is culturally unmarked, adult women's bodily fluids are seen as sexually dangerous and polluting to men (see also Clark 1997).

Another example of difference between men's and women's sexualities comes from China. During the nineteenth century in China the practice of marriage resistance and the creation of sisterhoods arose in the silk-producing province of Guangdon in south China (Sankar 1986; Topley 1975). Marriage, especially for young women in patriarchal China, was an oppressive institution. Men were entitled to control wives and family property. Due to the importance of reproducing the patrilineage and maintaining ancestor worship, arranged marriages were the norm; often the young couple did not meet before they were married. The new wife went to live in the household of her husband and was at first considered little more than a servant under the strict supervision of her mother-in-law. In the province of Guangdon, marriage presented an especially frightening prospect since women not only married out of their village but in many cases into enemy territory (Sankar 1986). With the development of the silk industry in Guangdon in the mid-1800s, many young unmarried women went to work in the silk factories, earning money for themselves as well as their families. With their own income, some of these women were able to postpone marriage indefinitely. Fathers supported this delay since the daughters provided income to their families.

Through the institution of silk work a tradition of marriage resistance developed, culminating in the creation of intimate sisterhoods by those who refused to marry. A woman who refused to marry took a public vow to remain unwed and not engage in sexual relations with men. This vow established her adult status, freeing her parents from any obligation to arrange a marriage and securing her rights to ancestor worship in her natal house (Sankar 1986). Sisterhoods of six to eight women each were formed with such names as "Golden Orchid Association" or "Association for Mutual Admiration." The sisters lived in cooperative houses and established joint funds to be used for holidays, emergencies, retirement, or death. Some houses were "vegetarian halls" where the women led a religious life; others were called "spinster halls." These halls were not so strictly religious and vegetarian, but heterosexual contacts were not allowed in either (Honig 1985; Sankar 1986; Smedley 1976; Topley 1975). According to some of the studies of this institution, sisters had sexual relations with each other; "larger sisterhoods may have contained several couples or ménage à trois" (Sankar 1986; see also Topley 1975). The sisterhoods were banned as "feudal remnants" after the victory of the Red Army in 1949, and many sisters fled to Malaysia,

Singapore, Hong Kong and Taiwan. Wieringa (1987), who conducted interviews with sisters living in a Buddhist temple in Singapore, notes that the abbess and the nuns spoke freely of their sexual relations and described their choices to enter a "vegetarian life" as a positive decision.

These sisterhoods were not simply the result of oppressive marriage conditions. A number of other sociocultural factors were important in the development of the sisterhoods. It was the custom in this region for the patrilineal kin group to build a girls' house for their adolescent and unmarried daughters (Topley 1975). Houses that were built for unmarried older daughters became known as spinster houses. Women past the age of marriage were given a spinster ceremony through which they attained adult status. Younger sisters and brothers, who were waiting until their elder sibling married, were then allowed to marry. Each of these practices played a significant role in the construction of sisterhoods, although without the silk work, they were probably not significant enough on their own to produce sisterhoods.

In the cases of the Chinese sisterhoods and the Papua New Guinea Sambia, the absence of a mirror image to men's or women's (homo)sexual practices underscores the prominence of cultural gender ideologies in constructing sexual practices. In the Sambia case a cultural practice rooted in an ideology of gender antagonism and the efficacy of bodily fluids legitimates particular insemination practices between men and boys. In China patriarchal institutions ensuring control of women produced public resistance by women to oppressive marital and economic conditions, leading to the establishment of separatist sisterhoods.

In these cases, gender ideologies create different sexual roles, behaviors, meanings and desires for women and men. Consequently, men and women in these cultures see themselves differently as sexual actors. For Sambian men, men's sexuality must be carefully sustained and enhanced, while women are constantly reminded that their sexual organs and fluids are debilitating and even dangerous to men. Historically in patriarchal China, men's sexual experiences and hence their desires were constructed broadly to include the practice of taking male consorts, particularly among upper-class men and royalty (Ng 1989). Women's sexual experiences were strictly limited to sexual relations with their husbands, unless they remained unmarried.

From these cases it is clear that gender ideologies are critical to the production of men's and women's sexualities. Gender ideologies construct what men and women are capable of sexually, limiting the heterosexual contacts of Sambian women, while prescribing frequent oral insemination for adolescent boys. It constructs what kinds of desires they are thought to have, as well as what kinds of experiences are actually possible, including the range of sexual partners permissible to Chinese men, the strict monogamy of Chinese wives, and the same-sex relations of unmarried Chinese women. By establishing certain ideas about who and what men and women are, gender ideologies create different possibilities for men's or women's understanding of their desires and their access to other sexual partners.

DECONSTRUCTING SEXUAL IDENTITIES

In the following section I will discuss in depth two cases of female same-sex relations that further complicate Western sexual categories. Studies of sexuality in Europe and America take for granted certain core assumptions about sexuality. Among those assumptions is the idea that individuals have fixed sexual object choices and sexual identities, defined typically as homosexual or heterosexual (with bisexual only recently getting attention). These assumptions turn out to have little cross-cultural reliability. Not all sexual practices across cultures fit neatly into the concept of sexual identities.

The following case concerns erotic attachments between women in Suriname, South America. The *mati* work, a widespread institution among Creole working-class women in Paramaribo, Suriname, is a sexual arrangement that is not based on a fixed notion of "sexual identity" (Wekker 1999).[6] *Mati*, although by no means a monolithic category, are women who have sexual relationships with men and with women; they may have a relationship with a man and a woman occurring at the same time or one at a time. While some *mati*, especially older women who have borne and raised their children, do not have sex with men any more, other, younger *mati* have a variety of arrangements with men, such as marriage, concubinage, or a visiting relationship. Women's relationships with women mostly take the form of visiting relationships, although a minority of women couples with their children live together in one household. These varied arrangements are made possible by the circumstance that most Creole, working-class women own or rent their own houses and are single heads of households (Wekker 1999).

The Afro-Surinamese folk religion, called Winti, provides the framework for the Creole concept of self and sexuality. Unlike the Western concept of the self as "unitary, authentic, bounded, static, trans-situational," the self in an Afro-Surinamese working-class universe is conceptualized as "multiplicitous, malleable, dynamic, and contextually salient" (Wekker 1999, 125). Winti religion pervades virtually all aspects of life, from before birth to beyond death. Within this framework both men and women are thought to be composed of male and female *winti*, gods. Both men and women are also deemed to be full sexual subjects, with their own desires and own possibilities to act on these desires. Sexual fulfillment per se is deemed important, while the gender of one's object choice is considered less important. According to one 84-year old *mati*, who had a variety of relationships with men in her life and bore a number of children, the "apples of her eye" throughout her long life were definitely women:

> I never wanted to marry or 'be in association with a man.' My 'soul.' / 'I' did not want to be

under a man. Some women are like that. I am somebody who was not greedy on a man, my 'soul,' I,' wanted to be with women. It is your 'soul' that makes you so. It is more equal when you are with a woman; the same rights you have, I have too. (Wekker 1999, 284)

Thus, a *mati* is conceptualized as a woman, part of whose "I" desires and is sexually active with other women. Since the "I" is multiply and openly conceived, it is not necessary to claim a "truest, most authentic kernel of the self," a fixed sexual "identity" that is oriented to other women. Rather, *mati* work is seen as a particularly pleasing and joyous activity, not as an identity (Wekker 1999).

Surinamese *mati* (and Lesotho *motsoalle*) do not see themselves as "lesbians" in the Western sense; they have sex with each other, but their relations with men, including husbands and boyfriends, are also part of their sexuality. According to Wekker (1999), sexuality in this working-class cultural nexus is multiply constructed through ideas about the self, sexuality, gender, and religion.[7] But *mati* work is not a sexual identity nor a distinct category of persons. It is produced through an ideology of sexuality in which men and women are seen as sexual beings whose sexuality is fluid and multiple.

TOMBOIS IN WEST SUMATRA

Taking one final example from my own work on *tombois* among the Minangkabau in West Sumatra, Indonesia (Blackwood 1998), I look more closely at the relation between sexuality and gender identity, one's sense of being either a man or woman.[8] In Indonesia the term *tomboi* (derived from the English word "tomboy") is used for a female acting in the manner of men (I use "female" here to refer to the physical sex of the body). Although *tombois* have female bodies, they are locally understood as female-bodied men who are attracted to (normatively gendered) women. In this overview I briefly explain the cultural factors that produce the *tomboi* gender identity and how this identity complicates any simple understandings of gender or sexuality.

Tombois pride themselves on doing things like Minangkabau (and Indonesian) men. They play *koa*, a card game like poker, which is perceived as a men's game. They smoke as men do; rural women rarely take up smoking. They go out alone, especially at night, which is men's prerogative. Like men, they drive motorcycles; women ride behind (women do drive motorcycles but in a mixed couple the man always drives).

Tombois construct their desire for and relationships with women on a model of normative genders, emphasizing their masculinity and their partner's femininity. *Tombois* say that their lovers are always feminine women, women, that is, who adhere to the codes of femininity assigned to female bodies. *Tombois* and their partners call each other *papi* and *mami*, and refer to other female couples as *cowok* and *cewek*, Indonesian words that have the connotation of "guy" and "girl." Their use of gender-marked terms to describe partners in a relationship reflect *tombois'* understanding of themselves as situated within the category "man" (*laki-laki*).

Certain key social processes (cultural ideologies) in West Sumatra are involved in the production of the *tomboi* identity. Central to these is a gender ideology that constructs two genders as mutually exclusive and distinct categories. Typical of many Islamic cultures, the Minangkabau believe that men and women have different natures.[9] Men are said to be more aggressive and brave than women. Boys are admonished not to cry—crying is what girls do. Women are expected to be modest, respectful, and humble, especially young, unmarried women. The Minangkabau maintain physical segregation of the sexes in most public spaces and events. This gender ideology constructs differences in rights and privileges between men and women, without, however, constituting men as superior (see Blackwood 2000).

Another key social process is a kinship ideology that situates women as the producers and reproducers of their lineages. The Minangkabau have a matrilineal form of kinship in which inheritance and property passes from mothers to daughters. In the context of a rural kin-based society, heterosexual marriages are the key to the maintenance of vital social and kin ties because they construct an extended network of kin and in-laws. For Minangkabau women the continuation of this kinship network through marriage and children is critical to their own standing and influence both in their kin groups and in the community. Because daughters are essential to the continuation of the lineage, young women are carefully monitored by their elders to ensure that they marry and marry well. Daughters are not just reproducers, however; they are also the leaders of the next generation of kin. Consequently, there are no acceptable fantasies of womanhood in rural villages that do not include marriage and motherhood.

The restrictive definitions and expectations of masculinity and femininity attached to male and female bodies help produce gender transgressions in the following way. If a young girl plays too roughly and enjoys boys' activities when little, she is called *bujang gadis*, a term meaning "boy-girl," which distinguishes her as different. Identified as masculine by others, *tombois* make sense of their own gender behavior as being that of a boy. Because their behavior falls outside the bounds of proper femininity, *tombois* deny their female bodies and produce the only other gender recognized in this two-gender system, the masculine gender. The persuasiveness of the dominant gender ideology circulating in West Sumatra means that other forms of womanhood, such as a "masculine" woman or an unmarried woman working in men's jobs, are unimaginable. Consequently, some females appropriate a masculine gender identity because it is the most suitable model available. This case illustrates the way gender as well as sexuality is culturally produced. *Tomboi* identity is negotiated and produced in a cultural context in which Minangkabau kinship and community, as well as Islam and the Indonesian state, all have a voice.

THE SOCIAL PRODUCTION OF SEXUALITIES

My discussion of the cultural processes that construct same-sex sexualities is based on a small but growing number of case studies. There has been no systematic effort to compare the cases of women's same-sex relations cross-culturally.[10] The availability of adequate information is one problem. The difficulties of coding the various types of behavior documented even in this short essay raise other problems for statistical analyses. Despite the problems of formulating comparative analyses, some consistencies appear among the cases that allow for generalization about the social processes at work.

The broader patterns that appear in the cultural construction of sexuality can be connected to different types of gender ideologies, kinship systems, and class societies. Earlier attempts at comparative theories suggested that where men have greater control over women, or in societies stratified by class and gender, women's same-sex practices are subject to more oppression than men's (Rubin 1975) or limited to clandestine relations or marginalized groups (Blackwood 1986a). Both these suggestions rely on a "constraint" theory of sexuality by implying that without men's control, women's same-sex relations would flourish. Reworking this earlier attempt with a more constructionist approach, I would suggest that in strict patrilineal class societies, such as India and China, where inheritance and property rights belong to men, an ideology of women's inferiority and the need to control women's sexuality help to produce a sexuality oriented to reproduction and men's desires.

The Chinese example of patriarchy suggests that men's sexual prerogatives combined with their control of wives constructs exclusive same-sex relations of the sisterhoods as both a resistance to marriage and a way to resolve the "threat" that an unmarried woman poses to men's control of their wives. Safeguards, such as chastity vows, were instituted to ensure that unmarried women with economic independence would not undermine marriage. For their part, women built on cultural expectations of close female bonds and the availability of economic resources to create sisterhoods and same-sex relationships.

In contrast, the cases of adolescent and ritual same-sex practices for the !Kung and Australian aborigines are produced in gender egalitarian, non-class societies. These societies have marriage requirements and prohibitions on certain forms of sexual relations. Yet, because they do not have the requirements about inheritance of property or rights of sexual access that are found in strict patrilineal societies, sexuality is constructed as something powerful, diverse, enjoyable, and explorable for both women and men. This is not to say that all non-class societies will produce multiple sexualities. In some societies same-sex relations may be culturally unintelligible (as certain groups have maintained to colonial superiors), but the evidence to back up such a statement with certainty is lacking. The important point is that many sociocultural processes work together to produce sexual meanings.

In sum, the cases presented here offer two important points. First, they provide evidence that the way sexuality is constructed—for instance, who is considered more sexually aggressive or more in need of sex—has everything to do with concepts of gender, selfhood, kinship (inheritance and property rights), and marriage. Second, they challenge the common assumption in the West that sexuality and sexual identity comprise stable, coherent categories. The cases mentioned above all show sexualities that fall outside of Western categories. If the very "nature" of sexuality derives from the cultural context, then what matters is how it is constructed in particular contexts, historical eras, or cultural domains. Consequently, careful ethnographic analysis that provides a cultural context for sexual practices will be the most productive way to further our understanding of women's sexualities.

NOTES

1. This discussion pertains to indigenous groups in Asia, Africa, the Pacific, Latin America, and native North America during colonial and post-colonial times. Because of space limitations I do not include material on white lesbians and lesbians of color in western Europe and the United States. For entry into the substantial scholarship on these groups, see Lewin 1996; Weston 1993.

2. Regarding the limitations of the anthropological record, see Blackwood and Wieringa 1999b.

3. The difficulties of categorizing something as a "sexual" relationship is exemplified in this case. Gay (1986) asked if young women in mummy-baby relationships make love like a man and a woman. Most women replied that the hugging and kissing of the mummy-baby relationship was different, distinguishing conceptually between what women do together sexually and what women and men do sexually.

4. This tradition appears to have died out after the 1950s (Kendall 1999). For a similar practice among Azande women, see Evans-Pritchard 1970.

5. For a similar ceremonial practice for women in the Solomon Islands in Melanesia, see Blackwood 1935.

6. Creoles, the second largest population group in Suriname, are the descendants of slaves brought from Africa and are mainly an urban group, also called Afro-Surinamese. They are distinguished culturally, psychologically, and ethnically from other blacks in Suriname, who are called the Maroons. The latter are the descendants of fugitive slaves who fled the plantations starting in the beginning of the seventeenth century (Wekker 1999).

7. Wekker also makes important connections between sexuality, colonial discourses, and colonial economic stratification that I do not have the space to discuss here.

8. For studies of other types of gender identities, such as the Native American two-spirit person, see Blackwood 1984b; Lang 1999.

9. Islam in West Sumatra is part of the everyday life of the Minangkabau, who generally see no conflict between *adat* (local customs, beliefs and laws) and Islam. The two have come to be mutually constructed (see Blackwood 2000).

10. In the research for my master's thesis (Blackwood 1984a) I surveyed a number of ethnographies, colonial records, and the Human Relations Area Files, and located reports of female same-sex practices in ninety-five indigenous cultures. This was not a comprehensive world survey and to my knowledge, no such survey has been done.

REFERENCES

Blacking, John. 1978. Uses of the Kinship Idiom in Friendships at Some Venda and Zulu Schools. In *Social System and Tradition in Southern Africa*. J. Argyle and E. Preston-Whyte, eds., pp. 101–117. Cape Town: Oxford University Press.

Blackwood, Beatrice. 1935. *Both Sides of Buka Passage*. Oxford: Clarendon Press.

Blackwood, Evelyn. 1984a. *Cross-Cultural Dimensions of Lesbian Relations*. Master's degree thesis, San Francisco State University.

———. 1984b. Sexuality and Gender in Certain Native American Tribes: The Case of Cross-Gender Females. *Signs: Journal of Women in Culture and Society* 10:27–42.

———. 1986a. Breaking the Mirror: The Construction of Lesbianism and the Anthropological Discourse in Homosexuality. In *The Many Faces of Homosexuality: Anthropological Approaches to Homosexual Behavior*. E. Blackwood, ed., pp. 1–17. New York: Harrington Park Press.

———, ed. 1986b. *The Many Faces of Homosexuality: Anthropological Approaches to Homosexual Behavior*. New York: Haworth.

———. 1998. Tombois in West Sumatra: Constructing Masculinity and Erotic Desire. *Cultural Anthropology* 13(4):491–521.

———. 1999. Indigenous Cultures. In *The Encyclopedia of Homosexuality*. B. Zimmerman, ed., Vol. 1 pp. 392–397. New York: Garland.

———. 2000. *Webs of Power: Women, Kin and Community in a Sumatran Village*. Lanham, MD: Rowman and Littlefield.

Blackwood, Evelyn, and Saskia E. Wieringa, eds. 1999a. *Female Desires: Same-Sex Relations and Transgender Practices Across Cultures*. New York: Columbia University Press.

———. 1999b. Sapphic Shadows: Challenging the Silence in the Study of Sexuality. In *Female Desires: Same-Sex Relations and Transgender Practices Across Cultures*. E. Blackwood and S.E. Wieringa, eds., pp. 39–66. New York: Columbia University Press.

Clark, Jeffrey. 1997. State of Desire: Transformations in Huli Sexuality. In *Sites of Desire, Economies of Pleasure: Sexualities in Asia and the Pacific*. L. Manderson and M. Jolly, eds., pp. 191–211. Chicago: University of Chicago Press.

Elliston, Deborah. 1995. Erotic Anthropology: "Ritualized Homosexuality" in Melanesia and Beyond. *American Ethnologist* 22(4):848–867.

Evans-Pritchard, E. E. 1970. Sexual Inversion among the Azande. *American Anthropologist* 72:1428–1434.

Gay, Judith. 1986. "Mummies and Babies" and Friends and Lovers in Lesotho. In *The Many Faces of Homosexuality: Anthropological Approaches to Homosexual Behavior*. E. Blackwood, ed., pp. 97–116. New York: Harrington Park Press.

Herdt, Gilbert. 1981. *Guardians of the Flute*. New York: McGraw-Hill.

Honig, Emily. 1985. Burning Incense, Pledging Sisterhood: Communities of Women Workers in the Shanghai Cotton Mills, 1919–1949. *Signs: Journal of Women in Culture and Society* 10(4):700–714.

Kaberry, Phyllis. 1939. *Aboriginal Woman, Sacred and Profane*. London: Routledge.

Kendall. 1999. Women in Lesotho and the (Western) Construction of Homophobia. In *Female Desires: Same-Sex Relations and Transgender Practices Across Cultures*. E. Blackwood and S.E. Wieringa, eds., pp. 157–180. New York: Columbia University Press.

Lang, Sabine. 1999. Lesbians, Men-Women, and Two-Spirits: Homosexuality and Gender in Native American Cultures. In *Female Desires: Same-Sex Relations and Transgender Practices Across Cultures*. E. Blackwood and S.E. Wieringa, eds., pp. 91–118. New York: Columbia University Press.

Lewin, Ellen, ed. 1996. *Inventing Lesbian Cultures in America*. Boston: Beacon.

Ng, Vivien W. 1989. Homosexuality and the State in Late Imperial China. In *Hidden from History: Reclaiming the Gay and Lesbian Past*. M. Duberman, M. Vicinus, and G.J. Chauncey, eds., pp. 76–89. New York: Meridian Books.

Nthunya, Mpho M'atsepo. 1997. *Singing Away the Hunger: The Autobiography of an African Woman*. Bloomington: Indiana University Press.

Povinelli, Beth. 1992. Blood, Sex, and Power: "Pitjawagaitj"/menstruation ceremonies and land politics in Aboriginal Northern Australia. Ninety-First Annual Meeting of the American Anthropological Association, San Francisco, 1992.

Roheim, Geza. 1933. Women and their Life in Central Australia. *Journal of the Royal Anthropological Institute of Great Britain and Ireland* 63:207–265.

Rubin, Gayle. 1975. The Traffic in Women: Notes on the Political Economy of Sex. In *Towards an Anthropology of Women*. R. Rapp, ed., pp. 157–211. New York: Monthly Review Press.

Sankar, Andrea. 1986. Sisters and Brothers, Lovers and Enemies: Marriage Resistance in Southern Kwangtung. In *The Many Faces of Homosexuality: Anthropological Approaches to Homosexual Behavior*. E. Blackwood, ed., pp. 69–83. New York: Harrington Park Press.

Shostak, Marjorie. 1983. *Nisa: The Life and Words of a !Kung Woman*. New York: Vintage Books.

Smedley, Agnes. 1976. *Portraits of Chinese Women in Revolution*. Westbury: The Feminist Press.

Topley, Marjorie. 1975. Marriage Resistance in Rural Kwangtung. In *Women in Chinese Society*. M. Wolf and R. Witke, eds., pp. 57–88. Stanford: Stanford University Press.

Wekker, Gloria. 1999. "What's Identity Got to Do with It?" Rethinking Identity in Light of the Mati Work in Suriname. In *Female Desires: Same-Sex Relations and Transgender Practices Across Cultures*. E. Blackwood and S.E. Wieringa, eds., pp. 119–138. New York: Columbia University Press.

Weston, Kath. 1993. Lesbian/Gay Studies in the House of Anthropology. *Annual Review of Anthropology* 22:339–67.

Wieringa, Saskia. 1987. *Uw Toegenegen Dora D.* Amsterdam: Furie.

Hijras: An "Alternative" Sex/Gender in India

Gayatri Reddy and Serena Nanda

In much of the current literature on sexual difference, hijras are represented as the principal "alternative" sex/gender identity in India—the

so-called "third sex," "eunuch-transvestite," or "intersexed" identity—a cultural definition that emphasizes hijras' status as "neither men nor women," as the title of Serena Nanda's (1999) book indicates. For the most part, hijras are phenotypic men who wear female clothing, and ideally renounce sexual desire and practice by undergoing a physical emasculation known as the *nirvan* or rebirth operation. This operation entails the sacrifice of male genitalia to the goddess Bahuchara or Bedhraj Mata, one of the many incarnations of Devi [Goddess] worshipped throughout India, in return for the divine power to bless or curse with fertility/infertility. As vehicles of this divine power, hijras engage in their "traditional" occupations of performing at the birth of a child, at marriages, and as servants of the goddess at Bedhraj Mata's temple (Vyas and Shingala 1987; Sharma 1989; Nanda 1999; Hall, 1997; Reddy 2000, 2003).

In addition to this idealized asexual role and in apparent contradiction to it, hijras also engage in prostitution or sex work with men. Those who engage in this activity, however, legitimize it through a life-cycle trajectory; according to them, all hijras start out as sex workers and it is only when their bodies and/or desires change that they become sexual renouncers and ritual performers. Whatever their occupation, unlike the commonly understood ascetic ideal, hijras lead their daily lives as a social group, inexorably tied to the [person]-in-the-world, to paraphrase Louis Dumont (1960). Hijras' position in Indian society thus shares features of both a caste within society, complete with rules of comportment, exchange, and hierarchies of moral value, as well as of (marginal) renouncers outside it. As individuals however, it is important to note that hijras represent a wide variety of desires, abilities, identities, and gender characteristics, and also vary widely in their constructions of self in relation to their culturally defined identity.

Since Serena Nanda's work, first published in 1990, much has been written about hijras in the context of sexual difference. Drawing on the anthropological fieldwork of both authors among hijras in South India, this article traces the construction of this category through three different lenses—sex/gender, religion, and politics. It challenges existing accounts of hijras that see them solely as a "traditional" sexual category, rather than a contemporary, politically engaged identity that is crosscut by a range of axes that shape their lives. As such, this article introduces readers to hijras with a descriptive account of them as the so-called "third sex" of India, as well as provides an introduction to the theoretical and methodological issues in the analysis of gender, sexuality, and identity construction in India.

HIJRAS AS A "THIRD" SEX AND GENDER

The popular understanding of hijras as an alternative sex and gender is predicated on a model of intersexuality—most typically, a *male* model of physical or functional anomaly of the reproductive and sexual system, although theoretically, women who do not menstruate can also become hijras. The word "hijra" is a masculine noun, widely translated into English as either "eunuch" or "hermaphrodite" (intersexed). Both these terms emphasize sexual impotence and are commonly understood in India to mean a physical defect impairing sexual function, both in the act of intercourse and in reproductive ability.

In much of the predominant literature, hijras are represented as sexually anomalous or impotent men who lack desire for women, an attribute often ascribed to their impaired reproductive capacity, or more specifically, their sexual organ. If a hijra is not born with a "defective" organ (and most are not), s/he must ideally make it so by emasculation, an act that is interpreted as a "rebirth"—from male to hijra. Whether hijras are "born" or "made," their identity is primarily envisioned in terms of a loss of virility, or as Wendy O'Flaherty (1973) puts it, they are "men minus men." But importantly, they are "men minus men" who perform many aspects of a female-gendered identity: they wear women's clothes, embody "feminine" gestures, movements and performative attributes, and adopt women's names. Importantly, this understanding is accompanied by the significant corollary that hijras are also 'not women,' their inability to bear children being the most significant marker of this construct. Hijras, in this scenario are therefore both 'not-women' and 'not-men,' often, though not always, identifying as an identity outside of the binary frame of gender (see Cohen (1995) for an alternative view that troubles the desire to locate hijras as an undeniably "third" category).

HIJRAS AND OTHER "NOT-MEN"

While hijras are clearly the most visible "alternative" sex/gender, they locate themselves within a larger spectrum of sexual and gender configurations in India. This spectrum, with its own social categories, lexicon, and criteria of membership, is indexed at the broadest level by the labels *kothi, panthi* and *naran* (cf. Hall, 1995; see Reddy, forthcoming, for an elaboration of this complex spectrum). In this conceptualization of sex/gender, *narans* are an undifferentiated category based primarily on gendered practice and the patriarchal naturalization of femaleness as reproductive capacity—that is, *all* women, in other words; *kothis* are those men who "like to do women's work" and desire the receptive position in same-sex encounters with other men; and *panthis* (or *giriyas* as they are referred to in north India) are the partners of *kothis* and/or *narans*, bounded both by their desire for penetrative sexuality, as well as their lack of desire for the constellation of "female" practices typically embodied by *kothis* and *narans*. In other words, the gender system in India appears to be divided on the basis of practice rather than anatomy, into "men" [*panthis*] and to use Don Kulick's phrase, "not-men" [*kothis* and *narans*] (Kulick 1998; Reddy forthcoming).

Within this sex/gender system, hijras identify themselves as one 'category' or branch of a broader spectrum of identities they refer to as their *kothi* "family." Hijras rank themselves as the most authentic of *kothis*, deserving of the most respect (*izzat*) in the community. They base this ranking on their formal kinship affiliation with hijra lineages and houses,

their absence of sexual desire, their modes of self-presentation including the kind of dress they wear, and their religious practice (Reddy 2001).

Perhaps one of the most important of these authenticating criteria for hijras is kinship. In this context, kinship is the affiliation and social obligation to one of the hijra houses or lineages in the community.[1] By engaging in a specific hijra kinship ritual, individuals not only acquire a *guru* or teacher within the community, but also signify their membership in the particular house/lineage to which the teacher belongs. This ritual not only denotes formal membership in the community, but also hierarchizes *kothis* along this axis of kinship. There are *kothis* (such as hijras) who are "official" kin—those who have engaged in this ritual kinship act—and those *kothis* who have not undertaken this formal ritual and therefore are only informally or unofficially related. While this does not prevent the latter from identifying/being identified as *kothis*, it places them lower in the *kothi* prestige hierarchy, according to hijras.

In addition to kinship, hijras' claim to asexuality—lacking sexual desire for either women or men—is another key element in their definition of themselves in relation to other *kothis* and *gandus* (a pejorative label applied to men who enjoy anal [*gand*] sex, a category which includes self-identified 'gay' men). Such *gandus* are defined not only by the *form* of their sexual desire, but more importantly, by its *excess*. Excessive sexual desire is a marker of inauthenticity that apparently defines *gandus* and by that token, separates them from the supposedly asexual hijras. An active symbol of hijras' essential *a*sexuality that is deployed for this purpose is the physical excision of their reproductive organs or the nirvan operation. One becomes resolutely and irrevocably a "real hijra" following this operation, serving by this

[1]Hijras are organized into formal groupings or lineages, each with its own leader (or *nayak*). Kinship obligations within these lineages are built on hierarchical principles of seniority, similar in some respects to that of Indian joint families (see Nanda 1999; Reddy forthcoming for elaborations on hijra kinship rules and obligations).

token to separate hijras from their libidinous fellow—*kothis*.

As mentioned earlier, hijras serve as the most strikingly visible dimension of *kothi* identity. For the most part, they are identifiable as "men" who grow their hair long, are clean-shaven, often adopt exaggerated "feminine" gestures and styles of self-presentation, and most importantly, wear saris, the most common dress worn by women in India. So important is this criteria that some hijras refer to themselves, in their own terminology, as sari-wearing *kothis* (*chatla kothi*) as opposed to other, non-sari-wearing (or *kada-chatla*) *kothis*.

Finally, in addition to sexual desire, kinship and sartorial presentation, religious practice is also a key dimension of hijras' self-image as the *kothis* most deserving of respect. Whether they identify as Hindu or Muslim (see below), most hijras claim to be blessed by (Hindu) gods/goddesses. Thereby, as vehicles of divine authority, hijras see themselves as having more respect (or *izzat*) than some of the other *kothi* identities, who they see as motivated solely by sexual desire rather than religious authenticity.

HIJRA RELIGIOUS AFFILIATION/PRACTICE

In addition to constructing identity through sex/gender difference, hijras also emphasize religious mythology and practice as an integral aspect of their identity-formation. Contrary to popular opinion, which identifies hijras as devotees of Bedhraj Mata and therefore as Hindus, many hijras in India also identify as Muslim. They do not see these identities as necessarily mutually contradictory, each identification in their eyes, providing different, contextually specific referents.

Hinduism and Hijra Mythology

In Hinduism, the complementary opposition of male and female, man and woman, represents a key symbolic referent. The interchange of male and female qualities,

transformations of sex and gender, and alternative sex and gender roles, both among deities and humans, are meaningful and positive themes in Hindu mythology, ritual and art, and are often drawn on in everyday constructions of self in India.

Hijras also draw on these mythological and divine themes and images to construct and present themselves, identifying with various gods and goddesses in this process. As "eunuch-transvestites" (Vyas and Shingala 1987), hijras identify most closely with Arjun, hero of the epic Mahabharata, who lives for a year in the guise of a "eunuch," wearing bangles, braiding [his] hair like a woman, dressing in female attire, and teaching the women of the King's court singing and dancing. In this gendered performance as a "eunuch-transvestite," Arjun participates in weddings and births, providing legitimacy for the ritual contexts in which hijras perform (Hiltelbeitel l980). The portrayal of Arjun in popular enactments of the Mahabharata in a vertically divided half-man/half-woman form highlights this identification.

This representation of Arjun resonates with the 'creative ascetic' Shiva, another key mythological/divine figure hijras identify with, especially in his appearance as Ardhanarisvara, a vertically divided half-man/half-woman (representing Shiva united with his female power or shakti). Shiva is one of the most important sexual/asexual figures in Hinduism, incorporating both male and female characteristics. He is an ascetic—one who renounces sex—and yet he appears in many erotic and procreative roles (O'Flaherty l973). His most powerful symbol and object of worship is the *linga*, or phallus, but the phallus is almost always set in the *yoni*, the symbol of the female genitals. The generative power of the phallus severed from the body is another important point of identification between Shiva and hijras, highlighting the latters' self-identification as ascetics or *sannyasis;* those who renounce sexuality and yet have the power to confer fertility.

Other Hindu deities, such as Vishnu, also have dual gender representations that are drawn on in public enactments of (hijra) self.

In one myth, the basis of a festival in South India attended by thousands of hijras, Vishnu comes to earth as a woman to marry a prince, who is, by this marriage, granted success in battle by the gods. However, although the prince is destined to win the battle against his enemies, it is also well known that he will be martyred in this process, rendering marriage to the prince undesirable for would-be brides, thereby necessitating Vishnu's performance of this role. During the festival, hijras enact the role of women who marry, and later, as widows, mourn the death of their husband, represented by the prince/god Koothandavur. Similarly, an important ceremony at the Jagannatha temple in Orissa involves a ritual in which Balabhadra, the ascetic older brother of the deity Jagannatha (commonly identified with Shiva), is seduced by a young man dressed as a female temple dancer (Marglin 1985). Ancient Hindu texts and origin myths likewise refer to androgynous, intersexed or "alternative" sexes and genders both among humans as well as deities (Bullough 1976; O'Flaherty 1980). The Kama Sutra, the classic Hindu 'treatise on love,' also specifically refers to those of a "third nature" and the particular sexual practices prescribed for them. In fact, as some authors contend, Hinduism is sometimes characterized as having a "propensity towards androygynous thinking" (Zwilling and Sweet 2000).

Islam and Hijra Practice

The Hindu religious context of alternative genders that provides a positive meaning for hijras is reinforced by the historical role of the 'eunuch' in the five hundred year history of Muslim court culture in India. This historical role has merged with those described in Hindu texts as a source of contemporary hijra identification. Indeed, while identifying with religious figures in Hinduism, hijras also identify as Muslims. The apparent paradox of hijras identifying with Hindu religious figures while also identifying as Muslim, is partly resolved by context, with claims to Muslim religious identity being constructed mainly through practice: through the acts that hijras employ, the proscriptions they are subject to, and the festivals that they celebrate. Although some hijras maintain that "religion does not matter for us,

all can join," many of them also say that when hijras join the community they "become Muslims." In many regions of India, hijras approximate the Islamic ideal in their custom of praying, using prescriptive Muslim greetings such as 'salam aleikhum,' undertaking the pilgrimage to Mecca, celebrating Muslim festivals, as well as engaging in certain commensal practices, sartorial prescriptions, circumcision rites, and (Muslim) burial practices. Clearly, however, hijras are not strictly "orthodox" religious practitioners. Apart from their worship of a Hindu goddess, hijras also blur the gender boundary in their practice of Islam, following rules of comportment specified by the shari'at for *both* men *and* women. Sometimes, in addition to the female names they choose at initiation, they may also choose male Muslim names. Hijra leaders (or *nayaks*) almost invariably are called by their Muslim names. Further, although not all hijras go on the Haj or pilgrimage to Mecca, those who do, go unescorted by male relatives, a prescription for post-pubescent and pre-menopausal women. In addition to these so-called "male" practices, hijras also follow Islamic practices enjoined on women, such as wearing the *burqa* on occasion (a garment that covers the entire body except for parts of the face), though they never wear this item of clothing when performing or entertaining. Though hijras also wear saris like all Indian women, for special occasions they wear green saris, as green is the color of Islam. Also, like some orthodox Muslim women, hijras are not permitted to wear *bindis* (the dot Hindu women wear on their foreheads).

Hijra practice reveals a pluralistic form of religion, which is arguably typical rather than unusual in Indian religious practice. Both Hindus and Muslims in India are characterized by an enormous diversity of communities, traditions, and customs, and religious pluralism has a long history in India. This pluralistic tradition, along with the ability to "compartmentalize" potentially conflictual beliefs and practices (Ramanujam 1990; Shweder and Bourne 1984), allows for a continuum rather than a dichotomy of religious thought, empowering hijras, amongst others, to practice their religion(s) without experiencing significant cognitive dissonance.

HIJRAS AND CONTEMPORARY POLITICS

The association of hijras with the power of (dis)embodied generativity is clearly related to their cultural identity as ritual performers at marriages and the birth of a child. It is these "traditional" roles for which they gain their respect or *izzat* in society. But recently, hijras have also gained visibility in another role, one that on the surface would seem to be in contrast to their marginalization in Indian society and culture.

This "new" role for hijras is in contemporary Indian politics. As one hijra stated during recent fieldwork, "Within this *kaliyug* (current cosmic period), hijras will become kings and rule the world. That is what [the god] Rama decreed thousands of years ago when he blessed us." Although hijras have not become kings, they have achieved notable political success. In recent years, hijras have been standing for and winning public election to local, state and even national office, and have been actively courted by mainstream political parties for these positions. Significantly, they are entering these new spheres as hijras, explicitly highlighting their identity as gender-neutral, asexual figures.

In the past few years, at least six hijras have been elected to public office at the local and state level, defeating more prominent candidates from national political parties such as Congress (I) and the Bharatiya Janata Party, and it is their transcendant morality *as* hijras that has been central to their success at the polls. Explicitly constructing themselves as individuals without the encumbrances of a family, gender, or caste affiliation, hijras emphasize that they are free from the impetus for nepotism, and therefore are the perfect antidotes to the rampant corruption and immorality of Indian politics. And indeed, the election of hijras can be viewed, at the most obvious level, as a revolt against upper-caste privilege, nepotism and corruption. In one of these elections, the hijra candidate was enthusiastically supported by an emerging political party formed to protect lower-caste and Dalit (formerly untouchable caste) interests, with her victory being hailed by the lower castes

and Dalits as a victory over the corrupt and exploitative upper castes. Hijras are also viewed as being more sensitive to issues of poverty and social stigma, and the electorate does seem to perceive hijras as more approachable and effective than other politicians. However, in the past year, the election of at least one hijra has been overturned by the lower courts in the north Indian state of Madhya Pradesh, on the grounds that hijras are in fact *men* (masquerading as women), and therefore cannot stand for election from seats reserved for women. This case is currently being appealed in the Supreme Court.

In their political campaigns, hijras selectively highlighted their resonance with the traditional *sannyasi* or ascetic identity, emphasizing religious and sexual renunciation as the source of their authenticity and *izzat* (Reddy 2003), even as this image marginalizes them in Indian society. This emphasis—on the connection between sexual renunciation and politics—has a long history in India, most prominently expressed by early Indian nationalists, Swami Vivekananda, and Mahatma Gandhi, but also by many contemporary Hindu politicians (cf. Basu 1995). The hijra political candidates also remained conspicuously silent in public on their Muslim identity, a seemingly paradoxical silence, given their articulated embrace of Islam.

An important question raised by the success of hijras in contemporary politics is what it heralds for the transformation of hijras from a culturally and socially marginalized community to a new position in Indian society (Reddy 2003). Indeed, we may look at this as part of the larger question of whether—or to what extent—gender ambiguous roles in all societies are a form of resistance that disrupts the gender and cultural status quo (Nanda 2000). Does this new role for hijras herald a "new chapter of enfranchisement in the history of India's eunuchs" as one news columnist claimed (Jacinto 2000)? Will it reformulate not only hijras' place in Indian society, but also prevailing constructions of Indian citizenship, sexuality, gender, and politics?

The answers are perhaps more ambiguous than the initial media enthusiasm suggests.

Not only has the recent legal verdict located hijras as inexorably *male,* a position that precludes the possibility of a more fluid identity and presentation of self, but a closer analysis suggests that rather than remaking normative institutions, hijra political campaigns and their subsequent election appear to have subtly played with "traditional" cultural values, thereby re-inscribing the dominant status quo. Indeed, contrary to popular representations, it seems to us that hijras were elected precisely because they did not disrupt the status quo, and in fact reinforced the prevailing politics of Hindu nationalism. This not only questions the emancipatory and subversive potential of the hijras, but in fact might actually reinforce the majoritarian (Hindu) view of politics and society. If, as one hijra campaign slogan contends, "you don't need genitals for politics," incorporating those without genitals in the "new" political order might not necessarily herald a radically new or liberal social and moral order in India (Reddy 2003).

Certainly at the most basic level, the initial mandate of the hijras did not emphasize their radical potential, but rather the public's denigration of their sexual ambiguity, viewing them as symbols of politicians' impotence and the publics' disillusionment with existing (male) politicians (who are often referred to as "eunuchs"). Their election therefore might have highlighted precisely the hijras' marginality—as a caricature of virile masculinity and the lack of political capability that this apparently symbolizes. By emphasizing the renunciate aspect of their identity, hijras are complicit in this construction—a construction that equates virile (hetero)masculinity with political competence—ultimately reinforcing rather than undercutting their marginalization in society (Reddy 2003).

HIJRAS AND CULTURAL CHANGE

Despite their marginalization, hijras have demonstrated a remarkable ability to survive throughout their long history in India. With the advent of British rule, the position of the hijras not only began to lose its traditional royal patronage, with the British ultimately removing this community from any state protection (Preston 1987), but hijras were also classified in the colonial hierarchy along with other "criminal castes," resulting in the confiscation of much of their property and the vilification of their status in society (Ayres, 1992; Reddy, forthcoming). Building on this colonial history, laws criminalizing sodomy and emasculation, specifically targeting hijras, were incorporated into the criminal code of independent India. While these state policies appear to have had little deterrent effect, combined with the declining opportunities and cultural interest in traditional performances of many kinds, hijras have had to creatively adapt to new situations to maintain their visibility and legitimacy in Indian society. Their entry into contemporary politics is perhaps one such creative re-crafting of themselves in response to changing historical and political circumstances. Despite the ambivalent feelings toward hijras, and the stigma, fear and ridicule that continues to surround them, their survival and vibrant identity is perhaps yet another powerful recognition of the *multiplicity* of differences and the complex history that goes to construct humanity, including, and perhaps especially, hijra identity.

REFERENCES

Ayres, Alyssa C.
1992.   A Scandalous Breach of Public Decency: Defining the Decent—Indian Hijras in the 19th and 20th Centuries. B.A. Honor's thesis. Harvard University.
Bullough, Vern
1976.   *Sexual Variance in Society and History.* Chicago: University of Chicago Press.
Cohen, Lawrence
1995.   "The Pleasures of Castration: The Postoperative Status of Hijras, Jankhas and Academics." In *Sexual Nature, Sexual Culture.* (eds.) P. Abramson, and S. Pinkerton. Chicago: University of Chicago Press.
Dumont, Louis
1960.   "World Renunciation in Indian Religions." *Contributions to Indian Sociology* 4: 33–62.

Hall, Kira
1995. Hijra/Hijrin: Language and Gender Identity. Ph.d diss., University of California,
Berkeley.

Hiltebeitel, Alf
1980. "Siva, the Goddess, and the Disguises of
the Pandavas and Draupadi." *History of
Religions*: 147–174.

Jacinto, Leela
2000. "Political Outing: Once Ostracized, India's
Secretive Eunuchs Get Enfranchised."
ABCNews.com, 30 November. <http://
abcnews.go.com/sections/world/dai-
lynews/ india_eunuch001129.html.>

Kulick, Don
1998. *Travesti: Sex, Gender, and Culture Among
Brazilian Transgendered Prostitutes*. Chicago:
University of Chicago Press.

Marglin, Frederique A
1985. *Wives of the God-King: The Rituals of the Devadasis of Puri*. Delhi: Oxford University Press.

Nanda, Serena
2000. *Gender Diversity: Cross-Cultural Variation*.
Prospect Heights, IL:Waveland Press.
1999 *Neither Man nor Woman: The Hijras of India*:
Belmont, CA:Wadsworth Press.

O'Flaherty, Wendy Doniger
1973. *Asceticism and Eroticism in the Mythology of
Siva*. London: Oxford University Press.
1980. *Women, Androgynes, and Other Mythical Beasts*.
Chicago: University of Chicago Press.

Preston, Laurence W.
1987. "A right to exist: Eunuchs and the state in
nineteenth-century India. "*Modern Asian
Studies*, 21 (2), pp. 371–387.

Ramanujam, A. K.

1990. "Is There an Indian Way of Thinking?
An Informal Essay." In *India Through
Hindu Categories*. M. Marriott (ed.), Delhi:
Sage Publications.

Reddy, Gayatri
Forthcoming. *With Respect to Sex: Charting Hijra
Identity in Hyderabad, India*. Chicago: Uni-
versity of Chicago Press.
2003. "'Men' Who Would Be Kings: Celibacy,
Emasculation and the Re-Production of
Hijras in Contemporary Indian Politics."
Social Research, 70 (1): 163–200.
2001   "Crossing 'Lines' of Subjectivity: The
Negotiation of Sexual Identity in Hyder-
abad, India," Special Issue 'Sexual Sites,
Seminal Attitudes: Sexualities, Masculini-
ties and Culture in South Asia,' *South Asia*
vol. XXIV: 91–101.

Sharma, Satish. K.
1989. *Hijras: The Labelled Deviants*. New Delhi:
Gian Publishing House.

Shweder, R. and E. J. Bourne
1984. Does the Concept of a Person Vary Cross-
culturally? In *Culture Theory: Essays of Mind,
Self, and Emotion*. Cambridge: Cambridge
University Press.

Vyas, S. and D. Shingala
1987. *The Life Style of the Eunuchs*. New Delhi:
Anmol Publications.

Zwilling, Leonard and Michael J. Sweet
2000. "The Evolution of Third-Sex Constructs in
Ancient India: A Study in Ambiguity" In
*Invented Identities: The Interplay of Gender,
Religion and Politics in India*. Julia Leslie and
Mary McGee, eds., New Delhi: Oxford Uni-
versity Press; pp. 99–132.

Measuring Up to Barbie: Ideals of the Feminine Body in Popular Culture

Jacqueline Urla and Alan C. Swedlund

It is no secret that thousands of healthy women in the United States perceive their bodies as defective. The signs are everywhere: from potentially lethal cosmetic surgery and drugs,

---

Adapted for this text from Jacqueline Urla and Alan C. Swedlund, "The Anthropometry of Barbie: Unsettling Ideals of the Feminine Body in Popular Culture", *Deviant Bodies: Critical Perspectives on Difference in Science and Popular Culture,* Jennifer Terry and Jacqueline Urla, eds. (Bloomington: Indiana University Press, 1995). Copyright by Indiana University Press.

to the more familiar routines of dieting, curling, crimping, and aerobicizing, women seek to take control over their unruly physical selves. Every year at least 150,000 women undergo breast implant surgery (Williams 1992), while Asian women have their noses rebuilt and their eyes widened to make themselves look "less dull" (Kaw 1993). Studies show the obsession with body size and sense of inadequacy starts frighteningly early; as many as 80% of 9 year old suburban girls are concerned about dieting and their weight (Bordo 1991:125). Reports like these, together with the dramatic rise in eating disorders among young women are just some of the more noticeable fall-out from what Naomi Wolf calls "the beauty myth." Fueled by the hugely profitable cosmetic, weight loss, and fashion industries, the beauty myth's glamorized notions of the ideal body reverberate back upon women as "a dark vein of self hatred, physical obsessions, terror of aging, and dread of lost control" (Wolf 1991:10).

It is this paradox—that female bodies are never feminine enough, that they require deliberate and oftentimes painful refashioning to be what "nature" intended—that motivates our inquiry into the feminine ideal. Neither universal nor changeless, idealized notions of both masculine and feminine bodies have a long history that shifts considerably across time, racial or ethnic group, class, and culture. Body ideals in twenty-first century North America are influenced and shaped by images from classical or "high art," the discourses of science and medicine, as well as a multitude of commercial interests, ranging from mundane life insurance standards, to the more high-profile fashion, fitness, and entertainment industries. Each have played contributing and sometimes conflicting roles in determining what counts as a desirable body for us today. In this essay, we focus our attention on the domain of popular culture and the ideal feminine body as it is conveyed by one of pop culture's longest lasting and most illustrious icons: the Barbie doll.

Making her debut in 1959 as Mattel's new teenage fashion doll, Barbie rose quickly to become the top selling toy in the United States. Several decades and a women's movement later, Barbie dolls remain one of Mattel's biggest selling items netting over one billion dollars in revenues worldwide (Adelson 1992), or roughly one Barbie sold every two seconds (Stevenson 1991).[1] By the nineties, Mattel was estimating that in the U.S. over 95% of girls between the ages of 3 and 11 own at least one Barbie and that the average number of dolls per owner is seven (Shapiro 1992). Barbie is clearly a force to contend with, eliciting, over the years, a combination of critique, parody, and adoration. A legacy of the post-war era, she remains an incredibly resilient visual and tactile model of femininity for pre-pubescent girls.

It is not our intention to settle the debate over whether Barbie is a good or bad role model for little girls. Though that issue surrounds Barbie like a dark cloud, we are more concerned with how Barbie has been able to survive and remain popular in a period marked by the growth of consumer society, intense debate over gender and racial relations, and changing notions of the body. Our aim, then, is not to offer another rant against Barbie, but to explore how this doll crystallizes some of the predicaments of femininity and feminine bodies in late twentieth-century North America.

A DOLL IS BORN

Parents thank us for the educational values in the world of Barbie ... They say that they could never get their daughters well groomed before—get them out of slacks or blue jeans and into a dress ... get them to scrub their necks and wash their hair. Well that's where Barbie comes in. The doll has clean hair and a clean face, and she dresses fashionably, and she wears gloves and shoes that match. (Ruth Handler 1964, quoted in Motz 1987:130)

Legend has it that Barbie was the brainchild of Mattel owner Ruth Handler, who first thought of creating a three dimensional fashion doll after seeing her daughter play with paper dolls. As an origin story, this one is touching and no doubt true. But Barbie was not the first doll of her kind nor was she just a mother's invention. Making sense of Barbie requires that we look to the larger socio-political and cultural milieu that made her genesis both possible and meaningful. Based on a German prototype, the "Lili" doll, Barbie was from "birth" implicated in the ideologies of the cold war and the research and technology exchanges of the military-industrial complex. Her finely crafted durable plastic mold was, in fact, designed by Jack Ryan, well known for his work in designing the Hawk and Sparrow missiles for the Raytheon Company. Conceived at the hands of a military weapons designer-turned-toy inventor, Barbie dolls came onto the market the same year as the infamous Nixon-Khrushchev "kitchen debate" at the American National Exhibition in Moscow. There, in front of the cameras of the world, the leaders of the capitalist and socialist worlds faced off, not over missile counts, but over "the relative merits of American and Soviet washing machines, televisions, and electric ranges" (May 1988:16). As Elaine Tyler May has noted in her study of the Cold War, this much celebrated media event signaled the transformation of American-made commodities and the model suburban home into key symbols and safeguards of democracy and freedom. It was thus with fears of nuclear annihilation and sexually charged fantasies of the perfect bombshelter running rampant in the American imaginary, that Barbie and her torpedo-like breasts emerged into popular culture as an emblem of the aspirations of prosperity, domestic containment, and rigid gender roles that were to characterize the burgeoning post-war consumer economy and its image of the American Dream.

Marketed as the first "teenage" fashion doll, Barbie's rise in popularity also coincided with and no doubt contributed to the post-war creation of a distinctive teenage lifestyle.[2] Teens, their tastes and behaviors, were becoming the object of both sociologists and criminologists, as well as market survey researchers intent on capturing their discretionary dollars. While J. Edgar Hoover was pronouncing "the juvenile jungle" a menace to American society, we have retailers, the music industry, and movie-makers declaring

the 13 to 19 year old age bracket "the seven golden years" (Doherty 1988:51–52).

Barbie dolls seemed to cleverly reconcile both of these concerns by personifying the good girl who was sexy, but didn't have sex, and was willing to spend, spend and spend. Amidst the palpable moral panic over juvenile delinquency and teenagers' new found sexual freedom, Barbie was a reassuring symbol of solidly middle-class values. Popular teen magazines, advertising, television and movies of the period painted a highly dichotomized world divided into good (i.e. middle class) and bad (i.e. working class) kids: the clean-cut college-bound junior achiever versus the street corner boy; the wholesome American Bandstander versus the uncontrollable bad seed (cf. Doherty 1988; and Frith 1981 for England). It was no mystery where Barbie stood in this thinly disguised class discourse. As Motz writes, Barbie's world bore no trace of the "greasers" and "hoods" that inhabited the many grade B films about teenage vice and ruin. In the life Mattel laid out for her in story books and comics, Barbie, who started out looking like a somewhat vampy, slightly Bardot-esque doll, was gradually transformed into a "'soc' or a 'frat'—affluent, well-groomed, socially conservative" (Motz 1987:130). In lieu of back-seat sex and teenage angst, Barbie had pajama parties, barbecues, and her favorite pastime, shopping.

Every former Barbie owner knows that to buy a Barbie was to lust after Barbie accessories: that matching pair of sandals and handbag, canopy bedroom set, or country camper. Both conspicuous consumer and a consumable item herself, Barbie was surely as much the fantasy of U.S. retailers as she was the panacea of middle class parents. For every "need" Barbie had, there was a deliciously miniature product to fulfill it. As Paula Rabinowitz has noted, Barbie dolls, with their focus on frills and fashion, epitomize the way that teenage girls and girl culture in general have figured as accessories in the historiography of post-war culture; that is as both essential to the burgeoning commodity culture as consumers, but seemingly irrelevant to the historical events defining cold war existence (Rabinowitz 1993).

Perhaps what makes Barbie such a perfect icon of late capitalist constructions of femininity is the way in which her persona pairs endless consumption with the achievement of femininity and the appearance of an appropriately gendered body. By buying for Barbie, girls practice how to be discriminating consumers knowledgeable about the cultural capital of different name brands, how to read packaging, and the overall importance of fashion and taste for social status (Motz 1987:131–132). Being a teenage girl in the world of Barbie dolls becomes quite literally a performance of commodity display requiring numerous and complex rehearsals. In making this argument, we want to stress that we are drawing on more than just the doll. "Barbie" is also the packaging, spin-off products, cartoons, commercials, magazines, and fan club paraphernalia, all of which contribute to creating her persona. Clearly, as we will discuss below, children may engage more or less with those products, subverting or ignoring various aspects of Barbie's "official" presentation. However, to the extent that little girls *do* participate in the prepackaged world of Barbie, they come into contact with a number of beliefs central to femininity under consumer capitalism. Little girls learn, among other things, about the crucial importance of their appearance to their personal happiness and ability to gain favor with their friends. Barbie's social calendar, like her closet, is constantly full, and the stories in her fan magazines show her frequently engaged in preparation for the rituals of heterosexual teenage life: dates, proms, and weddings. A perusal of Barbie magazines, and the product advertisements and pictorials within them, shows an overwhelming preoccupation with grooming for those events. Magazines abound with tips on the proper ways of washing hair, putting on make-up, and assembling stunning wardrobes. Through these play scenarios little girls learn Ruth Handler's lesson about the importance of hygiene, occasion-specific clothing, knowledgeable buying, and artful display as key elements to popularity and a successful career in femininity.

Barbie exemplifies the way in which gender has become a commodity itself, "something we can buy into . . . the same way we buy into a style" (Willis 1991:23). In her insightful analysis of the logic of consumer capitalism, cultural critic Susan Willis pays particular attention to the way in which children's toys like Barbie and the popular muscle-bound "He-Man" for boys link highly conservative and narrowed images of masculinity and femininity with commodity consumption (1991:27). Being or becoming a teenager, having a "grown-up" body, observes Willis, is presented as inextricably bound up with the acquisition of certain commodities, signaled by styles of clothing, cars, music, etc. In play groups and fan clubs (collectors are a whole world unto themselves) children exchange knowledge about the latest accessories and outfits, their relative merit, and how to find them. They become members of a community of Barbie owners whose shared identity is defined by the commodities they have or desire to have. The articulation of social ties through commodities is, as Willis argues, at the heart of how sociality is experienced in consumer capitalism. In this way, we might say that playing with Barbie serves not only as a training ground for the production of the appropriately gendered woman, but also as an introduction to the kinds of knowledge and social relations one can expect to encounter in late capitalist society.

BARBIE IS A SURVIVOR

For anyone tracking Barbie's history, it is abundantly clear that Mattel's marketing strategies have been sensitive to a changing social climate. When the women's movement gained momentum in the seventies, Barbie dolls became a target of criticism (Billyboy 1987; Lord 1994). Mattel responded by giving Barbie new outfits to "reflect the activities and professions that modern women are involved in" (quoted in Harpers, August 2, 1990, p. 20). Just as Barbie graduated from Candy striper and ballerina to astronaut and doctor, Mattel also tried to diversify her lily-white image beginning in 1967 with Barbie's first Black friend, "Colored Francie." With the expansion of sales worldwide, Barbie has acquired multiple national guises (Spanish Barbie, Jamaican Barbie, Malaysian Barbie, etc.).[3] In addition, her cohort of "friends" has become increasingly ethnically diversified, as has Barbie advertising, which now regularly feature Asian, Hispanic and Afro-American little girls playing with Barbie. Today, Barbie pals include a smattering of brown and yellow plastic friends, like Teresa, Kira, and Miko who appear on her adventures and, very importantly, can share her clothes.

Perhaps Mattel's most glamorous concession to multiculturalism was Shani who premiered at the 1991 Toy Fair with great fanfare and media attention. Unlike her predecessors who were essentially "brown plastic poured into blond Barbie's mold," Shani, together with her two friends, Asha and Nichelle (each a slightly different shade of brown), and boyfriend Jamal created in 1992, were decidedly Afro-centric, with outfits in "ethnic" fabrics rather than the traditional Barbie pink (Jones 1991). The packaging also announced that these dolls' bodies and facial features were meant to be more realistic of African American women, although as we will see, the differences, while meaningful, don't preclude interchanging clothes with Barbie. Now, Mattel announced, "ethnic Barbie lovers will be able to dream in their own image" (*Newsweek* 1990:48). Multiculturalism cracked open the door to Barbiedom and diversity could walk in as long as she was big busted, slim hipped, had long flowing hair, tiny feet, and was very very thin.[4]

In looking over the course of Barbie's career, it is clear that part of her resilience, continuing appeal and profitability stems from the fact that her identity is constructed primarily through fantasy and is consequently open to change and reinterpretation. As a fashion model, Barbie continually creates her identity anew with every costume change. In that sense, we might want to call Barbie emblematic of the restless desire for change that permeates post-modern capitalist society (Wilson 1985:63). Not only can her image be renewed with a change of clothes, Barbie is also seemingly able to clone herself effortlessly into new identities—"Malibu Barbie"; "Totally Hair Barbie"; "Teen Talk Barbie"; even Afro-centric Shani—without somehow suggesting a serious personality disorder. Furthermore, as a perpetual teenager, Barbie's owners are at liberty to fantasize any number of life choices for her; she might be a high-powered fashion executive or she just might marry Ken and "settle down" in her luxury condo. Her history is a barometer of changing fashions, changing gender and race relations, and a keen index of corporate America's anxious attempts to find new and more palatable ways of selling the beauty myth and commodity fetishism to new generations of parents and their daughters.

What is striking, then, is that while Barbie's identity may be mutable—one day she might be an astronaut, another a cheerleader—*her hyper-slender, big-chested body has remained fundamentally unchanged over the years*—a remarkable fact in a society that fetishizes the new and improved. Barbie, of course, did acquire flexible arms and legs as we know, her face has changed significantly, and her hair has grown by leaps and bounds (Melosh and Simmons 1986). But her body measurements, pointed toes, and proportions have not altered significantly. It is to that body and to the results of our class experiment in the anthropometry of Barbie that we now turn. But before taking out our calipers on Barbie and her friends to see how their bodies measure up, we want to offer a very brief historical overview of anthropometry to help us understand how the notion of the "average" American female body was debated in post-war United States.

THE MEASURED BODY: NORMS AND IDEALS

The paramount objective of physical anthropology is the gradual completion, in collaboration with the anatomists, the physiologists, and the chemists, of the study of the normal white man under ordinary circumstances.

Ales Hrdlicka, 1918

Anthropometry, the science of measuring human bodies, belongs to a long line of techniques of the 18th and 19th centuries—craniometry, phrenology, comparative anatomy—concerned with measuring, comparing, and interpreting variability in the physical dimensions of the human body. Early anthropometry shared with these early sciences the expectation that the body was a window into a host of moral, temperamental, racial, or gender characteristics. It sought to distinguish itself from its predecessors, however, by being more rigorous and standardized in its techniques (Hrdlicka 1939:12). Head shape, (especially cranial capacity), was a constant source of special fascination, but by the early part of this century, physical anthropologists, together with anatomists and medical doctors were developing a precise and routine set of measurements for the entire body that they hoped would permit systematic comparison of the human body across race, nationality, and gender.[5]

Anthropometry developed in the United States under the aegis of Ernest Hooton, Ales Hrdlicka, and Franz Boas, located respectively at Harvard, the Smithsonian, and Columbia University. Their main areas of interest were (1) identifying the physical features of racial and or national types, (2) the measurement of adaptation and "degeneracy," and (3) a comparison of the sexes. As is well documented by now, women and non-Europeans did not fare well in these emerging sciences of the body which held white males as the pinnacle of evolution (see the work of Blakey 1987; Gould 1981, Schiebinger 1989; Fee 1979; Russett 1989. Hooton, in his classic book, *Up from the Ape* (1931) regularly likened women and especially non-Europeans of both sexes to nonhuman primates. Similarly Hrdlicka's 1925 comparative study of male and female skulls went to rather extraordinary lengths to argue that women's brains (presumed at the time to be a sign of intelligence) were actually *smaller* than men's even though his measurements showed females to have a relatively *larger* cranial capacity than that of males.[6]

When it came to defining racial or national types, men, not women were the most commonly studied.[7] Although Hrdlicka and others considered it necessary to measure both males and females, early physical anthropology textbooks reveal that more often than not it was the biologically male body that was selected to visually represent a particular race or humanity as a whole. Males were, in short, the unspoken prototype, while women's bodies were understood as a sexual subset. Women's bodies were frequently described as deviations from the generic or ideal type: their body fat "excessive"; their pelvis maladaptive to a bipedal (i.e. more evolved) posture; their musculature weak. Scientists seem to agree that what most dictated a woman's physical shape was her reproductive function. All other features were subordinated to and could be explained by this capacity to bear children. Not surprisingly, given this assumption, it was women's, particularly African or non-European women's, reproductive organs, genitalia and secondary sexual characteristics, that were the most carefully scrutinized and measured (see Fausto-Sterling 1995).

In the United States, we begin to find an attempt to scientifically define a normative "American" female body in the late 19th and early twentieth centuries. By the 1860's, Harvard as well as other universities had begun to regularly collect anthropometric data on their male student populations, and in the 1890's comparable data began to be collected from the East Coast women's colleges as well. It was thus upper class, largely WASP, young people who were the basis of some of the early attempts to define the measurements of the "normal" American male and female. By basing themselves in elite colleges, "other" Americans—descendants of African slaves, North American Indians, and the many recent European migrants from Ireland, southern Europe, and eastern Europe—were effectively excluded from defining the norm. Rather, their bodies were more often the subject of racist evolutionary oriented studies concerned with "race crossing," degeneracy, and the effects of the "civilizing" process (see Blakey 1987).

Academia was not the only place where body standards were being developed. By the early part of the twentieth century industry began to make widespread commercial use of practical anthropometry: the demand for standardized measures of the "average" body manifested in everything from designs for labor-efficient workstations and kitchens to standardized sizes in the ready-to-wear clothing industry (cf. Schwartz 1986). Soon insurance companies would enter the scene. Between 1900 and 1920, the first medicoactuarial standards of weight and height began to appear. The most significant of these, the Dublin Standard Table of Heights and Weights, developed in 1908 by Louis Dublin, a student of Franz Boas and statistician for the Metropolitan Life Insurance Company, became the authoritative reference in every doctor's office (cf. Bennett and Gurin 1982:130–138). However, what began as a table of statistical averages, soon became a means of setting ideal 'norms'. Within a few years of its creation, the Dublin table shifted from providing a record of statistically "average" weights to becoming a guide to "desirable" weights which, interestingly enough, began to fall notably below the average weight for most adult women. Historian Joan Brumberg points to the Dublin Table, widely disseminated to doctors and published in popular magazines, together with the invention of the personal or bathroom scale, as the two devices most responsible in America for popularizing the notion that the human figure could be standardized and that abstract and often unrealistic norms could be uniformly applied (1988:232–235).

By the 1940s the search to describe the normal American male and female body in anthropometric terms was being conducted on many fronts fueled by a deepening concern about the physical fitness of the American people. Did Americans constitute a distinctive physical type? Were they physically stronger or weaker than their European ancestors? Could they defend themselves in time of war? And who did this category of "Americans" include? Questions such as these fed into an already long-standing preoccupation with defining a specifically American national character and, in 1945, led to the creation of some of the most celebrated and widely publicized life-size anthropometric statues of the century: Norm and Norma, the average American male and female. These statues, sculpted by Malvina Hoffman, were based on the composite measurements of thousands of white eighteen to twenty-five year old subjects. Both figures were put on display, but it was Norma who received the greatest media attention when the Cleveland Health Museum, which had purchased the pair, decided to sponsor a contest to find the woman in Ohio whose body most closely matched the dimensions of Norma. Under the catchy headline, "Are you Norma, Typical Woman?" the publicity surrounding this contest instructed women how to take their measurements for the contest. Within ten days, 3863 women had sent in their measurements to compete for the $100 prize in U.S. War Bonds that would go to the woman who most resembled the average American girl.

Besides bolstering the circulation of the *Cleveland Plain Dealer,* the idea behind the contest was to promote interest in physical fitness. Norma was described in the press as everything the young American woman should be in a time of war: fit, strong-bodied and at the peak of her reproductive potential. Newspaper articles emphasized that women had a national responsibility to be fit if America was to continue to excel after the war. Few contestants apparently measured up to the challenge (Shapiro 1945). Only one percent came close to Norma's proportions. Commenting on the search for Norma, Dr. Gebhard, director of the Cleveland Health Museum, was quoted in one of the many newspaper articles as saying that "if a national inventory of the female population of this country were taken there would be as many "4Fs" among the women as were revealed among the men in the draft" (Robertson 1945:4). The contest provided the occasion for many health reformers to voice their concern about the weakening of the "American stock" and to call for eugenic marital selection and breeding.

Norma and Norman were thus always more than statistical composites, they were prescriptive ideals that, like the college studies that preceded them, erased American's racial and ethnic differences. The "average American" of the post-war period was still imagined as a youthful white body. However, there were competing ideals. Health reformers, educators, and doctors who approved and promoted Norma as an ideal for American women were well aware that her sensible, strong, thick-waisted body differed significantly from the tall, slim-hipped bodies of fashion models in vogue at the time.[8] As the post-war period advanced, Norma would be overshadowed by the array of images of fashion models and pin up girls put out by advertisers, the entertainment industry, and a burgeoning consumer culture. These fashion images were becoming increasingly thin in the sixties and seventies while the "average" woman's body was in fact getting heavier.

THE ANTHROPOMETRY OF BARBIE: TURNING THE TABLES

Anthropometry, like the very notion of a "normal" body it has been used to construct, is part of an unsavory history. Nevertheless, in the contemporary cultural context where an impossibly thin image of women's bodies has become the most popular children's toy ever sold, it strikes us it might just be the power tool we need for destabilizing a fantasy spun out of control. It was with this in mind that we asked students in one of our social biology classes to measure Barbie to see how her body compared to the average measurements of young American women of the same period. Besides estimating what Barbie's dimensions would be if she were life-size, we see the experiment as an occasion to turn the anthropometric tables from disciplining the bodies of living women, to measuring the ideals by which we have come to judge ourselves and others. We also see it as an opportunity for students who have grown up under the regimes of normalizing science, students who no doubt have been measured, weighed, and compared to standards since birth, to use those very tools to unsettle a highly popular cultural ideal.

Our initial experiment involved measuring many Barbies and Kens from different decades as well as some of their friends. Here we will only report on the results for Barbie and Ken from the Glitter Beach collection, as well as Jamal and Shani, Barbie's more recent African-American friends. Mattel had marketed these latter dolls as having a more authentic African-American appearance and a "rounder more athletic" body, and we wanted to test that out.

After practicing with the calipers, discussing potential observational errors, and performing repeated trial runs, we began to record. In scaling Barbie to be life-sized, the students decided to translate her measurements using two standards: (a) If Barbie were a fashion model (5'10") and (b) if she were of average height for women in the United States (5'4"). We also decided to measure Ken, in the same way, using an average male stature, which we designated as 5'8", and the more "idealized" stature for men, 6'. We report here only the highlights of the measurements taken on the newer Barbie and newer Ken, Jamal, and Shani, scaled at the fashion-model height. For purposes of comparison, we include data on average body measurements from the standardized published tables of the 1988 Anthropometric Survey of the Army Personnel. We have dubbed these composites for the female and male recruits "Army Norma" and "Army Norm," respectively.

Both Barbie and Shani's measurements at 5'10" reveal the extreme thinness expected of the runway model. Both dolls have considerably smaller measurements than Army Norma *at all points*, even though they are six inches taller than her. When we scaled the dolls to 5'4"—the same as Army Norma—we can see just how skewed the dimensions are: Barbie's chest, waist, and hip measurements come out as 32"–17"–28," clinically anorectic to say the least. We also wanted to see if Mattel had physically changed the Barbie mold in making Shani. Most of the differences we could find

TABLE 1. Measurements of Glitter Beach Barbie, African-American Shani, and the Average Measurements of the 1988 U.S. Army Women Recruits.[1]

MEAS.	BARBIE	SHANI	U.S. ARMY "NORMA"
Height	5'10"	5'10"	5' 4"
Chest Circum.	35"	35"	35.7"
Waist Circum.	20"	20"	31"
Hip Circum[2]	32.50"	31.25"	38.10"
Hip Breadth	11.6"	11.0"	13.49"
Thigh Circum.	19.25"	20.00"	22.85"

[1] "Norma" is based on 2,208 army recruits, 1,140 of which were white, 922 of which were black.
[2] Hip circumference is referred to as "buttock circumference" in anthropometric parlance.

TABLE 2. Measurements of Glitter Beach Ken, African-American Ken, and the Average Measurements of the 1988 U.S. Army Male Recruits.[1]

MEAS.	KEN	JAMAL	U.S. ARMY "NORM"
Height	6' 0"	6' 0"	5' 9"
Chest Circum.	38.4"	38.4"	39.0"
Waist Circum.	28.8"	28.8"	33.1"
Hip Circum.[2]	36.0"	36.0"	38.7"
Hip Breadth	12.2"	12.2"	13.46"
Thigh Circum.	20.4"	20.4"	23.48"

[1] "Norm" is based on 1774 males, 1,172 of which were white and 458 of which were black.
[2] Hip circumference is referred to as "buttock circumference" in anthropometric parlance.

appeared to be in the face. Shani's nose is broader and her lips are slightly larger. The only significant difference we found in the bodies was that Shani's back is arched in such a way that it tilts her buttocks up, producing the visual illusion of a higher, rounder, butt . . . Perhaps this is what Mattel was referring to in claiming that Shani has a realistic or ethnically correct body (Jones 1991).

When it came to the male dolls, we did not find the same kind of dramatic difference between them and Army Norm as we did in the female dolls. As the table shows, Ken and Jamal were largely identical to each other, and they were only somewhat slimmer than the average soldier. Visually Ken and Jamal appear very tight and muscular and "bulked out," while the U.S. Army males tend to carry slightly more fat, judging from the photographs and data presented in the 1988 study.

OUR BARBIES, OUR SELVES

I feel like Barbie; everyone calls me Barbie; I love Barbie. The main difference is she's plastic and I'm real. There isn't really any other difference.

Hayley Spicer, winner of Great Britain's Barbie-Look-Alike competition

Our venture into anthropometry revealed that Barbie has a much more "abnormal" body than does Ken. But her hyper-thin body was by no means exceptional. Studies tracking the body measurements of *Playboy* magazine centerfolds and Miss America contestants show that between 1959 and 1978 the average weight and hip size for women in both of these groups has decreased steadily while the average weight of women was increasing (Wiseman, Gray, Mosimann and Ahrens 1992). A follow up study for the years 1979–1988 found this trend continuing into the eighties: approximately 69% of Playboy centerfolds and 60% of Miss America contestants were weighing in at 15% or more below their expected age and height category. In short, the majority of women presented to us in the media as having desirable feminine bodies, were, like Barbie, well on their way to qualify for anorexia nervosa.

On the surface, at least, it might seem that Barbie's signature thin body would seem at odds with the doll's seemingly endless desire for consumption and self-transformation. Being thin for most women requires repression of desire and self discipline, neither of which are traits we associate with the consummate shopper. And yet, as Susan Bordo (1990) has argued in regard to anorexia, these two phenomena hyper thin bodies and hyper consumption—are very much linked in advanced capitalist economies which depend upon commodity excess. Bodies, says Bordo, are where the regulation of desire is played out most keenly. The imperative to manage the body and to "be all that you can be"—in fact the idea that you can *choose* the body that you want to have—is a pervasive feature of consumer culture. Keeping control of one's body, not getting too fat or flabby, in other words, conforming to gendered norms of fitness and weight, have become signs of an individual's social and moral worth. But as Bordo, Sandra Bartky (1990), and other feminist scholars have been quick to point out, not all bodies are subject to the same degree of scrutiny or the same repercussions if they fail. It is women's bodies and desires in particular where the structural contradictions—the simultaneous incitement to consume and social condemnation for overindulgence—appear to be most acutely manifested in bodily regimes of intense self-monitoring and discipline. Just as it is women's appearance which is subject to greater social scrutiny, so it is that women's desires, hunger, and appetites which are seen as most threatening and in need of control in a patriarchal society.

This cultural context is relevant to making sense of Barbie and the meaning her body holds in late consumer capitalism. In dressing and undressing Barbie, combing her hair, bathing her, turning and twisting her limbs in imaginary scenarios, children acquire a very tactile and intimate sense of Barbie's body. Barbie is presented in packaging and advertising as a role model, a best friend or older sister to little girls. Television jingles use the refrain, "I want to be just like you," while look-alike clothes and look-alike contests make it possible for girls to live out the fantasy of being Barbie. In short, there is every reason to believe that girls (or adult women) link Barbie's body shape with her popularity and glamour.

This is exactly what worries many people. As our measurements show, Barbie's body differs wildly from anything approximating "average" female body weight and proportions. Over the years her wasp-waisted body has evoked a steady stream of critique for having a negative impact on little girls' sense of self-esteem. For example, the release of a Barbie aerobics work-out video for girls in 1992 was met with the following angry letter from an expert in the field of eating disorders:

> I had hoped these plastic dolls with impossible proportions would have faded away in this current health-conscious period; not at all. . . . Move over Jane Fonda. Welcome again, ever smiling, breast-thrusting Barbie with your stick legs and sweat-free aerobic routines. I'm concerned about the role model message she is giving our young. Surely it's hard to accept a little cellulite when the culture tells you unrelentingly how to strive for thinness and the perfect body. [Warner 1992][9]

There is no doubt that Barbie's body contributes to what Kim Chernin (1981) has called "the tyranny of slenderness." [10] But is repression all her hyper-thin body conveys? In her work on how anorectic women see themselves, Susan Bordo writes that, "for anorectics, [the slender ideal] may have a very different meaning; it may symbolize, not so much the containment of female desire, as its liberation from a domestic, reproductive destiny" (Bordo 1990:103).

Similar observations have been made about cosmetic surgery: women often explain their experience as one of empowerment, of taking charge of their bodies and lives (Balsamo

1993; Davis 1991). What does this mean for making sense of Barbie and her long lasting appeal? We would suggest that a sub-text of agency and independence, even transgression, accompanies this pencil-thin icon of femininity. On the one hand, one can argue that Barbie's body displays conformity to dominant cultural imperatives for a disciplined body and contained feminine desires. On the other hand, however, her excessive slenderness can also signify a rebellious manifestation of will-power, a refusal of the maternal ideal, symbolized by pendulous breasts, rounded stomach and hips. Hers is a body of hard edges, distinct borders, and self control. It is literally impenetrable. While the anorectic woman becomes increasingly androgynous the more she starves herself, Barbie, in the realm of plastic fantasy, is able to remain powerfully sexualized with her large gravity-defying breasts, even while she is distinctly non-reproductive. Like the "hard bodies" in fitness advertising, Barbie's body may signify for women the pleasure of control and mastery both of which are highly valued traits in American society and both of which are predominantly associated with masculinity (Bordo 1990:105). Putting these elements together with her apparent independent wealth can make for a very different reading of Barbie than that of bimbo. To paraphrase one Barbie doll owner: she owns a Ferrari and doesn't have a husband; she must be doing something right![11]

By invoking these testimonies of anorectic women, we are not trying to suggest that playing with Barbie, or trying to become like Barbie, are paths to empowerment for little girls. Rather we want to signal the complex and contradictory meanings that her body has in contemporary American society. And we also want to underscore that our bodies, whatever the reigning ideal might be, continue to function as a vitally important stage on which gender—as well as race and class—conformity and transgression are played out.[12] It is clear that a next step we would want to take in the cultural interpretation of Barbie is an ethnographic study of Barbie doll owners.[13] It is sensible to assume that the children who play with Barbie are themselves creative users who respond variously to the messages about femininity encoded in her fashions and appearance. In the hands of their adult and child owners, Barbies have become Amazon cave warriors, drag queens, dutiful mommies, and evil axe murderers.[14] As we consider Barbie's many meanings, we should also note that the doll has become a world traveler. A product of the global assembly-line, Barbie dolls owe their existence to the internationalization of the labor market and global flows of capital and commodities that today characterize the toy industry as well as other industries in the post-war era. Designed in Los Angeles, manufactured in Taiwan or Malaysia, distributed worldwide, Barbie TM is American-made in name only. Speeding her way into an expanding global market, Barbie brings with her some of the North American cultural subtext we have outlined in this analysis. How this teenage survivor has inserted herself into the cultural landscapes of Mayan villages, Bombay high rises, and Malagasy towns is a rich topic that begs to be explored.

ACKNOWLEDGMENTS

This essay is based on a longer piece of research first published in Urla and Swedlund (1995). Follow-up research we have carried out on the ideal of the thin waist will appear in Orgel, Urla, and Swedlund (in press).

NOTES

1. The statistics and figures provided on sales reflect research carried out in the nineties.
2. While the concept of adolescence as a distinct developmental stage between puberty and adulthood was not new to the fifties, Thomas Doherty (1988) notes that it wasn't until the end of World War II that the term "teenager" became standard usage in the American language.
3. More work needs to be done on how Barbie dolls are adapted to appeal to various national markets. For example, Barbie dolls manufactured in Japan for Japanese consumption are reputed to have noticeably larger, rounder

eyes than those marketed in the United States (see Billyboy 1987). For some suggestive thoughts on the cultural implications of the transnational flow of toys like Barbie dolls, TransFormers, and He-Man, see Carol Breckenridge's (1990) brief but intriguing editor's comment to *Public Culture.*

4. On Black Barbies see duCille 1995.

5. Though measurements of skulls, noses, facial angles for scientific comparison had been going on throughout the 19th century, it wasn't until the 1890's that any serious attempts were made to standardize anthropometric measurements of the living body. This culminated in the Monaco agreement of 1906, one of the first international meetings to standardize anthropometric measurement. For a brief review of the attempts to use and systematize photography in anthropometry see Spencer (1992).

6. Hrdlicka argued, rather fantastically, that there was more space between the brain and the cranium in women than in men. Michael Blakey refers to this as Hrdlicka's "air head" hypothesis (1987:16)

7. In her study of 18th century physical sciences, Schiebinger (1993) remarks that male bodies (skulls in particular) were routinely assumed to embody the prototype of their race in the various typologies devised by comparative anatomists of the period. "When anthropologists did compare women across cultures, their interest centered on sexual traits—feminine beauty, redness of lips, length and style of hair, size and shape of breasts or clitorises, degree of sexual desire, fertility, and above all the size, shape, and position of the pelvis" (1993:156). In this way, the male body "remained the touchstone of human anatomy," while females were regarded as a sexual subset of the species (1993:159–60).

8. Historians have noted a long-standing conflict between the physical culture movement, eugenicists and health reformers on the one hand, and the fashion industry on the other that gave rise to competing ideals in American society of the fit and the fashionably fragile woman (e.g. Banner 1983; Cogan 1989).

9. When confronted with these kinds of accusations, Mattel and the fashion industry protest that Barbie dolls, like fashion models, are about fantasy, not reality. "We're not telling you to be that girl" writes Elizabeth Saltzman, fashion editor for *Vogue*. "We're trying to show you fashion" (France 1992:22).

10. In response to this anxiety, Cathy Meredig, an enterprising computer software designer, created the "Happy to be Me" doll. Described as a healthy alternative for little girls, "Happy to be Me" has a shorter neck, shorter legs, wider waist and larger feet, and a lot fewer clothes, designed to make her look more like the average woman ("She's No Barbie, Nor Does She Care to Be." *New York Times*, August 15, 1991, C-11).

11. "Dolls in Playland." 1992. Colleen Toomey, producer. BBC.

12. For an illuminating case study of race, class, and gender codings of the female body, see Krause 1998.

13. While not exactly ethnographic, Hohmann (1985) offers a socio-psychological study of how children experiment with social relations during play with Barbies.

14. Barbie has become a somewhat celebrated figure among avant-garde and pop artists, giving rise to a whole genre of Barbie satire known as "Barbie Noire" (Kahn 1991; Ebersole and Peabody 1993). On queer appropriations of Barbie and Ken, see Rand (1995).

REFERENCES

Adelson, Andrea
1992   And Now, Barbie Looks Like a Billion. *New York Times.* Nov. 26. pg. D3.

Balsamo, Anne
1993   On the Cutting Edge: Cosmetic Surgery and the Technological Production of the Gendered Body. *Camera Obscura* 28:207–238.

Banner, Lois W.
1983   *American Beauty*. New York, Knopf.

Bartky, Sandra Lee
1990   "Foucault, Femininity, and the Modernization of Patriarchal Power." In *Femininity and Domination: Studies in the Phenomenology of Oppression.* pp. 63–82. New York: Routledge.

Bennett, William and Joel Gurin
1982   *The Dieter's Dilemma: Eating Less and Weighing More*. New York: Basic Books.

Billyboy
1987   *Barbie, her Life and Times, and the New Theater of Fashion*. New York: Crown Publishers.

Blakey, Michael L.
1987   Skull Doctors: Instrinsic Social and Political Bias in the History of American Physical Anthropology. *Critique of Anthropology* 7(2):7–35.

Bordo, Susan R.
1990   "Reading the Slender Body." In *Body/ Politics: Women and the Discourses of Science.* M. Jacobus, E. Fox Keller, and S. Shuttleworth, eds. pp. 83–112. New York: Routledge.

Bordo, Susan R.
1991   "'Material Girl': The Effacements of Post-modern Culture. In *The Female Body: Figures, Styles, Speculations.* L.Goldstein, ed. pp. 106–130. Ann Arbor, MI: The University of Michigan Press.

Breckenridge, Carol A.
1990   Editor's Comment: On Toying with Terror. *Public Culture* 2(2):i–iii.

Brumberg, Joan Jacobs
1988   *Fasting Girls: The History of Anorexia Nervosa.* New York: New American Library.

Chernin, Kim
1981   *The Obsession: Reflections on the Tyranny of Slenderness.* New York: Harper.

Cogan, Frances B.
1989   *All-American Girl: The Ideal of Real Woman-hood in Mid-Nineteenth Century America.* Athens and London: University of Georgia Press.

Davis, Kathy
1991   Remaking the She-Devil: A Critical Look at Feminist Approaches to Beauty. *Hypatia* 6(2):21–43.

Doherty, Thomas
1988   *Teenagers and Teenpics. The Juvenilization of American Movies in the 1950's.* Boston: Unwin Hyman.

DuCille, Ann
1995   "Toy Theory: Blackface Barbie and the Deep Play of Difference." In, *The Skin Trade: Essays on Race, Gender and Merchandising of Difference.* Cambridge: Harvard University Press.

Ebersole, Lucinda and Richard Peabody, eds.
1993   *Mondo Barbie.* New York: St. Martin's Press.

Fausto-Sterling, Anne
1995   "Gender, Race and Nation: The Comparative Anatomy of "Hottentot" Women in Europe, 1815–1817." In, *Deviant Bodies: Critical Perspectives on Difference in Science and Popular Culture.* J. Terry and J. Urla, eds. Bloomington: Indiana University Press.

Fee, Elizabeth
1979   Nineteenth Century Craniology: The Study of the Female Skull. *Bulletin of the History of Medicine* 53:415–433.

France, Kim
1992   "Tits 'R' Us." *Village Voice*, March 17, p. 22.

Frith, Simon

1981   *Sound Effects: Youth, Leisures, and the Politics of Rock'n'Roll.* New York: Pantheon.

Gould, Steven Jay
1981   *The Mismeasure of Man.* New York: Norton.

Hohmann, Delf Maria
1985   Jennifer and her Barbies: A Contextual Analysis of a Child Playing Barbie dolls. *Canadian Folklore Canadien* 7 (1–2): 111–120.

Hooton, E. A.
1931   Up from the Ape. New York: The MacMillan Company.

Hrdlicka, Ales
1925   Relation of the Size of the Head and Skull to Capacity in the Two Sexes. *American Journal of Physical Anthropology* 8:249–250.

Hrdlicka, Ales
1939   *Practical Anthropometry.* Philadelphia: Wistar Institute of Anatomy and Biology.

Jones, Lisa
1991   Skin Trade: A Doll is Born. *Village Voice.* March 26, p.36.

Kahn, Alice
1991   A Onetime Bimbo Becomes a Muse. *New York Times.* September 29.

Kaw, Eugenia
1993   Medicalization of Racial Features: Asian American Women and Cosmetic Surgery. *Medical Anthropology Quarterly* 7(1):74–89.

Krause, Elizabeth
1998.   A Bead of Raw Sweat in a Field of Dainty Perspirers: Nationalism, Whiteness and the Olympic Ordeal of Tonya Harding. *Transforming Anthropology* 7 (1).

Lawson, Carol
1993   Toys will be Toys: The Stereotypes Unravel. *New York Times.* February 11. C1, C8.

Lord, M.G.
1994   *Forever Barbie: The Unauthorized Biography of a Real Doll.* New York: William Morrow.

May, Elaine Tyler
1988   *Homeward Bound: American Families in the Cold War Era.* New York: Basic Books.

Melosh, Barbara and Christina Simmons
1986   "Exhibiting Women's History." In, *Presenting the Past: Essays on History and the Public.* Susan Porter Benson, Stephen Brier, and Roy Rosenzweig eds. Philadelphia: Temple University Press.

Motz, Marilyn Ferris
1983   "'I Want to Be a Barbie Doll When I Grow Up': The Cultural Significance of the Barbie Doll." In, *The Popular Culture Reader*, 3rd ed. Christopher D. Geist and Jack Nachbar,

eds. pp. 122–136. Bowling Green: Bowling Green University Popular Press.

Newsweek
1990   Finally, Barbie Dolls Go Ethnic. *Newsweek* (August 13), p. 48.

Orgel, Mary, Jacqueline Urla and Alan Swedlund
In press. Surveying a Cultural Waist-land: Biological Poetics and Politics of the Female Body. In, *Anthropology United: Challenging Bio-Social Reductivisms.* Susan McKinnon and Sydel Silverman, eds. University of Chicago Press.

Rabinowitz, Paula
1993   Accessorizing History: Girls and Popular Culture. Discussant Comments, Panel #150: "Engendering Post-war Popular Culture in Britain and America. Ninth Berkshire Conference on the History of Women. Vassar College, June 11–13, 1993.

Rand, Erica
1994   "We Girls Can Do Anything, Right Barbie? Lesbian Consumption in Postmodern Circulation." In *Lesbian Postmodern*, ed. Laura Doan, pp. 189–209. New York: Columbia.

Rand, Erica
1995.   *Barbie's Queer Accessories.* Durham and London: Duke University Press.

Robertson, Josephine
1945   Theatre Cashier, 23, Wins Title of "Norma." *Cleveland Plain Dealer.* September 21, pp. 1, 4.

Russett, Cynthia Eagle
1989   *Sexual Science: The Victorian Construction of Womanhood.* Cambridge, MA: Harvard University Press.

Schiebinger, Londa
1989   *The Mind has no Sex: Women in the Origins of Modern Science.* Cambridge: Harvard University Press.

Schwartz, Hillel
1986   *Never Satisfied: A Cultural History of Diets, Fantasies and Fat.* New York: The Free Press.

Shapiro, Eben

1992   'Total Hot, Totally Cool.' Long-Haired Barbie is a Hit. *New York Times.* June 22. p. D-9.

Shapiro, Harry L.
1945   Americans: *Yesterday, Today, Tomorrow.* Man and Nature Publications. (Science Guide No. 126). New York: The American Museum of Natural History.

Spencer, Frank
1992   "Some Notes on the Attempt to Apply Photography to Anthropometry during the Second Half of the Nineteenth Century. In *Anthropology and Photography: 1860–1920.* Elizabeth Edwards, ed. pp. 99–107. New Haven, CT: Yale University Press.

Stevenson, Richard
1991   Mattel Thrives as Barbie Grows. *New York Times.* December 2.

Urla, Jacqueline and Alan Swedlund
1995.   "The Anthropometry of Barbie: Unsettling Ideals of the Feminine Body in Popular Culture." In *Deviant Bodies: Critical Perspectives on Difference in Science and Popular Culture.* J. Terry and J. Urla, eds. pp. 277–313. Bloomington: Indiana University Press.

Warner, Patricia Rosalind
1992   Letter to the Editor. *Boston Globe.* June 28.

Williams, Lena
1992   Woman's Image in a Mirror: Who Defines What She Sees? *New York Times.* February 6. A1; B7.

Willis, Susan
1991   *A Primer for Daily Life.* London and New York: Routledge.

Wilson, Elizabeth
1985   *Adorned in Dreams: Fashion and Modernity.* London: Virago.

Wiseman, C., Gray, J., Mosimann, J. and Ahrens, A.
1992   Cultural Expectations of Thinness in Women: An Update. *International Journal of Eating Disorders* 11 (1):85–89.

Wolf, Naomi
1991   *The Beauty Myth: How Images of Beauty are Used Against Women.* New York: William Morrow.

VII

Gender, Property, and the State

The relationship between sexual inequality, the emergence of class structures, and the rise of the state has been an enduring interest in anthropological studies of gender. The subordination of women appears to emerge as an aspect of state formation. According to Gailey (1987: 6), "Institutionalized gender hierarchy . . . is created historically with class relations and state formative processes, whether these emerge independently, through colonization, or indirectly through capital penetration." We are led to ask what relationship class and state formation have with the oppression of women and, when gender hierarchy occurs, why women are the dominated gender. How does the state have power to penetrate and reorganize the lives of its members, whether in Sumerian legal codes decreeing monogamy for women or in welfare laws in the United States that influence household composition? Eventually, studying state formation may help us understand the origins and interrelationships of class and patriarchy, and the social reproduction of inequality.

Much discussion of this subject has centered on Engels' book *The Origin of the Family, Private Property, and the State*, a nineteenth-century text in which Engels argues that the emergence of the concept of private property and its ownership by men, as well as the development of a monogamous family, led to the subordination of women. In Engels' scheme, prior to this, gender relations were egalitarian and complementary. All production was for use, and people worked together for the communal household. Thus, changes in gender relations were linked to changes in material conditions because the ownership of productive property (initially domestic animals) was concentrated in the hands of men. This thesis has been influential in many Marxist and feminist analyses of women's subordination. For example, Leacock notes, "There is sufficient evidence at hand to support in its broad outlines Engels' argument that the position of women relative to men deteriorated with the advent of class society" (1973: 30).

Following Engels, Leacock observes that in early communal society the division of labor between the sexes was reciprocal, and a wife and her children were not dependent on the husband. Further, "The distinction did not exist between a public world of men's work and a private world of women's household service. The large collective household was the community, and within it both sexes worked to produce the goods necessary for livelihood" (1973: 33). In this view the oppression of women was built on the transformation of goods for use into commodities for exchange; the exploitation of workers and of women was generated by this process, which involved the emergence of the individual family as an isolated unit, economically responsible for its members, and of women's labor as a private service in the context of the family. This led to the "world historical defeat of the female sex" (Engels 1973: 120; Silverblatt 1988: 430).

In a reanalysis of Engels, Sacks agrees that women's position declined with the elaboration of social classes but disputes Engels' emphasis on the role of private property in this process (Sacks 1982). Rather, Sacks links state formation and the decline in the centrality of kinship groups to the deterioration in women's status. She delineates two relationships defining women in noncapitalist societies: sisterhood and wifehood. "Sister" refers to women's access to resources based on membership in a kin group. This relation implies autonomy, adulthood, and possible gender symmetry. "Wife," on the other hand, refers to a relationship of dependency on the husband and his kin. Sacks suggests that the development of states undermined women's status by dismantling the kin group corporations that formed the basis for sister relations (Sacks 1982).

However, critics of Sacks' position have argued that the process of state formation may involve uneven and contradictory developments. For example, elite women in the Kingdom of Dahomey, West Africa, challenged state imperatives by means of control of marketing associations. Thus, Silverblatt rebuts Sacks' evolutionary paradigm, suggesting the inevitability of the decline in women's status with state formation; instead, she suggests that we acknowledge the complex history of the emergence of elite privilege in the rise of the state. In addition, elite women such as the royalty of Dahomey may or may not share the goals of peasant women. They may instead join with the male elite in suppressing the authority and power of peasant market women. This illustrates the potential contradictions of gender affiliation on one hand, and class position on the other.

Several anthropologists have observed that Engels lacked reliable ethnographic information and oversimplified the complexities of gender relations in kinship societies and in precapitalist states (Gailey 1987: 15). In a critique of Engels, Moore argues against his essentialist assumption that there is a "natural" division of labor in which men are concerned with productive tasks and women with domestic ones. She also disagrees that an inevitable relationship will transpire between property, paternity, and legitimacy, in which men "naturally" want to transmit property to genetic offspring (1988: 47–48).

While Rapp (in this book) agrees with these criticisms, she points out that Engels addresses many current concerns, such as the relationship between women's participation in production and female status, and the implications of the separation of the domestic-public domains for women's roles in society (see also Silverblatt 1988: 432). She warns against overgeneralizing when trying to understand the origins of the state and ignoring the history and context in which political formations change. In her view, we must examine kinship structures that were supplanted with the rise of the state and replaced by territorial and class-specific politics. Kinship domains, formerly autonomous, were subjugated to the demands of emergent elites with repercussions for gender roles and relations.

Among the processes that we need to examine are the politics of kinship, the intensification of military complexes, the impact of trade on social stratification, and the changing content and role of cosmology. For example, in stratified societies the establishment of long-distance trade and tribute systems may affect elite marriage patterns, leading to the emergence of dowry and the exchange of women to cement male political alliances. Similar alliances are forged in societies that have experienced a rise in militarism. When economies change and demand increases for a traded commodity, exploitation of labor to produce it may also increase, and marriage systems that expand trading relations may be solidified through the exchange of women. Women themselves may be important figures in trading networks, as in West Africa and in Mesoamerica, where women are active in the marketplace.

Alternatively, the extension of the state into localized communities can significantly influence gender roles and relations. This occurs, for example, by undermining women's ritual responsibilities or by generating conflict between government policy and the respective interests of men and women (see Browner, this book). Finally, changes in political hierarchies were legitimated by cosmological explanations in early states such as those of the Inca and the Maya. For example, as Maya society became increasingly stratified, a category of elite rulers known as *ahaw* emerged. These rulers were legitimized by myths that established them as mediators between the natural and supernatural worlds and as protectors of the people. State ideology involved the celebration of both male and female forces, and the elite contained both men and women. Mothers of kings were always members of the high elite, and this class affiliation was also validated in myth (Schele and Freidel 1990, Freidel and Guenter, this book).

Ortner examines the process of state formation, with particular regard to its effect on gender ideology (1978). She analyzes the widespread ideology that associates the purity of women with the honor and status of their families. This pattern is evident in Latin America and the Mediterranean, and in societies of the Middle East, India, and China. Broad similarities exist in these varied societies. Ortner questions why the control of female sexual purity is such a ubiquitous and important phenomenon. She notes that all modern cases of societies concerned with female purity occur in states or systems with highly developed stratification, and they bear the cultural ideologies and religions that were part of the emergence of these states. She argues that no prestate societies manifest the pattern linking female virginity and chastity to the social honor of the group. Thus, concern with the purity of women was, in Ortner's view, structurally, functionally, and symbolically linked to the historical emergence of state structures.

The rise of the state heralds a radical shift in ideology and practice, with the emergence of the patriarchal extended family in which the senior man has absolute authority over everyone in the household. Women are brought under direct control of men in their natal families and later by their husbands and affinal kin. Ideologically women are thought to be in danger, requiring male protection; they are idealized as mothers and for their purity.

One of the central questions in the analysis of the impact of state formation is the role of hypergamy (up-status marriage, usually between higher-status men and lower-status women). Ortner (1978) suggests that a significant development in stratified society involves the transformation of marriage from an essentially equal transaction to a potentially vertical one, where one's sister or daughter could presumably marry into a higher strata (wife of a nobleman, consort of a king). Hypergamy may help explain the ideal of female purity because concepts of purity and virginity may symbolize the value of a girl for a higher-status spouse. Thus "a virgin is an elite female among females, withheld, untouched, exclusive" (Ortner 1981: 32).

Hypergamous marriages often involve the exchange of significant amounts of property, particularly in the form of dowry. The relationship between dowry, inheritance, and female status has been explored in a number of societies with varying marriage patterns. Dowry has been described as a form of premortem inheritance, parallel to men's rights in property accrued through inheritance after death of parents or other legators. However, considering dowry as a form of inheritance prior to death and as part of a woman's property complex obscures an important difference between the clear legal inheritance rights that men possess and the dowry that women may or may not receive (McCreery 1976; see also Stone and James in this book). Women obtain dowry at the discretion of their parents or brothers, and dowry is not based on the same rights as other forms of inheritance to which men have access.

Although dowry has been viewed as a form of inheritance for women, the dowry system in northern India has taken a pernicious turn as brides are burned to death, poisoned, or otherwise "accidentally" killed by husbands and in-laws who believe that the women have brought inadequate dowries. Conservative estimates are that at least 2,000 women die each year as a result of dowry murders (Stone and James in this book). Legislation enacted in 1961 banning dowries, and in 1986 amending the penal code to introduce a new offense, now known as dowry death, has been ineffective, and the dowry system continues to be deeply embedded in local culture (Koman 1996). Although the bestowing of dowry in India is centuries old, dowry murders are a recent social problem. Stone and James argue that dowry deaths represent a response to a growing materialist consumerism sweeping India that has stimulated demands for larger and ever-increasing dowries. They analyze these murders in the context of a patrilineal and patrilocal society with strongly prescribed subservience of wives to husbands and in-laws, in which parents prefer to see a daughter dead, rather than divorced. Women's fertility, which may once have been a source of power, is increasingly less valued. Even a woman who gives birth to sons is not protected from the risk of wife-burning. Thus women's relative lack of economic power and the loss of their one traditional source of leverage, their fertility, have heightened their vulnerability to violence.

Although the status of Indian women as reflected in the exchange of property at marriage appears to be deteriorating, in other parts of the world women's legal status and property rights have improved through state-sponsored changes in the judicial system. For example, Starr (1984) examines how in Turkey the impact of capitalistic agriculture and settled village life profoundly affected gender relations and women's access to property. These changes occurred in the cultural context of Islamic notions of male dominance and female submission and legislation giving equal rights to women.

Ottoman family law gave women rights to divorce and some protection against polygamous marriage, but inheritance practices remained constrained by Islamic law, in which women were under the authority of their husbands, had the status of a minor, received half the share of the patrimony obtained by their brothers, and had no rights to children of a marriage. According to Ataturk's secular reforms in the 1920s, women's rights were expanded to full adult status, women received equal rights to paternal inheritance, protection was granted to widows, and other legislation was enacted promoting equality for women. At first these state-initiated rights were incongruent with cultural practices, but by the late 1960s women had begun to use the courts to protect their rights to property and their reputations. Starr points out that although Engels emphasized the negative impact of private ownership on women's status, in this case law and culture played a positive counterbalancing role resulting in women's emancipation.

In her cross-cultural exploration of the political experiences of contemporary women, Caldwell Ryan (in this book) illustrates the ways in which women engage, respond to, or resist the state. She notes that women's interaction with the state may take the shape of voting, seeking political office, participating in women's movements or other forms of collective action, or individual action in response to state policies. A global perspective on women's encounters with the state suggests that although some women have experienced an increase in formal political rights and "real" power, others have seen their gains eroded by such forces as religious fundamentalism and global economic crises. Major world religions including Christianity, Hinduism, and Islam have experienced an increase in religious fundamentalism in the last thirty years. Accordingly, Caldwell Ryan traces the impact of religious fundamentalism in Iran, Afghanistan, and India on the status of women in those countries. She shows that it is useful to consider the specific circumstances of national histories and identities rather than focusing solely on religious doctrine to analyze the impact of religious fundamentalism on women in particular states.

Similarly, global economic upheavals have negatively affected women's everyday lives as well as demonstrating their limited political power. Structural adjustment policies initiated by the World Bank and the International Monetary Fund, for example, have led to higher prices for food and a decline in public spending on health and social services, all leading to increased burdens for women, who have been forced to take on a greater responsibility for providing for their families in response to economic austerity measures. Caldwell Ryan's discussion underscores the links between women's political empowerment and economic autonomy. Ultimately, one catalyst for global gender equity is the emergent international feminist movement, which has succeeded in putting gender on the agenda of nearly every state. Thus such issues as girls' education, female labor, child custody, and women's inheritance and property rights have emerged as matters for national debate and political action.

If the state can shape family and gender relations directly through legislation such as that determining rights to property, it may also have more indirect impact. Allison (in this book) argues that in Japan, boxed lunches (obentō), prepared by mothers for their children, are invested with a gendered state ideology. The state manipulates the ideological and gendered meanings associated with the box lunch as an important component of nursery school culture. Nursery schools, under state supervision, not only socialize children and mothers into the gendered roles they are expected to assume but also introduce small children to the attitudes and structures of Japanese education. The obentō, elaborately and artistically arranged, is intended to allow the mother to produce something of home and family to accompany the child into this new and threatening outside world. Embedded in the school's close scrutiny of obentō production and consumption is a message to obey rules and accept the authority of the school, and by extension, of the state. The obentō's message is also that mothers sustain their children through food and support state ideology as well.

In all the works included in this chapter we see the enduring influence of the issues raised by Engels with regard to the relationship between gender, property rights, and state structures. However, cross-cultural data demonstrate that this relationship is much more complex and varied than Engels' original formulation. Equally, universal evolutionary paradigms that posit a uniform impact of the rise of the state on gender roles cannot do justice to the myriad ways in which specific cultural histories, diverse social hierarchies, and systems of stratification affect gender relations and ideology. Thus, Silverblatt (1988: 448) asks, "What of the challenges that women and men, caught in their society's contradictions, bring to the dominant order of chiefs and castes, an order they contour and subvert, even as they are contained by it? And what of the other voices, the voices that chiefs and rulers do not (or cannot or will not) express?" The complex histories of the relationship between any particular state and gender relations in it show that while state formation has contributed to the definition of womanhood, women have also contributed to the definition of states (Silverblatt 1988: 452).

REFERENCES

Engels, Frederick. 1973. *The Origin of the Family, Private Property and the State.* New York: International Publishers.

Gailey, Christine Ward. 1987. *Kinship to Kingship: Gender Hierarchy and State Formation in the Tongan Islands.* Austin: University of Texas Press.

Koman, Kathleen. 1996. "India's Burning Brides." *Harvard Magazine* 98 (3): 18–19.

Leacock, Eleanor Burke. 1973. "Introduction." In Frederick Engels (ed.). *The Origin of the Family, Private Property and the State,* pp. 7–57. New York: International Publishers.

McCreery, John L. 1976. "Women's Property Rights and Dowry in China and South Asia." *Ethnology* 15: 163–174.

Moore, Henrietta L. 1988. *Feminism and Anthropology.* Minneapolis: University of Minnesota Press.

Ortner, Sherry. 1978. "The Virgin and the State." *Feminist Studies* 4 (3): 19–35.

——— 1981. "Gender and Sexuality in Hierarchical Societies: The Case of Polynesia and Some Comparative Implications." In Sherry B. Ortner and Harriet Whitehead (eds.). *Sexual Meanings: The Cultural Construction of Gender and Sexuality,* pp. 359–410. Cambridge: Cambridge University Press.

Sacks, Karen. 1982. *Sisters and Wives: The Past and Future of Sexual Equality.* Urbana: University of Illinois Press.

Schele, Linda and David Freidel. 1990. *A Forest of Kings.* New York: William Morrow.

Silverblatt, Irene. 1988. "Women in States." *Annual Review of Anthropology* 17: 427–461.

Starr, June. 1984. "The Legal and Social Transformation of Rural Women in Aegean Turkey. In Renee Hirschon (ed.). *Women and Property: Women as Property.* New York: St. Martin's Press, Inc.

Thinking About Women and the Origin of the State

Rayna Rapp

While anthropologists vary widely in their assessment of the autonomy of women in prestate societies, there seems to be a general consensus that with the rise of civilization, women as a social category were increasingly subjugated to the male heads of their households (Gailey 1987; Leacock 1978; Rohrlich 1980; Sacks 1982; Sanday 1981; Silverblatt 1988). This consensus is based, implicitly or explicitly, on a formulation developed by Frederick Engels in *The Origin of the Family, Private Property, and the State.* Engels linked the growth of private productive property to the

Revised by the editors with the permission and approval of the author.

dismantling of a system of communal kinship that existed in prestate societies. In this process, he argued, marriage grows more restrictive, legitimacy of heirs more important, and wives generally become means of reproduction to their husbands. At the same time, reciprocal relations among kin are curtailed, unequal access to strategic productive resources gradually develops, and estates or classes arise out of formerly kin-based social organizations. In this analysis, the creation of a class hierarchy is intimately linked to the creation of the patriarchal family and to restrictions on women's autonomy.

Engels' analysis provides the foundation for many themes concerning women that are currently being investigated: the relation between the economic roles of women, their control of resources, and their social status; the relation between the mode of production and the mode of reproduction;[1] and the effects of the separation or merger of domestic and public spheres of activity on the lives of women.[2] However, a thesis central to Engels' analysis—the link between class oppression and gender oppression—has remained less well examined. Drawing on a growing body of theory and data concerning state formation that has been amassed in recent years by twentieth-century archaeologists,[3] this article examines Engels' theory about the relationship between the subjugation of women, social stratification, and the rise of the state.

Most of the early theoretical work on emergence of state society was reductive, and it often condensed a multiplicity of processes into overly simplistic models. These theories ranged from a concentration on the extraction of social surplus (surplus material resources or labor beyond that needed for subsistence) via increasing division of labor and more productive technology (Childe 1950, 1952); to a focus on the emergence of central political authority to administer irrigation-based societies (Wittfogel 1955, 1957); to the effects of population pressure and warfare within circumscribed environments (Carneiro 1970, Harner 1970).

All of these theories tend to see the state as an inevitable and efficient solution to a particular set of problems. They ignore the specific historical, political, and economic contexts in which societies change.[4] Finally, they underplay the importance of kinship as a domain within which resistance to state formation is situated.[5] Not uncoincidentally, it is within the kinship domain that women's subordination appears to occur.

In recent years, a new set of theoretical and systemic formulations that are more processual have been developed. Such formulations offer fascinating hints about the role of kinship structure, and possibly women, in stratification. Some of the processes examined in state formation—the politics of kinship, the changing content and role of religious systems, the intensification of military complexes, and the role of trade in stimulating or increasing social stratification—are most pertinent to our interests here. I will discuss each of these briefly, suggesting some of the lines of inquiry they direct us to pursue.

THE POLITICS OF KINSHIP

Many anthropologists have examined the internal tensions of ranked kinship systems (Kirchoff 1959; Sahlins 1958; Fried 1967). In highly ranked kinship systems, the role of women is of crucial importance. Women not only transmit status, but may be contenders for leadership positions, either directly or through their children. This seems to be the case in Polynesia and in parts of Africa. As Gailey (1987) shows for Tonga, the existence of elite, ranked women became more problematic as stratification increased.

We need to know more about marriage patterns in such systems. In archaeology, ethnology, and Western history, we find that elite marriages may be implicated in the politics of establishing and maintaining long-distance trade and tribute systems.[6] Dowry is associated with highly stratified systems and dowered, elite women may appear as pawns in a classic case of male alliances formed via their exchange.[7] Ortner (1978) suggests that in state-organized systems, marriage may shift from horizontal alliances between individuals of similar social and economic backgrounds to vertical alliances between individuals of different backgrounds. In the latter situation there is a marked tendency toward hypergamy whereby lower-status women marry upper-status men. Ortner links these structural properties of the marriage system with ideologies requiring sexual purity and the protection of women (but not of men).

Silverblatt (1987), in a study of the Inca elite, suggests that as the Incas extended their rule, they required conquered communities to send women to Cuzco to serve in the temples, courts, and as noblemen's wives. For the conquered communities, this practice represented a loss of autonomy in marriage patterns, and a burden. At the same time, it made possible upward mobility to the specific males who sent sisters and daughters to Cuzco. The women themselves gained a great deal of prestige, but lost any control they might have had in arranging their own marriages and living within their natal communities.

CHANGING COSMOLOGIES

Both Silverblatt and Ortner draw our attention to the relationship between women and the religious systems in early states. They remind us that religious systems were the glue that cemented social relations in archaic societies. Such systems were used, as in the Inca case, to underwrite and justify changes in political hierarchies.

Tension about female status is often found within these religious systems. Eliade (1960) claims that the ritual expression of sexual antagonism and the existence of bisexual and/or androgynous gods accompanies the social organizational changes associated with the neolithic period. Male gods are often superimposed on female and androgynous gods. Evidence for this layering over of female and/or androgynous figures comes from Mesoamerica (Nash 1980), Peru (Silverblatt 1987), and is, of course, a favorite theme of classicists for early Greek society (Arthur 1976; Pomeroy 1975).

Pagels (1976), working with second-century A.D. Gnostic texts, analyzes the symbol system of sects in which the early Christian god was bisexual, and the Holy Family consisted of mother, father, and son. Such sects were organized into non-hierarchical religious communities, in which offices were rotated, and women participated in both teaching and preaching—a far cry from the ascendant Christian cosmology and practice which became the mainstream tradition. Cosmological changes are ideological precipitates of structural tensions; it is clear that their form and content have a great deal to tell us about class and gender.

INTENSIFICATION OF WARFARE

As early states became increasingly militaristic, social organization was transformed.[8] Several case histories lead us to believe that under conditions of intense warfare, men were not only burdened by conscription, but were blessed with increasing power as household heads (Muller 1987; Rohrlich 1980). Elite males may gain land, political domains, and alliance-forming wives in the process. Yet, sweeping statements about male supremacy and warfare (Divale and Harris 1976) are overgeneralized, and some evidence seems to contradict the association of warfare and an elevation of male status at the expense of female autonomy.

In the ancient West, for example, the correlation often works the other way: Spartan women held offices, controlled their own property, and had a great deal of sexual freedom, allegedly because they kept society functioning while the men were at war. Moreover, producing soldiers was considered as important as training them. In Athens, women's access to public places and roles seems to have increased a great deal during times of warfare. In Rome, during the Second Punic War, women gained in inheritance settlements and held public offices formerly closed to them (Pomeroy 1975). In the medieval Franco-Germanic world, noblewomen attained approximate parity in politics and property-management during the years of the most brutal military crisis (McNamara and Wemple 1973).

All these examples concern elite women only; we know very little about the effects of warfare on laboring women, who probably suffered then, as they do now. Nonetheless, it is not clear that warfare degrades women's status; the specific context within which military organization and practice occurs must be taken into account. Blood and gore clearly are not universal variables in theorizing about women's subordination.

TRADE

The role of trade in increasing and/or spreading stratification is an intriguing one.[9] Foreign-trade goods may be spread in many ways: by middlemen, via migrations, through central trading centers, and in marriage exchanges, to name but a few. Several studies suggest that the social relationships that surround production and distribution, and which undergird trade, may generate class and gender inequality (Adams 1974; Kohl 1975; Wiley 1974; Gailey and Patterson 1987). We need to know who produces goods, who appropriates them, and who distributes them. As demand for a trade commodity increases, exploitation of labor to produce it may arise. Marriage systems may also be intensified to expand the reproduction of trading alliances. Certainly there are numerous ethnographic examples of polygyny as a means to increase access to goods that wives produce. There are also many instances of increasing class division linked to increasing bridewealth.

But the control, ownership, and distribution of valued resources after they are produced is not exclusively a male function. In Mesoamerica and the Andes, to this day, women are active in the marketplace. Silverblatt (1978) suggests that they were important traders in early Incan times. Adams (1966) records their existence in Mesopotamia. And of course, their presence is felt in stratified groups throughout Africa and the Caribbean as well (Mintz 1971). Under what conditions does long-distance trade pass into the hands of men, and when is it possible for women to continue to perform it? When women are traders, do they constitute an elite, class-stratified group? To the extent that trade is implicated in the intensification of produc-

tion for exchange, women as producers, reproducers, and traders must be implicated too.

CONCLUSION: COLONIALISM, CAPITALIST PENETRATION, AND THE "THIRD WORLD"

As we come to identify the factors in state formation as they affect women, we must be careful to think in probabilistic rather than deterministic terms. We need to better understand the relative power of kinship and class, the interplay of household and public economic functions, the flexibility within religious systems, and the relative autonomy or subordination of women, in light of the possibilities open to each society. We should expect to find variations within state-making (and unmaking) societies over time, and between such societies, rather than one simple pattern.

Nowhere is this more evident than in analysis of the process of rapid penetration by patriarchal national states into the so-called Third World. While the history of such penetration varies from place to place and must be taken into account, certain patterns affecting the ways of life of women can be traced at a general level. Wherever women have been active horticulturalists of collective lands, the imposition of private property, taxation, labor migration, and cash cropping has had devastating effects. Their realm of productivity and expertise has been deformed and often destroyed (Blumberg 1976; Boserup 1970; Tinker 1976). Depending upon context, they may become either super-exploited, or underemployed, but always more dependent upon men.

The evidence also suggests a general pattern concerning political organization. Prior to colonial penetration, gender relations in indigenous cultures appear to have been organized along essentially parallel and complementary lines. Men and women had distinct but equally significant roles in production, distribution, and ritual activities.[10] Case histories from Africa, Asia, and the Americas suggest that patriarchal, colonizing powers rather effectively dismantled native work organizations, political structures, and ritual contexts. Leadership and authority were assigned to male activities, while female tasks and roles were devalued or obliterated. The complementary and parallel gender relations that characterized indigenous societies were destroyed. Several authors have gone so far as to argue that women, thus divested of their social organization and collective roles, have become like underdeveloped, monocrop regions. Once they lived in a diversified world; now they have been reduced to the role of reproducing and exporting labor power for the needs of the international world economy (Bossen 1973; Boulding 1975; Deere 1976).

State formation and penetration occurs over time; its form and force are highly variable, both within and between societies. Yet it is important to remember that the processes which began millennia ago are ongoing. Cumulatively, they continue to transform the lives of the masses of people who exist under their structures. It is a long way from the Sumerian law codes declaring monogamy for women to the welfare laws of the United States which affect parental relations and household structure. But in both cases, the power of the state to penetrate and reorganize the lives of its members is clear. As we seek to understand the complex, stratified societies in which we now operate, we are led to reflect on archaic societies in which the dual and intertwined processes of hierarchy we now retrospectively label "class" and "patriarchy" took their origins.

NOTES

1. Productive activities are those that generate income in cash, or other valued resources. Reproduction refers, broadly, to the set of activities encompassing domestic chores and other household activities such as childbearing, childrearing, and cooking.
2. For analyses implicitly or explicitly influenced by Origins see Brown 1975; Meillassoux 1975; Reiter 1975; Rubin 1975; Sacks 1974; Sanday 1974.
3. Summaries of the state formation literature may be found in Flannery 1972; Krader 1968; Service 1975; Webb 1975.
4. A less determinant and more processual perspective on stratification and state formation is set forth in Flannery 1972; Sabloff and Lamberg-Karlovsky 1975; and Tilly 1975. Such thinking also informs the corpus of Marxist historiography.
5. This has been a major thrust in Stanley Diamond's work (1951, 1974).
6. Such links are suggested in Flannery 1972; Wiley and Shimkin 1971; and by much of the literature on stratified chiefdoms (Sahlins 1958; Kirchoff 1959; and Fried 1967). In European history, we find instances in the international royal marriage patterns. See McNamara and Wemple (1973) for some of the implications of feudal marriage patterns.
7. See Arthur 1976; Ortner 1978; Goody and Tambiah 1973.
8. The temple and military complexes figure in the state formation schemes of Adams 1966; Steward 1955; and Wiley 1974 to name but a few.
9. The archaeology of trade is discussed in Sabloff and Lamberg-Karlovsky 1975, and is critically summarized in Adams 1974 and Kohl 1975. See also Wiley 1974.
10. Parallel and interarticulating forms of gender social organization are analyzed by Brown 1970; Silverblatt 1978; Siskind 1978; and Van Allen 1972.

REFERENCES

Adams, R. M. 1966. *The Evolution of Urban Society.* Chicago. Aldine.

———. 1974. "Anthropological Perspectives on Ancient Trade." *Current Anthropology* 15: 239–258.

Arthur, M. 1976. "Liberated Women: The Classical Era." In R. Bridenthal and C. Koontz (eds.). *Becoming Visible: Women in European History.* New York: Houghton and Mifflin.

Blumberg, R. 1976. "Fairy Tales and Facts: Economy, Fertility, Family and the Female." Unpublished paper.

Boserup, E. 1970. *Women's Role in Economic Development.* London: George Allen and Unwin.

Bossen, L. 1973. "Women in Modernizing Societies." *American Ethnologist* 2: 587–601.

Boulding, E. 1975. *Women, Bread, and Babies.* University of Colorado, Institute of Behavioral Sciences, Program on Research of General Social and Economic Development.

Brown, J. 1970. "A Note on the Economic Division of Labor by Sex." *American Anthropologist* 72: 1073–1078.

Brown, J. 1975. "Iroquois Women." In R. Reiter (ed.). *Toward an Anthropology of Women.* New York: Monthly Review Press.

Carneiro, R. J. 1970. "A Theory of the Origin of the State." *Science* 169: 733–738.

Childe, G. 1950. "The Urban Revolution." *Town Planning Review* 21 (3): 3–17.

Childe, G. 1952. "The Birth of Civilization." *Past and Present* 2: 1–10.

Deere, C. 1976. "Rural Women's Subsistence Production in the Capitalist Periphery." *Review of Radical Political Economics* 8: 9–18.

Diamond, S. 1951. *Dahomey: A Protostate in West Africa.* Ann Arbor: University of Michigan Press.

Diamond, S. 1974. *In Search of the Primitive: A Critique of Civilization.* New Brunswick, NJ: Transaction Books.

Divale, W., and M. Harris. 1976. "Population Warfare and the Male Supremacist Complex." *American Anthropologist* 78: 521–538.

Eliade, M. 1960. "Structures and Changes in the History of Religions." In C. Kraeling and R. Adams (eds.). *City Invincible.* Chicago: University of Chicago Press.

Flannery, K. 1972. "The Cultural Evolution of Civilizations." *Annual Review of Ecology and Systematics* 3: 399–426.

Fried, M. 1960. "On the Evolution of Social Stratification and the State." In S. Diamond (ed.). *Culture and History.* New York: Columbia University Press.

———. 1967. *The Evolution of Political Society.* New York: Random House.

Gailey, Christine Ward. 1987. *Kinship to Kingship: Gender Hierarchy and State Formation in the Tongan Islands.* Austin: University of Texas Press.

Gailey, Christine Ward, and Thomas C. Patterson. 1987. "Power Relations and State Formation." In Thomas C. Patterson and Christine W. Gailey (eds.). *Power Relations and State Formation,* pp. 1–26. Washington, DC: American Anthropological Association.

Goody, J., and S. Tambiah. 1973. *Bridewealth and Dowry.* Cambridge: Cambridge University Press.

Harner, M. 1970. "Population Pressure and Social Evolution of Agriculturalists." *Southwestern Journal of Anthropology* 26: 67–86.

Kirchoff, P. 1959. "The Principles of Clanship in Human Society." In M. Fried (ed.). *Readings in Anthropology* (Vol. 2). New York: Thomas Crowell.

Kohl, P. 1975. "The Archaeology of Trade." *Dialectical Anthropology* 1: 43–50.

Krader, L. 1968. *Formation of the State.* Englewood Cliffs: Prentice Hall.

Leacock, Eleanor. 1978. "Women's Status in Egalitarian Society: Implications for Social Evolution." *Current Anthropology* 19: 247–275.

McNamara, J., and S. Wemple. 1973. "The Power of Women through the Family in Medieval Europe: 500–1100." *Feminist Studies* 1: 126–141.

Meillassoux, C. 1975. *Femmes, greniers et capitaux.* Paris: Maspero.

Mintz, S. 1971. "Men, Women and Trade." *Comparative Studies in Society and History* 13: 247–269.

Muller, Viana. 1987. "Kin Reproduction and Elite Accumulation in the Archaic States of Northwest Europe." In Thomas C. Patterson and Christine W. Gailey (eds.). *Power Relations and State Formation.* pp. 81–97. Washington, DC: American Anthropological Association.

Nash, J. 1980. "Aztec Women: The Transition from Status to Class in Empire and Colony." In M. Etienne and E. Leacock (eds.). *Women and Colonization.* New York: Praeger.

Ortner, S. 1978. "The Virgin and the State." *Feminist Studies* 4 (3): 19–35.

Pagels, E. 1976. "What Became of God the Mother? Conflicting Images of God in Early Christianity" *Signs* 2: 293–303.

Pomeroy, S. 1975. *Goddesses, Whores, Wives and Slaves.* New York: Schoken Books.

Reiter, R. 1975. "Men and Women in the South of France." In R. Reiter (ed.). *Toward an Anthropology of Women,* pp. 252–282 New York: Monthly Review Press.

Rohrlich, Ruby. 1980. "State Formation in Sumer and the Subjugation of Women." *Feminist Studies* 6: 76–102.

Rubin, G. 1975. "The Traffic in Women." In R. Reiter (ed.). *Toward an Anthropology of Women.* New York: Monthly Review Press.

Sabloff, J., and C.C. Lamberg-Karlovsky. 1975. *Ancient Civilizations and Trade.* Albuquerque: University of New Mexico Press.

Sacks, K. 1974. "Engels Revisited." In Michelle Rosaldo and Louise Lamphere (eds.). *Woman, Culture and Society,* pp. 207–222. Stanford: Stanford University Press.

———. 1982. *Sisters and Wives: The Past and Future of Sexual Equality.* Urbana: University of Illinois Press.

Sahlins, M. 1958. *Social Stratification in Polynesia.* Seattle: University of Washington Press.

Sanday, Peggy. 1974. "Toward a Theory of the Status of Women." In Michelle Rosaldo and Louise Lamphere (eds.). *Woman, Culture and Society,* pp. 189–206. Stanford: Stanford University Press.

———. 1981. *Female Power and Male Dominance: On the Origins of Sexual Inequality.* Cambridge: Cambridge University Press.

Service, E. 1975. *Origins of the State and Civilization.* New York: Norton.

Silverblatt, Irene. 1978. "Andean Women in Inca Society." *Feminist Studies* 4 (3): 37–61.

———. 1987. *Moon, Sun, and Witches: Gender Ideologies and Class in Inca and Colonial Peru.* Princeton: Princeton University Press.

———. 1988. "Women in States." *Annual Review of Anthropology* 17: 427–461.

Siskind, J. 1978. "Kinship and Mode of Production." *American Anthropologist* 80: 860–872.

Steward, J. 1955. *The Theory of Culture Change.* Urbana: University of Illinois Press.

Tilly, C. 1975. "Reflections on the History of European State-Making." In C. Tilly (ed.). *The Formation of National States in Western Europe.* Princeton: Princeton University Press.

Tinker, I. 1976. "The Adverse Impact of Development on Women." In I. Tinker and M. Bramsen (eds.). *Women and World Development.* Washington, DC: Overseas Development Council.

Van Allen, J. 1972. "Sitting on a Man: Colonialism and the Lost Political Institutions of Igbo Women." *Canadian Journal of African Studies* 6: 165–181.

Webb, M. 1975. "The Flag Follows Trade." In J. Sabloff and C.C. Lamberg-Karlovsky (eds.). *Ancient Civilizations and Trade.* Albuquerque: University of New Mexico Press.

Wiley, G., 1974. "Precolumbian Urbanism." In J. Sabloff and C.C. Lamberg-Karlovsky (eds.). *Ancient Civilizations and Trade.* Albuquerque: University of New Mexico Press.

Wiley, G. and D. Shimkin. 1971. "The Collapse of the Classic Maya Civilization in the Southern Lowlands." *Southwestern Journal of Anthropology* 27: 1–18.

Wittfogel, K. 1955. "Oriental Society in Transition." *Far Eastern Quarterly* 14: 469–478.

———. 1957. *Oriental Despotism.* New Haven: Yale University Press.

Dowry, Bride-Burning, and Female Power in India

Linda Stone and Caroline James

Over the last two decades, the reports from India have shocked the world: married women murdered (usually burned to death) by their husbands and/or in-laws over the issue of inadequate dowry. These recent incidents of bride-burning are a shocking example of the new forms of violence against women which are arising in modern, or modernizing, settings in many areas of the world. In India, these events are occurring alongside the growth of feminist organizations, the expansion of educational and economic opportunities for women, and some societal questioning of traditional gender roles.

Reprinted from *Women's Studies International Forum*, Vol 18, No 2, Stone and James, "Dowry, Bridge-Burning and Female Power in India," pp. 125–135, © 1995, with permission from Elsevier.

This article examines the bride-burning problem in India by looking at recent changes which have occurred not only with respect to dowry transactions, but also with respect to more traditional sources of female domestic power. It is not possible here to consider all of the complex factors which are contributing to the dowry murders in India, but we suggest, though necessarily tentatively, that along with the traditional lack of female control over family property and marriage arrangements, the problem may be further compounded by a new loss of female power in another important sphere, namely the power women could traditionally exercise through their fertility.

The article draws upon published accounts of bride-burning combined with material from interviews with a bride-burning survivor carried out by one of the authors (James). This case emerged not from research focused on bride-burning, but rather as part of a larger study of literacy programs in adult education centers in Madhya Pradesh. In this study James (1988) found that many of the women who came to the adult education centers were fleeing dowry harassment or attempted burnings. The case we present here was selected for the depth and detail of information provided by the woman involved.

Before examining dowry murders, we offer some comments on dowry in India to place the issue in a broader cross-cultural perspective.

DOWRY IN INDIA

One feature of dowry systems in general which applies strongly to India is their association with socioeconomic stratification and the concerns of kin groups with maintaining or enhancing social status through marriage. In an historical treatment of dowry, Goody (1971, 1973, 1976) argued that in Eurasia, in contrast to Africa, intensive plow agriculture created differential wealth, promoting divisions between status groups. It then became important to perpetuate these divisions over the generations to insure that control over property remained within the status group. This was achieved in part by instituting "status group endogamy" through the mechanism of dowry marriage. Thus, "status group endogamy"

> . . . is not simply a question of the absence of marriage between groups . . . but of matching like for like, or getting an even better bargain. And the usual mechanism by which this is achieved is the matching of property, often by means of the dowry. . . . (Goody, 1973, p. 593)

Dowry, then, goes hand-in hand with a class system and with maintenance of the superiority of higher groups over lower. Here marriages, at least among the upper classes, must be well-controlled and, by extension, so must courtship. The roles of matchmaker and chaperone become important in this Eurasian context, along with a high value placed on female

virginity at marriage (Goody, 1976, p. 17). Women must be endowed with property in order to attract husbands of equal or higher rank, and their sexuality must be controlled in order to limit ". . . the possibility of conflicting claims on the estate in which a woman has rights" (Goody, 1976, p. 14). Schlegel (1991) has more recently confirmed the strong association between dowry transactions and cultural concerns with female premarital virginity, which, she argues, helps to prevent lower class males from claiming wealth through impregnating higher class females. Ultimately the whole complex of cultural values centering on female "purity" and the notion that the honor of male kin groups rests on the seclusion and sexual purity of its women (see Mandelbaum, 1988) is related to the institution of dowry as an instrument in preserving and perpetuating socioeconomic classes. As we shall see, both the themes of social status and female chastity recur through accounts of dowry murders.

There is, however, another common idea about dowry systems which does not apply well in India. This is the idea that dowry is a form of female property or wealth. Thus, Goody (1973) and others (e.g., Tambiah, 1973) have seen Eurasian dowry universally as "female inheritance"—women receive a portion of the family estate at marriage, rather than upon the death of the father or mother. This portion they receive as movable property rather than land which is left to sons. But many working in India, such as Miller (1981) and Sharma (1984), have convincingly shown that whereas this may be true in many areas of the world, in India dowry is property which passes from the bride's family to that of the groom, and that even if perceived to be "women's property" (*stridhan*) by some Indians themselves, in fact a bride does not have (and historically never had) genuine control over the use and distribution of this property. Women in the Indian dowry system should be seen as vehicles of property transmission rather than as true inheritors.

Madhu Kishwar (1986), who has written several articles on dowry for the Indian feminist magazine *Manushi*, has argued that Indian dowry effectively functions to disinherit women and promote their economic dependency on men, which in her view is the real crux of the modern problem of dowry murders. Although current law permits daughters to inherit from the father's estate, more often women are upon marriage made to sign over these rights to their brothers. As for the dowry itself, Kishwar (1986) writes:

> In actuality, a woman is seldom allowed to have control even over things that are supposedly for her personal use. Gold and other jewelry are traditionally supposed to be a woman's personal security, but, in practice, the gold usually stays in the custody of her mother-in-law or husband. It is up to them to give her what they wish for her personal use and daily wear . . . It is fairly common for certain items of her jewelry to be incorporated into her husband's sister's dowry. (pp. 6–7)

Moreover, Kishwar points out that were the point of Indian dowry to provide a daughter with some financial security, parents would give her productive assets such as land or a shop, rather than clothing and household goods, which depreciate in value.

Defining dowry as female inheritance, Goody (1976) saw it as a kind of economic "gain" for women. But the irony, to him, was that the system also entails a "loss" of women's control over their marriages or their sexual behavior:

> The positive control of marriage arrangements . . . is stricter where property is transmitted to women. It is a commentary on their lot that where they are more propertied they are initially less free as far as marital arrangements go. (Goody, 1976, p. 21)

But in the Indian context, it would appear that women lose on all counts. This context (and the whole question of sources, or lack of sources, of female power) is important to bear in mind in any discussion of dowry murders. In India dowry not only serves to promote status group endogamy (hypergamy) to maintain a class system, but it is now actively manipulated to serve new ends of status-seeking among individual families. In this modern context, women as vehicles of property transmission not only lack control over both property and marriage arrangements, as was largely the case previously, but may in fact suffer considerable harassment, physical abuse, and even murder in connection with their roles as bringers of dowry.

DOWRY MURDERS

From what is known about dowry deaths, it is possible to see some patterns, although exceptions exist in every case. They appear to be largely, though not exclusively, occurring in Northwest India, and they are largely, though no longer exclusively, among Hindu groups. They occur most often in cases of arranged marriages (the most common form of marriage in India) but have occurred in cases of a "love match," and they occur predominantly among the urban middle-class (Kumari, 1989; van Willigen & Channa, 1991). It is difficult to know how widespread the problem is, but most conservative estimates are that at least 2000 women are victims of dowry deaths per year in India (Chhabra, 1986, pp. 12–13). The area showing the greatest problem is New Delhi, with an estimated two dowry deaths per day (Bordewich, 1986, p. 21). The number of reported cases increases yearly. It is not known to what extent the increase reflects an increase in reporting rather than an increase in the crime. However, it may be that the crime is still underreported since the number of hospital cases of severe burns in young married women exceeds reports of violence against women by burning (Kumari, 1989, p. 24).

The preponderance of cases of bride-burning in North India is significant. This is also the area in which Miller (1981) finds significantly more males than females in juvenile age groups. This she attributes to neglect of female children, who are an economic liability relative to males. In the Northern region, too, dowry marriages are more common. The expense of providing dowry for daughters is one reason which Miller finds for the relatively intense preference for sons and relative neglect of female children in the North.

Sharma suggests that North Indian dowry has dramatically inflated as India has shifted to a market, cash economy over the last 50 years: ". . . dowry used to be more or less conventionally determined and many items could be made in whole or part by members of the bride's family themselves (e.g. rugs, clothing, bedding)" (Sharma, 1984, p. 70). But now, especially among the urban middle classes, expectations of televisions, motor scooters, refrigerators, large sums of cash, and so on are usual. Many observers related modern dowry and dowry deaths to the frustration of the urban middle class, caught in a new consumerism, status-seeking, and rising expectations of a life style they cannot on their own earning power quite afford (Bordewich, 1986, pp. 24–25).

Sharma's (1984) work on dowry has also cleared up one confusion, namely how it is that marriageable women appear to be in great supply (everyone is anxious to marry off a daughter and even accused dowry murderers manage to secure new brides!) even though there are far more males than females in the marriageable age groups in the North. Hypergamy (marriage of women upward into higher status groups) was traditionally common in the North and with modern dowry is becoming more so. In addition, lessening of caste restrictions in modern marriages promotes more hypergamous competition. Dowry givers are thus competing upwards for scarce grooms at the top (Sharma, 1984, p. 72).

Dowry and dowry murders continue despite the fact that dowry transactions have been illegal in India since the Dowry Prohibition Act of 1961.[1] As a result of pressure by women's organizations, subsequent amendments to the Act have even strengthened the laws against dowry and dowry harassment (Ghadially & Kumar, 1988, pp. 175–176). However, what is actually dowry can be legally claimed as "voluntary gifts" at marriage. Dowry persists not only because the law is ineffective or difficult to enforce, nor because of the pressures and demands of the groom's family, but also because the families of brides, in spite of growing public awareness of the tragic consequences, continue to give dowry. This may be due to concerns that otherwise a daughter could not be married at all (universally considered an undesirable event in India), or that the family could not secure an appropriate match. Also, parents of the bride may continue to believe that a lavish dowry will help to secure their daughter's favorable treatment in her in-laws' home, after which they may "yield to extortion out of fear for their daughter's safety . . . " (Bordewich, 1986, p. 24). Stein (1988) reports that many Indian women "still believe . . . that not only can dowry be used to overcome disadvantages in the marriage market, such as dark skin color, but it gives them dignity and status" (p. 485).

From the reported cases of dowry murders, it appears that the difficulties usually start early in the marriage. A new bride is harassed and criticized for the pitiful dowry she has brought. She is encouraged to wrangle more and more from her family, yet her in-laws remain unsatisfied until, at some point, the situation explodes into an attempt on her life. One woman ("Sita") whose husband attempted to burn her, reported the following:

> I got married when I was 23 years old to a person whose family was not as wealthy as our family. My father [a businessman] gave $8,000 cash as dowry. [He] gave me expensive clothes like 500 saris, 10 golden jewelry sets and one diamond set, all the pots and pans necessary for the house, a television set, wardrobe, freezer, cooler fan, double bed, furniture and other things he thought would be useful in the house. More than that, he used to send things from time to time, like on festivals. One year of my marriage has not passed when my in-laws and husband started giving me trouble every day for more dowry. My mother-in-law started telling my husband, "Leave this woman and we will get you another one, at least the other party will give us more and better dowry than what these people have given us. What her parents have given us is nothing. Moreover, this girl is ugly and she is dark."

Sita's reference to the relative wealth of her family and her detailed description of her lavish dowry appear to reinforce the same materialistic values which evidently lie behind dowry harassment and murders. Later she spoke with bitter resentment about her husband's new wife who "... is using all my things, like all my expensive saris, jewelry and other things." Her account also suggests a blatant economic motive for dowry murder—that it frees the woman's in-laws to get a new bride and an additional dowry. A similar idea reported in an article by Bordewich (1986) is expressed by the father of an allegedly murdered bride:

> ... as soon as we agreed on the marriage they started troubling us. First they told us to buy diamond rings instead of mere gold ones ... Then they insisted on a sofa bed for fifteen thousand rupees, but I could only afford one that cost seven thousand. Whatever was in my means I did, but they were always displeased ... they demanded a stereo and tape-cassette system, and then they asked for saris for the boy's sisters ... and then for a gas stove. I gave them ... I had read that there were so many tortures and murders of young women over dowry and I was afraid of what might happen to [my daughter]. I told them I would pay whatever I could ... But they didn't even wait for the money to come. They probably realized they had gotten all they could from us. A few days later [my daughter] was dead ... There has never been an investigation ... Now they can marry their son to another girl and get another dowry. (p. 25)

The most common means of murder is soaking the bride in kerosene and setting her aflame, with a report to the police of a suicide or an accident in the kitchen. Sita describes how this was attempted on her:

> [The winter my son was born] my mother-in-law started telling me not to wear so much gold jewelry at home, to remove it at night and keep it in the wardrobe. I did not understand why she was telling me this when she had not done so before. But I did what she asked. [Then] one evening my husband went into the kitchen and asked for a match box. My mother-in-law's sister-in-law gave him a match box which my husband then kept in the wardrobe very close to our bed. Then he left the house, saying he would be coming in late that night. That same evening, the electricity went off and my mother-in-law's

sister-in-law came to get the match box to light a lamp. She found the match box in the wardrobe and took it. My husband came in very late that night when my son and I were sound asleep. Due to the cold, I had pulled the covers up over our heads. Suddenly I felt that the quilt was wet and cold, but I thought it was just due to being cold at night. But when I removed the quilt from my face, there was a strong smell of kerosene. I got up quickly and saw my husband getting into bed and covering himself, pretending he was sound asleep ... he had been looking for the match box which he could not find. You can imagine that if he could have found the match box, my son and I would not have survived. We would have been burned to ashes.

One theme recurrent in many dowry murder cases is the issue of the bride's "reputation" and sexual "purity," which, as we saw in Goody's (1976) discussions of dowry, serves as a link between the institution of dowry, family concerns with status, and the perpetuation of socioeconomic classes. With respect to this issue, a woman facing dowry harassment is truly vulnerable as any suggestion of her "loose" character is an easy defense for her husband or in-laws. In the case above Sita reports that after fleeing from the bed,

> I started crying loudly, then my husband and mother-in-law came and started telling me to leave the house. I told them I would not step out of the house until my parents came, because if I would have left the house, they would have told the police and everybody that I was the one who wanted to leave the husband and the house, that it was my fault and not anyone else's in the family. They would have cooked up another story that I am a bad character and that that is why I left the house at that hour of the night (3:00 a.m.).

In a dowry murder case discussed by Kumari (1989), the husband accused of burning his young wife claimed that she had committed suicide because she could not forget her own "murky past" involving previous sexual activity (p. 64). Similarly, in newspaper accounts of dowry deaths it is common to find some innuendo of lapsed sexual behavior on the part of the victim.[2] Also illustrative is the following account, taken down by Bordewich (1986), from a woman who virtually sees a dowry murder:

> . . . In the house across the street we could see a man beating his wife. I went out onto the balcony and saw that the neighbors had gathered in the street to watch . . . A moment later I heard a scream . . . and there in front of me was the woman, burning in the window. She tried to wrap herself in the curtains, but they went up in flames. I ran into the street, but none of the neighbors seemed disturbed. People were saying it was "just a domestic issue" or that the woman must have had "a loose moral character." The woman died soon afterward in the hospital. The husband was never charged. (p. 26)

Dowry, Fertility, and Female Power

Dowry murders must be viewed within the context of Indian culture, which is characterized by patrilineal descent, patrilocality, the joint family, and strongly prescribed subservience of wives to husbands and in-laws. In both the popular press and scholarly literature, discussions of dowry murders incorporate these and other elements of Indian cultural traditions and women's roles within them. Certainly the association of death, fire, and female chastity or purity has caught the attention of writers who have drawn parallels between modern bride-burning and the ancient upper caste custom of *sati*, or the burning of a widow alive on her husband's funeral pyre. This was considered a (theoretically self-willed) act of great religious merit, only to be performed by a chaste wife in a state of ritual purity (Stein, 1988, p. 464). Again, in Hindu mythology, Sita must prove her chastity to her husband, Rama, through passing unburned through fire, and in another myth Sati Devi proves her loyalty to her husband, Shiva, by leaping to her death into the ceremonial fire of her father who insulted him.

Whatever deeper meaning all this may have within the Indian consciousness, Stein (1988) rightly points out that both the ancient sati and modern bride-burning reflect one clear fact of Indian life: the unacceptability of the unmarried adult woman. Thus sati was a way to dispose of the widow, who in earlier times among high castes, could not remarry, but who could, if alive, remain in society as a threatening, uncontrolled sexual woman. In the modern context, the existence of an unmarried adult daughter, with all the same connotations of uncontrolled, dangerous sexuality, brings shame and dishonor to her parents whose duty it is to marry her off, and who receive religious merit for doing so. So great is the pressure to marry the daughter (and keep her married, a divorced woman being equally unacceptable and threatening in Indian society) that a woman's parents remain in a weak and vulnerable position with respect to dowry harassment. Stein (1988) concludes:

> . . . marriage is still seen as the only way in which Indian women can be part of their own society, can function as social beings, even at the expense of their own personalities, and occasionally their lives. (p. 485)

The situation is compounded by another deep-rooted Indian tradition: the religious and social inferiority of the bride's family to that of the groom. In Hindu tradition a bride is a religious gift (*kanyadan*, gift of the virgin) and, as such, can only be given upward to those of higher rank, those to whom one must show perpetual deference and respect. The inferior and subservient position of a wife to her husband is on another level shared by the family who gives her. Thus "the subordination and frequently oppressed position of the daughter-in-law is exacerbated by the exclusion and deference of her own kin" (Stein, 1988, p. 476).

Kishwar (1986) also refers to these relationships in her discussions of dowry deaths, highlighting the powerless position of a bride and her parents. For her, dowry harassment is but one of many techniques by which a groom and his family can humiliate a bride to "accept a subordinate position within the family and feel grateful for being allowed to survive at all in the marital home" (p. 4). She also affirms that marriage of the daughter and dowry are matters of status and family honor, so that ". . . most parents would rather see their daughters dead than have them get a divorce and return permanently to the parental home" (p. 5).

Chhabra (1986), noting the many cases of dowry deaths which involve the mother-in-law, discusses the role of the traditionally problematic relationship between a woman and her daughter-in-law in India in terms of modern dowry harassment. Participating in or encouraging dowry harassment is the mother-in-law's way of rejecting the new bride, whom she perceives as a threat to her son's support and loyalty to herself (pp. 6–10).

All of these sociocultural factors and many more are fundamental to accounting for dowry deaths and, along with the inability of police and the courts to alleviate the problem, go a long way toward explaining why these deaths persist. However, most of these cultural traditions, which have in various ways, degrees, and combinations deeply shaped Indian women's lives, have been around for centuries, whereas dowry murders are apparently quite new, becoming a recognized social issue in India in the 1970s (Kumari, 1989). The concept of "dowry death" was only legally established in India in the 1980s (van Willigen & Channa, 1991, p. 371).

What has changed in Indian society to bring about this form of violence against women? Along with the new socioeconomic issues already referred to, it is important to ask also whether women in this modern context have lost sources of power which previously gave them some leverage. Despite all the constraints on women and the general sense of powerlessness which any account of the traditional Hindu woman's life will give, it was still the case that a new bride did not endlessly suffer ill-treatment from and subservience to in-laws, but gradually transformed herself from lowly bride to respected mother, perhaps eventually to become a powerful mother-in-law herself.[3] Regardless of however lowly the position of the affinal women in this strongly patrilineal society, she was, at worst, a necessary evil since she alone held the power to reproduce the husband's lineage. In a more traditional scenario, the adept Hindu woman tried to please her husband not only to express a culturally required subservience but also in order to become pregnant, as this would ultimately be her way out of misery and toward a rising status within the husband's household. With each sign of successful fertility, and particularly with the birth of sons, her position improved. As with many areas of Asia, sons were desired to continue the patrilineage, serve as heirs, perform important funeral rituals for parents, and to provide security in old age. Economically they contributed to home-based production or could bring in cash income.

A woman's fertility was the key to what can be considered a "great transition" in her status and identity. Summarizing this for the whole of India, Mandelbaum (1970) wrote of the bride that

> . . . the real relief comes when she becomes pregnant. Her mother-in-law can afford to relax a bit in her role as taskmistress; her husband is pleased; the men of the household are glad; there is an awakened interest in seeing that she eats well and rests easily. This first burgeoning also marks her first upward move in the family status hierarchy. . . .[then with childbirth] She is no longer the lowly probationer she was at first. If the child is a son, she has proved herself in the most important way of all and her confidence is the more secure. The son is her social redeemer and thenceforth her importance in the family tends gradually to increase. (pp. 88–89)

Raising this issue shifts the focus somewhat away from dowry, over which women evidently never had much control, and toward other sources of female power which may be changing, at least among the urban middle classes of the North. In a sense, female fertility, or the high value placed on women's successful reproduction, may have served as a "safety valve" for women in the past. But once this fertility value diminishes, women's position is indeed insecure. One startling feature of the dowry murder cases is the high number of women murdered who had already produced children, even sons. In one study 36% of the dowry murder cases involved women who had already produced children; another 11% of the women were pregnant at the time of death (Ghadially & Kumar, 1988, p. 168). Although she does not give numbers, Stein (1988) notes of dowry murder victims that ". . . a surprising number of them are pregnant when they die" (pp. 474–475).

Even victims of dowry harassment seem surprised to realize that childbirth and particularly the birth of a son does not alleviate their situation. Sita, in the case discussed earlier, remarked that after being harassed over dowry, "I gave birth to a male child. [But even with this] they did not want to keep me or the child either. They cared only for the dowry." Similarly in the case of Suman, described in the Indian feminist magazine Manushi, it was reported that

> . . . [The husband's] maltreatment of Suman continued to escalate. He pawned all her jewelry. Even the birth of her son did not improve the situation. When the son was a year old, Suman was once more beaten and thrown out of the house in the hope of pressuring her parents to give more dowry. (Kishwar, 1986, p. 8)

Demographic data from India supports the suggestion that the country's traditional strong value on high fertility may be changing. Fertility rates are declining and have been since the mid-1960s. An analysis of the 1981 census produced the following report:

> India, the second most populous country in the world, is experiencing the early stages of fertility transition. The unprecedented acceleration in the rate of growth of India's population, sparked off by declining mortality as early as 1921, has finally been arrested . . . It is beyond doubt that a significant contribution to this phenomenon lately has been from declining fertility, of which there is ample cumulative evidence. (Rele, 1987, p. 513)

One reason for the decline is undoubtedly urbanization, which tends to dampen fertility since the "cost" of children increases while their economic benefits decline. The above report also shows that the pace of decline is accelerating and that although the decline is occurring in both rural and urban

areas, urban fertility remains much lower than rural fertility. Other studies show that fertility rates are lower and declining faster among wealthier and more educated groups (Goyal, 1989). Along with fertility declines, some studies show declines in desired number of children, again most notable among urban, educated, and wealthier groups (Jejeebhoy & Kulkarni, 1989).

Could it be that changes in fertility values are taking place and that, however advantageous this may be for India's population problems, it may be a contributing factor to dowry murders? Demonstrating a significant change in fertility values (beyond merely showing a decline in fertility levels) and a definite connection with dowry murders would, of course, require much further research. Nevertheless, our inquiry into dowry murders, and discussion of the problem within the context of more traditional ways in which women acquired some domestic leverage, is suggestive. Previously through much of India a large joint family and the production of many sons was itself a source of prestige. Through successful reproduction, women could gain respect and greater security in the husband's household. In today's context, children and grandchildren, though undoubtedly still desired for all the same cultural reasons as before, become economically less important. At the same time a new urban consumerism and concern with material displays of wealth is widely reported in India and is directly referred to in all studies of dowry deaths. We suggest that insofar as these shifts in values may be occurring, they may diminish the domestic leverage women once exercised through reproduction.

WOMEN IN PRODUCTION AND REPRODUCTION

In his study of dowry systems, Goody (1976) incorporated the work of Boserup (1970), who distinguished systems of "female farming" (shifting cultivation), where women perform the major part of agricultural work, from "male farming" (plow agriculture) where male labor predominates. The latter is associated with private land ownership, a landless class of laborers, and dowry, as opposed to bridewealth marriages. Boserup saw the development of male farming in Asia, and the later shift to male farming in Africa, as detrimental to women since the diminution of their roles in production increased their economic and social marginalization.[4]

Boserup (1970) made the important point that in regions of female farming, women are valued both as workers and as child bearers, whereas in systems of male farming, they are valued as mothers only (p. 51). Applying these ideas to modern, urban India (where the valued economic activity is income-earning), it appears that a new problem facing women, at least among the middle classes, may be that women lack value, and therefore power, either as workers or as mothers. Of course middle class Indian women can and do make important contributions to household income, increasingly so in the modern context. But, as Sharma (1984) points out, we need to look at women's work in relation to the proportion of their economic potential relative to that of men:

> It might be possible to show that the expansion of dowry has been accompanied by a decline in women's capacity to contribute household income compared with that of men, even though there has been no absolute diminution of women's economic activity. New opportunities to earn cash wages in factories, in government employment and white collar occupations have expanded far more rapidly for men than for women . . . . (pp. 67–68)

Boserup's critics (Beneria & Sen, 1981) claim that one problem with her analysis is that she ignored women's roles in reproduction. Their point is that women's reproductive roles in many cases hinder their full or equal participation in wage labor or other socially valued economic activities, whereas Boserup laid the blame on sexually biased cultural values and changes in technology. In fact, however, Boserup did address women's roles in reproduction, though not quite in the way her critics would have liked to have seen. Writing before 1970, she seems to have foreseen that changes in fertility values could occur and could negatively impact women. Speaking in general of societies with male farming systems, where women have been devalued as workers but are still valued as mothers, she wrote: "There is a danger in such a community that the propaganda for birth control, if successful, may further lower the status of women both in the eyes of men and in their own eyes" (Boserup, 1970, p. 51). Whereas it is unlikely that "propaganda for birth control" alone would have this effect, it may be that in India, urbanization and the growth of the consumer economy are bringing about the same result.

CONCLUSION

Many observers of the problem of dowry murders in India have contributed to showing a powerful link between this form of violence against women and women's relative lack of economic power. With the urbanization and consumerism characterizing India today, women have not shared in access to new economic opportunities with men. We suggest that at the same time, their one traditional source of leverage, their fertility, has possibly diminished in value. Regrettably, women are valued for the dowry they will bring; but so long as their valuation rests primarily in their being vehicles of property transmission, they will remain vulnerable to dowry harassment and murder.

NOTES

1. In India there has been a long history of anti-dowry movements, and only recently have they concerned dowry harassment and murder issues. For discussion see Kumari (1989).
2. This observation was made by Frank Myka (personal communication) in his review of cases of dowry murders in the Hindustan Times during 1989.

3. For discussion of these aspects of women's lives in Hindu Nepal see Bennett (1983).
4. Boserup's work was an early contribution to what has become a vast literature that links female subordination to women's roles in production and women's access to property. Many of the arguments put forth in this line of research follow, with modification, Engels' (1884) treatise on the origin of the family. Important current studies can be found in Leacock and Safa (1986). Modern studies have in general emphasized that both the development of the world capitalist system and international development projects in the Third World have had adverse consequences for women. Today, different positions are taken within this framework. For a review of the literature see Tiano (1987).

REFERENCES

Beneria, Lourdes, and Sen, Gita. (1981). "Accumulation, Reproduction, and Women's Role in Economic Development: Boserup Revisited." *Signs*, 7, 279–298.

Bennett, Lynn. (1983). *Dangerous Wives and Sacred Sisters: Social and Religious Roles of High Caste Women in Nepal.* New York: Columbia University Press.

Bordewich, Fergus M. (1986). "Dowry Murders." *Atlantic Magazine,* July, pp. 21–27.

Boserup, Ester. (1970). *Women's Role in Economic Development.* London: George Allen & Unwin, Ltd.

Chhabra, Sagari. (1986). *Dowry Deaths in India: A Double Bind Perspective.* Unpublished master's thesis, Washington State University, Pullman.

Engels, Fredrich. (1884). *The Origin of the Family, Private Property, and the State.* New York: International.

Ghadially, Rehana, and Kumar, Promod. (1988). "Bride-burning: The Psycho-Social Dynamics of Dowry Deaths." In Rehana Ghadially (Ed.), *Women in Indian Society* (pp. 167–177). New Delhi: Sage Publications.

Goody, Jack. (1971). "Class and Marriage in Africa and Eurasia." *American Journal of Sociology.* 76, 585–603.

———. (1973). "Bridewealth and Dowry in Africa and Eurasia." Jack Goody and S. J. Tambiah (Eds.), *Bridewealth and Dowry* (pp. 1–58). Cambridge: Cambridge University Press.

———, Jack. (1976). *Production and Reproduction.* Cambridge: Cambridge University Press.

Goyal, R. S. (1989). "Social Inequalities and Fertility Behavior." In S. N. Singh, M. K. Premi, P.S. Bhatia, and Ashish Bose (Eds.), *Population Transition in India* (Vol. 2, pp. 153–161). New Delhi: B. R. Publishing Corporation.

James, Caroline. (1988). *People and Projects in Development Anthropology: A Literacy Project in Madhya Pradesh, India.* Unpublished Ph.D. dissertation, Washington State University, Pullman.

Jejeebhoy, Shireen J., and Sumati Kulkami. (1989). "Demand for Children and Reproductive Motivation: Empirical Observations from Rural Maharashtra." In Singh, M. K. Premi, P. S. Bhatia, and Ashish Bose (Eds.), *Population Transition in India* (Vol. 2; pp. 107–121). New Delhi: B. R. Publishing Corporation.

Kishwar, Madhu. (1986). Dowry: "To Ensure Her Happiness or to Disinherit her?" *Manushi*, 34, 2–13.

Kumari, Rajana. (1989). *Brides are Not for Burning: Dowry Victims in India.* London: Sangam Books Ltd.

Leacock, Eleanor, Safa, Helen, and contributors. (1986*). Women's Work, Development and the Division of Labor by Gender.* Boston: Bergin and Garvey Publishers, Inc.

Mandelbaum, David, (1970). "Society in India," Vol 1: *Continuity and Change.* Berkeley: University of California Press.

———, (1988). *Women's Seclusion and Men's Honor.* Tucson: University of Arizona Press.

Miller, Barbara. (1981). *The Endangered Sex.* Ithaca: Cornell University Press.

Rele, J. R. (1987). "Fertility Levels and Trends in India." *Population and Development Review*, 13, 513–530.

Schlegel, Alice. (1991). "Status, Property and the Value on Virginity." *American Ethnologist*, 18, 719–734.

Sharma, Ursula. (1984). "Dowry in North India: Its Consequences for Women." In Renee Hirschon (Ed.). *Women and Property—Women as Property* (pp. 62–73). New York: St. Martin's Press.

Stein, Dorothy. (1988). "Burning Widows, Burning Brides: The Perils of Daughterhood in India." *Pacific Affairs*, 61, 465–485.

Tambiah, S. J. (1973). "Dowry and Bridewealth and the Property Rights of Women in South Asia." In Jack Goody and S. J. Tambiah (Eds.), *Bridewealth and Dowry* (pp. 59–169). Cambridge, MA: Cambridge University Press.

Tiano, Susan. (1987). "Gender, Work and World Capitalism: Third World Women's Role in

Development." In Beth B. Hess and Myra Marx Ferree (Eds.), *Analyzing Gender: A Handbook of Social Science Research* (pp. 216–243) Newbury Park: Sage Publications.

van Willigen, John, and V.C. Channa, (1991). "Law, Custom, and Crimes Against Women: The Problem of Dowry Death in India." *Human Organization*, 50, 369–376.

Encountering the State: Cross-Cultural Perspectives on Women's Political Experience

Josephine Caldwell Ryan

In 1987, a Kenyan woman named Wambui Otieno became involved in a protracted legal battle that pitted her against her husband's family (Nzomo 1997, Nzomo and Staudt 1994). Otieno, a Christian Kikuyu, had married a Luo man who, suspecting that his family might attempt to dispossess his wife after his death, had asked to be buried on his farm near Nairobi. The case was decided in favor of Otieno's husband's relatives, and he was buried in his natal village instead. The case had clear implications for women's rights in customary law, a fact that was not lost on Otieno. According to the Washington Post she "warned Kenyan women that if she did not have the right to bury her husband, then they may not have the right to inherit their husband's property" (May 25, 1987, cited in Nzomo 1997:242).

In Wambui Otieno's case, she did retain control over property rights, but this is not always the outcome. In sub-Saharan African countries with plural legal systems, disputes may be settled in courts of statutory law, customary law, and in some cases, Islamic law. Zambia, for example, has a dual legal system in which both customary law and statutory laws apply to inheritance. Statutory law, which gives more consideration to women's inheritance rights, is frequently ignored in favor of customary law that privileges male kinship ties over conjugal ties should the husband die intestate. The specifics of

applicable customary law vary between ethnic groups, but in general, widows may be "inherited" as part of the estate or may be left destitute as a result of "property-grabbing" by the husband's family. New laws have attempted to address the problem by allowing men to designate women as heirs in their wills, but the problem persists. The Intestate Succession Act of 1989, for example, allows a woman to contest property-grabbing, yet a study by the Women in Southern Africa Research Trust has shown that most women do not take advantage of the law because of fear of witchcraft being worked against them by the husband's relatives (Munalula and Mwenda 1995:99).

The first case provides an example of a woman choosing to use a legal system to fight for her rights, while the second shows the failure of law to ensure that women's rights are protected even when that is the intent. This essay draws upon data from a variety of cultural contexts to illustrate ways in which women engage, respond to, or resist the state. Depending on their circumstances, women's interaction with the state may take the shape of formal participation (i.e., electoral politics), participation in women's movements or other forms of collective action with a political intent or effect, or individual responses to state policies that directly or indirectly affect quality of life for themselves and their families.

It is understood that the term "state" is not being considered as an impersonal,

Original material prepared for this text.

homogeneous force exclusively for evil or good but rather, as Waylen has observed, "a differentiated set of institutions, agencies, and discourses, and the product of a particular historical and political conjuncture (1998: 7). The term "political engagement" is also used in a broad sense. Since the 1970s Western feminist scholars have mounted a critique of male-dominated mainstream political practice and "politics" as an area of intellectual investigation. Deconstructing the androcentric biases inherent in the language and basic concepts of political science, they have argued for a broader definition of politics, one that would include activities of women not usually considered to be within the parameters of "conventional politics" (see for example volumes edited by Phillips 1998 and Randall and Waylen 1998, also Silverblatt 1988 and Waylen 1996). It is not the intention here to present a comprehensive survey of women's political activities or power; Silverblatt (1988: 452) is correct in her observation that "no uniform history of women in the state can account for the complex, often contradictory, histories of how women have engaged their particular political worlds."

CURRENT TRENDS AFFECTING WOMEN'S POLITICAL STATUS

With a few exceptions, women in contemporary states have the legal right to vote, but this does not mean it can always be exercised.[1] For example, Patience Ndetei, an elected member the Kenyan Parliament, made the following comments regarding the 1988 elections:

> My experience in the field was that a lot of women do not have the final say, especially at home as to whom they should vote for. I had a woman who was badly beaten by her husband and she had to run away from him simply because she was going to vote for me. . . . I confronted many other cases where women were not free (Daily Nation, April 30, 1988, cited in Nzomo 1997: 237).

Statistics on women's representation in politics indicate that in the last ten years there has been a dramatic increase in the number of women officeholders globally. The average percentage of women in national legislatures is nearly 11 percent, but this aggregate figure masks the real disparity between regions such as the Arab states, which have hovered around 3 percent for the last 25 years, and the Nordic states, which have seen an increase from 16.1 percent in 1975 to 36.4 percent in 1997. The opposite trend is present in the states that formerly comprised the Soviet Union and the Eastern bloc, which have seen female representation drop from an average of 23.3 percent in 1975 to 11.5 percent in 1997 (Inter-Parliamentary Union 1997, cited in Jaquette 1997).

Jane S. Jaquette notes that women's political participation and representation does not automatically result from having the right to vote, cannot be explained solely by cultural factors such as the degree of gender equality, and cannot be predicted by the level of economic development. In Japan, for example, less than 2 percent of legislators are women; in the U.S. women make up 11.2 percent of Congress. One mechanism for increasing women's political representation is the use of quota systems, adopted either by individual political parties, as in Mexico and Chile, or mandated by the state, as in Argentina, Taiwan, and Brazil. In Jaquette's view, if the present trends continue, women will soon achieve "critical mass" in many countries and be able to set the agenda for political change. Jaquette offers the following to account for the increase in female officeholders globally:

> Three interconnected reasons seem to stand out: First, the rise of the women's movement worldwide has heightened women's awareness of their political potential and developed new issues for which women are ready to mobilize. Second, a new willingness by parties and states to ease the constraints on women's access to politics, from increasing their recruitment pools to modifying electoral systems and adopting quotas. And third, as social issues supplant security concerns in the post-Cold War political environment, opportunities have opened for

new styles of leadership and have reordered political priorities (1997: 27).

The editors of a detailed comparative study of women's political engagement in forty-three countries open their introduction on a slightly less optimistic note, stating that the major finding is that "in no country do women have political status, access, or influence equal to men's" (Chowdhury et al. 1994: 3). Drawing on the findings from the individual case studies, they point to four major trends influencing the political participation of women at the national and subnational level: the rise of religious fundamentalism, the changing nature of nationalism, international economic forces, and the growth of international feminism (1994:4–10.)

RELIGIOUS FUNDAMENTALISM

Chowdhury et al. acknowledge an increase in religious fundamentalism in major world religions such as Christianity and Hinduism during the last three decades, but emphasize that Muslim fundamentalism has had the most significant impact (1994: 8). Two recent examples of Muslim fundamentalism linked to political power are the 1977–1979 Revolution in Iran, led by the party of the Ayatollah Khomeini, and the fall of the modernist People's Democratic Party of Afghanistan to fundamentalist Mujahideen revolutionaries in 1992. Both events resulted in immediate and dramatic shifts in the status of women in those countries.

In Iran, women's roles were dramatically restructured through a process of Islamicization after the 1979 Revolution, but as Parvin Paidar's study of gender and the political process in twentieth century Iran shows, women were granted legal and social rights "because they were mothers or potential mothers" (1995: 260). Ayatollah Khomeini adopted a policy of women's formal participation in national processes because:

. . . the political imperatives of revolutionary Iran convinced him that the very survival of the Islamic

Republic in its formative years depended upon the active participation of both men and women in society. This was why, contrary to many expectations, the establishment of a theocratic state did not result in outright prohibition of women from social activities (Paidar 1995: 303).

Valentine Moghadam's (1994) analysis shows that in Afghanistan, reform measures were introduced by the Marxist People's Democratic Party of Afghanistan (PDPA) which came to power in the Saur Revolution of 1978. These included campaigns to improve literacy rates and educational attainment for women, stop payment of bride price, the levirate, and coerced marriages, and end the exploitation of female labor. These measures met resistance because they posed a direct challenge to patriarchal values, economic practice, and the control of land. In the face of armed resistance and outside interference, the PDPA backed away from some of their original goals, and in the end the drive to raise the status of women failed. The Islamic opposition groups, known as the Mujahideen, received support from Pakistan, Saudia Arabia, Iran, and several other nations including the United States, and the result was a protracted period of internal conflict. In 1992 the Mujahideen assumed power; this signaled the beginning of a period of reversal of gains for women. Moghadam writes:

Once they came to power, the Mujahideen factions began to fight each other, but the men all agreed on the question of women. Thus the very first order of the new government was that all women should wear veils (1994:230).

In 1996 a group of religious students, called the Taleban, formed an opposition army and captured the capital, Kabul, after a bloody two year campaign. Raised in refugee camps in the 1980s, the men of the Taleban espoused a particularly conservative doctrine of Islam, and according to Moghadam, had "no conception of modern governance, democratic or participatory rule, or women's rights" (1999:180). The oppression of women in Afghanistan is now a matter of world attention, resulting in campaigns by both feminist and human rights organizations, such as the Feminist Majority Foundation.[2]

Moghadam points out that the level of modernization in Iran prior to the revolution in Iran has helped to liberalize the roles of women. But as the Islamic Republic has become less restrictive, the tribal patriarchal context of politics in Afghanistan has led to a dismal situation for women as a result of religious fanaticism (Moghadam 1999:172). Thus, specific circumstances of national histories and identities must be considered in comprehending the political status of women in any particular context, rather than using Islam or Islamicization as the sole explanatory factor. Deniz Kandiyoti's (1988) concept of the "patriarchal bargain" is also useful in understanding why women may act in ways that maintain the status quo of patriarchy; women pay the price of a patriarchal bargain, and in return get some degree of protection. According to Kandiyoti, different systems offer different sorts of "patriarchal bargains" to women, each with different "rules of the game and different strategies for maximizing security and optimizing their life options" (1988: 277).

Swarup et al. (1994: 375–376) provide two singular examples of growing religious fundamentalism in India. In contrast to decades of legislative action that outlawed *sati* (the immolation of widows), ended child marriage, and prohibited dowry, in 1986 the Indian government introduced the Muslim Women's (Protection of Rights in Divorce) Act. This law was intended to pacify leaders of conservative factions of the Muslim community who were outraged by the outcome of the Shah Bano case in which the Indian Supreme Court awarded alimony to the wife of a Muslim lawyer who had already married a much younger woman. The husband claimed that the Indian government was meddling in matters of Islam set forth in the *Sharia*.[3] The 1986 Act affirmed the primacy of *Sharia* law for Muslim women, and was opposed by women's rights groups and many educated Muslims. In the following year, a young widow was burned on her husband's funeral pyre. The act was condemned by

women's rights organizations and intellectuals, but thousands of Hindu men and women marched in support of *sati* as a matter of cultural and family right. The Indian government responded by enacting the Sati Prevention Measure of 1987, but pro-*sati* attitudes persist. Swarup et al. conclude:

> Thus, in the name of supporting traditional law and custom, Muslim and Hindu fundamentalists have tried to reinforce the loosening shackles of medieval paternalistic morality and preserve male supremacy. Although fundamentalists have so far been only somewhat successful, their power is increasing. This resurgence, coupled with the desire of the central government to maintain political stability at all costs, means that the influence of progressive and secular women is likely to be less powerful on this issue than on others (1994:377).

Historically, religion has often been a contentious issue for global feminists. For example, untangling the relationship between patriarchy and religion and refuting stereotypic depictions of Muslim women is a central theme in the writings of Nawal El Saadawi. Trained as a physician and a gifted writer, El Saadawi's activism on behalf of women's rights and other political issues in Egypt resulted in her being fired from her post as Director of Public Health and jailed by the government of Anwar Sadat. In 1982 she founded the Arab Woman's Solidarity Foundation, whose motto is "Power of Women-Solidarity-Unveiling of the Mind" (El Saadawi 1997). A controversial figure at home and abroad, El Saadawi consistently affirms her identity as an Arab woman and a Muslim while simultaneously denouncing religious fundamentalism and its subordinating effects on women.

THE CHANGING NATURE OF NATIONALISM

Modern nationalism is complex and variable in terms of fundamental concepts and practices, and the resulting configurations have different effects on women's status and political options. Chowdhury et al. (1994:6–8) note that the dominant themes during the period of decolonizing and rebuilding following World War II were achieving and strengthening the political power of the nation-state. In the process of state building most women in the world achieved formal (though not actual) legal equality. In addition, state secularism resulted in more opportunities for women as it weakened the power of gender hierarchy associated with religious denominations. In recent decades, however, state-focused nationalism has been challenged by the growth of ethnic, regional, and communal forces. The expansion of the European Economic Community on the one hand and the disintegration of the former Soviet Union on the other are recent examples of the trends of universalism and particularism at work.

Nations formed through revolution, such as the former Soviet Union, or decolonization, such as many countries in sub-Saharan Africa, have had to deal with serious internal ethnic and communal conflicts, and "often with only a thin veneer of representative government to find solutions" (Chowdhury et al. 1994:7). The recent ethnic fighting in the fragmented former Yugoslavia is one outcome of the trend toward particularism, and in that case, the deliberate use of rape as a weapon of war stands out as a singular example of the risks it can entail for women's status. According to Ruth Siefert, about 60,000 women in Bosnia-Herzegovina were victims of this form of warfare (Siefert 1996: 35.)

Another dimension of nationalism in African states is the effect of the colonial heritage on women's status. In an important article on women's politics in Africa, Staudt wrote that anthropological studies had provided "a vision of extensive female power as well as formal female authority in select areas of Africa" (1981: 2). She pointed out that colonialism affected women in two ways: first, colonial policies rendered women invisible and ignored any political authority they had possessed; second, the form of nationalist movements and the position of women within

them and the new governments themselves reflected the colonial overlay (Staudt 1981:5). The new socialist governments such as those of Angola, Ethiopia, Guinea, Mozambique, and Tanzania, were more likely to incorporate "emancipation ideology" in the state structures, explicitly mandating access to education and political participation for women, many of whom had participated in protests and guerilla movements in the nationalist cause. However, most failed to address women's roles in the domestic and subsistence spheres, which produced glaring contradictions, for example the inability of women in Tanzanian villages to access control over important resources, such as the control of land or money from crops they had farmed (Staudt 1981:8–10). Problems related to gender ideology and/or customary law persist into the present, as evidenced by a recent United Nations press release that describes women farmers as "invisible," noting that only 5 percent of the resources provided through extension services are available to women. On a more optimistic note, the press release also reports that in March 1999, Mozambique's parliament adopted a controversial land tenure law that stressed the equality of men and women in obtaining land titles (United Nations Africa Recovery 1999). As a participant at a 1998 leadership seminar held in Zimbabwe commented:

> In the African Women's Movement we have a troubled relationship with Nationalism. It is a relationship which binds us to certain loyalties, loyalties which are directly and indirectly connected by our subjective relationship with men who inherited the state at independence (Machipisa 1998).

In Africa and elsewhere, one of the most significant trends of the last two decades has been democraticization, a process that has significantly altered the political map of the world. The process has varied from region to region; in Latin America, dictatorships were replaced by popular sovereignty, while many European nations shook off the mantle of Soviet control. Women were participants in the transition in both cases, but there were differences too, as described by Jaquette and Wolchik:

> In Latin America, women organized to protest economic conditions and undermined the claims of authoritarian regimes that they were creating the necessary conditions for economic growth. In Central and Eastern Europe, women contributed to undermining support for the Communist regimes by fostering values in the home which were not approved by the Communist leadership. In Latin America these strategies of resistance resulted in the mobilization of women around gender issues, whereas the reverse was true in Central and Eastern Europe, where women's movements have been slow to organize after the transitions. There some women expressed their desire to return to the home; others voiced open skepticism about the value of equality in labor force participation and politics, the core goals of Western feminism (1998:4).

In summary, women's political engagement is shaped partially by the form of any particular nation-state as well as the historical circumstances that produced it. It thus both reflects and creates particular forms of gender relations and inequity (Waylen 1998:7).

INTERNATIONAL ECONOMIC FORCES

The relationship between economic status and political power is extremely complex. In their recent volume on the history of women and development in Africa, Snyder and Tadesse (1995) identify educational opportunities and economic empowerment as the two most pressing areas that must be addressed in Africa to improve women's status.

While acknowledging the importance of women's machinery within the government to insure women's voices are heard and ultimately to transform the institution, they also underline the idea that economic autonomy is a prerequisite for political empowerment (1995:182–184).

It is beyond the scope of this essay to review the large body of literature on gender and economic development (see Lockwood, this volume). Development theories have shifted several times since World War II, both with respect to economic development in general and with respect to women in particular (for recent perspectives on the latter see Kabeer 1994, Marchand and Parpart 1995, Snyder and Tadesse 1995). Suffice it to say that by the mid 1970s it was clear that both planned and unplanned economic development was not benefiting women and men equally and that in some cases women were actually losing ground (Boserup 1970, Tinker 1990). Trends and crises in the global economy in the 1970s exacerbated flawed development strategies, resulting in mounting debt, runaway inflation, and declining standards of living. These problems and others were addressed by policies introduced by the World Bank and the International Monetary Fund to promote macroeconomic stabilization and force internal structural transformation beginning in 1979. Loans were granted with conditions attached to them, which frequently created major economic upheavals as a result of mandatory devaluation of currency and belt-tightening of national budgets. Although the results varied from country to country, the overall pattern was that "structural adjustment" policies decreased public spending on education, health, and food subsidies and had the result of increasing the burden on women, who frequently had to work longer hours to absorb the cost of basic necessities, frequently in the informal sector of the economy.

In Ghana, for example, one result of economic stress in the last two decades is that women have been forced to take on a greater responsibility for providing for their families' needs. Work in the informal sector provides an important survival strategy for poor women, who gain income from subsistence farming, petty trading, food processing, and soap making, but it is complicated by social and infrastructural obstacles. Women work up to sixteen hours a day in economic activities. Whereas men are more likely to be involved in cash-cropping activities, 90 percent of women are subsistence farmers, meaning that they engage in small-scale hoe cultivation for survival needs. Women also work their husbands' farms and are responsible for transporting and marketing the farm produce of their husbands' farms. Women in rural Ghana have access to communal land through their male relatives, but have low levels of production because of heavy demands on their own labor and lack of capital to invest in production. They may cooperate with other women to share labor, or join a local credit pool to obtain capital, but are largely bypassed by extension agents and state resources. Their subsistence production is not acknowledged in official statistics and they are harassed by tax collectors and other state officials (Okine 1993).

Okine reports that the principal economic activity of poor urban women is petty trading and hawking. Although there is an upper echelon of traders who are large-scale wholesalers, they account for a tiny percentage of all traders, most of whom start with little or no capital at all. Many are the sole providers for their households. Because all vending and trading without a license is illegal, petty traders have to be wary of the police in order to avoid having their goods confiscated.

Okine points out that the economic activities of Ghanaian working women could hardly be described as liberating, in contrast to the way the economic productivity has been framed in Western Europe, and also that women's economic contributions are not recognized by policy makers or given any sort of meaningful state support. From this she concludes that the cause of the "persistent impoverishment" of Ghanaian women is not a male-dominated society, but rather "a lack of political power" (Okine 1993:191). The message in Okine's analysis is that the Ghanaian government must make changes to stop the economic exploitation of women and that women's organizations must be politically aware so that women will mobilize to pressure government; this is fundamentally a top-down approach.

Daises and Sadden (1993) also focus on women of the Third World, but their perspective on the responses of women to austerity measures associated with economic reform is somewhat different. They borrow Scott's (1985) concept of "everyday forms of resistance" to emphasize the agency that exists even in mundane, unorganized action with clearly defined, short-term objectives. They suggest that "even defensive struggles can, in the right circumstances, develop into more extensive forms of struggle with a greater capacity for expanding the room for maneuver and for changing the conditions within which struggle takes place" (Daises and Sadden 1993:11). They also discuss ways in which women use networks, associations, and diverse forms of protest to respond to austerity measures. One dramatic form of collective action is illustrated by "bread riots," which often develop from street protests over concerns about cost of living and increases in staple commodities. Women participated in a wave of bread riots that took place in the mid 1980s in the Middle East and several North African nations. The fact that such protests are spontaneous and based on immediate short-term objectives (economic relief) does not change the fact that they are political actions with the potential to change state policies.

WOMEN AND COLLECTIVE ACTION IN INTERNATIONAL FEMINISM

In September 1995, some 36,000 women from 189 nations met in Beijing, China for a much-anticipated United Nations Conference on Women, the fourth such conference to be held since 1975. Previous conferences had been held in Mexico City, Copenhagen, and Nairobi as part of the United Nations Decade on Women (1975–1985). In the two decades between the designation of 1975 as the Year of the Woman by the United Nations and the Beijing conference, a global institutional framework for empowering women was established, a complex process involving national governments, international agencies, nongovernmental organizations, activists, and scholars. In addition to creating the institutional structures for addressing gender issues at a global level, the process also involved reconciling a myriad of diverse national and regional identities and agendas, as well as exploring diverging conceptions of feminism.[4]

One result of the Beijing conference was the *Declaration and Platform for Action,* a sophisticated and comprehensive document that unequivocally situates gender inequality as a matter of human rights and social justice. It outlines a plan of action to create the conditions that will result in empowered girls and women achieving gender equity in all areas of life. It calls for national governments, the international community, and all segments of civil society to implement proposals and instruments from earlier conferences, such as the Convention on the Elimination of All Forms of Discrimination Against Women (CEDAW)[5] and to take immediate action in twelve "critical areas of concern." The increasing burden of poverty on women, inequality in access to equal and adequate education and training, inequality in economic structures and policies, and inequality between women and men in the sharing of power and decision making are among those so identified. In addition to putting gender issues on the global agenda, the Beijing document is testimony that the international women's movement has come of age. As the authors of a recent analysis of the events leading up to the Beijing conference note,

> The Beijing process marks a turning point in the development of the women's movement. It demonstrated the strength of coordinated action, the political creativity of the movement and its ability to appropriate and permeate both national and global spheres. In doing so, the women's movement manifested itself as a political movement with a global character (Lycklama a Nijeholt et al 1998: 43.)

An explicit agenda for creating gender equity is needed because even when communities have a strong tradition of single sex organizing (see Van Allen, this volume), it does not necessarily mean that women will use their mutual aid or social organizations effectively to express their political will (Staudt 1981). According to Staudt and Parpart, the overall picture for women in Africa is that despite high levels of organizational affiliation, "their gains in pressuring states have been minimal" (1989:8). Snyder and Tadesse point out that in Africa there has been an increase in professional women's organizations[6] and growth in coordinating organizations, but that "coalitions between grassroots women and educated women are still infrequent despite the great potential they hold for exerting pressure on governments to meet the immediate needs of rural women and to enact national policies that place human development and food security first" (1995:187).

Maxine Molyneaux has made a distinction between women's movements that are based on "practical" gender interests and address short-term, immediate concerns as opposed to those based on "strategic" interests; the latter derive "deductively from an analysis of women's subordination and from the formulation of a more satisfactory set of arrangements" (1985, cited in Waylen 1996: 20–22). Activities motivated by practical gender interests are diverse and take many forms, ranging from the "bread riots" discussed previously to communal kitchens, human rights campaigns, urban women's centers, and the like. Feminist movements involve women coming together self-consciously as women to press gender issues and are thus based on "strategic" gender interests. There is overlap between the two categories, but the scheme assists in understanding why women's movements do not necessarily involve a feminist consciousness.

The political participation of women in Argentina provides examples of both kinds of women's movements (Feijoo 1998). Although they were not enfranchised until 1947, Argentinean women were active in trade unions, anarchist and socialist movements, and other organizations. Before the 1976 military takeover, the women in various class and ethnic categories had been exposed to and had interacted with a variety of political ideologies, including international feminism in the 1970s, which resulted in the establishment of explicitly feminist organizations. The 1976 takeover introduced a period of state terrorism aimed at eliminating all dissident forces. Students, activists, and other "leftist" elements who posed a threat of popular mobilization were kidnapped and tortured, resulting in the "disappearance" of over 30,000 people (Feijoo 1989: 31–33). In response, women, generally mothers in their forties and fifties, engaged in increasingly large public demonstrations in the Plaza de Mayo, the main government square in Buenos Aires. Because they were acting in the role of mothers looking for their children, the military did not apply the usual punishments for subversion (Waylen 1996: 109). After the transition to democracy, however, the Madres distanced themselves from active political participation. Still their example was a model for similar movements in other Latin American dictatorships as well as for groups within Argentina seeking to cope with the difficult economic times that accompanied the transition.

In the process of constitutional reorganization, a quota law was passed requiring that 30 percent of upper level positions on party tickets be filled with women candidates; this has dramatically increased the formal participation of women. There has also been a resurgence of feminist organizing. It is thus ironic that as a result of the tendencies of President Menem to support the most conservative factions of women's organizations that the Argentinean delegation to the Beijing conference opposed policies favoring women's reproductive rights and "even questioned the use of the term 'gender'" (Feijoo 1989:43).

Further evidence of the overlap between practical and strategic gender interests in women's organizing is provided by Scarpaci's (1993) study of poor Chilean women under the Pinochet dictatorship (1973–1990). He interviewed members of a sewing cooperative formed to provide income from sewing tapestries and appliques to offset the costs of filing appeals on behalf of family members who had been detained by the state security forces. One finding was that the collective expanded to include literacy campaigns as well as discussion of women's issues. According to one member:

When I began working I realized that I contribute to my household. I contribute economically and therefore I don't find it fair that my husband should get upset because I participate in the [cooperative] and that he tells me I should do the wash and other things. I get upset, damn it, because I don't think only women should do these household chores (Scarpaci 1993:41).

In this case, it appears that a feminist consciousness was being produced through interaction in an organization that began as a response to a "practical" gender issue.

Understanding women's political motivation and mode of participation is no easier in countries with a longer history of liberal democracy, as in modern Japan. In a book remarkable for its innovative methodology as well as fresh thinking on the subject of women's political participation, Robin LeBlanc (1999) steps aside from the conventional studies of voter turnout and party platforms, waving on the "taxi" of political analysis and choosing a "bicycle" methodology to understand what citizenship means to Japanese housewives. LeBlanc was instructed by Japanese housewives how to ride a bicycle along paths and back alleyways quite different from the routes taxis took. In the process, she came to see the geography of her surroundings differently, and developed an awareness of the presence and activities of women from a new perspective. She notes that what one sees in the world of politics also depends on the social "transportation," or identity, one has. Ethnographic methods allowed LeBlanc to "follow" the paths Japanese housewives use as they confront the political system, producing information that would have been inaccessible from the "taxi" of formal political studies. Thus she provides a unique view into how Japanese women, alienated from the male world of elite politics and very conscious of themselves as "housewives," experience citizenship in a non-Western liberal democracy.

For example, she finds that participating in consumer cooperatives and volunteering "against" politics in activist causes are avenues through which housewives engage in collective action. She explores the interface between the public label of "housewife" and participation in the politics of the Netto party, which itself is the political wing of one such cooperative. Acknowledging that "bicycle citizenship" has its limitations in the present configuration of Japanese elite politics, she argues that this mode of citizenship is a facet of political organization that needs to be explored in other contexts as well.

THE GAP BETWEEN RHETORIC AND REALITY

As the foregoing discussion indicates, there are no easy generalizations about the nature or degree of political power of women. The last 25 years have been characterized by unprecedented global social, economic, and political change. Given that the obstacles to women's formal political participation have been removed (on paper at least) in most of the world's nations, does this mean that real political equity is in the near future for women?

Where women are disadvantaged educationally or struggle under entrenched patriarchal world views, political empowerment will not come easily. In Zimbabwe, for example, legislation was passed in the last two decades that permitted women to vote and made both men and women legally of age at 18. It also reformed divorce law for civil marriage, although marriage under customary law, which includes traditions of succession and inheritance, is also recognized. Before the years of structural adjustment, women also benefited from literacy campaigns and public health initiatives. Some state policies are less positive, such as the "clean up" campaigns that ostensibly target prostitutes. According to Jacobs, the 1983 campaign was directed against "younger, better-off-than-average women who appeared to be beyond 'traditional' patriarchal controls; that is, women for whom some employment opportunities have opened up recently" (1989:168).

The failure of the land tenure programs to consider gender as a factor has also had negative impact on women. The biggest such project in sub-Saharan Africa, Zimbabwe's program to redistribute land to landless poor,

takes two forms: in Model A projects, plots of land are distributed to heads of households, while in Model B projects, individuals own land communally. Jacobs found that resettlement benefited women in that it led to increased household incomes, but that women were excluded from holding title to individual plots. Unmarried women or widows can apply, but only small numbers actually receive title to the twelve acre plots. In case of divorce, a woman loses her right to remain on the land. One benefit that resettled women have that separates them from other Zimbabwean women is that rulings by resettlement officials have allowed wives, rather than brothers of the deceased, to inherit land. Thus, in Zimbabwe, gender ideology emphasizes the value of women who are rural producers, but state policy does not forbid their exclusion from the means of production. Polygyny rates are up in the resettlement areas, suggesting that junior wives are being used as laborers. Also, like urban women, resettlement women fear divorce because it will lead to poverty and loss of their children. For this reason, they are not likely to assert their demands (Jacobs 1998:129).

CONCLUSION

This overview of trends affecting women's political engagement shows that the goals and strategies of women's political struggles are diverse and that the results of their efforts show uneven progress. It is also clear that the growth of an international feminist movement, a measurable trend to include "women's rights machinery" in national governments, and even increased numbers of female officeholders, will not bring women political power by themselves. There are new tools, such as the growing international communications network, but "cybersisterhood" cannot reach those who lack access to computers.

Although she is speaking about Zambian women, Munachonga's observation that "discrepancies between formal support for women's development and actual practice will not disappear easily, because the attitudes underpinning this reality are not amenable to legislation," applies to politically disadvantaged women everywhere (1989: 140). She sees long-term political education, requiring the concerted efforts of women, as the only solution. The truth of Munachonga's assessment can be seen in the current controversy in Zimbabwe surrounding the Magaya vs. Magaya case, in which Venia Magaya, age 52, was disinherited of her father's estate in favor of her younger half-brother. In March 1999 the Supreme Court ruled that according to customary law women's rights to inheritance, ownership of property, and custody of children are inferior to men's. Infuriated by the ruling, women's groups are calling for constitutional reform (Bald 1999). There is no doubt that women in Zimbabwe, who were crucial in that country's struggle for independence, have the potential to reshape political and social institutions. The question in Zimbabwe and around the globe is simply, how long will it take to create gender equity?

NOTES

1. The government of Kuwait recently rejected a measure that would have given women the right to vote (New York Times, December 1, 1999).
2. The Feminist Majority Foundation has mounted a large-scale education and petition drive to raise global awareness of the situation in Afghanistan. See their homepage at www.feminist.org.
3. All Muslims are subject to the Sharia, the code of divine law derived from the Quran, teachings of the Prophet Mohammed, and other sources. The Sharia contains guidelines and rules for all aspects of a Muslim's life.
4. This process continues into the present. A recent issue of Women's Studies International Forum is devoted to the interface of local feminisms and the implication for global feminisms (Flew et al. 1999).
5. CEDAW was adopted in 1979, the U.N. General Assembly and is an international bill of rights for women. It defines what constitutes discrimination against women and sets up an agenda for national action to end it. An Optional Protocol to the Convention sets up procedures to make claims and to investigate cases of grave or systematic violations of women's rights is in process. (See the web site for United Nations Division for the Advancement of Women, www.un.or/womenwatch/daw).
6. Snyder and Tadesse cite a figure of 30,000 such groups in Kenya alone (1995:195).

REFERENCES

Bald, Margaret. 1999. "Second-Class Citizens." *World Press Review* 46(8):21.

Boserup, Esther. 1970. *Women's Role in Economic Development.* New York: St. Martin's Press.

Chowdhurry, Najma, and Barbara J. Nelson, with Kathryn A. Carver, Nancy J. Johnson, and Paula L. O'Loughlin. 1994. "Redefining Politics: Patterns of Women's Political Engagement from a Global Perspective." In Barbara J. Nelson and Najma Chowdhurry (eds.), *Women and Politics Worldwide*, pp. 3–24. New Haven: Yale University Press.

Daines, Victoria, and David Seddon. 1993. "Confronting Austerity: Women's Responses to Economic Reform." In Meredith Turshen and Briavel Holcomb (eds.), *Women's Lives and Public Policy: The International Experience*, pp. 3–32. Westport, Conn.: Praeger Publishers.

El Saadawi, Nawal. 1997. *The Nawal El Saadawi Reader.* London: Zed Books.

Feijoo, Maria del Carmen. 1998. "Democratic Participation and Women in Argentina. In Jane S. Jaquette and Sharon L. Wolchik (eds.), *Women and Democracy: Latin America and Central and Eastern Europe*, pp. 29–46. Baltimore: The Johns Hopkins Press.

Flew, Fiona, with Barbara Bagilhole, Jean Carabine, Natalie Fenton, Celia Kitzinger, Ruth Lister and Sue Wilkenson. 1999. Introduction: Local Feminisms, Global Futures. *Women's Studies International Forum* 22(4): 393–453.

Jacobs, Susan. 1989. "Zimbabwe: State, Class, and Gendered Models." In Jane L. Parpart and Kathleen A. Staudt (eds.), *Women and the State in Africa*, pp. 161–184. Boulder, Colorado: Lynne Rienner Publishers.

———. 1998. "The Gendered Politics of Land Reform: Three Comparative Studies". In Vicky Randall and Georgina Waylen (eds.), *Gender, Politics, and the State*, pp. 121–142. London: Routledge.

Jacquette, Jane S. 1997. "Women in Power: From Tokenism to Critical Mass." *Foreign Policy*, Fall 1997, pp. 23–37.

———— and Sharon L. Wolchik. 1998 "Women and Democratization in Latin America and Central and Eastern Europe: A Comparative Introduction." In Jacquette, Jane S., and Sharon L. Wolchik, (eds.), *Women and Democracy: Latin America and Central and Eastern Europe*, pp. 1–28. Baltimore, MD: John Hopkins University Press.

Kabeer, Nalia. 1994. *Reversed Realities: Gender Hierarchies in Development Thought*. London: Verso.

Kandiyoti, Deniz. 1988. "Bargaining with Patriarchy." *Gender and Society* 2(3):274–290.

LeBlanc, Robin M. 1999. *Bicycle Citizens: The Political World of the Japanese Housewife*. Berkeley: University of California Press.

Lycklama a Nijeholt, Joke Sweibel, and Virginia Vargas. 1998. The Global Institutional Framework: The Long March to Beijing." In Geertje Lycklama a Nijeholt, Virginia Vargas, and Saskia Wieringa (eds.), *Women's Movements and Public Policy in Europe, Latin America, and the Caribbean*, pp. 25–48. New York: Garland Publishing, Inc.

Machipisa, Lewis. 1998. "Rights-Africa: Women Groups Prepare for the Next Millennium." November 23, 1998. Interpress Service. *http://www.oneworld.org/ips2/nov98/16_48_060.html*

Marchand, Marianne H., and Jane L. Parpart (eds). 1995. *Feminism/Postmodernism/Development*. London: Routledge.

Moghadam, Valentine M. 1994. "Revolution, Islamist Recation, and Women in Afghanistan." In Mary Ann Tétrault (ed.), *Women and Revolution in Africa, Asia, and the New World*, pp. 211–235. Columbia, SC: University of South Carolina Press.

————. 1999. "Revolution, Religion, and Gender Politics: Iran and Afghanistan Compared. In *Journal of Women's History*, 10(4):172–195.

Molyneux, M. 1985. "Mobilization Without Emancipation? Women's Interest, the State and Revolution in Nicaragua." *Feminist Studies* 11(2):227–254.

Munachonga, Monica L. 1989. "Women and the State: Zambia's Development Policies and Their Impact on Women." In Jane L. Parpart and Kathleen A. Staudt (eds.), *Women and the State in Africa*, pp. 130–142. Boulder: Lynne Rienner Publishers.

Munalula, Margaret Mulela, and Winnie Sithole Mwenda. 1995. "Case Study: Women and Inheritance Law in Zambia." In Margaret Jean Hay and Sharon Stichter (eds.), *African Women South of the Sahara*, pp. 93–100. New York: Longman.

Nzomo, Maria. 1997. "Kenyan Women in Politics and Public Decision-Making." In Gwendolyn Mikell (ed.), *African Feminism: The Politics of Survival in Sub-Saharan Africa*, pp. 232–254. Philadelphia: University of Pennsylvania Press.

————, and Kathleen Staudt. 1994. "Man-Made Political Machinery in Kenya: Political Space for Women?" In Barbara J. Nelson and Najma Chowdhurry (eds.), *Women and Politics Worldwide*, pp. 416–433. New Haven: Yale University Press.

Okine, Vicky. 1993. "The Survival Strategies of Poor Families in Ghana and the Role of Women Therein." In Joycelin Massiah (ed.), *Women in Developing Economies: Making Visible the Invisible*, pp. 167–194. Providence, RI: Berg Publishers.

Paidar, Parvin. 1995. *Women and the Political Process in Twentieth-Century Iran*. Cambridge: Cambridge University Press.

Parpart, Jane L., and Kathleen A. Staudt. 1989. "Women and the State in Africa." In Jane L. Parpart and Kathleen A. Staudt (eds.), *Women and the State in Africa*, pp. 1–19. Boulder: Lynne Rienner Publishers.

Phillips, Anne. Ed. 1998. *Feminism and Politics*. New York: Oxford University Press.

Randall, Vicky, and Georgina Waylen (eds.) 1998. *Gender, Politics and the State*. London: Routledge.

Siefert, Ruth. 1996. "The Second Front: The Logic of Sexual Violence in Wars." *Women's Studies International Forum* 19(1–2): 35–43.

Silverblatt, Irene. 1988. "Women in States." *Annual Review of Anthropology* 17:427–461.

Scarpaci, Joseph L. 1993. "Empowerment Strategies of Poor Urban Women under the Chilean Dictatorship." In Meredith Turshen and Brian Holcomb (eds.), *Women's Lives and Public Policy*, pp. 33–50. Westport, Connecticut: Greenwood Press.

Scott, J.C. 1985. *Weapons of the Weak: Everyday Forms of Peasant Resistance*. New York and London: Yale University Press.

Snyder, Margaret C. and Mary Tadesse. 1995. *African Women and Development: A History*. London: Zed Books.

Staudt, Kathleen. 1981. "Women's Politics in Africa." *Studies in Third World Societies*, 16:1–28. Williamsburg, VA: College of William and Mary.

————, (ed.). 1990. *Women, International Development, and Politics*. Philadelphia: Temple University Press.

Swarup, Hem Lata, Niroj Sinha, Chitra Ghosh, and Pam Rajput. 1994. "Women's Political

Engagement in India: Some Critical Issues." In Barbara Nelson and Najma Chowdhury (eds), *Women and Politics Worldwide*, pp. 363–379. New Haven: Yale University Press.

Tinker, Irene (ed.). 1990. *Persistent Inequalities: Women and World Development.* New York: Oxford University Press.

United Nations. 1995. Report of the Fourth World Conference on Women, Beijing, 4–15 September 1995. A/CONF./177/20.

United Nations. 1999. "Women Farmers, the 'Invisible' Producers. *Africa Recovery*, vol. 11, no. 2.

Waylen, Georgina. 1996. *Gender in Third World Politics.* Boulder, Colorado: Lynne Rienner Publishers, Inc.

———. 1998. "Gender, Feminism, and the State: An Overview". In Vicky Randall and Georgina Waylen (eds.), *Gender, Politics and the State*, pp. 1–16. London: Routledge.

Japanese Mothers and Obentōs: *The Lunch-Box as Ideological State Apparatus*

Anne Allison

INTRODUCTION

Japanese nursery school children, going off to school for the first time, carry with them a boxed lunch (*obentō*) prepared by their mothers at home. Customarily these *obentōs* are highly crafted elaborations of food: a multitude of miniature portions, artistically designed and precisely arranged, in a container that is sturdy and cute. Mothers tend to expend inordinate time and attention on these *obentōs* in efforts both to please their children and to affirm that they are good mothers. Children at nursery school are taught in turn that they must consume their entire meal according to school rituals.

Food in an *obentō* is an everyday practice of Japanese life. While its adoption at the nursery school level may seem only natural to Japanese and unremarkable to outsiders, I will argue in this article that the *obentō* is invested with a gendered state ideology. Overseen by the authorities of the nursery school, an institution which is linked to, if not directly moni-

Reprinted with permission from *Anthropological Quarterly* 64: 195–208, 1991. Copyright © The Catholic University of America.

tored by, the state, the practice of the *obentō* situates the producer as a woman and mother, and the consumer, as a child of a mother and a student of a school. Food in this context is neither casual nor arbitrary. Eaten quickly in its entirety by the student, the *obentō* must be fashioned by the mother so as to expedite this chore for the child. Both mother and child are being watched, judged, and constructed; and it is only through their joint effort that the goal can be accomplished.

I use Althusser's concept of the Ideological State Apparatus (1971) to frame my argument. I will briefly describe how food is coded as a cultural and aesthetic apparatus in Japan, and what authority the state holds over school in Japanese society. Thus situating the parameters within which the *obentō* is regulated and structured in the nursery school setting, I will examine the practice both of making and eating *obentō* within the context of one nursery school in Tokyo. As an anthropologist and mother of a child who attended this school for fifteen months, my analysis is based on my observations, on discussions with other mothers, daily conversations and an interview with my son's teacher, examination of *obentō* magazines and cookbooks, participation in school rituals, outings, and Mothers' Association meetings, and the multifarious experiences of my son and myself as we faced the *obentō* process every day.

I conclude that *obentō* as a routine, task, and art form of nursery school culture are endowed with ideological and gendered meanings that the state indirectly manipulates. The manipulation is neither total nor totally coercive, however, and I argue that pleasure and creativity for both mother and child are also products of the *obentō*.

CULTURAL RITUAL AND STATE IDEOLOGY

As anthropologists have long understood, not only are the worlds we inhabit symbolically constructed, but also the constructions of our cultural symbols are endowed with, or have the potential for, power. How we see reality, in other words, is also how we live it. So the conventions by which we recognize our universe are also those by which each of us assumes our place and behavior within that universe. Culture is, in this sense, doubly constructive: constructing both the world for people and people for specific worlds.

The fact that culture is not necessarily innocent, and power not necessarily transparent, has been revealed by much theoretical work conducted both inside and outside the discipline of anthropology. The scholarship of the neo-Marxist Louis Althusser (1971), for example, has encouraged the conceptualization of power as a force which operates in ways that are subtle, disguised, and accepted as everyday social practice. Althusser differentiated between two major structures of power in modern capitalist societies. The first, he called, (Repressive) State Apparatus (SA), which is power that the state wields and manages primarily through the threat of force. Here the state sanctions the usage of power and repression through such legitimized mechanisms as the law and police (1971: 143–5).

Contrasted with this is a second structure of power—Ideological State Apparatus(es) (ISA). These are institutions which have some overt function other than a political and/or administrative one: mass media, education, health and welfare, for example. More numerous, disparate, and functionally polymorphous than the SA, the ISA exert power not primarily through repression but through ideology. Designed and accepted as practices with another purpose—to educate (the school system), entertain (film industry), inform (news media), the ISA serve not only their stated objective but also an unstated one—that of indoctrinating people into seeing the world a certain way and of accepting certain identities as their own within that world (1971: 143–7).

While both structures of power operate simultaneously and complementarily, it is the ISA, according to Althusser, which in capitalist societies is the more influential of the two. Disguised and screened by another operation, the power of ideology in ISA can be both more far-reaching and insidious than the SA's power of coercion. Hidden in the movies we watch, the music we hear, the liquor we drink, the textbooks we read, it is overlooked because it is protected and its protection—or its alibi (Barthes 1957: 109–111)—allows the terms and relations of ideology to spill into and infiltrate our everyday lives.

A world of commodities, gender inequalities, and power differentials is seen not therefore in these terms but as a naturalized environment, one that makes sense because it has become our experience to live it and accept it in precisely this way. This common-sense acceptance of a particular world is the work of ideology, and it works by concealing the coercive and repressive elements of our everyday routines but also by making those routines of the everyday familiar, desirable, and simply our own. This is the critical element of Althusser's notion of ideological power: ideology is so potent because it becomes not only ours but us—the terms and machinery by which we structure ourselves and identify who we are.

JAPANESE FOOD AS CULTURAL MYTH

An author in one *obentō* magazine, the type of medium-sized publication that, filled with glossy pictures of *obentōs* and ideas and recipes for successfully recreating them, sold in the bookstores across Japan, declares, ". . . the making of the *obentō* is the one most worrisome concern facing the mother of a child going off to school for the first time (*Shufunotomo* 1980: inside cover). Another *obentō* journal, this one heftier and packaged in the encyclopedic series of the prolific women's publishing firm, *Shufunotomo*, articulates the same social fact: "First-time *obentōs* are a strain on both parent and child" ("*hajimete no obentō wa, oya mo ko mo kinchō shimasu*") (*Shufunotomo* 1981: 55).

An outside observer might ask: What is the real source of worry over *obentō*? Is it the food itself or the entrance of the young child into school for the first time? Yet, as one look at a typical child's *obentō*—a small box packaged with a five or six-course miniaturized meal whose pieces and parts are artistically arranged, perfectly cut, and neatly arranged— would immediately reveal, no food is "just" food in Japan. What is not so immediately apparent, however, is why a small child with limited appetite and perhaps scant interest in food is the recipient of a meal as elaborate and as elaborately prepared as any made for an entire family or invited guests.

Certainly, in Japan much attention is focused on the *obentō,* investing it with a significance far beyond that of the merely pragmatic, functional one of sustaining a child with nutritional foodstuffs. Since this investment beyond the pragmatic is true of any food prepared in Japan, it is helpful to examine culinary codes for food preparation that operate generally in the society before focusing on children's *obentōs*.

As has been remarked often about Japanese food, the key element is appearance. Food must be organized, re-organized, arranged, re-arranged, stylized, and re-stylized to appear in a design that is visually attractive. Presentation is critical: not to the extent that taste and nutrition are displaced, as has been sometimes attributed to Japanese food, but to the degree that how food looks is at least as important as how it tastes and how good and sustaining it is for one's body.

As Donald Richie has pointed out in his eloquent and informative book *A Taste of Japan*

(1985), presentational style is the guiding principle by which food is prepared in Japan, and the style is conditioned by a number of codes. One code is for smallness, separation, and fragmentation. Nothing large is allowed, so portions are all cut to be bite- sized, served in small amounts on tiny individual dishes, and are arranged on a table (or on a tray, or in an *obentō* box) in an array of small, separate containers.[1] There is no one big dinner plate with three large portions of vegetable, starch, and meat as in American cuisine. Consequently the eye is pulled not toward one totalizing center but away to a multiplicity of de-centered parts.[2]

Visually, food substances are presented according to a structural principle not only of segmentation but also of opposition. Foods are broken or cut to make contrasts of color, texture, and shape. Foods are meant to oppose one another and clash: pink against green, roundish foods against angular ones, smooth substances next to rough ones. This oppositional code operates not only within and between the foodstuffs themselves, but also between the attributes of the food and those of the containers in or on which they are placed: a circular mound in a square dish, a bland colored food set against a bright plate, a translucent sweet in a heavily textured bowl (Richie 1985: 40–41).

The container is as important as what is contained in Japanese cuisine, but it is really the containment that is stressed, that is, how food has been (re)constructed and (re)arranged from nature to appear, in both beauty and freshness, perfectly natural. This stylizing of nature is a third code by which presentation is directed; the injunction is not only to retain, as much as possible, the innate naturalness of ingredients—shopping daily so food is fresh and leaving much of it either raw or only minimally cooked—but also to recreate in prepared food the promise and appearance of being "natural." As Richie writes, ". . . the emphasis is on presentation of the natural rather than the natural itself. It is not what nature has wrought that excites admiration but what man has wrought with what nature has wrought" (1985: 11).

This naturalization of food is rendered through two main devices. One is by constantly hinting at and appropriating the nature that comes from outside—decorating food with seasonal reminders, such as a maple leaf in the fall or a flower in the spring, serving in-season fruits and vegetables, and using season-coordinated dishes such as glassware in the summer and heavy pottery in the winter. The other device, to some degree the inverse of the first, is to accentuate and perfect the preparation process to such an extent that the food appears not only to be natural, but more nearly perfect than nature without human intervention ever could be. This is nature made artificial. Thus, by naturalization, nature is not only taken in by Japanese cuisine, but taken over.

It is this ability both to appropriate "real" nature (the maple leaf on the tray) and to stamp the human reconstruction of that nature as "natural" that lends Japanese food its potential for cultural and ideological manipulation. It is what Barthes calls a second order myth (1957: 114–7): a language which has a function people accept as only pragmatic—the sending of roses to lovers, the consumption of wine with one's dinner, the cleaning up a mother does for her child—which is taken over by some interest or agenda to serve a different end—florists who can sell roses, liquor companies who can market wine, conservative politicians who campaign for a gendered division of labor with women kept at home. The first order of language ("language-object"), thus emptied of its original meaning, is converted into an empty form by which it can assume a new, additional, second order of signification ("metalanguage" or "second-order semiological system"). As Barthes points out however, the primary meaning is never lost. Rather, it remains and stands as an alibi, the cover under which the second, politicized meaning can hide. Roses sell better, for example, when lovers view them as a vehicle to express love rather than the means by which a company stays in business.

At one level, food is just food in Japan—the medium by which humans sustain their nature and health. Yet under and through this code of pragmatics, Japanese cuisine carries other meanings that in Barthes' terms are mythological. One of these is national identity: food being appropriated as a sign of the culture. To be Japanese is to eat Japanese food, as so many Japanese confirm when they travel to other countries and cite the greatest problem they encounter to be the absence of "real" Japanese food. Stated the other way around, rice is so symbolically central to Japanese culture (meals and *obentōs* often being assembled with rice as the core and all other dishes, multifarious as they may be, as mere compliments or side dishes) that Japanese say they can never feel full until they have consumed their rice at a particular meal or at least once during the day.[3]

Embedded within this insistence on eating Japanese food, thereby reconfirming one as a member of the culture, are the principles by which Japanese food is customarily prepared: perfection, labor, small distinguishable parts, opposing segments, beauty, and the stamp of nature. Overarching all these more detailed codings are two that guide the making and ideological appropriation of the nursery school *obentōs* most directly: (1) there is an order to the food: a right way to do things, with everything in its place and each place coordinated with every other, and (2) the one who prepares the food takes on the responsibility of producing food to the standards of perfection and exactness that Japanese cuisine demands. Food may not be casual, in other words, nor the producer casual in her production. In these two rules is a message both about social order and the role gender plays in sustaining and nourishing that order.

SCHOOL, STATE, AND SUBJECTIVITY

In addition to language and second order meanings I suggest that the rituals and routines surrounding *obentōs* in Japanese nursery schools present, as it were, a third order, manipulation. This order is a use of a currency already established—one that has already appropriated a language of utility (food feeds hunger) to express and implant cultural behaviors. State-guided schools borrow this coded apparatus: using the natural convenience and cover of food not only to code a cultural order, but also to socialize children and mothers into the gendered roles and subjectivities they are expected to assume in a political order desired and directed by the state.

In modern capitalist societies such as Japan, it is the school, according to Althusser, which assumes the primary role of ideological state apparatus. A greater segment of the population spends longer hours and more years here than in previous historical periods. Also education has not taken over from other institutions, such as religion, the pedagogical function of being the major shaper and inculcator of knowledge for the society. Concurrently, as Althusser has pointed out for capitalist modernism (1971: 152, 156), there is the gradual replacement of repression by ideology as the prime mechanism for behavior enforcement. Influenced less by the threat of force and more by the devices that present and inform us of the world we live in and the subjectivities that world demands, knowledge and ideology become fused, and education emerges as the apparatus for pedagogical and ideological indoctrination.

In practice, as school teaches children how and what to think, it also shapes them for the roles and positions they will later assume as adult members of the society. How the social order is organized through vectors of gender, power, labor, and/or class, in other words, is not only as important a lesson as the basics of reading and writing, but is transmitted through and embedded in those classroom lessons. Knowledge thus is not only socially constructed, but also differentially acquired according to who one is or will be in the political society one will enter in later years. What precisely society requires in the way of workers, citizens, and parents will be the condition determining or influencing instruction in the schools.

This latter equation, of course, depends on two factors: (1) the convergence or divergence of different interests in what is desired as subjectivities, and (2) the power any particular interest, including that of the state, has in exerting its desires for subjects on or through the system of education. In the case of Japan, the state wields enormous control over the systematization of education. Through its Ministry of Education (Monbusho), one of the most powerful and influential ministries in the government, education is centralized and managed by a state bureaucracy that regulates almost every aspect of the educational process. On any given day, for example, what is taught in every public school follows the same curriculum, adheres to the same structure, and is informed by textbooks from the prescribed list. Teachers are nationally screened, school boards uniformly appointed (rather than elected), and students institutionally exhorted to obey teachers given their legal authority, for example, to write secret reports (*naishinsho*), that may obstruct a student's entrance into high school.[4]

The role of the state in Japanese education is not limited, however, to such extensive but codified authorities granted to the Ministry of Education. Even more powerful is the principle of the "*gakureki shakkai*" (lit. academic pedigree society) by which careers of adults are determined by the schools they attend as youths. A reflection and construction of the new economic order of post-war Japan,[5] school attendance has become the single most important determinant of who will achieve the most desirable positions in industry, government, and the professions. School attendance is itself based on a single criterion: a system of entrance exams which determines entrance selection and it is to this end—preparation for exams—that school, even at the nursery school level, is increasingly oriented. Learning to follow directions, do as one is told, and "*ganbaru*" (Asanuma 1987) are social imperatives, sanctioned by the state, and taught in the schools.

NURSERY SCHOOL AND IDEOLOGICAL APPROPRIATION OF THE *OBENTŌ*

The nursery school stands outside the structure of compulsory education in Japan. Most nursery schools are private; and, though not compelled by the state, a greater proportion of the three to six-year old population of Japan attends preschool than in any other industrialized nation (Tobin et al.1989; Hendry 1986; Boocock 1989).

Differentiated from the *hoikuen*, another pre-school institution with longer hours which is more like daycare than school,[6] the *yochien* (nursery school) is widely perceived as instructional, not necessarily in a formal curriculum but more in indoctrination to attitudes and structure of Japanese schooling. Children learn less about reading and writing than they do about how to become a Japanese student, and both parts of this formula—Japanese and student—are equally stressed. As Rohlen has written, "social order is generated" in the nursery school, first and foremost, by a system of routines (1989: 10, 21). Educational routines and rituals are therefore of heightened importance in *yochien,* for whereas these routines and rituals may be the format through which subjects are taught in higher grades, they are both form and subject in the *yochien.*

While the state (through its agency, the Ministry of Education) has no direct mandate over nursery school attendance, its influence is nevertheless significant. First, authority over how the *yochien* is run is in the hands of the Ministry of Education. Second, most parents and teachers see the *yochien* as the first step to the system of compulsory education that starts in the first grade and is closely controlled by Monbusho. The principal of the *yochien* my son attended, for example, stated that he saw his main duty to be preparing children to enter more easily the rigors of public education soon to come. Third, the rules and patterns of "group living" (shudanseikatsu), a Japanese social ideal that is reiterated nationwide by political leaders, corporate management, and marriage counselors, is first introduced to the child in nursery school.[7]

The entry into nursery school marks a transition both away from home and into the "real world," which is generally judged to be difficult, even traumatic, for the Japanese child (Peak 1989). The *obentō* is intended to ease a child's discomfiture and to allow a child's mother to manufacture something of herself and the home to accompany the child as s/he moves into the potentially threatening outside world. Japanese use the cultural categories of *soto* and *uchi; soto* connotes the outside, which in being distanced and other, is dirty and hostile; and *uchi* identifies as clean and comfortable what is inside and familiar. The school falls initially and, to some degree, perpetually, into a category of *soto.* What is ultimately the definition and location of *uchi,* by contrast, is the home, where family and mother reside.[8] By producing something from the home, a mother both girds and goads her child to face what is inevitable in the world that lies beyond. This is the mother's role and her gift; by giving of herself and the home (which she both symbolically represents and in reality manages)[9], the *soto* of the school is, if not transformed into the *uchi* of home, made more bearable by this sign of domestic and maternal hearth a child can bring to it.

The *obentō* is filled with the meaning of mother and home in a number of ways. The first is by sheer labor. Women spend what seems to be an inordinate amount of time on the production of this one item. As an experienced *obentō* maker, I can attest to the intense attention and energy devoted to this one chore. On the average, mothers spend 20–45 minutes every morning cooking, preparing, and assembling the contents of one *obentō* for one nursery school-aged child. In addition, the previous day they have planned, shopped, and often organized a supper meal with leftovers in mind for the next day's *obentō.* Frequently women[10] discuss *obentō* ideas with other mothers, scan *obentō* cookbooks or magazines for recipes, buy or make objects with which to decorate or contain (part of) the *obentō,* and perhaps make small food portions to freeze and retrieve for future *obentō.*[11]

Of course, effort alone does not necessarily produce a successful *obentō.* Casualness was never indulged, I observed, and even mothers with children who would eat anything prepared *obentō* as elaborate as anyone else's. Such labor is intended for the child but also the mother: it is a sign of a woman's commitment as a mother and her inspiring her child to being similarly committed as a student. The *obentō* is thus a representation of what the mother is and what the child should become. A model for school is added to what is a gift and a reminder from home.

This equation is spelled out more precisely in a nursery school rule—all of the *obentō* must be eaten. Though on the face of it this is petty and mundane, the injunction is taken very seriously by nursery school teachers and is one not easily realized by very small children. The logic is that it is time for the child to meet certain expectations. One of the main agendas of the nursery school, after all, is to introduce and indoctrinate children into the patterns and rigors of Japanese education (Rohlen 1989; Sano 1989; Lewis 1989). And Japanese education, by all accounts, is not about fun (Duke 1986).

Learning is hard work with few choices or pleasures. Even *obentōs* from home stop once the child enters first grade.[12] The meals there are institutional: largely bland, unappealing, and prepared with only nutrition in mind. To ease a youngster into these upcoming (educational, social, disciplinary, culinary) routines, *yochien obentōs* are designed to be pleasing and personal. The *obentō* is also designed, however, as a test for the child. And the double meaning is not unintentional. A structure already filled with a signification of mother and home is then emptied to provide a new form: one now also written with the ideological demands of being a member of Japanese culture as well as a viable and successful Japanese in the realms of school and later work.

The exhortation to consume one's entire *obentō*[13] is articulated and enforced by the nursery school teacher. Making high drama out of eating by, for example, singing a song; collectively thanking Buddha (in the case of Buddhist nursery schools), one's mother for making the *obentō*, and one's father for providing the means to make the *obentō*; having two assigned class helpers pour the tea, the class eats together until everyone has finished. The teacher examines the children's *obentōs*, making sure the food is all consumed, and encouraging, sometimes scolding, children who are taking too long. Slow eaters do not fare well in this ritual, because they hold up the other

students, who as a peer group also monitor a child's eating. My son often complained about a child whose slowness over food meant that the others were kept inside (rather than being allowed to play on the playground) for much of the lunch period.

Ultimately and officially, it is the teacher, however, whose role and authority it is to watch over food consumption and to judge the person consuming food. Her surveillance covers both the student and the mother, who in the matter of the *obentō*, must work together. The child's job is to eat the food and the mother's to prepare it. Hence, the responsibility and execution of one's task is not only shared but conditioned by the other. My son's teacher would talk with me daily about the progress he was making finishing his *obentōs*. Although the overt subject of discussion was my child, most of what was said was directed to me; what I could do in order to get David to consume his lunch more easily.

The intensity of these talks struck me at the time as curious. We had just settled in Japan and David, a highly verbal child, was attending a foreign school in a foreign language he had not yet mastered; he was the only non-Japanese child in the school. Many of his behaviors during this time were disruptive: for example, he went up and down the line of children during morning exercises hitting each child on the head. Hamada-sensei (the teacher), however, chose to discuss the *obentōs*. I thought surely David's survival in and adjustment to this environment depended much more on other factors, such as learning Japanese. Yet it was the *obentō* that was discussed with such recall of detail ("David ate all his peas today, but not a single carrot until I asked him to do so three times") and seriousness that I assumed her attention was being misplaced. The manifest reference was to box-lunches, but was not the latent reference to something else?[14]

Of course, there was another message, for me and my child. It was an injunction to follow directions, obey rules, and accept the authority of the school system. All of the latter were embedded in and inculcated through certain rituals: the nursery school, as any school (except such non-conventional ones as Waldorf and Montessori) and practically any social or institutional practice in Japan, was so heavily ritualized and ritualistic that the very form of ritual took on a meaning and value in and of itself (Rohlen 1989: 21, 27–8). Both the school day and school year of the nursery school were organized by these rituals. The day, apart from two free periods, for example, was broken by discrete routines—morning exercises, arts and crafts, gym instruction, singing—most of which were named and scheduled. The school year was also segmented into and marked by three annual events—sports day (*undōkai*) in the fall, winter assembly (*seikatsu happyōkai*) in December, and dance festival (*bon odori*) in the summer. Energy was galvanized by these rituals, which demanded a degree of order as well as a discipline and self-control that non-Japanese would find remarkable.

Significantly, David's teacher marked his successful integration into the school system by his mastery not of the language or other cultural skills, but of the school's daily routines—walking in line, brushing his teeth after eating, arriving at school early, eagerly participating in greeting and departure ceremonies, and completing all of his *obentō* on time. Not only had he adjusted to the school structure, but he had also become assimilated to the other children. Or restated, what once had been externally enforced now became ideologically desirable; the everyday practices had moved from being alien (*soto*) to familiar (*uchi*) to him, from, that is, being someone else's to his own. My American child had to become, in some sense, Japanese, and where his teacher recognized this Japaneseness was in the daily routines such as finishing his *obentō*. The lesson learned early, which David learned as well, is that not adhering to routines such as completing one's *obentō* on time leads to not only admonishment from the teacher, but rejection from the other students.

The nursery school system differentiates between the child who does and the child who does not manage the multifarious and constant rituals of nursery school. And for those who do not manage there is a penalty which the child learns either to avoid or wish to avoid. Seeking the acceptance of his peers, the student develops the aptitude, willingness, and in the case of my son—whose outspokenness and individuality were the characteristics most noted in this culture—even the desire to conform to the highly ordered and structured practices of nursery school life. As Althusser (1971) wrote about ideology: the mechanism works when and because ideas about the world and particular roles in that world that serve other (social, political, economic, state) agendas become familiar and one's own.

Rohlen makes a similar point: that what is taught and learned in nursery school is social order. Called *shudanseikatsu* or group life, it means organization into a group where a person's subjectivity is determined by a group membership and not "the assumption of choice and rational self-interest" (1989: 30). A child learns in nursery school to be with others, think like others, and act in tandem with others. This lesson is taught primarily through the precision and constancy of basic routines: "Order is shaped gradually by repeated practice of selected daily tasks . . . that socialize the children to high degrees of neatness and uniformity" (p. 21). Yet a feeling of coerciveness is rarely experienced by the child when three principles of nursery school instruction are in place: (1) school routines are made "desirable and pleasant" (p. 30), (2) the teacher disguises her authority by trying to make the group the voice and unit of authority, and (3) the regimentation of the school is administered by an attitude of "intimacy" on the part of the teachers and administrators (p. 30). In short, when the desires and routines of the school are made into the desires and routines of the child, they are made acceptable.

MOTHERING AS GENDERED IDEOLOGICAL STATE APPARATUS

The rituals surrounding the *obentō* consumption in the school situate what ideological meanings the *obentō* transmits to the child. The process of production within the home, by contrast, organizes its somewhat different ideological package for the mother. While the two sets of meanings are intertwined, the mother is faced with different expectations in the preparation of the *obentō* than the child is in its consumption. At a pragmatic level the child must simply eat everything in the lunch box, whereas the mother's job is far more complicated. The onus for her is getting the child to consume what she has made, and the general attitude is that this is far more the mother's responsibility (at this nursery school, transitional stage) than the child's. And this is no simple or easy task.

Much of what is written, advised, and discussed about the *obentō* has this aim explicitly in mind: that is, making food in such a way as to facilitate the child's duty to eat it. One magazine advises:

> The first day of taking *obentō* is a worrisome thing for mother and "*boku*" (child)[15] too. Put in easy-to-eat foods that your child likes and is already used to and prepare this food in small portions (*Shufunotomo* 1980: 28).

Filled with pages of recipes, hints, pictures, and ideas, the magazine codes each page with "helpful" headings:

- First off, easy-to-eat is step one.
- Next is being able to consume the *obentō* without leaving anything behind.
- Make it in such a way for the child to become proficient in the use of chopsticks.
- Decorate and fill it with cute dreams (*kawairashi yume*).
- For older classes (*nencho*), make *obentō* filled with variety.
- Once he's become used to it, balance foods your child likes with those he dislikes.
- For kids who hate vegetables. . . .
- For kids who hate fish. . . .
- For kids who hate meat. . . . (pp. 28–53)

Laced throughout cookbooks and other magazines devoted to *obentō*, the *obentō* guidelines issued by the school and sent home in the school flier every two weeks, and the words of Japanese mothers and teachers discussing

obentō, are a number of principles: (1) food should be made easy to eat: portions cut or made small and manipulable with fingers or chopsticks, (child-size) spoons and forks, skewers, toothpicks, muffin tins, containers, (2) portions should be kept small so the *obentō* can be consumed quickly and without any left-overs, (3) food that a child does not yet like should be eventually added so as to remove fussiness (*sukikirai*) in food habits, (4) make the *obentō* pretty, cute, and visually changeable by presenting the food attractively and by adding non-food objects such as silver paper, foil, toothpick flags, paper napkins, cute handkerchiefs, and variously shaped containers for soy sauce and ketchup, and (5) design *obentō*-related items as much as possible by the mother's own hands including the *obentō* bag (*obentōfukuro*) in which the *obentō* is carried.

The strictures propounded by publications seem to be endless. In practice I found that visual appearance and appeal were stressed by the mothers. By contrast, the directive to use *obentō* as a training process—adding new foods and getting older children to use chopsticks and learn to tie the *furoshiki*[16]—was emphasized by those judging the *obentō* at the school. Where these two sets of concerns met was, of course, in the child's success or failure completing the *obentō*. Ultimately this outcome and the mother's role in it, was how the *obentō* was judged in my experience.

The aestheticization of the *obentō* is by far its most intriguing aspect for a cultural anthropologist. Aesthetic categories and codes that operate generally for Japanese cuisine are applied, though adjusted, to the nursery school format. Substances are many but petite, kept segmented and opposed, and manipulated intensively to achieve an appearance that often changes or disguises the food. As a mother insisted to me, the creation of a bear out of miniature hamburgers and rice, or a flower from an apple or peach, is meant to sustain a child's interest in the underlying food. Yet my child, at least, rarely noticed or appreciated the art I had so laboriously contrived. As for other children, I observed that even for those who ate with no obvious "fussiness," mothers' efforts to create food as style continued all year long.

Thus much of a woman's labor over *obentō* stems from some agenda other than that of getting the child to eat an entire lunch-box. The latter is certainly a consideration and it is the rationale as well as cover for women being scrutinized by the school's authority figure—the teacher. Yet two other factors are important. One is that the *obentō* is but one aspect of the far more expansive and continuous commitment a mother is expected to make for and to her child. "*Kyōiku mama*" (education mother) is the term given to a mother who executes her responsibility to oversee and manage the education of her children with excessive vigor. And yet this excess is not only demanded by the state even at the level of the nursery school; it is conventionally given by mothers. Mothers who manage the home and children, often in virtual absence of a husband/father, are considered the factor that may make or break a child as s/he advances towards that pivotal point of the entrance examinations.[17]

In this sense, just as the *obentō* is meant as a device to assist a child in the struggles of first adjusting to school, the mother's role generally is perceived as being the support, goad, and cushion for the child. She will perform endless tasks to assist in her child's study: sharpen pencils and make midnight snacks as the child studies, attend cram schools to verse herself in subjects her child is weak in, make inquiries as to what school is most appropriate for her child, and consult with her child's teachers. If the child succeeds, a mother is complimented; if the child fails, a mother is blamed.

Thus at the nursery school level, the mother starts her own preparation for this upcoming role. Yet the jobs and energies demanded of a nursery school mother are, in themselves, surprisingly consuming. Just as the mother of an entering student is given a book listing all the pre-entry tasks she must complete, for example, making various bags and containers, affixing labels to all clothes in precisely the right place and with the size exactly right, she will be continually expected thereafter to attend Mothers' Association meetings, accompany children on fieldtrips, wash the clothes and indoor shoes of her child every week, add required items to a child's bag on a day's notice, and generally be available. Few mothers at the school my son attended could afford to work in even part-time or temporary jobs. Those women who did tended either to keep their outside work a secret or be reprimanded by a teacher for insufficient devotion to their child. Motherhood, in other words, is institutionalized through the child's school and such routines as making the *obentō* as a full-time, kept-at-home job.[18]

The second factor in a woman's devotion to over-elaborating her child's lunch-box is that her experience doing this becomes a part of her and a statement, in some sense, of who she is. Marx writes that labor is the most "essential" aspect to our species-being and that the products we produce are the encapsulation of us and therefore our productivity (1970: 71–76). Likewise, women are what they are through the products they produce. An *obentō* therefore is not only a gift or test for a child, but a representation and product of the woman herself. Of course, the two ideologically converge, as has been stated already, but I would also suggest that there is a potential disjoining. I sensed that the women were laboring for themselves apart from the agenda the *obentō* was expected to fill at school. Or stated alternatively, in the role that females in Japan are highly pressured and encouraged to assume as domestic manager, mother, and wife, there is, besides the endless and onerous responsibilities, also an opportunity for play. Significantly, women find play and creativity not outside their social roles but within them.

Saying this is not to deny the constraints and surveillance under which Japanese women labor at their *obentō*. Like their children at school, they are watched by not only the teacher but each other, and perfect what they create, partially at least, so as to be confirmed as a good and dutiful mother in the eyes of other mothers. The enthusiasm with which they absorb this task then is like my son's acceptance and internalization of the nursery school routines; no longer enforced from outside it becomes adopted as one's own.

The making of the *obentō* is, I would thus argue, a double-edged sword for women. By relishing its creation (for all the intense labor expended, only once or twice did I hear a mother voice any complaint about this task), a woman is ensconcing herself in the ritualization and subjectivity (subjection) of being a mother in Japan. She is alienated in the sense that others will dictate, inspect, and manage her work. On the reverse side, however, it is precisely through this work that the woman expresses, identifies, and constitutes herself. As Althusser pointed out, ideology can never be totally abolished (1971: 170); the elaborations that women work on "natural" food produce an *obentō* which is creative and, to some degree, a fulfilling and personal statement of themselves.

Minami, an informant, revealed how both restrictive and pleasurable the daily rituals of motherhood can be. The mother of two children—one, aged three and one, a nursery school student, Minami had been a professional opera singer before marrying at the relatively late age of 32. Now, her daily schedule was organized by routines associated with her child's nursery school: for example, making the *obentō*, taking her daughter to school and picking her up, attending Mothers' Association meetings, arranging daily play dates, and keeping the school uniform clean. While Minami wished to return to singing, if only on a part-time basis, she said that the demands of motherhood, particularly those imposed by her child's attendance at nursery school, frustrated this desire. Secretly snatching only minutes out of any day to practice, Minami missed singing and told me that being a mother in Japan means the exclusion of almost anything else.[19]

Despite this frustration, however, Minami did not behave like a frustrated woman. Rather she devoted to her mothering an energy, creativity, and intelligence I found to be standard in the Japanese mothers I knew. She planned special outings for her children at least two or three times a week, organized games that she knew they would like and would teach them cognitive skills, created her own stories and designed costumes for afternoon play, and shopped daily for the meals she prepared with her children's favorite foods in mind. Minami told me often that she wished she could sing more, but never once did she complain about her children, the chores of child-raising, or being a mother. The attentiveness displayed otherwise in her mothering was exemplified most fully in Minami's *obentōs*. No two were ever alike, each had at least four or five parts, and she kept trying out new ideas for both new foods and new designs. She took pride as well as pleasure in her *obentō* handicraft; but while Minami's *obentō* creativity was impressive, it was not unusual.

Examples of such extraordinary *obentō* creations from an *obentō* magazine include: (1) ("donut *obentō*"): two donuts, two wieners cut to look like a worm, two cut pieces of apple, two small cheese rolls, one hard-boiled egg made to look like a rabbit with leaf ears and pickle eyes and set in an aluminum muffin tin, cute paper napkin added, (2) (wiener doll *obentō*): a bed of rice with two doll creations made out of wiener parts (each consists of eight pieces comprising hat, hair, head, arms, body, legs), a line of pink ginger, a line of green parsley, paper flag of France added, (3) (vegetable flower and tulip *obentō*): a bed of rice laced with chopped hard-boiled egg, three tulip flowers made out of cut wieners with spinach precisely arranged as stem and leaves, a fruit salad with two raisins, three cooked peaches, three pieces of cooked apple, (4) (sweetheart doll *obentō* —*abekku ningyō* no *obentō*): in a two-section *obentō* box there are four rice balls on one side, each with a different center, on the other side are two dolls made of quail's eggs for heads, eyes and mouth added, bodies of cucumber, arranged as if lying down with two raw carrots for the pillow, covers made of one flower— cut cooked carrot, two pieces of ham, pieces of cooked spinach, and with different colored plastic skewers holding the dolls together (*Shufunotomo* 1980: 27, 30).

The impulse to work and re-work nature in these *obentōs* is most obvious perhaps in the strategies used to transform, shape, and/or disguise foods. Every mother I knew came up with her own repertoire of such techniques, and every *obentō* magazine or cookbook I examined offered a special section on these devices. It is important to keep in mind that these are treated as only flourishes: embellishments added to parts of an *obentō* composed of many parts. The following is a list from one magazine: lemon pieces made into butterflies, hard boiled eggs into *daruma* (popular Japanese legendary figure of a monk without his eyes), sausage cut into flowers, a hard-boiled egg decorated as a baby, an apple piece cut into a leaf, a radish flaked into a flower, a cucumber cut like a flower, a *mikan* (nectarine orange) piece arranged into a basket, a boat with a sail made from a cucumber, skewered sausage, radish shaped like a mushroom, a quail egg flaked into a cherry, twisted *mikan* piece, sausage cut to become a crab, a patterned cucumber, a ribboned carrot, a flowered tomato, cabbage leaf flower, a potato cut to be a worm, a carrot designed as a red shoe, an apple cut to simulate a pineapple (pp. 57–60).

Nature is not only transformed but also supplemented by store-bought or mother-made objects which are precisely arranged in the *obentō*. The former come from an entire industry and commodification of the *obentō* process: complete racks or sections in stores selling *obentō* boxes, additional small containers, *obentō* bags, cups, chopstick and utensil containers (all these with various cute characters or designs on the front), cloth and paper napkins, foil, aluminum tins, colored ribbon or string, plastic skewers, toothpicks with paper flags, and paper dividers. The latter are the objects mothers are encouraged and praised for making themselves: *obentō* bags, napkins, and handkerchiefs with appliquéd designs or the child's name embroidered. These supplements to the food, the arrangement of the food, and the *obentō* box's dividing walls (removable and adjustable) furnish the order of the *obentō*. Everything appears crisp and neat with each part kept in its own place: two tiny hamburgers set firmly atop a bed of rice; vegetables in a separate compartment in the box; fruit arranged in a muffin tin.

How the specific forms of *obentō* artistry— for example, a wiener cut to look like a worm

and set within a muffin tin—are encoded symbolically is a fascinating subject. Limited here by space, however, I will only offer initial suggestions. Arranging food into a scene recognizable by the child was an ideal mentioned by many mothers and cookbooks. Why those of animals, human beings, and other food forms (making a pineapple out of an apple, for example) predominate may have no other rationale than being familiar to children and easily reproduced by mothers. Yet it is also true that this tendency to use a trope of realism—casting food into realistic figures—is most prevalent in the meals Japanese prepare for their children. Mothers I knew created animals and faces in supper meals and/or *obentōs* made for other outings, yet their impulse to do this seemed not only heightened in the *obentō* that were sent to school but also played down in food prepared for other age groups.

What is consistent in Japanese cooking generally, as stated earlier, are the dual principles of manipulation and order. Food is manipulated into some other form than it assumes either naturally or upon being cooked: lines are put into mashed potatoes, carrots are flaked, wieners are twisted and sliced. Also, food is ordered by some human rather than natural principle; everything must have neat boundaries and be placed precisely so those boundaries do not merge. These two structures are the ones most important in shaping the nursery school *obentō* as well, and the inclination to design realistic imagery is primarily a means by which these other culinary codes are learned by and made pleasurable for the child. The simulacrum of a pineapple recreated from an apple therefore is less about seeing the pineapple in an apple (a particular form) and more about reconstructing the apple into something else (the process of transformation).

The intense labor, management, commodification, and attentiveness that go into the making of an *obentō* laces it, however, with many and various meanings. Overarching all is the potential to aestheticize a certain social order, a social order which is coded (in cultural and culinary terms) as Japanese. Not only is a mother making food more palatable to her nursery school child, but she is creating food as a more aesthetic and pleasing social structure. The *obentō's* message is that the world is constructed very precisely and that the role of any single Japanese in that world must be carried out with the same degree of precision. Production is demanding; and the producer must both keep within the borders of her/his role and work hard.

The message is also that it is women, not men, who are not only sustaining a child through food but carrying the ideological support of the culture that this food embeds. No Japanese man I spoke with had or desired the experience of making a nursery school *obentō* even once, and few were more than peripherally engaged in their children's education. The male is assigned a position in the outside world where he labors at a job for money and is expected to be primarily identified by and committed to his place of work.[20] Helping in the management of home and raising of children has not become an obvious male concern or interest in Japan, even as more and more women enter what was previously the male domain of work. Females have remained at and as the center of home in Japan and this message too is explicitly transmitted in both the production and consumption of entirely female-produced *obentō*.

The state accrues benefits from this arrangement. With children depending on the labor women devote to their mothering to such a degree, and women being pressured as well as pleasurized in such routine maternal productions as making the *obentō*— both effects encouraged and promoted by institutional features of the educational system heavily state-run and at least ideologically guided at even the nursery school level—a gendered division of labor is firmly set in place. Labor from males, socialized to be compliant and hard-working, is more extractable when they have wives to rely on for almost all domestic and familial management. And females become a source of

cheap labor, as they are increasingly forced to enter the labor market to pay domestic costs (including those vast debts incurred in educating children) yet are increasingly constrained to low-paying part-time jobs because of the domestic duties they must also bear almost totally as mothers.

Hence, not only do females, as mothers, operate within the ideological state apparatus of Japan's school system that starts semi-officially, with the nursery school, they also operate as an ideological state apparatus unto themselves. Motherhood is state ideology, working through children at home and at school and through such mother-imprinted labor that a child carries from home to school as with the *obentō*. Hence the post-World War II conception of Japanese education as being egalitarian, democratic, and with no agenda of or for gender differentiation, does not in practice stand up. Concealed within such cultural practices as culinary style and child-focused mothering, is a worldview in which the position and behavior an adult will assume has everything to do with the anatomy she/he was born with.

At the end, however, I am left with one question. If motherhood is not only watched and manipulated by the state but made by it into a conduit for ideological indoctrination, could not women subvert the political order by redesigning *obentō*? Asking this question, a Japanese friend, upon reading this paper, recalled her own experiences. Though her mother had been conventional in most other respects, she made her children *obentōs* that did not conform to the prevailing conventions. Basic, simple, and rarely artistic, Sawa also noted, in this connection, that the lines of these *obentōs* resembled those by which she was generally raised: as gender-neutral, treated as a person not "just as a girl," and being allowed a margin to think for herself. Today she is an exceptionally independent woman who has created a life for herself in America, away from homeland and parents, almost entirely on her own. She loves Japanese food, but the plain *obentōs* her mother made for her as a child, she is newly appreciative of now, as an adult.

The *obentōs* fed her, but did not keep her culturally or ideologically attached. For this, Sawa says today, she is glad.

ACKNOWLEDGMENTS

The fieldwork on which this article is based was supported by a Japan Foundation Post-doctoral Fellowship. I am grateful to Charles Piot for a thoughtful reading and useful suggestions for revision and to Jennifer Robertson for inviting my contribution to this issue. I would also like to thank Sawa Kurotani for her many ethnographic stories and input, and Phyllis Chock and two anonymous readers for the valuable contributions they made to revision of the manuscript.

NOTES

1. As Dorinne Kondo has pointed out, however, these cuisinal principles may be conditioned by factors of both class and circumstance. Her *shitamachi* (more traditional area of Tokyo) informants, for example, adhered only casually to this coding and other Japanese she knew followed them more carefully when preparing food for guests rather than family and when eating outside rather than inside the home (Kondo 1990: 61–2).

2. Rice is often, if not always, included in a meal: and it may substantially as well as symbolically constitute the core of the meal. When served at a table it is put in a large pot or electric rice maker and will be spooned into a bowl, still no bigger or predominant than the many other containers from which a person eats. In an *obentō* rice may be in one, perhaps the largest, section of a multi-sectioned *obentō* box, yet it will be arranged with a variety of other foods. In a sense rice provides the syntactic and substantial center to a meal yet the presentation of the food rarely emphasizes this core. The rice bowl is refilled rather than heaped as in the preformed *obentō* box, and in the *obentō* rice is often embroidered, supplemented, and/or covered with other foodstuffs.

3. Japanese will both endure a high price for rice at home and resist American attempts to export rice to Japan in order to stay domestically self-sufficient in this national food *qua* cultural symbol. Rice is the only foodstuff in which the Japanese have retained self-sufficient production.

4. The primary sources on education used are Horio 1988; Duke 1986; Rohlen 1983; Cummings 1980.

5. Neither the state's role in overseeing education nor a system of standardized tests is a new development in post-World War II Japan. What is new is the national standardization of tests and, in this sense, the intensified role the state has thus assumed in overseeing them. See Dore (1965) and Horio (1988).

6. Boocock (1989) differs from Tobin et al. (1989) on this point and asserts that the institutional differences are insignificant. She describes extensively how both yochien and hoikuen are administered (yochien are under the authority of Monbusho and hoikuen are under the authority of the Koseisho, the Ministry of Health and Welfare) and how both feed into the larger system of education. She emphasizes diversity: though certain trends are common amongst preschools, differences in teaching styles and philosophies are plentiful as well.

7. According to Rohlen (1989), families are incapable of indoctrinating the child into this social pattern of *shū ndanseikatsu* by their very structure and particularly by the relationship (of indulgence and dependence) between mother and child. For this reason and the importance placed on group structures in Japan, the nursery school's primary objective, argues Rohlen, is teaching children how to assimilate into groups. For further discussion of this point see also Peak 1989; Lewis 1989; Sano 1989; and the *Journal of Japanese Studies* issue [15(1)] devoted to Japanese preschool education in which these articles, including Boocock's, are published.

8. For a succinct anthropological discussion of these concepts, see Hendry (1987: 39–41). For an architectural study of Japan's management and organization of space in terms of such cultural categories as *uchi* and *soto,* see Greenbie (1988).

9. Endless studies, reports, surveys, and narratives document the close tie between women and home; domesticity and femininity in Japan. A recent international survey conducted for a Japanese housing construction firm, for example, polled couples with working wives in three cities, finding that 97% (of those polled) in Tokyo prepared breakfast for their families almost daily (compared with 43% in New York and 34% in London); 70% shopped for

groceries on a daily basis (3% in New York, 14% in London), and that only 22% of them had husbands who assisted or were willing to assist with housework (62% in New York, 77% in London) (quoted in *Chicago Tribune* 1991). For a recent anthropological study of Japanese housewives in English, see Imamura (1987). Japanese sources include *Juristo zokan sogo tokushu* 1985; *Mirai shakan* 1979; *Ohirasōri no seifu kenkyūkai* 3.

10. My comments pertain directly, of course, to only the women I observed, interviewed, and interacted with at the one private nursery school serving middle-class families in urban Tokyo. The profusion of *obentō*-related materials in the press plus the revelations made to me by Japanese and observations made by other researchers in Japan (for example, Tobin 1989; Fallows (1990), however, substantiate this as a more general phenomenon.

11. To illustrate this preoccupation and consciousness: during the time my son was not eating all his *obentō* many fellow mothers gave me suggestions, one mother lent me a magazine, his teacher gave me a full set of *obentō* cookbooks (one per season), and another mother gave me a set of small frozen food portions she had made in advance for future *obentōs*.

12. My son's teacher, Hamada-sensei, cited this explicitly as one of the reasons why the *obentō* was such an important training device for nursery school children. "Once they become *ichinensei* (first-graders) they'll be faced with a variety of food, prepared without elaboration or much spice, and will need to eat it within a delimited time period."

13. An anonymous reviewer questioned whether such emphasis placed on consumption of food in nursery school leads to food problems and anxieties in later years. Although I have heard that anorexia is a phenomenon now in Japan, I question its connection to nursery school *obentōs*. Much of the meaning of the latter practice, as I interpret it, has to do with the interface between production and consumption, and its gender linkage comes from the production end (mothers making it) rather than the consumption end (children eating it). Hence while control is taught through food, it is not a control linked primarily to females or bodily appearance, as anorexia may tend to be in this culture.

14. Fujita argues, from her experience as a working mother of a daycare (*hoikuen*) child, that the substance of these daily talks between teacher and mother is intentionally insignificant. Her interpretation is that the mother is not to be overly involved in, nor too informed about, matters of the school (1989).

15. "*Boku*" is a personal pronoun that males in Japan use as a familiar reference to themselves. Those in close relationships with males—mothers and wives, for example—can use *boku* to refer to their sons or husbands. Its use in this context is telling.

16. In the upper third grade of the nursery school (*nenchō* class; children aged five to six) my son attended, children were ordered to bring their *obentō* with chopsticks and not forks and spoons (considered easier to use) and in the traditional *furoshiki* (piece of cloth which enwraps items and is double tied to close it) instead of the easier-to-manage *obentō* bags with drawstrings. Both furoshiki and chopsticks (*o-hashi*) are considered traditionally Japanese and their usage marks not only greater effort and skills on the part of the children but their enculturation into being Japanese.

17. For the mother's role in the education of her child, see, for example, White (1987). For an analysis, by a Japanese of the intense dependence on the mother that is created and cultivated in a child, see Doi (1971). For Japanese sources on the mother-child relationship and ideology (some say pathology) of Japanese motherhood, see Yamamura (1971); Kawai (1976); Kyutoku (1981); *Sorifu seihonen taisaku honbuhen* (1981); *Kadeshobo shinsha* (1981). Fujita's account of the ideology of motherhood at the nursery school level is particularly interesting in this connection (1989).

18. Women are entering the labor market in increasing numbers yet the proportion to do so in the capacity of part-time workers (legally constituting as much as thirty-five hours per week but without the benefits accorded to full-time workers) has also increased. The choice of part-time over full-time employment has much to do with a woman's simultaneous and almost total responsibility for the domestic realm (*Juristo* 1985: see also Kondo 1990).

19. As Fujita (1989: 72–79) points out, its mothers are treated as a separate category of mothers, and non-working mothers are expected, by definition, to be mothers full time.

20. Nakane's much quoted text on Japanese society states this male position in structuralist terms (1970). Though dated, see also Vogel (1963) and Rohlen (1974) for descriptions of the social roles for middle-class, urban Japanese males. For a succinct recent discussion of gender roles within the family, see Lock (1990).

REFERENCES

Althusser, Louis. 1971. *Ideology and Ideological State Apparatuses (Notes toward an investigation in Lenin and philosophy and other essays).* New York: Monthly Review.

Asanuma, Kaoru. 1987. *"Ganbari" no Kozo (Structure of "Ganbari").* Tokyo: Kikkawa Kobunkan.

Barthes, Roland. 1957. *Mythologies.* Trans. by Annette Lavers. New York: Noonday Press.

Boocock, Sarane Spence. 1989. Controlled diversity: An overview of the Japanese preschool system. *The Journal of Japanese Studies* 15(1): 41–65.

Chicago Tribune. 1991. Burdens of Working Wives Weigh Heavily in Japan. January 27, Section 6, p. 7.

Cummings, William K. 1980. *Education and Equality in Japan.* Princeton NJ; Princeton University Press.

Doi, Takeo, 1971. *The Anatomy of Dependence: The Key Analysis of Japanese Behavior.* Trans. by John Becker. Tokyo: Kodansha Int'l. Ltd.

Dore, Ronald P. 1965. *Education in Tokugawa Japan.* London: Routledge and Kegan Paul.

Duke, Benjamin. 1986. *The Japanese School: Lessons for Industrial America.* New York: Praeger.

Fallows, Deborah. 1990. "Japanese Women." *National Geographic* 177(4): 52–83.

Fujita, Mariko. 1989. "It's All Mother's Fault": Childcare and the Socialization of Working Mothers in Japan. *The Journal of Japanese Studies* 15(1): 67–91.

Greenbie, Barrie B. 1988. *Space and Spirit in Modern Japan.* New Haven, CT: Yale University Press.

Hendry, Joy. 1986. *Becoming Japanese: The World of the Pre-School Child.* Honolulu: University of Hawaii Press.

———. 1987. *Understanding Japanese Society.* London: Croom Helm.

Horio, Teruhisa. 1988. *Educational Thought and Ideology in Modern Japan: State Authority and Intellectual Freedom.* Trans. by Steven Platzer. Tokyo: University of Tokyo Press.

Imamura, Anne E. 1987. *Urban Japanese Housewives: At Home and in the Community.* Honolulu: University of Hawaii Press.

Juristo zōkan Sōgōtokushu. 1985. Josei no Gensai to Mirai (The present and future of women). 39.

Kadeshobo shinsha. 1981. *Hahaoya (Mother).* Tokyo: Kadeshobo shinsha.

Kawai, Hayao. 1976. *Bosei shakai nihon no Byōri (The Pathology of the Mother Society—Japan).* Tokyo: Chuo Koronsha.

Kondo, Dorinne K. 1990. *Crafting Selves: Power, Gender, and Discourses of Identity in a Japanese Workplace.* Chicago, IL: University of Chicago Press.

Kyū toku, Shigemori. 1981. *Bogenbyo (Disease Rooted in Motherhood).* Vol. II. Tokyo: Sanma Kushuppan.

Lewis, Catherine C. 1989. From Indulgence to Internalization: Social Control in the Early School Years. *Journal of Japanese Studies* 15(1): 139–157.

Lock, Margaret. 1990. Restoring Order to the House of Japan. *The Wilson Quarterly* 14(4): 42–49.

Marx, Karl, and Frederick Engels. 1970 (1947). *Economic and Philosophic Manuscripts,* ed. C.J. Arthur. New York: International Publishers.

Mirai shakan. 1979. Shufu to onna (Housewives and Women). Kunitachishi Komininkan Shimindaigaku Semina-no Kiroku. Tokyo: Miraisha.

Mouer, Ross and Yoshio Sugimoto. 1986. *Images of Japanese Society: A Study in the Social Construction of Reality.* London: Routledge and Kegan.

Nakane, Chie, 1970. *Japanese Society.* Berkeley: University of California Press.

Ohirasōri no Seifu kenkyūkai. 1980. Katei Kiban no Jujitsu (The Fullness of Family Foundations). (Ohirasōri no Seifu Kenkyūkai-3). Tokyo: Okurashō Insatsukyōku.

Peak, Lois. 1989. "Learning to Become Part of the Group: The Japanese Child's Transition to Preschool Life." *The Journal of Japanese Studies* 15(1): 93–123.

Ritchie, Donald. 1985. *A Taste of Japan: Food Fact and Fable, Customs and Etiquette, What the People Eat.* Tokyo: Kodansha International Ltd.

Rohlen, Thomas P. 1974. *The Harmony and Strength: Japanese White-Collar Organization in Anthropological Perspective.* Berkeley: University of California Press.

———. 1983. *Japan's High Schools.* Berkeley: University of California Press.

———. 1989. "Order in Japanese Society: Attachment, Authority and Routine." *The Journal of Japanese Studies* 15(1): 5–40.

Sano, Toshiyuki. 1989. "Methods of Social Control and Socialization in Japanese Day-Care Centers. *The Journal of Japanese Studies* 15(1):125–138.

Shufunotomo Besutoserekushon shiri-zu. 1980. Obentō 500 sen. Tokyo: Shufunotomo Co., Ltd.

Shufunotomohyakka shiri-zu. 1981. 365 nichi no obentō hyakka. Tokyo: Shufunotomo Co.

Sōrifu Seihonen Taisaku Honbuhen, 1981. Nihon no kodomo to hahaoya (Japenese mothers and children): Kokusaihikaku (international comparisons). Tokyo: Sōrifu Seishonen Taisaku Honbuhen.

Tobin, Joseph J., David Y. H. Wu, and Dana H. Davidson. 1989. *Preschool in Three Cultures: Japan, China, and the United States*. New Haven, CT: Yale University Press.

Vogel, Erza. 1963. *Japan's New Middle Class: The Salary Man and His Family in a Tokyo Suburb*. Berkeley: University of California Press.

White, Merry. 1987. *The Japanese Educational Challenge: A Commitment to Children*. New York: Free Press.

Yamamura, Yoshiaki. 1971. *Nihonjin to Haha: Bunka Toshite No Haha no Kannen Ni Tsuite no Kenkyu (The Japanese and Mother: Research on the Conceptualization of Mother as Culture)*. Tokyo: Toyo-shuppansha.

VIII

Gender, Household, and Kinship

The study of kinship has been central to cross-cultural research. Marriage customs, systems of descent, and patterns of residence have been described and compared in a range of societies around the world. At the heart of traditional studies of kinship is the opposition between the domestic domain on the one hand and the public, political, and jural domain on the other. Anthropologists, particularly those working in Africa, studied kinship in this latter domain. They delineated large corporate descent groups called lineages that managed property and resources and that were the basic building blocks of political organization (Fortes 1949, 1953). Marriage, for some kinship theorists, is a political transaction, involving the exchange of women between men who wish to form alliances (Levi-Strauss 1969; see also Ortner 1978). A woman, from this perspective, is a passive pawn with little influence over kinship transactions. She is viewed "in terms of the rights her kin have to her domestic labor, to the property she might acquire, to her children, and to her sexuality" (Lamphere 1974: 98). The dynamic, affective, and even interest-oriented aspects of women's kinship are essentially ignored in an approach that is rooted in androcentric principles: Women have the children; men impregnate the women; and men usually exercise control (Fox 1967).

   Recent critiques of the traditional study of kinship have pointed out that it is "no longer adequate to view women as bringing to kinship primarily a capacity for bearing children while men bring primarily a capacity for participation in public life" (Collier and Yanagisako 1987: 7). A gendered approach to kinship takes a number of different directions but focuses on the status of men and women in different kinship systems and on the power (defined as the ability to make others conform to one's desires and wishes) that accrues to women through their manipulation of social relations (Maynes et al. 1996). Cross-cultural variations in the status of men and women have been examined in relation to rules of descent and postmarital residence (Martin and Voorhies 1975; Friedl 1975). Among horticulturalists, for example, women have higher status in societies characterized by matrilineal descent (descent through the female line from a common female ancestor) and matrilocal residence (living with the wife and her kin after marriage) than in societies characterized by patrilineal descent (descent through the male line from a common male ancestor) and patrilocal residence (living with the husband and his kin after marriage). In matrilineal systems, descent group membership, social identity, rights to land, and succession to political office are all inherited through one's mother.

When matrilineality is combined with matrilocal residence, a husband marries into a household in which a long-standing domestic coalition exists between his wife and her mother, sisters, and broader kin relations (Friedl 1975). These women cooperate with one another in work endeavors and provide mutual support. Although in a matrilineal system a man retains authority over his sisters and her children, the coalitions formed by kin-related women can provide them with power and influence both within and beyond the household (Brown 1970; Lamphere 1974) and also with a degree of sexual freedom. The important issue for women's status, as Schlegel (1972: 96) has argued, is not the descent system per se but the organization of the domestic group.

In this book, Menon discusses a classic anthropological case of matrilineality—the Nayar of South India. The Nayar are perhaps best known for their marriage system, which could be both polygynous (a man with several wives) or polyandrous (a woman with several husbands). Traditional Nayar women went through two forms of marriages, one the *tali-tying* (the tali is a gold ornament), and the other the *sambandam,* or joining together with one or more visiting husbands (See Gough 1961 for further discussion). Both these ceremonies legitimized reproduction for the matrilineal descent group or *taravad.* Menon (this book) focuses not only on the status and roles of women within the traditional matrilineal *taravads,* but also on how a slow shift from matriliny to patriliny (itself the result of broader social and economic changes) has opened other avenues for women. Among modern-day Nayar, *tali-tying* no longer exists, marriages are monogamous, and couples live in nuclear family households. While some authors have suggested that the status and autonomy accorded Nayar women under the traditional system has declined with these changes, Menon argues that both class and kinship position influenced the relative autonomy of women within the *taravad* just as they do in the new monogamous and nuclear family system.

In contrast to matrilineal and matrilocal systems, in patrilineal and patrilocal societies women do not have their own kin nearby. A woman enters her husband's household as a stranger. Separated from her own kin, she cannot forge lateral alliances easily. However, other opportunities are open to women that enhance their power and status in patrilineal and patrilocal societies. Taiwanese women, for example, marry into the households of their husbands (Wolf 1972). A Taiwanese wife must pay homage to her husband's ancestors, obey her husband and mother-in-law, and bear children for her husband's patrilineage. According to Wolf (1972: 32), "A woman can and, if she is ever to have any economic security, must provide the links in the male chain of descent, but she will never appear in anyone's genealogy as that all-important name connecting the past to the future."

After a Taiwanese wife gives birth to a son, her status in the household begins to change, and it improves during her life course as she forges what Wolf calls a uterine family—a family based on the powerful relationship between mothers and sons. The subordination of conjugal to intergenerational relationships that is exemplified by the Taiwanese case, as well as the opportune ways in which women take advantage of filial ties to achieve political power within and beyond the household, are apparent in other societies around the world—for example, in sub-Saharan Africa (Potash 1986).

When a Taiwanese wife becomes a mother-in-law she achieves the greatest power and status within her husband's household. Wolf (1972: 37) concludes that "the uterine family has no ideology, no formal structure, and no public existence. It is built out of sentiments and loyalties that die with its members, but it is no less real for all that. The descent lines of men are born and nourished in the uterine families of women, and it is here that a male ideology that excludes women makes its accommodations with reality." Similarly, Hausa trading women in West Africa are able to compensate for an ideology that keeps them in residential seclusion by depending on their children to distribute their goods, provide information on the world outside the household, and help with child care and cooking (Schildkrout 1983).

Wolf's research on Taiwanese women substantiates Lamphere's (1974: 99) observation that "the distribution of power and authority in the family, the developmental cycle of the domestic group, and women's strategies are all related." By "strategies" Lamphere is referring to the active ways in which women use and manipulate kinship to their own advantage. The strategic use of kinship is a mechanism for economic survival among the African-American families of a Midwestern town described by Stack (in this book). The households of these families are flexible and fluid; they are tied together by complex networks of female kinship and friendship. If the boundaries of the household are elastic, the ties that unite kin and friends are long-lasting. Through these domestic networks, women exchange a range of goods and services including child care. They rely on one another and through collective efforts keep one another afloat. When one member of the network achieves a degree of economic success she can choose to withdraw from kin cooperation to conserve resources. However, by reinitiating gift-giving and exchange, at some point she can easily reenter the system. Stack's research shows one example of a strategy pursued by many families in the United States who must cope with urban poverty and the constant threat of unemployment.

A similar approach is shown in research on Afro-Caribbean families, who also live in conditions of economic uncertainty and stress. This research has generated a vigorous debate about a complex of characteristics, including female-headed households, women's control of household earnings and decision making, kinship networks linked through women, and the absence of resident men. This complex of characteristics has been referred to as matrifocality. Drawing on data from her research in Jamaica, Prior (in this book) reviews the concept of matrifocality, a concept first introduced by Raymond Smith in 1956 to describe the central position and power of the mother within the household. Rather than viewing these households as disorganized or pathological results of slavery and colonialism, anthropologists recently have stressed their adaptive advantages (Bolles and Samuels 1989) for women who are both mothers and economic providers. Furthermore, as Prior suggests, the composition of households in the Caribbean is fluid; they can be female-headed at one point in time and nuclear at another. Arguing against a widely held conception within anthropology, Prior suggests that fathers and male partners are by no means marginal to the household.

Prior points out that very little work has been done on the relations between men and women in such households because men were always assumed to be absent. One neglected aspect of male–female household relations is domestic violence. Such violence often emerges because the expectations that women hold for men, whether they are monetary contributions to the household or fidelity, are not fulfilled. The potential for violence that can erupt when women challenge men about these unfulfilled obligations can undercut the power that women otherwise maintain within the household.

Women-centered families like those of African-Americans and Afro-Caribbeans have been described for other parts of the world (Tanner 1974). Both Brettell (1986) and Cole (1991) find such families among populations in northern Portugal and link them to a long history of male emigration. Whether in agriculture or in fishing, many women in northern Portugal must fulfill both male and female roles within the household.

In this region women often inherit significant property and there is a tendency for matrilocal residence or neolocal residence near the wife's kin. This matrilateral bias is also apparent among Japanese-American immigrants in the urban United States (Yanagisako 1977). Manifested in women-centered kin networks, this bias influences patterns of co-residence, residential proximity, mutual aid, and affective ties. Rather than stressing the economic reasons for the maintenance of kinship ties, Yanagisako draws attention to the role of women as kin keepers who foster and perpetuate channels of communication and who plan and stage elaborate family rituals.

The social and ritual importance of kinship is precisely what di Leonardo (in this book) focuses on in her discussion of the female world of cards and holidays. The Italian-American women she describes work in the labor market and at home, but they are also engaged in "kin work." Kin work is women's work and involves maintaining contact through all kinds of mechanisms with family members who are deemed important. Unlike child care and house cleaning, it is a task that has to be carried out by the woman herself. Though it is often burdensome, women undertake kin work, according to di Leonardo, because through it they can set up a chain of valuable and long-term obligations within a wide circle of social relations.

Although di Leonardo identifies other parts of the developed world in which women have greater kin knowledge than men and work hard at maintaining kinship networks (for example, Lomnitz and Perez-Lizaur 1987), several questions are open to further empirical investigation. For example, why does kin work take on ritual significance in some societies, and why is it culturally assigned to women in some contexts and to men in others? Di Leonardo interprets the emergence of gendered kin work in association with a relative decline in importance of the domain of public male kinship that is found, for example, in African societies characterized by a powerful principle of descent. The shift, she suggests, is part of the process of capitalist development. Enloe (1990) has taken these arguments much further by demonstrating how both global politics and global economics are engendered. Without kin work, for example, Hallmark (the card manufacturer) would be out of business.

Collier and Yanagisako (1987) have argued that gender and kinship are mutually constructed and should be brought together into one analytic field (see also Stone 1997). Kinship and gender are closely allied because they are both based in, but not exclusively determined by, biology and because what it means to be a man or a woman is directly linked to the rules of marriage and sexuality that a culture constructs. As Lindenbaum (1987: 221) has observed, "Relations of kinship are in certain societies, relations of production. If kinship is understood as a system that organizes the liens we hold on the emotions and labors of others, then it must be studied in relation to gender ideologies that enmesh men and women in diverse relations of productive and reproductive work. The variable constructions of male and female that emerge in different times and places are central to an understanding of the character of kinship."

REFERENCES

Bolles, A. Lynn and Deborah d'Amico Samuels. 1989. "Anthropological Scholarship on Gender in the English-Speaking Caribbean." In Sandra Morgen (ed.). *Gender and Anthropology*, pp. 171–188. Washington, DC: American Anthropological Association.

Brettell, Caroline B. 1986. *Men Who Migrate, Women Who Wait: Population and History in a Portuguese Parish.* Princeton: Princeton University Press.

Brown, Judith K. 1970. "Economic Organization and the Position of Women Among the Iroquois." *Ethnohistory* 17: 151–167.

Collier, Jane Fishburne and Sylvia Junko Yanagisako. 1987. *Gender and Kinship: Essays Toward a Unified Analysis.* Stanford: Stanford University Press.

Cole, Sally. 1991. *Women of the Praia: Work and Lives in a Portuguese Coastal Community.* Princeton: Princeton University Press.

Enloe, Cynthia. 1990. *Bananas, Beaches and Bases: Making Feminist Sense of International Politics.* Berkeley: University of California Press.

Fortes, Meyer. 1949. *The Web of Kinship Among the Tallensi. London: International African Institute,* Oxford University Press.

———. 1953. "The Structure of Unilineal Descent Groups." *American Anthropologist* 55: 25–39.

Fox, Robin. 1967. Kinship and Marriage: An Anthropological Perspective. Harmondsworth: Penguin.

Friedl, Ernestine. 1975. *Women and Men: An Anthropologist's View.* New York: Holt, Rinehart and Winston.

Gough, Kathleen. 1961. "Nayar: Central Kerala." In David M. Schneider and Kathleen Gough (eds.) *Matrilineal Kinship,* pp 298–384. Berkeley: University of California Press.

Lamphere, Louise. 1974. "Strategies, Cooperation, and Conflict Among Women in Domestic Groups." In Michelle Z. Rosaldo and Louise Lamphere (eds.). *Woman, Culture, and Society,* pp. 97–112. Stanford: Stanford University Press.

Levi-Strauss, Claude. 1969. *The Elementary Structures of Kinship.* Boston: Beacon Press.

Lindenbaum, Shirley, 1987. "The Mystification of Female Labors." In Jane Fishburne Collier and Sylvia Junko Yanagisako (eds.). *Gender and Kinship: Essays Toward a Unified Analysis.* Stanford: Stanford University Press.

Lomnitz, Larissa and Marisol Perez-Lizaur. 1987. *A Mexican Elite Family ,1820–1980.* Princeton: Princeton University Press.

Martin, M. Kay and Barbara Voorhies. 1975. *Female of the Species.* New York: Columbia University Press.

Maynes, Mary Jo, Ann Waltner, Birgitte Soland, and Ulrike Strasser. 1996. *Gender, Kinship, Power: A Comparative and Interdisciplinary History.* New York: Routledge.

Ortner, Sherry. 1978. "The Virgin and the State." *Feminist Studies* 4 (3): 19–35.

Potash, Betty (ed.). 1986. *Widows in African Societies.* Stanford: Stanford University Press.

Schildkrout, Enid. 1983. "Dependence and Autonomy: The Economic Activities of Secluded Hausa Women in Kano." In Christine Oppong (ed.). *Female and Male in West Africa.* Winchester, MA: Allen and Unwin.

Schlegel, Alice. 1972. *Male Dominance and Female Autonomy: Domestic Authority in Matrilineal Societies.* New Haven: Human Relations Area Files.

Smith, Raymond. 1956. *The Negro Family in British Guiana: Family Structure and Social Status in the Villages.* London: Routledge and Kegan Paul.

Stone, Linda. 1997. *Kinship and Gender: An Introduction.* Boulder, CO.: Westview Press.

Tanner, Nancy. 1974. "Matrifocality in Indonesia and Africa and Among Black Americans." In Michelle Z. Rosaldo and Louise Lamphere (eds.). *Woman, Culture, and Society,* pp. 129–156. Stanford: Stanford University Press.

Wolf, Margery. 1972. *Women and the Family in Rural Taiwan.* Stanford: Stanford University Press.

Yanagisako, Sylvia Junko. 1977. "Women-Centered Kin Networks in Urban Bilateral Kinship." *American Ethnologist* 2: 207–226.

Male Authority and Female Authority: A Study of the Matrilineal Nayars of Kerala, South India

Shanti Menon

In the winter of 1990, I was travelling on a train from Trichur to Madras in South India. My travelling companion was a middle-aged Nayar businessman, a widower. We got into a discussion about my research in Kerala. He was surprised that I was even considering studying Nayar women on the subject of female empowerment. "You are wasting your time," he said, with an arrogance that is typical of upper class Nayar men.

> Our women are really very well off, they are treated with great respect and they wield a lot of power. You should be studying the lower castes. Their women are treated like cattle. The men treat them like pieces of property which they own. They are not like us. That is the difference between matrilineality and patrilineality. Our women are in a very fortunate situation.

Later that evening he talked about his attempts to arrange a marriage for his son.

> All we want is a girl with a college degree and from an upper middle-class family. We want a girl who will stay at home and take care of things. I can't believe how difficult that is. Today, the moment a girl has a college degree she wants to go out and work. And once she starts earning some money she becomes very headstrong and self-willed. She starts placing her interests before that of the men in the household, and that's when the problems start. I know a lot of marriages that are breaking up because of this reason. We want to avoid that. Today girls are very different from what they were when I was young.

From Mary Jo Maynes, Ann Waltner, Birgitte Soland, and Ulrike Strassed, eds. *Gender, Kinship and Power: A Comparative and Interdisciplinary History*. New York: Routledge.

I found it interesting that he did not see the contradiction between the two sets of statements that he had made, a tension between beliefs and practices that characterizes the situation of women within the Nayar matrilineal kinship system. In this paper I propose to explore these tensions and the relationship between the dominant discourse on gender and kinship on the one hand and women's agency on the other. As Foucault (1978) states, "where there is power, there is resistance and yet, or rather consequently, this resistance is never in a position of exteriority in relation to power." I argue, through a narration of women's experiences, that Nayar matrilineality, like patrilineal kinship systems, operates within the structures of patriarchy. Nayar women covertly contest and disrupt this script in their everyday lives. They do not, however, openly challenge it.

In the public domain, Nayar women's speech and actions are framed within the terms of the dominant discourse. Scott (1990, p. 4) states that "situations of domination produce a public transcript in close conformity with how the dominant group would wish to have things appear. The dominant never control the stage absolutely, but their wishes normally prevail. In the short run, it is in the interest of the subordinate to produce a more or less credible performance, speaking the lines and making the gestures he knows are expected of him." This is a tactic that Nayar women adopt in their dealings with men. The "hidden transcript" is revealed in their private behavioral practices, at variance with their speech and actions in the public sphere.

In the first section of this article, I will describe the Nayar matrilineal kinship system and the transformation of this institution. In the second section, I will narrate, through Nayar women's "voices," their experiences of living within this kinship system, and what the changes mean in the context of their lives. In the final section, I will analyze women's contestation and disruption of the dominant gender and kinship ideology.

The accounts of women's lives are based on my fieldwork in Alanthara village in Trichur District, Central Kerala. Situated three miles from Trichur town, the district headquarters, Alanthara has expanded considerably over the past thirty years. Traditionally, the village has been an agricultural community. The land reform laws of the 1960s, which included a limit on the size of landholdings and redistribution of excess land among the landless laborers, brought radical changes in the economic pattern in the village. Tenant farming was abolished, and tenants were given the rights to the land that they cultivated. The Nayar households in the village, most of whom were landowners, lost a significant part of their holdings. Today agriculture is no longer a viable primary source of income for most families. Many of the young men work in urban areas, either within the state or outside. The expanding economy in the Middle East, following the oil boom, has provided laboring jobs for several young men in the village. The large sums of money that they send home to their families have drastically affected not only the class structure within the village but also the quality of life that people lead and their expectations and aspirations for the future.

I spent one year living in the village and talking with women from the "old" families. "Old" is a term used by the villagers when speaking of established families who have lived in the village for two generations or more, as opposed to those who have moved into the village in the recent past. In narrating the accounts of Nayar women's lives, I speak from my specific location as a Nayar woman whose family has lived in Alanthara for generations. Though I did not grow up in the village, I have strong ties with the place; it is my "home" in India.

Though the experiences narrated in these accounts are true for many Nayar women living in rural Central Kerala, they cannot be extended to Nayar women living in other regions in the state. Women's experiences within the matrilineal tradition vary across the state depending on socioeconomic and cultural factors.

NAYAR MATRILINEALITY IN CENTRAL KERALA

The Nayars of Central Kerala, a dominant caste group, traditionally "exemplified an extremely matrilineal form of social organization" (Moore 1986, p. 523). This was reflected primarily in their laws of inheritance and marriage systems. The Nayars lived in matrilineal joint families called *taravads*. A traditional *taravad* usually consisted of a set of matrilineally related kin, both male and female. This would include sisters and brothers, the sisters' children and their daughters' children. The property was owned communally by all the members of the family but it was managed by the most senior male member of the family, called the *karanavan*. He had no right to sell or give the property away; this could only be done with the consent of all the members of the *taravad*, but his authority regarding the management of the property and decisions taken within the *taravad* was absolute. Descent was traced through the female line, and property passed from a mother to her children, both male and female. A son had no right to pass his inheritance on to his children. On his death it reverted back to his *taravad*.

The marriage system (*sambandham*) of the matrilineal Nayars was characterized by loose marital ties, expressed in serial and simultaneous polyandry and polygyny and hypergamy, that is to say both men and women had multiple spouses, and women married men of a higher caste or class. Hypergamy was encouraged by the *taravad* because such a union raised its "prestige." The men lived in their own *taravads*, with their mothers and sisters, and visited their wives in the evening. They had no rights or responsibilities over their children. A woman's children were the responsibility of her *taravad*. There were no fathers or in-laws in a *taravad*, and little importance was attached to a relationship between husband and wife or father and children (Mencher 1965).

In the second half of the nineteenth century, the "impact of a cash economy, western style education, improved communication and a British inspired system of law" (Jeffrey 1976, p. xiv) led to major social and political changes. This in turn led to a popular demand for laws changing traditional matrilineal practices. A series of legislative measures stretching from 1896 to 1976, relating to personal and inheritance laws, slowly eroded matrilineal practices in Central Kerala (Jeffrey 1990). The changes were a result of "massive economic, ideological and legislative pressures (Mies 1980, p. 89) aimed at bringing the group in line with the dominant patrilineal system that existed in the rest of India. This has resulted in a redefinition of Nayar women's positions. In the following section of this paper, I narrate women's accounts of their experiences within this rapidly changing system. In doing so, my intention is not to reproduce the workings of the matrilineal system, but to explore ways in which matrilineality and patrilineality mirror one another. I examine women's locations within matrilineal kinship groups and the implications of these locations for the degree of autonomy that women exercise both within private spaces and in the public domain.

WOMEN'S VOICES AND THE "EXPERIENCE" OF MATRILINEALITY

Though legislation has effectively abolished matrilineal practices in Kerala, the Nayars, like my travelling companion on the train, still regard themselves and are seen by other castes as a matrilineal group. Though they occupy a subordinate position within the kinship group, Nayar women do not experience some of the oppressive situations faced by women in patrilineal kinship groups. Kandiyoti (1988, p. 278) describes the control and manipulation of women under "classic" Indian patriarchy:

Girls are given away in marriage at a very young age into households headed by their husband's father. There, they are subordinate not only to

all the men but also to the more senior women, especially their mother-in-law . . . The young bride enters her husband's household as an effectively dispossessed individual who can establish her place in the patriliny only by producing male offspring. The patrilineage totally appropriates both women's labor and progeny and renders their work and contribution to production invisible.

Nayar women in Alanthara do not face similar situations. A woman owns property, and is never placed in a subservient position in her husband's home. A girl is not seen as a burden on her family, and there are no social pressures on her to bear sons. Her *taravad* is always her "home," and provides a great deal of security:

It makes a difference when we are living in our own homes, we have greater autonomy because it is our place. The men may have more power than the women, often they only seem to take all the decisions in the family. What many people do not realize is that very often it is the women "within" the home who are the real decision makers, the men merely carry them out. But as we all know, it is important to project the men as the "real" figures of authority, to the world at large. This is necessary for the prestige of the *taravad*. However, being on our own ground gives us great strength. We have the freedom to speak freely without bothering about formal niceties. We have to deal with people related to us by blood, our mothers, our brothers, they are all "ours." That is not so with our husband's families. It is easier to deal with our own, to express needs and opinions and take actions that are related to our life. It is different with a set of people who we are connected with by marriage ties. Our strength lies in our own home. (Girija, age twenty-eight)

The *taravad* provides women with a space from which they can challenge the dominant gender ideology and exercise a certain degree of autonomy.

The Nayars are not a homogenous group, and a woman's influence within her kinship group is mediated by the socioeconomic class in which her *taravad* is situated. Women from landowning families are far more dependent on and controlled by the men in their *taravads* than women who are members of less affluent *taravads*. This is often ignored by writers when discussing the situation of Nayar women within the matrilineal kinship system. In 1901, the Cochin Census Commissioner, M. Sankara Menon (a Nayar), wrote:

> The condition of women under this complicated system requires to be specially noticed. The two sexes are nearly on a par as to inheritance of property. Again conjugal freedom also being not all on one side, the relations of the sexes appear to be more rational than amongst most other communities . . . Further, the woman is free to enjoy the pleasures of social life, as it seldom falls to her lot to be worried with the miseries of domestic seclusion (Fuller 1976, p. 6).

This picture was almost never completely accurate. The *karanavan* had considerable authority over all the members of the *taravad*, and women's movements outside the *taravad* and their sexuality were controlled. The extent of autonomy wielded by Nayar women is mediated both by their family organization and by their locations within a hierarchical class structure. Following Dyson and Moore (1983, p. 45) I define female autonomy as women's:

> capacity to manipulate [their] personal environment. Autonomy indicates the ability . . . to obtain information and to use it as the basis for making decisions about [their] private concerns and those of [their] intimates. Autonomy, in other words, relates directly to human agency.

In the traditional Nayar extended family, like in the patrilineal extended family, the oldest male member, the *karanavan*, was in a position of authority. Upper-class Nayar women, like the women in the other dominant castes and classes in patrilineal India, lived very circumscribed lives, controlled by their male kin. Kalyaniamma, a seventy-three-year-old matriarch of one of the leading *taravads* in Alanthara, described what it was like for her to live and grow up in a rural, landowning, upper-class *taravad*.

> I grew up in a joint family which included my grandmother, my mother, my mother's brother who was the *karanavan* of the *taravad*, and the five of us children—my four siblings and I. For many years my uncle's wife and their children also lived in our taravad. This was very unusual, but then the social practices had slowly begun to change at this time.
>
> My uncle, the *karanavan*, managed all the affairs of the household, including the finances. He would give the women money to run the household, and they were accountable to him for every *paise* that they spent.
>
> Though we women had some degree of freedom within the house, we were in charge of running the household and seeing to it that everything worked smoothly, our lives were very restricted. Most of the time we were confined to the physical space within the *taravad*. We had no access to the front of the house, and as a young girl I was not allowed to meet with male visitors to the *taravad*. The only time we went out of the *taravad* was to visit the temples, and at this time we were closely supervised by the older women. On rare occasions we visited the homes of other members of the family, but this did not happen often. We did not go to the stores, that was absolutely out. Everything that we wanted, including our clothes, was bought for us by the men. We had no choice but to like the clothes that they bought for us. No one asked us for an opinion anyway, and we never thought to give one. It was not our place. It is so different today. Women move around and there aren't as many restrictions as there were when I was young. My daughters had greater control over their lives when they were young than I ever did. That may have been because the *taravad* had broken up at the time they were growing up, and they lost their father when they were very young. It is easier dealing with a woman than negotiating with an autocratic male. (Kalyaniamma, age seventy-three)

The women in Kalyaniamma's *taravad* had a limited degree of autonomy in the management of "domestic" affairs, but on the whole their lives were controlled by the *karanavan*. The transformation of matrilineality within a brief time span is reflected in her description of the differences between her life and that of her daughters.

Kalyaniamma belongs to an affluent, landowning family in the village, a family that has the financial resources that enables it to seclude its women physically. Her kinswoman, Gowriamma, a member of a distant and less affluent branch of the same *taravad*, had greater autonomy in the management of her affairs. Her relatively lower class status placed far fewer social constraints on her life than that experienced by Kalyaniamma:

My father died when I was around thirteen years old. My mother became mentally unstable, and we were very badly off financially. The *karanavans* in the main *taravad* helped us quite a bit, but there was only so much that they could do, after all they had their own responsibilities. So my brother and I started working. I went out to work. That was quite unusual, in these parts at least. There were very few Nayar women in the job force; it is not like it is today. Today a lot of Nayar women are employed. When I was young only women from poor families went out to work. Families that had some income and could maintain a minimum standard of living, families where the members had something to eat everyday, and clothes to wear, in such families, the women stayed at home, they did not go out to work. I went to work because I had to; I had no choice, but I was an exception. Even many educated Nayar women stayed at home. The families felt that it was a matter of the *taravad* honor, it was a disgrace to send the women out of the home. I have been managing this household from a very young age, after all I helped to raise my siblings. I make all the decisions in this family. I am used to it, I cannot live any other way. (Gowriamma, age sixty-five)

Kalyaniamma and Gowriamma belong to different branches of the same *taravad*. The difference in their class positions influenced the control that each woman had over her life. There were far fewer physical and social constraints in Gowriamma's life than there were in Kalyaniamma's.

Women who lived in small *taravads* where there was no *karanavan* in residence also had a greater degree of autonomy. This fact was alluded to by all the women with whom I spoke:

It is easier for women to live together without men, especially when it is mother and daughters. The house is ours, and it is a very warm and supportive environment. (Janakiamma, age sixty-five)

My father died when I was very young and I lived here with my mother. My uncles did not live with us. We had a very close relationship, I could discuss everything with her. We made all the decisions regarding the household together. . . . There are all the little things that women share with each other, especially mothers and daughters. It is a special relationship. In many respects my life was a lot easier than that of women in some of the other *taravads* where the *karanavans* took all the decisions and the women were expected to follow directions. I had a great deal of freedom. (Sharadaamma, age sixty-five)

Within the matrilineal tradition, the Nayars were both polygynous and polyandrous. Theoretically this meant that a woman could form and break alliances with men. However, in practice this, like the other aspects of her life, was mediated by her class position. For upper-class Nayar women, whose lives were strictly regulated by a set of rigid social codes, the opportunity to form independent relationships with men was practically nonexistent. The *karanavan* controlled the alliances that were formed. It is very likely that, similar to patrilineal kinship systems, women were used in forging male kinship networks and to further the interests of the male members of the *taravad*. The social control of women, through control of their sexuality, differs by class, and has different implications for women depending on their class status. Kalyaniamma describes the situation in her *taravad* in these words:

My mother and my grandmother had *sambandham* relationships. The trend shifted with our generation—we had monogamous marriages. There were monogamous marriages even in my mother's time, but in our *taravad* my mother and grandmother had polyandrous unions. . . . I have heard it said that after the five of us, my brothers, sister and I, were born our uncles decided that there were enough children in the *taravad*. They felt that the children were depleting the resources of the *taravad*, that they could not afford to economically support any more children. So they stopped the men from visiting my mother. That was the end of her *sambandham* relationships. . . . Our marriages were all arranged by the family. At this time it had become customary for the boy and girl to meet before the marriage was settled. I remember my husband came to visit us and I did meet with him before we were married. Of course the decision to accept the proposal was taken by the older members of the family, my grandmother and my uncle. I was not asked or expected to express an opinion. (Kalyaniamma, age seventy-three)

In this case, the men in the *taravad* had rights over their female kin, and they exercised rights to form social links and build power networks. The women had control over the marriage arrangements, and their dependence on the *taravad* left them with no choices or alternative courses of action.

Gowriamma, on the other hand, was economically independent. She worked to support her siblings, and the absence of a male authority figure gave her greater freedom. She had two children out of wedlock, and has been living with a man whom she has not married. Though this is common knowledge in the village, she is not ostracized, and is accepted by all the Nayar families.

Stolcke (1981) argues that in caste and lineage societies, where members' positions are determined by birth, marriage patterns and rules of inheritance either partially or totally define a person's social condition. Class and caste supremacy is maintained by endogamous marriages and the control of women's sexuality in them. Though the Nayars were hypergamous, marriage between individuals of widely different social classes was frowned upon. For example, Janakiamma, whose family owned a small store in the village, wanted to marry Raghu, a member of one of the landowning families. The idea was met with stiff opposition by both families:

Raghu and I wanted to marry each other but the families were absolutely against it. His family belonged to a higher social class. Even though we are both Nayars, the *karanavan* in his *taravad* made it known to the *karanavan* in our *taravad* that they would not accept our marriage. We lived in a joint family at that time, and

my uncle made all the decisions in the family. He did not want to do anything that would antagonize Raghu's family, after all their status was higher than ours. So I was married off to a man working in Madras, I suppose they thought that was far enough to keep us apart. (Janakiamma, age sixty-five)

A marriage alliance not only brings two individuals together, but also links families and establishes genealogical status. For a couple to challenge this arrangement would lead to a disruption of class hierarchies, and was therefore actively discouraged.

Janakiamma returned to the village a few years later. Her *taravad* had split up by this time and they were no longer under the control of her uncle. She and Raghu started a relationship that lasted till his death a few years ago. Speaking about this she said:

I think women today have a lot more freedom than when I was young. I feel that if it had been today, we would not have to go through all that we did, we would have gone ahead and got married, and the families would have eventually come around. My mother was sympathetic but she was powerless, there was little that she could do. . . . In a way I think the system today is much better. It is easier to talk with and persuade a husband, rather than a brother. I think most women have some degree of power over men in a situation where they are sexually involved, and that is not the case with brothers. There is always a distance and it is impossible to talk with them beyond a point. (Janakiamma, age sixty-five)

It is significant that Janakiamma recognizes that, with the changing times, the control of women has passed from brothers to husbands. Women still do not have the autonomy, within the kinship system, to negotiate relationships for themselves, unless they step out of the sphere of male influence. Today, marriages are still arranged among the Nayars, but many more women have the freedom to refuse a match, and they are no longer governed by a tradition that demanded silence and absolute obedience to the will of the *karanavan*:

Today marriage proposals are discussed with the young girls, and they have the freedom to turn down an alliance that they do not want. There is a lot of pressure on couples today to make a marriage work, and I think with a little bit of give and take most marriages can be made to work out. There are very few options for women if they walk out of a marriage, it is less socially acceptable to do so. It was easier to walk away from a marriage when I was young than it is today. (Janakiamma, age sixty-five)

The shift from matrilineality to patrilineality and monogamous marriages has meant that the "ownership" of a woman has passed from her *taravad* to her husband. It has also brought with it social and cultural pressures on women to adapt and conform to the patrilineal and patriarchal image of the "ideal" Indian woman, one who is loyal and submissive to her husband. It is no longer considered "respectable" for a woman to divorce her husband, and it is difficult for a woman to remarry, whether she is divorced or widowed.

Women from lower socioeconomic families are still in a vulnerable position and are often "used" to enhance the status of their *taravads*. Sudha was married at the age of eighteen to a young man in the village who is mentally retarded. She did not want the marriage, but was powerless to do anything about it. With little education and a job as a housemaid, she was pressured by her family to accept the match because:

My family thought this marriage would get them out of the circle of poverty. Sunil's is an old *taravad*, and the marriage would raise our status. Everyone told me not to be selfish and think only of myself. So my life was sacrificed in the larger interests of the family. (Sudha, age twenty-eight)

The marriage alliance enabled Sudha's family to establish kinship connections that would have been impossible any other way. A few years later, her *taravad* was able to capitalize on this connection when they arranged a marriage for her younger sister to a man who belonged to a higher socioeconomic class. Sudha's better economic situation enabled her to pay some of the wedding expenses.

The shift towards patrilineality and the nuclear family has resulted in a different kind of control over women's sexuality. As Kalyaniamma describes it:

Today if a woman is widowed, her chances of remarrying are very limited. That was not an issue when I was a child. By the time I was an adolescent there was also a stigma attached to unmarried women who had children. I think it went hand in hand with the spread of monogamous marriages. The women were not ostracized or anything, but people talked about it very disparagingly. Now of course, it is very difficult. It would be really hard on a woman if she has an illegitimate child, no matter to which class she belongs. (Kalyaniamma, age seventy-three)

Janakiamma's relationship with Raghu attracted some comment, but was accepted by the people in the village. Today, a woman in a similar situation would be ostracized irrespective of her caste and class situation.

Today polyandry and polygyny are nonexistent in Kerala. Male role definitions have shifted, and the husband, rather than the brother, is central to a woman's life. With the shift in the location of power, a woman's relationship with her husband and his family has taken on a significance that was absent within the *taravad* system:

When my daughters come home for the vacations, they spend more time with their husbands' families than they do here. That is a big change in our residence patterns. We do not say anything. Times have changed, and we feel that once the girls are married they ought to follow the wishes of their husbands. . . . And since the men stay in their homes, they expect their wives to do the same. (Veena, age forty-two)

This change in residence patterns has further weakened the Nayar matrilineal kinship system.

The social and economic changes that have resulted in the slow shift from matriliny to patriliny have also opened up new avenues for women. Today Nayar women are no longer constrained by the rigid traditions and practices that existed in the *taravad*. They have greater access to the world outside the four walls of their home, and increasing numbers are joining the work force.

MALE AUTHORITY AND FEMALE AUTONOMY

The narratives in the previous section are expressions of the "public" discourse on gender and kinship. They provide only a partial picture of individual women's lives within the matrilineal system. Women's agency and their subversion of the dominant discourse are obscured in this picture. It hides the fact that within their separate sphere women create a space from which they can resist male authority in subtle and silent ways. This resistance is never articulated; it is a shared secret among women. To voice it would be to bring out into the open, to make public the contradictions within which they operate— contradictions which they accept as part of their everyday lives.

The fact that Nayar women lived in *taravads* with related kin made it easy for women to forge bonds and work together to subvert male authority. For example, Janakiamma and Raghu could not influence the *karanavans* in both their *taravads* to arrange their marriage. However, in spite of all the restrictions on her movement, Janakiamma frequently met with Raghu, and at one time the two of them even contemplated eloping. When I asked her how she did this, she laughed and said:

> There are ways and ways. Do you really believe that the men know everything that goes on in a household? The women do. The women would have liked to arrange this marriage, my mother was sympathetic but there was little that she could do. Marriages are negotiated between two families and the women were helpless . . . After my marriage ended, I returned home. My uncles had moved out of the *taravad* by then, and there was only my mother and I. It was easy for Raghu and I to start a relationship. My mother was very supportive, and we did not have to fear anyone. (Janakiamma, age sixty-five)

The strategies women employ to undermine the dominant ideology lurk in the background and are embedded within the contradictions in their narratives. For example, when talking about the control of resources in her *taravad*, Kalyaniamma said:

> In our families it is the men who control the money. They keep the money with them and give it out to the women to run the household. In many instances the women had to account to the men for the money that they spent. My mother did not have to do that. But we had to ask the men for money. (Kalyaniamma, age seventy-three)

Later, when we discussed decision-making within the household, she presented a very different picture:

> I am in charge of everything in this household. I control the money, I make the decisions. I think in most *taravads* it is the women who make the decisions. Of course, the men like to think that they do, and we let it seem that way (laughs), but when you get down to the bottom of it, it is the women who are in control. (Kalyaniamma, age seventy-three)

In this instance Kalyaniamma informally subverted the authority of the men in the family. She recognized that this has to be done covertly and within the private space of the family. The men accept this fact, as long as their authority is not publicly challenged and both sides pretend that it is the men who are in charge of affairs. As Scott (1991, p. 779) points out, the fact that women's power can only be exercised within the private domain of the household "reaffirms men's official rule as powerholders [and] is a tribute . . . to men's continued control of the public transcript."

Women also employ strategies of submission and silence in order to negotiate positions of autonomy for themselves. Neeta, a young woman who works as a clerk in a government office, described the financial arrangements in her family in these words:

> My husband makes almost all the decisions in the household, and I go along with him. . . . It is not really as difficult as it sounds. I hand my

paycheck to him every month, he controls the money and the expenses for the household. I like it that way, it saves me a lot of bother. (Neeta, age twenty-seven)

In this statement she lays out the traditional position that places men in control of household resources. Later, talking about her job, she says:

I do not think I could ever give up my job. I enjoy the independence it gives me. . . . I do not have to depend on anyone for money, I do not have to ask someone for every little thing that I need.
I: But you told me earlier that you handed your paycheck to your husband?
N: I do that, but I do not give him everything. I keep some money aside for my use and give him the rest. This money is mine to do with as I please. I do not spend it on the household or on the children; that has to come out of the money in the bank. I am sure that my husband knows that I do not give him all my salary, but he has never asked me about it and I see no need to discuss it with him. There are some things that are best not spoken about, we all know that don't we? (laughs) (Neeta, age twenty-seven)

In this instance Neeta has created a space for herself by not directly confronting her husband's authority. In this situation her submission and silence are temporary holding positions rather than markers of oppression.

My intention in this paper is not to argue that Nayar women are able to resist or counteract all forms of male domination. However, I would like to contradict the suggestion made by some writers (Mies 1980; Liddle and Joshi 1986) that matrilineal kinship systems gave women a considerable degree of autonomy. As these narratives show, women's lives are made up of overlapping and intersecting layers within which they negotiate specific positions, depending on their class locations and the particular historical moment.

Dorothy Smith (1987) argues that our view of the world is not built upon our experiences. Instead it is constructed on the silence of women, by men who occupy positions of power. In this paper, I have attempted to represent the voices of a few Nayar women, to capture some of the tensions of their experiences as they have lived and articulated them. However, "it is not individuals who have experience, but subjects who are constituted through experience" (Scott 1991, p. 779). The evidence presented in these separated yet related narratives offers complex yet partial insights into individual women's lives. Their subversion of the dominant gender and kinship ideology that places them in subordinate positions is embedded in silence and contradictions. They do not offer any critique of their situation or directly challenge male authority. Instead they work around it, and in so doing perpetuate gender hegemonies. In many significant ways, patrilineality and matrilineality, at least as practiced among the Nayars, are two sides of the same coin, particularly with regard to the power relationships within which women are located. Women's resistance to these power relationships may take on new meanings within changing contexts as matrilineality is further transformed and redefined by historical forces and dominant ideologies.

ACKNOWLEDGMENT

The fieldwork on which this paper is based was carried out in Alanthara village, Trichur District, Kerala during 1990 and 1991. It was supported by a grant from the American Institute of Indian Studies, Chicago. I would like to thank Sari Biklen, Susan Wadley, Jyotsna Singh and Deborah Neff for comments on earlier drafts of this article.

REFERENCES

Dyson, Tim, and Mick Moore. "On Kinship Structure, Female Autonomy, and Demographic Behavior in India." *Population and Development Review*, Vol. 9, No. I (March 1983): 35–60.

Foucault, Michel. *The History of Sexuality Vol. 1: An Introduction.* New York: Random House, 1978.

Fuller, C.J. *The Nayars Today.* Cambridge: Cambridge University Press, 1976.

Jeffrey, Robin. *The Decline of Nayar Dominance.* New York: Holmes & Meier Publishers Inc., 1976.

Jeffrey, Robin. "Matriliny, Women, Development—and a Typographical Error." *Pacific Affairs* 63 (Fall 1990): 373–377.

Kandiyoti, Deniz. "Bargaining with Patriarchy." *Gender and Society,* Vol. 2, No. 3 (September 1988):274–290.

Liddle, Joanna, and Rama Joshi. *Daughters of Independence.* London: Zed Books Ltd., 1986.

Mencher, Joan P. "The Nayars of South Malabar." In *Comparative Family Systems,* ed. M.F. Nimkoff. Boston: Houghton Mifflin Company, 1965, pp. 163–191.

Mies, Maria. Indian Women and Patriarchy. *Conflicts and Dilemmas of Working Women.* New Delhi: Concept Publishing Company, 1980.

Moore, Melinda A. "A New Look at the Nayar Taravad." *Man* (N.S.) 20 (1986): 523–541.

Omvedt, Gail. "'Patriarchy': The Analysis of Women's Oppression," *The Insurgent Sociologist.* Vol. 13, No. 3 (1986): 30–50.

Scott, James C. *Domination and the Art of Resistance.* New Haven: Yale University Press, 1990.

Scott, James W. "A New Look at the Nayar Taravad," *Man* (N.S.) 20 (1986): 523–541.

Scott, Joan W. "The Evidence of Experience." *Critical Inquiry* 17 (1991): 773–797.

Smith, Dorothy. *The Everyday World as Problematic. A Feminist Sociology.* Boston: Northeastern University Press, 1987.

Stolcke, Verena. "Women's Labours: The Naturalisation of Social Inequality and Women's Subordination." In *Of Marriage and the Market: Women's Subordination Internationally and its Lessons,* eds. Kate Young, Carol Wolkowitz and Roslyn McCullagh. London and New York: Routledge, 1981, pp.159–177.

Domestic Networks: "Those You Count On"

Carol Stack

In The Flats the responsibility for providing food, care, clothing, and shelter and for socializing children within domestic networks may be spread over several households. Which household a given individual belongs to is not a particularly meaningful question, as we have seen that daily domestic organization depends on several things: where people sleep, where they eat, and where they offer their time and money. Although those who eat together and contribute toward the rent are generally considered by Flats residents to form minimal domestic units, household changes rarely affect the exchanges and daily dependencies of those who take part in common activity.

The residence patterns and cooperative organization of people linked in domestic networks demonstrate the stability and collective power of family life in The Flats. Michael Lee grew up in The Flats and now has a job in Chicago. On a visit to The Flats, Michael described the residence and domestic organization of his kin. "Most of my kin in The Flats lived right here on Cricket Street, numbers sixteen, eighteen, and twenty-two, in these three apartment buildings joined together. My mama decided it would be best for me and my three brothers and sister to be on Cricket Street too. My daddy's mother had a small apartment in this building, her sister had one in the basement, and another brother and his family took a larger apartment upstairs. My uncle was really good to us. He got us things we wanted and he controlled us. All the women kept the younger kids together during the day. They cooked together too. It was good living."

Yvonne Diamond, a forty-year-old Chicago woman, moved to The Flats from Chicago with her four children. Soon afterward they were evicted. "The landlord said he was going to build a parking lot there, but he never did. The old place is still standing and has folks in it today. My husband's mother and father took me and the kids in and watched over them while I had my baby. We stayed on after my husband's mother died, and my husband joined us when he got a job in The Flats."

When families or individuals in The Flats are evicted, other kinsmen usually take them in. Households in The Flats expand or contract with the loss of a job, a death in the family, the beginning or end of a sexual partnership, or the end of a friendship. Welfare workers, researchers, and landlords have long known that the poor must move frequently. What is much less understood is the relationship between residence and domestic organization in the black community.

The spectrum of economic and legal pressures that act upon ghetto residents, requiring them to move—unemployment, welfare requirements, housing shortages, high rents, eviction—are clear-cut examples of external pressures affecting the daily lives of the poor. Flats residents are evicted from their dwellings by landlords who want to raise rents, tear the building down, or rid themselves of tenants who complain about rats, roaches, and the plumbing. Houses get condemned by the city on landlords' requests so that they can force tenants to move. After an eviction, a landlord can rent to a family in such great need of housing that they will not complain for a while.

Poor housing conditions and unenforced housing standards coupled with overcrowding, unemployment, and poverty produce hazardous living conditions and residence changes. "Our whole family had to move when the gas lines sprung a leak in our apartment and my son set the place on fire by accident," Sam Summer told me. "The place belonged to my sister-in-law's grandfather. We had been living there with my mother, my brother's eight children, and our eight children. My father lived in the basement apartment 'cause he and my mother were separated. After the fire burned the whole place down, we all moved to two places down the street near my cousin's house."

When people are unable to pay their rent because they have been temporarily "cut off aid," because the welfare office is suspicious of their eligibility, because they gave their rent money to a kinsman to help him through a crisis or illness, or because they were laid off from their job, they receive eviction notices almost immediately. Lydia Watson describes a chain of events starting with the welfare office stopping her sister's welfare checks, leading to an eviction, co-residence, overcrowding, and eventually murder. Lydia sadly related the story to me. "My oldest sister was cut off aid the day her husband got out of jail. She and her husband and their three children were evicted from their apartment and they came to live with us. We were in crowded conditions already. I had my son, my other sister was there with her two kids, and my mother was about going crazy. My mother put my sister's husband out 'cause she found out he was a dope addict. He came back one night soon after that and murdered my sister. After my sister's death my mother couldn't face living in Chicago any longer. One of my other sisters who had been adopted and raised by my mother's paternal grandmother visited us and persuaded us to move to The Flats, where she was staying. All of us moved there—my mother, my two sisters and their children, my two baby sisters, and my dead sister's children. My sister who had been staying in The Flats found us a house across the street from her own."

Overcrowded dwellings and the impossibility of finding adequate housing in The Flats have many long-term consequences regarding where and with whom children live. Terence Platt described where and with whom his kin lived when he was a child. "My brother stayed with my aunt, my mother's sister, and her husband until he was ten, 'cause he was the oldest in our family and we didn't have enough room—but he stayed with us most every weekend. Finally my aunt moved into the house behind ours with her husband, her brother, and my brother; my sisters and brothers and I lived up front with my mother and her old man."

KIN-STRUCTURED LOCAL NETWORKS

The material and cultural support needed to absorb, sustain, and socialize community members in The Flats is provided by networks of cooperating kinsmen. Local coalitions formed from these networks of kin and friends are mobilized within domestic networks; domestic organization is diffused over many kin-based households which themselves have elastic boundaries.

People in The Flats are immersed in a domestic web of a large number of kin and friends whom they can count on. From a social viewpoint, relationships within the community are "organized on the model of kin relationships" (Goodenough 1970, p. 49). Kin-constructs such as the perception of parenthood, the culturally determined criteria which affect the shape of personal kindreds, and the idiom of kinship, prescribe kin who can be recruited into domestic networks.

There are similarities in function between domestic networks and domestic groups which Fortes (1962, p. 2) characterizes as "workshops of social reproduction." Both domains include three generations of members linked collaterally or otherwise. Kinship, jural and affectional bonds, and economic factors affect the composition of both domains and residential alignments within them. There are two striking differences between domestic networks and domestic groups. Domestic networks are not visible groups, because they do not have an obvious nucleus or defined boundary. But since a primary focus of domestic networks is child-care arrangements, the cooperation of a cluster of adult females is apparent. Participants in domestic networks are recruited from personal kindreds and friendships, but the personnel changes with fluctuating economic needs, changing life styles, and vacillating personal relationships.

In some loosely and complexly structured cognatic systems, kin-structured local networks (not groups) emerge. Localized coalitions of persons drawn from personal kindreds can be organized as networks of kinsmen. Goodenough (1970, p. 49) correctly points out that anthropologists frequently describe "localized kin groups," but rarely describe kin-structured local groups (Goodenough 1962; Helm 1965). The localized, kin-based, cooperative coalitions of people described in this chapter are organized as kin-structured domestic networks. For brevity, I refer to them as domestic networks.

RESIDENCE AND DOMESTIC ORGANIZATION

The connection between households and domestic life can be illustrated by examples taken from cooperating kinsmen and friends mobilized within domestic networks in The Flats. Domestic networks are, of course, not centered around one individual, but for simplicity the domestic network in the following example is named for the key participants in the network, Magnolia and Calvin Waters. The description is confined to four months between April and July 1969. Even within this short time span, individuals moved and joined other households within the domestic network.

THE DOMESTIC NETWORK OF MAGNOLIA AND CALVIN WATERS

Magnolia Waters is forty-one years old and has eleven children. At sixteen she moved from the South with her parents, four sisters (Augusta, Carrie, Lydia, and Olive), and two brothers (Pennington and Oscar). Soon after this she gave birth to her oldest daughter, Ruby. At twenty-three Ruby Banks had two daughters and a son, each by a different father.

When Magnolia was twenty-five she met Calvin, who was forty-seven years old. They lived together and had six children. Calvin is now sixty-three years old; Calvin and Magnolia plan to marry soon so that Magnolia will receive Calvin's insurance benefits. Calvin has two other daughters, who are thirty-eight and forty, by an early marriage in Mississippi. Calvin still has close ties with his daughters and their mother who all live near one another with their families in Chicago.

Magnolia's oldest sister, Augusta, is childless and has not been married. Augusta has maintained long-term "housekeeping" partnerships with four different men over the past twenty years, and each of them has helped her raise her sisters' children. These men have maintained close, affectional ties with the family over the years. Magnolia's youngest sister, Carrie, married Lazar, twenty-five years her senior, when she was just fifteen. They stayed together for about five years. After they separated Carrie married Kermit, separated from him, and became an alcoholic. She lives with different men from time to time, but in between men, or when things are at loose ends, she stays with Lazar, who has become a participating member of the family. Lazar usually resides near Augusta and Augusta's "old man," and Augusta generally prepares Lazar's meals. Ever since Carrie became ill, Augusta has been raising Carrie's son.

Magnolia's sister Lydia had two daughters, Lottie and Georgia, by two different fathers, before she married Mike and gave birth to his son. After Lydia married Mike, she no longer received AFDC benefits for her children. Lydia and Mike acquired steady jobs, bought a house and furniture, and were doing very well. For at least ten years they purposely removed themselves from the network of kin cooperation, preventing their kin from draining their resources. They refused to participate in the network of exchanges which Lydia had formerly depended upon; whenever possible they refused to trade clothes or lend money, or if they gave something, they did not ask for anything in return. During this period they were not participants in the domestic network. About a year ago Lydia and Mike separated over accusations and gossip that each of them had established another sexual relationship. During the five-month-period when the marriage was ending, Lydia began giving some of her nice clothes away to her sisters and nieces. She gave a couch to her brother and a TV to a niece. Anticipating her coming needs, Lydia attempted to reobligate her kin by carrying out the pattern which had been a part of her daily life before her marriage. After Lydia separated from her husband, her two younger children once again received AFDC. Lydia's oldest daughter, Lottie, is over eighteen and too old to receive AFDC, but Lottie has a three-year-old daughter who has received AFDC benefits since birth.

Eloise has been Magnolia's closest friend for many years. Eloise is Magnolia's first son's father's sister. This son moved into his father's household by his own choice when he was about twelve years old. Magnolia and Eloise have maintained a close, sisterly friendship. Eloise lives with her husband, her four children, and the infant son of her oldest daughter, who is seventeen. Eloise's husband's brother's daughter, Lily, who is twenty, and her young daughter recently joined the household. Eloise's husband's youngest brother is the father of her sister's child. When the child was an infant, that sister stayed with Eloise and her husband.

Billy Jones lives in the basement in the same apartment house as Augusta, Magnolia's sister. A temperamental woman with three sons, Billy has become Augusta's closest friend. Billy once ran a brothel in The Flats, but she has worked as a cook, has written songs, and has attended college from time to time. Augusta keeps Billy's sons whenever Billy leaves town, has periods of depression, or beats the children too severely.

Another active participant in the network is Willa Mae. Willa Mae's younger brother, James, is Ruby's daughter's father. Even though James does not visit the child and has not assumed any parental duties toward the child, Willa Mae and Ruby, who are the same age, help each other out with their young children.

Calvin's closest friend, Cecil, died several years ago. Cecil was Violet's husband. Violet, Cecil, and Calvin came from the same town in Mississippi and their families have been very close. Calvin boarded with Violet's family for five years or so before he met Magnolia. Violet is now seventy years old. She lives with her daughter, Odessa, who is thirty-seven, her two sons, Josh, who is thirty-five and John, who is forty, and Odessa's three sons and daughter. Odessa's husband was killed in a fight several years ago and ever since then she and her family have shared a household with Violet and her two grown sons. Violet's sons Josh and John are good friends with Magnolia, Ruby, and Augusta and visit them frequently. About five years ago John brought one of his daughters to live with his mother and sister because his family thought that the mother was not taking proper care of the child; the mother had several other children and did not object. The girl is now ten years old and is an accepted member of the family and the network.

Chart 1 shows the spatial relations of the households in Magnolia and Calvin's domestic network in April 1969. The houses are scattered within The Flats, but none of them is more than three miles apart. Cab fare, up to two dollars per trip, is spent practically every day, and sometimes twice a day, as individuals visit, trade, and exchange services. Chart 2 shows how individuals are brought into the domestic network.

The following outline shows residential changes which occurred in several of the households within the network between April and June 1969.

April 1969

Household Domestic Arrangement

1. Magnolia (38) and Calvin (60) live in a common-law relationship with their eight children (ages 4 to 18).
2. Magnolia's sister Augusta and Augusta's "old man," Herman, share a two-bedroom house with Magnolia's daughter Ruby (22) and Ruby's three children. Augusta and Herman have one bedroom, the three children sleep in the second bedroom, and Ruby sleeps downstairs in the living room. Ruby's boyfriend, Art, stays with Ruby many evenings.
3. Augusta's girlfriend Billy and Billy's three sons live on the first floor of the house. Lazar, Magnolia's and Augusta's ex-brother-in-law, lives in the basement alone, or from time to time, with his ex-wife Carrie. Lazar eats the evening meal, which Augusta prepares for him, at household #2.

4. Magnolia's sister Lydia, Lydia's "old man," Lydia's two daughters, Georgia and Lottie, Lydia's son, and Lottie's three-year-old daughter live in Lydia's house.
5. Willa Mae (26), her husband, her son, her sister Claudia (32), and her brother James (father of Ruby's daughter) share a household.
6. Eloise (37), her husband Jessie, their four children, their oldest daughter's (17) son, and Jessie's brother's daughter Lily (20), and Lily's baby all live together.
7. Violet (70), her two sons, Josh (35) and John (40), her daughter Odessa (37), and Odessa's three sons and one daughter live together. Five years ago John's daughter (10) joined the household.

June 1969

Household Domestic Arrangement

1. Household composition unchanged.
2. Augusta and Herman moved out after quarreling with Ruby over housekeeping and cooking duties. They joined household #3. Ruby and Art remained in household #2 and began housekeeping with Ruby's children.
3. Billy and her three sons remained on the first floor and Lazar remained in the basement. Augusta and Herman rented a small, one-room apartment upstairs.
4. Lottie and her daughter moved out of Lydia's house to a large apartment down the street, which they shared with Lottie's girl friend and the friend's daughter. Georgia moved into her boyfriend's apartment. Lydia and her son (17) remained in the house with Lydia's "old man."
5. James began housekeeping with a new girl friend who lived with her sister, but he kept most of his clothes at home. His brother moved into his room after returning from the service. Willa Mae, her husband, and son remained in the house.
6. Household composition unchanged.
7. Odessa's son Raymond is the father of Clover's baby. Clover and the baby joined the household which includes Violet, her two sons, her daughter, Odessa, and Odessa's three sons and one daughter and John's daughter.

Typical residential alignments in The Flats are those between adult mothers and sisters, mothers and adult sons and daughters, close

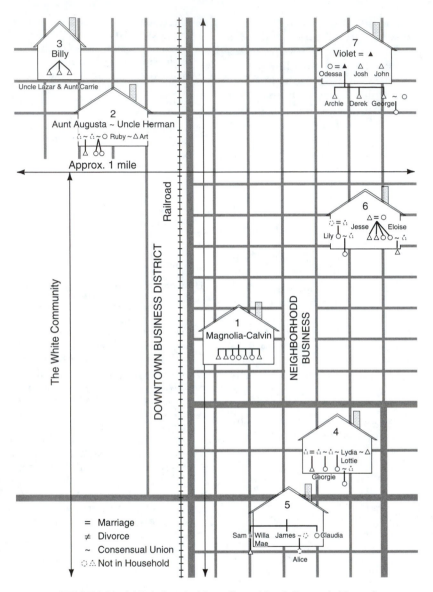

CHART 1 Spatial Relations in Magnolia and Leo's Domestic Network

adult female relatives, and friends defined as kin within the idiom of kinship. Domestic organization is diffused over these kin-based households.

Residence patterns among the poor in The Flats must be considered in the context of domestic organization. The connection between residence and domestic organization is apparent in examples of a series of domestic and child-care arrangements within Magnolia and Calvin's network a few years ago. Consider the following four kin-based residences among Magnolia and Calvin's kin in 1966.

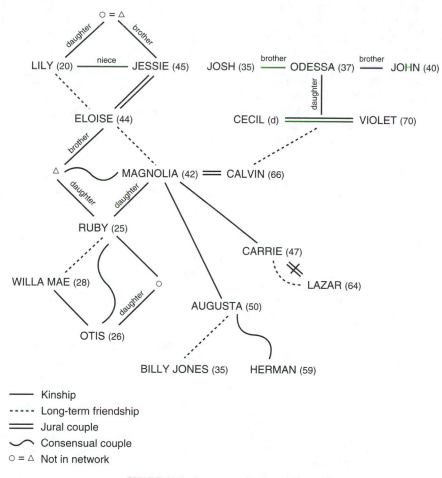

CHART 2 Kin-Structured Domestic Network

Household Domestic Arrangement

1. Magnolia, Calvin, and seven young children.
2. Magnolia's mother, Magnolia's brother, Magnolia's sister and her sister's husband, Magnolia's oldest daughter, Ruby, and Ruby's first child.
3. Magnolia's oldest sister, Augusta, Augusta's "old man," Augusta's sister's (Carrie) son, and Magnolia's twelve-year-old son.
4. Magnolia's oldest son, his father, and the father's "old lady."

Household composition *per se* reveals little about domestic organization even when cooper-

ation between close adult females is assumed. Three of these households (1, 2, 3) were located on one city block. Magnolia's mother rented a rear house behind Magnolia's house, and Magnolia's sister Augusta lived in an apartment down the street. As we have seen, they lived and shared each other's lives. Magnolia, Ruby, and Augusta usually pooled the food stamps they received from the welfare office. The women shopped together and everyone shared the evening meal with their men and children at Magnolia's mother's house or at Magnolia's. The children did not always have a bed of their own or a bed which they were expected to share with another child. They fell asleep and slept through the night wherever the late evening visiting patterns of the adult females took them.

The kinship links which most often are the basis of new or expanded households are those links children have with close adult females such as the child's mother, mother's mother, mother's sister, mother's brother's wife, father's mother, father's sister, and father's brother's wife.

Here are some examples of the flexibility of the Blacks' adaptation to daily, social, and economic problems (Stack 1970, p. 309).

Relational Link	Domestic Arrangement
Mother	Viola's brother married his first wife when he was sixteen. When she left him she kept their daughter.
Mother's mother	Viola's sister Martha was never able to care for her children because of her nerves and high blood. In between husbands, her mother kept her two oldest children, and after Martha's death, her mother kept all three of the children.
Mother's brother	A year after Martha's death, Martha's brother took Martha's oldest daughter, helping his mother out since this left her with only two children to care for.
Mother's mother	Viola's daughter (20) was living at home and gave birth to a son. The daughter and her son remained in the Jackson household until the daughter married and set up a separate household with her husband, leaving her son to be raised by her mother.
Mother's sister	Martha moved to Chicago into her sister's household. The household consisted of the two sisters and four of their children.
Father's mother	Viola's sister Ethel had four daughters and one son. When Ethel had a nervous breakdown, her husband took the three daughters and his son to live with his mother in Arkansas. After his wife's death, the husband took the oldest daughter, to join her siblings in his mother's home in Arkansas.
Father's mother	When Viola's younger sister, Christine, left her husband in order to harvest fruit in Wisconsin, Christine left her two daughters with her husband's mother in Arkansas.
Father's sister	When Viola's brother's wife died, he decided to raise his two sons himself. He kept the two boys and never remarried although he had several girl friends and a child with one. His residence has always been near Viola's and she fed and cared for his sons.

The basis of these cooperative units is mutual aid among siblings of both sexes, the domestic cooperation of close adult females, and the exchange of goods and services between male and female kin (Stack 1970). R.T. Smith (1970, p. 66) has referred to this pattern and observes that even when lower-class Blacks live in a nuclear family group, what is "most striking is the extent to which lower-class persons continue to be involved with other kin." Nancie Gonzalez (1970, p. 232) suggests that "the fact that individuals have simultaneous loyalties to more than one such grouping may be important in understanding the social structure as a whole."

These co-residential socializing units do indeed show the important role of the black female. But the cooperation between male and female siblings who share the same household or live near one another has been underestimated by those who have considered the female-headed household and the grandmother-headed household (especially the mother's mother) as the most significant domestic units among the urban black poor.

The close cooperation of adults arises from the residential patterns typical of young adults. Due to poverty, young females with or without children do not perceive any choice but to remain living at home with their mother or other adult female relatives. Even if young women are collecting AFDC, they say that their resources go further when they share goods and services. Likewise, jobless males, or those working at part-time or seasonal jobs, often remain living at home with their mother or, if she is dead, with their sisters and brothers. This pattern continues long after men have become fathers and have established a series of sexual partnerships with women, who are living with their own kin, friends, or alone with their children. A result of this pattern is the striking fact that households almost always have men around: male relatives, by birth or marriage, and boyfriends. These men are often intermittent members of the households, boarders, or friends who come and go; men who usually eat, and sometimes sleep, in the households. Children have constant and close contact with these men, and especially in the case of male relatives, these relationships last over the years.

The most predictable residential pattern in The Flats is that men and women reside in one of the households of their natal kin, or in the households of those who raised them, long into their adult years. Even when persons temporarily move out of the household of their mother or of a close relative, they have the option to return to the residences of their kin if they have to.

GENEROSITY AND POVERTY

The combination of arbitrary and repressive economic forces and social behavior, modified by successive generations of poverty, make it almost impossible for people to break out of poverty. There is no way for those families poor enough to receive welfare to acquire any surplus cash which can be saved for emergencies or for acquiring adequate appliances or a home or a car. In contrast to the middle class, who are pressured to spend and save, the poor are not even permitted to establish an equity.

The following examples from Magnolia and Calvin Waters' life illustrates the ways in which the poor are prohibited from acquiring

any surplus which might enable them to change their economic condition or life style.

In 1971 Magnolia's uncle died in Mississippi and left an unexpected inheritance of $1,500 to Magnolia and Calvin Waters. The cash came from a small run-down farm which Magnolia's uncle sold shortly before he died. It was the first time in their lives that Magnolia or Calvin ever had a cash reserve. Their first hope was to buy a home and use the money as a down payment.

Calvin had retired from his job as a seasonal laborer the year before and the family was on welfare. AFDC allotted the family $100 per month for rent. The housing that the family had been able to obtain over the years for their nine children at $100 or less was always small, roach-infested, with poor plumbing and heating. The family was frequently evicted. Landlords complained about the noise and often observed an average of ten to fifteen children playing in the household. Magnolia and Calvin never even anticipated that they would be able to buy a home.

Three days after they received the check, news of its arrival spread throughout their domestic network. One niece borrowed $25 from Magnolia so that her phone would not be turned off. Within a week the welfare office knew about the money. Magnolia's children were immediately cut off welfare, including medical coverage and food stamps. Magnolia was told that she would not receive a welfare grant for her children until the money was used up, and she was given a minimum of four months in which to spend the money. The first surplus the family ever acquired was effectively taken from them.

During the weeks following the arrival of the money, Magnolia and Calvin's obligations to the needs of kin remained the same, but their ability to meet these needs had temporarily increased. When another uncle became very ill in the South, Magnolia and her older sister, Augusta, were called to sit by his side. Magnolia bought round-trip train tickets for both of them and for her three youngest children. When the uncle died, Magnolia bought round-trip train tickets so that she and Augusta could attend the funeral. Soon after his death, Augusta's first "old man" died in The Flats and he had no kin to pay for the burial. Augusta asked Magnolia to help pay for digging the grave. Magnolia was unable to refuse. Another sister's rent was two months overdue and Magnolia feared that she would get evicted. This sister was seriously ill and had no source of income. Magnolia paid her rent.

Winter was cold and Magnolia's children and grandchildren began staying home from school because they did not have warm winter coats and adequate shoes or boots. Magnolia and Calvin decided to buy coats, hats, and shoes for all of the children (at least fifteen). Magnolia also bought a winter coat for herself and Calvin bought himself a pair of sturdy shoes.

Within a month and a half, all of the money was gone. The money was channeled into the hands of the same individuals who ordinarily participate in daily domestic exchanges, but the premiums were temporarily higher. All of the money was quickly spent for necessary, compelling reasons.

Thus random fluctuations in the meager flow of available cash and goods tend to be of considerable importance to the poor. A late welfare check, sudden sickness, robbery, and other unexpected losses cannot be overcome with a cash reserve like more well-to-do families hold for emergencies. Increases in cash are either taken quickly from the poor by the welfare agencies or dissipated through the kin network.

Those living in poverty have little or no chance to escape from the economic situation into which they were born. Nor do they have the power to control the expansion or contraction of welfare benefits (Piven and Cloward 1971) or of employment opportunities, both of which have a momentous effect on their daily lives. In times of need, the only predictable resources that can be drawn upon are their own children and parents, and the fund of kin and friends obligated to them.

REFERENCES

Fortes, Meyer. 1962. "Marriage in Tribal Societies." *Cambridge Papers in Social Anthropology, No. 3.* Cambridge: Cambridge University Press.

Gonzalez, Nancie. 1970. "Toward a Definition of Matrifocality." In *Afro-American Anthropology: Contemporary Perspectives*, eds. N. E. Whitten and John F. Szwed. New York: The Free Press.

Goodenough, Ward H. 1962. "Kindred and Hamlet in Lakalai, New Britain." *Ethnology* 1:5–12.

———. 1970. *Description and Comparison in Cultural Anthropology.* Chicago: Aldine Publishing Company.

Helm, June. 1965. "Bilaterality in the Socio-Territorial Organization of the Arctic Drain Age Dene." *Ethnology*, 4:361–385.

Piven, Frances Fox and Richard A. Cloward. 1971. *Regulating the Poor: The Functions of Public Welfare.* New York: Vintage Books.

Smith, Raymond T. 1970. "The Nuclear Family in Afro-American Kinship." *Journal of Comparative Family Studies* 1(1):55–70.

Stack, Carol B. 1970. "The Kindred of Viola Jackson: Residence and Family Organization of an Urban Black American Family." *In Afro-American Anthropology: Contemporary Perspectives*, eds. N. E. Whitten and John F. Szwed. New York: The Free Press, pp. 303–312

Matrifocality, Power, and Gender Relations in Jamaica

Marsha Prior

Anthropologists have long recognized kinship units in which women maintain considerable

Original material prepared for this text.

control over the household earnings and decision making. While numerous studies have provided pertinent data and have contributed to the theory of social organization, the subject of female-focused kinship units has always been controversial, subject to bias, and confusing. The variations in terminology and a preoccupation with the origin of these units is responsible for much of the confusion. In addition, two biases, prevalent throughout the twentieth century, have influenced our understanding and acceptance of female-focused units. One bias has been the predominant view that nuclear families are "normal"; the other bias is the failure to recognize the full extent of female roles in society. The unfortunate result of this is that very little is known about the dynamics within and between female-focused kinship units.

The term *matrifocal*, which is most commonly used to refer to households composed of a key female decision maker, was coined by R.T. Smith in 1956. Recognition of such households precedes the usage of this term, however. As early as the 1930s scholars noted that African-American and African-Caribbean households were not composed of nuclear families as were the majority of middle-class households in the United States and Great Britain. Observers were struck by the authoritative role of women in these households and the limited role of the father in the family. Mothers controlled the earnings brought into the household and made key decisions. Fathers were either absent or did not appear to play a major role in economic contributions and in household decision making. However, attempts to address this situation reveal more the attitudes and biases prevalent at that time—many of which remain with us today—than any real insight as to the nature of such units. These *maternal families*, as they were often called during this early period, were viewed by scholars as deviant structures (Mohammed 1988). The high rate of illegitimacy and instability among mating partners was cited as proof that these families were disorganized and detrimental to the well-being of their members (Henriques 1953; Simey 1946; see also Moynihan 1965).

The bias toward nuclear family organization that dominated early studies stems from nineteenth-century evolutionists who viewed the nuclear family as a superior system of kinship organization and from Malinowski who argued that nuclear families are universal (Collier, Rosaldo, and Yanigisako 1982). Thus, societies that exhibited large numbers of non-nuclear households were considered abnormal, and it was essential that their development be explained.

Scholars naturally turned to the common characteristics of these female-focused societies, noting that they were former slave societies from Africa. One explanation, suggested by Frazier (1939), held that maternal families were an adaptive strategy to the slave system that defined slaves as individual property who could be traded to another plantation at any time. Nuclear families would have been torn apart with frequent trading of adult slaves. Plantation owners were less likely, though, to tear apart mother-child dyads, at least until the child reached adolescence. Thus, the stable unit in a slave system was a household consisting of mothers and their children. The other explanation common during this time period, argued that the maternal family stemmed from the traditional African system that survived in spite of the Africans' forced migration and subsequent integration into the slave system (Herskovits 1941). These two theories enjoyed a lively debate until the mid-1950s when scholars moved away from historical explanations and emphasized the role of present social or economic conditions.

M.G. Smith (1962) argued that family structure in the West Indies was determined by the already existing mating systems that vary somewhat throughout the region. Clarke (1957), R.T. Smith (1956), and Gonzalez (1960) focused more on the effect that the current economic system had on household organization. The prevalent household structure found among African descendants in the United States and the Caribbean was viewed as an adaptive strategy to poverty, unemployment, or male migration. Nuclear families with only two working adults per household are believed by some to be at risk in socioeconomic environments in which poverty conditions exist, unemployment is high, and adult men must migrate to find work (see Durant-Gonzalez 1982; Gonzalez 1970:242). Thus, in such societies we are more likely to see households composed of a mother, a grandparent, and children; a mother and children; adult siblings and their children; or adult siblings, their children, and a grandparent.

The emphasis placed on the socioeconomic environment marked a new trend in matrifocal studies whereby the relationship between men and women took a more prominent position. However, the studies placed more emphasis on the "marginal" or absent man than on the ever-present woman and were criticized for ignoring the wide range of roles and tasks performed by women. Furthermore, Smith noted (1962:6) specific ethnographic data were used to generalize about matrifocal societies throughout the Caribbean. This proved to be problematic in understanding matrifocal societies theoretically, and it generated confusion as scholars used different terms to refer to similar types of kinship and household organizations.

R.T. Smith used the term *matrifocal* to refer to the type of structure he originally witnessed among lower class British Guianese (1956). Taking a developmental approach, Smith noted that matrifocal households arise with time after a man and woman begin to cohabit. Early in the cycle the woman is economically dependent on the male partner. Her primary role is to provide care for the children, but as the children grow older and earn money for small tasks and labor it is the mother who controls their earnings. The father, meanwhile, has been unable to make significant contributions to the household economy due to his overall low status within a society that maintains prejudicial hiring policies. Smith's concept of matrifocality focuses on two criteria—the salience of women in their role as mothers and the marginality of men (i.e., their inability to contribute economically to the household) (1956; 1973; 1988).

The study of household structure conducted by Gonzalez on the Garifuna (Black Carib) of Guatemala was not intended, nor originally identified, as a study on matrifocality per se, but Gonzalez did note the effect that male emigration had on household structure (1960). Gonzalez observed that households were comprised of members who were related to each other consanguineally (through blood); no two members of the household were bound by marriage. These consanguineal households developed in response to a socioeconomic environment that encouraged men to migrate as they sought employment (see also Gonzalez 1984 for comments regarding the applicability of dividing households into consanguineal and affinal types).

The terms and definitions for the household structures observed by R.T. Smith and Gonzalez were created to fit specific ethnographic data. They were later applied by various scholars to other societies that exhibited similar structures, which created confusion (see Kunstadter 1963; Randolph 1964; M.G. Smith 1962:6; and R.T. Smith 1973:126) and was exacerbated by the use of other terms to rectify the problem (e.g., the use of matricentric or female-headed). Thus, in the literature we see these terms used interchangeably to refer to structures in which women control household earnings and decision making and men are viewed as marginal, though the impetus behind such household formation may differ from one society to the next. The whole concept became so clouded with terms and biases that Gonzalez astutely noted that depending on which scholar one is reading, matrifocality can suggest (1) that women are more important than the observer had expected, (2) that women maintain a good deal of control over money in the household, (3) that women are the primary source of income, or (4) that there is no resident male (1970:231–232).

Recent authors have criticized the emphasis on men's marginality and the focus on women's domestic tasks that arose in the study of matrifocality (Barrow 1988; Mohammed 1988; Tanner 1974). Concentration on women's *domestic* tasks ignores the full extent of women's networks, their access to resources, control over resources, relations with men, and relationship between household and society, all of which are important considerations when discussing matrifocality. Male marginality is problematic in part because the term is difficult to define. Does it mean that the father does not live in the household? Has he migrated out of the community? Does he contribute sporadically, or not at all, to the household economy? Is he not around to make household decisions?

As Tanner has remarked, matrifocality should not be defined in "negative terms" (i.e., by the absence of the father). Instead, we should focus on the role of women as mothers, and note that in matrifocal systems mothers have at least some control over economic resources and are involved in decision making. According to Tanner, however, matrifocality goes beyond these two criteria. To be matrifocal a society must culturally value the role of mother—though not necessarily at the expense of fathers. In matrifocal societies the woman's role as mother is central to the kinship structure, but Tanner does not limit this role to domestic tasks. As mothers women may participate in cultivation, petty marketing, wage labor, in rituals, and so forth (1974). This broader definition allows us to recognize matrifocal units within a variety of kinship systems. Matrifocal units can exist in matrilineal or patrilineal societies, within nuclear families, and in bilateral systems. In any society with an emphasis on the mother-child dyad where this unit is culturally valued and where the mother plays an effective role in the economy and decision making of the unit, that unit can be defined as matrifocal (Tanner 1974:131–132).

Tanner's definition finally allows us to avoid some of the problems that previous studies encountered and permits us to further address issues pertinent to matrifocal units. We can examine gender relations within the context of gender hierarchies and the broader socioeconomic environment of which matrifocal households are a part. One area that has received little attention is the relationship between physical violence against women and matrifocality. Violence against women and matrifocality seem to contradict each other due to the assumptions regarding power and the authoritative role of women in matrifocal households.

Women, having access to and control over resources and authority to make household decisions, are viewed as powerful. This view has been particularly evident in studies of women in the Caribbean where a large number of matrifocal households exist (Massiah 1982). Caribbean women are frequently portrayed as powerful, autonomous individuals (Ellis 1986; Powell 1982, 1986; Safa 1986). Although Caribbean women's control and power over resources and decisions is not to be discounted, fieldwork in a low-income community in Jamaica suggests that matrifocality and physical violence against women are not mutually exclusive. To understand the relationship between these two phenomena requires knowledge of sociocultural elements that affect both gender relations and matrifocal household organization.

The community of study is a low-income urban neighborhood approximately 0.05 square miles located in the parish of St. Andrew, Jamaica. During the time at which data were collected, 1987 to 1988, there were an estimated 210 households with a population of 1,300. The majority of the households were of wooden construction, many without electricity, and very few with running water. Some of the wealthier residents maintained houses constructed of concrete. No telephones were present in any household because telephone lines were not available.

Within the community a variety of household organizational units were observed. Nuclear families based on common-law marriage, legal marriage, or coresidency existed. There were also single female-headed households, single male-headed households, and a variety of extended and collateral arrangements. Finally, there were households whose membership included kin and nonkin (i.e., a friend or acquaintance may reside in the household). This range in domestic organization demonstrates that household membership may vary in response to economic and social conditions.

What makes these arrangements more interesting is that the households are subject to change. During the course of the fieldwork households altered their membership; thus, a nuclear arrangement would shift to single female-headed with children as the father moved out, and it might have shifted again if a grandmother or sister moved in. Regardless of the various household arrangements, matrifocality was observed. Women certainly maintained control over the economic resources and were responsible for many household decisions. Women as mothers were structurally central to the kinship units, and mothers were culturally valued as indicated by both male and female informants.

Although Caribbean women are portrayed as powerful and autonomous, male–female relations, as anywhere in the world, are based on some form of interdependence. Within this community social and economic status are intricately tied to gender relations. Both genders support the basic notion that women are to provide sexual services and domestic labor for men, and men are to provide women with money and gifts. However, the relationships are not a simple equation whereby women provide sexual services and domestic labor in exchange for money. Women often spoke of sexual activity as something that they desired and enjoyed, and men felt free to request money from women with whom they have had relations (especially if she is the mother to any of his children). Nevertheless, there is an understanding that if a woman will not provide sexual services or domestic labor or if the man does not provide cash or gifts from time to time, the relationship will end. These expectations played key roles in understanding gender relations and the behavior of men and women.

In addition to these expectations, adult status is primarily attained by the birth of a child. At this socioeconomic level higher educational degrees, prestigious employment, and ownership of cars and houses are out of most community members' reach. Both men and women view the birth of a child as an opportunity to announce their own adult status. Thus, children are normally desired and are a source of pride for both the mother and father.

The instability that marks male–female relationships is recognized by community members and can be related to cultural values as well as to the socioeconomic environment that encourages men and women to seek more resourceful partners. Male and female informants readily acknowledged the shifting allegiances between men and women. Men were known to keep several girlfriends at one time, and marriage, common-law or legal, was no guarantee that monogamy will follow. Women also admitted to keeping an eye out for a better partner and said they would initiate a change if they so desired. Couples tended to set up visiting relationships whereby the couple did not coreside. Children, of course, may be born from these unions. If a Jamaican woman of this socioeconomic class married at all, it was more likely to occur after the age of thirty (see Brody 1981:253–255).

As households were observed and data collected through the course of fieldwork, it became apparent that fathers and male partners were not marginal to the households. Whether or not they resided in the same household as the woman, they could potentially be very influential. It also became clear that in certain situations female control over household issues could be jeopardized. A brief look at some of the households and the gender relations among men and women will demonstrate these points.

MARY'S HOUSEHOLD

Mary is a twenty-seven-year-old mother occupying a one-room wooden house—no electricity or running water—with four children. The two oldest children were fathered by one man; the youngest two were fathered by another. Sexual relations with the first father had ceased several years ago; however, Mary does maintain sexual relations with the younger children's father, though he keeps other girlfriends.

Mary's primary source of income stems from sporadic petty marketing. When Mary has the capital to invest in goods, she sells clothing and shoes in a downtown Kingston stall that is rented by her mother. Mary is very much involved in politics; she attends meetings, distributes literature, and talks to anyone about her party's political candidates and officials. She was able to work for a few months as an enumerator during a national campaign to register voters. Mary depends on contributions from the two fathers of her children. The first father rarely comes to visit, but he is in the National Guard, draws a steady paycheck, and consistently sends money for the children.

The father of her two youngest children, who works as a cook and a driver, is usually good about bringing money but has, on occasion, lapsed. Such lapses can be a severe stress on Mary's limited household budget and were the source of domestic violence on one occasion. Earl, the father of Mary's youngest children, had promised to bring some money. When he showed up at her doorstep she asked for the money, and he told her that he didn't have any. This made her angry so she began yelling at him, and a fight ensued. They began hitting each other with their fists, but the fight escalated when Earl picked up a shovel and hit Mary on the wrist. Mary fought back by taking a cutlass and striking him on the shoulder. Earl then left the premises, and Mary sought medical treatment for the pain in her wrist.

This was the first and only act of violence between the two in a seven-year period. Mary stated that they rarely even quarrel. Though not typical, the violence demonstrates the economic dependence of Mary on the contributions of the fathers and the stress that can surface when she is threatened by the lack of such contributions. Mary admitted that she was extremely angry when he told her that he had no money to give her because he had promised earlier that he would bring her some. She was convinced that he had the money to give but was holding out on her.

DORA'S HOUSEHOLD

Dora, twenty-eight years old, lives under similar circumstances as Mary and has had comparable experience regarding fathers and money. Dora is the mother of three children. Two live with her; one stays with relatives in the country. Dora's one-room house has neither electricity nor running water.

The father of Dora's first two children provides some money to the household. Dora is almost totally dependent on these contributions because she is confined to the house and cannot work due to a crippling disease. Ned, the father of her youngest child, provides nothing to the household, which is a continuous source of grief to Dora. Dora is quiet and normally avoids conflict. Her one attempt to address Ned's negligence resulted in violence, as had Mary's. Dora had decided that because Ned did not provide clothes or money for their son, Michael, he did not deserve to see the child. She packed up Michael's belongings and sent him over to Ned's sister's house for a short while, believing that the sister would feed Michael and buy him some clothes. When Ned arrived to take Michael for a visit to his own house, he questioned the child's whereabouts and became angry when Dora told him that he had been sent to Ned's sister's house. Ned began hitting Dora. She struck back once but relented when Ned punched her in the side and ran off. She did not see him again for several days. This incident occurred six months prior to our interview, and Dora has not asked Ned for anything since and vows that she never will.

RITA'S HOUSEHOLD

Rita lives in a household consisting of six members, including herself. Two of her four children, a granddaughter, a friend of her daughter, and Rita's boyfriend occupy a three-room apartment without electricity or running water. Rita is thirty-nine years old. Her boyfriend, Tom, is 40 and has lived with her for four years. They have no common children.

Rita runs a successful neighborhood bar, giving her control over the major portion of the household budget. She receives some financial contribution from the father of one daughter. Rita and Tom have established a reciprocal relationship regarding money. She does expect him to contribute from his earnings as a taxi driver when he is able, but she may be just as likely to provide Tom with money when he is in need. Rita is aware of Tom's other girlfriends and realizes that a good deal of his earnings go to entertaining these women. With her own successful business Rita is less financially dependent on her male partner than other women. She does look to Tom, however, for companionship and emotional support. The time he spends with other women is reluctantly accepted, though on one occasion his infidelities did result in conflict. One night, as he came home late, Rita began cursing Tom and made derogatory remarks about Tom's other girlfriend. Tom responded by punching Rita. She fought back for a few minutes then they both simply let it go. In the past year Rita has avoided comment on Tom's affairs and is determined to put up with it, for now at least, because she is not ready to end the relationship. Rita's attitude is that most men do this, so there is little point in severing this relationship to find another boyfriend who will do the same.

HANNAH'S HOUSEHOLD

Thirty-six-year-old Hannah is an articulate and ambitious woman. She lives in a two-room house with seven other people (five of her six children live with her along with a friend her age and a friend of one of her daughters). Hannah worked as a domestic but lost her job during my stay in the community. She did have a job lined up, cleaning the office of a dentist.

Hannah's first three children were fathered by one man; her fourth child was fathered by another man; and her last two children were fathered by a third man. The first man to father her children is now sick and unable to work. He does not provide any financial support to Hannah's household. The other two fathers help out every now and then, but the support is not enough for her to rely on. She rarely sees any of her chil-

dren's fathers now, but Hannah did relate an incident involving the last father, Gerald, that occurred nearly five years prior to our interview. At the time of the incident Hannah and Gerald were still intimately involved but did not coreside. Hannah had grown dissatisfied with the relationship because Gerald provided no support for herself or his children. Thus, she had decided to break off the relationship. When Gerald learned of her decision he became angry and abusive. One night after everyone had gone to bed, he came to her house, began yelling at her, and proceeded to destroy some of her belongings: He broke a lamp and smashed a small table. Another night he came to her window, tore off the screen, and began yelling at her again. He threw a bucket of water on her and the children and threw stones. Hannah, not wanting the children to get hurt, went outside to confront him, and he began physically assaulting her. Hannah managed to grab a broken bottle and cut him with it. Gerald then left the premises, never bothering her much afterwards.

SUMMARY

Although women in matrifocal households often maintain control over resources and decision making within the household, the previous data indicate that the power associated with such control and authority can be compromised. Power, as defined by Adams, is the control over one's environment and the ability to control the environment of others based on access and control of resources that are of value to the other (1975:12). In the cases cited above the interdependence between men and women and the access that men have to certain resources must be addressed to understand female power and domestic violence.

As indicated previously, both genders view women as exercising control over sexual services and domestic labor, and men have access to some (though not all) of the economic resources that women need. At this socioeconomic level men may not be able to contribute significantly to the household economy. Nevertheless, women view men as a source of monetary and material needs and feel they have the right to demand these resources. Though women are constantly seeking ways to earn money and often don't want to rely on contributions from male partners, many, again due to the socioeconomic environment, are dependent on male contributions, no matter how small. The data suggest that while men are dependent on women, they can more easily circumvent the control that female partners have over desired resources than women can circumvent the resources that men control. In this culture it is acceptable for men to have more than one female partner. While women complain of this it is expected and negates the control that individual women can exert. Women, on the other hand, may try to circumvent male control over economic resources, but they are also subjected to an economic system that exploits the lower class for their cheap labor and that offers high unemployment. In addition to this interdependence these women are members of a culture that may value women as *mothers,* but women in general do not necessarily enjoy a high status. In other words the *mother* role is valued, but women are overall subordinate to men (Henry and Wilson 1975). Male informants felt it was their right to physically coerce or punish women as they saw fit, but a man would almost never physically abuse his own mother.

In relating the cases cited previously the intent is not to suggest that the women were weak, powerless, and always dominated by men. Women often fought back and worked to become as independent as possible. These cases are also not intended to promote negative images of men. I recount incidences of abuse to demonstrate the extreme to which men can affect matrifocal households, but I must emphasize that male influence can also be positive and rewarding for members of the household. Fathers were observed visiting their children, taking them to the health clinic, and providing money, food, and clothing.

The data collected from this study remind us that, in spite of a long interest in matrifocality, we still have much to learn. We must rid ourselves of biases that narrow our focus. Just as it was wrong to assume that men are marginal, that women perform only domestic tasks, and that the nuclear family is "normal," we must not assume that women in matrifocal societies are *always* powerful or that they consistently enjoy a high status within that society. The power that women exert must be documented and integrated into the overall cultural context that would also note gender relations, the socioeconomic environment, the political environment, and cultural values. Only then can studies on matrifocality provide us with a better understanding of human behavior.

REFERENCES

Adams, Richard N. 1975. *Energy and Structure: A Theory of Social Power.* Austin: University of Texas Press.

Barrow, Christine. 1988. Anthropology, the Family and Women in the Caribbean. In Patricia Mohammed and Catherine Shepherd (eds.). *Gender in Caribbean Development*, pp. 156–169. Mona, Jamaica: University of West Indies.

Brody, Eugene B. 1981. *Sex, Contraception, and Motherhood in Jamaica.* Cambridge, MA: Harvard University Press.

Clarke, Edith. 1957. *My Mother Who Fathered Me.* London: George Allen & Unwin.

Collier, Jane, Michelle Rosaldo, and Sylvia Yanagisako. 1982. Is There a Family? New Anthropological Views. In Barrie Thorne (ed.). *Rethinking the Family: Some Feminist Questions*, pp. 25–39. New York: Longman.

Durant-Gonzalez, Victoria. 1982. The Realm of Female Familial Responsibility. In Joycelin Massiah (ed). *Women and the Family*, pp. 1–27. Cave Hill, Barbados: University of the West Indies, Institute of Social and Economic Research.

Ellis, Pat. 1986. Introduction: An Overview of Women in Caribbean Society. In Pat Ellis (ed.). *Women of the Caribbean*, pp. 1–24. Kingston: Kingston Publishers.

Frazier, E. Franklin. 1939. *The Negro Family in the United States.* Chicago: Chicago University Press.

Gonzalez, Nancie L. 1960. Household and Family in the Caribbean. *Social and Economic Studies* 9: 101–106.

———. 1970. Toward a Definition of Matrifocality. In Norman E. Whitten, Jr. and John F. Szwed (eds.). *Afro-American Anthropology*, pp. 231–244. New York: The Free Press.

———. 1984. Rethinking the Consanguineal Household and Matrifocality. Ethnology 23(1): 1–12.

Henriques, Fernando M. 1953. *Family and Colour in Jamaica*. London: Eyre and Spottiswoode.

Henry, Frances and Pamela Wilson. 1975. The Status of Women in Caribbean Societies: An Overview of Their Social, Economic and Sexual Roles. *Social and Economic Studies* 24(2): 165–198.

Herskovits, Melville J. 1941. *The Myth of the Negro Past*. New York: Harper & Brothers.

Kunstadter, Peter. 1963. A Survey of the Consanguine or Matrifocal Family. *American Anthropologist* 65: 56–66.

Massiah, Joycelin. 1982. Women Who Head Households. In Joycelin Massiah (ed.). *Women and the Family*, pp. 62–130. Cave Hill, Barbados: University of West Indies, Institute of Social and Economic Research.

Mohammed, Patricia. 1988. The Caribbean Family Revisited. In Patricia Mohammed and Catherine Shepherd (eds.). *Gender in Caribbean Development*, pp. 170–182. Mona, Jamaica: University of West Indies.

Moynihan, Daniel P. 1965. *The Negro Family: The Case for National Action*. U.S. Department of Labor, Washington, D.C.

Powell, Dorian. 1982. Network Analysis: A Suggested Model for the Study of Women and the Family in the Caribbean. In Joycelin Massiah

(ed.). *Women and The Family*, pp. 131–162. Cave Hill, Barbados: University of the West Indies, Institute of Social and Economic Research.

———. 1986. Caribbean Women and Their Response to Familial Experiences. *Social and Economic Studies* 35(2): 83–130.

Randolph, Richard R. 1964. The "Matrifocal Family" as a Comparative Category. *American Anthropologist* 66: 628–31.

Safa, Helen. 1986. Economic Autonomy and Sexual Equality in Caribbean Society. *Social and Economic Studies* 35(3): 1–21.

Simey, Thomas. 1946. *Welfare Planning in the West Indies*. Oxford: Clarendon Press.

Smith, M.G. 1962. *West Indian Family Structure*. Seattle: University of Washington Press.

Smith, Raymond T. 1956. *The Negro Family in British Guiana: Family Structure and Social Status in the Villages*. London: Routledge and Kegan Paul.

———. 1973. The Matrifocal Family. In Jack Goody (ed.). *The Character of Kinship*, pp. 121–144. London: Cambridge University Press.

———. 1988. *Kinship and Class in the West Indies: A Genealogical Study of Jamaica and Guyana*. New York: Cambridge University Press.

Tanner, Nancy. 1974. Matrifocality in Indonesia and Africa and Among Black Americans. In Michelle Zimbalist Rosaldo and Louise Lamphere (eds.). *Woman, Culture, and Society*, pp. 129–156. Stanford: Stanford University Press.

The Female World of Cards and Holidays: Women, Families, and the Work of Kinship

Micaela di Leonardo

Why is it that the married women of America are supposed to write all the letters and send all the cards to their husbands' families? My old man is a much better writer than I am, yet he expects me to correspond with his whole family. If I asked him to correspond with mine, he would blow a gasket.

Letter to Ann Landers

Women's place in man's life cycle has been that of nurturer, caretaker, and helpmate, the weaver of those networks of relationships on which she in turn relies.

Carol Gilligan, In a Different Voice[1]

Feminist scholars in the past fifteen years have made great strides in formulating new understandings of the relations among gender, kinship, and the larger economy. As a result of this pioneering research, women are newly visible and audible, no longer submerged within their families. We see households as loci of political struggle, inseparable parts of the larger society and economy, rather than as havens from the heartless world of industrial capitalism.[2] And historical and cultural variations in kinship and family forms have become clearer with the maturation of feminist historical and social-scientific scholarship.

Two theoretical trends have been key to this reinterpretation of women's work and family domain. The first is the elevation to visibility of women's nonmarket activities— housework, child care, the servicing of men, and the care of the elderly—and the definition of all these activities as *labor,* to be enumerated alongside and counted as part of overall social reproduction. The second theoretical trend is the nonpejorative focus on women's domestic or kin-centered networks. We now see them as the products of conscious strategy, as crucial to the functioning of kinship systems, as sources of women's autonomous power and possible primary sites of emotional fulfillment, and, at times, as the vehicles for actual survival and/or political resistance.[3]

Recently, however, a division has developed between feminist interpreters of the "labor" and the "network" perspectives on women's lives. Those who focus on women's work tend to envision women as sentient, goal-oriented actors, while those who concern themselves with women's ties to others tend to perceive women primarily in terms of nurturance, other-orientation—altruism. The most celebrated recent example of this division is the opposing testimony of historians Alice Kessler-Harris and Rosalind Rosenberg in the Equal Employment Opportunity Commission's sex discrimination case against Sears Roebuck and Company. Kessler-Harris argued that American women historically have actively sought higher-paying jobs and have been prevented from gaining them because of sex discrimination by employers. Rosenberg argued that American women in the nineteenth century created among themselves, through their domestic networks, a "women's culture" that emphasized the nurturance of children and others and the maintenance of family life and that discouraged women from competition over or heavy emotional investment in demanding, high-paid employment.[4]

I shall not here address this specific debate but, instead, shall consider its theoretical background and implications. I shall argue that we need to fuse, rather than to oppose, the domestic network and labor perspectives. In what follows, I introduce a new concept, the work of kinship, both to aid empirical feminist research on women, work, and family and to help advance feminist theory in this arena. I believe that the boundary-crossing nature of the concept helps to confound the self-interest/altruism dichotomy, forcing us from an either-or stance to a position that includes both perspectives. I hope in this way to contribute to a more critical feminist vision of women's lives and the meaning of family in the industrial West.

In my recent field research among Italian-Americans in Northern California, I found myself considering the relations between women's kinship and economic lives. As an anthropologist, I was concerned with people's kin lives beyond conventional American nuclear family or household boundaries. To this end, I collected individual and family life histories, asking about all kin and close friends and their activities. I was also very interested in women's labor. As I sat with women and listened to their accounts of their past and present lives, I began to realize that they were involved in three types of work: housework and child care, work in the labor market, and the work of kinship.[5]

By kin work I refer to the conception, maintenance, and ritual celebration of cross-household kin ties, including visits, letters, telephone calls, presents, and cards to kin; the organization of holiday gatherings; the creation and maintenance of quasi-kin relations; decisions to neglect or to intensify particular ties; the mental work of reflection about all these activities; and the creation and communication of altering images of family and kin vis-à-vis the images of others, both folk and mass media. Kin work is a key element that has been missing in the synthesis of the "household labor" and "domestic network" perspectives. In our emphasis on individual women's responsibilities within households and on the job, we reflect the common picture of households as nuclear units, tied perhaps to the larger social and economic system, but not to *each other*. We miss the point of telephone and soft drink advertising, of women's magazines' holiday issues, of commentators' confused nostalgia for the mythical American extended family: it is kinship contact *across households*, as much as women's work within them, that fulfills our cultural expectation of satisfying family life.

Maintaining these contacts, this sense of family, takes time, intention, and skill. We tend to think of human social and kin networks as the epiphenomena of production and reproduction: the social traces created by our material lives. Or, in the neoclassical tradition, we see them as part of leisure activities, outside an economic purview except insofar as they involve consumption behavior. But the creation and maintenance of kin and quasi-kin networks in advanced industrial societies is *work*; and, moreover, it is largely women's work.

The kin-work lens brought into focus new perspectives on my informants' family lives. First, life histories revealed that often the very existence of kin contact and holiday celebration depended on the presence of an adult woman in the household. When couples divorced or mothers died, the work of kinship was left undone; when women entered into sanctioned sexual or marital relationships with men in these situations, they reconstituted the men's kinship networks and organized gatherings and holiday celebrations. Middle-aged businessman Al Bertini, for example, recalled the death of his mother in his early adolescence: "I think that's probably one of the biggest losses in losing a family—yeah, I remember as a child when my Mom was alive . . . the holidays were treated with enthusiasm and love . . . after she died the attempt was there but it just didn't materialize." Later in life, when Al Bertini and his wife separated,

his own and his son Jim's participation in extended-family contact decreased rapidly. But when Jim began a relationship with Jane Batemen, she and he moved in with Al, and Jim and Jane began to invite his kin over for holidays. Jane single-handedly planned and cooked the holiday feasts.

Kin work, then, is like housework and child care: men in the aggregate do not do it. It differs from these forms of labor in that it is harder for men to substitute hired labor to accomplish these tasks in the absence of kinswomen. Second, I found that women, as the workers in this arena, generally had much greater kin knowledge than did their husbands, often including more accurate and extensive knowledge of their husbands' families. This was true both of middle-aged and younger couples and surfaced as a phenomenon in my interviews in the form of humorous arguments and in wives' detailed additions to husbands' narratives. Nick Meraviglia, a middle-aged professional, discussed his Italian antecedents in the presence of his wife, Pina:

NICK: My grandfather was a very outspoken man, and it was reported he took off for the hills when he found out that Mussolini was in power.

PINA: And he was a very tall man; he used to have to bow his head to get inside doors.

NICK: No, that was my uncle.

PINA: Your grandfather too, I've heard your mother say.

NICK: My mother has a sister and a brother.

PINA: Two sisters!

NICK: You're right!

PINA: Maria and Angelina.

Women were also much more willing to discuss family feuds and crises and their own roles in them; men tended to repeat formulaic statements asserting family unity and respectability. (This was much less true for younger men.) Joe and Cetta Longhinotti's statements illustrate these tendencies. Joe responded to my question about kin relations: "We all get along. As a rule, relatives, you got nothing but trouble." Cetta, instead, discussed her relations with each of her grown children, their wives, her in-laws, and her own blood kin in detail. She did not hide the fact that relations were strained in several cases; she was eager to discuss the evolution of problems and to seek my opinions of her actions. Similarly, Pina Meraviglia told the following story of her fight with one of her brothers with hysterical laughter: "There was some biting and hair pulling and choking . . . it was terrible! I shouldn't even tell you. . . ." Nick, meanwhile, was concerned about maintaining an image of family unity and respectability.

Also, men waxed fluent while women were quite inarticulate in discussing their past and present occupations. When asked about their work lives, Joe Longhinotti and Nick Meraviglia, union baker and professional, respectively, gave detailed narratives of their work careers. Cetta Longhinotti and Pina Meraviglia, clerical and former clerical, respectively, offered only short descriptions focusing on factors of ambience, such as the "lovely things" sold by Cetta's firm.

These patterns are not repeated in the younger generation, especially among younger women, such as Jane Batemen, who have managed to acquire training and jobs with some prospect of mobility. These younger women, though, have *added* a professional and detailed interest in their jobs to a felt responsibility for the work of kinship.[6]

Although men rarely took on any kin-work tasks, family histories and accounts of contemporary life revealed that kinswomen often negotiated among themselves, alternating hosting, food-preparation, and gift-buying responsibilities—or sometimes ceding entire task clusters to one woman. Taking on or ceding tasks was clearly related to acquiring or divesting oneself of power within kin networks, but women varied in their interpretation of the meaning of this power. Cetta Longhinotti, for example, relied on the "family Christmas dinner" as a symbol of her central kinship role and was involved in painful negotiations with her daughter-in-law over the issue: "Last year she insisted—this is

touchy. She doesn't want to spend the holiday dinner together. So last year we went there. But I still had my dinner the next day. . . . I made a big dinner on Christmas Day, regardless of who's coming—candles on the table, the whole routine. I decorate the house myself too . . . well, I just feel that the time will come when maybe I won't feel like cooking a big dinner—she should take advantage of the fact that I feel like doing it now." Pina Meraviglia, in contrast, was saddened by the centripetal force of the developmental cycle but was unworried about the power dynamics involved in her negotiations with daughters- and mother-in-law over holiday celebrations.

Kin work is not just a matter of power among women but also of the mediation of power represented by household units.[7] Women often choose to minimize status claims in their kin work and to include numbers of households under the rubric of family. Cetta Longhinotti's sister Anna, for example, is married to a professional man whose parents have considerable economic resources, while Joe and Cetta have low incomes and no other well-off kin. Cetta and Anna remain close, talk on the phone several times a week, and assist their adult children, divided by distance and economic status, in remaining united as cousins.

Finally, women perceived housework, child care, market labor, the care of the elderly, and the work of kinship as competing responsibilities. Kin work was a unique category, however, because it was unlabeled and because women felt they could either cede some tasks to kinswomen and/or could cut them back severely. Women variously cited the pressures of market labor, the needs of the elderly, and their own desires for freedom and job enrichment as reasons for cutting back Christmas card lists, organized holiday gatherings, multifamily dinners, letters, visits, and phone calls. They expressed guilt and defensiveness about this cutback process and, particularly, about their failures to keep families close through constant contact and about their failures to create perfect holiday celebrations. Cetta Longhinotti, during the period when she was visiting her elderly mother every weekend in addition to working a full-time job, said of her grown children, "I'd have the whole gang here once a month, but I've been so busy that I haven't done that for about six months." And Pina Meraviglia lamented her insufficient work on family Christmases, "I wish I had really made it traditional . . . like my sister-in-law has special stories."

Kin work, then, takes place in an arena characterized simultaneously by cooperation and competition, by guilt and gratification. Like housework and child care, it is women's work, with the same lack of clear-cut agreement concerning its proper components: How often should sheets be changed? When should children be toilet trained? Should an aunt send a niece a birthday present? Unlike housework and child care, however, kin work, taking place across the boundaries of normative households, is as yet unlabeled and has no retinue of experts prescribing its correct forms. Neither home economists nor child psychologists have much to say about nieces' birthday presents. Kin work is thus more easily cut back without social interference. On the other hand, the results of kin work—frequent kin contact and feelings of intimacy—are the subject of considerable cultural manipulation as indicators of family happiness. Thus, women in general are subject to the guilt my informants expressed over cutting back kin-work activities.

Although many of my informants referred to the results of women's kin work—cross-household kin contacts and attendant ritual gatherings—as particularly Italian-American, I suggest that in fact this phenomenon is broadly characteristic of American kinship. We think of kin-work tasks such as the preparation of ritual feasts, responsibility for holiday card lists, and gift buying as extensions of women's domestic responsibilities for cooking, consumption, and nurturance. American men in general do not take on these tasks any more than they do housework and child care—and probably less, as these tasks have not yet been the subject of intense public debate. And my informants' gender breakdown in relative articulateness on kinship and workplace themes reflects the still prevalent occupational segregation—most women cannot find jobs that provide enough pay, status, or promotion possibilities to make them worth focusing on—as well as women's perceived power within kinship networks. The common recognition of that power is reflected in Selma Greenberg's book on nonsexist child rearing. Greenberg calls mothers "press agents" who sponsor relations between their own children and other relatives; she advises a mother whose relatives treat her disrespectfully to deny those kin access to her children.[8]

Kin work is a salient concept in other parts of the developed world as well. Larissa Adler Lomnitz and Marisol Pérez Lizaur have found that "centralizing women" are responsible for these tasks and for communicating "family ideology" among upper-class families in Mexico City. Matthews Hamabata, in his study of upper-class families in Japan, has found that women's kin work involves key financial transactions. Sylvia Junko Yanagisako discovered that, among rural Japanese migrants to the United States, the maintenance of kin networks was assigned to women as the migrants adopted the American ideology of the independent nuclear family household. Maila Stivens notes that urban Australian housewives' kin ties and kin ideology "transcend women's isolation in domestic units."[9]

This is not to say that cultural conceptions of appropriate kin work do not vary, even within the United States. Carol B. Stack documents institutionalized fictive kinship and concomitant reciprocity networks among impoverished black American women. Women in populations characterized by intense feelings of ethnic identity may feel bound to emphasize particular occasions—Saint Patrick's or Columbus Day—with organized family feasts. These constructs may be mediated by religious affiliation, as in the differing emphases on Friday or Sunday family dinners among Jews and Christians. Thus the personnel involved and the amount and kind of labor considered necessary for the satisfactory performance of particular kin-work tasks are likely to be culturally constructed.[10] But while the kin and quasi-kin universes and the ritual calendar may vary among women according to race or ethnicity, their general responsibility for maintaining kin links and ritual observances does not.

As kin work is not an ethnic or racial phenomenon, neither is it linked only to one social class. Some commentators on American family life still reflect the influence of work done in England in the 1950s and 1960s (by Elizabeth Bott and by Peter Willmott and Michael Young) in their assumption that working-class families are close and extended, while the middle class substitutes friends (or anomie) for family. Others reflect the prevalent family pessimism in their presumption that neither working- nor middle-class families have extended kin contact.[11] Insofar as kin contact depends on residential proximity, the larger economy's shifts will influence particular groups' experiences. Factory workers, close to kin or not, are likely to disperse when plants shut down or relocate. Small businesspeople or independent professionals may, however, remain resident in particular areas—and thus maintain proximity to kin—for generations, while professional employees of large firms relocate at their firms' behest. This pattern obtained among my informants.

In any event, cross-household kin contact can be and is effected at long distance through letters, cards, phone calls, and holiday and vacation visits. The form and functions of contact, however, vary according to economic resources. Stack and Brett Williams offer rich accounts of kin networks among poor blacks and migrant Chicano farmworkers functioning to provide emotional support, labor, commodity, and cash exchange—a funeral visit, help with laundry, the gift of a dress or piece of furniture.[12] Far different in degree are exchanges such as the loan of a vacation home, a multifamily boating trip, or the provision of free professional services—examples from the kin networks of my wealthier informants. The point is that households, as labor- and income-pooling units, whatever their relative wealth, are somewhat porous in relation to others with whose members they share kin or quasi-kin ties. We do not really know how class differences operate in this realm; it is possible that they do so largely in

terms of ideology. It may be, as David Schneider and Raymond T. Smith suggest, that the affluent and the very poor are more open in recognizing necessary economic ties to kin than are those who identify themselves as middle class.[13]

Recognizing that kin work is gender- rather than class-based allows us to see women's kin networks among all groups, not just among working-class and impoverished women in industrialized societies. This recognition in turn clarifies our understanding of the privileges and limits of women's varying access to economic resources. Affluent women can "buy out" of housework, child care—and even some kin-work responsibilities. But they, like all women, are ultimately responsible, and subject to both guilt and blame, as the administrators of home, children, and kin network. Even the wealthiest women must negotiate the timing and venue of holidays and other family rituals with their kinswomen. It may be that kin work is the core women's work category in which all women cooperate, while women's perceptions of the appropriateness of cooperation for housework, child care, and the care of the elderly varies by race, class, region, and generation.

But kin work is not necessarily an appropriate category of labor, much less gendered labor, in all societies. In many small-scale societies, kinship is the major organizing principle of all social life, and all contacts are by definition kin contacts.[14] One cannot, therefore, speak of labor that does not involve kin. In the United States, kin work as a separable category of gendered labor perhaps arose historically in concert with the ideological and material constructs of the moral mother/cult of domesticity and the privatized family during the course of industrialization in the eighteenth and nineteenth centuries. These phenomena are connected to the increase in the ubiquity of productive occupations for men that are not organized through kinship. This includes the demise of the family farm with the capitalization of agriculture and rural-urban migration; the decline of family recruitment in factories as firms grew, ended child labor, and began to assert bureaucratized forms of control; the decline of artisanal labor and of small entrepreneurial enterprises as large firms took greater and greater shares of the commodity market; the decline of the family firm as corporations—and their managerial work forces—grew beyond the capacities of individual families to provision them; and, finally, the rise of civil service bureaucracies and public pressure against nepotism.[15]

As men increasingly worked alongside of non-kin, and as the ideology of separate spheres was increasingly accepted, perhaps the responsibility for kin maintenance, like that for child rearing, became gender-focused. Ryan points out that "built into the updated family economy . . . was a new measure of voluntarism." This voluntarism, though, "perceived as the shift from patriarchal authority to domestic affection," also signaled the rise of women's moral responsibility for family life. Just as the "idea of fatherhood itself seemed almost to wither away" so did male involvement in the responsibility for kindred lapse.[16]

With postbellum economic growth and geographic movement, women's new kin burden involved increasing amounts of time and labor. The ubiquity of lengthy visits and of frequent letter-writing among nineteenth-century women attests to this. And for visitors and for those who were residentially proximate, the continuing commonalities of women's domestic labor allowed for kinds of work sharing—nursing, childkeeping, cooking, cleaning—that men, with their increasingly differentiated and controlled activities, probably could not maintain. This is not to say that some kin-related male productive work did not continue; my own data, for instance, show kin involvement among small businessmen in the present. It is, instead, to suggest a general trend in material life and a cultural shift that influenced even those whose productive and kin lives remained commingled. Yanagisako has distinguished between the realms of domestic and public kinship in order to draw attention to anthropology's relatively "thin descriptions" of

the domestic (female) domain. Using her typology, we might say that kin work as gendered labor comes into existence within the domestic domain with the relative erasure of the domain of public, male kinship.[17]

Whether or not this proposed historical model bears up under further research, the question remains, Why do women do kin work? However material factors may shape activities, they do not determine how individuals may perceive them. And in considering issues of motivation, of intention, of the cultural construction of kin work, we return to the altruism-versus-self-interest dichotomy in recent feminist theory. Consider the epigraphs to this article. Are women kin workers the nurturant weavers of the Gilligan quotation, or victims, like the fed-up woman who writes to complain to Ann Landers? That is, are we to see kin work as yet another example of "women's culture" that takes the care of others as its primary desideratum? Or are we to see kin work as another way in which men, the economy, and the state extract labor from women without a fair return? And how do women themselves see their kin work and its place in their lives?

As I have indicated previously, I believe that it is the creation of the self-interest/altruism dichotomy that is itself the problem here. My women informants, like most American women, accepted their primary responsibility for housework and the care of dependent children. Despite two major waves of feminist activism in this century, the gendering of certain categories of unpaid labor is still largely unaltered. These work responsibilities clearly interfere with some women's labor force commitments at certain life-cycle stages; but, more important, women are simply discriminated against in the labor market and rarely are able to achieve wage and status parity with men of the same age, race, class, and educational background.[18]

Thus for my women informants, as for most American women, the domestic domain is not only an arena in which much unpaid labor must be undertaken but also a realm in which one may attempt to gain human satisfactions—and power—not available in the labor market. Anthropologists Jane Collier and Louise Lamphere have written compellingly on the ways in which varying kinship and economic structures may shape women's competition or cooperation with one another in domestic domains.[19] Feminists considering Western women and families have looked at the issue of power primarily in terms of husband–wife relations or psychological relations between parents and children. If we adopt Collier and Lamphere's broader canvas, though, we see that kin work is not only women's labor from which men and children benefit but also labor that women undertake in order to create obligations in men and children and to gain power over one another. Thus Cetta Longhinotti's struggle with her daughter-in-law over the venue of Christmas dinner is not just about a competition over altruism, it is also about the creation of future obligations. And thus Cetta's and Anna's sponsorship of their children's friendship with each other is both an act of nurturance and a cooperative means of gaining power over those children.

Although this was not a clear-cut distinction, those of my informants who were more explicitly antifeminist tended to be most invested in kin work. Given the overwhelming historical shift toward greater autonomy for younger generations and the withering of children's financial and labor obligations to their parents, this investment was in most cases tragically doomed. Cetta Longhinotti, for example, had repaid her own mother's devotion with extensive home nursing during the mother's last years. Given Cetta's general failure to direct her adult children in work, marital choice, religious worship, or even frequency of visits, she is unlikely to receive such care from them when she is older.

The kin-work lens thus reveals the close relations between altruism and self-interest in women's actions. As economists Nancy Folbre and Heidi Hartmann point out, we have inherited a Western intellectual tradition that both dichotomizes the domestic and public domains and associates them on exclusive axes such that we find it difficult to see self-interest in the home and altruism in the workplace.[20] But why, in fact, have women fought for better jobs if not, in part, to support their children? These dichotomies are Procrustean beds that warp our understanding of women's lives both at home and at work. "Altruism" and "self-interest" are cultural constructions that are not necessarily mutually exclusive, and we forget this to our peril.

The concept of kin work helps to bring into focus a heretofore unacknowledged array of tasks that is culturally assigned to women in industrialized societies. At the same time, this concept, embodying notions of both love and work and crossing the boundaries of households, helps us to reflect on current feminist debates on women's work, family, and community. We newly see both the interrelations of these phenomena and women's roles in creating and maintaining those interrelations. Revealing the actual labor embodied in what we culturally conceive as love and considering the political uses of this labor helps to deconstruct the self-interest/altruism dichotomy and to connect more closely women's domestic and labor-force lives.

The true value of the concept, however, remains to be tested through further historical and contemporary research on gender, kinship, and labor. We need to assess the suggestion that gendered kin work emerges in concert with the capitalist development process; to probe the historical record for women's and men's varying and changing conceptions of it; and to research the current range of its cultural constructions and material realities. We know that household boundaries are more porous than we had thought—but they are undoubtedly differentially porous, and this is what we need to specify. We need, in particular, to assess the relations of changing labor processes, residential patterns, and the use of technology to changing kin work.

Altering the values attached to this particular set of women's tasks will be as difficult as are the housework, child-care, and occupational-segregation struggles. But just as feminist research in these latter areas is complementary and cumulative, so researching kin work should help us to piece together the home, work, and public-life landscape—to see the female world of cards and holidays as it is constructed and lived within the changing political economy. How female that world is to remain, and what it would look like if it were not sex-segregated, are questions we cannot yet answer.

ACKNOWLEDGMENT

Many thanks to Cynthia Costello, Rayna Rapp, Roberta Spalter-Roth, John Willoughby, and Barbara Gelpi, Susan Johnson, and Sylvia Yanagisako of Signs for their help with this article. I wish in particular to acknowledge the influence of Rayna Rapp's work on my ideas.

Acknowledgment and gratitude to Carroll Smith-Rosenberg for my paraphrase of her title, "The Female World of Love and Ritual: Relations between Women in Nineteenth-Century America," *Signs: Journal of Women in Culture and Society* 1, no. 1 (Autumn 1975): 1–29.

NOTES

1. Ann Landers letter printed in *Washington Post* (April 15, 1983); Carol Gilligan, *In a Different Voice* (Cambridge, Mass.: Harvard University Press, 1982), 17.
2. Heidi I. Hartmann, "The Family as the Locus of Gender, Class, and Political Struggle: The Example of Housework," *Signs* 6, no. 3 (Spring 1981): 366–94; and Christopher Lasch, *Haven in a Heartless World: The Family Besieged* (New York: Basic Books, 1977).
3. Representative examples of the first trend include Joann Vanek, "Time Spent on Housework," *Scientific American* 231 (November 1974): 116–20; Ruth Schwartz Cowan, "A Case Study of Technological and Social Change: The Washing Machine and the Working Wife," in *Clio's Consciousness Raised*, ed. Mary Hartmann and Lois Banner (New York: Harper & Row, 1974), 245–53; Ann Oakley, *Women's Work: The Housewife, Past and Present* (New York: Vintage, 1974); Hartmann; and Susan Strasser, *Never Done: A History of American Housework* (New York: Pantheon Books, 1982). Key contributions to

the second trend include Louise Lamphere, "Strategies, Cooperation and Conflict among Women in Domestic Groups," in *Woman, Culture and Society*, ed. Michelle Zimbalist Rosaldo and Louise Lamphere (Stanford, Calif.: Stanford University Press, 1974), 97–112; Mina Davis Caulfield, "Imperialism, the Family and the Cultures of Resistance," *Socialist Revolution* 20 (October 1974): 67–85; Smith-Rosenberg; Sylvia Junko Yanagisako, "Women-centered Kin Networks and Urban Bilateral Kinship," *American Ethnologist* 4, no. 2 (1977): 207–26; Jane Humphries, "The Working Class Family, Women's Liberation and Class Struggle: The Case of Nineteenth Century British History," *Review of Radical Political Economics* 9 (Fall 1977): 25–41; Blanche Weisen Cook, "Female Support Networks and Political Activism: Lillian Wald, Crystal Eastman, Emma Goldman," in *A Heritage of Her Own*, ed. Nancy F. Cott and Elizabeth H. Pleck (New York: Simon & Schuster, 1979); Temma Kaplan, "Female Consciousness and Collective Action: The Case of Barcelona, 1910–1918," *Signs* 7, no. 3 (Spring 1982): 545–66.
4. On this debate, see Jon Weiner, "Women's History on Trial," *Nation* 241, no. 6 (September 7, 1985): 161, 176, 178–80; Karen J. Winkler, "Two Scholars' Conflict in Sears Sex-Bias Case Sets Off War in Women's History," *Chronicle of Higher Education* (February 5, 1986), 1, 8; Rosalind Rosenberg, "What Harms Women in the Workplace," *New York Times* (February 27, 1986); Alice Kessler-Harris, "Equal Employment Opportunity Commission vs. Sears Roebuck and Company: A Personal Account," *Radical History Review* 35 (April 1986): 57–79.
5. Portions of the following analysis are reported in Micaela di Leonardo, *The Varieties of Ethnic Experience: Kinship, Class and Gender among California Italian-Americans* (Ithaca, N.Y.: Cornell University Press, 1984), chap. 6.
6. Clearly, many women do, in fact, discuss their paid labor with willingness and clarity. The point here is that there are opposing gender tendencies in an identical interview situation, tendencies that are explicable in terms of both the material realities and current cultural constructions of gender.
7. Papanek has rightly focused on women's unacknowledged family status production, but what is conceived of as "family" shifts and varies (Hanna Papanek, "Family Status Production: The 'Work' and 'Non-Work' of Women," *Signs* 4, no. 4 [Summer 1979]: 775–81).
8. Selma Greenberg, *Right from the Start: A Guide to Nonsexist Child Rearing* (Boston: Houghton

Mifflin Co., 1978), 147. Another example of indirect support for kin work's gendered existence is a recent study of university math students, which found that a major reason for women's failure to pursue careers in mathematics was the pressure of family involvement. Compare David Maines et al., *Social Processes of Sex Differentiation in Mathematics* (Washington, D.C.: National Institute of Education, 1981).

9. Larissa Adler Lomnitz and Marisol Pérez Lizaur, "The History of a Mexican Urban Family," *Journal of Family History* 3, no. 4 (1978): 392–409, esp. 398; Matthews Hamàbata, Crested Kimono *Power and Love in the Japanese Business Family* (Ithaca, N.Y.: Cornell University Press, 1990); Sylvia Junko Yanagisako, "Two Processes of Change in Japanese-American Kinship," *Journal of Anthropological Research* 31 (1975): 196–224; Maila Stivens, "Women and Their Kin: Kin, Class and Solidarity in a Middle-Class Suburb of Sydney, Australia," in *Women United, Women Divided,* ed. Patricia Caplan and Janet M. Bujra (Bloomington: Indiana University Press, 1979), 157–84.

10. Carol B. Stack, *All Our Kin: Strategies for Survival in a Black Community* (New York: Harper & Row, 1974). These cultural constructions may, however, vary within ethnic/racial populations as well.

11. Elizabeth Bott, *Family and Social Network,* 2d ed. (New York: Free Press, 1971): Michael Young and Peter Willmott, *Family and Kinship in East London* (London: Routledge & Kegan Paul, 1957), and *Family and Class in a London Suburb* (London: Routledge & Kegan Paul, 1960). Classic studies that presume this class difference are Herbert Gans, *The Urban Villagers: Group and Class in the Life of Italian-Americans* (New York: Free Press, 1962); and Mirra Komarovsky, *Blue-Collar Marriage* (New York: Random House, 1962). A recent example is Ilene Philipson, "Heterosexual Antagonisms and the Politics of Mothering," *Socialist Review* 12, no. 6 (November–December 1982): 55–77. Edward Shorter, *The Making of the Modern Family* (New York: Basic Books, 1975), epitomizes the pessimism of the "family sentiments" school. See also Mary Lyndon Shanley. "The History of the Family in Modern England: Review Essay," *Signs* 4, no. 4 (Summer 1979): 740–50.

12. Stack; and Brett Williams, "The Trip Takes Us: Chicano Migrants to the Prairie" (Ph.D. diss., University of Illinois at Urbana-Champaign, 1975).

13. David Schneider and Raymond T. Smith, *Class Differences and Sex Roles in American Kinship and Family Structure* (Englewood Cliffs, N.J.: Prentice-Hall, Inc., 1973), esp. 27.

14. See Nelson Graburn, ed., *Readings in Kinship and Social Structure* (New York: Harper & Row, 1971), esp. 3–4.

15. The moral mother/cult of domesticity is analyzed in Barbara Welter, "The Cult of True Womanhood, 1820–1860," *American Quarterly* 18, no. 2 (Summer 1966): 151–74; Nancy Cott, *The Bonds of Womanhood: "Women's Sphere" in New England, 1780–1835* (New Haven, Conn.: Yale University Press, 1977); and Ruth Bloch, "American Feminine Ideals in Transition: The Rise of the Moral Mother, 1785–1815," *Feminist Studies* 4, no. 2 (June 1978): 101–26. The description of the general political-economic shift in the United States is based on Harry Braverman, *Labor and Monopoly Capital: The Degradation of Work in the Twentieth Century* (New York: Monthly Review Press, 1974); Peter Dobkin Hall, "Family Structure and Economic Organization: Massachusetts Merchants, 1700–1850," in *Family and Kin in Urban Communities, 1700–1950,* ed. Tamara K. Hareven (New York: New Viewpoints, 1977), 38–61; Michael Anderson, "Family, Household and the Industrial Revolution," in *The American Family in Social-Historical Perspective,* ed. Michael Gordon (New York: St. Martin's Press, 1978), 38–50; Tamara K. Hareven, Amoskeag: *Life and Work in an American Factory City* (New York: Pantheon Books, 1978); Richard Edwards, Contested Terrain: *The Transformation of the Workplace in the Twentieth Century* (New York: Basic Books, 1979); Mary Ryan, *The Cradle of the Middle Class: The Family in Oneida County,* New York, 1790–1865 (Cambridge: Cambridge University Press, 1981); Alice Kessler-Harris, *Out to Work: A History of Wage-earning Women in the United States* (New York: Oxford University Press, 1982).

16. Ryan, 231–32.

17. Sylvia Junko Yanagisako, "Family and Household: The Analysis of Domestic Groups," *Annual Review of Anthropology* 8 (1979): 161–205.

18. See Donald J. Treiman and Heidi I. Hartmann, eds., *Women, Work and Wages: Equal Pay for Jobs of Equal Value* (Washington, D.C.: National Academy Press, 1981).

19. Lamphere (n. 4 above); Jane Fishburne Collier, "Women in Politics," in Rosaldo and Lamphere, eds. (n. 4 above), 89–96.

20. Nancy Folbre and Heidi I. Hartmann, "The Rhetoric of Self-Interest: Selfishness, Altruism, and Gender in Economic Theory," in *The Consequences of Economic Rhetoric,* ed. Arjo Klamer and Donald McCloskey (New York: Cambridge University Press, 1988).

IX

Gender, Ritual, and Religion

In many non-western societies women's ritual roles are central and indispensable to community cohesion and well-being. In contrast, in Anglo-European cultures women's religious activities tend to be secondary and marginal because of the pre-eminence of men in both organizational hierarchies and doctrine. Anthropological research has long recognized that religious systems reflect, support, and carry forward patterns of social organization and central values of a society. What has not been sufficiently recognized is the interrelationships of men and women in the perpetuation of social life through religious activities and the relationship between gender stratification and gendered religious symbolism.

The study of the ritual activities of women has often been embedded in analyses of life cycle events, such as the Nkang'a girl's puberty ritual among the Ndembu of Central Africa (Turner 1968: 198) or pregnancy and childbirth rituals in Asia (Jacobson 1989; Laderman 1983). With the exception of these areas of research, the study of women and religion has often been neglected, despite the fact that women are prominent in religious activities. As a result of a renewed interest in the study of gender in various cultures, scholars have begun to explore how the religious experience of women is different from that of men; whether and how women become ritual specialists; what religious functions they perform and the degree to which these are private or public; and finally, what implications these ritual activities have for women's prestige and status.

This has led, in some cultural contexts, to an attempt to formulate a more complete ethnographic picture. For example, in the literature on Australian aborigines, where there is a good deal of debate about gender roles, a number of ethnologists have asserted that the dominance of senior men is sustained by their control of sacred knowledge and that their position is recognized by both men and women in the culture (Warner 1937; White 1975; Bern 1979). This viewpoint has been challenged by Diane Bell (1981, 1983), who notes that male anthropologists have underestimated and under-reported the religious life of Australian aboriginal women. She argues that "Both men and women have rituals that are closed to the other, both men and women allow the other limited attendance at certain of their rituals, and, finally, there are ceremonies in which both men and women exchange knowledge and together celebrate their membership in one society and their duty to maintain the law of their ancestors" (1981: 319).

Bell focuses in particular on the love rituals of women, rituals that originally were viewed by ethnologists as magic and therefore deviant, unimportant, and marginal to the central decision-making realm of men. In contrast, Bell suggests that in the celebration of these rituals, used by women to establish and maintain marriages of their own choosing, "Women clearly perceived themselves as independent operators in a domain where they exercised power and autonomy based on their dreaming affiliations with certain tracts of land. These rights are recognized and respected by the whole society" (1981: 322). The love rituals of Australian aboriginal women are, in short, by no means peripheral to the society. They are underwritten by Dreamtime Law and feared by men who are often unaware that they are being performed and unable to negate their power. Through their rituals some Australian aboriginal women have, as Hamilton (1981) suggests, a mechanism with which to challenge the ideology of male superiority that is expressed in male ritual.

Mathews (1985) provides us with another example of an important arena of religious activity—the civil-religious hierarchy or cargo system in Mesoamerica—that has long been considered a public and exclusively male arena. If women were mentioned at all in studies of the cargo system, it was for their peripheral roles in food preparation. Based on her research in the state of Oaxaca in Mexico, Mathews begins by pointing out that an application of the domestic-public model (see Section III) to an understanding of these religious ceremonies obscures the significant ritual roles of women because it places the cargo system in the public sphere of activity and fails to acknowledge the importance of the household unit. Rather than oppose men and women within a rigid domestic-public model, Mathews emphasizes the parallel and interdependent roles of men and women in the execution of cargo. Male cargo holders (mayordomos) organize and coordinate the activities of men, and female cargo holders (mayordomas) organize and coordinate the activities of women. At the end of their year of responsibility, both share in the prestige gained from service.

If Oaxacan women have an important and prestige-conferring role within the religious sphere of cargo activity, similar opportunities are denied them within the civil sphere. Thus Mathews explores the impact of the penetration of the state (see Section VII) on the lives of women. A sexual divide-and-rule state policy, she argues, makes men into social adults and women into domestic wards whose dealings with the public sphere become restricted. Prestige in local institutions is undermined by its absence in extracommunity institutions, and as civil offices assume increasing importance at the expense of cargo offices, the position of women is eroded.

In contrast to the underestimation of women's religious roles in the literature on Australian aborigines and the Mesoamerican cargo system, studies of sub-Saharan Africa have long recognized that the ritual life of women is both significant and highly elaborated. In this region, women are involved in complex ceremonies of initiation; they are engaged in witchcraft and divination (Mendonsa 1979; Ngubane 1977); they act as spirit mediums and healers (Green 1989; Sargent 1989); they lead and participate in possession cults (Berger 1976); and they form their own secret societies (MacCormack 1979).

Boddy (in this book) discusses the role of women in the zar spirit possession cult of northern Sudan. In particular she emphasizes how zar serves as a cultural resource mobilized by individuals, particularly women, under certain conditions. Boddy argues that the Sudanese women in the village of Hofiriyat where she conducted her research view themselves in a complementary rather than inferior or subordinate position vis-à-vis men. This complementarity in gender relations is reflected in the dialectical relationship between zar and Islam. "If women are constrained by their gender from full participation in Islam, men are constrained by theirs from full participation in the zar" (Boddy 1989:60). Zar is not, in Boddy's view, a "peripheral cult" (Lewis 1971).

In a range of cultural contexts, anthropologists have argued that women use spirit possession and trance as an outlet for the stress that results from their social and material deprivation and subordination (Broch 1985; Hamer and Hamer 1966; Lewis 1966, 1986; Morsy 1979; Pressel 1973). As Danforth (1989: 99) argues with regard to firewalking (Anastenaria) in northern Greece, "Through these rituals women seek to address the discrepancies that characterize the relationship between an official ideology of male dominance and a social reality in which women actually exercise a significant degree of power. Spirit possession . . . provides a context for the resolution of conflict often associated with gender roles and gender identity." Boddy views the zar cult in more nuanced terms. Although she acknowledges that some of her informants use zar to improve their subordinate status, she emphasizes that women are more susceptible to spirit attack (as illness episode) "as a function of their femininity." Zar is a form of feminist discourse for women with marital or fertility problems. Close to 50 percent of Hofriyati women who were ever or are married have succumbed to possession. "Spirits, villagers assert, rarely trouble themselves with the unwed" (Boddy 1989:166).

Discourse, in the form of sexually explicit funerary songs and dances performed by women, is also the subject of McIntosh's analysis (in this book) of death rituals among the Giriama of Kenya. McIntosh begins by noting that many ritual forms, particularly in sub-Saharan Africa, lend themselves to unruliness, turning the normative social world upside down (see also Davis 1971, 1975). But, she asks, does such ritual behavior really pose a threat to patriarchal orders and how can it be understood from an insider's perspective? Have these perceptions changed in conjunction with the arrival of Western lifestyles and tourism? McIntosh argues that in a gender-neutral sense the sexual license of funerary songs is a mechanism by which the Giriama can confront the power of death. Grief and sexual expression are assimilated such that a funeral becomes like a wedding: "the last wedding of the deceased." However, the persistence of this "tradition" occurs in a society where women's sexuality is still controlled by a set of popular expectations about female modesty and yet simultaneously challenged by the growth of a "sex safari" industry. The obscenities expressed by women in the funerary rituals are thus viewed with ambivalence—innocuous tradition on the one hand; a training ground for real sexual promiscuity and misconduct on the other. Today women are frequently derided for, if not prohibited by their husbands from participating in these unruly rituals.

The relationship between women's religion and sexuality is equally central to Kendall's discussion (in this book) of Korean shamans but in this case she wonders whether this is an appropriate interpretation of what is going on and suggests that it is an interpretation rooted in western culture. While she acknowledges that the belief that shamanic experience implies a sexual union between the female shaman and her guardian god "lurks in some corners of the Korean popular imagination", she emphasizes that Korean shamanistic rituals are less about repressed sexuality than they are about expressive bodily play and challenges to gender oppression.

This essay also introduces us to the concept of female religious practitioners (healers and shamans) more generally. Such women frequently transcend local cultural definitions of womanhood and are recognized as having extraordinary characteristics. Korean women who become mansin (shamans) stand above the social and economic constraints generally imposed on a proper Korean wife and mother.

The mansin occupies an ambiguous status similar to that of other "glamorous but morally dubious female marginals, the actress, the female entertainer, and the prostitute" (Kendall 1985). Though not always accorded respect, the mansin wears the costumes and speaks with the authority of the gods. Mansin and their rituals are, in Kendall's view, "integral components of Korean family and village religion. Within this religious system, women and shamans perform essential ritual tasks that complement men's ritual tasks" (1985: 25). Korean housewives come to the mansin for therapeutic answers to a range of personal and household problems; for divinations about the future and prospects for the coming year; and for female solidarity and a "venting of the spleen" (Kendall 1985: 25). Women's rituals in Korea, like those in some other parts of the world, are both practical and expressive.

Mama Lola, the Vodou priestess (manbo) described by Brown (in this book) is a ritual specialist, diviner, and healer working in New York who, when she is possessed, "acts out the social and psychological forces that define and often contain the lives of contemporary Haitian women." Through ritual, Mama Lola empowers her clients. This phenomenon of psychological empowerment is characteristic of other religious systems; it is described by Danforth (1989) in his discussion of the New Age Firewalking cult in the United States and by Wadley (1989) in her analysis of the active control over their lives that north Indian village women gain through their ritual activities.

Mama Lola maintains a very personal relationship with two female spirits. To one she stands in the role of child to a spiritual mother, thereby metaphorically expressing an important bond within Haitian culture and society that is manifested in her own relationship with her daughter Maggie. This ritually embedded mother–child metaphor can be found in other parts of the world where women healers meet the physical and emotional needs of their patients just as mothers meet the needs of their children (Wedenoja 1989; Kerewsky-Halpern 1989). If one of Mama Lola's female spirits represents the nurturing side of women in relation to their children, the other represents the romantic side in relation to men.

In Haitian Vodou the diverse roles of women are projected into the religious sphere. This is equally true of other religious traditions. In Catholic cultures values about ideal womanhood are sanctified by the image of the Virgin Mary, who represents submission, humility, serenity, and long suffering (Stevens 1973). In Mexico, for example, Eve and the Virgin Mary are contrasting images that "encode the cycle of reproduction within the domestic group. When a woman is nursing and sexually continent she resembles the Virgin. When she submits to sex, she is more like Eve" (Ingham 1986: 76). Hindu goddesses are also multifaceted; they are mothers, mediators, and protectresses. According to Preston (1985: 13), there is a connection "between the role of women in Indian life and the special position of female deities in the Hindu pantheon. Though Indian women are supposed to be absolutely devoted to their husbands who are respected as embodiments of the deity, women may also reign supreme in their own domains as mothers of their children." In Dinaan Hinduism the Great Goddess takes several forms, some good and some evil. Babb (1975: 226) suggests that these two aspects reflect an opposition in male and female principles: "When female dominates male, the pair is sinister; when male dominates female the pair is benign."

In this book, we have taken the approach that what it means to be male and female (i.e., gender) is learned and shaped within a cultural context. Religious symbols are a powerful mechanism by which culturally appropriate gender messages are transmitted. As Bynum observes, "It is no longer possible to study religious practice or religious symbols without taking gender—that is, the cultural experience of being male or female—into account" (1986: 1–2). In addition, through participation and leadership in ritual, women may enhance or challenge their socially-defined position. Involvement in religious activities may also generate a sense of female or community solidarity through membership in a congregation or participation in ritual functions. And in many cultures there are parallel religious traditions. If possession is more characteristic of women than it is of men it is precisely because it provides an outlet for ritual expression. This is as true in the simpler societies as it is in state societies with masculinist or patriarchal religions. Thus, Michael Lambek (1993) has described a symbiotic relationship between Islam on the one hand and the spirit possession rituals of women on the other on the island of Mayotte off the coast of Tanzania in Africa. While men are "expected and enabled to display their moral concerns in the universalistic arena provided by Islam" women, through mediumship, "can exercise their authority and play a significant role in the *mraba* (their family) and the community. This can protect or further their own interests, for example, enabling sisters to continue to lay immoral claims upon their brothers after their parents' death" (Lambek 1993: 335, 334). These symbiotic relationships are certainly worthy of further exploration.

REFERENCES

Babb, Lawrence. 1975. *The Divine Hierarchy*. New York: Columbia University Press.

Bell, Diane. 1981. "Women's Business Is Hard Work: Central Australian Aboriginal Women's Love Rituals." *Signs* 7: 314–337.

———. 1983. *Daughters of the Dreaming*. London: George Allen and Unwin.

Berger, Iris. 1976. "Rebels or Status-Seekers? Women as Spirit Mediums in East Africa." In Nancy J. Hafkin and Edna G. Bay (eds.). *Women in Africa*, pp. 157–182. Stanford: Stanford University Press.

Bern, J. 1979. "Ideology and Domination: Toward a Reconstruction of Australian Aboriginal Social Formation." *Oceania* 50: 118–132.

Boddy, Janice. 1989. *Wombs and Alien Spirits: Women, Men, and the Zar Cult in Northern Sudan*. Madison: University of Wisconsin Press.

Broch, Harald Meyer. 1985. "'Crazy Women Are Performing in Sombali': A Possession-Trance Ritual on Bonerate, Indonesia." *Ethos* 13: 262–282.

Bynum, Caroline Walker. 1986. "Introduction: The Complexity of Symbols." In Caroline Walker Bynum, Steven Harrell, and Paula Richman (eds.). *Gender and Religion: On the Complexity of Symbols*, pp. 1–20. Boston: Beacon.

Danforth, Loring M. 1989. *Firewalking and Religious Healing: The Anastenaria of Greece and the American Firewalking Movement*. Princeton: Princeton University Press.

Davis, Natalie Zemon. 1971. "The Reasons of Misrule: Youth Groups and Charivaris in Sixteenth-Century France." *Past and Present* 50:41–75

———. 1975. "Women on Top." In Natalie Zemon Davis, *Society and Culture in Early Modern France*, pp. 124–151. Stanford: Stanford University Press.

Fox, Margery. 1989. "The Socioreligious Role of the Christian Science Practitioner." In Carole Shepherd McClain (ed.). *Women as Healers: Cross-Cultural Perspectives*, pp. 98–114. New Brunswick, NJ: Rutgers University Press.

Green, Edward C. 1989. "Mystical Black Power: The Calling to Diviner-Mediumship in Southern Africa." In Carole Shepherd McClain (ed.). *Women as Healers: Cross-Cultural Perspectives*, pp. 186–200. New Brunswick, NJ: Rutgers University Press.

Hamer, J. and I. Hamer. 1966. "Spirit Possession and its Socio-Psychological Implications among the Sidamo of Southwest Ethiopia." *Ethnology* 5: 392–408.

Hamilton, Annette. 1981. "A Complex Strategical Situation: Gender and Power in Aboriginal Australia." In N. Grieve and P. Grimshaw (eds.). *Australian Women: Feminist Perspectives*, pp. 69–85. Melbourne: Oxford University Press.

Ingham, John. 1986. *Mary, Michael and Lucifer.* Austin: University of Texas Press.

Jacobson, Doranne. 1989. "Golden Handprints and Red-Painted Feet: Hindu Childbirth Rituals in Central India." In Nancy Auer Falk and Rita M. Gross (eds.). *Unspoken Worlds: Women's Religious Lives*, pp. 59–71. Belmont, CA: Wadsworth Publishing Co.

Kendall, Laurel. 1985. *Shamans, Housewives, and Other Restless Spirits: Women in Korean Ritual Life.* Honolulu: University of Hawaii Press.

Kerewsky-Halpern, Barbara. 1989. "Healing with Mother Metaphors: Serbian Conjurers' Word Magic." In Carole Shepherd McClain (eds.). *Women as Healers: Cross-Cultural Perspectives*, pp. 115–135. New Brunswick, NJ: Rutgers University Press.

Laderman, Carol. 1983. *Wives and Midwives: Childbirth and Nutrition in Rural Malaysia.* Berkeley: University of California Press.

Lambek, Michael. 1993. *Knowledge and Practice in Mayotte: Local Discourses of Islam, Sorcery and Spirit Possession.* Toronto: University of Toronto Press.

Lewis, L. M. 1966. "Spirit Possession and Deprivation Cults." *Man* 1: 307–329.

———. 1971. *Ecstatic Religion: An Anthropoligical Study of Spirit Possession and Shamanism.* Baltimore: Penguin Books.

———. 1986. *Religion in Context: Cults and Charisma.* Cambridge: Cambridge University Press.

MacCormack, Carol P. 1979. "Sande: The Public Face of a Secret Society." In Bennetta Jules-Rosette (ed.). *New Religions of Africa*, pp. 27–39. Norwood, NJ: Ablex.

Mathews, Holly F. 1985. "'We are Mayordomo': A Reinterpretation of Women's Roles in the Mexican Cargo System." *American Ethnologist* 12 (2): 285–301.

Mendonsa, Eugene L. 1979. "The Position of Women in the Sisala Divination Cult." In Bennetta Jules-Rosette (ed.). *The New Religions of Africa*, pp. 57–67. Norwood, NJ: Ablex.

Mernissi, Fatima. 1978. "Women, Saints and Sanctuaries." *Signs* 3: 101–12.

Morsy, Soheir. 1979. "Sex Roles, Power, and Illness." *American Ethnologist* 5: 137–150.

Ngubane, H. 1977. *Body and Mind in Zulu Medicine: An Ethnography of Health and Disease In Nyuswa-Zulu Thought and Practice.* New York: Academic Press.

Pressel, Ester. 1973. "Umbanda in Sao Paulo: Religious Innovations in a Developing Society." In Erika Bourguignon (ed.). *Religion, Altered States of Consciousness and Social Change*, pp. 264–318. Columbus: Ohio State University Press.

Preston, James J. 1985. *Cult of the Goddess: Social and Religious Change in a Hindu Temple.* Prospect Heights, IL: Waveland. (Orig pub. 1980.)

Sanday, Peggy. 1974. "Female Status in the Public Domain." In Michelle Z. Rosaldo and Louise Lamphere (eds.). *Woman, Culture, and Society*, pp. 189–206. Stanford: Stanford University Press.

Sargent, Carolyn. 1989. "Women's Roles and Women Healers in Contemporary Rural and Urban Benin." In Carole Shepherd McClain (ed.). *Women as Healers: Cross-Cultural Perspectives*, pp. 204–218. New Brunswick, NJ: Rutgers University Press.

Stevens, Evelyn. 1973. "Marianismo: The Other Face of Machismo in Latin America." In Ann Pescatello (ed.). *Female and Male in Latin America*, pp. 89–101. Pittsburgh: University of Pittsburgh Press.

Turner, Victor. 1968. *Drums of Affliction.* Oxford: Clarendon Press.

Wadley, Susan S. 1989. "Hindu Women's Family and Household Rites in a North Indian Village." In Nancy Auer Falk and Rita M. Gross (eds.). *Unspoken Worlds: Women's Religious Lives*, pp. 72–81. Belmont, CA: Wadsworth.

Warner, William Lloyd. 1937. *A Black Civilization: A Study of an Australian Tribe.* New York: Harper & Row.

Wedenoja, William. 1989. "Mothering and the Practice of 'Balm' in Jamaica." In Carole Shepherd McClain (ed.). *Women as Healers: Cross-Cultural Perspectives*, pp. 76–97. New Brunswick, NJ: Rutgers University Press.

White, I. 1975. "Sexual Conquest and Submission in the Myths of Central Australia." In L. Hiatt (ed.). *Australian Aboriginal Mythology*, pp. 123–142. Canberra: Australian Institute of Aboriginal Studies.

Spirit Possession and Gender Complementarity: Zâr in Rural Northern Sudan

Janice Boddy

July 20, 1976, 4:00 P.M. The door to my hôsh bangs open. Asia ducks beneath the lintel, lifts the water container from her head, and pours its contents into my zîr. Her face is seamed with sweat. "Allaaah!" she exclaims, "The land is hot today! Shufti, ya Janice, I've heard they are drumming in Goz. Do you want to go?"

Of course!—a zâr is on. But the walk in this heat is a long one, and my leg has been badly swollen for several days.

"Sadig is borrowing camels from his cousin. You must ride."

Moments later I am teetering sidesaddle, following the equally inexpert Sadig along a trail that hems some withered fields of maize. My camel munches lazily at each low acacia, and I am soon covered in scratches from their thorns. Prodding seems only to anger the beast, and I fear a painful bite; it would have been faster to walk. Still beyond sight of Goz we are reached by the deep bass of drumming, fitful through the sultry air. The camels perk, raise their heads, start trotting toward the sound.

Goz is a newish settlement, an odd assortment of square thatched huts, thorn corrals, and a couple of half-completed mud-brick hôshs. The drumming comes from one of these. Hofriyati[1] arriving by foot have preceded my arrival; the zâr has just begun. Ideally a zâr should take place in the room of a house, if capacious, but because of the heat, today's has been mounted in the yard.

A litany of greetings over, I am seated near the dancing grounds an open area (mîdân) bounded on three sides by palm-fiber ground mats. Here sit several dozen chanting women: the spirit-possessed. Now and then one rises to her knees and begins to move her upper body in time with the sonorous beat. In the center of the mîdân stands the shaykha—zâr practitioner or "priestess"—a forceful, brawny woman in an electric-pink pullover, tôb[2] tied loosely at her waist. She is arguing with a woman just as brash as she, who, between expletives, puffs furiously on a cigarette. I learn that the shaykha speaks not to the woman but to her spirit, in an effort to diagnose the source of the woman's complaint. Observing from the side is a tall, very black, incongruously muscled figure clad in a tôb, large wristwatch, and hairnet—the shaykha's reputedly transvestite assistant from south of Shendi. In contrast, the "ayâna—"sick woman" and focus of the ceremony—is frail, elderly. She rests quietly on a pillow next to the musicians, facing the front of the hôsh, arms and legs curled tight against her white-tôbed body.

The shaykha concludes her discussion, sits down, and starts to drum. Using only the tips of her fingers, she beats a large earthen dallûka stretched with goat hide, its whitened flanks boldly adorned with mauve geometric designs. Another dallûka responds in shifted accents, joined half a second later by the nugarishan, a tall brass mortar that rings, when struck, like a cowbell, only deeper. A fourth woman beats a complementary rhythm on an inverted aluminum washtub or tisht. The result is a complicated syncopation, its underlying pattern one long beat, three short. The sound is less soothing than cacophonous, yet endlessly repeated and accompanied by reiterative chants, the effect is indeed soporific. The chants, I learn, are called "threads"—khuyût (singular is khayt)—and when sung they are said to be "pulled."

The rhythm intensifies; the ayâna rises to dance. Now visible over her tôb is a red sash attached to a reddish waist cloth in the style of a Sam Browne belt. She is possessed, my companions say, by Khawâja (Westerner) spirits: a doctor, lawyer, and military officer—all of these at once. Yet it is the lattermost she appears to manifest in dance. Her tôb is folded cowl-like over her head, obscuring her face; she flourishes a

---

This chapter is excerpted from Janice Boddy, *Women, Men and the Zâr Cult in Northern Sudan* (University of Wisconsin Press, 1989) and adapted for this volume.

cane—hooked, as in vaudevillian burlesque. Her dance is a slow, rhythmic walk crisscrossing a chimeric square, feet first moving side to side, then forward and back. With a leap of the imagination she is an officer of the desert corps conducting drill. Every so often she bends rigidly at the hip and, cane pressed to her forehead, bobs her torso up and down. I am told that her spirits have requested the white tôb, cane, cigarettes, "European" belt, and yet to be purchased, a radio.

The band takes up the chant of another zâr. The ayâna sits; the shaykha leaves her drum and starts to dance, tôb covering her head. Suddenly, the tôb is thrown off. She turns on her heel, goose-steps the length of the mîdân, stops before me, abruptly pulls herself to attention. She salutes me three or four times, stiffly, eyes glazed and staring, a grin playing wildly on her face. Her left hand grips a sword within its sheath; with her right she grasps my own with unusual strength and pumps it "Western style" in time to the drums. I am shaken by this treatment and by thoughts of her sword. The chant sounds like a military march: I recognize the British Pasha spirit, Abu Rîsh Ya Amîr ad-Daysh ("Owner of Feathers, O Commander of the Army"). The drums desist. At once my hand is released. The shaykha's features assume a more dignified composure and she returns to the center of the mîdân.

Evening falls. Women rise to dance—or "descend" (nazal), as the zâr step is called—throughout the night. Others respond to the spirits' chants from a kneeling position, bobbing up and down from the waist, tôbs covering their heads like so many Halloween ghosts. One who stands has mounted a zâr in the past: she has "slaughtered" (dabahat, for dhabahat) for the spirits, thus confirming relations with those by which she is possessed. A woman who remains sitting or kneeling has yet to sacrifice; though acknowledged to be possessed, and perhaps even aware of the types of zayran that bother her, she remains somewhat uncertain of her spirits and limited to kneeling at their ceremonies until she undertakes a cure. Yet she is no less an adept for this.

In the waning, eerie light I see a woman—spirit—performing a strange pantomime with a sword, crouching low, sweeping the flat of the weapon back and forth along the ground. She dashes through these postures with skill and grace; I am reminded of a hunter flushing game, or a soldier wary of enemies lying hidden in dense vegetation.

At the start of another chant a tall older woman dressed in red lights a cigarette. She struts down the mîdân, smoking, walking stick held perpendicular to the ground at the end of an outstretched arm, pompous, indifferent, mandarinlike. Some chants later she reappears, transmogrified. Now she and the transvestite stage a sword fight closely resembling the men's dance of a nearby desert people. The combatants leap at each other with apparent abandon, landing within inches of the audience, their sharp unsheathed blades swooping dangerously from aloft. Spectators shrink in terror at their bravado. The two are possessed, I learn, by zâyran of the Arab (Nomad) species.

Occasionally during the evening's drumming, the shaykha dances around the ayâna, encircling her with her arms, coaxing a seemingly reluctant spirit to enter its host and fully reveal itself before the assembly. But the ayâna has not risen since her foray into the mîdân at the start. She sits, silently watching.

I notice at the end of each chant that several who have "descended"—standing or kneeling— begin to scratch themselves, and hiccup and burp indiscriminately. Zaineb tells me these reactions signify the spirit's departure from the body of its host, of a woman's leaving trance.

July 24, 5:30 PM. Last day of the ceremony. The sacrificial ram is led into the mîdân, and a red and gold cloth—a garmosîs or bridal shawl—is placed over its back and head. The musicians play a chant. Incense is freshly lit, and the brazier thrust beneath the shawl. The animal is forced to inhale the smoke, then led from the mîdân and slaughtered by the ayâna's son. Blood spurting from its throat is collected in a bowl and placed before the drums. The ayâna crosses seven times over the carcass before it is dragged off to be butchered. With the others I now step forward to deposit a few piasters in the victim's congealing blood. Someone whispers an invitation to drink araki (liquor) . . . being khawâja (a westerner) I am expected to imbibe. The possessed anoint themselves with blood, some also take a sip; the shaykha daubs it on herself and the ayâna's feet and arms. Drumming and chanting recommence. Still wearing her stigmata of the zâr the ayâna rises to dance.

A woman "descends" with a prayer shawl round her neck, holding its fringed ends in her hands, rocking to and fro as she paces the mîdân. The gesture echoes that of men at a zikr, a "remembrance" ceremony of the Islamic (sûfî) fraternities from whose membership women are excluded.

Later another woman (Zaineb's cousin and sister-in-law) dances briskly wearing trousers of a European cut; she is possessed, I learn, by the Airplane Captain zâr.

Later still, an older lady performs the local "pigeon dance," concluding with a shabâl[3] to the dancer in the Mediterranean head scarf. She has been seized by Muna, Sitt ash-Shabâl, a southern prostitute zâr given to mimicking village women when appearing in their midst.

An unwed girl now rises, snatches up the bridal shawl, and flings it over her head. She shuffles forward, out of time with the chant. Onlookers gasp. This is the costume of Lulîya, the Ethiopian prostitute fond of Hofriyati weddings whose thread was sung some time ago; it is unlikely that She[4] would return so soon, and uninvited. The audience tries to dissuade the girl without success. It is not right, they say, for an unmarried girl to dance so like a bride, in public. Has she no shame? Beside me a woman snaps, "That virgin is not possessed (mazûr). She just wants a husband!"

Night falls; a pressure lamp is placed on a low table near the musicians. The mîdân is a pond of light shallowing to darkness at its sides. Dancers cast weird shadows on the sand, eyes in faces lit from below appear enormous, wild. Drums throb without flagging; redolent smoke of incense clouds the evening. The atmosphere is tense, intoxicating, eerie.

A piercing cry—a uniformed schoolgirl nine or ten years old has sprawled forward into the mîdân, upheld on all four limbs, body jerking rapidly up and down from the shoulders. Immediately, she is led off by some older women, told it is not proper for a child to behave this way at a zâr. But she does not stop. Outside the mîdân the women try to calm her. Now she is sobbing and has gone quite limp. When efforts to revive her fail she is dragged, resisting, back into the center. She balks at attempts to bring her to the shaykha and is deposited before the drums. The shaykha approaches; the girl cringes. The shaykha censes her, covers her with a white tôb, and asks, "What do you want? Who are you?" No response.

Onlookers taunt the intrusive zâr, trying vainly to garner its sympathy: "Ah, her father is poor! Her mother is blind! Her brother is ill!" The shaykha sends for the girl's father. He is brought into the mîdân and made to give his daughter's spirit ten piasters (about twenty-five cents). Still there is no word from the zâr; the girl remains limp, appearing deeply entranced.

It is getting late. Smells of cooking waft through the mîdân, and laughter from the kitchen. More drumming and dancing are called for. The shaykha requests certain threads to test for various species of zayran, hoping the presumptuous spirit will be drawn to identify itself. She blows into the schoolgirl's ears and behind her neck, she pulls at her limbs, whips her softly with a length of rope, beats her lightly with an iron spear. She censes her, rolls her head along the girl's body. She takes the girl in her arms and dances to and fro, blowing a whistle to the incessant beat. She leads the girl around the mîdân and is twice successful in getting her to move briefly of her own accord. At last the girl jogs back and forth through the open space, one arm pumping like the wheel of a locomotive, the other, raised and crooked at elbow, sounding an imagined alarm. The shaykha blows her pipe whistle in accompaniment. The troublesome spirit is identified: Basha-t-Adil the Khawâja railway engineer.

Still the episode continues. For over an hour the shaykha tries every technique in her repertoire, aiming to convince the implacable zâr to abandon his newfound host and refrain from bothering her again until she is a woman and married. Finally the shaykha guides the girl out of the mîdân and out of the hôsh. They cross the threshold, the khashm al-bayt,[5] backwards, facing the assembly; they remain in the path for several minutes, then return as they had left facing the mîdân. The girl, now calmed and weeping softly, is brought to sit near me—a human khawâja—but placed with her back to the ritual.

Soon the sacrificial meal is served and proceedings brought to a close. It is almost 2:00 A.M. The ayâna is now formally well, though tomorrow she must eat the head meat of the ram in a private ceremony followed by a procession to the Nile. Several people approach the ayâna, touch her right shoulder and say "Insha 'allâh byinf'ik, "God willing, it is benefiting you." In the company of my neighbors I return, exhausted, to Hofriyat.

ZÂR AND ZAYRAN

Smoking, wanton dancing, flailing about, burping and hiccuping, drinking blood and alcohol, wearing male clothing, publicly threatening men with swords, speaking loudly lacking due regard for etiquette: these are hardly the behaviors of Hofriyati women for whom dignity and propriety are leading concerns. But in the context of a *zâr* they are common and expected. The ceremony is rich in complex imagery and movement. Yet it has none of the solemn pageantry of a Mass, nor the predictable, repetitive manipulation of symbols which I, raised as a Catholic, might have found familiar. The tone of a zâr resembles neither the subdued formality of a Muslim Friday prayer, nor the unorchestrated ceremoniousness of life cycle rites in Hofriyat. It is closer in character to *zikrs* of the Qadriya and Khatmiya sûfî orders in Sudan, but lacks their cohesion and transcendent focus. What is singular about a *zâr* is its spontaneity, its imagination, whose basis nonetheless is a comprehensive repertoire of symbols and spirit roles—a resource on which participants draw for inspiration. Moves are lightly choreographed—improvisations on well-known themes; "players" are interchangeable, costumes readily borrowed and exchanged. But during the performance, neither players' bodies nor their costumes belong to village women—they belong, instead, to *zayran*. *Zâr* rituals are always fraught with tension and surprise, for at any moment a woman might be "seized" by a spirit that Hofriyati did not before know existed, or she did not know she had.

How is all of this to be understood? What is this phenomenon; who or what are these spirits that so dramatically appear in women's bodies?

THE POSSESSION CONCEPT

Zâr refers to a type of spirit, the illness such spirits can cause by possessing humans, and the rituals necessary to their pacification. The cult[6] is found throughout the northern Sudan and variations of the same name appear in Egypt, Ethiopia, Somalia, (where it is called *sâr*), Arabia, and southern Iran.[7]

In writing of spirit "possession" in Hofriyat, I am using indigenous terms. When someone is considered to be affected by a *zâr*, people say of her, *inda rih*, *inda zâr*, or *inda dastûr*[8]— "she has a spirit." Alternatively, they say she is *mazûr* or *madastîr*—"with spirit," possessed. *Zâr* influence, being possessed of and by a spirit, is considered an affliction and expressed as illness. A spirit causes its novice host to suffer; however initial misery should be surpassed by a more positive concern on the part of the spirit for its host's well-being as their relationship progresses. Once possessed, always possessed: zayran never wholly abandon those they have chosen as their hosts.

Someone diagnosed as *zâr* possessed is liable to be affected by her spirit(s) at any time. *Zayran* are able to infiltrate the bodies of their hosts at will, a move which villagers say always coincides with the latter's entrancement. According to Hofriyati, possession trance (*ghaybîya* or *ghaybûba*) is a state induced by the spirit's forceful entry into the body, which displaces or shifts the person's human self to another perceptual plane. It is, as Bourguignon (1973: 12–13) suggests, "a radical discontinuity of personal identity"; yet in contrast to her model, the distortion of perception this entails pertains not only to the self but to other entities as well.

Still, trance is only one manifestation of possession in Hoftiyat, for *zayran* affect their hosts in countless additional ways (see also Constantinides 1972, 1977; Cloudsley 1983:81). They are always near, or in local parlance "above" (*fôg*), their human hosts, whence they might influence people's perceptions and behaviors in the course of daily life. Further, despite the acknowledged powers of *zayran*, possession trance rarely occurs unpremeditatedly, outside of ritual contexts. Here one is not diagnosed as possessed because she becomes entranced; rather, she becomes entranced because she is possessed. Schoolgirl mishaps notwithstanding, the possessed rarely enter trance spontaneously; this is something one must learn to do in the course of a curing ceremony in order to negotiate an appropriate relationship with instrusive *zayran*. As adepts put it, one must learn how not to resist a spirit's attempts to enter the human world through the medium of her body. The implicit link to ideas about sexual intercourse in Hoftiyat is striking and reiterated in the fact that a woman should be married before she becomes possessed.

Thus trance is in no way aberrant; it is a practiced behavior which the possessed are expected to display under certain conditions. Although an integral part of possession therapy and relapse prophylaxis, it is not consistently evinced by the possessed during ceremonies, and when evinced, it is variable in apparent depth and duration from one episode or individual to the next. Since it is considered inappropriate to be entered by a spirit (or a husband) while menstruating, a woman at a *zâr* signals *zayran* of her condition by tying a knot in her braids, so constraining the spirits' activity. Moreover, because it must conform to prescribed patterns of "spiritness," trance performance requires skill and considerable control. Thus it is not, as some would assert, a spontaneous neurological manifestation of nutritional deficiency which (at least originally) is accounted for after the fact as possession (e.g., Kehoe and Giletti 1981). Such models betray their foundation in a Western rationalism which derogates any mode of consciousness other than that of critical self-awareness. In the search for reductive biological explanations as to why trance should occur, trance itself is misconstrued, parted from its cultural context. Here an essential point is missed. For villagers the system of meaning—possession—is both logically and contextually prior to the behavior—trance—through which it finds expression (cf. Lambek 1981:7).

This is not to deny that biological factors might affect the proclivity to enter trance or the ease with which the behavior is learned. Some of the possessed initially experience difficulty in becoming lost from themselves and allowing their spirits to assume control; others do not. Here perhaps one's nutritional status plays a role. Still, it must be stressed that Hofriyati generally enter trance after having been diagnosed as possessed or, if undiagnosed, when attending a spirit ritual. And in either case, an individual's trance behavior is learned (cf. Bourguignon 1973:4–15, 1976: 37 ff.), shaped by her knowledge of *zayran* and their provenance. It may be novel and unexpected, but must be

consistent with villagers' understanding of spirits to be accepted as legitimate possession and not considered dissimulation or idiosyncratic madness. The few women who do enter trance spontaneously—apparently uninduced, in nonceremonial situations—are hardly neophytes. Rather, they are long-term adepts of the *zâr* who, in the course of their possession careers, have become progressively more skilled at alternating modes of consciousness and allowing the spirits to exhibit themselves through their bodies (see also Besmer 1983:24).

According to Hofriyati, the fact that possession trance typically must be induced and is rare apart from public ritual has less to do with human ability or volition than with spirit caprice. Humans convoke *zayran* through ritual drumming and singing, and normally the spirits—for whom access to the human world is a principal motive for possession—are willing to oblige. Indeed, they regard such invitations as their due, in partial fulfillment of bargains struck with humans, and are likely to become disgruntled and dangerous when neglected or put off. If the possessed take care to mollify them, spirits ought to respond by confining their appearance to ritual contexts where they can frolic and be entertained. Yet none of this is certain. Spirits are willful, and for sport or revenge might "descend" into their hosts without benefit of prior summons. So despite the controlled nature of possession trance and spirit display, the startling possibility exists that at any moment a woman might not be who she usually is.

In Hofriyat possession is a matter of fact. Here the reality of spirits and their powers goes unchallenged, even by villagers who have no firsthand experience of them and regardless of how hotly they dispute the proper therapy for possession affliction, discussed later. Clearly, Hofriyati, like the rest of us, face doubts concerning their beliefs from time to time. But cosmological mavericks they are not. Doubts, like beliefs, are grounded in a social context. Zayran are immanent in the world of Hofriyat; sceptic and zealot, both, are canopied by their existence.

THE POSSESSED

In Hofriyat, as elsewhere in Sudan, possession activity is mainly, but not exclusively, the province of women.[9] Somewhat more than 40 percent of Hofriyati women ever married and over the age of fifteen (N = 129 [1977] and 135 [1984]) claim a *zâr* affliction. Marital status is a significant factor in possession illness: spirits, villagers assert, rarely trouble themselves with the unwed—with women whose fertility has yet to be activated.[10] Most affected are those between the ages of thirty-five and fifty-five, two-thirds of whom have spirits. This proportion is due to a cumulative effect: once possessed a woman is always possessed thereafter.

By contrast, only a handful of men from the entire village area are publicly acknowledged to be possessed. In Hofriyat itself only four men (about 5 percent of the resident adult male population) are considered adepts of the *zâr*; three have undergone the requisite ceremonies, one when only thirteen years of age. Two men born in the village but now living elsewhere are known to have spirits, and I obtained information concerning ten others from the vicinity, five of whom were deceased prior to fieldwork. During my six-year absence from the village, only one man had become possessed, in contrast to sixteen women. In 1984, several male acquaintances privately declared themselves to be possessed and confessed admiration for the *zâr,* but would not publicly seek to confirm their afflictions for fear of losing face.

Why is this the case? Why, assuming that possession is a public idiom for the articulation and interpretation of experience,[11] should there exist sexual disproportion among those who acknowledge having spirits? An obvious approach is to ask whether the range of experience that possession constructs is more common to Hofriyati women than to men. This I think to be the case, mainly because possession is closely linked to fertility with which women are identified and for which they bear responsibility. I do not agree with I. M. Lewis (1971, 1986) on this issue, who, arguing from a sociological perspective, suggests that *zâr* possession is a strategy which women use in an oblique attempt to redress the effects of their subordinate social status. Lewis holds that since spirits demand desiderata which husbands must provide if their wives are to regain well-being, possession can be seen as a measure of gender conflict: it is a strategic evocation of shared beliefs by women wishing to mitigate their subordination to men.

The perspective is illuminating, but presents a number of difficulties. First, it places unwarranted emphasis on the assumed intentionality of women and thus insidiously underestimates the factuality of spirits in the Sudanese world. Words like strategy imply volition, which may certainly be present and, if so, motivated by status considerations in some cases of possession but certainly not in all. Moreover, Lewis's deprivation hypothesis appears to presume that women seek the same status held by men, which , since men have deprived them of it, was originally within their purview. Such assumptions fail to bear scrutiny in Hofriyat, where the social worlds of men and women are largely separate and distinct, a condition due not to happenstance or the prevailing wills of men, but to cultural design. Wilson's (1967) critique of the model tries to address this problem by shifting the locus of proposed status competition from intersex to intrasex relations and, in so doing, is sympathetic to the Sudanese context. However, it shares with Lewis's theory the drawback of a conflict orientation to social interaction that is firmly rooted in Western premises of individualism,[12] whose validity in non-Western cultures must be open to debate (cf Morsy 1978; Boddy 1988). Even granting that status may be a consideration in certain episodes of possession illness, the sociological argument cannot account for the *zâr* in its entirety. It glosses over the issue of belief and is therefore unable to explain or interpret possession forms (for example, the characteristics of spirits, the nature and variety of possession symptoms) and processes (such as the reevaluation of one's past that acquiring a spirit entails). Such factors, however important to the possessed, are implicitly deemed incidental when the investigator's focus is competition.[13] The social status model is unidimensional, at once too general in application and too narrow in concern to deal adequately with the complexities of *zâr*.

It is imperative to ask why so many scholars—among them Kehoe and Giletti (1981)—are committed to viewing possession as a consequence of women's deprivation rather than their privilege, or perhaps their inclination. Such explanations consistently mislocate the question of why women should be more susceptible to possession than men. Especially in his early work, Lewis (1971:77), for example, suggests that joining a *zâr* coterie enables women to express solidarity vis-à-vis men, who are seen as their oppressors. Men have Islam, which excludes women from active participation; hence women, who are socially peripheral, must resort to the equally peripheral cult of *zâr* both to mitigate their subordination and to express religious fervor (Lewis 1971: 66–99; see also Lewis 1986:23–50, 102–5). This is a classic but unhappily androcentric portrayal of women, who are forever seen as reacting to men rather than acting for themselves within a specific cultural context.

To avoid such pitfalls, we need to examine closely how the sexes in Hofriyat conceive of their interrelations both collectively and individually. Judging from my informants, some women—by no means all or only those who are possessed—clearly feel subordinate to men, resent their positions, and are not consistently above vituperation. However, their feelings seem to derive less from their status as women than from the specific actions of individual men, notably husbands. And the problem these men pose is not that they deny women, as a class, an elevated social position, but that they sometimes—often inadvertently— thwart individual women's legitimate attempts to achieve it. The reverse can also be said for women, who may frustrate the status aspirations of men. Both sexes are active participants in the social life of Hofriyat, bisected as it is into gender-distinct yet partially overlapping spheres. If men are central and women peripheral with respect to Islam and

external relations, women are central and men peripheral when it comes to physical, social, and cultural reproduction: the worldliness of village life. Although men and women are subject to different constraints, the actions of each bear consequence for those of the other.

Indeed, whatever consciousness women have of themselves as a group is hardly one of inferiority and wholescale subordination to men, but of complementarity. As villagers see it, the sexes are engaged—not in a war—but in a dialectical relationship of qualitatively disparate yet socially equivalent parts, each commanding certain resources but reliant on the other for fulfillment. They do not conceive of themselves as locked in a struggle between classes, hierarchically understood. Although a Marxist critique might legitimately consider this to be a mystification of political realities, it cannot be ignored if we are truly concerned with the meaning of *zâr* to women and men in Hofriyat. Political relations are mystified for both within the Hofriyati universe of meaning.

When properly situated in the framework of sexual complementarity, the question of why women as a category should be more likely than men to interpret certain experiences as possession expands to two: Why women? Why not men? As Kapferer (1983:98) astutely argues with respect to women's preponderance in Sri Lankan exorcisms, such questions cannot be resolved by focusing on the possessed's motives and intentions alone, independent of the cultural constructs that inform them. We need to consider the qualities that define the sexes in Hofriyat, the typifications each sex holds of the other, the components of gender identity (see also Nelson 1971). Only then might we have a basis for deciding whether a particular incidence of possession constitutes attempted cross-sex or intrasex status manipulation, or something else—an expression of psychological or social disturbance (cf. Crapanzano 1973, 1977b, 1980; Obeyesekere 1970,1981; Kapferer 1983, 1986), cross-sex communication (cf. Lambek 1980, 1981), religious experience (cf. Constantinides 1972, 1977; Lewis 1986), a form of play, dramatic allegory, or all of these and more. Its cultural underpinnings—idioms of the everyday world, prosaic conceptualizations of gender—empower possession as a form of social discourse.

Thus put, a focus on the articulatory potential of possession instead of on the status aspirations of individuals possessed changes the tenor of the analytic enterprise. It widens the interpretive net and does not attempt to simplify matters where simplicity belies the facts. Rather, it makes possible a variety of explanations at different levels of analysis and experience, all of them immanent in the *zâr* as a system of meaning, all of them potentially relevant to any specific episode of possession.

Returning to Hofriyati gender constructs and the *zâr*, both sexes allege that women are naturally more vulnerable to spirit attack as a function of their femininity.[14] Spirits are attracted to women—and married women in particular—for it is they who use henna, perfumes, soaps, and scented oils; wear gold jewelry and diaphanous wraps, all human finery which spirits are known to covet. The proclivities of *zayran* are symmetrical to those of Hofriyati women: both are regarded as consumers of goods provided by men.

Although many questions remain to be addressed, this goes some way toward explaining why women interpret certain experiences and illness episodes as possession. It also suggests why, in this sexually polarized community, men do not. But here more remains to be said. A common characterization of women that they do not completely share is that because they are wanting in *'aql* (reason or social sense), they lack sufficient moral strength to uphold the tenets and ideals of Islam. According to local religious authorities it is reprehensible and abhorrent—though not, strictly speaking, *haram* (forbidden)—for Muslims to traffic with spirits. They say that each individual has the responsibility to steer a proper course of spirit avoidance, something women find more difficult to do than men. Women's perceived inability to resist and so deny *zayran* access to earthly pleasures is put down to their inherent moral frailty, notwithstanding that they are more likely to encounter jinn

than men. Just as the public identity of women accounts for their greater participation in the *zâr* so the public identity of men as pious Muslims accounts, in part, for their forbearance (see also Lambek 1981:62–64).

The last is solely a masculine perspective. Women see no incompatibility between the *zâr* and Islam: to them possession ritual is part of a general religious enterprise (cf. Constantinides 1972:98). Hofriyati culture therefore contains conflicting interpretations of the relationship between possession and Islam. These, in turn, have divergent implications for the handling of troublesome spirits.

EXORCISM VERSUS ACCOMMODATION

Where men hold the reputedly orthodox view that intrusive spirits can and must be dislodged from the body by force, women maintain that *zayran* cannot be got rid of at all.[15] Adepts insist that if one's illness is caused by a *zâr*, no amount of Islamic or even Western medicine will effect a cure. Attempts to exorcise the spirit serve merely to exacerbate the patient's condition. Symptom remission alone can be achieved, and only if the afflicted agrees to hold a propitiatory ceremony on behalf of the as yet unnamed *zâr*. During this ceremony, often held long after her initial illness has dissipated, the possessed enters into a contractual relationship with the spirit(s) responsible for her lapse from health. There, in response to drumming and singing chants associated with the various named *zayran*, she ideally enters trance: a spirit's chant is an invitation to "descend" (*nazal*) and enter the body of its host, where its identity can be affirmed and its demands revealed.[16] In return for certain offerings, acquisitions, and observances, the invasive spirit agrees to restore, and refrain from further jeopardizing, its host's well-being.

Henceforward, human host and possessive *zâr* are joined in continuous but unequal partnership. The spirit remains above her, able to exert its influence or infiltrate her body at will. To some extent the possessed can rely on the spirit's compliance in maintaining her health, but only so long as she regularly attends the ceremonies of others, abstains from traditional mourning behavior, associates herself with clean and sweet-smelling things, and is not given over to strong emotion. A violation of these provisions renders her vulnerable to relapse. Yet the curing rite has opened communications between the two entities, and it is hoped that any future problems can be dealt with expeditiously. From the spirit's perspective, contracts with humans are infinitely renegotiable, so if the possessed wishes to allay further attack from her *zâr*, she must take scrupulous care to mollify it. If all goes well, what begins as an uneasy truce between a willful spirit and its initially reluctant host might graduate to positive symbiosis as their relationship stabilizes and matures. Alleviating the symptoms of possession illness is a matter of establishing reciprocal obligations between spirit and host; their relationship should become, like that between partners in a marriage, one of complementarity, exchange, and mutual accommodation.

Although the majority of men denounce the propitiation of *zayran*, this is not because they deny that such spirits exist. In Hofriyat, *zayran* comprise a distinct class of *jinn*,[17] mischievous invisible beings that populate a world that is parallel to our own and contiguous with it but imperceptible to humans most of the time. Typical of their exceptional attributes, jinn can transform themselves into animals, assume human form (but incompletely so, for their feet are always hooved), or take possession of live human bodies at will. *Jinn* are mentioned in the Quran (Suras 6, 17, 18, 34, 37, 46, 55, 72, and 114); they are a constant if often low-key part of both men's and women's daily lives.

Further, should a man become ill there is a chance that the diagnosis will be possession regardless of its feminine associations. Men recognize the powers of *zayran* and acknowledge that even the most pious among them occasionally succumbs to spirit attack. But this is where their public support for the cult stops: most insist that, despite a practiced

resistance, *zayran*, like other jinn, must eventually capitulate to the powerful exorcistic techniques of Islamic medicine. In the company of their fellows they decry as un-Islamic women's ceremonial attempts to assuage and socialize the spirits.

In face of such weighty opposition the *zâr* cult thrives, and its rites are attended even by the most submissive and religious of wives. For women, *zâr* falls squarely within the purview of Islam. And when arguing their position with men (something I witnessed only twice), women said that Allah expects the afflicted to seek respite from their suffering—clearly, it is better to be healthy than "broken" by spirits or overzealous efforts to dislodge them. Perhaps men are right that involvement in the cult imperils one's prospect of a pleasurable afterlife, but then, is Allah not merciful?

Men, for their part, though publicly adamant that only exorcism is correct in the eyes of Islam, are privately not so intractable (cf. Barclay 1964:206; Constantinides 1982). Often hesitant, concerned, uncertain that Islamic medications will effect a cure or fearing reprisals of a powerful spirit if it is put off, most do not interfere when their womenfolk conduct propitiatory ceremonies, and provide money to meet the spirits' demands. Here perhaps, as Lewis (1971: 88) suggests, men tacitly recognize the contradiction between the formal ideology of male supremacy and the social (and cultural) importance of women. Intriguing, too, in the light of the ethnographic situation in Hofriyat, is Lewis's more recent view that woman's participation in the *zâr* might offer men "the privilege of vicarious participation in what they ostensibly condemn as superstition and heresy. Thus, if there is a dual spiritual economy [male and female], its two branches are interdependent and complementary" (Lewis 1986:106). It seems plausible that just as men's religious devotions count also for their womenfolk (1986:106), so women's *zâr* devotions might count indirectly for their men. As noted earlier, several male informants confided in 1984 that they believe themselves incurably possessed by *zayran*. These men enjoy listening to spirit rituals from afar or watching *bi shubbak* ("through a window"), but do not openly attend for fear of ridicule. Such peripheral and vicarious participation echoes that of women at a *zikr*—the "dervish" rite of Islamic fraternities whose membership in Sudan is exclusively male.

GLOSSARY

dallûka	large pottery drum used in weddings and zâr ceremonies
hôsh	house yard and/or wall that encloses it
shabâl	woman's gesture of flicking her hair at an approaching man in the context of a wedding dance; said to confer luck
shaykha	female curer of the zâr cult
zâr	a type of spirit, the illness it can cause, and the ritual by which the illness is assuaged; more generally, the "cult" that surrounds such spirits
zikr	remembrance: ceremony of the Islamic fraternities
zîr	large water jar

NOTES

1. Hofriyat is a pseudonym for the Sudanese village where I began conducting field work in 1976. "Hofriyati" refers to the people of the village, all of whom speak Arabic and profess Islam. The village is located on the Nile, a little over 120 miles (200 km) north and east of Khartoum.
2. A woman's modesty garment, consisting of some nine meters of cloth wound around the body and covering the head.
3. A flick of the hair, a movement said to confer luck on the recipient.
4. I use an initial capital letter (e.g. He, She) when referring to a specific spirit in order to indicate its sex while distinguishing it from its human host.
5. Literally, mouth of the house.
6. For a discussion of the cult's possible origins see Boddy 1989 and Constantinides 1991.
7. On northern Sudan see Constantinides 1977, 1982, 1991; Kenyon 1991, 2000. On zar in Egypt see Al-Guindi 1978; Kennedy 1978; Saunders 1977; in Ethiopia, Leiris 1958; Young 1975; in Somolia, where it is better known as sar, Lewis 1971, 1986; in Arabia, Trimingham 1965:258; and in southern Iran, Modarressi 1968.

8. This term literally means "statute" or "constitutional law," and colloquially, "permission" (Wehr 1976:281). In northern Sudan, however, the term also refers to a door jamb (Constantinides 1977:65–66, n. 6) or a bolt (Hillelson 1930: 35). The reference to doorways is significant, and discussed in Boddy 1989.
9. See Barclay (1964:196–206); Cloudsley (1983: 67–87); Constantinides (1972, 1977); Trimingham (1965:174–77); Zenkovsky (1950).
10. For a discussion of the relationship between female fertility and possession see Boddy 1989.
11. See Crapanzano 1977. This point is more fully developed in Boddy 1989.
12. Although the fluctuating kinship networks of Hofriyati are individualistic this is not to say that the individual is the focal social unit in Hofriya. Hofriyati women and men are always subordinate to a range of collective interests: family, lineage, village, religious group, etc.
13. Lewis (1971:30, 1983) certainly does not consider other factors unimportant, yet they do not figure into his analysis to the same extent as does the question of cross-sex competition.
14. See Kapferer (1983:100–110) for a similar view of the susceptibility of Sri Lankan women.
15. Interestingly, this is similar to the situations of men and women in a marriage: although men may divorce an unwanted wife at will, women must accommodate themselves to the marriage, however unhappy.
16. Spirits are hardly inanimate or genderless, as my use of the impersonal pronoun implies. But when not referring to specific spirits and possession episodes, I use the neuter form to avoid confusion between humans and *zayran*.
17. However, the classification of spirits varies somewhat from area to area in Sudan, and in some places (though not in Hofriyat or its environs) *zayran* and jinn are considered different forms of spirit being. On this issue see Constantinides (1972:102–4), and Trimingham (1965:177 ff.).

REFERENCES

Al-Guindi, Fadwa. 1978. *The Angels of the Nile: A Theme in Nubian Ritual. In Nubian Ceremonial Life*, edited by John Kennedy, pp. 104–113. Berkeley: University of California Press.

Barclay, Harold. 1964. Buurri al-Lamaah: *A Suburban Village in Sudan*. Ithaca, NY: Cornell University Press.

Besmer, Fremont E. 1983. *Horses, Musicians, and Gods: The Hausa Cult of Possession-Trance.* South Hadley, Mass: Bergin and Garvey.

Boddy, Janice. 1988. Spirits and Selves in Northern Sudan. The Cultural Therapeutics of Possession and Trance. *American Ethnologist* 15(1): 4–27.

———. 1989. *Wombs and Alien Spirits: Women, Men and the Zâr Cult in Northern Sudan.* Madison: University of Wisconsin Press.

Bourguignon, Erika. 1973. Introduction: A Framework for the Comparative Study of Altered States of Consciousness. In *Religion, Altered States of Consciousness, and Social Change,* edited by Erika Bourguignon, pp. 3–35. Columbus: Ohio State University Press.

———. 1976. *Possession.* San Francisco: Chandler and Sharp.

Brown, Karen M. 1990. *Mama Lola: A Vodou Priestess in Brooklyn.* Berkeley: University of California Press.

Cloudsley, Ann. 1983. *Women of Omdurman: Life, Love, and the Cult of Virginity.* London: Ethnographica.

Constantinides, Pamela. 1972. Sickness and the Spirits: A Study of the "Zâr" Spirit Possession Cult in Northern Sudan. Ph.D. dissertation, University of London.

———. 1977. "Ill at Ease and Sick at Heart": Symbolic Behavior in a Sudanese Healing Cult. In *Symbols and Sentiments,* edited by Ian M. Lewis, pp. 185–205. Bloomington: Indiana University Press.

———. 1982. Women's Spirit Possession and Urban Adaptation in the Muslim Northern Sudan. In *Women United, Women Divided: Comparative Studies of Ten Contemporary Cultures,* edited by P. Caplan and D. Bujra, pp. 141–76. New York: John Wiley.

———. 1991. "The History of Zâr in the Sudan." In I. M. Lewis, Ahmed al-Safi and Sayyid Hurreiz, Editors. *Women's Medicine: The Zâr-Bori Cult in Africa and Beyond,* pp. 83–99. Edinburgh: International African Institute, Edinburgh University Press.

Crapanzano, Vincent. 1973. *The Hamadsha: A Study in Moroccan Ethnopsychiatry.* Berkeley: University of California Press.

———. 1977a. Mohammed and Dawua: Possession in Morocco. In *Case Studies of Spirit Possession,* edited by Vincent Crapanzano and Vivian Garrison, pp. 141–76. New York: John Wiley.

———. 1977b. *Introduction to Case Studies of Spirit Possession,* edited by Vincent Crapanzano and Vivian Garrison, pp. 1–39. New York: John Wiley.

———. 1980. *Tuhami: Portrait of a Moroccan.* Chicago: University of Chicago Press.

Hillelson, S. 1930. *Sudan Arabic, English Arabic Vocabulary.* 2nd ed. London: Sudan Government.

Kapferer, Bruce. 1983. *A Celebration of Demons: Exorcism and the Aesthetics of Healing in Sri Lanka.* Bloomington: Indiana University Press.

———. 1986. Performance and the Structure of Meaning and Experience. In *The Anthropology of Experience,* edited by V. W. Turner and E. M. Bruner, pp188–206. Chicago: University of Illinois Press.

Kehoe, Alice B., and Dody H. Giletti. 1981. Women's Preponderance in Possession Cults: The Calcium Deficiency Hypothesis Extended. *American Anthropologist* 83(3): 549–61.

Kennedy, John G. 1978. *Nubian Ceremonial Life,* edited by John Kennedy. Berkeley: University of California Press.

Kenyon, Susan. 1991. *Five Women of Sennar.* New York: Oxford University Press.

———. 2000. " [title to follow]" In Heike Behrend and Ute Luig, editors. *Spirit Possession, Modernity, and Power in Africa.* Madison: University of Wisconsin Press.

Lambek, Michael. 1980. Spirits and Spouses: Possession as a System of Communication among the Malagasy Speakers of Mayotte. *American Ethnologist* 7(2):318–31.

———. 1981. *Human Spirits: A Cultural Account of Trance in Mayotte.* New York: Cambridge University Press.

Leiris, Michel. 1958. *La Possession et ses aspects théâtraux chez les Ethiopiens de Gondar.* L'Homme: Cahiers d'ethnologie, de géographie et de linguistique. Paris: Plon.

Lewis, I. M. 1971. *Ecstatic Religion: An Anthropological Study of Spirit Possession and Shamanism.* Baltimore, Md.: Penguin Books.

———. 1986. *Religion In Context: Cults and Charisma.* Cambridge: University of Cambridge Press.

Modaressi, Tahgi. 1968. *The Zar Cult in South Iran. In Trance and Possession States,* edited by Raymond Prince, pp. 149–55. Montreal: R. M. Bucke Memorial Society.

Morsy, Soheir. 1978. Sex Roles, Power, and Illness in an Egyptian Village. *American Ethnologist,* 5:137–50.

Nelson, Cynthia. 1971. Self, Spirit Possession, and World-View: An Illustration from Egypt. *International Journal of Psychiatry* 17:194–209.

Obeyesekere, Gananath. 1970. The Idiom of Possession. *Social Science and Medicine* 4:97–111.

———. 1981. *Medusa's Hair: An Essay on Personal Symbols and Religious Experience.* Chigago: University of Chicago Press.

Saunders, Lucie Wood. 1977. Variants in Zar Experience in an Egyptian Village. In *Case Studies in Spirit Possession,* edited by Vincent Crapanzano and Vivian Garrison, pp. 177–91. New York: John Wiley.

Trimingham, J. Spencer. 1965. *Islam in the Sudan.* 1949. Reprint. London: Oxford University.

Vantini, Giovanni. 1981. *Christianity in the Sudan.* Bologna, Italy: EMI Press.

Wehr, Hans. 1976. *A Dictionary of Modern Written Arabic.* 3rd ed. Edited by J. Milton Cowan. Ithaca, N.Y.: Spoken Language Services.

Wilson, Peter. 1967. Status Ambiguity and Spirit Possession. *Man,* n.s. 2:366–78.

Young, Allan. 1975. Why Amhara Get Kureynya: Sickness and Possession in an Ethiopian Zar Cult. *American Ethnologist* 2(3):567–84.

Zenkovsky, Sophie. 1950. Zar and Tambura as Practiced by the Women of Omdurman. *Sudan Notes and Records.* 31(1): 65–81.

"Tradition" and Threat: Women's Obscenity in Giriama Funerary Rituals

Janet McIntosh

INTRODUCTION

It is midday in the Giriama village outside the town of Malindi, Kenya, and women are gathering on one side of a well-swept clearing framed by mud and thatch huts. They sit with their legs stretched before them, comparing their finery —flamboyant *leso* cloths; clean, bright polyester blouses from town; and the customary bustles of grass and cotton that accentuate their hips. My black skirt and T-shirt seem dull by comparison, but as always the women greet me warmly, seating me on a woven mat on the earth next to them. We are assembling to mark the passing of a young woman who died in childbirth; her body lies in the center of the clearing, cradled by a bed of woven sisal ropes. Her mother and three elderly women flank the bed, waving small handkerchiefs in desultory motions to chase off the flies. They have not slept since the tragic night before, but some of them are capable of laughter as well as tears, and occasionally break into a low-key song and dance, swishing

their handkerchiefs rhythmically. Other female kin are out of sight, gathered in a nearby hut where they will receive well-wishers during the next five days of ceremony. And at the other side of the homestead the men carry out their tasks: six or seven take turns digging a grave, while others decide where they will buy the planks to build a coffin. Most sit on mats, drinking from small gourds of palm wine, discussing local politics, and comparing the jobs they have lost and gained in town.

Word has gone out through the neighboring communities that a funeral has begun, and the crowd swells to about two hundred as the afternoon wears on. When a male song leader arrives and positions himself near the corpse, ten or fifteen enthusiastic women gather around him. At his cue, several of them begin to jangle winnowing trays laden with broken glass, creating a silvery percussive effect. The rest break into song and dance, shuffling in a circle, shimmying their hips emphatically, and punctuating their movement now and then by falling forward and catching themselves with a well placed step. Some of their songs speak to

Original material prepared for this text.

death and decay: "Fly away, housefly. You can't land on this body, because it's covered with rashes." But many of the lyrics are teasing and a little startling: "Mother's clothes are falling off," quips one song. As the singers warm to their task, the lyrics become graphic:

> May I screw you? May I screw you?
> An unmarried non-virgin will be screwed
> A man's wife is maize meal and meat
> I will die and stop screwing

One by one, women and girls from the surrounding crowd join in, and the circle widens to accommodate them. Soon they put aside the winnowing trays, clapping with enthusiasm as they sing and shuffle around the corpse and its tenders, who continue to whisk the flies away. From time to time the dancers stop in their tracks and face the center of the circle, clapping loudly. Several women leap into the middle and begin to gyrate their pelvises, inching up to the others to simulate sexual contact and intercourse. Normal decorum is abandoned; a seventy-year-old woman grinds against a thirty-year-old male song leader, while a young woman simulates sex with her mother-in-law. A woman with gray hair organizes a stunt, placing a giant wooden pestle upside down by the head of the corpse, climbing onto it and moving her pelvis in quick circles, barely keeping her balance. I turn to my neighbor, a married woman holding a baby, and remark: "I have talked to many people about your funerals, but I still wonder why the women perform these songs and dances."

"It's just our tradition," she says with a gentle smile, adding: "They are trying to distract the bereaved people from their pain." I ask why she doesn't join in. "My husband doesn't like me to," she replies, "He thinks the women who do the dances have no respect for their men." Another woman inside the circle, an unmarried forty-something, mimes a sex act with more zeal than most. A young man from the village passes me and whispers in my ear snidely: "That one is a prostitute; she keeps a lot of men happy." Another song begins:

> Mr. Charo Baya knows how to screw
> Finish fast; I want to get home and cook!

> My husband doesn't screw me that way.
> Charo Baya you've won me—Your penis is big;
> my hips can't hold you.

As the dancing grows louder and more exuberant, three giggling teenagers pull me into the fray and prod me before them, daring me to perform the dance moves. An old woman glares at us from just outside the circle; like some other elders, she objects to the participation of young unmarried women, and I wonder if her ire is directed partly at me. I clap and step my way around the corpse until shyness gets the better of me and I withdraw to the margins, craning my neck to take in the scene. I can see the men still clustered on their side of the homestead, drinking, talking, and observing the grave-diggers, who sweat profusely as they struggle to complete their job before nightfall. A few young men stand on the edge of the dancing circle, looking on with small gourds of palm wine in their hands, ogling and occasionally lunging at the women they admire the most. One of the men plunges in and is set on by two women who gyrate against his side and back until he extricates himself, laughing. The circle closes again, a riot of stepping, clapping women, who seem to delight as each new song ups the ante of bawdy suggestion.

A Giriama funeral in the Malindi area is a momentous event, a protracted ritual far longer, more expensive, and better attended than any other rite in Giriama custom. Social life is magnified during these gatherings: men gain and lose prestige in displays of generosity; commerce in food, palm wine, and property quickens; old friends strike up new relations; and enemies settle their grudges, sometimes violently. Above all, women's funerary songs and dances escalate into lewd rebellions that, like the above scenario, far outstrip normal expectations for female behavior. What does this sexual performance by women signify? Is it considered mere "tradition," a benign ritual release, as the young woman above and many others wanted me to believe? Or do the currents of disapproval— her husband's denunciation of the dancing women, the passing young man's whisper, and the old woman's stare—suggest another level of interpretation, one that takes the rebellious overtones of the songs and dances more seriously?

These questions have a precedent in a broader literature that explores the relationship between gender, power, and ritual. Much of this literature emphasizes the unique opportunity that ritual offers subordinate groups, particularly women, to violate custom and express discontent. Ritual spirit possession, for example, has been heralded as a means of "[expressing] dissatisfaction with existing patterns" (Bourguignon 1973: 33), especially in cultures where other avenues of redress are not available (Lewis 1971). Possession can also open a space for violations of sexual protocol redolent of those in Giriama funerals; in Danforth's account of possession by St. Constantine among Anastenaridien Greeks, possessed women engage in "flamboyant, demonstrative, even flirtatious behavior that is considered more appropriate for men" (1989: 100). By becoming "symbolically male" through possession, Danforth says, such women garner publicity while enhancing their power and status beyond the domestic sphere (100). Whereas spirit possession partakes of its own special devices—including the appropriation of the agency and powers of the possessing spirit—other types of ritual offer women additional opportunities for misbehavior. In numerous sub-Saharan African rituals, for example, normative arrangements are turned upside-down and subordinate groups, women in particular, may temporarily take on the roles of their social superiors (Gluckman 1963). Ritual form, then, seems to lend itself to unruliness like that in Giriama women's funerary song and dance.

While it may provide a useful emotional outlet for women's frustrations, the enduring question is whether unruly ritual behavior poses a substantial threat to patriarchal orders. When there is no possessing spirit from which to borrow prestige, do the exceptional events within a ritual confer any new powers on the participants? Do ritual acts really challenge the tenets of social life once the ritual moment has passed? Social theorists have tended to address this issue in general terms. Mary Douglas, for example, sees ritual misbehavior as universally beguiling and potentially threatening to the status quo: "We seek to create order," she writes, "[yet] we do not simply condemn disorder. We recognise that it is destructive to existing patterns; also that it has potentiality. It symbolizes both danger and power" (Douglas 1966: 94). In his analysis of medieval carnivals, Mikhael Bakhtin interprets ritual bawdiness as a moment of freedom that just might have enduring effects; a "true feast of becoming, change, and renewal" (Bakhtin 1962: 18). Although such readings credit unruly ritual with liberating potential, others doubt that it poses a genuine threat or challenge to the powers that be. According to Gluckman, a ritual of rebellion that takes place within a strong social structure is but an ineffectual gesture; a form of "instituted protest [that] in complex ways renews the unity of the system" (1954: 3).

In this article, I approach the question of ritual power from a somewhat different angle. Rather than asking whether Giriama women's funerary songs and dances actually change the social system, I instead explore how Giriama themselves perceive them. And in a parallel to the tension between theorists like Douglas and Gluckman, I detect two conflicting interpretations of funerary obscenity among Giriama in the Malindi area. At one level, the women's performance is publicly couched as Gluckman might have predicted: a harmless "tradition" and a salubrious tool of emotional healing. Yet another, less formal discourse implies that the songs and dances threaten the sexual dignity of Giriama women. Although Douglas might locate this threat in some generic danger inherent to unruly ritual, "danger" is always construed in light of tensions specific to a given social moment. In fact, I argue, Giriama women's funerary songs have long been obscene, yet the current disapproval among Giriama in Malindi is distinctly colored by a development that is both modern and local: the arrival of Western lifestyles and tourism on the Kenya coast, and the corresponding emergence of a fraught sexual ethos in society-at-large.

GIRIAMA, PAST AND PRESENT

The Giriama are the largest of nine related Bantu groups called the Mijikenda, who live in a 5,000-square mile strip in the coastal hinterland of eastern Kenya. According to Mijikenda oral history, their people dwelled as subsistence farmers for centuries while based in fortified villages called *kaya* that were governed by male elders and organized by sacred spaces, age-set rituals, and semi-secret societies termed *mwanza*. The *kaya* dispersed in the nineteenth century, and since then Mijikenda culture has been subject to forces that threaten older ways of life. But like all self-told histories, Mijikenda accounts are both reflections of the past and "statements of what informants feel it should be" (Willis 1993: 44). *Kaya* are often invoked as part of a nostalgic call for unity and "authenticity" in moments of social, economic, and political insecurity (Parkin 1991; Mazrui 1997), yet stories of isolated life in the *kayas* obscure the fact that for centuries, coastal Mijikenda have interacted with wealthier town-dwelling Arab and Swahili Muslims in fluid economic, religious, and even kin relations. And in the colonial and post-colonial eras, Mijikenda have endured difficult integration into a multicultural coastal economy of Europeans, Asians, Arabs, Swahili, and upcountry Kenyans. Today, cash is increasingly important for the essentials of life in and near Malindi, making wage labor a virtual necessity, yet many Giriama who seek jobs are hampered by lack of training and employer prejudice. Education is perceived as a key to wealth, but school fees are out of reach for many Giriama families. Now as then, few Mijikenda own land or large businesses, and other ethnic groups on the coast regard them as a low-status, "backward" people. Such economic and ideological pressures have resulted in numerous Giriama conversions to Islam or Christianity, yet aggressive assertions of Giriama "tradition" still play a role in local and governmental politics. And rituals such as

funerals remain popular despite Muslim and Christian censure.[1]

SEX AND DEATH IN FUNERARY RITUAL

The two major funerary song-and-dance types for Giriama women in the Malindi area, termed *kifudu* and *kihoma,* are considered "traditional," yet oral histories indicate that both originated outside of Giriama funerals. *Kifudu* songs are accompanied by the rhythmic shaking of shells or broken glass in a broad winnowing tray, and the dances involve much shimmying of the breasts and hips. According to Giriama elders, *kifudu* emerged from a women's fertility cult called *mwanza wa kifudu* that dates back to the *kaya* era. In the *mwanza wa kifudu,* women kept sacred clay pots that were named after their deceased former custodians and believed to have a life force of their own. Since *kifudu* pots could either protect or destroy women's health and reproductive capacities, they were supplicated at every new moon: removed from their shrines to be spoken to, sung and danced to, and "played" by blowing air over their openings. The supplicatory songs and dances were called *kifudu cha tsongo,* and, according to anthropologist Monica Udvardy, were characterized by "obscene or ludicrous" lyrics and correspondingly "suggestive movements" (Udvardy 1990b: 142). These songs were imported into the funerals of members of the *mwanza wa kifudu* but at some point, for unknown reasons, they were generalized to funerals at large. The propitiation of *kifudu* pots still takes place in some Giriama homesteads further inland, but in many areas, including Malindi, the tradition has dwindled, and the *kifudu* fertility medicines have been dispersed among and reinterpreted by individual diviner/healers (Thompson 1990).[2] Yet *Kifudu* songs endure, and some women still compose new ones that address two major themes: death and grief, and bawdy sexual antics. *Kifudu* songs are customarily sung by post-menopausal women (Udvardy 1990a: 145), but in the Malindi area the sanctions for their performance have been blurred, and young women and even pubescent girls participate, to the dismay of some elders.

The second variety of funerary song, called *kihoma*, is said to be more obscene than *kifudu*. *Kihoma* involves a slightly different dance style accompanied by vigorous clapping and, unlike *kifudu*, is totally prohibited after the corpse has been buried. Men as well as women compose these songs, and the lyrics discuss graphic sexual themes from both male and female points of view.[3] In some Giriama groups, men occasionally dance to *kihoma* songs as well, but among Giriama close to Malindi, women and girls dominate the dancing almost exclusively. Giriama informants claim that *kihoma* songs originated with another Mijikenda group, the Chonyi, and some elders suggest they have been popularized in recent years by young funeral participants who are excessively zealous about their sexual content. But while elders distinguish between *kifudu* and *kihoma* and decry the changes in funerary performance, most youth are only dimly aware of the songs' histories, and are hard-pressed to categorize individual songs as either *kifudu* or *kihoma*. I will return to the subject of how elders regard changes in funerary songs below, for their disapproval signals more holistic changes in Giriama life.

Leaving these controversies aside for the moment, I want to explore Giriama explanations for why sexual songs should be performed at funerals in the first place. Anthropologists van Gennep (1960) and Victor Turner (1967) have written at length about the "liminal" phase in rites of passage, in which normal social rules are suspended and ritual participants behave in unorthodox ways. In many sub-Saharan funerals, liminality takes the specific form of inversion: a reversal of ordinary hierarchies and taboos.[4] In Giriama funerals, the visibility of the corpse defines the boundaries of the liminal phase; Giriama say that its uncanny presence opens behavioral possibilities that are curtailed off from everyday experience.[5] And, in keeping with the sub-Saharan funerary theme of inversion, *kifudu* and *kihoma* song and dance upend customary expectations with

implications of female promiscuity, female sexual aggression, incest, adultery, and homosexuality.[6] Yet funerary inversions in other African cultures include all kinds of reversals, including turning clothing inside out, moving in a counterclockwise direction, and slandering local rulers. So why should sexual license be the inversion of choice for Giriama? Giriama explain that sex has an antithetical relation to death, a tension that lends sexual imagery a special emotional charge. The funerary songs and dances, they say, "mock" death by confronting its power with defiant expressions of sexual pleasure. For those who remember that *kifudu* performances emerge from a fertility cult, the songs and dances also invoke reproductive capacity, the continuation of life even in the presence of its end. And the ecstatic and ridiculous elements of the songs and dances are said to "change the minds" of the bereaved, distracting them from their grief by presenting them with images pleasurable, extreme, and, sometimes, silly.[7] Witty double-entendres such as the line: "I'll bury something in you!" instantaneously defuse the miseries of death and burial by rhetorically transforming the death rite into a sexual encounter.

Yet there is another, more paradoxical relationship between death and sexual permissiveness at these funerals, in which they are not so much juxtaposed as aligned.[8] The dancing circle where the corpse lies is referred to as a "bad place" with negative supernatural overtones, and this "bad place," say informants, is a place in which "bad things can happen." The corpse, then, is both a signal that existential normalcy has vanished and a prompt to wreak further havoc, as the *kifudu* and *kihoma* songs and dances do with their dissolute symbolism. One Giriama man aligns the destruction of death with the disgrace of sexual abandon; when I asked him to explain *kifudu* and *kihoma* to me, he replied: "Someone has died! Things have already turned to shit, so why not let everything run to ruin?" Other informants assimilate grief and sexual expression on the emotional level, saying: "When someone has died, and your grief is so bad, what can you do but laugh and celebrate?" Such utterances surely have performative elements, as expressions of wishful thinking that might help to create the kind of celebration they describe and in so doing help the bereaved to forget their sorrow. But they also contain an implicit theory, a strange emotional geometry in which extreme grief passes beyond sorrow and travels full circle to the giddy version of joy seen in *kifudu* and *kihoma* performances. This paradox is echoed in the expression of some funeral participants: "A funeral is like a wedding; the last wedding of the deceased."

GENDER, SEXUALITY, AND CHANGE IN GIRIAMA LIFE

The sexual content of *kifudu* and *kihoma* songs and dances appears to play an important role in processing and transforming the emotions that accompany death, but it is also a pivotal site for complex and changing gender relationships among Giriama in the Malindi area. Before discussing local interpretations of women's funerary performances, I offer here a brief history of the shifting gender dynamics that underlie them. Since the nineteenth century, the patriarchal household arrangements of the *kaya* era have undergone considerable change in many Giriama communities, yet the theme of male dominance persists. Homesteads in the *kaya* model are made up of several polygynous households headed by a senior man who makes decisions about property allocation, conflicts, and patrilineal rituals. Parents and other elders oversee marital arrangements, including bride-price transactions, and women's rights to resources are severely constrained by a patrilineal inheritance system. These structures endure in some Giriama communities, but in others, economic changes and cultural contact have destabilized older ways of life. In the small villages flanking Malindi town, for example, household arrangements have an improvisational feel. Young men may split off from their father's homestead in search of economic opportunities closer to town, squatting

on land owned by Muslims or upcountry Kenyans with other Mijikenda hopefuls, and building one or two huts for their wife or wives. In cases of divorce or abandonment, some women choose to live on their own, supporting themselves and their children rather than returning to their natal homestead. But shifting household arrangements have not greatly enhanced women's economic opportunities. Although men venture into town to seek wage labor, and may aspire to private investments and property ownership, women rarely accumulate capital or property of their own, tending to remain close to home as they raise children and till the family's small subsistence farm plot. For income they may sell domestic animals, firewood, thatch, deep-fried goods, and the surplus from their small farming plots, but such enterprises rarely yield a large profit. A significant number of women become professional diviner-healers, an increasingly popular choice that can lead to prestige and a limited degree of financial power (Thompson 1990). Yet even such creative pursuits do not weaken the pervasive gender ideology that limits girls' and women's prospects. Many parents prefer to spend their limited school fee money on their sons, a pattern that perpetuates both economic and ideological inequities. One man justifies the limitations on girls' education with the assertion that "our women are pure womanhood in its natural state." In Giriama discourse, this "natural state" is deemed servile, irresponsible, and capricious, while men, by contrast, are considered strong, brave, and more intellectual (McIntosh 1996; Thompson 1990).

The sexual customs that emerged from the *kaya* era have also changed in the Malindi area, yet a powerful residue of sanctions and proscriptions remains. According to *kaya* custom, sexual courtship and behavior should be highly discreet. Sex itself must be engaged in with care because it is believed to be linked to supernatural powers. Ritual sexual intercourse, for example, is said to bring prosperity and purification when performed at moments of significant social transition (Udvardy 1990a, 1990b). Termed "*mathumia*," these rites between spouses can mark the "coming out" ceremony of a newborn, the circumcision of a son, and the various training phases of a diviner-healer. They may sanction a child's marriage arrangement, or purify individuals in a compromised state (a widow, for example, should have ritual intercourse with another man if her husband dies an inauspicious death). Senior males are pivotal figures in *mathumia* rites; when an individual in a homestead dies, for example, or when a homestead relocates, the senior male must perform *mathumia* with his first wife before other homestead members can resume normal sexual relations. When a couple violates *mathumia* restrictions, their children are believed susceptible to illness and death. Udvardy suggests that *mathumia* rites underscore the "mutual dependence of the genders for the prosperous enactments of creation, recreation, and transformation" (Udvardy 1990a: 87), but, she adds, the rites often depend on the leadership of male homestead heads, and therefore re-inscribe their seniority. Meanwhile, the Giriama belief in women's "greater potential to cause disorder" (Thompson 1990) generates additional constraints for female sexuality. Unmarried girls are expected to protect their chastity, and married women (not men) who are unfaithful may inflict their children with a supernaturally borne illness termed *kirwa*.

With cultural contact and change, Giriama communities everywhere have altered some or all of these customs, yet women's sexuality is still policed by popular expectation. Christianity and Islam, of course, do not recognize *mathumia* or *kirwa* beliefs, but both portray premarital sex and overt expressions of sexuality as sinful, particularly among women. Among Giriama who do not consider themselves Muslim or Christian, *kirwa* beliefs and *mathumia* proscriptions are followed only erratically by members of the younger generation. In fact, popular expectations in Malindi operate primarily by means of secular ideologies. Whereas today's men are said to be more sexually aggressive than in the past, women are still expected to resist advances, defining their decency through modesty. In conversation this

theme occasionally appears through trope of hunting: men play the role of predator, women of prey, and the ones with integrity elude capture until they can run no more. And while they may desire sex, women are constrained by an unwritten rule of silence: unlike men, women should not initiate sexual liaisons verbally. "A woman can say it [express desire] with her body," my informants tell me, "but not with her mouth." The female body's language, furthermore, should be subtle and indirect: a glance, a fleeting half-smile, or a slight, sinuous motion. The burden of sexual comportment, hence, has largely shifted from both sexes (as seen in *mathumia* proscriptions) to women and girls alone.

If sexual expectations continue their policing function, sexual behavior in Malindi town constantly threatens to violate these proscriptions. While Giriama communities everywhere are faced with sexual changes, Malindi's economic and cultural situation has created exceptional tensions. In recent decades, numerous upcountry Kenyans have moved to the coast for economic opportunities, bringing versions of modernity in tow, including nuclear family structure, consumerist aspirations, and "Western" sexual behavior with demonstrative premarital passion. The last twenty years have also brought a high volume of European and American tourists, who flock to the palm-lined beaches of the Indian Ocean in a display of wealth, hedonism, and exposed flesh. Malindi has become a popular "sex safari" destination, with visitors of both sexes searching for an exotic fling. This clientele has lured many young African men and women into hustling and prostitution in Malindi's casinos, hotels, and beaches. Even Giriama who rarely enter town are aware of the changing sexual habits in urban centers, reading about them in the newspapers, and noting the sexual lyrics of the urban-based music that pumps from young men's boom boxes. And the practice of exchanging sex for cash has filtered into the surrounding villages, where some women have begun to solicit local clients, often because of economic need. In one village on the outskirts of Malindi town, a sixty-year-old

Giriama man was recently arrested for paying a thirteen-year-old girl for sex; she capitulated, she said, because her single mother had no source of income for food. Several elder women told me stories of schoolgirls selling their bodies to teachers and other students—narratives that entwine the elders' anxieties about the lures of prostitution and the perils of a Western-style education. Even Giriama women who do not sell sex are also said to be changing their sexual habits. One Giriama man in his late thirties, for example, told me that he had recently propositioned a woman for sexual relations, but was so shocked and revolted when she accepted on the spot (rather than putting him off time and again as he expected) that he withdrew the suggestion. Evidently, expectations of female modesty are alive in Giriama ideology in the Malindi area, but are constantly challenged and changed. This tension sets the stage for local interpretations of funerary songs.

WOMEN'S RITUAL LICENSE: CONFLICTING INTERPRETATIONS

On the face of it, *kifudu* and *kihoma* performances offer Giriama women a unique opportunity to express their desires and decry male power while asserting their own self-worth. At a funeral, any woman—old, young, married or single—can intone a sexual invitation ("May I screw you?") and exult in the imagined pleasures of adultery ("Charo Baya knows how to screw!") While they flout conventions verbally, the women enact further obscenities with their bodies by dancing suggestively and simulating sexual intercourse with partners normally forbidden to them. But *kifudu* and *kihoma* performances do not simply play with expressions of desire; they also enact women's rivalry with and resentment against men. Whereas Giriama men compete with other men during funerary "prestige competitions" (Parkin 1972: 81), women bond with one another in their funerary songs, directing antagonism and rivalry outward toward men and toward women from neighboring areas. Sexual derision is a popular weapon: "My husband doesn't

know how to screw me," complains one lyric. Another song mocks jealous husbands while belittling their genitalia: "A jealous husband will not grow fat/He only has thin legs and long testicles." Still another song degrades women from a rival community, then berates an elderly man for being an inept provider: "You don't clothe me or feed me, grandfather. You know, you're just yoghurt." In a way, these songs are the symbolic antithesis of *mathumia*: they desacralize sex, they flout the order of sexual custom, they put a thumb in the eye of male elders, and they stress antagonism between genders rather than interdependence. In a culture where women's power, sexual autonomy, and general worth are constrained and demeaned, these full-throated testimonies of anger, sexual agency, and pride are surely emotionally significant gestures of resistance.

But can we assume that onlookers, and the singers themselves, understand the women's words and actions as an important and enduring statement of rebellion? *Kifudu* and *kihoma* take place within a ritual frame, and like all rituals, this one sets up an extra-ordinary and perplexing relationship between the ritual participants and what they are saying and doing. In his exploration of this relationship, Gluckman analyses numerous rituals of rebellion that flout the existing power structure through blasphemy, humor, and obscenity (Gluckman 1954; 1965). Using ethnographic evidence from Zulu and other African cultures, he concludes that participation in such rituals does not constitute a threat to the status quo. In fact, he argues, such rituals often emerge from a strong social order, and further solidify it:

> The acceptance of the established order as right and good, and even sacred, seems to allow unbridled license, very rituals of rebellion, for the order itself keeps this rebellion within bounds. Hence to act the conflicts, whether directly or by inversion or in other symbolical forms, emphasizes the social cohesion within which the conflicts exist (1965: 125).

The "ritual of rebellion," then, is a kind of cage for disorder, particularly in societies where social structure is already strong. If anything, Gluckman implies, rebellion is less likely after such rituals, for rebellious impulses are restricted to a socially sanctioned time and place, and thus reminded of their impotence.

At the same time that the ritual context brackets antisocial behavior, ritual form can also defuse subversive messages by virtue of the fact that most ritual behaviors are second-hand. Anthropologist Lila Abu-Lughod makes a related observation in her account of Egyptian Bedouin women's poetry (Abu-Lughod 1986). Bedouin women recite poetry to express feelings of grief and self-pity that would normally be unacceptable because in Bedouin culture, stoicism and emotional self-control are considered essential to social dignity. Abu-Lughod suggests that a poem is an acceptable medium of expression because it offers the woman who recites it a kind of alibi: if the woman reciting the poem did not author it, she cannot be fully credited with the sentiments in the text. As a result, a woman performing poetry is exempt from normal critiques of emotional expression, being evaluated instead by a "different set of standards regarding conformity to societal ideals" (207). While Abu-Lughod's analysis does not directly concern ritual, we can extrapolate her analysis to ritual form, in which participants' acts and utterances have a pre-scripted, second-hand quality similar to that of poetic recitation.

If we combine Gluckman's and Abu-Lughod's accounts, we can interpret ritual as doubly qualified to defuse potentially subversive messages. First, ritual is sharply bracketed from everyday life by a special space, time, and behavioral protocol; its boundaries might be likened to quotation marks that set it off from the continuous stream of ordinary happenings. Second, the content of ritual does not spring anew from the agency and opinions of ritual participants, but instead is derivative of rituals past, and as such, resembles reported speech more than first-hand utterance. If these devices are central to local interpretations of *kifudu* and *kihoma*, we might expect the performances to pose no threat to Giriama social order, and the singers themselves to be treated no differently for

participating. And indeed, this is a common account of *kifudu* and *kihoma* among Giriama near Malindi. In interviews, I asked numerous informants whether women's funerary songs are permissible given the overarching expectation of female sexual modesty, and was repeatedly told that the songs are "just tradition," and hence do not constitute a genuine rebellion against social expectations. This reassurance was often delivered in a quick and patterned fashion, rather like a stock response designed to strip the performances of any significance beyond their generic status as "tradition," and, perhaps, to preclude further inquiry by this probing outsider.[9] These stock dismissals of *kifudu* and *kihoma* may have a protective function for the Giriama community at large, for they emphasize that such behaviors are restricted to the ritual frame and hence pre-empt accusations that their non-ritual social habits are primitive and debased. And women defend their performances as "just tradition" with special alacrity, guarding their most privileged moment of expression by denying that real expression is involved at all.

But are Giriama women's funerary utterances and actions completely absolved by the ritual context? Are women really free to say and do anything in ritual without consequence? Despite the public sanction for *kifudu* and *kihoma*, unofficial currents of ambivalence and disapproval run through the Giriama communities near Malindi town. In informal contexts such as casual conversations, gossip sessions, and whispered asides like that of the man who passed me during the funeral, men of all ages and elder women voice anxiety about *kifudu* and *kihoma* performances today. A number of young men say that although they might be tempted to sleep with a woman who enjoys performing the songs and dances, they would not marry her—implying that the free sexual expression in the performances is sexually attractive, but suggests inferior virtue. Still other men, like the husband of the woman I spoke to at the funeral above, forbid their wives to participate in the singing and dancing at all, seeming to fear either that stigma will attach to their wives, or that the performance might augur actual promiscuity. Meanwhile, older women complain that the young girls who participate in funerary songs and dances "don't respect their elders anymore" and are prone to promiscuity and prostitution. In such discussions, *kifudu* and *kihoma* are portrayed not as meaningless ritual behaviors, but instead as a kind of training ground for real sexual misconduct. Apparently, Giriama detect the seeds of genuine danger and resistance described by Douglas and Bakhtin, and fear that these might escape the ritual boundary, putting down roots in ordinary life.

Where does this tension between stock approval of funerary obscenity and informal disapproval emerge from? The moralizing forces of Islam and Christianity doubtless contribute to the discourse of danger, since both religions construe Giriama rituals as heathenistic and corrupt. But those who regard the rituals with suspicion include numerous Giriama who do not call themselves converts—in fact some of them, including some elderly women, openly despise the influence of world religions on their milieu. Although Mary Douglas might ascribe their disapproval of funerary ritual to the inherent dangers of "disorder," she may undervalue the ways in which culturally specific anxieties define "disorder" as "dangerous." Interestingly, Gluckman anticipates the importance of context in construals of unruly ritual, though he deals with it only indirectly. Where there is little threat of misconduct outside of the ritual context, he says, ritual rebellion will not affect the extant social order. But, he predicts, "where the [social] relationships involved are weak, there cannot be license in ritual" (1965: 132). Gluckman does not explain the concept of "weak relationships" in great detail, but the fraught sexual issues in the Malindi area surely bring Giriama society under this rubric. While the homestead breaks apart, women and girls are loosed from the mast, and through a kind of *bricolage* of the examples that surround them, improvise new sexual identities. Male homestead heads in the Malindi area no longer orchestrate sexual conduct through *mathumia,* and as supernatu-

ral proscriptions for sexual transgression fade, fears of adultery mount. Women's potential promiscuity spells a drop in male control over female sexuality (and, by implication, paternity), giving men reason for discomfort.[10] Meanwhile, the elders' authority is shunted to the side, making both elder men and elder women uncomfortable as they watch old hierarchies of respect and resource distribution crumble.

As these social anxieties grow, the membrane surrounding the ritual becomes permeable in two directions. Sexual threats run from the outside in, as growing numbers of girls join the obscene dancing circles—a violation of previous ritual guidelines that the elders link to their exposure to promiscuity and prostitution in daily life. In turn, the portrayal of sexual dissolution in the ritual threatens, in the popular imagination, to spill beyond its bounds and influence daily behavior. Since the acts and utterances in funerary songs and dances have begun to speak of possible rather than unlikely behavior, the ritual content is no longer totally dismissed as a benign kind of reported speech. Instead, currents of suspicion frame the ritual content as a first-hand report of the unruly desires of women participants. Thus ritual participants are caught between two interpretations of their actions: although they are partially absolved by the protective cloak of tradition, they also risk the labels of promiscuity or unmarriageability. In funerary ritual today, an expressive space for women is offered with one hand and revoked with the other.

I would like to return briefly to a subject I mentioned earlier: the elder women's claim that funerary songs are now revoltingly obscene compared to the gentler, more graceful performances of their youth. Although this complaint may have an element of truth, I do not take it entirely at face value. First, I witnessed some of the same elderly women who complain about funerary obscenity participating in the lewdest songs and dances with delight; evidently, the style was not as alien to them as they suggested. Secondly, early missionary and colonial reports of *kifudu* song and dance suggest that it was obscene long before these women were young. Ludwig Krapf, the first missionary to East Africa, mentions "immoralities and abominations" practiced at a *mwanza wa kifudu* ceremony he witnessed in 1847, noting that "[these] are well known to every one" (Krapf 1968 [1860]: 162). The colonial officer Arthur Champion, writing around 1914, describes one *kifudu* dance as "demoniacal" and "frenz[ied]" (26), and relates that "[another] dance performed by two old women over the grave was of an extremely sensual character. This unseemly dance produced great mirth amongst the mourners" (Champion 1967: 28). Although these accounts are colored by an overarching colonialist horror toward African rites, and although they do not rule out the possibility that the rituals contain more brazen material now than then, they do suggest that overtly sexual material in funerary songs and dances is not new. It is possible, then, that the elder women's complaints are about something more than obscenity within ritual. Although the obscene signifiers within funerary ritual may not have changed significantly, the social context for their interpretation has changed, lending the sexual phenomena signified in the ritual a more real and threatening cast. The elder women's nostalgia, then, may not be for another kind of song, but for another way of life altogether.

CONCLUSION

Sex is considered "appropriate" subject matter at a Giriama funeral for gender-neutral reasons. It symbolizes the extremity of life's borders, it distracts the mourners from their misery, and it mocks the despair and the finality of death. Yet in their songs and dances, women magnify these sexual elements and direct them at male targets, giving funerary rituals acute significance for Giriama gender politics. Through these ritual moments women assert female unity and pride, vent their complaints about male power, and convey their joy in breaking through the sexual decorum normally expected of them.

Given all of this, what should we make of the original tension between Douglas' and Gluckman's accounts of ritual license? Gluckman's insistence that rituals of rebellion are benign is echoed by Giriama themselves when they attest that their funerals are "just tradition." But although the protective ritual frame may render their acts partially permissible, the women's fulminating grievances do not go unacknowledged. Douglas' suggestion that ritual disorder spells "danger" also circulates among Malindi-based Giriama as an interpretive possibility. Thus, for the ambivalent onlooker at a funeral, an archetypical expression of Giriama "tradition" threatens to encourage, if not serve as a catalyst for a transformation in the gendered order.

As I have suggested, the perceived "danger" in women's funerary songs stems not simply from the presence of disorder in the ritual, but largely from changes in the surrounding social context that influence the interpretation of that disorder. The new sexual options in Malindi both vex the patriarchal order and challenge the "official" notion that ritual can successfully contain its own subversive strains. But I don't mean to imply that Malindi is the only site of such contests over ritual meaning. Giriama everywhere interact with other cultures, creating local social tensions that could challenge the security of the ritual frame—a pattern that may reach into the past as well. Although elders idealize the virtuous sexual codes of their youth, their memories are shaped by nostalgia, raising the possibility that sexual behavior has long run up against customary expectations, and that a double discourse about women's funerary performances has obtained for some time. We might, in fact, expand this argument outward, into a general suggestion. Perhaps Gluckman idealizes the "official" discourses of social unity in the African societies he studies, and in so doing, overlooks the changes, tensions, and fault lines elemental to all societies. If this is the case, if no society is so intact, then disorderly ritual moments are potentially as uniformly "dangerous" as Mary Douglas posits—only the degree and shape of danger will be locally construed, and presumably construed differently by various groups within a given society. The mere presence of "danger" in ritual, then, should not encourage theoreticians to leap to a universally triumphant narrative of female ritual unruliness, for such a leap would overlook the nuance and force of local interpretations of the ritual and its relationship to everyday life. In the Giriama case, such interpretations limit the practical efficacy of women's ritual gestures, for either the ritual gestures are not taken seriously or they are taken seriously and met with the sort of redress we have seen (derision or prohibition). What women can accomplish through unruly ritual, then, remains an open question that can only be addressed case by case, with close attention to the local anxieties that define the perplexing relationship between the mundane social world and the exhilarating alternatives encoded in ritual.

ACKNOWLEDGMENTS

I would like to thank Jennifer Dickinson, Rachel Heiman, Larry Hirschfeld, Penelope Papailias, and Gaye Thompson for their valuable feedback on a draft of this essay. Gaye Thompson provided rich insights into Giriama society, as did Kainga Kalume Tinga. My research assistant, Maxwell Phares Kombe, supported me with astonishing patience and intelligence, for which I will always be grateful. The people who assisted me along the way are far too numerous to name but they include many Giriama, Swahili, and Europeans who welcomed me, talked to me, and tolerated me, often with kindness and good humor. Thanks are also due to the Malindi Museum Society and Fort Jesus Museum, Mombasa for their interest and support. This research was carried out with a grant from the Fulbright-Hays Foundation.

NOTES

1. Although Giriama have partially internalized the message that they are "backward," they counter it with themes of rebellion against the groups who have scorned them. A number of funerary songs, which I do not present here, are laced with expressions of defiance against Muslims, Christians, and upcountry tribes. The strategic use of a stigmatized "tradition" as a tool of vengeance has important implications for Giriama political ideology, but these are beyond the scope of this article.

2. Udvardy notes that despite their importance, the *kifudu* secret societies are "not much talked about" (1990b: 151) by comparison to men's cults, lending them a "muted" quality common to female-dominated institutions (Ardener 1977). Perhaps this relative silence has facilitated their rapid transformation and quick disappearance from memory. Most Giriama under thirty in Malindi know *kifudu* as funerary song and dance only, not as a secret society—despite the fact that the *kifudu* society is still active several kilometers West of the town.

3. The dual narrative perspective of funerary songs is important to their significance, but it introduces complexities beyond the scope of this article. Briefly, I think that the songs' narrative volatility helps to construct the "ritual alibi" I discuss later in this article, by making the songs seem more like reported speech than first person expression. Yet, clearly, this alibi is not sufficient to defuse all suspicion toward the women who participate.

4. A survey of texts on East Africa, conducted over forty years ago, found more than 600 sources describing inversions in connection with death rituals (Berglund 1957).

5. Kihoma songs must cease the instant the corpse has been buried, suggesting that the visibility of the corpse defines the boundaries of the liminal period. This seems a fitting criterion, given that a corpse appears to embody liminality itself: the dead person is neither here nor there, for breath and mind have vanished, yet the flesh, bafflingly, remains.

6. Despite the fact that women may dance against one another in a sexually suggestive way at funerals, I found no evidence that lesbian sex is a Giriama cultural category. While they are aware that female–female sexual relations can occur among their Swahili and Arab neighbors, they have no term for it in their mother tongue. Informants tell me that if a woman loves another woman, she will sexualize the relationship not through direct contact but by arranging an affair between her husband and the female object of her affection. Homosexual sex between men, on the other hand, is acknowledged and condemned.

7. In a village about fifty kilometers Southwest of Malindi, Udvardy reports that Giriama considered funerary songs "entertainment for the departing spirit . . . the songs must be sung to accompany the spirit, so that it knows it is not alone and need not be sad" (Udvardy 1990a: 145–146). In Malindi, however, the emphasis is entirely on the emotions of those still living. This discrepancy may reflect a gradual move away from customary ancestor propitiation in Malindi; those who decline to consider the departing spirit set a precedent for neglecting the ancestral spirit as well.

8. The alignment of sex and death has been suggested too by Western avant-garde theorists such as Georges Bataille (1897–1962), who posited a fundamental kinship between sex and death in the human psyche. According to Bataille (1962), sex and death are conceptually aligned for existential reasons: both can dissolve the social self, lifting the boundary between individual subjectivity and the rest of the world. Bataille's theory emerges from a particular moment in Western history—after Renaissance writers had construed orgasm as a "small death"; after de Sade made his mark with his sex- and violence-ridden fiction; and after Freud suggested that orgasm resolves both life and death instincts—so should be applied with caution to other cultural contexts. Yet it does seem that numerous cultures have drawn some kind of symbolic equivalence between sex and death, suggesting that their sign qualities lend them to symbolic interplay.

9. The category of "tradition" has strategic dimensions in numerous colonial and post-colonial contexts. It may, for example, be used to protect or decry a given cultural practice; to sanction new forms of authority; or to confer an aura of unquestionability upon an otherwise contentious act. For more on such processes, see Hobsbawm and Ranger (1983).

10. It is worth noting that male objections to funerary songs primarily address their obscene contents, and not the contents that articulate a female–male rivalry. I suggest this discrepancy emerges from the fact that at the economic and political levels, patriarchy among Giriama remains intact and so is not threatened by the songs that express rivalry per se. Male control over female sexuality, on the other hand, is under threat. Men's disapproval of funerary performances, then, is correspondingly focused on female sexual expression.

REFERENCES

Abu-Lughod, Lila. 1986. *Veiled Sentiments: Honor and Poetry in a Bedouin Society.* Berkeley: University of California Press.

Ardener, Edwin. 1977. "Belief and the Problem of Women," in Shirley Ardener, ed., *Perceiving Women.* New York: John Wiley and Sons.

Bakhtin, M. M. 1962. *Rabelais and His World.* Transl. Helene Iswolsky. Cambridge: MIT Press.

Bourguignon, Erika, Ed. 1973. *Religion, Altered States of Consciousness, and Social Change.* Columbus: Ohio State University Press.

Bataille, Georges. 1962. *Death and Sensuality: A Study of Eroticism and the Taboo.* New York: Walker and Company.

Berglund, A. I. 1957. *Some African Funerary Inversions.* Unpublished M.A. Thesis. Uppsala: Department of Cultural Anthropology, Library of the African Research Programme.

Champion, A. M. 1967. *The Agiriama of Kenya.* London: Royal Anthropological Institute.

Danforth, Loring M. 1989. *Firewalking and Religious Healing: The Anastenaria of Greece and the American Firewalking Movement.* Princeton: Princeton University Press.

Douglas, Mary. 1966. *Purity and Danger: An Analysis of the Concepts of Pollution and Taboo.* London: Routledge.

Gluckman, Max. 1954. *Rituals of Rebellion in South-East Africa.* Manchester: Manchester University Press.

———. 1965. *Custom and Conflict in Africa.* Oxford: Basil Blackwell.

Hobsbawm, Eric and Terence Ranger. 1983. *The Invention of Tradition.* Cambridge: Cambridge University Press.

Krapf, J. Lewis. 1968. *Travels, Researches, and Missionary Labors during an 18 Years' Residence in Eastern Africa.* Missionary Researches and Travels Nr. 2. London: Frank Cass and Co.

Lewis, I. M. 1971. *Ecstatic Religion: A Study of Shamanism and Spirit Possession.* London: Routledge.

Mazrui, Alamin M. 1997. *Kayas of Deprivation, Kayas of Blood: Violence, Ethnicity, and the State in Coastal Kenya.* Nairobi: Human Rights Commission.

McIntosh, Janet S. 1996. Professed Disbelief and Gender Identity on the Kenya Coast. In Natasha Warner et al., eds. *Gender and Belief Systems.* Berkeley, California: Berkeley Women and Language Group, University of California.

Parkin, David J. 1972. *Palms, Wine, and Witnesses: Public Spirit and Private Gain in an African Farming Community.* London: Intertext Books.

————. 1991. *Sacred Void: Spatial Images of Work and Ritual among the Giriama of Kenya.* Cambridge: Cambridge University Press.

Thompson, Sally Gaye. 1990. *Speaking "Truth" to Power: Divination as a Paradigm for Facilitating Change among Giriama in the Kenyan Hinterland.* Unpublished Doctoral dissertation in Anthropology, presented to the School of African and Oriental Studies, University of London.

Turner, Victor. 1967. *The Forest of Symbols.* Ithaca, NY: Cornell University Press.

Udvardy, Monica. 1990a. *Gender and the Culture of Fertility among the Giriama of Kenya.* Unpublished

Doctoral dissertation in Anthropology, presented to the University of Uppsala, Sweden.

————. 1990b. "Kifudu: A Female Fertility Cult among the Giriama." In Anita Jacobson-Widding and Walter van Beek, eds., *The Creative Communion: African Folk Models of Fertility and the Regeneration of Life.* Uppsala: Academiae Ubsaliensis. Distributed by Almquist and Wiksell International, Stockholm, Sweden.

van Gennep, Arnold. 1960. *The Rites of Passage.* Transl. Monika B. Vizedom and Gabrielle L. Caffee. Chicago: University of Chicago Press.

Willis, Justin. 1993. *Mombasa, the Swahili, and the Making of the Mijikenda.* Oxford: Clarendon Press.

Mama Lola and the Ezilis: Themes of Mothering and Loving in Haitian Vodou

Karen McCarthy Brown

Mama Lola is a Haitian woman in her mid-fifties who lives in Brooklyn, where she works as a Vodou priestess. This essay concerns her relationship with two female *lwa,* Vodou spirits whom she "serves." By means of trance states, these spirits periodically speak and act through her during community ceremonies and private healing sessions. Mama Lola's story will serve as a case study of how the Vodou spirits closely reflect the lives of those who honor them. While women and men routinely and meaningfully serve both male and female spirits in Vodou, I will focus here on only one strand of the complex web of relations between the "living" and the Vodou spirits, the strand that connects women and female spirits. Specifically I will demonstrate how female spirits, in their iconog-

raphy and possession-performance, mirror the lives of contemporary Haitian women with remarkable specificity. Some general discussion of Haiti and of Vodou is necessary before moving to the specifics of Mama Lola's story.

Vodou is the religion of 80 percent of the population of Haiti. It arose during the eighteenth century on the giant sugar plantations of the French colony of Saint Domingue, then known as the Pearl of the Antilles. The latter name was earned through the colony's veneer of French culture, the renowned beauty of its Creole women, and most of all, the productivity of its huge slave plantations. Haiti is now a different place (it is the poorest country in the Western hemisphere) and Vodou, undoubtedly, a different religion from the one or ones practiced by the predominantly Dahomean, Yoruba, and Kongo slaves originally brought there. The only shared language among these different groups of slaves was French Creole, yet they managed before the end of the eighteenth century to band together (most

Reprinted with permission from Nancy Falk and Rita Gross (eds.), *Unspoken Worlds: Women's Religious Lives* (Belmont, Calif.: Wadsworth Publishing Co.), pp. 235–245. The main ideas in this article are developed further in a chapter of *Mama Lola: Vodou Priestess in Brooklyn* (Berkeley: University of California Press, 1991).

likely through religious means) to launch the only successful slave revolution during this immoral epoch. As contemporary Haitian history has made amply clear, a successful revolution did not lead to a free and humane life for the Haitian people. Slave masters were quickly replaced by a succession of dictators from both the mulatto and black populations.

Haitians started coming to the United States in large numbers after François Duvalier took control of the country in the late 1950s. The first wave of immigrants was made up of educated, professional people. These were followed by the urban poor and, most recently, the rural poor. All were fleeing dead-end lives in a society drenched in corruption, violence, poverty, and disease. There are now well over one-half million Haitians living in the U.S.

Alourdes, the name by which I usually address Mama Lola, came to New York in 1963 from Port-au-Prince, the capital of Haiti and a city of squalor and hopelessness where she had at times resorted to prostitution to feed three small children. Today, twenty-five years later, Alourdes owns her own home, a three-story row house in the Fort Greene section of Brooklyn. There she and her daughter Maggie run a complex and lively household that varies in size from six people (the core family, consisting of Alourdes, Maggie, and both their children) to as many as a dozen. The final tally depends on how many others are living with them at any given time. These may be recent arrivals from Haiti, down-on-their-luck friends and members of the extended family, or clients and members of the extended family, or clients of Alourdes's Vodou healing practice.

Maggie, now in her thirties, has been in the United States since early adolescence and consequently is much more Americanized than her mother. She is the adult in the family who deals with the outside world. Maggie does the paperwork which life in New York requires and negotiates with teachers, plumbers, electricians, and an array of creditors. She has a degree from a community college and currently works as a nurse's aide at a New York hospital.

Most of the time Alourdes stays at home where she cares for the small children and carries on her practice as a *manbo*, a Vodou priestess. Many Haitians and a few others such as Trinidadians, Jamaicans, and Dominicans come to her with work, health, family, and love problems. For diagnostic purposes, Alourdes first "reads the cards." Then she carries out healing "work" appropriate to the nature and severity of the problem. This may include: counseling the client, a process in which she calls on her own life experience and the shared values of the Haitian community as well as intuitive skills bordering on extrasensory perception; administering baths and other herbal treatments; manufacturing talismans; and summoning the Vodou spirits to "ride" her through trance-possession in order that spiritual insight and wisdom may be brought to bear on the problem.

Vodou spirits (Haitians never call them gods or goddesses) are quite different from deities, or even saints, in the way that we in North America usually use those terms. They are not moral exemplars, nor are their stories characterized by deeds of cosmic or even heroic proportion. Their scale (what makes them larger than life though not other than it) comes, on the one hand, from the key existential paradoxes they contain and, on the other, from the caricature-like clarity with which they portray those pressure points in life. The *lwa* are full-blown personalities who preside over some particular social arena, and the roles they exemplify contain, as they do for the living who must fill them, both positive and negative possibilities.

Trance-possession within Vodou is somewhat like improvisational theater.[1] It is a delicate balancing act between traditional words and gestures which make the spirits recognizable and innovations which make them relevant. In other words, while the character types of the *lwa* are ancient and familiar, the specific things they say or do in a Vodou ritual unfold in response to the people who call them. Because the Vodou spirits are so flexible and responsive, the same spirit will manifest in different ways in the north and in the south of Haiti, in the countryside and in the cities, in Haiti and among the immigrants in New York. There are even significant differences from family to family. Here we are considering two female spirits as they manifest through a heterosexual Haitian woman who has lived in an urban context all her life and who has resided outside of Haiti for a quarter of a century. While most of what is said about these spirits would apply wherever Vodou is practiced, some of the emphases and details are peculiar to this woman and her location.

Vodou is a combination of several distinct African religious traditions. Also, from the beginning, the slaves included Catholicism in the religious blend they used to cope with their difficult lives. Among the most obvious borrowings were the identifications of African spirits with Catholic saints. The reasons why African slaves took on Catholicism are complex. On one level it was a matter of habit. The African cultures from which the slaves were drawn had traditionally been open to the religious systems they encountered through trade and war and had routinely borrowed from them. On another level it was a matter of strategy. A Catholic veneer placed over their own religious practices was a convenient cover for the perpetuation of these frequently outlawed rites. Yet this often cited and too often politicized explanation points to only one level of the strategic value of Catholicism. There was something deep in the slaves' religious traditions that very likely shaped their response to Catholicism. The Africans in Haiti took on the religion of the slave master, brought it into their holy places, incorporated its rites into theirs, adopted the images of Catholic saints as pictures of their own traditional spirits and the Catholic calendar as descriptive of the year's holy rhythms, and in general practiced a kind of cultural judo with Catholicism. They did this because, in the African ethos, imitation is not the sincerest form of flattery but the most efficient and direct way to gain understanding and leverage.

This epistemological style, exercised also on secular colonial culture, was clearly illustrated when I attended Vodou secret society[2] ceremonies in the interior of Haiti during the 1983 Christmas season. A long night of thoroughly African drumming and dancing included a surprising episode in which the drums went silent, home-made fiddles and brass instruments emerged, and a male and female dancer in eighteenth-century costume performed a slow and fastidious *contradans*. So eighteenth-century slaves in well-hidden places on the vast sugar plantations must have incorporated mimicry of their masters into their traditional worship as a way of appropriating the masters' power.

I want to suggest that this impulse toward imitation lies behind the adoption of Catholicism by African slaves. Yet I do not want to reduce sacred imitation to a political maneuver. On a broader canvas this way of getting to know the powers that be by imitating them is a pervasive and general characteristic of all the African-based religions in the New World. Grasping this important aspect of the way Vodou relates to the world will provide a key for understanding the nature of the relationship between Alourdes and her female spirits. When possessed by her woman spirits, Alourdes acts out the social and psychological forces that define, and often confine, the lives of contemporary Haitian women. She appropriates these forces through imitation. In the drama of possession-performance, she clarifies the lives of women and thereby empowers them to make the best of the choices and roles available to them.

Sacred imitation is a technique drawn from the African homeland, but the kinds of powers subject to imitation shifted as a result of the experience of slavery. The African religions that fed into Haitian Vodou addressed a full array of cosmic, natural, and social forces. Among the African spirits were those primarily defined by association with natural phenomena such as wind, lightning, and thunder. As a result of the shock of slavery, the lens of African religious wisdom narrowed to focus in exquisite detail on the crucial arena of social interaction. Thunder and lightning, drought and pestilence became pale, second-order threats compared with those posed by human beings. During the nearly 200 years since their liberation from slavery, circumstances in Haiti have forced Haitians to stay focused on the social arena. As a result, the Vodou spirits have also retained the strong social emphasis gained during the colonial period. Keeping these points in view, I now turn to Alourdes and two female Vodou spirits she serves. They both go by the name Ezili.

The Haitian Ezili's African roots are multiple.[3] Among them is Mammy Water, a powerful mother of the waters whose shrines are found throughout West Africa. Like moving water, Ezili can be sudden, fickle, and violent, but she is also deep, beautiful, moving, creative, nurturing, and powerful. In Haiti, Ezili was recognized in images of the Virgin Mary and subsequently conflated with her. The various manifestations of the Virgin pictured in the inexpensive and colorful lithographs available throughout the Catholic world eventually provided receptacles for several different Ezilis as the spirit subdivided in the New World in order to articulate the different directions in which women's power flowed.

Alourdes, like all Vodou priests or priestesses, has a small number of spirits who manifest routinely through her. This spiritual coterie, which differs from person to person, both defines the character of the healer and sets the tone of his or her "temple." Ezili Dantor is Alourdes's major female spirit, and she is conflated with Mater Salvatoris, a black Virgin pictured holding the Christ child. The child that Dantor holds (Haitians usually identify it as a daughter!) is her most important iconographic detail, for Ezili Dantor is above all else the woman who bears children, the mother par excellence.

Haitians say that Ezili Dantor fought fiercely beside her "children" in the slave revolution. She was wounded, they say, and they point to the parallel scars that appear on the right cheek of the Mater Salvatoris image as evidence for this. Details of Ezili Dantor's possession-performance extend the story. Ezili Dantor also lost her tongue during the revolution. Thus Dantor does not speak when she possesses someone. The only sound the spirit can utter is a uniform "de-de-de." In a Vodou ceremony, Dantor's mute "de-de-de" becomes articulate only through her body language and the interpretive efforts of the gathered community. Her appearances are thus reminiscent of a somber game of charades. Ezili Dantor's fighting spirit is reinforced by her

identification as a member of the Petro pantheon of Vodou spirits, and as such she is associated with what is hot, fiery, and strong. As a Petro spirit Dantor is handled with care. Fear and caution are always somewhere in the mix of attitudes that people hold toward the various Petro spirits.

Those, such as Alourdes, who serve Ezili Dantor become her children and, like children in the traditional Haitian family, they owe their mother high respect and unfailing loyalty. In return, this spiritual mother, like the ideal human mother, will exhaust her strength and resources to care for her children. It is important to note here that the sacrifice of a mother for her children will never be seen by Haitians in purely sentimental or altruistic terms. For Haitian women, even for those now living in New York, children represent the main hope for an economically viable household and the closest thing there is to a guarantee of care in old age. The mother–child relationship among Haitians is thus strong, essential, and in a not unrelated way, potentially volatile. In the countryside, children's labor is necessary for family survival. Children begin to work at an early age, and physical punishment is often swift and severe if they are irresponsible or disrespectful. Although in the cities children stay in school longer and begin to contribute to the welfare of the family at a later age, similar attitudes toward childrearing prevail.

In woman-headed households, the bond between mother and daughter is the most charged and the most enduring. Women and their children form three- and sometimes four-generation networks in which gifts and services circulate according to the needs and abilities of each. These tight family relationships create a safety net in a society where hunger is a common experience for the majority of people. The strength of the mother–daughter bond explains why Haitians identify the child in Ezili Dantor's arms as a daughter. And the importance and precariousness of that bond explain Dantor's fighting spirit and fiery temper.

In possession-performance, Ezili Dantor explores the full range of possibilities inherent in the mother–child bond. Should Dantor's "children" betray her or trifle with her dignity, the spirit's anger can be sudden, fierce, and uncompromising. In such situations her characteristic "de-de-de" becomes a powerful rendering of women's mute but devastating rage. A gentle rainfall during the festivities at Saut d'Eau, a mountainous pilgrimage site for Dantor, is readily interpreted as a sign of her presence but so is a sudden deluge resulting in mudslides and traffic accidents. Ezili's African water roots thus flow into the most essential of social bonds, that between mother and child, where they carve out a web of channels through which can flow a mother's rage as well as her love.

Alourdes, like Ezili Dantor, is a proud and hard-working woman who will not tolerate disrespect or indolence in her children. While her anger is never directed at Maggie, who is now an adult and Alourdes' partner in running the household, it can sometimes sweep the smaller children off their feet. I have never seen Alourdes strike a child, but her wrath can be sudden and the punishments meted out severe. Although the suffering is different in kind, there is a good measure of it in both Haiti and New York, and the lessons have carried from one to the other. Once, after Alourdes disciplined her ten-year-old, she turned to me and said: "The world is evil. . . . You got to make them tough!"

Ezili Dantor is not only Alourdes's main female spirit, she is also the spirit who first called Alourdes to her role as priestess. One of the central functions of Vodou in Haiti, and among Haitian emigrants, is that of reinforcing social bonds. Because obligations to the Vodou spirits are inherited within families, Alourdes's decision to take on the heavy responsibility of serving the spirits was also a decision to opt for her extended family (and her Haitian identity) as her main survival strategy.

It was not always clear that this was the decision she would make. Before Alourdes came to the United States, she had shown little interest in her mother's religious practice, even though an appearance by Ezili Dantor at a family ceremony had marked her for the priesthood when she was only five or six years old. By the time Alourdes left Haiti she was in her late twenties and the memory of that message from Dantor had either disappeared or ceased to feel relevant. When Alourdes left Haiti, she felt she was leaving the spirits behind along with a life marked by struggle and suffering. But the spirits sought her out in New York. Messages from Ezili and other spirits came in the form of a debilitating illness that prevented her from working. It was only after she returned to Haiti for initiation into the priesthood and thus acknowledged the spirits' claim on her that Alourdes's life in the U.S. began to run smoothly.

Over the ten years I have known this family, I have watched a similar process at work with her daughter Maggie. Choosing the life of a Vodou priestess in New York is much more difficult for Maggie than it was for her mother. To this day, I have yet to see Maggie move all the way into a trance state. Possession threatens and Maggie struggles mightily; her body falls to the floor as if paralyzed, but she fights off the descending darkness that marks the onset of trance. Afterwards, she is angry and afraid. Yet these feelings finally did not prohibit Maggie from making a commitment to the *manbo's* role. She was initiated to the priesthood in the summer of 1982 in a small temple on the outskirts of Port-au-Prince. Alourdes presided at these rituals. Maggie's commitment to Vodou came after disturbing dreams and a mysterious illness not unlike the one that plagued Alourdes shortly after she came to the United States. The accelerated harassment of the spirits also started around the time when a love affair brought Maggie face to face with the choice of living with someone other than her mother. Within a short period of time, the love affair ended, the illness arrived, and Maggie had a portentous dream in which the spirits threatened to block her life path until she promised to undergo initiation. Now it is widely acknowledged that Maggie is the heir to Alourdes's successful healing practice.

Yet this spiritual bond between Alourdes and Maggie cannot be separated from the social, economic, and emotional forces that hold them together. It is clear that Alourdes and Maggie depend on one another in myriad ways. Without the child care Alourdes provides, Maggie could not work. Without the check Maggie brings in every week, Alourdes would have only the modest and erratic income she brings in from her healing work. These practical issues were also at stake in Maggie's decision about the Vodou priesthood, for a decision to become a *manbo* was also a decision to cast her lot with her mother. This should not be interpreted to mean that Alourdes uses religion to hold Maggie against her will. The affection between them is genuine and strong. Alourdes and Maggie are each other's best friend and most trusted ally. In Maggie's own words: "We have a beautiful relationship . . . it's more than a twin, it's like a Siamese twin. . . . She is my soul." And in Alourdes's: "If she not near me, I feel something inside me disconnected."

Maggie reports that when she has problems, Ezili Dantor often appears to her in dreams. Once, shortly after her arrival in the United States, Maggie had a waking vision of Dantor. The spirit, clearly recognizable in her gold-edged blue veil, drifted into her bedroom window. Her new classmates were cruelly teasing her, and the twelve-year-old Maggie was in despair. Dantor gave her a maternal backrub and drifted out the window, where the spirit's glow was soon lost in that of a corner streetlamp. These days, when she is in trouble and Dantor does not appear of her own accord, Maggie goes seeking the spirit. "She don't have to talk to me in my dream. Sometime I go inside the altar, just look at her statue . . . she says a few things to me." The image with which Maggie converses is, of course, Mater Salvatoris, the black virgin, holding in her arms her favored girl child, Anaise.

It is not only in her relationship with her daughter that Alourdes finds her life mirrored in the image of Ezili Dantor. Ezili Dantor is also the mother raising children on her own, the woman who will take lovers but will not marry. In many ways, it is this aspect of Dantor's story that most clearly mirrors and maps the lives of Haitian women.

In former days (and still in some rural areas) the patriarchal, multigenerational extended family held sway in Haiti. In these families men could form unions with more than one woman. Each woman had her own household in which she bore and raised the children from that union. The men moved from household to household, often continuing to rely on their mothers as well as their women to feed and lodge them. When the big extended families began to break up under the combined pressures of depleted soil, overpopulation, and corrupt politics, large numbers of rural people moved to the cities.

Generally speaking, Haitian women fared better than men in the shift from rural to urban life. In the cities the family shrank to the size of the individual household unit, an arena in which women had traditionally been in charge. Furthermore, their skill at small-scale commerce, an aptitude passed on through generations of rural market women, allowed them to adapt to life in urban Haiti, where the income of a household must often be patched together from several small and sporadic sources. Urban women sell bread, candy, and herbal teas which they make themselves. They also buy and re-sell food, clothing, and household goods. Often their entire inventory is balanced on their heads or spread on outstretched arms as they roam through the streets seeking customers. When desperate enough, women also sell sex. They jokingly refer to their genitals as their "land." The employment situation in urban Haiti, meager though it is, also favors women. Foreign companies tend to prefer them for the piecework that accounts for a large percentage of the jobs available to the poor urban majority.

By contrast, unemployment among young urban males may well be as high as 80 percent. Many men in the city circulate among the households of their girlfriends and mothers. In this way they are usually fed, enjoy some intimacy, and get their laundry done. But life is hard and resources scarce. With the land gone, it is no longer so clear that men are essential to the survival of women and children. As a result, relationships between urban men and women have become brittle and often violent. And this is so in spite of a romantic ideology not found in the countryside. Men are caught in a double bind. They are still reared to expect to have power and to exercise authority, and yet they have few resources to do so. Consequently, when their expectations run up against a wall of social impossibility, they often veer off in unproductive directions. The least harmful of these is manifest in a national preoccupation with soccer; the most damaging is the military, the domestic police force of Haiti, which provides the one open road toward upward social mobility for poor young men. Somewhere in the middle of this spectrum lie the drinking and gambling engaged in by large numbers of poor men.

Ezili Dantor's lover is Ogou, a soldier spirit sometimes pictured as a hero, a breathtakingly handsome and dedicated soldier. But just as often Ogou is portrayed as vain and swaggering, untrustworthy and self-destructive. In one of his manifestations Ogou is a drunk. This is the man Ezili Dantor will take into her bed but would never depend on. Their relationship thus takes up and comments on much of the actual life experience of poor urban women.

Ezili Dantor also mirrors many of the specifics of Alourdes's own life. Gran Philo, Alourdes's mother, was the first of her family to live in the city. She worked there as a *manbo*. Although she bore four children, she never formed a long-term union with a man. She lived in Santo Domingo, in the Dominican Republic, for the first years of her adult life. There she had her first two babies. But her lover proved irrational, jealous, and possessive. Since she was working as hard or harder than he, Philo soon decided to leave him. Back in Port-au-Prince, she had two more children, but in neither case did the father participate in the rearing of the children. Alourdes, who is the youngest, did not know who her father was until she was grown. And when she found out, it still took time for him to acknowledge paternity.

In her late teens, Alourdes's fine singing voice won her a coveted position with the Troupe Folklorique, a song and dance group that drew much of its repertoire from Vodou. During that period Alourdes attracted the attention of an older man who had a secure job with the Bureau of Taxation. During their brief marriage Alourdes lived a life that was the dream of most poor Haitian women. She had a house and two servants. She did not have to work. But this husband, like the first man in Philo's life, needed to control her every move. His jealousy was so great that Alourdes was not even allowed to visit her mother without supervision. (The man should have known better than to threaten that vital bond!) Alourdes and her husband fought often and, after less than two years, she left. In the years that followed, there were times when Alourdes had no food and times when she could not pay her modest rent but, with pride like Ezili Dantor's, Alourdes never returned to her husband and never asked him for money. During one especially difficult period Alourdes began to operate as a Marie-Jacques, a prostitute, although not the kind who hawk their wares on the street. Each day she would dress up and go from business to business in downtown Port-au-Prince looking for someone who would ask her for a "date." When the date was over she would take what these men offered (everyone knew the rules), but she never asked for money. Alourdes had three children in Haiti, by three different men. She fed them and provided shelter by juggling several income sources. Her mother helped when she could. So did friends when they heard she was in need. For a while, Alourdes held a job as a tobacco inspector for the government. And she also dressed up and went out looking for dates.

Maggie, like Alourdes, was married once. Her husband drank too much and one evening, he hit her. Once was enough. Maggie packed up her infant son and returned to her mother's house. She never looked back. When Maggie talks about this marriage, now over for nearly a decade, she says he was a good man but alcohol changed him. "When he drink, forget it!" She would not take the chance that he might hit her again or, worse, take his anger and frustration out on their son.

Ezili Dantor is the mother—fierce, proud, hard-working, and independent. As a religious figure, Dantor's honest portrayal of the ambivalent emotions a woman can feel toward her lovers and a mother can feel toward her children stands in striking contrast to the idealized attitude of calm, nurture, and acceptance represented by more standard interpretations of the Holy Mother Mary, a woman for whom rage would be unthinkable. Through her iconography and possession-performances, Ezili Dantor works in subtle ways with the concrete life circumstances of Haitian women such as Alourdes and Maggie. She takes up their lives, clarifies the issues at stake in them, and gives them permission to follow the sanest and most humane paths. Both Alourdes and Maggie refer to Ezili Dantor as "my mother."

Vodou is a religion born of slavery, of wrenching change and deep pain. Its genius can be traced to long experience in using the first (change) to deal with the second (pain). Vodou is a religion in motion, one without canon, creed, or pope. In Vodou the ancient African wisdom is preserved by undergoing constant transformation in response to specific life circumstances. One of the things which keeps Vodou agile is its plethora of spirits. Each person who serves the spirits has his or her own coterie of favorites. And no single spirit within that group can take over and lay down the law for the one who serves. There are always other spirits to consult, other spirit energies to take into account. Along with Ezili Dantor, Alourdes also serves her sister, Ezili Freda.

Ezili Freda is a white spirit from the Rada pantheon, a group characterized by sweetness and even tempers. Where Dantor acts out women's sexuality in its childbearing mode, Freda, the flirt, concerns herself with love and romance. Like the famous Creole mistresses who lent charm and glamour to colonial Haiti, Ezili Freda takes her identity and worth from her relationship with men. Like the mulatto elite in contemporary Haiti who are the heirs of those Creole women, Freda loves fine clothes and jewelry. In her possession-performances, Freda is decked out in satin and lace. She is given powder and perfume, sweet smelling soaps and rich creams. The one possessed by her moves through the gathered community, embracing one and then

another and then another. Something in her searches and is never satisfied. Her visits often end in tears and frustration.[4]

Different stories are told about Freda and children. Some say she is barren. Others say she has a child but wishes to hide that fact in order to appear fresher, younger, and more desirable to men. Those who hold the latter view are fond of pointing out the portrait of a young boy that is tucked behind the left elbow of the crowned Virgin in the image of Maria Dolorosa with whom Freda is conflated. In this intimate biographical detail, Freda picks up a fragment from Alourdes's life that hints at larger connections between the two. When Alourdes was married she already had two children by two different men. She wanted a church wedding and a respectable life, so she hid the children from her prospective in-laws. It was only at the wedding itself, when they asked about the little boy and girl seated in the front row, that they found out the woman standing before the altar with their son already had children.

Alourdes does not have her life all sewn up in neat packages. She does not have all the questions answered and all the tensions resolved. Most of the time when she tells the story of her marriage, Alourdes says flatly: "He too jealous. That man crazy!" But on at least one occasion she said: "I was too young. If I was with Antoine now, I never going to leave him!" When Alourdes married Antoine Lovinsky she was a poor teenager living in Port-au-Prince, a city where less than 10% of the people are not alarmingly poor. Women of the elite class nevertheless structure the dreams of poor young women. These are the light-skinned women, who marry in white dresses in big Catholic churches and return to homes that have bedroom sets and dining room furniture and servants. These are the women who never have to work. They spend their days resting and visiting with friends and emerge at night on the arms of their men dressed like elegant peacocks and affecting an air of haughty boredom. Although Alourdes's tax collector could not be said to be a member of the elite, he provided her with a facsimile of the dream. It stifled her and confined her, but she has still not entirely let go of the fantasy. She still loves jewelry and clothes and, in her home, manages to create the impression, if not the fact, of wealth by piling together satin furniture, velvet paintings, and endless bric-a-brac.

Alourdes also has times when she is very lonely and she longs for male companionship. She gets tired of living at the edge of poverty and being the one in charge of such a big and ungainly household. She feels the pull of the images of domesticity and nuclear family life that she sees every day on the television in New York. Twice since I have known her, Alourdes has fallen in love. She is a deeply sensual woman and this comes strongly to the fore during these times. She dresses up, becomes coquettish, and caters to her man. Yet when describing his lovable traits, she always says first: "He help me so much. Every month, he pay the electric bill," and so forth. Once again the practical and the emotional issues cannot be separated. In a way, this is just another version of the poor woman selling her "land." And in another way it is not, for here the finances of love are wound round and round with longing and dreams.

Poor Haitian women, Alourdes included, are a delight to listen to when their ironic wit turns on what we would label as the racism, sexism, and colonial pretense of the upper-class women Freda mirrors. Yet these are the values with power behind them both in Haiti and in New York, and poor women are not immune to the attraction of such a vision. Ezili Freda is thus an image poor Haitian women live toward. She picks up their dreams and gives them shape, but these women are mostly too experienced to think they can live on or in dreams. Alourdes is not atypical. She serves Freda but much less frequently than Dantor. Ezili Dantor is the one for whom she lights a candle every day; she is the one Alourdes turns to when there is real trouble. She is, in Alourdes' words, "my mother." Yet I think it is fair to say that it is the tension between Dantor and Freda that keeps both relevant to the lives of Haitian women.

There is a story about conflict between the two Ezilis. Most people, most of the time, will say that the scars on Ezili Dantor's cheek come from war wounds, but there is an alternative explanation. Sometimes it is said that because Dantor was sleeping with her man, Maria Dolorosa took the sword from her heart and slashed the cheek of her rival.

A flesh-and-blood woman, living in the real world, cannot make a final choice between Ezili Dantor and Ezili Freda. It is only when reality is spiced with dreams, when survival skills are larded with sensuality and play, that life moves forward. Dreams and play alone lead to endless and fruitless searching. And a whole life geared toward survival becomes brittle and threatened by inner rage. Alourdes lives at the nexus of several spirit energies. Freda and Dantor are only two of them, the two who help her most to see herself clearly as a woman.

To summarize the above discussion: The Vodou spirits are not idealized beings removed from the complexity and particularity of life. On the contrary, the responsive and flexible nature of Vodou allows the spirits to change over space and time in order to mirror people's life circumstances in considerable detail. Vodou spirits are transparent to their African origins and yet they are other than African spirits. Ancient nature connections have been buried deep in their iconographies while social domains have risen to the top, where they have developed in direct response to the history and social circumstances of the Haitian people. The Vodou spirits make sense of the powers that shape and control life by imitating them. They act out both the dangers and the possibilities inherent in problematic life situations. Thus, the moral pull of Vodou comes from clarification. The Vodou spirits do not tell the people what should be; they illustrate what is.

Perhaps Vodou has these qualities because it is a religion of an oppressed people. Whether or not that is true, it seems to be a type of spirituality with some advantages for women. The openness and flexibility of the religion, the multiplicity of its spirits, and the detail in which those spirits mirror the lives of the faithful makes women's lives visible in ways they are not in the so-called great religious traditions. This visibility can give women a way of working realistically and creatively with the forces that define and confine them.

NOTES

1. I use terms such as possession-performance and theater analogies in order to point to certain aspects of the spirits' self-presentation and interaction with devotees. The terms should not be taken as indicating that priestesses and priests simply pretend to be spirits during Vodou ceremonies. The trance states they enter are genuine, and they themselves will condemn the occasional imposter among them.
2. In an otherwise flawed book, E. Wade Davis does a very good job of uncovering and describing the nature and function of the Vodou secret societies. See *The Serpent and the Rainbow* (New York: Simon and Schuster, 1985).
3. Robert Farris Thompson traces Ezili to a Dahomean "goddess of lovers." *Flash of the Spirit: African and Afro-American Art and Philosophy* (New York: Random House, 1983), p. 191.
4. Maya Deren has drawn a powerful portrait of this aspect of Ezili Freda in *The Divine Horsemen: The Living Gods of Haiti* (New Paltz, N.Y.: Documentext, McPherson and Co., 1983), pp. 137–45.

FURTHER READINGS

Brown, Karen McCarthy. "The Center and the Edges: God and Person in Haitian Vodou." *The Journal of the Interdenominational Theological Center* 7, no. 1 (Fall 1979).

———. "Olina and Erzulie: A Woman and a Goddess in Haitian Vodou." Anima, Spring 1979.

———. "Systematic Forgetting, Systematic Remembering: Ogou in Haiti." In *Africa's Ogun: Old World and New.* Ed. by Sandra T. Barnes. Bloomington, Ind.: University of Indiana Press, 1988.

———. "Alourdes: A Case Study of Moral Leadership in Haitian Vodou." In *Saints and Virtues,* ed. by John S. Hawley. Berkeley, Calif.: University of California Press, 1987.

———. "Afro-Caribbean Spirituality." *In Caring and Curing: Health and Medicine in the Western Religious Traditions,* ed. by Lawrence Eugene Sullivan. New York: Macmillan Press, 1988.

———. "The Power to Heal: Reflections on Women, Religion and Medicine." In *Shaping New Vision: Gender and Values in American Culture.* Ann Arbor, Mich.: UMI Press, 1987.

Deren, Maya. *Divine Horsemen: The Living Gods of Haiti.* New Paltz, N.Y.: Documentext, McPherson and Co., 1983.

Metraux, Alfred. *Voodoo in Haiti.* New York: Schocken Books, 1972.

Thompson, Robert Farris. *Flash of the Spirit: African and Afro-American Art and Philosophy.* New York: Random House, 1983.

Shamans, Bodies, and Sex: Misreading a Korean Ritual

Laurel Kendall

"But isn't it sexual?" This paper owes its genesis to the presentation of another—"Of Gods and Men: Performance, Possession, and Flirtation in Korean Shaman Ritual"—to the questions it raised, and to my bemusement when more than one respondent, on more than one occasion, insisted that sexuality "explained" the activities of female Korean shamans.[1] Speaking of the a modern, Western intellectual tradition, Michel Foucault describes sexuality as, "the general and disquieting meaning that pervades our conduct . . . a general signification, a universal secret, an omnipresent cause, a fear that never ends."[2] This chapter illustrates how this pervasive and common sense notion of sexuality gets in the way of ethnographic clarity.

The shamans who are the subjects of this paper are women. Indeed, most Korean shamans are women and the minority of male shamans dress in traditional women's clothing before donning the spirits' robes for a ritual. Shamans are chosen by the spirits; women experience this calling as frighteningly vivid dreams and visions, manic behavior, and compulsions to wander. They also experience misfortunes, both personally, and within their families, which recur until they accept their calling and are initiated. The initiation enables the shaman to call on the spirits for inspiration and visions which she will use to prognosticate both during divination sessions and when speaking in the persona of the spirits during minor and major rituals. Through her ability to make this connection with the spirits, the Korean shaman secures their favor on behalf of her clients. Ill health, problematic personal relations, and increasingly, business reverses, cause clients to seek out shamans, obtain divinations, and sponsor rituals. In addition to performing divinations, newly-initiated shamans can, with a minimum of training, perform simple prayer ceremonies for the good fortune of a client's family or business. The client makes offerings to the spirits and the shaman makes a petition on behalf of the client, then briefly manifests the spirits, offering in the voices of household gods and ancestors advice and cautions for all members of the client's family. With more training and observation of experienced shamans, the initiate learns to perform more complicated rituals for healing, business success, success in finding a marriage partner, and conceiving a child.[3]

The most elaborate, potent, and expensive ritual that Korean shamans perform is called *kut*. In *kut*, shamans wear clothing associated with the gods and ancestors and through song and dance, summon these spirits, in proper sequence, to the ritual space, manifesting them in their own bodies. In the persona of demanding gods and tearful ancestors, they scold, banter and commiserate with the clients, offer advice and prognostications, and depart with promises to help the family move toward a more optimistic future. The *kut* satisfies the appetites and demands of household gods and the worldly cravings of ancestors so that the troubling emotions they have vented toward the living family are transformed into good will and promises of future blessing and protection. Ominous forces are expelled and the path to an auspicious fortune is opened wide. The work of successful shamanship, closely bound with the successful performance of *kut*, requires a range of skills: singing, dancing, miming, playing the drum and percussive instruments, arranging elaborate offerings, and above all, providing canny divinations and convincing spirit manifestations. How was sexuality read into my description of these activities?

THE ETHNOGRAPHIC PROBLEM: "AMBIGUOUS SEXUALITY WAFTING"

The problem was of my own making. In my earlier ethnography, I had written that "an element of ambiguous sexuality wafts about the *mansin*'s (shaman's) performance."[4] "Of Gods and Men" explored the sources of that ambiguity. The presentation began with a disturbing memory from the field of a male spectator pinching the breast of a dancing shaman while he secured a thousand-*won* bill under her chest band. I used this image to approach a nagging question: why is the Korean shaman profession constructed as both disreputable and a service to the gods? I located my answer in the domain of dance. Dance, a source of pleasure and play, becomes in shaman ritual an amusement for the gods as well as the spectators, all of whom are said "to play" (*nolda*). As a gateway for the release of playful impulses and powerful emotions and as a sign and instrument of healing, dance also carries the danger of emotional abandon and disgrace. In extreme cases, the gods seize the dancing woman and claim her as a shaman.

A colleague wrote to thank me for a copy of my paper on "erotic dance." Erotic dance? What had I said?

I had included dancers' descriptions of a sense of joy, mirth, or excitement rising from the belly to the chest[5] and noted that this rising of spirited feelings (*hung, sinparam*) mapped the same trajectory as that taken by the personal body-governing gods who rise up when clients borrow shamans' costumes to dance, and by choking, potentially fatal emotions of rage and frustration that rise to the chest in "fire sickness" (*hwabyong*) when they have been held too long inside. I had written that in shaman rituals, the dance becomes a gateway for the expression of strong emotion in the idiom of spirits who, when they "play" in the person of a shaman or a client, vent their desires and appetites and attain (temporary) satisfaction. Korean shaman rituals dramatize the obverse of the Buddhist ideal of transcendence and of the Confucian injunction to controlled moderation; they deal with the consequences of worldly craving, using the dance as one idiom of both symptom and cure. I suggested that these associations, and the attendant possibility of being possessed by either spirits or compulsions and consequently disgraced, vested both dancing and the women who dance for a living with an aura of moral ambivalence (Kendall 1991).

"It must be sexual."

One respondent to an oral presentation of my paper insisted that sexual cravings necessarily explained the sensations Koreans described as rising from the belly. In a dialogue that exhausted the question-and-answer period, I was equally stubborn in my insistence that dancing Koreans did not read these experiences as sexual, that sexual desire—expressed most explicitly in the dancing compulsion—was but one of several emotions that Koreans expressed through the dancing, possessed or otherwise. Was lust more profound than the other bundled appetites and cravings that even nominal Korean Buddhists would recognize as obstacles to enlightenment or, in popular religion, as burdens weighing upon the restless dead? Is sexuality the engine that propels the dancer and runs the dance? A classic Freudian reading would have it so. Is the power that shamans claim through their danced possession by (mostly but not exclusively) male gods the regenerative power of sexuality turned to ritual ends? This is what

respondents to my paper seemed to insist upon. One discussant even delicately suggested that I should "not be afraid" to give my ethnography a sexual gloss. Why hadn't I seen it? Was I "hung up?" I was challenged, aware of corroborating examples elsewhere in the world, but I maintained an abiding unease with what seemed to be a reductionistic interpretation of the Korean material.

WOMEN, BODIES, AND SEX

In the 1970s, anthropologists concerned with what were then called "sex roles" asked, "Is female to male as nature is to culture?" Sherry Ortner, who phrased the question, argued that while the symbolic relegation of women to a lower order of existence is necessarily a cultural construct, the near universality of such perceptions is grounded in "the body and the natural procreative functions specific to women alone."[6] Much subsequent anthropological writing echoed this assumption that disparate cultures constructed women within the biological "givens" of the female body.[7] While Sherry Ortner and Harriet Whitehead,[8] as well as Bryan Turner[9] all explicitly eschew a simple biological determinism, they nevertheless assume that much of the anxious life of a given society is constructed around women's bodies as instruments of sexuality and reproduction. This is the obverse and conscious rejection of an abiding but more simplistic assumption, sometimes encountered in the literature on women and spirit possession (see below) that sexual repression is a common female problem.

Michel Foucault speaks of the "hysterization of women's bodies," the notion that women's sexuality as innately problematic and that women's problems are innately sexual," as a historical development of the early modern West.[10] The publication of Foucault's *The History of Sexuality* prompted a veritable cottage industry in social and historical writings about the body as a site through which social discipline is imposed and social power is affirmed.[11] These efforts have opened the question of gender to complex historical and cultural analyses—how are different notions of "masculity" and "femininity" experienced through male and female bodies that are made to act in socially prescribed ways? A few voices of caution have been raised against the ease with which such endeavors might slide into an older tendency to define "woman" through the body, sex, and reproduction to the exclusion of other dimensions of experience.[12]

In emphasizing that the men's and women's bodily experiences are redefined through history, Foucault offered liberation from, in Gayle Rubin's words, "the traditional understanding of sexuality as a natural libido yearning to break free of social constraint."[13] Sexualities could now be seen as multiple and both culturally and historically constituted, rather than simply "natural."[14] Eroticism is thus one dimension of a larger question posed by Clifford Geertz and restated by Nancy Scheper-Hughes and Margaret Lock as, ". . . whether any expression of human emotion and feeling—whether public or private, individual or collective, whether repressed or explosively expressed is ever free of cultural shaping and cultural meaning. The most extreme statement of Geertz's position, shared by many of the newer psychological and medical anthropologists, would be that without culture we would simply not know how to feel."[15]

What does this material bring to the question, "But isn't it sexual?" First, recognizing the importance of contemporary studies that regard women, and in particular the sexuality of women, as culturally and historically constituted, it simultaneously recognizes a deep-rooted impulse in Western social science writing to approach the question of women through sexuality and reproduction, an impulse that may obscure other possible readings.[16] Second, a plea for the recognition of culturally-constituted ideologies of eroticism, or any other expression of human feeling, is a plea for ethnographic precision and imagination and an honest recognition of the profound difficulty of interpreting human motivation in the absence of confident psychobiological "givens."

And now to Korea.

IS POSSESSION EROTIC?

The idea that shamanic experience implies a sexual union between the female shaman and her guardian god does seem to lurk in some corners of the Korean popular imagination. In the film version of "Portrait of a Shaman" (*Munyodo*), released in the 1970s, but *not* in Kim Tongni's original novella, the seasoned shaman and her initiate periodically ingest a blood-red concoction of Chinese medicine, whereupon they emit orgasmic shrieks while painted images of brawny gods leer up in front of the camera. In fact, the use of hallucinogens is unknown in Korean shamanic practice. More recently, an initiate who came to the shaman profession after attending graduate school in the United States and reading Eliade, evolved a signature dance style that required her to kneel in front of the altar and bend her torso backward, gestures which Western observers readily interpreted as a sexual reception of the god. Her Korean shaman colleagues found these same movements strange and referred to her performance as the "vagina dance" (*poji chum*).[17] Both portrayals suggest the influence of foreign notions of an eroticized shamanism.

Shamans have told me that because *most* (but not all) of the gods are male, or *if* predominantly male gods possess a shaman (rather than female gods or divine couples), a shaman will have a troubled marital history. Some shamans claim that jealous gods prevent them from having marital relations with their husbands, but other *mansin* scoff at this.[18] Songjuk Mansin told me, "Male gods don't like what is between man and woman," a statement that suggested her own agreement. Similarly, Okkyong's Mother, who enjoys the most stable marriage of all of the shamans I know well, affirmed that she sleeps upstairs in her shrine while her husband sleeps on the ground floor. A shaman colleague, describing a similar arrangement, asserted that "men stink" (a literal translation).

Yongsu's Mother complained that her dead husband, installed as a guardian god in her shrine, had prevented her from marrying again after an early widowhood, but she made it clear that the god was no substitute for a flesh and blood husband, that she would have preferred not to live alone. An aged shaman, initiated while still a young woman, wept when she described her many long years without a mate. A young married shaman described the stress of periods of enforced abstinence before performing significant rituals. In sum, *mansin* may boast of their gods' jealousy as a measure of their gods' power, an attribute of the shaman's own professional success. The gods may drive living husbands away, but they do not, in most instances, replace absent husbands as sexual partners. If some shamans use the gods as a justification for avoiding sexual contact with their husbands, this seems more an expression of distaste than a divine cure for or sublimation of repressed sexuality. This material counters what Pat Caplan has dubbed "the so-called 'hydraulic' model of sexuality,"[19] the Freudian assumption that an innate and problematic sexual drive must necessarily find expression or sublimation, if not in men, then in gods. The Korean material contains only the thinnest and most idiosyncratic suggestion that these needs might ever find expression in some Korean shamans' experience of possession.

Among the many scholars who have published on the subject of Korean shamanism, to my knowledge only Jung Young Lee has attempted to make a case for "a fundamental motive in Korean shamanism through a study of sexual repression."[20] Lee's study suffers from an excess of innuendo and inaccuracy—old men encountered in dreams are necessarily objects of sexual attraction, prayers for fertility are ultimately expressions of thwarted sexuality (rather than thwarted desires for sons), and the installation of guardian deities (who need not be male) in the initiate's shrine invariably establishes a sexual relationship between shaman and deity. The first two claims are unsubstantiated, either in the body of Lee's work or elsewhere in the literature on Korean shamanism. The third rests on the testimony of one shaman informant, possessed by a divine general, who "dreamed that she went to bed with the general."[21]

It is revealing that Lee utterly confuses the term "sexual repression"—the forcing of inexpressible sexual needs and desires into the subconscious mind—with "sexual oppression"—the systematic subjugation of women on the basis of gender.[22] This is an honest mistake insofar as psychological interpretations of female trance phenomena reveal an almost unconscious tendency to dissolve the social into the sexual. Consider, for example, psychiatrist and medical anthropologist Arthur Kleinman's field observation of a Taiwanese possession cult:

> Informants described it [possession] to me as one of the most exciting experiences they had ever witnessed or participated in. This must have been especially true for lower-class mothers and grandmothers, ordinarily trapped in the physical confines and daily routines of their homes. Cult members did not merely trance: they danced, jumped around, sang, exhibited glossolalia, gave voice to strong emotions, and sometimes engaged in activities with strong sexual overtones. For example, men and women touched and massaged each other; they jumped around together; women rubbed the inside of their thighs and men exhibited rapid thrusting movements of the pelvis; at times the ecstatic frenzy of the trances resembled orgasmic behavior.[23]

In this passage, "orgasmic behavior" and "sexual overtones" are the judgments of a clinical observer who deems the excitement of possession "especially true for lower-class mothers and grandmothers" as a release from "the physical confines and daily routines of their homes." The passage makes a reflex link between social constraints, sexual repression, and ritual release, and again, finds a locus in the problematic bodies of women, although pelvis-thrusting men were also present. Consider also Melford Spiro's well-known description of women in Burmese *nat* cults:

> Restricting this discussion to female shamans, it will be recalled that, typically, females are possessed by a *nat* [spirit], and/or decide to marry a *nat* who had previously possessed them, either in adolescence or in or near menopause. These are females, in short, who are either first experiencing the mounting pressures of sexual desire

and therefore—especially in Burma, where any physical contact with the opposite sex is prohibited—of sexual frustration, or they are females who, at menopause, are experiencing a heightening of their sex drives combined with the fear of losing their sexual attractiveness. The attendant frustration of the menopausal females is further intensified (in a large percentage of cases) by marriages with socially weak and sexually inadequate husbands. Add to this a previous observation, *viz.*, that the majority of those possessed, being of lower-class origin, are also suffering from status deprivation, and it then becomes at least plausible that one explanation for the differential effect of *nat* festivals is differential drive-intensity. That is, it is the women with the strongest frustrations (sexual, prestige, etc.) who are most susceptible to possession.[24]

By Spiro's logic, Burmese women respond to menarche and menopause with an emotional script that would not be out of place in an American women's magazine. And as in American women's magazines, "sexual attractiveness" is assumed to be at least as important to a woman's esteem as "prestige, etc." The contribution of Burmese culture to these constructions of self is that of a restrictive sluice gate, imposing sexual segregation upon the torrents of spring. The passage assumes a clinical familiarity with the subjects' "sexual frustration," "heightening of their sex drives," and "marriages with socially weak and sexually inadequate husbands," but elsewhere Spiro implies that these deductions must necessarily have been commonsensical, "When interviewed, these shamans describe the onset of possession as a highly pleasurable physical act, accompanied by deep and accelerated breathing, palpitations, and tingling of the flesh. The descriptions sounded very much like the description of sexual orgasm, but I could not pursue this line of inquiry because of *the near impossibility in Burma of discussing sexual matters with females*" (emphasis added).[25]

Spiro, at least, asked the shamans what the sensations of trance felt like. Gregory Bateson and Margaret Mead made inductive associations in their description of the Balinese trance dancer fallen backward onto the ground "writhing in some sort of orgasmic climax."[26]

Perhaps possession behavior and erotic experience have so thoroughly bled together within the ethnographic gaze because, as Scheper-Hughes and Lock suggest, "It is sometimes during the experience of sickness, as in moments of deep trance or sexual transport, that mind and body, self and other become one."[27] For their part, Scheper-Hughes and Lock maintain a distinction between different kinds of experiences that may "sometimes" be equivalent in their consequences. They urge that such experiences be studied as part of an ambitious project to understand "the mindful body, as well as the self, social body, and body politic."[28] Such challenges are foreclosed when one domain of experience, "deep trance," is subordinated to the explanatory power of another, "sexual transport." The association of possession and sexual experience is compounded when the subject is a woman who dances. The Western tradition has long associated dancing with sexual expression.[29] The Korean tradition also views the dancing woman as at least potentially sexually available but in very specific contexts.

To summarize, the question "But isn't it sexual?" seems to have been provoked by strong (Western) associations. In the literature, possession experiences have sometimes been described as "erotic" or equivalent to "orgasm," a particularly tempting association where those possessed are women, socially oppressed, and consequently (it is assumed) sexually repressed. Most Korean shamans are women and most (but not all) of the gods who claim any one shaman are male. Therefore (by the logic of a flawed deduction) shamans experience possession either sexually or as sublimation. The sex question is posed primarily because Korean shamans are women.

This path of association—women, possession, dance, sex—is at least loosely "Freudian;" ultimate causes are situated in the individual subconscious, in drives that find expression, satisfaction, or sublimation through ritual participation, dance, and the experience of possession. But "Isn't it sexual?" may also indicate a different and more subtle line of interpretation. Mikhail Bakhtin's characterized aspects of medieval and renaissance folk culture as a celebration of the regenerative power of the body and bodily life." In carnivalistic portrayals of eating, drinking, copulation, and defecation, visions of a regenerated world were brought close to human experience through the body.[30] Bakhtin inverts the Freudian premise that all things come from psychobiological drives; rather, it is the body that takes the world into itself and reconstitutes it in performance."[31] Jean Comaroff describes the organizing sexual metaphors of a Tswana dance, performed to welcome male initiates after their return from the bush, as a regenerative replication of the Tswana social world. The different positions assumed by the dancing men and women and the different movements they assumed in the dance, the lateral rolling motions of the women and the vertical, or phallic movement of the upright sticks held by the men "implied not only the complementarily of male-female sexuality but the distinction between agnatic rank and matrilineality. . . . The map of the dance floor also replicated the spatial order of the social world, its organization of center and periphery, its opposed yet complementary relations between male and female."[32] Jean Comaroff postulates a widespread use of bodily metaphors in such world-defining dance forms, citing a similar emphasis on male "phallic" leaps and female lateral swaying in a fertility ritual of the Umeda people of the West Sepik District of New Guinea, described by Alfred Gell,[33] and Eric Ten Raa's description of mimed copulation in a ritual performed by the Sandawe of central Tanzania for the purpose of making the country fertile.[34] As Judith Lynn Hanna observes, dance is a particularly powerful medium for focusing awareness on the body and its associations.[35] Comaroff notes that danced celebrations of sexuality and Bakhtinean "bodily life" were precisely what provoked missionary ire in many parts of the world and, in some instances, resulted in local denials of prior practices.[36]

When an indigenous intelligentsia internalizes Western judgments, the result may be expurgated reinscriptions of custom. Frederique Marglin describes the nearly vanished devadasis of Puri, temple dancers and ritual specialists who celebrate the auspicious dimensions of female sexuality and fertility: "well-being and health or more generally . . . all that creates, promotes, and maintains life."[37] The devadasi's identity as a sexual being, as reflected in the link between temple dancing and prostitution, is central to Marglin's analysis of the devadasi's auspicious associations. To reach this understanding, Marglin first found it necessary to read through a process of historical reinterpretation. Indian reformers had attempted to retrieve Indian dance as an art form distinct from the onus of prostitution. It was claimed that the devadasi were originally chaste virgins, meant only for the gods, who were later debased by degenerate rulers and rich and powerful men, or that economic hardship had forced the devadasis into prostitution.[38]

We turn again to the Korean material with an awareness both of the expressive potential of the danced body, and of the likelihood of denials and redefinitions. Indeed, for the last twenty-five years, I have listened with amusement to emphatic denials of the existence of a living, vital, Korean shaman tradition. Over less than a decade in the 1970s, I saw elements of Bakhtinian body humor—mimed phallic display, defecation, and the unceremonious tossing away of a soiled baby—disappear from the performance of a rural masked dance tradition as it gained popularity among students and urbanites and was no longer performed as a celebration punctuating the agricultural cycle. Are the auspicious forces engendered by a Korean shaman's *kut* (her major ritual) in any sense generated by a danced and performed expression of positive sexual forces? Here, as elsewhere, the shamanic experience is realized in the performing body of the shaman.[39] Drumming and percussion inspire lively dancing and the inspiration to speak "the true words of the spirits." A successful *kut* resolves, in an atmosphere of play, the vexations (*soksanghada*) of the gods and ancestors and satisfies their tremendous appetites (*yoksim*). But are these "vexations" and "appetites," expressed through the dancing, miming, and speaking body of the shaman, innately sexual? Is there any evidence at all that this should be the cause? This passage caused some of my readers to think so:

The *mansin* (shaman) who performs the Official's play (the segment of a shaman ritual that appeases a particularly greedy god) is . . . encouraged to dance her way to the far sidelines and coax the men into accepting an empty wine cup which she fills to the brim. . . . Her gesture is suggestive. To fill a man's cup outside the intimacy of kinship suggests the behavior of a woman paid to serve men's pleasure, the hospitality offered in a wine house . . . [during the Official's play] the *mansin* who distributes the [Official's] . . . wine encourages a spectator of either sex to dance a few bars with her in the enthusiasm of the moment.[40]

The few bars of dance described here are distinct from the jumps, accompanied by percussive drum beats, that bring on possession.[41] When shamans dance a few steps while selling the Official's wine, and when they dance a slow and graceful prelude to the jumping dance of possession, they execute the basic steps performed at Korean country celebrations, arms stretched out from the shoulders and bent slightly at the elbows to gesture rhythmically as the dancer takes slow steps with slight bends of the knee. The grace of the dancer is in her arms, her strength and flexibility in her shoulders. Women dance this way with each other, and men with men. Indeed, the women with whom I danced at a village Mother's Day picnic told me that they could not imagine how Americans had any fun at parties where, as I had told them, men and women "played together."

Such dancing, in and of itself, is neither explicitly gendered nor erotically charged. To dance at a *kut* or a country party is to "play" (*nolda*), to amuse oneself in a relatively unrestrained and pleasurable moment. Sexual expression, danced or otherwise, is euphemized as "play," but certainly as a subset and not a generative form.[42] Between women and men, dancing takes on a flirtatious cast (but can we call it "erotic"?) when a woman—a *kisaeng* or a shaman—invites a man to dance and pours him a cup of wine. In the Official's play, the gesture is ambiguous, since the shaman acts in the persona of a masculine god, a "man" dancing with a man.[43]

In her *Dance, Sex and Gender*, Judith Hanna cites selections from my 1985 ethnography to present the interactions of Korean shamans and male spectators as one among many other examples of "aphrodisiac dancing . . . which conveys the gender role of sexual object or partner."[44] The reader might never realize that this material comes from an ethnography subtitled *Women in Korean Ritual Life*, that it is the men who are marginal at Korean shaman rituals. Taken as a whole, Hanna's ethnographic overview of sexual expression through dance unravels some of the many different contexts, stakes, and consequences of such expression: in courtship, in prostitution, as an expression of union with the sacred, as a means of coping with supernatural forces, as a sex-role script, or as a sublimation. Her interpretation of dance as the gendered body's mediation of an "instinctual sexual drive," however, leads her to appropriate decontextualized data in support of a universal psychobiological "truth." Hanna links "the sexuality of dance and its potential to excite" to her quantifiable, verifiable observation that "Dancing can lead to altered states of consciousness (with changed physiological patterns in brain wave frequency, adrenalin, and blood sugar) and hence to altered social action."[45]

My Korean data appears in Hanna's study under the heading "Seduction of Forces and Female Shamans," a section intended to illustrate that dance not only can be "performed to arouse the passion of a human lover, but it has sexual overtones in relationship to overcoming the forces of nature."[46] The selling of a cup of wine, a mildly nuanced flirtation, becomes, in this appropriation, an act of sexual arousal equivalent to a striptease. A marginal bit of business becomes the central encounter of a complex ritual process. What is assumed to happen between female shamans and male spectators "explains" what must then necessarily happen between shamans and gods.

Some representations in Korean popular culture—and, I suspect, many Korean men—assume that shamans are sexually promiscuous.[47] Recall that it was a male spectator's tweak of a shaman's breast that caused me to write about "performance, possession, and flirtation" in the first place. The stereotype is a function both of what shamans do—their public performance—and who they are (by virtue of what they do)—women who earn a livelihood outside the constraints and protections of respectable family life and who are simultaneously independent and vulnerable to harassment. Shamans whom I have known seem anxious to preserve their reputations and genuinely vexed by importunate men.[48] Is this flirtation/harassment a necessary part of the *kut*? From at least the turn of the century, some *kut* were always performed in shrines away from home, sometimes without the knowledge of the sponsor's husband, a tendency that may be even more pronounced today when *kut* are performed in commercial shrines rather than in cramped apartments where neighbors, particularly Christian neighbors, might complain about the noise of drum and symbols.[49] *Kut* were performed within the women's quarters of the palace and,[50] if we are to believe an old genre painting, in the segregated women's quarters of elite eighteenth-century homes. Thus, while shamans may, on the one hand, exploit the men's presence by selling lucky wine, and on the other, risk the men's harassment, the men's presence with its potential for play is not essential to the successful performance of a Korean shaman ritual. An efficacious, auspicious ritual does not require the energies unleashed by a brief heterosexual danced encounter. Rather it is the gods and ancestors who must play and feast to their satisfaction while spectators, particularly the sponsoring woman, are encouraged to dance to satisfy their own body-governing spirits.

Korean shaman rituals do include some more general representations of Bakhtinian "bodily life," most notably in the final send-off of wandering ghosts (*yongsil*) in which the performing shaman mimics the manner of their death, clutching her throat and rolling her eyes for the hanged, pantomiming dysentery, or simulating childbirth by dropping a metal bowl with a clatter from under her skirts.[51] In this exorcistic sequence, the shaman's play suggests not so much the cele-

bration of a regenerative life force as a comfortingly humorous acknowledgment of the terrors of the mortal body.

Manifestations of sexual appetite are mimed in a small bit of business when a shaman seizes a dried fish, drumstick, or gong mallet, thrusts it out from the vicinity of her well-clothed genitals, and draws it up, usually pointing in the direction of the ritual's female sponsor. Sometimes the phallus (I think we can safely call it a phallus) is manipulated under the shaman's costume to suggest an erection. This is a bit of improvisational business, not a requisite element of the formal structure of the *kut* as recorded by folklorists. (So far as I know, folklorists have not bothered to record it.) The gesture is sharp and quick, always too quick for my camera. However often performed, it is almost invariably met with giggles from the spectators and an exchange of smirks among the shaman team. When Songjuk Mansin wrapped the dried fish in her costume vest and proceeded to rub it, Yongsu's mother expressed humorously exaggerated disgust, swatting with her drumstick at Songjuk's hands and at the makeshift phallus. At another *kut,* Yongsu's mother complained to Songjuk Mansin that the Spirit Warrior, manifested by a third shaman, was making too many demands of the client. To underscore her point, she improvised a phallus with a length of twisted towel, held out taught, and muttered "too much of this" as she gave it a thrust and a jerk.

What does this body play signify? The gods who receive a phallus in passing are among the most stereotypically demanding (the Official and the Spirit Warrior), not the highest gods (the Mountain God, the Heavenly King, the House Lord) whose dignified portrayals in *kut* are briefer and far less amusing to the spectators. Gods of middling rank have less shame and are consequently more active in stirring up trouble in client households. When they appear in *kut* they level outrageous and comically executed demands for food, music, and cash, and are met with equally stubborn resistance from the female spectators. The shaman's humorous portrayals make it possible for shamans and clients to engage the gods in a bargaining, bantering process of reconciliation. In caricature, the god's phallus is less an instrument of domination, or object of desire, than one more comic sign of a demanding, overbearing appetite, "too much of this." Could the gesture and the remark just possibly be a shaman's comment upon the masculine gender? When I saw a shaman, in the persona of the Official, playfully tweak a client's breast, I began to wonder.

CONCLUSION

Is it sexual? If so, then not in predictable ways. It would be difficult to read the phallic play described above as an expression of repressed sexual desire, or view these tumescent gods as idealized alternatives to mortal men. Indeed, they seem very much the opposite. If, as late twentieth century anthropological writing would have it, expressions of bodily life make statements about social relationships, then the gods' phallic exhibitionism underscores the general tenor of their dealings with mortals; they are, like lusty mortal men, bothersome and demanding,. This is a measure of their power and of their obvious foibles. The "drag" act, Judith Butler suggests, is the "site of a certain ambivalence" against the order of things that can be both an expression of surrender and of insurrection,[52] but Rosalind Morris's cautions that this playful parody should not be over read as a serious act of resistance.[53]

Let us not, once again, mistake a part for the whole. That some shamans sometimes improvise phalluses adds a gloss to their portrayal of a particular category of masculine gods and gendered relationships more generally. These comic portrayals no more "explain" the sum of shamanic performance in sexual terms than does the shaman's occasional harassment by men or the selling of cups of wine. Such phenomena might, however, contribute to an analysis of gendered perceptions of a sexual Other. Performance offer a rich and subtle ground for such a project, as the work of Judith Butler, Linda Williams, Jennifer Robertson, and others suggests,[54] but this ground is also mined with booby traps. Ritual,

myth, and art may, in Geertzian terms, show us "how people feel about things"[55] but interpretation comes through the reading eye, and there's the rub. The burden is on the anthropologist to provide the best and most valid reading possible, knowing that if it is worth considering, it is also worthy of contestation.

In other places, I have offered my own reading of the Korean shaman's relationship with her gods.[56] In this essay, I have been concerned with misreading, with how an observer, influenced by psychobiological interpretations of human—and particularly female—behavior could draw commonsensical but ultimately unfounded conclusions about sexual expression in Korean shaman rituals. I have also considered recent studies that regard social phenomena as "embodied," expressed by and through the body and its imagery. Specifically, I explored a possible interpretive link between those ritual dances observed elsewhere in the world that create and regenerate social worlds through their portrayal of heterosexual sexuality, encounters between female Korean shamans and male spectators, and instances of phallic play in shamanic ritual. I found this particular association weak as an overarching explanation but useful in one restricted case of performance business. A further consideration of the body and expressions of body life in Korean shaman ritual, in folk dramas, and in jokes and conversations, may offer other kinds of insights into the operation of gender and sexuality in Korean popular culture. But "Korean popular culture" is itself a moving target. The particular shamans who are the subjects of this paper inhabit a very different world of experience from that of media-savvy young Korean women who, in the 1990s, have begun to articulate totally new and unabashedly explicit discourses of sexuality.[57] The argument is for more, better, and more varied fieldwork.

This paper originally appeared in French in *Anthropologie et Societes*. vol. 22, n.2, 1998, as "Mais n'est-ce pas "seuxel, Le lapsus derriere le regard ethnographique," and in English as "'But Isn't it Sexual?' The Freudian Slip beneath the Ethnographic Gaze" in *Gender/Bodies/Religions*, edited by Sylvia. Marcos., Ed., 2000).

It is reprinted here in English with the permission of *Anthropologie et Societes* and Adler Publications. My observations are drawn from several field trips to Korea, initially supported by the Institute for International Education (Fulbright) and the Social Science Research Council, more recently by the Belo-Tanenbaum Fund of the American Museum of Natural History. I am grateful for the many provocative comments on my earlier work that inspired me to write this paper; those by Jean Comaroff were particularly inspiring. An early version was originally written for the "Workshop on the construcition of Gender and Sexuality" in East and Southeast Asia at the University of California, Los Angeles in December, 1990. The three anonymous readers who reviewed this article for *Anthropology et Societes* were extremely useful in forcing me to clarify my intentions. I, of course, am responsible for the shortcomings of this effort.

NOTES

1. Laurel Kendall, "Of Gods and Men: Performance, Possession, and Flirtation in Korean Shaman Ritual, *Cahiers d'Extreme-Asie*, (special issue on Korean Ritual, Alex Guillemoz, ed.), vol. 3, (1991/2) no. 2, pp. 185–202.

2. Michel Foucault, *The History of Sexuality, Volume I: An Introduction,* New York, Vintage Books, 1980, p. 69.

3. These are described in Laurel Kendall, *Shamans, Housewives, and Other Restless Spirits: Women in Korean Ritual Life,* Honolulu, University of Hawaii Press, 1985, p. 61.

4. Laurel Kendall, *Shamans, Housewives, and Other Restless Spirits: Women in Korean Ritual Life,* Honolulu, University of Hawaii Press, 1985, p. 61.

5. Cho Dongwha, cited in Alan C. Heyman, *Dances of the Three-Thousand-League Land,* Seoul, Dong-A Publishing Co, p. 5.

6. Sherry B. Ortner, "Is Female to Male as Nature Is to Culture?" in *Women, Culture, and Society,* M. Z. Rosaldo and L. Lamp here, eds., 1974, Stanford, Stanford University press, pp. 67–87.

7. Judith Hock-Smith and Anita Spring, eds., *Women in Ritual and Symbolic Roles,* New York and London, Plenum Press, 1978, p. 3.

8. Sherry B. Ortner and Harriet Whitehead eds., *Sexual Meanings: The Cultural Construction of Gender and Sexuality,* New York, Cambridge University Press, 1981, pp. 3, 19.

9. Sherry B. Ortner and Harriet Whitehead eds., *Sexual Meanings: The Cultural Construction of Gender and Sexuality,* New York, Cambridge University Press, 1981, pp. 3, 19.

10. Foucault, *op. cit.,* especially pp. 104, 153. See also Pat Caplan, "Introduction," in *The Cultural Construction of Sexuality,* P. Caplan, ed., London and New York, Tavistock, 1987, pp. 1–30.

11. As a bellwether, in 1990 the American Ethnological Society took "the body" as the theme of its annual meeting. In this same year, the journal *History of Religions* devoted a theme issue to "the body." For a critical review of anthropological approaches to the body, see Nancy Scheper-Hughes and Margaret Lock, "The Mindful Body: A Prolegomenon to Future Work in Medical Anthropology," *Medical Anthropology Quarterly* vol. 1, no.1, 1987, pp. 6–41. For an overview of historical writing on sexuality and of anthropological thinking on this topic see Caplan, *op. cit.*

12. See in particular Gesela Bock, "Women's History and Gender History: Aspects of an International Debate," *Gender and History,* vol. 1, no. 1, 1989, pp. 7–29; and Jane Flax, "Postmodernism and Gender Relations in Feminist Theory," *Signs: Journal of Women in Culture and Society,* vol., 12 no. 4, pp. 621–643.

13. Gayle Rubin, "Thinking sex: Notes for a Radical Theory Rubin, Thinkingsex: Notes for a Radical Theory Rubin, Thinkingsex: Notes for a Radical Theory Rubin, Thinking sex: Notes for a Radical Theory Rubin, Thinking sex: Notes for a Radical Theory of the Politics of Sexuality," in *Pleasure and Danger: Exploring Female Sexuality,* C. Vance, ed., Boston, Routledge and Paul, 1984, pp. 287–319.

14. See Judith Butler, *Bodies that Matter: on the Discursive Limits of "Sex,"* New York, Routledge, 1993; Caplan, *op. cit.,* Teresa De Laruetis, ed., *Technologies of Gender,* Bloomington, University of Indiana Press, 1986; and Sherry B. Ortner, *Making Gender: The Politics and Erotics of Culture,* Boston, Beacon Press, 1996.

15. Scheper-Hughes and Locke, *op. cit.,* p. 28.

16. This tendency is not exclusively Western. Earlier generations of Japanese historians and folklorists regarded women as "mothers," a tendency that has lingering influence upon the historical study of Japanese women. See Helen Hardacre, "Sex and Gender in Women's History

in Japan," paper presented to the Annual Meeting of the Association for Asian Studies, Chicago, April 8, 1990.

17. Chungmoo Choi, personal communication.

18. Youngsook Kim Harvey, *Six Korean Women: the Socialization of Shamans*, St. Paul, West Publishing Company, 1979, p. 200.

19. Caplan, *op. cit.*, p. 1.

20. Jung Young Lee, *Korean Shamanistic Rituals*, The Hague, Mouton, 1981.

21. Ibid., p. 174.

22. Ibid., pp. 167–170.

23. Arthur Kleinman, *Patients and Healers in the Context of Culture: An Exploration of the Borderland between Anthropology, Medicine, and Psychiatry*, Berkeley and Los Angeles: University of California Press, 1980. p. 315. "Sexual oppression" has been widely offered as an ultimate, and ultimately circular, explanation for the ethnographic predominance of women in spirit possession. For the most synthesized and intellectually provocative statement of this approach, see I. M. Lewis's, *Ecstatic Religion*, Harmondsworth, Penguin, 1969. The women are assumed to be manipulative, their possession a coercive strategy, although whether this is a conscious or a subconscious motivation is seldom made explicit. For a critique which, like much recent writing on religious activities, argues that possession activities should be understood through the meanings imparted to them by the participants, see Anita Spring, "Epidemiology of Spirit Possession among the Luvale of Zambia," in *Women in Ritual and Symbolic Roles,* J. Hock-Smith and A Spring, eds, New York and Longdon, Plenum Press, pp. 165–190. For a critique specific to the Korean material, see Kendall, 1985, *op. cit.*

24. Melford E. Spiro, *Burmese Supernaturalism*, Englewood Cliffs, New Jersey: Prentice-Hall, Inc., p.223.

25. Ibid., p. 122.

26. Gregory Bateson and Margaret Mead, *Balinese Character: a Photographic Analysis,* Special Publications of the New York Academy of Sciences, vol. 2, 1942, p. 168.

27. Scheper-Hughes and Lock, *op. cit.*, p. 29.

28. Ibid.

29. Judith Lynne Hanna, *Dance, Sex, and Gender: Signs of Identity, Dominance, Defiance, and Desire*, Chicago and London, University of Chicago Press. 1988, p. 19.

30. Mikhail Bakhtin, *Rabelais and His World*, H. Isowolsky, trans., Cambridge, Mass., MIT Press, 1968 [1965], pp. 38–39.

31. Jean Comaroff, 1985, *Body of Power, Spirit of Resistance: The Culture and History of a South African People*, Chicago, University of Chicago Press, pp. 6–7.

32. Comaroff, *op. cit.*, p. 111.

33. Alfred Gell, *Metamorphosis of the Cassowaries: Umeda Society, Language, and Ritual*, New Jersey, Humanities Press Inc., 1975, p. 234.

34. Eric Ten Raa, "The Moon as a Symbol of Life and Fertility in Sandawe Throught," *Africa, vol.* 39, 1969, p. 38.

35. Hanna, 1988, *op. cit., p. 13.*

36. Comaroff, *op. cit.*, p. 151.

37. Frederique Apffel Marglin, *Wives of the God-king: The Rituals of the Devadasis of Puri*, Delhi, Oxford University Press, 1985, p. 19.

38. Ibid., pp. 8–9. As in India, Korean dance has been recontextualized as an icon of "Korean tradition," taught to respectable young women in studios and university dance departments. Following Foucaultian logic, dancing could now be viewed as an instrument of discipline in the construction of Korean or Indian femininity.

39. Amanda Porterfield, "Shamanism: A Psychosocial Definition," *Journal of the American Academy of Religion*, vol. 55, no. 4, 1987, pp. 721–739.

40. Kendall, 1991, *op. cit.*

41. In summoning the gods, the shaman begins a slow and ordinary dance, broken by a sudden leap encouraged by a sudden burst of rapid drumbeats. The dancer continues to jump, rotating on the balls of her feet, pumping her arms up and down. When the dancer is a client who has borrowed the shaman's costume to entertain her personal spirits, this activity is sufficient. The client jumps to exhaustion, save on those rare occasions where her body-governing god chooses to gesture or speak. When the shaman stops jumping, however, she mimes, sings, and speaks in the persona of the god.

42. One can find explicit representations of sexual acts and possible erotic glosses in some more specialized Korean dances. Korean masked dance dramas seem to suggest sexual intercourse when two characters place their arms on each others' shoulders and rock from side to side, provoking humor rather than titillation. The multi-drum dance, performed as the grand finale of nearly every recital of "traditional Korean dance," has erotic overtones. The dance is said to express the Buddhist initiate's religious fervor but is also associated with the legend of a famous courtesan who performed it to the distraction of a hypocritically

lustful monk, as described by Alan C. Heyman, *op. cit.* It is almost invariably performed by a woman, but is taught now at dancing schools servicing the middle class and in university dance departments.

43. As the shaman Yongsu's Mother said, after knocking an importunate male customer against the wall, "Oh, that wasn't me, it was the honorable Official [the possessing spirit] who did that." See Kendall, 1985, *op. cit.*, p. 61.

44. Hanna, *op. cit.*, pp. 46, 71–72.

45. Ibid., p. 22.

46. Ibid., p. 70.

47. Ch'oe and Chang indicate that men used to gather and amuse themselves at the home of the *mansin*, Cho Yong-ja, until her son took up residence. The *mansin* recalls the village chief's proposition as a grievous insult. See Ch'oe Kil-sÚng and Chang Chu-gun, *KyÚnggido chiyÚk musok* (Regional shaman practices of KyÚnggi Province), Seoul, Ministry of Culture, 1967, pp. 32–33, 54). In folklore circles I have heard it said that shamans used also to serve as itinerant prostitutes, but I have no corroborating evidence. The novels of Kim Tongni portray the shaman as a woman who casually enters sexual liaisons.

48. See Kendall, 1985, *op. cit.*, pp. 61–62.

49. See "Korean Mudang and Pansu," *Korea Review*, vol.3, 1903, p. 147.

50. For descriptions of shamanic practices in dynastic times, as gleaned from old records, see Yi Nung-hwa, *ChosÚn musok ko* (Reflections on Korean shamanism), translated into modern Korean by Yi Chae-gon, Seoul, Paengnôk, 1976 [1927]. In historical references to shaman rituals on Cheju Island before the ChosÚn period (1392–1910), men and women together celebrated communal rituals "in the form of gregarious songs and dances." See Chang Chu-gun, *Kankoku no mingan sinko* (Korean Folk Beliefs), Tokyo, Kinkasha, 1973, English summary, p. 12. Chang argues that the gendered dichotomy of

Confucian rites for men and folk religious practices for women was a consequence of the Confucian transformation of Korean society during the ChosÚn period. If this local example can be expanded, and if these heterosexual songs and dances can be shown as fundamental to the ritual and not the sideline activities of more recent times, then perhaps one finds the Korean equivalent of a Bakhtinian carnival undermined by the imposition of a new moral hegemony. This would be an intriguing example, innocent of missionary influence and Western-derived values.

51. Watching one such performance, I realized that the shaman had borrowed some of the lines from the childbirth scene in the Yangju Masked Dance Drama which is still, despite self-censorship, a creditably Bakhtinian celebration of bodily life. In abbreviated contemporary *kut*, the final send-off of wandering ghosts is greeted with sighs of impatience from other members of the shaman team, anxious to finish up and get home.

52. Butler, *op. cit.*, p. 124.

53. Rosalind C. Morris, " ALL MADE UP: Performance Theory and the New Anthropology of Sex and Gender," *Annual Review of Anthropology*, vol. 24, 1995, pp. 567–592.

54. Butler, *op. cit.*; Williams, *op. cit.*; and also Jennifer Robertson, "Doing and Undoing 'Female' and 'Male' in Japan: The Takarazuka Revue," in *Japanese Social Organization*, Takie Sugiyama Lebra, ed., Honolulu, University of Hawaii Press, 1992, pp. 79–107.

55. Clifford Geertz, *The Interpretation of Culture*, New York, Basic Books, 1973, p. 82.

56. Kendall 1991/2 *op. cit.*

57. For the changing sexual discourses of young Korean women, see So-Hee Lee, "The Concept of Female Sexuality in Korean Popular Culture," in *Under Construction: The Gendering of Modernity, Class, and Consumption in the Republic of Korea*, L. Kendall, ed., Unpublished ms.

X

Gender, Politics, and Reproduction

All human reproductive behavior is culturally patterned. This cultural patterning includes menstrual beliefs and practices; restrictions on the circumstances in which sexual activity may occur; beliefs and practices surrounding pregnancy, labor, and the postpartum period; understanding and treatment of infertility; and the significance of menopause. Although research on human biological reproduction has been dominated by medical concerns such as normal and abnormal physiological functioning, an increasing anthropological literature emphasizes the centrality of reproduction to global social, political, and economic processes (Ginsburg and Rapp 1995; Sargent and Brettell 1996). Biological reproduction refers to the production of human beings, but this process is always a social activity, leading to the perpetuation of social systems and social relations. The ways in which societies structure human reproductive behavior reflect core social values and principles, informed by changing political and economic conditions (Browner and Sargent 1990: 215).

Much of the available anthropological data on reproduction prior to 1970 is to be found within ethnographies devoted to other subjects. For example, Montagu (1949) analyzed concepts of conception and fetal development among Australian aborigines, and Malinowski (1932) wrote about reproductive concepts and practices among the Trobriand Islanders. Several surveys of ethnographic data on reproduction were compiled, such as Ford's (1964) study of customs surrounding the reproductive cycle or Spencer's (1949–1950) list of reproductive practices around the world.

In the past twenty-five years anthropologists have sought to use cross-cultural data from pre-industrial societies to help resolve women's health problems in the industrialized world (Davis-Floyd and Sargent 1997; Jordan 1978). For example, comparative research on birth practices has raised questions regarding the medicalization of childbirth in the United States. Anthropologists have also involved themselves in international public health efforts to improve maternal and child health around the world. In addition, anthropological research has helped clarify the relationship between population growth and poverty. While some analysts have held the view that overpopulation is a determinant of poverty and the poor must control their fertility to overcome impoverishment, others argue the reverse: People have many children because they are poor (Rubinstein and Lane 1991: 386).

Concern with population growth has often focused on women as the potential users of contraceptives, although women's personal desires to limit fertility may not be translated into action because of opposition from husbands, female relations, or others with influence or decision-making power. In this area of research anthropologists have an important contribution to make in examining such factors as cultural concepts regarding fertility and family size, the value of children, dynamics of decision making within the family and community, and the relationship between women's reproductive and productive roles.

Since the 1970s anthropological interest has turned to the linkages between cultural constructions of gender, the cultural shaping of motherhood, and reproductive beliefs and practices. In many societies throughout the world the relationship between women's social positions and maternity is clear: A woman becomes adult by childbearing, and her prestige may be greatly enhanced by bearing numerous male children (Browner and Sargent 1990: 218). Thus, in the Middle East a woman is "raised for marriage and procreation [and] acquires her own social status only by fecundity" (Vieille 1978: 456), while in parts of Africa pressures to be prolific weigh heavily on women (Sargent 1982).

In much of the world infertility is dreaded by men and women alike but is a particular burden to women (Browner and Sargent 1990: 219; Inhorn and Van Balen 2002). Such pressure to reproduce is especially intense in agrarian societies, which have a high demand for labor. However, in many hunter-gatherer and horticultural societies, motherhood and reproduction are less emphasized. As Collier and Rosaldo observe, "Contrary to our expectation that motherhood provides women everywhere with a natural source of emotional satisfaction and cultural value, we found that neither women nor men in very simple societies celebrate women as nurturers or women's unique capacity to give life" (1981: 275).

Just as beliefs and practices regarding fertility are culturally patterned, birth itself is a cultural production (Jordan 1978). As Romalis notes, "The act of giving birth to a child is never simply a physiological act but rather a performance defined by and enacted within a cultural context" (1981: 6). Even in advanced industrial societies such as the United States, childbirth experiences are molded by cultural, political, and economic processes (Oakley 1980; Martin 1987; Michaelson et al. 1988). Studying the cultural patterning of birth practices can illuminate the nature of domestic power relations and the roles of women as reproductive health specialists, and it can increase our understanding of the relations between men and women cross-culturally.

Davis-Floyd (in this book) illustrates how gender ideology is revealed in the management of American pregnancy and birth. Childbirth in the United States is routinized, and it is usually highly technological. Davis-Floyd argues that core beliefs in American society about science, technology, and patriarchy shape American birth. Through the normalizing of high-tech childbirth, a message is conveyed to American women that their bodies are defective machines and that they must therefore rely on more efficient machines to give birth. Drawing on centuries-old Western European notions of nature, culture, and society, today's dominant medical model regards the male body as the ideal body-machine, while the female body is considered abnormal and inherently inadequate. Hospital birth "rituals" work to transform the birthing woman into an "American mother," who has been socialized through the birth experience to accept core values of the society. Thus birth is a cultural rite of passage, in which the patriarchal status quo is reproduced and reaffirmed.

Although reproduction is culturally patterned, not all individuals in a society share reproductive goals. As Browner (in this book) points out, reproductive behavior is influenced by the interests of a woman's kin, neighbors, and other members of the community, and these interests may conflict. Government policies regarding the size and distribution of population may differ from the interests of reproducing women. Women's goals in turn may not be shared by their partners or other individuals and groups in the society. Browner examines the ways in which access to power in a society determines how conflicts concerning reproduction are carried out and dealt with by analyzing population practices in a Chinantec-Spanish-speaking township in Oaxaca, Mexico.

In this community the government's policy to encourage fertility reduction was imposed on a pre-existing conflict between the local community as a whole, which encouraged increased fertility, and women of the community, who sought to limit family size. Women and men manifested very different attitudes concerning fertility desires: Women sought much smaller families than men. As children increasingly attended school their economic benefits appeared slight to their mothers. Further, women viewed pregnancy as stressful and debilitating. Yet despite these negative views, women felt they could not ignore pressures to reproduce.

Such pressure came from community men, who valued a large population for the defense and well-being of the collectivity, and from women, who, while not desiring more children themselves, wanted other women to bear children in the interests of the group. In spite of the ease of obtaining government contraceptives, women rejected their use. In this cultural, political, and economic context, local women experienced conflict between personal desires to have few children and local pressures to be prolific.

Personal desires for children together with a pronatalist culture and advances in reproductive technology have generated consumer demand for surrogate motherhood in the United States, according to Ragoné's research (in this book). Ragoné explores surrogates' stated motivations for becoming surrogate mothers as well as the details of their actual experiences. She describes surrogates' explanations as a cultural script reflecting widely accepted ideas about reproduction, motherhood, and family. In contrast to popular opinion, surrogates deny being motivated by financial gain. Rather, they conceptualize surrogacy as a "gift," a priceless donation to the commissioning couple. The apparent "commodification" of women's bodies represented in surrogate motherhood remains a troubling issue, however. In addition, the recent shift from traditional surrogacy (in which the surrogate contributes an ovum) to gestational surrogacy, where the surrogate gestates the couples' embryos, raises important questions about what constitutes "real" parenthood. Surrogacy challenges the Euro-American emphasis on genetic relatedness and the biological basis of kinship, and creates potential conflicts surrounding the claims of different kinds of biological and non-biological mothers and fathers. Thus surrogacy poses profound challenges to our understandings of kinship, family, and reproduction.

Advanced reproductive technologies, including fetal diagnostic testing and surveillance technologies such as amniocentesis and ultrasound imaging continue to change values and expectations associated with conception, pregnancy, and birth (Rapp 1999). Critical feminist writings have questioned the excessive medicalization of women's reproductive processes, moving from the earlier focus on technocratic birth described by Davis-Floyd to the rapid developments in reproductive science and technology such as gestational surrogacy. These technologies, more widely available in industrialized societies, are increasingly accessible to populations in other countries as well, where they pose challenging ethical dilemmas as well as opportunities.

Women and men confronting infertility, for example, look to sophisticated medical interventions in the hope of a successful pregnancy outcome (Inhorn and Van Balen 2002; Layne 1999). Inhorn's (1994) rich account of Egyptian women's attempts to overcome infertility inaugurated the expanding anthropological literature on infertility in societies with high-technology medical systems as well as in poorer countries where low-income populations have access principally to low-technology biomedical treatment. Globally, feminists have expressed concern at the gap between the growing availability of the technology, and the public understanding of its social, legal, and moral implications. The low success rates of infertility technologies, the high expense, and the physical toll on women have prompted concerns that women's bodies are objectified as sites of medical experimentation.

Ginsburg (1987) also discusses reproduction as a domain of contested moral and medical meanings, using the example of abortion in American culture. She suggests that the focus of this conflict of interests is the relationship between reproduction, nurturance, sex, and gender. Using life histories of pro-life and pro-choice activists in Fargo, North Dakota, she reveals how different historical conditions affect reproductive decisions. The activist protesters in Fargo vie for the power to define womanhood in light of a basic American cultural script in which, in the context of marriage, pregnancy results in childbirth and motherhood. Ginsburg argues that the struggle over abortion rights is a contest for control over the meanings attached to reproduction in America and suggests that "female social activism in the American context operates to mediate the construction of self and gender with larger social, political, and cultural processes."

Similarly, Whitbeck argues that controversy over abortion rights in the United States must be understood in relation to a cultural context that neglects women's experiences and the status of women as "moral individuals." Rather, American culture regards women and women's bodies as "property to be bartered, bestowed, and used by men" (Whitbeck 1983: 259). Concern with restricting access to abortions derives from the interest of the state or others in power to control women's bodies and their reproductive capacity (Whitbeck 1983: 260).

Whereas Ginsburg discusses how abortion activists seek to define American womanhood in relation to cultural ideals of motherhood and nurturance, Gruenbaum (in this book) shows that cultural expectations of marriage and motherhood in Sudan form the context for the deeply embedded practice of female genital cutting (FGC). FGC is reported to exist in at least twenty-eight countries, and current estimates are that between 200,000 and one million girls experience some form of genital cutting annually. Other estimates suggest that as many as 5 million children are operated on each year (Kouba and Muasher 1985; Sargent 1991; Toubia 1994). The various forms of FGC present serious risks, such as infection and hemorrhage at the time of the procedure, and future risks to childbearing; therefore, social scientists, feminists and other local activists, and public health organizations have opposed the practices. However, as Gruenbaum observes, female genital cutting remains highly valued and continues to be most strongly defended by women, who carry out the practice.

Women in Sudan derive status and security as wives and mothers. Virginity is a prerequisite for marriage, and in this context clitoridectomy and infibulation, the major forms of FGC, are perceived as protecting morality. Thus, these practices persist because they are linked to the important goal of maintaining the reputa-tion, marriageability, and longterm economic security of daughters. Forty years of policy formulated by the Sudanese government and by international health organizations emphasizing the physically dangerous dimensions of FGC and prohibiting the most extensive forms of the practice have not resulted in its elimi-nation, although conditions seem ripe for change. For anthropologists, FGC has tested the limits of cultural relativism and generated continuing debate about how to respect cultural difference while taking a stance in accord with one's own moral positions.

Miller's discussion of female infanticide and child neglect in North India (1987) is also set in a strongly patrilineal, patriarchal society and again dramatic-ally illustrates ethical conflicts that emerge from prevailing gender ideologies that favor sons and the associated devaluation of daughters. In North India family survival depends on the reproduction of sons for the rural labor force, and prefer-ence for male children is evident in substantial ethnographic data documenting discrimination against girls. In this region preferences for male children result in celebrations at the birth of a boy, while a girl's birth goes unremarked. Sex-selective child care and female infanticide also indicate cultural favoring of male children.

Reports of female infanticide in India have occurred since the eighteenth cen-tury. There is evidence that a few villages in North India have never raised one daughter. In spite of legislation prohibiting female infanticide, the practice has not totally disappeared, although Miller argues that direct female infanticide has been replaced by indirect infanticide or neglect of female children. Indirect female infanticide is accomplished by nutritional and health care deprivation of female children, a phenomenon also discussed by Charlton (1984). Miller argues that the strong preference for sons in rural North India is related to their economic and social functions.

The preference for male children has important repercussions in the increas-ing demand for abortion of female fetuses following amniocentesis. For example, in one clinic in North India 95 percent of female fetuses were aborted following prenatal sex determination. Thus, new reproductive technologies such as amnio-centesis are seen to be manipulated by patriarchal interests. Miller suggests that, ultimately, understanding the patriarchal culture of north India may help promote more effective health care and enhanced survival chances for female children.

The readings in this section illustrate the ways in which human reproductive behavior is socially constructed and influenced by global economic and politi-cal processes (Ginsburg and Rapp 1991). Rather than perceiving reproductive health in a narrow biological or purely personal framework, cross-cultural research suggests that women's health needs should be addressed in the con-text of their multifaceted productive, reproductive, and social roles. Conse-quently, decisions about such reproductive health issues as family size and composition are never left to the individual woman, but are influenced by kin, community, and state interests. These interests are often contested with the introduction of new reproductive technologies enabling sophisticated prenatal testing, treatment for infertility, and surrogate mothering. As these technolo-gies increasingly spread throughout the world, their availability will raise impor-tant questions regarding cultural definitions of family, gender ideology, and reproductive health.

REFERENCES

Browner, Carole and Carolyn Sargent. 1990. "Anthropology and Studies of Human Repro-duction." In Thomas M. Johnson and Carolyn Sargent (eds.). *Medical Anthropology: Con-temporary Theory and Method*, pp. 215–229. New York: Praeger Publishers.

Charlton, Sue Ellen M. 1984. *Women in Third World Development*. Boulder, CO: Westview Press.

Collier, Jane F. and Michelle Z. Rosaldo. 1981. "Politics and Gender in Simple Societies." In Sherry B. Ortner and Harriet Whitehead (eds.). *Sexual Meanings: The Cultural Construction of Gender and Sexuality*, pp. 275–329. Cambridge: Cambridge University Press.

Davis-Floyd, Robbie and Carolyn Sargent. 1997. "Introduction: The Anthropology of Birth." In Robbie Davis-Floyd and Carolyn Sargent (eds.). *Childbirth and Authoritative Knowledge*, pp. 1–51. Berkeley: University of California Press.

Ford, Clellan Stearns. 1964. "A Comparative Study of Human Reproduction." *Yale University Publications in Anthropology* No. 32: Human Relations Area Files Press.

Ginsberg, Faye. 1987. Procreation Stories: Reproduction, Nurturance, and Procreation in Life Narratives of Abortion Activists. *American Ethnologist* 14 (4): 623–636.

Ginsburg, Faye and Rayna Rapp. 1991. "The Politics of Reproduction." *Annual Review of Anthropology* 20: 311–43.

———. (eds.). 1995. *Conceiving the New World Order: The Global Politics of Reproduction*. Berkeley: University of California Press.

Jordan, Brigitte. 1978. *Birth in Four Cultures*. Montreal: Eden Press Women's Publications.

Inhorn, Marcia and Frank Van Balen. 2002. *Infertility Around the Globe*. Berkeley: University of California Press.

Inhorn, Marcia. 1994. *Quest for Conception*. Philadelphia: University of Pennsylvania Press.

Kouba, Leonard J. and Judith Muasher. 1985. "Female Circumcision in Africa: An Overview." *African Studies Review* 28 (1): 95–110.

Layne, Linda. 1999. "I Remember the Day I Shopped for Your Layette." In L. Morgan and M. Michaels (eds.). *Fetal Subjects, Feminist Positions*. Philadelphia: University of Pennsylvania Press.

Malinowski, Bronislaw. 1932. *The Sexual Life of Savages in Northwestern Melanesia*. London: Routledge and Kegan Paul.

Martin, Emily. 1987. *The Woman in the Body: A Cultural Analysis of Reproduction*. Boston: Beacon Press.

Miller, Barbara. 1987. "Female Infanticide and Child Neglect in Rural India." In Nancy Scheper-Hughes (ed.), *Child Survival*, pp. 95–112. Dordrecht: D. Reidel Publishing.

Michaelson, Karen, et al. 1988. *Childbirth in America: Anthropological Perspectives*. South Hadley, MA: Bergin and Garvey.

Montagu, M. F. Ashley. 1949. "Embryology from Antiquity to the End of the 18th Century." *Ciba Foundation Symposium* 10 (4): 994–1008.

Oakley, Ann. 1980. *Women Confined: Towards a Sociology of Childbirth*. New York: Schocken Books.

Rapp, Rayna. 1999. *Testing Women, Testing the Fetus: The Social Impact of Amniocentesis in America*. New York: Routledge.

Romalis, Shelly (ed.). 1981. *Childbirth: Alternatives to Medical Control*. Austin: University of Texas Press.

Rubinstein, Robert A. and Sandra D. Lane. 1991. "International Health and Development." In Thomas M. Johnson and Carolyn Sargent (eds.). *Medical Anthropology: Contemporary Theory and Method*, pp. 367–391. New York: Praeger Publishers.

Sargent, Carolyn. 1982. *The Cultural Context of Therapeutic Choice*. Dordrecht, Holland: D. Reidel Publishing Company.

———. 1991. "Confronting Patriarchy: The Potential for Advocacy in Medical Anthropology." *Medical Anthropology Quarterly* 5 (1): 24–25.

Sargent, Carolyn F. and Caroline B. Brettell (eds.). 1996. *Gender and Health: An International Perspective*. Upper Saddle River, NJ: Prentice Hall, Inc.

Spencer, Robert. 1949–1950. "Introduction to Primitive Obstetrics." *Ciba Foundation Symposium* 11 (3): 1158–88.

Toubia, Nahid, M.D. 1994. "Female Circumcision as a Public Health Issue." *The New England Journal of Medicine* 331 (11).

Gender and Ritual: Giving Birth the American Way

Robbie E. Davis-Floyd

Although the array of new technologies that radically alter the nature of human reproduction is exponentially increasing, childbirth is still an entirely gendered phenomenon. Because only women have babies, the way a society treats pregnancy and childbirth reveals a great deal about the way that society treats women. The experience of childbirth is unique for every woman, and yet in the United States childbirth is treated in a highly standardized way. No matter how long or short, how easy or hard their labors, the vast majority of American women are hooked up to an electronic fetal monitor and an IV (intravenously administered fluids and/or medication), are encouraged to use pain-relieving drugs, receive an episiotomy (a surgical incision in the vagina to widen the birth outlet in order to prevent tearing) at the moment of birth, and are separated from their babies shortly after birth. Most women also receive doses of the synthetic hormone pitocin to speed their labors, and they give birth flat on their backs. Nearly one-quarter of babies are delivered by Cesarean section.

Many Americans, including most of the doctors and nurses who attend birth, view these procedures as medical necessities. Yet anthropologists regularly describe other, less technological ways to give birth. For example, the Mayan Indians of Highland Chiapas hold onto a rope while squatting for birth, a position that is far more beneficial than the flat-on-your-back-with-your-feet-in-stirrups (lithotomy) posi-

tion. Mothers in many low-technology cultures give birth sitting, squatting, semi-reclining in their hammocks, or on their hands and knees, and are nurtured through the pain of labor by experienced midwives and supportive female relatives. What then might explain the standardization and technical elaboration of the American birthing process?

One answer emerges from the field of symbolic anthropology. Early in this century, Arnold van Gennep noticed that in many societies around the world, major life transitions are ritualized. These cultural rites of passage make it appear that society itself effects the transformation of the individual. Could this explain the standardization of American birth? I believe the answer is yes.

I came to this conclusion as a result of a study I conducted of American birth between 1983 and 1991. I interviewed over 100 mothers, as well as many of the obstetricians, nurses, childbirth educators, and midwives who attended them.[1] While poring over my interviews, I began to understand that the forces shaping American hospital birth are invisible to us because they stem from the conceptual foundations of our society. I realized that American society's deepest beliefs center on science, technology, patriarchy, and the institutions that control and disseminate them, and that there could be no better transmitter of these core values and beliefs than the hospital procedures so salient in American birth. Through these procedures, American women are repeatedly told, in dozens of visible and invisible ways, that their bodies are defective machines incapable of giving birth without the assistance of these other, male-created, more perfect machines.

RITES OF PASSAGE

A *ritual* is a patterned, repetitive, and symbolic enactment of a cultural belief or value; its primary purpose is alignment of the belief system of the individual with that of society. A *rite of passage* is a series of rituals that move individuals from one social state or status to another as, for example, from girlhood to womanhood, boyhood to manhood, or from the womb to the world of culture. Rites of passage transform both society's perception of individuals and individuals' perceptions of themselves.

Rites of passage generally consist of three stages, originally outlined by van Gennep: (1) *separation* of the individuals from their preceding social state; (2) a period of *transition* in which they are neither one thing nor the other; and (3) an *integration* phase, in which, through various rites of incorporation, they are absorbed into their new social state. In the year-long pregnancy/childbirth rite of passage in American society, the separation phase begins with the woman's first awareness of pregnancy; the transition stage lasts until several days after the birth; and the integration phase ends gradually in the newborn's first few months of life, when the new mother begins to feel that, as one woman put it, she is "mainstreaming it again."

Victor Turner, an anthropologist famous for his writings on ritual, pointed out that the most important feature of all rites of passage is that they place their participants in a transitional realm that has few of the attributes of the past or coming state. Existing in such a non-ordinary realm, he argues, facilitates the gradual psychological opening of the initiates to profound interior change. In many initiation rites involving major transitions into new social roles (such as military basic training), ritualized physical and mental hardships serve to break down initiates' belief systems, leaving

them open to new learning and the construction of new cognitive categories.

Birth is an ideal candidate for ritualization of this sort, and is, in fact, used in many societies as a model for structuring other rites of passage. By making the naturally transformative process of birth into a cultural rite of passage, a society can ensure that its basic values will be transmitted to the three new members born out of the birth process: the new baby, the woman reborn into the new social role of mother, and the man reborn as father. The new mother especially must be very clear about these values, as she is generally the one primarily responsible for teaching them to her children, who will be society's new members and the guarantors of its future.

THE CHARACTERISTICS OF RITUAL

Some primary characteristics of ritual are particularly relevant to understanding how the initiatory process of cognitive restructuring is accomplished in hospital birth. We will examine each of these characteristics in order to understand (1) how ritual works; (2) how the natural process of childbirth is transformed in the United States into a cultural rite of passage; and (3) how that transformation works to cement the patriarchal status quo.

Symbolism

Above all else, ritual is symbolic. Ritual works by sending messages in the form of symbols to those who perform and those who observe it. A *symbol* is an object, idea, or action that is loaded with cultural meaning. The left hemisphere of the human brain decodes and analyzes straightforward verbal messages, enabling the recipient to either accept or reject their content. Complex ritual symbols, on the other hand, are received by the right hemisphere of the brain, where they are interpreted holistically. Instead of being analyzed intellectually, a symbol's message will be *felt* through the body and the emotions. Thus, even though recipients may be unaware of incorporating the symbol's message, its ultimate effect may be extremely powerful.

Routine obstetric procedures are highly symbolic. For example, to be seated in a wheelchair upon entering the hospital, as many laboring women are, is to receive through their bodies the symbolic message that they are disabled; to then be put to bed is to receive the symbolic message that they are sick. Although no one pronounces, "You are disabled; you are sick," such graphic demonstrations of disability and illness can be far more powerful than words. Suzanne Sampson told me:

> I can remember just almost being in tears by the way they would wheel you in. I would come into the hospital, on top of this, breathing, you know, all in control. And they slap you in a wheelchair! It made me suddenly feel like maybe I wasn't in control any more.

The intravenous drips commonly attached to the hands or arms of birthing women make a powerful symbolic statement: They are umbilical cords to the hospital. The cord connecting her body to the fluid-filled bottle places the woman in the same relation to the hospital as the baby in her womb is to her. By making her dependent on the institution for her life, the IV conveys to her one of the most profound messages of her initiation experience: In American society, we are all dependent on institutions for our lives. The message is even more compelling in her case, for *she* is the real giver of life. Society and its institutions cannot exist unless women give birth, yet the birthing woman in the hospital is shown, not that she gives life, but rather that the institution does.

A Cognitive Matrix

A *matrix* (from the Latin *mater*, mother), like a womb, is something from within which something else comes. Rituals are not arbitrary; they come from within the belief system of a group. Their primary purpose is to enact, and thereby, to transmit that belief system into the emotions, minds, and bodies of their participants. Thus, analysis of a culture's rituals can lead to a profound understanding of its belief system.

Analysis of the rituals of hospital birth reveals their cognitive matrix to be the *technocratic model* of reality which forms the philosophical basis of both Western biomedicine and American society. All cultures develop technologies. But most do not supervalue their technologies in the particular way that we do. This point is argued clearly by Peter C. Reynolds (1991) in his book *Stealing Fire: The Mythology of the Technocracy* (a *technocracy* is a hierarchical, bureaucratic society driven by an ideology of technological progress). There he discusses how we "improve upon" nature by controlling it through technology. The technocratic model is the paradigm that charters such behavior. Its early forms were originally developed in the 1600s by Descartes, Bacon, and Hobbes, among others. This model assumes that the universe is mechanistic, following predictable laws that the enlightened can discover through science and manipulate through technology, in order to decrease their dependence on nature. In this model, the human body is viewed as a machine that can be taken apart and put back together to ensure proper functioning. In the seventeenth century, the practical utility of this body-as-machine metaphor lay in its separation of body, mind, and soul. The soul could be left to religion, the mind to the philosophers, and the body could be opened up to scientific investigation.

The dominant religious belief systems of Western Europe at that time held that women were inferior to men—closer to nature and feebler both in body and intellect. Consequently, the men who developed the idea of the body-as-machine also firmly established the male body as the prototype of this machine. Insofar as it deviated from the male standard, the female body was regarded as abnormal, inherently defective, and dangerously under the influence of nature.

The metaphor of the body-as-machine and the related image of the female body as a defective machine eventually formed the philosophical foundations of modern obstetrics. Wide cultural acceptance of these metaphors accompanied the demise of the midwife and the rise of the male-attended, mechanically manipulated birth. Obstetrics was thus enjoined by its own conceptual origins to develop tools and technologies for the manipulation and improvement of the inherently defective, and therefore anomalous and dangerous, process of birth.

The rising science of obstetrics ultimately accomplished this goal by adopting the model of the assembly-line production of goods as its template for hospital birth. Accordingly, a woman's reproductive tract came to be treated like a birthing machine by skilled technicians working under semiflexible timetables to meet production and quality control demands. As one fourth-year resident observed:

> We shave 'em, we prep 'em, we hook 'em up to the IV and administer sedation. We deliver the baby, it goes to the nursery, and the mother goes to her room. There's no room for niceties around here. We just move 'em right on through. It's hard not to see it like an assembly line.

The hospital itself is a highly sophisticated technocratic factory; the more technology the hospital has to offer, the better it is considered to be. Because it is an institution, the hospital constitutes a more significant social unit than an individual or a family. Therefore it can require that the birth process conform more to institutional than personal needs. As one resident explained,

> There is a set, established routine for doing things, usually for the convenience of the doctors and the nurses, and the laboring woman is someone you work around, rather than with.

The most desirable end-product of the birth process is the new social member, the baby; the new mother is a secondary by-product. One obstetrician commented, "It was what we were all trained to always go after—the perfect body. That's what we were trained to produce. The quality of the mother's experience—we rarely thought about that."

Repetition and Redundancy

Ritual is marked by repetition and redundancy. For maximum effectiveness, a ritual concentrates on sending one basic set of messages, repeating it over and over again in different forms. Hospital birth takes place in a series of ritual procedures, many of which convey the same message in different forms. The open and exposing hospital gown, the ID bracelet, the intravenous fluid, the bed in which she is placed—all these convey to the laboring woman that she is dependent on the institution.

She is also reminded in myriad ways of the potential defectiveness of her birthing machine. These include periodic and sometimes continuous electronic monitoring of that machine, frequent manual examinations of her cervix to make sure that it is dilating on schedule, and, if it isn't, administration of the synthetic hormone pitocin to speed up labor so that birth can take place within the required 26 hours.[2] All three of these procedures convey the same messages over and over: *Time is important, you must produce on time, and you cannot do that without technological assistance because your machine is defective.* In the technocracy, we supervalue time. It is only fitting that messages about time's importance should be repeatedly conveyed during the births of new social members.

Cognitive Reduction

In any culture, the intellectual abilities of ritual participants are likely to differ, often markedly. It is not practical for society to design different rituals for persons of different levels of intellectual ability. So ritual utilizes specific techniques, such as rhythmic repetition, to reduce all participants to the same narrower level of cognitive functioning. This low level involves thinking in either/or patterns that do not allow for consideration of options or alternative views.

Four techniques are often employed by ritual to accomplish this end. One is the *repetition* already discussed above. A second is *hazing*, which is familiar to undergraduates who undergo fraternity initiation rites but is also part of rites of passage all over the world. A third is *strange-making*—making the commonplace appear strange by juxtaposing it with the unfamiliar. Fourth is *symbolic inversion*—metaphorically turning things upside-down and inside-out to generate, in a phrase coined by Roger Abrahams (1973), "The power attendant upon confusion."

For example, in the rite of passage of military basic training, the initiate's normal patterns of action and thought are turned topsy-turvy. He is made strange to himself: His head is shaved, so that he does not even recognize himself in the mirror. He must give up his clothes, those expressions of his past individual identity and personality, and put on a uniform identical to that of the other initiates. Constant and apparently meaningless hazing, such as orders to dig six ditches and then fill them in, further breaks down his cognitive structure. Then through repetitive and highly symbolic rituals, such as sleeping with his rifle, the basic values, beliefs, and practices of the Marines are incorporated into his body and his mind.

In medical school and again in residency, the same ritual techniques that transform a youth into a Marine are employed to transform college students into physicians. Reduced from the high status of graduate to the lowly status of first-year medical student, initiates are subjected to hazing techniques of rote memorization of endless facts and formulas, absurdly long hours of work, and intellectual and sensory overload. As one physician explained:

> You go through, in a six-week course, a thousand-page book. You have pop quizzes in two or three courses every day the first year. We'd get up around 6, attend classes till 5, go home and eat, then head back to school and be in anatomy lab working with a cadaver, or something, until 1 or 2 in the morning, and then go home and get a couple of hours sleep, and then go out again.

Subjected to such a process, medical students often gradually lose any broadminded goals of "helping humanity" they had upon entering medical school. A successful rite of passage produces new professional values structured in accordance with the technocratic and scientific values of the dominant medical system. The emotional impact of this cognitive narrowing is aptly summarized by a former resident:

> Most of us went into medical school with pretty humanitarian ideals. I know I did. But the whole process of medical education makes you inhuman. . . . you forget about the rest of life. By the time you get to residency, you end up not caring about anything beyond the latest techniques and most sophisticated tests.

Likewise, the birthing woman is socialized by ritual techniques of cognitive reduction. She is made strange to herself by being dressed in a hospital gown, tagged with an ID bracelet, and by the shaving or clipping of her pubic hair, which symbolically de-sexualizes the lower portion of her body, returning it to a conceptual state of childishness. (In many cultures, sexuality and hair are symbolically linked.) Labor itself is painful, and is often rendered more so by the hazing technique of frequent and very painful insertion of someone's fingers into her vagina to see how far her cervix has dilated. This technique also functions as a strange-making device. Since almost any nurse or resident in need of practice may check her cervix, the birthing woman's most private parts are symbolically inverted into institutional property. One respondent's obstetrician observed, "It's a wonder you didn't get an infection, with so many people sticking their hands inside of you."

Cognitive Stabilization

When humans are subjected to extremes of stress and pain, they may become unreasonable and out of touch with reality. Ritual assuages this condition by giving people a conceptual handle-hold to keep them from "falling apart" or "losing it." When the airplane starts to falter, even passengers who don't go to church are likely to pray! Ritual mediates between cognition and chaos by making reality appear to conform to accepted cognitive categories. In other words, to perform a ritual in the face of chaos is to restore order to the world.

Labor subjects most women to extremes of pain, which are often intensified by the alien and often unsupportive hospital environment. They look to hospital rituals to relieve the distress resulting from their pain and fear. They utilize breathing rituals taught in hospital-sponsored childbirth education classes for cognitive stabilization. They turn to drugs for pain relief, and to the reassuring presence of medical technology for relief from fear. LeAnn Kellog expressed it this way:

> I was terrified when my daughter was born. I just knew I was going to split open and bleed to death right there on the table, but she was coming so fast, they didn't have any time to do anything to me. . . . I like Cesarean sections, because you don't have to be afraid.

When you come from within a belief system, its rituals will comfort and calm you. Accordingly, those women in my study who were in basic agreement with the technocratic model of birth before going into the hospital (70%) expressed general satisfaction with their hospital births.

Order, Formality, and a Sense of Inevitability

Its exaggerated and precise order and formality set ritual apart from other modes of social interaction, enabling it to establish an atmosphere that feels both inevitable and inviolate. To perform a series of rituals is to feel oneself locking onto a set of "cosmic gears" that will safely crank the individual through danger to safety. For example, Trobriand sea fishermen described by anthropologist Bronislaw Malinowski (1954) regularly performed an elaborate series of rituals on the beach before embarking. The fishermen believed that these rituals, when carried out with precision, would obligate the gods of the sea to do their part to bring the fishermen safely home. Likewise, obstetricians, and many birthing women, feel that correct

performance of standardized procedures ought to result in a healthy baby. Such rituals generate in humans a sense of confidence that makes it easier to face the challenge and caprice of nature.

When women who have placed their faith in the technocratic model are denied its rituals, they often react with fear and a feeling of being neglected:

> My husband and I got to the hospital, and we thought they would take care of everything. I kept sending my husband out to ask them to give me something for the pain, to check me, but they were short-staffed and they just ignored me until the shift changed in the morning.

Hospital rituals such as electronic monitoring work to give the laboring woman a sense that society is using the best it has to offer—the full force of its technology—to inevitably ensure that she will have a safe birth.

However, once those "cosmic gears" have been set into motion, there is often no stopping them. The very inevitability of hospital procedures makes them almost antithetical to the possibility of normal, natural birth. A "cascade of intervention" occurs when one obstetric procedure alters the natural birthing process, causing complications, and so inexorably "necessitates" the next procedure, and the next. Many of the women in my study experienced such a "cascade" when they received some form of pain relief, such as an epidural, which slowed their labor. Then pitocin was administered through the IV to speed up the labor, but pitocin very suddenly induced longer and stronger contractions. Unprepared for the additional pain, the women asked for more pain relief, which ultimately necessitated more pitocin. Pitocin-induced contractions, together with the fact that the mother must lie flat on her back because of the electronic monitor belts strapped around her stomach, can cause the supply of blood and oxygen to the fetus to drop, affecting the fetal heart rate. In response to the "distress" registered on the fetal monitor, an emergency Cesarean is performed.

Acting, Stylization, Staging

Ritual's set-apartness is enhanced by the fact that it is usually highly stylized and self-consciously acted, like a part in a play. Most of us can easily accept this view of the careful performances of TV evangelists, but it may come as a surprise that those who perform the rituals of hospital birth are often aware of their dramatic elements. The physician becomes the protagonist. The woman's body is the stage upon which he performs, often for an appreciative audience of medical students, residents, and nurses. Here is how one obstetrician played to a student audience observing the delivery he was performing:

"In honest-to-God natural conditions babies were *sometimes* born without tearing the perineum and without an episiotomy, but without artificial things like anesthesia and episiotomy, the muscle is torn apart and if it is not cut, it is usually not repaired. Even today, if there is no episiotomy and repair, those women quite often develop a rectocoele and a relaxed vaginal floor. This is what I call the saggy, baggy bottom." (Laughter by the students. A student nurse asks if exercise doesn't help strengthen the perineum.) "No, exercises may be for the birds, but they're not for bottoms. . . . When the woman is bearing down, the leveator muscles of the perineum contract too. This means the baby is caught between the diaphragm and the perineum. Consequently, anesthesia and episiotomy will reduce the pressure on the head, and hopefully, produce more Republicans." (More laughter from the students) (Shaw 1974: 90).

Cognitive Transformation

The goal of most initiatory rites of passage is cognitive transformation. It occurs when the symbolic messages of ritual fuse with individual emotion and belief, and the individual's entire cognitive structure reorganizes around the newly internalized symbolic complex. The following quote from a practicing obstetrician presents the outcome for him of such transformative learning:

I think my training was valuable. The philosophy was one of teaching one way to do it, and

that was the right way. . . . I like the set hard way. I like the riverbanks that confine you in a direction. . . . You learn one thing real well, and that's the way.

For both nascent physicians and nascent mothers, cognitive transformation of the initiate occurs when reality as presented by the technocratic model, and reality as the initiate perceives it, become one and the same. This process is gradual. Routine obstetric procedures cumulatively map the technocratic model of birth onto the birthing woman's perceptions of her labor experience. They align her belief system with that of society.

Take the way many mothers come to think about the electronic fetal monitor, for example. The monitor is a machine that uses ultrasound to measure the strength of the mother's contractions and the rate of the baby's heartbeat through electrodes belted onto the mother's abdomen. This machine has become the symbol of high technology hospital birth. Observers and participants alike report that the monitor, once attached, becomes the focal point of the labor.[3] Nurses, physicians, husbands, and even the mother herself become visually and conceptually glued to the machine, which then shapes their perceptions and interpretations of the birth process. Diana Crosse described her experience this way:

As soon as I got hooked up to the monitor, all everyone did was stare at it. The nurses didn't even look at me anymore when they came into the room—they went straight to the monitor. I got the weirdest feeling that *it* was having the baby, not me.

This statement illustrates the successful conceptual fusion between the woman's perceptions of her birth experience and the technocratic model. So thoroughly was this model mapped on to her psyche that she began to feel that the machine was having the baby, that she was a mere onlooker. Soon after the monitor was in place, she requested a Cesarean section, declaring that there was "no more point in trying."

Consider the visual and kinesthetic images that the laboring woman experiences—herself in bed, in a hospital gown, staring up at an IV pole, bag, and cord, and down at a steel bed and a huge belt encircling her waist. Her entire sensory field conveys one overwhelming message about our culture's deepest values and beliefs: Technology is supreme, and the individual is utterly dependent upon it.

Internalizing the technocratic model, women come to accept the notion that the female body is inherently defective. This notion then shapes their perceptions of the labor experience, as exemplified by Merry Simpson's story:

> It seemed as though my uterus had suddenly tired! When the nurses in attendance noted a contraction building on the recorder, they instructed me to begin pushing, not waiting for the urge to push, so that by the time the **urge** pervaded, I invariably had no strength remaining but was left gasping and dizzy. . . . I felt suddenly depressed by the fact that labor, which had progressed so uneventfully up to this point, had now become unproductive.

Note that she does not say "The nurses had me pushing too soon," but "My uterus had tired," and labor had "become unproductive." These responses reflect her internalization of the technocratic tenet that when something goes wrong, it is her body's fault.

Affectivity and Intensification

Rituals tend to intensify toward a climax. Behavioral psychologists have long understood that people are far more likely to remember, and to absorb lessons from, those events that carry an emotional charge. The order and stylization of ritual, combined with its rhythmic repetitiveness and the intensification of its messages, methodically create just the sort of highly charged emotional atmosphere that works to ensure long-term learning.

As the moment of birth approaches, the number of ritual procedures performed upon the woman will intensify toward the climax of birth, whether or not her condition warrants such intervention. For example, once the woman's cervix reaches full dilation (10 cm), the nursing staff immediately begins to exhort the woman to push with each contraction, whether or not she actually feels the urge to push. When delivery is imminent, the woman must be transported, often with a great deal of drama and haste, down the hall to the delivery room. Lest the baby be born *en route,* the laboring woman is then exhorted, with equal vigor, *not* to push. Such commands constitute a complete denial of the natural rhythms of the woman's body. They signal that her labor is a mechanical event and that she is subordinate to the institution's expectations and schedule. Similar high drama will pervade the rest of her birthing experience.

Preservation of the Status Quo

A major function of ritual is cultural preservation. Through explicit enactment of a culture's belief system, ritual works both to preserve and to transmit the culture. Preserving the culture includes perpetuating its power structure, so it is usually the case that those in positions of power will have unique control over ritual performance. They will utilize the effectiveness of ritual to reinforce both their own importance and the importance of the belief and value system that legitimizes their positions.

In spite of tremendous advances in equality for women, the United States is still a patriarchy. It is no cultural accident that 99 percent of American women give birth in hospitals, where only physicians, most of whom are male, have final authority over the performance of birth rituals—an authority that reinforces the cultural privileging of patriarchy for both mothers and their medical attendants.

Nowhere is this reality more visible than in the lithotomy position. Despite years of effort on the part of childbirth activists, including many obstetricians, the majority of American women still give birth lying flat on their backs. This position is physiologically dysfunctional. It compresses major blood vessels, lowering the mother's circulation and thus the baby's oxygen supply. It increases the need for forceps because it both narrows the pelvic outlet and ensures that the baby, who must follow the curve of the birth canal, quite literally will be born heading upward, against gravity. This lithotomy position completes the process of symbolic inversion that has been in motion ever since the woman was put into that "upside-down" hospital gown. Her normal bodily patterns are turned, quite literally, upside-down—her legs are in the air, her vagina totally exposed. As the ultimate symbolic inversion, it is ritually appropriate that this position be reserved for the peak tranformational moments of the initiation experience—the birth itself. The doctor—society's official representative—stands in control not at the mother's head nor at her side, but at her bottom, where the baby's head is beginning to emerge.

Structurally speaking, this puts the woman's vagina where her head should be. Such total inversion is perfectly appropriate from a social perspective, as the technocratic model promises us that eventually we will be able to grow babies in machines—that is, have them with our cultural heads instead of our natural bottoms. In our culture, "up" is good and "down" is bad, so the babies born of science and technology must be delivered "up" toward the positively valued cultural world, instead of down toward the negatively valued natural world. Interactionally, the obstetrician is "up" and the birthing woman is "down," an inversion that speaks eloquently to her of her powerlessness and of the power of society at the supreme moment of her own individual transformation.

The episiotomy performed by the obstetrician just before birth also powerfully enacts the status quo in American society. This procedure, performed on over 90 percent of first-time mothers as they give birth, expresses the value and importance of one of our technocratic society's most fundamental markers—the straight line. Through episiotomies, physicians can deconstruct the vagina (stretchy, flexible, part-circular and part-formless, feminine, creative, sexual, non-linear), then reconstruct it in accordance with our cultural belief and value system. Doctors are taught (incorrectly) that straight cuts heal faster than the small jagged tears that sometimes occur during birth. They learn that straight cuts will prevent such tears, but in fact, episiotomies often cause severe tearing that would not otherwise occur (Klein 1992; Shiono et al. 1990; Thorp and Bowes 1989; Wilcox et al. 1989[4]). These teachings dramatize our Western belief in the superiority of culture over nature. Because it virtually does not exist in nature, the line is most useful in aiding us in our constant conceptual efforts to separate ourselves from nature.

Moreover, since surgery constitutes the ultimate form of manipulation of the human body-machine, it is the most highly valued form of medicine. Routinizing the episiotomy, and increasingly, the Cesarean section, has served both to legitimize and to raise the status of obstetrics as a profession, by ensuring that childbirth will be not a natural but a surgical procedure.

Effecting Social Change

Paradoxically, ritual, with all of its insistence on continuity and order, can be an important factor not only in individual transformation but also in social change. New belief and value systems are most effectively spread through new rituals designed to enact and transmit them; entrenched belief and value systems are most effectively altered through alterations in the rituals that enact them.

Nine percent of my interviewees entered the hospital determined to avoid technocratic rituals in order to have "completely natural childbirth," yet ended up with highly technocratic births. These nine women experienced extreme cognitive dissonance between their previously held self-images and those internalized in the hospital. Most of them suffered severe emotional wounding and short-term post-partum depression as a result. But 15 percent did achieve their goal of natural childbirth, thereby avoiding conceptual fusion with the technocratic model. These women were personally empowered by their birth experiences. They tended to view technology as a resource that they could choose to utilize or ignore, and often consciously subverted their socialization process by replacing technocratic symbols with self-empowering alternatives. For example, they wore their own clothes and ate their own food, rejecting the hospital gown and the IV. They walked the halls instead of going to bed. They chose perineal massage instead of episiotomy, and gave birth like "primitives," sitting up, squatting, or on their hands and knees. One of them, confronted with the wheelchair, said "I don't need this," and used it as a luggage cart. This rejection of customary ritual elements is an exceptionally powerful way to induce change, as it takes advantage of an already charged and dramatic situation.

During the 1970s and early 1980s, the conceptual hegemony of the technocratic model in the hospital was severely challenged by the natural childbirth movement which these 24 women represent. Birth activists succeeded in getting hospitals to allow fathers into labor and delivery rooms, mothers to birth consciously (without being put to sleep), and mothers and babies to room together after birth. They fought for women to have the right to birth without drugs or interventions, to walk around or even be in water during labor (in some hospitals, Jacuzzis were installed). Prospects for change away from the technocratic model of birth by the 1990s seemed bright.

Changing a society's belief and value system by changing the rituals that enact it is possible, but not easy. To counter attempts at change, individuals in positions of authority often intensify the rituals that support the status quo. Thus a response to the threat posed by the natural childbirth movement was to intensify the use of high technology in hospital birth. During the 1980s, periodic electronic monitoring of nearly all women became standard procedure, the epidural rate shot up to 80 percent, and the Cesarean rate rose to nearly 25 percent. Part of the impetus for this technocratic intensification is the increase in malpractice suits against physicians. The threat of lawsuit forces doctors to practice conservatively—that is, in strict accordance with technocratic standards. As one of them explained,

> Certainly I've changed the way I practice since malpractice became an issue. I do more C-sections . . . and more and more tests to cover myself. More expensive stuff. We don't do risky things that women ask for—we're very conservative in our approach to everything. . . . In 1970 before all this came up, my C-section rate was around 4 percent. It has gradually climbed every year since then. In 1985 it was 16 percent, then in 1986 it was 23 percent.

The money goes where the values lie. From this macro-cultural perspective, the increase in malpractice suits emerges as society's effort to make sure that its representatives, the obstetricians, perpetuate our technocratic core value system by continuing through birth rituals to transmit that system. Its perpetuation seems imperative, for in our technology we see the promise of our eventual transcendence of bodily and earthly limitations—already we replace body parts with computerized devices, grow babies in test tubes, build space stations, and continue to pollute the environment in the expectation that someone will develop the technologies to clean it up!

We are all complicitors in our technocratic system, as we have so very much invested in it. Just as that system has given us increasing control over the natural environment, so it has also given not only doctors but also women increasing control over biology and birth. Contemporary middle-class women do have much greater say over what will be done to them during birth than their mothers, most of whom gave birth during the 1950s and 1960s under general anesthesia. When what they demand is in accord with technocratic values, they have a much greater chance of getting it than their sisters have of achieving natural childbirth. Even as hospital birth still perpetuates partriarchy by treating women's bodies as defective machines, it now also reflects women's greater autonomy by allowing them conceptual separation from those defective machines.

Epidural anesthesia is administered in about 80 percent of American hospital births. So common is its use that many childbirth educators are calling the 1990s the age of the "epidural epidemic." As the epidural numbs the birthing woman, eliminating the pain of childbirth, it also graphically demonstrates to her through lived experience the truth of the Cartesian maxim that mind and body are separate, that the biological realm can be completely cut off from the realm of the intellect and the emotions. The epidural is thus the perfect technocratic tool, serving the interests of the technocratic model by transmitting it, and of women choosing to give birth under that model, by enabling them to use it to divorce themselves from their biology:

> Ultimately the decision to have the epidural and the Cesarean while I was in labor was mine. I told my doctor I'd had enough of this labor business and I'd like to . . . get it over with. So he whisked me off to the delivery room and we did it. (Elaine)

For many women, the epidural provides a means by which they can actively witness birth while avoiding "dropping into biology." Explained Joanne, "I'm not real fond of things that remind me I'm a biological creature— I prefer to think and be an intellectual emotional person." Such women tended to define their bodies as tools, vehicles for their minds. They did not enjoy "giving in to biology" to be pregnant, and were happy to be liberated from biology during birth. And they welcomed advances in birth technologies as extensions of their own ability to control nature.

In dramatic contrast, six of my interviewees (6 percent), insisting that "I am my body," rejected the technocratic model altogether. They chose to give birth at home under an alternative paradigm, the *holistic model*. This model stresses the organicity and trustworthiness of the female body, the natural rhythmicity of labor, the integrity of the family, and self-responsibility. These homebirthers see the safety of the baby and the emotional needs of the mother as one. The safest birth for the baby will be the one that provides the most nurturing environment for the mother.[5] Said Ryla,

> I got criticized for choosing a home birth, for not considering the safety of the baby. But that's exactly what I was considering! How could it

possibly serve my baby for me to give birth in a place that causes my whole body to tense up in anxiety as soon as I walk in the door?

Although homebirthers constitute only about 2 percent of the American birthing population, their conceptual importance is tremendous, as through the alternative rituals of giving birth at home, they enact—and thus guarantee the existence of—a paradigm of pregnancy and birth based on the value of connection, just as the technocratic model is based on the principle of separation.

The technocratic and holistic models represent opposite ends of a spectrum of beliefs about birth and about cultural life. Their differences are mirrored on a wider scale by the ideological conflicts between biomedicine and holistic healing, and between industrialists and ecological activists. These groups are engaged in a core value struggle over the future—a struggle clearly visible in the profound differences in the rituals they daily enact.

CONCLUSION

Every society in the world has felt the need to thoroughly socialize its citizens into conformity with its norms, and citizens derive many benefits from such socialization. If a culture had to rely on policemen and make sure that everyone would obey its laws, it would disintegrate into chaos, as there would not be enough policemen to go around. It is much more practical for cultures to find ways to socialize their members from the *inside*, by making them *want* to conform to society's norms. Ritual is one major way through which such socialization can be achieved.

American obstetrical procedures can be understood as rituals that facilitate the internalization of cultural values. These procedures are patterned, repetitive, and profoundly symbolic, communicating messages concerning our culture's deepest beliefs about the necessity for cultural control of natural processes. They provide an ordered structure to the chaotic flow of the natural birth process. In so doing, they both enhance the natural affectivity of that process and create a sense of inevitability about their performance. Obstetric interventions are also transformative in intent. They attempt to contain and control the process of birth, and to transform the birthing woman into an American mother who has internalized the core values of this society. Such a mother believes in science, relies on technology, recognizes her biological inferiority (either consciously or unconsciously), and so at some level accepts the principles of patriarchy. She will tend to conform to society's dictates and meet the demands of its institutions, and will teach her children to do the same.

Yet it is important to note that human beings are not automatons. Human behavior varies widely even within the restraints imposed by particular cultures, including their rituals. As July Sanders sums it up:

> It's almost like programming you. You get to the hospital. They put you in this wheelchair. They whisk you off from your husband, and I mean just start in on you. Then they put you in another wheelchair, and send you home. And then they say, well, we need to give you something for the depression. [Laughs] Get away from me! That will help my depression!

Through hospital ritual procedures, obstetrics deconstructs birth, then inverts and reconstructs it as a technocratic process. But unlike most transformations effected by ritual, birth does *not* depend upon the performance of ritual to make it happen. The physiological process of labor itself transports the birthing woman into a naturally transitional situation that carries its own affectivity. Hospital procedures take advantage of that affectivity to transmit the core values of American society to birthing women. From society's perspective, the birth process will not be successful unless the woman and child are properly socialized during the experience, transformed as much by the rituals as by the physiology of birth. In the latter half of this century, women have made great strides in attaining equality with men on many cultural fronts. Yet, as I noted at the beginning, the cultural treatment of birth is one of the most revealing indicators about the status of women in a given society. In the United States, through their ritual transformation during birth, women learn profound lessons about the weakness and defectiveness of their bodies and the power of technology. In this way, every day in hospitals all over the country, women's status as subordinate is subtly reinforced, as is the patriarchal nature of the technocracy.

NOTES

1. The full results of this study appear in Davis-Floyd 1992.
2. In Holland, by way of contrast, most births are attended by midwives who recognize that individual labors have individual rhythms. They can stop and start; can take a few hours or several days. If labor slows, the midwives encourage the woman to eat to keep up her strength, and then to sleep until contractions pick up again (Beatriz Smulders, Personal Communication, 1994; Jordan 1993).
3. As is true for most of the procedures interpreted here as rituals, there is no scientific justification for the routine use of the electronic fetal monitor: Numerous large-scale studies have shown no improvement in outcome (Leveno et al. 1986; Prentice and Lind 1987; Sandmire 1990; Shy et al. 1990). What these studies do show is that a dramatic increase in the rate of Cesarean section accompanies routine electronic monitoring. Most commonly, this increase is due both to the occasional malfunctioning of the machine, which sometimes registers fetal distress when there is none, and to the tendency of hospital staff to overreact to fluctuations on the monitor strip.
4. See Goer 1995: 274–284 for summaries and interpretations of these studies and others concerning electronic fetal monitoring.
5. For summaries of studies that demonstrate the safety of planned, midwife-attended home birth relative to hospital birth, see Davis-Floyd 1992, Chapter 4, and Goer 1995.

REFERENCES

Abrahams, Roger D. 1973. "Ritual for Fun and Profit (or The Ends and Outs of Celebration)." Paper delivered at the Burg Wartenstein

Symposium No. 59, on "Ritual: Reconciliation in Change." New York: Wenner-Gren Foundation for Anthropological Research.

Davis-Floyd, Robbie E. 1992. *Birth as an American Rite of Passage.* Berkeley: University of California Press.

Goer, Henci. 1995. *Obstetric Myths Versus Research Realities: A Guide to the Medical Literature.* Westport, CT: Bergin and Garvey.

Jordan, Brigitte. 1993. *Birth in Four Cultures: A Cross-Cultural Investigation of Birth in Yucatan, Holland, Sweden and the United States* (4th edition revised). Prospect Heights: Waveland Press.

Klein, Michael et al. 1992. "Does Episiotomy Prevent Perineal Trauma and Pelvic Floor Relaxation?" *Online Journal of Current Clinical Trials* 1 (Document 10).

Leveno K. J., F. G. Cunningham, S. Nelson, M. Roark, M. L. Williams, D. Guzick, S. Dowling, C. R. Rosenfeld, A. Buckley. 1986. "A Prospective Comparison of Selective and Universal Electronic Fetal Monitoring in 34,995 Pregnancies." *New England Journal of Medicine* 315 (10): 615–619.

Malinowski, Bronislaw. 1954. (orig. pub. 1925). "Magic, Science, and Religion." In *Magic, Science and Religion and Other Essays*, pp. 17–87. New York: Doubleday/Anchor.

Prentice, A. and T. Lind. 1987. "Fetal Heart Rate Monitoring During Labor—Too Frequent Intervention, Too Little Benefit." *Lancet* 2: 1375–1877.

Reynolds, Peter C. 1991. *Stealing Fire: The Mythology of the Technocracy.* Palo Alto, CA: Iconic Anthropology Press.

Sandmire, H. F. 1990. "Whither Electronic Fetal Monitoring?" *Obstetrics and Gynecology* 76 (6): 1130–1134.

Shaw, Nancy Stoller. 1974. *Forced Labor: Maternity Care in the United States.* New York: Pergamon Press.

Shiono, P., M. A. Klebanoff, and J. C. Carey. 1990. "Midline Episiotomies: More Harm Than Good?" *American Journal of Obstetrics and Gynecology* 75 (5): 765–770.

Shy, Kirkwood, David A. Luthy, Forrest C. Bennett, Michael Whitfield, Eric B. Larson, Gerald van Belle, James P. Hughes, Judith A. Wilson, Martin A. Stenchever. 1990. "Effects of Electronic Fetal Heart Rate Monitoring, as Compared with Periodic Auscultation, on the Neurologic Development of Premature Infants." *New England Journal of Medicine* 322 (9): 588–593.

Thorp, J. M. and W. A. Bowes. 1989. "Episiotomy: Can Its Routine Use Be Defended?" *American Journal of Obstetrics and Gynecology* 160 (5Pt1): 1027–1030.

Turner, Victor. 1979. (orig. pub. 1964). "Betwixt and Between: The Liminal Period in Rites de Passage." In W. Lessa and E. Z. Vogt (eds.). *Reader in Comparative Religion*, pp. 234–243. 4th edition. New York: Harper and Row.

van Gennep, Arnold. 1966. (orig. pub. 1908). *The Rites of Passage.* Chicago: University of Chicago Press.

Wilcox, L. S. et al. 1989. "Episiotomy and Its Role in the Incidence of Perineal Lacerations in a Maternity Center and a Tertiary Hospital Obstetric Service." *American Journal of Obstetrics and Gynecology* 160 (5Pt1): 1047–1052.

The Politics of Reproduction in a Mexican Village

Carol H. Browner

Although women in all societies bear children in private, or with only a select few present, human reproduction is never entirely a personal affair. Kin, neighbors, and other members of the larger collectives of which women are a part seek to influence reproductive behavior in their groups. Their concerns, however, about who reproduces, how often, and when frequently conflict quite sharply with the desires of the reproducers themselves.[1] At the

Reprinted with permission of The University of Chicago Press from *Signs* 11(4):710–724, 1986 © 1986 by The University of Chicago. All rights reserved.

state level, governments develop policies with which they try to shape the size, composition, and distribution of their populations. These policies inevitably seek to influence the reproductive activities of individuals. They may be directed toward the fertility of the whole society or selectively imposed on particular classes, subcultures, or other internal groups,[2] but they are usually promoted without much consideration for the individual women who bear and raise the children, and, as a result, they may not be embraced by their target groups. Further, state-initiated population policies are sometimes challenged by internal groups whose objectives differ from those of the state.[3]

It is surprising that conflicts between the reproductive desires of a society's fecund women and the demographic interests of other individuals, groups, and political entities are rarely explored. After a comprehensive review of research in demography, population studies, and the anthropology and sociology of reproduction, Rosalind Pollack Petchesky reports, "Utterly lacking [in these fields] is any sense that the methods and goals of reproduction, and control over them, may themselves be a contested area within [a] culture."[4] Also absent from this research is the recognition that differential access to a society's sources of power determines how conflicts over reproduction are conducted and resolved, and even whether resolution ever occurs.

The following account analyzes the relationship between the population practices in one indigenous community in Mexico and the Mexican government's recent effort to reduce population growth. It shows that the government's fertility-reducing policy was superimposed on a long-standing local conflict between this community's women, who wished to limit the size of their own families, and the community as a whole, which wanted all of its female members to reproduce abundantly. Despite their apparent concordance with the goals of the state, the women refused the government's contraceptive services. They continued to have many children instead. The discussion will consider both why these indigenous rural women did not act on the fertility desires they expressed and why the demographic policies of Mexico have met

uncertain success; for the two are outcomes of the same phenomenon: an overriding cultural prohibition in that community against any kind of fertility control.

BACKGROUND

The data presented here were collected in 1980–81 in a community I will call San Francisco, a Chinantec-Spanish-speaking *municipio* (township) located five hours by bus from the capital of the state of Oaxaca. The *municipio* was made up of a *cabecera* (head town) and a number of *ranchos* (hamlets) spread over a fifty-kilometer range. A year's participant observation was combined with interviews from a sample selected from the 336 adult women who lived in San Francisco. This sample consisted of 180 women selected to represent the age, residence, and linguistic background of the women. The husbands of the married women were also interviewed, a total of 126 men.

Historically, an important element in women's attempts to control their fertility was the use of medicinal plants. In addition to learning the respondents' reproductive desires and attitudes toward childbearing and child rearing, one aim of the interviews was to determine how the knowledge and use of such plants for management of reproduction and the maintenance of reproductive health were distributed and what might be the social implications of this distribution of knowledge before and after the Mexican government's introduction of modern birth control techniques. Demographic, economic, and health data were also obtained.

The *municipio* consisted of just over three hundred families of subsistence farmers who lived dispersed over its 18,300 hectares. Nearly two-thirds of the households (65 percent) cultivated the community's abundant communal landholdings in the tropical lowlands thirty miles east of the *cabecera*, or three hours from there by bus. The remainder used private plots located either in the *cabecera* or in the highland territory that individual Franciscanos purchased in 1930 from a neighboring *municipio*, or they farmed in both places. About a third of the families (32 percent) lived permanently on lowland ranches while most of the rest divided their time between the town center and the lowlands. Although only 5 percent of the households worked solely for wages, another 80 percent reported cash income from at least occasional wage labor.

Most full-time *rancho* residents had regular contact with the *cabecera*. Men made the trip several times each year to attend mandatory town assemblies. Men were also required to reside in the head town during their terms of civil and/or religious community service (cargos), which required several years of full-time commitment over the course of their lifetimes. Women had no formal reason for regular visits to the *cabecera*, but they sometimes went during holidays. In addition, they were expected to help their husbands carry out cargo responsibilities and often moved with them to the *cabecera* during their husbands' terms of office.

Until about 1965, the *municipio* fit the model of a closed corporate peasant community,[5] maintaining only sporadic contact with the world outside. Since that time, San Francisco's isolation had been sharply reduced by mandatory primary education, the construction of the Oaxaca-Tuxtepec highway and a feeder road connecting the *cabecera* in it, and a growing stream of migrants leaving the area for Oaxaca City, Mexico City, and the United States. Nevertheless, for many residents, daily life was much as it had always been: 42 percent of the women interviewed and 16 percent of the men had never been more than a few miles outside the community.

WOMEN'S ATTITUDES TOWARD PREGNANCY AND CHILDREN

Women in San Francisco expressed sharply negative attitudes about childbearing and child rearing, an unexpected finding that is contrary to the results of most other studies of peasants' attitudes toward fertility in Latin America.[6] While most research has suggested that peasant women want fewer children than

they actually have, it has also suggested that, among these women, three to five children is considered the ideal family size and childlessness is considered a great misfortune. In San Francisco, a very different picture emerged. Among my study population, it was not unusual for women to volunteer that they would have preferred to remain childless or to have far smaller families than they did have. (Sixty of the 180 women interviewed had five or more children.) Sixty-three percent believed that there were women in their community who would choose childlessness if they could. As one informant explained, "The women without children, they're the smart ones"; and yet, as we shall see, choosing childlessness was socially very problematic.[7]

The differences in fertility desires between women and men in San Francisco underscored the women's negative attitudes. Respondents were asked whether they wanted to have more children. The majority of both sexes who still considered themselves of childbearing age said they wanted no more (see table 1), but women were satisfied with far smaller families than were men. The overwhelming majority of the women (80 percent) who had at least one living child said they were content with their present family size. Moreover, of the small number of childless women (N = 9), one-third indicated that they were satisfied to remain so. However, most of the men who were satisfied with family size had at least four children (60 percent), and of the childless men (N = 6), none indicated that he was satisfied.

Women with large families said they resented the demands of child care and the limitations it placed on them. Many saw children as a burden. They considered them too much work, too hard to raise, a source of problems, "war," and domestic strife. They viewed children as pesky disturbances who kept them tied to the house. One woman told me, "[The people of the community] want us to have many children. That's fine for them to say. They don't have to take care of them and keep them clean. My husband sleeps peacefully through the night, but I have to get up when the children need something. I'm the one the baby urinates on; sometimes I have to get out of bed in the cold and change both our clothes. They wake me when they're sick or thirsty, my husband sleeps through it all."

This resentment was balanced to some extent by the women's perception of advantages associated with children. They particularly valued the physical and emotional companionship of their children, in part because the women were extremely reluctant to be at home alone, especially at night. They feared ghosts, phantoms, and spirits and worried about drunks reputed to harass solitary women. Women also tried to avoid going alone on errands out of town, for they feared wild animals and unknown men. They always sought out a child—their own or someone else's—if no other companion could be found.

Overall, however, most Franciscanas did not perceive much practical advantage in rearing large families. There was little economic benefit seen, for the women considered their offspring lazy or too busy with other activities to be of much help. Since mandatory school attendance was strictly enforced in San Francisco, and children were encouraged by school authorities to attend frequent after-school activities, mothers often felt saddled with chores that their children should have done. Although women hoped their offspring would care for them in their old age, the expectation that they would actually do so was changing as children left the village to find employment elsewhere. Interestingly, mothers expressed greater support for their children's migration than did fathers.[8] Nevertheless, the women felt disappointed when they realized that they had been forgotten at home.

In addition to resenting the hard work of raising children and the frustrations of its uncertain rewards, the women in this sample saw frequent pregnancies as physically stressful and even debilitating. In their view, much of a woman's blood supply during pregnancy was devoted to nourishing the developing fetus. This left their own bodies unbalanced and susceptible to the large number of disorders that could be caused by penetration of cold and aire (air, winds). They also saw parturition as a threat to their health, believing that, during childbirth, the womb—and the rest of the body—must "open" to expel the newborn and that this process increased the body's already heightened vulnerability to aire.

Postpartum complications were common among Franciscanas. Of the 180 interviewed, two-thirds reported at least one. They ranged from conditions the women considered relatively minor, such as facial swelling and backaches, to such serious conditions as uterine prolapse and uncontrolled bleeding. Emotional complications were sometimes mentioned as well. For instance, one woman reported that, after the birth of her second child, she was unable to tolerate criticism from her husband's relatives, with whom she and her family then lived. "I wanted to get up and run and run, I had no idea to where," she told me. In addition to the complications of pregnancy per se, women also feared that frequent childbirth and short birth intervals caused menstrual hemorrhaging, exhaustion, and early death. There are no reliable data on postpartum mortality for this particular population, but examples existed in the memories of all women interviewed.

The women's illness experiences that were not related to pregnancy reinforced their understanding that frequent pregnancies harmed their general health. Those who had had four or more pregnancies were significantly more likely than the rest to report at least one serious illness ($c^2 = 7.06$, $P < .001$). Even when age was controlled for, this pattern occurred. Women with four or more pregnancies were also significantly more likely to report a greater number of minor health problems overall, including headaches, backaches, breast problems, and coraje (anger sickness; $c^2 = 6.38$, $P < .025$). Again with age controlled for, women who had had four or more pregnancies were less healthy overall than women who had had fewer pregnancies.

THE CASE FOR LARGE FAMILIES

Despite the desires of many Franciscanas to have few (or no) children, they did not think that they could actually do so. The pressures on them to reproduce were simply too great to ignore. These pressures came most often and overtly from the community's men, who argued that a populous community was vital to the defense of the collectivity and its interests. Women were another source of pressure. Although most wanted few children themselves, they felt that other women were obligated by the needs of the collectivity to bear many children.

Maintaining a sufficient population base was a constant source of concern. San Francisco was surrounded by communities that coveted its comparatively large landholdings. It needed a sizable male population to defend its borders in case of armed attack by neighboring enemy communities who still threatened the *municipio*. One particularly bloody battle in the 1950s claimed the lives of thirteen Franciscanos. Residents also felt threatened by indications that the federal government might resettle members of other communities or ethnic groups onto San Francisco's lands or allocate territory to other *municipios* that were litigating for it because, unlike many rural *municipios*, San Francisco had more land than its population required. Residents were also concerned about the regional government's proposals to consolidate San Francisco with neighboring *municipios* because it was considered far too small to remain independent. The most likely of these plans would combine San Francisco with its most hated and feared enemy.

A number of endogenous factors also threatened the community's population base. Despite the presence in the *cabecera* of two government health centers, disease continued to take a significant toll. The rate of infant mortality in the state was one of Mexico's highest. On average, deaths from all causes in San Francisco had not declined during the past fifteen years.[9] Migration from the community to the state and national capitals and to the United States was also taking increasing numbers of the most able-bodied women and men. In the past two decades, the state of Oaxaca had experienced Mexico's highest rate of outmigration, suffering a net population loss of 290,000 between 1960 and 1970 alone.

Because this trend had continued, Oaxaca's population had grown more slowly than that of any other Mexican state.[10] San Francisco had been acutely affected by these broader demographic trends. Of the women interviewed whose children were grown, nearly two-thirds reported having at least one child who resided outside the *municipio*, and more than one-fourth reported that all their grown children lived elsewhere.

Half of San Francisco's adult population was now over forty years old. As a result of this aging trend, an increasing proportion of the population were experiencing declining physical strength and productivity, which residents felt boded ill for the community's future. One concrete and very important manifestation of these difficulties was the inability of the *municipio* to find enough men to fill the annual eighteen-man quota for civil and religious cargo positions. Moreover, there had been increasing pressure for independence from San Francisco on the part of some of the lowland *rancho* subcommunities (*agencias*); two had already won semiautonomous status from the regional government, and at least one of these was continuing to press for even greater independence.[11] All of these trends led residents of San Francisco to worry about the collectivity's future and to seek ways to diminish the impact of depopulation.

THE BIRTH CONTROL TREE

Although some of the reasons for the depopulation of San Francisco were new, concern about the size and strength of the collectivity was not. The conflict between the collective desire for a large and populous community and individual women's wishes to have few children had had a long, dramatic history in the *municipio*.

On many occasions during my fieldwork, men told me how, some twenty years before, they had cut down a tree whose bark was used by women as a contraceptive. They needed to eliminate the tree, they said, because so many women were refusing to bear children. This is the story the men told: Not far from the town center and just off a popular path to the low-land hamlets was a tree without a name. Its bark turned red when stripped from its trunk and was said to prevent conception. The large old tree was the only one of its kind known to the people of San Francisco. "Who knows where the seed came from," said one elderly resident; "strange it was the only one." Women who wished to avoid pregnancy brewed tea from the bark and drank it prior to intercourse. This would "burn" their wombs and render them temporarily sterile. This tea was dangerous and powerful, "like poison," some said. It could kill an incautious user. Women who drank the tea several times grew emaciated and weak. Even if they subsequently wished to bear children, as many as eight years might pass before a pregnancy.

Some said the users went secretly at night to get bark from the tree. Others thought that itinerant peddler women from an enemy town secretly sold Franciscanas strips of the dried bark along with other wares. Said one man, "It was they who deceived our women into not wanting children because they didn't want our town to grow."

A group of San Francisco's men were at work one day cutting back brush from the path that passed near the tree. They could see it from where they worked, almost stripped of its bark from frequent use. "Let's get rid of it," one of them said quietly; "we must have more children in this town." The others quickly agreed. "So," explained one who had been there, "we cut down the tree and tore its roots right out." They used the trunk to restore a nearby bridge in disrepair and returned home tired but satisfied with their work. (In an alternate version of the story, the men saw the tree, were angered, and stripped it entirely of its bark, causing it to die.)

I asked some of the men who said they were responsible for the act why they had killed the tree. "We were angry," one told me. "The women weren't having babies. They were lazy and didn't want to produce children." Another said that the women "had stopped making children. We were working hard with our men's work, but they weren't doing any of their women's work." One who

said he remembered the incident explained that "the town was small and we wanted it to grow. We wanted a big town and we needed more people. But the women wouldn't cooperate." A woman I interviewed saw the men's motives differently. "The men depended on the women," she said. "They couldn't have their children by themselves. But the women were walking free. The men pulled out the tree to control the women so they'd have children for them."

My research in San Francisco led me to ask often about the birth control tree. Every man I asked had heard of it although none could tell me its name or show me one like it. These days, they explained, people seldom passed the spot where it had grown because a better road to the lowlands had been built. After weeks of asking, I nearly concluded that the tree was only a myth. Persistence finally led me to a woman who said her husband could show me the tree. He was more than reluctant to comply. "What if people found out that it has grown back?" he said. "What if they began to use it again? Then what would happen to the town?"

I continued to press him. Finally, he said he would not show me the tree but would take my field assistant's nine-year-old son to see it. The boy could later lead me to the spot. During the same period, one of the men who said he had participated in the destruction of the tree agreed to see if it had possibly regenerated. During different weeks, each of the two informants independently led me to the same clump of *Styrax argenteus*. As the second man showed me the abundant young growth, he expressed surprise that several had grown where only one had been.

The women I asked about the tree were consistently less informative than the men. While all the men knew of the birth control tree, the majority of women said they had never even heard of it, let alone used it to avoid pregnancy. The men did not believe the women were as ignorant as they claimed. I asked one man how the men had learned of the tree if the women had used it only in secret. He replied, "Of course the women think they have their secrets. But we men were able to find out. They have no secrets from us."

THE WOMEN'S RESPONSES
TO PRESSURES TO REPRODUCE

There are several morals to this story, but the inevitability of negative reactions to behaviors that place individual interests above those of the collectivity is a very important one. In San Francisco, married women with few or no children were seen as selfish and socially negligent regardless of whether their low fertility was natural or willfully induced. Such women were particularly vulnerable to gossip, much of which centered on their fertility behavior. They were sharply and repeatedly criticized for causing miscarriages and using contraceptives. Some were even accused of infanticide. All of their acts were carefully monitored by relatives and other interested parties to detect any efforts to avoid pregnancy. For example, lemon juice was widely regarded as a contraceptive and an abortifacient.[12] After failing to conceive during her first year of marriage, one woman fell subject to her mother-in-law's constant gossip and criticism for avoiding her reproductive responsibilities by eating too much of the fruit. Another woman determinedly broke her young daughter of the habit of enjoying lemons, for she feared that they would damage her daughter's fertility.

Women with small families were susceptible to gossip about marital infidelity, which diminished the social status of their husbands as well. As a middle-aged mother of six explained, "The women who are most likely to go with other men are the ones who don't have much work to do. They have time for sex. But if you have a lot of kids like I do, you have to work very hard all the time. The tiredness takes over at the end of the day and you don't have time to think about the husbands of other women. You don't have time to go out looking for men." The targets of such gossip attributed it to envy of the relative wealth and freedom they enjoyed as a result of having small families— and they adamantly denied that their low fertility was due to contraceptives.

Contraceptives were, however, readily available at the town's two government-run health centers; one even provided the services free of charge. The Mexican government's interest in lowering its national birth rate had led it since 1972 to promote family planning aggressively.[13] The walls of both clinics were decorated almost exclusively with posters demonstrating the benefits of small families and *paternidad responsable* (responsible parenthood).[14] They were written in simple language with humorous illustrations. The text of a typical one read: "What will happen when we are more? We will have less money . . . less food . . . less education . . . less space . . . less clothing . . . less peace. You can avoid these problems if you plan your family. Now planning is easier! Consult the family doctor at the Social Security Clinic although you may not be insured. *The consultation is free.*"[15] Each clinic assigned its staff monthly inscription quotas for new contraceptive users. Health center personnel were expected to undertake house-to-house campaigns to introduce fecund women to modern birth control techniques.

Overwhelmingly, Franciscanas rejected these government services. For the period between January 1980 and February 1981, records from the two clinics indicated that thirteen Franciscanas initiated contraceptive use—only 7 percent of women between the ages of eighteen and forty-five. These women used contraceptives for an average of just 3.5 months before stopping, and only one continued using contraceptives for longer than six months.

When I asked several who said they wanted no more children why they did not seek the means to avoid pregnancy, they revealed an extreme reluctance to engage in socially disapproved behavior. Some indicated they would never consider obtaining birth control from government clinics because they would be ashamed to be publicly "registered" as a user of contraceptives. This same fear of community censure led women to avoid other means of fertility control and even the kinds of behavior that could be construed as attempts at fertility limitation. When I naively asked one of the town midwives if she had ever been asked to perform an abortion, she looked at me and said, "They wouldn't dare." Similarly, a Franciscana suffering from menstrual delay was afraid to inquire locally for a remedy. Even though she was convinced that she was not pregnant, she was sure she would be accused of abortion if she took a remedy to induce menstrual bleeding.

The women responded to these pressures to reproduce not simply by refusing to use contraceptives but also by denying they knew anything whatsoever about ways to limit fertility. It seemed they felt that merely possessing information would be interpreted as evidence of their malevolent intentions. When I asked women the direct question, "Do you know of any herbs or other remedies that can be used to avoid pregnancy?" only 11 percent mentioned specific techniques such as the infamous birth control tree. Another 6 percent said they believed that ways existed but knew of none themselves. The remaining 83 percent said they believed there were no traditional ways to avoid getting pregnant. An even larger proportion (86 percent) said they knew no ways to induce an abortion. Even Franciscanas who considered themselves authorities on a great many subjects pleaded ignorance when it came to birth limitation.

Denial, however, did not necessarily imply ignorance. Probes revealed that 60 percent who had initially said they knew no ways to limit births had at least heard of the existence of techniques for fertility limitation. The vast majority of these respondents named modern rather than traditional methods and the responses were often quite oblique. For example, to the questions, "Is there anything that can be done to not have children if one doesn't want to have them? If so, what things?" typical responses were: "Yes, in the health center"; "I know the doctor has some"; "They say there are pills, medicines." Other replies explicitly identified the government as the source of contraceptives, shifting the question away from indigenous techniques for birth limitation to methods made available from outside the community. For example, "These days the government doesn't allow people to have so many children. It gives them medicines so they won't"; and "There used to be lots of herbs. Now, the government sends us doctors."

Yet none of the affirmative responses to the questions about knowledge of birth control could be interpreted as endorsements of contraceptive use. No respondent seemed to regard the available fertility-limiting techniques as liberating or as helping them to achieve their expressed goals of having small families. In fact, when responding affirmatively to the probe concerning their knowledge of contraceptives, the women would frequently volunteer a disclaimer in an apparent effort to dissociate themselves even further from the information, even though the probe did not concern their own experiences with contraceptives. For instance; "Well, yes, I have heard that there are medicines available, but I haven't tried them"; "Yes, there are remedies in the health center, but I haven't looked into it"; and, "They say there are medicines in the health center, but I myself haven't used any." Even most of those few in my study population (four out of six women) whose health center records revealed a history of contraceptive use strenuously denied use when directly asked during interviews.

Others told me with extreme caution what they knew about contraception. Some who during interviews had denied all knowledge of contraceptive methods subsequently came to my house to tell me about plants or other techniques that had previously "escaped" their memories. Even knowledge that seemed to me benign was very reluctantly conveyed if it pertained to birth limitation. For example, after initially denying she knew any remedies to induce an abortion, one woman reconsidered and whispered, "I don't know if this would really work, but some say that it can: carrying heavy loads, carrying heavy tumplines of firewood every day, doing a lot of laundry. It's said this can make one abort." Although this idea might be inferred from the circumstances under which miscarriages were observed to have occurred, women carefully guarded even this much knowledge, for they feared it would be incriminating.

IMPLICATIONS OF THE RESEARCH

These data shed light on the context in which a national population planning program was experienced in a rural indigenous community. The context was political, economic, civic, and cultural. On the part of the Mexican government, the decision to promote family planning among indigenous populations was politically delicate, for many Mexican nationalists regard the preservation of their Indian cultural heritage as fundamental to their cultural identity as Mexicans, and aggressive programs to limit the growth of indigenous groups may be perceived as cultural genocide.[16] However, because economic development could not keep pace, the need to check population growth proved more pressing than the state's concerns with the politics of ethnic preservation. Terry L. McCoy has shown, moreover, that the recognition that the government could be destabilized by unchecked growth among less than fully loyal social classes and cultural groups provided significant impetus for the Mexican population policy.[17] In Mexico, as in other developing countries, such policies are used to further state consolidation.

A reduction in San Francisco's rate of population growth was, as we have seen, the last thing the male guardians of the collectivity wanted. While appreciating the value of birth control for the nation in the abstract, and in some cases even wishing for relatively small families themselves, the men unambivalently rejected family planning for the people of San Francisco. In contrast, the women were caught between their desires to have very few children and inexorable local social pressures to be prolific. Because of this pressure, government family planning services could not help the women achieve their own fertility goals. In fact, the existence of these services may have made it even more difficult for the women to practice covert fertility limitation: with the availability of modern contraceptives in the community, women fell under even more suspicion than before.

It has all too often been assumed that women's reproductive goals could be understood by analyzing those of the larger collectivities of which they are a part. However, when collectivities have specific fertility goals, it is reasonable to expect that these goals will conflict with the reproductive desires of at least some of the female members of the group. The extent to which women successfully implement their individual fertility goals depends on a number of factors that vary according to the characteristics of the particular society in which they live. These include the nature of the gender-based power relations and the extent to which women feel they can support one another in controversy. In stratified societies, issues related to social class and ethnicity also play a part, and women may be torn by conflicting sets of interests.[18] Studies that fail to consider *both* these broad sociopolitical conditions and the interests and desires of individual women will understate the complexity, misrepresent the realities, and yield questionable conclusions about reproductive policy and reproductive behavior.

Support for this research was generously provided by grants from the National Science Foundation (BNS-8016431), National Institute for Child Health Development (HD-04612), and the Wenner-Gren Foundation for Anthropological Research (3387). Arthur J. Rubel provided truly valuable assistance during all phases of this research, including the production of this report. Judith Friedlander's suggestions also contributed importantly to the manuscript.

NOTES

1. Burton Benedict, "Social Regulation of Fertility," in *The Structure of Human Populations*, ed. G. A. Harrison and A. J. Boyce (Oxford: Clarendon Press, 1972), 73–89; Carole Browner, "Abortion Decision Making: Some Findings from Colombia," *Studies in Family Planning* 10, no. 3 (1979): 96–106; Thomas K. Burch and Murray Gendall, "Extended Family Structure and Fertility: Some Conceptual and Methodological Issues," in *Culture and Population: A Collection of Current Studies*, ed. Steven Polgar (Cambridge, Mass.: Schenkman Publishing Co.; Chapel Hill, N.C.: Carolina Population Center, 1971), 87–104; Ronald Freedman, "The Sociology of Human Fertility: A Trend Report and Bibliography," *Current Sociology* 10/11, no. 2 (1961–62): 35–121; Frank Lorimer, *Culture and*

Human Fertility: A Study of the Relation of Cultural Conditions to Fertility in Nonindustrial and Transitional Societies (Paris: Unesco, 1958); John F. Marshall, Susan Morris, and Steven Polgar, "Culture and Natality: A Preliminary Classified Bibliography," *Current Anthropology* 13, no. 2 (April 1972): 268–78; Moni Nag, *Factors Affecting Human Fertility in Nonindustrial Societies: A Cross-cultural Study* (New Haven, Conn.: Human Relations Area Files Press, 1976); Steven Polgar, "Population History and Population Policies from an Anthropological Perspective," *Current Anthropology* 13, no. 2 (April 1972): 203–11.

2. Bernard Berelson, *Population Policy in Developed Countries* (New York: McGraw-Hill Book Co., 1974); J. C. Caldwell, "Population Policy: A Survey of Commonwealth Africa," in *The Population of Tropical Africa*, ed. John C. Caldwell and Chukuka Okonjo (New York: Columbia University Press, 1968), 368–75; Leslie Corsa and Deborah Oakley, *Population Planning* (Ann Arbor: University of Michigan Press, 1979), chap. 5, 155–94; William L. Langer, "Checks on Population Growth, 1750–1850," *Scientific American* 226, no. 2 (1972): 92–99; Benjamin White, "Demand for Labor and Population Growth in Colonial Java," *Human Ecology* 1, no. 3 (1973): 217–39.

3. Ad Hoc Women's Studies Committee Against Sterilization Abuse, *Workbook on Sterilization and Sterilization Abuse* (Bronxville, N.Y.: Sarah Lawrence College, 1978); Toni Cade, "The Pill: Genocide or Liberation?" in *The Black Woman*, ed. Toni Cade (New York: New American Library, 1970), 162–69; Lucinda Cisler, "Unfinished Business: Birth Control and Women's Liberation," in *Sisterhood Is Powerful: An Anthology of Writings from the Women's Liberation Movement*, ed. Robin Morgan (New York: Vintage Books, 1970), 245–89; Sally Covington, "Is 'Broader' Better? Reproductive Rights and Elections '84," *Taking Control: The Magazine of the Reproductive Rights National Network* 1, no. 1 (1984): 6–8; Boston Women's Health Book Collective, *Our Bodies, Ourselves: A Book by and for Women* (New York: Simon & Schuster, 1971); Reproductive Rights National Network, "Caught in the Crossfire: Third World Women and Reproductive Rights," *Reproductive Rights Newsletter* 5, no. 3 (Autumn 1983): 1–13; Helen Rodriguez-Trias, *Sterilization Abuse* (New York: Barnard College, Women's Center, 1978).

4. Rosalind Pollack Petchesky, *Abortion and Woman's Choice: The State, Sexuality, and Reproduction Freedom* (New York and London: Longman, Inc., 1984), esp. 10.

5. Eric R. Wolf, "Types of Latin American Peasantry: A Preliminary Discussion," *American Anthropologist* 57 (1955): 452–71, and "Closed Corporate Peasant Communities in Mesoamerica and Central Java," *Southwestern Journal of Anthropology* 13 (1957): 1–18.

6. Clifford R. Barnett, Jean Jackson, and Howard M. Cann, "Childspacing in a Highland Guatemala Community," in *Polgar*, ed. (n. 1 above), 139–48; Paula H. Hass, "Contraceptive Choices for Latin American Women," *Populi* 3 (1976): 14–24; Jenifer Oberg, "Natality in a Rural Village in Northern Chile," in *Polgar*, ed., 124–38; Michele Goldzieher Shedlin and Paula E. Hollerbach, "Modern and Traditional Fertility Regulation in a Mexican Community: The Process of Decision-Making," *Studies in Family Planning* 12, no. 6/7 (1981): 278–96. John Mayone Stycos, *Ideology, Faith, and Family Planning in Latin America: Studies in Public and Private Opinion on Fertility Control* (New York: McGraw-Hill Book Co., 1971).

7. It should be noted that the women's professed negative attitudes toward childbearing and child rearing generally were not apparent in their behavior toward their children.

8. C. H. Browner, "Gender Roles and Social Change: A Mexican Case," *Ethnology* 25, no. 2 (April 1986): 89–106.

9. Arthur J. Rubel, "Some Unexpected Health Consequences of Political Relations in Mexico" (paper presented at the eighty-second annual meeting of the American Anthropological Association, Chicago, 1983).

10. Consejo Nacional de Población México (CONAPO), *México Demográfico: Breviario* (Mexico City: CONAPO, 1979), 52, 78. More recent statistics on out-migration are not available.

11. Anselmo Hernandez Lopez, personal communication, Oaxaca, Mexico, 1981.

12. C. H. Browner and Bernard Ortiz de Montellano, "Herbal Emmenagogues Used by Women in Colombia and Mexico," in *Plants Used in Indigenous Medicine: A Biocultural Approach*, ed. Nina Etkin (New York: Docent Publishers, 1986), 32–47.

13. Victor Urquidi et al., *La explosión humana* (Mexico City: Litoarte, 1974); Frederick C. Turner, *Responsible Parenthood: The Politics of Mexico's New Population Policies* (Washington, D.C.: American Enterprise Institute for Public Policy Research, 1974).

14. This official slogan of the government's population control program was chosen to emphasize the concrete advantages of small

families to individual couples rather than the macrodemographic benefits of a reduced national birth rate (Terry L. McCoy, "A Paradigmatic Analysis of Mexican Population Policy," in *The Dynamics of Population Policy in Latin America*, ed. Terry L. McCoy [Cambridge, Mass.: Ballinger Publishing Co., 1974], 377–408, esp. 397).

15. Mexico City: Instituto Mexicano de Seguro Social (IMSS); italics in original. In the mid-1960s, the government's Social Solidarity Program (Solidaridad Social) extended the social security health system to cover the health needs of some rural areas. Family planning services were part of the coverage.

16. [Gonzalo] Aquirre Beltrán, *Obra polémica* (Mexico City: Instituto Nacional de Antropología e Historia, 1976); Luis Leñero Otero, *Valores ideológicos y las políticas de población en México* (Mexico City: Editorial Edicol, 1979), 115–17.

17. McCoy, 377–408.

18. Floya Anthias and Nira Yuval-Davis, "Contextualizing Feminism: Gender, Ethnic and Class Divisions," *Feminist Review* 15 (Winter 1983): 62–75, esp. 70–71.

Surrogate Motherhood: Rethinking Biological Models, Kinship, and Family

Heléna Ragoné

In the wake of publicity created by the Baby M Case[1] it seems unlikely that anyone in the United States can have remained unfamiliar with surrogate motherhood or can have failed to form an opinion. The Baby M Case raised, and ultimately left unanswered, many questions about what constitutes motherhood, fatherhood, family, reproduction, and kinship. When I began my field research in 1987, surrogate mother programs and directors had already become the subject of considerable media attention, a great deal of it sensationalized and negative in character. Much of what has been written about surrogate motherhood, has, however, been largely speculative or polemic in nature. Opinions have ranged from the view that surrogate motherhood is symptomatic of the dissolution of the American family[2] and the sanctity of motherhood, to charges that it reduces or assigns women to a breeder class structurally akin to prostitution (Dworkin 1978), or that it constitutes a form of commercial baby selling (Annas 1988; Neuhaus 1988).

Data for this chapter derive from nine years of ongoing ethnographic research.

Original material prepared for this text.

Twenty-eight formal interviews with traditional surrogates and twenty-six with gestational surrogates were conducted, as well as twenty-six interviews with individual members of couples (i.e., individuals who had enlisted the services of traditional as well as gestational surrogates) and five interviews with ovum donors. Aside from these formal interviews I also engaged in countless conversations with surrogates, observing them as they interacted with their families, testified before legislative committees, worked in surrogate programs, and socialized at program gatherings with directors and others. The opportunity to observe the daily workings of the surrogate mother programs provided me with invaluable data on the day-to-day operations of such programs. I attended the staff meetings of one such program on a regular basis and observed the consultations in which prospective couples and surrogates were interviewed singly by such members of the staff as the director, a psychologist, a medical coordinator, or the administrative coordinator.

In addition to these formal interviews I conducted thousands of hours of participant observation and was able to observe numerous consultations between program staff, intending couples, and prospective surrogate mothers. I have attempted, whenever possible, to select individuals from the various phases of the traditional and gestational surrogacy process: those individuals who have not yet been matched, those who are newly matched and are attempting "to get pregnant," those who have confirmed pregnancies, and those who have recently given birth, as well as those for whom several years have elapsed since the birth of their child. My decision to interview individuals in all stages of the process has been motivated by my wish to assess what, if any, shifts individuals might experience as they go through the process.

Historically there have been three profound shifts in the Western conceptualization of the categories of conception, reproduction, and parenthood. The first occurred in response to the separation of intercourse from reproduction through birth control methods (Snowden et al. 1983), a precedent that may have paved the way for surrogate motherhood in the 1980s (Andrews 1984:xiii). A second shift occurred in response to the emergence of assisted reproductive technologies (ARTs) and to the subsequent fragmentation of the unity of reproduction, when it became possible for pregnancy to occur without necessarily having been "preceded by sexual intercourse" (Snowden et al. 1983:5). The third shift occurred in response to further advances in reproductive medicine that called into question the "organic unity of fetus and mother" (Martin 1987:20). It was not, however, until the emergence of reproductive medicine that the fragmentation of motherhood became a reality; with that historical change what was once the "single figure of the mother is dispersed among several potential figures, as the functions of maternal procreation—aspects of her physical parenthood—become dispersed" (Strathern 1991:32).

TRADITIONAL SURROGACY

There are two types of surrogate mother programs: "open" programs, in which surrogate and couple select one another and interact throughout the insemination and the pregnancy, and "closed" programs, in which couples select their surrogates from biographical and medical information and a photograph of the surrogate is provided to them by programs. After the child is born in a "closed" program, the couple and surrogate meet only to finalize the step-parent adoption. Due to advances in reproductive medicine and to consumer demand, there are now also two types of surrogacy: traditional surrogacy in which the surrogate contributes an ovum to the creation of the child, and gestational or in-vitro fertilization (IVF) surrogacy where the surrogate gestates the couple's embryos.

Studies of the surrogate population tend to focus, at times exclusively, on surrogates' stated motivations for becoming surrogate mothers (Parker 1983). Their stated reasons include the desire to help an infertile couple start a family, financial remuneration, and a love of pregnancy (Parker 1983:140). Soon after I began my own research, I observed a remarkable degree of consistency or uniformity in surrogates' responses to questions about their initial motivations for becoming surrogates. It was as if they had all been given a script in which they espoused many of the motivations earlier catalogued by Parker: motivations that also, as I will show, reflect culturally accepted ideas about reproduction, motherhood, and family.

I also began to uncover several areas of conflict between professed motivations and actual experiences, discovering, for example, that although surrogates claim to experience "easy pregnancies" and "problem-free labor," it was not unusual for surrogates to have experienced miscarriages, ectopic pregnancies, and related difficulties. For example, Jeannie, age 36, divorced with one child, described the ectopic pregnancy she experienced while she was a traditional surrogate in this manner: "*I almost bled to death: I literally almost died for my couple.*" Nevertheless, she was again inseminated a second time for the same couple. As this and other cases demonstrate, even when their experiences are at odds with their stated motivations, surrogates tend not to acknowledge inconsistencies between their initially stated motivations and their subsequent experiences. This reformulation of motivations can be seen in the following instance. Fran, age 27, divorced with one child, described the difficulty of her delivery in this way: "*I had a rough delivery, a C-section, and my lung collapsed because I had the flu but it was worth every minute of it. If I were to die from childbirth, that's the best way to die. You died for a cause, a good one.*" As both these examples illustrate, some surrogates readily embrace the idea of meaningful suffering, heroism, or sacrifice, and although their stated motivations are of some interest they do not adequately account for the range of shifting motivations uncovered in my research.

One of the motivations most frequently assumed to be primary by the casual observer is remuneration and I took considerable pains in trying to evaluate the influence of monetary rewards on surrogates. In all programs, surrogates receive between $10,000 and $15,000 (for three to four months of insemination and nine months of pregnancy, on average), a fee that has changed only nominally since the early 1980s. As one program psychologist explained, the amount paid to surrogates is intentionally held at an artificially low rate so as to screen out women who might be motivated by monetary gain alone. One of the questions I sought to explore was whether surrogates were denying the significance of remuneration in order to cast their actions in the more culturally acceptable light of pure altruism, or whether they were motivated, at least in part, by remuneration and in part by other factors with the importance of remuneration decreasing as the pregnancy progressed, the version of events put forth by both program staff and surrogates.

The opinion popular among both scholars and the general population, that surrogates are motivated primarily by financial gain, has tended to result in oversimplified analyses of surrogate motivations. More typical of surrogate explanations for the connection between the initial decision to become a surrogate and the remuneration received are comments such as those expressed by Fran. "*It [surrogacy] sounded so interesting and fun. The money wasn't enough to be pregnant for nine months.*" Andrea,

age 29, who was married with three children, said "*I'm not doing it for the money. Take the money: that wouldn't stop me. It wouldn't stop the majority.*" Sarah, age 27, who attended two years of college, and was married with two children, explained her feelings about remuneration in the following way: "*What's $10,000 bucks? You can't even buy a car. If it was just for the money you will want the baby. Money wasn't important. I possibly would have done it for expenses, especially for the people I did it for. My father would have given me the money not to do it.*"

The issue of remuneration proved to be of particular interest in that, although surrogates do accept monetary compensation for their reproductive work, its role is a multifaceted one. The surrogate pregnancy, unlike a traditional pregnancy, is viewed by the surrogate and her family as work; as such, it is informed by the belief that work is something that occurs only within the context of a paid occupation (Ferree 1984:72). It is interesting to note that surrogates rarely spend the money they earn on themselves. The majority of surrogates I interviewed spent their earnings on home improvement, gifts for their husbands, a family vacation, or simply to pay off "family debts."

One of the primary reasons that most surrogates do not spend the money they earn on themselves alone appears to stem from the fact that the money serves as a buffer against and/or reward to their own families, particularly to their husbands who must make a number of compromises as a result of the surrogate arrangement. One of these compromises is obligatory abstention from sexual intercourse with their wives from the time insemination takes place until a pregnancy has been confirmed (a period that lasts on average from three to four months in length, but that may be extended for as long as one year).

The devaluation of the amount of the surrogate payment by the surrogates themselves as insufficient to compensate for "nine months of pregnancy" serves several important purposes. First, this view is representative of the cultural belief that children are "priceless" (Zelizer 1985); in this sense surrogates are merely reiterating a widely held cultural belief when they devalue the amount of remuneration they receive. For example, when the largest and one of the most well-established surrogate mother programs changed the wording of its advertising copy from "Help an Infertile Couple" to "Give the Gift of Life," the vastly increased volume of response revealed that the program had discovered a successful formula with which to reach the surrogate population. With surrogacy, the gift is conceptualized as a child, a formulation that is widely used in Euro-American culture—for example, in blood donation (Titmuss 1971) and organ donation (Fox and Swazey 1992).

The gift formulation holds particular appeal for surrogates because it reinforces the idea that having a child for someone is an act for which one cannot be compensated. As I have already mentioned, the gift of life narrative is further enhanced by some surrogates to include the near-sacrifice of their own lives in childbirth (Ragoné 1996, 1999). Fran, whose dismissal of the importance of payment I have already quoted, also offered another, even more revealing account of her decision to become a surrogate mother: "*I wanted to do the ultimate thing for somebody, to give them the ultimate gift. Nobody can beat that, nobody can do anything nicer for them.*" Stella, age 38, married with two children, noted that the commissioning couples "*consider it [the baby] a gift and I consider it a gift.*" Carolyn, age 33, married with two children, discussed her feelings about remuneration and having a surrogate child in these terms: "*It's a gift of love. I have always been a really giving person, and it's the ultimate way to give. I've always had babies so easily. It's the ultimate gift of love.*" For Euro-Americans it is "gift relations" rather than economic exchanges that characterize the family (Carrier 1990:2). Thus, when surrogates minimize or dismiss the importance of money, they are on the one hand reiterating cultural beliefs about the pricelessness of children, and they are on the other hand suggesting that the exchange of a child for money is not a relationship of reciprocity but of kinship.

Once a surrogate enters a program, she also begins to recognize just how important having a child is to the commissioning couple. She sees with renewed clarity that no matter how much material success the couple has, their lives are emotionally impoverished because of their inability to have a child. In this way the surrogate's fertility serves as a leveling device for perceived, if unacknowledged, economic differences, and many surrogates begin to see themselves as altruistic or heroic figures who can rectify the imbalance in a couple's life. The surrogate's sense of place and her social network are greatly enlarged as she receives telephone calls from the program, rushes to keep doctor's appointments, meets with prospective couples (she may even be flown to other cities to meet couples), and later on attends (in the open programs) monthly or semi-monthly surrogate support-group meetings. In some programs she may attend individual therapy sessions. She is often taken out socially by her couple, she may receive gifts from them for herself and her children, be telephoned regularly by them or receive cards and letters from them, and she attends holiday parties and other social events hosted by the program. Her sense of importance is also enhanced when she tells others about her new and unusual work. Once a surrogate meets, selects, and is selected by her couple and begins insemination—another rite of passage that confers additional status upon her—the couple becomes central to her life, adding an important steady source of social interaction and stimulation.

The entire surrogate experience serves to alter the balance of power in the surrogate's personal life, giving her entrée to a more public role and creating new and exciting demands upon her time. From the moment she places a telephone call to a surrogate mother program to the moment she delivers a child, the balance of power in a surrogate's personal life is altered radically. Her time can no longer be devoted exclusively to the care and nurture of her own family because she has entered into a legal and social contract to perform an important and economically rewarded task: helping an infertile couple to begin a family of their own. Unlike other types of employment, this activity cannot be regarded as unfeminine, selfish, or nonnurturant.

In this sense, we can see how surrogacy assists surrogates in their efforts to transcend the limitations of their domestic roles by high-lighting "their differences from men . . . [b]y accepting and elaborating upon the symbols and expectations associated with their cultural definition" (Rosaldo 1974:37), for example, motherhood. The gravity of the task provides the surrogate with an opportunity to do more than care for her family alone, and surrogates often report feeling that they are undertaking a task laden with importance, a project that fills them with a sense of pride and self-worth. Sally, age 33, married with two children and a full-time homemaker, discussed how surrogacy provided her with a feeling of unique accomplishment: *"Not everyone can do it. It's like the steelworkers who walk on beams ten floors up; not everyone can do it, not everyone can be a surrogate."*

GESTATIONAL SURROGATES

From 1987 to 1993 over 95 percent of all surrogacy arrangements were traditional. As of 1994 a profound shift occurred with 50 percent of all surrogacy arrangements gestational and as of 1999 that percentage continues to increase at the largest surrogate mother program (which is also the largest ovum donation program). With the advent of gestational surrogacy, however, reproduction is not only separated from sexual intercourse and motherhood but from pregnancy as well. In addition, gestational surrogacy creates three discernible categories of motherhood where there was previously only one: (1) the biological mother, the woman who contributes the ovum (traditionally assumed to be the "real mother"); (2) the gestational mother, the woman who gestates the embryos but who bears no genetic relationship to the child; and (3) the social mother, the woman who raises or nurtures the child.

The growing prevalence of gestational surrogacy is, in part, guided by recent legal precedents in which a surrogate who does not contribute an ovum toward the creation of a child has a significantly reduced possibility of being awarded custody in the event that she

reneges on her contract and attempts to retain custody of the child. However, although legal factors have certainly contributed to the meteoric rise in the rates of gestational surrogacy, it should be remembered that for couples the ability to create a child genetically related to both parents is the primary reason that gestational surrogacy continues to grow in popularity.

But not all gestational surrogate arrangements involve the couple's embryos; numerous cases involve the combination of donor ova and the intending father's semen. Why then do couples pursue gestational surrogacy when traditional surrogacy provides them with the same degree of biogenetic linkage to the child, has a higher likelihood of being successful, and costs less? Several reasons are cited by the staff of the largest surrogate mother program. The primary reason is that many more women are willing to donate ova than are willing to serve as surrogate mothers. This surrogate program is now also the largest ovum donation program in the U.S. with over 300 screened donors on file. The second reason, as previously mentioned, is that the U.S. courts would, in theory, be less likely to award custody to a gestational surrogate than to a traditional surrogate who contributed her own ovum to the creation of the child.[3] But perhaps most importantly, when commissioning couples choose donor ova/gestational surrogacy, they sever the surrogate's genetic link to and/or claim to the child. By contrast, with traditional surrogacy the adoptive mother must emphasize the importance of nurturance and social parenthood, while the surrogate mother deemphasizes her biogenetic tie to the child.

An additional reason, and one of critical importance, is that couples from certain racial, ethnic and religious groups (e.g., Japanese, Taiwanese, and Jewish) could find women who were willing to donate their ova, but were rarely able to locate women who were willing to serve in the capacity of surrogate. Thus, couples from particular ethnic/racial/religious groups who are seeking donors from those groups often pursue ovum donation/gestational surrogacy.[4]

The gestational surrogate's articulated ideas about relatedness (or more accurately, the presumed lack thereof) also produce a shift in emphasis away from potentially problematic aspects of gestational surrogacy, such as race and ethnicity. Unlike traditional surrogate arrangements in which the majority of couples and surrogates are Euro-American, it is not unusual for gestational surrogates and commissioning couples to come from diverse racial, ethnic, religious and cultural backgrounds. In fact, approximately 30 percent of all gestational surrogate arrangements at the largest program now involve surrogates and couples matched from different racial, ethnic, and cultural backgrounds. I have, over the last four years, interviewed a Mexican-American gestational surrogate who was carrying a child for a Japanese couple; an African-American gestational surrogate who had attempted several embryo transfers unsuccessfully for both a Japanese couple and a Euro-American couple; a Euro-American gestational surrogate who had delivered twins for a Japanese couple; and a Taiwanese couple looking for an Asian American ovum donor and gestational surrogate.

When I questioned Carole, an African-American gestational surrogate (who at twenty-nine was single, with one child, and had yet to sustain a gestational pregnancy) about the issue of racial difference (between herself and her couple), she stated: "*I had friends who had a problem because [they thought] I should help blacks. And I told them, Don't look at the color issue. If a white person offered to help you, you wouldn't turn them down.*" However, the following statement by Carole reveals that the issue of racial difference is further nuanced as a positive factor, one that actually facilitates the surrogate/child separation process: *My mom is happy the couple is not black because she was worried I would want to keep it [the baby]. The first couple I was going to go with was black. I don't want to raise another kid.*

When I questioned Linda, a thirty-year old Mexican-American woman pregnant with a child for a couple from Japan, about this issue, her reasoning illustrated how beliefs concerning racial difference can be used by surrogates (and couples) to resolve any conflicting feelings about the child being related to a surrogate by virtue of having been carried in her body: "*No, I haven't [thought of the child as mine], because she's not mine, she never has been. For one thing, she is totally Japanese. It's a little hard for me. In a way she will always be my Japanese girl; but she is theirs.*" In this quote, we can see how Linda recapitulates one of the initial motivations cited by gestational surrogates, the desire to bear a child for an infertile couple while highlighting the lack of physical and racial resemblance, or biogenetic tie. "*If I was to have a child, it would only be from my husband and me. With AI [traditional surrogacy], the baby would be a part of me. I don't know if I could let a part of me. . . . AI was never for me; I never considered it.*"

Carole and Linda are aware, of course, as are other gestational surrogates, that they do not share a genetic tie with the children they produce as gestational surrogates. But concerns such as Carole's about raising an African-American couple's child reveal how racial resemblance raises certain questions about relatedness even when there is no genetic tie.[5] Although she knows that the child is not genetically hers, certain boundaries become blurred for her when an African-American couple is involved whereas with a Euro-American couple the distinction between genetic/nongenetic or self/other is clear. Cultural conceptions such as this about the connection between race and genetics deserve further exploration.

Not surprisingly, the shift from traditional to gestational surrogacy has attracted a different population of women. Overall, women who elect to become gestational surrogates tend to articulate the belief that traditional surrogacy, even though less medically complicated[6] is not an acceptable option for them because they are uncomfortable with the prospect of contributing their own ovum to the creation of a child. They also cannot readily accept the idea that a child who is genetically related to them would be raised by someone else. In other words, they explicitly articulate the opinion in traditional surrogacy (where the surrogate contributes an ovum) that the surrogate is the mother of the child, whereas in gestational surrogacy (where she does not contribute an ovum) she is not. They are nonetheless interested in participating in gestational surrogacy because it provides them with access to the world of surrogacy.[7] This often includes, interestingly enough, women who have been voluntarily sterilized (tubal ligations). For example, Barbara, age 30, married with three children, a Mormon and a two-time gestational surrogate (now planning a third pregnancy) stated: "*The baby is never mine. I am providing a needed environment for it to be born and go back to mom and dad. It's the easy kind of babysitting.*"

Oddly enough, the beliefs of IVF surrogates run contrary to current legal opinion as expressed in the findings of both Britain's Warnock Report and the Australian Waller Commission's report that "when a child is born to a woman following the donation of another's egg the woman giving birth should, for all purposes, be regarded in law as the mother of that child" (Shalev 1989:117). It should be noted that the opinion expressed in both the Warnock Report and the Waller Commission contradicts not only the views expressed by IVF surrogates but also by commissioning couples who choose gestational surrogacy precisely because it eliminates the issue of genetic relatedness for them. It also contradicts Euro-American kinship ideology, specifically the continued emphasis on the importance of biogenetic relatedness.[8] However, this effort to expand our definition of biological relatedness, which has until recently depended on a genetic component, runs contrary to the Euro-American emphasis on biogenetic relatedness, in which genetic parents are legally and socially considered the "real" parents. This fragmentation or dispersal of parenthood, a byproduct of reproductive technologies, has resulted in what Marilyn Strathern has describes as the "claims of one kind of biological mother against other kinds of biological and nonbiological mothers" (1992:32) and fathers.

How then to account for the gestational surrogate's motivations? Should a gestational surrogate's maternal rights be "modeled on the law of paternity, where proof of genetic parentage establishes . . . parentage, or . . . on the nine month experience of pregnancy as establishing the preponderant interest of . . . parentage" (Hull 1990:152). It is of fundamental importance to gestational surrogates to circumvent the biogenetic tie to the child, and they do so in spite of the greatly increased degree of physical discomfort and medical risk they face in IVF procedures (as compared to risks associated with traditional surrogacy, which are the same as those faced in traditional pregnancy).[9] Any effort, legal or ethical, to argue that pregnancy is a determining factor in parenthood not only fails to consider Euro-American kinship ideology but perhaps most importantly neglects to consider the position of the gestational surrogate and commissioning couple.

The medical procedures commonly encountered by gestational surrogates [the self-administration of hormonal medications] can cause considerable discomfort. In the following example, Barbara discussed her experience: "*After a while you dread having to do it; I had lumps from all those injections. Two times a day and twice a week, three injections a day. If you don't do it, the pregnancy would be lost. . . . You are just [as] concerned with the pregnancy as if it's your own, sometimes more.*" Vicky, age 33, Euro-American, married with three children, who had given birth three weeks earlier, explained how she was able to sustain her motivation and commitment throughout the difficult medical procedures: "*It was hard, but it needed to be done for the baby's sake. All the shots [were] on a daily basis. I didn't mind it at all, but it had to be at a certain time. It was like a curfew. Sure it was painful, but it does go away.*"

The sentiments expressed by Barbara and Vicky are similar to those expressed by traditional surrogates who have experienced difficult, sometimes life-threatening pregnancies and deliveries. Both cast these experiences in terms of meaningful or heroic suffering (Ragoné 1996). The vastly increased physical discomfort and scheduling difficulties are, however, a price that gestational surrogates are willing to endure in order to circumvent what they regard as the problematic biogenetic tie.

Barbara expressed a belief shared by many gestational surrogates about their pregnancies when she stated: *"I separate AI [artificial insemination] and IVF completely, almost to the point I don't agree with AI. I feel like that person is entering into an agreement to produce a child to give to someone else. I feel it is her baby she is giving away"* [emphasis mine]. In a similar fashion, Lee, age 31, married with two children, Euro-American, who was waiting for an embryo transfer, discussed the differences between traditional (AI) and gestational surrogacy. *"Yes, it's [the fetus] inside my body, but as far as I am concerned, I don't have any biological tie. The other way [AI], I would feel that there is some part of me out there."*

This view of surrogacy differs in several important ways from the one expressed by traditional surrogates, who advance the idea that the term "parent" should be applied only to individuals who actually choose to become engaged in the process of raising a child, regardless of the degree of relatedness. They achieve this perspective in part by separating motherhood into two components: biological motherhood and social motherhood. Only social motherhood is viewed by traditional surrogates as "real" motherhood; in other words, nurturance is held to be of greater importance than biological relatedness. In this respect, it is the gestational surrogate, not the traditional surrogate, who tends to subscribe to a decidedly more traditional rendering of relatedness.

It was perhaps impossible to predict with any degree of certainty that advances in reproductive medicine coupled with an increase in consumer demand would produce such a profound shift in the rates of traditional (AI) and gestational surrogacy. Assistive reproductive technologies, e.g., surrogate motherhood, ovum donation, and sperm donation, have called into question what was once understood to be the "natural" basis of parenthood. As we have seen, traditional surrogates underplay their own biological contribution in order to bring to the fore the importance of the social, nurturant role played by the adoptive mother. In this way motherhood is reinterpreted as primarily an important social role

in order to sidestep problematic aspects of the surrogate's biogenetic relationship to the child and the adoptive mother's lack of a biogenetic link. For traditional surrogates nurture takes precedence and ascendancy over nature; motherhood is understood as a social construct rather than a biological phenomenon. Gestational surrogates however, interestingly remain committed to the genetic model of parenthood,[10] reasoning that "real" parenthood is in fact genetic.

Many of the early theories about the future of surrogacy focused, at times exclusively, upon its potential for exploitation, but they failed to take into consideration the fact that both fertility and infertility must be contextualized: both are embedded in a series of personal, social, historical, and cultural processes and practices. Within surrogates' statements, assessments, and questions is testimony to the plasticity and resilience of family, which in spite of these seemingly odd changes, persists.

ACKNOWLEDGMENTS

I owe a very special thank you to Dr. Sydel Silverman of the Wenner Gren Foundation for Anthropological Research for her support. An additional thank you is also owed to the University of Massachusetts–Boston for ongoing support in the form of Faculty Development Grants. I am especially indebted to the women and men who have shared their experiences with me over the last ten years; their belief in and commitment to this research has made it an engaging and rewarding experience. I would also like to extend very special and heartfelt thanks to the directors, psychologists, and surrogate program staff who have over the years generously given of their time and their expertise.

NOTES

1. A couple, Elizabeth and William Stern, contracted with a surrogate, Mary Beth Whitehead, to bear a child for them because

Elizabeth Stern suffered from multiple sclerosis, a condition that can be exacerbated by pregnancy. Once the child was born, however, Whitehead refused to relinquish the child to the Sterns, and in 1987, William Stern, the biological father, filed suit against Whitehead in an effort to enforce the terms of the surrogate contract. The decision of the lower court to award custody to the biological father and to permit his wife to adopt the child was overturned by the New Jersey Supreme Court, which then awarded custody to William Stern, prohibiting Elizabeth Stern from adopting the child while granting visitation rights to Mary Beth Whitehead. These decisions mirrored public opinion about surrogacy (Hull 1990: 154).

2. See Rapp (1978: 279) and Gordon (1988:3) for a historical analysis of the idea of the demise of the American family.

3. In June 1993, the California Supreme Court upheld the decisions of both the lower court and the court of appeals with respect to gestational surrogacy contracts. In Anna Johnson v Mark and Crispina Calvert, Case #SO 23721, a case involving an African American gestational surrogate, a Filipina American mother and a Euro-American father, the gestational surrogate and commissioning couple both filed custody suits. Under California law, both of the women could, however, claim maternal rights: Johnson, by virtue of being the woman who gave birth to the child; and Calvert, who donated ovum, because she is the child's genetic mother. In rendering their decision, however, the court circumvented the issue of relatedness, instead emphasized the "intent" of the parties as the ultimate and decisive factor in any determination of parenthood. The court concluded that if the genetic and birth mother are not one and the same person then "she who intended to procreate the child—that is, she who intended to bring about the birth of a child that she intended to raise on her own—is the natural mother under California law."

4. Why women from certain cultural groups are willing to donate ova but not serve as surrogates is a subject of considerable interest. Since gestational surrogates reason that they (unlike traditional surrogates and ovum donors) do not part with any genetic material, they are able to deny that the child(ren) they produce are related to them. Given the parameters of Euro-American kinship ideology, additional research will be required to ascertain why ovum donors do not perceive their donation of genetic material as problematic.

5. During the course of the interview, I specifically asked her what her feelings and ideas were about having a child for a couple from another racial background (I also asked this question of all the surrogates who were matched with couples from different racial backgrounds).

6. Gestational surrogates often complain about the discomfort they experience as a result of having to self-inject two or three times per day for as long as three to four months of the pregnancy. They report that progesterone is especially painful, since it is oil-based and has a tendency to pool and lump under the skin. Even though the largest of the surrogate programs claims to inform gestational surrogates about the need to self-administer shots, several gestational surrogates reported that they had not anticipated either the frequency or the discomfort of the injections.

7. I have discussed elsewhere in great detail the system of rewards that makes surrogate motherhood attractive to this group of women (Ragoné 1994; 1996, 1999).

8. While there are in fact observable differences in family patterns within the U.S., most notably among poor and working poor African-Americans whose alternative models of mothering/parenting may stem from "West African cultural values" as well as "functional adaptations to race and gender oppression" (Collins 1988: 119; Stack 1974), we should not lose sight of the fact that such perceived differences in family patterns do not necessarily weaken Euro-American kinship ideology. They continue to privilege the biogenetic model of family.

9. Aside from studies of the increased rates of multiple births there are few longitudinal studies on the effects of infertility treatments. Research does, however, suggest that infertility patients have an increased risk of ovarian cancer (Jensen, Riis, et al. 1987). The question remains: although an infertile woman knowingly accepts the risks associated with infertility treatments, do surrogacy and ovum donation programs provide their populations with adequate information about the possibility of long-term risk?

10. Once a gestational surrogate has begun to develop a relationship with her couple and has experienced several unsuccessful embryo

transfers, she may begin to reformulate or revise her initial beliefs concerning relatedness and family. An unsuccessful gestational surrogate may, for example, opt to become what is referred to in surrogate-mother programs as a "cross-over," someone who chose initially to participate in gestational surrogacy but then decided to become a traditional surrogate.

REFERENCES

Andrews, Lori. 1984. *New Conceptions: A Consumer's Guide to the Newest Infertility Treatments.* New York: Ballantine.

Annas, George. 1988. "Fairy Tales Surrogate Mothers Tell." In *Surrogate Motherhood: Politics and Privacy.* Larry Gostin, ed., pp. 43–55. Bloomington: Indiana University Press.

Carrier, James. 1990. Gifts in a World of Commodities: The Ideology of the Perfect Gift in American Society. *Social Analysis* 29:19–37.

Collins, Patricia Hill. 1988. *Black Feminist Thought: Knowledge, Consciousness and the Politics of Empowerment.* New York: Routledge.

Dworkin, Andrea. 1978. *Right-Wing Women.* New York: Perigee Books.

Ferree, Myra. 1984. Sacrifice, Satisfaction and Social Change: Employment and the Family. In *My Troubles are Going to Have Trouble with Me.* Karen Sacks and Dorothy Remy, eds., pp. 61–79. New Brunswick, NJ: Rutgers University Press.

Fox, Renee and Judith Swazey. 1992. *Spare Parts: Organ Replacement in American Society.* New York and Oxford: Oxford University Press.

Gordon, Linda. 1988. *Heroes of Their Own Lives.* New York: Viking.

Hull, Richard. 1990. Gestational Surrogacy and Surrogate Motherhood: In *Ethical Issues in the New Reproductive Technologies,* Richard Hull, ed., pp. 150–155. Belmont, CA: Wadsworth Publishers.

Jensen, P., Riis, B., Rodbro, P., Stram, V., and Christiansen, C. 1987. Climacteric symptoms after oral and percutaneous hormone replacement therapy. *Matvritas* 9: 207–215.

Martin, Emily. 1987. *The Woman in the Body: A Cultural Analysis of Reproduction.* Boston: Beacon Press.

Neuhaus, Robert. 1988. Renting Women, Buying Babies and Class Struggles. *Society* 25(3):8–10.

Parker, Phillip. 1983. Motivation of Surrogate Mothers: Initial Findings. *American Journal of Psychiatry* 1 40:117–119.

Ragoné, Heléna. 1994. *Surrogate Motherhood: Conception in the Heart.* Boulder, CO, and Oxford: Westview Press/Basic Books.

———. 1996. Chasing the Blood Tie: Surrogate Mothers, Adoptive Mothers and Fathers. *American Ethnologist* 23(2): 352–365.

———. 1998. Incontestable Motivations. In *Reproducing Reproduction: Kinship, Power, and Technological Innovation.* Sarah Franklin and Heléna Ragoné, eds., Philadelphia: University of Pennsylvania Press.

———. 1999. The Gift of Life: Surrogate Motherhood, Gamete Donations and Constructions of Altruism. In *Transformative Mothering: On Giving and Getting, in a Consumer Culture.* Linda Layne (ed.). pp. 132–176. New York: New York University Press.

———. 2000. Of Likeness and Difference: How Race is Being Transfigured by Gestational Surrogacy. In *Ideologies and Technologies of Motherhood: Race, Class, Sexuality and Nationalism.* Heléna Ragoné and France Winddance Twine, eds. New York and London: Routledge.

Rapp, Rayna. 1978. Family and Class in Contemporary America: Notes Toward an Understanding of Ideology. *Science and Technology* 42(3)278–300.

Rosaldo, Michelle. 1974. Woman, Culture and Society: A Theoretical Overview. In *Woman, Culture and Society,* M. Rosaldo and L. Lamphere, eds. Stanford, CA: Stanford University Press.

Shalev, Carmel. 1989. *Birth Power: The Case for Surrogacy.* New Haven: Yale University Press.

Snowden, R. Mitchell, G., and Snowden, E. 1983. *Artificial Reproduction: A Social Investigation.* London: Allen and Unwin.

Stack, Carol. 1974. *All Our Kin.* New York: Harper & Row.

Strathern, Marilyn. 1991. The Pursuit of Certainty: Investigating Kinship in the Late Twentieth Century. Distinguished Lecture. Society of the Anthropology of Europe.

———. 1992. *Reproducing the Future: Anthropology, Kinship and the New Reproductive Technologies.* Manchester: Manchester University Press.

Titmuss, Richard. 1971. *The Gift Relationship: From Human Blood to Social Policy.* New York: Pantheon Books.

Warnock, Mary. 1984. *The Warnock Report: Report of the Committee of Inquiry into Human Fertilisation and Embryology.* London: Her Majesty's Stationery Office.

Zelizer, Viviana. 1985. *Pricing the Priceless Child.* New York: Basic Books.

Female Genital Cutting: Culture and Controversy

Ellen Gruenbaum

"Get away! What's the matter with you? You kids are behaving like a bunch of animals!" an older Sudanese woman yelled from inside the adobe brick room where the circumcision was to take place. She slapped the wire netting that screened the window and stomped outside to chase the small throng of laughing, curious children away from the window where they were peeking inside. She rounded the corner of the well-built rectangular adobe house and accosted the boys and girls at the window in a high-pitched, agitated voice, "Move on! See this switch? Let's go!" She smacked the ground threateningly with her long, thin stick, the sort commonly used to prod a wayward donkey or goat.

The children scattered. An older, more sensible boy took up a position near the window where he could keep the others away. The woman adjusted her long tobe, the over garment that covers the hair and body but not the face, and returned to the other women inside, who were preparing for the circumcisions. They had already moved one bed, made of wood and woven rope, into the center of the room where the trained midwife would have good light. The cotton mattresses on three beds where the children would recuperate were covered with clean cotton sheets and pillows. The midwife directed them to cover the bed for the surgeries with a red oilcloth over a cotton pillow and a pile of clean cloth scraps that could support a girl gently, and wash it with soap and water. They boiled water in a kettle on the charcoal fire, and the midwife prepared her instruments to be sterilized in an enamel bowl: a hypodermic, two sharp new razors, a curved suture needle, suturing thread, and a small scissors.

"Come, sit right close to me so you can see everything!" the midwife urged, motioning me to a small, low stool beside her. I hesitated, wondering if I would be able to watch the little girls experience the cutting that awaited them, known locally as "Pharaonic circumcision." But as an anthropologist doing research on rural health services and women's roles in this Sudanese village, I wanted this opportunity to observe, to be better able to understand and describe this important experience in the lives of girls. What I was about to witness was the most severe form of female genital cutting and closure (infibulation) found anywhere in Africa.

CLITORIDECTOMY, EXCISION, AND INFIBULATION

The term "female genital mutilation," or FGM, has been widely used in recent years, to describe various forms of "female circumcision" that are found in many countries. "Mutilation" is technically accurate for most variants of the practices since they entail damage to or removal of healthy tissues or organs. The provocative term, as well as the realities it conveys, has stimulated great international concern and action against the practices.

But since "mutilation" connotes intentional harm, its use is tantamount to accusing the women who do it of harmful intent. Some people, even those who favor stopping the practices, have been deeply offended by the term FGM, arguing that it is not women's intent to mutilate their daughters but to give them proper, socially expected treatment. Their intent is simply to "circumcise" or "purify." The words commonly used for female genital cutting in Arabic-speaking countries, *tahur* or *tahara*, means "purification," that is, the achievement of cleanliness through a ritual activity. "Female circumcision," however, echoes the term for the removal of the foreskin in the male, which has been considered non-mutilating (Toubia 1993:9)—at least until the recent movement to end that practice as well (see the work of the organization NOCIRC)—and is therefore rejected by many people, since it seems to trivialize the damage done and the huge scale of the practices. I prefer the term "Female Genital Cutting," or "FGC," which has become well established in international discourse: it avoids disparaging the practitioners yet does not minimize the seriousness of the issue.

There are several types of cutting and removal of tissues of genitalia of young girls and women, done to conform to social expectations in communities of many different religions and ethnicities. The form varies not only from one sociocultural context to another but even within a single village, such as the Sudanese village just described, where different ethnic groups do different types of cutting. Forms vary between families, too, with some preferring their ethnic group's traditional forms while other families seek less harmful forms. Also, trained midwives and other practitioners (including traditional birth attendants, other older women, barbers, and even medical doctors) have their own individual techniques of doing the procedures, resulting in varying amounts of tissue taken and various levels of hygiene. (In most countries, medical doctors are now strongly discouraged or forbidden by their professional organizations and governments from doing *any* form of FGC.)

In some cultural contexts, it is very young children who are cut, including infants or toddlers (Shandall 1967, Toubia 1993, 1994, Abdal Rahman 1997). Anne Jennings reported southern Egyptian girls undergoing genital cutting at age 1 or 2 (1995:48). Most commonly, it is done to young girls between the ages of 4 and 8. But in some cultural contexts (e.g. the Maasai of East Africa), cutting is delayed until a young woman is in her teens and about to be married (14–15 or even older).

In the past few years the World Health Organization has developed a comprehensive typology that technical experts use for the different types. People who practice female genital cutting have their own terms for different types in their many languages, of course, which may or may not fit well with the World Health Organization's four types. Researchers can, however, place the range of the practices into the following categories.

Clitoridectomy. The World Health Organization's Type I includes both the partial and total removal of the clitoris, called clitoridectomy, and also the less severe forms of the operations, such as the cutting away of part or all of the clitoral prepuce, or "hood," analogous to the foreskin removal of male circumcision. Removal of only the prepuce seems to be very rare, but partial removal of the clitoris is fairly common.

Clitoridectomy, whether partial or total, is often referred to by Muslims and others as "*sunna* circumcision" or "*sunna* purification." In my experience doing ethnographic research in Sudan, the term "*sunna* circumcision" was in fact applied to a wide variety of surgeries, perhaps because of the positive association between that word and Muslim religious values.

Excision. The World Health Organization's Type II is called "excision." In this type, the cutting goes further than clitoridectomy to include removal of the prepuce, the entire clitoris, and partial or total excision of the labia minora (the smaller inner lips of the vaginal opening). In Sudan this form is usually also called "*sunna*," even though it is more damaging than what some people mean by "*sunna*." They are grouped in common parlance because there are just two basic folk terms—*sunna* and pharaonic circumcision—and they use the "*sunna*" terminology for both clitoridectomy and excision. In fact, it is often applied to any circumcisions that are not "pharaonic." Imprecise terms (such as *nuss* for "half") are also used for some of the in-between forms that would be included in Type II.

Infibulation and reinfibulation. The most severe cutting occurs with Type III, or infibulation. It is the main type in Sudan, where it is commonly called "pharaonic circumcision." People think it dates back to the days of the Pharaohs. In Egypt, where this severe infibulation is rare, it is called "Sudanese circumcision." In this type, part or all of the external genitalia—prepuce, clitoris, labia minora, and all or part of the labia majora—are removed and the raw edges are infibulated (held together by stitching or thorns). When healed, infibulation leaves a perfectly smooth vulva of skin and scar tissue with only a single tiny opening for urination and menstrual flow, preserved during healing by the insertion of a small object such as a piece of straw. In a variation of infibulation that is slightly less severe, the trimmed labia minora are sewn shut but the labia majora are left alone. In either case, it is essential that a midwife be present for childbirth to make an incision in the tissue to allow the baby to be born. The new mother is then reinfibulated by the midwife, a practice that is repeated after each pregnancy. The new mother often asks the midwife to make the opening very small, "like a virgin," to enhance her husband's sexual pleasure. This is analogous to, although more severe than, what some North American obstetricians do: take an extra stitch, called "the husband's stitch," when doing an episiotomy, for the purpose of restoring tightness to the opening.

Other variations. Others that do not include tissue removal are grouped as Type IV. This includes practices such as pricking, piercing, incision, stretching of the clitoris or labia, cauterization, cuts or scrapes on the genitalia, or the use of harmful substances in the vagina. Labia stretching to pursue culturally preferred aesthetics of the body is not particularly harmful, but other variations can be painful or damaging. In some East African countries, some men's preference for "dry sex" has resulted in the introduction of dangerous or uncomfortable astringents into the vagina to dry it out before intercourse, which is included in Type IV. In Europe and North America, the fad of labia piercing could be included as a Type IV practice.

HARMFUL EFFECTS

The harmful effects of these forms differ, but all forms—from clitoridectomy to infibulation—create risks for the girls at the time of cutting. Medical reports document cases of excess bleeding (hemorrhage), infections, blood poisoning (septicemia), retention of urine, or shock. Such complications can be life-threatening. Later on, the infibulated state sometimes results in retention of menses (if the vagina is blocked by scar tissue), difficulty in urination (if there is excess scar tissue

around or over the urethra), and a high incidence of urinary tract and chronic pelvic infections. At first intercourse, the extremely small size of the opening created by infibulation presents a barrier which can make first sexual intercourse very difficult or impossible. Often the scar tissue around the opening must be painfully ruptured or is cut by the husband, a midwife, or a doctor. During childbirth, the inelastic scar tissue of infibulation must be cut by the birth attendant at the right time so labor will not be obstructed. Not only is obstructed labor dangerous to the baby, but also the mother's internal tissues can be damaged, creating a fistula (opening in the tissue separating the vagina from the urinary bladder), which can result in an embarrassing condition with constantly leaking urine (Shandall 1967, Shell-Duncan & Hernlund 2000b:14–18, Gruenbaum 2001, Toubia 1994).

The psychological effects are less well understood, not systematically researched, and no doubt differ a great deal from one situation to another. There is anecdotal evidence of adverse psychological effects, perhaps particularly if it comes without warning and seems a betrayal of trust. Yet many women simply accept the experience as just part of becoming a woman.

Damage to sexual responsiveness is suspected for many women, yet there is also data that suggests the frequency and extent of problems vary greatly. Many women do not lose sexual interest and retain the ability to achieve sexual satisfaction and orgasms, even among the infibulated (Gruenbaum 2001, chapter 5, and Lightfoot-Klein 1989). Sexual responsiveness could be affected differently depending on which tissues are cut and how, whether the surrounding or underlying tissues retain sensitivity, whether there is severe infibulation, and of course whether the emotional attachment of the partners is strong and the relationship loving and supportive. Some midwives have been careful to avoid cutting too much of the sensitive tissue (clitoris and erectile tissue) hoping to preserve sensitivity, but still make the result look like an infibulation by joining the labia across the opening.

It is therefore erroneous to assume that all women who have been cut have lost their sexual responsiveness. Similarly, although many experience very harmful medical consequences, many do not, so one cannot generalize about the effects without reference to the specific practices and circumstances.

BUT WHY?

Indeed, the world wonders how loving parents can allow their daughters to be held down and cut, usually causing fear, pain, and possible major damage to health and physical functions, immediate or long-term. It seems incongruous and shocking to imagine a six-year-old girl enduring such pain and indignity, particularly at the hands of those she trusts.

Yet current estimates are that somewhere between 200,000 and a million girls experience some form of female genital cutting each year (Yoder 2003), mostly in 28 countries in Africa, and many millions of women and girls are living with FGC's life-long effects. In addition, the practices are found in other countries where they have spread by immigration or due to adoption of genital cutting if they believe it is associated with their religion. Why do women continue to arrange for these practices to be done to their daughters?

Is it because of any particular religion? No. The practices are found in many countries and among people of widely different ethnic groups and religions, including Judaism, Christianity, Islam, and traditional African religions. Yet it often happens that people who follow circumcision traditions often *do* associate the practices with their own religious beliefs.

For example, although many learned religious scholars have declared that infibulation has no place in Islam, and others say that no form whatsoever should be permitted, other teachers consider female circumcision as an "ennobling" act that is very proper for Muslims, so long as they don't go beyond clitoridectomy, which is usually called "*sunna* circumcision.*" The basic meaning of the Arabic word "*sunna*" is "tradition," which usually connotes the traditions of the Prophet Mohammed, i.e., those things that he did or advocated during his lifetime (570–622 C.E.), handed down through oral tradition and the writings know as the *Hadith*. Muslims believe the Holy Qur'an to be God's direct revelation, and the first source of guidance for righteous living, and it is silent on female circumcision. But Muslims also respect the sayings and actions attributed to the Prophet Mohammed during his lifetime as a secondary source of guidance. Although disputes remain among Muslims about which stories and quotations offer the most reliable versions of the Prophet's advice and how the sayings and stories should be interpreted, many Muslims have concluded that the Prophet Mohammed's words on the subject— "Reduce but do not destroy"—mean that only the less severe cutting is acceptable, though not required. Others believe the Prophet actually advocated it, making it either an obligation or at least a blessing to do it. Others believe Muslims should avoid female circumcision completely, since it is not mentioned in the Qur'an as a duty of the faithful. Using the term *sunna*, then, seems to imply that it is expected of Muslims, and while the term may help convince Muslims to give up infibulation, it may reinforce their continuing clitoridectomy. No doubt there will be many lively discussions among Muslim scholars in the coming years!

How about male dominance—is that the cause of this practice? Many analysts have noted that female genital cutting forms a part of the subordination of women where it is found. While of course not all strongly patriarchal societies of the world utilize female genital cutting, where it is found it is indeed embedded in the patriarchal structures of male domination of the lives of women and girls (Gruenbaum 2001, Shell-Duncan & Hernlund 2000a, Assaad 1980, Hayes 1975, El Saadawi 1980.) That is not to say that women do not have any control or influence on the decisions, types, and timing of the cutting. And that does not mean it is always men who are pushing for it. Rather, the conditions of women's lives often encourage their participation in and celebration of the cutting, their advocacy or their tolerance of the rituals, and their willingness to endure or accept the health risks.

In analysis of several case examples, including my Sudanese research, the manifestation of male dominance is primarily in disparate economic and social circumstances of women and men. While women are usually economically productive (whether for the market economy or for subsistence), carry out important services in the domestic sphere, and have some distinctive rights in each of the different cultures of Africa, most societies nevertheless accord greater political and economic power to men, especially older and more dominant and successful men. Economic and social situations of women vary a great deal—traders/market women have their own incomes to spend and farming women may have sources of income they use to help support their families or provide for their personal needs, but in many cultures, a woman's access to economic resources is mediated by men. In Islamic law, Muslim women are entitled to own and manage property, but the inheritance rules favor men—a daughter receives half the share of a son, for example. Even then, local groups often expect daughters not to claim shares, so that their brothers can be more secure, arguing that women are entitled to rely on husbands and male kin for support and should not need separate holdings. In other cultures, women may be dependent on men for access to land, livestock, foodstuffs, a share of a husband's income, and old-age support by sons. But women are vulnerable to divorce or polygyny that might reduce their security. If economic security and socially-approved reproduction are mediated by the dominant roles of men, women clearly need to conform to whatever rules the culture requires, including varying expectations for virginity, excision, or infibulation in order to have successful marriages and child-bearing. Their enculturation process must prepare girls for their subordinate roles.

Women's consciousness regarding their positions may range from strong belief in the moral superiority of men, to wry acceptance of the role disparity, to willingness to challenge the status quo in favor of better futures. But given the power of social pressure and the rewards of acceptance of genital cutting—propriety, marriage, children, and financial support—it should not be surprising that most women have not yet jumped on the bandwagon of abandoning female genital cutting.

CULTURAL CONTEXTS AND PEOPLE'S REASONS

The explicit reasons people give for circumcising their daughters are varied, depending on the cultural contexts in which FGC practices occur. For some, genital cutting is a rite of passage to marriageable womanhood. The Maasai of Kenya, for example, usually wait until a girl's marriage has been arranged, and she is then excised (Type II) and her head is shaved during the weeks of marriage preparations. After she has healed she goes to her husband and new home ready for womanhood.

Female genital cutting often plays a role in gender identity. Some even use terms like "male parts" for the clitoris and labia, saying removal of them results in a more feminine and aesthetically pleasing body. In many of the Nile Valley cultures of Egypt and Sudan, genital cutting helps to define feminine gender and is considered an essential prerequisite to marriage. Nile Valley girls are cut at earlier ages, so that they will be known to be virgins and ready for socially approved marriage when old enough.

The type of circumcision done sometimes defines ethnic identity. Even within a single village, such as the Sudanese village described above, different ethnic groups do different types of cutting. Thus, the Zabarma and Hausa minorities who have immigrated to Sudan anywhere from a century ago to more recent decades have usually resisted adopting infibulation, yet some have also adopted it along with other changes as part of their cultural and linguistic acculturation to the dominant Arab-Sudanese culture.

Some practitioners in Sudan advocated genital cutting as a way to preserve virginity. Not only is cutting expected to reduce some sexual sensitivity, thought to help girls and wives resist improper sexual relationships by taming what are thought to be overly powerful female sexual impulses, but also the infibulation is an actual barrier to penetration, preventing pre-marital pregnancy. People have even speculated, without any confirmation, that the practice may have developed in ancient times as a measure to prevent rape by strangers passing through on trade routes.

THE BIG DAY

The morning cool was beginning to fade, and the day promised to be hot and dry, as usual. The midwife washed her hands thoroughly with soap and water, shook off the water, and let them dry. The two pretty little girls were guided through the door by their mother. Recently bathed, hair freshly plaited and dotted with some henna paste, the girls wore colorful new dresses and special ornaments known as *jirtig*, as protection against excessive blood loss or the harm that might be done by spirits (*jinn*). The family's gold jewelry was ready for them to put on during recovery. They looked proud, though a little anxious, about this first time to be treated as such special people.

Their male cousin, about 7, lay silently on a bed in the corner, his face to the wall. Earlier in the morning he had been taken by car to the small hospital in a town several kilometers away to be circumcised by a medical assistant. When he returned, he was greeted with celebratory ululations and helped into a bed in the corner of this room to recover.

As the dozen women present greeted the mother and girls with smiles and encouragement, the mother hesitated, reconsidering the wisdom of doing the younger, who looked to be only about four years old. The other was six, the best age to be able to complete healing before starting school. But there were many advantages to cutting three children the same day, since the families could share the expenses of the celebration and not have to do it again in two years for the younger one. The midwife and the others quickly overcame the mother's hesitation, urging her to do it right away. Don't worry, it will soon be over, she's already prepared, and, as the saying goes, "You grow up, you forget" (*Tekbara, tensa*). Outside, other relatives and neighbors were cooking over charcoal fires, preparing a dried meat and yogurt stew, beans, bread, tea, and sweets for the well-wishers expected to begin arriving soon. The ceremony would not be easily delayed.

So, both girls were cut, the younger first. Thankfully the midwife's methods were fairly hygienic, not like the old methods, when the cutting was done using broken glass or an unsterilized knife with thorns for sutures. This midwife's better techniques were respected, as her patients usually avoided the worst complications. The first girl was washed carefully, held by loving but firm arms of the women, and injected—painfully—with the local anesthetic xylocaine into her clitoris, prepuce, and labia to deaden the feeling. A few minutes later, she was cut carefully, avoiding major arteries. She did not feel any pain when her prepuce, clitoris, and labia minora (inner lips) were cut off with one of the sterilized razor blades. Her labia majora (outer lips) were trimmed slightly and the two sides sutured together with the curved needle so they could heal with a smooth surface, leaving just one opening for urine and future menstrual flow. The second girl was done the same way, and after each cutting, the midwife rinsed the wound with an antiseptic, sprinkled the wound with antibiotic powder, and gave the girl some aspirin. Amid celebratory ululating, each girl was moved to a side bed to recover.

As soon as the work was completed, the bed cleaned up, and bowl with the discarded tissues carried out, adult well-wishers, both men and women, began arriving. They congratulated each child and tucked a little money under their pillows, then moved outside to share in the breakfast meal that the families had prepared. It was a joyful occasion of visiting and drinking tea. Meanwhile, as the local anesthetic wore off, the newly circumcised children endured their pain with aspirin and loving mothers.

BUT WHAT ABOUT GIRLS' AND WOMEN'S HUMAN RIGHTS?

Did these young girls consent to this cutting? They appeared to be willing. Of course in other places where girls are not informed beforehand, the practice is to surprise the girl and circumcision is carried out by force (see for example El-Saadawi for Egypt) it is obvious that such girls did not consent. But it is also quite common in Sudan and other countries for older girls to make fun of younger uncircumcised girls, teasing them with peer pressure until the younger girls' enviousness of being a big girl (i.e., circumcised) leads them to nag their mothers to let them be cut. Or suppose you grow up simply knowing that it will happen, and when your mother prepares the new dress, fusses over getting you ready, and tells you the big day has arrived, you go willingly, trusting your mother that it is for the best? Have you given your informed consent?

People concerned about the human rights of children would say no. At 5 or 6 years of age, one is by no means fully informed about the risks and consequences. A girl probably has no idea about sexual pleasure or infections or childbirth. Similarly, if you live in a culture where arranged marriages are common, and at 13 your father and mother arrange for you to get married to a groom they have selected for you, would you be able to speak up for yourself? Like so many other girls, you would probably feel you had no choice, or you would trust that your parents know best and accept the situation.

Both are violations of what have come to be understood as human rights for girls—the right to bodily integrity (that is, not to have her body permanently altered) and the right to consent to or decline to marry. Both of these clearly have not always been accepted as rights and certainly are not yet accepted in many societies. But should they be rights? The international community increasingly agrees that they should be, although there is no general agreement on what the age of consent should be: 16? 18? Most of the world's countries are signatories to agreements like the Convention on Elimination of All Forms of Discrimination Against Women, the Convention on the Rights of the Child, and other international agreements that stand against violations of girls' and women's rights, but not all enforce them.

Bodily integrity is something an adult woman can decide for herself. In the United States or Europe, it is accepted that someone over 18 is free to get tattoos or consent to having her labia pierced if she wishes. But to impose a decision on a child that will permanently alter her body, even if she is passively acquiescing, is to deny her right to make that decision when she is old enough to understand the consequences.

SO, WHAT'S BEING DONE ABOUT FEMALE GENITAL CUTTING?

As you might expect, many who learn about female genital cutting practices respond with outrage and take strong positions against the practices. Outsiders often have evoked horrible stereotypes of malicious intent, condemning the people who practice such genital cutting of girls as intending to "torture" females or "deprive women of their sexuality."

Local reformers sometimes engage in similar strongly worded condemnations in international discourse. But grassroots change agents realize that inflammatory rhetoric and "preaching" alone are not likely to change strongly held values and traditions. Reformers recognize that it may take some time to enlist local practitioners in the change process, so they have patiently promoted health education that they hope will lead people to voluntarily abandon female genital cutting. Others have introduced alternate rituals that contribute to the social goals, for example a rite of passage for maturing girls that substitutes for a traditional ritual of circumcision, but without the physical harm of cutting. Meanwhile, a large number of countries are also pursuing legal reforms and policy changes to criminalize or otherwise discourage the cutting of underage girls. (See Rahman and Toubia, 2000, for an international comparison of laws and policies on female genital cutting.)

But the first step in changing anything is to understand what it means to the people who do it. With more insight, we can better understand why people have resisted widespread change and why some are now pursuing change. Many writers, particularly social scientists and public health researchers, have tried to improve the understanding of people's reasons for genital cutting without condemning the people who have followed their traditional practices (Boddy 1982, Cloudsley 1983, Gruenbaum 1982, 1996, 2001, El Dareer 1982, Obermeyer 2003).

In the Sudanese villages I studied, female genital cutting still persists, but change is in progress. In one village in the Gezira area, over the past twenty years female circumcision has become an increasingly important topic for discussions. Some mothers have quietly arranged to have their daughters be cut less severely, moving from severe infibulation to preserving more of the tissue and not closing the opening as much. Others have gone further, dropping infibulation and doing only Type II or Type I, resisting the social pressure to conform.

A few years later, when I interviewed the midwife from the descriptions above on a return visit, she said she hoped to change over to doing only the milder *sunna*, but the vast majority of her clients still wanted infibulations. Her changing attitude was encouraged by the government trained medical assistant at their local clinic, who was taking an active role in persuading people to stop infibulating. The public health discussions that have been held separately among the women, among the men, among school boys, and among girls, have resulted in greater willingness to talk about modification, a moderate change, though not total abandonment. Throughout the country, doctors and other medical personnel havedecided to actively oppose all forms of female genital cutting. A law against the severe form, dating back to 1946, had seldom been enforced, but recently, the government of Sudan is showing renewed interest in enforcement of the laws against all forms of female genital cutting.

Stated intentions, of course, are not always realized, especially when there is such opposition. Nevertheless it is encouraging that grassroots developments, education, and organized public health education are having an effect to reduce the incidence of new cases.

SOCIAL MOVEMENTS FOR CHANGE

Successful social change requires widespread support, not merely written laws and policies. How will that support be won? Reformers need to endeavor to fully understand people's reasons. As Gerry Mackie has noted, "The followers of mutilation are good people who love their children; any campaign that insinuates otherwise is doomed to provoke defensive reaction" (Mackie 1996: 1015).

But remaining detached and uninvolved with this serious problem tests the ethical limits of "cultural relativism" (the respect that anthropologists use to try to understand each culture in its own terms rather than to judge it ethnocentrically by the values of another culture). The World Health Organization, the United Nations Children's Fund (UNICEF) and United Nations Population Fund issued a joint statement in 1996:

> It is unacceptable that the international community remain passive in the name of a distorted vision of multiculturalism. Human behaviours and cultural values, however senseless or destructive they may appear from the personal and cultural standpoint of others, have meaning and fulfil a function for those who practise them. However, culture is not static but it is in constant flux, adapting and reforming. People will change their behaviour when they understand the hazards and indignity of harmful practices and when they realize that it is possible to give up harmful practices without giving up meaningful aspects of their culture.

Both elements are necessary to a successful change effort aimed at a cultural practice: a deep understanding of people's reasons and motivations for keeping a practice, yet recognition of the flexibility of culture. People have demonstrated many times that cultures can adapt, and people can make changes when convinced of the need without losing cultural identity and meaning. Ultimately, it is up to them to decide when the time is ripe, but can efforts within a cultural group and efforts from outside accelerate the process?

Opinion leaders and grassroots activists, working in different ways, are vital to social change. An outspoken critic of the Islamist government of Sudan and a long-time supporter of the leftist movement there, Fatima Ibrahim challenged the government's interpretation of Islam, and argued that the Islamic religion can be used to *support* women's rights and social justice. The Medical Assistant who holds discussions about FGC in the village where he works, the doctor who studies Islamic texts to help her clarify the limits of *sunna* circumcision to the medical establishment, the midwife who tries to convince her clients to do milder forms or none at all—all of these that I observed in Sudan are helping to prepare for change.

In the past two decades organized efforts for change throughout the African countries affected have accelerated dramatically, as international and non-governmental organizations have become involved and as African women have moved into leadership positions in speaking out about female genital cutting. International organizations, such as the Inter-African Committee Against Harmful Traditional Practices, have taken a lead role in conducting public health education by organizing discussion groups in towns and villages. The World Health Organization has taken on the anti-circumcision work, as have other international organizations. Can such a message be carried forward effectively, so that female circumcision might actually be ended soon?

OBSTACLES TO CHANGE: RISK OF *NOT* CUTTING

The social conditions that act as barriers to parents taking the risk of leaving their daughters uncircumcised help to explain resistance to change (Gruenbaum 1996). No matter how clever the public health education message on the hazards of cutting or how authoritative the religious sources that say it is unnecessary, parents know that it *is* necessary if it is the prerequisite for their daughter's marriageability and long-term social and financial security. Even when the religious authorities speak against the practices and medical risks are known, these may not be sufficient reasons for parents to risk their daughters' marriageability and long-term security.

To counteract the social risks there are a number of possible directions for policymakers and change agents to address. One is to reduce the economic dependency of women. Better educational opportunities and employment opportunities would allow young women and their families to see delayed marriage as something other than a disaster. Daughters could be encouraged more in their education and careers, secure in the knowledge that although marriage is desirable, failure to marry or loss of spouse will not necessarily result in penury and dependence on male relatives. Better support for inheritance rights of women might help.

This is indeed a part of the change process that I have observed in Sudan. The teachers, professors, public health workers, students and other activists now working on reform are, as a result of their awareness, literacy, and cosmopolitan outlook, better able to confidently state that female circumcision can be left behind, that it is both harmful to health and not Islamic. Such women are confident that they will have a say in the decision on the circumcision of daughters, and they endeavor to provide their daughters with the educational opportunities needed to be self-reliant.

But even educated and confident women cannot be certain their uncircumcised daughters will be marriageable. If the young men in the community remain committed to marrying infibulated brides, a daughter's education may preserve her from poverty, but it will not assure her of marriage and children. The risk is lessened if there are social and familial ties to progressive families where men prefer *sunna* or no circumcision.

But as this cultural debate unfolds (Gruen-baum 1996), it is encouraging that some young men do state their preference for unin-fibulated brides. One educated young man I knew in Khartoum told me he had insisted that the family not infibulate his sister, and he swore he would not marry an infibulated woman, even if she were a cousin. But will he or others like him actually refuse to marry a cousin the family expects him to marry? Or would he refuse to marry the young woman who has caught his eye, simply because she is infibulated? And can young men effectively prevent their sisters' circumcisions? How do families cope with the risk that there may not be men like this for their daughters to marry?

Risk avoidance remains the most significant factor to explaining why otherwise well-informed families cling to female genital cut-ting practices. Gerry Mackie offered a provocative exploration of the risks involved in such social changes by comparing efforts to end infibulation and excision in Africa with the process of ending the painful, crippling foot-binding of girls (i.e., tightly binding their small feet so they would not grow) practiced in China for centuries. Footbinding, which lasted until the early 20th century, was also related to mak-ing daughters marriageable (Mackie 1996).

While there had been efforts to change foot-binding historically, parents were afraid to be the first to change, since men sought to marry women with tiny feet only. However, once a critical mass of people was persuaded of its harm through educational campaigns, they found they could take the risk of change when, with other parents, they pledged not to let their daughters' feet be bound nor let their sons marry women with bound feet. The movement led to wholesale abandonment of footbinding in a single generation (Mackie 1996:1001). Pledge groups do function in African societies for various purposes, so now that there is grow-ing awareness of the risks of female genital cut-ting, perhaps people will develop this pledge idea for female genital cutting as well.

Thus, despite the spread of female genital cutting and its tenacity, there is no reason to conclude that it cannot change rapidly in the coming years, when people have learned enough about the issue and when they believe the risks of not doing it are not too high. The conditions are ripe for change in infibulation and excision practices in Africa. The interna-tional activism, the efforts at culturally appro-priate approaches, and the emergence of, and a degree of support for, indigenous lead-ers of the movement make this an excellent time, if the additional resources can be mobi-lized, for rapid change to occur. Indeed, the World Health Organization, UNICEF, and the United Nations Population Fund have announced a joint plan to "significantly curb female genital mutilation over the next decade and completely eliminate the practice within three generations" (Reaves 1997).

To mobilize the Islamic religious arguments against infibulation—i.e., claiming only *sunna* is permitted for Muslims—often results in peo-ple favoring *sunna*, allowing them to continue to reject total abandonment of all forms. Reformers debate the wisdom of this: although abandoning infibulation constitutes a definite improvement in the health of women and girls, what public health officials have often advocated as "harm reduction," it might result in even stronger belief in the Islamic rightness of the remaining form, clitoridectomy, which might delay the demise of *all* forms.

ALTERNATIVE RITES

Even where circumcisions continue in Sudan, the celebration of it has lessened. Whether that indicates a decline in importance of the event or is due to harsh economic conditions is not clear, but even wealthy families have curtailed the celebrations. Reduction in cele-brations suggests that cutting is beginning to lose its symbolic power, and might in a few years decline.

An extremely positive development in the last few years has been even more explicit changes in the way circumcision is celebrated in several areas where activists have been at work. Recognizing that circumcision is a rite of pas-sage in many of the places where it is practiced, reformers have begun to introduce alternative ways to mark these important life transitions without involving the usual genital cutting. One good example comes from Kenya, where rural families have been adopting an alternative rite to circumcision over the last few years, known as "Circumcision Through Words" (*Ntanira na Mugambo*). As described by Malik Stan Reaves (1997), groups of families have participated in bringing together their appropriate-aged daughters to spend a week of seclusion learning their traditions concerning women's roles as adults and as future parents. The Kenyan national women's group, Maendeleo ya Wanawake Organization, worked with international collaborators to develop this program to include self-esteem and dealing with peer pressure, along with traditional values, as well as messages on personal health and hygiene, reproductive issues, and communications skills. At the end of the week of seclusion, a community celebration of feasting, singing, and dancing affirms the girls' transition to their new status.

Such approaches recognize that female circumcision has deep cultural significance, and if that significance can be preserved while the actual cutting is discontinued, there is strong hope that change can be rapid. Indeed, Reaves quotes the Chair of the Maendeleo ya Wanawake Organization, Zipporah Kittonysaid, as saying she was "overjoyed" to see the positive response and believes it was a critical achievement toward the eradication of female circumcision (Reaves 1997). This project serves as an excellent example of combining local initiative, international expertise, preparatory research and community discussion, and support from private foundations (including the Moriah Fund, Ford, Population Action International/Wallace Global Fund, and Save the Children–Canada) to accomplish a culturally sensitive alternative to female circumcision.

PUBLIC HEALTH EDUCATION

Poster campaigns, teachers on lecture tours, training for health workers, and public health announcements in the media have all been used at various times and places for several decades to spread the word on the dangers of female genital cutting. In the past two decades, the movement has accelerated, with more respectful and effective teaching tools and methods available. The Inter-African Committee, for example, uses a technique that involves sending a woman health worker into a marketplace where women are found, and striking up a discussion. She asks questions like "What do you think, is female circumcision a good tradition?" Rather than preaching, she listens to what they have to say, what their beliefs are. "Are you aware of the hazards?" leads to a discussion of the short and long term complications.

The educator encourages women to bring up their beliefs and then discusses them respectfully. For example, there is an erroneous belief in some countries that if the clitoris touches the baby's head at birth the baby will die. An educator brought the idea up in one such discussion filmed by the Inter-African Committee for their film *Female Circumcision: Beliefs and Misbeliefs* (1992), and the health worker explained that that was not possible. She also discussed other potentially harmful traditional practices such as nutritional taboos and marrying too young, encouraging the women to offer opinions and discuss their ideas with each other.

The work of national women's organizations in the countries affiliated with the Inter-African Committee is having a positive effect. Through such means as community discussions, formal classes with anatomical teaching aids, and organizing in villages willing to undergo friendly "inspections" of their baby girls, to show the success of the message, each national committee is reporting progress. The Sudan National Committee for Traditional Harmful Practices, for example, has many rural branches now, and although their efforts were met with resistance initially, their work is now better received according to the Executive Secretary, Amna Abdel Rahman Hassan (2002). Rogaia Abusharaf noted that the Sudan National Committee consistently avoids making female circumcision a separate issue, but always discusses it as one among several reproductive health issues (1999). Discussing child spacing, contraceptive use, and maternal and child health first, women are better prepared to consider not only the anti-circumcision message but also their well-being and rights.

TAKING A STANCE?

Regardless of the emotional or moral response one may feel about these situations, it is my opinion that those who are committed to improving the lives of women and girls must channel their responses into change efforts that are culturally informed and socially contextualized if they are to be effective. Anthropologists commonly advocate using cultural relativism to encourage people to overcome their prejudicial and ethnocentric tendencies and learn to understand cultures in their own terms. People who have been raised with the values and practices of their own culture, values and practices that have developed in adaptation to their own environment and social experiences, can be expected to have great faith in their own traditions. People are usually very unwilling to be judged according to, or expected to conform to, some other culture's values. So anthropologists rely on the mental exercise and teaching tool of cultural relativism to cultivate respect for cultural difference and enhance our ability to be analytical rather than ethnocentrically judgmental.

But that does not mean that we cannot discuss cultural practices in terms of their consequences, whether apparently neutral, helpful to some (e.g., to the preservation of identity), or harmful in certain respects (e.g., resulting in increased rates of infections). Indeed, most cultural practices are contested even within a cultural group: women and men may see things differently. Calm elders and testosterone-influenced youth may differ on when to fight. Men of a culture may like the "double standard" of sexual liberty for themselves but faithfulness for their wives, while the women have a different view of this.

As our human dialogs among cultures expand among societies and we humans try to agree on health protection measures or human rights protections, each culture must stretch a little as new information, experiences, and knowledge affect them. Once we have accepted that culture is dynamic and each of us is a citizen of a multi-cultural planet, it becomes easier to engage in respectful discussion, rather than the denunciation or preaching that often results from those who take a strong, absolute position in their interactions.

What feminist does not have respect for women's voices and their process of setting their own priorities, whether it be to end a war, get clean water, or change a traditional practice they have been questioning? What humanist can refuse to listen to the voices of women telling us of *their* priorities? And often anthropologists and public health workers, aware of possible harm from a practice, conduct a respectful dialog about it with people of another culture? Many anthropologists choose to advocate respectfully for change, and that is entirely in keeping with professional work in applied anthropology. But at other times an anthropologist steps back to observe, understand, and analyze in a non-interfering fashion, knowing that could be useful both for promoting mutual understanding and for assisting change agents.

As I see it, female genital cutting practices are changing and appear to be on their way to eventual abandonment as people become more knowledgeable, have alternative options that serve the same identity goals and promote values concerning morality, and become better able to resist the risks of change. Outsiders can help most effectively by offering understanding, respect, and support for grassroots and international change efforts, not only on female genital cutting but also on the *many* issues faced by the women and children of poor countries. It's fine to take a strong position ("I think people should stop doing this!"). But it's equally important to learn respectful dialog for those who do not see it your way.

My personal view is one of respectful challenge. As an anthropologist, my first commitment is to research and promote understanding, but as a humanist, I do not recoil from engagement in fostering improvements of the human condition. Female genital cutting practices vary so much that they clearly are not equally harmful. But because they are performed on non-consenting children, the human rights stance of total opposition to all forms, based on a right to bodily integrity, is ultimately hard to refute. [That principle would also prohibit male infant circumcision and ear-piercing of babies and toddlers, perhaps even extraction of a 12-year-old's teeth for orthodontia, so there are many ethical discussions to be had!] At the same time, my cultural relativism leads me to respect the values people choose to live by, recognizing that people themselves will make their future and choose when and how to change.

Thus, for outsiders, it has little practical consequence whether one is "for it" or "against it," since it is only the practitioners themselves who are in a position to abandon female genital cutting. What really matters is that we engender the respect and understanding for dialog to take place. That requires a respectful "cultural relativist" understanding on which to build the dialog for change, but anthropologists also recognize that "culture" is always contested and changing. Change is inevitable, and the world community should offer practitioners of female genital cutting not racist or ethnocentric condemnation, but understanding and listening. The international community can foster respectful dialog, help deliver information, and offer help with alternatives and improvement of underlying conditions that perpetuate the practices. Women and children living in poverty or marginal economic circumstances without the comforts of clean water, decent housing, adequate food resources, educational opportunities, job opportunities, electricity, or immunizations and basic health services may have social change agendas for their lives that do not list ending female genital cutting as their top priority. The international community would be wise to listen to African women and offer international assistance for their highest priorities as well.

While students, policy-makers, and the general public engage in disputes about female genital cutting, listening to the ideas of those affected and including attention to questions of context, motive, perspective, and the process of persuasion can only help. Change will need deep thinkers with passionate hearts and caring words.

BIBLIOGRAPHY

Abdalla, Raqiya Haji Dualeh. 1982. *Sisters in Affliction: Circumcision and Infibulation of Women in Africa.* London: Zed Press.

Abdal Rahman, Awatif. 1997. Member of the Sudan National Committee on Harmful Traditional Practices, quoted in Reuter report, "Sudan Tackles 'Silent Issue' of Female Circumcision," Feb. 20.

Abusharaf, Rogaia. 1999. Personal communication, Nov. 18.

Assaad, Marie Bassili. 1980. "Female Circumcision in Egypt: Social Implications, Current Research, and Prospects for Change." *Studies in Family Planning* 11, No. 1:3–16.

Cloudsley, Anne. 1983. *Women of Omdurman: Life, Love, and the Cult of Virginity.* London: Ethnographia.

Boddy, Janice. 1989. *Wombs and Alien Spirits: Women, Men, and the Zar Cult in Northern Sudan.* Madison: University of Wisconsin Press.

El Dareer, Asma. 1982. *Woman, Why Do You Weep? Circumcision and Its Consequences.* London: Zed Press.

El Sadaawi, Nawal. 1980a. "Creative Women in Changing Societies: A Personal Reflection." *Race and Class* 22, No. 2:159–82.

———. 1980b. *The Hidden Face of Eve: Women in the Arab World.* London: Zed Press.

Gruenbaum, Ellen. 1982. "The Movement Against Clitoridectomy and Infibulation in Sudan. *Medical Anthropology Newsletter* 13, no. 2:4–12. (Reissued in 1997 in *Gender in Cross-Cultural Perspective*, 2d ed., ed. Caroline Brettell and Carolyn Sargent, pp. 441–53. Upper Saddle River, N.J.: Prentice Hall.)

Gruenbaum, Ellen. 1996. "The Cultural Debate Over Female Circumcision: The Sudanese Are Arguing This One Out for Themselves." *Medical Anthropology Quarterly* 10, no. 4:455–75.

———. 2001. *The Female Circumcision Controversy: An Anthropological Perspective.* Philadelphia: University of Pennsylvania Press.

Hassan, Amna Abdal Rahman, Executive Secretary of the Sudan National Committee Against Harmful Traditional Practices, personal communication, 2002.

Jennings, Anne. 1995. *The Nubians of West Aswan: Village Women in the Midst of Change.* Boulder, CO: Lynne Rienner.

Mackie, Gerry. 1996. "Ending Footbinding and Infibulation." *American Sociological Review* 61: 991–1017.

———. 2000. "Female Genital Cutting: The Beginning of the End." *In* Shell-Duncan and Hernlund 2000: 253–281.

Obermeyer, Carla Maklouf. 2003. "The Health Consequences of Female Circumcision: Science, Advocacy, and Standards of Evidence," *Medical Anthropology Quarterly.*

Rahman, Anika, and Nahid Toubia. 2000. *Female Genital Mutilation: A Guide to Worldwide Laws and Policies.* London: Zed Press.

Reaves, Stanley. 1997. "Alternative Rite to Female Circumcision Spreading in Kenya." *Africa News Services.* Nov. 19.

Shandall, Ahmed Abu El Futuh. 1967. "Circumcision and Infibulation of Females." *Sudan Medical Journal* 5, no. 4:178–212.

Shell-Duncan, Bettina, and Ylva Hernlund, eds. 2000a. *Female "Circumcision" in Africa: Culture, Controversy, and Change.* Boulder, CO: Lynne Rienner.

Shell-Duncan, Bettina, and Ylva Hernlund. 2000b. "Female 'Circumcision' in Africa: Dimensions of the Practice and Debates." *In* Shell-Duncan and Hernlund, eds., 2000a:1–40.

Toubia, Nahid. 1993. *Female Genital Mutilation: A Call for Global Action.* New York: Women, Ink.

———. 1994. "Female Circumcision as a Public Health Issue." *New England Journal of Medicine* 331, no. 11 (Sept. 15):712–16.

———. 1996. Interview on "Fresh Air." National Public Radio.

Yoder, Stan. 2003. Personal communication, July 29.

XI

Culture Contact, Development, and the Global Economy

We live today in a global world based on complex political and economic relationships. There are few places that remain untouched by international markets, the mass media, geopolitics, or economic aid. However, the global world, particularly the global economy, is not a new phenomenon. It has its roots in the sixteenth century, when the powerful countries of Western Europe began to colonize populations in Asia, Africa, and the Americas. Part of this process involved the extraction of raw materials such as gold, sugar, rubber, and coffee, and the exploitation of the labor of indigenous populations for the profit of the colonizing nations.

Although most of the colonized world achieved independence by the 1960s, the economic domination of the capitalist world system that was initiated during the colonial period has not been significantly altered. In the late twentieth century an imbalanced relationship between the countries of the industrial, or "developed," world and the developing, or Third World, remains. How have the men and women of the developing world experienced the continuing impact of the penetration of capitalism and the integration of their societies into the global economy?

This question has been addressed in particular with regard to women, and two opposing views have been formulated. Chaney and Schmink (1980), in a review of studies on women and modernization, describe a minority position suggesting that women in the Third World are downtrodden and that capitalist development can help them improve their situation. Those who hold this opinion emphasize that women's economic and social status can be enhanced by an increase in female labor-force participation. Another perspective, stimulated by Ester Boserup's argument that in the course of economic development women experience a decline in their relative status within agriculture (1970: 53), suggests that culture contact, colonialism and development have introduced "a structure and ideology of male domination" (Leacock 1979: 131). In many parts of the world, originally egalitarian gender relationships have been replaced by more hierarchical ones, and women have consequently been marginalized and removed from the positions of economic and political decision making that they held in the precolonial period.

Researchers have demonstrated the negative effects of colonialism and capitalist penetration in a number of different historical contexts. Silverblatt (1980: 160), for example, portrays the Spanish conquest of the Andes as a "history of the struggle between colonial forces which attempted to break down indigenous social relations and reorient them toward a market economy and the resistance of the indigenous people to these disintegrating forces." Her focus is on the impact of this struggle on the lives of Andean women.

In the pre-Inca and Inca periods Andean women had status and power that were manifested in their customary usufruct rights to land and in their ability to organize labor. After the conquest, Spanish law came up against Andean custom with regard to the property rights of women. In addition, "The Spanish system . . . ignored the deeply embedded Andean conception of the household embodying the necessary complementarity of male and female labor" (Silverblatt 1980: 168). The result of Spanish colonialism in the Andes was the strengthening of patrilineal and patrilocal ties at the expense of matrilineal and matrilocal ties. Women became both politically and religiously disenfranchised. Indeed, women who continued to practice traditional religion were persecuted. Despite this persecution, the religious practices survived and became a very important mechanism of cultural resistance and defense (Silverblatt 1980: 179).

Etienne and Leacock (1980) have suggested that in many historical contexts women resisted colonization and acted to defend themselves. This was true, for example, of Seneca women in Pennsylvania and New York who withstood the attempts of Quakers to put agricultural production in the hands of men, to individualize land tenure, and to deny them political participation (Rothenberg 1980). A similar resistance to change has been documented for several other North American Indian groups (Grumet 1980). According to Weiner (1980: 43), the colonial period did not diminish the economic power of women in the Trobriand Islands in Melanesia "because no one ever knew that banana leaves had economic value." Women's wealth withstood a number of Western incursions and, as a result, "served to integrate new kinds of Western wealth, as well as individual economic growth, into the traditional system."

The impact of culture contact and colonialism on the lives of women in the developing world has not been uniform. Indeed, Silverblatt (1980) stresses class distinctions—elite Inca women had different experiences from peasant women. However, it is evident that one aspect of colonialism was the imposition of European and American ideas about the appropriate roles of men and women, an issue that Lockwood addresses in her essay in this volume. Programs designed to stimulate economic development in Third World societies continue to perpetuate culturally rooted assumptions about gender and the division of labor, particularly the definition of men as breadwinners and women as homemakers (Charleton 1984). Based on these assumptions, development planners, often with the support of local elites, direct their efforts at providing new skills and technology to men, even when women are the ones involved in subsistence production and trade (Chaney and Schmink 1980). As Schrijvers (1979: 111–112) has observed, "If women got any attention, it was as mothers and housekeepers in family-planning projects and in training programs for home economics. . . . Male-centered development programs often resulted in new divisions of labor between the sexes, by which the dependency of women on men greatly increased."

Lockwood (in this book) reviews the literature on the differential effects of the penetration of capitalism and development around the world, which sometimes work to the benefit of women and sometimes to their detriment. More specifically, she explores the relationships among gender ideology, women's control of material resources, family and kinship structures, and capitalist development. Based on a comparative analysis of two Tahitian cases where development programs were introduced in the 1960s, she argues that a gender ideology that empowers women is not sufficient to counter the increasing dependence on men that often results from developmental change. Rather, women must also control strategic resources in order to maintain status and power in both household and community in the face of capitalist penetration.

Like Lockwood, Wilson-Moore (in this book) shows that under certain conditions development programs can have a positive impact on women and their families. She explores the viability of homestead gardening as an economic strategy for women in Bangladesh where both men and women are involved in gardening, but use different methods and cultivate different crops. Women's gardens can be an effective foundation for the nutritional well-being of family members and do not necessarily have to compete with those of men. Development, in Wilson-Moore's view, is as much about feeding as it is about profit, and any program that is introduced should take into account the importance of subsistence as well as cash cropping in the context of the complementary gender roles in the local social system.

Agribusiness and multinational industrial production are other forms of global capitalism that bring mixed benefits for women in developing countries. Arizpe and Aranda (1981) argue that strawberry agribusiness, although a major employer for women in Zamora, Mexico, does not enhance women's status or create viable new opportunities for women. These researchers examine why women comprise such a high proportion of the employees in this business and cite cultural factors that constrain opportunities for women and continue to define women's work as temporary and supplementary. Employers take advantage of these constraints—they permit them to keep wages low and work schedules flexible. Arizpe and Aranda's conclusions support those of other researchers who point to a range of phenomena that make a female labor force attractive to multinational business and industry. "Women's socialization, training in needlework, embroidery and other domestic crafts, and supposedly 'natural' aptitude for detailed handiwork, gives them an advantage over men in tasks requiring high levels of manual dexterity and accuracy; women are also supposedly more passive—willing to accept authority and less likely to become involved in labour conflicts. Finally, women have the added advantage of 'natural disposability'—when they leave to get married or have children, a factory temporarily cutting back on production simply freezes their post" (Brydon and Chant 1988: 172).

As with agribusiness, the internationalization of capitalist production has led to the relocation in developing countries of many labor-intensive and export-oriented manufacturing and processing plants owned by multinational corporations. Many of these have provided new opportunities for employment, primarily for women. For example, in some electronics factories in Southeast Asia, women make up 80 percent to 90 percent of the labor force (Brydon and Chant 1988). However, just as with the assessment of the impact of development schemes on the lives of women in the developing world, there are two opposing views about the effect of multinationals. Some emphasize the benefits of jobs that provide women with greater financial stability (Lim 1983), while others see multinationals perpetuating or even creating new forms of inequality as they introduce young women to a new set of individualist and consumerist values. The sexually segregated work force remains in place within paternalistic industrial contexts that encourage turnover and offer no opportunities for advancement (Nash and Fernandez-Kelly 1983).

Fernandez-Kelly (1984) analyzes workers' responses to the international political and economic system at the levels of household and factory along the Mexican side of the U.S.–Mexico border, where more than 100 assembly plants (maquiladoras) have been established. These industries primarily employ women. By working herself in the apparel industry, Fernandez-Kelly documented hiring practices and working conditions of factory women. Low wages, oppressive working conditions, lack of job mobility, and insecure job tenure make maquiladoras a precarious option, selected by women with few alternatives. Factory workers also suffer from the contradictions between idealized notions of women's roles and their actual involvement in wage labor, which causes conflict over mores and values.

In this book, Cairoli describes how young unmarried Moroccan women employed in the export garment industry in Fez, Morocco, reconcile some of the contradictions between the cultural values and role expectations for women and the reality of their industrial employment. Inspired by Aihwa Ong's (1991: 280) emphasis on the "experiential and interpretive dimensions of work relations," Cairoli discusses how these female laborers transform their workplace into an interior domestic space, operating in it as they would in their own household. "They model their position in the factory hierarchy on their role in the household and so are able not only to accept the domination of the factory, but to find in that domination their own sources of personal self-worth and power." Factory owners become like fathers who guard the virtue of their female workers. Fellow garment workers are like sisters and thus the authority of a female supervisor is akin to the authority of the eldest sister. As in the Moroccan home, female space in the factory is separated from male space.

Mills (in this book) takes up similar issues, but in relation to young women who migrate from rural areas in Thailand to Bangkok to find employment. In recent years the literature focused on the impact of migration on gender roles and gender ideologies has grown significantly (Brettell 2003; Pessar 2003). This reflects the increasing numbers of women involved in both internal and international population flows, a phenomenon that has led some scholars to speak of the 'feminization of migration'. These female migrants have become domestic workers in households as far afield as Washington, DC, Los Angeles, Italy, Kuwait, and Malaysia. They have become factory workers on the global assembly lines located along the US–Mexican border or throughout Asia and Southeast Asia—that is, working for multinational industries that are especially dependent on a mobile female labor force. They have become garment workers in the gateway cities of the United States. And migrant women, some of them very young, have become prostitutes in the cities of both the developed and developing world, part of the growing global sex industry.

Mills tells us that when she began her research she assumed that she would find that female migrants were being 'victimized' by "Thailand's headlong pursuit of national development: their entry into urban labor markets a sacrifice demanded by rural families desperate to make ends meet." She discovered that although these young women encounter difficulties in the city and in their urban jobs, and although they have a powerful sense of duty toward their parents, they are also able to fulfill certain desires for being a modern woman. They achieve independence, and they become involved in consumption activities that are sometimes focused on their own attractiveness and efforts to keep 'up-to-date' (*thansamay*). And yet, they are also ambivalent about urban life and believe that "a return to the village household remains their most reliable source of economic security as they age, and particularly when they marry."

By contrast, Zimmer-Tamakashi (in this book) describes a situation where the introduction of wage labor and the shift from household to factory industry have problematic social implications, particularly for gender relations. She discusses the sexual politics of Papua New Guinea's educated elite, and the sexual competition among men of different tribal and national backgrounds. In a situation where men have access to cash and women have become more dependent on them, cases of domestic violence have increased. Women are experiencing a growing sense of gender oppression, and rape and violence against women have become "women's issues" largely ignored by male politicians. Those women who themselves enter the cash economy may experience more autonomy, but this too may generate domestic violence from men motivated by a fear of women's independence and their own economic uncertainty.

Although Cairoli's work, coupled with that of Ong (1987), show examples of adaptation and resistance in the face of global capitalism, in the final analysis, much of the work on women in development tends to support Leacock's (1979) rather pessimistic assessment. Real development, from her perspective, "would mean bringing an end to the system whereby the multinational corporations continue to 'underdevelop' Third World nations by consuming huge proportions of their resources and grossly underpaying their workers" (1979: 131). This will require a truly international effort. The gendered approach to culture contact, colonialism and development has demonstrated the close relationship between capitalist penetration, patriarchal gender ideologies, and the sexual division of labor. This relationship has been present since the early days of colonialism and has been perpetuated by a global economy that has created an international division of labor often oppressing both men and women, but especially women. As Chaney and Schmink (1980: 176) put it, development policies and programs frequently lead "not only to the degradation of the physical environment but also of the social environment, as various groups are systematically excluded from the tools of progress and their benefits."

REFERENCES

Arizpe, Lourdes and Josefina Aranda. 1981. "The 'Comparative Advantages' of Women's Disadvantages: Women Workers in the Strawberry Export Agribusiness in Mexico." *Signs* 7: 453–473.

Boserup, Esther. 1970. *Woman's Role in Economic Development.* New York: St. Martin's Press.

Brettell, Caroline B. 2003. "Gender and Migration." In Caroline B. Brettell, *Anthropology and Migration: Essays on Transnationalism, Ethnicity, and Identity,* pp. 139–151. Walnut Creek, CA: Altamira Press.

Brydon, Lynne and Sylvia Chant. 1988. *Women in the Third World: Gender Issues in Rural and Urban Areas.* New Brunswick, NJ: Rutgers University Press.

Chaney, Elsa M. and Marianne Schmink. 1980. "Women and Modernization: Access to Tools." In June Nash and Helen I. Safa (eds.). *Sex and Class in Latin America,* pp. 160–182. South Hadley, MA: J.F. Bergin Publishers.

Charlton, Sue-Ellen M. 1984. *Women in Third World Development.* Boulder, CO: Westview Press.

Etienne, Mona and Eleanor Leacock. 1980. "Introduction." In Mona Etienne and Eleanor Leacock (eds.). *Women and Colonization: Anthropological Perspectives,* pp. 1–24. New York: Praeger.

Fernandez-Kelly, Maria Patricia. 1984. "Maquiladoras: The View From the Inside." In Karen Brodkin Sacks and Dorothy Remy (eds.). *My Troubles are Going to Have Trouble With Me,* pp 229–246. New Brunswick, NJ: Rutgers Press.

Grimshaw, Patricia. 1989. "New England Missionary Wives, Hawaiian Women and the Cult of True Womanhood." In Margaret Jolly and Martha MacIntyre (eds.), *Family and Gender in the Pacific: Domestic Contradictions and the Colonial Impact*, pp. 191–44. Cambridge: Cambridge University Press

Grumet, Robert Steven. 1980. "Sunksquaws, Shamans, and Tradeswomen: Middle Atlantic Coastal Algonkian Women During the 17th and 18th Centuries." In Mona Etienne and Eleanor Leacock (eds.). *Women and Colonization: Anthropological Perspectives*, pp. 43–62. New York: Praeger.

Leacock, Eleanor. 1979. "Women, Development, and Anthropological Facts and Fictions." In Gerrit Huizer and Bruce Mannheim (eds.). *The Politics of Anthropology: From Colonialism and Sexism Toward a View from Below*, pp. 131–142. The Hague: Mouton.

Lim, Linda Y. C. 1983. "Capitalism, Imperialism, and Patriarchy: The Dilemma of Third-World Women Workers in Multinational Factories." In June Nash and Maria Patricia Fernandez-Kelly (eds.). *Women, Men and the International Division of Labor*, pp. 70–91. Albany: State University of New York.

Nash, June and Maria Patricia Fernandez-Kelly (eds.). 1983. *Women, Men and the International Division of Labor*. Albany: State University of New York.

Ong, Aihwa. 1987. *Spirits of Resistance and Capitalist Discipline: Factory Women in Malaysia*. Albany: State University of New York Press.

———. 1991. "The Gender and Labor Politics of Post-Modernity." *Annual Review of Anthropology* 20:279–309.

Pessar, Patricia. 2003. "Anthropology and the Engendering of Migration Studies," In Nancy Foner (ed.). *American Arrivals: Anthropology Engages the New Immigration*, pp. 75–98. Santa Fe, NM: School of American Research Press.

Rothenberg, Diane. 1980. "The Mothers of the Nation: Seneca Resistance to Quaker Intervention." In Mona Etienne and Eleanor Leacock (eds.). *Women and Colonization: Anthropological Perspectives*, pp. 63–87. New York: Praeger.

Schrijvers, Joke. 1979. "Viricentrism and Anthropology." In Gerrit Huizer and Bruce Mannheim (eds.). *The Politics of Anthropology: From Colonialism and Sexism Toward a View from Below*, pp. 97–115. The Hague: Mouton.

Silverblatt, Irene. 1980. "Andean Women Under Spanish Rule." In Mona Etienne and Eleanor Leacock (eds.). *Women and Colonization: Anthropological Perspectives*, pp. 149–185. New York: Praeger.

Weiner, Annette. 1980. "Stability in Banana Leaves: Colonization and Women in Kiriwina, Trobriand Islands." In Mona Etienne and Eleanor Leacock (eds.). *Women and Colonization: Anthropological Perspectives*, pp. 270–293. New York: Praeger.

The Impact of Development on Women: The Interplay of Material Conditions and Gender Ideology

Victoria S. Lockwood

During the colonial era, European nations expanded their cultural, economic, and political hegemony over much of the non-western world (see Wolf 1982). To gain access to the material wealth of their colonies, the Europeans established conditions under

Original material prepared for this text.

which native populations had little choice but to produce crops or other commodities for markets, or to work for wages on European plantations or in mines. As these processes escalated and other western interventions intensified, capitalist relations of production began to subsume indigenous economies in most parts of the world.

Since that time, capitalism has proven a versatile, dynamic, and ever-expanding political economic system. Today, even the most remote and isolated village has been touched and transformed by it. The general terms often applied to that transformation—"development" and "modernization"—describe not only the processes of market integration (and shifts to capitalist production relations), but also the dynamic restructuring of social institutions, social relations, and world view that accompanies it.

Although there is great diversity in how this structural and ideological transformation has taken place around the world, research focused on gender issues in development has identified several important themes. First, men and women rarely participate in development the same way; in other words, they do not have access to the same kinds of development-generated opportunities and choices. Second, men and women rarely share equally in the various "costs" and "benefits" of development. Indeed, a growing number of studies suggest that women's social, economic, and political position relative to that of men actually deteriorates with capitalist development, or that, at best, its effects on women are highly mixed (Boserup 1970; Etienne and Leacock 1980; Nash 1977; Fernandez-Kelly 1981; Charleton 1984; Bossen 1975, 1984; Caulfield 1981; Afonja 1981).

At the same time, a number of cases in which women's position and status have improved show that there are important exceptions to this general trend. In other words, it is clear that, "The changes brought about by colonialism, or, later, capitalist productive relations, are not automatically detrimental to women" (Rapp 1979: 505, cited in Di Leonardo 1991: 15; my emphasis). Thus, ". . . we must be wary of simplistically portraying men as the winners and women as the losers" (Moore 1988: 79). As

the rapidly growing body of literature on women and development points out, the situation is much more complex than that.

The highly variable impact of development on non-western women raises a number of important questions. How, specifically, does development (capitalist integration) differentially affect men and women, and why does women's position frequently deteriorate? And, in those cases where women's position has improved, is it possible to identify particular material/structural or ideological factors that have contributed in the development process to maintaining women's position or to promoting gender equity?

My goal in this article is twofold: first, to discuss these questions in the context of recent research; and second, to present a comparative case study of two rapidly modernizing, neighboring Tahitian islands[1] that sheds light on these issues.

VARIABILITY IN DEVELOPMENT'S IMPACT ON WOMEN

Most scholars agree that it is difficult to generalize about the impact of development on non-western women. As Moore (1988: 74) notes, "Women are not a homogeneous category, and the circumstances and conditions of their lives in the varying regions of the world are very different." Nevertheless, it is possible to identify the factors that play a major role in shaping how women in any particular society are affected by integration into capitalist markets and production systems. These factors interact in highly complex ways to shape the choices and options—the "opportunity structures"—open to women.

But first, in order to understand how men and women—even husbands and wives in the same family—can differentially experience development, it is important to remember that families are internally stratified units and that family members do not necessarily share the same priorities or goals (see Wilk 1989). Gender and age differences structure patterns of unequal access to authority, decision-making prerogatives, and control over family activities and resources. Those that do have access—most often senior males or male heads of households—may be in a favored position to participate in new and prestigious economic activities (e.g., commercial agriculture). In contrast, other family members, such as wives, may find that "modernization" simply means working longer hours at devalued household tasks that bring in little or no money, and having less say over the affairs of their families.

Forms of Capitalist Integration

One of the key factors affecting women's position is the manner in which different communities participate in capitalist markets and are integrated into global capitalism (see Mukhopadhyay and Higgins 1988). In rural areas, previously subsistence-based families may begin producing cash crops for local or export markets, become involved in other kinds of commodity production (i.e., crafts), or seek jobs in nearby towns. If jobs are available, families may abandon agriculture wholly or in part. As they become more dependent on money and imported foods and the cost of living increases, some rural villagers leave the countryside, migrating to nearby cities in search of wage work. Sometimes the search for work ultimately takes rural migrants to foreign industrialized nations where they are absorbed into the low-skilled, low-paid urban work force.

Each of these forms of capitalist integration has different implications for men and women depending on how the sexual division of labor is renegotiated to reflect new economic conditions; that renegotiation will be shaped by ideological notions of the types of work "appropriate" for men and women. Cash-crop agriculture may be defined as the domain of men, while women continue to produce food crops. Women may specialize in the production and sale of crafts if craft production was a female activity before market integration. If men migrate to find wage jobs, women may be left at home to feed and support families. If families migrate, men may find work in the city, but women who cannot find jobs may resort to street peddling or other marginal activities in the urban informal sector.

Degree of Structural Transformation

The *degree* to which a particular society has been incorporated into capitalist relations of production also plays a role in shaping how women are affected by development. Some communities have resisted or avoided full incorporation and maintained pre-capitalist institutions and values (see, for example, Rodman 1993; Petersen 1993); this is true in many rural "peasant" communities in the Third World where families produce for markets or hold wage jobs, yet simultaneously maintain kin-based relations of production and property ownership. In other communities, pre-capitalist institutions have largely been replaced by capitalist relations of production; this is true in areas of the most extensive commercial and missionary intervention.

These structural changes include shifts from kin- or family-based systems of property ownership to individual ownership. Land and labor become commodified and production becomes oriented to market sales and making money; wealth accumulation becomes a major goal. Those who are able to accumulate capital become an elite who are in a position to concentrate control over land and the other means of production. These processes result in the formation of class structures and the promotion of individualistic, competitive, and profit-oriented value systems characteristic of capitalist societies.

The impact of development on women will, in part, be shaped by how far this structural transformation has advanced. If, for example, increasing pressure on land has caused a system of land tenure to shift from matriclan ownership to individual ownership, women may find that they have lost control over land while men who participate in cash-cropping or other market-oriented activities are increasingly gaining individual control. On the other hand, where communities have resisted this shift to individual ownership, women may find that their property rights have not diminished.

Existing Systems of Gender, Family, and Social Relations

Another critical factor shaping the impact of development on women is the local system of gender and family relations, including patterns of gender stratification and ideology. There is great diversity in these systems around the world ranging from the relatively egalitarian, horticultural societies of island New Guinea (Lepowsky 1993), to the highly gender stratified and segregated Islamic societies of the Middle East (see Abu-Lughod 1986). Variability in gender structures is accompanied by fundamental differences in how different societies conceive of femaleness and maleness, and in what they perceive to be the basic mental and physical capabilities of men and women. Gender ideology, as well as family and kinship structures, will play a major role in determining the kinds of behaviors and socioeconomic roles that are considered appropriate (and consistent with family responsibilities) for women.

The Western Gender Bias in Development

Appreciating the complexity of forces that shape the options open to men and women as their communities develop explains little, however, about the frequently negative impact of development on women. If development were in fact a gender-neutral phenomenon, one would expect that the *relative* social, economic, and political position of men and women would remain the same—both men's and women's situations would either improve or deteriorate in more or less the same ways. But this rarely happens. Numerous studies now point to several important processes of gender discrimination embedded in western-style, capitalist development, processes that have contributed to women's deteriorating position in many developing regions. In some cases, development has introduced forms of gender bias that did not previously exist in non-western communities; in others, introduced gender biases have intensified existing gender asymmetries.

Women and "Modernization"

Prior to the 1970s and the surge of scholarly interest in women's issues, it was widely (and ethnocentrically) assumed that modernization ("westernization") promoted more egalitarian gender relations, and greater rights and freedoms for women. In an influential article, Laurel Bossen (1975) noted, "The Western industrialized nations [were] thought to be closest to an ideal of modern egalitarian treatment for women. . . . Hence modern changes that [brought] societies closer to the Western pattern and standard [were] presented as advantageous to women" (1975: 587). Evidence of women's increasing equality included legal freedoms; the right to vote, run for office, and own property; as well as greater participation in the wage labor force. The latter was thought to promote female economic independence from "traditional family structures." In contrast, women in rural developing areas were thought to be "servile, dependent, and decidedly inferior to . . . men" (1975: 587).

Bossen effectively argues that neither the egalitarian view of western gender relations nor the servile, inferior view of Third World women reflects reality. Although western women may possess certain legal rights, they do not enjoy full equality with men, nor are they as socially valued or esteemed as men. At the same time, research in less technologically sophisticated, non-western cultures has shown that, in some cases, women may be highly valued and possess many of the same socioeconomic and political prerogatives as men (see Lepowsky 1993 on the Vanatinai of New Guinea; Geertz 1961 on the Javanese; Kluckhohn and Leighton 1946 on the Navajo; and Etienne and Leacock 1980). Thus, as Bossen (1975: 589) notes ". . . it does not follow that the greater wealth and superior technology controlled by modern societies corresponds to greater equality among its members, female or otherwise."

"Modernized Patriarchy"

The gender biases that characterize western capitalist societies—and which were more severe in the Victorian era—were first introduced in many non-western regions during the colonial era. They have continued to reappear, however, as one "subtext" of many western-designed or-oriented development programs.

One of these gender biases is a structural feature of western, capitalist relations of production in which the formal economic ("productive") and domestic/reproductive spheres are artificially distinguished, and the latter is devalued. In capitalist societies, "The concept of labor [is] reserved for activity that produces surplus value" (i.e., cash-earning activities) (Mies 1982a: 2; see also Sacks 1974). Thus, "work" becomes commodity or cash-crop production, or wage employment, activities that were typically dominated by men after their introduction; men, then, become associated with a formal, "productive" sphere that is often physically (spatially) separated from the activities of the household/domestic sphere.

Many of the typical activities of women—giving birth to and caring for children, maintaining the household and its affairs, production for family use/consumption—are not defined as "productive" in capitalist systems because they generate nothing of monetary value, and thus women do not "work." Thus much of the work that women do perform in the domestic domain becomes "invisible." An important example of this is that agricultural development efforts in Africa and elsewhere have frequently focused on men, even though "invisible" women farmers actually produce 50 percent of the world's food for direct consumption (Escobar 1995: 172–173).

Capitalist enterprises benefit from the structural separation of the productive and domestic domains because, since women do no work, they do not have to be compensated for their labor; they also benefit in that women (and sometimes children) serve as a relatively inexpensive, available, and easily dismissed pool of labor. If the demand for labor increases in the capitalist system or families cannot support themselves on one income, women may move into wage labor, but they are typically paid less than men. The rationale of capitalist employers is that women are "temporary" (and less skilled) workers who really belong at home with the children.

This capitalist economic rationale for the devaluation and domestication of women was reinforced during the colonial era (and since) by patriarchal, Victorian-era notions of appropriate male/female activities and relations, and by notions of female inferiority (physically and intellectually). In the Society Islands, for example, English missionaries believed that cultivation (previously practiced by both Tahitian men and women) was "unsuitable to [the female] sex" and that pre-contact women's other economic activities were "derogatory to the female and inimical to an improvement in morals"; they decided that "men should dig, plant, and prepare the food, and the women make cloth, bonnets, and attend to the householdwork" (Ellis 1981, III: 392–393, cited in Thomas 1987). Being relegated to making bonnets at home was quite a step down, particularly for high-ranking Tahitian women, who had figured prominently in the affairs and sociopolitical machinations of their chiefdoms—and sometimes even led warriors into battle—before the arrival of the Europeans (Oliver 1974; Lockwood 1988).

The model of Christian family life advanced by missionaries and colonial officials provided a supporting ideological framework for the structural separation of the male-dominated productive domain and the devalued, female domestic domain. The Bible describes the moral and correct family as consisting of a male head of family who is father and provider, and a female wife and mother who is his helpmate and subordinate. Women's financial dependence on the male "breadwinner" is a cornerstone of their secondary status.

Western gender biases not only domesticated non-western women, they frequently also introduced a "value structure that defines women's primary task in society as biological and social reproduction"; when this occurs in conjunction with a system—capitalism—that "allocates higher rewards to production roles in the public domain . . . men [achieve] an edge over women" (Afonja 1986: 134). That edge frequently supported patriarchal gender and family systems.

Relegation to a devalued, "nonproductive" domestic sphere was frequently accompanied in many cases by women's loss of control over productive resources and property; these were vested in the male "breadwinner" and head of the family. And that loss of control had a critical, negative impact on women's social position, authority, and status. In capitalist systems, control over the means of production (resources, capital, technology) is the material basis of differential authority and power; this is true not only in the community at large, but also in the internally stratified family. Following Schlegel (1977), "power" can be defined as the ability to control one's own and others' persons and activities, as well as the ability to make the decisions and shape the affairs/policies of the family or social group. Where women do not participate in productive activities or control resources or income, they are not only financially dependent on men, they are also relatively powerless and politically subordinate to men (see Freidl 1975, 1991).

By introducing structures and ideologies that privilege men and "domesticate" women, western-style development has frequently limited the options available to women and contributed to a decline in their status in the family and community.[2] In these cases, development becomes more than simply a means for promoting market integration or raising the standard of living, it becomes a vehicle for institutionalizing "modernized" patriarchy (Escobar 1995: 177).

Contemporary Negative Trends for Women

Several of the major trends in Third World development today reflect these gender biases. In rural areas, the devaluation and domestication of women has contributed to the *feminization of subsistence agriculture.* When new cash crops and technologies were introduced (during the colonial era and more recently), it was typically assumed that men were the farmers, and new opportunities, credits, and modern technology were made

available to them. In many areas of Africa and Latin America where women had in fact been the major farmers, women were pushed into subsistence cultivation for family consumption. Defined as part of the "domestic" domain, subsistence production became both devalued and "invisible." As women assumed "the burden for providing for 'family' consumption" they were "often prevented from engaging in cash-crop production themselves, and the frequent bias of government schemes and incentives in favour of male farmers (and the cash crops they produce) lead to further discrimination and disadvantage for women" (Moore 1988: 75). The cost to women of the feminization of subsistence agriculture was often exacerbated by changes in land tenure and other systems of property rights that effectively negated women's rights and institutionalized systems of individual (often male) ownership and inheritance.

Women are frequently pushed into subsistence production not only by male domination of cash-crop production (and of resources and technology), but also by male domination of most wage jobs and by male out-migration. In rural areas, where jobs are available on plantations or on commercial farms, women are typically hired as lowly-paid domestics, while men have access to the higher-paying and more prestigious jobs. When men migrate from rural areas to towns in search of wage work, rural women are frequently left at home with the double burden of caring for the house and children, and fulfilling familial subsistence needs.

Not only does subsistence production become devalued and invisible in the domestic domain, but women's other productive—and even cash-earning—activities frequently do as well. In many developing regions, women have found ways to earn small amounts of cash income by producing marketable crafts or other commodities (i.e., prepared foods) in their homes ("cottage industries").

In the Yucatan, for example, Mayan women weave hammocks (Littlefield 1978), and in India women make lace (Mies 1982b). But these women's situation is much like that of other poor, female commodity producers who work out of their homes. They are dependent on outside suppliers who bring them the raw materials for their craft, and they are exploited by commercial middlemen and exporters who pay them little yet reap large profits for themselves. Because women have few income-earning options outside the domestic domain and are largely bound to this domain by gender and family structures, they are unable to alter the conditions of that exploitation. Because this work is frequently defined as "domestic activity women do in their spare time," instead of as productive labor (Moore 1988: 84 citing Mies 1982b), these contributions to family livelihood are devalued and become invisible.

It is important to note that in both the cases where rural women seek wage jobs or produce commodities at home, the prevailing perception that women are domestics who make no productive contributions to the family has little to do with reality. Indeed, the entire artificial conceptualization of a female "domestic" domain in opposition to a formal, male "productive" domain is largely a myth in most developing regions (see Lamphere in this volume). Nevertheless, the "myth" remains strong and western gender ideology supports it. The dual beneficiaries are men, whose dominant position as "provider" and head of the family remains intact and unthreatened, and capitalist enterprises, which hire female "domestics" cheaply.

Another major trend in Third World development has been the *feminization of the industrial labor force.* It has been estimated that 80 percent of the workers in world market factories (typically owned by western multinational corporations) are young women (13–25 years old) (Moore 1988: 100; see also Nash and Fernandez-Kelly 1983). Young women are hired because of their ". . . apparently innate capacities for the work—'nimble fingers'—their docility, their disinclination to unionize, and the fact that women are cheap because, while men need an income to support a family, women do not" (Moore 1988: 101). Women are also paid less (as noted above), and hired at the lowest levels (skilled and management positions go to men), because they are seen as temporary workers. It appears that wage

earning and financial contributions to families frequently do enhance young women's personal autonomy (see Ong 1987; Kung 1994). But often there are also significant social costs, and rarely does women's position improve in the male-dominated family.

These cases suggest that even though women's income earning is a *potential* material foundation for enhanced authority and status in the household, that potential may not be realized. Young female Taiwanese factory workers, for example, turn over their wages to their fathers, the heads of patriarchal Chinese families (Kung 1994). And in other cases, women's income may be so meager (due to low wages) or devalued that it is seen only as a "domestic supplement." Thus gender ideologies and family structures may redefine or "mystify" women's actual productive and income contributions—effectively negating them.

MAINTAINING WOMEN'S POSITION: THE INTERPLAY OF MATERIAL CONDITIONS AND GENDER IDEOLOGY

The relatively smaller number of cases in which women's position has not deteriorated illustrates how key material factors, supported by prevailing gender ideology and family systems, have worked to enhance women's autonomy, authority, and power in the family and community. In rural Java, for example, shifts to an export agricultural economy during the Dutch colonial period (and since) were not associated with major changes in the sexual division of labor, or in women's relatively high status and economic independence (Stoler 1977). Both men and women played important roles in labor-intensive, wet rice cultivation, and women were also significantly involved in trading activities. Through agricultural wage labor and trading, women became significant income earners in the household: ". . . women clearly control family finances and dominate the decision-making process" in the domestic domain, but Stoler notes that the domestic and public domains actually merge and overlap (1977: 85). In poorer households, women's income gives them both independence and authority in the family; in wealthier households, women's earnings could become the "material basis for social power" (84); where they are able to buy land or expand lucrative trading operations, women achieved both economic and political power.

Similarly, women in male-dominated Yoruba society (Nigeria) have achieved economic independence by participating in commercial enterprises and trade, and by owning houses (Barnes 1990). In this society where marriages are brittle and women do not inherit property from husbands, owning a house is an important form of social security for women. Income from commercial enterprises is used to purchase a house; the house then generates capital from rents. By owning the house, Yoruba women achieve the status of senior authority figure in the household. This is possible because even though Yoruba gender and family structures strongly favor men, women and men "are [seen as] equally capable of performing society's valued and essential tasks" (Barnes 1990: 255). Thus, when a woman owns a house, she is able to undermine the conditions that promote her structural subordination and achieve some social power. Female "home owners" also achieve political clout in their urban neighborhoods and sometimes become community leaders.

All the cases that have been cited in which development-related socioeconomic change did not promote women's increasing subordination have two significant characteristics in common. First, women were able to exert control over strategic productive resources (usually through ownership), and/or they were able to earn and control cash income (capital). And second, prevailing gender ideologies supported (did not redefine or negate) female participation in production and income earning, as well as female control over the products of their labor, including income. Whether women's productive efforts take place in the "formal" public domain or in the domestic domain (or in that large amorphous area where the two domains are actually one in many cases), they are socially defined as "producers," and they control key resources and income.

The cases of rural Tahitian women on the islands of Tubuai and Rurutu (Austral Islands, French Polynesia) show how different forms of market integration may have strikingly different consequences for women (even in the same society). They also show how women's control of resources and income plays a critical role in shaping their differential authority, decision making, and "power" in the household and community.

DIFFERENT OUTCOMES FOR WOMEN ON NEIGHBORING TAHITIAN ISLANDS

Rurutu and Tubuai are neighboring islands in rural French Polynesia. They are culturally similar, sharing the relatively homogeneous, Neo-Tahitian sociocultural patterns that coalesced in the region following centuries of French colonial and Christian missionary intervention. They have also both experienced the intense French government efforts to "modernize" and develop its overseas Pacific territory over the last three decades. In addition, the islands are similar in their geographic and population sizes (about 2,000 people, 300 households).

The push for regional development began in the early 1960s. In the rural outer islands, development programs were aimed at modernizing agriculture by transforming Tahitian taro farmers and fishermen into export producers for the rapidly growing Papeete market. Various heavily subsidized projects were implemented on different islands; they included copra and coffee production, European vegetable cultivation, and other kinds of commodity production (e.g., crafts).

Rural modernization also included the building of schools and clinics, rural electrification and telephone services (late 1980s), and integration of rural populations into the French family welfare and legal systems. Each rural island was designated a "municipality" and provided with a budget to employ a significant number of islanders on the government payroll (as road or maintenance workers, clerks, teachers, or secretaries). In the absence of commercial and tourist development on these remote islands, there are few other kinds of jobs. Today, about 45 percent of all families on Rurutu and Tubuai include an employed member, usually the male household head; about 25 percent of all jobs are held by women. Despite income earning from jobs or commodity production, most families continue to rely on agriculture/fishing to fulfill their subsistence needs.

Through their various cash-earning activities, as well as government social programs, many rural Tahitian families have achieved relatively high incomes and a level of material affluence unknown in many parts of the "developing" world (see discussion later in this chapter). At the same time, however, the cost of living in this import-dependent society is extremely high, and consumption standards are constantly rising. Consequently, and despite their high incomes, cash is ever-scarce and highly coveted. Most families today pursue any and all economic activities possible to generate cash income.

Pre-Modernization Gender Relations and Stratification

Before the introduction of development programs in the 1960s, rural families on both Tubuai and Rurutu mainly cultivated gardens (taro and other root crops, coconuts, bananas) and fished to fulfill subsistence needs. Small amounts of cash were earned through copra production or vanilla cultivation, or from sporadic sales of manioc starch, fresh foods, or pandanus craft items to passing schooners. Land was owned jointly by cognatic groups of kin; both men and women inherited rights in the land owned by their parents and grandparents.

Patterns of Tahitian domestic organization and gender relations reflected French colonial and Christian missionary efforts to transform Tahitians in their own images. As noted earlier, missionaries specifically sought to bring Tahitian society more into line with Victorian-era mores and practices (Thomas 1987). In accord with those patterns, as well as with Christian precepts, men were defined as the "breadwinners," "providers," and heads of their families. Men performed most agricultural labor and fished. Women's appropriate (and moral) domain was the household, where they spent their time caring for children, doing the housework, and weaving pandanus mats (and making bonnets) (Ellis 1981, III: 392–393, cited in Thomas 1987). Islanders today sometimes describe women's domain as "interior" (household) and men's domain as "exterior," the fields and ocean.

Men dominated cash-earning opportunities where they were available. Men processed copra and planted vanilla gardens, and controlled the cash earnings (see Lockwood 1988; Oliver 1981). Although women's efforts were concentrated in the household itself, they also worked in their husbands' gardens, fished from the reef, and performed many other kinds of "productive" labor. Nevertheless, a general pattern of male authority and preeminence (and female subordination) in the household was promoted by Christian teachings and the Bible, and by male control of increasingly coveted cash income. Although wives were usually in charge of daily expenditures for food and other necessities, husbands dispersed these monies to their wives as they saw fit.

Despite these structural changes, Tahitians somehow failed to become indoctrinated in Victorian-era attitudes about women's relative inferiority. Although Tahitians were (and are) devout believers in the familial/domestic prescriptions of the Bible, their own understandings of the nature of men and women differed substantially from those of the French and the missionaries. Most importantly, they did not have a belief in individuals' superiority or inferiority based on gender criteria.[3] This was reflected in a psychological study of Tahitian men and women conducted in the early 1960s (Levy 1973). Levy (1973: 236) concluded that in the Tahitian world view, women and men are seen to be much alike in their capabilities and talents, and to have no major personality, behavioral, or intellectual differences. He noted that Tahitians acknowledged that men's and women's lives were different—because of women's role in reproduction and because they perform different tasks—but that's all.

Indeed, one of the major themes of Tahitian gender ideology is male/female interdependence, and not hierarchy (superiority/ inferiority) as in many western societies. Thus, although Tahitian women were economically and politically subordinate in the post-contact, male-dominated household, they were not (and are not today) treated as inferiors. In contemporary communities, women receive a great deal of respect and admiration from both men and other women for their roles as managers of the family and domestic domain, and for their devoted care of their children (see Langevin 1990). Despite their "domesticity," they are outspoken at community meetings and exhibit little deference to men.

Rural Development: Differing Paths for Tubuai and Rurutu

The economic profiles of Tubuai and Rurutu began to diverge in the early 1960s when government development planners charted different courses for each island. Tubuai was chosen as a major target for agricultural development, specifically European green vegetable and potato cultivation. It also became the administrative center for the five Austral Islands, and the site for the one high school in the group. A small airstrip was built to facilitate transport and contact with Tahiti.

Today, Tubuai Islanders are heavily involved in commercial agriculture, as well as other kinds of commodity production and export; these activities are largely the domain of men, although women are needed to perform substantial amounts of secondary labor in agricultural fields. Tubuai is today the regional potato producer, exporting over 1,200 tons (metric) to Papeete each year; it also exports about 550 tons of vegetables annually. The commodification of land and labor, shifts to individual land ownership (from the previous kin-based system), and the spread of new ethics of wealth accumulation and consumerism are increasingly observable. Of all of the Austral Islands, Tubuai is the most developed and affluent; in 1994, average familial income was about $2,000/month

(Lockwood 1993). It is also the most westernized as measured in the number of islanders who have attended the French-staffed high school and who aspire to a western material lifestyle.

In the mid-1980s and despite the fact that they were not "farmers," Tubuai women began to sign up with the Agricultural Service in large numbers to plant potatoes. Women's access to land was assured by their own familial lands, and they also had access to the same financial subsidies and credits as male farmers. By the early 1990s, 43 percent of all potato farmers were women (Lockwood 1993).

Tubuai women had always earned small amounts of money from selling crafts or a few vegetables to other families, and a few held jobs as teachers, secretaries, or maintenance workers. But, for most women, potato cultivation was the first opportunity to earn significant amounts of income of their own; most women—who typically cultivate on a smaller scale than men—earn between $1,000 and $1,500 during the three-month potato season. Because Tahitians believe that income earned by an individual belongs to that individual, wives are able to make their own independent decisions about how their money will be expended. Indeed, many female potato farmers explain that they decided to plant potatoes to have their own money to do as they like; women's money is, however, almost always used to buy food, clothes, and other items for their families.

Thus by the early 1990s, Tubuai women were adopting new "modern" socioeconomic roles and breaking down barriers in the traditional sexual division of labor that defined women as "domestics." They had also achieved a level of financial autonomy.

The Island of Rurutu

The island of Rurutu's development trajectory has been significantly different. Because of its rugged interior terrain, agricultural development projects were not promoted, although in recent years limited efforts have been made to expand the potato project and green vegetable cultivation there. (In 1990, islanders exported about 35 tons of onions and 60 tons of taro, tarua, and bananas.) A small airstrip was built on the island, and government services and jobs were created much as on Tubuai.

Most families on Rurutu earn money from the craft production of their female members and craft items are Rurutu's major export. Crafts include pandanus mats, satchels, and hats, Tahitian quilts (*tifaifai*), and shell and flower necklaces—items once made exclusively for household use. Rurutu women produce crafts as part of their domestic work in their own households, or while participating in a *pupu*, a cooperative work group of ten to twenty women who usually belong to the same church. Their reputation for fine craft production extends throughout the territory.

Rurutu women have organized cooperatives to help sell their crafts, and these are supported and subsidized by various government programs. (Craft cooperatives are present on most outer islands, but they are most highly developed on Rurutu.) Women are active agents in making arrangements to sell their items in Papeete though relatives, or if necessary, through a retailer at the central urban market. The minimal use of non-kin middlemen means that female producers retain almost all of the market price of their products. In the early 1990s, Rurutu's annual craft exports were valued at about $400,000 (one-third the value of Tubuai's potato crop).

How Rurutu women came to specialize in craft production to an extent that far exceeds that of other rural islands, however, is not clear (and informants could not explain it). As noted earlier, most rural Tahitian women weave mats and make quilts for household use. This specialization probably began to emerge in the pre-development decades; at that time, the populations of neighboring islands earned small amounts of cash selling copra, coffee, or manioc starch. Rurutu families had little of these items to sell; they could, however, sell mats and hats to the local Chinese family-owned general stores for export to Papeete. Thus, in the absence of other significant options, it is likely that women launched themselves into commercial craft production and in so doing, they became central agents in the generation of their families' incomes.

Although Rurutu is integrated into regional markets through craft and other kinds of small-scale production, it is today less "westernized" than Tubuai. As commercial agriculture is little developed, the traditional, family-based system of land ownership is not threatened by the kinds of changes taking place on Tubuai. Ethics of familial sharing and participation in cooperative work groups (*pupus*) are widespread on Rurutu, but have generally disappeared on Tubuai. Because families do not participate in potentially lucrative vegetable exports, most make significantly less money than Tubuai families (the average monthly income is $1,500). Consequently, there is less western-style consumerism. And because until recently, Rurutu children were required to board at the Tubuai high school in order to attend it, fewer Rurutu Islanders have received as many years of formal French education as Tubuai Islanders.

And clearly, on Rurutu, there has been little change in the traditional division of labor. The division between the female's "interior" world and the male's "exterior" world is strictly maintained. Interestingly, it is women who chastise other women who violate these "proper" roles by "doing men's work" in the gardens; women are highly protective of their domain. Compared to more "modern" Tubuai women, then, Rurutu women appear to be both "traditional" and domestic.

THE GENDER CONSEQUENCES OF DIFFERENT DEVELOPMENT PATHS

Although Rurutu women may not be doing anything "new," they have achieved an important role in income generation (and control) that is unparalleled on the more modernized Tubuai.[4] Careful examination of household budgets and income on both islands revealed that women on Rurutu are indeed significant "providers." On Rurutu, women bring in more than 50 percent of all income in almost half of all families (45.5 percent). In other

TABLE 1   Comparison of Rurutu and Tubuai: Development and Gender

	RURUTU	*TUBUAI*
Percent of families with female breadwinners	45.5%	26%
Economic status of women	"Providers"	Not "Providers"
Degree of female financial dependence on males	Low	High
Household headship		
Male household head	49%	68%
Joint male/female heads	41%	25%
Women's household decision making	High	Moderate
Women's community political participation	Moderate	Low

words, it is almost equally likely in Rurutu families that the wife/mother is the breadwinner as it is that the husband/father is the breadwinner. On Tubuai, women are the breadwinners in only 26 percent of all families[5] (see Table 1).

And in this society where women *retain control* of the income they generate, Rurutu women are given credit for their productivity. This was summed up by one Rurutu man who said that women today differed from those of his grandmother's generation because they helped to "provide" for the family (the male role). I had not heard Tubuai women described this way, although they are certainly involved in many productive activities. It became clear that a general ethic of women as "providers" existed on Rurutu that was not articulated on Tubuai.

Rurutu women's status as "providers" was reflected in a subtle shift away from the typical pattern of husbands as heads of families to "joint husband/wife" family heads. In 49 percent of all Rurutu families the husband was declared head of the family, while in 41 percent, husbands and wives were joint household heads. In comparison, Tubuai had a much higher proportion of male household heads (68 percent) and husbands and wives were "joint" heads in only 25 percent of all families.[6] Rurutu women also played a greater role than Tubuai women in decision making about household budgets and expenditures[7] (differences between the two islands are summarized in Table 11.1).

There were also significant differences between the two islands in how women and

men were perceived and valued. Informants were asked to compare men and women in terms of various characteristics including intelligence, who worked harder, and several other personality traits. They were also asked who was "superior": men, women, or both (equal). Tubuai and Rurutu islanders generally agreed on most of the characteristics of men and women, with the exception of intelligence and superiority. On Rurutu, the majority of informants (58 percent) thought that women were more intelligent, while on Tubuai, the majority (64 percent) thought that men and women were equally intelligent.[8] (Only 29 percent of Tubuai Islanders thought that women were more intelligent.) And, on both Rurutu and Tubuai, the majority thought that men and women were "equal" (56 percent and 82 percent respectively); but on Rurutu, 23 percent of all informants thought that women were superior, whereas this was true of only 2 percent of all Tubuai informants. (It is also interesting to note that no one thought men worked hardest; both sets of islanders thought either women worked hardest, or that men and women worked equally hard.)

The higher valuation of Rurutu women can also be seen in women's greater political participation on the island. In 1994, three women served on the 16-member, island municipal council; one woman had been elected as a district mayor (the island has three districts). On Tubuai, islanders could remember no woman ever serving on the municipal council, and no woman has ever been elected mayor or district mayor.

There was also a tendency for both male and female Rurutu Islanders to extol the virtues of women to a greater extent than on Tubuai, although women were clearly held in high regard on both islands. When asked to compare the thoughts and mentality of men and women, Rurutu informants (male and female) described women as more expressive and outgoing (men were reserved), as better organizers, and generally as "seeing farther" than men. Women were described as more active in church and community groups than men, and they tended to take on the organizational roles in those activities. Both men and women described men's thoughts as centered on their taro gardens and fishing; once these tasks were successfully accomplished, men relaxed or got together with other men to drink; they were described as having "few concerns" other than farming and fishing. Women, however, were described as constantly thinking about how to make ends meet, how to generate the money that was needed for a household purchase, or how to organize the next church event. They "saw further" in that they were constantly contemplating the future needs of their families.

It should be noted that although Rurutu women's economic roles and income generation have promoted greater gender equity in familial authority and decision making and in community leadership than on Tubuai, they are not associated with other differences in family organization, fertility, or gender-based land-use patterns. On both islands, most families are nuclear in structure (about two-thirds of all families), have an average household size of five to six people, and produce approximately five children. Between 20 and 30 percent of all families reside on and cultivate the wife's land (most familial); the rest utilize the husband's land.

CONCLUSION

As the discussion has shown, many of the western gender biases described above were introduced into Tahitian society, promoting the structural domestication of women, including their economic dependence on male "providers" and heads of families. But at the ideological level, Tahitians never accepted notions of male superiority and female inferiority, continuing to see men and women in a largely egalitarian, interdependent way that afforded mutual respect for both. Consequently, and despite other kinds of changes in their society, women never lost their rights to own and control land and other resources, they were never divested of the right to control the income they earned, and they were given credit for the productive contributions they made regardless of their "domesticity."

But because development took different courses on Rurutu and Tubuai, its impact on women has been different. On Rurutu, island women appear to be "traditional" and have continued to perform domestic roles, including craft production. Because of a lack of other major cash-earning opportunities, women's craft earnings have become a major component of total familial cash income and women are increasingly seen as family "provisioners" (the male role). As women have been credited with that status, there has been an increase in women's authority and decision-making in the household and community, as evidenced mainly in the large number of families in which both husbands and wives are considered to be joint household heads (see Table 11.1). Interesting, Jennings (1995) describes a similar phenomenon among the Sudanese Baggara, an Islamic pastoral society; when Baggara women's income from selling milk and butter became a significant component of family income, they began to have greater say in important family and community decisions, including herd movement.

If one compares the situation on Rurutu to Tubuai, is appears that Tubuai women—unlike the more "domestic" Rurutu women — are performing new kinds of economic roles and making inroads into lucrative, male-dominated development projects (potato cultivation). While this is certainly true, they are actually able to earn only a small percentage of what men are able to earn. Thus, in the vast majority of families, women are not family breadwinners, as they are on Rurutu, and most women are financially dependent on husbands. Since they are not breadwinners, they are not viewed as "provisioners" (women's income continues to be a household supplement) and they have not experienced the added clout that being a family provisioner brings (increased decision-making and authority). Consequently, on Tubuai, most families are led by male household heads, and not by joint teams of husbands and wives (as on Rurutu). The fact that Tubuai women are participating in a new, development-oriented activity (potatoes) while Rurutu women are performing a traditional domestic role (craft production) appears to have virtually no impact on women's evolving status; the key factors are relative contribution to familial income ("breadwinning" or not) and being credited with the status of "provisioner."

The cases of Tubuai and Rurutu highlight the interplay of both material conditions and gender ideology in shaping how capitalist development affects women. They suggest that a gender ideology that "empowers" women (i.e., Tahitian women's generally high status found on both Tubuai and Rurutu) is *not* sufficient—in and of itself—to ensure that women will not be subordinate to, and dependent on, men in developing regions of the world. The Rurutu data reinforce the conclusion drawn from other cases where women's position has not deteriorated: Women's control of strategic material resources and capital—the material basis of "power" in all capitalist systems—is a necessary condition for achieving a position of relative authority and power in both the household and community. It is important to note, however, that the extent to which women are able to control resources and capital will in part be determined by prevailing gender ideologies and family structures. Thus one can conclude that where women in developing regions are able to produce a strong material base, and where gender ideology empowers them to control it for their own ends, they will be in a position to achieve greater gender equity with men.

NOTES

1. In 1994–1995, a comparative study of the differential impact of capitalist development on women was undertaken on the neighboring Tahitian islands of Tubuai, Rurutu, and Raivavae. Two other anthropologists, Jeanette Dickerson-Putman and Anna Laura Jones, contributed to the project. The study was funded by a gratefully acknowledged grant from the National Science Foundation (SBR-9311414).

2. Women's relative lack of opportunity compared to men can also be seen in their strikingly lower rates of literacy and educational attainment (particularly in Latin America, the Middle East, and Africa) (see Moore 1988), as well as in higher rates of female morbidity and mortality (Charleton 1984).

3. Pre-contact Tahitians (both male and female) were ranked relative to one another in terms of the amount of *mana*, or supernatural power, they possessed (see Oliver 1974). *Mana*, and thus social rank, was determined by birth and genealogical distance from high-ranking chiefs; males and females were ranked in this highly stratified society by these criteria and not by gender. High-ranking women clearly dominated lower-ranking men.

4. In this comparative study, 164 Tubuai households and 181 Rurutu households were included (approximately 55–60 percent of all island households). These households were chosen to be representative of the populations at large in terms of two criteria: 1) major household economic activity/socioeconomic status (income), and 2) stage in the developmental cycle of the family (young, middle, elderly families). Informants included male and female household heads, as well as couples.

5. Tubuai households (N = 139): In 103 (74 percent) women earn less than half of all income; in 36 (26 percent) women earn more than half of all income. Rurutu households (N = 134): In 73 (54.5 percent) women earn less than half of all income; in 61 (45.5 percent) women earn more than half of all income. This is a statistically significant difference: Chi-square = 11.47; p < .00071; df = 1. (Families of single male or female heads were not included.)

6. For Tubuai (N = 134 households), husbands were declared head of the family in 91 households (68 percent), husbands and wives were joint heads in 34 households (25 percent), and wives were declared the head in 9 households (7 percent). For Rurutu (134 households),

husbands were declared head in 66 households (49 percent), husbands and wives were joint heads in 55 households (41 percent), and wives were declared the head in 13 households (10 percent). The difference between the two islands is statistically significant (Chi-square = 9.66; p < .0079; df = 2). (Households of single household heads were not included in the analysis.)

7. Although on both islands the predominant pattern is for either wives, or husbands and wives together, to oversee day-to-day household expenditures, this is more often true on Rurutu (82 percent of all families) than on Tubuai (74 percent). Similarly, wives contribute to decision-making about large consumer purchases in 87 percent of all Rurutu families, but in 75 percent of Tubuai families.

8. Tubuai informants (N = 58): Most intelligent—women (17 or 29 percent); men (4 or 2 percent), both (37 or 64 percent). Rurutu informants (N = 33): Most intelligent—women (19 or 58 percent), men (2 or 6 percent), both (12 or 36 percent). The difference between the two islands is statistically significant (Chi-square = 7.20, p < .0272; df = 2).

REFERENCES

Abu-Lughod, Lila. 1986. *Veiled Sentiments: Honor and Poetry in a Bedouin Society.* Berkeley: University of California Press.

Afonja, Simi. 1986. "Changing Modes of Production and the Sexual Division of Labor Among the Yoruba." In E. Leacock and H. Safa (eds.). *Women's Work: Development and the Division of Labor by Gender.* S. Hadley: Bergin & Garvey.

Barnes, Sandra. 1990. "Women, Property and Power." In P. Sanday and R. Goodenough (eds.). *Beyond the Second Sex,* pp. 253–280. Philadelphia: University of Pennsylvania Press.

Boserup, Ester. 1970. *Women's Role in Economic Development.* London: George Allen and Unwin.

Bossen, Laurel. 1975. "Women in Modernizing Societies." *American Ethnologist* 2 (4): 587–601.

———. 1984. *The Redivision of Labor: Women and Economic Choice in Four Guatemalan Communities.* Albany: State University of New York Press.

Caulfield, Mina. 1981. "Equality, Sex, and the Mode of Production." In G. Berreman (ed.). *Social Inequality: Comparative and Developmental Approaches,* pp. 201–219. New York: Academic Press.

Charleton, Sue Ellen. 1984. *Women in Third World Development.* Boulder, CO: Westview.

Di Leonardo, Michaela, ed. 1991. *Gender at the Crossroads of Knowledge: Feminist Anthropology in the Postmodern Era.* Berkeley: University of California Press.

Escobar, Arturo. 1995. *Encountering Development: The Making and Unmaking of the Third World.* Princeton, NJ: Princeton University Press.

Etienne, M. and E. Leacock, eds. 1980. *Women and Colonization: Anthropological Perspectives.* Cambridge: J.F. Bergin.

Fernandez-Kelly, Maria P. 1981. "The Sexual Division of Labor, Development, and Women's Status." *Current Anthropology* 22 (4): 414–419.

Friedl, Ernestine. 1975. *Women and Men: An Anthropologist's View.* Prospect Heights, IL: Waveland Press.

———. 1991. "Society and Sex Roles." In E. Angeloni (ed.). *Annual Editions, Anthropology 91/92,* pp. 112–116. Guilford, CT: Dushkin Publishing.

Geertz, Hildred. 1961. *The Javanese Family.* New York: Free Press.

Jennings, Anne M. 1995. *The Nubians of West Aswan.* Boulder, CO.: Lynne Rienner.

Kluckhohn, C. and D. Leighton. 1946. *The Navaho.* Cambridge, MA: Harvard University Press.

Kung, Lydia. 1994. *Factory Women in Taiwan.* New York: Columbia University Press.

Langevin, Christine. 1990. *Tahitiennes de la Tradition a l'Integration Culturelle.* Paris: Editions L'Harmattan.

Lepowsky, Maria. 1993. *Fruit of the Motherland: Gender in an Egalitarian Society.* New York: Columbia University Press.

Levy, Robert. 1973. *Tahitians: Mind and Experience in the Society Islands.* Chicago: University of Chicago Press.

Littlefield, Alice. 1978. "Exploitation and the Expansion of Capitalism: The Case of the Hammock Industry of Yucatan." *American Ethnologist* 5 (3): 495–508.

Lockwood, Victoria. 1988. "Capitalist Development and the Socioeconomic Position of Tahitian Peasant Women." *Journal of Anthropological Research* 44 (3): 263–285.

———. 1989. "Tubuai Women Potato Planters and the Political Economy of Intra-Household Gender Relations." In R. Wilk (ed.). *The Household Economy: Reconsidering the Domestic Mode of Production,* pp. 197–220. Boulder, CO: Westview.

————. 1993. *Tahitian Transformation: Gender and Capitalist Development in a Rural Society*. Boulder, CO: Lynne Rienner.

Mies, Maria. 1982a. "The Dynamics of the Sexual Division of Labor and the Integration of Rural Women into the World Market." In L. Beneria (ed.). *Women and Development: The Sexual Division of Labor in Rural Societies*, pp. 1–28. New York: Praeger.

————. 1982b. *The Lace Makers of Narsapur*. London: Zed Press.

Moore, Henrietta. 1988. *Feminism and Anthropology*. Minneapolis: University of Minneapolis Press.

Mukhopadhyay, C. and P. Higgins. 1988. "Anthropological Studies of Womens' Status Revisited: 1977–1987." *Annual Review of Anthropology* 17: 461–495.

Nash, June. 1977. "Women and Development: Dependency and Exploitation." *Development and Change* 8: 161–182.

Nash, June and Maria Fernandez-Kelly, eds. 1983. *Women and Men and the International Division of Labor*. Albany: State University of New York Press.

Oliver, Douglas. 1974. *Ancient Tahitian Society*. (3 vols.) Honolulu: University of Hawaii Press.

————. 1981. *Two Tahitian Villages: A Study in Comparison*. Honolulu: The Institute for Polynesian Studies.

Ong, Aihwa. 1987. *Spirits of Resistance and Capitalist Discipline: Factory Women in Malaysia*. Albany: State University of New York Press.

Petersen, Glenn. 1993. "Some Pohnpei Strategies for Economic Survival." In *Contemporary Pacific Societies: Studies in Development and Change*, V. Lockwood, et al., eds., pp. 185–196. Englewood Cliffs, N.J.: Prentice-Hall.

Rapp, Rayna. 1979. "Anthropology: Review Essay." *Signs* 4 (3): 497–513.

Rodman, Margaret. 1993. "Keeping Options Open: Copra and Fish in Rurual Vanuatu." In *Contemporary Pacific Societies: Studies in Development and Change*, V. Lockwood, et al., eds., pp. 171–184. Englewood Cliffs, N.J.: Prentice-Hall.

Sacks, Karen. 1974. "Engels Revisited: Women, the Organization of Production and Private Property." In *Woman, Culture and Society*, M. Rosaldo and L. Lamphere, eds., pp. 207–222. Stanford: Stanford University Press.

Schlegel, Alice. 1977. *Sexual Stratification: A Cross-Cultural View*. New York: Columbia University Press.

Stoler, Ann. 1977. "Class Structure and Female Autonomy in Rural Java." *Signs* 3: 74–89.

Strathern, Marilyn. 1984. "Domesticity and the Denigration of Women." In O'Brien, D. and S. Tiffany (eds.). *Rethinking Women's Roles: Perspectives from the Pacific*. Berkeley: University of California Press.

Thomas, Nicholas. 1987. "Complementarity and History: Misrecognizing Gender in the Pacific." *Oceania* 57 (4): 261–270.

Wilk, Richard, ed. 1989. *The Household Economy: Reconsidering the Domestic Mode of Production*. Boulder, CO: Westview Press.

Wolf, Eric. 1982. *Europe and the People Without History*. Berkeley: University of California Press.

Doing Their Homework: The Dilemma of Planning Women's Garden Programs in Bangladesh

Margot Wilson-Moore

Recently a number of development agencies in Bangladesh (for example, CARE, CIDA, Helen Keller International, the Mennonite Central Committee, Save the Children, UNICEF, USAID) have planned and implemented independent projects or program components directed specifically toward homestead gardening as an alternative to field crop production. For the growing cadre of marginal and landless farmers with little or no cultivable

Original material prepared for this text.

land outside of the household, homestead gardening constitutes a subsistence strategy with considerable potential for improving family nutrition and cash generation.

Traditionally a complement to field crop production, homestead gardens provide a much-needed supply of nutritious, interesting, and vitamin-rich foods for home consumption. In addition, the sale of homestead garden produce makes substantial amounts of cash available for rural farm families. The discussion that follows considers homestead gardening within the broad context of international development in Bangladesh and more particularly in relation to the burgeoning literature on the role of women in development. This discussion focuses specifically on homestead gardening as a viable development strategy for rural women.

International development aid constitutes a major influence for change today. In Bangladesh millions of foreign aid dollars comprise a large proportion of the national budget. Since 1974 to 1975, Bangladesh has received not less than $700 million from the United States each year in international aid, and these donations represent two-to three-and-one-half times the total revenue budget generated in-country. However, the results in terms of quantifiable improvements are relatively few, and despite these substantial foreign aid contributions Bangladesh continues to demonstrate a negative balance of payments (greater than $5 million in 1984 to 1985) and a negative balance of trade ($135 million US in 1984 to 1985).

Environmental stress, population pressure, illiteracy, and historical explanations such as exploitation and isolation have been espoused as general causes for the persistent poverty in Bangladesh. Similarly, behavioral causes, such as a closely structured hierarchy and system of patronage, rugged individualism, and failure of Bangladeshis to "trust" one another and work cooperatively, have been offered as causes of the destitution and privation that characterize daily life in Bangladesh (Maloney 1986).

Whatever the causes, pervasive poverty and widespread destitution are commonplace, and in terms of standard "development" criteria, such as per capita income, literacy rate,

mortality and fertility rates, economic diversification, and physical and social infrastructure, Bangladesh can only be termed a development failure. Historically, vast transfers of resources out of the area have significantly depleted the resource base while more recent problems of overpopulation, land fragmentation, and environmental disasters have drawn the attention of the international aid community.

Women's issues have received considerable attention from the international donor community in recent years, but to understand the "state of the art" of women and development research[1] in Bangladesh, it is necessary to trace its roots in broader issues of development theory and feminism. Early development theory tended to overlook the special needs of women, anticipating perhaps a "trickle-down" of benefits from men toward whom most programs are directed. Feminist critiques of development theory revolve primarily around this issue—the failure of development theory to address the problems of women directly. Women are either categorized with men or ignored altogether. Women are routinely subsumed within the rubric of more general development processes that are expected to address the issues of both men and women.

A variety of critiques of development theory exist (for an in-depth discussion see Jaquette 1982; Barnes-McConnell and Lodwick 1983; Wilson-Moore 1990), and the ongoing dialogue among these critiques has generated a vast and critical literature addressing the issue of women and development in the Third World. The feminist critique of development theory is firmly grounded in feminist thought, and the theoretical perspectives that have emerged in feminist development theory clearly reflect theoretical underpinnings in feminist theory. Feminist theoretical models predict relationships between various spheres of women's lives[2] and generate research questions and information useful, indeed imperative, for appropriate development planning for women.

Too often, however, women and development researchers fail to incorporate feminist theory into their research designs or neglect to articulate the underlying feminist assumptions that influence their work. Theorizing is, in large part, left to feminist academicians who usually rely on ethnographic (rather than development) literature for constructing and testing their models. As a result feminist theory, women, and development research have progressed, in recent years, along separate and divergent paths. Despite the actuating influence of feminist theory on women and development research and their common concerns with the situation of women, discourse between these two bodies of literature is remarkably scant.

Women and development research tends to be of a highly practical nature, concentrating on the immediate and pragmatic problems faced by women in developing nations. Resources and institutional support are then directed toward these identified needs. A women's component may be incorporated into existing development programs, or alternatively projects may be designed specifically and solely for women. Often, however, development programs do not meet the needs of the women for whom they are designed. Many focus on "individual solutions," such as education to improve women's opportunities for urban wage employment, increase their access to innovative technology, or improve their subsistence production skills. Too often the systemic constraints on Third World people in general and on women in particular, such as high rates of unemployment and lack of child-care facilities, are overlooked.

The role of women in socioeconomic development has been the subject of much interest in Bangladesh (cf. Hossain, Sharif, and Huq 1977; Islam 1986) and has focused the attention of the aid community on those development issues particular to women, especially those at the lowest economic levels who are often the poorest of the poor. Khan et al. (1981) have shown that in 1981 326 government and nongovernment programs for women were registered with the Ministry of Women's Affairs. The majority provide training in knitting, sewing, embroidery, handicrafts, and garment-making. Unfortunately, however, although directed toward poor and destitute women, the income-generating potential of these skills is minimal (Khan et al. 1981:24) and the emphasis on low payment and domestic-like work only serves to perpetuate women's subordinate status and economic circumstance.

In 1986 Schaffer found that the focus of more than 100 development projects directed specifically toward women had expanded to include self-help and income generation, family planning and health, education and literacy, agriculture development projects, rural employment and industry, and female leadership training. The majority of these projects focus on integrating women into existing programs, although a few "women only" projects exist. Most donor agencies philosophically support development activities for women (Schaffer 1986:4); however, a number of cultural attitudes toward women constrain them. The view of women's work as minimal and unimportant is compounded by the women's own perception of their work as noneconomic and therefore without value.

Beyond this, religious proscriptions that predicate family honor on women's virtue and legislate women's appropriate place as inside the household necessitate development on an outreach basis (providing inputs and training to women in their own homes), while effectively preventing agencies from recruiting female staff to provide that outreach service.

Initially, little specific information was available about women in Bangladesh, and the resulting imperative for more and better data regarding women's roles, statuses, and activities generated a predominantly descriptive focus in the early research. This is especially true in the rural areas where early village studies (cf. Raper 1970; Zaidi 1970) provided only brief references to women's activities. Other village studies followed (cf. Arens and Van Beurden 1980; BRAC 1983; Chowdhury 1978; Hartmann and Boyce 1983; Mukherjee 1971), but still little direct reference was made to women.

More recently a number of authors have commented on the "invisibility" of women's economic contribution in Bangladesh (cf. Chen 1986; Huq 1979; Islam 1986; Smock

1977; Wallace et al. 1987). Women's labor routinely includes postharvest processing of field crops, such as rice, jute, mustard seed, lentils, and millet; care of animals; homestead gardening; and minor household maintenance, to name only a few. Because the labor of rural women takes place primarily inside the household, it often goes unnoticed. Nevertheless, their economic contribution is substantial (Chen 1986; Wallace et al. 1987). The importance of these kinds of studies is in shifting the focus away from the view of women as dependent and helpless. Instead, they are recognized as actors, engaged in economic pursuits in both rural and urban areas. As such they cease to be "welfare cases" and become instead an appropriate target for "mainstream" development processes.

In addition to their traditional domestic roles increasing numbers of women from landless and marginal families are being forced by economic circumstance to leave their homes to seek wage labor. At the same time technology, especially mechanized rice processing, is displacing rural women from their traditional roles in postharvest processing of field crops (Begum 1989). Cooperative programs are encouraging and supporting female entrepreneurs, but the success of these schemes often accrues from their constituting an extension of existing female roles that do not "encroach upon the traditional domain of men . . . [and are] not conceived as a threat to men's interests" (Begum 1989: 527).

Homestead gardening as a development strategy for women fits easily within these dictates because it neither encroaches on nor threatens men's traditional subsistence activities. Homestead gardening is an integral part of women's work in Bangladesh (cf. Chen 1983; Hannan 1986; Hassan 1978; Huq 1979; Hussain and Banu 1986; Scott and Carr 1985) and provides an opportunity for women to make sizable contributions to the rural farm family in terms of nutritious food for consumption as well as income generated from the sale of excess produce.

Homestead gardening is not the exclusive purview of women, although much of the research to date suggests that it is (Chen 1986;

Huq 1979). This misconception is likely a result of research bias toward women. In Bangladesh women's issues have become a primary concern of development planners, and as a result women's roles are often considered without reference to other members of the community and to men in particular. The result is a misrepresentation of women as the principal, even exclusive, actors in certain sectors of the subsistence economy; in this case as the cultivators of homestead gardens. By contrast data from my own research (Wilson-Moore 1989, 1990) show that both men and women are involved in vegetable cultivation, although some clear differences exist between what men and women do in the garden.

Men and women grow different crop varieties at different times of the year—men in winter, women in summer. The fact that the crops grown by women tend to be more indigenous in nature and those cultivated by men more likely to be imported varieties may be an artifact of men's more active participation in the public sphere. Because men are active in the marketplace, they may simply be exposed to new varieties of vegetables most often and are therefore more predisposed to experimentation. In a similar vein it may be argued that women are in some sense a reservoir of traditional information and cultivation patterns, reflective of a time before imported varieties and development inputs were available.

A clear distinction also exists between male and female patterns of vegetable cultivation in which men's patterns are reminiscent of field crop production patterns characterized by monocropping and the rows and beds of European gardens. Women's gardens, by contrast, have a jumbled appearance and may represent the indigenous patterns commonly in practice prior to outside influence (for a discussion of cross-cultural gardening traditions see Brownrigg 1985).

Women's gardens are found inside or immediately adjacent to the household. Requirements for housing, cooking, stabling of animals, and postharvest processing and storage of field crops necessitate that individual plants or small clusters of plants be scattered throughout the homestead, dotted around the central courtyard and household structures. Small plots may be located around the periphery of larger homesteads, usually immediately outside of the circle of infacing buildings.

Gourds are encouraged to grow over trellises, along the walls, and across the roofs of buildings. Other climbing plants may be trained to grow up the trunks of nearby trees. Shade-loving plants are grown under the cover of fruit and fuelwood trees, and those more tolerant of direct sun are planted in the clear places.

Plant species are highly diverse. Because there are no beds or rows, tall and medium height trees, smaller bushy shrubs, upright plants, creepers, and root crops form the horizontal layers characteristic of this type of garden. Weeding is infrequent, and it is often difficult to differentiate the homestead garden from the surrounding undergrowth. In fact an untrained observer might not recognize this type of homestead garden at all.

Husbands often fail to recognize the gardening efforts of their wives, even when the proof was crawling across the roofs and walls of the homestead and into the cooking pot at meal times. That men fail to acknowledge women's productive labor in gardens may lie partially in more general societal attitudes toward women as producers (they are not seen as such) but also in the scattered appearance of their homestead gardens, which prevents their immediate recognition by uninterested, or uninitiated, observers, be they husband, anthropologist, or development worker.

Women cultivate vegetable varieties that spring up readily, can be produced from seed preserved from the previous year, and are well-adapted to the seasonal vagaries of the climate, flourishing inside and around the homestead with a minimum of care or input. Women often stagger the planting times so that everything does not mature at once. In fact related women in separate households may coordinate their planting times, as well as the varieties planted, to maximize their production through sharing.

Vegetable gardens cultivated by women tend to have a high diversity of plant species but a small number of plants of any particular type. Accordingly, the quantities are smaller yet more varied, and they are intended for family consumption. High diversity and low volume production is the predominant characteristic of women's gardening patterns in Bangladesh and throughout Asia, a strategy well-suited to fulfilling family consumption needs.

It is no coincidence that the vegetables grown most commonly in homestead gardens are the ones villagers prefer to eat. These vegetables can be eaten on a daily basis without becoming unappetizing. Alternatively the diversity of vegetables produced in the homestead garden also helps to offset the boredom of eating the same food every day. In fact villagers prefer to have a variety of foods, even if that means eating something that they dislike from time to time.

In this way the garden acts as a living larder, providing fresh produce on a daily basis. As individual plants become ripe the women harvest them and prepare them for consumption. If more vegetables become ripe than can be consumed within the household at one time, they may be given away, traded with neighbors, or sent to the market for sale.

Homestead gardening as a development strategy for women is predicated on a view of women's production as valuable and essential to the nutritional and economic welfare of the rural farm family. Furthermore, the minimal overlap between men's and women's gardening patterns ensures that as a development strategy homestead gardening also does not compete with men's traditional activities in field crop cultivation or vegetable production. Thus, homestead gardening conforms to two primary stipulations (Begum 1989; Schaffer 1986) for success and would seem an ideal development strategy for women.

Unfortunately, these stipulations do not necessarily guarantee a positive result, and outcomes of garden programming may prove surprising if the planners have not "done their homework" prior to implementation. In this regard Brownrigg has (1985) emphasized the necessity of in-depth locally based research and observes that when such research is omitted or conducted in a cursory manner programs often fail to meet the needs of the target population. Barnett (1953) has argued that acceptance of innovation is based on the ability of recipient populations to analyze new ideas and technologies and to identify some similarity with existing culture traits. Accordingly, the more identifiable an innovation is, the more easily it can be matched with a trait already existing in the cultural lexicon, and the more readily it will be adopted.

Social science, and anthropology in particular, has much to contribute. Participant observation is a field methodology well-suited to producing detailed information about existing indigenous practices; information often not available through any other means; and information appropriate, perhaps imperative, for planners who wish to build on and enhance those existing practices. By focusing on extant patterns planners can effectively determine which goals are attainable and which populations are most appropriately targeted.

In the context of Bangladesh, for example, homestead garden programs intended to improve family nutrition and increase consumption of vitamin-rich vegetables are most appropriately directed toward women because their production is intended, in the first instance, for home consumption. If, on the other hand, program goals include increasing family income through sale of garden produce, men may constitute a more appropriate target group because their vegetable production is traditionally intended for the market. Finally, a program goal of increased access to cash for women requires careful consideration because women's limited access to the market and ramifications of cash generation on family nutrition are two important, potentially negative, dimensions of income-generating schemes for women.

Women routinely remain secluded within the household in Bangladesh. As a result, marketing of women's garden produce constitutes something of a dilemma. Produce must be transported and sold by a male family member or neighbor. Women are able to retain control over the cash generated in this way by providing a shopping list (for household essentials such as oil or kerosene) when they turn over the produce for sale. Accordingly, the money is recycled back into the family budget on a daily basis and does not accumulate. It fails to be assigned a "value" by men or women and as a result goes unrecognized. That this particular economic contribution fails to affect women's status in any appreciable way has been discussed elsewhere (Wilson-Moore 1989).

Beyond the lack of recognition that greets women's economic enterprise in the garden, Boserup (1970) has shown that when women's economic activities become profitable (especially in terms of cash generation), men tend to take them over (see also Chaney and Schmink 1976). Male takeovers of the income-generating component of women's homestead gardening and the displacement of women from their traditional roles in vegetable production necessitates only a small shift in production activities. However, the ramifications in terms of family nutritional well-being may be far-reaching. Rural farm families depend on women's homestead production for a ready supply of varied and vitamin-rich vegetable foods, a complement nutritionally and aesthetically to the masebhate (rice and fish) mainstays of the Bangladeshi diet.

Redirecting women's vegetable production toward the market would necessitate a change in production technique, disrupting the traditional patterns of women's homestead garden production and interfering with that ready supply of vegetable foods. The traditional pattern that produces small quantities of diverse vegetable foods intended for consumption within the homestead would have to be replaced by high-output, low-diversity cropping. Furthermore, there is little evidence to suggest that rural families would use the cash earned in this way to "buy back" or replace vegetable foods in the diet. Rather, high-status processed foods such as tea, white sugar, white flour, and bread are more apt to make an appearance when cash becomes available for their purchase.

Maintaining a balance between growing vegetable crops in large volume for sale and in sufficient variety for home consumption represents a problem in terms of the space and time constraints of homestead production. However, the existing, complementary yet rarely overlapping patterns of men's and women's traditional vegetable production seems well-suited to the respective cash generation and consumption needs of the family. Accordingly, planners concerned with pervasive poverty and widespread nutritional deficiency diseases in Bangladesh may wish to consider the benefits of developing each of these gardening strategies as they mutually, yet independently, support the rural farm family.

NOTES

1. Throughout this paper the terminology women and development has been used as a generic term for women's development in an effort to avoid more specific references such as women in development (WID) or development for women. These advocate, in the first case, the incorporation of a women's component into existing programs and, in the second, separate programming by women for women (see Jaquette 1982; Barnes-McConnell and Lodkwick 1983; Wilson-Moore 1990 for a more comprehensive discussion of these terms).

2. For example, see Boserup (1970), Friedl (1975), and Sanday (1973, 1974) for models that predicate women's status on women's participation in the work force and their economic contribution to the family.

REFERENCES

Arens, Jenneke and Jos Van Beurden. 1980. *Jhagrapur: Poor Peasants and Women in a Village in Bangladesh*. Calcutta: Orient Longman.

Barnes-McConnell, Pat and Dora G. Lodwick. 1983. *Working with International Development Projects: A Guide for Women–in–Development*. East Lansing: Michigan State University, Office of Women in International Development.

Barnett, Homer. 1953. *Innovation: The Basis of Culture Change*. New York: McGraw-Hill.

Begum, Kohinoor. 1989. "Participation of Rural Women in Income-Earning Activities: A Case Study of a Bangladesh Village." *Women's Studies International Forum* 12(5):519–528.

Boserup, Ester. 1970. *Women's Role in Economic Development*. New York: St. Martin's Press.

BRAC (Bangladesh Rural Advancement Committee). 1983. *Who Gets What and Why: Resource Allocation in a Bangladesh Village*. Dhaka: BRAC Publication.

Brownrigg, Leslie. 1985. *Home Gardening in International Development: What the Literature Shows*. Washington, DC: League for International Food Education.

Chaney, Elsa and Marianne Schmink. 1976. "Women and Modernization: Access to Tools." In June Nash and Helen Safa (eds.). *Sex and Class in Latin America*. New York: Praeger.

Chen, Martha Alter. 1986. *A Quiet Revolution: Women in Transition in Rural Bangladesh*. Cambridge: Schenkman Publishing.

Chowdhury, Anwarullah. 1978. *A Bangladesh Village: A Study of Social Stratification*. Dhaka: Centre for Social Studies.

Friedl, Ernestine. 1975. *Women and Men: An Anthropologist's View*. New York: Holt, Rinehart and Winston.

Hannan, Ferdouse H. 1986. *Past, Present and Future Activities of Women's Desk*. Comilla: Bangladesh Academy for Rural Development.

Hartmann, Betsy and James K. Boyce. 1983. *A Quiet Violence: Views from a Bangladesh Village*. London: Oxford University Press.

Hassan, Nazmul. 1978. *Spare Time of Rural Women: A Case Study*. Dhaka: University of Dacca, Institute of Nutrition and Food Science.

Hossain, Monowar, Raihan Sharif, and Jahanara Huq (eds.). 1977. *Role of Women in Socio-Economic Development in Bangladesh*. Dhaka: ABCO Press.

Huq, Jahanara. 1979. "Economic Activities of Women in Bangladesh: The Rural Situation." In Women for Women (eds.). *The Situation of Women in Bangladesh*, pp. 139–182. Dhaka: BRAC Printers.

Hussain, S. and S. Banu. 1986. *BARD Experiences in Organization of Women in their Involvement in Agricultural Related Activities*. Comilla: Bangladesh Academy for Rural Development.

Islam, Shamima. 1986. "Work of Rural Women in Bangladesh: An Overview of Research." Paper presented at workshop on women in agriculture. Comilla: Bangladesh Academy for Rural Development.

Jaquette, Jane S. 1982. "Women and Modernization Theory: A Decade of Feminist Criticism," *World Politics* 34(2):267–284.

Khan, Salma, Jowshan Rahman, Shamima Islam, and Meherunnessa Islam. 1981. *Inventory for Women's Organizations in Bangladesh.* Dhaka: UNICEF.

Maloney, Clarence. 1986. *Behavior and Poverty in Bangladesh.* Dhaka: University Press Limited.

Mukherjee, Ramkrishna. 1971. *Six Villages of Bengal.* Bombay: Popular Prakashan.

Raper, Arthur. 1970. *Rural Development in Action: The Comprehensive Experiment at Comilla, East Pakistan.* Ithaca: Cornell University Press.

Sanday, Peggy. 1973. "Toward a Theory of the Status of Women." *American Anthropologist* 75(5): 1682–1700.

————. 1974. "Female Status in the Public Domain." In Michelle Z. Rosaldo and Louise Lamphere (eds.). *Woman, Culture, and Society,* pp. 189–206. Stanford, CA: Stanford University Press.

Sattar, Ellen. 1979. "Demographic Features of Bangladesh with Reference to Women and Children." In Women for Women (eds.). *The Situation of Women in Bangladesh,* pp. 1–22. Dhaka: BRAC Printers.

Schaffer, Teresita C. 1986. *Survey of Development Project and Activities for Women in Bangladesh.* Dhaka: Provatee Printers.

Scott, Gloria L. and Marilyn Carr. 1985. *The Impact of Technology Choice on Rural Women in Bangladesh: Problems and Opportunities.* Washington, DC: World Bank Working Paper No. 731.

Smock, Audrey Chapman. 1977. "Bangladesh: A Struggle with Tradition and Poverty." In Janet Z. Giele and Audrey C. Smock (eds.). *Women: Roles and Status in Eight Countries,* pp. 83–126. New York: John Wiley and Sons.

Wallace, Ben J., Rosie M. Ahsan, Shahnazz H. Hussain, and Ekramul Ahsan. 1987. *The Invisible Resource: Women and Work in Rural Bangladesh.* Boulder, CO: Westview Press.

Wilson-Moore, Margot. 1989. "Women's Work in Homestead Gardens: Subsistence, Patriarchy, and Status in Northwest Bangladesh." *Urban Anthropology* 18(203):281–297.

————. 1990. "Subsistence, Patriarchy, and Status: Women's Work in Homestead Gardens in Northwest Bangladesh." Ph.D. dissertation, Southern Methodist University, Dallas, Texas.

Zaidi, S. M. Hafeez. 1970. *The Village Culture in Transition: A Study of East Pakistan Rural Society.* Honolulu: East-West Press.

Factory as Home and Family: Female Workers in the Moroccan Garment Industry

M. Laetitia Cairoli

My factory is better . . . because every girl in it is like a daughter of the owner.

Thus, one Fez clothing factory worker explained why she had remained at her job for four years, despite the notoriously low pay and constant overtime demanded there. In the past two decades the Moroccan garment industry has developed into one of the country's most significant export trades and Moroccan females have become the labor power for cloth-

Reproduced by permission of the Society for Applied Anthropology from *Human Organization* vol. 57, no. 2, 1998.

ing manufacture. Although their role in the garment factories is widely regarded as exploitative and demeaning, the workers themselves continue to use the idiom of family to describe their relationships to factory owners, administrators, supervisors, and their fellow workers. In the course of a year of ethnographic research in the city of Fez, I began an exploration of how garment factory workers make sense of their labor on the shop floor.

Inside one Fez garment factory, where I worked during a three-month period, I observed workers as they sought to impose their own assumptions and values upon the factory system and thereby render their labor meaningful. Nearly all of Morocco's garment factory workers are female and most are unmarried.[1] They confront the factory with a set of cultural values that order their social world, central to which is their identity as kinswoman, a self-perception workers believe to be ordained by Islam. Despite their engagement with the factory, workers continue to perceive themselves first and foremost as daughters, sisters, and perhaps wives and mothers in a patriarchal family. As such, they presume that their rightful place is in the private sphere of the home, which is the arena of their most noble efforts. Thus, they transform the workshop floor into an interior space, recast factory staff into family, and operate in the factory as they would in the household. In this way they retain their prized identity as kinswoman, even within the factory, and they convert factory labor into work that is significant to them.[2] In doing so, however, they render themselves more amenable to the factory's exploitation.

There are, of course, limits to the workers' re-creation of the factory: for Moroccan females, the garment factory is a new kind of public space with characteristics unlike the private arena of the home. In some instances, workers find that their efforts to impose the blueprint of home and family on the factory fall short, and they confront what they recognize to be foreign work regimes and excessive domination. When this occurs, workers resist. I do not see this behavior as contradictory; rather, I assert that the workers' ability to comply with factory domination (which occurs far more frequently than does resistance) is rooted in their conversion of factory into home. Here I explore how this transformation is enacted.

THE "GLOBAL FACTORY"

Any study of Moroccan female garment workers must be set in the context of the recent literature on the phenomenon of women's participation in factory production. Over the past two decades, this scholarship has explored the effects of global capitalism on the definitions and meanings of gender. Two central questions have been posed: the first concerns the impact of women's participation in industrialization on the women themselves, on the men, on the family, and on the local culture. The second question is whether this impact—and the very participation of women in factories worldwide—is intrinsic to factory technology itself and/or capitalism, or if it results from local culture (Warren and Borque 1989). Researchers have sought to understand whether women's participation in these new forms of labor marks their liberation from local "patriarchy," or marks a new kind of enslavement to the demands of foreign capital. Those arguing the former possibility have pointed to ways in which factory work provided women an escape from the confines of home and new opportunities for personal autonomy (Lim 1983; Salaff 1981). Other researchers have emphasized, instead, the exploitation in modern production systems that is particularly detrimental to female status (Nash and Fernandez-Kelly 1983).

The literature on women and technology has demonstrated that women's entry into capitalist wage work affects the nature of gender roles and relations in complex and contradictory ways. As Nash (1981) notes, female participation in new forms of capitalist wage labor intensifies existing forms of gender subordination, while simultaneously decomposing and recomposing them. The roots of these transformations are found both in local patriarchies and in global capitalism. While the literature on women in the global factory has illuminated critical aspects of gender transformations which accompany the movement of global capital, much of the early research was limited in scope.

A particular weakness in the literature is its relative lack of detailed cultural analysis of what Ong (1991:280) calls the "experiential and interpretive dimensions of work relations." Much of the earliest research overlooked the unique ways in which workers transform capitalist work regimes and formulate their own kinds of meanings. This limitation in the literature was partly a result of the analysts' perspective on the nature of capitalism. Characterizing the capitalist system as powerful and deterministic, theorists often assumed that the methods and relations of production associated with high-tech factories would occur wherever these factories were established (Blim 1992). Theorists would then analyze the new industrialization as an effect of a standard logic, or as the result of the intersection of capitalism and a local patriarchal system.

More recent conceptualizations of the global capitalist system stress the flexibility of capitalist processes and allow for a new interpretation of the effects of industrialization (Blim 1992; Ong 1991). Capitalism (including its associated technology) is no longer seen as a homogenizing agent that flattens local systems into replicas of each other. Instead, capitalism is now understood to merge with indigenous values and practices and thus to proliferate new kinds of labor processes and relations.

If this particular perspective on capitalism is adopted, the phenomenon of the factory, and the lives of its workers, can be studied as a cultural process linked to other local cultural forms, rather than as a consequence of capitalist production (Calagione and Nugent 1992). With this perspective, the local particulars in the worker's experience of industrialization become central; indeed, they become the focus of the study. Here, I follow this approach and discuss the Moroccan clothing factory as another expression of specifically Moroccan cultural values. Workers experience their labor according to Moroccan categories already familiar to them, and use their own cultural meanings to interpret the garment factory. The Fez garment factory is thoroughly "Moroccanized" despite imported technology and systems of production.

Inside the factory, the garment workers struggle to retain a notion of themselves as family members, specifically as daughters (or sometimes as wives) in patriarchal households. They have accepted a notion of themselves as subservient and dutiful long before they enter the garment factory. They model their position in the factory hierarchy on their role in the household and so are able not only to accept the domination of the factory, but to find in that domination their own sources of personal self-worth and power. Thus, workers transform colleagues into loyal sisters and factory owners into concerned fathers. They are able to accept the constraints that the factory imposes by assimilating the owners' dominance into other, more acceptable forms of relationships. This re-molding of relationships formed inside the factory to fit the prototypes of ties formed outside ultimately makes the workers available for increased exploitation. Persons with authority in the factory capitalize on workers' interpretations of their roles to maximize production and ultimately increase profit.

RESEARCH METHODS

I conducted the fieldwork for this study in the city of Fez from August 1994 to August 1995. The fieldwork involved intensive ethnography, which included formal interviews of Fez factory owners, formal and informal interviews of workers and their families, two random surveys carried out in separate garment factories in the city, and three months of participant observation inside one of those garment factories. The factory where I worked, which I call "Confection," employs some 150 workers and has been in operation for some six years. It is typical in size and operation of garment factories in Fez. At Confection I worked in the packaging department, where finished garments are tagged and prepared for shipment. This experience provided me a position from which to observe everyday work routines, the nature of the work process, staff hierarchies, and personal interactions inside the factory. It was through "acting like a worker" that I began to understand something of what factory work means to Moroccan factory girls.

THE ECONOMIC CONTEXT OF GARMENT PRODUCTION

Today clothing manufacture is one of Morocco's chief export industries, and garments account for a quarter of the country's exports (Leymarie and Tripier 1992). Conservative estimates suggest that Morocco's garment factories employ close to a quarter of the country's factory workers: some 95,000 of the country's total 444,000 industrial workers produce garments. Virtually all of these workers are female (Ministère du Commerce 1994).[3]

The importance of the garment industry to the Moroccan economy is a recent phenomenon. Before the 1980s, garment manufacture was relatively insignificant. Between 1981 and 1991 the production of garments more than quadrupled (Leymarie and Tripier 1992) and, although males had formerly predominated in the garment factories, it was females who were hired, en masse, to staff the new enterprises.[4] The boom in the Moroccan garment business, and the concomitant employment of females, was fueled by several factors. These included the government economic readjustment program, trade agreements with the European Economic Community, and the movement of European production "off-shore."

The Moroccan government economic readjustment program, instituted in 1983, was a primary catalyst of the new trend (Leymarie and Tripier 1992). Before the institution of the readjustment program, Moroccan industry consisted largely of state-owned, high-tech enterprises with little capacity for generating employment. These included such industries as phosphate mining and production of thread and cloth. The program sought to replace such industries with private, low capital, labor-intensive ones. This change in Moroccan industry marked a shift in the gender of the country's work-force. As Morocco turned to light manufacturing for export, including garment production, food processing and electronics manufacturing, females flooded into factories. This employment of female factory workers is characteristic of export-oriented industries across the globe (Nash and Fernandez-Kelly 1983; Rothstein and Blim 1992; Ong 1987, 1991, Nash 1981).

European sub-contractors (predominantly French), motivated by favorable trade conditions and the desire for "off-shore" production sights, became involved in the industry in the late 1970s. They sought out Moroccan enterprises that could supply them with low cost labor, they sent in raw materials needed for production and exported the final products. These subcontractors encouraged the wide scale employment of females, enjoying greater profits because women would accept far lower wages than the salaries men demanded (Joekes 1982a, 1982b, 1985). Thus, the nature and structure of the Moroccan garment industry is defined by the relationship between the European contractors and private Moroccan industrialists.

Moroccan garment factories are generally small, family-owned businesses with staffs of 50 employees or less, flexible enough to respond to a foreign, somewhat volatile, market. Because of their relatively small size they can, and often do, elude government regulation. The garment factories commonly do not heed Moroccan labor law, which in part accounts for their poor working conditions. The factories open and close rapidly and unexpectedly, with fluctuations in the external market. Thus, Moroccan females labor in an industry that provides them insecure positions and relatively poor conditions (Leymarie and Tripier 1992).

Originally, Morocco's garment factory workers, like all Moroccan factory hands, were predominantly male. Before the 1980s, female garment factory workers did unskilled work on the margins of production, but they did not operate sewing machines. Today, however, women and girls fill nearly all positions in the garment factories. The wide-scale employment of females as garment factory workers takes on new meanings in the Moroccan context.

The Social Context of Garment Production

In my research I found that garment factory workers are, for the most part, unmarried young girls who live at home with their parents and unmarried siblings. This fact is widely recognized in Morocco. The workers are generally daughters of lower class households which, in comparison with others of their class, are relatively poor and suffer high rates of male unemployment. (I herein refer to the house-holds where garment workers live as "factory households"). The vast majority of garment workers contribute all or at least part of their earnings to household support and are significant wage-earners.[5]

Despite their positions as breadwinners, factory workers retain a fierce hold on the value of the patriarchal family. Both in word and action, they revere the traditional hierarchy that establishes males as protectors and females as dependents. Garment workers speak of factory labor as a temporary aberration they must tolerate until a successful marriage places them in the position of non-working wife and mother (married workers, a minority, are often young and as yet childless; workers with children generally work because they are destitute).

In their homes, garment workers enact the rituals of subservience that confirm and reinforce their positions as daughters, or sometimes as wives, in either case female and junior members of the household. In spite of their engagement with the factory, workers strive to maintain their identity as kinswoman because this identity is more central to them than their self-perception as workers.[6]

Local ideologies of gender, to which workers adhere, reinforce the patriarchal structure of factory households. Male authority in the family is legitimized by an ideology that defines women as economically dependent, subservient, and in need of control. According to the Moroccan gender code, a woman's proper role is that of wife and mother, a position that is essentially non-economic and properly played out in the privacy of the domestic sphere. Men appropriately take the position of breadwinner and operate in the economic sphere outside the home. Thus, women are symbolically associated with the home and with private, interior domestic space. A family's honor is embedded in its ability to keep women inside and protected, thus maintaining the divide between male and female that is at once a separation between inside and outside, private and public, kin and non-kin, home and business.[7]

The favored portrayal of female activities as home-bound, kin-related and non-economic obscures the fact that Moroccan women have always been active in the economy (Beneria 1984, Davis 1983). Today, the economic participation of Moroccan females represents 36% of national economic activity (Direction de la Statistique 1994), although it goes largely unrecognized. Still, the above-described gender code retains its position as an ideal, rooted in the popular understanding of Islam. The mass entry of Fez's women into the garment factories blatantly contradicts the pervasively held Moroccan notions of family and gender. In this article, I explore how factory workers live with this contradiction.

The Factory in Fez

Fez is an ancient city, revered among Moroccans as a spiritual capital and regarded as a bulwark of Islam and Muslim society. Traditionally, Fez has been an important artisanal center. Today it is a textile town. At independence, the Moroccan government established its largest public cloth spinning and weaving factories in Fez, which were (and are today) staffed by men. During the 1980s garment manufacturing emerged as the city's principal industry and today the sewing factories of Fez employ more than a third of all Fez factory workers, nearly all of them women (Ministère du Commerce 1995a, 1995b). This is a vivid contrast to the situation that existed less than three decades ago, when the town's textile enterprises were the province of men.

Industrial enterprises are scattered throughout the city of Fez, although most industry is located in three industrial quarters. Small factories and artisanal workshops producing for the local market and the tourist trade are found in the ancient medina. Other modest-sized factories exist in the city's newer sections, including the Ville Nouvelle and the recently developed urban periphery. The bulk of Fez's industry, including the largest and most "modern" factories, many of which produce for export, is located in the city's industrial quarters. These include the oldest and largest, Quartier Industriel Sidi Brahim, the industrial quarter of Doukkarat, and the most recently created quarter in Ben Souda. Three-quarters of Fez's factory workers labor in these districts (Fejjal 1987).

The majority of Fez's garment factories are privately owned by a class of Moroccan elite, known as the Fassi. The term *"Fassi"* is used throughout the country to describe a group of influential families originally native to the city of Fez, who control much of Morocco's wealth and political power. The Fassi are at the top of the local class structure, which includes a middle level of educated bureaucrats and a lower level made up of the majority of city dwellers, who are relatively poor and uneducated. This lower class is the class with which garment workers identify.

THE LABOR PROCESS AND FACTORY STAFF

The labor process in Fez garment factories involves six separate steps, which precede and follow upon the actual sewing of the garments. They include, in sequential order: the intake and inventory of fabric and supplies imported from Europe; the cutting of the fabric; the actual sewing of the garments, carried out by workers seated in rows ("sewing lines"); the ironing of finished products; the final inspection of completed garments; and packaging and shipment. This production sequence is carried out in the same manner, using the same kind of technology, in garment factories throughout the world.

These production tasks are carried out by factory staff who labor in a hierarchy of authority. At the top of this hierarchy are the factory owners, who are either upper-class Moroccans (generally the above-described Fassi) or Europeans; in both cases, those at the top owners of the factory hierarchy are most frequently men.[8] Owners generally leave the daily direction of the factory to be handled by administrators, the garment manufacturing technicians who plan and supervise production. Like the owners, these individuals are upper-class Moroccan men (often of the owner's family) or Europeans.[9] A workshop director, generally a Moroccan man,

oversees the management of all factory staff on the workshop floor. Next in the hierarchy are the workshop supervisors, who manage each particular production process; there are, for instance, one or two line supervisors for each sewing line. These supervisors are generally Moroccan males or females, of the same class as the workers. Finally, at the bottom of the factory hierarchy, are the mass of factory workers, who are Moroccan females of the lower class.

On the margins of production are the factory mechanics, transport bus drivers, secretaries and maids. The mechanics and bus drivers are Moroccan lower-class men, the former considered relatively skilled. The secretaries are Moroccan females who, because they are literate and not engaged in manual work, hold relatively high status within the factory. The maids, unskilled and impoverished females in a demeaned occupation, occupy the lowest position in the hierarchy.

Factory staff rely on familiar and valued models of relationships to interact with each other and with those who control them. I will explore how local assumptions about home and family, assumptions that are themselves infused with ideas about gender, inform the workers' attempts to transform factory relations into meaningful intercourse.

Factory as Home and Family

I like this factory very, very much. The people here are nice, it is like a family. There are hardly any men working here . . . so it is like being in your own house . . . If I ever left this job, I would go straight back home.

The gendering of the workshop floor as female transforms what might have been a public and immoral space into a private and acceptable one. As Emen, a seven-year employee of the Confection expressed it above, the fact that garment factories hire (nearly) only females makes the work that goes on in them somewhat more respectable. The factory is a private space, like a house, because it is a female space, a space free from the threat of illicit sexuality. Whatever transpires inside the factory is less morally questionable because the shop floor is imagined to be a private rather than a public arena. As one worker explained with pride, "one girl passes her cloth to another girl, and we are at ease, because we are all girls."

Garment factory workers are generally demeaned by Fez inhabitants for their participation in factory labor. Factory labor is in itself poorly regarded because it is manual labor, neither autonomous nor artisanal, and participation in factory work connotes a low class status. But for females, it suggests as well a lack of family honor and the real or potential loss of personal virtue. Girls who engage in factory labor are assumed to be related to males who are unable to appropriately support and protect them. The glaring presence of factory girls on the streets of Fez is often cited as proof of the inability of families to control and monitor their daughters. In response to such deprecating images, garment workers take refuge in the fact that they work in a safe, protected, all-female environment.

The actual physical construction of the factories and the way workers approach and understand factory space expresses the notion of factory as home. The factories producing for export, situated in Fez's three industrial districts, are large, low-lying structures that look like warehouses. Rows of narrow windows parallel the factory roofs but are almost unnoticeable from outside. The windows are generally too high for a passerby to see inside and, unlike the male-staffed cement and construction factories (where metal doors are often left open and interior courtyards are visible to the outside), the garment factories in the same districts housing Moroccan girls are shut tight to the stranger's eye. They look at first glance as if they are unoccupied.

Large metal doors mark the entrance to the factories and a guardian sits directly behind these doors. The doors open into a courtyard where the trucks that transport materials to and from Europe load and unload. The factory men—the guardian, mechanics and drivers—often remain in this open, transitional space. On arrival workers file through the courtyard and directly into the workshop. This is an area separate from the courtyard, located behind it, or up a flight of stairs. Once they have arrived inside the factory, workers may not leave the building without permission (often written) from their supervisors. At the Confection factory, workers who became ill during the work day required written authorization to get past the guardian and walk out of the building. Even if a worker wished to quit the job permanently, she could not leave the premises with written permission. The factory is a private space, tightly enclosed and closely monitored.

Altogether, then, the garment factory is a concrete structure built around an open courtyard, monitored by a male guardian, in which women remain protected from view and separate from males present. This description of place is reminiscent of the traditional Fez household (Mernissi 1994), in which a male slave prevented the entrance of strangers, and where women remained protected inside, carrying out the labor specific to them. While such households may have existed only rarely and for the wealthy few, the notion of the home as a private, enclosed and specifically female space remains a Moroccan ideal. The female garment factory is modeled on this prototype.

Unlike Moroccan female bureaucrats who wear European business suits, or university students who wear western style skirts or jeans on campus,[10] garment factory workers do not don "professional" or western dress to go to work. They travel to and from the factory in the modest jellaba, a long, loose fitting robe worn in public spaces by traditional Moroccan women. Their retention of the jellaba signals identification with conventional Moroccan womanhood, as opposed to "modern" working women or with university girls (two other groups of women in transition). Inside the factories, workers are dressed in the informal clothing Moroccan women wear in the privacy of the home: baggy, pajama-like dresses or skirts or blue jeans in distinctive Moroccan combinations of style and color (in some factories workers must wear regulation smocks). Most wear plastic sandals on their bare feet, as they would at home. In summer the workshops can be stiflingly hot, and workers who take pains to dress modestly in the public arena of the streets labor in a minimum of clothing in the factory, as if confident that they are not exposed to a stranger's view.

Inside this production center imagined as domestic space, factory owners and workers alike assert that they work together "as a family"; owners claim to treat workers "as daughters." Workers identify the owners in a protective role that their fathers might hold, and assert that all fellow garment workers are "sisters."[11] Even where workers recognize the discontinuities between ties formed inside the factory and those formed at home, the analogy to family life is implicit. For example, one worker, who detested the factory, claimed she would prefer to stay at home because her mother, as she said, "would never yell at (her) the way this administrator does."

The factory is the home and family is the idiom through which factory personnel think about their relations to each other. The gendered dimension of family relationships is evident in the way female factory workers approach owners, co-workers and supervisors, male and female.

In using the metaphor of family, workers quite consciously help owners in their achievement of production goals. Despite a skill hierarchy among them, they treat each other as "sisters" and thus with relative equality. Workers vehemently assert that they support each other in the accomplishment of factory tasks. Repeatedly, I was told stories of lines of machine operators who had stayed late in order to help one of their slower members, or of individual machine operators who had fallen behind in their own tasks in order to assist an inexperienced newcomer. Workers emphasized their willingness to work well with each other, taking pride in their ability to behave in a sisterly fashion. At Confection (as at many other Fez factories) workers ate lunch together from communal plates, just as they would at home, making evident their attempts to replicate the atmosphere of the home inside the factory.

The sisterly relations among workers is perhaps most evident in the way they interact with their supervisors, particularly in their defiance of factory demands. Females are increasingly being placed in supervisory positions inside Fez factories and the majority of sewing line supervisors today are female. At Confection, workers were relatively free in directly challenging female supervisors; they seemed to fear these supervisors less than they feared supervisory males.

Disputes between workers and female supervisors were not uncommon and often took the form of loud and sudden outbursts of resistance from workers in response to unbearable production pressures. Before such exchanges became problematic, however, the defiant worker's co-workers would often intervene, attempting to assuage the stressed worker's feelings and encourage her compliance. In one such case, I watched as a put-upon worker argued with her supervisor, refusing to complete a particular task. When the other workers tried to calm this worker and urge her compliance, the worker asked, "Why should she be allowed to boss me?" In response, her colleague asserted, "If Hakima cannot boss us, then who will?" The annoyed worker ultimately complied.

Co-workers had reminded the rebellious worker of the validity of the hierarchy among them, one not foreign to the mode of control used within the family. An age-hierarchy among siblings is accepted in traditional Moroccan homes, and it is recognized that the eldest sister has the authority to lead her younger sisters in the housework. Verbalization of defiance and argument is not uncommon among siblings in a household. Neither is the eventual cooperation attained through a common acknowledgement of, and respect for, a universally recognized hierarchy, The authority of the female supervisor gains validity because it is reminiscent of the authority of the eldest sister. This argument, like others between workers and their female supervisors, is reminiscent of arguments between sisters in a household. Arguments with male supervisors take on a different tone, as discussed below. First, however, it is necessary to discuss the position of males in the factory.

Workers and workshop-level supervisors are today nearly exclusively female. Still, there are some males present inside the factories and on the workshop floor. The men may be the factory owners, high level administrators, the workshop director, supervisors, or the male service workers (who include the factory transport drivers, guardians, and mechanics). It is now rare to find men on the sewing lines; three was the greatest number of male sewing machine operators I could identify in any Fez factory, and most have none.

In general, the factory men attempt to separate themselves from the females. Factory guardians and transport drivers generally remain in the courtyard, separate from the workshop floor and the females there. The mechanics' duties compel them to be present on the workshop floor amidst the females. At Confection, they did not dally on the floor and remained in a separate room when possible. The factory men took lunch together, eating only after the mass of workers had left the lunch room. Just as men in Moroccan homes often remove themselves after meals to retreat to the all-male public cafes and street corners, men in the factory did not linger with women in a space that was clearly female.

The men present on the workshop floor are most often the workshop director and the supervisors directing the labor of the female machine operators. As noted above, the majority of line supervisors in Fez factories today are female; still, most factories retain at least several men in the position of sewing line supervisor. Almost all factories have retained men in the position of cutting supervisor (a post requiring technical training largely unavailable to lower-class Moroccan females). All the Fez factories I visited retained a male as workshop director, the position of greatest authority on the workshop floor. Workshop directors are always men, one informant explained, because "a man can make the girls afraid, but a woman cannot."

This hierarchy of gender authority on the factory floor reflects the hierarchy within the domestic sphere, where women carry out the daily labor and men retain the authority,

The organization and use of space inside the factory makes explicit a gender hierarchy taken for granted. The few men who are present on the workshop floor (either administrators, supervisors or mechanics) are free to move about the factory at will. The female workers, however, are not permitted to leave their positions without authorization; a pass is required even to use the restroom. Workers must remain in place until production quotas are met and often do not know when the workday will end. Officially, they are not permitted to speak while they work.[12]

Thus, the very few males present on the workshop floor are upright figures standing and moving with relative self-control across a space in which females are fixed. It appears that males control females in an otherwise all-female space. The apparent immobilization of women in fixed places inside the factory parallels the limits placed on their freedom of movement in the culture generally. It also reiterates the local gender ideology that defines women as subservient and men as in control.

Given this presumed hierarchy of authority between male and female, the female garment workers directly confront male supervisors less often than female supervisors. In one case I observed a young packaging worker carrying heavy boxes down a staircase while the male workshop supervisor stood by, watching her without assisting. When the task was done the worker complained to her colleagues that the supervisor had done nothing to help. One colleague responded, "What business does a man have working in this factory?" and the other coworkers agreed that a man has no compelling interest in factory work. The demeaned labor in the garment factory is not worthy of a man's time or energy. It is common in Moroccan households to watch females toil while males relax, and factory families invariably defend this as natural. Just as a girl would not expect her father, or even her brother, to help her carry out her household tasks, so a garment factory worker ought not to expect assistance from males on the workshop floor. Garment factory work is degraded work and it is the work of females.

Nonetheless, workers do occasionally resist the authority of men in the factory; they are, however, sanctioned for it. In one case at Confection, a sewing line operator asked her male supervisor for permission to use the restroom. When he refused her, she stood up to leave her seat nonetheless. He slapped her and she, in return, slapped him. She was fired for her deed. In explaining to me why the worker was forced to leave, one girl said, "In Morocco a man can hit a woman but a woman must never, ever, hit a man. Even if he hits her, she must not hit him back." These customs prevail on the shop floor.

Factory owners, almost always male, are removed from everyday interactions on the shop floor, and thus are not engaged in the quotidian labor process. According to the dominant metaphor, factory owners are fathers and the mass of females who toil on the workshop floor, daughters. Cast in the role of fathers, owners take their positions as guardians of female virtue seriously. They provide transportation so that workers can travel to and from the factory in the protected space of factory vans (which are frequently all-female spaces; male workers often travel separately). In this way, owners curb the workers' wanderings on the streets of Fez, like fathers protecting their chastity.[13] In many factories, owners required the workers to remain inside while awaiting the arrival of the company vans, thereby preventing their unnecessary exposure on the street. At Confection the owner instituted a rule forbidding workers from travelling to and from the factory on public transportation and requiring all workers to commute in the company vans. The rule was put in place when the owner discovered that young men were frequenting the local streets in the early evening, hoping to socialize with workers leaving the factory.

Thus, the owners' control of workers reaches beyond service inside the factory. The owners' efforts to monitor female comportment on the streets of Fez were approved by community members and workers as well. Owners themselves used the idiom of family to characterize their relations with workers. One owner described himself as the workers' "father, brother, uncle, friend." He reported that he gave extra money to the neediest workers, and he claimed to buy many of them the rams needed for the ritual annual sacrifice. Although it was impossible to corroborate his story, owners cultivated the loyalty of workers by presenting themselves as concerned and watchful fathers.

Typically, workers verbalized feelings of fondness and respect for the factory owners. Concerning the above-mentioned transportation regulations at Confection, many workers defended the restrictions placed on their movements outside the factory, claiming that such controls helped maintain their reputations and assure the community that they were honorable girls. In a similar way, I found that Moroccan girls who chafed at the restrictions their fathers and brothers placed upon them would nonetheless defend these men against criticism and readily portray their influence as a form of protection or an expression of concern. Thus, workers justified the owners' increased control just as they might justify the limits placed on them by male kin as the men's attempt to guard and shelter them. Workers, perceiving themselves as "daughters," were compelled by a sense of family obligation to comply with the limits imposed on them.

This rich and meaningful basis for relationship binds girls to the factory in a sort of moral obligation that many workers acknowledge. Work becomes a commitment to the father and, through fulfilling it, a worker demonstrates her high moral standing as a female, and as a member of the community. One worker at a Fez garment factory described the working of overtime as a kind of moral obligation, a burden necessary to bear. "If the boss needs us to stay and work till seven o'clock in the evening, we must stay. We have to help him keep his commitments with people overseas." She explained how a fellow worker got fired: one evening when they were working overtime, the girl just got up from her machine and said to the owner, "Just give me my money for my hours worked." She then left the factory without waiting to be certain the export truck was ready to go, unwilling to help the owner meet his deadlines.

"One must not speak like that," the first worker said, criticizing the actions of her colleague. "It sounds hard, as if you do not trust that the boss will give you what he owes you." Although workers frequently see little of the factory owners, the relationship between worker and owner is phrased as highly personalized and based on trust.

Another worker described an incident that forced her to miss the seven-day naming ceremony for her sister's first-born child, which she sorely regretted. In recounting how this had come to pass, she emphasized the cooperative and dutiful quality of her own response:

> On the day of the naming ceremony, I went to the director and said, "Today is the seventh-day naming ceremony for my sister's first child, I want to leave early to attend." The director pleaded with me "Please, we cannot let you go early today. Please, don't go. You understand we need you, don't you?" I answered, "Yes, no problem."

In continuing, the worker explained that she could have feigned illness in order to be released from the factory that day, but she would not do so because she was an honest and trustworthy person. Although I prompted her, the worker would express no resentment or anger at this sequence of events. According to her interpretation, she was never forbidden to leave the factory but rather was begged to stay and help. And to this appeal she responded. She missed her sister's party because she was obliged to answer a higher duty.

This worker's description of loyalty to the factory is a familiar form of discourse among workers, and it precisely parallels the way in which relations with family are described. For instance, another worker described to me her premature departure from school, which came about when her father approached her and (by her account) said, "my little daughter. . . you can see the situation we are in. Please, can you leave school and try to get work to help us?" The worker emphasized that her father had never commanded her but rather had pleaded with her. As she recounted his words, the worker imitated her father's begging voice and placed her fingertips over her mouth and

kissed them, mimicking the gesture her father had used to signal a request.

Within the family, workers do not experience authority simply as a gripping hold on their liberties and personal autonomy. Instead, in submitting to authority, they perceive themselves as providing a needed response to a call for service. The assistance they provide to the owners, and to their male kin as well, is in some ways a source of personal power, for it is these females alone who can answer the males' call for assistance. They interpret their own compliance as a moral obligation, and in cooperating they display their own good character and worthiness as daughters or wives.[14]

As the worker/owner relationship gets carried out in terms of the code associated with father/daughter, parent/child or possibly husband/wife, what might appear as domination or exploitation of workers by owners often gets reconfigured into something more acceptable. By thinking in terms of the family model, workers can experience owners and administrators not as dominating, but as begging or pleading for their cooperation and assistance. In cooperating with the owner, they assert their own moral rectitude as loyal, principled individuals who understand the importance of preserving the social tie above all else.

CONCLUSION

It is young unmarried women who staff the garment factories of Morocco. Fez locals, and Moroccans generally, claim that the low pay, long hours, and unpaid overtime associated with garment factory labor are accepted by these young girls because they work "only for clothes and make-up." As daughters (or sometimes wives), workers are presumed to be supported by family males; they are believed to contribute minimally, at most, to household support. As noted above, contrary to public opinion, research indicates that garment factory workers are an important source of household support.

Nonetheless, the local understanding of women's participation in low-paid factory labor coincides with Marxist feminist explanations of female employment on the global assembly line (Elson and Pierson 1981). From both perspectives, it is women's role in reproduction, and their position as dependent daughters, wives, and/or mothers, that explains their vulnerability to and acceptance of low-wage work.

Here, I have attempted to explore how Moroccan understandings of home, family and gender render females willing workers on the garment factory shop floor. Workers transform the public space of the factory into the private space of the home in an attempt to assuage the contradiction inherent in their presence inside the factory, outside the home, in a role ideologically reserved for men. They behave inside this "home" as kinswoman, using the assumptions and practices associated with family to regulate their comportment inside factory walls. They approach owners much like fathers, and supervisors like parents or elder sisters. They treat each other like siblings. They accept factory hierarchies based on their understanding of, and reverence for, the patriarchal family and the gender order it endorses.

Local meanings and values thus mediate the workers' approach to the factory. Their transformation of factory into a home allows them to accommodate the owners' power with little resistance. They willingly accept the factory administration's power as they would accept the authority of their own fathers, in their role as daughters, or that of their husbands in the role of wife. In this way, the owners are able to appropriate labor at a low cost without risking resistance. To some extent, workers and their families are willing accomplices in the factory's exploitation, because this exploitation gets phrased in terms that are not only accepted, but revered.

NOTES

1. Here, the word "workers" refers to the female garment factory workers of Fez. I refer to the workers as "girls" rather than women because the vast majority of them are unmarried and thus defined, in Morocco, as girls, or *binet*. The residents of Fez, Moroccans generally, and the workers themselves refer to garment factory workers as girls.

2. Here I contrast the idea of "labor" with that of "work" as in Comaroff and Comaroff (1987) and Walman (1979).

3. The accuracy of these numbers is questionable. The figures are based on government census materials and reflect only the factories officially registered with the government. It is widely understood in Morocco, however, that many industrial operations are unregistered and "hidden." Factory owners prefer to keep their operations unnoticed by the government to avoid the financial and legal implications that are inherent in official recognition. Even where the factory itself is recognized by the government, many of its workers may not be. Factory owners often regard even permanent, full-time employees as seasonal workers, temporary staff, or apprentices, and thus deny them the work papers that would ensure them the benefits prescribed by law. Obviously, government data cannot account for such employees. One economist in Morocco suggested that government figures be doubled to arrive at a more accurate count of industrial workers in Fez. During one year in Fez, I met few garment workers who held work registration papers. None of the 150 workers in the factory where I worked had working papers.

4. Moroccan men were slowly replaced by women in the garment industry. Throughout the 1980s females were hired to replace departing males in existing factories and most workers hired in new factories were female. Females were frequently hired to replace males involved in labor unrest. Fez factory owners recounted that males working in Fez garment factories before the general workers strike of 1990 were replaced by females. Morocco suffers high rates of unemployment, and male joblessness has not been alleviated by the boom in the garment industry.

5. According to my survey research, 76% of workers surveyed were never-married females, 16% were married and 8% were divorced. Nearly all of the workers surveyed (92%) were between the ages of 13 and 25. Never-married and divorced workers (84% of the total) almost invariably lived as daughters in their natal households (divorced young women return to their natal homes when possible). Married

workers lived either in their husband's natal home or in a separate conjugal home. The majority of married workers were newly married women who had worked in the factory before marriage. Most of the married workers who continued working after having children were destitute women whose husbands were unable to work. Workers earned anywhere from 300 to 800 dirhams per month, and 89% of workers reported contributing some or all of their salary to the family. These salaries were considered significant in lower class households in which men found difficulty securing steady work.

6. Although I am not in any way suggesting a privileged relationship between Islam and women's subjugation to factory labor, other researchers have investigated women's participation in wage labor with focus on the Muslim context (Hijab 1988; Ibrahim 1985; Macleod 1991; Ong 1987; and White 1994).

7. Abu Lughod (1986) provides a complex exploration of the notion of honor, and an early, comprehensive collection on the notion of honor is found in Peristiany (1966). See Dwyer 1978, Mernissi 1987, Sabbah 1984 and Combs-Schilling 1989 for discussions of specifically Moroccan notions of honor as they pertain to gender and gender relations.

8. Related women—the wives and sometimes daughters of the owners—are prominent in the operation of a few Fez factories. But it is most frequently men who play the day-to-day role of factory owner and administrator.

9. It is interesting to note that many of the European technical directors are female while Moroccan technical directors are almost exclusively male.

10. There is a growing number of university students who today dress in distinctively Islamic robes, but I do not consider them here.

11. This situation is reinforced by the fact that many workers are related to each other through biological kinship. High level factory staff are often relatives of the factory owner (Fejjal 1987) so that there is a sense in each factory that this is a family enterprise. Personal ties are key in the recruitment of new workers: factory owners and administrators give the relatives and friends of trusted workers preference in hiring. It is common for sisters, cousins, even mother and daughter to work in the same factory, either at the same time or sequentially. At Confection, 10% of the workers had sisters or cousins working contemporaneously with them; others reported that their relatives had worked there previously. Nearly 20% of the workers surveyed had sisters who worked in other garment factories in Fez. Biological kin ties among the workers help contribute to making the idiom of family a reality.

12. Moroccans, men in particular, characterize women as "full of empty talk." Their propensity to be engaged in meaningless speech is prohibited on the factory floor.

13. There are economic reasons for providing transport as well: for many workers, the cost of public transportation to and from the factory would represent such a large percentage of the salary as to make working purposeless. The father of one former worker laughed wryly when he explained that his daughter's month of factory work had actually cost the family money; the girl's salary did not cover her bus fare to and from the factory. (She was considered an apprentice, which explains her absurdly low salary.)

14. Abu Lughod (1986) explores the dimensions of the authority relationship between Bedouin men and women.

REFERENCES

Abu Lughod, Lila. 1986. *Veiled Sentiments.* Berkeley: University of California Press.

Beneria, Lourdes. 1984. Women and Rural Development: Morocco. *Cultural Survival Quarterly* 8(2):30–32.

Blim, Michael L. 1992. Introduction: The Emerging Global Factory and Anthropology. In *Anthropology and the Global Factory: Studies of the New Industrialization in the Late Twentieth Century.* M.L. Blim and F.A. Rothstein, eds., pp. 1–30. New York: Bergin and Garvey.

Calagione, John and Daniel Nugent. 1992. Workers' Expressions: Beyond Accommodation and Resistance on the Margins of Capitalism. In *Worker's Expressions: Beyond Accommodation and Resistance.* J. Calagione and D. Nugent, eds., pp. 1–34. Albany: SUNY Press.

Comaroff, John L. and Jean Comaroff. 1987. The Madman and the Migrant: Work and Labor in the Historical Consciousness of a South African People. *American Ethnologist* 14(2): 191–209.

Combs-Schilling, M. Elaine. 1989. *Sacred Performances: Islam, Sexuality and Sacrifice*. New York: Columbia University Press.

Davis, Susan S. 1983. Patience and Power: *Women's Lives in a Moroccan Village*. New York: Schenkman.

Dwyer, Daisy H. 1978. *Images and Self-Images: Male and Female in Morocco*. New York: Columbia University Press.

Direction de la Statistique de Maroc. 1994. *Femme et Condition Feminine au Maroc*. Rabat: Les Editions Guessous.

Elson, Diane and Ruth Pierson. 1981. The Subordination of Women and the Internationalisation of Factory Production. In *Of Marriage and the Market: Women's Subordination in International Perspective*. Kate Yound, ed., pp. 144–166. London: CSE Books.

Fejjal, Ali. 1987. Industrie et Industrialisation à Fes. *Revenue de Geographie Marocaine Nouvelle Serie* 11(2): 55–70.

Fernandez-Kelly, Maria P. 1983. *For We Are Sold, I and My People: Women and Industry in Mexico's Frontier*. Albany: State University of New York Press.

Hijab, Nadia. 1988. *Womanpower: The Arab Debate on Women at Work*. Cambridge: Cambridge University Press.

Ibrahim, Beth. 1985. "Cairo's Factory Women". *In Women and the Family in the Middle East*. Elizabeth Fernea, ed., pp. 293–299. Austin: University of Texas Press.

Joekes, Susan. 1982a. *The Multifibre Arrangement and Outward Processing: The Case of Morocco and Tunisia*. In EEC and the Third World. C. Stevens, ed., pp. 102–112. London: Hodder and Soughton.

———. 1982b. Female-led Industrialization and Women's Jobs in Third World Export Manufacturing: The Case of the Moroccan Clothing Industry. *Brighton: Institute of Development Studies Research Reports* No. 15.

———. 1985. Working for Lipstick? Male and Female Labour in the Clothing Industry in Morocco. In *Women, Work and Ideology in the Third World*. H. Afshar, ed., pp. 183–214. London: Tavistock Publications.

Leymarie, Serge and Jean Tripier. 1992. *Maroc: Le Prochain Dragon?* Casablanoa: Editions Eddif Maroc.

Lim, Linda Y.C. 1993. Capitalism, Imperialism and Patriarchy: The Dilemma of Third-World Women Workers in Multinational Factories. In *Women, Men, and the International Division of Labor*. June Nash and M.P. Fernandez-Kelly, eds., pp. 205–223. Albany: State University of New York Press.

Macleod, Arlene E. 1991. *Accommodating Protest: Working Women, the New Veiling, and Change in Cairo*. New York: Columbia University Press.

Mernissi, Fatima. 1987. *Beyond the Veil: Male-Female Dynamics in a Modern Muslim Society*. Bloomington: Indiana University Press.

———. 1994. *Dreams of Trespass: Tales of a Harem Girlhood*. New York: Addison-Wesley Publishing Company.

Ministère du Commerce de L'Industrie et de la Privatisation. 1994. Situation des Industries de Transformation. Rabat: Dèlegation de Commerce et de l'Industrie de la Wilaya de Fes.

Nash, June. 1981. Ethnographic Aspects of the World Capitalist System. *Annual Review of Anthropology* 10:393–424.

Nash, June and Maria P. Fernandez-Kelly eds., 1983. *Women, Men and the International Division of Labor*. Albany: State University of New York Press.

Ong, Aibwa. 1987. *Spirits of Resistance and Capitalist Discipline: Factory Women in Malayisia*. Albany: State University of New York Press.

———. 1991. The Gender and Labor Politics of Postmodernity. *Annual Review of Anthropology* 20:279–309.

Peristiany, J.G. 1966. *Honor and Shame: The Values of Mediterranean Society*. Chicago: University of Chicago Press.

Rothstein, Francis A. and Michael L. Blim, eds., 1992. *Anthropology and the Global Factory: Studies of the New Industrialization in the Late Twentieth Century*. New York: Bergen and Garvey.

Sabbah, Fatna. 1984. *Woman in the Muslim Unconscious*. New York: Oxford Pergamon Press.

Salaff, Janet. 1981. *Working Daughters of Hong Kong: Filial Piety or Power in the Family?* New York: Cambridge University Press.

Wallman, Sandra, ed. 1979. *The Social Anthropology of Work*. London: Academic Press.

Warren, Kay B. and Susan C. Bourque. 1989. Women, Technology and Development Ideologies: Frameworks and Findings. In *Gender and Anthropology*. S. Morgen, ed., pp. 382–411. Washington: American Anthropological Association.

White, Jenny B. 1994. *Money Makes Us Relatives: Women's Labor in Urban Turkey*. Austin: University of Texas Press.

Consuming Desires, Contested Selves: Rural Women and Labor Migration in Thailand

Mary Beth Mills

A friend who had been working in Bangkok came back to visit [our village]. She wore beautiful clothes. When she saw me, her greeting was, "Oh ho! How did you get so run-down looking? Want to come work with me?" . . . [That night] I lay thinking, "I ought to go give it a try." dreamed that I would go [to the city], work really hard and save money to help my family. I lay unable to stop thinking about this until I slept. I got up early in the morning and at once rushed to find my friend. I was so happy that I could go with her. I got my clothes ready and said goodbye to my brothers, sisters, father and mother.

Khem, Bangkok textile worker, age 21.[1]

In this brief passage, a young Thai labor migrant gives an account of how she left home to begin urban employment at the age of sixteen. Central to this narrative is the moral obligation of a dutiful daughter—"I would work really hard and save money to help my family"—anchoring Khem's story in the intimate world of village kinship and rural poverty. But this projection of virtue and self-sacrifice stands alongside a portrait of the confident returning migrant with her "beautiful clothes" and teasing disdain for the sorry existence of her friend. It is this image of urban sophistication and accumulation, as much as her concern for household needs, that occupies Khem's waking thoughts before sleep and propels her rapid departure the next morning.

Khem's narrative, placing kinship-based morality alongside desires for autonomy and commodified display, highlights widespread themes within rural-urban migration in contemporary Thailand. In these few sentences Khem constructs two potential selves: the

"good daughter" motivated by emotional ties and a deep sense of responsibility to rural family, and the "modern woman" whose independence and mobility are tied to her experience with urban society. For Khem and thousands of other young women working in the capital city of Bangkok, both these self-images are desirable, both play a key role in their decisions to leave home; however, both are also potentially at odds. Each rests on a different set of priorities: saving money to assist family or spending it to acquire the commodities and experiences associated with urban status and modern style. Consequently, rural-urban migration involves much more than a shift in physical location. As young Thai women move into Bangkok employment they also engage in a process of self-construction, laying claim to, negotiating and at times contesting these different aspects of gender identity.

Khem is but one among the hundreds of thousands of rural women whose labor in Bangkok manufacturing and service jobs has sustained Thailand's successful drive to attract global capital investment and compete with other industrializing nations around the world.[2] Rural agricultural households have played an essential part in the rapid expansion of Thailand's urban industrial economy. First, they provide a highly flexible pool of labor through out-migration; second, the continuing economic ties between workers and their village homes bear part of the cost of maintaining and reproducing this labor force, thereby allowing urban employers to pay lower wages and fewer benefits (Porpora and Lim 1987).[3] Indeed, women like Khem—unmarried, in their late teens and early twenties—now constitute the preferred work force of many Bangkok employers. Few if any communities in rural

Thailand remain untouched by this youthful outflow. In many rural areas it is a virtual cliché to observe that "there is no one left in the villages but the old people and little children." While it is by no means true that all young people leave the countryside for urban employment, still the high rates at which they are leaving often makes it more meaningful to ask not whether adolescent children will go to Bangkok but when.[4]

At one level, this exodus represents yet another example of how an expanding global economy of "flexible accumulation" has targeted young, rural women as an easily controlled and relatively inexpensive work force (Harvey 1989:153–155). Young women without the responsibilities of a family are expected to have a limited commitment to wage employment, working for a few months or years before marriage, and consequently can be expected to put up with low pay, limited benefits, and job insecurity. Their youth and gender also suggest a work force already schooled in obedience to (parental) authority, hard work, and the patience and dexterity required for many domestic chores (such as weaving and sewing). Women's character and skills are seen by employers to be particularly well-suited for the fine detail and endless repetition of textile and electronics manufacturing, industries that have dominated the shift to globally dispersed production sites.

However, if young women in Thailand and elsewhere appeal to employers as a presumably quiescent and inexpensive labor force, this tells us little about why women themselves take up wage work nor how they understand their experiences of it. To try and answer these questions I conducted anthropological fieldwork with rural-urban migrants both in Bangkok's industrial zones and in rural sending communities in Thailand's northeastern region during the late 1980s and early 1990s.[5] When I began this research I expected to find that young women moving into Bangkok were the unwitting victims of their country's headlong pursuit of national development: their entry into urban labor markets a sacrifice demanded by rural families desperate to make ends meet. While the difficulties women encountered in urban

jobs and their obligations to family were certainly significant parts of the migration story, it soon became clear that this was only part of the picture.

Although they were well aware of the hardships they encountered as low wage laborers, the women I met certainly did not see themselves as victims. Rather, young women like Khem almost always took credit for the decision to leave the village and find urban work, sometimes with the active support of their parents, sometimes quite the opposite. Nor were the economic returns to rural households from daughters' employment always clear; parents with whom I spoke often complained about infrequent or inadequate wage remittances. Furthermore, women's out-migration was not limited to the more impoverished segments of a community but involved families across social strata: poor, middle, and even quite well-off peasant households. I quickly realized that the entry of young rural women into urban labor was a product of complex motivations. As Khem's words themselves reveal, labor mobility reflects social and cultural tensions within households and within the individual herself. Women's migration is not just a response to dominant ideals of filial obligation (to "save money to help my family") but to equally powerful perceptions of status lost to already mobile peers and desires for "beautiful clothes" and other commodified signifiers of urban glamour and sophistication. In other words, the movement of young women into Bangkok has as much to do with aspirations for particular kinds of personhood as with specific material goals.

Cynthia Enloe makes the obvious but often overlooked point that young women around the globe enter and stay in new types of employment—despite low wages, harsh labor discipline, and unhealthy working conditions—not solely for the money earned but also to achieve more complex social goals: "Without women's own needs, values, and worries, the global assembly line would grind to a halt" (Enloe 1989:16–17). For Khem and others like her, the "needs, values, and worries" behind their migration revolve not only around familiar meanings of family and community but also newly imagined needs and possibilities. In particular, the idea of working in Bangkok offers young rural women an experience of personal independence that is largely unavailable to them within the village setting as unmarried daughters subordinate to parents and other elders.[6] For the adolescent whose peers are all working in Bangkok, the tales told by friends on visits home invoke images of glamour and style she might otherwise only see on television broadcasts.

MIGRATION AND DISCOURSES OF MODERNITY

When young migrants speak of their decision to go to Bangkok, as in Khem's account, their stories almost always invoke the gendered imagery of "good daughters" and "modern women." As daughters, migrants respond to obligations of respect and gratitude owed by all children to their parents; from this perspective migration to Bangkok is an important means for youth to acknowledge their debts to parents by earning money to send home. This is especially significant for young women who, unlike their brothers, cannot take the vows of a Theravada Buddhist monk to earn religious merit for their parents. Spending a few months in the monastic discipline of a Buddhist temple remains among the most important obligations a son has to his mother and father, one that can take precedence over economic contributions. Daughters, however, are raised to express their gratitude and loyalty by caring for the day-to-day needs of household members. They are expected to be more industrious and responsible in such matters than their brothers. According to Nid, whose Bangkok wages as a maid in a tourist guest house paid for the care of a seriously ill father, young men in the village only "play and run around." They may go off, she argued, for days, weeks, or months, sleeping in the temple or at a friend's house; they don't see what the family needs or what they are going without. "Men don't see, they don't pay attention. But women are responsible, they see what's missing; they know when there's not enough rice. Women have to look after the family." Urban wages allow young rural women to fulfill these expectations in a form that is both concrete and highly valued by family at home.

Just as powerful in shaping migration decisions is an explicit desire to be "up-to-date" (*thansamay*), to participate in Thai "modernity." Let me be clear that by "modernity" I am not referring to an objective social or cultural state of being but rather to a powerful field of popular discourse and cultural imagery. Around the world, ideas about "modernity" are closely linked to participation in an increasingly globalized capitalist economy; however, these broadly-based processes can provoke different responses in different contexts. The result is what Michael Watts identifies as the "production of . . . new, local modernities" out of the historical experiences and the cultural and symbolic resources available to people in specific settings (in Pred and Watts 1992:18). In contemporary Thailand, symbols and activities linked to notions of modernity are a part of everyday life. People at all levels of Thai society are familiar with and employ a language of "being modern" (*khwaam pen thansamay*, literally "being up-to-date"), "newness" (*samay may*, "new times"), and "progress" (*khwaam caroen*) to discuss and at times critique perceptions and experiences of social and cultural change. For example, the urban elite, scholars, and policy makers frequently debate whether national political and economic development has meant too much "modernity" (i.e., at the expense of "traditional values"). To rural producers the images of urban wealth and commodified "progress" that pervade Thai popular culture pose models of consumption and social status that, even if difficult to achieve, are impossible to ignore. In particular, the ownership and display of new technologies and consumer commodities are increasingly valued as symbols of "up-to-date" (*thansamay*) success and social status throughout Thailand.

Most rural youth, then, see the move to Bangkok at least in part as an opportunity to be at the center of contemporary Thai society—to "open their ears and eyes" (*poet huu poet taa*)— and to earn the cash necessary to purchase the commodity emblems of a *thansamay*, "up-to-date" identity. Young rural women confront these seductive attributes of "modern" *thansamay* self-hood in a strikingly gendered form: throughout Thailand images of the beautiful *thansamay* woman—on billboards, television ads, serial dramas, and in many other formats—set powerful standards for defining this status. Moreover city life provides a multitude of settings and social institutions—from beauty parlors and shopping malls, to movie theaters and nightclubs—where migrants can observe and pursue "modern" womanhood for themselves.

Part of what draws young rural women into the city is an unspoken but powerful suggestion that there they can be at once beautiful, modern and mobile. With an urban income they can enhance their own beauty and modernity; they can participate in the adventure, excitement and independence of modern city life. Indeed, one of the most valued benefits for migrants is that urban employment allows them to work indoors, away from the skin darkening effects of the sun. White skin is a crucial marker of physical beauty in both urban and rural Thai aesthetic systems. Older villagers often describe women and men moving into Bangkok as "going to get [white] skin" (*pay aw phiw*). While some offered these comments as a disparagement of youthful vanity, migrants on return visits were frequently complimented on their pale skin. At the same time that they acquire such signs of modern attractiveness, young migrants also hope that by sending money back to parents and siblings, they can maintain their standing within the home community as good women and daughters.

Thansamay beauty and urban consumer lifestyles present seductive models for how young women might retain and enhance their youthful beauty while exercising their own independence and mobility. Nevertheless, aspects of *thansamay* womanhood contrast sharply with household-based values of maidenly modesty, virginal beauty, and constraints

on female spatial mobility. The portrayal of women and women's bodies in the dominant urban-centered culture, linking beauty with modernity and active sexuality, flirts dangerously with equally powerful ideas about beauty predicated upon women's sexual propriety and modesty. Highly sexualized images of women's bodies, already familiar to villagers from television, movies and other media, are reinforced in urban settings by the proliferation of commercial enterprises—shopping malls, salons, nightclubs, discos, massage parlors, go-go bars, and more—many of which link the celebration of modern female beauty to the actual sale of women's sexual services (Van Esterik 1988, 2000). This association of commercial sex work with popular and contemporary images of femininity points to a less celebrated side of modern Thai womanhood. The stigmatized figure of the prostitute stands as a reminder of the disreputable consequences that being too "modern," too "up-to-date" may entail for the unwary.[7]

In sum, migration decisions involve a fragile convergence between young women's sense of duty and desires for adventure. Working in the city promises a level of personal autonomy unavailable to young women in the village prior to marriage and motherhood, without having to deny their obligations to family. Once in the city, however, the realities of low wages, minimal benefits and often harsh working and living conditions mean that daughterly responsibilities and the pursuit of *thansamay* ideals of autonomy and material display frequently come into conflict. Migrants' hopes to be both modern women and good daughters are not so easily achieved in the face of Bangkok realities.

BEING UP-TO-DATE—MIGRANTS, WORK, AND COMMODITY CONSUMPTION

The young women that I knew both in Bangkok and in rural communities found these images of *thansamay* identity compelling and the prospect of remaining at home dull by comparison. When describing their experiences before coming to the city, many migrants alluded to feelings of boredom: "In the village there's nothing to do." The Bangkok they see on nightly television broadcasts and hear about from friends is, by contrast, a place of boundless novelty and excitement. As one young textile worker explained, "I had to go see for myself." Perhaps more importantly, Bangkok is also where they can earn the money needed to actively enjoy the style and amenities of an "up-to-date" identity. Thip, a textile worker who left her village home at age 19, wanted to work in Bangkok because "at home there was no money and nothing to do. I wanted to have lots of money, money to send home and to buy things for myself as well."

Cash wages, or more particularly what those wages can buy, may be the key attraction of urban employment; however, in some ways young women's desires to be "up-to-date" can be addressed through the work experience itself, especially when they find employment in Bangkok's industrial manufacturing sector. In contrast to the decidedly "old-fashioned" drudgery of family-based rural agriculture (hard, heavy physical labor, largely unmechanized and performed out-of-doors), urban factories in themselves carry an attractive aura of participation in *thansamay* society (performing lighter, even if highly repetitive tasks, involving impressive new technologies, and located indoors out of the sun and rain).

But if factories can project an image of "up-to-date" agency and status to employees, this is not always easy to sustain, especially as migrants struggle to cope with low wages and limited benefits. Employees in large manufacturing companies generally earn the legal minimum (just under US$4.00 per day in 1990, and only rising to about US$6.00 daily by 1996) but even after many years of service few workers' wages rise much above this rate.[8] Many more women in Bangkok earn even less. Fifty or sixty baht per day (US$2.00–2.50) was not an uncommon wage for workers on temporary or probationary contracts in the late 1980s, an employment status that until the passage of legislation in 1990 could be prolonged for months and sometimes years. Lower than minimum wages were reported frequently by the women I interviewed, especially those working in small garment factories or piece-rate sweat shops; particularly low wages were the rule for women employed as domestic servants.[9] In larger industrial companies, where employers were mostly likely to pay workers the legal minimum, many women reported that their wages could be docked for numerous reasons including fines for lateness, failure to make production quotas, or minor infractions of shop floor regulations.

In addition to low wages, young migrants must also learn to cope with new strictures and forms of authority including the rigid time-discipline of urban manufacturing. For example, Bangkok's large garment industry includes thousands of small shops subcontracting for larger companies; these enterprises typically pay employees on a piece-rate basis (e.g., a set amount per finished garment) and work days can last twelve hours or more, especially when an order is due. Larger manufacturing enterprises have standard eight-hour shifts; however, mandatory overtime can be frequent and may involve anywhere from two to eight additional hours of work.[10] Moreover, the largest factories tend to operate in three shifts around the clock. Shifts rotate once a week forcing workers into a new cycle of sleep and eating every seven days. Even without the strains of overtime, this constant upheaval in daily routines frequently results in health problems: disrupted menstruation, headaches and insomnia, intestinal problems and ulcers. In addition, women may confront a variety of other dangers in the workplace such as toxic chemicals and gases, accidents due to improperly maintained machinery or worker fatigue, or respiratory infections from poorly ventilated work sites. Adding to these complaints, young female workers are also potential targets for sexual harassment and other forms of intimidation by male supervisors and other figures of authority at work.

While acknowledging the hardships of long hours and often unpleasant, if not unsafe, working conditions, many of the migrants I interviewed appreciated their relative freedom after working hours. Living conditions in company dormitories or rented rooms in the slums are often crowded, hot, and dirty, still they offer the chance to escape from direct supervision on the shop floor. It is here, at the end of the shift and outside the factory gates, that migrants are best able to explore and absorb images of sophisticated urban lifestyles by watching television and popular movies or going to department stores, entertainment parks and the like. For many young women, these ventures into urban consumer culture are particularly valued aspects of their time in the city.

The young women to whom I spoke were often reluctant to reveal exactly how much they spent in the city, especially on non-essential items; yet any visit to the rooms of young workers reveals the importance given to commodity purchases and display. Ut and Tiw's small lodging is a case in point. From May to November of 1990, I made regular visits to the two sisters at their rented room, one of four tiny partitions on the second floor of an old wooden house. It measured about 2.5 meters across and 4 meters long. One corner was walled off as a tiny bath and toilet area, another was used as a makeshift "kitchen" with a few pots and dishes, an electric rice cooker, and a small gas ring. The rest of the room was furnished with several blankets and cushions along with Ut and Tiw's few other possessions. An electric fan sat in one corner, usually idle unless the sisters were entertaining visitors. On a set of shelves by one wall a small tape deck stood next to a row of cassettes by well-known Thai vocal performers and pop-rock stars. A half-dozen small photo albums and a camera occupied another shelf, while yet another held a haphazard collection of cosmetics, a bottle or two of deodorants, powders, and lotions along with combs, brushes, and small novelty items, hair clips and ribbons. Not long after I first began to visit Ut and Tiw, I arrived one week to discover a small color television had been added to their belongings, the culmination of nearly three years' effort. The sisters had saved the 7500 baht (US$300) purchase price out of their wages and by taking on occasional piece-rate assembly work given out by Tiw's company for those wanting to earn extra money on their own time.

In addition to acquiring new mass-market commodities, many rural-urban migrants are eager to join in new commodified forms of leisure and entertainment. At home a young village woman is enmeshed in an intense web of social relations that include parents, elders, and neighbors as well as siblings and friends, all of whom can observe, comment upon, and potentially influence her behavior; as factory workers in the city, migrants' primary social interaction is with friends and co-workers, most of whom are of similar age and background. The expectations and interests of their peers play an important role in shaping the consumption behavior of many migrants.

Working side-by-side, sharing a rented room or living in the common quarters of factory dormitories, young women find themselves in an intense world of peer-oriented companionship, far removed from the authority of parents and elders that would frame and intersect such ties in the village setting. Friendly pressures to participate in common activities—such as shared meals and outings—place steady demands upon the cash earnings of young workers. Many of the young women that I knew in Bangkok described themselves as "great spenders" (*chay ngoen keng*, literally "good at using money" [rather than saving it]). Money, they said, is hard to hang onto, not because of large or flamboyant purchases but because of the everyday demands of urban existence including their desires to hang out and "have fun" with friends. Almost inevitably these interactions involve some form of consumption: whether gatherings revolve around purchased meals, trips to local markets, or, more rarely, spending a day at one of the city's commercial amusement parks (such as "Happyland" or the part-zoo/part-rock concert venue, "The Crocodile Farm").

These peer group "outings" (*pay thiaw*) in search of fun and entertainment are, for many migrants, among the most satisfying experiences of life in Bangkok. Given migrants' limited leisure hours and low wages, a *thiaw* is usually brief—an afternoon's trip to the market, a shopping mall, or a park; but it may also be a much longer excursion, perhaps over a holiday weekend, to the beach or (more commonly) to a friend's home in a distant and unfamiliar province. Such outings offer a dramatic break from the tedium and exhaustion of factory shifts. They are also the best chances for most migrants by their own actions to approximate dominant images of a truly "modern" lifestyle. For example, participating in these peer group activities requires investing in certain kinds of *thansamay* commodity display. Young women dress carefully for these events, usually in blue jeans and colorful blouses or t-shirts. Other commodities like cameras can also be in high demand especially on longer trips.[11]

Even a small *thiaw* involves the mobilization of such commodity symbols of *thansamay* self-presentation. One Sunday afternoon (the day most factory workers have free) I was visiting Ut and several other women from her village who all worked at the same Bangkok textile factory. We had gathered in Ut's rented room but soon decided to go visit some young men also from the same village, who were living in a one-room flat about thirty minutes away by bus. In preparation, two of the women had to go back to their dormitory rooms to change out of the casual shorts they had on; I stayed with Ut and her friend, Noi, who had suggested the outing. While we waited, Noi looked over Ut's small collection of cosmetics and began to try on two different colors of lipstick. When she turned back to us, Ut had finished changing into a pair of black stretch slacks. Noi scolded her, "Don't you want to wear something more up-to-date [*thansamay*]? You look like a country hick [*duu baan nohk loey*]." Ut quickly changed into a pair of blue jeans, even though they were not quite dry from the morning's laundry.

URBAN DILEMMAS— CONFRONTING AMBIVALENCE AND MARGINALITY

While the acquisition and display of commodities in these ways provide crucial demonstrations of *thansamay* identity and status among migrant peers, within the broader urban setting these claims receive little recognition. Amid Bangkok's exploding consumerism migrants' consumption patterns—restricted as they are by low wages and limited leisure time—offer only a weak approximation of truly "up-to-date" urban living. There are always more and newer commodities to acquire, more places to see, more outings to take. Wearing jeans and cosmetics, taking trips to the Crocodile Farm or an air-conditioned department store are pleasant and attractively *thansamay* activities; nevertheless, surrounded by the city's hypermodernity and intense commercialization, rural women's access to and control over the extensive cultural repertoire of "being up-to-date" is partial at best.

It is not surprising, then, that the women I knew in Bangkok almost universally expressed ambivalence about their experiences in the city. And their unease tended to increase over time. Many migrants acknowledged the positive aspects of urban life: the city is a place of "progress" (*khwaam caroen*) and "development" (*kaan phattana*). Living there had taught them a great deal, it had "opened the ears, opened the eyes." They appreciated the many "conveniences" and "comforts" (*khwaam saduak sabaay*) of city life: easy access to running water, electricity, transportation, markets and entertainment. And central to these advantages was the fact that, "In the city there's money, in the village there's none." Just as recognizable, however, were Bangkok's less pleasant dimensions. The city was polluted, noisy, and congested. Workers lived in crowded dormitories or cheap rented rooms in which, nevertheless, it was very easy to feel alone and isolated. On the job, too, they endured insecure, often unhealthy and oppressive working conditions. Among the women I knew, whether they had worked in Bangkok for six months or sixteen years, enthusiasm for the *thansamay* qualities of city living was always tempered by unease over its alien and alienating aspects. In some cases these tensions can lead to an explicit critique of unjust circumstances, prompting some migrants to become active in trade unions and labor protest (see Brown 2001;

Mills 1999a). However, labor organizing is a difficult and risky venture. Nor is it an option readily available to most migrants. Only a tiny minority of urban workers even have access to independent union institutions or understand their rights within the labor laws. Instead, the vast majority of migrants in Bangkok respond to the ambivalence engendered by their urban experiences with less radical actions, neither outright "resistance" nor passive acquiescence, but what might better be described as "coping strategies" (see Lamphere 1987:30). A major focus of these is the maintenance of connections with rural kin and community.

The continuing strength of migrants' identification with rural family and community—i.e., what informs the "good daughter" imagery of Khem's and other migrants' stories—is at least partly rooted in pragmatic assessments of their longer term insecurity as urban laborers. For example, migrants know that few Bangkok factories will hire women over the age of 25 and some restrict new hires to 21 or younger. Women who stay in the city after their mid-twenties are very careful not to lose their current employment lest they find themselves choosing between a premature return home or poorly paid informal sector work such as domestic service or sweatshop subcontracting labor. Similar fears underlie a widespread reluctance among migrant women to marry and start a family in the city. Workers know well that urban employers tend to prefer not only youthful but also unmarried, unencumbered employees. A woman who marries and especially a woman with children to care for is at a significant disadvantage in the labor market. Consequently many rural women believe that a return to the village household remains their most reliable source of economic security as they age, and particularly when they marry. Poor married women in Bangkok are often relegated to a secondary labor market of insecure, low paying jobs such as scavenging, small-scale cottage industries, and vending (Thorbek 1987: 61ff., 72–75). The insecurity and hardship of such a future was widely acknowledged by the migrants I met.

But this generalized perception of long-term vulnerability in the city does not mean that the prospect of a return home is without problems. If the idea of settling in the city is fraught with difficulty, going home to a future of rice farming and motherhood raises a different set of concerns, ones linked to migrants' ongoing aspirations for *thansamay* forms of success and autonomy. The wages they can earn in Bangkok, limited though they may be, provide a steady and individualized source of cash income, unlike the more irregular, often unpredictable, and collective earnings that characterize household agricultural production. A former textile worker in her mid-twenties, having returned to her village in preparation for marriage to a local man, was quick to identify the unfortunate consequences that this move was going to have. She was happy with her prospective husband, but their union would put an end to her time in Bangkok; from then on she would be "only a mother and housewife." Her sense of loss was shared by many young women as they contemplated when to leave urban work and take up the burdens of raising their own family.

One response among migrant women is to plan for a return home but to do so in a way that will preserve some of their hard-won *thansamay* status and autonomy. A common ambition is to open a small shop or food vending enterprise. Others who are able to marshal their resources and energy during their limited leisure hours choose to invest in further education or vocational training. Maew, an employee in a leather bag factory, at age nineteen decided to drastically reduce both her expenditures in the city and remittances home, in order to pay for a high school education. When I met her she had been taking adult education classes every Sunday for the past two years; she expected to complete her diploma in another two or three years. She was also saving money in a bank account so that when she left Bangkok to go home she would be able to continue her education at the provincial teacher's college. In a similar case, Lek, a textile worker from the same village as Maew, saved her wages until she could pay the 7000 baht (US$280) tuition at a Bangkok beauty school. On her days off from the factory she attended classes and practiced the skills of hairdressing and cosmetic application. Although Lek did not think that she could make a living in this way in her village, she thought she might be able to find a job in a hair shop in a nearby town.

Lek and Maew were somewhat unusual in their ability to marshal their resources towards such specific long-term future goals. For Maew this decision resulted in an ongoing conflict with family in the village, particularly her mother who regularly requested that Maew contribute money to the rural household and periodically threatened to travel to Bangkok (and did so on at least one occasion) to get the money from Maew herself. Most of the rural-urban migrants that I knew either had less concrete plans for their future or were unable or unwilling to ignore parental expectations so consistently. Nevertheless, they too hoped to be more than just "rice and upland crop farmers" (*chaaw naa chaaw ray*) when they left the city. Achieving this goal is more difficult—and even Maew and Lek wondered if their educational investments would really pay off in the end. Moreover, young women who plan and work towards a "successful" return to the village may find that circumstances intervene. A sudden illness, an accident on the job, factory layoffs, a family crisis, or the compelling demands and expectations of parents—any of these or similar events can quickly force a woman to make a difficult choice.

All migrant women I knew confronted this dilemma to some degree during their time in the city. Attempts to pursue *thansamay* aspirations are fundamentally at odds with young women's obligations to rural kin. Whatever the purpose of their urban expenditures (personal items, daily needs, entertainment with friends, education or vocational training) every baht spent in Bangkok is, at least in theory, one less available to assist family at home. New patterns of commodity consumption, while necessary for the pursuit of a *thansamay* sense of self, confront migrants both with their own marginal status within the dominant, commodified culture of Bangkok and with their potential

(or actual) failure to maintain the ideal image of a "good daughter." Although, among the women I interviewed, the economic hardships of rural households were rarely the primary motivating factor in their migration decisions, all recognized the moral force of family obligations. Women who described themselves as "good spenders" (*chay ngoen keng*) often did so in the context of explaining their irregular remittances to village kin. The amounts and frequency of migrants' contributions to rural households varied widely among the women I interviewed; self-reporting commonly elicited contributions totaling anywhere from 30% to 80% of monthly income but these initial claims were usually revealed later on to represent much more occasional remittances. There were very few women who would admit to never having sent money but most agreed that they would rather wait and save a particular sum (often 2000 or 3000 baht, US$80–$120) over several months which they could then take home on a visit instead of sending back smaller but more frequent contributions.[12]

In part this allowed the women to exercise greater control over the use of their earnings by saving toward particular consumption projects, the most common being the purchase of materials to use in building their parents a new house. These goals were often supported by rural kin but they could also be frustrated by periodic demands for increased or immediate contributions. Some of these requests come at predictable intervals: calls for help with harvest or transplanting expenses, or younger siblings' school costs at the beginning of term (e.g., uniforms, books, high school tuition, etc.). At other times migrants will be called upon to help out in a household emergency, particularly when a sudden or severe illness strikes. Although young women may complain amongst themselves that people in the village think only about money, most migrants do their best to comply with requests from home. But sometimes daughters find themselves in the position of censoring the consumption demands of their own parents. For example, when Lan's mother asked for a color television to replace the black-and-white set that Lan and a sister (also working in the city) had bought a few years before, Lan responded with some exasperation: "I'm saving now for the cost of building her a new house. [My sister and I] bought the supporting posts last year. Mother will have to wait for the television."

If the demands of urban consumption styles jeopardize the fragile balance of migrants' desires to be both "modern women" and "good daughters," there are moments when migrants can confront these tensions and rework them to their own benefit. Here the importance of maintaining ties to rural kin can be seen as not only a matter of migrants' pragmatic concerns for the future but also because it is through trips home, bringing money, wearing new clothes and accompanied by new friends that migrants can lessen, if only briefly, the strains of urban life and project a solid identity of both *thansamay* success and filial respect and gratitude. These tensions, and migrants' attempts to resolve them, are an important aspect of one of the most popular activities in which rural-urban migrants engage: organizing (and participating in) elaborate ceremonial trips to make ritual donations to village temples. Although framed within the Buddhist merit-making language of popular Thai religious beliefs, the enthusiasm with which migrants participate in these events often has less to do with desires to add to their store of karmic merit (although such goals are by no means irrelevant) than with the opportunities that these trips provide to resolve (if only temporarily) some of the tensions that arise during the course of their urban experiences. Specifically, these merit-making trips are occasions when migrants' *thansamay* consumption practices parallel and even support their commitment to the village home.

On these occasions several people, usually from the same village, will plan an excursion, rent a bus and recruit friends in the city to come along. Both women and men migrants participate (indeed the mixed sex format is an added attraction for many young people); however, it is often the women who attend to the time-consuming details. Passengers pay a fare for the bus trip and contribute to a merit fund which will be offered to the community temple. These trips are organized around significant temple ceremonies: an ordination, commonly held at the beginning of the Buddhist lenten season; a *thoht kathin*, the ritual presentation of new robes to monks at the end of this period, or most often a *thoht phaa paa* ("offering of forest robes"), which may be held at almost any time of the year. All involve rituals during which significant offerings can be made to the host temple in addition to the presentation of robes and other items to resident monks. In this way a donation of several thousand baht may be collected, usually with a particular purpose in mind such as the construction of new temple buildings.

But organizing a merit-making trip, as the women I knew quickly pointed out, is a lot of work. A successful trip (i.e., one that raises a substantial amount of money) depends on recruiting many participants. Migrants from the same village must coordinate among themselves, not an easy task when they may live and work in opposite ends of Bangkok and seldom have access to private telephone lines, which could facilitate contact. A rented bus must be reserved for the occasion, invitations to participants and envelopes for their contributions must be printed, donors must be solicited. This last task is often the most troublesome. One worker in a large cotton factory complained that every year so many ceremonies took place she was reluctant to ask her friends to contribute to yet another one. "If you ask them they try to give something but it may only be 10 baht [US$0.40]. And finding people to be *kamakaan* ('committee members') is really hard." This latter category is largely an honorary position for which the individual gets his or her name printed on the official invitations and any other documents acknowledging key participants. However, in return for this honor, the "committee member" is expected to contribute a significant sum of money; in 1990, this usually meant giving at least 100 baht (about US$4.00), slightly more than a day's pay at the time for many workers. They should also attend the ceremony in person, although this is not considered essential.

If the trip's organizers cannot recruit enough people to be *kamakaan* then the chances of collecting a respectable donation are seriously reduced. Should this happen, I was told, the organizers would lose face at home for bringing in a disappointing amount. For example, when Ut and her friends—all from the same village in northeastern Thailand—were approached in the fall of 1990 by their community's leaders to help organize a *thoht phaa paa* from Bangkok, they were less than enthusiastic. The village was planning to build a new temple *saalaa* (meeting hall), the full cost of which was expected to be close to $10,000 (several hundred thousand baht). Although the *thoht phaa paa* was not expected to raise anywhere near the full amount, the women were clearly reluctant to take on the task: "We just did one last year," several told me, "and already they want another one!" They were not sure it would be worth all the time and effort.

It is clear from such comments that these ceremonial trips do not completely erase the tensions young women confront as rural-urban migrants; however, in the actual performance of these events participants can enact the close convergence of ongoing ties to kin and community with their claims to *thansamay* autonomy and urban success. On the several merit-making trips I attended, a large passenger bus, packed with people, and decorated on one side with a long banner proclaiming the destination and ceremonial objective of its purpose, left Bangkok in the evening, usually on a Saturday at the end of the afternoon factory shift. We traveled all night, arriving at the host community sometime in the early to mid-morning. Each time the journey began in an atmosphere of celebration and revelry that continued throughout the night, fueled in part by a steady flow of alcohol (consumed mainly but not exclusively by the male passengers), along with soft drinks and other treats purchased by passengers in anticipation of the evening's festivities. Those who tried to rest their heads against seat backs and windows hoping to catch a little sleep were loudly serenaded by their more energetic companions usually with the aid of a microphone hooked into the

bus's internal sound system and backed by drums and cymbals brought along by the celebrants. Sometime during the night the organizers of the trip passed through the bus collecting envelopes they had distributed earlier and that passengers had filled with cash contributions. The amounts would later be recorded along with participants' names for the final offering at the temple.

The ceremony itself took place soon after reaching the host community. On one *thoht phaa paa* to a village in the northeastern province of Khon Kaen, we arrived in time to complete the *phaa paa* presentation before the daily offering of the monks' late morning meal, the food for which had been prepared in large quantities by villagers in order that everyone attending could share once the monks had eaten. The presentation of money to the temple was the focus of the ritual but it also included offerings of commodity items for the personal use of resident monks: robes, bath and laundry soap, toilet paper, packaged drinks and drink mixes such as Ovaltine. These were presented in elaborate cellophane wrapped bundles, a format that has been standardized by urban stores specializing in such ready-to-go merit packages. The ceremony concluded with speeches by community leaders and the most senior organizers of the *thoht phaa paa*, as well as ritual chants and blessings led by the temple monks. Meanwhile the final amount of money donated had been tallied and was announced for everyone to hear.

When the ritual itself was finished the merit-makers could finally relax. Migrants visited with family and introduced the friends who had accompanied them from Bangkok. Fresh from the successful display of devotion to temple and community concerns, they could enjoy their status (however temporary) as good daughters (and sons) whose successful sojourns as modern wage workers in the nation's capital had made possible their contributions to the prosperity of their community and its temple. The congratulatory atmosphere continued well into the evening with the perfomance by a folk-opera (*moh lam*) troupe hired by the host community for the occasion. The next morning it was time to get back on the bus and return to the city.

Young people working in Bangkok acknowledge the religious merit that participants earn on these excursions but also emphasize that the trips are fun and entertaining. This combination of spiritual and worldly purposes in merit-making ceremonies is a key part of their power to defuse ongoing conflicts, at least temporarily, between migrants' aspirations for achievement within the dominant culture of urban "modernity" and their continuing attachments to village family and community. *Thoht phaa paa* and other ceremonial trips provide an opportunity to display success and to show off urban friends to people back home, as well as to renew and affirm solidarity with the rural community and its moral focus, the temple. It is one of the few moments when fulfilling one's obligations as a good village daughter (or son) and the pursuit of a *thansamay* identity appear to coincide.

CONCLUSION

In a variety of ways, rural migrants' sense of self as "up-to-date" or "modern" is denied or marginalized within the dominant Bangkok setting. The exploitation and discipline of industrial work as well as low wage rates pose serious constraints throughout young women's time in the city. Moreover, by pursuing new forms of urban commodity consumption, women can quickly threaten their ability to fulfill the economic contributions expected of them by people at home and that they themselves acknowledge. Nevertheless, for women working in Bangkok, commodity consumption (both of material goods and of commodified images and events) presents a desirable set of practices through which they can confront and attempt to rework the tensions and contradictions that underlie their status as urban wage laborers. By looking carefully at how migrants use their hard-earned wages—for commodity purchases, for entertainment, for merit-making trips, as well as for cash remittances—we can begin to see

that consumption offers a range of strategies by which young rural women can pursue their own interests and stretch, if only temporarily, the limits of their subordination within the wider Thai society. Viewing migrants as consumers (and not only as workers) reveals more complex dimensions of women's urban employment and personal agency. In effect, labor migrants' consumption practices are one of the few available avenues through which they can exercise new forms of autonomy and seek to construct socially satisfying and valued identities.[13]

As they move between rural and urban settings, young Thai women must negotiate not only shifts in space but also shifting identities and social relations. In this context, rural-urban mobility must be recognized as more than a strategy for economic survival or accumulation; it is also a vehicle through which migrants struggle over what it means to be "modern" in contemporary Thai society and how to reconcile these aspirations and images with equally compelling concerns for and moral commitments to rural kin and community. In the midst of these complex demands, it is little wonder that women should experience the movement into urban employment in highly ambivalent ways. Nevertheless, this ambivalence cannot be taken as passivity or a failure to recognize the inequities they encounter. Throughout their time in the city, young women make very real efforts to maintain a sense of meaning and purpose despite the many difficulties they face. Young women in Bangkok are often torn between duty and affection for rural kin on the one hand, and personal desires for autonomy and urban adventure on the other. The choices they make, however, are shaped not only by the structural disparities of Thai society and a globalized economy but also by the cultural resources that are available to them and through which they seek to understand who they are and who they wish to become.

This article has been revised and condensed from an earlier publication (Mills 1997).

NOTES

1. Khem is a pseudonym, as are the names of all informants cited in the text. Her statement is my own translation from a short autobiographical narrative written during the time I was interviewing her in 1987–88. Parts of her narrative were published in the February 1988 newsletter [*chotmaay khaaw phúan ying*] of Friends of Women, a Thai women's rights organization.

2. In the late 1980s annual GDP growth in Thailand averaged over 10% falling only slightly in the early and mid-1990s (Pasuk and Baker 1995: 152–523; Warr 1993: 53, 56–157). Although these rates dropped considerably following the Asian financial crisis that began in 1997, Thailand's cheap and flexible (i.e., easily replaceable) migrant labor force remains crucial to attracting international investment.

3. Thus, for example, men and women working in Bangkok may receive supplements of rice, other foods and even cash from rural households; children born to urban workers are frequently sent home to be raised by grandparents or other kin in the countryside; rural households also provide care and support to migrant members in cases of illness, unemployment or other crises they may encounter while working in the city.

4. Bangkok was the only significant destination for industrial labor migrants in the 1980s but by the 1990s migrants were also traveling to find work in new industrial zones established in several different regions of the country (see, for example, Theobald 2002).

5. For a more detailed discussion of these findings, focusing on one particular sending community where I lived in 1989–90, see Mills 1999b.

6. It is widely acknowledged that Thai women enjoy a high degree of autonomy as economic actors and household decision makers (at least relative to more rigidly patriarchal cultures in other parts of Asia) but these are generally the by-products of age, marriage, and motherhood. The extent to which Thai women do in fact enjoy a high social "status" has been the subject of considerable debate. See, for example, Van Esterik 1982, Keyes 1984, Kirsch 1982 and 1985.

7. Thailand's well-known sex industry is connected to the more respectable marketing of modern female beauty in many ways. For instance, popular beauty contests are commonly believed to be arenas for recruiting high-class escort and call-girl services. Although some women in the sex industry may enter or continue in this work at least partly because their earnings allow for enhanced commodity display and accumulation (e.g., Lyttleton 1994:267), the linkages between prostitution and "modern" womanhood remain problematic for migrants in other occupations and within the wider society. Sex work was very much stigmatized among the industrial laborers I interviewed. For analyses of the cultural contradictions which frame the experiences of some women sex workers in Thailand see Muecke 1992 and Lyttleton 1994.

8. Bangkok minimum wage was 97 baht in 1990; it rose to 110 baht (US$4.40) in 1993 and was nearly 150 baht in 1996, changes that came about after sustained campaigns by labor rights groups and unions. Minimum wage rates are set by region and somewhat lower rates apply in most parts of the country outside Bangkok. Exchange rates are based on the baht's pre-1997 value.

9. A 1980 survey of northeastern women working in Bangkok found that domestic servants earned a mean monthly income, including payments in kind, of 800 baht or $32 (U.S.) while those with factory jobs averaged 1200 baht (US$48) per month (Pawadee 1982: 103). While similar survey data on income in the late 1980's and early 1990's is unavailable, anecdotal reports by migrants indicate that domestic service remained very poorly paid. The greatest earning potential for migrants can be the sex trade; however, this depends upon highly variable working conditions ranging from relatively autonomous enterprise to virtual slave labor (see Truong 1990:185–88).

10. Many migrant women actively seek overtime. Given low base wages, overtime hours are often the only way to earn enough to cover their living expenses while also saving money to send home or to purchase valued commodity items.

11. Of course most leisure time is not spent on such outings. Many migrants spend much of their time outside of work doing laundry and other chores, and generally "resting." However, the latter often includes visiting with friends, chatting or watching television and perhaps sharing a meal, activities that also involve commodity consumption though on a smaller scale than the more intensely consumption-oriented *thiaws*.

12. In fact few of the migrants I knew made regular monthly remittances to village families. Those who did were usually working to support a child left at home in the care of grandparents.

13. Other scholars working in different parts of the world have also found that new forms of commodity consumption play an important role in women's responses to new kinds of wage labor (see, for example, Freeman 2000; Lynch 1999; Silvey 2000).

REFERENCES

Brown, Andrew 2001 "After the Kader Fire: Labour Organising for Health and Safety Standards in Thailand." IN J. Hutchison and Andrew Brown, eds. *Organising Labour in Globalising Asia*. London/New York: Routledge, pp. 127–46.

Enloe, Cynthia 1989 *Bananas, Beaches and Bases: Making Feminist Sense of International Politics*. Berkeley: University of California Press.

Freeman, Carla 2000 *High Tech and High Heels in the Global Economy: Women, Work, and Pink-Collar Identities in the Caribbean*. Durham, NC: Duke University Press.

Friends of Women 1988 *Friends of Women Newsletter [chotmaay khaaw phúan ying]*. Bangkok, Friends of Women Group. February.

Harvey, David 1989 *The Condition of Postmodernity*. Cambridge, MA: Blackwell.

Keyes, Charles F. 1984 "Mother or Mistress but Never a Monk: Buddhist Notions of Female Gender in Rural Thailand." *American Ethnologist* 11(2):223–41.

Kirsch, A. Thomas 1982 "Buddhism, Sex-Roles and the Thai Economy." In *Women of Southeast Asia*. Penny Van Esterik, ed. Pp. 16–41. DeKalb, IL: Northern Illinois University, Center for Southeast Asian Studies.

———. 1985 "Text and Context: Buddhist Sex Roles/Culture of Gender Revisted." *American Ethnologist* 12(2):302–20.

Lamphere, Louise 1987 *From Working Daughters to Working Mothers: Immigrant Women in a New England Industrial Community*. Ithaca, NY: Cornell University Press.

Lynch, Caitlin 1999 "The 'Good Girls' of Sri Lankan Modernity: Moral Orders of Nationalism and Capitalism." *Identities* 6:55–89.

Lyttleton, Chris 1994 "The Good People of Isan: Commercial Sex in Northeast Thailand." *The Australian Journal of Anthropology* 5(3):257–79.

Mills, Mary Beth 1997 "Contesting the Margins of Modernity: Women, Migration, and Consumption in Thailand." *American Ethnologist* 24(1):37–61.

———. 1999a "Enacting Solidarity: Unions and Migrant Youth in Thailand." *Critique of Anthropology* 19(2):175–91.

———. 1999b. *Thai Women in the Global Labor Force: Consuming Desires, Contested Selves*. New Brunswick, NJ: Rutgers University Press.

Muecke, Marjorie 1992 "Mother Sold Food, Daughter Sells Her Body: The Cultural Continuity of Prostitution." *Social Science and Medicine* 35(7):891–901.

Pasuk Phongpaichit and Chris Baker 1995 *Thailand: Economy and Politics*. Kuala Lumpur, Oxford, and New York: Oxford University Press.

Pawadee Tongudai 1982 Women, Migration and Employment: A Study of Migrant Workers in Bangkok. Ph.D. dissertation, New York University.

Porpora, Douglas, and Lim Mah Hui 1987 "The Political Economic Factors of Migration to Bangkok." *Journal of Contemporary Asia* 17(1):76–89.

Pred, Allan and Michael John Watts 1992 *Reworking Modernity: Capitalisms and Symbolic Discontent*. New Brunswick, NJ: Rutgers University Press.

Silvey, Rachel 2000 "Diasporic Subjects: Gender and Mobility in South Sulawesi." *Women's Studies International Forum* 23(4):501–15.

Theobald, Sally 2002 "Working for Global Factories: Thai Women in Electronics Export Companies in the Northern Regional Industrial Estate." IN *Women and Work in Globalising Asia*, eds. Dong-Sook S. Gills and Nicola Piper. London: Routledge, pp. 131–53.

Thorbek, Susanne 1987 *Voices From the City: Women of Bangkok*. London: Zed Press.

Truong, Thanh-Dam 1990 *Sex, Money and Morality: Prostitution and Tourism in Southeast Asia*. London: Zed Books Ltd.

Van Esterik, Penny 1982 "Laywomen in Theravada Buddhism." IN *Women of Southeast Asia*. P. Van Esterik, ed. pp. 55–78. DeKalb, IL: Center for Southeast Asian Studies, Northern Illinois University.

———. 1988 "Gender and Development in Thailand: Deconstructing Display." Toronto: York University, Department of Anthropology, Thai Studies Project Report.

———. 2000 *Materializing Thailand*. Oxford, UK: Berg.

Warr, Peter G. 1993 "The Thai Economy." IN Peter G. Warr (ed) *The Thai Economy in Transition*. Melbourne and Cambridge: Cambridge University Press, pp. 1–80.

"Wild Pigs and Dog Men": Rape and Domestic Violence as "Women's Issues" in Papua New Guinea

Laura Zimmer-Tamakoshi

INTRODUCTION

Male violence against women is a concern of feminists in both developed and developing countries (Counts, Brown & Campbell 1992; Davies 1994). Leaders in many developing countries, however, have been slow in recognizing the extent and nature of the problem. This is in part because of insufficient research and cultural norms allowing for a "certain amount of wife-beating" and forced sex within marriage (United Nations 1989). It is also the result of women's weaker political presence in developing countries and male resentment over a few women's gains in economic and social independence. Nevertheless, prompted by alarm over increased violence against women, concern over the deleterious effects of violence on women's participation in development, and negative images of Papua New Guinea in the world press, in 1982 the Papua New Guinean government directed its Law Reform Commission to begin research into domestic violence. The resulting, and for a developing country, unprecedented publications revealed that a majority of Papua New Guinean wives have been hit by their husbands, most more than once a year, with urban wives suffering a higher level of violence than their rural counterparts (Toft, ed. 1985, 1986a, 1986b; Toft and Bonnell 1985). Less systematically researched, rape is also a concern as Papua New Guinea tops the United States with a reported rate of 45 rapes per 100,000 persons versus 35 per 100,000 in the United States and well above the lower incidences of reported rapes in Japan and other industrial and non-industrial nations (Herman 1989: 23). In 1990 there were, 1,896

Original material prepared for this text.

rapes reported in Papua New Guinea, a country with less than 4 million in population (Dinnen 1993). Such statistics do not capture the severity of the problem, however, as most of these rapes were committed by three or more rapists (with more than 15, 20, or 40 males participating in any particular gang rape), and, as in the United States and elsewhere, many rapes are unreported, especially those committed by the victims' husbands, lovers, dates, or close relatives (Dinnen 1996; Finkelhor and Yllo 1985; Russell 1984; Toft 1985; Toft 1986a; Zimmer 1990).

This chapter examines violence against women in Papua New Guinea, reviewing past and present patterns of rape and domestic violence and adding to a multidimensional theory concerning the prevalence and increase of such violence. Although traditional attitudes toward violence contribute to its acceptance, recent research has targeted the psychological and economic pressures of development and inequality as fueling violence against women, particularly as they have different effects on the circumstances and attitudes of males and females. Josephides (n.d.), for example, argues that in Papua New Guinea, "Much of men's violence towards women is motivated by a fear that women are gaining a new kind of independence," and that men's violence is an attempt to terrify and control the women. Both Josephides and Bradley (1994), who worked at the Papua New Guinea Law Reform Commission from 1986 to 1990, see the violence as stemming not only from men's insecurities about their wives' potential independence but also their own uncertain situations and the effects of urban lifestyles (including alcohol abuse and reduced social support networks) on male–female relations. Other factors are increased eroticism and sexual conflicts as old taboos disappear and men (and sometimes women) place greater demands on their spouses and sexual partners (Jenkins 1994; Rosi and Zimmer-Tamakoshi 1993).

Supporting these arguments with cases and other material, I also develop a needed political dimension to better understand violence against women in Papua New Guinea (and elsewhere, as I discuss in the concluding section of this chapter). While individuals commit violence and it is individuals who experience the traumas and dislocations of change and development, the intersection of sex and class politics also informs and fuels sexual and domestic violence. With a small number of Papua New Guineans enjoying an elite lifestyle and under pressure from the "grassroots" to bring about an economic miracle on their behalf, elite women have become targets of disaffection not only from men and women in the lower classes but also from men in their own class. Feeling harassed on all sides, by unsympathetic constituents and, from their perspective, "demanding" or bikhet (uncontrollable, conceited) wives and girlfriends, many elite males have taken the path of least resistance and higher political capital, scapegoating elite women and using violence to assert control over them (Rosi and Zimmer-Tamakoshi 1993; Zimmer-Tamakoshi 1993b and 1995). Thus, I not only contend, along with others, that 1) women's opportunities for self-expression and economic independence threaten the self-esteem and security of men who do not have such opportunities and 2) that such men use violence against women to assert or regain a sense of dominance. I also argue that 3) violence against women is rife among Papua New Guinea's elite (a fact demonstrated by the Law Reform Commission reports) even when one excludes what Josephides has referred to in person as antifeminist rascals (or criminals) some of who are members of elite society (as has been reported by Dinnen 1993; Harris 1988; and Zimmer-Tamakoshi n.d.) and 4) that the violence is partly motivated by class and sexual tensions that paint elite females as symbols of all that is wrong with contemporary Papua New Guinean society. Finally, violence against women does not occur in isolation from other forms of violence. Political tensions in Papua New Guinea are grounded in a weak state that is unable to ensure even basic services to its population or to control public disturbances such as tribal conflicts over land. As has been argued for Papua New Guinea (A. Strathern 1993) and other parts of the world (Riches 1986), expressions of conflict such as the resumption of tribal warfare in the New Guinean highlands have strategic value in the context of a weak state. In a weak state violence may be a rational means of social advantage when there are no higher-level powers strong enough or interested enough in interfering with lower-level clashes. In the case of violence against women, men who want to can assert their dominance over women with little fear of resistance as long as there is widespread envy or fear of those women, and state officials charged with protecting them are unable or unwilling to do so.

WILD PIGS AND DOG MEN

Rape and domestic violence are not common in every New Guinean society (see Goodale 1980 and Mitchell 1992), but, fearing violence, most Papua New Guinean women walk in groups when going to and from their gardens or to office, school, or marketplace. Because husbands and boyfriends are likely perpetrators of violence against them, women also seek the protective company of family and friends when they are at home. Women's fear of violence, especially sexual violence, is fanned with vivid stories of past attacks on women and fresh accounts in the daily press. Around village hearths in the night, women and girls listen to the hushed and often admonitory tones of older persons telling them tales (captured in early anthropological monographs) of gang rape and mutilation of women's genitals as ways men "used to" punish errant wives and daughters (Meggitt 1964: 204, 207; Newman 1964: 266; Read 1952: 14); how wife-swapping or preying on other men's wives were tolerated as long as neither was too blatant an attack on a man's self-esteem (Berndt 1962: 160 Brown 1969: 94; Langness 1969: 45 and 1974: 204; Read 1954: 866); and how rape did and does occur in the varied contexts of women being found alone on a garden path or at work in their gardens, in war, and when a man tires of his lover, wishes to end an adulterous affair or lessen his culpability in either case by instigating a gang rape of the woman (Berndt 1962: 168). Outside the highlands, Tolai women shudder when they hear how Tolai men's cults once celebrated masculinity with the sexual abuse of widows and other women without male protection (Bradley 1982, 1985; Parkinson 1907: 473). And in West New Britain, Lakalai women do not mourn changes in the men's ceremonial season, which once included the casual rape of women in their own villages (Chowning 1985: 85).

Although many men's cults and their predations on women have died out as Christianity has taken over (Bradley 1985 and Chowning 1985), violence against women continues. Today, the contexts in which violence occurs are more but there are parallels in the circumstances of some of the victims and the motivations of their attackers. Finding a woman alone on a garden path is now varied in cases like one in 1983 in which a former rugby league star and two other assailants beat and raped a three-months-pregnant woman when they found her alone on the Daulo Pass where she was stranded after the vehicle in which she was a passenger broke down (PNG *Post Courier* 1984a). Tiring of his lover, a young man may arrange to have her gang-raped as did a young man in the city of Lae when he forced his girlfriend to have sex with his friends after he had sex with her (PNG *Post Courier* 1984c). Another traditional form of violence—humiliating the enemy by raping their women—was echoed in the same month when a man was held by two assailants and forced to watch while a third man raped his wife in Rabaul village (PNG *Post Courier* 1984g). In the same month, a gang of about 15 youths, all under the age of 20, raped a nine-year-old girl, her mother, and another woman while the women's husbands were beaten and held at knife-point. The gang then broke into a nearby house and stole $6,000 worth of cash and goods (PNG *Post Courier* 1984b, d, e, f, g). The gangs' actions replicated attacks against the enemies' women in warfare, but in this instance there was the added twist that some of the younger rapists were trying to prove their right to membership in the gang by raping white women (see Harris 1988 on *rascal* gang entry requirements). Echoes of using rape and beatings to punish errant wives or daughters abound in the case of "Bill and Maria" (Case 2 below) in which "Bill" (all names are pseudonyms for obvious reasons) rapes his wife in a public carpark as a means of asserting his dominance and punishing her independence.

In many traditional Papua New Guinean societies, particularly in the Highlands, violence against women was part of a sociopolitical context in which political eminence was achieved through the control and distribution of wealth, and older men and women controlled access to land and marriage, two main ingredients in the acquisition of wealth. Marriage was important for both males and females for it was through marriage that one acquired a helpmate, produced children, and paid off one's debts to society. For men of ambition, marrying several women was virtually the only means of becoming a "Big Man," as women's gardening and pig-raising activities and daughters' brideprices brought men the necessary "wealth" (pigs, yams, shells) to fund networks of supporters and to outgive competitors within and outside their clans. To marry at all required the support of older men and women, who gathered together the brideprice. The process of attracting brideprice supporters began during a man's childhood and youth, when he and his peers participated in lengthy initiations designed to test and strengthen their obedience and relationships to their supporters. During initiation, young men were told many falsehoods about women as a way of keeping them away from women until their elders were ready to support their marriages. Such fabrications included depictions of women, particularly young women, as dangerous and untrustworthy creatures who were to be feared and avoided if possible (Counts 1985;

Dickerson-Putman n.d.; Faithorn 1976; Gelber 1986; Zimmer-Tamakoshi 1996a). Boys learned that "over-indulgence in sexual relations with women depletes a man's vital energies leaving his body permanently exhausted and withered" (Meggitt 1964: 210) and that contact of any kind with women causes a man "to accumulate debilitating dirt in his body" (Newman 1964: 265). Young women's powers of seduction were portrayed as so great that young men were warned not to look at a young woman because "if you look at her, and she looks at you, then you will copulate" (Berndt 1962: 103; Read 1954: 867; Langness 1967: 165).

Part of the ideology initiates learned included notions of male superiority and dominance over women. Men's superiority was said to reside in their greater capacity for self-control. Initiates were taught that mature men do not act "like wild pigs" having sex indiscriminately or like "women" acting on whim and self-interest rather than promoting the social good (Gelber 1986, Chapter Two; Lindenbaum 1976: 56). Young men who were disrespectful of or doubted their elders' injunctions risked permanent bachelorhood as they depended on older men and women for brideprice help (Bowers 1965; Glasse 1969: 26; Waddell 1972: 46), and few prospective in-laws would allow their daughters to marry "dog men," men with inordinate desires for sex who spent their lives "sniffing" after other men's wives and destroying the village peace.

Promoting male solidarity, notions of male superiority allowed for effective regulation of access to and control over women. In most Papua New Guinean societies, the importance of female labor to men was such—and still is—that men have variously portrayed women as men's "hands" (Lindenbaum 1976: 59), "tradestores" (M. Strathern 1972: 99), "tractors" (Langness 1967: 172), and "capital assets" (Cook 1969: 102). Recent ethnographies suggest it was more young women's sexuality and labor than older women's that was at issue, as older women had rewards and reasons of their own to support their husbands' activities and to promote the well-being of their children's clans as well

as their own (Counts 1985; Dickerson-Putman n.d.; M. Strathern 1980; Zimmer-Tamakoshi 1996a). Just as parents warned sons against the dangers of women, so too did they warn daughters against unregulated association with young men. They also taught their daughters that safety lay in cooperating with their elders to achieve fruitful marriages and honorable lives. Women—young or old—who rebelled against such beliefs or interfered with men's activities and plans, risked beatings and punitive rapes (Berndt 1962; Josephides 1985; Meggitt 1964; Read 1954; and M. Strathern 1972). Believing women to be weak-willed, husbands justified beating their wives fairly regularly as a way of getting them to fulfill their obligations to them. Also believing women to be by nature deceitful and seductive, men readily blamed rape victims for bringing the rapes on themselves. Women were thus wise to build large networks of supporters in their own and their husbands' groups who might rise to their defense in the case of rape or an overzealous wife-beater.

Today, introduced notions of women's inferiority and men's right to dominate them, men's greater access to cash incomes and women's increasing dependence on men, the weakening of parents' economic control over sons and daughters (especially those living and working in urban areas), and opportunities (primarily through education) for a few women to achieve both economic and social independence all contribute to an increasing incidence of violence against women in Papua New Guinea. Grafted onto old beliefs, the views of some Christian missions—that women be subservient to and mindful at all times of their husbands' and, much less so, their parents' wishes—and foreign media portrayals of women as erotic sex objects, docile housewives, or man-eaters, further alienate young Papua New Guineans from one another as women are shrouded in further mystifications. During my first year of fieldwork with a group of Highlanders known as the Gende, an urban gang member bragged to me about his sexual exploits which included kidnapping and raping young girls and even a married woman. In response to my shocked expression, he assured me that "They liked it! It was like it is in a James Bond movie—sexy! The woman fights with James Bond and tries to kill him and then he forces her to have sex with him and she is his woman from then on. Sometimes he kills her if she is a really bad woman." When I asked if he had killed anyone, he said he had killed the one woman because he feared she would tell her husband that he had raped her (which he denied, insisting that it wasn't rape and that "She liked it! I'm sexy!").

In the material realm, men's control of economic resources has tightened in both village and town as the proceeds from most cash crops are controlled by men, men dominate the job market, and men's educational opportunities are greater than women's. Women's dependence on men is greatest among urban women. One result of this dependence is that urban husbands—especially prosperous ones—are more likely to fight with their wives, to cheat on them, and to abuse them both physically and sexually (Ranck and Toft 1986; Rosi and Zimmer-Tamakoshi 1993; Zimmer-Tamakoshi 1993a). Several Gende women I know left husbands who beat them, drank too much, and wasted their salaries on other women, saying they'd rather marry a village husband who worked with them in the gardens and not against them in town. In the case of low-income husbands who are less attractive to other women, a wife's threat to return to the village to find another husband is taken very seriously, and such a husband is less likely even than a villager to beat his wife (Ranck and Toft 1986; Zimmer-Tamakoshi 1996b).

The weakening of parental control over the beliefs and actions of the younger generation and its relationship to violence against women can be illustrated in the experience of another Gende woman. This young woman's husband, also Gende, grew up in Port Moresby and is more western in his outlook on life than she is. Jealous of his womanizing and pressured by her relatives to get him to pay off the remaining brideprice he owes them, she has stayed in town, playing cards most of the time her husband is working and being the butt of his

anger or lust whenever he is home. Although she usually suffers his abuse quietly, on one occasion he forced her to have sex during her period, a heinous act in the eyes of more traditional Gende. Hysterical and threatening suicide, the young woman cut off one of her fingers with an axe, thereby demonstrating her shame. A parallel experience occurred a generation before to the girl's aunt. Married to a migrant but living in the village, the aunt was forced by her young husband—on a rare visit home—to have sex during her period. Ashamed and angry, the aunt moped around the village for a day and then left for her garden house—several miles distant from the village—where she hung herself. Unsuspecting, her family did not find her until it was too late. When the women cleaned her body for burial, they discovered menstrual blood mixed with semen smeared over her lower body and skirt as well as bruises on her arms and chest where her husband had apparently held her down forcefully. Although such actions would have resulted in the young man's death in the past, the aunt's husband stayed in town, away from the girl's parents and male relatives, hiding behind the power of Australian colonial law and her parents' belief that the young man would be more useful to them if he continued working and paid them a large compensation payment for their daughter's death.

How far outside the normal realm of parental control (and protection) young persons can get is illustrated in "Violet's" case. In this case, parental pressures and absence are only part of the story. Other factors responsible for "Violet's" fate are her naive hopes for love and romance, and a sociocultural environment in which many young men no longer fear women so much as see them as sexual prey.

Case 1—"Violet"

I have written elsewhere on the motives and circumstances of young village women moving to town in the hope of attracting suitors who can pay the large brideprices expected by the women's families and fulfill women's dreams of a prosperous lifestyle (Zimmer-Tamakoshi

1993a). Living with younger kinsmen, married sisters, or even non-relatives, these girls are poorly chaperoned and often end up victims of sexual assault and bondage. One such victim was Violet. When she first came to Port Moresby, Violet stayed with an older sister and brother-in-law in a house provided by the company her brother-in-law worked for. Violet spent her days looking after her sister's children while her sister worked as a checker in a local supermarket. Evenings, Violet attended the local movie theater with girlfriends or stayed home to watch T.V. with her sister's family. As soon as she moved in with her sister, Violet became the target of her brother-in-law's unwanted sexual advances. On numerous occasions, feigning illness in order to spend the day at home and threatening to kill her if she revealed what he was doing, Violet's brother-in-law had sex with Violet. When Violet became pregnant, her sister wanted to send her back to the village, but Violet feared the censure and disappointment of her parents. Violet obtained an illegal abortion and moved in with a girlfriend.

Supporting herself by prostitution and frequenting the notorious "Pink Pussycat" and other cocktail lounges, Violet continues to hope that she will one day meet and marry a "nice man" who will take her out of her misery. The types of men Violet is most likely to meet, however, are married men looking for an evening's distraction or university students preying on naive husband-hunters. The violent and sexually-charged atmosphere of both the University and the city are well-known to anyone who has spent time in either location. In a paper on the situations of women students at the University of Papua New Guinea, Joan Oliver reported that "women students had a pervasive fear of attack, harassment, threats, bashings, rape and breaking into rooms by male students or strangers" (1987: 159; see also Still and Shea's report of 1976). She further reported that because of their fears many women either drop out of school or become engaged to male protectors who not infrequently soon have the women pregnant (1987: 170).

With the proportion of female students at UPNG hovering at 10 percent, male students are in keen competition with one another for the friendship of female classmates. The competition works itself out along divisions of language and region as, for example, Chimbu *wantoks* (persons who speak Chimbu) jealously attempt to guard all Chimbu girls for themselves and Papuans (from southern Papua New Guinea) fight off any non-Papuans who might try to have a relationship with a Papuan girl. Since having sex with a female student risks reprisal from her campus *wantoks*—but not the police!—many University men satisfy their sexual desires by visiting Port Moresby's night spots and bringing back girls like Violet to the University playing fields and dorms where they have sex with them—often forced. These escapades may also bring reprisals, of course, as happened when a gang of University students raped a young girl from a nearby squatter settlement on the University football field while her younger brother was made to watch. Class antagonism as well as ethnic outrage was evident as men and boys from the settlement stalked the campus paths and housing areas for weeks after threatening to rape female students and teachers at UPNG for what the "spoiled, *bikhet* school boys" had done.

Meri Wantok and Meri Universiti

As suggested in the previous paragraph, a broad set of factors that seems conducive to high levels of violence against women in Papua New Guinea is the extra-local politics of sexuality. This set of factors includes the intersections of elite and urban sexual politics with nationalist and class interests and rhetoric. In a paper on nationalism and sexuality in Papua New Guinea, I argued that the practice of holding educated women, or *meri universiti*, responsible for all that is wrong with contemporary Papua New Guinean society is both a political maneuver to ease class and interethnic tensions and jealousies in Papua New Guinea's culturally diverse society (Zimmer-Tamakoshi 1993b) and a satisfying fiction for the majority of Papua New Guineans who feel left out of "progress" and "development." Symbolizing privilege and, in some instances, sexual freedom (or anarchy), *meri universiti* and *skull meri* (school girls) are both envied for their perceived opportunities and hated as selfish betrayers of their cultural roots, while "grassroots" women and more circumspect elite women who show (or appear to show) greater concern for their kin and language groups are accorded respect as *meri wantok* and *meri bilong ples*.

There is as much diversity within the elite as without, particularly between educated men and women. Unlike their male counterparts, who come from all parts of the nation, Papua New Guinea's small class of educated elite women come almost entirely from coastal and off-shore island areas that have been long involved with the outside world. As a result, they are more likely than their male peers to come from educated and economically privileged backgrounds, and as a group they are more western in demeanor and appearance than most Papua New Guinean women. Another difference between educated men and women (and between educated women and the majority of Papua New Guinea's population) is that many educated elite women come from matrilineal societies in which women's status tends to be higher relative to many patrilineal societies and women are freer in their relations with men. On one occasion, when I was having dinner at the Bird of Paradise hotel in Goroka, I was surprised to learn that the couple at the table beside me were married (but not to each other!), were travelling together throughout the Highlands on government business, and that their spouses on Bougainville Island were satisfied with the phone calls the pair made at each stop on their tour of duty. It was difficult to imagine such easy professionalism in a partnership involving a Highlands man and woman. Rumors and jealous spouses would prevent this as Highlanders (and many other Papua New Guineans) believe it is impossible for men and women to be together for long without engaging in sex. Unusual, such behavior becomes a focus of the anger and jealousies that exist between the sexes and between class, ethnic, and racial groupings in Papua New Guinea.

Increasing the distance between elite men and themselves some elite women have opted for marriage with non-Papua New Guineans or to forgo marriage entirely. Several examples are two of the three women to ever sit as members of National Parliament and a former president of the National Council of Women, all married to or in long-term relationships with white, expatriate males. Such high-profile interracial relationships on the part of women embarrass the male leadership as the majority of Papua New Guineans see them as signs of elite immorality and weakness (e.g., elite men's inability to control their women) and collaboration of the elite with outsiders and former colonials. There have been attempts to control elite women's freedoms at all levels of Papua New Guinean society from the government down, including public censure, violence, and the refusal of full citizenship rights to foreign spouses and recurrent threats to disenfranchise the children of mixed marriages.

An example of the public scapegoating of elite or educated women is the "mini-skirt debate." The "mini-skirt debate" began back in the early seventies—prior to Papua New Guinea's independence in 1975—with Tolai religious and political leaders in East New Britain calling for a campaign against immodest dress and claiming that school girls and young women were provoking an increasing incidence of rape and STDs in East New Britain by wearing provocative western-style clothing and makeup. The debate entered the pages of Papua New Guinea's *Post Courier* where it has continued off and on for years. The response of young women to men's condemnation of their dress is summed up in one early letter to the editor signed "Four Tolai Girls" (PNG *Post Courier* 1973a). As quoted in Hogan (1985: 56–57):

[The young women] had no doubts that the banning of mini-skirts would have wider implications. For its writers, wearing mini-skirts signified that they wanted greater control over their lives. They accused the initiators of the circular of having political motivations—of using the issue of public morality for their own political purposes . . . and [of knowing] that with education women would be able to judge the decisions of men.

Three male Tolai students at the University of Papua New Guinea added their opinions to the debate by writing that the four Tolai girls were blindly following the dictates of western culture and wanting "to keep on 'pleasing' and 'praising' the colonial administration without stopping and asking themselves a single question" (PNG *Post Courier* 1973b).

The political advantages of focusing on the behaviors of a few elite women and suggesting that they are the root cause of problems both for women and the country as a whole are the obvious appeal to the masses, the small cost of blaming persons who do not constitute a large constituency, and the ease of following a time-honored tradition of blaming women for problems that men create or holding them up as suspicious characters bent on interfering in men's relations with one another. The anti-colonial sentiment and racial undercurrents in elite men's condemnation of elite women is also a popular cause in a nation that is trying to unite a diversity of regions and language groups into one strong nation (see Lindstrom 1992).

Two cases that illustrate the sexual politics of Papua New Guinea's educated elite and the sexual competition among men of different tribal and national backgrounds are the cases of "Bill and Maria" and "Lita." Although their cases are well-known to me, I can only sketch in the barest of details here in this brief chapter. Readers who wish to read more detailed cases are referred to Susan's Toft's harrowing account of marital violence of two couples living in Port Moresby (1985) and Andrew Strathern's grisly report on sadistic rape in Hagen (1985).

Case 2—"Bill and Maria"

I have written about Bill and Maria in a paper on love and marriage among the educated elite in Port Moresby (Rosi and Zimmer-Tamakoshi 1993). I described how this young couple—both highlanders, both finishing their education at UPNG and the parents of two young children—were suffering severe pressures and tensions in their marriage, with the result that they fought often and violently. Much of the tension was caused by in-laws: Maria's father demanding a large brideprice for his educated daughter, and Bill's village-based family critical of Maria's lack of traditional skills and anxious that the couple pay most of the brideprice and child-wealth payments themselves. Raised on a government station and exposed in her religious and educational experience to western ideas about appropriate and desirable marital relations, Maria was hurt and angered by Bill's drinking, numerous infidelities, and by his toying with the idea of marrying a second wife back in the highlands to raise pigs for exchange purposes.

What I did not discuss in that paper was the fact that Bill ended most arguments with his wife by raping her, sometimes in public places. On one occasion, after coming home drunk and disheveled in the early morning hours, Bill dragged Maria out of bed and raped her—spread-eagled over a car hood in a University parking lot—while loudly accusing her of being the cause of all his troubles, of having affairs with other men, and of dressing and behaving too provocatively to be a good wife. While there was little truth to his accusations, his use of these particular criticisms to justify his brutality reveals important contradictions in the lives of educated men, contradictions arising from the complex politics of sexuality in contemporary Papua New Guinea. On many occasions, Bill expressed pride in Maria's education and her poise in social situations involving both Papua New Guineans and expatriates. At one large garden party, for example, at which scores of University professors and students had gathered, Bill and Maria joined easily into the festivities, eating, drinking, dancing, and talking with the other guests—together and singly. As the evening progressed, however, Bill began following Maria around, demanding that she join the group of women who were sitting on woven mats on the perimeter of the night's action. These women—the wives of older and more conservative faculty and staff—were dressed modestly in *meri wantok* fashion in form-hiding *meri blouses* and ankle-length *laplaps*, and spent the evening quietly talking with one another and tending small children they had brought with them to the party. Also on the fringes, but drinking heavily, were some of Bill's male relatives—several students and several older men who did maintenance work at the university. These men ogled skimpily dressed expatriate women and the more daring *meri universiti* at the same time they criticized Bill for allowing Maria to wear a short, tight skirt and form-revealing blouse.

At the University club and at parties, I many times heard men slander particular women, their clothing choices, and their alleged sexual habits. If the women were not related to the men, they would also discuss ways of going about seducing or raping the woman. Add to this the disapproving and often envious statements of men's lesser-educated kin—telling their more advantaged brothers to avoid marrying women who waste money on makeup and fancy clothes like spoiled white women at the same time as they express their desire to have sex with such women—and a situation arises in which it seems impossible for men like Bill to have it both ways—a wife who is attractive in new and sophisticated ways but one who does not attract the desire or censure of men who are her husband's associates, friends, relatives, or enemies.

Case 3—"Lita"

Further illuminating the sexual side of interethnic and interracial politics in urban Papua New Guinea, Lita's case is interesting because she is one of a small number of Papua New Guinean women who have discarded traditional relationships in order to express themselves in new and unusual ways. Pretty, bright, and poised in the presence of men of all ages and nationalities, Lita was engaged to a middle-aged expatriate when I first met her in one of the classes I was teaching at UPNG. Spurning her age-mates and vocal about her preference for white men—whom she claimed were gentler and more supportive of women's interests (for similar sentiments see the case of

"Barbara" in Rosi and Zimmer-Tamakoshi 1993)—Lita accepted the gifts and attentions of her lover while at the same time playing the field at local discos and bars frequented by expatriate and Papua New Guinean businessmen and leaders.

Halfway through the semester, Lita began a secret love affair with one of her teachers at UPNG—an expatriate who was much younger than her fiance. When the affair became public knowledge and both expatriate lovers were spying on the other and attempting to engage the sympathies and help of Lita's friends, Lita's *wantoks* abducted her from her apartment, severely beat her and raped her, warning her to cease having affairs with either man and to choose someone from her own ethnic and racial background to marry. When I learned about the attack from some of Lita's classmates, I was dismayed by their lack of sympathy for her. Saying that she should not have embarrassed her *wantoks* and other Papua New Guineans by choosing white lovers over black, the majority felt she had only gotten what she deserved and that she was lucky her *wantoks* had not killed her.

Lita's social background is similar to Maria's in that both women were raised in urban or peri-urban settings by parents who are employed in the government sector and who—in their commitment to a more western, or "modern" ethic—have raised their daughters to expect more egalitarian and open relations with men than is the norm in most parts of Papua New Guinea. Unfortunately for both young women, most of their *wantoks* do not agree and feel that the young women's "immodest" and "loose" behavior is injurious to ethnic and racial pride. Furthermore, both young women's *wantoks* are for the most part far less prosperous than either young woman's family, and there are economic and class tensions to contend with. When Lita informed her parents she was engaged to a foreigner, they at first protested it would never work. Promised a large brideprice, however, they and many of their village *wantoks* allowed that the marriage might be a good idea. Lita's *wantoks* at UPNG, however, took her engagement as an insult to them as more suitable partners, and when she compounded the insult by having affairs with two expatriates at the same time, it was too much to bear. In Maria's case, while her father and brothers have threatened to have her husband arrested for his repeated brutality, her *wantoks* side with Bill, contending that Maria is at least partly to blame for his behavior and that her husband and father should see to it that she conform to the clothing and behavioral norms of most highlanders rather than some small segment of PNG and expatriate society.

RAPE AND DOMESTIC VIOLENCE AS "WOMEN'S ISSUES"

As the foregoing suggests, violence against women has long been accepted in many Papua New Guinean societies as a legitimate means of controlling women and expressing or affecting men's relations with other men. From studies done in the 1980s by the Law Reform Commission (Toft, ed. 1985, 1986b) and other ethnographic sources we know that in the past both women and men agreed to men's right to chastise women with beatings and sometimes rape. Today, when some women's increased opportunities for self-expression and economic independence are perceived as threatening men's relations and the general good, many men and even many women consider violence to be an acceptable "comeuppance" for young women like Maria and Lita, and a means of preserving ethnic and national unity and pride. Nevertheless, there has been a sea change in women's attitudes toward violence against them and not only amongst elite women. Since the Second World War and the expansion of Papua New Guinea's towns and cities, urban dwellers have voiced their concerns over high rates of urban crime and domestic violence. Urban women have been especially concerned with the ever-present threat of pack rape and domestic violence associated with urban men's greater alcohol consumption, male sexual jealousy, and money problems (Toft 1986a: 12–14). In 1981, the National Council of Women passed a resolution stating that crimes against women seemed to be increasing and that there were inadequate controls to protect women. The Council then requested the government to investigate the problem, and on August 18, 1982, the Papua New Guinea Minister for Justice passed to the Law Reform Commission a Reference on Domestic Violence (Toft, ed. 1986a). The ensuing studies revealed many things about the nature, extent, and causes of domestic violence in Papua New Guinea as well as changing attitudes toward violence against women. Positive correlations were shown to exist, for example, between a decreasing acceptance of domestic violence and a person's sex, degree of urbanization, and levels of education and income (Toft 1986a: 23–26). Significantly, both urban low-income women and elite women are far less prepared than rural women to admit fault in failing to meet obligations to their husbands or to believe they "deserve" occasional beatings. Although the majority of urban men— especially educated men—also say it is unacceptable to hit wives, their apparent change in attitude is not reflected in their behavior.

Statistics are a weak measure of reality, however, and it is in case studies that we learn the depth of experience and motivations behind women's change of attitudes. In a study of two cases of marital violence in Port Moresby, Toft (1985) shows how men's violence against women interferes with the women's abilities, needs, and desires to function well in urban environments. One informant, "Rose," was regularly hit by her husband, who also phoned her at work in jealous piques and sometimes beat her so badly she could not work or take care of their young children. In a paper on Gende women in town, I make the point that while many urban women are technically unemployed, they fulfill many obligations to their village kin and in-laws and must be free to move about the urban environment without fear (Zimmer-Tamakoshi 1996b). Women in low-income households, for example, are almost always in town to protect their husbands' incomes from dissipation (e.g., alcohol, cards, prostitutes) and to see that their children get a better education than is always possible in the village. To achieve these ends, women meet husbands at their place of work on pay day for the handing over of the pay packet, they search the urban markets and stores for bargains to make their husbands' small incomes pay for both household and extra-household exchange demands, and they do without their school-age children's help in the daily round of collecting firewood and water for use in sub-standard squatter settlements at the edge of town. Such women have little patience with violent husbands whose utility to them is marginal at best. Women with more education have potentially greater opportunities to live life differently than their mothers' generation. Often, however, their desires and potential are not realized as violence, and fear of violence, keeps them out of work. Female graduates of Papua New Guinea's teachers' colleges, for example, rarely teach for more than a year or so after graduating, even though they express, during their training, a strong desire and ability to be career teachers. A major constraint against their fulfilling their self-expectations is the threat of male violence against them, causing many to flee into early marriages and the comparative safety of compliance with men's wishes (Wormald and Crossley 1988).

Women's growing sense of gender oppression and their anger over their wasted potential reveals itself in diverse and often unusual ways. Young women like "Violet," impregnated by her brother-in-law and more or less abandoned by her family, may turn to prostitution to earn a living and make men pay for what they would otherwise take anyway. In urban contexts where women and girls have few options, "selling their bodies" to husbands or customers makes economic sense however much self-violence it represents (see also Borrey 1994). Cases like "Donna's" (see below), in which women are packraped because they represent a threat to men's interests or, as in this case, a threat to Papua New Guinean pride, are more and more seen as deliberate assaults against women as a whole and not individual women.

Case 4—"Donna"

Donna was a successful Filipina business woman married to one of the expatriate lecturers at UPNG and living on campus in one of the homes provided for UPNG faculty and their families. Resentment against expatriate women is high in Papua New Guinea, because most expatriate women live enviable lifestyles and many fill full- or part-time positions in the work force that Papua New Guineans feel should be given to Papua New Guinean workers, especially male workers. Openly critical of what she felt were lax working habits on the part of her Papua New Guinean employees, Donna earned even more enmity than usual.

Sometime in the late 1980s, Donna and her husband were eating dinner when a gang of rascals broke through their dining room windows, beat the husband, and abducted Donna. Taking Donna by car to a remote location, the gang raped her and then left her, naked and badly injured. After crawling and stumbling back to the University, Donna left the country to be joined soon after by her husband. Newspapers and gossip revealed that Donna had been the victim of a pay-back rape for her racial slurs and her successful competition against Papua New Guinean businessmen. Although her rape shocked the University community, particularly the expatriates, many persons—expatriate and Papua New Guinean, male and female—blamed Donna for being too outspoken and too obviously successful for a female expatriate business woman.

As time went on, however, public outcry began to divide itself along sexual rather than racial lines, and all women were more fearful as they went about their daily activities. In another much-reported case in the city of Lae, several Papua New Guinean men raped and then murdered a respected and well-liked white helicopter pilot when the man she was trying to sell her car to drove her to a secluded place where he was joined by the other men. During the trial, there were demonstrations throughout Papua New Guinea in favor of a strong penalty—"Death," "*Katim bol bilong ol*" ("cut their balls off!")—and when the defendants were let off with light sentences there was a spontaneous demonstration of several thousand women in Port Moresby protesting "men's disregard for women."

Although in the mid-1980s Papua New Guinea's male-dominated government supported the Law Reform Commission studies and a subsequent public awareness campaign on violence against women, rape and domestic violence are now "women's issues" in Papua New Guinea and no longer even a small part of male politicians' rhetoric. This shift became brutally apparent in 1987 when an all-male Parliament booed Rose Kekedo and other women from the floor when they tried to present the Law Reform Commission's interim report on domestic violence (*The Times of Papua New Guinea* 1992). In 1987 and since there have been no women in Papua New Guinea's Parliament. Papua New Guinea has never had more than a few women in higher government positions, and at most there have been only three Papua New Guinean women in Parliament at the same time (1977–1982). Significantly, none of these women ever felt the need to run a feminist campaign, until recently that is. Since 1987, as the numbers of female candidates and winners continues to shrink (Wormald 1992), female leaders such as former Parliamentarians Josephine Abaijah and Nahau Rooney have taken public positions on women's issues, focusing most on the concerns of "grassroots" women as crucial to Papua New Guinea's future and, of course, their own re-election. Rape and domestic violence top the list of concerns, however, as they affect all women (Waram 1992a and 1992b). Women's organizations have joined the campaign against violence with women leaders in Port Moresby choosing the theme "Violence Against Women" for their May 1993 International Women's Day Celebration (*The Times of Papua New Guinea* 1993b) and provincial women's leaders in East New Britain embarking on a campaign against violence and making plans to open a women's crisis center by 1994 (*The Times of Papua New Guinea* 1993a).

Similar situations exist in other Pacific countries where violence against women is less prevalent but nonetheless serious and feared by women who see it destroying their families and any hopes they have for establishing new opportunities and relationships for themselves (Dominy 1990; Lateef 1990; Ralston 1993; Trask 1989; Zimmer-Tamakoshi 1993b and 1995). Women in Vanuatu and the Solomon Islands have been especially vocal, decrying the effects of colonialism and modernity on their societies (most notably alcohol abuse, consumerism, gambling, and class and sex inequalities), but, above all, the impact of male dominance on women's hopes and aspirations (see Billy, Lulei, and Sipolo 1983; Griffen 1976; Molisa 1983, 1987, 1989). Asserting what it is that women want, Vanuatu poet and feminist Grace Mera Molisa both unites and speaks for women throughout the Pacific in her poem "Colonised People" (1987: 9–13), part of which is reprinted here:

> Women too
> have a right
> to be Free.
>
> Free to think
> Free to express
> Free to choose
> Free to love
> and be loved
> as Woman Vanuatu.

She does not, however, any more than my argument has, lay the blame for women's plight simply on the shoulders of men. While she blasts male leaders for scapegoating female politicians who threaten their grasp of power in "Hilda Lini" (1987: 26–27), she also condemns women for envying other women's successes and going along with men's definitions of things in "Delightful Acquiescence" (1989: 24):

> Half of Vanuatu
> is still colonized
> by her self.
>
> Any woman
> showing promise
> is clouted
> into acquiescence.

REFERENCES

Berndt, Ronald M. 1962. *Excess and Restraint: Social Control among a New Guinea Mountain People*. Chicago: University of Chicago Press.

Billy, A., H. Lulei, and J. Sipolo, eds. 1983. *"Mi Mere": Poetry and Prose by Solomon Islands Women Writers*. Honiara.

Borrey, Anou. 1994. "Youth, Unemployment, and Crime." Paper presented at the National Employment Summit, 11–12 May, Port Moresby.

Bowers, Nancy. 1965. "Permanent Bachelorhood in the Upper Kaugel Valley of Highland New Guinea." *Oceania* 36: 27–37.

Bradley, Christine. 1982. "Tolai Women and Development." University College of London. Unpublished Ph.D. Thesis.

———. 1985. "Attitudes and Practices Relating to Marital Violence Among the Tolai of East New Britain." In Susan Toft (ed). *Domestic Violence in Papua New Guinea*, pp. 32–71. Port Moresby: Papua New Guinea Law Reform Commission Monograph No. 3.

———. 1994. "Why Male Violence Against Women is a Development Issue: Reflections from Papua New Guinea." In Miranda Davies (ed). *Women and Violence*, pp. 10–26. London: Zed Books, Ltd.

Brown, Paula. 1969. "Marriage in Chimbu." In R.M. Glasse and M.J. Meggitt (eds.). *Pigs, Pearlshells, and Women: Marriage in the New Guinea Highlands*, pp. 77–95. New Jersey: Prentice Hall, Inc.

Chowning, Ann. 1985. "Kove Women and Violence: The Context of Wife-Beating in a West New Britain Society." In Susan Toft (ed.). *Domestic Violence in Papua New Guinea*, pp. 72–91. Port Moresby: Papua New Guinea Law Reform Commission Monograph No. 3.

Cook, E. A. 1969. "Marriage Among the Manga." In R.M. Glasse and M.J. Meggitt (eds.). *Pigs, Pearlshells, and Women: Marriage in the New Guinea Highlands*, pp. 96–116. New Jersey: Prentice Hall, Inc.

Counts, Dorothy Areyers. 1985. "Tamparonga: 'The Big Women' of Kaliai." In J.K. Brown, Virginia Kerns, and Contributors. In *Her Prime: A New View of Middle-Aged Women*, pp. 49–64. South Hadley, MA: Bergin and Garvey Publishers, Inc.

Counts, Dorothy Ayers, Judith K. Brown, and Jacquelyn C. Campbell, eds. 1992. *Sanctions and Sanctuary: Cultural Perspectives on the Beating of Wives*. Boulder: Westview Press.

Davies, Miranda, ed. 1994. *Women and Violence: Realities and Responses Worldwide*. London: Zed Books Ltd.

Dickerson-Putman, Jeanette. 1996. "From Pollution to Empowerment: Women, Age, and Power Among the Bena Bena of the Eastern Highlands." In J. Dickerson-Putman (ed.). *Women, Age, and Power: The Politics of Age Difference Among Women in Papua New Guinea and Australia. Pacific Studies* 19 (4): 41–70

Dinnen, Sinclair. 1993. "Big Men, Small Men and Invisible Women." *Australian and New Zealand Journal of Criminology* (March 1993) 26: 19–34.

———. 1996. "Law, Order, and State." In Laura Zimmer-Tamakoshi (ed.). *Modern PNG Society*. Bathurst, Australia: Crawford House Press.

Dominy, Michelle. 1990. "Maori Sovereignty: A Feminist Invention of Tradition." In J. Linnekin and L. Poyer (eds.). *Cultural Identity and Ethnicity in the Pacific*, pp. 237–257. Honolulu: University of Hawaii Press.

Faithorn, Elizabeth. 1976. "Women as Persons: Aspects of Female Life and Male-Female Relations Among the Kafe." In P. Brown and G. Buchbinder (eds.). *Man and Woman in the New Guinea Highlands*, pp. 86–95. Washington, DC: American Anthropological Association.

Finkelhor, David and Kersti Yllo. 1985. *License to Rape: Sexual Abuse of Wives*. New York: Holt, Rinehart, and Winston.

Gelber, Marilyn G. 1986. *Gender and Society in the New Guinea Highlands: An Anthropological Perspective on Antagonism Toward Women*. Boulder, CO: Westview Press, Inc.

Glasse, R. M. 1969. "Marriage in South Fore." In R.M. Glasse and M.J. Meggitt (eds.). *Pigs, Pearlshells, and Women: Marriage in the New Guinea Highlands*, pp. 16–37. Englewood Cliffs, NJ: Prentice Hall, Inc.

Goodale, Jane C. 1980. "Gender, Sexuality, and Marriage: A Kaulong Model of Nature and Culture." In C. MacCormack and M. Strathern (eds.). *Nature, Culture and Gender*, pp. 119–142. Cambridge: Cambridge University Press.

Griffen, V., ed. 1976. *Women Speak Out! A Report of the Pacific Women's Conference, October 27–November 2*. Suva.

Harris, Bruce. 1988. *The Rise of Rascalism—Action and Reaction in the Evolution of Rascal Gangs*. Port Moresby: Papua New Guinea Institute of Applied Social and Economic Research.

Herman, Dianne F. 1989. "The Rape Culture." In Jo Freeman (ed.). *Women: A Feminist Perspective*, pp. 20–44. Mountain View, California: Mayfield Publishing Company.

Hogan, Evelyn. 1985. "Controlling the Bodies of Women: Reading Gender Ideologies in Papua New Guinea." In Maev O'Collins et al. *Women in Politics in Papua New Guinea*, pp. 54–71. Working Paper No. 6. Canberra Department of Political and Social Change, Australian National University.

Jenkins, Carol (and The National Sex and Reproduction Research Team). 1994. *National Study of Sexual and Reproductive Knowledge and Behaviour in Papua New Guinea*. Papua New Guinea Institute of Medical Research Monograph 10.

Josephides, Lisette. 1985. *The Production of Inequality: Gender and Exchange Among the Kewa*. London: Tavistock.

———. n.d. "Gendered Discourses of Tradition and Change." Unpublished paper.

Langness, L. 1967. "Sexual Antagonism in the New Guinea Highlands: A Bena Bena Example." *Oceania* 37: 61–177.

———. 1969. "Marriage in Bena Bena." In R.M. Glasse and M.J. Meggitt (eds.). *Pigs, Pearlshells, and Women: Marriage in the New Guinea Highlands*, pp. 38–55. Englewood Cliffs, NJ: Prentice Hall, Inc.

———. 1974. "Ritual, Power, and Male Dominance." *Ethos* 2: 189–212.

Lateef, S. 1990. "Current and Future Implications of the Coups for Women in Fiji." *The Contemporary Pacific* 2 (1): 113–130.

Lindenbaum, Shirley. 1976. "A Wife is the Hand of Man." In P. Brown and G. Buchbinder (eds.). *Man and Woman in the New Guinea Highlands*, pp. 54–62. Washington, DC: American Anthropological Association.

Lindstrom, Lamont. 1992. *Pasin Tumbuna: Cultural Traditions and National Identity in Papua New Guinea. Culture and Communications Working Paper*. Honolulu: Institute of Culture and Communications, East-West Center.

Meggitt, Mervyn J. 1964. "Male-Female Relationships in the Highlands of Australian New Guinea." *American Anthropologist* 66: 204–224.

Mitchell, William E. 1992. "Why Wape Men Don't Beat Their Wives: Constraints Toward Domestic Tranquility in a New Guinea Society." In Counts, Brown, and Campbell (eds.). *Sanctions and Sanctuary: Cultural Perspectives on the Beating of Wives*, pp. 89–98. Boulder, CO: Westview Press.

Molisa, Grace Mera. 1983. *Black Stone*. Suva.

———. 1987. *Colonised People*. Port Vila, Vanuatu.

———. 1989. *Black Stone II*. Port Vila, Vanuatu.

Newman, Philip L. 1964. "Religious Belief and Ritual in a New Guinea Society." *American Anthropologist* 66: 257–272.

Oliver, Joan. 1987. "Women Students at the University of Papua New Guinea in 1985." In S. Stratigos and P.J. Hughes (eds). *The Ethics of Development: Women as Unequal Partners in Development*, pp. 156–172. Port Moresby: University of Papua New Guinea Press.

Parkinson, R. 1907. Thirty Years in the South Seas (trans. by N.C. Barry from Dreissig Jahre in der Sudsee). Stuttgart: Strecker and Schroder. Typescript in the Papua New Guinea Collection, University of Papua New Guinea.

PNG Post Courier. 1973a. "Four Tolai Girls." June 13.

———. 1973b. "Three Mataungan Students." June 28.

———. 1984a. "Gang Rapist Jailed for Seven Years." April 13, p. 9.

———. 1984b. "Pack Rape! Horror Attack on Two Families." October 4, p. 1.

———. 1984c. "Two More Attacks." October 23, p. 2.

———. 1984d. "Another Youth is Charged." October 25, p. 2.

———. 1984e. "Badili Horror: Sixth Youth Charged." October 26, p. 2.

———. 1984f. "Badili Attack Man Charged." October 30, p. 2.

———. 1984g. "Young Girl Raped." October 31, p. 2.

Ralston, Caroline. 1993. "Maori Women and the Politics of Tradition: What Roles and Power Did, Do, and Should Maori Women Exercise?" *The Contemporary Pacific* 5 (1): 23–44.

Ranck, Stephen and Susan Toft. 1986. "Domestic Violence in an Urban Context with Rural Comparisons." In S. Toft (ed.). *Domestic Violence in Urban Papua New Guinea*, pp. 3–51. Law Reform Commission of Papua New Guinea, Occasional Paper No. 19.

Read, Kenneth E. 1952. "Nama Cult of the Central Highlands, New Guinea." *Oceania* 23: 1–25.

———. 1954. "Marriage Among the Gahuka-Gama of the Eastern Central Highlands, New Guinea." *South Pacific* 7: 864–871.

Riches, David, ed. 1986. *The Anthropology of Violence*. Oxford: Basil Blackwell.

Rosi, Pamela and Laura Zimmer-Tamakoshi. 1993. "Love and Marriage Among the Educated Elite in Port Moresby." In R. Marksbury (ed.). *The Business of Marriage: Transformations in Oceanic Matrimony*, pp. 175–204. The University of Pittsburgh Press.

Russell, Diana E. H. 1984. *Sexual Exploitation*. Beverly Hills, CA: Sage Publications.

Still, K. and J. Shea. 1976. *Something's Got to be Done So We Can Survive in This Place: The Problem of Women Students at UPNG*. Education Research Unit Research Report 20. Port Moresby: University of Papua New Guinea.

Strathern, A. 1985. "Rape in Hagen." In S. Toft (ed.). *Domestic Violence in Papua New Guinea*, pp. 134–140. Law Reform Commission of Papua New Guinea Monograph No. 3.

———. 1993. "Violence and Political Change in Papua New Guinea." *Pacific Studies* 16 (4): 41–60.

Strathern, M. 1972. *Women in Between: Female Roles in a Male World*, Mt. Hagen, New Guinea. London: Seminar Press.

———. 1980. "No Nature, No Culture: The Hagen Case." In C. MacCormack and M. Strathern (eds.). *Nature, Culture and Gender*, pp. 174–222. Cambridge: Cambridge University Press.

The Times of Papua New Guinea. 1992. "The Status of Women in Papua New Guinea." 9 January, p. 19.

———. 1993a. "East New Britain Women Embark on Campaign Against Violence." 4 March, p. 5.

———. 1993b. "Women Celebrate Their Day on Monday." 4 March, p. 2.

Toft, Susan. 1985. "Marital Violence in Port Moresby: Two Urban Case Studies." In S. Toft (ed.). *Domestic Violence in Papua New Guinea*, pp. 14–31. Papua New Guinea Law Reform Commission Monograph No. 3.

Toft, Susan, ed. 1985. *Domestic Violence in Papua New Guinea.* Papua New Guinea Law Reform Commission Monograph No. 3.

———. 1986a. *Domestic Violence in Urban Papua New Guinea.* Papua New Guinea Law Reform Commission Occasional Paper No. 19.

———. 1986b. *Marriage in Papua New Guinea.* Papua New Guinea Law Reform Commission Monograph No. 4.

Toft, Susan and S. Bonnell, eds. 1985. *Marriage and Domestic Violence in Rural Papua New Guinea.* Papua New Guinea Law Reform Commission Occasional Paper No. 18.

Trask, Haunani-Kay. 1989. "Fighting the Battle of Double Colonization: The View of an Hawaiian Feminist." *Ethnies* 8–9–10 (1): 61–67.

United Nations. 1989. *Violence Against Women in the Family.* Vienna: Centre for Social Development and Humanitarian Affairs.

Waddell, Eric. 1972. *The Mound Builders: Agricultural Practices, Environment and Society in the Central Highlands of New Guinea.* Seattle: University of Washington Press.

Waram, Ruth. 1992a. "Violence: A Crime Against Women." Papua New Guinea *Post Courier* 13 February, 24–25.

———. 1992b. "Women's Day Snubbed, While Many Centres Go Without Celebrations." Papua New Guinea *Post Courier* 26 March, 25 and 28.

Wormald, Eileen. 1992. "1992 National Election—Women Candidates in the Election." *The Times of Papua New Guinea* 28 May, 23–26.

Wormald, Eileen and Anne Crossley, eds. 1988. *Women and Education in Papua New Guinea and the South Pacific.* Port Moresby: University of Papua New Guinea Press.

Zimmer, Laura J. 1990. "Sexual Exploitation and Male Dominance in Papua New Guinea." In a special issue on Human Sexuality. *Point* 14: 250–267.

Zimmer-Tamakoshi, Laura. 1993a. "Bachelors, Spinsters, and 'Pamuk Meris.'" In R. Marksbury (ed.). *The Business of Marriage: Transformations in Oceanic Matrimony*, pp. 83–104. University of Pittsburgh Press.

———. 1993b. "Nationalism and Sexuality in Papua New Guinea." *Pacific Studies* 16 (4): 61–97.

———. 1995. "Passion, Poetry, and Cultural Politics in the South Pacific." In R. Feinberg and L. Zimmer-Tamakoshi (eds.). Politics of Culture in the Pacific Islands, special issue *Ethnology* 34 (2 & 3): 113–128.

———. 1996a. "Empowered Women." In W. Donner and J. Flanagan (eds.). *Social Organization and Cultural Aesthetics: Essays in Honor of William H. Davenport*, pp. 84–101. University of Pennsylvania Press.

———. 1996b. "Papua New Guinean Women in Town: Housewives, Homemakers, and Household Managers." In L. Zimmer-Tamakoshi (ed.). *Modern PNG Society.* Bathurst, Australia: Crawford House Press.

———. n.d. "Patterns of Culture in the Tower of Babel: Letters from Port Moresby, Papua New Guinea." Accepted for publication in *Journal de la Societe des Oceanistes.*

Film Bibliography

GENERAL FILMS

The Gender Tango. Films for the Humanities & Sciences. 1997. 47 minutes.

Looks at the way that women define themselves and are defined by others. Includes sections on a young beauty contest contestant in the U.S., a Latin American woman who sells cosmetics "hut to hut" in the Amazon; a woman who masqueraded as a man to gain acceptance in the male-dominated world of jazz music; and two contrasting aboriginal societies: in one, women are seen as evil and polluting and in the other, they are treated as valuable, powerful members of the tribe.

Cross-Cultural Comparisons: Gender Roles. Western Illinois University (distributed by Insight Media). 1995. Two volumes, 60 minutes each.

Compares gender roles in several countries. The first part discusses Hindu, Chinese, and Islamic gender roles, examining cultural practices that give men authority over women. The second part focuses on societies that have tried to remedy gender inequalities with specific policies and changes in law. Examples from China, the former Soviet Union, and Sweden are presented.

Gender Matters. A production for the Open University by the BBC. 1992. 24 minutes.

Examines gender subordination, probing its effects on both individuals and societies. Profiling individual women, it looks at their varied roles and proposes that future development policies focus on changing existing forms of control while maintaining cultural sensitivity.

In My Country: An International Perspective on Gender. Utah Valley State College. 1993. Two volumes, 91 minutes total.

This video is designed to be used as a resource for studying cultural attitudes related to gender. Divided into sections by topic, it covers division of household labor, types of discipline for boys and girls, marriage decisions, control of money, and society's view on rape, care of the elderly, and attitudes toward homosexuals. Features interviews with people from Zaire, El Salvador, St. Vincent, England, Taiwan, Sweden, Lebanon, Japan, India, China, the Fiji Islands, and Mexico.

Girls Around the World. Women Make Movies. 1998–2000. 6 parts, 30 minute, each.

A collection of six documentaries that examine the hopes, dreams, and views of a diverse group of 17-year-old girls from Benin, Peru, Germany, Finland, Pakistan, and China.

Women Organize! Women Make Movies. 2000. 32 minutes.

Portrays women organizers across the U.S. who are involved in the global struggles for racial, social, and economic justice.

BIOLOGY, GENDER, AND HUMAN EVOLUTION

Jane Goodall Studies of the Chimpanzee. "Tool Using." National Geographic Society. 1978. 24 minutes.

Describes how young chimpanzees play with objects and how this play prepares them for making and using tools as adults.

Among the Wild Chimpanzees. National Geographic Society. 1984. 59 minutes.

Features Jane Goodall as researcher and examines infant chimpanzee development and behavior, male–female dominance, and hunting.

Brain Sex: Brain Architecture and the Sexes. Discovery Communications. 1992. 3 volumes, 52 minutes each.

This series examines differences between male and female learning patterns, appetites, expectations, and behaviors, exploring how fetal sex hormone levels affect later behavior. It considers evidence that men and women use different parts of the brain to carry out similar functions, probes evolution's role in shaping gender differences, and looks at differences in attitudes towards love and sex. Series titles include: 1. Sugar and Spice: The Facts Behind Sex Differences; 2. Anything You Can Do, I Can Do Better: Why the Sexes Excel Differently; and, 3. Love, Love Me Do: How Sex Differences Affect Relationships.

Sex and Gender with Evelyn Fox Keller. PBS Video. 1990. 30 minutes.

Evelyn Fox Keller, a theoretical physicist and feminist historian of science, describes how gender plays a significant role in Western scientific theory and method.

The Long-Haired Warriors. University of California Extension Center for Media and Independent Learning. 1998. 60 minutes.

This documentary introduces a number of Vietnamese women who were active in the National Liberation Front and shows the major role played by Vietnamese women in the Vietnamese Conflict and the historical precedents for same. In this video, Vietnamese women tell of their war experiences during the Vietnamese Conflict: their active participation, their involvement, the tortures they endured, the effects of the Vietnamese Conflict to this day.

The Dream Becomes Reality? Nation Building and the Continued Struggle of the Women of the Eritrean People's Liberation Front: A Documentary. University of California Extension Center for Media and Independent Learning. 1995. 43 minutes.

Features 6 Eritrean women who participated in the 30-year military struggle for independence from Ethiopia. During the war these women fought and worked in various aspects of the revolutionary media as members of the Eritrean People's Liberation Front. Now in post-war Eritrea the women speak about the war, the gender egalitarianism among the liberation forces, and their thoughts about the current situation of women in post-war Eritrea. Includes significant background on the liberation struggle.

The Gay Gene. Films for the Humanities & Sciences. 1998. 29 minutes.

Focuses on the science behind the controversial genetic research into the so-called "gay gene." A geneticist explains how the study was carried out, from the initial interviews with gay men and their families, to the plotting of family trees, the extraction of DNA, and the analysis of samples in the lab. The program also considers the findings of the research: that homosexuality is, in part, genetically determined. It discusses whether these finds will advance the cause of gay rights and promote tolerance and understanding in society at large.

DOMESTIC WORLDS AND PUBLIC WORLDS

Kypseli: Women and Men Apart—A Divided Reality. University of California, Berkeley. 1976. 40 minutes.
Examines gender roles in a Greek peasant village.

Afghan Women. University of California, Berkeley. 1975. 17 minutes.
Examines the role of women in a rural community in northern Afghanistan.

Some Women of Marrakech. Granada Disappearing World Series. Thomas Howe Associates. 1976. 55 minutes. Re-edited for Odyssey, 1981.
Discusses the importance of marriage and family for women in Morocco and shows the impact of religion and class on women's lives.

Women, Work and Babies. NBC production. 1985. 60 minutes.
Discusses gender ideology in the United States and problems of working mothers.

The Double Day. IWFP. Cinema Guild. 1975. 51 minutes.
Discusses burdens of working women in Latin America.

Clotheslines. Filmmaker's Library. 1981. 32 minutes.
Shows the love–hate relationship that women have with cleaning the family clothes.

Not Baking. University of California. 1995. 9 minutes.
A woman explores her inability to bake. Archival footage demonstrates the tremendous force of America's baking tradition.

Power Plays. Corporation for Community College Television. 1988. 30 minutes.
Explores the relationship of gender to conjugal power, both traditionally and as it exists today. It shows how conjugal power varies in different socioeconomic strata and considers how relative conjugal power varies between public and private spheres. It also discusses factors that increase equality between spouses and describes alternatives to power politics in a marriage.

Defying the Odds: Women Around the World Create New Roles. Filmmakers Library. 1996. 29 minutes.
This film was produced for the Beijing Women's Conference and focuses on the lives of four women of diverse ages and backgrounds who have broken ground in new fields. They are questioning age-old traditions as they forge careers in their respective societies.

The Double Shift. Films for the Humanities & Sciences. 1996. 47 minutes.
Most women who have careers and raise families do a "double shift"—they hold one job for which they are paid and another for which they are not. This program examines that reality and whether or not women can ever be equal in this situation.

A Man in a Woman's World. Huby's Ltd. 1997. 18 minutes.
This video explores the stereotypes that surround men who choose an occupation traditionally

filled by women. Men explain the challenges and rewards of working in such traditionally female dominated jobs as nurse or flight attendant.

The Double Burden: Three Generations of Working Mothers. New Day Films. 1992. 56 minutes.

Portrays the lives of three families—one Mexican-American, one Polish-American, and one African-American—each with three generations of women who have worked outside the home while raising families.

A Female Cabby in Sidi Bel-Abbes. First Run/Icarus Films. 2000. 52 minutes.

Focuses on the life of Soumicha, a mother of three and the only woman taxi driver in Sidi Bel-Abbes (Algeria). Her interactions with her passengers bring out contradictory aspects of Algerian society.

Miyah: The Life of a Javanese Woman. Insight Media. 1999. 30 minutes.

Dscribes the lives of millions of rural dwellers whose work in cities supports Asia's economies through an examination of one woman's experiences. Miyah is employed as a servant and cook for a prominent Jakarta family.

EQUALITY AND INEQUALITY: THE SEXUAL DIVISION OF LABOR AND GENDER STRATIFICATION

Hunters and Gatherers

N!ai: The Story of a !Kung Woman. Penn State University. 1980. 59 minutes.

Features the biography of a !Kung woman from early childhood to middle age and the impact of colonial penetration on her life.

The Warao. University of California, Berkeley. 1978. 57 minutes.

Ethnographic account of division of labor among the Warao of the Orinoco River Delta in Venezuela.

Before We Knew Nothing. World Cultures on Film and Video, U. of California. 1989. 62 minutes.

An exploration of the roles and activities of Ashaninka women in the Amazon rain forest.

Horticulturalists

Seasons of the Navajo. PBS Video. Peace River Films. 1984. 60 minutes.

Presents one family's kinship with the earth through seasons, touching briefly on Navajo matriliny and women's work and craft responsibilities.

The Trobriand Islanders of Papua New Guinea. Films Incorporated Video. 1990. 52 minutes.

Focuses on the distribution of women's wealth after a death and the month of celebration following the yam harvest.

Agriculturalists

Luisa Torres. Chip Taylor Communications. 1980. 28 minutes.

The recollections of a Hispanic woman in northern New Mexico; discusses division of labor, marriage, use of medicinal plants, and other aspects of daily life.

Kheturni Bayo: North Indian Farm Women. Penn State. 1980. 19 minutes.

Examines the roles and the duties of the women in a typical extended family of land-owning peasants in Gujarat, India.

Seed and Earth. Filmmakers Library. 1994. 36 minutes.

Portrays everyday life in rural West Bengal. Shows how gender and age determine work, ritual, and leisure activities.

The Ladies of the Lake: A Matriarchial Society. Filmmakers Library. 1998. 20 minutes.

Looks at a rare matriarchal community in southwest China. The Mosuo culture has survived both the time of the concubines and the cultural revolution but is now being threatened by Beijing's one-child-per-family policy. In this culture power is handed from the matriarch to the most intelligent daughter.

Pastoralists

Masai Women. Thomas Howe Associates. 1983. 52 minutes.

Examines the role of women among pastoralists in Kenya.

Women of the Toubou. University of California, Berkeley. 1974. 25 minutes.

Examines gender roles among nomads of the Sahara.

Boran Women. University of California, Berkeley. 1975. 18 minutes.

Shows women's daily work in Kenyan society, including caring for cattle, milk storage, and child care.

Deep Hearts. University of California, Berkeley. 1980. 53 minutes.

Documentary on the Bororo Fulani in Niger, Africa. Focuses on ritual dances in which men compete in a beauty contest.

Hamar Trilogy. Filmmakers Library. 1994/1991/1994. 55 minutes each.

Trilogy focuses on the Hamar, an isolated people of southwestern Ethiopia whose traditional lifestyle has barely been touched by war and the famine in the north. The films concentrate on the powerful and outspoken Hamar women. Titles include *The Women Who Smile; Two Girls Go Hunting; and Our Way of Loving.*

Miscellaneous

Asante Market Women. Penn State. 1983. 52 minutes.
Power of Ghanaian market women from a matrilineal and polygynous society.

From the Shore. Indiana University. 1989. 17 minutes.
Explores the formation of a fishing cooperative among women in the coastal village of Shimoni, Kenya, in defiance of the traditional roles of women.

Maids and Madams. Filmmakers Library. 1985. 52 minutes.
Describes the plight of Black female domestic servants in South Africa and analyzes the relationship between gender, class, and apartheid.

A Kiss on the Mouth. Women Make Movies. 1987. 30 minutes.
Examines female prostitution in urban Brazil.

My Husband Doesn't Mind if I Disco. World Cultures on Film and Video, University of California. 1995. 28 minutes.
Examines the negotiation of role and gender ideology in Tibet.

Mamma Benz: An African Market Woman. (Also titled: *God Gave Her a Mercedes Benz.*) Filmmakers Library. 1992/1993. 48 minutes.
The markets of Africa are dominated by strong older women. They control the price and determine who can buy their goods. These women rule the markets and are treated with deference. This film focuses on one of these women who presides over the cloth market in Lomé, Togo.

A Little for My Heart and a Little for My God: A Muslim Women's Orchestra. Filmmakers Library. 1993. 60 minutes.
Since in Algeria women are traditionally not allowed to mix with men, female orchestras customarily entertain gatherings of women. This film is a portrait of one of these orchestras. (In French with English subtitles.)

THE CULTURAL CONSTRUCTION OF PERSONHOOD

A Man, When He Is a Man. Women Make Movies. 1982. 66 minutes.
Set in Costa Rica, this film illuminates the social climate and cultural traditions that nurture machismo and allow the domination of women to flourish in Latin America.

Sexism in Language: Thief of Honor, Shaper of Lies. University of California. 1995. 29 minutes.
Analyzes the gender bias that permeates everyday language.

Small Happiness. Women of a Chinese Village. New Day Films. VHS Video cassette. 1984. 58 minutes.
Provides historical perspective on marriage, birth control, work, and daily life.

The Women's Olamal: The Organization of a Maasai Fertility Ceremony. Documentary Educational Resources. 1984. 115 minutes.
Presents a picture of women's lives in the male-dominated society of the Maasai in Kenya.

Rights of Passage: Four Stories of Survival. Filmmakers Library. 1994. 30 minutes.
This film gives the stories of four young women coming of age in different parts of the world and looks at what can be the personal cost of this transition.

Maasai Manhood. ISHI. 1983. 53 minutes.
Describes a male initiation ritual among the pastoral Maasai of Kenya.

Beyond Macho. Films for the Humanities and Sciences. 1985. 26 minutes.
Explores roles for men that have evolved in response to feminism and economic changes in the United States through an examination of the lives of two men, one a nurse and the other a "house-husband."

Men and Masculinity. OASIS. 1990. 30 minutes.
Covers the thirteenth National Conference on Men and Masculinity and discusses a broad range of men's movement issues in the United States, including antipornography activism, challenges to homophobia, and domestic violence.

Stale Roles and Tight Buns. OASIS. 1988. 29 minutes.
Uses advertising images to show how men are stereotyped in the media and how myths develop that limit men's and women's roles.

Becoming a Woman in Okrika. Filmmakers Library. 1990. 27 minutes.
Covers a coming-of-age ritual in a village in the Niger Delta.

Surname Viet Given Name Nam. Women Make Movies. 1989. 108 minutes.
Explores the multiplicity of identities of Vietnamese women in Vietnam and in California.

The Smell of Burning Ants. Film Arts Foundation. 1995. 21 minutes.
The film depicts the often painful aspects of male socialization in the west.

Tough Guise: Media Images & the Crisis in Masculinity. Wellesley Centers for Women. 1999. 40 minutes.

Although femininity has been widely examined, the dominant role of masculinity has until recently remained largely invisible. Tough Guise is the first program to look systematically at the relationship between the images of popular culture and the social construction of the masculine identities in the United States in the late 20th century.

Growing Up and Liking It: The Menstruation Myth. Filmmakers Library. 1991. 28 minutes.

The monthly menstruation cycle, a natural occurrence that from time immemorial has made women the object of taboo and superstition, is the subject of this video. We meet women of varying ages and cultural backgrounds who share with us the vivid and often disturbing memories coming of age.

Guardians of the Flutes: The Secrets of Male Initiation. BBC Television. 1996. 55 minutes.

Among the Sambia, the roles of men and women are sharply delineated. They live in separate spaces in their round huts. Male children live with their mothers until they are old enough to move into the boys' house. This period of transition is marked by physical violence and sexual rites.

Man Oh Man—Growing Up Male in America. New Day Films, Inc. 1987. 19 minutes.

Focuses on being a man in contemporary American society, with an emphasis on the difficulties of living up to cultural ideals of manhood.

Sexuality in MesoAmerica: Machismo and Marianismo. Cinema Guild. 1996. 33 minutes.

Describes how machismo and marianismo shape sexual behavior and identity in Mesoamerica. Shows the historical and cultural antecedents of these models, illustrates how they are integrated in different social sectors, and explores how they are being redefined by contemporary revolutionary movements.

CULTURE, SEXUALITY AND THE BODY

Killing Us Softly III. Cambridge Documentary Films. 1999. 30 minutes.

Details psychological and sexual themes in American advertising. In this film, Kilbourne updates the classic film and looks at how the image of women in advertising has changed over the last 20 years.

Slim Hopes. Media Education Foundation. 1995. 30 minutes.

Offers a new way to think about eating disorders such as anorexia and bulimia and provides a critical perspective on the social impact of advertising. New film by Jean Kilbourne.

Women Like Us. Women Make Movies. 1990. 49 minutes.

Portrays older lesbian women in Great Britain, their feelings and lifestyles, and discusses the implications of sexual orientation for family and work relations.

Juggling Gender. Women Make Movies. 1992. 27 minutes.

Through a focus on a bearded lesbian performer, the film explores the fluidity of gender and the construction of gender identity.

On Being Gay. TRB Productions. 1986. 80 minutes.

Through a monologue by Brian McNaught, this film addresses myths about homosexuality and such topics as growing up gay in a straight world, Bible-based bigotry, stereotypes, transvestism, transsexualism, and AIDS.

Georgie Girl. Women Make Movies. 2001. 70 minutes.

In 1999, Georgina Beyer became the first transgendered person to hold national office in New Zealand. This film shows her life story from growing up on a small farm to becoming a celebrity in the cabaret circuit in Auckland.

Metamorphosis: Man into Woman. Filmmakers Library. 1990. 58 minutes.

Features a transsexual confronting gender stereotypes in society.

Multiple Genders: Mind and Body in Conflict. Films for the Humanities & Sciences. 1997/1998. 40 minutes.

Looks at whether or not there are only two sexes. A transsexual doctor contends that there are more and that transsexuals and hermaphrodites at least constitute two others. A theologian addresses the moral implications of multisexual orientation, while a physician and polygendered people ask: Is sex the same as gender? Are inter-sexes mistakes or parts of nature?

Barbie Nation: An Unauthorized Tour. New Day Films. PBS. 1998. 54 minutes.

Plumbs the cult of the Barbie Doll, telling the Barbie stories of diverse men, women, and children. It is about the creation of femininity and the marking—and subversion—of femininity's icon.

De Mujer a Mujer. Women Make Movies. 1995. 46 minutes.

Latina women discuss their experiences and feelings about sexuality and maturation.

Friends and Lovers. World Cultures on Film and Video, University of California. 1994. 28 minutes.

Gay men discuss their feelings about intimacy in an age of AIDS and challenge our assumptions about relationships and sexuality.

The Remarkable Case of John/Joan. Canadian Broadcasting Corporation. Filmmakers Library. 1997. 30 minutes.

Eight-month-old John was the victim of an accident during circumcision which left him with almost no penis. The next year when he was almost two it was decided to have his testicles removed and bring him up as a girl following the theory that environment was more important in creating sexual identity than biology. When he was an adolescent John learned the truth about his birth and having been miserable as a girl, he underwent reconstructive surgery to return himself to being a man.

Honored by the Moon. Women Make Movies. 1989/1990. 15 minutes.

Addresses issues of homophobia within the American Indian community. Native American lesbians and gay men speak of their unique historical and spiritual role.

Beauty Before Age: Growing Old in Gay Culture. New Day Films. 1997. 22 minutes.

Explores the power of youth and beauty in the gay community. A diverse group of men, ages 19 to 77, navigate their fears of becoming old, undesirable, and alone. Offers a male perspective on a traditionally female issue, and illuminates the larger societal obsession with physical appearance.

I'm not a Common Woman (Yo No Soy Una Qualquiera). Women Make Movies. 1989. 20 minutes.

In Argentina, "qualquiera" means many things: a nobody, a thing, a Jane Doe. However in slang its meaning is clear—whore. This video exploits the double entendre to its fullest, creating a provocative portrait of Latin machismo and female resistance.

Sunflowers. University of California Extension Center for Media and Independent Learning. 1997. 50 minutes.

Portrait of a spirited community of gay men in a rural town in the Philippines. The Sunflowers, as they are called locally, have since 1975 performed in drag the town's most important annual Christian festival.

I, Doll: The Unauthorized Biography of America's 11½ Sweetheart. Women Make Movies. 1996. 57 minutes.

Examines the Barbie phenomenon. Includes interviews with fans and critics, who express their feelings about the 6 ounces of plastic that became a national icon.

Not Simply a Wedding Banquet. Third World Newsreel. 1997. 50 minutes.

Shows the story of the first gay couple to have a public wedding in Taiwan in November 1996. It also focuses on the public's reaction to the event.

Our House: Lesbians and Gays in the Hood. Third World Newsreel. 1993. 28 minutes.

Interviews with African-American gays and lesbians provides an uncompromising look at homophobia, racism, alienation and empowerment.

Paradise Bent. Filmmakers Library. 2000. 50 minutes.

Explores the lives of Samoan *fa'afafines,* boys who are raised as girls.

Shinjuku Boys. Women Make Movies. 1995. 53 minutes.

Introduces three onnabes, women who live as men and have girlfriends, yet do identify as lesbians. Shows the complexity of female sexuality in Japan today.

Two Spirits: Native American Lesbians and Gays. Third World Newsreel. 1994. 28 minutes.

Explores the Native American belief in "Two Spirit" human androgyny. Includes interviews with Native Americans from throughout the Americas and works to redefine difference and the complexities of sexuality and culture.

GENDER, PROPERTY, AND THE STATE

No Longer Silent. International Film Bureau. 1986. 57 minutes.

Analyzes dowry deaths in India, as well as the cultural preference for boys and female infanticide.

Modern Brides. South Asian Area Center, University of Wisconsin. 1985. 30 minutes.

Features two young women, one with an arranged marriage and one with a "love match," and discusses the bride's capacity to work as a substitute for dowry.

Las Madres: The Mothers of Plaza de Mayo. Direct Cinema Ltd. 1986. 64 minutes.

Focuses on Argentinean mothers who, beginning in 1977, defied laws against civil demonstrations to protest the disappearance of their children under the military dictatorship.

Donna: Women in Revolt. Women Make Movies. 1980. 65 minutes.

An examination of the history and development of Italian feminism through the personal stories of women involved in the women's rights movement at the turn of the century and the resistance during World War II and of present-day feminists.

Weaving the Future: Women of Guatemala. Women Make Movies. 1988. 28 minutes.

A perspective on women in Guatemala's liberation struggle, exploring the pivotal role of women in building a just society amid political strife and poverty.

Gabriella. Women Make Movies. 1988. 67 minutes.
Examines the work of a mass organization of diverse women's groups in the Philippines.

Women of Niger: Between Fundamentalism and Democracy. Women Make Movies. 1993. 26 minutes.
Niger is a traditionally Islamic country where women are not allowed to vote for themselves and those who speak out about their rights have been physically attacked and excommunicated. Muslim Fundamentalism clashes with the country's struggle for democracy, of which women are among the most ardent defenders. This film deals with human rights and the impact of fundamentalism on women.

Our Honor and His Glory: Honor Killing in the Palestine Zone. Filmmakers Library. 1997. 28 minutes.
In some areas of North Africa, the Middle East, and Asia, honor is deemed of such importance that a father, a brother or a cousin is entitled by tribal custom to kill a woman, often a young girl, who is suspected of having sullied the family's honor. This film documents two cases in Palestinian villages.

Keep Her Under Control: Law's Patriarchy in India. University of California Extension Center for Media and Independent Learning. 1998. 52 minutes.
This film explores the role of women in a Muslim-dominated village in Rajasthan, in northern India. It focuses on the story of a single woman who refuses to live by the moral and legal codes of the village's Islamic patriarchy.

To Walk Naked. Third World Newsreel. 1995. 12 minutes.
In 1990, a group of women protested the destruction of their homes in the squatter camps of Dobsonville, by the then Afrikaaner National government. They reflect on their experiences including the social stigma of stripping themselves naked to protest their oppression.

Where is Grandma Zheng's Homeland? First Run/Icarus Films. 2000. 90 minutes.
During World War II, thousands of Korean and Chinese women were forced to serve Japanese servicemen as "comfort women." This documentary focuses on one such woman, Grandma Zheng Shunyi.

The Women Outside. Third World Newsreel. 1995. 60 minutes.
Documents the lives of women who work in the South Korean military brothels and clubs where over 27,000 women "service" the 37,000 American soldiers. It raises questions about U.S. military policy, South Korean governmental policy, and their dependence on the sexual labor of women.

GENDER, HOUSEHOLD, AND KINSHIP

Dadi's Family. Odyssey. 1981. 58 minutes.
Describes family tensions in a patrilineal joint household in northern India.

A Wife Among Wives. University of California, Berkeley. 1981. 70 minutes.
Turkana women discuss polygyny.

Tobelo Marriage. University of California, Berkeley. 1990. 106 minutes.
Chronicles a marriage ritual in Eastern Indonesia, including exchange of valuables, negotiations, and preparatory activities.

Asian Heart. Filmmakers Library. 1987. 38 minutes.
Deals with marriage brokering between clients from Denmark and Filipino "mail order brides."

A Village in Baltimore. Doreen Moses. 1730 21st St. N.W. Washington, DC 20009. 1981. 63 minutes.
Conveys the problems and conflicts of changing identities and traditions among Greek immigrants in the United States, focusing on dowry, marriage, and other social events.

All Dressed in White. University of California. 1994. 18 minutes.
Explores the complex relationships among religion, ethnicity, and gender by investigating one key symbol: the wedding dress. Based on stories of four women in a Catholic Indian family from Goa who have migrated to Singapore and then to California.

Chronicle of a Savanna Marriage. Filmmakers Library. 1997. 56 minutes.
Follows the marriage of one girl for 15 years starting from when she was promised to her future husband through her circumcision, marriage, and the addition of additional wives to the household.

Not Without My Veil: Among the Women of Oman. Filmmakers Library. 1993. 29 minutes.
Examines the view of Muslim women as oppressed and confined. The practice of wearing the traditional veil symbolizes this for many westerners, but this video shows a different reality. It shows these women as educated, professional women who choose to wear the veil as a symbol of their origins and their identities.

Just Mom and Me: Single Motherhood. Filmmakers Library. 2000. 60 minutes.
This film interweaves the stories of five single mothers in vastly different circumstances.

Filmed over three years, this is a realistic portrayal of the financial and emotional challenges of single parenting. It also gives voice to the children who reflect on the realities of not having a father in the home.

Single Dads. Huby's; Distributed by The School Co. 1997. 18 minutes.

Are single dads treated differently from single moms? Are there government and community resources available to single dads? This program focuses on the special challenges of being a single father, looking at how single fathers balance family and job responsibilities.

The Polygamists. Films for the Humanities & Sciences. 1998. 52 minutes.

This documentary takes place in Mant, Utah, and follows several of the 450 families who practice plural marriage in the town.

Fighting Grandpa. Greg Pak. Filmmakers Library. 1999. 21 minutes.

The filmmaker tells the story of his Korean immigrant grandmother's seventy-year struggle with her husband. Forced to give up her dream of becoming a nurse, she is left with their four children for ten years while her husband studied in the U.S., and finally brought to America to endure her husband's parsimonious ways, she had every right to be bitter.

A Day Will Come: Change and Tradition in Pakistani Marriage. Filmmakers Library. 2000. 28 minutes.

Follows the engagement of two children of a middle class family in Quetta, Pakistan. The two engagements could not be more different because one of the engagements is a traditional, arranged marriage to a woman that the groom has never met, while the second engagement is a love match.

Saheri's Choice: Arranged Marriages in India. Films for the Humanities & Sciences. 1998. 25 minutes.

Examines the custom of arranged marriages in India. It follows the story of one girl and her family as they confront the reality of an impending marriage that was arranged when the girl was barely six. An overview of the custom shows it to be widely practiced by all castes although many Indians view it negatively.

The Afar Tribe: A Bride's Story. Films for the Humanities and Sciences. 60 minutes.

Presents the story of Fatuma, who is the daughter of the clan chief and her arranged marriage to her first cousin.

Divorce Iranian Style. Women Make Movies. 1998. 80 minutes.

Chronicles the experiences of Iranian women who are seeking divorce under Islamic law.

Without Fathers or Husbands. Insight Media. 1995. 26 minutes

The Na, an ethnic group in southeast China, have a matrilineal social organization. They have developed an unusual family structure in which all members of a household are consanguineous relatives. Issues concerning incest and sexual relationships are explored.

GENDER, RITUAL, AND RELIGION

Out of Order. Icarus Films. 1983. 88 minutes.

Presents personal narratives of six women in various stages of convent life.

The Living Goddess. University of California, Berkeley. 1979. 30 minutes.

Studies the Newar of Nepal, focusing on a ritual cult in which young virgin girls are thought to embody the spirits of goddesses.

A Sense of Honor. Films Incorporated. 1984. 55 minutes.

Made by an Egyptian anthropologist, the film describes the impact of Islamic fundamentalism on the lives of women in Egypt.

Rastafari: Conversations Concerning Women. Eye in I Filmworks. 1984. 60 minutes.

Examines the roles and relations of men and women in the Jamaican Rastafarian movement.

Keep Her Under Control: Law's Patriarchy in India. University of California Extension Center for Media and Independent Learning. 1998. 52 minutes.

Explores the role of women in a Muslim-dominated village in Rajasthan, in northern India. The documentary focuses on the story of a woman, named Hurmuti, who refuses to live by the moral and legals codes of the village's Islamic patriarchy.

A Veiled Revolution. Icarus. 1982. 27 minutes.

Attempts to discern the reasons behind the movement in Egypt by young educated women to resume wearing traditional Islamic garb.

An Initiation Kut for a Korean Shaman. Laurel Kendall and Diana Lee and the Center for Visual Anthropology. University of Hawaii Press. 1991. 36 minutes.

Portrays the initiation of Chini, a young Korean woman demonstrating her ability to perform as a shaman and shouting out the spirit's oracles.

Mammy Water: In Search of Water Spirits in Nigeria. University of California. 1991. 59 minutes.

Focuses on the worship of a local water goddess by the Ibibio-, Ijaw-, and Igbo-speaking people of southeastern Nigeria.

Hidden Faces. Women Make Films. 1990. 52 minutes.
Examines the conflict between feminist ideals and Islamic values and traditions of the veil and clitoridectomy.

Beyond the Veil: Are Iranian Women Rebelling? Films for the Humanities & Sciences. 1997. 22 minutes.
In this program a female reporter dons the hijah—"modest dress"—and goes undercover to find out how Iranian women feel about the government-enforced dress code and about their diminished role in Iranian society.

Who Will Cast the First Stone? Cinema Guild. 1989. 52 minutes.
Examines the impact of Islamization on women in Pakistan, in particular the Hudood Ordinances under which adultery, rape, or extramarital sex are considered a crime against the state, punishable by stoning to death.

Daughters of the Nile (Dochters van de Nijl). Distributed by Filmmakers Library. 1992. 46 minutes.
This film about Egypt's women captures their separate and subordinate life under the Islamic code. Men and women speak about their traditions, expectations, and patterns of life.

Monday's Girls. California Newsreel. 1994. 50 minutes.
Follows two young Nigerian women's different experiences of a traditional rite of passage. Young virgins spend five weeks in "fattening rooms," emerging to dance before the villagers and to be married.

Father, Son and Holy War. First Run Icarus Films. 1994. 120 minutes.
Examines the connections between religion, violence, and male identity in India.

Flowers for Guadalupe: The Presence of the Virgin of Guadalupe in Mexican Women's Lives. Filmmakers Library. 1995. 57 minutes.
Explores the importance of the Virgin of Guadalupe as a liberating symbol for Mexican women.

Nailed. Third World Newsreel. 1992. 50 minutes.
A Filipina explores the roles of the Catholic Church and 400 years of colonialism in the Pacific region. This documentary is inspired by Lucy Reyes, a woman who has been reenacting the Crucifixion for 16 years by being nailed to a cross.

Trokosi: Wife of the Gods. The Cinema Guild. 1994. 25 minutes.
Focuses on the West African religious institution of *trokosi,* in which young women are chosen to serve a period of servitude for crimes committed by their grandparents or great-grandparents. They must also submit sexually to the priests, becoming a "wife of the gods."

GENDER, POLITICS, AND REPRODUCTION

No Longer Silent. International Film Bureau. 1986. 57 minutes.
Discusses dowry deaths in India, as well as the cultural preference for boys and female infanticide.

Rites. Filmmakers Library. 1990. 52 minutes.
Considers three major contexts in which female "genital mutilation" occurs: cosmetic, punitive, and rite of passage. Particularly emphasizes the health risks and psychological consequences of female circumcision.

China's One-Child Policy. Nova Special. 1985. 60 minutes.
A documentary on China's population policy, its implementation, unpopularity, and its relation to gender ideology.

Nyamakutaù: The One Who Receives: An African Midwife. Filmmakers Library. 1989. 32 minutes.
Portrays a traditional African midwife who incorporates pharmaceuticals with local practices to improve health standards in her village.

Birth and Belief in the Andes of Ecuador. University of California. 1995. 28 minutes.
A portrait of women in four Andean communities, documenting their beliefs and practices surrounding childbirth and infant care.

On the Eighth Day. Women Make Movies. 1992. Two parts, 51 minutes each.
A two-part film series which explores the social, economic, and political influences and impacts of new reproductive and genetic technologies.

Something Like War. Women Make Movies. 1991. 52 minutes.
The film explores the intersection of the reality of women's lives and the family planning project enforced by the government.

Birth Stories. Cinema Guild. 1994. 30 minutes.
Blends women's personal stories of pregnancy and birth with footage of actual birth.

Whose Bodies, Whose Rights. University of California Extension Center for Media and Independent Learning. 1996. 56 minutes.
Explores the growing debate over male circumcision in America, showing that the practice has only the flimsiest medical rational and is primarily a repressive social custom based on medical and cultural myths.

Fire Eyes: Female Circumcision. Filmmakers Library. 1994. 60 minutes.
Presents an African viewpoint on the culturally explosive issue of female circumcision. Testimony from doctors details the various forms of female circumcision and the ob/gyn problems that

result, and several women who have experienced it speak out about their experiences and their views on the practice for their daughters.

Gift of a Girl: Female Infanticide. Filmmakers Library. 1997. 24 minutes.

Explores the complexity of female infanticide in southern India and shows steps that are being taken to eradicate the practice.

Abortion: Stories From the North and South. Cinema Guild. 1984. 55 minutes.

Filmed in Ireland, Japan, Thailand, Peru, Columbia, and Canada, this cross-cultural survey shows how abortion transcends race, religion, and social class and how differences in the practice and perception of abortion are mainly in the degree of secrecy and danger accompanying it.

La Operacion. Cinema Guild. 1982. 40 minutes.

Examines the controversial use of female sterilization as a means of population control in Puerto Rico, which has the highest incidence of sterilization in the world.

The Desired Number. Women Make Movies. 1995. 28 minutes.

Focuses on the Ibu Eze ceremony, which celebrates women who have given birth to large numbers of children, to highlight how family planning issues often conflict with traditional family values.

The Pill. PBS Home Video. 2003. 56 minutes.

Presents interviews with the first generation of women to have access to the Pill. It chronicles how harnessing female hormones into a little pill unleashed a social revolution.

Six Billion and Beyond. University of California Extension Center for Media and Independent Learning. 1999. 56 minutes.

Examines how young people in India, China, Mexico, Italy, Kenya, and the USA are making decisions about their lifestyles, patterns of consumption, and reproductive choices.

COLONIALISM, DEVELOPMENT, AND THE GLOBAL ECONOMY

Women at Risk. Filmmakers Library. 1991. 56 minutes.
Presents portraits of women refugees in Asia, Africa, and Latin America.

The Global Assembly Line. New Day Films. 1986. 58 minutes.

A portrayal of the lives of working women and men in the "free-trade zones" of developing countries and North America. Focuses on Mexico and the Philippines.

Bringing It All Back Home. Women Make Movies. 1987. 48 minutes.

Analyzes how the patterns of international capital investment and the exploitation of Third World women workers in free-trade zones is being brought home to the First World, as Britain's declining industrial regions have been designated "enterprise zones" to attract the multinationals.

A State of Danger. Women Make Movies. 1989. 28 minutes.

Offers a perspective on the Intifada, presenting women's testimonies on their experiences with the Israeli military.

Hell to Pay. Women Make Movies. 1988. 52 minutes.
Presents an analysis of the international debt situation through the eyes of the women of Bolivia.

Holding Our Ground. International Film Bureau, Inc. 1988. 51 minutes.

Features women and children in the Philippines who pressure the government for land reform, establish their own money lending system, and build shelters for street children.

Maria's Story. Filmmakers Library. 1990. 53 minutes.
Portrays an FMLN guerilla, Maria Serrano, who has been living in the countryside for 11 years. Discusses her role in the revolution as well as the impact of the revolution on her family.

Time of Women. Women Make Movies. 1988. 20 minutes.

A portrait of the life of women in an Ecuadorian village where men are absent as migrants. The film looks at the impact of national economic policies on these rural women.

Fair Trade. Indiana University. 1989.

Profiles Tanzanian women and their struggle to become small entrepreneurs, and looks at the impact of development organizations and the aid that they extend to women through capital loans.

Where Credit Is Due. Indiana University. 1989.

Features the problem that Kenyan women have with the banking system, which generally refuses loans to women, and describes the Kenya Women's Finance Trust as an example of a credit cooperative for women borrowed from rural traditions of Women's support groups.

Once This Land Was Ours. Women Make Movies. 1991. 19 minutes.

The feminization of poverty in rural agricultural India.

Troubled Harvest. Women Make Movies. 1990. 30 minutes.

This documentary traces the female workers' experience with the fruit industry in Mexico and Latin America.

Modern Heroes, Modern Slaves. Filmmakers Library. 1997. 45 minutes.

Starting from the case of Flor Contemplacion, a Philippine maid hanged in Singapore for killing her abusive employer, this film shows the human and sometimes tragic side of this organized labor trade: failed marriages, family break-ups, and exploitation and abuse at the hands of unscrupulous employers.

Behind the Smile. Filmmakers Library. 1993. 46 minutes.

Hundreds of thousands of young Thai women leave their rural homes and work in the factories of Bangkok. This film explores the lives of these young women who live in crowded dormitories or shacks with few possessions, homesick for their families.

In Danku the Soup Is Sweeter: Women and Development in Ghana. Filmmakers Library. 1992. 30 minutes.

In this village in the north of Ghana, as in many African villages, women carry the burden of caring for the children, raising food, and trying to make a better life for their families. Through a special project, the women were given access to credit for the first time. This aid allowed them to become "entrepreneurs," and the film follows two women in their new enterprises as they struggle to make their enterprises work and to pay back their loans.

Sisters and Daughters Betrayed: The Trafficking of Women and Girls and the Fight to End It. University of California Extension Center for Media and Independent Learning. 1995. 28 minutes.

Sex trafficking is a global—and especially Asian—crisis of growing dimensions. Millions of women and young girls have been illegally transported from rural to urban areas and across national borders for the purpose of prostitution. This video explores the social and economic forces that drive this lucrative underground trade and the devastating effect it has on women's lives.

Daughters of Ixchel: Maya Thread of Change. University of California Extension Center for Media and Independent Learning. 1993. 29 minutes.

Explores the lives of Maya women today, portrays their ancient weaving processes, and examines the economic, political, and cultural forces that are profoundly affecting the women and their weaving.

The Women's Bank of Bangladesh. Films for the Humanities & Sciences. 1997. 47 minutes.

Describes the philosophy, development, and function of the Grameen Bank, and then follows three women who have taken out loans to fund their cottage industries. Islamic leaders and most males oppose the bank as being contrary to Islamic law, but the bank's founder defends the bank and its policy saying that women in the region are more competitive in business than men.

Women of the Earth: Australian Aborigines. Films for the Humanities & Sciences. 1998. 56 minutes.

Portrays Australia's Aborigines through the eyes of aboriginal women. Archival footage, excellent narration, and storytelling by the women themselves reveal the tribes' struggle for land rights, and the even greater struggle to retain their traditional lifestyles and customs in a world that is fast disappearing.

Woman by Woman: New Hope for the Villages of India. Insight Media. 2001. 30 minutes.

Documents progressive change for women in rural India. It illustrates how women have fought for their rights, become community leaders, and begun to tackle taboo subjects such as reproductive rights.

Made in Thailand. Women Make Movies. 1999. 33 minutes.

This documentary is about women factory workers and their struggle to organize unions. It examines the profound impact of the New World Order on the populations that provide the global economy with cheap labor.

Ouvrières du Monde (Working Women of the World). First Run/Icarus Films. 2000. 53 minutes.

Focuses on Levi Strauss & Co. and the relocation of its garment production from Western countries to nations such as Indonesia, the Philippines, and Turkey.

Señorita Extraviada. Independent Television Service (ITVS). 2001. 74 minutes.

Chronicles the story of the more than 200 kidnapped, raped, and murdered young women of Juarez, Mexico. This video presents the testimonies of victims' families and their search for truth while it examines Juarez's role as job center in the global economy.

Sixteen Decisions. University of California Extension Center for Media and Independent Learning. 2000. 59 minutes.

Presents the human face of the Grameen Bank in Bangladesh. It focuses on the everyday life of 18-year-old Selina, a mother of two, and the key issues facing her, such as dowry, housing, and her children's futures.

Women in Action. Insight Media. 1992. 30 minutes.

Focuses on projects centered on women and work in Dominica, Jamaica, and Guyana.